Handbook of
Rehabilitation
Psychology

Handbook of Rehabilitation Psychology

Edited by

Robert G. Frank and
Timothy R. Elliott

American Psychological Association
Washington, DC

Published by
American Psychological Association
750 First Street, NE
Washington, DC 20002

Copies may be ordered from
APA Order Department
P.O. Box 92984
Washington, DC 20090-2984

In the U.K., Europe, Africa, and the Middle East, copies may be ordered from
American Psychological Association
3 Henrietta Street
Covent Garden, London
WC2E 8LU England

Typeset in Century Schoolbook by EPS Group Inc., Easton, MD

Printer: Data Reproductions Corporation, Auburn Hills, MI
Dust jacket designer: Naylor Design Inc., Washington, DC
Technical/Production Editor: Amy J. Clarke

The opinions and statements published are the responsibility of the authors, and such opinions and statements do not necessarily represent the policies of the American Psychological Association.

Library of Congress Cataloging-in-Publication Data
Handbook of rehabilitation psychology / edited by Robert G. Frank and
    Timothy R. Elliott.—1st ed.
      p. cm.
    Includes bibliographical references and index.
    ISBN 1-55798-644-4 (casebound : acid-free paper)
      1. Clinical health psychology—Handbooks, manuals, etc.
  2. Medical rehabilitation—Psychological aspects—Handbooks, manuals, etc.
  I. Frank, Robert G., 1952–   . II. Elliott, Timothy R.

    R726.7.H366 2000
    617′.03′019—dc21

                                99-087407

British Library Cataloguing-in-Publication Data
A CIP record is available from the British Library.

Printed in the United States of America
First Edition

*To my father, Fred J. Frank, a truly noble person who shaped my thinking
and identity with love and compassion, and
John P. Gluck, first my mentor and now my mentor and friend*
RGF

*To my long-time friend, Jeff Douglas, whose experience along
life's pathway helped me find direction, inspiration, and meaning in my own*
TRE

Contents

Contributors

Glenn S. Ashkanazi, PhD, Department of Clinical and Health Psychology, University of Florida, Gainesville

Faye Z. Belgrave, PhD, Department of Psychology, Virginia Commonwealth University, Richmond

Erin D. Bigler, PhD, Department of Psychology, Brigham Young University, Provo, UT

Stephen M. Bloomfield, MD, Department of Neurosurgery, West Virginia University School of Medicine, Morgantown

Neil Bockian, PhD, Illinois School of Professional Psychology, Chicago

Charles H. Bombardier, PhD, Department of Rehabilitation Medicine, University of Washington School of Medicine, Seattle

Gary R. Bond, PhD, Department of Psychology, Indiana University–Purdue University, Indianapolis

Dawn E. Bouman, PhD, Department of Psychology, Drake Center, Inc., Cincinnati, OH

Bruce Caplan, PhD, independent practice, Wynnewood, PA

Kathleen Chwalisz, PhD, Department of Psychology, Southern Illinois University, Carbondale

Joe Cioffi, MEd, consultant, New York, NY

Tim Conway, MA, Department of Clinical and Health Psychology, University of Florida, Gainesville

Pamela A. Corbin, PhD, NorthKey Community Care, Covington, KY

Nancy Crewe, PhD, Department of Counseling, Educational Psychology, and Special Education, and Department of Physical Medicine and Rehabilitation, Michigan State University, East Lansing

Bruce Crosson, PhD, Department of Clinical and Health Psychology, University of Florida, Gainesville

Gerald M. Devins, PhD, Culture, Community, and Health Studies, Centre for Addiction and Mental Health (Clarke Division), and Department of Psychiatry and Psychology, Toronto Hospital, University of Toronto, Toronto, Ontario, Canada

Daniel M. Doleys, PhD, Pain and Rehabilitation Institute, Birmingham, AL

Dana S. Dunn, PhD, Department of Psychology, Moravian College, Bethlehem, PA

Timothy R. Elliott, PhD, Spain Rehabilitation Center, University of Alabama at Birmingham

Janet E. Farmer, PhD, Department of Physical Medicine and Rehabilitation, School of Medicine, University of Missouri—Columbia

Frank A. Fee, PhD, AdCare Health Systems, Inc., Springfield, OH

Greg R. Ford, PhD, Department of Rehabilitation Medicine, University of Washington School of Medicine, Seattle

Robert G. Frank, PhD, Department of Clinical and Health Psychology, University of Florida, Gainesville

Robert L. Glueckauf, PhD, Center for Research on Telehealth and Healthcare Communications, Department of Clinical and Health Psychology, University of Florida, Gainesville

Robert Guenther, PhD, Department of Clinical and Health Psychology, College of Health Professions, University of Florida, Gainesville

Kristofer J. Hagglund, PhD, Department of Physical Medicine and Rehabilitation, School of Medicine, University of Missouri—Columbia

Stephanie L. Hanson, PhD, College of Health Professions, University of Florida, Gainesville

Dennis C. Harper, PhD, Department of Pediatrics, College of Medicine, University of Iowa, Iowa City

Jennifer S. Haut, PhD, Department of Behavioral Medicine and Psychiatry, West Virginia University School of Medicine, Morgantown

Marc W. Haut, PhD, Department of Behavioral Medicine and Psychiatry, West Virginia University School of Medicine, Morgantown

Allen W. Heinemann, PhD, Department of Physical Medicine and Rehabilitation, Northwestern University Medical School, Chicago, and Rehabilitation Institute of Chicago

S. Lisbeth Jarama, PhD, Survey Research Lab, Virginia Commonwealth University, Richmond

Brick Johnstone, PhD, Department of Physical Medicine and Rehabilitation, School of Medicine, University of Missouri—Columbia

Jody Kashden, PhD, independent consultant, Morgantown, WV

Thomas Kerkhoff, PhD, Shands Rehabilitation Hospital, University of Florida, Gainesville

Donald G. Kewman, PhD, Department of Physical Medicine and Rehabilitation, University of Michigan Medical Center, Ann Arbor

Peter A. Lichtenberg, PhD, Institute of Gerontology and Department of Physical Medicine and Rehabilitation, Wayne State University School of Medicine, Detroit, MI

Marcia Liss, PhD, independent consultant, Coventry, RI

Susan E. MacNeill, PhD, Department of Physical Medicine and Rehabilitation, Wayne State University School of Medicine, Detroit, MI

James F. Malec, PhD, Department of Psychiatry and Psychology, Mayo Medical Center and Medical School, Rochester, MN

Mary McAweeney, PhD, School of Public Health, University of Michigan, Ann Arbor

Ilene D. Miner, CSW, League for the Hard-of-Hearing, New York, NY

Steve Moelter, MS, Department of Psychology, Sociology, and Anthropology, Drexel University, Philadelphia, PA

Alberto I. Moran, BA, School of Psychology, Farleigh Dickinson University, Teaneck, NJ

Laura Muhlenbruck, MA, Department of Psychology, University of Missouri—Columbia

John J. Nicholas, MD, Department of Physical Medicine and Rehabilitation, Temple University School of Medicine, Philadelphia, PA

David R. Patterson, PhD, Department of Rehabilitation Medicine, University of Washington School of Medicine, Seattle

David B. Peterson, PhD, Department of Health Studies, New York University, New York

Christopher A. Pierce, MA, Department of Psychiatry and Behavioral Science, University of Washington, Seattle

Robert Q Pollard, Jr., PhD, Department of Psychiatry, University of Rochester Medical Center, Rochester, NY

Jennie L. Ponsford, PhD, Department of Psychology, Monash University, and Bethesda Rehabilitation Research Unit, Melbourne, Australia

Cynthia L. Radnitz, PhD, School of Psychology, Farleigh Dickinson University, Teaneck, NJ

Sandra G. Resnick, MS, Department of Psychology, Indiana University–Purdue University, Indianapolis

J. Scott Richards, PhD, Department of Physical Medicine and Rehabilitation, University of Alabama at Birmingham

Joseph Ricker, PhD, Kessler Medical Rehabilitation Research and Education Corporation, West Orange, NJ

Mitchell Rosenthal, PhD, Kessler Medical Rehabilitation Research and Education Corporation, West Orange, NJ, and Department of Physical Medicine and Rehabilitation, University of Medicine and Dentistry of New Jersey, Newark

Bruce Rybarczyk, PhD, Departments of Psychology and Physical Medicine and Rehabilitation, Rush–Presbyterian–St. Luke's Medical Center, Chicago

Laura H. Schopp, PhD, Department of Physical Medicine and Rehabilitation, School of Medicine, University of Missouri—Columbia

Richard Shewchuk, PhD, Department of Health Services Administration, School of Health Related Professions, University of Alabama at Birmingham

Cheryl L. Shigaki, PhD, Older Adult Services, Pine Rest Christian Mental Health Services, Grand Rapids, MI

Zachary M. Shnek, PhD, Department of Psychology, Toronto General Hospital, and Department of Public Health Sciences, University of Toronto, Toronto, Ontario, Canada

Edna Mora Szymanski, PhD, College of Education, University of
  Maryland, College Park
Lynda Szymanski, PhD, Department of Psychology, College of
  St. Catherine, St. Paul, MN
Edward Taub, PhD, Department of Psychology, University of Alabama at
  Birmingham
Gitendra Uswatte, MA, Department of Psychology, University of
  Alabama at Birmingham
Alan Vaux, PhD, Department of Psychology, Southern Illinois University,
  Carbondale

Handbook of
Rehabilitation
Psychology

Rehabilitation Psychology: Hope for a Psychology of Chronic Conditions

Robert G. Frank and Timothy R. Elliott

Rehabilitation psychology is concerned with the treatment and science of disabling and chronic health conditions. Rehabilitation psychology was one of the first applied clinical specialties in professional psychology; it was recognized as a division of the American Psychological Association more than 40 years ago. Yet the specialty has rarely occupied center stage in American psychology. This may have been due, in part, to the multidisciplinary nature of rehabilitation and the many outlets for publications by influential pioneers in rehabilitation (Shontz & Wright, 1980). However, the field has grown tremendously over the past two decades, and a brief review of the research and clinical activities of rehabilitation psychologists reveals a huge domain, vastly exceeding any traditional definition of professional psychology. Rehabilitation psychology now encompasses aspects of social psychology, clinical health psychology, clinical and counseling psychology, health policy, and the psychology of chronic health conditions. The intermingling of these complex areas requires a diverse yet comprehensive fund of knowledge. Rehabilitation psychology now has increasingly diverse applications in an array of clinical settings, ranging from inpatient rehabilitation hospitals to outpatient and community-based facilities.

Field theory concepts enriched our appreciation of the impact of the group and the situation on the individual with a disability. Behavioral approaches guided tremendous strides in understanding the maintenance of disabling behaviors (Fordyce, 1976) and the treatment of symptoms driven by psychophysiological mechanisms (Ince, 1980). Elegant demonstrations of theory from the laboratory to the clinic have had radical effects on physical functioning (e.g., see Chapter 22). Psychological expertise in research method and evaluation has been pivotal in the rise of large-scale research programs that amassed data eventually used in the development of multidisciplinary intervention programs for low-incidence, high-impact, and high-cost disabilities such as spinal cord injuries (Zasler & Kreutzer, 1994). More recently, the specialty has achieved diplomate status from the American Board of Professional Psychology, which has affirmed the ascendancy of rehabilitation psychology within the ranks of professional psychology.

Opportunities for Rehabilitation Psychology in the New Health Care Environment

The "corporatization" of health care in the United States and the recognition of limited resources for health care expenditures in publicly funded delivery systems (e.g., Medicare, Medicaid) have redefined the typical clinical activities of many practicing psychologists. Rehabilitation settings have not been exempted from the changes brought on by changes in publicly financed health systems. The impact of recent changes in the financing systems have created a chaotic environment in rehabilitation programs. Psychologists, who had previously been blissfully unaware of finance systems, have become financial payment experts. The rapidity of the changes and the ambiguous role of psychologists in the emerging systems have created concerns for most psychologists. The eclectic and diverse identity of rehabilitation psychology has encountered this evolution with a sense of confidence not shared by those in more traditional roles.

There are three overarching reasons why rehabilitation psychology should sense opportunity in the face of evolving health care. First, the majority of health care expenditures are associated with the care and management of chronic disease and disability and with the acute episodes of care associated with these conditions (Frank, in press). In both public and private health care systems there is increased emphasis on the containment of costs and the need to prevent, contain, and treat chronic conditions and their symptoms in a cost-efficient manner. Rehabilitation psychologists are more familiar and expert in addressing the needs and issues of people with these conditions, perhaps more so than specialists in any other discipline within psychology.

Second, the prevailing emphasis on primary care, primary and secondary prevention, and multidisciplinary approaches are congruent with the routine research and practice interests of rehabilitation psychologists (Frank, 1999; Klapow, Pruitt, & Epping-Jordan, 1997). Throughout its existence, rehabilitation psychology has worked shoulder-to-shoulder with colleagues in medicine, nursing, and education to address the varied health and social concerns of persons with disabilities. These relationships have been solidified in professional multidisciplinary organizations, such as the American Congress of Rehabilitation Medicine, the National Rehabilitation Association, and the American Association of Spinal Cord Injury Psychologists and Social Workers, in which rehabilitation psychologists have assumed key leadership roles.

Rehabilitation psychologists have demonstrated and used their considerable research expertise in working with federal funding agencies that address established service and research priorities germane to persons with disabilities. Rehabilitation psychologists have assumed similar roles with private funding agencies, such as the Paralyzed Veterans of America and have collaborated with these organizations to develop multidisciplinary clinical practice guidelines.

In concert with these agencies, rehabilitation psychologists have shown a keen interest and active involvement in the public and health policy-making process (Frank, Sullivan, & DeLeon, 1994). These activities can elevate the status and impact of rehabilitation psychology on resource allocation and the dispersion of funds for subsequent research and practice (Johnstone et al., 1995). These activities are also fundamental for psychologists to assist health care systems with a science-based model of behavioral health care (Leviton, 1996; Sanderson, Riley, & Eshun, 1997).

Third, rehabilitation psychology—by virtue of its accomplishments in research and practice—embodies the emergence of professional psychology as a health profession rather than a profession mired in the murky and crowded waters of mental health. Rehabilitation psychology directly affects outcomes that are beyond the circumscribed definitions of traditional mental health practice (e.g., individual therapy for emotional adjustment). Rehabilitation psychologists are involved in resolving issues with physical health and health-related quality of life and are well acquainted with biopsychosocial mechanisms associated with disease, injury, disability, and well-being in a fashion other psychological disciplines could emulate.

As we have described, rehabilitation psychology has evolved in a consistent manner, with rapid expansion during the past 2 decades. In the past 20 years, growth in rehabilitation has produced more jobs for psychologists than have other clinical sectors (Frank, Gluck, & Buckelew, 1990). Now, however, changes in financing of health services have shaken the rehabilitation delivery systems. As acute medicine changed a decade earlier with movement to the prospective payment system, rehabilitation is now changing. As in all chaotic changes, there is great peril and true opportunity. Much has been written of the peril; we add little to that voice in this text. The opportunities, assuming that organized psychology, training programs, and practitioners are capable of exploiting the moment, are the target of this text.

During the next 30 years, the "graying of America" (Frank et al., 1990) will significantly alter health care needs in the United States. The aging of the American population coincides with an increase in chronic health conditions. In 1995, as many as 1 million Americans had chronic health conditions. The per capita cost for individuals with chronic health conditions are three times higher than for individuals without (Hoffman, Rice, & Sung, 1996). Individuals with chronic health conditions, and consequent limitations in activity, comprise about 17% of the population but account for more than 47% of medical expenditures, according to Hoffman et al.

As noted by Frank (1999), individuals with chronic disorders comprise the original roots of rehabilitation psychology. The discipline has since narrowed its focus from the emphasis on chronic care to a specific disabling condition. This shift has moved the discipline to a narrow perspective just as the changes in demographics demand attention to chronic health conditions. By focusing on the broader concept of chronic health conditions that may lead to disability, rehabilitation psychology can be poised to provide comprehensive psychological and community integration services to a population with many real needs. In essence, this focus on chronic conditions creates a psychology of primary care with emphasis on chronicity as the defining variable (Frank, 1999). However, primary care models are likely to be less prevalent in the future. It makes little sense for rehabilitation psychology, or any psychological discipline, to copy medical delivery models. Despite this caveat, all health care delivery systems are likely to emphasize comprehensive care that includes community reintegration—a major feature in every aspect of rehabilitation psychology.

Increasingly, the failures of the acute medical model have been recognized and often lamented. The increased emphasis on efficiency in the delivery of health care has exacerbated the bias of medicine to focus on symptoms instead of the whole person. Rehabilitation psychology has the potential to establish fundamental services for individuals with chronic conditions. To do this, the discipline must focus on the psychology of the individual (including the psychology of disability), as well as life styles, prevention, coping, and community integration; most of these tasks are inherent to current practice in the discipline. There is no small irony that, by embracing these areas, rehabilitation psychology returns to its roots and recognizes the social, vocational, and clinical psychological aspects of the individual. By coming full circle, rehabilitation psychology asserts its rightful role as the provider of a broadly based primary care service for individuals requiring chronic care.

The elements inherent to this approach are described in this text. At the same time, the more recent emphasis of the discipline on significant disabling conditions, such as spinal cord or brain injury, have also been addressed. Thus, we believe and hope that this text offers an integration and a review of the tremendous strides within the discipline as well as the challenges for the next epoch. Rehabilitation psychology provides the ideal template for professional psychology. The discipline is practiced in health care settings, an area of huge growth. Rehabilitation psychology taxes the entire wealth of clinical skills applicable to professional psychology from individual psychotherapy to neuropsychological assessment to group therapy to consultation.

Scope of the Text

Despite the growth and success of rehabilitation psychology, the discipline lacks a comprehensive, up-to-date text that conveys its richness and potential. The *Handbook of Rehabilitation Psychology* was developed to document the enormous breadth and depth of rehabilitation psychology and to provide a contemporary perspective of the specialty. As changes in the financing and delivery of health care have transformed professional psychology, models for the effective delivery of psychological services are rare. Rehabilitation psychology has much to offer the larger profession. For example, rehabilitation psychology is an ideal vehicle for a primary care psychology focusing on chronic health conditions (Frank, 1999). In this handbook we bring together the steady progress of the field of rehabilitation psychology and its potential to serve as a template for applied psychology.

In designing the text, we were guided by respect for the evolutionary path of the discipline, while recognizing the panorama of opportunity in the present. The breadth of rehabilitation psychology requires that we divide the material into four sections.

Section I, Clinical Conditions, addresses topics and areas that have defined the field of rehabilitation psychology such as spinal cord injury, traumatic brain injury, amputation, and stroke. To these core areas, we have added critical areas reflecting the growth of the discipline, such as geriatrics, burn, pain, psychiatric rehabilitation, multiple sclerosis, sensory impairment, and issues in the rehabilitation of children.

Section II, Critical Factors, provides an overview of essential skill areas for the field. Included are works discussing functional status and quality-of-life measures, assessment of personality and psychopathology, outcomes, neuropsychological assessment in children and neurorehabilitation, forensic evaluations, and rehabilitation of individuals with brain tumors. Also included in this section are descriptions of unique rehabilitation issues such as postacute programs for brain injury. Alcohol abuse plays a critical role in traumatic injury and rehabilitation and is discussed. Application of magnetic resonance imaging (MRI) to the dynamic brain may prove to be the ultimate rehabilitation outcome predictor; functional MRI (fMRI) is described in this section. Another innovative rehabilitation method, constraint-induced movement, is also reviewed.

Section III, Social Interpersonal Issues, addresses the importance of the behavioral ecosystem to rehabilitation outcomes. Included are chapters addressing disability and vocation, social support and disability, family caregiving, culture, and social psychological factors affecting rehabilitation. Also in this section is a discussion of issues involved in the prevention of injury.

Section IV, Professional Issues, includes chapters that review new payments systems on rehabilitation, ethical issues in rehabilitation, and education issues for psychologists. The handbook also includes resources for quick and informative reference: a list of additional resources (e.g., Web sites, national organizations), a list of frequently used acronyms, and a glossary.

Even with this division of material, several important topics, such as sexuality and the Americans With Disabilities Act of 1990 (P. L. 101-336), were omitted. These omissions are regrettable, but reflect the diversity of the field. Undoubtedly, there are other omissions—the field has grown too large for one text to cover every aspect. Although we recognize that the text is not comprehensive, we believe that the material included provides a broad view of the field 40 years into its evolution. We hope that this text provides a blueprint for the next epoch of rehabilitation psychology.

References

Americans With Disabilities Act of 1990, P. L. 101-336, 104 Stat. 327.

Fordyce, W. E. (1976). *Behavioral methods for chronic pain and illness.* St. Louis, MO: Mosby.

Frank, R. G. (1999). Organized delivery systems: Implications for clinical psychology services or we zigged when we should have zagged. *Rehabilitation Psychology, 44*(1), 36–51.

Frank, R. G. (in press). Rehabilitation. In A. Baum, T. Revenson, & J. Singer (Eds.), *Handbook of health psychology.* Mahwah, NJ: Erlbaum.

Frank, R. G., Gluck, J. P., & Buckelew, S. P. (1990). Rehabilitation: Psychology's greatest opportunity? *American Psychologist, 45,* 757–761.

Frank, R. G., Sullivan, M., & DeLeon, P. (1994). Health care reform in the states. *American Psychologist, 49,* 855–867.

Hoffman, C., Rice, D., & Sung, H. Y. (1996). Persons with chronic conditions: Their prevalence and costs. *Journal of the American Medical Association, 276,* 1473–1479.

Ince, L. P. (1980). *Behavioral psychology in rehabilitation medicine.* Baltimore: Williams & Wilkins.

Johnstone, B., Frank, R. G., Belar, C., Berk, S., Bieliauskas, L. A., Bigler, E. D., Caplan, B., Elliott, T. R., Glueckauf, R. L., Kaplan, R. M., Kreutzer, J. S., Mateer, C. A., Patterson, D., Puente, A. E., Richards, J. S., Rosenthal, M., Sherer, M., Shewchuk, R., Siegel, L. J., & Sweet, J. J. (1995). Psychology in health care: Future directions. *Professional Psychology: Research and Practice, 26,* 341–365.

Klapow, J. C., Pruitt, S. D., & Epping-Jordan, J. E. (1997). Rehabilitation psychology in primary care: Preparing for a changing health care environment. *Rehabilitation Psychology, 42,* 325–335.

Leviton, L. C. (1996). Integrating psychology and public health: Challenges and opportunities. *American Psychologist, 51,* 42–51.

Sanderson, W. C., Riley, W. T., & Eshun, S. (1997). Report of the working group on clinical services. *Journal of Clinical Psychology in Medical Settings, 4,* 3–12.

Shontz, F., & Wright, B. (1980). The distinctiveness of rehabilitation psychology. *Professional Psychology, 11,* 919–924.

Zasler, N. D., & Kreutzer, J. S. (1994). Model systems of care. *NeuroRehabilitation, 4*(2), 4–80.

Part I

Clinical Conditions

1

Spinal Cord Injury

J. Scott Richards, Donald G. Kewman, and Christopher A. Pierce

Spinal cord injury (SCI) resulting from trauma imposes major and permanent life changes on the predominantly young male population who receive these injuries. Although recent improvements in medical care have improved life expectancy, social, attitudinal, and architectural integration have often lagged behind. In this chapter we review the changing demographics of this population and then consider the role of traditional clinical and counseling techniques in assessment and treatment that apply to SCI rehabilitation. Activities unique to SCI in clinical, counseling, and behavioral health practice are discussed. Finally, we address the importance of environmental factors with regard to long-term adjustment such as vocational and educational issues.

Etiology and Demographics

A great deal of what is known about the demographics and etiology of SCI comes from the collaborative database derived from the Model SCI Systems of Care Program funded by the National Institute on Disability and Rehabilitation Research. From that source, we know that more than half of all injuries occur in the 16- to 30-year-old age group and that men make up 82% of the cases (Go, DeVivo, & Richards, 1995). This percentage has changed little in the more than 20 years that the database has been in operation (Stover & Fine, 1986).

The ethnic makeup of the SCI population does not appear to correspond to that of the general population. In 1990 the proportion of White people in the Model SCI Systems database was 70% (Go et al., 1995). This is considerably lower than the 80% found in the 1990 national census. In addition, African Americans with SCI represent 20% of individuals listed in the database, although they are only 12% of the general population.[1]

---

[1] These percentages may not present an accurate picture of the ethnic makeup of the SCI population. The national database distinguishes Hispanic patients from other groups, whereas the census classifies these patients as belonging to another ethnic group (i.e., White, African American, Asian American, or American Indian). Another reason for this discrepancy may be that the database collects its information from systems based in large urban areas that do not necessarily capture the national ethnic distribution.

The educational level of people with SCI tends to be lower than that of the population in general, even when taking the median age of this population into consideration. For instance, 66% of patients with SCI ages 18–21 are at least high school graduates, whereas for the same age group in the general population the figure is 86% (Go et al., 1995). This same pattern is supported by population-based estimates from the state registries of Colorado, Georgia, and Virginia.

Most people with SCI are single (i.e., never married) at the time of injury. For the national database, this figure is 54% (Go et al., 1995). This is congruent with the relatively young age at which most injuries occur. This percentage varies somewhat for state registries (Georgia, 43%; Colorado, 48%; Virginia, 50%).

Assessment and Treatment Issues

Psychological Adjustment Following SCI

Depression in its several forms is probably the most common behavioral disorder within the general population. This likely holds for people with SCI as well. Severe depression can limit a person's functioning and quality of life and strain health resources. In a rehabilitation setting, people who experience depression tend to have less functional independence and mobility when discharged (Umlauf & Frank, 1983). Depressive behavior has been associated with longer hospital stays and fewer improvements during rehabilitation (Malec & Neimeyer, 1983). Depression has also been associated with the occurrence of preventable secondary complications such as pressure sores and urinary tract infections (Herrick, Elliott, & Crow, 1994). Nonhospitalized individuals who have SCI and high levels of depressive behavior spend more days in bed, have fewer days out of the home, use more paid attendants, and incur increased overall medical expenses (Tate, Forchheimer, Maynard, & Dijkers, 1994).

When assessing depression in people with SCI it is important to use appropriate diagnostic criteria (Elliott & Frank, 1996). Depressed mood alone, which may be a common consequence of trauma, does not constitute diagnosable depression. In addition, diagnoses other than major depression may be more appropriate (e.g., dysthymic disorder, depressive disorder not otherwise specified, or one of the bipolar disorders). A number of personal factors may contribute to depression in people with SCI. People with premorbid histories of maladjustment, psychological disorders, and alcohol use are often prone to depressive behavior following SCI (Judd, Stone, Webber, Brown, & Burrows, 1989; Tate, 1993). These are pre-injury characteristics of a disproportionate number of persons with SCI. In general, difficulty coping with life may lead to difficulty coping with SCI. However, good problem-solving skills are associated with lower depression scores (Elliott, Godshall, Herrick, Witty, & Spruell, 1991). Hope and goal-directed energy are also associated with lower distress (Elliott, Witty,

Herrick, & Hoffman, 1991). These behaviors and cognitive strategies can be targets for intervention.

Pharmacotherapy for the treatment of clinical depression in people with SCI should be efficacious. However, the efficacy of antidepressant medication has not been adequately studied in double-blind, randomized trials in the SCI population (Elliot & Frank, 1996). Consequently, conclusions about what medications effectively alleviate depression while maintaining good side-effect profiles cannot be drawn. Tricyclic antidepressants often produce side effects that could be especially problematic for people with SCI. Consequently, selective serotonin reuptake inhibitors and other nontricyclic antidepressants are more typically the treatment of choice. As a result of the lack of a research base and the possible deleterious side effects of antidepressant medications, the psychologist's role in medication management is to consult regarding the need for antidepressants and to help monitor efficacy and side effects. Because side-effect profiles have not been established in the SCI population, the psychologist must be alert for unanticipated effects.

One outcome of depression that must be monitored is suicide. Many people with SCI may consider suicide when setbacks interfere with their quality of life. Suicide can take the form of overt action, self-neglect, or refusal of required care (Dijkers, Abela, Gans, & Gordon, 1995). Suicides as a percentage of all deaths for people with SCI are reported at 5–10% (DeVivo, Kartus, Stover, Rutt, & Fine, 1989; Geisler, Jousse, Wynne-Jones, & Breithaupt, 1983; Nyquist & Bors, 1967). The suicide rate for the population as a whole is only slightly above 1% of all deaths. The suggested risk factors for suicide in people with SCI are alcohol and drug abuse, psychiatric history, criminal history, family dysfunction, and suicide attempts prior to the injury or during hospitalization (Charlifue & Gerhart, 1991). Dijkers et al. found that the suicide rate for people with SCI was highest among young adults, men, and White people. Suicide rates were highest for people with incomplete (sensory or motor sparing below the neurologic spinal cord lesion) paralegia (injury to the thoracic cord or lower resulting in normal arm-hand function and paralysis of the legs). The authors also found that the rate of suicide diminishes by year postinjury, dropping off considerably after the 5th year. This suggests that for those who learn to cope early, the rate of suicide approaches that of the general population. It also suggests the possibility of developing programs targeted for the first few years postdischarge for monitoring and reducing risk factors.

Anxiety disorders have not been studied as thoroughly as depression among people with SCI. Therefore, their incidence and prevalence are uncertain. Anxiety is a logical possibility considering the traumatic circumstances often associated with the onset of SCI and the physical and psychological sequelae associated with acute care, rehabilitation, and community re-entry, which can also induce distress (Radnitz et al., 1995).

Over the first year postinjury, Hancock, Craig, Dickson, Chang, and Martin (1993) found that anxiety levels were significantly higher for people with SCI than for a control group. In their sample, 25% of people with

SCI scored one standard deviation above the cutoff score for their anxiety measure as compared with 5% of the control sample. In addition, anxiety did not decrease over the course of the year. Looking at the same individuals 2 years later, Craig, Hancock, and Dickson (1994) found that anxiety levels were still elevated compared with the control sample and had not decreased. Frank, Elliott, Buckelew, and Haut (1988) found that age was not related to level of general anxiety, but anxiety was related to the amount of life stress their sample of people with SCI had endured.

Social anxiety and social phobia can develop in people with SCI. Dunn (1977) analyzed anxiety and avoidance in social situations by age, type of injury (paraplegia vs. tetraplegia), and time since injury. He found that social anxiety was related to age but not type of injury or time since injury. Specifically, regardless of type of injury or time since injury, older individuals endorsed more social discomfort than did younger ones. Dunn, Van-Horn, and Herman (1981) have evaluated techniques and materials for social skills development in people with SCI that can reduce social discomfort and avoidance.

The traumatic nature of SCI would appear to place such individuals at risk for posttraumatic stress disorder (PTSD). Radnitz et al. (1995) assessed the current and lifetime diagnosis of PTSD in a group of veterans with SCI. Using a PTSD scale and a structured interview based on criteria of the third revised edition of the *Diagnostic and Statistical Manual of Mental Disorders (DSM–III–R*; American Psychiatric Association, 1987), they found a current diagnosis rate of 14–17% and a lifetime diagnosis rate of 34–35%, depending on the instrument used. The authors reported that these rates are similar to those of other traumatized groups. Further research should confirm the extent to which anxiety disorders are problematic and the efficacy of pharmacologic and behavioral interventions.

Cognitive Deficits

Because rehabilitation involves relearning or new learning following SCI, it is important to ascertain that the person with SCI has sufficient cognitive capacity to learn and retain what is required for effective and healthy postrehabilitation living. Assessment of cognitive difficulties in this population has been given considerable focus in the literature, much of that focus primarily being directed toward the identification of possible concomitant traumatic brain injury (TBI). Given that traumatic onset SCI by definition occurs most often through a rapid deceleration event (e.g., motor vehicle crash, diving injury, fall) and in other instances may be associated with a period of anoxia (surgical complications, cardiopulmonary arrest at onset), the possibility of concomitant cognitive deficits has been well recognized (Davidoff, Roth, & Richards, 1992). In addition to injury-related events that could compromise cognitive functioning, preinjury events likewise can lead to lingering cognitive difficulties. For example, persons may have prior histories of TBI, learning disability, or prolonged alcohol or drug abuse. A number of postinjury factors could also compromise neuropsychological test performance, suggesting cognitive deficits that may or may not be significant. For example, depression, preoccupation with the impact of injury, pain, medications, or lack of cooperation with testing may present as cognitive deficits. If a patient also has low intellectual ability and educational achievement, it can be problematic for the clinician to draw unequivocal inferences about possible TBI that may have occurred at the time of SCI.

However, the importance of moderate to severe TBI with respect to lingering cognitive and behavioral difficulties has been well explicated (Dikmen, Machamer, Winn, & Temkin, 1995). Almost 50% of people with SCI experience loss of consciousness or significant posttraumatic amnesia associated with their injury (Davidoff et al., 1992; Dowler et al., 1997; Richards, Brown, Hagglund, Bua, & Reeder, 1988). The presence of such findings should raise the suspicion of a concomitant TBI and encourage the psychologist to pursue evaluation of cognitive abilities and deficits. Such deficits, if present, are likely to be diffuse rather than focal, if the SCI was the result of a rapid deceleration event in an individual without a prior history of cortical insult (Gennarelli, 1993).

Given the importance of learning ability in rehabilitation, the rehabilitation psychologist working on the SCI unit is well advised to routinely carry out at least some rudimentary assessment of cognitive ability, with more in-depth formal neuropsychological evaluations considered for those who show evidence of significant impairment. Because much of the information presented in rehabilitation is presented verbally and less in written format, some assessment of verbal learning ability (e.g., California Verbal Learning Test; Delis, Kramer, Kaplan, & Ober, 1987) is helpful. Limited hand function in persons with tetraplegia precludes the use of many neuropsychological tests that assume intact motor function. Several authors have devised comprehensive neuropsychological test batteries that do not require hand function and can be considered when more in-depth evaluation is indicated (Dowler et al., 1997; Richards et al., 1988). It is important not to overestimate or underestimate the significance of cognitive deficits and the possibility of TBI in this population. Mild concomitant TBI may have few long-term implications. In more moderate and severe cases of concomitant TBI, however, cognitive and behavioral difficulties may persist over time, with significant implications for personal and social functioning of the person with SCI in the interpersonal context (Dowler et al., 1997; Richards et al., 1991).

Pain

Pain following SCI is a perplexing and vexing complication, with prevalence estimates ranging from 48 to 94% (Ragnarsson, 1997). Variations in prevalence estimates are likely a function of differences in sample populations and pain assessment methods (Richards, 1992). It is not clear why some individuals develop this problem following SCI and others do not (Beric, 1997). Although post-SCI pain is receiving appropriate increased attention with respect to biomedical theories of its origin (Beric, 1997; Yezierski, 1996), patients with SCI who have to cope with this complication on a day-to-day basis experience pain as an "insult added to injury." In a recent study of nonhospitalized persons with SCI a median of 2.3 years postinjury, presence of chronic pain was the only complication that predicted lower quality-of-life scores (Lundquist, Siösteen, Blomstrand, Lind, & Sullivan, 1991). Biomedical approaches to understanding and treating pain following spinal cord injury are needed, but those experiencing this complication daily can benefit from psychological assessment and assistance with management of this complication.

Several SCI pain classification schemes have been proposed (Beric, 1997; Siddall, Taylor, & Cousins, 1997), with no uniform agreement on subtypes and their definitions. This problem complicates the clinician's ability to summarize the available literature and conduct clinical studies. In the meantime, the major subtypes of pain, cutting across different classification schemes, include overuse and mechanical pain, root pain, and dysesthetic or central pain. Some have proposed other subtypes: psychogenic pain, visceral pain, and referred pain (Siddall et al., 1997). Purely psychogenic pain is nearly nonexistent. It is important for a psychologist working with this population to realize that pain can be "referred," that is, experienced in one body part but originating elsewhere (e.g., ruptured appendix experienced as shoulder pain) and that pain can reflect correctable (e.g., overuse, unstable fracture) and dangerous conditions (e.g., ascending syrinx). The importance of working with a competent physician in the evaluation of these complaints cannot be overstated. In some cases (e.g., root, dysesthetic pain), post-SCI pain becomes a chronic condition that does not yield easily to physical, medical, or surgical intervention.

Although it is always difficult to determine causation, psychosocial factors are inextricably linked with chronic pain in this population as in others. People injured from gunshot are more likely to develop post-SCI pain (Richards, Stover, & Jaworski, 1990) and are more likely to be of minority status from lower socioeconomic status levels (Go et al., 1995). Substance abuse is a factor in the onset of many SCIs, and a return to substance abuse after rehabilitation is also frequent (Heinemann, Mamott, & Schnoll, 1990). The potential for abuse of narcotics or other medications with abuse potential (e.g., Valium) is high in this population. "Self-medication" for pain through alcohol use and abuse also should be monitored.

Cognitive–behavioral and operant strategies for assessing SCI pain have been developed, and treatment approaches have been broadly outlined (Umlauf, 1992). Most authors suggest a multi-axial assessment approach involving self-report pain measures (e.g., visual analog scale, McGill Pain Questionnaire; Melzack, 1975), coping scales (e.g., Rosenstiel & Keefe, 1983), structured clinical interview (e.g., Kerns, Turk, & Rudy, 1985), and personality measures. A comprehensive assessment should be used to select treatment approaches (Wegener & Elliott, 1992) so that patients with SCI pain who are also depressed receive different interventions than those with an ongoing substance abuse problem, family stress, or secondary gain component. Unfortunately, there are no well-controlled outcome studies of psychosocial interventions for SCI pain. In the absence of such data, the clinician is left with techniques that have proven efficacious with other chronic pain populations with appropriate modifications for people with SCI. Operant learning techniques aimed at modifying reinforcement contingencies in the environment, cognitive–behavioral and pharmacologic treatment of depression and anxiety, family therapy, relaxation training, biofeedback, and hypnosis can be helpful. Goal setting, problem solving, assertiveness and other skills training, substance abuse treatment, and even treatment of sexual dysfunction and general counseling regarding adjustment and future plans may also be helpful in individual cases in which chronic pain is problematic.

Substance Abuse

Substance abuse, both alcohol and drug related, is often a vexing problem for many people with SCI both pre- and postinjury. Heinemann et al. (1990) found that people with SCI from a predominantly veteran's population reported substantially higher lifetime and immediate preinjury frequency of substance abuse compared to an age-matched nondisabled control population. In some cases acute postinjury care and rehabilitation hospitalization become a de facto detoxification program. In the rehabilitation setting, patients are not usually receptive to counseling about substance abuse. Their typical belief is that they do not need treatment because they have been "without" for several weeks. Empirical data indicate, however, that there is a rapid return to substance abuse after rehabilitation (Heinemann, Keen, Donohue, & Schnoll, 1988). Most SCI rehabilitation programs address this important issue individually and in psychoeducational groups. However, with the resistance of most patients, and with increasingly short rehabilitation stays, formal treatment programs for substance abuse incorporated into the initial rehabilitation process have been few. More recent developments in the substance abuse intervention literature hold some promise. Motivational interviewing, for example, is a brief and efficient intervention with some early evidence of efficacy in other disability groups (Bombardier, 1995).

Obtaining reliable data concerning substance abuse is always a problem. Information derived from self-report or questionnaire data, in the absence of confirming or denying data from a well-informed other, has questionable reliability. Many of the commonly used substance abuse screening instruments have obvious item content (e.g., Michigan Alcoholism Screening Test; Selser, 1971); hence, they are subject to potential sources of self-report bias. Scales with more subtle content may be more beneficial.

The potential for prescription drug abuse is also present. Such medications as Valium (often prescribed for spasticity), narcotic-based analgesics for pain, and anxiolytic and other psychotropic medications have the potential for abuse. Given the absence of a highly effective treatment for central pain, treating physicians are often faced with continuous pressure from patients to prescribe strong narcotics. If this occurs, some of these individuals can develop tolerance and may eventually require detoxification.

Sexuality

Perhaps because of the predominance of men in the SCI population, more has been written about sexuality for men with SCI than for women, although that trend is changing (e.g., Krotoski, Nosek, & Turk, 1996). Depending on the level of the neurologic deficit and extent, SCI can have a profound impact on sexual physiology, or the "mechanics" of sexuality. The goal of assessment and treatment in this important arena of life functioning, as in other aspects of rehabilitation, is optimal adaptation and accommodation to changes in the physical aspects of sexuality.

For men following SCI, impairment in obtaining psychogenic erections (i.e., erections solely triggered by mental or nontactile stimulation) is probable. In a large case series, Bors and Comarr (1960) found a relationship between upper and lower motor neuron status and the likelihood of reflex or psychogenic erections. Patients with complete upper motor reuron lesions are very likely to have reflex erections (i.e., automatic erections typically stimulated by contact, which can occur in the absence of arousal). However, these may not be sufficiently firm, or last long enough for intercourse. Ejaculation and psychogenic erection are unlikely in this group. Men with complete lower motor neuron injuries are somewhat more likely to have psychogenic erections (1 in 4) and much less likely to have reflex erections. About 1 in 5 are able to ejaculate. The ability of clinicians to predict erectile response and ejaculation becomes far less certain for men with incomplete lesions. Fertility remains problematic: If ejaculation can occur during intercourse, the viability and quality of sperm are often low. Some success (Ayers, Moinipanah, Bennett, Randolph, & Peterson, 1988) has occurred with the use of electroejaculation and externally applied vibration to extract semen and produce pregnancy through artificial insemination. Penile prostheses, both fixed and inflatable, were the major recourse to improve erectile dysfunction in the 1960s and 1970s. Externally applied vacuum devices, oral medications (e.g., Viagra) and injections recently have become available. Although not without risk, these devices are safer and far less costly and have been proven beneficial with regard to sexual behavior and satisfaction (Richards, Lloyd, James, & Brown, 1992).

For women, changes in sexual physiology equivalent to those of men are thought to be lubrication (parallel to erection) and uterine and vaginal contractions (parallel to ejaculation; Sipski & Alexander, 1992). Sipski, Alexander, and Rosen (1995) demonstrated in unique laboratory settings that women with SCI are capable of achieving orgasm and that some, but not all, of the physiological changes that occur in women without SCI also occur in women with SCI. However, the work of Jackson, Wadley, Richards, and DeVivo (1995) suggested that participation in sexual intercourse diminishes somewhat postinjury for women and that self-reported orgasm decreases markedly. These two lines of research suggest the possibility (untested in controlled studies) that a substantial proportion of women with SCI could be taught self-stimulation or other techniques that would substantially improve sexual response and experience (the same is likely true for men with SCI).

Temporary disruption in hormonal and menstrual cycles in women with SCI is common, and the need for appropriate birth control counseling therefore should be emphasized. In the absence of information to the contrary and in the absence of pelvic sensation and early postinjury menstruation, some women with SCI may conclude erroneously that they are not capable of becoming pregnant. Successful pregnancies do occur, but the possibility of unique complications argues for careful follow-up during pregnancy and delivery by an obstetrician familiar with SCI (Jackson, 1995).

The role of the psychologist with regard to sexual dysfunction can range from education to active sex therapy. The role of sex educator, however, can be assumed by several different professionals in the rehabilitation setting. The rehabilitation psychologist should be familiar and comfortable with the topic and address it directly when it is broached. One area in which psychologist involvement in education could be productive is the prevention of sexually transmitted disease (STDs). Because discomfort (a common symptom of STDs) may not be felt by the person with SCI, the presence of an STD may go undetected. In addition to education, people with SCI may need specific suggestions regarding exploration and renewal of their sexuality. Sensate focus activities coupled with a prohibition of attempts at intercourse are an effective method for couples to reduce performance anxiety and learn to focus on sexual communication and mutual pleasuring. Social skills training may be helpful so that the person with SCI is more comfortable initiating contact with others. Proper assessment and treatment of other psychosocial problems that might impede sexual readjustment is also in order (e.g., depression, substance abuse, proper hygiene, bowel and bladder accidents).

Sexuality following SCI has been widely explored, and numerous excellent written and audiovisual resources are available to help the rehabilitation psychologist become more knowledgeable and effective in this arena (e.g., Ducharme & Gill, 1996; Sipski & Alexander, 1997; Tepper, 1997). Formal training in sex counseling and therapy is also available (e.g., with the American Association of Sex Educators, Counselors and Therapists).

Intervention Strategies

Psychoeducational Approaches

We cannot describe all of the possible intervention approaches that have been used with people with SCI. Trieschmann (1988) and, more recently,

McAweeney, Tate, and McAweeney (1997) summarized the intervention literature for this population. We briefly describe unique characteristics and issues that occur when providing intervention services in the rehabilitation environment for people with SCI and suggest approaches that have been successful.

The clinician may experience a general resistance or reluctance to engage actively in psychotherapeutic interventions by many people with acute-onset SCI. From the patient's perspective, the primary reason for being in a rehabilitation hospital is not for mental health purposes but to achieve maximal physical independence. Compounding this reality is the fact that many men who acquire SCI are not typically introspective individuals (Rohe & Krause, 1993). For many, being seen by a psychologist, particularly when such a service is not requested, may have a stigmatizing effect.

To counteract some of these issues, a number of practitioners in inpatient SCI rehabilitation settings have developed practical alternative service delivery models. One suggestion would be to work with the physicians and other staff so that all people with recent-onset SCI are routinely referred to the psychologist. Psychological services are therefore presented as part of the overall "rehabilitation package." A routine referral can help destigmatize the process and reduce resistance. Traditional, insight-oriented psychotherapy, either on an individual or group basis, is not routinely practiced in rehabilitation settings. A structured psychoeducational group experience for acutely injured people with SCI is frequently offered. Descriptions of such approaches can be found by Trieschmann (1988). In these approaches, each group session, rather than being unstructured or insight or affect oriented, addresses topics reflective of the new realities with which the person with SCI must cope. Information is presented in a didactic fashion with group discussion afterward. The presence of an effective peer coping model who has an SCI often facilitates discussion. Family members are invited to attend as well, and sessions are often led by the members of the rehabilitation team. The psychologist's role may consist of organizing the group schedule, facilitating discussion, and presenting information for one or more sessions. With the reduction in the length of inpatient rehabilitation in recent years, the number of sessions needs to be limited, with constant recycling. A list of topics could include such issues as the search for a cure for SCI, sexuality and fertility, social skills and assertiveness, disability legislation, architectural and attitudinal barriers, travel, recreational opportunities, managing personal care attendants, bowel and bladder functioning, diet, skin care, medication use and abuse, and substance abuse.

Reasonable goals for the psychologist during the initial rehabilitation phase should be focused around assessment of history, personality, and behavioral style; development of rapport; and participation in the psychoeducational process outlined above. If these goals are accomplished, the individual with SCI and family member may be more likely to contact the psychologist postdischarge if difficulties develop. This could allow more indepth individual work with that psychologist or permit a referral to an independent living center (ILC) or mental health resource in the patient's community.

Peer Counseling

Exposure to peers or people with similar injuries has been considered beneficial to adjustment to SCI through modeling and emotional support. Such exposure may take place informally by virtue of receiving rehabilitation in a setting with other people with SCI. More formal interaction with a peer who provides information or counseling is often integrated into the rehabilitation process as part of a purposefully designed program (Tate, Rasmussen, & Maynard, 1992). This is sometimes done in a group format with experienced peers leading a discussion of a topic related to independent living. Group learning for adults with SCI in rehabilitation facilities has the advantage of providing peer support and opportunities to share problems, reducing isolation, and increasing motivation (Payne, 1995). However, one-to-one counseling by a peer may be the most frequently used delivery model for such services. Often these services are obtained through a community-based ILC from peers who have received some orientation and training to become peer counselors.

The timing of peer counseling is another subject of interest. Psychologists may be involved in deciding the best timing for introducing a peer counselor. In some settings, the psychologist may brief or debrief the peer counselor to optimize this kind of intervention and better coordinate psychological care.

Vocational and Educational Issues

For young people, going to school is an important social role. Following graduation from school, entering the workforce becomes a pre-eminent social role. Participation in these roles is associated with superior psychosocial adjustment for adults with SCI compared to nonstudents and people who are unemployed (Krause & Anson, 1997).

Most children with SCI attend school. Because of federal legislation (most notably Section 504 of the Rehabilitation Act of 1973, Education for All Handicapped Children Act of 1975, Education of the Handicapped Act Amendment of 1975, and Individuals With Disabilities Education Act of 1990), many are mainstreamed in regular classrooms with various accommodations and additional services where needed. Psychologists can serve as advocates for children with SCI and their families by educating them regarding the special education process and applicable laws. In addition, psychologists may offer recommendations to the school regarding academic accommodations and social reintegration issues. Psychologists sometimes discuss with a teacher methods for reintroducing the child into the social environment of the classroom, such as having the teacher or child discuss aspects of SCI with their classmates in a matter-of-fact way.

The rates of post high school education for those injured as children appear to be much higher than rates for people injured as adults (22% in one study; Kewman & Forchheimer, 1997). This same study also highlighted the important role that education plays in postinjury employment; education was found to be the strongest predictor of employment. Seventy-seven percent of people with post-high school training were employed, but only 37% of people with less education obtained paid employment, for an overall employment rate of 46%.

Completion of a vocational education program may boost the likelihood of employment. Unfortunately, few youngsters with SCI receive vocational planning, vocational education, or community work experiences (Massagli, Dudgeon, & Ross, 1996). Furthermore, these same authors pointed out that accommodations made to allow completion of school may not be sufficient for the demands of the competitive workplace. The number of adults in one study receiving state vocational rehabilitation services at discharge from inpatient rehabilitation was 45% and declined thereafter (Dijkers et al., 1995).

Vocational interest testing and discussion of options for acquiring needed skills are frequently provided by psychologists working in SCI care. In part, this preliminary vocational counseling serves to convey and validate the message that working after sustaining an SCI is a viable goal. To some degree, the effort to promote post high school education and vocational productivity may be hindered by specific personality styles characteristic of many people with SCI. Compared to the general population, male individuals with SCI have been shown to be more introverted and interested in working with things rather than with people or data (Rohe & Athelstan, 1982). This interest pattern is at odds with the majority of jobs that may be available to people with physical limitations and emphasizes the need for careful educational and career planning to maximize the chances of a successful vocational placement.

Pediatrics

Most SCIs in children occur at the high cervical levels, rendering a disproportionate number tetraplegic (Dickman & Rekate, 1993). The literature about the psychosocial effects of SCI on children is limited and mostly theoretical (Richards, Elliott, Cotliar, & Stevenson, 1995). Risk factors for adjustment problems are probably similar to the general population of children with chronic illness and disability and include patients' pre-injury psychological status, parents' psychological status, family stress, and family cohesion (Warschausky, Engel, Kewman, & Nelson, 1996).

There has been speculation that impaired mobility of children growing up with an SCI may negatively affect curiosity and initiation (Johnson, Berry, Goldeen, & Wicker, 1991; Zejdlic, 1992). Lollar (1994) assessed cognitive function in 145 children and adolescents (mean age = 15.9 years) with SCI. Although they presented stronger overall intellectual functioning and better mental flexibility, their social awareness and judgment was poorer than their able-bodied, age-matched peers. Kewman, Warschausky, and Engel (1995) discussed how children with SCI may be at risk for social integration difficulties as a result of social stigma. Psychological intervention aimed at teaching and promoting specific social skills such as how to enter peer interactions or cope with teasing or avoidance by peers is an important therapeutic goal.

Conclusion

Traditionally trained psychologists who become involved in the rehabilitation of people with SCI have opportunities to use all of the assessment and therapy skills at their command as well as acquired knowledge and skills specific to the rehabilitation setting. Problems encountered in the general mental health field such as depression, anxiety, suicide, and substance abuse are encountered in the SCI population as well. However, skills unique to practice with people who have sustained an SCI must be developed, such as assessment and treatment of chronic pain, neurologically based sexual dysfunction, and secondary conditions. A broader perspective than a focus on the individual with SCI is also necessary; caregiver concerns and the impact of the social (culture) and physical (environmental barriers) environment often place intervention outside the individual with a focus on minimizing or eliminating barriers to social reintegration. The psychologist also needs to learn that he or she may not always be the best source of therapeutic intervention; referral to peer counselors or ILCs may be important adjunct or primary sources for help. Perhaps more than in traditional mental health fields, adjusting to SCI needs to be considered a lifelong process; issues and interventions change as a function of time postinjury and age.

Changes in health care reimbursement and delivery can be seen as both a threat and an opportunity. The threat is associated with decreased lengths of stay and a seemingly endless stream of services (including psychological services) that are no longer covered by third-party payers or reimbursed at such low rates and with such limits as to make adequate service delivery impossible through traditional venues. However, the challenge is in coping actively with these trends by designing assessment and intervention approaches that are demonstrably valid, clearly articulated so as to be transmittable to other clinicians, and cost effective. Using nontraditional and low-cost providers under the direction of a clinical psychologist and moving into the community using interactive video ("telehealth" or "telerehabilitation") and other technologies to deliver service remotely represent directions to explore. In a related way, identifying oneself more strongly with behavioral medicine than with traditional mental health service delivery is consonant with the continuing need for creative and effective ways to prevent or treat the secondary conditions that compromise quality of life and the need for better ways to maintain wellness, once it is achieved.

The need continues for effective, well-trained clinicians who can work with people with SCI, and there is an even greater need for clinician–

researchers. Psychologists have lagged behind in attempts to rigorously evaluate the efficacy of their interventions. In an era of increasing scrutiny of health care practice and outcomes, a profession without a substantial research base documenting the efficacy of its interventions can be marginalized by those who design health care plans. Psychologists are better equipped than most if not all of their rehabilitation team colleagues to carry out such research. The complexity of such endeavors notwithstanding, clinical intervention research by rehabilitation psychologists must be undertaken with rigor and urgency to preserve their place in the rewarding arena of rehabilitation and lifelong care of people with SCIs.

References

American Psychiatric Association. (1987). *Diagnostic and statistical manual of mental disorders* (3rd ed., rev.). Washington, DC: Author.

Ayers, J. W. T., Moinipanah, R., Bennett, C. J., Randolph, J. F., & Peterson, E. P. (1988). Successful combination therapy with electroejaculation and in vitro fertilization–embryo transfer in the treatment of a paraplegic male with severe oligosthenospermia. *Fertility and Sterility, 49*, 1089–1090.

Beric, A. (1997). Post-spinal cord injury pain states. *Pain, 72*, 295–298.

Bombardier, C. (1995). Alcohol use and traumatic brain injury. *Western Journal of Medicine, 162*, 150–151.

Bors, E., & Comarr, A. E. (1960). Neurological disturbances of sexual function with special reference to 529 patients with spinal cord injury. *Urologic Surveys, 10*, 191–197.

Charlifue, S. W., & Gerhart, K. A. (1991). Behavioral and demographic predictors of suicide after traumatic spinal cord injury. *Paraplegia, 72*, 488–492.

Craig, A. R., Hancock, K. M., & Dickson, H. G. (1994). A longitudinal investigation into anxiety and depression in the first 2 years following a spinal cord injury. *Paraplegia, 32*, 675–679.

Davidoff, G. N., Roth, E. J., & Richards, J. S. (1992). Cognitive deficits in spinal cord injury: Epidemiology and outcome. *Archives of Physical Medicine Rehabilitation, 73*, 275–284.

Delis, D. C., Kramer, J. H., Kaplan, E., & Ober, B. A. (1987). *The California Verbal Learning Test, research edition.* New York: The Psychological Corporation.

DeVivo, M. J., Kartus, P. L., Stover, S. L., Rutt, R. D., & Fine, P. R. (1989). Cause of death in patients with spinal cord injuries. *Archives of Internal Medicine, 149*, 1761–1766.

Dickman, C. A., & Rekate, H. L. (1993). Spinal trauma. In M. R. Eichelberger (Ed.), *Pediatric trauma: Prevention, acute care, rehabilitation* (pp. 362–377). St. Louis, MO: Mosby-Year Book.

Dijkers, M. P., Abela, M. B., Gans, B., & Gordon, W. A. (1995). The aftermath of spinal cord injury. In S. L. Stover, J. A. DeLisa, & G. G. Whiteneck (Eds.), *Spinal cord injury: Clinical outcomes from the model systems* (pp. 185–212). Gaithersburg, MD: Aspen.

Dikmen, S. S., Machamer, J. E., Winn, H. R., & Temkin, N. R. (1995). Neuropsychological outcome at one year post injury. *Neuropsychology, 9*, 80–90.

Dowler, R. N., Herrington, D. L., Haaland, K. Y., Swanda, R. M., Fee, F., & Fiedler, K. (1997). Profiles of cognitive functioning and chronic spinal cord injury and the role of moderating variables. *Journal of the International Neuropsychological Society, 3*, 464–472.

Ducharme, S. H., & Gill, K. M. (1996). *Sexuality after spinal cord injury.* Baltimore: Brookes.

Dunn, M. (1977). Social discomfort in the patient with spinal cord injury. *Archives of Physical Medicine and Rehabilitation, 58*, 257–260.

Dunn, M., VanHorn, R. E., & Herman, S. H. (1981). Social skills and spinal cord injury: A comparison of three training procedures. *Behavior Therapy, 12*, 153–164.

Education for All Handicapped Children Act of 1975, P. L. 94-142, 89 Stat. 773.

Education of the Handicapped Act Amendments of 1986, P. L. 99-457, 100 Stat. 1145.

Elliott, T. R., & Frank, R. G. (1996). Depression following spinal cord injury. *Archives of Physical Medicine and Rehabilitation, 77,* 816–823.

Elliott, T. R., Godshall, F., Herrick, S., Witty, T., & Spruell, M. (1991). Problem-solving appraisal and psychological adjustment following spinal cord injury. *Cognitive Therapy Research, 15,* 387–398.

Elliott, T. R., Witty, T., Herrick, S., & Hoffman, J. (1991). Negotiating reality after physical loss: Hope, depression, and disability. *Journal of Personality and Social Psychology, 61,* 608–613.

Frank, R. G., Elliott, T. R., Buckelew, S. P., & Haut, A. E. (1988). Age as a factor in response to spinal cord injury. *American Journal of Physical Medicine and Rehabilitation, 67,* 128–131.

Geisler, W., Jousse, A., Wynne-Jones, M., & Breithaupt, D. (1983). Survival in traumatic spinal cord injury. *Paraplegia, 21,* 364–373.

Gennarelli, T. A. (1993). Cerebral concussion and diffuse brain damage. In T. R. Cooper (Ed.), *Head injury* (3rd ed., pp. 137–158). Baltimore: Williams & Wilkins.

Go, B. K., DeVivo, M. J., & Richards, J. S. (1995). The epidemiology of spinal cord injury. In S. L. Stover, J. A. DeLisa, & G. G. Whiteneck (Eds.), *Spinal cord injury: Clinical outcomes from the model systems* (pp. 21–55). Gaithersburg, MD: Aspen.

Hancock, F. M., Craig, A. R., Dickson, H. G., Chang, E., & Martin, J. (1993). Anxiety and depression over the first year of spinal cord injury: A longitudinal study. *Paraplegia, 31,* 349–357.

Heinemann, A. W., Keen, M., Donohue, R., & Schnoll, S. (1988). Alcohol use by persons with recent spinal cord injury. *Archives of Physical Medicine Rehabilitation, 69,* 619–624.

Heinemann, A. W., Mamott, B. D., & Schnoll, S. (1990). Substance use by persons with recent spinal cord injuries. *Rehabilitation Psychology, 35,* 217–228.

Herrick, S., Elliott, T. R., & Crow, F. (1994). Social support and the prediction of health complications among persons with spinal cord injuries. *Rehabilitation Psychology, 39,* 231–250.

Individuals With Disabilities Education Act of 1990, P. L. 101-476, 104 Stat. 1142.

Jackson, A. J. (1995). Obstetrical outcomes in women with spinal cord injury [Abstract]. *Journal of Spinal Cord Medicine, 18,* 141.

Jackson, A. J., Wadley, V. G., Richards, J. S., & DeVivo, M. J. (1995). Sexual behavior and function among spinal cord injured women [Abstract]. *Journal of Spinal Cord Medicine, 18,* 141.

Johnson, K. M. S., Berry, E. T., Goldeen, R. A., & Wicker, E. (1991). Growing up with a spinal cord injury. *Spinal Cord Injury Nursing, 8,* 11–19.

Judd, F. K., Stone, J., Webber, J. E., Brown, D. J., & Burrows, G. D. (1989). Depression following spinal cord injury: A prospective in-patient study. *British Journal of Psychiatry, 154,* 668–671.

Kerns, R. D., Turk, D., & Rudy, T. (1985). The West Haven–Yale Multidimensional Pain Inventory (WHYMPI). *Pain, 23,* 345–356.

Kewman, D. G., & Forchheimer, M. (1997, September). *Factors predicting return to work 3 to 6 years following spinal cord injury.* Poster session presented at the annual meeting of the American Association of Spinal Cord Injury Psychologists and Social Workers, Las Vegas, NV.

Kewman, D. G., Warschausky, S. A., & Engel, L. (1995). Juvenile rheumatoid arthritis and neuromuscular conditions: Scoliosis, spinal cord injury, and muscular dystrophy. In M. C. Roberts (Ed.), *Handbook of pediatric psychology* (2nd ed., pp. 384–402). New York: Guilford Press.

Krause, J. S., & Anson, C. A. (1997). Adjustment after spinal cord injury: Relationship to participation in employment or educational activities. *Rehabilitation Counseling Bulletin, 40,* 202–214.

Krotoski, D., Nosek, M., & Turk, M. (1996). *Women with physical disabilities.* Baltimore: Brookes.

Lollar, D. J. (1994). Psychological characteristics of children and adolescents with spinal cord injury. *SCI Psychosocial Process, 7,* 55–59.

Lundquist, C., Siösteen, A., Blomstrand, C., Lind, B., & Sullivan, M. (1991). Spinal cord injuries: Clinical, functional, and emotional status. *Spine, 16*, 78–83.

Malec, J., & Neimeyer, R. (1983). Psychologic prediction of duration of inpatient spinal cord injury rehabilitation performance of self care. *Archives of Physical Medicine and Rehabilitation, 64*, 359–363.

Massagli, T. L., Dudgeon, B. J., & Ross, B. W. (1996). Educational performance and vocational participation after spinal cord injury in childhood. *Archives of Physical Medicine and Rehabilitation, 77*, 995–999.

McAweeney, M. J., Tate, D. G., & McAweeney, W. (1997). Psychosocial interventions in the rehabilitation of people with spinal cord injury: A comprehensive methodological injury. *SCI Psychosocial Process, 78*, 58–66.

Melzack, R. (1975). The McGill pain questionnaire: Major properties and scoring methods. *Pain, 1*, 277–299.

Nyquist, R., & Bors, E. (1967). Mortality and survival in traumatic myelopathy during 19 years from 1946–1965. *Paraplegia, 5*, 22–48.

Payne, J. A. (1995). Group learning for adults with disabilities or chronic disease. *Rehabilitation Nursing, 20*, 268–272.

Radnitz, C. L., Schlein, I. S., Walczak, S., Broderick, C. P., Binks, M., Tirch, D. D., Willard, J., Perez-Strumolo, L., Festa, J., Lillian, L. B., Bockian, N., Cytryn, A., & Green, L. (1995). The prevalence of posttraumatic stress disorder in veterans with spinal cord injury. *SCI Psychological Process, 8*, 145–149.

Ragnarsson, K. T. (1997). Management of pain in persons with spinal cord injury. *The Journal of Spinal Cord Medicine, 20*, 186–199.

Richards, J. S. (1992). Chronic pain and spinal cord injury: Review and comment. *The Clinical Journal of Pain, 8*, 119–122.

Richards, J. S., Brown, L., Hagglund, K., Bua, G., & Reeder, K. (1988). Spinal cord injury and concomitant traumatic brain injury: Results of a longitudinal investigation. *American Journal of Physical Medicine and Rehabilitation, 67*, 211–216.

Richards, J. S., Elliott, T. R., Cotliar, R., & Stevenson, V. (1995). Pediatric medical rehabilitation. In M. C. Roberts (Ed.), *Handbook of pediatric psychology* (pp. 703–722). New York: Guilford Press.

Richards, J. S., Lloyd, L. K., James, J. W., & Brown, J. (1992). Treatment of erectile dysfunction secondary to spinal cord injury: Sexual and psychosocial impact on couples. *Rehabilitation Psychology, 37*, 205–213.

Richards, J. S., Osuna, F. J., Jaworski, T. M., Novack, T. A., Leli, D. A., & Boll, T. J. (1991). The effectiveness of different methods of defining traumatic brain injury in predicting post discharge adjustment in a spinal cord injury population. *Archives of Physical Medicine Rehabilitation, 72*, 275–279.

Richards, J. S., Stover, S. L., & Jaworski, T. (1990). Effect of bullet removal or subsequent pain in persons with spinal cord injury secondary to gunshot wound. *Journal of Neurosurgery, 73*, 401–404.

Rohe, D. E., & Athelstan, G. T. (1982). Vocational interests of persons with spinal cord injury. *Journal of Counseling Psychology, 29*, 283–291.

Rohe, D. E., & Krause, J. S. (1993, August). *The five factor model of personality: Findings among males with spinal cord injury.* Paper presented at the 101st Annual Convention of the American Psychological Association, Toronto, Ontario, Canada.

Rosenstiel, A. K., & Keefe, F. J. (1983). The use of coping strategies in chronic low back pain patients: Relationship to patient characteristics and current adjustment. *Pain, 17*, 33–44.

Section 504 of the Rehabilitation Act of 1973, P. L. 93-112, 87 Stat. 355.

Selser, M. L. (1971). The Michigan Alcoholism Screening Test (MAST): The quest for a new diagnostic instrument. *American Journal of Psychiatry, 3*, 176–181.

Siddall, P. J., Taylor, D. A., & Cousins, M. J. (1997). Classification of pain following spinal cord injury. *Spinal Cord, 35*, 69–75.

Sipski, M. L., & Alexander, C. J. (1992). Sexual function and dysfunction after spinal cord injury. *Physical Medicine and Rehabilitation Clinics of North America, 3*, 811–828.

Sipski, M. L., & Alexander, C. J. (1997). *Sexual function in people with disability and chronic illness: A health professional's guide.* Gaithersburg, MD: Aspen.

Sipski, M. L., Alexander, C. J., & Rosen, R. C. (1995). Physiologic responses associated with orgasm in SCI women [Abstract]. *Journal of Spinal Cord Medicine, 18,* 140.

Stover, S. L., & Fine, P. R. (1986). *Spinal cord injury: The facts and figures.* Birmingham: University of Alabama at Birmingham.

Tate, D. G. (1993). Alcohol use among spinal cord injured patients. *American Journal of Physical Medicine and Rehabilitation, 72,* 192–195.

Tate, D. G., Forchheimer, M., Maynard, F., & Dijkers, M. (1994). Predicting depression and psychological distress in persons with spinal cord injury based on indicators of handicap. *American Journal of Physical Medicine and Rehabilitation, 73,* 175–183.

Tate, D. G., Rasmussen, L., & Maynard, F. (1992). Hospital to community: A collaborative medical rehabilitation and independent living program. *Journal of Applied Rehabilitation Counseling, 23,* 18–21.

Tepper, M. C. (1997). *Providing comprehensive sexual health care in spinal cord injury rehabilitation.* Huntington, CT: Sexual Health Network.

Trieschmann, R. B. (1988). *Spinal cord injuries: Psychological, social, and vocational rehabilitation* (2nd ed.). New York: Demos.

Umlauf, R. L. (1992). Psychological interventions for chronic pain following spinal cord injury. *The Clinical Journal of Pain, 8,* 111–118.

Umlauf, R. L., & Frank, R. G. (1983). A cluster-analytic description of patient subgroups in the rehabilitation setting. *Rehabilitation Psychology, 28,* 157–167.

Warschausky, S., Engel, L., Kewman, D., & Nelson, V. S. (1996). Psychosocial factors in rehabilitation of the child with a spinal cord injury. In R. R. Betz & M. J. Mulcahey (Eds.), *The child with a spinal cord injury* (pp. 471–482). Rosemont, IL: American Academy of Orthopaedic Surgeons.

Wegener, S. T., & Elliott, T. R. (1992). Pain assessment in spinal cord injury. *The Clinical Journal of Pain, 8,* 93–101.

Yezierski, R. (1996). Pain following spinal cord injury: The clinical problem and experimental studies. *Pain, 68,* 185–194.

Zejdlic, C. P. (1992). *Management of spinal cord injury.* Boston: Jones & Bartlett.

2

Limb Amputation

Bruce Rybarczyk, Lynda Szymanski, and John J. Nicholas

Limb amputation is a common condition, but advances in prosthetic technology often make it invisible to the general public. Estimates of the prevalence of limb amputation in the United States vary greatly, from 358,000 (National Center for Health Statistics, 1991) to as many as 2.5 million people (American Amputation Foundation, 1997; Winchell, 1995). The larger estimates would mean that more than 1 in 100 Americans have had an amputation. Despite a pioneering study of adjustment to "misfortune" among war veterans with amputations conducted 50 years ago (Dembo, Leviton, & Wright, 1956, 1975), rehabilitation psychologists have had only limited involvement with this population.

The most common type of amputation (90%) is the removal of a lower extremity (Bradway, Malone, Racy, Leal, & Poole, 1984; Wilson, 1989). Men are more likely to have amputations than women (Winchell, 1995), and the majority of amputations (75%) are performed on people older than age 65 (Clark, Blue, & Bearer, 1983). There is a high mortality rate among individuals with an amputation; 40–60% of people with lower extremity amputations die within 2 years of their surgery (Cutson & Bongiorni, 1996). Most of the deaths occur in older adults with multiple medical illnesses and are secondary to cardiac complications. Moreover, the risk of losing the contralateral leg following a unilateral amputation is 15–20% and approximately 40% two and four years after the amputation, respectively (Cutson & Bongiorni, 1996).

There are four primary etiological factors that necessitate the amputation of one or more limbs: (a) vascular disease and infection, (b) trauma, (c) tumors, and (d) congenital deformities or abnormalities. The majority of amputations are a result of vascular disease (Buttenshaw, 1993; Frierson & Lippmann, 1987) and lead to the removal of a lower extremity (Williamson & Walters, 1996). There are several levels of lower limb amputation, including removal of one or more toes, amputations through the foot (transmetatarsal, Lisfranc, and Chopart), ankle disarticulation (Syme), transtibial amputations (below the knee), knee disarticulation

This chapter was adapted from "Coping With a Leg Amputation: Integrating Research and Clinical Practice," by B. Rybarczyk, J. J. Nicholas, and D. Nyenhuis (1997), *Rehabilitation Psychology*, *42*(3), 241–256. Copyright 1997 by Springer. Adapted with permission.

(amputation at the knee), transfemoral amputation (above the knee), hip disarticulation (removal of the femur), and hemipelvectomy (removal of half of the pelvis; Wilson, 1989). There also are several types of upper extremity amputations, including removal of individual or multiple digits, wrist disarticulation (removal of hand at wrist joint), below-elbow amputation, elbow disarticulation (removal of forearm), above-elbow amputation, shoulder disarticulation (removal of entire arm), and forequarter amputation (removal of arm, clavicle, and scapula; Wilson, 1989).

Following an amputation, patients usually are referred to a *prosthetist*, a health professional who specializes in the creation and fitting of artificial limbs. Proper rehabilitation training is required for those with amputations to learn to use the prosthesis to engage in daily tasks such as walking. Using a prosthesis to walk requires significantly more physical energy than walking with both natural limbs. For example, amputations that are unilateral below the knee, bilateral below the knee, bilateral below the knee, and bilateral above the knee require 40–60%, 90–120%, 60–100%, and at least 200% more energy, respectively, than is required with both lower extremities intact (Cutson & Bongiorni, 1996; Waters, Perry, Antonelli, & Hislop, 1976).

In addition to being physically demanding, undergoing an amputation and prosthesis training can be a psychologically distressing experience. Shukla, Sahu, Tripathi, and Gupta (1982) studied 72 people with recent amputations ages 10–60+ and found many experiencing sadness (62%), anxiety (53%), crying spells (53%), and insomnia (47%). Furthermore, it is well documented that individuals with amputations experience high rates of clinical depression, with estimates ranging from 21% to 35% (Kashani, Frank, Kashani & Wonderlich, 1983; Rybarczyk, Nyenhuis, Nicholas, Cash, & Kaiser, 1995; Rybarczyk et al., 1992; Williamson, Schulz, Bridges, & Behan, 1994). All people with amputations must come to terms in some way with the loss of their limb and the related functional limitations. The significance of this loss was documented by Parkes (1975), who found that widows demonstrated more overt distress immediately following their spouse's death than did people experiencing recent limb loss. However, the distress level of the widows significantly decreased 1 year after the loss, whereas people with amputations did not experience a significant decrease in distress during the same period.

Factors in Adjustment to an Amputation

One unique aspect of a leg amputation is the wide spectrum of psychological responses that can be associated with the experience. These responses range from viewing the amputation as a great personal tragedy to seeing it as a new lease on life. The response depends on a complex interplay between objective physical factors and individual psychosocial factors. For this reason, it is critical for clinicians to understand the issues that are known to affect adjustment and to undertake a thorough assessment of these issues with each individual who is seeking services from a mental health professional. We focus on adjustment to lower extremity amputations because they are more prevalent and have generated more research than arm amputations.

Medical

One factor that would presumably play a role in adjustment is the medical cause of an amputation (e.g., congenital condition, cancer, diabetes, vascular disease, war time injury, or trauma). However, two studies (Rybarczyk et al., 1992, 1995) tested this variable and found that no particular cause stands out as a predictor of poor adjustment. Even if a significant relationship were found, it would be difficult to interpret because of confounding factors. For example, one would not be able to tell the extent to which the negative psychological responses are connected to the amputation itself or the coexisting chronic conditions that preceded the amputation (e.g., cancer, diabetes, chronic pain). Each of the most common comorbid conditions has been independently linked to increased susceptibility to depression (Cassileth et al., 1984). Conversely, it has been suggested that individuals who endure chronic illness for many years have the opportunity to gradually habituate to decreases in functional status and therefore may adjust better to an amputation (Williamson et al., 1994).

In a number of situations, quality of life actually improves following an amputation and subsequent adaptation to walking with a prosthesis; this is most often the case for an individual who undergoes an amputation after experiencing years of vascular-related chronic pain or undergoing repeated surgical attempts to save the leg. In Parkes's 1975 study, patients reported an average of 2.6 surgeries prior to an amputation. Indeed, in a recent study diabetic patients with amputations were found to be better adjusted than a matched group of diabetic patients with chronic foot ulcerations (Carrington, Mawdsley, Morley, Kincey, & Boulton, 1996). Foot ulcerations often take months to heal and usually are treated with decreased weight bearing and prolonged bed rest. Such events may recur repeatedly, diminishing an individual's quality of life and leading to a sense of helplessness and despair.

Another medical variable that would seem to be important in coping with an amputation is the length of time since the amputation. The popular wisdom, supported by limited research only (e.g., Heinemann, Bulka, & Smetak, 1988), is that the more time that goes by after an acquired disability the more likely the person is to cope effectively. Yet in four studies examining this variable, Frank et al. (1984), Rybarczyk et al. (1992, 1995), and Williamson et al. (1994) found either no connection or only a small correlation (~.20) between adjustment and time since an amputation.

In our clinical work, which covers both outpatient and inpatient care, we often see individuals who exhibit an initial sense of relief at the time of the amputation and only later experience grief over their losses. In a study of older adults with amputations, only 23% reported that the initial period following their amputation was the most distressing time (Mac-

Bride, Rogers, Whylie, & Freeman, 1980). These authors also noted that in many cases older adults have the opportunity for "anticipatory grief" during the months or years preceding an amputation when they are given increasingly dire warnings by their physicians regarding the possibility of losing a leg. Sometimes the most negative response comes when the individual is fitted with a prosthesis and subsequently discovers that it does not function as effectively as he or she had hoped or had been led to believe by a health care provider.

Several reports indicate that phantom limb pain (PLP) is a significant risk factor for poor adjustment following an amputation (Katz, 1992; Lindesay, 1985; Pell, Donnan, Fowkes, & Ruckley, 1993). Most individuals with amputations experience some type of phantom limb sensation or physical feeling of the amputated limb; in fact, the prevalence of phantom limb sensation is between 90 and 100% (Jensen, Krebs, Nielsen, & Rasmussen, 1984; Krane & Heller, 1995). Phantom limb sensations are not painful and usually decrease in duration, frequency, and intensity over time (Jensen, Krebs, Nielsen, & Rasmussen, 1985; Winchell, 1995). PLP, however, is the subjective experience of pain in the limb that has been amputated; it occurs in 60–90% of all people with amputations (Buchanan & Mandel, 1986; Sherman & Sherman, 1983; Shukla et al., 1982; Winchell, 1995). Notably, these high percentages are based on survey responses and not on the number of patients presenting to their physician complaining of PLP.

The quality of PLP varies but most commonly is described as intermittent cramping or burning (Krane & Heller, 1995). PLP in adults can be continuous or episodic and is most frequently experienced during the first 6 months postsurgery (Jensen et al., 1984; Krane & Heller, 1995; Sherman, 1997). Sherman, Sherman, and Parker (1984) found that 50% of patients with PLP reported that their symptoms decreased somewhat over time, but the remaining patients experienced either no relief at all or an exacerbation of pain. PLP often decreases in frequency and intensity during the first 6 months postsurgery (Jensen et al., 1985). Carlen, Wall, Nadvorna, and Steinbach (1978) noted that PLP often remits within a few months after surgery without any intervention. When it lasts longer than 6 months, it is difficult to treat and often becomes chronic (Jensen et al., 1985).

Although the pathophysiology of PLP is not well understood, peripheral, spinal cord, and cerebral neuronal factors are thought to contribute to this phenomenon (Jensen et al., 1984). Notably, PLP is more frequent in patients who had the amputation secondary to blood clots (Weiss & Lindell, 1986) and in those who experienced more preamputation pain and postamputation stump pain (Jensen et al., 1985). Gerhards, Florin, and Knapp (1984) found that patients with more social support had less PLP than those with fewer social resources.

Disability

One common assumption regarding disability is that more physical impairment leads to poorer psychological adjustment. In the case of amputation, the degree of impairment is substantially less with a below-knee amputation compared to an above-knee amputation (Medhat, Huber, & Medhat, 1990) and even more so compared with bilateral amputations. However, in two studies, Rybarczyk et al. (1995) and Williamson et al. (1994) found no connection between the level of amputation and physical impairment.

One conclusion from these amputation studies and the wider research on adjustment to disability is that the degree of impairment, irrespective of other factors, is too simplistic to serve as an important predictor of an individual's overall adjustment. However, the conceptual distinction made among impairment, disability, and handicap (World Health Organization, 1980) has created an opportunity for more precise studies of the adjustment process. In this model *impairment* is defined as dysfunction at the organ level (e.g., the amputation itself), *disability* as the effects of the impairment on performance and behavior in everyday life (e.g., walking), and *handicap* as the effects of impairment on fulfillment of social roles (e.g., employment). Although impairment may have a significant impact on an individual's self-concept (e.g., body image), experiencing oneself as disabled or handicapped is more likely to play a pivotal role in the adjustment process.

Williamson et al. (1994) tested the relationship between a self-rated measure of "activity restriction," which encompasses both disability and handicap and adjustment to an amputation. They found that the extent to which an individual reports that his or her activities are restricted was significantly (.32) correlated with adjustment as defined by scores on the Center for Epidemiologic Studies–Depression Scale (Radloff, 1977). In contrast, several other measures that provided an approximate measure of impairment (e.g., level of amputation) had no direct relation to adjustment. According to the theory, when activities that are essential to an individual's identity and self-worth (i.e., self-care, other-care, work, recreation, and friendships) are threatened, the individual feels demoralized and eventually becomes depressed. Conversely, an individual may not have as much difficulty adjusting to an amputation if he or she has fewer activities that are restricted. For instance, someone with a sedentary lifestyle, a single-story home, a network of friends who are easy to access, a desk job, or leisure pursuits that do not involve extensive leg movement is less likely to have difficulty adjusting than someone with a more active lifestyle. In fact, in our practice we encounter many individuals who choose not to wear their prosthesis very often and spend most of their time in a wheelchair for the sake of convenience, without any appreciable impact on their chosen activities.

Age Related

Children and Adolescents

Research indicates that young children cope fairly well with the loss of a limb (Atala & Carter, 1992) and that adapting to limb loss becomes more difficult as age increases (Tebbi & Mallon, 1987). In a review article, Tyc (1992) identified several psychosocial factors that can contribute to a child's positive adjustment to a limb amputation, including family cohesion, good social support, and low levels of family conflict. High daily stressors, parental depression, and medical problems predicted poor adjustment (Tyc, 1992).

Assessment of adolescents' coping with limb loss should address concerns specific to their developmental level. Tebbi and Mallon (1987) reported that the primary concerns for early, middle, and late adolescents are body image, peer relationships, and independence and autonomy, respectively. Amputation during these sensitive developmental years can have a significant impact on social functioning, such as increased high school dropout rates because of concern over cosmetic appearances among teenagers with upper-limb amputations (Scotland & Galway, 1983). Prospects for normal long-term adjustment may be be more promising, as evidenced by a study that found no significant differences in marital status or number of offspring between those who had amputations prior to age 16 and a matched sample of the general population (Jorring, 1971).

Walters (1981) identified four primary stages through which an adolescent progresses when adjusting to an amputation: (a) impact, (b) retreat, (c) acknowledgment, and (d) reconstruction. Adolescents tend to feel depressed, discouraged, and angry (impact stage) and become more withdrawn and despondent (retreat stage) when they begin to mourn the loss of their limb. During the acknowledgment and reconstruction stages, they accept their new appearance and any related functional implications and express a willingness to reintegrate with their social system and participate in their rehabilitation.

Phantom limb sensations and PLP in children and adolescents have received little attention because of the popular belief that children rarely experience these phenomena (Krane & Heller, 1995; McGrath & Hillier, 1992). Krane and Heller disputed this common misperception by reporting phantom limb sensation in 100% and PLP in 82% of the children and adolescent patients who underwent amputations. Their study shows that PLP in children and adolescents tends to decrease in frequency and intensity over time more so than in adults.

Older Adults

The majority of people undergoing amputations are 60 years old or older (Buttenshaw, 1993). Older adults generally have more medical problems and are less physically resilient than are younger adults. Several studies indicate that older adults often discard their prostheses within months of rehabilitation training because the physical demands are high (e.g., Cutson & Bongiorni, 1996). Thus, when older adults undergo an amputation it often is complicated by several other ongoing coping issues related to physical frailty and chronic illness.

Three studies with adults have found limited support for the hypothesis that older adults (age 65+) with amputations are less prone to psychological adjustment problems compared with younger adults (Dunn, 1994; Frank et al., 1984; Williamson et al., 1994). Thus, one could theorize that older adults do not have as strong a reaction as younger adults because they view the amputation and attendant changes in mobility and body image as an undesirable but relatively "on-time" event (i.e., common for their age). However, our most recent study found a relation between older age and fewer body image concerns, but older adults with amputations were not found to be better adjusted in either study (Rybarczyk et al., 1992, 1995).

Williamson et al. (1994) hypothesized that activity restrictions are not as likely to lead to depression in older adults as in younger adults. They obtained a similar finding that older cancer patients were not as depressed as a matched group of younger cancer patients (Williamson & Schulz, 1995) and reasoned that, in general, older adults do not perceive losses in activity to be as critical because of age-related psychological changes. In part, they based this hypothesis on developmental theories (e.g., Neugarten, 1968) and posited that older adults move away from an overall emphasis on active mastery (i.e., directly changing the environment to suit one's needs and desires) and move toward a more passive–accommodative approach to the world. In addition, Schulz, Heckhausen, and O'Brien (1994) suggested that many older adults compensate for this loss of external control by exerting more "secondary control" over their internal (i.e., psychological) world.

Body Image

It has been noted that individuals with amputations must reconcile three different images of their body: (a) before the amputation, (b) without a prosthesis, and (c) with a prosthesis. Some individuals with amputations develop negative attitudes about themselves as a result of their altered body and consequent disability. As demonstrated in a previous study (Rybarczyk et al., 1995), individuals with amputations sometimes express embarrassment, shame, or even revulsion about their own bodies. We viewed this as self-stigmatization, in the sense that an individual is internalizing the social stigma that often is applied to individuals who are viewed as abnormal in some significant way. One depressed older woman with bilateral leg amputations stated it poignantly: "I feel like I am only half a person" (Rybarczyk, Nicholas, & Nyenhuis, 1997, p. 249). In a milder form, others report that they do not like to look at their prosthesis or leg and do not like it when others ask about their amputation.

In both studies (Rybarczyk et al., 1992, 1995), these negative self-perceptions were significantly predictive of depression, lower ratings of adjustment by the individual's prosthetist, and lower overall quality of life. Similarly, Williamson (1995) found that greater self-consciousness in public situations was significantly correlated with activity restriction among older adults with amputations. Furthermore, self-perceptions can have direct social effects because an individual's poor self-image is communicated to others in subtle ways (Winchell, 1995).

The feeling of self-stigma should be differentiated from grieving over a lost part of the self, which often is expressed by individuals with a new amputation. The feeling that something is missing tends to occur during the initial period of adjustment and then passes quickly, whereas feelings of self-stigma are as common among individuals who have had amputations for many years as they are for those who recently underwent an amputation (Rybarczyk et al., 1995). Although gender is known to play an important role in body image, in both studies we conducted there was also no relationship between gender and body image concerns, or adjustment in general (Rybarczyk et al., 1992, 1995). In only one study has adjustment to an amputation been correlated with gender; women were more likely to be depressed than were men (Kashani et al., 1983).

Interpersonal Factors

Perceived Negative Attitudes

The most common interpersonal issue expressed by individuals with amputations is that others view them as inferior in ways other than lower extremity functioning. Social psychologists refer to this "power of single characteristics to evoke inferences about a person" (Wright, 1983, p. 32) as the "spread effect." Numerous studies document that the nondisabled public holds a range of prejudicial attitudes toward people with disabilities (Yuker, 1994). Similarly, the well-meaning public frequently makes the mistake of assuming that individuals who undergo an amputation see it as a negative event. The cumulative effect of these attitudes can be a sense of isolation in individuals with a disability.

Being aware of the negative biases commonly held by the public and learning to not personalize these biases often is promoted as a healthy approach for individuals with disabilities (e.g., Winchell, 1995). This perspective is evident in the following comment: "In general, I find the attitudes of others to be more amusing than troubling. People who know me well don't even think of me as disabled, as an 'amputee'" (age 32; Rybarczyk et al., 1997, p. 247). Similarly, Chaiklin and Warfield (1973) conducted one of the earliest adjustment studies with 24 patients with amputations and found that those who denied the existence of any kind of a social stigma were less likely to make good progress in a rehabilitation program (no psychological measures of adjustment were included). The authors suggested that awareness is a first step toward "managing" or "neutralizing" stigma.

Despite the popular notion that it is adaptive to be aware of discrimination and stigma, our research found that individuals who reported being more stigmatized by others were more likely to be depressed (Rybarczyk et al., 1995). High levels of perceived social stigma also were linked to poorer overall adjustment, as rated by the individual's prosthetist. In effect, it seemed more adaptive to be less attuned to the negative biases that others might hold, regardless of whether these biases were taken personally. An alternative explanation of this finding would be that these respondents were accurately perceiving a greater degree of bias from others because individuals with disabilities who have depression may actually elicit much stronger negative stereotypes and reactions from people without disabilities (Elliott & Frank, 1990). If this is the case, then it would be important for psychologists and other professionals to help these individuals differentiate between the negative responses they are getting in relation to their mood from those they are getting as a result of their amputation.

Feeling Vulnerable to Victimization

In general, it has been noted that individuals with physical disabilities often present to rehabilitation professionals with issues related to fears regarding violence, property crime, and sexual victimization (Goodwin & Holmes, 1988). In particular, individuals with amputations frequently report a heightened sense of vulnerability to personal crime (Williamson, 1995). This can either be a specific concern (e.g., about being mugged) or a global sense of fear about "being taken advantage of" following an amputation. Some individuals experience a realistic concern that leads them to take appropriate precautions, whereas others have an exaggerated concern that results in excessive avoidant behaviors, a diminished quality of life, and poorer health (Ross, 1993). An unpublished analysis of the data from two previous studies (Rybarczyk et al., 1992, 1995) reveals that a large percentage of individuals reported feeling more "vulnerable to becoming a crime victim" and "less able to defend yourself." These individuals had significantly higher depression scores, greater social isolation, lower ratings of adjustment by their prosthetist, and an overall lower quality of life than those not feeling vulnerable. Likewise, Williamson (1995) also showed that feelings of vulnerability among older adults with amputations were strongly related to activity restriction ($r = .46$) and not feeling comfortable in public ($r = .37$).

The following brief list made by a 44-year-old woman who had an amputation in childhood illustrates that an increased sense of vulnerability is sometimes based on real events: "Had my purse snatched. Hit by a hit-and-run driver. Fell down two flights of stairs" (Rybarczyk et al., 1997, p. 249). This woman drew the conclusion that all of these events were somehow related to her amputation. Sexual victimization also can be a realistic concern, as was documented by a 48-year-old woman:

> A 'counselor' got a group of young women together with below knee amputations and I feel, in looking back, that he was using us. He later phoned me, took me to lunch, and tried to have an affair with me. I was young (in my 20s) and naive. (p. 249)

Fear of crime or other types of harm can become a significant factor in the development of excess disability. A kind of vicious cycle develops as the individual gradually becomes deconditioned, feels even more vulnerable, and then further restricts activities. The 44-year-old woman cited in the previous paragraph made it clear how feeling more vulnerable directly affects functional status: "Because of these and other experiences, my greatest fear is that something bad is going to happen to me in public. This has become a detriment to my progress" (p. 249).

Positive Coping

With one recent exception (Dunn, 1997), no research focuses on the qualities that are instrumental in a positive adjustment to an amputation. This bias is probably related to a strong emphasis in the stress and coping research on measuring negative affect as the exclusive outcome measure. An alternative theoretical model, sometimes referred to as "crisis theory," places an equal emphasis on the potential for learning and growth following adverse life events. In this vein, several pioneering researchers have explored the factors that contribute to positive adjustment to both disability (e.g., Wright, 1983) and life-threatening illness (e.g., Taylor, 1997).

The limited research on positive adjustment to disability has focused on the changes that take place in an individual's value system. Specific value changes that are thought to be necessary for positive adjustment include moving away from basing one's worth on either physical qualities or comparative value (e.g., "I am a valuable person because I'm a better athlete than most people"; Keany & Glueckauf, 1993; Wright, 1983). Positive adjustment occurs when the individual shifts to basing his or her self-worth on nonphysical qualities and on a sense of intrinsic value (e.g., "I'm as important as any other person because of my uniqueness"). This intrinsic-value perspective, for instance, is present when the individual comes to see his or her prosthesis in a positive light because of what it enables him or her to do rather than in a negative light because of its inferiority to the lost limb. Interestingly, these shifts in values parallel many of those proposed as being critical to the intrapsychic developmental changes of late adulthood. For example, Peck (1968) suggested that learning to value wisdom over physical powers is a healthy developmental change that begins at midlife.

Although the "search for meaning" in traumatic life events has been a long-standing theme in the nonscientific literature, it only recently has become a topic of study among behavioral scientists. A recent group of researchers addressing how individuals cope with life-threatening illness has established a relation between finding meaning and positive adaptation (e.g., Taylor, 1983). Individuals who find something positive (i.e., a silver lining) in an undesirable medical event appear to have a better adjustment and survive longer. The range of positive changes that occur as a result of serious illness include reordering priorities, deciding to spend more time on important relationships, having an enhanced sense of living in the present, seeing a need for more enjoyment in life, and seeing life as precious and fragile (Taylor, 1997). Rather than one point of view being linked to better adjustment, it appears that having any sense of positive personal change is an important factor in adaptation.

Dunn (1997) investigated the issue of finding positive meaning among a sample of predominantly well-educated male members of an amputee golf league. He found that 77% of the 138 study participants reported that something positive happened as a result of their amputation. There was a significantly lower rate of depression among those who reported that something positive happened compared to those who said that nothing positive happened. In a similar vein, Dunn confirmed the findings of an earlier study (Schulz, 1992) that individuals who were predisposed to optimism were more positively adjusted to their amputation. The following comments (Rybarczyk et al., 1997, p. 250) illustrate positive changes among individuals with amputations:

> Most of my experiences related to having an amputation have been positive, and often very humorous. I think it has enabled me to reach out to people in a special way, with a heightened sense of empathy and understanding. (age 46)

> *   *   *

> I think it takes great strength to go through what I and all amputees have gone through. I think people recognize that strength in me and appreciate me for it. (age 23)

> *   *   *

> I became a good basketball player because of my amputation. I had to push myself extra hard ever since I was a kid to prove that I could do it. It taught me determination and how to set goals. (age 19)

Dunn (1994) pointed out that this ability to find a silver lining in misfortune is sometimes viewed negatively, as evidence of living in a state of denial or holding on to an illusion. However, a body of research shows that positive illusions are in fact linked to psychological well-being in all individuals (e.g., Taylor & Brown, 1988) and appear to contribute to positive health outcomes in life-threatening illness. For example, individuals with AIDS who had a more realistic appraisal of their level of control of their disease actually had decreased survival time, after other factors were controlled (Reed, Kemeny, Taylor, Wang, & Visscher, 1994). Moreover, cognitive psychotherapists encourage depressed clients to "reframe" negative life events in a neutral or positive light, which can be construed as an effort to create positive illusions. Another example of positive reframing in its most dramatic form came from a patient with a bilateral amputation who said, "I'm feeling optimistic now because they've taken both my legs and now I've got nothing more to lose."

Another cognitive perspective issue that has been proposed as relevant to the psychological adjustment process to illness and disability is downward social comparison. Seeing oneself as lucky or blessed in comparison to others who have had greater misfortune has been linked to adjustment to a range of negative events (Taylor & Lobel, 1989). For example, a person with a below-knee amputation might consider himself lucky compared to a friend with an above-knee amputation or might feel lucky to have survived an accident. The comment of a 60-year-old man captured this perspective: "Since my amputation is a result of war, I consider myself fortunate to even be alive." On the other hand, when individuals who are in the midst of adverse events seek social support from others, affiliating with those who are more fortunate appears to be important for increasing hope and motivation (Taylor & Lobel, 1989). Thus, an individual who is striving to adjust to an amputation would want to establish supportive relationships with individuals who have already made a positive adjustment to their amputation.

Older adults also have a similar social comparison coping method available to them that may be instrumental in viewing an amputation as less of a misfortune than if it occurs earlier in life. Heckhausen and Brim (1997) showed that older adults, in general, use more social downgrading than do younger adults. This occurs when individuals see "most people their age" as having more problems than they do in a variety of domains of life (e.g., health, marriage, leisure). Furthermore, there is a tendency for this downgrading to be more pronounced in domains in which an individual has particular problems (e.g., mobility).

Religion and spirituality are now receiving greater recognition from psychologists as crucial factors in adjustment to chronic illness and disability (see Pargament, 1997). However, these variables only recently have been translated into useful clinical constructs that can be assessed with valid and reliable instruments. Rybarczyk and Nicholas were coinvestigators on a study examining the impact of religion and spirituality on the adjustment of 96 rehabilitation patients with a wide range of medical conditions (15 with amputations; Fitchett, Rybarczyk, DeMarco, & Nicholas, 1999). The correlational findings showed that various measures of religion and religious coping were positively correlated with adjustment and health. However, when these variables were included in a longitudinal analysis of adjustment over a 4-month period which controlled for the impact of other variables, no support was found for religiosity being predictive of better adjustment. In contrast, the results show that higher scores on a measure of negative religious coping (e.g., feeling angry at or estranged from God or one's religious community as a result of a negative event) were predictive of diminished physical recovery. This finding suggests that clinicians should inquire about these issues and address them when they are present. In fact, in this study, there was a strong positive correlation between psychologists asking about religion and spiritual issues and how helpful the patients found the counseling they received from that psychologist on the rehabilitation service.

Intervention Issues

Many factors in adjustment outlined in the previous section are not discussed with family members, friends, or health care providers; they are experienced privately by the individual with an amputation. This isolation often is enhanced by the fact that individuals with amputations do not necessarily reveal their disability to those around them—they can "pass" in the nondisabled world—partly because of the increasing effectiveness of prosthetic technology in creating a natural-looking leg. So the burden often falls on clinicians to begin a dialogue about adjustment issues. They can play a key role in normalizing the feelings and experiences of individuals with amputations.

Normalization may be accomplished by meeting and talking with others who have a similar physical condition and experiences. In addition, these contacts provide the opportunity to see how others find meaning in their amputation experience. Even though there are perhaps more than a million individuals with leg amputations in the United States, ironically they are largely "hidden" from each other because of prosthetic technology. Support groups are an important bridge to finding others who are in a similar situation. In the Chicago area alone, there are perhaps a dozen or more groups for individuals with amputations (e.g., a ski club, a family group). However, for reasons that are not apparent, individuals who need them the most often have trouble finding their way to them. In our second study (Rybarczyk et al., 1995), in the Chicago area, 50% of the patients who had significant levels of depression reported that they were not in a support group even though they wanted to be in one. One reason that some individuals may avoid support groups is the divergent psychological responses that can sometimes limit the amount of "common ground" in a group.

As an alternative to support groups, the self-help book *Coping With Limb Loss* (Winchell, 1995) can be an excellent first step for an individual with an amputation. This book includes a great deal of useful information for people with a new amputation as well as essential information for family members. Another excellent resource is the videotape series *Life Without a Limb: Amputees Speak Out* about adjustment to an amputation, which includes commentary by a psychologist and poignant testimony by individuals who have gone through the experience (Riggert & Butterbaugh, 1991). When significant levels of depression or anxiety are present, a referral should be made for individual psychotherapy.

Children

Pediatric psychology has much to offer children with medical illnesses, such as those with a medical illness or trauma meriting amputation. Because a review of child clinical psychology principles would be beyond the scope of this chapter, we focus on a few studies that specifically address amputation. Atala and Carter (1992) reviewed several treatments that effectively help children prepare for and cope with amputations, including play therapy, modeling, emotive imagery, relaxation techniques, and mastery and behavioral rehearsal. Denton (1988) strongly recommended formal parent support groups to assist the family in coping with the child's amputation.

Phantom Limb Pain

Psychologists can play an important role in helping patients cope with PLP. Many individuals with amputations feel embarrassed about phantom limb experiences and do not discuss these phenomena with their physicians. Surprisingly, one study reported that 69% of 2,700 veterans were told by their physicians, directly or implicitly, that their phantom pain was "just in their heads" (Sherman, Ernst, & Markowski, 1986, cited in Sherman, 1977). There are several strategies that can be used to prevent the occurrence of PLP. Altering surgical procedures by administering epidural agents prior to amputation has demonstrated limited but promising beneficial results (e.g., Bach, Noreng, & Tjellden, 1988). Sherman suggested that all patients be well informed prior to surgery about phantom limb sensations to prevent undue anxiety associated with this unfamiliar experience.

Although PLP sometimes can be prevented, many individuals with amputations continue to experience it. Treatments that temporarily reduce PLP are available, but there is only limited evidence to suggest that treatments are effective at a 1-year follow-up (Sherman & Tippens, 1982). Treatment is most beneficial when matched to the specific type of pain. For example, burning PLP is best targeted with interventions that increase blood flow to the residual limb (e.g., temperature biofeedback, thermal imagery), whereas cramping PLP is most responsive to treatments that decrease tension in the muscles of the limb (e.g., relaxation strategies, tension biofeedback; Sherman, 1977). No systematic studies exist comparing the effectiveness of various treatment strategies for PLP. In addition to biofeedback and relaxation strategies, Sherman and Tippens (1982) recommended considering pharmacological agents (e.g., muscle relaxants, vasodilators), sympathetic blocks, prosthetic refitting, transcutaneous electrical stimulation, and ultrasounds to help alleviate PLP. Unfortunately, some patients do not experience relief from any of the above treatments; these patients should be treated with the same cognitive–behavioral approaches used with patients with other types of chronic pain (e.g., Caudill, 1999).

Sexual Functioning

One area that is frequently not addressed by clinicians who work with people with amputations is sexual functioning. Williamson and Walters (1996) found that only 9% of the sample that they assessed were given any information or opportunities to ask questions about sexual functioning after an amputation, which mirrors a general neglect in health care settings of this critical aspect of health. Interventions aimed at decreasing the impact of an acquired disability on sexuality typically involve providing instruction on how to remain sexually active within the limitations of a disability and how to initiate a dialogue with a partner. Considerable dialogue with a partner often is necessary when an individual is newly disabled because of required changes in sexual positioning and the need to be reassured about continued sexual attractiveness. Increasing the comfort level of the health care provider is another effective target area for intervention.

Williamson and Walters (1996) found that older age predicted a more negative impact of an amputation on the individual's sexual activity. This may be explained by the possibility that the current cohort of older adults may not be as likely to engage in open discussions about sexual issues with their partners. In the absence of clinical intervention, this cohort may refrain from activity because they simply do not know how to negotiate changes in their sexual practice.

Future Directions

Given the comparative size of this disability group and the frequency of adjustment problems identified in studies, more attention is warranted from researchers studying psychological interventions for facilitating adjustment to an acquired disability. Investigators and funding agencies should focus on controlled clinical intervention studies. Our recommendation would be to develop and test a screening method directed at individuals who recently underwent an amputation. (The critical period when an individual begins to settle into a coping style appears to be at about the time of being fitted for a prosthesis). The screening would identify those who have a clinical depression or test positive for variables shown to be correlated with poor adjustment (e.g., activity restriction, negative body image, perceived social stigma). Cognitive–behavioral interventions appear to be highly appropriate for this population, given the cognitions (e.g., self-evaluation, perceptions of others) that have been linked to positive adjustment.

Another approach would be to develop a cost-effective group intervention modeled after successful mind–body well interventions aimed at facilitating coping and increasing self-management of chronic health problems (e.g., Caudill, Schnable, Zuttermeister, Benson, & Friedman, 1991; Lorig & Holman, 1993). These multicomponent group interventions typically include several of the following elements: instruction on the mind–body connection, relaxation training, cognitive–behavioral approaches to managing pain, anxiety and depression, problem-solving, effective communication and information on nutrition, sleep, exercise, and disease-specific topics. This type of approach would focus on issues that are common to all individuals with amputations, including ways to effectively deal with negative stereotypes. A sensible approach would be to provide the program at a prosthetics clinic, which often becomes the primary care setting for any amputation-related health issues, and to have the group coled by a psychologist and lay person with an amputation. This latter approach to leadership has been used with success in the arthritis self-help programs developed by Lorig and colleagues (e.g., Lorig & Holman, 1993).

Conclusion

Individuals with leg amputations constitute a larger, more diverse, and relatively "invisible" group compared to more publicized disabilities (e.g., spinal cord injury). Yet the available data suggest that they experience levels of depression and other adjustment problems that are comparable to those found among individuals with other life-changing acquired disabilities.

The diversity of medical, developmental, and other life circumstances leading up to an amputation results in a wide spectrum of psychological responses, ranging from viewing it as only a moderately significant event or even a life-improving surgery to seeing it as a catastrophic event. Several factors have been found to be related to poorer adjustment to an amputation: little or no history of significant medical problems prior to the amputation, the presence of long-term PLP, a significant degree of activity restriction resulting from the amputation, adolescence, persistent body image or social stigma concerns, and feeling vulnerable to victimization. Coping factors that may contribute to positive adjustment to an amputation include finding positive aspects of the experience, using humor, measuring oneself against those who are less fortunate (downward social comparison), having someone who is well adjusted to a similar disability as a role model, and seeing oneself as doing well compared with most others in one's age group.

Psychosocial interventions for individuals with new amputations should include several of the following components: matching the person to a community online support group, or an individual peer counselor with an amputation who can serve as a role model of adjustment, providing information that helps normalize the many potential feelings and stages associated with limb loss, providing tools for self-monitoring symptoms of depression and potential treatment referrals for any depression that may occur after discharge, and providing prompt pain treatment interventions for individuals who have PLP that lasts longer than a few weeks. Families of children and adolescents should be provided with similar information. Much of the information presented may not be used until a later date when the individual faces new adjustment problems or when he or she reaches a point of being psychologically ready for it.

The majority of individuals with amputations are well adjusted and have come to see their amputation not as a defining characteristic but as one of many challenges faced in their lives. Psychologists can still provide a service to these individuals by helping to empower them to take a consumer approach to such issues—obtaining the best prosthesis technology possible and working to increase accessibility where it is limited.

References

American Amputee Foundation, Inc. (1997). *Fact sheet*. Little Rock, AK: Author.

Atala, K. D., & Carter, B. D. (1992). Pediatric limb amputation: Aspects of coping and psychotherapeutic intervention. *Child Psychiatry and Human Development, 23*, 117–130.

Bach, S., Noreng, M. F., & Tjellden, N. U. (1988). Phantom limb pain in amputees during the first 12 months following limb amputation, after preoperative lumbar epidural blockade. *Pain, 33,* 291–301.

Bradway, J. K., Malone, J. M., Racy, J., Leal, J. M., & Poole, J. (1984). Psychological adaptation to amputation: An overview. *Orthotics and Prosthetics, 38,* 46–50.

Buchanan, D. C., & Mandel, A. R. (1986). The prevalence of phantom limb experiences in amputees. *Rehabilitation Psychology, 31,* 183–188.

Buttenshaw, P. (1993). Rehabilitation of the elderly lower limb amputee. *Reviews in Clinical Gerontology, 3,* 69–84.

Carlen, P. L., Wall, P. D., Nadvorna, H., & Steinbach, T. (1978). Phantom limbs and related phenomena in recent traumatic amputations. *Neurology, 28,* 211–217.

Carrington, A. L., Mawdsley, S. K. V., Morley, M., Kincey, J., & Boulton, A. J. M. (1996). Psychological status of diabetic people with or without lower limb disability. *Diabetes Research and Clinical Practice, 32,* 19–25.

Cassileth, B. R., Lusk, E. J., Strouse, T. B., Miller, D. S., Brown, L. L., Cross, P. A., & Tenaglia, A. N. (1984). Psychosocial status in chronic illness: A comparative analysis of six diagnostic groups. *New England Journal of Medicine, 311,* 506–511.

Caudill, M. (1999). *Managing pain before it manages you.* New York: Guilford Press.

Caudill, M., Schnable, R., Zuttermeister, P., Benson, H., & Friedman, R. (1991). Decreased clinic use by chronic pain patients: Response to behavioral medicine intervention. *Clinical Journal of Pain, 7,* 305–310.

Chaiklin, H., & Warfield, M. (1973). Stigma management and amputee rehabilitation. *Rehabilitation Literature, 34,* 162–167.

Clark, G. S., Blue, B., & Bearer, J. B. (1983). Rehabilitation of the elderly amputee. *Journal of the American Geriatrics Society, 31,* 439–448.

Cutson, T. M., & Bongiorni, D. R. (1996). Rehabilitation of the older lower limb amputee: A brief review. *Journal of the American Geriatric Society, 44,* 1388–1393.

Dembo, T., Leviton, G. L., & Wright, B. A. (1975). Adjustment to misfortune: A problem of social–psychological rehabilitation. *Rehabilitation Psychology, 22,* 1–100.

Denton, J. R. (1988). Traumatic amputation in childhood: Functional psychosocial aspects. *Loss, Grief, and Care, 2,* 1–10.

Dunn, D. S. (1994). Positive meaning and illusion following disability: Reality negotiation, normative interpretation, and value change. *Journal of Social Behavior and Personality, 9*(5), 123–138.

Dunn, D. S. (1997). Well-being following amputation: Salutary effects of positive meaning, optimism, and control. *Rehabilitation Psychology, 41,* 285–302.

Elliott, T., & Frank, R. G. (1990). Social and interpersonal responses to depression and disability. *Rehabilitation Psychology, 35,* 135–147.

Fitchett, G., Rybarczyk, B., DeMarco, G., & Nicholas, J. J. (1999). The role of religion in medical rehabilitation outcomes: A longitudinal study. *Rehabilitation Psychology, 44,* 333–353.

Frank, R. G., Kashani, J. H., Kashani, S. R., Wonderlich, S. A., Umlauf, R. L., & Ashkanazi, G. S. (1984). Psychological response to amputation as a function of age and time since amputation. *British Journal of Psychiatry, 144,* 493–497.

Frierson, R. L., & Lippmann, S. B. (1987). Psychiatric consultation for acute amputees. *Psychosomatics, 28,* 183–189.

Gerhards, F., Florin, I., & Knapp, T. (1984). The impact of medical, reeducational, and psychological variables on rehabilitation outcome in amputees. *International Journal of Rehabilitation Research, 7,* 379–388.

Goodwin, L. R., & Holmes, G. E. (1988). Counseling the crime victim: A guide for rehabilitation counselors. *Journal of Applied Rehabilitation Counseling, 19,* 42–47.

Heckhausen, J., & Brim, O. G. (1997). Perceived problems of self and others: Self-protection by social downgrading throughout adulthood. *Psychology and Aging, 12,* 610–619.

Heinemann, A. W., Bulka, M., & Smetak, S. (1988). Attributions and disability acceptance following traumatic injury: A replication and extension. *Rehabilitation Psychology, 33,* 195–199.

Jensen, T. S., Krebs, B., Nielsen, J., & Rasmussen, P. (1984). Non-painful phantom limb phenomena in amputees: Incidence, clinical characteristics and temporal course. *Acta Neurologica Scandinavia, 70,* 407–414.

Jensen, T. S., Krebs, B., Nielsen, J., & Rasmussen, P. (1985). Immediate and long-term phantom limb pain in amputees: Incidence, clinical characteristics, and relationship to pre-amputation limb pain. *Pain, 21,* 267–278.

Jorring, K. (1971). Amputation in children. *Acta Orthepedica Scandinavia, 42,* 178–186.

Kashani, J. H., Frank, R. G., Kashani, S. R., & Wonderlich, S. A. (1983). Depression among amputees. *Journal of Clinical Psychiatry, 44,* 256–258.

Katz, J. (1992). Psychophysiological contributions to phantom limb. *Canadian Journal of Psychiatry, 37,* 282–298.

Keany, K. C., & Glueckauf, R. L. (1993). Disability and value change: An overview and reanalysis of acceptance of loss theory. *Rehabilitation Psychology, 38,* 199–210.

Krane, E. J., & Heller, L. B. (1995). The prevalence of phantom sensation and pain in pediatric amputees. *Journal of Pain and Symptom Management, 10,* 21–29.

Lindesay, J. E. (1985). Multiple pain complaints in amputees. *Journal of Rehabilitation and Social Medicine, 78,* 452–455.

Lorig, K., & Holman, H. R. (1993). Arthritis self-management studies: A twelve-year review. *Health Education Quarterly, 20,* 17–28.

MacBride, A., Rogers, J., Whylie, B., & Freeman, S. J. J. (1980). Psychosocial factors in the rehabilitation of elderly amputees. *Psychosomatics, 21,* 258–265.

McGrath, P. A., & Hillier, L. M. (1992). Phantom limb sensations in adolescents: A case study to illustrate the utility of sensation and pain logs in pediatric clinical practice. *Journal of Pain and Symptom Management, 7,* 46–53.

Medhat, A., Huber, P. M., & Medhat, M. A. (1990). Factors that influence the level of activities in persons with lower extremity amputation. *Rehabilitation Nursing, 15,* 13–18.

National Center for Health Statistics. (1991). [National Health Interview Survey obtained from the Orthotics and Prosthetics National Office]. Unpublished raw data.

Neugarten, B. (1968). *Personality in middle and late life.* New York: Atherton Press.

Pargament, K. I. (1997). *The psychology of religion and coping: Theory, research and practice.* New York: Guilford Press.

Parkes, C. M. (1975). Psycho-social transitions: Comparison between reactions to loss of a limb and loss of a spouse. *British Journal of Psychiatry, 127,* 204–210.

Peck, R. C. (1968). Psychological development in the second half of life. In B. L. Neugarten (Ed.), *Middle age and aging* (pp. 88–92). Chicago: University of Chicago Press.

Pell, J. P., Donnan, P. T., Fowkes, F. G. R., & Ruckley, C. V. (1993). Quality of life following lower limb amputation for peripheral arterial disease. *European Journal of Vascular Surgery, 7,* 448–451.

Radloff, L. S. (1977). The CES-D scale: A self-report depression scale for research in the general population. *Applied Psychological Measurement, 1,* 385–401.

Reed, G. M., Kemeny, M. E., Taylor, S. E., Wang, H.-Y. J., & Visscher, B. R. (1994). "Realistic acceptance" as a predictor of decreased survival time in gay men with AIDS. *Health Psychology, 13,* 299–307.

Riggert, S., & Butterbaugh, R. (Producers). (1991). *Life without a limb: Amputees speak out* [Videotape]. Louisville, KY: Frazier Rehabilitation Center.

Ross, C. E. (1993). Fear of victimization and health. *Journal of Quantitative Criminology and Health, 9,* 159–175.

Rybarczyk, B., Nicholas, J. J., & Nyenhuis, D. (1997). Coping with a leg amputation: Integrating research and clinical practice. *Rehabilitation Psychology, 42*(3), 241–256.

Rybarczyk, B., Nyenhuis, D. L., Nicholas, J. J., Cash, S., & Kaiser, J. (1995). Body image, perceived social stigma, and the prediction of psychosocial adjustment to leg amputation. *Rehabilitation Psychology, 40,* 95–110.

Rybarczyk, B. D., Nyenhuis, D. L., Nicholas, J. J., Schulz, R., Alioto, R. J., & Blair, C. (1992). Social discomfort and depression in a sample of adults with leg amputations. *Archives of Physical Medicine and Rehabilitation, 73,* 1169–1173.

Schulz, R. (1992, November). *Limb amputation among the elderly.* Paper presented at the annual meeting of the Gerontological Society of America, Washington, D.C.

Schulz, R., Heckhausen, J., & O'Brien, A. T. (1994). Control and disablement process in the elderly. *Journal of Social Behavior and Personality, 9*(5), 139–152.

Scotland, T. R., & Galway, H. R. (1983). A long-term review of children with congenital and acquired upper limb deficiency. *Journal of Bone and Joint Surgery, 65-B,* 346–349.

Sherman, R. (1977). *Phantom pain.* New York: Plenum Press.

Sherman, R., & Sherman, C. (1983). Prevalence and characteristics of chronic phantom limb pain among American veterans: Results of a trial survey. *American Journal of Physical Medicine, 62,* 227–238.

Sherman, R., Sherman, C., & Parker, L. (1984). Chronic phantom and stump pain among American veterans: Results of a survey. *Pain, 18,* 83–95.

Sherman, R., & Tippens, J. (1982). Suggested guidelines for the treatment of phantom limb pain. *Orthopedics, 5,* 1595–1600.

Shukla, G. D., Sahu, S. C., Tripathi, R. P., & Gupta, D. K. (1982). A psychiatric study of amputees. *British Journal of Psychiatry, 141,* 50–53.

Taylor, S. E. (1983). Adjustment to threatening events: A theory of cognitive adaptation. *American Psychologist, 38,* 1161–1173.

Taylor, S. E. (1997, April). *Psychosocial factors in the course of disease.* Paper presented at the annual meeting of the Society for Behavioral Medicine, San Francisco, CA.

Taylor, S. E., & Brown, J. (1988). Illusions and well-being: A social psychological perspective on mental health. *Psychological Bulletin, 103,* 193–210.

Taylor, S. E., & Lobel, M. (1989). Social comparison activity under threat: Downward evaluation and upward contacts. *Psychological Review, 96,* 569–575.

Tebbi, C. K., & Mallon, J. C. (1987). Long-term psychosocial outcome among cancer amputees in adolescence and early adulthood. *Journal of Psychosocial Oncology, 5,* 69–82.

Tyc, V. L. (1992). Psychosocial adaptation of children and adolescents with limb deficiencies: A review. *Clinical Psychology Review, 12,* 275–291.

Walters, J. (1981). Coping with a leg amputation. *American Journal of Nursing, 81*(7), 1349–1352.

Waters, R. L., Perry, J., Antonelli, D., & Hislop, H. (1976). Energy cost of walking of amputees: The influence of level of amputation. *Journal of Bone and Joint Surgery, 58-A,* 42–46.

Weiss, S. A., & Lindell, B. (1986). Phantom limb pain and etiology of amputation in unilateral lower extremity amputees. *Journal of Pain and Symptom Management, 11,* 3–17.

Williamson, G. M. (1995). Restriction of normal activities among older adult amputees: The role of public self-consciousness. *Journal of Clinical Geropsychology, 1,* 229–242.

Williamson, G. M., & Schulz, R. (1995). Activity restriction mediates the association between pain and depressed affect: A study of younger and older adult cancer patients. *Psychology and Aging, 10,* 369–378.

Williamson, G. M., Schulz, R., Bridges, M. W., & Behan, A. M. (1994). Social and psychological factors in adjustment to limb amputation. *Journal of Social Behavior and Personality, 9,* 249–268.

Williamson, G. M., & Walters, A. S. (1996). Perceived impact of limb amputation on sexual activity: A study of adult amputees. *Journal of Sex Research, 33,* 221–230.

Wilson, A. B. (1989). *Limb prosthetics* (6th ed.). New York: Demos.

Winchell, E. (1995). *Coping with limb loss.* Garden City Park, NY: Avery.

World Health Organization. (1980). *International classification of impairments, disabilities, and handicaps. A manual of classification relating to the consequences of disease.* Geneva: Author.

Wright, B. A. (1983). *Physical disability: A psychological approach.* New York: Harper & Row.

Yuker, H. E. (1994). Variables that influence attitudes toward persons with disabilities: Conclusions from the data. *Journal of Social Behavior and Personality, 9*(5), 3–22.

3

Traumatic Brain Injury

Mitchell Rosenthal and Joseph Ricker

Within the past 2 decades, traumatic brain injury (TBI) has become a primary diagnostic entity treated in medical rehabilitation facilities. Only 7–10% of inpatient rehabilitation unit patients have TBIs, but specialized brain injury rehabilitation programs at the inpatient and postacute level are far more numerous for them than are accredited rehabilitation programs for spinal cord injury (SCI) or chronic pain patients (Commission on Accreditation of Rehabilitation Facilities [CARF], 1997). Given the high incidence of TBI, estimated recently to be 102.1/100,000 population in the United States (Centers for Disease Control and Prevention [CDC], 1997), and the common pattern of neurobehavioral, cognitive, and psychosocial disabilities that result, it is not surprising that psychologists play an important role in the treatment of this multifaceted disability.

Epidemiology of Traumatic Brain Injury

The research literature describing the epidemiology of TBI is somewhat confusing, in part because of differing definitions of TBI. In this chapter, TBI is defined as it is in the Traumatic Brain Injury Model Systems National Database (Harrison-Felix, Newton, Hall, & Kreutzer, 1996): "Damage to brain tissue caused by an external mechanical force, as evidenced by loss of consciousness due to brain trauma, posttraumatic amnesia (PTA), skull fracture, or objective neurological findings that can be reasonably be attributed to TBI on physical examination or mental status examination" (p. 2). The incidence of brain injury has been estimated from 100–392/100,000 U.S. population (Kraus & McArthur, 1998), with the most often-cited estimate of 200/100,000 population. Analysis of the National Health Interview Survey (NHIS) data indicate that approximately 1.9 million Americans sustain a TBI each year (Collins, 1993). Furthermore, an estimated 50,000–75,000 experience moderate to severe disability resulting from the TBI. Recent estimates, however, by the CDC (Thurman, Alverson, Dunn, Guerrero, & Sniezek, 1999) suggest that the overall incidence rate has diminished to less than 100/100,000, possibly because

The writing of this chapter was supported in part by the National Institute on Disability and Rehabilitation Research, U.S. Department of Education Grant H133A20016.

individuals with very mild injuries tend to be seen in emergency rooms and released without being hospitalized. Given the pressures in recent years to decrease inpatient bed use, this trend is likely to continue. Another factor that may be responsible for decreased incidence is the increased use of seat belts, air bags, child car seat restraints, bicycle helmets, or other protective devices. In terms of prevalence, Kraus and McArthur (1998) used an estimation formula and found that the total new cases of disability resulting from brain injury in the United States in 1995 would be 73,152, or 28 cases per 100,000 population.

TBI is related to a variety of key demographic and etiologic factors. Recent studies have confirmed that the peak age for TBI remains between 15 and 24 (176.7/100,000) and over age 75 years (186.2/100,000; CDC, 1997). Approximately 2–3 times more male than female individuals sustain TBIs. Some studies have reported a significantly greater incidence of TBI in ethnic minority populations (Cooper et al., 1983; Whitman, Coonley-Hoganson, & Desai, 1984), but concerns regarding the accuracy of the data have been noted (Kraus & McArthur, 1998) and are related to inconsistent hospital reporting procedures. However, lower socioeconomic status has been found to be a risk factor for a greater incidence of TBI (Collins, 1993). Primary etiologies for TBI include motor vehicle crashes, assaults, falls, and sports or recreation-related injuries.

Those who work directly with TBI often note that individuals who experience a TBI are not representative of the general population in a number of ways. First, the incidence of positive blood alcohol findings (found to exceed 50% in most studies and often significantly beyond the legal intoxication limit) in motor vehicle crashes and violence-related TBI represents an important risk factor (Kraus, Fife, Conroy, & Nourjah, 1989). This observation is likely as relevant in cases of illicit drug use. Second, it appears that a high proportion of individuals who sustain TBI have a criminal history. For example, Kreutzer, Marwitz, and Witol (1995) found that 20% of 327 consecutive admissions for TBI had a preinjury criminal record; in a smaller study, Thomsen (1987) reported that almost half of her patients (20/40 cases) had a preinjury history of problems with the law.

Initial Presentations

Nature and Pathology of Injuries

The role of the rehabilitation psychologist or neuropsychologist is not to determine the nature of the underlying neuropathology. No neuropsychological tests or patterns are typical for or indicative of any particular neuropathology following TBI. Rather, the psychologist may incorporate neuropathologic issues and theories in her or his overall formulation of the critical dependent variables of functional disability status and restoration of function. To do this, it is important for psychologists who work with survivors of TBI to have a basic understanding of the possible neurobiological substrates underlying brain injury.

The neuropathological effects of TBI can be grossly classified as anatomic or biochemical. This distinction may not be useful clinically, however, as anatomic and biochemical changes may coexist and interact. For example, a sudden impact to the head may result in a localized contusion (an anatomic event) impact depolarization of neurons (a biochemical event), which may lead to toxic levels of calcium influx (further biochemical events), which may result in eventual diffuse changes to a nerve cell's axon (further anatomic changes). Given these potential interactions, it may be more useful clinically to conceptualize neuropathological events as primary or secondary.

Primary Injuries

The brain is suspended within cerebrospinal fluid, surrounded by three layers of meninges (pia, arachnoid, and dura) and encased in the skull. In general, the human brain is very well protected from everyday mechanical forces. Mechanical trauma to the head can, however, cause the brain to become damaged. One obvious way in which this can occur is from the skull and brain being penetrated, for example, from a gunshot wound or assault with an object such as a screwdriver. Blunt trauma to the head may also result in penetrating brain injury as the result of a skull fracture that displaces pieces of bone into cerebral tissue. Although penetrating injuries often exert their greatest neurobehavioral effects in a manner consistent with their anatomic focus, there may also be widespread effects in other brain regions.

In addition to actual penetration of the skull case, the mechanical forces to which the brain may be subjected during a fall, assault, or motor vehicle accident may cause structural damage to the brain itself without causing penetration or damage to the skull. Sufficient inertial loading (i.e., the speed at which the head—and therefore the brain—is moving; often referred to as *acceleration*) combined with a sudden stop (i.e., head impact or abrupt change in the direction of the head's movement; often referred to as *deceleration*) may cause the brain to come into abrupt contact with one or more internal surfaces of the skull. Because the posterior areas within the skull are relatively smooth, primary contusion injuries in the posterior portions of the brain are unusual in deceleration events (although direct trauma to the posterior regions of the head can result in posterior trauma). More frequently, however, the anterior portions of the brain (the frontal poles, orbitofrontal cortex, and anterior temporal lobes) become contused against the bony prominence of the skull (e.g., sphenoid wing; temporal fossa). This may result in localized contusions of the cerebral cortex and immediate underlying white matter.

Focal lesions and cortical contusions are not the only forms of pathology in TBI and may not represent the most debilitating of the neuropathologic outcomes. The brain can move within the skull, which may result in twisting of ascending and descending axonal pathways. Furthermore, commisural fibers (e.g., the corpus callosum) and other fiber tracts (e.g., the fornices) may also become stretched or torn as the result of differential deceleration of the brain within the skull case. This widespread disruption of axonal tracts is typically referred to as *diffuse axonal injury* (DAI) and is thought to underlie many of the chronic neurocognitive and neurobehavioral consequences of TBI.

In earlier conceptualizations of DAI (e.g., Strich, 1961), axonal injuries were assumed to be immediate and the sole result of direct mechanical forces that would tear or shear axons. It has been more recently established, however, that the permanent neuropathology of DAI occurs many hours or days following the event as the result of biochemical cascades (Novack, Dillon, & Jackson, 1996). DAI may mediate many of the long-term neurobehavioral phenomena observed following moderate and severe levels of brain injury by causing widespread disconnection of brain regions.

Secondary Injuries

Edema is a frequent secondary complication of moderate and severe brain injuries. Edema occurs when there is an increase in water concentration within cells, between cells, or both. It may be caused by direct mechanical trauma, or it may be the result of altered vascular permeability. Consequently, increased intracranial pressure (ICP) can result, which may lead to further cerebral disruption and damage.

Cardiac and respiratory changes can also result from either TBI or other aspects of trauma that resulted in TBI. For example, blunt force to the chest during a motor vehicle accident may result in cardiac or pulmonary contusions. Cardiopulmonary dysfunction or damage may then lead to additional cerebral disruption from cardiac arrest or hypoxia. Transient hypertension may follow TBI secondary to the hyperrelease of catecholamines (endogenous neurotransmitters that mediate a host of functions). TBI survivors with tracheotomies may also develop pulmonary and other respiratory complications.

Infection may follow a head injury, often as the result of septic skull penetration. In addition to systemic effects, infections may also lead to focal processes (e.g., cerebral abscesses) that may exacerbate cognitive impairment (or produce novel cognitive impairment).

Following TBI there is a hyperrelease of the catecholamines norepinephrine and epinephrine. This can result in changes in glucose, cortisol, and thyroid hormones. Furthermore, because of the mechanical forces on the brain the pituitary may become damaged or dysfunctional. The infundibulum or stalk of the pituitary may become stretched, resulting in mechanical deformation and possible shearing.

Seizures may follow focal contusions or penetrating injuries. They are not known to be caused by DAI. Seizure vulnerability and prophylaxis are frequently discussed in TBI care, and occurrence varies with severity of injury. In a population-based study, 5-year cumulative probabilities for seizure following brain injury were as follows: after severe brain injury, 10%;

after moderate brain injury, 1%; and after mild brain injury, <1% (Annegers, Hauser, Coan, & Rocca, 1998).

Consciousness and Coma

In general, loss of consciousness is a typical finding following significant TBI. Exceptions occur in instances of focal injuries, and loss of consciousness does not always occur in penetrating injuries. Nevertheless, although formal *coma* (defined as an absence of eye opening, no following of commands, and no understandable speech; also defined by a Glasgow Coma Scale [GCS; Teasdale & Jennett, 1974] score of 8 or less) need not be present in TBI, the depth of lost consciousness is a generally accepted indicator of brain injury severity, particularly in cases of suspected diffuse cerebral injury. The use of length of coma and duration of unconsciousness in predicting outcome is discussed later in this chapter.

Vegetative States and Minimal Consciousness

About 20% of severely injured TBI survivors remain at an unresponsive level at 30 days postinjury (Braakman, Jennett, & Minderhoud, 1988). Although the term *coma* is used frequently in the popular parlance, coma can last for only several weeks. An individual who has spontaneous sleep–wake cycles but no apparent level of conscious awareness is typically said to be in a persistent vegetative state (PVS). PVS patients are observed to maintain relatively normal sleep–wake patterns. This may be particularly troubling for family members who observe that the patient "appears" awake but does not interact. Because of this wakefulness, family members may also be susceptible to believing that the patient is conscious and aware.

Posttraumatic Amnesia

PTA refers to the period of time following head trauma during which an individual demonstrates an impaired sensorium. It has been suggested that length of PTA is a useful clinical indicator of outcome when used in combination with immediate injury severity variables (Levin, Benton, & Grossman, 1982). Although PTA is useful when properly measured and tracked regularly during the course of recovery (e.g., using the Galveston Orientation and Amnesia Test [GOAT]; Levin, O'Donnell, & Grossman, 1979), retrospective estimates of PTA by patients or clinicians are unreliable (Gronwall & Wrightson, 1981). Many factors that are independent of brain injury can interfere with even measurement or estimation of PTA (e.g., alcohol or other chemical substances at the time of injury; pain distraction caused by other injuries; metabolic disturbances from other physical injuries; emotional trauma or shock at the time of the accident; retelling of the story with inaccuracies accumulating over time).

Medical Complications and Neurocognitive and Neurobehavioral Sequelae

Although the primary injury in TBI is typically the brain injury itself, it is important to be aware that there are many additional medical problems that often occur. The comorbid complications can not only exacerbate the primary brain injury, but can also interfere with goal attainment in the rehabilitation process. (For more information, see Hammond & McDeavitt, 1999; or Zafonte, Elovic, O'Dell, Mysiw, & Watanabe, 1999.)

Because of the differing etiologies and diffuse nature of brain dysfunction following a given TBI, it is difficult to predict the specific neuropsychological sequelae for a given individual. In general, the following types of cognitive impairments are often observed following TBI: deficits in arousal, attention, memory, capacity for new learning; problems in initiating, maintaining, organizing, or engaging in goal-directed behavior; self-monitoring and awareness of deficits; impaired language and communication; visuoperceptual deficits; and agitation, aggression, disinhibition, and depression. The nature, severity, and chronicity of these deficits are highly variable between individuals and dependent on the interaction between a variety of factors, including the nature of the brain dysfunction; time since injury; preinjury neuropsychological and psychological status; family support; and receptivity of the physical, psychological, and social environments. A challenge for psychologists in TBI rehabilitation is to select those measures that are both sensitive and specific to the effects of TBI and show the strongest predictive relationship with acute and long-term outcome.

Measurement in TBI Rehabilitation

The psychologist working in brain injury must be familiar with several scales and measures. Even though many of these indices are not the responsibility of psychologists to apply to patients, having a working knowledge of each is critical to provide valid and clinically meaningful interpretations and predictions of functional status and future outcome.

Glasgow Coma Scale

The GCS, an ordinal scale, assesses a patient's behavioral responses within the domains of eye movement, motor functions, and vocalization (Teasdale & Jennett, 1974). The total score ranges from 3 to 15, with lower scores representing increased depth of unconsciousness. Clinically, scores of 13 to 15 are considered to represent mild injury. Scores from 9 to 12 are used to classify moderate injuries. Scores of 8 and below typically represent severe brain injuries. In general, the GCS is an adequate gross predictor of outcome at 6-months postinjury (Jennett & Teasdale, 1981). There is some degree of variability in the predictive power of the GCS, however. For example, individuals with an initial GCS in the 13 to 15 range who also demonstrate focal lesions on neuroimaging often have outcomes more comparable with patients with GCS totals in the 9 to 12 range (Williams, Levin, & Eisenberg, 1990). Furthermore, an initial GCS may be lowered by factors other than the primary brain injury (e.g., the presence of significant amounts of alcohol in one's system at the time of injury; experiencing an acute medical crisis; Zafonte, Hammond, & Peterson, 1996).

A modification to the GCS, the Glasgow–Liege Score, has been used to improve outcome classification on the basis of initial presentation (Born, Albert, Hans, & Bonnal, 1985). The Glasgow–Liege assesses several brainstem reflexes in addition to gross verbal, motor, and eye-opening responses.

Rancho Los Amigos Levels of Cognitive Functioning Scale

The RLAS (Hagen, Malkmus, & Durham, 1972) is an ordinal scale with anchor points reflecting levels of behavior and gross cognition. The RLAS ranges from Level I (no response) to Level VIII (purposeful and appropriate behavior). This scale is based on behavioral observations and is not as useful in clinical prediction as other measures.

Galveston Orientation and Amnesia Test

The GOAT (Levin et al., 1979) was designed to be a more objective way of measuring presence and depth of PTA. The GOAT asks patients to provide detailed information related not only to temporal orientation (day, date, place, time of day), but also to recall of the trauma including events immediately prior to and following its onset.

Glasgow Outcome Scale

The GOS (Jennett & Bond, 1975) is an ordinal scale that provides a global evaluation of outcome. Patients are rated from 1 to 5 (1 = *death*; 2 = *persistent vegetative state*; 3 = *severe disability*; 4 = *moderate disability*; 5 = *good recovery*). The GOS is widely used and is related to the GCS and PTA in terms of outcome prediction (Jennett & Teasdale, 1981).

Disability Rating Scale

The DRS (Rappaport, Hall, Hopkins, Belleza, & Cope, 1982) was developed for the purpose of assessing disability in the continuum of care from coma to community. It has been used in many studies of TBI and has been shown to correlate with the GOS (Rappaport et al., 1982). The DRS has a greater psychometric range than the GOS, however, and has been demonstrated to have interrater reliabilities between .97 and .98 (Gouvier, Blanton, Laporte, & Nepomuceno, 1987).

Functional Independence Measure

The FIM (Hamilton, Granger, Sherwin, Zielenzy, & Tashman, 1987) is an 18-item ordinal scale designed to provide a standard measure of functional independence, regardless of specific disability. The FIM can be divided into two subscales: Motor (self-care, sphincter control, mobility) and Cognition (communication, psychosocial adjustment, cognitive function). A recent study has validated the use of the FIM with the TBI population (Corrigan, Smith-Knapp, & Granger, 1997). However, the FIM and similar functional rating scales may not be specific enough to index particular cognitive or other neurobehavioral changes, particularly beyond the inpatient rehabilitation phase of recovery from TBI.

Community Integration Questionnaire

The CIQ (Willer, Rosenthal, Kreutzer, Gordon, & Rempel, 1993) was developed to assess the degree of disability experienced by an individual with a TBI on return to community living. It is a 15-item scale that can be divided into three subscales: Home Integration, Social Integration, and Productivity. The CIQ has proven to be useful in research efforts as a measure of quality of life and level of social and vocational functioning, but it has received some criticism as to its psychometric properties, sensitivity to change over time, and reliability for individuals with severe cognitive deficits (Dijkers, 1997).

Levels of Brain Injury Severity and Corresponding Presentations

A brain injury that is classified initially as severe does not invariably result in total and permanent disability. Of note also is the degree of variability in outcome that may occur. For example, a brain injury that is initially classified as severe may result in a variety of outcomes, from death to surprisingly good recovery. Prolonged impairments in consciousness (i.e., coma and PTA) are common following severe TBI. Approximately 30–50% of individuals who sustain an initially severe TBI die; of those who survive severe TBI, about 20% remain in an unresponsive state 30 days postinjury (Braakman et al., 1988). The initial recovery process may be prolonged, and these individuals may not be amenable to extensive psychometric assessment or higher level rehabilitation interventions during their acute rehabilitation stay.

Individuals who sustain brain injuries of moderate initial severity may show a great deal of variability in their presentation. For example, individuals who sustain relatively mild brain injuries (in terms of GCS score) but who also have focal lesions (e.g., from a discrete penetrating injury such as that inflicted by an ice pick) are often classified as having sustained moderate TBI, but these individuals typically have good recovery.

In recent years, mild brain injury has been a topic of growing interest as well as controversy. This has no doubt been prompted by increased research, increased numbers of outpatient brain injury rehabilitation programs, and increased personal injury litigation. From a prospective and empirical viewpoint, the literature suggests that the usual course following mild head impact is that of complete or nearly complete recovery (Binder, 1997). Nonetheless, there appears to be a small percentage of individuals whose symptoms persist well beyond what empirical and clinical research would predict. In a meta-analytic review, Binder, Rohling, and Larrabee (1997) suggested that little of neurobehavioral phenomena reported following mild head impact could be attributed to brain damage. Yet there appears to be a minority of individuals who continue to report symptoms and disability for many months or years following mild head trauma. Cullum and Thompson (1997), who provided a thoughtful review of the literature, concluded that multiple factors must be considered when interpreting cognitive and emotional symptoms after mild head impact.

Assessment and Intervention

Role of the Psychologist in the Acute Stage

At the acute stage of recovery, the primary focus of care is at the level of sustaining life and addressing very early medical issues and initial consultations and referrals. Nevertheless, rehabilitation psychologists can play an important role. Psychologists can use early assessment instruments (e.g., GOAT, Levin et al., 1979; Coma–Near-Coma Scale, Rappaport, Dougherty, & Kelting, 1992) to assist other health care professionals in making realistic early treatment plans. Psychologists can also be a resource for family education and support during the acute phase of brain injury. Early rehabilitation intervention is the standard of care in the model system approach to TBI rehabilitation (Ragnarsson, Thomas, & Zasler, 1993); however, studies do not demonstrate the efficacy of early intervention by psychology (or any other discipline).

Role of the Psychologist in the Postacute Stage

Psychologists have multiple roles in the successful rehabilitation of individuals who have sustained a brain injury. Heinemann, Hamilton, Linacre, Wright, and Granger (1995) analyzed outcome data from 140 patients with TBI and 106 patients with SCI, contributed by eight hospitals that subscribed to the Uniform Data System for Medical Rehabilitation. Although patients were enrolled in comprehensive multidisciplinary rehabilitation programs, the intensities of physical therapy, occupational therapy, or speech therapy were not associated with changes in functional outcome, even after controlling for factors such as age, admission status, and length of stay. Only the intensity of psychological services had any relationship with functional gains. This finding appeared to be specific to cognitive functioning among patients with brain injury.

Neuropsychological Assessment

In the context of rehabilitation, neuropsychological assessment can provide a wealth of information to the treating team, patient, and family. It is important to recognize that formal neuropsychological assessment in a rehabilitation setting is rarely purely diagnostic (i.e., TBI or not). Typically, the diagnosis is already established. Rather, neuropsychological assessment can assess the level of disability and assist in formulating realistic rehabilitation goals, assessing changes in status, and making realistic discharge plans.

Formal assessment may be flexible or based on a battery of tests. The most widely used formal battery of neuropsychological tests is most likely the Halstead–Reitan Neuropsychological Test Battery (Reitan & Wolfson, 1993), although most psychologists do not use this battery in its complete form. Given its length and heavy reliance on sensorimotor functioning, however, this battery may not be the most appropriate one for TBI inpatients.

The National Institute on Disability and Rehabilitation Research (NIDRR) Traumatic Brain Injury Model Systems of Care (Ragnarsson et al., 1993) has also established a battery of neuropsychological tests that have been studied during both inpatient and outpatient rehabilitation. This battery includes the GOAT (Levin et al., 1979), Symbol Digit Modalities Test (Smith, 1991), the Token Test (Benton, Hamsher, & Sivan, 1994), Wechsler Memory Scale—Revised Logical Memory I and II (Wechsler, 1987), Wechsler Adult Intelligence Scale—Revised Digit Span and Block Design (Wechsler, 1981), Grooved Pegboard (Matthews & Klove, 1964), Visual Form Discrimination Test (Benton, Hamsher, Varney, & Spreen, 1983), Controlled Oral Word Association Test (Benton et al., 1994), Rey Auditory Verbal Learning Test (Rey, 1964), Trail Making Test (Army Individual Test Battery, 1941), and Wisconsin Card Sorting Test (Grant & Berg, 1948). At 1-year follow-up, improvements in neuropsychological functioning were noted in the majority of these formal tests, with the most improvement noted on tests of attention, concentration, and verbal learning (Kreutzer, Gordon, Rosenthal, & Marwitz, 1993).

For detailed descriptions of these and other tests, as well as batteries designed to assess specific neurocognitive domains (e.g., language, visual information processing), the reader is referred to existing compendia of tests (e.g., Spreen & Strauss, 1998).

Behavior Management

Patients who sustain TBI often have behavioral disturbances. Although some aspects of their behavior may be related to nonbehavioral factors (e.g., biologically mediated agitation), many other issues may be at least partially addressed through the application of behavior modification approaches. It must be noted, however, that traditional approaches to behavior modification are based on learning theory, and learning is typically impaired among TBI survivors. Thus, successful behavior management with TBI survivors may need to focus more on stimulus control (i.e., environmental factors) than operant learning (i.e., recalling relationships between behaviors and their consequences). Several useful manuals have been published that detail the application of behavior management techniques with the TBI population (Jacobs, 1993; Matthies, Kreutzer, & West, 1997).

Patient and Family Education and Support

Rehabilitation psychologists who work in TBI rehabilitation are frequently called on to provide education and support to patients and families. Survivors of TBI may become more dependent on family members (Jacobs, 1987), and this perceived level of burden may not decrease with time (Brooks, Campsie, Symington, Beattie, & McKinlay, 1986). Patient and family education may occur through a variety of approaches, ranging from formal interdisciplinary family conferences and educational groups to supportive counseling and formal family therapy (Muir, Rosenthal, & Diehl, 1990).

Psychopharmacological Management

Although psychologists do not directly prescribe medications or directly recommend specific psychopharmacologic regimens for patients, it is important to have familiarity with the drugs that are currently used in the treatment and management of TBI. For a comprehensive review of psychopharmacological treatment following brain injury, see Zafonte et al. (1999).

Psychostimulants, such as methlyphenidate (best known as Ritalin), amantadine, and bromocriptine, are used with TBI patients. Such drugs may be of particular use in increasing the tonic (i.e., general) arousal of TBI patients. Antiseizure medications are used to prevent seizure or to control a known seizure disorder. They are also used in some TBI patients to manage agitation, regardless of whether the cause is seizure related. Antiseizure medications are also gaining popular use among individuals who do not have TBI and as a primary or adjunctive treatment for mood disorders (e.g., bipolar disorder). Antipsychotic medications are often used to control agitated behavior in non-TBI populations. Their use with TBI survivors is more controversial, however, and may exacerbate the neurobehavioral symptoms of TBI and thus interfere with the rehabilitation process.

Cognitive Rehabilitation

The use of behavioral or learning-based procedures to improve cognitive functioning has a long history (see Boake, 1991), but systematic studies are far more recent. Cognitive rehabilitation is arguably one of the more controversial areas within TBI rehabilitation (Bergquist & Malec, 1997). The term *cognitive rehabilitation* is broad and typically encompasses endeavors including cognitive retraining, cognitive remediation, and compensatory strategy training. Cognitive rehabilitation is often divided into two major approaches: *restorative* and *compensatory* (Ben-Yishay & Diller, 1993). Restorative approaches (e.g., having patients practice memorizing lists of words to improve verbal learning) focus on intervening at the level of areas of impaired cognitive functioning. Compensatory approaches (e.g., teaching someone with poor verbal memory to rely on visual memory skills) are focused on functional goals, and interventions are designed to teach the individual how to reach goals using residual abilities and relative strengths.

Direct retraining techniques are perhaps the most common cognitive rehabilitation approach. This approach is based on practice, with the assumption that practicing various cognitive tasks results in general improvements in cognition. Examples include having individuals memorize lists or generate solutions to hypothetical problems. Although patients generally show improvement on tasks that they are required to practice, there is insufficient evidence to support generalization to real-world tasks or functional domains apart from the specific target areas (Harrell, Parente, Bellingrath, & Lisicia, 1992). Potential exceptions to this are process-specific training approaches that derive from direct training, but specific skills are targeted for improvement. Skills that have been shown to be positively affected by intervention include visual scanning (Weinberg et al., 1977), attention and concentration (Sohlberg & Mateer, 1989), and spatial organization (Weinberg et al., 1979). True treatment effects are difficult to determine, however, as follow-up studies have suggested that untreated patients eventually show similar improvements (Gordon et al., 1985). It has also been suggested that with some types of interventions, the effects are minimal to nonexistent once natural recovery and practice effects are considered (Ponsford & Kinsella, 1988).

The most common approaches to compensatory device training involves the use of cognitive memory "orthoses" such as planners, tape recorders, or calendars. Although their functional effectiveness is fairly well established, there is little evidence that the use of such devices results in a meaningful improvement in the underlying core cognitive abilities (Parente & Stapleton, 1997). In addition, the efficacy and benefit of personal organization and time management products are hardly limited to individuals with acquired cerebral impairment.

Although cognitive rehabilitation is often applied as a specific intervention for impairments, some centers have taken a more programmatic approach. In such programs, cognitive rehabilitation is seen as a process that occurs within the context of a therapeutic milieu (i.e., treatment is seen as "holistic") rather than in the context of specific time-delimited sessions. The results of many programmatic approaches are generally in a positive direction, but improvement has been difficult to attribute solely to specific cognitive interventions. Prigatano, Fordyce, and Seiner (1984) found that TBI rehabilitation resulted in significant improvements in functional abilities, but there was minimal increase in actual neurocognitive abilities. TBI patients who received an outpatient holistic cognitive rehabilitation (Ben-Yishay, Silver, & Piasetsky, 1987) showed a significant increase in resumption of work at long-term follow-up, but the specific relationship between cognitive skills acquisition and outcome is not clear.

Prognostication of Long-Term Outcome

Empirical prediction of long-term outcome poses several challenges in the TBI populations. The first issue is related to the variable or set of variables one is using for prediction. Length of coma has been found to be a good predictor of return to work at 6 months (Ruff et al., 1993), but this assumes that a reliable index of coma (e.g., the GCS) is used. Length of PTA is also used in prediction of outcome. Jennett and Teasdale (1981) found that when PTA is less than 14 days, the 6-month outcome is "good" (according to the GOS) in 83% of patients and "moderate" in 17%. Between 15 and 28 days of PTA, 66% were rated as having a good outcome, 31% a moderate level of disability, and 3% severe disability.

Return to work has frequently been used as a dependent variable in outcome prediction studies. For example, data from the TBI Model Systems of Care has indicated that higher levels of injury severity (GCS, length of coma, and length of PTA), physical functioning (indexed with the FIM and DRS), cognitive functioning (delayed verbal recall), and behavioral functioning (RLAS) predicted successful return to work at 1-year post-TBI (Cifu et al., 1997).

Using a multivariate prediction model, Dikmen et al. (1994) examined return to work at 1–2 years postinjury. In this model, relatively accurate predictions regarding return to work could be made on the basis of education, preinjury work history, severity of brain injury, neuropsychological functioning (as measured with the Halstead–Reitan Neuropsychological Test Battery), and severity of other (nonhead) injuries.

Much is still not known about long-term outcome following brain injury. For example, long-term improvement following brain injury is not uncommon beyond the general clinically accepted cutoff of 12–18 months. More studies also need to be conducted on predicting long-term outcome using multivariate models of acute factors. Furthermore, the critical role of preinjury medical, educational, and psychosocial variables in long-term outcome needs further investigation.

Postacute Issues

Following acute neurorehabilitation, a variety of treatment options are available to an individual with a TBI, depending on severity and type of disability, financial resources, access to transportation, and support and family system. In addition, although there are a large number of brain injury programs in the United States, certain types of programs are not equally distributed in urban and rural areas and in certain parts of the country. Given the decreasing length of stay in acute inpatient rehabilitation hospitals, access to postacute (or subacute) rehabilitative services is becoming increasingly important to optimize long-term outcome for the person with a brain injury and the family.

Salcido, Moore, Schleenbaker, and Klim (1996) defined subacute rehabilitation (SR) as

> a level of rehabilitation care designed to meet the needs of patients who medically and physically are too frail to participate in the rigors of a conventional inpatient physical rehabilitation program (i.e. 3 hours or more of daily therapy). SR also may be appropriate for patients who do not require intense multiple therapies but may have medical comorbidities and complicating factors that require the medical supervision of a physiatrist. (p. 60)

Patients receive the same types of rehabilitation services as in acute rehabilitation (i.e., physical, occupational and speech therapy), but with lesser intensity and often provided by paraprofessionals or health care workers with less specialized experience. Psychologists typically provide services within a brain injury SR program but often as consultants (see Rosenthal and Lichtenberg, 1998). For patients who are deemed "slow to recover" (i.e., remain in a minimally responsive state for weeks or months after injury or individuals who make very slow progress in rehabilitation therapy), SR is often recommended either immediately after acute neurotrauma care or after comprehensive inpatient rehabilitation has been completed. For low-level patients, a focus of rehabilitative therapy is on sensory stimulation and continual assessment of the patient's responsiveness to the environment. SR may also be viewed as a more cost-effective alternative for older adults with TBI who are capable of significant gain in functional outcome but may take twice as long to achieve such gains because of comorbidities and reduced capacities in speed of learning (Cifu et al., 1996; Reeder, Rosenthal, Lichtenberg, & Wood, 1996). Although studies done with hip fracture and stroke patients have suggested similar outcomes following acute or subacute rehabilitation, this finding has not been systematically investigated to date with the TBI population. Some individuals who are minimally responsive after acute rehabilitation require a more chronic, long-term treatment program. This type of program is usually located in a nursing home and provides primarily medical, nursing, and custodial care with therapy provided to maintain function and prevent further deterioration in the individual's physical condition.

Perhaps the most pervasive forms of postacute rehabilitation are outpatient therapy and day treatment. Outpatient therapy can consist of a single or combination of therapies (e.g., physical therapy, occupational therapy, speech-language therapy, psychotherapy) that an individual may receive at a rehabilitation center or specialized brain injury rehabilitation program. In all but the mildest of cases, a period of outpatient therapy is recommended after inpatient rehabilitation to assist people with a TBI in reaching their highest level of physical and psychological functioning. This is often accompanied by periodic medical monitoring, usually by a physiatrist, and follow-up neuropsychological evaluation after 6 months or longer to assess level of recovery and residual impairments. Day treatment is a form of outpatient treatment in which a full array of treatment services are provided to individuals who often attend 3–5 days per week for 4–6 hours per day. The duration of day treatment programs is generally 3–6 months. These programs, which are often accredited by CARF as "community-integrated programs," provide the standard array of rehabilitation services with ongoing medical supervision; cognitive rehabilitation; case management; vocational rehabilitation services; and individual, family, and group psychotherapy. Many of these programs are psychologist led or managed and are termed *holistic* or *neuropsychological rehabilitation* programs and have produced impressive outcomes (see Malec & Basford, 1996).

Transitional-living programs are designed for higher functioning individuals who are ready to learn independent-living skills in a community setting. Often, such individuals have completed an extensive therapy program and are medically stable. Transitional-living programs usually are located in single or multifamily dwellings in the community, and staffed by counselors or therapists who may be affiliated with a brain injury rehabilitation program. Because of a variety of cognitive and behavioral problems, residents in a transitional-living program need some training to develop or regain skills in community mobility, shopping, managing personal finance, job-seeking, use of leisure time, and developing appropriate interpersonal relationships.

For individuals with chronic, severe behavior problems, a neurobehavioral residential treatment program is often a desired placement. This type of program may be hospital-based with a focus on a high degree of structure, systematic use of behavioral management, physical management, and psychopharmacology. Individuals who exhibit severe disinhibition, agitation (beyond the acute phase of recovery), and antisocial behavior (including the threat of potential harm to self or others) are likely candidates to receive treatment in these settings.

Community Reintegration

Family Reintegration

Families are often characterized as the "second victim" of a TBI. The catastrophic nature of the injury and its residual sequelae, accompanied by the circumstances surrounding it (i.e., often a motor vehicle crash or violent encounter) creates difficulties in acceptance and coping with "life after brain injury." Yet the family is a critical element in efforts to achieve successful community integration. The typical adult with brain injury is unmarried and lives alone prior to the injury. Quite often, he or she returns to the family of origin, who assume the primary role of caregiver. This poses considerable problems for the family, who are unaccustomed to their new roles and experience a great deal of burden, which may even increase over the years postinjury (Brooks et al., 1986). In other cases, a person with a TBI returns to a spouse, who may accurately perceive their partner as a significantly different person or even as a child. This can create tremendous stress on the caregiving spouse and in some cases on parent–child relationships. Serio, Kreutzer, and Gervasio (1995) found in their study of family needs following brain injury that the need for emotional support is most frequently unmet, in comparison with needs for medical information, professional support, and instrumental support. Rosenthal and Young (1988) outlined a multifaceted model of family intervention strategies that may be used by psychologists and other rehabilitation team members to optimize family adaptation.

Vocational Reintegration

For many survivors of brain injury, the process of re-entering competitive employment is one of the greatest obstacles and likely factors contributing to a sense of quality of life. Despite the catastrophic nature of TBI, many survivors have sufficiently recovered basic physical and cognitive skills within 6–12 months postinjury to begin the process of vocational rehabilitation. The first step is usually a referral from the rehabilitation facility to the state vocational rehabilitation agency. Many state offices have counselors who specialize in TBI. After establishing eligibility for services, an individualized written rehabilitation plan may be established, consisting of a variety of elements: (a) comprehensive extended evaluation, which may include up-to-date medical, neuropsychological, and vocational interest or aptitude examinations; (b) referral to a specialized brain injury rehabilitation program that has a vocational rehabilitation component; (c) contact with preinjury employer and attempts to assist the client to return to the same or, more typically, reduced job; and (d) referral to a supported employment program, which may be administered by the state agency or by a vocational rehabilitation company or brain injury rehabilitation program. The supported-employment model, which is known as a *place-train model*, is one in which clients are placed in a competitive work setting with a job coach, who works alongside the employee until the employee no longer needs the cuing or guidance that has been provided. Initially developed with the psychiatric population, it has appeared to be an effective model for the brain injury population as well (Wehman et al., 1989). For some individuals, the level of residual deficits is so severe that a return to work is not feasible. They should be referred to the Disability Determination Service for evaluation of eligibility for long-term disability payments through the social security system.

Academic Reintegration

For children or young adults who sustain a TBI, an important goal is resumption of school or academic activities. In the past decade, the federal and state education agencies have recognized TBI as a distinct entity. Children and adolescents who experience a TBI are eligible to receive special education services under the Individuals With Disabilities Education Act (IDEA, P. L. 101-456), which was initially enacted in 1990 and revised in 1997. In some rehabilitation programs, educational tutoring is initiated during the inpatient hospitalization. When discharge approaches, the rehabilitation team (frequently the psychologist or social worker) often works directly with the individual's local school district to develop a transition plan to enable a child to reestablish an educational program. An individualized educational plan is developed, which may include homebound tutoring, part-time in-school schedule, use of compensatory strategies or devices, modified curriculum, assistive technology, special transportation, and similar services. This plan is subject to review on a yearly basis or more often as needed. Some large school districts even have a designated special education person with expertise in TBI, who oversees the educational programming of children with TBI. Many universities also offer services for students with disabilities.

Sexuality

The combination of physical, neuropsychological, and behavioral sequelae following TBI result in a variety of social disabilities, including the challenges of reestablishing meaningful social relationships, particularly of an intimate nature. Self-image often is significantly impaired following TBI, even in cases in which changes in physical appearance are minor. Problems in accurately perceiving and expressing emotion, as well as physical limitations, can pose obstacles for individuals attempting to engage in sexual behavior. On a more basic level, feelings of unattractiveness and awareness of one's disability may impede the capacity to establish satisfying intimate relationships. Sexual education, assertiveness training, and couples counseling are some of the techniques that are useful in assisting the person with TBI to resume an identity as a "sexual being" (Griffith & Lemberg, 1993).

Substance Abuse

A major risk factor for successful community reintegration following TBI is the use and abuse of alcohol and drugs. A recent study examined cross-sectional ($n = 322$) and longitudinal samples ($n = 73$) from the TBI Model Systems of Care programs up to 4 years postinjury (Kreutzer et al., 1996). The investigators found that those who used alcohol excessively prior to the injury remained heavy drinkers at follow-up several years postinjury. Other investigators have identified substance abuse as a major impediment to participation in supported employment programs and job retention (Sale, West, Sherron, & Wehman, 1991). In a recent study, Bogner, Corrigan, Spafford, and Lamb-Hart (1997) demonstrated the effectiveness of a community-based model, termed the "TBI network," in increasing the productivity and decreasing the level of substance use in 72 individuals who sustained severe TBI. Although many rehabilitation psychologists do not have advanced training in substance abuse treatment, screening measures such as the Brief MAST (Michigan Alcoholism Screening Test; Pokorney, Miller, & Kaplan, 1972) or the CAGE Questionnaire (cut down, annoyed, felt guilty, and eye opener; Ewing, 1984) can be used to correctly identify those who used substances excessively and may be likely to abuse substances following discharge into the community. It would also be important for the rehabilitation psychologists to identify, educate, and refer to community providers who can treat substance abuse problems in people with TBI.

Models and Standards of Care

Commission on Accreditation of Rehabilitation Facilities

The only widely accepted standards of care for TBI are those promulgated by CARF (1998). These standards were originally developed by the Brain Injury Special Interest Group of the American Congress of Rehabilitation Medicine and later adopted by CARF in 1985. The initial set of standards were designed only to cover comprehensive inpatient rehabilitation. In 1988, standards were developed for the rapidly expanding field of post-acute brain injury rehabilitation. The standards were termed "community integrative" and intended to include programs that provided a structured brain injury rehabilitation program in an outpatient, day treatment, or residential setting. Psychological services, such as neuropsychological assessment, cognitive rehabilitation, behavioral management, and patient and family counseling, are identified in the standards as integral to brain injury rehabilitation service delivery.

From a consumer protection standpoint, the adoption of standards of care was an important development in providing to individuals with brain injuries and their families a guide for selection and evaluation of the quality of a program. The addition of specific ethical standards to the brain injury rehabilitation standards in the early 1990s was, in part, a response to the many allegations of fraud and abuse among brain injury service providers (Kerr, 1992). Despite these "safeguards," the existence of such standards of care cannot prevent unscrupulous providers from engaging in misleading or deceptive practices or providing exorbitantly expensive, unnecessary, or ineffective treatment. The CARF standards are in a continuous state of evolution and are revised every 3 years.

Psychologists have been instrumental in the promulgation and refinement of CARF standards. Nevertheless, the forces of managed care and concerns about economic survival have pressured CARF to "dilute" these standards, particularly in relationship to the necessity for a comprehensive, interdisciplinary rehabilitation team. In recent years, the role of the psychologist (and other rehabilitation disciplines) as a compulsory member of the rehabilitation team has been challenged. To date, the importance of psychological factors in medical rehabilitation and position as member of the core rehabilitation team have been successfully maintained. Yet as the essential characteristics of comprehensive rehabilitation continue to be questioned, rehabilitation psychologists must be vigilant to these potential threats and provide sufficient evidence to document the relationship between their contributions and optimal rehabilitation outcomes.

Traumatic Brain Injury Model Systems of Care

In 1987, shortly after the development of CARF standards, NIDRR announced funding for a new program of service demonstration and research —the TBI model systems of care. This program was modeled after the already existing SCI model systems of care, which had been initiated in 1971 (see chapter 2). A *model system of care* has been described as a system of service delivery that provides "an entire spectrum of care— emergency evacuation and advanced life support at the accident scene, intensive care, comprehensive physical and psychosocial rehabilitation and long-term community follow-up" (Ragnarsson et al., 1993, p. 3). The overall objectives of the TBI model systems of care program are (a) to develop and demonstrate a model system of care for people with TBI, stressing continuity and comprehensiveness of care; and (b) to develop and maintain a standardized national database for innovative analyses of TBI treatments and outcomes (Harrison-Felix et al., 1996; Ragnarsson et al., 1993). The major issues to be addressed in this project include (a) demographics of the population; (b) causes of injury; (c) nature of diagnoses, including severity, level of impairment, disability, and handicap; (d) types of services and treatment; (e) the costs of treatment; and (f) measurement and prediction of outcome. Recently, a substantial boost in federal funding allowed an increase from 5 to 17 model systems. Psychologists serve as the principal investigator or coprincipal investigator on most of these grants.

In addition to the aforementioned general objectives, the following priorities have recently been added to the scope of the program: (a) investigate the efficacy of alternative methods of service delivery intervention after inpatient rehabilitation discharge and other postacute pathways; (b) identify and evaluate interventions, including those involving emerging technology, that can improve vocational outcomes and community integration; (c) develop key predictors of rehabilitation outcome, including subjective well-being at hospital discharge and at long-term follow-up; (d) determine relationships between cost of care, specific treatment interventions, and functional outcomes; (e) examine the implications of violence as a cause of TBI on treatment interventions, rehabilitation costs, and long-term outcomes; and (f) investigate the outcome of alternative pathways of postacute treatment, such as skilled nursing facilities, SR facilities, and home care.

A major focus of the model systems has been an emphasis on outcomes measurement. Studies have been performed to assess the reliability and validity of well-known measures such as the DRS, FIM, and Functional Assessment Measure (Hall et al., 1996) and newly developed instruments such as the CIQ (Willer et al., 1993).

Economic Issues Following Traumatic Brain Injury

In addition to personal disruption in the areas of cognition, vocation, and family, survivors of disabling TBI can encounter significant financial costs. One obvious cost is that of medical rehabilitation care. For severe TBI, High et al. (1996) reported that the average cost to provide just the initial inpatient rehabilitation care and services to one individual may cost more than $85,000. Financial costs are not limited to medical rehabilitation, however. TBI survivors may also incur costs related to lost wages and loss of future financial security for families. Overall, it has been estimated that there is a total lifetime expense of $44 billion in United States for all head injuries, of which $4.5 billion are from direct treatment costs (Max, MacKenzie, & Rice, 1991). In addition, it has also been estimated that brain-injury-related work loss and disability result in a total cost of $20.6 billion.

Given these cost issues, as well as concerns in recent years about fraud and abuse in the head injury rehabilitation industry, one justifiable question is whether TBI rehabilitation is truly cost effective. In one of the earlier investigations of cost effectiveness, Aronow (1987) matched 60 patients from a comprehensive inpatient TBI rehabilitation program with TBI patients from a neurotrauma program without formal rehabilitation services. Patients who received inpatient TBI rehabilitation were significantly improved on scales of functional status, living arrangement, vocational status, and self-care abilities. Although the rehabilitation costs of the comprehensive rehabilitation group totaled approximately $1 million for the 60 patients, these patients had lower care costs on discharge. A total care cost saving of $335,842 across patients per year was calculated. Later, Cope, Cole, Hall, and Barkan (1991) studied a total of 192 patients, with follow-up on 145 members from the original sample. Treatment gains were maintained for approximately 2 years following residential TBI rehabilitation. The greatest annual cost saving, as indexed by the cost reduction in attendant care needs, was in the most severely injured group, with an average cost reduction of $41,228. Individuals who sustained mild TBI demonstrated the smallest annual savings benefit of $2,696. Johnston and Lewis (1991) examined the effects of residential TBI rehabilitation with 82 patients from nine residential TBI rehabilitation programs. They found that this form of treatment decreased the need for later care, with more acutely treated cases demonstrating greater benefit.

Although it appears that TBI rehabilitation works and that intensive early rehabilitation increases its efficacy, increased amounts of rehabilitation do not necessarily lead to improved outcome. Johnston (1991) conducted a follow-up evaluation with the patients of Johnston and Lewis's (1991) study. He found that there was no difference in longer term outcome between patients who had received a few months of residential rehabilitation and those who had received years of similar treatment. The amount of money spent on treatment also did not correlate with outcome. Putnam and Adams (1992) examined this issue in a unique study of TBI rehabilitation efforts. In their study, the investigators had access to complete treatment and cost data from the Michigan Catastrophic Claims Association. Michigan is unique in that its no-fault automobile insurance provisions (at the time that their study was conducted) provided claimants with unrestricted access to multidisciplinary rehabilitation without annual or lifetime capitations on services or benefits. Putnam and Adams randomly sampled 100 records of individuals who had sustained TBI. Of interest is that the poorest outcomes were noted among individuals who had received the greatest amount of treatment and highest money expenditure. The findings of this study are sobering in that they clearly suggest that there are not infinite gains associated with increasing amounts of rehabilitation expenditure.

Ricker (1998) reviewed the empirical literature regarding TBI rehabilitation, with specific attention given to cost issues. His conclusion to the question "TBI rehabilitation: Is it worth the cost?" was "Yes! However. . . ." It was clear that TBI rehabilitation could positively affect functional outcome by reducing the need for supervision, improving vocational reintegration, and increasing the ability to perform activities of daily living. With regard to the qualification in the above response, it was pointed out that the majority of endeavors in TBI rehabilitation were clearly occurring outside of the types of settings that were described in the clinical studies. Also, at the time of the review, there was essentially no empirical research that directly addresses the issue of cost benefit (or potentially the lack thereof) specifically for clinical neuropsychological or rehabilitation psychology services in the context of TBI rehabilitation.

Conclusion

We provided a brief overview of the nature of TBI and its short- and long-term physical, cognitive, and neurobehavioral consequences. A framework has been provided to understand the multiple roles of psychologists in assessing and managing the deficits and the rehabilitation process, both for the survivor with brain injury and significant others. Within the past two decades, TBI has become a central core of most rehabilitation programs in the United States and has received increasing interest internationally. Psychologists have been instrumental in establishing innovations in clinical practice and in engaging in critical research to establish the validity of new techniques of assessment (e.g., neuropsychological assessment) and rehabilitation treatment (e.g., cognitive rehabilitation). In addition, psychologists have been actively involved in treatment efficacy research, which has become of increased salience in the era of health care reform and managed care. Psychologists have been at the forefront in model systems of care for people with TBI and in developing standards of care. Future developments in the art and science of brain injury rehabilitation will likely continue to be dependent, in part, on the substantial contributions of psychologists committed to the concerns of people with brain injury and their families.

References

Annegers, J. F., Hauser, W. A., Coan, S. P., & Rocca, W. A. (1998). A population-based study of seizures after traumatic brain injuries. *New England Journal of Medicine, 338*, 20–24.

Army Individual Test Battery. (1941). *The Trail Making Test*. Washington, DC: Department of Defense.

Aronow, H. U. (1987). Rehabilitation effectiveness with severe brain injury: Translating research into policy. *Journal of Head Trauma Rehabilitation, 2*, 24–36.

Benton, A. L., Hamsher, K. de S., & Sivan, A. B. (1994). *Multilingual aphasia examination* (3rd ed.). Iowa City, IA: AJA Associates.

Benton, A. L., Hamsher, K. de S., Varney, N. R., & Spreen, O. (1983). *Contributions to neuropsychological assessment*. New York: Oxford University Press.

Ben-Yishay, Y., & Diller, L. (1993). Cognitive remediation in traumatic brain injury: Update and issues. *Archives of Physical Medicine and Rehabilitation, 74*, 204–213.

Ben-Yishay, Y., Silver, S. M., & Piasetsky, E. (1987). Relationship between employability and vocational outcome after intensive holistic cognitive rehabilitation. *Journal of Head Trauma Rehabilitation, 2*, 35–48.

Bergquist, T. F., & Malec, J. F. (1997). Current practice and training issues in treatment of cognitive dysfunction. *Neurorehabilitation, 8*, 49–56.

Binder, L. M. (1997). A review of mild head trauma: Part II. Clinical implications. *Journal of Clinical and Experimental Neuropsychology, 19*, 432–457.

Binder, L. M., Rohling, M. L., & Larrabee, J. (1997). A review of mild head trauma. Part I: Meta-analytic review of neuropsychological studies. *Journal of Clinical and Experimental Neuropsychology, 19*, 421–431.

Boake, C. (1991). History of cognitive rehabilitation following head injury. In J. S. Kreutzer, P. H. Wehman, et al. (Eds.), *Rehabilitation for persons with traumatic brain injury: A functional approach* (pp. 3–12). Baltimore: Brookes.

Bogner, J. A., Corrigan, J. D., Spafford, D. E., & Lamb-Hart, G. L. (1997). Integrating substance abuse treatment and vocational rehabilitation after traumatic brain injury. *Journal of Head Trauma Rehabilitation, 12*(5), 57–71.

Born, J. D., Albert, A., Hans, P., & Bonnal, J. (1985). Relative prognostic value of best motor response and brain stem reflexes in patients with severe head injury. *Neurosurgery, 16*, 595–600.

Braakman, R., Jennett, W. B., & Minderhoud, J. M. (1988). Prognosis of the posttraumatic vegetative state. *Acta Neurochirgica, 95*, 49–52.

Brooks, N., Campsie, L., Symington, C., Beattie, A., & McKinlay, W. (1986). The five year outcome of severe blunt head injury: A relative's view. *Journal of Neurology, Neurosurgery and Psychiatry, 49*, 764–770.

Centers for Disease Control and Prevention. (1997, January 10). Traumatic brain injury—Colorado, Missouri, Oklahoma, and Utah, 1990–1993. *Morbidity and Mortality Weekly Report, 48*(1), 8–11.

Cifu, D. X., Keyser-Marcus, L., Lopez, E., Wehman, P., Kreutzer, J. S., Englander, J., & High, W. (1997). Acute predictors of successful return to work 1 year after traumatic brain injury: A multicenter analysis. *Archives of Physical Medicine and Rehabilitation, 78*(2), 125–131.

Cifu, D. X., Kreutzer, J. S., Marwitz, J. H., Rosenthal, M., Englander, J., & High, W. (1996). Functional outcomes of older adults with traumatic brain injury: A prospective, multicenter analysis. *Archives of Physical Medicine and Rehabilitation, 77*(9), 883–888.

Collins, J. G. (1993). Types of injuries by selected characteristics: United States. 1986–1988. National Center for Health Statistics. *Vital Health Statistics, 2*(182), 1–87.

Commission on Accreditation of Rehabilitation Facilities. (1997). *Directory of accredited programs*. Tucson, AZ: Author.

Commission on Accreditation of Rehabilitation Facilities. (1998). *Standards for medical rehabilitation programs*. Tucson, AZ: Author.

Cooper, K. D., Tabbador, K., Hauser W. A., Schulman, K., Feiner, C., & Factor, P. R. (1983). The epidemiology of head injury in the Bronx. *Neuroepidemiology, 2*, 70–88.

Cope, D. N., Cole, J. R., Hall, J. M., & Barkan, H. (1991). Brain injury: Analysis of outcome in a post-acute rehabilitation system: Part I. General analysis. *Brain Injury, 5*, 111–125.

Corrigan, J. D., Smith-Knapp, K., & Granger, C. V. (1997). Validity of the Functional Independence Measure for persons with traumatic brain injury. *Archives of Physical Medicine and Rehabilitation, 78*, 828–834.

Cullum, C. M., & Thompson, L. L. (1997). Neuropsychological diagnosis and outcome in mild traumatic brain injury. *Applied Neuropsychology, 4*(1), 6–16.

Dijkers, M. (1997). Measuring the long-term outcomes of traumatic brain injury: A review of the Community Integration Questionnaire. *Journal of Head Trauma Rehabilitation, 12*(6), 74–91.

Dikmen, S. S., Temkin, N. R., Machamer, J. E., Holubkov, A. L., Fraser, R. T., & Winn, R. (1994). Employment following traumatic head injuries. *Archives of Neurology, 51*, 177–186.

Ewing, J. A. (1984). Detecting alcoholism: The CAGE Questionnaire. *Journal of the American Medical Association, 252*, 1905–1907.

Gordon, W. A., Hibbard, M. R., Eglko, S., Diller, L., Shaver, M. S., Lieberman, A., & Ragnarsson, K. (1985). Perceptual remediation in patients with right brain damage: A comprehensive program. *Archives of Physical Medicine and Rehabilitation, 66*, 353–359.

Gouvier, W. D., Blanton, P., Laporte, K., & Nepomuceno, C. (1987). Reliability and validity of the Disability Rating Scale and the Levels of Cognitive Functioning Scale in monitoring recovery from severe head injury. *Archives of Physical Medicine and Rehabilitation, 68*, 94–97.

Grant, D. A., & Berg, E. A. (1948). A behavioral analysis of the degree of reinforcement and ease of shifting to new responses in a Weigl-type card sorting problem. *Journal of Experimental Psychology, 38*, 404–411.

Griffith, E. R., & Lemberg, S. (1993). *Sexuality and the person with traumatic brain injury: A guide for families*. Philadelphia: F.A. Davis.

Gronwall, D., & Wrightson, P. (1981). Memory and information processing after closed head injury. *Journal of Neurology, Neurosurgery, & Psychiatry, 44*, 889–895.

Hagen, C., Malkmus, D., & Durham, P. (1972). *Levels of cognitive functioning*. Downey, CA: Rancho Los Amigos Hospital.

Hall, K. M., Mann, N., High, W. M., Wright, J., Kreutzer, J. S., & Wood, D. (1996). Functional measures after traumatic brain injury: Ceiling effects of FIM, FIM + FAM, DRS and CIQ. *Journal of Head Trauma Rehabilitation, 11*(5), 27–39.

Hamilton, B. B., Granger, C. V., Sherwin, F. S., Zielenzy, M., & Tashman, J. S. (1987). A uniform national data system for medical rehabilitation. In M. Fuhrer (Ed.), *Rehabilitation outcome analysis and measurement*. Baltimore: Paul Brookes.

Hammond, F. M., & McDeavitt, J. T. (1999). Medical and orthopedic complications. In M. Rosenthal, E. Griffith, J. S. Kreutzer, & B. Pentland (Eds.), *Rehabilitation of the adult and child with traumatic brain injury* (3rd ed., pp. 53–73). Philadelphia: Davis.

Harrell, M., Parente, R., Bellingrath, E. G., & Lisicia, K. A. (1992). *Cognitive rehabilitation of memory: A practical guide*. Rockville, MD: Aspen.

Harrison-Felix, C., Newton, N., Hall, K. M., & Kreutzer, J. S. (1996). Descriptive findings from the Traumatic Brain Injury Model Systems National Data Base. *Journal of Head Trauma Rehabilitation, 11*(5), 1–14.

Heinemann, A. W., Hamilton, B., Linacre, J. M., Wright, B. D., & Granger, C. (1995). Functional status and therapeutic intensity during inpatient rehabilitation. *American Journal of Physical Medicine and Rehabilitation, 74*, 315–326.

High, W. M., Hall, K. M., Rosenthal, M., Mann, N., Zafonte, R., Cifu, D. X., Boake, C., Bartha, M., Ivanhoe, C., Yablon, S., Newton, C. N., Sherer, M., Silver, B., & Lemkuhl, L. D. (1996). Factors affecting hospital length of stay and charges following traumatic brain injury. *Journal of Head Trauma Rehabilitation, 11*(5), 85–96.

Individuals With Disabilities Education Act of 1990, P. L. No. 101-476, 104 Stat. 1142.

Jacobs, H. E. (1987). The Los Angeles head injury survey: Project rationale and design implications. *Journal of Head Trauma Rehabilitation, 2*, 37–50.

Jacobs, H. E. (1993). *Behavior analysis guidelines and brain injury rehabilitation*. Gaithersburg, MD: Aspen.

Jennett, B., & Bond, M. R. (1975). Assessment of outcome in severe brain damage: A practical scale. *Lancet, 1*, 480–484.

Jennett, B., & Teasdale, G. (1981). *Management of head injuries*. Philadelphia: Davis.

Johnston, M. V. (1991). Outcomes of community re-entry programmes for brain injury survivors: Part 1. Independent living and productive activities. *Brain Injury, 5*, 141–154.

Johnston, M. V., & Lewis, F. D. (1991). Outcomes of community re-entry programmes for brain injury survivors: Part 2. Further investigations. *Brain Injury, 5*, 155–168.

Kerr, P. (1992, March 16). Centers for head injury accused of earning millions for neglect. *New York Times*, p. 1.

Kraus, J., Fife, D., Conroy, C., & Nourjah, P. (1989). Alcohol and brain injuries: Persons blood-tested, prevalence of alcohol involvement, and early outcome following injury. *American Journal of Public Health, 79*, 294–299.

Kraus, J. S., & McArthur, D. L. (1998). The epidemiology of traumatic brain injury. In M. Rosenthal, E. Griffith, J. Kreutzer, & B. Pentland (Eds.), *Rehabilitation of the adult and child with traumatic brain injury* (3rd ed.). Philadelphia: F.A. Davis.

Kreutzer, J. S., Gordon, W. A., Rosenthal, M., & Marwitz, J. (1993). Neuropsychological characteristics of patients with brain injury: Preliminary findings from a multicenter investigation. *Journal of Head Trauma Rehabilitation, 8*, 47–59.

Kreutzer, J. S., Marwitz J. H., & Witol, A. D. (1995). Interrelationships between crime, substance abuse, and aggressive behaviors among persons with traumatic brain injury. *Brain Injury, 9*, 757–768.

Kreutzer, J. S., Witol, A. D., Sander, A. M., Cifu, D. X., Marwitz, J. H., & Delmonico, R. (1996). A prospective longitudinal multicenter analysis of alcohol use patterns among persons with traumatic brain injury. *Journal of Head Trauma Rehabilitation, 11*(5), 58–69.

Levin, H. S., Benton, A., & Grossman, M. (1982). *Neurobehavioral consequences of closed head injury*. New York: Oxford University Press.

Levin, H. S., O'Donnell, V. M., & Grossman, R. G. (1979). The Galveston Orientation and Amnesia Test: A practical scale to assess cognition after head injury. *Journal of Nervous and Mental Disease, 167*, 675–684.

Malec, J. F., & Basford, J. S. (1996). Post-acute brain injury rehabilitation. *Archives of Physical Medicine and Rehabilitation, 77*, 198–207.

Matthews, C. G., & Klove, H. (1964). *Instruction manual for the Adult Neuropsychology Test Battery*. Madison: University of Wisconsin Medical School.

Matthies, B. K., Kreutzer, J. S., & West, D. D. (1997). *The behavior management handbook: A practical approach to patients with neurological disorders*. San Antonio, TX: Therapy Skill Builders.

Max, W., MacKenzie, E. J., & Rice D. P. (1991). Head injuries: Costs and consequences. *Journal of Head Trauma Rehabilitation, 6*(2), 876–941.

Muir, C. A., Rosenthal, M., & Diehl, L. N. (1990). Methods of family intervention. In M. Rosenthal, E. R. Griffith, M. R. Bond, & J. D. Miller (Eds.), *Rehabilitation of the adult and child with traumatic brain injury* (2nd ed., pp. 433–448). Philadelphia: Davis.

Novack, T. A., Dillon, M. C., & Jackson, W. T. (1996). Neurochemical mechanisms in brain injury and treatment: A review. *Journal of Clinical and Experimental Neuropsychology, 18*, 685–706.

Parente, R., & Stapleton, M. (1997). History and systems of cognitive rehabilitation. *Neurorehabilitation, 8*, 3–11.

Pokorney, A. D., Miller, B. A., & Kaplan, H. B. (1972). The Brief MAST: A shortened version of the Michigan Alcoholism Screening Test. *American Journal of Psychiatry, 129*, 342–343.

Ponsford, J. L., & Kinsella, G. (1988). Evaluation of a remedial programme for attentional deficits following closed-head injury. *Journal of Clinical and Experimental Neuropsychology, 10*, 693–708.

Prigatano, G. P., Fordyce, D. J., & Seiner, H. K. (1984). Neuropsychological rehabilitation after closed head injury in young adults. *Journal of Neurology, Neurosurgery, and Psychiatry, 47*, 505–513.

Putnam, S. H., & Adams, K. M. (1992). Regression-based prediction of long-term outcome following multidisciplinary rehabilitation for traumatic brain injury. *The Clinical Neuropsychologist, 6*, 383–405.

Ragnarsson, K. T., Thomas, J. P., & Zasler, N. D. (1993). Model systems of care for individuals with traumatic brain injury. *Journal of Head Trauma Rehabilitation, 8*, 1–11.

Rappaport, M., Dougherty, A., & Kelting, D. (1992). Evaluation of coma and the vegetative states. *Archives of Physical Medicine and Rehabilitation, 73*, 628–634.

Rappaport, M., Hall, K. M., Hopkins, H. K., Belleza, T., & Cope, D. N. (1982). Disability Rating Scale for severe head trauma: Coma to community. *Archives of Physical Medicine and Rehabilitation, 63*, 118–123.

Reeder, K., Rosenthal, M., Lichtenberg, P., & Wood, D. (1996). Impact of age on functional outcome following traumatic brain injury. *Journal of Head Trauma Rehabilitation, 11*(3), 22–31.

Reitan, R. M., & Wolfson, D. (1993). Halstead–Reitan Neuropsychological Test Battery. Tucson, AZ: Neuropsychology Press.

Rey, A. (1964). *L'examen clinique en psychologie* [The clinical psychological exam]. Paris: Presses Universitaires de France.

Ricker, J. H. (1998). Traumatic brain injury rehabilitation: Is it worth the cost? *Applied Neuropsychology, 5*(4), 184–193.

Rosenthal, M., & Lichtenberg, P. A. (1998). Subacute rehabilitation: New opportunities and challenges for rehabilitation psychologists. *Rehabilitation Psychology, 43*, 63–73.

Rosenthal, M., & Young, T. (1988). Effective family intervention after traumatic brain injury. *Journal of Head Trauma Rehabilitation, 3*(4), 42–50.

Ruff, R. M., Marshall, L. F., Crouch, J., Klauber, M. R., Levin, H. S., Barth, J., Kreutzer, J., Blunt, J. A., Foulkes, M. A., & Eisenberg, H. M. (1993). Predictors of outcome following severe head trauma. *Brain Injury, 7*(2), 101–111.

Salcido, R., Moore, R. W., Schleenbaker, R. E., & Klim, G. (1996). The physiatrist and subacute rehabilitation. *Physical Medicine Clinics of North America, 7*(1), 55–81.

Sale, P., West, M., Sherron, P., & Wehman, P. H. (1991). Exploratory analysis of job separations from supported employment for persons with traumatic brain injury. *Journal of Head Trauma Rehabilitation, 6*(3), 1–11.

Serio, C. D., Kreutzer, J. S., & Gervasio, A. H. (1995). Predicting family needs after brain injury: Implications for intervention. *Journal of Head Trauma Rehabilitation, 10*(2), 32–45.

Smith, A. (1991). *Symbol Digit Modalities Test*. Los Angeles: Western Psychological Services.

Sohlberg, M. M., & Mateer, C. A. (1989). *Introduction to cognitive rehabilitation: Theory and practice*. New York: Guilford Press.

Spreen, O., & Strauss, E. (1998). *A compendium of neuropsychological tests* (2nd ed.). New York: Oxford University Press.

Strich, S. (1961). Shearing of nerve fibres as a cause of brain damage due to head injury. *The Lancet, 2*, 443–448.

Teasdale, G., & Jennett, B. (1974). Assessment of coma and impaired consciousness. *Lancet,* 2, 81–84.

Thomsen, I. V. (1987). Late psychosocial outcome in severe blunt head trauma. *Brain Injury,* 1(2), 131–143.

Thurman, D. J., Alverson, C., Dunn, K. A., Guerrero, J., & Sniezek, J. (1999). Traumatic brain injury in the United States: A public health perspective. *Journal of Head Trauma Rehabilitation,* 14(6), 602–615.

Wechsler, D. (1981). *Wechsler Adult Intelligence Scale—Revised.* San Antonio, TX: The Psychological Corporation.

Wechsler, D. (1987). *Wechsler Memory Scale—Revised.* San Antonio, TX: The Psychological Corporation.

Wehman, P., Kreutzer, J., West, M., Sherron, P., Diambra, J., Fry, R., Groah, C., Sale, P., & Killam, S. (1989). Employment outcomes of persons following traumatic brain injury: Preinjury, postinjury and supported employment. *Brain Injury, 3,* 397–412.

Weinberg, J., Diller, L., Gordon, W. A., Gerstman, L. J., Lieberman, A., Lakin, P., Hodges, G., & Ezrachi, O. (1977). Visual scanning training effect on reading-related tasks in acquired right brain damage. *Archives of Physical Medicine and Rehabilitation, 58,* 479–486.

Weinberg, J., Diller, L., Gordon, W. A., Gerstman, L. J., Lieberman, A., Lakin, P., Hodges, G., & Ezrachi, O. (1979). Training sensory awareness and spatial organization in people with right brain damage. *Archives of Physical Medicine and Rehabilitation, 60,* 491–496.

Whitman, S., Coonley-Hoganson, R., & Desai, B. T. (1984). Comparative head trauma experience in two socioeconomically different Chicago-area communities: A population study. *American Journal of Epidemiology, 4,* 570–580.

Willer, B., Rosenthal, M., Kreutzer, J. S., Gordon, W. A., & Rempel, R. (1993). Assessment of community integration following rehabilitation for traumatic brain injury. *Journal of Head Trauma Rehabilitation, 8*(2), 75–87.

Williams, D. H., Levin, H. S., & Eisenberg, H. M. (1990). Mild head injury classification. *Neurosurgery, 27*(3), 422–428.

Zafonte, R. D., Elovic, E., O'Dell, M., Mysiw, W. J., & Watanabe, T. (1999). Pharmacology in traumatic brain injury: Fundamentals and treatment strategies. In M. Rosenthal, E. Griffith, J. S. Kreutzer, & B. Pentland (Eds.), *Rehabilitation of the adult and child with traumatic brain injury* (3rd ed., pp. 536–555). Philadelphia: Davis.

Zafonte, R. D., Hammond, F. M., & Peterson, J. (1996). Predicting outcome in the slow to respond traumatically brain injured patient: Acute and subacute parameters. *Neuro-Rehabilitation, 6,* 19–32.

4

Stroke

Bruce Caplan and Stephen Moelter

Stroke constitutes the major cause of paralysis in the United States, and its survivors comprise the largest diagnostic category of referrals to rehabilitation hospitals (Granger, Hamilton, & Gresham, 1988). It is estimated that more than two-thirds of stroke patients have consequent limitations in major functional activities (Baum, 1982), placing stroke among the primary etiologies of disability in adults. As the "graying" of the population continues, stroke will surely remain a major public health problem well into the 21st century.

Rehabilitation psychological assessment and intervention with stroke survivors demands a broad range of knowledge and skills reflecting the multiple consequences precipitated by the neurological event. "Stroke psychologists" must be well versed in both neuropsychology and traditional rehabilitation psychology to assist patients (as well as family members and the treating team) in dealing with the cognitive, emotional, physical, social, sexual, and vocational ramifications of stroke. Our use of the term *rehabilitation psychologist* should therefore be understood to imply a substantial degree of neuropsychological expertise and familiarity with certain principles and practices (e.g., treatment adherence, stress management) of what has traditionally been considered "health psychology."

In this chapter, we range widely (and necessarily to a relative extent superficially) over the facts and abilities that one must possess to work effectively with stroke survivors. We urge interested readers to consult related works (e.g., Bornstein & Brown, 1991; Delaney & Ravdin, 1997; Gresham, 1995b; Lezak, 1995; Mora & Bornstein, 1998) for greater depth of discussion of particular topics. We first provide an overview of epidemiological factors, economic impact, types of stroke, and the characteristics of particular regional syndromes. We then discuss selected issues of phenomenology and the assessment and treatment of stroke as they typically arise in the acute medical, acute rehabilitation, and postacute phases, respectively.

It should be noted that the subsample of individuals with stroke that receives rehabilitation tends to include those in the middle range of impairment. Those with milder strokes are often discharged and sent directly to their homes, perhaps with recommendations for outpatient therapies or a home program. More severely affected individuals who cannot tolerate (or are judged unlikely to benefit from) a rigorous inpatient rehabilitation program may be destined for a nursing home or skilled care facility, increasing numbers of which offer some therapeutic services. Protocols are now emerging (e.g., Stineman, Maislin, Fiedler, & Granger, 1997; Ween, Alexander, D'Esposito, & Roberts, 1996) that may permit empirically based placement decisions.

Overview

Stroke is "an acute neurological dysfunction of vascular origin with sudden (within seconds) or at least rapid (within hours) occurrence of symptoms and signs corresponding to the involvement of focal areas of the brain" (World Health Organization, 1989, p. 1412). Stroke has also been called a "brain attack" to draw the etiological parallel between stroke and heart attack, both of which often result from atherosclerotic processes (American Heart Association, 1998).

It is important to distinguish *stroke* from related terms. *Transient ischemic attacks* (TIAs) are episodes of focal neurologic dysfunction that typically last 2–15 minutes and resolve fully within 24 hours. *Reversible ischemic neurologic deficits* (RINDs) are symptomatically similar to TIAs but of longer duration—from 24 hours to 1–3 weeks. (The uniqueness of this entity is a controversial topic; see Yatsu, Grotta, & Pettigrew, 1995.) When symptoms persist beyond 3 weeks, the term *stroke* unequivocally applies.

Stroke is poorly understood by the general public. Pancioli et al. (1998) found that only 57% of their telephone survey respondents could identify 1 of 5 established warning signs of stroke (unilateral weakness–paralysis, sudden onset of blurred vision, difficulty speaking, dizziness–loss of balance and coordination, severe headache), and only 8% could list 3 signs. Only 66% could identify 1 stroke risk factor, and those at greater risk for stroke (older people, men, and African Americans) knew fewer risk factors.

Epidemiology

The most recent epidemiological study derives an estimated annual incidence of over 700,000 first and recurrent strokes (Broderick et al., 1998). Broad population values are somewhat misleading, however, because the incidence of stroke varies substantially as a function of age, type of stroke, gender, and ethnic group. For instance, stroke incidence increases steadily with age (Terent, 1993), particularly for ischemic events (Wolf, 1997). Men have incidence rates that are 30% (Wolf, 1997) higher than those of women, and African Americans are at greater risk of stroke than White Americans (288 vs. 179 first strokes per 100,000, respectively; Broderick et al., 1998).

Studies of stroke prevalence (i.e., the number of stroke survivors at any given time) reveal that over 3 million Americans are disabled as a result of stroke (Terent, 1993). In 1994, 154,350 Americans died from stroke, 75% of them older people (Bonita & Beaglehole, 1993). According to Bonita and Beaglehole, men have a higher death rate than women (42 vs. 33 per 100,000). The mortality rate from stroke is declining in most industrialized countries because of both decreasing incidence and increased survival. However, stroke remains the third most common cause of death in industrialized countries, trailing only heart disease and cancer (Bonita & Beaglehole, 1993).

Economic Impact

Stroke has a huge economic impact on the individual and family, the medical community, and society. Estimates of annual stroke-related costs (both direct and indirect) have risen from approximately $7 billion in 1976 (Adelman, 1981) to $30 billion in 1993 (Dobkin, 1995). The per person lifetime cost of stroke varies considerably by stroke type: subarachnoid hemorrhage, $228,030; intracranial hemorrhage, $123,565; ischemic stroke, $90,981. Over half of the total costs are incurred during the period beginning more than 2 years after onset, highlighting the persistent economic consequences for patient and family (Taylor et al., 1996). Such long-term costs have been shown to be reduced by prevention of initial or recurrent stroke (by modification of risk factors; see below), limiting of common secondary complications (Goldberg & Berger, 1988), and multidisciplinary rehabilitation (Dobkin, 1995).

Risk Factors

Risk factors for stroke may be divided into those that are modifiable (e.g., hypertension, diabetes mellitus, atrial fibrillation, alcohol use, and smoking) and those that are not (e.g., prior stroke, age, sex, race–ethnicity, and family history). Wolf (1997) categorized stroke risk factors into those related to living habits (e.g., smoking, diet, exercise), atherogenic processes, or disease states. Manipulation of modifiable risk factors may have dramatic effects on the incidence, prevalence, and economic and personal costs of stroke. Gorelick (1994) estimated that 378,500 strokes could be prevented each year through treatment of hypertension, cigarette smoking, atrial fibrillation, and heavy alcohol consumption.

Brown, Baird, Shatz, and Bornstein (1996) concluded from their review that studies of stroke risk factors "have begun to provide some consistent evidence of an association with cognitive deficit . . . most clearly demonstrated in relation to hypertension" (p. 358). Subtle cognitive decline resulting from undetected hypertension-induced vascular compromise may thus be a harbinger of clinically significant stroke.

Clinical and Anatomical Correlates of Stroke

Stroke is not a single condition but a collection of cerebrovascular disorders. The two major categories of cerebrovascular disease that result in stroke are (a) cerebral infarction or ischemic stroke secondary to thrombosis (occlusion of blood vessels) or embolism (abrupt blockage of a vessel by a fragment of thrombus that has broken off and traveled to the site), which both account for over 80% of first stroke (Terent, 1993); and (b) hemorrhage, either intracerebral or subarachnoid (11% and 6% of first strokes, respectively). These conditions stand in stark opposition, as the former results from insufficient blood reaching the brain, whereas the latter is produced by excessive blood in the cranium. Early identification of the responsible mechanism is vital, because treatments are substantially different. Recently developed interventions for acute ischemia (e.g., tissue plasminogen activator), which seek to enhance blood flow, are clearly contraindicated in hemorrhagic conditions (Alberts, 1998).

The two categories of stroke differ in incidence and early mortality but not in long-term outcome. In general, hemorrhage is less common but more fatal in the short term. Recent findings reveal a 30-day case fatality rate of 45% for subarachnoid hemorrhage (SAH), 52% for intracerebral hemorrhage (ICH), and about 10% for thrombotic–embolic stroke (Bamford, Dennis, Sandercock, Burn, & Warlow, 1990). Self-perceived quality of life (de Haan, Limburg, Van der Meulen, Jacobs, & Aaronson, 1995) as well as neurologic and functional outcome do not appear to differ between groups with hemorrhage or infarction, but the former may improve at a more rapid rate (Chae, Zorowitz, & Johnston, 1996).

Ischemic Stroke

Cerebral ischemia occurs when blood flow is reduced to a level insufficient to maintain the physiological requirements of the nerve cell; infarction results when diminished blood flow causes cell death (Welch & Levine, 1991).

The most common cause of ischemia and subsequent infarction is atherosclerosis, a noninflammatory, progressive disease (beginning in childhood and peaking between the ages of 50 and 70) that may affect any artery in the body; it is the most common vascular disorder. Fatty deposits build up on the arterial wall, producing a thrombus that gradually narrows the arterial passage until the vessel becomes sufficiently occluded to produce stroke. With complete deprivation of blood flow beyond several minutes, permanent damage generally ensues (Welch & Levine, 1991). Because the buildup of plaque occurs slowly, compensatory blood flow through collateral vessels may be adequate to delay onset or diminish severity of symptoms.

Another type of ischemic event—lacunar stroke—occurs when small penetrating branches of the major cerebral arteries become clogged, resulting in thrombotic infarction (Adams, Victor, & Ropper, 1997). These small occlusions frequently affect the basal ganglia, internal capsule, thalamus, and pons. Some authors have described location-specific syndromes following lacunar infarcts including pure motor or sensory stroke, dysarthric stroke, and hemiparesis with ataxia (Adams et al., 1997). A series of lacunar strokes may produce an accumulation of deficits resulting in multi-infarct dementia (Cummings & Mahler, 1991).

Embolic stroke is produced by abrupt interruption of blood supply by bits of thrombus that have broken loose and lodged in a "downstream" vessel. This mechanism causes rapid onset of (usually focal) symptoms with little opportunity for compensation through collateral blood supply. Embolism may account for as many as 20% of all strokes with approximately half of the emboli emanating from cardiac sources such as atrial fibrillation, myocardial infarction, or mitral valve prolapse. When the embolus becomes lodged in an arterial vessel, ischemic factors (similar to those in thrombotic stroke) begin to operate.

Hemorrhagic Stroke

Hemorrhagic stroke occurs when a blood vessel in the brain ruptures, often (but not always) resulting in dramatic onset of symptoms. Hemorrhagic strokes are typically classified according to the anatomical locus of the bleeding (i.e., extradural, subdural, subarachnoid, intercerebral, intracerebral, and cerebellar). We briefly consider two primary mechanisms of hemorrhage: primary intracerebral and subarachnoid.

Primary ICH, the third most common cause of stroke (following thrombotic and embolic stroke; Adams et al., 1997), results from degeneration and rupture of a penetrating cerebral artery, often because of hypertension. In this type of hemorrhage, the blood rarely reaches the surface of the cortex; in about 90% of patients, it enters the cerebrospinal fluid (Adams et al., 1997). Significant compression of brainstem structures may prove fatal.

The fourth most common cause of stroke is SAH, caused by a ruptured saccular aneurysm. An *aneurysm* is a small ballooning of the wall of an artery that weakens the vessel, leaving it prone to rupture and hemorrhage. In SAH, blood leaks into the subarachnoid space (i.e., between the external surface of the brain and the arachnoid meningeal layer).

In contrast to the insidious onset of thrombotic stroke and the abrupt appearance of symptoms caused by embolism, hemorrhagic stroke may announce itself in either an acute or gradual fashion according, in large part, to the size of the ruptured vessel and the size of the rupture itself. With rapid onset, the consequences are often severe. Dramatic elevation in intracranial pressure resulting from the outpouring of blood into the brain is the primary life-threatening process in hemorrhagic stroke.

Regional Syndromes

The neurobehavioral effects of stroke are primarily determined by the location and size of the lesion, and these, in turn, depend largely on the artery that is involved. Individual differences in cerebral organization of functions produce some unpredictability, as does the existence and extent of temporarily dysfunctional (but potentially viable) regions ("ischemic penumbra"; Hakim, 1998). Nonetheless, certain symptoms tend to accompany damage to particular cortical regions. What follows is a brief overview of the most common deficits following stroke affecting major anatomical landmarks.

Anterior Cerebral Artery Stroke

Arising from the ends of the anterior communicating artery within the Circle of Willis, the left and right anterior cerebral arteries (ACAs) supply the anterior-medial aspects of each cerebral hemisphere. This distribution includes cortical regions such as the medial orbital divisions of the frontal lobe and the frontal pole, and subcortical territory including anterior portions of the corpus callosum, internal capsule, caudate nucleus, and globus pallidus. Lesions limited to the ACA are relatively rare and most often cooccur with middle cerebral artery (MCA) infarction. Typically, there is contralateral lower extremity motor impairment, with relative sparing of upper extremities. Other effects may include incontinence, motor aphasia, and affective and behavioral changes associated with orbital and medial frontal-lobe damage (e.g., poor decision making, personality change, affective lability, loss of initiative and spontaneity).

Middle Cerebral Artery Stroke

The left and right MCA have the largest distribution of any cerebral artery, supplying the lateral aspects of each cerebral hemisphere. This distribution includes the cortical and subcortical portions of the lateral frontal lobe and parietal lobe, as well as the superior aspects of the temporal lobe and insula. The penetrating branches of the MCA also irrigate the basal ganglia.

The classic picture of total MCA occlusion is contralateral hemiplegia of face, arms, and legs; hemisensory deficits; and loss of vision in the field contralateral to the lesion. Various forms of aphasia follow occlusion of particular left MCA branches, whereas right MCA stroke may cause deficits in visual spatial, constructional, and attentional processes (including neglect), as well as unawareness of deficits (anosognosia) and aprosodia (impaired understanding or expression of the emotional components of language). Many of these are similar to the deficits associated with internal carotid artery (ICA) stroke; however, MCA strokes typically have a more rapid onset and produce greater disability because few adequate collateral sources are available. Visual field cuts, including superior quadrantanopia (visual defect involving an upper quadrant) and homonymous hemianopsia (visual defect involving the right or left half of the visual field for both eyes), are common following infarction of either hemisphere.

Internal Carotid Artery Stroke

The ICA, along with the external carotid, arises from the common carotid artery and is the primary conduit for blood to the ACAs and MCAs. One might expect severe consequences to follow carotid stroke because of the breadth of blood distribution that may be affected, but this is not necessarily the case. The redundancy of the cerebral vascular system permits blood flow to be maintained to tributaries of the ICA, thereby limiting the functional consequences.

At greatest risk are the border-zone (watershed) regions between areas of arterial perfusion (i.e., at the border of the superior parietal and superior frontal lobe and within the deep portions of each hemisphere). The behavioral effects of ICA stroke depend on the aspect of the middle cerebral, anterior cerebral, or deep penetrating branches that is most affected. Effects similar to those seen in MCA infarction are common.

Posterior Cerebral Artery Stroke

The vertebral arteries join at the level of the brain stem to form the basilar artery. Branches of the vertebrobasilar circulation irrigate the medulla, pons, midbrain, and cerebellum; as such, stroke in this region can be life threatening. Beyond the brain stem level, the basilar artery bifurcates into left and right posterior cerebral arteries (PCAs), which feed the inferomedial and medial temporal regions, the primary and secondary visual cortices, and much of the thalamus, substantia nigra, and midbrain.

PCA stroke that affects thalamic regions may result in a wide variety of deficits, the most problematic of which is severe sensory loss across all modalities. Other deficits associated with subcortical damage include oculomotor palsy and cerebellar ataxia. Cortical infarcts of the PCA may result in achromatopsia (loss of color vision), tunnel vision (i.e., inability to see objects not centrally located), alexia without agraphia, and memory impairment. For the medical aspects of stroke, see Adams et al. (1997) on more comprehensive treatments.

Psychological Assessment and Intervention

Stroke rehabilitation should be viewed as a multistage process similar to the contemporary conceptualization of multidisciplinary traumatic brain injury rehabilitation as a continuum "from coma to community" (see chap. 3). The importance of psychological assessment and treatment is supported by the Framingham Study finding that psychosocial disabilities were more common than physical ones following stroke (Gresham et al., 1975). Stroke psychologists assess cognitive and emotional functioning, contribute to judgments about patients' suitability for rehabilitation, monitor and treat psychological and social factors that affect recovery, advise other members of the treating team, educate patients and relatives, and offer referrals and recommendations for postdischarge living (Kelly-Hayes & Paige, 1995). The following section describes the what and how of "stroke psychology" in the acute medical, acute rehabilitation, and post-acute phases.

Acute Assessment and Treatment

The first encounter with a stroke patient is likely to occur in the intensive care unit. Some hospitals have designated stroke units, many operating according to a detailed treatment protocol or "critical pathway" (Wentworth & Atkinson, 1996). The value of such special units in the short term has been partially supported (e.g., Ronning & Guldvog, 1998; Stroke Unit Trialists Collaboration, 1997), but whether patients maintain gains over time remains uncertain (Dijkerman, Wood, & Hewer, 1996). Recent data from Norway suggest better quality of life 5 years after stroke in patients who received care in a stroke unit than in those treated in a general ward (Indredavik, Bakke, Slordahl, Rokseth, & Haheim, 1998).

The rehabilitation psychologist's contribution to stroke patient care at this point includes preliminary cognitive and emotional assessment, counseling of patient and family, and consultation to staff. Patients seen in such circumstances may be suboptimally responsive because of direct effects of the stroke (e.g., depressed arousal, aphasia) or secondary consequences (e.g., medication, sleep deprivation). Although formal neurobehavioral evaluation may be difficult, some attempt should be made to assess the patient's cognitive and emotional status, even if all that can be concluded is that they are "not yet testable." Multiple visits may be required because waxing and waning of mental status is common. The patient's chart should be regularly reviewed for pertinent observations by other staff members. Physician notes may include the results of a mental status evaluation. Nursing reports often include a section on patient behavior and may describe statements or questions asked by the patient providing evidence of language impairment, memory deficit, or level of insight into his or her condition.

Several brief, yet reasonably broad, cognitive screening measures are available, but all lack the depth and detail of the more extensive neuropsychological evaluation that may be indicated at a later point. Screening tests permit only tentative inferences, not conclusive diagnostic or prognostic statements.

Two instruments mentioned in the *Post-Stroke Rehabilitation: Clinical Practice Guideline* developed by the Agency for Health Care Research and Quality (AHCRQ; Gresham, 1995a) are the Mini-Mental State Examination (MMSE; Folstein, Folstein, & McHugh, 1975) and the Neurobehavioral Cognitive Status Examination (NCSE; Kiernan, Mueller, Langston, & Van Dyke, 1987), which is now marketed under the name Cognistat. The MMSE is heavily weighted with language-based tasks, rendering it of limited applicability with aphasic (language-disordered) patients, and only a single summary score is derived. An expanded version of the MMSE (Modified MMSE, or 3MS; Teng & Chui, 1987) has greater sensitivity and a lower false-negative rate than the original version and also better predictive value for functional outcome. The NCSE samples a broad array of cognitive functions in an efficient fashion, yielding separate scores for individual domains. However, it has not yet been widely used in controlled investigations of stroke. One discouraging finding is the

NCSE's failure to distinguish between groups of patients with left- and right-hemisphere lesions (Osmon, Smet, Winegarden, & Gandhavadi, 1992). Moreover, because both the MMSE and NCSE show education effects, they may underestimate impairment in well-educated people and overestimate deficits in those with less education.

In seeking evidence of stroke-related cognitive loss, one must recall that strokes tend to affect older individuals, many of whom have medical problems that compromise cognitive abilities; intellectual decline, therefore, may have already begun, creating a fragile baseline on which stroke-related cognitive deficits are superimposed. For example, Phillips and Mate-Kole (1997) found a pattern of neuropsychological impairment in patients with peripheral vascular disease that was "highly similar" to that exhibited by those with cerebral infarcts. Henon et al. (1997) reported a 16% incidence of prestroke dementia (as assessed by informant questionnaire) in 202 consecutive patients, virtually none of whom had been formally diagnosed as demented. Of those diagnosed with poststroke dementia, nearly 40% had experienced cognitive loss before stroke onset (Pohjasvaara, Erkinjuntti, Vataja, & Kaste, 1997).

Neuropsychological evaluation in acute care must assess rehabilitation potential. Rentz (1991) argued that successful treatment can be achieved in patients who possess only rudimentary cognitive abilities: attention, procedural learning, and capacity to imitate or follow nonverbal instructions. Assessment of memory and perceptual functioning are particularly relevant at this phase. Given that much of rehabilitation requires learning new ways to manage daily life activities, the patient's memory capacity—both acquisition (which is understood to encompass the ability to attend to new material) and retention—is clearly of paramount importance. Furthermore, perceptual deficits such as unilateral neglect have been shown to have profound implications for treatment and outcome (e.g., Gialanella & Mattioli, 1992).

Because of the considerable emotional stress produced by stroke, supportive and educational counseling of patient and family constitutes perhaps the most important role of the rehabilitation psychologist at this time. It may not be possible to evaluate the affective state of an acutely ill cognitively impaired stroke patient who cannot understand or reliably respond to interview questions. Furthermore, behaviors or symptoms (e.g., sleep disturbance, poor appetite) that might signify depression or anxiety in healthy individuals may not have the same diagnostic meaning for a hospitalized stroke patient (Woessner & Caplan, 1996). Nonetheless, clinicians should be alert for less ambiguous indicators of distress. Although effective psychological counseling of the patient may not be feasible under these constraints, frequent visits will make the psychologist a "familiar face," building a foundation for future intervention and easing the transition into rehabilitation.

The psychologist's interactions with the patient's relatives are of great importance as well (Evans, Hendricks, Haselkorn, Bishop, & Baldwin, 1992). An acute-onset illness such as stroke may disrupt a long-standing psychosocial equilibrium, eliciting anxiety about the uncertain future. A spouse may feel anger at the patient for not having modified risk behaviors or guilt about having provoked an argument that (he or she fears) caused the stroke. Such worries and misperceptions often diminish with brief discussion about the causes and consequences of stroke and some preparation about prognosis, even if this has not yet been determined. Nonetheless, it may be useful to advise the family about the factors that complicate early prediction and the time frame within which prognosis may become clearer. Relatives can be relieved to hear explanations of such peculiar and troubling phenomena as neglect, aphasia, or aprosodia. This information may need to be repeated several times because its complexity and novelty tax even intelligent nonspecialists. Furthermore, the emotional response to receiving unpleasant and unwanted news may create additional barriers to understanding.

Family members benefit from reassurance that the range of "normal" emotional reactions (their own and those of their affected relative) is vast; in addition to struggling with the primary distress caused by this frightening event, they should not be further burdened with worrying whether their reactions are "appropriate." They can also be made aware of the existence of support groups for stroke survivors and their relatives. Some may find value in selected reading material (Lezak, 1978; Clark & Bray, 1984).

Acute Rehabilitation Assessment and Treatment

Many stroke survivors are transferred to rehabilitation units, and this relocation may produce problematic emotional and cognitive responses. McCaffrey and Fisher (1987) described the constellations of losses (e.g., dignity, self-efficacy, self-reliance, financial independence) and fears (e.g., death, dependence, recurrent stroke) that may become apparent to the stroke survivor, engendering strong emotional reactions. Constant confrontation with the disabilities of other people on the unit may be demoralizing as well. In light of the importance of psychological care in rehabilitation, it is discouraging to note Lewinter and Mikkelsen's (1995) finding that patients from an experimental stroke rehabilitation unit reported that treatment of nonphysical factors (e.g., psychological, social, and sexual phenomena) received insufficient attention.

Following the patient's transfer to rehabilitation, the psychologist's activity accelerates because more extensive evaluations of cognitive functioning and emotional status are generally possible. However, the patient's productive time is likely to be limited by both fatigue and the competing demands of other staff members. If extended testing is not feasible following taxing physical and occupational therapy regimens, multiple brief (20–30 minutes) stints may be required.

A strong case can be made for the value of psychological and neuropsychological assessment in rehabilitation treatment planning for stroke survivors. The AHCPRQ guideline (Gresham, 1995a) asserts that those patients who exhibit evidence of cognitive or emotional problems on clinical examination or on screening measures should be given tests that "sample key cognitive, emotional, behavioral, and motivational domains. Cognitive elements include attention, orientation, memory, language, reasoning, judgment, spatial skills, motor coordination, and social skills" (p. 91). Patients should be evaluated for the presence of depression, anxiety, extent of awareness of deficits and their implications, and level of commitment to the rehabilitation program. The guideline also requires a complete neuropsychological examination in those instances "when more precise understanding of deficits will facilitate treatment" (p. 91). We believe that this applies to the great majority of stroke survivors seen in rehabilitation units, given the incidence of higher cognitive deficits and emotional distress. Findings are routinely shared directly with other members of the treating team during team rounds and other face-to-face discussion, as well as through chart notes.

In addition to the importance of psychological and neuropsychological data for shaping treatment (Caplan, 1982), there is considerable empirical support for its predictive value (Galski, Bruno, Zorowitz, & Walker, 1993; Sundet, Finset, & Reinvang, 1988). In particular, depression (Angeleri, Angeleri, Foschi, Giaquinto, & Nolfe, 1993; Morris, Robinson, Andrzejewski, Samuels, & Price, 1993; Robinson, Starr, Lipsey, Rao, & Price, 1984) and unilateral neglect (Kotila, Niemi, & Laaksonen, 1986; Paolucci et al., 1996) are negative prognostic indicators, unless successfully treated (Gonzalez-Torrecillas, Mendlewicz, & Lobo, 1995).

Space does not permit an extensive treatment of the common neuropsychological deficits and emotional reactions demonstrated by stroke patients. We briefly discuss several of the more common problems, and Exhibit 4.1 contains definitions of many pertinent disorders. See Bornstein and Brown (1991), Delaney and Ravdin (1997), and Lezak (1995) for valuable discussions of the phenomena and pertinent assessment methods.

Neuropsychological Disorders and Rehabilitation

Because stroke tends to be a focal phenomenon, the accompanying deficits of higher cognitive function may be exquisitely selective. Indeed, the growing enterprise of cognitive neuropsychology (e.g., Margolin, 1992) has devoted substantial effort to the fractionation of cognitive functions through intensive single-case or small-group studies of individuals with cognitive deficits, often following stroke. Clinical neuropsychologists have repeatedly demonstrated that lateralized lesions tend to produce certain predictable symptoms: Left-hemisphere lesions compromise language skills (Benson & Ardila, 1996) but leave spatial–perceptual abilities relatively intact, whereas right-hemisphere lesions result in the opposite pattern (e.g., Hier, Mondlock, & Caplan, 1983).

Intrahemispheric localization is relevant as well. For example, anterior left-hemisphere injury generally produces nonfluent aphasia characterized by effortful, halting, agrammatic speech that contains a preponderance of "high-information" words (i.e., so-called "telegraphic speech");

Exhibit 4.1.   Neuropsychological Disorders Secondary to Stroke

Syndrome	Structure involved
Dominant hemisphere syndromes	
Aphasia: impairment of language comprehension or production	LH
• Broca's (expressive) aphasia—nonfluent output characterized by poor articulation but adequate comprehension	Left FL, IFG
• Wernicke's (receptive) aphasia—fluent output with poverty of content and poor comprehension	Left posterior TL, STG
• Conduction aphasia—fluent output and adequate comprehension with poor repetition and difficulty with auditory–verbal memory span	PL, SMG
• Global aphasia—significant impairment of both expressive and receptive language functions.	LH
• Anomic aphasia—deficit in word-finding with fluent language and good comprehension and repetition	LH
Pure alexia: deficit in reading and visual processing such that perceptual aspects of the word are not matched with the internal representation of the word	Posterior LH
Agraphia: disorders of writing and spelling. May be limited to writing and spelling or include deficits in reading (i.e., alexia with agraphia)	Posterior LH AG
Apraxia: inability to correctly perform skilled movements that is not a result of weakness, sensory loss, or tremor	LH
• Ideomotor apraxia—difficulty in performing overlearned actions particularly when asked to pantomime them	Anterior CC, Left PL, PM
• Ideational apraxia—difficulty in performing sequences of actions to achieve a goal	Left PL
Acalculia: impairment in the ability to calculate arithmetic problems	Left PL, AG, MG
Perceptual and attentional syndromes	
Agnosia: partial or complete inability to recognize sensory stimuli, not explainable by defects in basic sensation or diminished alertness	Varies by subtype
• Visual—impairment of visual object recognition	Left or right OT
• Auditory—inability to recognize sounds in the presence of otherwise intact hearing	Left or right TL
• Somatosensory—difficulty perceiving objects through tactile stimulation, despite otherwise intact somatosensory capacity	PL
Visuospatial and constructional disorders: impairment in using the spatial properties of objects (location, orientation, and space relationships)	RH
• Disorders of perception—difficulty in localizing, describing, and using relationships among objects in space	Right PL
• Constructional apraxia—inability to copy drawings or three-dimensional figures secondary to visuoperceptual impairment	Right PL

Exhibit 4.1.   *(Continued)*

Syndrome	Structure involved
Body perception disturbances: impairment in knowledge about the arrangement of body parts and their spatial relationship to objects in the environment	PL
• Right–left disorientation—difficulty recognizing the right and left sides of the patient's or another person's body	Left PL
• Autopagnosia—inability to localize and name the parts of one's own body or on another person's body	Left posterior PL
• Finger agnosia—inability to identify one's own fingers or those of another person	Left and right PL
Neglect: failure of a patient to report, respond, or orient to stimuli presented contralateral to a lesion	Right IPL, FL, SC
• Sensory neglect—failure to detect sensory stimuli presented on the side contralateral to a lesion	Right IPL
• Spatial neglect—difficulty orienting one's body in space or solving problems with a spatial component as a result of neglect of one side of space	Right IPL
Anosognosia: unawareness of neurological deficits or illness	Right PL
Memory disturbances	
Working memory disturbance: difficulty holding information in short-term memory while engaging in other cognitive tasks	DLPFC
Amnestic syndromes: impairment in the ability to learn or recall information	MTL, BF, TH
Frontal-lobe syndromes	
Disinhibition syndrome: disinhibition in social and sexual activity with dramatic changes in affect or impaired judgment and insight	OFL
Executive function syndrome: deficiency in planning, initiating, monitoring, and maintaining flexibility in behavior	DLPFC
Apathetic syndromes: generalized apathy in motivation and spontaneous actions with indifference	ML
Disturbances of emotional functioning	
Emotional disorders: alteration in emotional functioning	RH
Poststroke depression: appearance of symptoms of depression secondary to stroke that are primarily attributed to the location of the damage and only partially as reaction to injury	Anterior LH, BG / Anterior RH
Aprosody: difficulty in producing and comprehending the affective components of language	RH, IFG, IPL, STG

Note. LH = left hemisphere, RH = right hemisphere, FL = frontal lobe, TL = temporal lobe, PL = parietal lobe, IFG = inferior frontal gyrus, STG = superior temporal gyrus, AG = angular gyrus, CC = corpus callosum, PM = premotor cortex, MG = marginal gyrus, OT = occipital temporal region, IPL = inferior parietal lobe, SC = subcortical structures, DLPFC = dorsolateral prefrontal cortex, MTL = medial temporal lobe, BF = basal forebrain, TH = thalamus, OFL = orbital frontal lobe, BG = basal ganglia, SMG = supramarginal gyrus. For more information, see Feinberg and Farah (1997), Filley (1995), Kolb and Whishaw (1990), and Williams (1993).

comprehension is better preserved than expression. Posterior lesions of the left hemisphere, by contrast, are accompanied by fluent prosodic speech (albeit of impoverished content) but impaired comprehension.

Furthermore, certain phenomena may occur (although with dissimilar frequencies) following damage to either hemisphere, but they take different forms and show varying associated features, depending on the involved side. For instance, constructional apraxia (impaired capacity to copy or assemble structures in two or three dimensions; not the result of motor dysfunction) has been viewed as primarily a perceptual impairment in cases of right-hemisphere lesions but a "dysexecutive deficit" when it follows left-hemisphere damage (Kirk & Kertesz, 1989). Moreover, contralateral neglect has been repeatedly shown to occur far more frequently with right- than left-hemisphere cortical involvement (and also with subcortical lesions), but the accompanying reading disorders (alexia) may differ. Right-hemisphere patients do not read material on the left side of the page (or even the left-sided portion of individual words) and commit other perceptual errors; individuals with left-hemisphere lesions may omit right-sided material but also commit other alexic errors that parallel their spontaneous speech (Caplan, 1987; Coslett, 1997).

Given the routine nature of neuroradiological examination in acute stroke care, the rehabilitation psychologist typically knows from the outset the location of lesion and hence is likely to have formed some hypotheses about the expected test profile. These expectations also derive from testing already performed by other team members such as speech pathologists and occupational therapists. The logistics of the contemporary rehabilitation unit, where psychological and neuropsychological evaluation and treatment constitute only one arm of the armamentarium, further induce adoption of the "flexible" or "hypothesis-testing" approach. That patients are typically "available" (physically and mentally) for, at most, 1 hour at a time confers the luxury of being able to administer a selection of tests, score them and review the results, and consider what the day's findings dictate for the next day's session.

In the initial contact with the patient (and visiting relatives or friends), rehabilitation psychologists should state that they are members of the treating team and that referral for psychological services is common or even routine. The emotional stress of acute illness and hospitalization should be acknowledged and "normalized," and clinicians' availability to listen, support, and educate should be made clear. Clinicians should offer some brief description of the brain basis of various cognitive, memory, perceptual, and linguistic functions and how these might have been affected by the stroke. They should explain the importance of identifying any neuropsychological deficits so that these can be considered in planning the rehabilitation program and so that the patient is aware of and participates in learning to compensate for them. The patient and family members can be asked whether they have noticed any such difficulties. A plan for the first formal session should be proposed and the patient's agreement secured to reinforce the collaborative nature of the assessment.

At the end of this discussion, the psychologist ought to have formed an impression of the level at which testing should begin. We draw a broad distinction between those individuals who require a lower level screening (such as the NCSE) and those who can tackle more challenging tasks. In the latter instance, we often begin with several short, multifactorial tasks (e.g., Trail Making Test, Symbol Digit Modalities), coupled with selected subtests of the Wechsler scales (e.g., Information, Digit Span, Similarities) and brief measures of reading (because of its association with premorbid intellect and its sensitivity to visual neglect) and memory (because of the above-noted central role of learning and recall in the rehabilitation process). Preliminary results dictate selection of subsequent measures. In each session, tests on which success is anticipated are mixed with those that are expected to reveal the patient's deficits; an evaluation that only documents areas of difficulty simply frustrates and demoralizes the patient. Depending on the length of stay, selective retesting may be valuable to quantify progress and to be able to make recommendations for post-discharge activities on the basis of the most current information. For further description of the process of neuropsychological evaluation in rehabilitation, see Caplan (1982), Caplan and Shechter (1995), and Lezak (1987).

There is considerable merit in supplementing one's experience of the patient's performance during formal testing with observation of their behavior, achievements, and difficulties in other therapies and on the nursing unit. Salient differences in environments (e.g., lighting, noise, presence of others), motivation, and task complexity may lead to varying levels of behavioral adequacy, early recognition of which permits adjustment of the treatment program.

Given the multiple roles of the stroke psychologist, it is advisable to complete the bulk of testing as quickly as possible. The emphasis can then shift to the affective, behavioral, familial, and vocational realms where the need exists and (assuming need, expertise, and resources) to neuropsychological rehabilitation.

The historically pessimistic view of the permanence of neurologically based cognitive deficits began to give way in the 1980s to a more adventurous, interventionist posture (see Diller & Gordon, 1981). Among the targets of treatment have been deficits in attention, memory, visual scanning, and executive functions.

The need for theoretical bases for interventions has been debated, and some vital practical lessons have been learned. For example, one cannot assume that training effects automatically carry over to related tasks; rather, one must plan for and train toward generalization. Also, rote drill alone is of limited usefulness. Multimodal intervention is desirable, as is psychological counseling, especially when the patient's diminished awareness of deficits (see below) is a limiting factor.

The practice of neuropsychological rehabilitation continues to grow, the literature proliferates, and professional training and practice guidelines emerge (Calvanio, Levine, & Petrone, 1993; Gouvier et al., 1997; Riddoch & Humphreys, 1994; Robertson, 1993; von Steinbuchel, von Cramon, & Poppel, 1992).

Impaired Awareness

The phenomenon of impaired awareness (anosognosia) has a long, vexing, but nonetheless edifying history (McGlynn & Schacter, 1989). Several facts now seem clear. First, unawareness may involve any of a variety of deficits including (but not limited to) hemiplegia, sensory deficits, and various cognitive abilities. The term *denial* in isolation carries little meaning because global denial is rare; failure to identify what is being denied leads to misinterpretation, misunderstanding, and (possibly) mistreatment. Furthermore, patients may be selectively anosognosic, oblivious to hemiplegia but distressed by other disabling consequences of their stroke. Berti, Ladavas, and Della Corte (1996) recently reported dissociations for awareness of upper- and lower-limb weakness within the same patient and also for verbal and behavioral indicators of awareness.

Unawareness occurs more often with right (especially parietal and basal ganglia) than left-hemisphere dysfunction and, as such, is often (although not invariably) found in association with unilateral neglect (e.g., Ellis & Small, 1997). Cutting (1978) reported an incidence of 58% among right-hemisphere lesion patients and 14% in the left-hemisphere group. Cognitive impairment may coexist with anosognosia (Levine, Calvanio, & Rinn, 1991), but it does not seem to be a requisite (Small & Ellis, 1996). Starkstein, Federoff, Price, Leiguarda, and Robinson (1992) found mild, moderate, and severe anosognosia in 10, 11, and 13% of their series, respectively. Anosognosia is more common and of greater intensity in the early phase and tends to moderate over time (Weinstein, 1991); what begins as florid denial may evolve to acknowledgment of the existence of the impairment but denial or minimization of the implications of the condition (anosodiaphora). Persistent anosognosia may be more common in those with severe hemisensory deficit, spatial neglect, and intellectual deficits (Levine et al., 1991).

The impact of both neurological and psychological factors needs to be explored in individual cases. As noted above, there should be a high index of suspicion for patients with right-hemisphere lesions. However, one should also ask relatives or knowledgeable others about the individual's habitual coping styles and strategies (which may have included denial, avoidance, or some related tactic). Structured interviews assist in establishing degree and content of anosognosia (Starkstein et al., 1992).

Staff must be sensitive to the conflict that patients face in having to acknowledge either neurological or psychological defects. The former may be less amenable to treatment, but the latter connote a sort of character flaw, immaturity, or other undesirable trait. Another "no-win" situation confronting the stroke survivor is the implicit choice between depression and denial: If one does not appear depressed, one must be "in denial," and when one relinquishes denial, one must necessarily become depressed. Here again, the situation is more complicated and variable. Denial does not immunize against depression (Starkstein et al., 1992), and signs of depression may be interspersed among assertions of unrealistic expectations that staff interpret as denial.

In considering how best to manage anosognosia, one must recognize the distinction between *verbal denial* and *behavioral denial*. We encourage staff to finesse direct confrontation of patients' overt verbal expressions of unawareness as long as patients are engaging in therapies, for this participation reflects some degree of insight into deficits that require treatment. We believe that attacking denial, forcing patients and families to acceptance of a grim prognosis, yields a pointless "victory" for staff. Those whose unawareness creates a consistent barrier to participation in therapy, however, may require repeated gentle demonstrations of the functional consequences of their difficulties, coupled with discussion of available interventions and the promise of the therapist's best efforts. Nonetheless, for some individuals, unawareness may preclude optimal rehabilitation. See the work of Langer and Padrone (1992) and Crosson et al. (1989) for interventions derived from particular conceptualizations of "awareness."

Emotional Disorders

Depression. Investigations of poststroke depression (PSD) have proliferated in the past 15 years (Gordon & Hibbard, 1997). PSD may derive from (a) structural alterations to the brain, (b) the patient's emotional response to sudden and disabling illness, or (c) a combination of the two. Researchers have examined the incidence, course, associated symptoms, cerebral lateralization and localization, and treatment of PSD. Robinson and Starkstein (1990) concluded that approximately 40% of acute-stroke patients exhibit diagnosable depression; Gordon and Hibbard (1997) found reported prevalences to range from 25% to 79%.

Studies of PSD have been inconclusive. Morris, Robinson, Raphael, and Hopwood (1996) reported that the highest incidence of PSD has typically been found among patients with left anterior lesions or left basal ganglia involvement; Schwartz et al. (1993) found individuals with right-hemisphere lesions to have the greater incidence; and Gainotti, Azzoni, Gasparini, Marra, and Razzano (1997) found nonsignificant differences between the two laterality groups.

There are conflicting findings regarding the causes, characteristics, and course of major and minor PSD. For example, the underlying causes may differ as a function of chronicity—acute depression being attributable to biological factors (e.g., location of lesion, depletion of norepinephrine and serotonin), whereas depression during rehabilitation might stem from growing awareness of functional limitations, with chronic phase depression deriving from the socially handicapping consequences of stroke. Consensus is also lacking regarding the relevance of somatic symptoms in the diagnosis of PSD (Robinson & Starkstein, 1990; Stein, Sliwinski, Gordon, & Hibbard, 1996). A further point of dispute involves the impact of PSD on cognitive functioning, with some (Robinson, Bolla-Wilson, Kaplan, Lipsey, & Price, 1986) arguing for a "dementia syndrome of depression" in stroke survivors, whereas others (e.g., House, Dennis, Warlow, Hawton, &

Molyneux, 1990) have claimed to find, at most, only a weak association between depression and higher cognitive deficit.

Studies suggest that PSD may prolong hospitalization, limit the ultimate level of functional recovery, and compromise social reintegration (e.g., Angeleri et al.,1993; Feibel & Springer, 1982; Parikh et al., 1990; Ramasubbu, Robinson, Flint, Kosier, & Price, 1998; Zalewski, Keller, Bowers, Miske, & Gradman, 1994). There is also the startling finding that those who exhibited either major or minor depression in the postacute period had a mortality rate 3.4 times higher during the subsequent decade than did those who were not depressed (Morris et al., 1993).

As noted above, assessment of emotional state in this population remains complicated. Most common diagnostic instruments were not constructed with stroke patients in mind (but see Nelson, Mitrushina, Satz, Sowa, & Cohen, 1993). Although several measures (e.g., observer rating scales and a self-report instrument with stylized "happy" and "sad" faces at opposite ends of a line) have recently been developed for use with neurologically compromised individuals (e.g., Gainotti et al., 1997; Stern & Bachman, 1991), these have not yet been widely adopted. Furthermore, aphasic patients may not be able to communicate their emotional state; indeed, the common practice of excluding many (if not most) aphasic patients from studies of PSD clearly limits the generalizability of the findings.

Evidence suggests that affective information provided by stroke survivors in general is unreliable (Toedter et al., 1995); fatigue, confusion, diminished concentration or other cognitive problems, lowered arousal level with consequent impaired perception of emotional state, and impaired awareness may all detract from the accuracy of patient self-report (Hibbard, Gordon, Stein, Grober, & Sliwinski, 1993; Spencer, Tompkins, & Schulz, 1997). In addition, patients whose speech is aprosodic (i.e., uninflected, lacking the usual rhythm and "melody") may be mistakenly viewed as depressed because they "sound sad," even if their statements and behavior do not conform to that diagnosis (Ross, 1997).

Given these obstacles, we endorse a multimodal approach to diagnosing PSD. Depending on the individual case, this involves some combination of administration of standardized self- and observer-report instruments (with awareness of the caveats for interpretation offered by Woessner & Caplan, 1996), interview of both patient and family members, and behavioral observations by multiple staff in multiple contexts. Clinicians should also take note of the suggestions of Ross and Rush (1981), who argued that depression in stroke (and head injury) patients might be signified by poor or erratic recovery, noncompliance with the rehabilitation program, "management difficulties," and deterioration from a previously stable level.

There is remarkably little research on the efficacy of psychological treatments of PSD. This may be due, in part, to the historical view of poststroke depression as a natural, unavoidable (even necessary or desirable) response, with the result that referrals for treatment were infrequent. Nonetheless, in an early unpublished study, Latow (1983) suggested that individual psychotherapy during rehabilitation could be effective. More recently, Grober, Hibbard, Gordon, Stein, and Freeman (1993) described some success with adaptations of cognitive–behavioral therapy techniques (see especially their Table 11-2 for detailed treatment strategies). This remains an area with much research potential.

Pharmacologic treatment of PSD has been investigated more extensively and has met with greater success. Following a report of positive impact of nortryptiline (Lipsey, Robinson, Pearlson, Rao, & Price, 1984), investigators described encouraging results with other tricyclics such as imipramine (Lauritzen et al., 1994) and amitryptiline, as well as selective serotonin reuptake inhibitors (SSRIs; Andersen, Vestergard, & Lauritzen, 1994). The newest drugs of this type, Paxil and Prozac, have just begun to be studied in PSD (Miyai & Reding, 1998). Small-scale studies support the effectiveness of stimulants such as methylphenidate and dextroamphetamine (see Kraus, 1995, for review). Electroconvulsive therapy has been used in cases of severe refractory depression following stroke (Currier, Murray, & Welch, 1992), but this remains an infrequent treatment in light of the potential for complications.

Anxiety. Poststroke anxiety appears to be less common than PSD, but it is disabling nonetheless. Starkstein et al. (1990) found generalized anxiety disorder (GAD) in 24% of acute-GAD stroke patients, most of whom also showed evidence of major depression; only 6% had GAD alone. Castillo and Robinson (1993) reported an 11% rate of GAD among nondepressed stroke survivors. Shimoda and Robinson (1998) found that GAD in association with major depression delayed recovery from depression and also compromised resumption of social functioning and activities of daily living (ADL); the presence of GAD alone, however, did not have the same disabling impact.

In a longitudinal study, Astrom (1996) identified 20 cases of GAD among 71 acute-stroke patients (28%), 11 of whom also had a diagnosis of major depression. Prevalence remained high at 3 months (31%), 1 year (24%), 2 years (25%), and 3 years (19%), and in each instance, more than half had comorbid depression.

In three studies (Burvill et al., 1995; O'Rourke, MacHale, Signorini, & Dennis, 1998; Sharpe et al. 1990), researchers found agoraphobia to be the most common subtype of anxiety disorder, although the actual incidence was only about 7–8%. Burvill et al. found women to be four times as likely as men to be diagnosed as agoraphobic. There is often associated fear of recurrent stroke or of falling while away from home and being stranded (Sharpe et al., 1990).

Burvill et al. (1995) noted that depression is generally held to result from the experience of "loss" but that anxiety is more often produced by "threat." They proposed that stroke is more frequently construed as a threat (fear of additional strokes, further disability, financial troubles). It would be of interest to investigate the perspectives of stroke survivors on perceived losses and threats accompanying their condition and the association of these views with symptoms of depression or anxiety.

Given its association with dependence in ADL and social dysfunction, poststroke GAD is clearly an understudied problem. Few suggestions have been offered for effective treatment. However, in some instances, anxiety stems from unwarranted or exaggerated fears about imagined post-discharge problems; in these cases, supportive counseling, coupled with frank and specific problem-focused discussion, can alleviate some anxiety.

Apathy. The presence of apathy might seem to be an exclusionary criterion for admission to rehabilitation, because one would not expect apathetic patients to exhibit the requisite motivation for therapy. How-ever, patients may be admitted primarily for the purpose of training family members who will provide care at home. Also one must be cautious not to conclude that an aprosodic individual is apathetic. Starkstein, Federoff, Price, Leiguarda, and Robinson (1993) reported a 23% incidence of apathy among 80 patients studied within 10 days after stroke. Half of these also showed (primarily major) depression, but the others exhibited apathy alone; the latter group had a high frequency of lesions affecting the pos-terior portion of the internal capsule. Apathetic patients without depres-sion were also more cognitively impaired and functionally disabled.

Given the widespread belief that the indifference reaction is associ-ated with right-hemisphere injury (e.g., Gainotti, 1972), it is notable that no hemispheric differences were reported. Starkstein et al. (1993) did not offer treatment suggestions. Okada, Kobayashi, Yamagati, Takahashi, and Yamaguchi (1997) found a 50% incidence of apathy among patients with subcortical infarction, 40% of whom also exhibited depression. Bilateral frontal and anterior temporal hypoactivity (measured by regional cerebral blood flow) characterized this group. Okada et al. opined that poststroke apathy results from cortical serotonergic deficits and that dopaminergic and serotonergic agents might be effective treatments. Marin, Fogel, Haw-kins, Duffy, and Krupp (1995) described a series of 7 apathetic patients with heterogeneous etiologies (4 of them vascular) who were successfully treated pharmacologically, several with stimulants. Other forms of emo-tional disorder may follow stroke such as mania (Starkstein, Federoff, Ber-thier, & Robinson, 1991), atypical psychosis, delusional behavior (Signer, Cummings, & Benson, 1989), and pathological emotionalism (Allman, 1991; Andersen, Vestergaard, & Riis, 1993; Robinson, 1998).

Intervention With Family and Staff

The rehabilitation psychologist can assist in managing the sometimes frac-tious relations that develop among staff, patient, and family, fostering bet-ter communication and understanding of the other "team's" stresses, mo-tivations, concerns, and behavior (Caplan & Reidy, 1996). Simply reframing or rephrasing certain comments or actions may be sufficient. For example, staff can be advised to view "intrusive" family members as "concerned" and "involved" (albeit perhaps overwhelmed), and relatives can be assisted in grasping that seemingly "indifferent" staff are "efficient."

If the patient's relatives display persistent distress, additional educational and supportive counseling should be offered. Evans, Matlock, Bishop, Stranahan, and Pederson (1988) demonstrated the value of instructional classes and cognitive–behavioral counseling in limiting deterioration of family functioning in the year following onset. The rehabilitation psychologist also plays a significant role in discharge planning, whatever the destination. Although transfer to a nursing home or assisted-living facility may, in fact, be permanent, it is often not a certainty at the time. Thus, one can say (without being misleading) that what is being decided is where the individual should go next, not necessarily forever. One can also emphasize that improvement need not end with rehabilitation discharge. Neurological and functional recovery are not invariably parallel processes. Furthermore, one must distinguish among "recovery" at the levels of impairment, disability, and handicap. Certainly, a stable neurologic deficit does not preclude further reduction of disability or improvement in social functioning (Roth et al., 1998).

Postacute Assessment and Treatment

Increasing numbers of stroke survivors are being discharged from rehabilitation units before they have "plateaued," thus creating a continuum between inpatient and outpatient treatment. Although some of these discharges are no doubt driven by cost consciousness, the physical comforts of home, the opportunity to put therapy lessons to use in the real world, and the resumption of aspects of control of one's life and activities also support the move to limit inpatient rehabilitation stays. It is also at this point that emotional and psychosocial rehabilitation assumes paramount importance, as survivors and their families struggle with re-establishing their lives, taking into account the survivor's residual limitations and continuing needs. They must confront the "new normal." Of the many topics relevant to this phase, we briefly consider four—driving, sexual functioning, caregiver burden, and vocational prospects—for which psychological expertise may be sought.

Driving

In contemporary society, the ability to drive represents freedom and independence; exclusion from driving can therefore be devastating, not only for one's self-image but also because of the social, recreational, and vocational limitations that follow. Restrictions should not be imposed lightly nor should approval be given in a cavalier fashion.

Resumption of driving seems to be irrelevant for the majority of stroke survivors. Legh-Smith, Wade, and Hewer (1986) found that two-thirds of their sample had stopped driving before their illness and of the remainder, 58% did not resume afterward; Fisk, Owsley, and Pulley (1997) reported that only 30% of prestroke drivers resumed driving after discharge from rehabilitation. Legh-Smith et al. found nondrivers to be less socially active and (perhaps as a result) more depressed than more mobile peers. Some rehabilitation facilities have driving specialists that conduct detailed evaluations including on-road tests, but these are relatively rare; Fisk et al. (1997) noted that only 5% of their sample of 290 had undergone a road test. In the absence of such services, the team and family may look to the rehabilitation psychologist for guidance. Clearly, information from a recent neuropsychological evaluation is most pertinent, particularly with respect to the domains of attention, perception, speed of response, and judgment.

Formal testing may identify such profound levels of deficit (e.g., gross distractibility, severe unilateral neglect), in the face of which a road test would be ill advised. For such people, specific training may be beneficial. However, the authors of the AHCRQ guidelines (Gresham, 1995a) cited studies demonstrating that poor performance on testing does not necessarily translate to impaired behavior behind the wheel (e.g., Brooke, Questad, Patterson, & Valois, 1992). Despite the apparent importance of intact language functioning (for reading street signs, speedometers, etc.), in two studies (Golper, Rau, & Marshall, 1980; Lebrun, Leleux, Fery, Domes, & Buyssens, 1978), researchers found that language ability alone did not predict driving performance in people with aphasia.

Nonetheless, the final decision on an individual's license to drive resides with the state Department of Motor Vehicles. Psychologists should know their obligation under state law to report individuals with conditions that might compromise their ability to operate a vehicle in a safe manner (Poser, 1993). Regardless of state law, we believe that patients should be advised to undergo evaluation for their own protection and peace of mind. They should be cautioned about the potential financial risks if they fail to notify their insurance company of their medical condition and subsequently are involved in an accident.

Sexual Functioning

Sexual dysfunction is common in both men and women following stroke (Boldrini, Basaglia, & Calanca, 1991; Bray, DeFrank, & Wolfe, 1981), but clinicians often do not address the issue because of simple oversight, discomfort with the topic, or stereotypic notions about the asexuality of older people. Although sexual activity may indeed decline with age, this is not invariably the case, and the status and needs of each individual and his or her partner should be evaluated as such. Fugl-Meyer and Jaasko (1980) found that 83% of their patients had been sexually active prior to stroke, but at 1-year follow-up, about 33% were completely inactive, 33% reported decreased frequency, and the remainder had returned to prestroke levels. Monga, Lawson, and Inglis (1986) found that incidences of sexual inactivity increased from 11% to 64% in men and 29% to 54% in women after stroke onset. Little longitudinal work has been conducted on this topic, but Hawton (1984) provided some encouraging findings, noting return of libido at about 6 months after onset in the majority of his sample that had been premorbidly sexually active. Erectile ability returned at approximately 7 weeks, and intercourse resumed at an average of 11 weeks.

Causes of poststroke sexual disturbances include physiological dysfunctions such as diminished erectile capacity in men or lubrication in women, comorbid diseases such as diabetes, reduced sensory or motor function, and the impact of medications. In addition, one must consider factors such as loss of self-esteem, depression, reduced level of desire, fear of precipitating another stroke, role shifts, concern about the partner's response, performance anxiety, limited mobility, communication difficulties, and cognitive deficits (Good, 1997).

The rehabilitation psychologist's role in sexual counseling is outlined by Ducharme (1987). Much of what he recommended is educational in nature, and he listed the many topics that merit discussion, including role changes, fears of recurrence, and guilt. A model of sexual counseling (Annon, 1974) provides a useful framework. At a minimum, during rehabilitation, the first two components (*permission*, *limited information*) should be completed. Simply raising the topic, thereby legitimizing discussion and questioning (i.e., giving permission) and offering a few basic facts, does an immense service. It is our belief that virtually all team members should be capable of handling these two steps. As requested, *specific suggestions* may be given regarding adaptive techniques, and audiovisual resources may be recommended. *Intensive therapy* should generally be provided only by those with specific training (PLISSIT).

We urge clinicians to keep in mind the distinction drawn by Trieschmann (1980) among sex drives, sex acts, and sexuality. She cited Romano's (1973) statement (which dealt specifically with women) that "sexuality includes a range of behaviors from smiling to orgasm" (p. 28). This typology is useful in identifying the locus of dysfunction and determining suitable interventions.

Caregiver Burden

In recent years, the multiple burdens that accompany the caregiving role have begun to receive attention. In view of the shift toward outpatient care, it is vital to attend to the needs of the person who may be the linchpin of the stroke survivor's posthospital life—the spouse (although children may be called on as well). The best discharge plan will disintegrate if too great a load is placed on the primary caregiver.

The potential physical burdens are obvious: providing assistance with transfers, pushing the wheelchair, monitoring ambulation, and so on. These tasks can be draining on older people, especially those with health problems of their own. At least as taxing as the physical demands are the emotional strains—dealing with a spouse who may have been "characterologically altered" (Lezak, 1978) by the stroke, one who exhibits cognitive deficits or behavioral change, who cannot fulfill the same social roles, make financial decisions, share driving, and so on. Caregivers have greater difficulty dealing with these cognitive–behavioral consequences of stroke than the physical ones (Anderson, Linto, & Stewart-Wynne, 1995). The result can be a deteriorating spiral of social isolation, emotional distress, and functional decline for both partners. Investigations of the emotional impact of caregiving burden following stroke have not yet yielded a coherent body of findings. However, it is clear that caregiving is associated with disturbing levels of several forms of distress as well as disruption of lifestyle (e.g., anxiety, depression, frustration, and social isolation; Macnamara, Gummow, Goka, & Gregg, 1990). Stein, Berger, Hibbard, and Gordon (1993) provided a good overview of the problem and discussed some possible interventions.

We endorse Macnamara et al.'s (1990) proposal that institutions adopt an activist attitude, reaching out to caregivers instead of simply sending information or announcing educational opportunities or support groups. Respite care programs or day hospitals may provide some relief, but caregivers often must be reassured that these do not constitute abandonment. Caregivers must be reminded of the importance of self-care so that they may continue to provide good care to their affected partner (Lezak, 1978). Once again, "giving permission" is an important psychological service. For discussion of extreme caregiver burden in rehabilitation, see Chapter 26.

Vocational Functioning

Although stroke primarily afflicts the elderly population, a significant proportion of survivors are of traditional working age. Weinfeld (1981) found that approximately 25% of strokes affect people between ages 45–65, and Becker et al. (1986) reported that 27% of their multicenter sample of stroke patients were younger than age 65. Furthermore, as more older workers remain on the job, either from necessity or by choice, the possibility of returning to work should be considered for ever more stroke survivors. However, there are few studies of poststroke vocational restoration, and they are difficult to compare because of methodological differences including the fundamental one of the variable definition of *work*.

Weisbroth, Esibill, and Zuger (1971) discovered that over one-third of their sample under age 65 returned to work, albeit some at a lesser level; women were more likely to return to work; age and education had little effect. However, Smolkin and Cohen (1974) discovered that those who did not complete high school were less likely to resume work than were high school graduates, especially if they were women. Professionals had a higher return-to-work rate than did less skilled workers—a conclusion also reached by Howard, Till, Toole, Matthews, and Truscott, (1985).

In a long-term (3–8 years postonset) follow-up study of individuals who were under age 65 at the time of their stroke, Coughlan and Humphrey (1982) found only a 30% rate of employment among men who were under age 65 at follow-up; of women under age 60, only 17% were working. Gresham, Phillips, and Wolf (1979) reported that "decreased level of vocational function" (p. 955) was the most prevalent functional limitation at 6 months or more postonset but that removing the influence of comorbid conditions (e.g., arthritis) reduced the incidence of vocational impairment from 65% to 38%, thereby demonstrating the more limited vocational impact of stroke per se.

Many stroke patients considering returning to work can benefit from a comprehensive neuropsychological evaluation (Caplan & Shechter,

1991), despite the limitations on "ecological validity" that have been discussed (Sbordone & Long, 1996); Merceier et al. (1991) found neuropsychological test performance to be the best predictor for return to work of all factors they considered. Test results should be conveyed to the patient, family, and vocational counselors, and possible "reasonable accommodations" to the workplace may be discussed. According to Black-Schaffer and Lemieux (1994), most accommodations fall into one of five categories: (a) physical access to the work facility, (b) use of technological equipment or modifications, (c) personal assistance services, (d) flexible scheduling, and (e) restructuring of responsibilities.

Few programs exist whose purpose is vocational restoration of the stroke survivor. Kempers (1994) and Black-Schaffer and Lemieux (1994) described services at the Rehabilitation Institute of Chicago and New England Rehabilitation Hospital, respectively. The former is considered prevocational, whereas the latter appears more comprehensive. Data on inpatient treatment show that about half of their clients returned to some form of productive activity; aphasia, substance use (alcohol and smoking), and inability to drive were associated with lesser likelihood of return to work (Black-Schaffer & Osberg, 1990). The efficacy of supported-employment procedures (job-site strategies implemented by professional staff such as employer education, performance feedback to the client, and task-specific cognitive rehabilitation), used with individuals with traumatic brain injury (see chapter 2) and other disabilities (e.g., Wehman et al., 1989), should be fully examined in stroke survivors.

Conclusion

The term *stroke* is sadly apt in its connotation of a rapid-onset event that affects a range of domains of functioning at individual, familial, and societal levels. Although improved pharmacologic treatment of acute stroke may improve outcome for some individuals, the increasing number of aging people virtually guarantees the persistence of stroke rehabilitation. In addition to continuing to fulfill the roles outlined in this chapter, rehabilitation psychologists can contribute to the refinement of stroke treatment in a number of ways. In this section, we note several relevant aims and activities.

As discussed above, there is a distressingly low level of public knowledge about the risk factors and early-warning signs of stroke. Psychologists can contribute to public education (both large scale and at the individual client level) aimed at both minimizing risk and ensuring prompt treatment. Behavioral management strategies (pioneered by health psychologists) can assist in reducing such modifiable risk factors as smoking and alcohol consumption and in promoting adherence to medical treatment of diabetes and hypertension.

Rehabilitation psychologists can also be instrumental in strengthening the link between neuropsychological assessment and functional treatment. Clearly, there would be great value in more precise determination of the predictive validity of particular measures to establish early prognosis and select suitable treatment. The value of the algorithm of Ween et al. (1996) discussed above might be improved by the addition of neuropsychological data.

Equally important is the need for documenting the "ecological validity" of later testing to provide a sound basis for recommendations about such postdischarge activities as driving and returning to work. This warrants major attention in the near future, because third-party payers are increasingly unwilling to support services that are not demonstrably cost-efficient, if not essential. The "neurofunctional evaluation" used at MossRehab Hospital is a novel grafting of traditional neuropsychological perspective onto a set of rehabilitation activities (Ferraro & Nagele, 1989; Mayer, Keating, & Rapp, 1986).

Similarly, proponents of the plethora of tactics that fall under the rubric of "neuropsychological rehabilitation" must redouble their efforts to demonstrate meaningful impact on ADL. Admittedly, this is still a new endeavor and, as such, there is merit in determining what techniques are ineffective as well as identifying those that are. Here again, the "neurofunctional" point of view may open new avenues of intervention with practical payoff.

Lewinter and Mikkelsen (1995) suggested a troubling level of patient dissatisfaction with the extent to which emotional needs are addressed during stroke rehabilitation, and Feibel, Joynt, and Berk (1979) found that unmet psychosocial needs persist. Accurate assessment of the stroke survivor's emotional state can present multiple challenges, but this should inspire creative approaches, not resignation. Reliable and valid behavioral indicators need to be identified, and new assessment tools evaluated in depth.

Rehabilitation psychologists must serve as advocates for treatment of depression, anxiety, and other forms of emotional disturbance that are too often viewed by staff as "understandable" and are therefore ignored. There are disturbingly few formal investigations of the efficacy of psychological treatments of poststroke distress in either individual or group formats; given the multiple ways in which it can sabotage rehabilitation, such affective disorders as persistent depression and anxiety must be recognized and addressed. Rehabilitation psychologists should work to counter the perception that emotional distress is a peripheral issue.

There is an evident contemporary trend toward outpatient care, and stroke rehabilitation is no exception. Rehabilitation psychologists need to ensure that their expertise is recognized and applied in this venue. Many of the strategies proposed by Stiers and Kewman (1997) are pertinent and include serving as case managers, supervising paraprofessionals, developing treatment protocols, advocating for provision of services guaranteed under the Americans With Disabilities Act of 1990 (P. L. 101-336), conducting (or consulting in) research, and lobbying for enlightened public policy on issues affecting people with disabilities. Funding agencies must be shown the need for increased research support. The model systems approach that has succeeded with spinal cord injury and traumatic brain injury ought to be extended to stroke.

In discussing reasonable responses to the recent paradigm shift in health care, Johnstone et al. (1995) suggested that psychologists should consider redirecting their clinical emphasis from one-on-one care toward consultation and education with frontline staff. They also pointed out the need for continuing care during community re-entry because patients and caregivers encounter problems that can subvert long-term adjustment. Here again, forceful advocacy (and research) may help convince third-party payers that counseling of the stroke survivor's primary caregiver is an important prophylactic measure, helping to foster successful long-term outcome, and should therefore be a reimbursable service.

Finally, rehabilitation psychologists must work to influence various agencies including those that accredit health care organizations. It will be necessary to remain vigilant to ensure continuing recognition of the impact of psychological factors on rehabilitation success and to maintain psychologists' place as members of the core treating team. The historical view of rehabilitation as the multidisciplinary process par excellence developed for good reason. Contemporary pressures to impose bidisciplinary treatment must be resisted.

References

Adams, R. D., Victor, M., & Ropper, A. H. (1997). *Principles of neurology* (6th ed.). New York: McGraw-Hill.

Adelman, S. M. (1981). National survey of stroke: Economic impact. *Stroke, 12*(Suppl. 1), I-69–I-88.

Alberts, M. J. (1998). TPA in acute ischemic stroke: United States experience and issues for the future. *Neurology, 51*(Suppl. 3), S53–S55.

Allman, P. (1991). Depressive disorders and emotionalism following stroke. *International Journal of Geriatric Psychiatry, 6,* 377–383.

American Heart Association. (1998). *Heart and stroke A–Z guide.* Dallas, TX: Author.

Americans With Disabilities Act of 1990, P. L. 101-336, 104 Stat. 327.

Anderson, G., Linto, J., & Stewart-Wynne, E. (1995). A population-based assessment of the impact and burden of caregiving for long-term stroke survivors. *Stroke, 26,* 843–849.

Andersen, G., Vestergaard, K., & Lauritzen, L. (1994). Effective treatment of poststroke depression with selective serotonin reuptake inhibitor citalopram. *Stroke, 25* 1099–1104.

Andersen, G., Vestergaard, K., & Riis, J. (1993). Citalopram for post-stroke pathological crying. *Lancet, 342,* 837–839.

Angeleri, F., Angeleri, V. A., Foschi, N., Giaquinto, S., & Nolfe, G. (1993). The influence of depression, social activity, and family stress on functional outcome after stroke. *Stroke, 24,* 1478–1483.

Annon, J. (1974). *The behavioral treatment of sexual problems.* Honolulu, HI: Enabling Systems.

Astrom, M. (1996). Generalized anxiety disorder in stroke patients: A 3-year longitudinal study. *Stroke, 27,* 270–275.

Bamford, J., Dennis, M., Sandercock, P., Burn, J., & Warlow, C. (1990). The frequency, causes and timing of death within 30 days of stroke: The Oxfordshire Community Stroke Project. *Journal of Neurology, Neurosurgery, and Psychiatry, 53,* 824–829.

Baum, H. (1982). Stroke prevalence: An analysis of data from the 1977 National Health Interview survey. *Public Health Reports, 97,* 24–30.

Becker, C., Howard, G., Leroy, K. R., Yatsu, F. M., Tooler, J. F., Coull, B., Feibel, J., & Walker, M. (1986). Community hospital-based stroke programs: North Carolina, Oregon, and New York—Part II. *Stroke, 17,* 285–293.

Benson, D. F., & Ardila, A. (1996). *Aphasia: A clinical perspective.* New York: Oxford University Press.

Berti, A., Ladavas, E., & Della Corte, M. (1996). Anosognosia for hemiplegia, neglect dyslexia, and drawing neglect: Clinical findings and theoretical considerations. *Journal of the International Neuropsychological Society, 2,* 426–440.

Black-Schaffer, R. M., & Lemieux, L. (1994). Vocational outcome after stroke. *Topics in Stroke Rehabilitation, 1,* 74–86.

Black-Schaffer, R. M., & Osberg, J. (1990). Return to work after stroke: Development of a predictive model. *Archives of Physical Medicine and Rehabilitation, 71,* 285–290.

Boldrini, P., Basaglia, N., & Calanca, M. C. (1991). Sexual changes in hemiparetic patients. *Archives of Physical Medicine and Rehabilitation, 72,* 202–207.

Bonita, R., & Beaglehole, R. (1993). Stroke mortality. In J. P. Whisnant (Ed.), *Stroke: Populations, cohorts, and clinical trials* (pp. 59–79). Boston: Butterworth-Heinemann.

Bornstein, R., & Brown, G. (Eds.). (1991). *Neurobehavioral aspects of cerebrovascular disease.* New York: Oxford University Press.

Bray, G., DeFrank, R., & Wolfe, T. (1981). Sexual functioning in stroke survivors. *Archives of Physical Medicine and Rehabilitation, 62,* 286–288.

Broderick, J., Brott, T., Kothari, R., Miller, R., Khoury, J., Pancioli, A., Gebel, J., Mills, D., Minneci, L., & Shukla, R. (1998). The Greater Cincinnati/Northern Kentucky Stroke Study: Preliminary first-ever and total incidence rates of stroke among blacks. *Stroke, 29,* 415–421.

Brooke, M., Questad, K., Patterson, D., & Valois, T. (1992). Driving evaluation after traumatic brain injury. *American Journal of Physical Medicine and Rehabilitation, 71,* 177–182.

Brown, G. G., Baird, A. D., Shatz, M. W., & Bornstein, R. A. (1996). The effects of cerebral vascular disease on neuropsychological functioning. In I. Grant & K. A. Adams (Eds.), *Neuropsychological assessment of neuropsychiatric disorders* (pp. 343–378). New York: Oxford University Press.

Burvill, P. W., Johnson, G. A., Jamrozik, K. D., Anderson, C. S., Stewart-Wynne, E. G., & Chakera, T. M. H. (1995). Anxiety disorders after stroke: Results from the Perth Community Stroke Study. *British Journal of Psychiatry, 166,* 328–332.

Calvanio, R., Levine, D., & Petrone, P. (1993). Elements of cognitive rehabilitation after right hemisphere stroke. *Neurologic Clinics, 11,* 25–63.

Caplan, B. (1982). Neuropsychology in rehabilitation: Its role in evaluation and intervention. *Archives of Physical Medicine and Rehabilitation, 63,* 362–366.

Caplan, B. (1987). Assessment of unilateral neglect: A new reading test. *Journal of Clinical and Experimental Neuropsychology, 9,* 359–364.

Caplan, B., & Reidy, K. (1996). Staff–patient–family conflicts in rehabilitation: Sources and solutions. *Topics in Spinal Cord Injury, 2,* 21–33.

Caplan, B., & Shechter, J. A. (1991). Vocational capacity with cognitive impairment. In S. J. Scheer (Ed.), *Medical perspectives in vocational assessment of impaired workers* (pp. 149–172). Gaithersburg, MD: Aspen.

Caplan, B., & Shechter, J. (1995). The role of neuropsychological assessment in rehabilitation: History, rationale, and examples. In L. A. Cushman & M. J. Scherer (Eds.), *Psychological assessment in medical rehabilitation* (pp. 359–391). Washington, DC: American Psychological Association.

Castillo, C. S., & Robinson, R. G. (1993). Focal neuropsychiatric syndromes after cerebrovascular disease. *Current Opinion in Psychiatry, 6,* 109–112.

Chae, J., Zorowitz, R. D., & Johnston, M. V. (1996). Functional outcome of hemorrhagic and nonhemorrhagic stroke patients after in-patient rehabilitation. *American Journal of Physical Medicine and Rehabilitation, 75,* 177–182.

Clark, G., & Bray, G. (Eds.). (1984). *A stroke family guide and resource.* Springfield, IL: Charles C Thomas.

Coslett, H. B. (1997). Acquired dyslexia. In T. E. Feinberg & M. J. Farah (Eds.), *Behavioral neurology and neuropsychology* (pp. 197–208). New York: McGraw-Hill.

Coughlan, A., & Humphrey, M. (1982). Presenile stroke: Long term outcome for patients and their families. *Rheumatology and Rehabilitation, 21,* 115–120.

Crosson, B., Barco, P. P., Velozo, C. A., Bolesta, M. M., Cooper, P. V., Werts, D., & Brobeck, T. C. (1989). Awareness and compensation in postacute head injury rehabilitation. *Journal of Head Trauma Rehabilitation, 4,* 46–54.

Cummings, J., & Mahler, M. (1991). Cerebrovascular dementia. In R. Bornstein & G. Brown (Eds.), *Neurobehavioral aspects of cerebrovascular disease* (pp. 131–149). New York: Oxford University Press.

Currier, M. B., Murray, G. B., & Welch, C. C. (1992). Electroconvulsive therapy for poststroke depressed geriatric patients. *Journal of Neuropsychiatry and Clinical Neurosciences, 4,* 140–144.

Cutting, J. E. (1978). Study of anosognosia. *Journal of Neurology, Neurosurgery, and Psychiatry, 41,* 548–555.

de Haan, R. J., Limburg, M., Van der Meulen, J. H., Jacobs, H. M., & Aaronson, N. K. (1995). Quality of life after stroke. Impact of stroke type and lesion location. *Stroke, 26,* 402–408.

Delaney, R. C., & Ravdin, L. D. (1997). The neuropsychology of stroke. In P. D. Nussbaum (Ed.), *Handbook of neuropsychology and aging* (pp. 315–330). New York: Plenum Press.

Dijkerman, H., Wood, V., & Hewer, R. L. (1996). Long-term outcome after discharge from a stroke rehabilitation unit. *Journal of the Royal College of Physicians of London, 30,* 538–546.

Diller, L., & Gordon, W. A. (1981). Rehabilitation and clinical neuropsychology. In S. B. Filskov & T. J. Boll (Eds.), *Handbook of clinical neuropsychology* (pp. 702–733). New York: Wiley.

Dobkin, B. D. (1995). The economic impact of stroke. *Neurology, 45*(Suppl. 1), S6–S9.

Ducharme, S. (1987). Sexuality and physical disability. In B. Caplan (Ed.), *Rehabilitation psychology desk reference* (pp. 419–435). Gaithersburg, MD: Aspen.

Ellis, S., & Small, M. (1997). Localization of lesion in denial of hemiplegia after acute stroke. *Stroke, 28,* 67–71.

Evans, R. L., Hendricks, R. D., Haselkorn, J. K., Bishop, D. S., & Baldwin, D. (1992). The family's role in stroke rehabilitation: A review of the literature. *American Journal of Physical Medicine and Rehabilitation, 71,* 135–139.

Evans, R. L., Matlock, A. L., Bishop, D. S., Stranahan, S., & Pederson, C. (1988). Family intervention after stroke: Does counseling or education help? *Stroke, 19,* 1243–1249.

Feibel J., & Springer, C. (1982). Depression and failure to resume social activities after stroke. *Archives of Physical Medicine and Rehabilitation, 63,* 276–278.

Feibel, J., Joynt, R., & Berk, S. (1979). The unmet needs of stroke survivors [Abstract]. *Neurology, 29,* 592.

Feinberg, T., & Farah, M. (Eds.). (1997). *Behavioral neurology and neuropsychology.* New York: McGraw-Hill.

Ferraro, M., & Nagele, D. (1989). Applying neuropsychological principles to functional assessment and intervention in brain injury rehabilitation. *Rehabilitation Report, 5,* 4–6.

Filley, C. M. (1995). *Neurobehavioral anatomy.* Niwot: University of Colorado Press.

Fisk, G. D., Owsley, C., & Pulley, L. V. (1997). Driving after stroke: Driving, exposure, advice, and evaluations. *Archives of Physical Medicine and Rehabilitation, 78,* 1338–1345.

Folstein, M. F., Folstein, S. E., & McHugh, P. R. (1975). Mini-mental state. *Journal of Psychiatric Research, 12,* 189–198.

Fugl-Meyer, A., & Jaasko, L. (1980). Post-stroke hemiplegia and sexual intercourse. *Scandinavian Journal of Rehabilitation Medicine, 7*(Suppl.), 158–165.

Gainotti, G. (1972). Emotional behavior and hemispheric side of lesion. *Cortex, 8,* 41–55.

Gainotti, G., Azzoni, A., Gasparini, F., Marra, C., & Razzano, C. (1997). Relation of lesion location to verbal and nonverbal mood measures in stroke patients. *Stroke, 28,* 2145–2149.

Galski, T., Bruno, R. L., Zorowitz, R., & Walker, J. (1993). Predicting length of stay, functional outcome, and aftercare in the rehabilitation of stroke patients: The dominant role of higher-order cognition. *Stroke, 24,* 1794–1800.

Gialanella, B., & Mattioli, F. (1992). Anosognosia and extrapersonal neglect as predictors of functional recovery following right hemisphere stroke. *Neuropsychological Rehabilitation, 2,* 169–178.

Goldberg, G., & Berger, G. G. (1988). Secondary prevention in stroke: A primary rehabilitation concern. *Archives of Physical Medicine and Rehabilitation, 69,* 32–40.

Golper, L., Rau, M., & Marshall, R. (1980). Aphasic adults and their decisions on driving: An evaluation. *Archives of Physical Medicine and Rehabilitation, 61,* 34–40.

Gonzalez-Torrecillas, J. L., Mendlewicz, J., & Lobo, A. (1995). Effects of early treatment of poststroke depression on neuropsychological rehabilitation. *International Psychogeriatrics, 7,* 547–560.

Good, D. (1997). Sexual dysfunction following stroke. In M. Aisen (Ed.), *Sexual and reproductive neurorehabilitation* (pp. 145–167). Totowa, NJ: Humana Press.

Gordon, W. A., & Hibbard, M. R. (1997). Poststroke depression: An examination of the literature. *Archives of Physical Medicine and Rehabilitation, 78,* 658–663.

Gorelick, P. B. (1994). Stroke prevention: An opportunity for efficient utilization of health care resources during the coming decade. *Stroke, 25,* 220–224.

Gouvier, W. D., Ryan, L. M., O'Jile, J. R., Parks-Levy, J., Webster, J. S., & Blanton, P. D. (1997). Cognitive retraining with brain-damaged patients. In A. M. Horton, D. Wedding, & J. Webster (Eds.), *The neuropsychology handbook: Vol. 2. Treatment issues and special populations* (pp. 3–46). New York: Springer.

Granger, C., Hamilton, B., & Gresham, G. (1988). Stroke rehabilitation outcome study: Part 1. General description. *Archives of Physical Medicine and Rehabilitation, 68,* 506–509.

Gresham, G. E., Fitzpatrick, T. E., Wolf, P. A., McNamara, P. M., Kannel, W. B., & Dawber, T. R. (1975). Residual disability in survivors of stroke—The Framingham Study. *New England Journal of Medicine, 293,* 954–956.

Gresham, G., Phillips, T., & Wolf, P. (1979). Epidemiologic profile of long-term stroke disability: The Framingham study. *Archives of Physical Medicine and Rehabilitation, 60,* 487–491.

Gresham, G. E. (Chair). (1995a). *Post-stroke rehabilitation. Clinical practice guideline* (AHCRQ Pub. No. 16). Rockville, MD: U.S. Department of Health and Human Services, Public Health Service, Agency for Health Care Policy and Research

Gresham, G. E. (Chair). (1995b). *Post-stroke rehabilitation: Patient and family guide* (AHCRQ Publication). Rockville, MD: U.S. Department of Health and Human Services, Public Health Service, Agency for Health Care Policy and Research.

Grober, S., Hibbard, M., Gordon, W., Stein, P., & Freeman, A. (1993). The psychotherapeutic treatment of post-stroke depression with cognitive behavioral therapy. In W. A. Gordon (Ed.), *Advances in stroke rehabilitation* (pp. 215–241) Andover, MA: Andover Medical.

Hakim, A. M. (1998). Ischemic penumbra: The therapeutic window. *Neurology, 51*(Suppl. 3), S44–S46.

Hawton, K. (1984). Sexual adjustment of men who have had strokes. *Journal of Psychosomatic Research, 28,* 243–249.

Henon, H., Pasquier, F., Durieu, I., Godefroy, O., Lucas, C., Lebert, F., & Leys, D. (1997). Preexisting dementia in stroke patients: Baseline frequency, associated factors, and outcome. *Stroke, 28,* 2429–2436.

Hibbard, M., Gordon, W., Stein, P., Grober, S., & Sliwinski, M. (1993). A multi-modal approach to the diagnosis of post-stroke depression. In W. Gordon (Ed.), *Advances in stroke rehabilitation* (pp. 185–214). Andover, MA: Andover Medical.

Hier, D. B., Mondlock, J., & Caplan, L. R. (1983). Behavioral abnormalities after right hemisphere stroke. *Neurology, 33,* 337–344.

House, A., Dennis, M., Warlow, C., Hawton, K., & Molyneux, A. (1990). The relationship between intellectual impairment and mood disorder in the first year after stroke. *Psychological Medicine, 20,* 805–814.

Howard, G., Till, J., Toole, J., Matthews, C., & Truscott, L. (1985). Factors influencing return to work following cerebral infarction. *Journal of the American Medical Association, 253,* 226–232.

Indredavik, B., Bakke, F., Slordahl, S. A., Rokseth, R., & Haheim, L. L. (1998). Stroke unit treatment improves long-term quality of life: A randomized controlled trial. *Stroke, 29,* 895–899.

Johnstone, B., Frank, R. G., Belar, C., Berk, S., Bieliauskas, L. A., Bigler, E. D., Caplan, B., Elliott, T., Glueckauf, R., Kaplan, R. M., Kreutzer, J., Mateer, C., Patterson, D., Puente, A., Richards, J. S., Rosenthal, M., Sherer, M., Shewchuk, R., Siegel, L., & Sweet, J. J. (1995). Psychology in health care: Future directions. *Professional Psychology: Research and Practice, 26,* 341–365.

Kelly-Hayes, M., & Paige, C. (1995). Assessment and psychologic factors in stroke rehabilitation. *Neurology, 45*(Suppl. 1), S29–S32.

Kempers, E. (1994). Preparing the young stroke survivor for return to work. *Topics in Stroke Rehabilitation, 1,* 65–73.

Kiernan, R. J., Mueller, J., Langston, J. W., & Van Dyke, C. (1987). The Neurobehavioral Cognitive Status Examination: A brief but quantitative approach to cognitive assessment. *Annals of Internal Medicine, 107,* 481–485.

Kirk, A., & Kertesz, A. (1989). Hemispheric contributions to drawing. *Neuropsychologia, 27,* 881–886.

Kolb, B., & Whishaw, I. Q. (1990). *Fundamentals of human neuropsychology* (3rd ed.). New York: Freeman.

Kotila, M., Niemi, M.-L., & Laaksonen, R. (1986). Four-year prognosis of stroke patients with visuospatial inattention. *Scandinavian Journal of Rehabilitation Medicine, 18,* 177–179.

Kraus, M. F. (1995). Neuropsychiatric sequelae of stroke and traumatic brain injury: The role of psychostimulants. *International Journal of Psychiatry in Medicine, 25,* 39–51.

Langer, K. G., & Padrone, F. J. (1992). Psychotherapeutic treatment of awareness in acute rehabilitation of traumatic brain injury. *Neuropsychological Rehabilitation, 2,* 59–70.

Latow, J. (1983, August). *Effectiveness of psychotherapy for stroke victims during rehabilitation.* Paper presented at the 91st Annual Convention of the American Psychological Association, Anaheim, CA.

Lauritzen, L., Bjerg Bendsen, B., Vilmar, T., Bjerg Bendsen, E., Lunde, M., & Bech, P. (1994). Post-stroke depression: Combined treatment with imipramine or desipramine and mianserin. *Psychopharmacology, 114,* 119–122.

Lebrun, Y., Leleux, C., Fery, C., Domes, M., & Buyssens, E. (1978). Aphasia and fitness to drive. In *Clinical Aphasiology Conference proceedings.* Minneapolis, MN: BRK.

Legh-Smith, J., Wade, D. T., & Hewer, R. L. (1986). Driving after stroke. *Royal Society of Medicine, 79,* 200–203.

Levine, D. N., Calvanio, R., & Rinn, W. E. (1991). The pathogenesis of anosognosia for hemiplegia. *Neurology, 41,* 1770–1781.

Lewinter, M., & Mikkelsen, S. (1995). Patients' experience of rehabilitation after stroke. *Disability and Rehabilitation, 17,* 3–9.

Lezak, M. D. (1978). Living with the characterologically altered brain-injured patient. *Journal of Clinical Psychiatry, 39,* 592–598.

Lezak, M. D. (1987). Assessment for rehabilitation planning. In M. Meier, A. Benton, & L. Diller (Eds.), *Neuropsychological rehabilitation* (pp. 41–58). New York: Oxford University Press.

Lezak, M. D. (1995). *Neuropsychological assessment* (3rd ed.). New York: Oxford University Press.

Lipsey, J. R., Robinson, R. G., Pearlson, G. D., Rao, K., & Price, T. (1984). Nortriptyline treatment for poststroke depression: A double-blind trial. *Lancet, 1,* 297–300.

Macnamara, S. E., Gummow, L. J., Goka, R., & Gregg, C. H. (1990). Caregiver strain: Need for late poststroke intervention. *Rehabilitation Psychology, 35,* 71–78.

Margolin, D. I. (1992). *Cognitive neuropsychology in clinical practice.* New York: Oxford University Press.

Marin, R. S., Fogel, B. S., Hawkins, J., Duffy, J., & Krupp, B. (1995). Apathy: A treatable syndrome. *Journal of Neuropsychiatry and Clincal Neurosciences, 7,* 23–30.

Mayer, N., Keating, D., & Rapp, D. (1986). Skills, routines, and activity patterns of daily living: A functional nested approach. In B. Uzzell & Y. Gross (Eds.), *Clinical neuropsychology of intervention* (pp. 205–222). Boston: Martinus Nijhoff.

McCaffrey, R. J., & Fisher, J. M. (1987). Cognitive, behavioral and psychosocial sequelae of cerebrovascular accidents and closed head injuries in older adults. In L. L. Carstensen & B. A. Edelstein (Eds.), *Handbook of clinical gerontology* (pp. 277–288). New York: Pergamon Press.

McGlynn, S., & Schacter, D. (1989). Unawareness in neuropsychological syndromes. *Journal of Clinical and Experimental Neuropsychology, 11,* 143–205.

Mercier, P., LeGall, D., Aubin, G., Joseph, P., Alhayek, G., & Guy, G. (1991). Value of the neuropsychological evaluation in cerebral arterial aneurysms surgically treated. *Neurochirurgie, 37,* 32–39.

Miyai, I., & Reding, M. J. (1998). Effects of antidepressants on functional recovery following stroke: A double-blind study. *Journal of Neurologic Rehabilitation, 12,* 5–13.

Monga, T., Lawson, J., & Inglis, J. (1986). Sexual dysfunction in stroke patients. *Archives of Physical Medicine and Rehabilitation, 67,* 19–22.

Mora, C., & Bornstein, R. A. (1998). Evaluation of cerebrovascular disease. In G. Goldstein, P. D. Nussbaum, & S. R. Beers (Eds.), *Neuropsychology* (pp. 171–186). New York: Plenum Press.

Morris, P. L. P., Robinson, R. G., Andrzejewski, P., Samuels, J., & Price, T. R. (1993). Association of depression with 10-year poststroke mortality. *American Journal of Psychiatry, 150,* 124–129.

Morris, P. L. P., Robinson, R. G., Raphael, B., & Hopwood, M. J. (1996). Lesion location and poststroke depression. *Journal of Neuropsychiatry and Clinical Neurosciences, 8,* 399–403.

Nelson, L., Mitrushina, M., Satz, P., Sowa, M., & Cohen, S. (1993). Cross-validation of the neuropsychology behavior and affect profile in stroke patients. *Psychological Assessment, 5,* 374–376.

Okada, K., Kobayashi, S., Yamagati, S., Takahashi, K., & Yamaguchi, S. (1997). Poststroke apathy and regional cerebral blood flow. *Stroke, 28,* 2437–3441.

O'Rourke, S., MacHale, S., Signorini, D., & Dennis, M. (1998). Detecting psychiatric morbidity after stroke. *Stroke, 29,* 980–985.

Osmon, D. C., Smet, I. C., Winegarden, B., & Gandhavadi, B. (1992). Neurobehavioral cognitive status examination: Its use with unilateral stroke patients in a rehabilitation setting. *Archives of Physical Medicine and Rehabilitation, 73,* 414–418.

Pancioli, A. M., Broderick, J., Kothari, R., Brott, T., Tuchfarber, A., Miller, R., Khoury, J., & Jauch, E. (1998). Public perception of stroke warning signs and knowledge of potential risk factors. *Journal of the American Medical Association, 279,* 1288–1292.

Paolucci, S., Antonucci, G., Gialloretti, L. E., Traballesi, M., Lubich, S., Pratesi, L., & Palombi, L. (1996). Predicting stroke inpatient rehabilitation outcome: The prominent role of neuropsychological disorders. *European Neurology, 36,* 385–390.

Parikh, R. M., Robinson, R. G., Lipsey, J. R., Starkstein, S. E., Federoff, J. P., & Price, T. R. (1990). The impact of poststroke depression on recovery in activities of daily living over a 2-year follow-up. *Archives of Neurology, 47,* 785–789.

Phillips, N. A., & Mate-Kole, C. C. (1997). Cognitive deficits in peripheral vascular disease: A comparison of mild stroke patients and normal control subjects. *Stroke, 28,* 777–784.

Pohjasvaara, T., Erkinjuntti, T., Vataja, R., & Kaste, M. (1997). Dementia three months after stroke: Baseline frequency and effect of different definitions of dementia in the Helsinki Stroke Aging Memory Study (SAM) cohort. *Stroke, 28,* 785–792.

Poser, C. (1993). Automobile driving fitness and neurological impairment. *Journal of Neuropsychiatry and Clinical Neurosciences, 5,* 342–348.

Ramasubbu, R., Robinson, R. G., Flint, A. J., Kosier, T., & Price, T. R. (1998). Functional impairment associated with acute poststroke depression: The stroke data bank study. *Journal of Neuropsychiatry and Clinical Neurosciences, 10,* 26–33.

Rentz, D. M. (1991). The assessment of rehabilitation potential: Cognitive factors. In R. J. Hartke (Ed.), *Psychological aspects of rehabilitation* (pp. 97–114). Gaithersburg, MD: Aspen.

Riddoch, M. J., & Humphreys, G. W. (1994). *Cognitive neuropsychology and cognitive rehabilitation.* Hillsdale, NJ: Erlbaum.

Robertson, I. H. (1993). Cognitive rehabilitation in neurologic disease. *Current Opinion in Neurology, 6,* 756–760.

Robinson, R. G. (1998). *The clinical neuropsychiatry of stroke.* New York: Cambridge University Press.

Robinson, R. G., Bolla-Wilson, K., Kaplan, E., Lipsey, J., & Price, T. (1986). Depression influences intellectual impairment in stroke patients. *British Journal of Psychiatry, 148,* 541–547.

Robinson, R. G., & Starkstein, S. E. (1990). Current research in affective disorders following stroke. *Journal of Neuropsychiatry and Clinical Neurosciences, 2,* 1–14.

Robinson, R. G., Starr, L. B., Lipsey, J. R., Rao, K., & Price, T. (1984). A 2-year longitudinal study of poststroke mood disorders: Dynamic changes in associated variables over the first 6 months of follow-up. *Stroke, 15,* 510–517.

Romano, M. (1973, Winter). Sexuality and the disabled female. *Accent on Living,* pp. 27–34.

Ronning, O. M., & Guldvog, B. (1998). Stroke unit versus general medical wards: II. Neurological deficits and activities of daily living. *Stroke, 29,* 586–590.

Ross, E. (1997). The aprosodias. In T. Feinberg & M. Farah (Eds.), *Behavioral neurology and neuropsychology* (pp. 699–709). New York: McGraw-Hill.

Ross, E., & Rush, A. (1981). Diagnosis and neuroanatomical correlates of depression in brain-damaged patients. *Archives of General Psychiatry, 38,* 1345–1354.

Roth, E. J., Heinemann, A. W., Lovell, L. L., Harvey, R. L., McGuire, J. R., & Diaz, S. (1998). Impairment and disability: Their relation during stroke rehabilitation. *Archives of Physical Medicine and Rehabilitation, 79,* 329–335.

Sbordone, R. J., & Long, C. J. (1996). *Ecological validity of neuropsychological testing.* Delray Beach, FL: GR Press/St. Lucie Press.

Schwartz, J. A., Speed, N. M., Brunberg, J. A., Brewer, T. L., Brown, M., & Greden, J. F. (1993). Depression in stroke rehabilitation. *Biological Psychiatry, 33,* 694–699.

Sharpe, M., Hawton, K., House, A., Molyneux, A., Sandercock, P., Bamford, J., & Warlow, C. (1990). Mood disorders in long-term survivors of stroke: Associations wih brain lesion location and volume. *Psychological Medicine, 20,* 815–828.

Shimoda, K., & Robinson, R. G. (1998). Effect of anxiety disorder on impairment and recovery from stroke. *Journal of Neuropsychiatry and Clinical Neurosciences, 10,* 34–40.

Signer, S., Cummings, J. L., & Benson, D. F. (1989). Delusions and mood disorders in patients with chronic aphasia. *Journal of Neuropsychiatry and Clinical Neurosciences, 1*(1), 40–45.

Small, M., & Ellis, S. (1996). Denial of hemiplegia: An investigation into the theories of causation. *European Neurology, 36,* 353–363.

Smolkin, C., & Cohen, B. (1974). Socioeconomic factors affecting the vocational success of stroke patients. *Archives of Physical Medicine and Rehabilitation, 55,* 269–271.

Spencer, K. A., Tompkins, C. A., & Schulz, R. (1997). Assessment of depression in patients with brain pathology: The case of stroke. *Psychological Bulletin, 122,* 132–152.

Starkstein, S. E., Cohen, B. S., Federoff, P., Parikh, R. M., Price, T. R., & Robinson, R. G. (1990). Relationship between anxiety disorders and depressive disorders in patients with cerebrovascular injury. *Archives of General Psychiatry, 47,* 246–251.

Starkstein, S. E., Federoff, P., Berthier, M. L., & Robinson, R. (1991). Manic-depressive and pure manic states after brain lesions. *Biological Psychiatry, 29,* 149–158.

Starkstein, S. E., Federoff, J. P., Price, T. R., Leiguarda, R., & Robinson, R. G. (1992). Anosognosia in patients with cerebrovascular lesions: A study of causative factors. *Stroke, 23,* 1446–1453.

Starkstein, S. E., Federoff, J. P., Price, R., Leiguarda, R., & Robinson, R. G. (1993). Apathy following cerebrovascular lesions. *Stroke, 24,* 1625–1630.

Stein, P., Berger, A., Hibbard, M., & Gordon, W. (1993). Interventions with the spouses of stroke survivors. In W. Gordon (Ed.), *Advances in stroke rehabilitation* (pp. 242–257). Andover, MA: Andover Medical.

Stein, P., Sliwinski, M., Gordon, W., & Hibbard, M. (1996). The discriminative properties of somatic and non-somatic symptoms for post-stroke depression. *The Clinical Neuropsychologist, 10,* 141–148.

Stern, R. A., & Bachman, D. L. (1991). Depressive symptoms following stroke. *American Journal of Psychiatry, 148,* 351–356.

Stiers, W., & Kewman, D. (1997). Psychology and medical rehabilitation: Moving toward a consumer driven health care system. *Journal of Clinical Psychology in Medical Settings, 4,* 167–179.

von Steinbuchel, N., von Cramon, D., & Poppel, E. (Eds.). (1992). *Neuropsychological rehabilitation.* Berlin, Germany: Springer-Verlag.

Stineman, M., Maislin, G., Fiedler, R., & Granger, C. (1997). A prediction model for functional recovery in stroke. *Stroke, 28,* 550–556.

Stroke Unit Trialists' Collaboration. (1997). How do stroke units improve patient outcomes? A collaborative systematic review of the randomized trials. *Stroke, 28,* 2139–2144.

Sundet, K., Finset, A., & Reinvang, I. (1988). Neuropsychological predictors in stroke rehabilitation. *Journal of Clinical and Experimental Neuropsychology, 10,* 363–379.

Taylor, T. N., Davis, P. H., Torner, J. C., Holmes, J., Meyer, J. W., & Jacobson, M. F. (1996). Lifetime cost of stroke in the United States. *Stroke, 27,* 1459–1466.

Teng, E. L., & Chui, H. C. (1987). The Modified Mini-Mental State (3MS) Examination. *Journal of Clinical Psychiatry, 48,* 314–318.

Terent, A. (1993). Stroke morbidity. In J. P. Whisnant (Ed.), *Stroke: Populations, cohorts, and clinical trials* (pp. 37–58). Boston: Butterworth-Heinemann.

Toedter, L. J., Reese, C. A., Berk, S. N., Schall, R. R., Hyland, D. T., & Dunn, D. S. (1995). The reliability of psychological measures in the assessment of stroke patients: Caveat inquisitor? *Archives of Physical Medicine and Rehabilitation, 76,* 719–725.

Trieschmann, R. B. (1980). *Spinal cord injuries.* New York: Pergamon Press.

Ween, J. E., Alexander, M. P., D'Esposito, M., & Roberts, M. (1996). Factors predictive of stroke rehabilitation outcome in a rehabilitation settting. *Neurology, 47,* 388–392.

Wehman, P., West, M., Fry, R., Sherron, P., Groah, C., Kreutzer, J., & Sale, P. (1989). Effect of supported employment on the vocational outcomes of persons with traumatic brain injury. *Journal of Applied Behavior Analysis, 22,* 395–405.

Weinfeld, F. (1981). The national survey of stroke. *Stroke, 12*(Suppl.), 1–71.

Weinstein, E. (1991). Anosognosia and denial of illness. In G. Prigatano & D. Schacter (Eds.), *Awareness of deficit after brain injury* (pp. 240–257). New York: Oxford University Press.

Weisbroth, S., Esibill, N., & Zuger, R. (1971). Factors in the vocational success of hemiplegic patients. *Archives of Physical Medicine and Rehabilitation, 52,* 441–446.

Welch, K., & Levine, S. (1991). Focal brain ischemia: Pathophysiology and acid-base status. In R. Bornstein & G. Brown (Eds.), *Neurobehavioral aspects of cerebrovascular disease* (pp. 17–38). New York: Oxford University Press.

Wentworth, D., & Atkinson, R. (1996). Implementation of an acute stroke program decreases hospitalization costs and length of stay. *Stroke, 27,* 1040–1043.

Williams, J. M. (1993). *Clinical neuropsychology.* Woodsboro, MD: Cool Springs Software.

Woessner, R., & Caplan, B. (1996). Emotional distress following stroke: Interpretive limitations of the SCL-90-R. *Assessment, 3,* 291–305.

Wolf, P. A. (1997). Epidemiology and risk factor management. In K. M. A. Welch, L. R. Caplan, D. J. Reis, & B. K. Siesjo (Eds.), *Primer on cerebrovascular diseases* (pp. 751–757). San Diego, CA: Academic Press.

World Health Organization. (1989). Stroke 1989: Recommendations on stroke prevention, diagnosis, and therapy. *Stroke, 20,* 1407–1431.

Yatsu, F., Grotta, J., & Pettigrew, L. (1995). *Stroke: 100 maxims.* St. Louis, MO: Mosby.

Zalewski, C., Keller, B., Bowers, C., Miske, P., & Gradman, T. (1994). Depressive symptomatology and post-stroke rehabilitation outcome. *The Clinical Gerontologist, 14,* 52–67.

5

Geriatric Issues

Peter A. Lichtenberg and Susan E. MacNeill

The number of older adults requiring medical rehabilitation has increased significantly in the 1980s and 1990s, and this area of subspecialization within rehabilitation psychology is likely to continue to evolve. This chapter is designed to introduce rehabilitation psychologists to the unique aspects of geriatric rehabilitation. Medical rehabilitation with older adults remains focused on improving functional abilities, particularly activities of daily living (e.g., ADL; bathing, dressing, grooming, transferring) and instrumental ADL (e.g., financial management, shopping, medication management, driving), as well as returning older adults into independent-living arrangements. The challenge and opportunities for psychologists lie in defining how mental health issues affect these important rehabilitation outcomes. We explore these issues by examining the history of geriatric rehabilitation, the impact of mental health problems on health outcomes in older adults, and the assessment and treatment of psychological disorders in rehabilitation settings. A model for working with medically ill geriatric patients is presented.

History

Current models of geriatric rehabilitation have arisen primarily from patient need and financial reimbursement issues rather than from a theoretically driven model of care. Haffey and Welsh (1995) reviewed the major financial forces behind the incredible growth of rehabilitation services to older adults. During the 1980s, the advent of the prospective payments to hospitals for diagnosis-related groups (DRGs) triggered the use of rehabilitation hospitals for admission and treatment of older adults who could not yet function independently at home. With DRGs for instance, acute care hospitals were paid a set amount per primary diagnosis no matter what secondary diagnoses existed. Thus, patients were discharged from hospitals quicker and sicker. If patients had functional deficits, they could be discharged to rehabilitation centers, which could receive reimbursement from Medicare for continued inpatient stays. However, given the relatively high cost of the inpatient rehabilitation service, cost shifting in the 1990s resulted in reduced lengths of stays in acute rehabilitation hospitals and the development of a number of subacute rehabilitation programs located in nursing homes. The combined economic realities of the 1980s and 1990s propelled geriatric rehabilitation into its current level of prominence.

In addition to financial impacts, a second trend that has contributed to the growth of geriatric rehabilitation has been demographic. In the 1980s the fastest growing segment of the population consisted of those ages 85 years and older, and the number of centenarians doubled over the decade. This group represented the frailest of the older adults and the ones who would need the most assistance in regaining independent functioning. These demographic trends are predicted to continue in the coming decades.

Kemp (1990) was the first to highlight the psychological aspects of geriatric rehabilitation. According to Kemp, the purpose of geriatric rehabilitation was not only to improve function and promote independence in older adults but also to improve life satisfaction and self-esteem. The major focus of geropsychology in the rehabilitation setting was to help patients adjust to their disabilities. Kemp identified stages of adjustment as including acute shock and denial followed by acknowledgment of losses and the need to compensate for them. Psychological aspects pertinent to medical rehabilitation were motivation, cognitive ability, depression, and personality traits. Kemp foreshadowed what remain as some of the major roles engaged in by rehabilitation psychologists working with older adults.

Unique Aspects

Kemp's (1990) conceptualization focusing on the adjustment to disability has remained a cornerstone of geriatric rehabilitation. In this conceptualization, psychological issues are not assumed to emerge until after the disability has occurred. Thus, the model posited that patients function and cope well until faced with abrupt trauma, at which point they must develop new coping techniques. This model may be considered relevant for geriatric patients only to the extent that rehabilitation psychologists view medically ill older adults as analogous to younger adults experiencing spinal cord injuries or traumatic brain injuries. In this chapter, we challenge rehabilitation psychologists to relinquish this model in their work with older adults. A rudimentary adjustment model does not take into account the complexities seen with medically ill older adults. Although an elementary model no doubt holds true for certain older adults entering rehabilitation, we provide evidence that pre-existing psychological issues, systemic diseases, and variations across the age span affect recovery over the course of rehabilitation.

Pre-Existing Psychological Disorders

Frequently occurring psychological problems including both cognitive and depressive disorders are directly associated with the medical syndromes that result in admissions to medical rehabilitation units (Lichtenberg, 1998). In a 5-year study of 812 geriatric rehabilitation patients, Hanks and Lichtenberg (1996) demonstrated the comorbidity of physical and mental health problems. Cognitive impairment was present in 40% of all patients, and 34% scored in the depressed range on the Geriatric Depression Scale (GDS; Brink et al., 1982; Yesavage et al., 1983). This pattern of results can be starkly contrasted with community base rates of cognitive deficits in only 15% of older adults (Evans et al., 1989); Hanks and Lichtenberg found a prevalence of 40% for similar aged rehabilitation patients. The trend for an increased prevalence of depression was also found in medical rehabilitation patients. Furthermore, Hanks and Lichtenberg reported the prevalence of depression at 34% for all age groups compared to community estimates of 15% (Blazer, Hughes, & George, 1987).

Systemic Diseases

Chronic medical diseases have tremendous impact on recovery from all primary rehabilitation diagnoses. Systemic diseases such as hypertension, diabetes mellitus, arthritis, and congestive heart failure affect recovery from stroke or hip fracture and health outcomes. In the data set mentioned above, for example, 64% had hypertension and 34% had diabetes. The accumulation of severe comorbid disease was found to be the most powerful predictor of mortality as compared with demographic data 1 year following rehabilitation (Arfken, Lichtenberg, & Kuiken, 1998). Moore and Lichtenberg (1995) demonstrated that the severity of comorbid medical conditions was the single best predictor of functional outcome in a double cross-validation study with older medical rehabilitation patients.

Variation Across the Age Span

The young-old (ages 60–79), and the older-old (those over age 80) may represent different types of aging individuals. In the Hanks and Lichtenberg (1996) study, for example, the young-old patients, contrary to our hypothesis, had more severe medical comorbidities than did the older-old patients. In comparison to community samples of young-old, the age-matched rehabilitation sample had several times the rate of cognitive impairment, depression, and alcohol abuse. In contrast, the older-old group had only slightly higher rates of cognitive impairment, depression, and alcohol abuse as compared to community samples. These data suggest that the young-old patients admitted to a rehabilitation facility represent an extreme sample from this age category. They have more severe illnesses and physical disabilities than their peers. Mental and physical health problems coexist at high levels within this group. These individuals are not likely to be seen as rehabilitation patients in their later 80s and 90s because of the high mortality associated with their combined medical and psychological conditions (Arfken et al., 1998).

The older-old group, on the other hand, represents a group of survivors, who were more likely to be quite healthy in their 60s and 70s. Their rehabilitation problems of lower extremity fractures, joint replacements, and strokes represent the wearing out of their bodies. They often have limited physical functioning skills both at admission and discharge. This group, by virtue of advanced age and weakened condition, is more likely than other groups to enter nursing homes following medical rehabilitation.

Stroke Rehabilitation

Geriatric issues refer to the presence of comorbid conditions, including medical, neurological, and psychological conditions. In this section, we illustrate how clinicians need to conduct their assessments with an eye toward understanding the multiple systems that are impaired in a single individual. Because stroke is primarily a geriatric issue, we explore rehabilitation with stroke patients as a prominent aspect of medical rehabilitation with older adults. In one of the first conceptualizations of stroke as a geriatric issue, Rusin (1990) emphasized the importance of cognitive and affective functioning, as well as caregiving issues with stroke patients. However, Rusin provided no empirical data, nor have empirical studies to date provided an explanation of exactly how stroke rehabilitation is influenced by geriatric issues.

Recovery from stroke is significantly affected by the prevalence of comorbid medical diseases. Diabetes, hypertension, and heart disease are the most common chronic diseases in older adults, increasing their susceptibility to stroke. In a study evaluating the impact of disease on disability, Campbell et al. (1994) found that 79% of an older community sample had at least two chronic conditions, and 36% had more than three. Not only do these chronic diseases increase the risk of stroke, but they also have a tremendous influence on the recovery process during stroke rehabilitation. Because of the interrelationships between heart disease and stroke, they have been most extensively studied. Patients with heart disease are more likely to experience clinical manifestations of disease during rehabilitation and, thus, a more complicated rehabilitation course (Roth, 1994). Diabetes has also been identified as an independent risk factor for stroke and is furthermore a risk factor for mortality following stroke (Tuomilehto, Rastenyte, Jousilahti, Sarti, & Vartiainen, 1996).

Neurological syndromes such as dementia and delirium are also important comorbid conditions to attend to; they are common in older adults and especially in stroke patients. Recent evidence has implicated stroke as a core part of the behavioral expression of Alzheimer's disease. Two recent studies highlighted the high intercorrelation between Alzheimer's disease and stroke. Snowden et al. (1997) found that stroke was central to an observable dementia syndrome in those older individuals with confirmed postmortem evidence of Alzheimer's disease. In a retrospective study of 25 years, Kokmen, Whisnant, O'Fallon, Chu, and Beard (1996) reported that overall dementia rates for stroke patients was 20% but the rate of stroke in people with Alzheimer's disease was greater than predicted. These findings suggest that dementia in older stroke patients may be less related to characteristics of a new-onset stroke (e.g., size or location) and more closely associated with the general integrity of the central nervous system (e.g., presence of cerebral damage). Delirium is also a frequent concomitant of stroke and is closely associated with worse outcome following stroke. These findings emphasize the role of clinical geriatric assessment for clinicians working in stroke rehabilitation. Because of the high occurrence of these neurological processes, clinicians in stroke rehabilitation must be proficient with assessment of both delirium and dementia.

Poststroke depression (PSD) and depression in dementia have been focused on as key to stroke rehabilitation for a long time (Robinson, Kubos, Starr, Rao, & Price, 1984; Robinson, Starr, Kubos, Price, 1983). Depression is a syndrome with many causes; some appear clearly related to neuroanatomical functioning, whereas others may be related to adjustment issues and coping (Hartke, 1991). The literature addressing PSD includes lengthy discussions of the etiology and relationship to location of injury. Whatever the cause, depression has been found to be associated with worse outcome following stroke.

The prevalence of these geriatric factors in stroke rehabilitation was recently investigated by our research team (Mast, MacNeill, & Lichtenberg, 1999). In a study of 97 consecutive stroke rehabilitation patients referred between 1995 and 1997, rates of dementia, depression, and alcohol abuse were calculated. The average age for this cohort of stroke patients was 75 years (SD = 8 years), and their average level of education was 9 years (SD = 4 years). Psychological disturbance was high in both the groups with dementia and those without. More than 50% of the stroke patients had dementia, and 30% of all patients had depression. In the group without dementia, 17% had cognitive impairment.

Impact of Mental Health Problems on Health Outcomes

The relationship between mental health problems and health outcomes, including independence with self-care abilities, is poorly understood. It is incumbent on rehabilitation psychologists to provide evidence that mental health problems are relevant to the outcomes of medical rehabilitation: functional abilities and living independently. Our brief review of research provides empirical support for the importance of rehabilitation psychology with older adults.

Cognition and Health Outcome

Some studies examine the relationship between cognition and ADL abilities in specific populations, such as stroke, geropsychiatric, and Alzheimer's disease patients. Titus, Gall, Yerxa, Roberson, and Mack (1991) compared perceptual abilities in 25 stroke patients with 25 control patients and then correlated these abilities with a performance-based measure of basic ADL tasks. Their sample was relatively young (mean age = 59 years) and well educated (60% completed high school or greater). Whereas only one test was related to dressing skills (visual discrimination, $r = .47$; $p < .01$), several cognitive tests were related to upper extremity hygiene, eating, and total ADL scores. Correlations ranged from .41 to .57.

Nadler, Richardson, Malloy, Marran, and Brinson (1993) examined the relationship of the Mattis Dementia Rating Scale (DRS; Mattis, 1988) to self-care skills in 50 psychogeriatric patients. This sample had a mean age of 75 years and a mean educational level of 10.8 years. A performance-based measure of ADL abilities from the occupational therapy field was used. The DRS total score was significantly related to hygiene skills ($r = .57$). In an extension of this study, Richardson, Nadler, and Malloy (1995) investigated the relationship between several neuropsychological measures (not including the DRS this time) and ADL abilities. A total of 108 psychogeriatric patients participated, with a mean age of 74 years and a mean educational level of 10.6 years. In this study, cognitive tests were unrelated to ADL abilities.

Other researchers have continued to investigate the relationship between neuropsychological performance and everyday functioning (Tupper & Cicerone, 1990, 1991). Tuokko and Crockett (1991) reported on a large study of neuropsychological measures, patient self-ratings, and caregiver ratings in older individuals with and without dementia. They reported that basic self-care skills were the last functions to be affected by dementia. In a medical rehabilitation setting, however, where patients have to learn new techniques and skills for basic self-care, the relationship of cognition to basic self-care skills may emerge as an important one.

Many of the studies cited above have methodological weaknesses. Shortcomings include reliance on self-report or caregiver report of ADL abilities, small sample sizes, and a failure to measure potential mediator variables such as age and education. Two of our studies on the prediction of ADL functioning in urban older medical rehabilitation patients are described below. In these studies, we have attempted to overcome methodological problems cited in research. Specifically, the Functional Independence Measure (FIM) was used as a standardized tool to measure ADL skills (see Lichtenberg, 1998).

Cognition and Recovery of ADL Functioning Over the Course of Rehabilitation

In a first study (Lichtenberg, 1998) on the relationship of mental health problems and health outcome, older medical rehabilitation patients were evaluated on the ADL components of the FIM, with the cognitive components removed (e.g., memory problem solving). The ADL components include seven items measuring feeding, grooming, bathing, dressing upper and lower body, and transferring to toilet and to tub.

A total of 426 consecutive patient admissions to the geriatric rehabilitation unit over a 2½-year period were included in the study. Mean patient age was 78 years (SD = 7.4), mean educational level was 9.8 years (SD = 3.5), mean length of stay was 18.4 days (SD = 7.1), and the mean number of chronic health conditions was 7.5 (SD = 1.5). One-third of the patients were admitted for a lower extremity fracture, one-third for lower extremity weakness or gait disturbance, and one-third for a central nervous system disorder such as a stroke. On admission, the patient's mean functioning for ADL was in the range of modified dependence, which improved to modified independence on discharge. Forty-four percent of the patients scored in the cognitively impaired range on the DRS, and 56% scored in the cognitively unimpaired range, using a cutoff score of 123.

Hierarchical regression analysis was used to evaluate the predictors of change in FIM over the course of rehabilitation. ADL scores at admission were entered first, demographic variables second (age, race, education, and gender), and number of existing medical conditions and length of stay were entered third. Cognition was entered last. Admission ADLs accounted for 53% of the variance in discharge ADL skills. Variables in Steps 2 and 3 did not significantly add to the prediction of discharge ADL scores. Cognition, however, contributed 3% of unique variance in prediction. Results of this study provide evidence that cognition is related to physical recovery during medical rehabilitation. Moore and Lichtenberg (1995) provided further evidence for the importance of cognition in relearning ADL skills during medical rehabilitation in their double cross-validation study.

Predictors of Return to Independent Living

Evaluating the ability to return to independent living, particularly for those patients living alone prior to admission, is a frequent referral question for neuropsychologists in health care settings. Despite the importance of this question, we found only one published study that specifically investigated the relationship between cognitive factors and return to living alone. Friedman (1993) studied 178 older adults who were living alone and had had a stroke. The patients were interviewed at 2, 6, and 12 months poststroke. Thirty-three percent of the patients were discharged back to living alone, and this number remained constant throughout the 12-month follow-up period. In comparing those who returned to living alone with those who did not, ADL abilities, Mini-Mental State Score, and type of stroke (lacunar vs. nonlacunar) were the most powerful predictors of ability to return home alone. This study was conducted in New Zealand, however, and thus has limited generalizability in the United States because the health care systems of the two countries is dramatically different.

MacNeill and Lichtenberg (1997) conducted a study designed to better assess the relationship among cognition, ADL abilities, and return to living alone in a geriatric medical rehabilitation sample. The base rate for living alone prior to admission was 37% for patients over the age 60. A total of 372 patients who entered the hospital and were living alone prior to admission were studied. Similar to our other studies this group had a mean age of 78 years (SD = 7.9) and consisted of 75% women and 66% African American.

One-hundred-forty-six (39%) patients returned to living alone after their hospitalization. Logistic regression with a forward-selection forced-entry method was used to identify the best predictors of return to living alone. When ADL and ambulation abilities from the FIM were entered first, there was a 63% overall correct rate of classification. Demographic variables and comorbid medical disease were entered on the next two steps but did not improve prediction. Finally, the DRS total score was entered. Classification improved by 9% overall to 72% correct classification. Further analysis indicated that both groups performed similarly on motor items of the FIM. We concluded that cognitive deficits are the significant limiting factor in preventing older adults from returning to living alone.

Impact of Depression on Health Outcome

Just as cognition has been related to health outcome, depression has also been identified as having a significant impact on health outcome. Livingston-Bruce, Seeman, Merrill, and Blazer (1994) used community-based cohorts from the National Institute on Aging's Established Populations for Epidemiological Studies of the Elderly to follow 1,189 older adults. The cohort was interviewed in 1988 and again approximately 2.5 years later. Patient mortality from refusals and deaths was 6% (n = 73). Initially, all patients were independent in all ADL. At the second interview, 6% of men and 4% of women had disabilities with regards to ADLs. For both men and women, when controlling for other medical factors, depression emerged as a significant predictor of disability onset.

Depression also appears to be a significant factor in long-term recovery among geriatric stroke patients. Depression may be twice as common in poststroke patients as it is in the older community population (Primeau, 1988). Parikh et al. (1990) studied the relationship of depression to ADL functioning 2 years following the initial stroke. Patients who had been depressed in the hospital were significantly more impaired in physical activities 2 years after their stroke than were the nondepressed patients. Bacher, Korner-Bitensky, Mayo, Becker, and Coopersmith (1990) reported similar findings in their 12-month study of 48 poststroke patients. In none of the above studies, however, did the researchers control for demographic influences on recovery or investigate the role of rehabilitation in recovery.

Other researchers have demonstrated a relationship between functional recovery and depression in geriatric patients following orthopedic injuries. Reduced recovery from hip fracture was associated with depression in a number of studies. Among these, Cummings et al. (1988) provided a 6-month follow-up of 92 patients with hip fracture. Depressive symptomatology was associated with poorer outcome in basic and advanced ADLs

1 year after hip fracture in a sample of 536 geriatric patients assessed by Magaziner, Simonsick, Kashner, Hebel, and Kenzora (1990).

Diamond, Holroyd, Macciocchi, and Felsenthal (1995) investigated the effects of depression on functional outcome during geriatric physical rehabilitation. Depression was prevalent in 29% of the sample at admission and in 22% of the sample at discharge after a 25-day rehabilitation stay. Although the patients with and without depression did not differ on functional abilities at admission, the depressed patients made fewer gains at discharge. Note that without any treatment during their rehabilitation, patients usually remained depressed.

Again methodological weaknesses of the above studies were numerous. Most important, these studies did not control for potential moderator variables such as age, education, sex, and the severity of patients' medical problems. With the exception of the Diamond et al. (1995) study, none of the researchers investigated the role of rehabilitation in the depression–functional recovery relationship. Our research focuses on this issue with a sample of 423 patients. The demographic characteristics of this sample was described in the section on cognition.

In this study, depression among older adults was found to be an important risk factor for failure to recover following illness or injury. In regression analysis, order of variable entry included first demographic variables, length of stay, and number of comorbid medical conditions, followed by a measure of cognitive functioning. Depression was entered in the fourth block of the analysis. The results indicate that whereas depression was not a significant predictor of ADL on admission to rehabilitation, it was a predictor of discharge ADL. Thus, levels of depression were a significant predictor of functional recovery during rehabilitation.

The effects of depression on survival in our geriatric medical rehabilitation population was assessed by examining survival up until 1996 for a sample of older rehabilitation patients admitted between 1991 and 1993 (Arfken, Lichtenberg, & Tancer, 1999). A total of 455 patients, representing consecutive admissions to the geriatric rehabilitation program who received both a cognitive assessment (DRS) and an affective assessment (GDS), were entered into the survival analysis. The researchers examined univariate and multivariate predictors of survival. The yearly mortality rate was 19%, with an overall mortality rate of 36%. Predictor variables included demographic variables, medical burden, ADL abilities, length of stay, and DRS and GDS scores. In the multivariate analysis only two variables predicted survival: a lower depression score and female gender. Lack of depression was the best predictor of survival when compared to all other predictor variables. The relative risk of dying was 38% higher for those with higher GDS scores.

Treatment Issues

Ever-decreasing lengths of stay and shift for neuropsychologists to a consultant role in subacute rehabilitation (e.g., rehabilitation units located in long-term care facilities) are reducing the abilities of psychologists to provide extensive treatment in stroke rehabilitation. In one viable model of treatment under this current system, psychologists create plans for the treatment of psychological disorders, which are then carried out by nonmental health therapists in the rehabilitation team under the psychologist's supervision. This model of treatment was found to be highly effective in the following study.

Lichtenberg, Kimbarow, Morris, and Vangel (1996) developed and carried out a treatment study to evaluate the usefulness of behavioral treatment for depression in older medical rehabilitation inpatients. The major tasks of this study were to develop a treatment protocol that could be delivered by nonmental health professionals in a medical rehabilitation hospital, to specify the treatment in such detail that it could be replicated, and to evaluate the effectiveness of the treatment. Because many hospital or rehabilitation settings do not have the requisite number of psychologists to deliver depression treatment, two behavioral treatment protocols were created: (a) treatment delivered by the psychologist and (b) treatment delivered by trained occupational therapists. Participants in these groups were then compared with a no-treatment control group. The results provided evidence for validity of the treatment.

Clinical Tools

Tools for neuropsychological assessment in the medical rehabilitation of older adults must incorporate three elements. First, the tools must be validated on older populations. Normative data on older adults are essential to the interpretation of any assessment results. Second, the tools must be efficient; the amount of time allowed for psychological services in medical rehabilitation is shrinking as a result of decreased lengths of stay and downsized health care systems. Third, tools must be scrutinized for their validity with minority populations. Validating assessment tools with diverse patient populations must be a priority for rehabilitation psychology. In the following section, we briefly review the tools for the assessment of cognition, depression, and alcohol abuse.

Normative Studies Research Project Test Battery

The NSRP is a brief cognitive test battery requiring between $1\frac{1}{4}$ and 2 hours to complete (Lichtenberg, 1998). Assessment of all aspects of memory is emphasized. Also included in the NSRP battery are tests that tap into the domains of language, visuospatial skills, and executive functioning. An important inclusion to the NSRP battery is a test of reading as a brief assessment of premorbid functioning. A sample of 237 patients were given the following tests: DRS, Boston Naming Test, Hooper Visual Organization Test, Visual Form Discrimination Test, and Logical Memory I and II to examine clinical value of the NSRP battery. Of the 237 patients,

74 were cognitively intact and fully independent in ADL abilities, 89 were cognitively impaired and had deficiencies in at least 3 ADL, and the the remaining 73 patients were either cognitively intact but had ADL deficiencies or cognitively impaired but had few ADL limitations. As with any good cognitive assessment in older adults, the NSRP incorporates assessments of depression and alcohol abuse. The data summarized in Lichtenberg (1998) found the NSRP to be a valid assessment battery.

Geriatric Depression Scale

The GDS was created in the early 1980s (Brink et al., 1982; Yesavage et al., 1983) and was the first screening measure developed for and validated on older people. The GDS is composed of 30 yes–no self-referent statements. An advantage of the GDS over other self-report measures is its omission (on an empirical basis) of somatic items. The GDS has been found to be a highly reliable and valid measure of depression in the older population. Acceptable levels of reliability have been reported by Brink et al. and by Rapp, Parisi, Walsh, and Wallace (1988). This scale has also been demonstrated to be useful in detecting depression in medically ill older patients with improved sensitivity and specificity data compared with other self-report measures (Norris, Gallagher, Wilson, & Winograd, 1987; Rapp, Parisi, & Walsh, 1988). There is also considerable evidence that the GDS is valid when used with cognitively compromised patients (Lichtenberg, Marcopulos, Steiner, & Tabscott, 1992; Parmelee, Katz, & Lawton, 1989), although these findings are not unequivocal (Kafonek et al., 1989).

CAGE Questionnaire

Curtis, Geller, Stokes, Levine, and Moore (1989) investigated physician detection of the alcohol abuse. Forty-five percent of nonelderly alcohol abusers were correctly identified by physicians, whereas only 27% of older alcohol abusers were correctly identified. Gender effects were striking in that no older women were diagnosed as alcoholic individuals by the house physician. Similarly, Schuckit, Atkinson, Miller, and Berman (1980) found that physicians did not detect 90% of older alcoholic individuals in their sample.

The CAGE Questionnaire was developed in 1970 and is a most efficient and effective alcohol-screening device (Ewing, 1984). The questionnaire is made up of four simple questions about attitudes and behaviors related to the individual's drinking habits. (The name of the questionnaire refers to four areas tapped by the following questions: Have you ever tried to *c*ut down on your drinking? Do you get *a*nnoyed when you are criticized for your drinking? Do you ever feel *g*uilty about your drinking? Do you ever have a drink first thing in the morning to steady your nerves, as an *e*ye opener.) A score of two affirmative responses raises the suspicion of alcoholism, whereas a score of three of four affirmative responses is almost always a sure sign of alcoholism. The original data gathered on the CAGE consisted of comparing responses of 16 alcoholic individuals with 114 non-alcoholic randomly selected medical patients. A second study of 166 alcoholic men revealed the CAGE to be a valid screening instrument, with a sensitivity of 85% and specificity of 100%. Bush, Shaw, Cleary, Delbanco, and Aronson (1987) prospectively studied 518 patients admitted to the orthopedic and medical services of a community hospital during a 6-month period. The criterion measure used for alcohol abuse was the standard criteria from the *Diagnostic and Statistical Manual of Mental Disorders,* third edition (American Psychiatric Association, 1980). The CAGE and three laboratory tests were compared for their ability to detect alcohol abuse. The laboratory tests were very insensitive, whereas the CAGE Questionnaire was highly valid. The CAGE had a sensitivity of 85% and specificity of 89%. Curtis et al. (1989) found the CAGE to be highly useful in detecting alcohol abuse in older people.

Conclusion

Medical rehabilitation with older adults is one of the mainstays of rehabilitation psychology, despite a lack of empirical research in this area. In this chapter, we discussed specific geriatric issues, including medical, neurological, and psychological comorbidities frequently accompanying geriatric rehabilitation patients. We reviewed the past research findings as well as data from our research group to illustrate the complex nature of geriatric rehabilitation and emphasized the need for focused assessment and treatment of cognitive and psychological factors. In the face of tremendous downsizing of medical rehabilitation, psychologists continue to play a critical role in evaluation and team decision making. In light of current changes in medical rehabilitation for older adults, we explored assessment techniques that can accommodate a faster moving, downsized market.

References

American Psychiatric Association. (1980). *Diagnostic and statistical manual of mental disorders* (3rd ed.). Washington, DC: Author.

Arfken, C. L., Lichtenberg, P. A., & Kuiken, T. (1998). Importance of comorbid illnesses in predicting mortality for geriatric rehabilitation. *Topics in Geriatric Rehabilitation, 13,* 69–76.

Arfken, C. L., Lichtenberg, P. A., & Tancer, M. E. (1999). Cognitive impairment and depression predict mortality in medically ill older adults. *Journal of Gerontology: Medical Sciences, 54A,* M152–M156.

Bacher, Y., Korner-Bitensky, N., Mayo, N., Becker, R., & Coopersmith, H. (1990). A longitudinal study of depression among stroke patients participating in a rehabilitation program. *Canadian Journal of Rehabilitation, 1,* 27–37.

Blazer, D., Hughes, D., & George, L. (1987). The epidemiology of depression in an elderly community population. *The Gerontologist, 27,* 281–287.

Brink, T., Yesavage, J., Lum, G., Heersema, P., Addey, M., & Rose, T. (1982). Screening tests for geriatric depression. *Clinical Gerontologist, 1,* 37–41.

Bush, B., Shaw, S., Cleary, P., Delbanco, T. L., & Aronson, M. D. (1987). Screening for alcohol abuse using the CAGE Questionaire. *American Journal of Medicine, 82,* 231–235.

Campbell, A. J., Busby, W. J., Robertson, M. C., Lum, C. L., Langlois, J. A., & Morgan, F. C. (1994). Disease, impairment, disability and social handicap: A community based study of people aged 70 years and over. *Disability and Rehabilitation, 16,* 72–79.

Cummings, S., Phillips, S., Wheat, M., Black, D., Goosby, E., Wlodarcyzk, D., Trafton, P., Jergesen, H., Winograd, C., & Hulley, S. (1988). Recovery of function after hip fracture: The role of social supports. *Journal of the American Geriatrics Society, 36,* 801–806.

Curtis, J. R., Geller, G., Stokes, E., Levin, D. M., & Moore, R. D. (1989). Characteristics, diagnosis, and treatment of alcoholism in elderly patients. *Journal of the American Geriatrics Society, 37,* 310–316.

Diamond, P. T., Holroyd, S., Macciocchi, S. N., & Felsenthal, G. (1995). Prevalence of depression and outcome on the geriatric rehabilitation unit. *American Journal of Physical Medicine & Rehabilitation, 74,* 214–217.

Evans, D. A., Funkenstein, H. H., Albert, M. S., Scherr, P. A., Cook, N. R., Chown, M. J., Hebert, L. E., Hennekens, C. H., & Taylor, J. O. (1989). Prevalence of Alzheimer's disease in a community population of older persons. *Journal of the American Medical Association, 262,* 2551–2556.

Ewing, J. A. (1984). Detecting alcoholism: The CAGE Questionaire. *Journal of the American Medical Association, 252,* 1905–1907.

Friedman, P. J. (1993). Stroke outcome in elderly people living alone. *Disability and Rehabilitation, 17*(2), 90–93.

Haffey, W. J., & Welsh, K. J. (1995). Subacute care: Evolution in search of value. *Archives of Physical Medicine and Rehabilitation, 76,* 2–4.

Hanks, R. A., & Lichtenberg, P. A. (1996). Physical, psychological and social outcomes in geriatric rehabilitation patients. *Archives of Physical Medicine and Rehabilitation, 77,* 783–792.

Hartke, R. J. (1991). *Psychological aspects of geriatric rehabilitation.* Gaithersburg, MD: Aspen.

Kafonek, S., Ettinger, W. H., Roca, R., Kittner, S., Taylor, N., & German, P. S. (1989). Instruments for screening for depression and dementia in a long-term care facility. *Journal of the American Geriatrics Society, 37,* 29–34.

Kemp, B. (1990). The psychosocial context of geriatric rehabilitation. In B. Kemp, K. Brummel-Smith, & J. W. Ramsdell (Eds.), *Geriatric rehabilitation* (pp. 41–57). Boston: College Hill Press.

Kokmen, E., Whisnant, J. P., O'Fallon, W. M., Chu, M. S., & Beard, C. M. (1996). Dementia after ischemic stroke. *Neurology, 19,* 154–159.

Lichtenberg, P. A. (1998). *Mental health practice in geriatric health care settings.* Binghamton, NY: Haworth Press.

Lichtenberg, P. A., Kimbarow, M. L., Morris, P., & Vangel, S. J. (1996). Behavioral treatment of depression in predominantly African American medical patients. *Clinical Gerontologist, 17,* 15–33.

Lichtenberg, P. A., Marcopulos, B. A., Steiner, D., & Tabscott, J. (1992). Comparison of the Hamilton Depression Rating Scale and the Geriatric Depression Scale: Detection of depression in dementia patients. *Psychological Reports, 70,* 515–521.

Livingston-Bruce, M. L., Seeman, T. E., Merrill, S. S., & Blazer, D. G. (1994). The impact of depressive symptomatology on physical disability: MacArthur studies on successful aging. *American Journal of Public Health, 84,* 1796–1799.

MacNeill, S. E., & Lichtenberg, P. A. (1997). Home alone: The role of cognition in return to independent living. *Archives of Physical Medicine & Rehabilitation, 78,* 755–758.

Magaziner, J., Simonsick, E. M., Kashner, T. M., Hebel, J. R., & Kenzora, J. E. (1990). Predictors of functional recovery one year following hospital discharge for hip fracture. *Journal of Gerontology, 45,* M101–M107.

Mast, B. T., MacNeill, S. E., & Lichtenberg, P. A. (1999). Geropsychological problems in medical rehabilitation: Dementia and depression among stroke and lower extremity fracture patients. *Journal of Gerontology: Medical Sciences, 54A,* M607–M612.

Mattis, S. (1988). *Dementia Rating Scale*. Odessa, FL: Psychological Assessment Resources.

Moore, C. A., & Lichtenberg, P. A. (1995). Neuropsychological prediction of independent functioning in a geriatric sample: A double cross validational study. *Rehabilitation Psychology, 41,* 115–130.

Nadler, J., Richardson, E. D., Malloy, P. F., Marran, M. E., & Brinson, M. E. (1993). The ability of the Dementia Rating Scale to predict everyday functioning. *Archives of Clinical Neuropsychology, 8,* 449–460.

Norris, J. T., Gallagher, D., Wilson, A., & Winograd, C. H. (1987). Assessment of depression in geriatric medical outpatients: The validity of two screening measures. *Journal of the American Geriatrics Society, 35,* 989–995.

Parikh, R., Robinson, R., Lipsey, J., Starkstein, S., Federoff, J., & Price, T. (1990). The impact of poststroke depression on recovery in activities of daily living. *Archives of Neurology, 47,* 785–789.

Parmelee, P. A., Katz, I. R., & Lawton, M. P. (1989). Depression among institutionalized aged: Assessment and prevalence estimation. *Journal of Gerontology, 44,* M22–M29.

Primeau, F. (1988). Post-stroke depression: A critical review of the literature. *Canadian Journal of Psychiatry, 33,* 757–765.

Rapp, S. R., Parisi, S. A., & Walsh, D. A. (1988). Psychological dysfunction and physical health among elderly medical inpatients. *Journal of Consulting and Clinical Psychology, 56,* 851–855.

Rapp, S. R., Parisi, S. A., Walsh, D. A., & Wallace, C. E. (1988). Detecting depression in elderly medical inpatients. *Journal of Consulting and Clinical Psychology, 56,* 509–513.

Richardson, E. D., Nadler, J. D., & Malloy, P. F. (1995). Neuropsychologic prediction of performance measures of daily living skills in geriatric patients. *Neuropsychology, 9,* 565–572.

Robinson, R. G., Kubos, K. L., Starr, L. B., Rao, K., & Price, T. R. (1984). Mood disorders in stroke patients: Importance of location of lesion. *Brain, 107,* 81–93.

Robinson, R. G., Starr, L. B., Kubos, K. L., & Price, T. R.. (1983). A two-year longitudinal study of post-stroke mood disorders: Findings during the initial evaluation. *Stroke, 14,* 736–741.

Roth, E. J. (1994). Heart disease in patients with stroke: Part II. Impact and implications for rehabilitation. *Archives of Physical Medicine and Rehabilitation, 75,* 94–101.

Rusin, M. J. (1990). Stroke rehabilitation: A geropsychological perspective. *Archives of Physical Medicine & Rehabilitation, 71,* 914–922.

Schuckit, M. A., Atkinson, J. H., Miller, P. L., & Berman, J. (1980). A three year follow-up of elderly alcoholics. *Journal of Clinical Psychiatry, 41,* 412–416.

Snowden, D. A., Greiner, L. H., Mortimer, J. A., Riley, K. P., Greiner, P. A., & Markesbury, W. R. (1997). Brain infarction and the clinical expression of Alzheimer's disease: Findings from the nun study. *Journal of the American Medical Association, 277,* 813–817.

Titus, M., Gall, N., Yerxa, E., Roberson, T., & Mack, W. (1991). Correlation of perceptual performance and activities of daily living in stroke patients. *The American Journal of Occupational Therapy, 45,* 410–418.

Tuokko, H. A., & Crockett, D. J. (1991). Assessment of everyday functioning in normal and malignant memory disordered elderly. In D. E. Tupper & K. D. Cicerone (Eds.), *The neuropsychology of everyday life: Issues in development and rehabilitation* (pp. 135–182). Boston: Kluwer Academic.

Tuomilehto, J., Rastenyte, D., Jousilahti, P., Sarti, C., & Vartiainen, E. (1996). Diabetes mellitus as a risk factor for death from stroke. *Stroke, 27,* 210–215.

Tupper, D. E., & Cicerone, K. D. (Eds.). (1990). *The neuropsychology of everyday life: Assessment of basic competencies*. Boston: Kluwer Academic.

Tupper, D. E., & Cicerone, K. D. (Eds.). (1991). *The neuropsychology of everyday life: Issues in development and rehabilitation*. Boston: Kluwer Academic.

Yesavage, J., Brink, T., Rose, T., Lum, O., Huang, V., Adez, M., & Leirer, V. (1983). Development and validation of a geriatric depression screening scale: A preliminary report. *Journal of Psychiatric Research, 17,* 37–49.

6

Neuromuscular and Musculoskeletal Disorders in Children

Dennis C. Harper and David B. Peterson

Neuromuscular and musculoskeletal disorders of childhood remain one of the major challenges for rehabilitation psychologists in the next century. Assistance for those children with congenital or acquired disorders involves the efforts of a vast array of professionals whose goals are to minimize chronic health impairment, maximize functional life skills, and promote a person-driven quality of lifestyle by enhancing the individual's choice (Livneh & Antonak, 1997). Many children born with lifelong diseases and physical impairments can and do enjoy a high quality of life because of the advances in the medical and behavioral sciences that have evolved over the past decade (Stein, 1989).

We focus on the key medical and psychosocial aspects of a selected group of physical disabilities that are either congenital or typically occur in childhood and have a lifelong impact. Many children and youth with these neuromuscular and musculoskeletal diseases may experience a different social reality as they mature (Harper, 1991a, 1991b), which can significantly affect their ultimate levels of life functioning (Cadman, Boyle, & Szatmri, 1987; Wallander, Varni, Babani, Banis, & Wilcox, 1989). We discuss three disorders—cerebral palsy, spina bifida, and juvenile rheumatoid arthritis (JRA)—that involve multiple systems of the body; cerebral palsy and spina bifida involve the central nervous system and its impact on the movement of muscular system, and JRA involves the skeleton and muscular systems. We selected these conditions because they represent the more frequent disorders in the neuromuscular and musculoskeletal categories, and they can be viewed as presenting a variety of common elements among such disorders in children and youth.

Historical Trends and Contemporary Issues in Adaptation and Adjustment to Chronic Physical Impairments

Within the past 10 years the models or paradigms for describing and defining disability have undergone some interesting changes. The following paragraphs briefly trace historical notions of disability and adjustment, present some key contemporary concepts and challenges to the earlier views, and subsequently identify several key concepts regarding the psychosocial impact of childhood physical disability. This review provides an important theoretical template for the treatment of and research on children and youth with chronic neuromuscular and musculoskeletal impairments.

Historical Views

Children and youth with an observable neuromuscular or musculoskeletal impairment often experience a social reality that differs from that of their nonphysically impaired peers. Until recently, research and the psychological adjustment of those with physical impairments have been characterized as a search for syndrome-specific personality types (e.g., the "blind personality," the "epileptic personality") and locating psychopathological characteristics associated with particular disabled populations (Harper, 1991b; Harper & Richman, 1978). Disability was viewed as misfortune, which must negatively affect life adjustment for those with such obvious and visible physical differences. The difference was located within the person (Rusk, 1958). The degree of impairment or severity of disability broadly defined was viewed as an indicator of potential psychopathology for the individual; certainly the more physically impaired the person, the more maladjusted he or she should appear. This person-based psychopathology has not been successful in relating the extent of disability or the presence of physical involvement to the degree of psychosocial adjustment (Harper, 1991b, 1996). Medical diagnostics did not seem to capture the essence of what was related to differences in functional capabilities as well as individual personal views of disability. These earlier views were dominant in studying the adjustment of those with physical impairment and chronic disorders and to a large extent evolved out of a "psychopathological model" and regarded disability as "disease and illness" exclusively (Harper, 1991b). This viewpoint is relevant historically but lacks empirical support.

Contemporary Models

Contemporary research on the adjustment and adaptation of children with physical impairment and chronic health disorders is sophisticated in its design, methodology, and ability to ask complicated questions involving interactions between the person and the environment. Disability is no longer viewed as a static concept (Polloway, Smith, Patton, & Smith, 1996). People change, situations change, and the impact of disability changes as well. Researchers in the late 1970s and the 1980s began to explore disability from interactionist (interplay between the person and the environment) and developmental perspectives. Harper (1991b, 1996) and others (e.g., Livneh & Antonak, 1997) have noted that there is tremendous variation within and between particular physical disorders. Heterogeneity of adjustment is the more common outcome for all types of physical disorders.

Contemporary work focusing on family studies of youth with physical impairments and chronic disability has also begun to identify the necessary family resources and social supports that can reduce psychosocial morbidity (Sorensen, 1993). This research attempts to define risk resistance factors in the family and identify the important use of positive coping skills (Livneh & Antonak, 1997). This research is also characterized by an interactionist perspective that examines a combination of parental and child background traits to explain particular reactions to particular disabilities for children and adults at different developmental intervals. Disability functioning is related to existing environmental and psychological supports and is, in part, defined by the presence or absence of such supports.

Finally, a more current examination of the rehabilitation literature presents a changing view in the understanding of the idea of adjustment to physical impairments like cerebral palsy and spina bifida. This contemporary view suggests that psychosocial adjustment is not a static concept, but rather a process of adaptation and coping at various stages to chronic physical and health disorders (Livneh & Antonak, 1997). This implies that pediatric rehabilitation for those with neuromuscular and musculoskeletal disorders is a developmental process and requires periodic readjustment and support at different times in an individual's life. Most important this conceptualization removes rehabilitation from a disease or illness-deficit model to an ongoing management perspective in relation to coping skills over the life span. Guidance is based on what you (the individual with the difference) need to know to enhance and empower yourself to make choices on an ongoing basis within a particular social context at different times. Physical "disability" is not an immutable trait but rather a more fluid state. As a state, physical differences are always contextual and in flux (Harper, 1997b).

Developmental–Biosocial Framework

The interplay between the chronic disease and its potential impact on children is mediated in part by the following: the child's age at onset, the severity of the disease from a medical and functional vantage, duration and fluctuations, manifest physical symptoms, observability of illness, and the history and type of family disruption and financial burden. In addition, the individual child and parental characteristics are important in this equation, such as intellectual and developmental level, personality characteristics, coping skills, and type and availability of social supports (Harper, 1991a, 1991b). This array represents a complicated evolving set of variables that change over time and is a multifactorial equation (Harper & Aylward, 1993).

Of particular importance to a pediatric rehabilitation psychologist is approaching the child and the chronic health disorder within a developmental framework as the basic clinical template. This orientation is fundamental in the assessment, treatment, and amelioration of chronic illnesses. It implies the application of treatment and practice in ways that differ completely from those used with adults (Eiser, 1990; Harper, 1991a, 1991b; Kazdin, 1989). This emphasis implies a specific need for knowledge about children's needs and skills in a disease-free state (i.e., normative child development) and an awareness of the particular tasks of childhood and developmental stages common to all children and youth. Developmental parameters define the characteristics and are the critical factors in assessing the impact of a given chronic illness in a particular child at a certain time in development. This developmental and life span focus also implies an awareness of the fluid and evolving nature of child and adolescent growth while continuing to emphasize the particular age or stage of the individual child's current physical, cognitive, and social—environmental status.

The developmental focus has wide-ranging implications for the practitioner's understanding and treatment of childhood disability. An illness or a chronic disability may interfere with the child's efforts to master the developmental agenda of biobehavioral organization (Garrison & McQuiston, 1989). *Biobehavioral organization* refers to the interactive and reciprocal interplay of behavioral life experiences and the biological structure of the human (e.g., heredity, developmental level). This suggests that an illness may interfere with mastery and disturb the equilibrium of development and normative flow of many of the common tasks of childhood and adolescence. A particular disability or chronic illness may slow, delay, or interrupt this normative and evolving growth process either on a temporary or more or less permanent basis. In addition, the child's response to treatments and procedures, in terms of understanding and cooperation (adherence), is also related to his or her developmental awareness capability (Eiser, 1990). This developmental perspective suggests an awareness or knowledge of factors about illness and their effect on the child's personality and self-esteem (Sorensen, 1993).

The developmental variation that may occur in relation to a particular illness or chronic disability also needs to be understood in relation to the parental caregiving and its potential altering effect, both quantitatively and qualitatively, on this family relationship (Bradford, 1997). Children develop within families and often with siblings. Family transactions and caregiving need to be framed within different developmental levels and time frames (Harper, 1991a, 1991b).

In summary, developmental status is a complex distillation of age, cognitive level, adaptive maturity, and individual experience related to the particular chronic illness. Therefore, developmental adaptation becomes key in judging the child's personal response to illness and disability, the child's participation in ameliorative health management or maintenance, the family members' responses to caregiving, and the idiosyncratic shape that future adaptive skills may take.

Two questions are of major importance when conceptualizing psychological health care of children with physical disabilities: (a) Did the biological problem interfere with the developmental growth agenda? and (b) What has occurred in the form of compensatory growth in this change from the usual growth pattern? (*Growth* here is broadly conceived to reflect physical, psychological, and social changes.) These are the fundamental questions that are basic to a developmental framing of any specific childhood neuromuscular and musculoskeletal disorder. This developmental–biosocial orientation is an essential framework of child health psychology (Harper, 1997b). The next section highlights the application of a developmental–clinical template for the practice of pediatric rehabilitation as it relates to chronic illness in children and youth.

Theoretical Models as the Clinical Template for Practice and Research

Developmental Adaptation

"The way we see the problem (childhood disability/illness) is the problem" (Harper, 1991a, p. 534). How we conceptualize human difference and the process of adaptation is a problem. A theoretical model is an important part of practice and research in understanding the psychosocial effects in chronic physical disorders. A theoretical approach dictates in varying degrees a plan, a mind-set of integrating information, or at least some consequences and shared consensus within the professional community.

What model or theory should be endorsed when exploring how children and families traverse life when one member happens to have a chronic physical disorder? Stage models of adjustment have been viewed as rather static (Livneh & Antonak, 1997) and have been replaced by models of adaptation, viewed as an evolving and reciprocating process with multiple factors (Harper, 1991a). In fact, Harper (1991b) defined a complex set of interactions among the array of both illness- and disability-related variables to be considered in conceptualizing chronic illness in children. Such conceptualizing of the psychosocial impact implies a bidirectional set of relationships among these variables, such as observability–appearance, chronological age, functional limitations, adjustment and personality styles, life experiences, peer social interactions, and family functioning. There are complex relationships among these variables between their rate of progression, pattern and sequence, level, type, and context of adaptive functioning. Individual differences and variation is the rule between individuals with common phenotypic, chronic physical disorders.

The fundamental notion of the "developmental adaptation" paradigm is evolving change or variable adaptation to the direct effects of the physical disorder and the indirect effects, often the psychosocial consequences. Development sets limits at particular times that change as a function of biosocial growth and evolving mastery. Assessment of adaptive functioning within this paradigm needs to be both time referenced and context defined. What the child is doing and where the child needs to do it are the overall focus. Adaptive functioning is like a snapshot in a particular place and time. Such pictures tell only part of the story of the life cycle. Multiple snapshots in a longitudinal path are needed to unravel the idiosyncratic nature of disability and its consequences over time for the individual. This developmental adaptation framework is consistent with the view of disability as a "state" variable as opposed to a "trait" variable (Luckasson et al., 1992) and places human difference in a social and cultural framework as well. Functional impact of human difference is in part related to environmental and psychological supports.

Clinical Template and Clinical Strategies

There are several fundamental notions of assisting and understanding children and young people with chronic neuromuscular and musculoskeletal disorders that are implied in this foregoing discussion of developmental adaptation. First, a chronic disability is not the central organizing principle of the person (Wright, 1983). Children with visible physical differences learn about themselves largely in a social context (Harper, Wacker, & Seaborg-Cobb, 1986). Certainly the physical condition may bring with it certain unique aspects, but the physical condition takes its impact in the "field" and the interaction with the social and physical demands. The physical impairments discussed in this chapter are based on a biological reality but are defined and characterized within a social context. These differences are a function of person factors, disease factors, and environmental factors and their interaction. Children with chronic disorders would benefit from treatment, assessment, and amelioration integrated more thoroughly in a developmental adaptation framework. This framework or clinical template stresses children's understanding of their health problem and the meaning that chronic disorder has for them during maturation.

Parental Information and Knowledge of Disability and Health Status

The child's understanding of particular health-related problems is a function of individual child developmental–cognitive awareness variables, broad family responses reflective of their views of the chronic illness, and the child's idiosyncratic reactions to past history with the particular chronic health problem (Eiser, 1990; Jones et al., 1984; Lemanek, 1994; Wallander et al., 1989). Initial counseling with parents and discussion of their child's chronic health problems during their initial understanding of the affects are among the key elements in the child's adaptation to the ongoing health problem. Several excellent resources are available: *Counseling Parents of Children With Chronic Illness or Disability* (Davis, 1993), *Coping with Cerebral Palsy* (Schleichkorn, 1993), *Coping in Young Children* (Zeitlin & Williamson, 1994), and *Counseling the Chronically Ill Child* (O'Dougherty, 1983). The authors of these books provide a comprehensive overview of the practice and necessary support issues for children and families. The majority of these authors underscored the importance of helping parents and children "make sense" out of their situation, both explicitly and implicitly, by building a "conceptual system" about the disease process and its place in their life (Davis, 1993, p. 19). Viewing the child within the context of this process reveals that the chronic health problem is a new and unknown situation that often places the progress of developmental status and outcomes (e.g., future) in a state of ambiguity. The parent can no longer use typical child growth trajectories as a guide for future developmental outcomes. Ambiguity is often the hallmark of chronic disease (Davis, 1993; Harper, 1991b). These experts uniformly testified to the importance of being prepared to tell others about their child (what does my child have?) and the child's evolving need to have the same skill and knowledge to pass this on when interacting with peers and others.

Knowledge of the child's difference needs to be addressed as soon as possible, and parents and children benefit by specific rehearsal of how to explain the health problems to otherss. This dialogue should be specific and address the unsaid queries as well (e.g., she can learn, he or she understands, we are not devastated, he or she is growing fine). Family rehearsal of these statements can be both therapeutic and empowering for parents and siblings. The child with the health condition benefits from having a prerehearsed explanation to offer their peers. These dialogues can and should be rehearsed with the child at their level awareness and understanding and skill. This type of explanation evolves as the child matures, asks additional questions, and encounters new questions and situations in contacts with peers.

Child Self-Disclosure

The issue of what to tell others should be discussed with all children who have a chronic illness, explanations and understandings should be reviewed periodically, and each individual should be given a specific set of explanatory strategies to offer to peers and friends. These explanations obviously require some individualized tailoring for the child or adolescent related to his or her conceptual level, current and ongoing medical condition, prior experiences and understanding of the disorder, and social and emotional status. They should be rehearsed to ensure that the dialogue is used and easy to deliver. The "tone" of these dialogues has a major impact on these social interactions with peers; how one says something may be more crucial than what one says.

Many visible disabilities are also characterized by a range of attributions from peers and others, which often are negative and illogical (Harper, 1996, 1997a) and can pervade the status of the child with chronic illness or disability (Wright, 1983). These negative attributions are known to "spread" and devalue the person's perceived status and worth (Jones et al., 1984; Yuker, 1988). The essence of this characterization often attributes a stigma (Wright, 1983) to a particular disease or condition and the person. Practically, this means that children see physical impairments in peers as limiting their functional social-play participation (Harper, 1997a; Harper et al., 1986) and often add on other presumed but unsubstantiated negatives (e.g., "looks handicapped, must be retarded"). In fact, the link between visible physical impairments as viewed by peers without a disability clearly suggests that this phenomena of negative spread is a universal characteristic in many cultures (Harper, 1995, 1997a).

The type of explanation offered to a child as well as to a parent must (a) anticipate these queries; (b) provide a clear message at the appropriate level; (c) deliver the statement in a positive, affirmative tone; and (d) anticipate other unsaid attributions toward the child with the chronic visible health condition. For example, a child between ages 5 and 8 years with cerebral palsy might respond by saying, "I have cerebral palsy, a part of my brain does not make my legs work right, but I am smart"; a similarly aged child with spina bifida might offer, "I have spina bifida, which means part of my spine stops my legs from working, but I am smart." A similarly aged child with Duchenne muscular dystrophy might say, "My muscles are getting weaker, so I might need to use a wheelchair, but I am smart." A child with JRA might offer, "My joints have problems working, I need to take medicines, this hurts a lot, but I am smart, and I can do my school work." The pairing of a reasonable and straightforward explanation describing the chronic illness with positive cognitive skills is essential in dealing with frequent assumptions that if you look different you must also be less smart or even retarded (Harper, 1997a). Generally, strategies need to be individually tailored as well as updated and reinterpreted as the child's understanding matures and as questions change over time.

Noncategorical Approach to Psychosocial Consequences

Numerous authors (Drotar & Crawford, 1985; Livneh & Antonak, 1997; Pless & Pinkerton, 1975; Stein, 1989) have noted that psychosocial outcomes are not disease specific. Instead, many adjustment and adaptive processes are related to a number of cross-disease dimensions (Stein, 1989), which encompass the dimensions of onset, prognosis and course, predictability, adaptive impact of treatments, and visibility of the condition (Jones et al., 1984; Stein & Jessop, 1984). These commonalities are part of the clinical template, the noncategorical perspective for focusing on functional interventions, and reflect a fundamental view of understanding the psychosocial impact of chronic physical disorders in children and their families.

Consistent with this change is the contemporary noncategorical perspective on "why some children and families do better with a chronic health disorder than others" irrespective of medical diagnostic categories. This search for positive variables (Livneh & Antonak, 1997; Wright, 1983, 1988) is an important shift in the social psychology of dealing with human difference. Such perspective was noted historically by Wright (1983) and reflects a fundamental view that a person's disability is frequently not the first or primary organizing principle of personhood. This does not reduce the importance of particular diagnostic categories and the diagnostic process, but it places the issue of personal identification and disability in a broader perspective and promotes a more idiosyncratic study of human differences. This orientation reflects the seminal view that human difference is a variable state and in part contextually defined (Harper, 1996) and related to existing physical, psychological, and environmental supports. The search for valid empirically determined treatments and interventions is now more person and situation specific (Fonagy, 1995).

Children's Developmental Views of Illness

Children's views of illness or their physical state can have significantly affect all aspects of their psychological and social adjustment (Bennett, 1994; Eiser, 1990; Lavigne & Faier-Routman, 1992). The physical disorders reviewed here restrict physical activities, often require various medications and multiple surgical procedures, may result in diminished energy and declining stength, and frequently cause chronic pain, all of which may interfere with developing children's sense of mastery and control over their bodies. These issues for the most part affect all the physical disorders reviewed in this chapter and are often evident from birth or from the early toddler years (Capute & Accardo, 1996). Children with congenital illnesses often have no experience of being free of disease. Their view of their body is "cultured" in part by the physical disorder. The fears, anxieties, pain, and restrictions can interfere with the growth of their developmental agenda (Eiser, 1990).

Coping and adjustment–adaptation is a multifactorial array of person factors, general and specific disease factors, and environmental factors that reciprocally interact to result in varying degrees of adaptation and adjustment over time (Bradford, 1997; Wallander et al., 1989). Developmental stages and behavioral descriptions can be used as guidelines while recognizing that these periods represent a balance between chronological age, mental age, stage, and unique prior experience.

Although enjoying widespread attention, the stage model used to explain a child's understanding of illness has been criticized by Eiser (1990) and Livneh and Antonak (1997), and newer theoretical models have been proposed (Lemanek, 1994). These newer paradigms or models emphasize a bidirectional interaction between multiple factors that interact to produce levels of varying adaptation (Wallander et al., 1989), interaction between perceived stress and resultant coping (Lazarus & Folkman, 1984), and a noncategorical approach to illness that assumes that children with chronic illness have common life experiences and problems stemming from generic medical conditions (general limitations) rather than just specific illnesses (Lemanek, 1994). Such factors as observability of the condition, illness path, origin, illness severity, multiple or sensory impairments, and self-attributions (Jones et al., 1984; Lemanek, 1994) interact in an evolving fashion over time. All of these conceptualizations are filtered through an evolving cognitive mind-set, and the stage model appears somewhat limited in explaining why some children develop complex understandings of their illnesses at a very young age despite predictions of a limited awareness of illness based on a linear cognitive stage model.

These developmental conceptualizations of "how the child's mind works" suggests the following practice clinical implications: (a) Stage–age theories are a beginning marker for explanations, treatments, and approaches to the child directly; (b) children's prior experiences and what they know about their health disorders should be reviewed and acknowledged in assessing their understanding of the impact of chronic illness; and (c) the explanations, treatments, and procedures offered to children and youth regarding their chronic illnesses need periodic review, reformulation, and more complex levels (perhaps irrespective of stage) of interpretation on an ongoing basis from health care providers (Eiser, 1990).

The developmental time frames and concerns presented in Exhibit 6.1 highlight key factors in the process of growing up with a chronic physical disorder. The developmental concerns are selected from among the key issues of disability's impact on children and youth with neuromuscular and musculoskeletal impairments during their developmental years. Disability factors are always framed in a developmental and evolving context, and these topics should be reviewed and monitored for these children and their families at these specified intervals. More comprehensive sources reviewing developmental issues and disability include Davis (1993), Eiser (1990), O'Dougherty (1983), and Schleichkorn (1993).

Selected Physical Disorders

Cerebral Palsy

Definition

Approximately 9,000 children are diagnosed with cerebral palsy each year in the United States, and about 1 million individuals have the disease (Livneh & Antonak, 1997). A number of different definitions for cerebral palsy are provided in the professional literature, each reflecting diverse professional orientations toward the disorder (Kopriva & Taylor, 1993). According to Bleck (1975), "cerebral palsy is a non-progressive disorder of movement and is caused by a malfunctioning of, or damage to, the brain (cerebral dysfunction)" (p. 59). Kopriva and Taylor (1993) drew together features that are common to the disorders known as cerebral palsy: "(a) aberrant control of movement or posture; (b) early onset; and (c) no recognized underlying progressive pathology" (p. 520). Alternatively, *cerebral palsy* (literally, "brain weakness") has been defined as a generic term referring to a family of impairments of muscle tone and control or of locomotion resulting from permanent and nonprogressive defects or lesions of the immature brain (Falvo, 1991; Livneh & Antonak, 1997).

In addition to the primary symptoms noted above, cerebral palsy typ-

Exhibit 6.1. Developmental Time Frame and Concerns for Growing Up With a Chronic Physical Disorder

Infancy (0–1½ years)

Primary goal is establishing trust and attachment.

Regular and close physical contact is important and needed.

Children with neuromuscular disability may be hard to hold and comfort; parents need to know how to hold and comfort their child.

Parents may view physical differences and awkward movements as rejection of their affections.

Separations related to hospitalizations can increase dependency.

Parental initial reactions to physical differences are important.

Children should be encouraged to have active contact with the environment.

Toddlers (1½–3 years)

The major developmental task is establishing autonomy and independence.

Children should be encouraged to undertake independent efforts ("you do it," "try it").

Doing "too much" for child promotes passivity and limits self-esteem.

Children begin to ask questions about how the body works.

Let the child explore and do not overprotect or overcontrol.

Preschool (3–5 years)

Morality and sense of right and wrong are developing.

The child may attribute disability to personal actions ("Why is this happening to me, what did I do?").

Children at this time have vague ideas about body functioning; misinterpretations are common.

Observable physical differences become an issue with peers and may bring about the first signs of rejection.

Children need knowledge about physical differences and what to say to peers.

Parents should have information for sharing with family and friends.

Elementary (6–12 years)

Issues of mastery–achievement, self-motivation, and increasing autonomy are the main developmental goals.

Social skills are key to facilitate peer acceptance.

Physical differences need more explanation at their current level of understanding.

The child needs to become more involved in hospital and medical care.

The child should be making choices and decisions with parental support.

Coping strategies can be taught to the child directly.

Peer inquiries may become more severe (e.g., "what's wrong with you?").

What and how the child tells others needs practice.

Adolescence (12–16 years)

The body, dating, and gender identity are key issues.

Maturing ideas about sexuality may need clarification.

Independence requires parents to "let go."

Physical attractiveness, "looks," are a key issue in peer interactions.

Independence can generate fears of being on one's own.

Assuming major decisions and choice for medical care plans is the goal.

Fears of "being different" can be intense.

Guided vocational–educational planning is needed.

Supportive and explorative counseling is often helpful; helping with self-concerns; "who am I?", reframing "differences" related to disabilities.

ically involves secondary disabilities, including sensory disorders, seizures, cognitive impairment, heart defects, asthma, dental abnormalities,
and speech and language disabilities (Gold, 1993; Kohn, 1990; Livneh &
Antonak, 1997). Cognitive functioning for children with cerebral palsy varies from above average to mental retardation (approximately half to three-
quarters of those studied with cerebral palsy had some form of mental
retardation; Kopriva & Taylor, 1993). Caution must be used to avoid mis-
interpreting physiological neuromuscular symptoms for cognitive ones.
For example, the effects of motor impairment may be misleading (e.g.,
dysarthria, or lack of speech fluency, is not the same as language impairment).

Cerebral palsy can be divided into two major categories on the basis
of locus of structural central nervous system change (Batshaw & Perret,
1992; Kopriva & Taylor, 1993). In cerebral palsy involving pyramidal
tracts (pathways) of the nervous system, damage occurs in the motor cortex or pyramidal tract of the brain, resulting in spasticity as the predominant symptom. The pyramidal tract is involved with the voluntary control
of muscles in the arms and legs (initiating movement). Damage to the
nerve fibers or cells in this area results in spastic paralysis. Symptoms
vary depending on the region of the brain affected (e.g., hemiplegia, quadriplegia). Extrapyramidal cerebral palsy is associated with difficulty in
regulating movement and maintaining posture. The most common form of
extrapyramidal cerebral palsy is choreoathetoid, marked by abrupt, involuntary movement of the extremities (Batshaw & Perret, 1992).

Assessment

The American Academy for Cerebral Palsy and Developmental Medicine
adopted Dr. Winthrop Phelps' classification system in 1956, which was
based on manifestations of cerebral palsy by way of location, cause of damage, and development of the brain at the time in which the damage occurred (Kopriva & Taylor, 1993).

Immediate postnatal assessment of cerebral palsy is difficult given the
maturational state of the infant's central nervous system. Several behavioral symptoms may indicate the existence of cerebral palsy: excessive
sleepiness, irritability on waking, weak cries and poor sucking, apathy
toward environment, and unusual sleep position ("rag-doll" or extended-
arch position; Batshaw & Perret, 1992). Pediatricians who have thorough
knowledge of cerebral palsy are able to make a clinical diagnosis, but most
often the delayed motor development of speech is detected by a concerned
parent and brought to the attention of the family practitioner. Spastic
cerebral palsy may be identifiable in the first few months of life, but choreoathetoid movements may not be detectable for over 18 months (Batshaw & Perret, 1992).

Prevention

Three distinct groups of factors—prenatal, perinatal, and postnatal—delineate causes of cerebral palsy, each having different associations with

respect to prevention of the disorder and amelioration of contributory factors influencing the condition. Prenatal causes comprise 44% and include genetic syndromes, teratogens (agents causing physical defects of the embryo), chromosomal abnormalities, brain malformations, intrauterine infections, and placental malfunctioning. Perinatal causes include (27%) pre-eclampsia, complications of labor–delivery, major infection, central nervous system infections, asphyxia, and prematurity. Postnatal causes (5%) include meningitis, traumatic brain injury, and toxins. Finally, 24% of causes of cerebral palsy remains unknown (Kopriva & Taylor, 1993; Livneh & Antonak, 1997; Pellegrino, 1997).

Amelioration and Treatment

Early detection of cerebral palsy enhances the rehabilitation process (Kopriva & Taylor, 1993). Commencing therapy (physical, early cognitive stimulation) within the first few weeks of life increases the probability that motor and developmental function develop optimally.

Cerebral palsy may be associated with expressive language difficulty. Manual communication may compensate for this functional limitation, but motor deficits associated with cerebral palsy may limit this compensatory strategy. Augmentative communication devices such as electronic communication boards and computers with synthetic voice capability are very useful in promoting language use and socialization. Voice-activated technology, such as lights, televisions, curtains, doors, and telephones, can assist with controlling the environment. Depending on the child's clarity of speech, a child may be able to use voice-activated word-processing programs.

Rehabilitation psychologists can play a significant role in the family's adjustment to disability. It is important for psychologists working with families of children with cerebral palsy to help the family develop realistic expectations regarding development, based on several evaluations over time. In addition, parents may be susceptible to despair and denial, which may be ameliorated with psychoeducational and supportive therapy techniques. Parent groups are especially useful for information and support.

In the past, treatment incorporated orthopedic surgery techniques, but these have given way to early diagnosis and intervention, placing more emphasis on global remediation of developmental deficits through a variety of physical therapy, occupational therapy (orthotic devices such as braces), medication (to reduce spasticity), and in some instances surgical interventions (e.g., for hydrocephalus, vascular abnormalities, cysts, or tumors or to correct residual deformities).

Surgical intervention is common for children with cerebral palsy to ameliorate strabismus (deviation of eye gaze caused by muscle imbalance) and cleft lip and palate. Children very likely need orthopedic surgery as they mature. Two state-of-the-art techniques involve the injection of botulinium toxin (Botox) and selective neurosurgery of the spinal nerve roots (dorsal rhizotomy). These procedures show promise for reducing spasticity, increasing range of motion, and increasing functional skills. The efficacy of both of these techniques is not yet established with respect to significant and longer term increases in functional adaptive skills (Forssberg & Tedroff, 1997).

Spina Bifida

Definition

The term *spina bifida* refers to a separation of the bones in the spinal column (Charney, 1992). Spina bifida is accompanied by *myelomeningocele*, a fluid-filled sac that protrudes from the malformed spine, containing the spinal cord. A portion of the spinal cord is visible at birth, and the nerve development below the opening is incomplete, resulting in paralysis and absence of sensation (Charney, 1992). The sequelae of spina bifida with myelomeningocele include impairments in ambulation, gastrointestinal complications, bowel difficulties and impactions, urinary tract infections (secondary to catheterization), and symptomatic hypercalcemia (causing anorexia, vomiting, constipation, polyuria [excessive urination], polydypsia [excess water drinking]).

Spina bifida with myelomeningocele belongs to a family of neural tube defects that can range from benign meningocele (protruding sac surrounds a normal spinal cord, with no resulting neurological deficits) to anencephaly (absence of cerebral cortex, which is invariably fatal). Prevalence of neural tube defects is approximately 1 in 1,000 births in the United States (Hobbins, 1991). Survival to adulthood has been estimated at about 85% (McLone, 1989).

Children with myelomeningocele tend to have congenital malformations of the brain (Charney, 1992). Arnold–Chiari type II malformation of the hindbrain is a malformation of the brain stem and part of the cerebellum, where both are drawn down toward the neck rather than remaining in the skull. For 60–95% of children with myelomeningocele, this displacement interferes with cerebrospinal fluid flow and results in enlarged ventricles (hydrocephalus). Other consequences may include difficulties with breathing, swallowing, vocal cord function, and strabismus. The combination of neural tube defect, hydrocephalus, and other neuropathological abnormalities of the brain can result in deficits in mobility, musculoskeletal deformities, spinal malformations, bladder and bowel dysfunction, skin sores, obesity, seizure disorders, and visual (strabismus) and cognitive deficits (33% usually have mild mental retardation; Charney, 1992). Decubiti (deep skin lesions) require close monitoring and treatment before infection becomes acute. Chronic pain may be a serious problem related to extent and level of the lesion, and narcotic analgesics should be avoided.

Assessment

Measuring levels of alpha-fetoprotein in the mother's amniotic fluid during the second trimester of pregnancy can help detect neural tube defects.

High-resolution ultrasonography can visualize vertebral malformation (Nadel, Green, Holmes, Frigoletto, & Benacerraf, 1990). Ultrasound can also be used to diagnose hydrocephalus in newborns with spina bifida.

Amelioration and Treatment

The cause of neural tube defects is unclear, and therefore prevention and treatment are difficult. It has been hypothesized that there are both environmental and genetic influences involved. Prenatal treatment with folic acid has been successful in preventing recurrences of neural tube defects, and avoidance of antiepileptic drugs during the first trimester of pregnancy decreases the risk of occurrence (Main & Mennuti, 1986; Rosa, 1991). The incidence of spina bifida declined in the 1980s, although the reason remains unclear (Edmonds & James, 1990).

Because of the complex nature of neural tube defects and the concomitant deficits, a multidisciplinary treatment approach is useful. Closure of the malformation is usually performed within the first few days of life to prevent infection. Unfortunately, this has no effect on neurological functioning (Charney, 1992). Impairment of areas of functioning is based on the location of the defect on the spine.

Depending on the level of the lesion, periodic or intermittent catheterization may be a necessary technique to ensure that the bladder is empty on a regular basis. This area of assistance requires skill, sensitivity, and repeated practice on the part of parents and other caregivers. Elementary-aged children require specific assistance with this process throughout the school day. By the time the child is approximately 8–10 years old, self-training programs for intermittent clean catheterization can be attempted and are usually successful (Wong & Whaley, 1990). Bowel regulation and urinary tract maintenance can be facilitated by nursing and occupational therapy staff on a multidisciplinary team.

Some children with spina bifida and associated hydrocephalus demonstrate unusual language and learning problems. Neuropsychological assessment of these children frequently identifies isolated skills in memory and excessive verbal fluency–verbosity, with limited comprehension of general language function. This has been called "hyperverbal behavior" (Charney, 1992). These somewhat cheeky language styles tend to give false impressions of skill levels, and consequently such children should receive extensive neuropsychological assessment.

Sex education and counseling becomes a critical issue as the child approaches adolescence. Sensation of the scrotum, penis or clitoris, perianal area, volitional control of sphincter muscle, ability to achieve erection and ejaculation, and orgasm should be carefully evaluated, and an optimistic attitude toward sexuality should be encouraged. Broader concepts of sexuality beyond a simple genital focus may need to be incorporated into a sex education program.

Juvenile Rheumatoid Arthritis

Definition

JRA is the most common joint disease of childhood, affecting between 60,000 and 200,000 children in the United States (Cassidy & Petty, 1995; Erlandson, 1989; Koch, 1992). JRA, a disease of the connective tissues of the body manifesting as sudden and unexpected exacerbations and remissions of joint inflammation, is a chronic, systemic (bodywide) disorder of unknown origin, which requires intensive daily treatment regimens of medicine and specialized exercise, exacting a heavy burden on family caregiving (Falvo, 1991; Kopriva & Taylor, 1993). High fever and rash are prominent in children with JRA.

There are three subtypes of JRA. Systemic onset disease occurs in 20% of children with JRA, presenting with fever of unknown origin, rash, enlarged lymph nodes, infection of the covering of the heart, pneumonia, enlarged liver and spleen, and associated acute abdominal pain (Koch, 1992). Systemic symptom, which include growth retardation, delayed sexual maturation, and reduced red blood cells, may recur and subside or develop into polyarticular arthritis (see below), and a quarter of children with this subtype of JRA manifest permanent joint deformity (Kredich, 1992).

The second subtype, polyarticular disease, affects 40% of all children with JRA, with five or more joints affected (Koch, 1992). Symptoms may manifest as low-grade fever and slight enlargement of the liver and spleen, mild reduced red blood cells, malaise, and weight loss. The cervical spine, wrists, hips, and knees may be affected by pain, decreased range of motion, and stiffness, along with symmetrical involvement of the small joints of the hands and feet.

The third subtype is pauciarticular disease, which affects approximately 40% of children with JRA and involves four or fewer joints within the first 6 months of onset of JRA (Koch, 1992). The hands and feet are rarely involved, and girls are more likely than boys to develop this subtype of JRA. A subgroup of this subtype affects mostly boys over the age of 8 and primarily involves the lower extremities. Between 10–50% of children with this subtype of JRA develop iridocyclitis (infection of the iris of the eye), leading to permanent visual loss in one or both eyes (Koch, 1992).

The disease process attacking the joint in JRA attacks the joint and adjacent supporting structures (e.g., synovium or joint lining), which become chronically inflamed, eroding cartilage, bone, and supportive tissues and producing heat, swelling, and loss of motion. The etiology of JRA is unknown but may result from infection, autoimmunity, trauma, or genetic predisposition (Cassidy & Petty, 1995). Research in the past 10 years has focused on the relationship of JRA with viruses, bacteria, immunodeficiency, stress, and trauma (Erlandson, 1989).

Assessment

There is no formal laboratory assessment for JRA (Koch, 1992). Laboratory studies typically used for adults often show negative results in children with JRA. Radiological studies are able to identify only advanced articular destruction in children. Most frequently, evaluation of JRA involves the examination of individual joints and overall functional status (e.g., degree of fatigue and length of morning stiffness; Koch, 1992). Physical and occupational therapy and assessment are important, observing posture in sitting and standing and any abnormalities in alignment or gait. Strength, dexterity, and mobility may change as the disease progresses.

Amelioration and Treatment

Currently there are no curative treatments for JRA. Early identification and treatment serve to ameliorate the ravages of the disease. Various drugs can be used to control inflammation and systemic complications: intrajoint injection of steroids for pain or flexion; aspirin for inflammation and pain (however, this increases the risk of Reye's syndrome); and immunization against infections on an annual basis (Koch, 1992).

For acute symptoms, bed rest, splinting, and range of motion therapy can be used to facilitate recovery of the damaged joint by decreasing inflammation and preventing additional damage (Koch, 1992). Prolonged inactivity is contraindicated because it leads to muscle wasting.

The use of heat and light massage may promote relaxation and increased elasticity around affected joints, providing symptomatic relief (Koch, 1992). For the pauciarticular subtype of JRA, frequent ophthalmological examinations must be regular and frequent to monitor for development of iridocyclitis. Medical monitoring of a multitude of other systemic disorders may best be managed by a multidisciplinary treatment team.

Extended hospitalizations associated with the implementation of medical technology to the treatment of JRA have significant psychosocial ramifications. The use of splints, braces, or other supportive technology can also have an isolating effect in a child's social life, with predictable responses by children to someone who is "different." This can negatively affect educational functioning; children with JRA appear to have a greater risk for academic underachievement, high absenteeism, associated fatigue, and disease-related distractibility and irritations (e.g., morning stiffness, inflammatory-related pain). These children experience difficulty with fine motor coordination and can appear awkward, adding further psychosocial stigma. Parent and peer psychoeducation and supportive psychotherapy for children maturing with such social pressures may facilitate optimal social adjustment (Batshaw & Perret, 1992).

Hagglund et al. (1996) developed an innovative family-based comprehensive intervention program for children with JRA and their families. This treatment program recognizes the importance of using behavioral contracting strategies to reinforce treatment adherence, a major problem in the treatment of JRA (Rapoff, 1996). These behavioral methods focus on all aspects of treatment for the child with JRA and are likely among the more promising innovations in this chronic disorder's future. A related and important treatment focuses on pain management. Cognitive–behavioral techniques for pain reduction, distraction, relaxation, and mental imagery have all been shown to have significant benefits. Clay, Harper, and Varni (1999) developed a computer-based system to treat chronic pain in children and youth. This multimodal system is being piloted at the University of Iowa hospitals and clinics and consists of an interactive CD-ROM detailing relaxation skills and coping methods for pain reduction.

Conclusion

This chapter focused on the psychosocial consequences of selected neuromuscular and musculoskeletal disorders in children. The theoretical and clinical understanding of the psychosocial impact of physical disability has undergone redefinition in the past decade. Personality development and adjustment to physical disorders focused on a search for disability-specific or disease syndrome differences. A person-based locus of psychopathology related degree of body disfigurement in a direct way to adjustment outcomes. Contemporary research on the adjustment and adaptation of children with physical impairment and chronic health disorders is sophisticated in its design, methodology and focus; researchers are exploring more complicated interactions among the person, the family, and the environment. The psychosocial impact of disability is now viewed as a variable state and defined in part by time, in a certain context, and a particular social field; coping with disability changes over time, and so does its impact on the person.

Our central thesis is that a developmental interactionist focus is imperative in the assessment, treatment, and amelioration of chronic illness in children and youth. Understanding adaptation to illness is aided by viewing the child and the family through a developmental and evolving lens. Chronic health impairments clearly can influence the biobehavioral agenda of physical and psychosocial growth and the child's evolving mastery over these differences. A developmental adaptation model conceptualizes the child's accommodation to chronic illness and is presented as a key theoretical paradigm to approach the practice and research for chronic neuromuscular and musculoskeletal disorders in children. This model conceptualizes the psychosocial impact of chronic illness and physical impairment as a reciprocal set of relationships among such variables as observability and appearance of the person with the chronic health and physical concerns, chronological and developmental age, functional limitations, coping and personality styles, life experiences, ongoing peer social interactions, and family functioning. There are complex evolving relationships between these variables among their rate of progression, pattern and sequence, level, type, and the context of adaptive functioning. Individuals with similar phenotypic, chronic disorders usually present with individual differences and variation. Disabilities can be conceptualized as noncategorical with many psychosocial outcomes across physical disabilities that are often not disease specific. Functional impairment from the person's perspective is a key to understanding adjustment and accommodation to chronic illness and physical disorders.

The child and parent's view and response to chronic illness and physical disorders are key in shaping ongoing adaptation. Early offering of disability information to parents should emphasize, in part, "making some sense" out of the disability and potential long-term outcomes. Explanations of the health problem, how to approach others with this information, and the child's understanding of the disorder and its disclosure to peers are all key elements in the rehabilitation process. Observable differences can dramatically affect a peer's perception of the child with a disability and subsequently the child's self-esteem. Strategies for ameliorating the effects of stigma of disability involve disclosure and affirmation of disabilities to peers and others. Parents and children need supportive guidance and rehearsal in this process of telling others about disabilities and strengths.

Cerebral palsy, spina bifida, and JRA require a "team approach" to rehabilitation involving many health practitioners. Cerebral palsy is a neuromuscular disorder that can have an effect on many different body systems. Independent mobility is a common challenge. The neuromuscular disorder often impairs expressive communication, making social interaction difficult. Early counseling promoting independence is often needed. Spina bifida, also present at birth, often impairs walking, affects bowel and bladder functioning, and in some cases causes learning disabilities. Prenatal treatment with folic acid has been successful in reducing this neural tube disorder. Mobility training, counseling on sexuality, and vocational guidance are needed to promote maximum independence. JRA is the most common joint disease of childhood. This chronic disease has no known cure and often impairs children from daily functioning because of chronic pain. Children need early, intensive, and broad-based rehabilitation to assist with long-term accommodation to their chronic health concerns.

Our central thesis is that understanding psychosocial adaptation to chronic illness and physical impairment in children requires a complex and evolving perspective by the rehabilitation psychologist. A strategy for assessment, treatment, and amelioration that is based on a developmental adaptation paradigm may assist children and youth in reaching their optimal quality of life.

References

Batshaw, M. L., & Perret, M. A. (1992). *Children with disabilities: A medical primer* (3rd ed.). Baltimore: Brookes.

Bennett, D. (1994). Depression among children with chronic medical problems: A meta-analysis. *Journal of Pediatric Psychology, 19,* 149–169.

Bleck, E. E. (1975). Cerebral palsy. In E. E. Bleck & D. A. Nagel (Eds.), *Physically handicapped children: A medical atlas for teachers* (pp. 37–89). New York: Grune & Stratton.

Bradford, R. (1997). *Children, families and chronic disease: Psychological models and methods of care.* New York: Routledge.

Cadman, D., Boyle, M., & Szatmri, P. (1987). Psychological distress in mothers of disabled children. *Pediatrics, 79,* 805–813.

Capute, A. J., & Accardo, P. J. (1996). *Developmental disabilities in infancy and childhood* (Vol. 1 & 2). Baltimore: Brookes.

Cassidy, J. T., & Petty, R. E. (1995). *Textbook of pediatric rheumatology* (3rd ed.). Philadelphia: W. B. Saunders.

Charney, E. B. (1992). Neural tube defects: Spina bifida and myelomeningocele. In M. L. Batshaw & M. A. Perret (Eds.), *Children with disabilities: A medical primer* (pp. 471–488). Baltimore: Brookes.

Clay, D. L., Harper, D. C., & Varni, J. W. (1999, April). *Use of emerging technologies to address barriers to treatment research in pediatric chronic pain.* Paper presented at the 7th Florida Conference on Child Health Psychology, Gainesville, FL.

Davis, H. (1993). *Counseling parents of children with chronic illness or disability.* Baltimore: Brookes.

Drotar, D., & Crawford, P. (1985). Psychological adaptation of siblings of chronically ill children: Research and practice implications. *Developmental and Behavioral Pediatrics, 6,* 355–362.

Edmonds, L. D., & James, L. M. (1990). Temporal trends in the prevalence of congenital malformations at birth based on the Birth Defects Monitoring Program, United States, 1979–1987. *Mortality and Morbidity Weekly Report, 39,* 19–23.

Eiser, C. (1990). *Chronic childhood disease. An introduction to psychological theory and research.* New York: Cambridge University Press.

Erlandson, D. M. (1989). Juvenile rheumatoid arthritis. In M. K. Logigian & J. D. Ward (Eds.), *A team approach for therapists: Pediatric rehabilitation* (pp. 195–227). Boston: Little, Brown.

Falvo, C. R. (1991). *Medical and psychosocial aspects of chronic illness and disability.* Gaithersburg, MD: Aspen.

Fonagy, P. (1995). Is there an answer to the outcome research question? Waiting for Godot. *Changes, 13,* 168–179.

Forssberg, H., & Tedroff, K. B. (1997). Botulinum toxin treatment in cerebral palsy: Intervention with poor evaluation? *Developmental Medicine and Child Neurology, 39,* 635–640.

Garrison, W. T., & McQuiston, S. (1989). *Chronic illness during childhood and adolescence: Psychological aspects.* Newbury Park, CA: Sage.

Gold, J. T. (1993). Pediatric disorders: Cerebral palsy and spina bifida. In M. G. Eisenberg, R. L. Glueckauf, & H. H. Zaretsky (Eds.), *Medical aspects of disability: A handbook for the rehabilitation professional* (pp. 281–306). New York: Springer.

Hagglund, K. J., Doyle, N. M., Clay, D. L., Frank, R. G., Johnson, J. C., & Pressly, T. A. (1996). A family retreat as a comprehensive intervention for children with arthritis and their families. *Arthritis Care and Research, 9*(1), 35–41.

Harper, D. C. (1991a). Paradigms for investigating rehabilitation and adaptation to childhood disability and chronic illness. *Journal of Pediatric Psychology, 16,* 533–542.

Harper, D. C. (1991b). Psychosocial aspects of physical differences in children and youth. In K. Jaffe (Ed.), *Physical medicine and rehabilitation clinics of North America* (Vol. 2, pp. 765–779). Philadelphia: W. B. Saunders.

Harper, D. C. (1995). Children's attitudes towards physical differences among youth from western and non-western cultures. *Cleft Palate–Craniofacial Journal, 32,* 114–119.

Harper, D. C. (1996). The social psychology of physical difference. *The Iowa Psychologist, 2,* 7–8.

Harper, D. C. (1997a). Children's attitudes toward physical disability in Nepal. A field study. *Journal of Cross-Cultural Psychology, 28,* 710–729.

Harper, D. C. (1997b). Pediatric psychology: Child health in the next century. *Journal of Clinical Psychology and Medical Settings, 4,* 179–190.

Harper, D. C., & Aylward, G. (1993, September). *Social skill development and assessment in children and adolescents with developmental disabilities.* Paper presented at the annual meeting of the American Academy for Cerebral Palsy and Developmental Medicine, Nashville, TN.

Harper, D. C., & Richman, L. C. (1978). Personality profiles of physically impaired adolescents. *Journal of Clinical Psychology, 34,* 336–342.

Harper, D. C., Wacker, D., & Seaborg-Cobb, L. (1986). Children's social preferences towards peers with visible physical differences. *Journal of Pediatric Psychology, 11,* 323–342.

Hobbins, J. C. (1991). Diagnosis and management of neural-tube defects today. *New England Journal of Medicine, 324,* 690–691.

Jones, E., Farina, A., Hastorf, A., Marbus, H., Mitler, D., Scott, R., & French, R. (1984). *Social stigma: The psychology of marked relationships.* New York: Freeman.

Kazdin, A. E. (1989). Developmental psychopathology: Current research, issues and directions. *American Psychologist, 44,* 180–187.

Koch, B. M. (1992). Rehabilitation of the child with joint disease. In G. E. Molnar (Ed.), *Pediatric rehabilitation* (2nd ed., pp. 293–333). Baltimore: Williams & Wilkins.

Kohn, J. G. (1990). Issues in the management of children with spastic cerebral palsy. *Pediatrician, 17,* 230–236.

Kopriva, P., & Taylor, J. R. (1993). Cerebral palsy. In M. G. Brodwin, F. Tellez, & S. K. Brodwin (Eds.), *Medical, psychosocial, and vocational aspects of disability* (pp. 519–536). Athens: Elliott & Fitzpatrick.

Kredich, D. (1992). Rheumatic disease of childhood. In R. E. Behrman & R. M. Kliegman (Eds.), *Nelson's textbook of pediatrics* (pp. 281–295). Philadelphia: W. B. Saunders.

Lavigne, J. V., & Faier-Routman, J. (1992). Psychological adjustment to pediatric physical disorders: A meta-analysis review. *Journal of Pediatric Psychology, 17,* 133–157.

Lazarus, R. S., & Folkman, S. (1984). *Stress, appraisal and coping.* New York: Springer.

Lemanek, K. L. (1994). Editorial: Research on pediatric chronic illness: New directions and current confounds. *Journal of Pediatric Psychology, 19,* 143–148.

Livneh, H., & Antonak, R. (1997). *Psychosocial adaptation to chronic illness and disability.* Gaithersburg, MD: Aspen.

Luckasson, R., Coulter, D. L., Polloway, E. A., Reiss, S., Shalock, R. L., Snell, M. E., Spitalnik, D. M., & Stark, J. A. (1992). *Mental retardation: Definition, classification, and systems of support* (9th ed.). Washington, DC: AAMR.

Main, D. M., & Mennuti, M. T. (1986). Neural tube defects: Issues in prenatal diagnosis and counseling. *Obstetrics and Gynecology, 67,* 1–16.

McLone, D. G. (1989). Spina bifida today: Problems adults face. *Seminars in Neurology, 9,* 169–175.

Nadel, A. S., Green, J. K., Holmes, L. B., Frigoletto, F. D., Jr., & Benacerraf, B. R. (1990). Absence of need for amniocentesis in patients with elevated levels of maternal serum alpha-fetoprotein and normal ultrasonographic examinations. *New England Journal of Medicine, 323,* 557–561.

O'Doughetry, M. (1983). *Counseling the chronically ill child: Psychological impact and intervention.* Boston, MA: Lewis.

Pellegrino, L. (1997). Cerebral palsy. In M. L. Batshaw (Ed.), *Children with disabilities* (4th ed., pp. 499–528). Baltimore: Brookes.

Pless, I. B., & Pinkerton, P. (1975). *Chronic childhood disorder—Promoting patterns of adjustment.* London: Kimpton.

Polloway, E. A., Smith, J. D., Patton, J. R., & Smith, T. E. C. (1996). Historical changes in mental retardation and developmental disabilities. *Education and Training in Mental Retardation and Developmental Disabilities, 31,* 3–12.

Rapoff, M. A. (1996). Adherence. In S. T. Wegener, B. L. Belza, & E. P. Gall (Eds.), *Clinical care in the rheumatic diseases* (pp. 137–140). Atlanta, GA: American College of Rheumatology.

Rosa, F. W. (1991). Spina bifida in infants of women treated with carbamazepine during pregnancy. *New England Journal of Medicine, 324,* 674–677.

Rusk, H. A. (Ed.). (1958). *Rehabilitation medicine.* St. Louis, MO: Mosby.

Schleichkorn, J. (1993). *Coping with cerebral palsy*. Austin, TX: Pro-Ed.

Sorensen, E. S. (1993). *Children's stress and coping. A family perspective*. New York: Guilford Press.

Stein, E. K., & Jessop, D. J. (1984). Relationship between health status and psychological adjustment among children with chronic conditions. *Pediatrics, 73*, 169–174.

Stein, E. K. (1989). *Caring for children with chronic illness: Issues and strategies*. New York: Springer.

Wallander, J. L., Varni, J. W., Babani, L., Banis, H. T., & Wilcox, K. (1989). Family resources as resistance factors for psychological maladjustment in chronically ill and handicapped children. *Journal of Pediatric Psychology, 14*, 157–173.

Wong, D., & Whaley, L. (1990). *Clinical manual of pediatric nursing*. Philadelphia: Mosby.

Wright, B. A. (1983). *Physical disability—A psychosocial approach* (2nd ed.). New York: Harper & Rowe.

Wright, B. A. (1988). Attitudes and the fundamental negative bias: Conditions and correlations. In H. E. Yuker (Ed.), *Attitudes toward persons with disabilities* (pp. 3–21). New York: Springer.

Yuker, H. E. (Ed.). (1988). *Attitudes toward persons with disabilities*. New York: Springer.

Zeitlin, S., & Williamson, G. G. (1994). *Coping in young children: Early intervention practices to enhance adaptive behavior and resilience*. Baltimore: Brookes.

7

Burn Injuries

David R. Patterson and Greg R. Ford

The physical and psychological needs of individuals who require burn injury rehabilitation have received inadequate attention. Burn injuries are a common form of trauma in the United States. Brigham and McLoughlin (1996) estimated that such trauma accounts for 54,000 hospital admissions, 500,000 emergency room visits, and 5,500 deaths annually in the United States alone. Severe burn injuries are almost always treated in surgical units and preferably in multidisciplinary burn centers. Early medical care typically involves intravascular fluid resuscitation, nutritional support, topical antibacterial agents, skin substitutes, and early excision and grafting (Caldwell, Wallace, & Cone, 1996). The quality of care has increased dramatically over the past three decades (Currerie, Luterman, Braun, & Shires, 1980) and has resulted in increased survival rates across all age groups (Nguyen, Gilpin, Meyer, & Herndon, 1996). A *burn injury of moderate severity* is defined as an open wound which, if not treated adequately, can lead to infection, amputation, and eventually death. The practice of many burn centers is to debride (scrape off dead portions of) burned skin on a daily or twice-daily basis. Burn injuries that lack potential to heal on their own are typically treated with skin grafts. Such wound cleaning and grafting procedures are frequently painful for a period of weeks. Such pain can be worse than that experienced in the initial burn injury and can wear on the best of a patient's coping mechanisms.

Although only a small percentage of patients with burn injuries require an extensive inpatient rehabilitation stay after their acute burn care has concluded, such injuries can result in a variety of rehabilitation issues. Sustained hospitalization in itself may result in deterioration of every organ system, even in healthy college students (Bortz, 1984). Burn patients are exposed to disuse associated with bed rest, a variety of painful procedures, and nutritional and hydration challenges. A severe burn that is left to heal on its own will scar. Even if the burn site is grafted, some scarring still results. Scarring can result in permanent disfigurement and can affect a burn survivor's emotional outcome, independent of the size or location of the injury. Burn injuries that occur at any joint have the potential to result in impaired mobility. As scar tissue over a joint contracts, flexibility is increasingly compromised. Splinting, vigorous stretching therapies, and surgical releases are often necessary to maintain mobility. Severe burn injuries also can result in amputations, neuropathies, and heterotopic ossification (calcification of bone joints; Hurren, 1995). All of these complications can have an emotional and physical effect on patients (Patterson, Ptacek, & Esselman, 1997–98).

The emotional needs of patients with burn injuries have long been overshadowed by the emphasis on survival. As such, research and theory on the psychological care of patients with burns are rudimentary relative to the general history of providing care for this type of trauma. Like many areas of disability, early reports on the psychological care of patients with burns are largely dominated by medical and psychoanalytic models. Such models have led to several misleading assumptions about the outcome of burn patients. Bernstein must be credited for taking a very sensitive initial look at patients with severe burns; his *Emotional Care of the Facially Burned and Disfigured* (1976) greatly facilitated the profession's attention to the emotional needs of patients. However, the psychoanalytic perspective is accompanied by the belief that burn injuries inevitably create intrapsychic conflicts in patients that lead to alterations in personality functioning (Bernstein, 1976). Early outcome studies on burn survivors were often driven by psychiatric models, with outcome measured in psychopathologic terms. The reliance on formal diagnosis to capture the outcome of burn survivors led investigators to overlook substantial portions of patients' experience. Furthermore, the medical model led to the assumption that the nature and size of a burn injury would predict emotional impact. More powerful determinants of emotional outcome such as preinjury adjustment or social support are often ignored when outcome is viewed through such models. Almost all of the early work done on the psychological care of burn patients has been dominated by medical models which, as discussed below, are simplistic and erroneous.

An additional problem with the early burn outcome literature is that reports rely excessively on the subjective opinion of the clinician. A number of recent studies have used objective measures to track the outcomes of burn survivors. Like other areas of disability (Trieschmann, 1988), more rigorous research demonstrates that severe burn injuries do not result inevitably in depression and that early research described emotional outcome far too pessimistically. Adcock, Goldberg, and Patterson (in press) demonstrated that health care professionals on burn units tend to overestimate psychological distress and that this discrepancy between staff and patient perceptions is larger in staff members with more experience. More current research also indicates that the nature of a burn injury alone has little to do with how well a patient eventually adjusts. Adjustment to a burn injury appears to involve a complex interplay between the preinjury characteristics of the survivor, the moderating environmental factors (e.g., social support), and the nature of the injury and ensuing medical care (Patterson et al., 1993).

Despite substantial improvements, even the most recent studies have severe limitations. Burn outcome studies are seldom driven by sophisticated biosocial models, and good longitudinal designs are a rarity. Although outcome measures are more psychometrically robust, they are often driven by models of psychopathology. For example, determining whether patients meet the criteria of the *Diagnostic and Statistical Manual of Mental Disorders* (4th ed. [*DSM–IV*]; American Psychiatric Association, 1994) for posttraumatic stress disorder (PTSD), a popular theme in recent studies, is of some utility but may overlook the "subclinical suffering" experienced by a number of patients. The authors of most current studies do not acknowledge that patients' emotional status may actually improve after such trauma; they also do not integrate general measures of health-determined quality of life. Therefore and despite improvements in the objectivity of burn outcome research, researchers would benefit from more sophisticated models, sensitive measures, and longitudinal designs.

Psychological Outcome

In a review of the literature on the psychological impact of burn injuries, Patterson et al. (1993) divided the available studies into three categories. The first group examined premorbid psychopathology in people who have sustained severe burn injuries. A second group examined patients' psychological reactions during hospitalization, and the third focused on long-term adjustment in burn patients after hospital discharge.

Premorbid Psychopathology

Several studies focus on the issue of premorbid psychopathology in people presenting at hospitals for burn care. Available research largely supports conjecture that individuals with burns severe enough to warrant hospital care often have preexisting chaos and dysfunction in their lives. In a review of the literature, Kolman (1983) concluded that the incidence of mental illness and personality disorders was higher in burn unit patients than in the general population. In a more recent review, Patterson et al. (1993) also supported the contention that the incidence of prior psychiatric disorders is higher among burn unit patients as compared with expected levels in the general population, with estimates ranging from 28% to 75%. The most common diagnoses identified in these studies include depression, character disorder, and substance abuse. These studies also document several ways in which prior psychopathology has an adverse impact on hospital course, including increasing the likelihood that patients stay longer on a burn unit and that they develop more serious psychopathology. Moreover, individuals with pre-existing psychopathology are described as coping with hospitalization through previously established dysfunctional, and often disruptive, patterns. Patterson et al. (in press) reported that a sample of 199 patients with burns had higher estimates of problems on the Rand Mental Health Inventory when compared with the general population, even after they had been screened for previous psychiatric diagnoses.

Psychological Reactions During Hospitalization

Hospitalization for burn injuries may vary in length from less than 1 week to several months, depending on the severity of burn and the presence of other medical complications. The hospitalization period can be broken into two distinct stages: (a) the critical stage, typically spent in the intensive care unit, and (b) the acute care stage of recovery, which occurs when patients are medically stable and able to begin rehabilitation (Avni, 1990; Patterson, 1987). Each setting represents a distinct medical, environmental, and psychological context and presents the patient with a unique set of challenges.

Characteristics of the critical care stage include uncertainty regarding outcome and a struggle for survival, particularly in the case of severe burn injuries. During this phase, patients typically undergo repeated medical procedures and must contend with severe physiological stresses, including anoxia (lack of oxygen which results in cerebral damage), electrolyte imbalance, infections, and edema (swelling), while residing in an environment that is alternately overstimulating and understimulating (Steiner & Clark, 1977). Under such frightening and unusual environmental conditions, mild disorientation, confusion, illusions, or hallucinations may represent functional conditions caused by sensory deprivation and overload, sleep deprivation, or the shock of extremely threatening events (Patterson, 1987). Delirium and brief psychotic reactions may also be seen as adaptive psychological defense mechanisms during extreme stress (Hamburg, Hamburg, & deGoza, 1953). However, it is most likely that distinct changes in mental status result from pathophysiological causes, such as infections, alcohol withdrawal, or metabolic complications (Perry & Blank, 1984).

The incidence of true delirium among burn patients was estimated at 19% in a study by Perry and Blank (1984), the most methodologically sound study to date on this topic. In this study, delirium was found to be associated with being male and having a history of alcohol or drug abuse, having larger burns, and having an increased likelihood of a fatal outcome. Delirium can perhaps best be thought of as an early reaction limited to the immediate postburn phase that often indicates important medical complications.

In contrast to the often frightening environment during the critical phase, patients move to an environment that is more consistent, familiar, and less intrusive during the acute phase of recovery. Despite these changes in environment and mental status, patients must continue to undergo painful procedures on a daily basis, including debridement and dressing changes, and must face further plastic surgery, grafting, and aggressive therapies. Moreover, patients are increasingly aware of the physical and psychological impact of their injuries (Patterson, 1987).

Psychological difficulty common in the acute phase of recovery includes depression and anxiety, both general anxiety and PTSD. The literature indicates estimates of moderate depression ranging from 23 to 61%, general anxiety from 13 to 47%, and PTSD of 30% (the anxiety described in these studies is usually not described in enough detail to provide a specific diagnosis; however, the anxiety is clinically significant and enough to warrant pharmacological intervention; Patterson et al., 1993). Studies on both depression and anxiety among hospitalized burn patients are beset by methodological difficulties that limit the conclusions that can be drawn from these estimates of incidence. With regard to depression, investigators have usually not distinguished between clinically diagnosable depression and depressive symptoms. Nonetheless, these studies show that the average of self-reported depressive symptoms fall in the mildly depressed range and that severity of depressive symptoms are associated with resting pain (Choiniere, Melzack, Rondeau, Girard, & Paquin, 1989) and family or marital problems (Andreasen & Norris, 1972).

Studies of anxiety disorders among burn patients have achieved greater methodological sophistication and have distinguished between general anxiety and PTSD or acute stress disorder (ASD). In general, researchers looking at general anxiety suggest that anxiety symptoms in burn patients become increasingly less common over time (e.g., decreasing from nearly 50% prevalence at Week 1 to 13% at Week 4) and are comparable with anxiety symptoms among medical and surgical patients but less severe than those of psychiatric patients (Patterson et al., 1993). Available research on PTSD has suggested that burn patients with this diagnosis had more severe pain, had larger burn areas, expressed more guilt about the precipitating event, and were more likely to have experienced a delirium. In a study of 54 consecutively admitted burn patients assessed daily for symptoms of PTSD, Patterson, Carrigan, Robinson, and Questad (1990) found that 63% of patients endorsed intrusive, recurrent memories of the burn events, but only 30% met full criteria of the third revised *Diagnostic and Statistical Manual of Mental Disorders* for PTSD during their hospital stay, and none met diagnostic criteria at discharge. More recently, Ehde, Patterson, Wiechman, and Wilson (1999, in press) found similar rates of ASD (inpatient) and PTSD (outpatient) with substantially larger numbers of patients. However, in more recent studies using superior measures (*DSM–III–R*; American Psychiatric Association, 1987), Perry, Difede, Musngi, Frances, and Jacobsberg (1992) found an actual increase in PTSD as time progresses after hospitalization.

To summarize, distress is common among many people hospitalized following burn injuries, but symptoms often do not reach diagnostically significant levels. Rates of depression and generalized anxiety are similar to those found in other hospitalized patients (Choiniere et al., 1989). Delirium and PTSD, although occurring more frequently in burn patients than in other patients, are often transient reactions, limited to the critical or early acute phases of recovery. Early research, plagued by methodological limitations, seems to have overestimated the prevalence of psychopathology.

Long-Term Effects of Burn Injuries in Adults

Health care professionals may tend to assume that severely burned individuals experience long-term and relatively permanent declines across multiple areas of functioning. However, these assumptions may be based largely on their observations of these patients at discharge and immediately thereafter and might not reflect the actual long-term course of adjustment. In fact, it is widely observed that the first year after hospitalization is a psychologically unique period of high distress not seen afterward. In addition to the high demands of rehabilitation, patients must deal with secondary stressors including family strains and disruption in daily life. Whatever the reason, the literature suggests that many of these symptoms are transient.

Available research suggests that symptoms of anxiety and depression, which commonly occur together during the first year after hospitalization, tend to decrease thereafter, particularly after 1-year postinjury (Patterson et al., 1993). In addition, there is evidence of a corresponding improvement with time in adjustment to burn injuries, quality of life, and self-esteem, independent of size or severity of burn injuries. Most often quality of life is reported to improve with time. The minority of burn survivors who express a lowered quality of life often also have limited range of motion and subsequent, lasting decreased functional capacity. Problems of noncompliance with medical staff during hospitalization and reliance on avoidance coping styles also are reported to be associated with diminished quality of life. Whereas available studies do not conclusively link depressive or anxiety symptoms to size or severity of burn, there is some suggestion that decreased awareness and recollection of circumstances surrounding the burn injury may provide a buffer against the development of psychopathology. Social support likewise has been found to serve as a buffer against the development of psychological difficulty, particularly family support.

In terms of social adjustment, the majority of patients who sustain burn injuries return to work, although 50–60% require some sort of change in job status. Following burn-related hospitalization, social interaction patterns often change such that survivors increase socializing with the family and spend less time interacting with nonfamily members. There is little evidence that burn injuries lead to increased marital conflict in married burn victims, relative to their nonburned counterparts. However, decreased sexual satisfaction is a common finding among burn patients, especially women (Patterson et al., 1993).

General Implications

Psychological distress during and after hospitalization may be likely in cases in which emotional dysfunction preceded burn injury. Once hospitalized for burn care, patients often experience transient emotional distress, independent of their premorbid status. Depression and anxiety symptoms commonly cooccur during the acute phase of recovery and may persist for the first year after discharge, but they do not occur at a higher rate in burn victims relative to other hospitalized patients. Delirium, which is commonly confined to the critical phase of recovery, and PTSD or ASD symptoms, which may persist during the acute phase and after discharge, are more commonly seen in burn patients but tend to be relatively transient. Overall, for the majority of people hospitalized, a burn represents a painful but temporary disruption of life's routine, after which they eventually resume their normal preinjury functioning, largely independent of burn area or location. However, for the subgroup of patients who have been found to experience long-term disruption in social, vocational, and physical functioning, services such as long-term psychotherapy, vocational counseling, and intensive outpatient physical rehabilitation should be considered.

Clinical Treatment

Survivors of severe burn injuries must endure a unique set of physical, environmental, and emotional challenges during each phase of recovery. As outlined earlier, psychological sequalae of burn injuries during the recovery phase include delirium, anxiety, depression, and pain. Yet available research supports a more hopeful view of long-term psychological recovery. This research has important implications for treating patients during the three phases of physical recovery. The following sections contain recommendations for patient management based on our clinical experience in a burn setting and previous writings (Moss, Everett, & Patterson, 1994; Patterson et al., 1993).

Early Stage of Recovery

The early stage of burn recovery typically occurs in an intensive care unit, where a patient faces uncertain survival in a highly invasive and confusing environment. These characteristics of the environment and patient physical status have important implications for the clinician attempting to intervene on the patient's behalf. First, direct or high-level psychological intervention during this phase is often of minimal value. Patients are typically drowsy, confused, disoriented, and intubated, which substantially reduces the possibility of direct communication.

Moreover, focusing on past or future concerns can be counterproductive even when patients are more alert. Patients typically should be encouraged to cope with the frighteningly unusual circumstances of the intensive care unit through whatever defenses are available to them, even primitive strategies such as denial and repression. Some clinicians argue that patient delirium and brief psychotic reactions, although upsetting to staff and the patient's family, should be seen as patient coping attempts. Direct confrontation of issues related to the causes or ramifications of the injury can easily overwhelm coping resources that are needed to facilitate the patient's primary task during this phase—physical survival. Instead, supportive psychological interventions should focus on immediate concerns (e.g., assuring the patient that outside matters are being addressed) and protecting and sanctioning the coping strategies being used by the patient.

The clinician can also effectively intervene during the early stage of recovery by working through the patient's family members. Understandably, family members may be anxious and distressed while observing the patient's often tenuous grip on life (Shelby, 1992). Wheras the presence of family members and friends can promote a sense of familiarity in patients and thus can alleviate anxiety and agitation, such individuals should be encouraged to intervene in a supportive and limited manner. Moreover, because of reduced cognitive abilities, the patient's coping ability is often influenced by cues received from significant others. As family members express high levels of anxiety and stress, the patient may pick up on these cues and behave accordingly. Helping these individuals to instead convey a sense of hope and calmness can allow the patient's behavior to reflect these emotions.

Intervention, including both education and emotional support, might also be directed at the staff. In particular, educating staff about the transient nature of delirium and helping them distinguish between distress and the syndrome of depression can allay their concerns about the patient's mentation and mental health. Finally, it is not uncommon for nurses and other medical staff to project onto patients their own feelings (e.g., feelings of inadequacy in the face of uncertain physical status). Helping staff members understand and deal effectively with these issues, if done in a gentle and supportive manner and in the spirit of "educating" them, can help them monitor and gain insight into these potentially counterproductive reactions.

A related issue that may arise in the critical care burn setting is the need for support and debriefing of staff members. Because of the close involvement with patients and their families in the context of providing frontline care to medically compromised patients, nurses may be particularly prone to having significant psychological reactions warranting supportive intervention. Staff reactions may be particularly pronounced following the death of a patient who had been making steady improvement. Nurses may need focused grief counseling in such instances, separately or as a group. Another instance in which staff debriefing can be helpful is when overstressed family members begin to lash out at staff. Helping staff understand that these hostile reactions often represent displacement of anger and helplessness onto them can reduce both distress and tendency to retaliate and become punitive.

Intermediate Stage of Recovery

The intermediate (or acute care) stage begins when the patient is medically stabilized and is thus able to undergo the rehabilitative phase of recovery, which lasts for the remainder of the patient's inpatient stay. (With decreased hospital stays, however, the distinction between acute and rehabilitative stages of care is becoming less dependent on whether the patient is hospitalized.) With issues of survival largely resolved, healing takes precedence. Along with improvement in physical status comes improved cognitive clarity and more regular sleep. Patients also experience less frequent surgical procedures. However, they must continue to endure wound care, including debridement and dressing changes, often with less sedation. As such, anxiety and distress during procedures are commonly seen. As an additional source of pain and anxiety, patients must undergo increasingly intense daily physical rehabilitation, such as ranging, exercising, and splinting. These procedures often cause a significant level of physical discomfort and pain.

Two distinct psychological reactions are common during this phase. First, despite improved physical status, the patient with severe burns may cope by remaining in a state of psychological shock (i.e., dissociated state). Because dissociated states usually diminish with time and are gradually replaced by coping with pragmatic concerns, psychological intervention is often not necessary. This reaction can essentially be thought of as a continuation of coping strategies used in the critical care setting and should be supported by psychological staff as long as the patient continues to make adequate progress in rehabilitation.

Increased patient distress and grief represent a second common constellation of reactions. For many patients, distress increases as they are more able to focus on the impact of burn injuries on their lives. A friend, family member, or pet may have died in the accident. Patients also must cope with the loss of their homes or personal properties. In addition to these external losses, patients often are forced to grieve their former life (e.g., job, mobility, physical abilities). Besides depression, symptoms of ASD, including nightmares and intrusive thoughts of the accident, are the most common psychological problem in the acute care stage of recovery. Anxiety and regression are also common, along with behavioral problems such as hostility and dependence.

In the acute care setting, distress or depressive symptoms are more common than the syndrome of clinical depression. Although brief psychological counseling can be helpful, medications may be necessary, particularly when suicidal ideation or diagnostic criteria for a major depressive disorder are present. When offering counseling to a patient, it is often helpful to normalize the patient's depressive symptoms and to provide reassurance that symptoms often diminish on their own, particularly if the patient has not been prone to depression prior to the current circumstances. Clinicians should be mindful that hospitalizations of over 1 month and repeated medical setbacks have been found to be associated with increased depression (Andreasen & Norris, 1972). The severity of depressive episodes has also been related to a patient's level of resting pain (that occurring between procedures) and the pressure of family and marital problems (Andreasen, Norris, & Hartford, 1971; Tempereau, 1989).

ASD symptoms can be thought of as a predictable psychological response to the abnormal stressor (i.e., burn trauma) recently experienced. As described in *DSM-IV* (American Psychiatric Association, 1994), ASD involves a constellation of symptoms experienced in response to a traumatic event involving a severe threat to the physical integrity of self or others and to which one responded with intense fear, helplessness, or horror. Foa, Hearst-Ikeda, and Perry (1995) found a brief prevention program to be effective in reducing PTSD symptoms in women who have been assaulted. Treatment included exposure, relaxation training, and cognitive restructuring. The authors attributed treatment success to instituting treatment 2 weeks posttrauma rather than immediately after the trauma. We have found that an effective initial approach involves normalizing symptoms for patients (e.g., assuring them that symptoms often abate on their own); helping them talk through the events repeatedly; and providing the opportunity for confronting, rather than avoiding, reminders of the trauma. Whereas an approach combining normalizing symptoms and education may be the most effective treatment for many patients initially, a combined counseling (e.g., Foa et al., 1995) and medication treatment approach is helpful when symptoms do not abate after a short period.

Generalized anxiety and nightmares are other common psychological complaints. Both of these symptoms are often seen during the first few weeks of hospitalization, with symptoms typically decreasing thereafter, particularly after 1 month. Informing patients that dreams are normal and typically subside in about a month can help allay concerns of abnormality and refocus patients' mental energy on other areas of recovery.

Long-Term Recovery

The long-term stage of recovery typically begins when patients leave the hospital and reintegrate into society. For patients with severe burns, this stage likely involves continued physical rehabilitation on an outpatient basis, along with possible continuation of procedures (e.g., dressing changes) begun in the hospital or a return for further cosmetic surgery. Patients may encounter daily pain during rehabilitation, and they must confront cosmetic or other existential concerns. Patients also face a remarkable number of daily hassles (e.g., compensating for inability to use hands) during this phase. This is a period when patients slowly regain a sense of competence while simultaneously adjusting to the practical limitations of a burn injury, such as limited range of motion or adjustment to prosthetic devices (e.g., artificial limbs or adaptive aids). In addition, a significant number of patients with burns may continue to have vivid memories of the accident and may experience changes in family and occupational roles. It is not surprising, then, that the first year following discharge is usually the most difficult for burn patients. Furthermore, the increase in symptoms of PTSD noted by some researchers after discharge is understandable (Perry et al., 1992). It can be helpful to make followup calls to patients after discharge with referrals for outpatient psychotherapy available on request. Moreover, repeated or more frequent calls may be helpful for patients with identified risk factors for more prolonged depression.

In terms of vocational status, patients often face an extended period of outpatient recovery before being able to return to work. In addition, some patients choose to change jobs, but others experience undesirable changes in their employment status such as a job reassignment or reduced work time. A significant number of patients go through vocational challenges, which make a vocational counselor a valuable member of the burn team.

Adjustment difficulties that persist after the 1-year postdischarge usually involve perceptions of a diminished quality of life and lowered self-esteem. Some studies suggest that a general trend of the impact of burn disfigurement is decreased self-esteem in women and social withdrawal in men. It is also likely that a subset of burn patients withdraw from society because of their disfigurement and are captured neither by outcome studies nor outpatient psychological treatment. Such individuals may have been essentially "normal" (i.e., lacking premorbid psychopathology) before, and thus may be particularly challenged by the notion of seeking psychological help to facilitate coping with their disfigurement. A variety of theoretical approaches are available to address cosmetic concerns in those who do present in the treatment setting (see Pruzinsky & Cash, 1990).

A successful program designed to enhance self-esteem is the Changing Faces program in Great Britain (Partridge, 1997), which includes a hospital-based image enhancement and social skills program, along with a series of publications for patients dealing with aspects of facial disfigurement. The hospital-based component provides patients with image-enhancement methods, which include corrective cosmetic techniques, color analysis and clothing coordination, and behavioral and social skills training. Education in image enhancement methods can help a patient take cosmetic steps to cope with facial disfigurement, particularly that which is no longer amenable to plastic and reconstructive surgery. Specific suggestions are made in a number of areas including using makeup, selecting glasses frames and clothing, and styling hair.

Behavioral and social skills training can help the burn survivor develop practical communication strategies to deal with difficult social situations and can thereby help prevent social isolation (Partridge, 1997). Specific strategies to help patients manage their thoughts and respond appropriately in difficult situations are provided, with an emphasis on dealing with prolonged staring and intrusive questions. For example, patients are provided with several possible responses to intrusive questions that allow them to end the conversation graciously; for example, "I was hurt in an accident, but it was a long time ago, and I don't dwell on it at all now" (Partridge, 1997, p. 12). Patients are also given suggestions for managing the difficult process of returning to intimate relationships. Little outcome research has been conducted on programs such as Changing Faces. However, available reports link these programs to increased self-esteem and social comfort and reduced depression (Partridge, 1997).

A final note relates to the importance of using ancillary resources such as support groups and peer counseling with burn survivors. Major burn facilities ideally have a network of burn survivors who are willing to talk with patients in the hospital. Peer counseling can be particularly helpful for burn patients, many of whom have had little exposure to or inclination to work with mental health professionals in the past. Survivor support is also readily available to patients by telephone through such organizations as the Phoenix Society in the United States and the Changing Faces program. Support groups for patients and family members can also be immensely helpful.

Pain Control

It is impossible to comprehensively address psychological and rehabilitation care of patients with burns without considering the issue of pain control. Sustaining a severe burn is one of the most painful experiences a person may experience in a lifetime; yet, typical burn care inflicts more pain than does the initial trauma. Once or twice daily, patients have their dressings removed, necrotic skin debrided, and stinging antiseptic agents applied. This process may continue for weeks or even months. Although pain gradually decreases over time (Ptacek, Patterson, Montgomery, Ordonez, & Heimbach, 1995), anticipatory anxiety does not. Ptacek, Patterson, and Doctor (in press) indicated that the pain reported by a patient varies substantially from day to day, does not follow a uniform pattern between individuals, and is not related to the size of the burn injury. One largely predictable element of burn pain is that procedural pain (pain that occurs during a medical procedure) is of greater intensity and shorter duration than background pain (that which the patient experiences during rest). Perry, Heidrich, and Ramos (1981) indicated that patients with burns reported procedural pain as excruciating, despite receiving morphine during their wound care. It is clear from the work of Perry (1984) and others (e.g., Choiniere et al., 1989) that opioid analgesic drugs do not control all burn pain, and an effective strategy often includes a variety of approaches.

Treatment of burn pain can generally be divided into pharmacologic and nonpharmacologic approaches. Pharmacologically, opioid agonists (those agents that bind with receptors) are the most commonly used analgesics because they are potent forms of pain control, are familiar to most caregivers, and provide a dose-dependent degree of sedation that is useful both to patients and the staff members treating them (Patterson & Sharar, 1997). Typical opioid analgesics (morphine-based drugs) used on burn units include morphine, hydromorphone, methadone, meperidine, codeine, oxycodone, and fentanyl. Although physical dependence on opioid analgesics is to be expected with prolonged use, psychological dependence (addiction) is a rarity in patients being treated for burn pain. Estimates of such addiction in opioid-naive patients is 1 in 3,000 (Porter & Jick, 1980). As such, one role of the psychologist is to assure patients that taking opioid analgesics is not a sign of weakness and that fears of addiction are unwarranted.

Opioid analgesics may be supplemented with other pharmacologic approaches, including nonsteroidal anti-inflammatory agents or inhaled nitrous oxide (Filkins, Cosgrav, & Marvin, 1981). Anxiolytics such as lorazepam (a benzodiazepine class drug) have been recently found to lessen burn pain, largely by treating accompanying acute anxiety (Patterson, Ptacek, Carrougher, & Sharar, 1997). For particularly challenging wound care, anesthetic agents that result in conscious sedation (i.e., levels of consciousness are decreased enough so that patients are unaware of pain) may be warranted. Agents such as ketamine, propofol, and inhaled desflurane have been found to be useful in this regard (Patterson & Sharar, 1997).

Cognitive–behavioral interventions and hypnosis are often well suited for patients who are undergoing painful medical procedures. In looking at cognitive–behavioral approaches, it is useful to determine whether patients tend to be sensitizers who focus their attention on the painful procedures, or if they are repressors who like to turn their attention away. Sensitizing patients can benefit from coping strategies that allow them to reinterpret the meaning or sensation of their pain. Repressing patients are likely to benefit more from approaches that allow them to dissociate from their experience such as deep relaxation and imagery (Everett, Patterson, & Chen, 1990). In any case, it is usually helpful to patients to learn to discriminate *hurt* from *harm* and to understand that burn pain of great intensity is always temporary and that the presence of pain usually indicates that the tissue is viable and healing (Patterson, 1995).

Hypnosis is an appealing psychological approach on the burn unit because it can be applied quickly, often with dramatic results. Patients in burn units might be unusually good candidates for hypnosis because they are emotionally regressed from trauma care, dissociated by virtue of sustaining trauma, and motivated to comply because of their high levels of pain (Patterson, Adcock, & Bombardier, 1997). Hypnosis is probably best applied before a patient undergoes a painful procedure. There are several controlled studies to indicate that such an approach reduces reports of pain, particularly in those patients with high levels of pain (Patterson, Everett, Burns, & Marvin, 1992; Patterson, Goldberg, & Ehde, 1996; Patterson, Ptacek, et al., 1997). Ewin (1979, 1986) presented compelling anecdotal evidence that early implementation of burn care (e.g., within 4 hours of the burn injury) can retard the progression of a thermal injury, although his findings need to be substantiated in a controlled study.

Management of Self-Inflicted Burns and Axis II Disorders on a Burn Unit

Burn units are often charged with managing patients with characterological behavioral issues, including self-inflicted burns. Available estimates of rates of self-inflicted burn admissions range from .67% (Daniels, Fenley, Powers, & Cruse, 1991) to 9% (Skully & Hutcherson, 1983). There is also some evidence to suggest that rates of suicide attempts from self-inflicted burns have increased over the past 10 years (Castellani, Beghini, Barisoni, & Marigo, 1995). Patients who intentionally inflict burns for psychological reasons other than suicide (parasuicide) often carry the *DSM-IV* (American Psychiatric Association, 1994) diagnosis of borderline personality disorder. Scant research attention has been directed to this difficult population and the techniques helpful in managing their behavior on the burn unit. In a review of admissions to burn center over 13 years, Wiechman, Ehde, Patterson, and Wilson (in press) found that although very few patients were admitted each year for self-inflicted burns, these patients were often admitted repeatedly and therefore represented a disproportionate number (28%) of admissions.

Several principles are critical to management of patients presenting with self-inflicted burns or, more generally, with significant characterological issues. First, consistent, early application of behavior modification principles, as outlined earlier, can be helpful. Second, it is essential to work closely with staff on the development and implementation of a behavioral plan. It can be helpful to work with staff to help them view difficult behavior as a part of the patient's pathology rather than as a personal affront. It is also important to help staff predict patient behavioral problems (e.g., discharge is likely to be viewed by the patient as abandonment, leading to escalation of behavioral difficulties). Clinicians can also help educate staff about the need to minimize and limit contact with such patients (e.g., responding to patient concerns on a time-contingent basis.) In particularly difficult cases, staff can be coached to have patients direct questions of a psychological nature to the clinician. Often a skilled clinician can discuss issues with the patient in a flexible, supportive, yet firm manner, and can thereby help minimize staff splitting (Stoudemire & Thompson, 1982). Centralization of care and consistency are particularly important in managing patients with chaotic lives; patient questions can then be directed to that person or persons charged with directing their care, and opportunities for staff splitting can be further minimized. Another critical role for the clinician is to work with other disciplines (e.g., social work) to get the patient into long-term psychotherapy after discharge. A clear distinction is made between the burn unit, where the goal is optimal, rapid burn care, and outpatient psychotherapy, where the goal often is symptom uncovering within the context of long-term care. Finally, staff should be cautioned against undermedicating pain because of the aversiveness of the patient.

Using a Quota System to Facilitate Rehabilitation

As stated earlier, patients with severe burns undergo prolonged hospitalization and are particularly prone to developing distress. Withdrawal, passivity, anxiety, and decreased social interaction are common behaviors and often represent a syndrome that is difficult to distinguish from depression. This syndrome, which can be termed "helplessness," resembles the "learned helplessness" phenomenon first elucidated by Seligman (1975).

The quota system is a treatment approach to the helplessness phenomenon that is successfully used in the rehabilitation and chronic pain fields (Fordyce, 1976). The goals of this approach are to help patients gain a sense of predictability and control while minimizing the overwhelming nature of rehabilitation through systematic, gradual increases in expected behaviors.

The quota system approach includes separate baseline and program phases. In the baseline phase, a series of behaviors are identified and measured for 3–5 days prior to implementing the quota system. Targeted behaviors, which must be readily quantifiable and observable, can include any task perceived by the patient to be difficult or overwhelming. Common examples in the burn setting include sitting tolerance, walking, range of motion exercises, pressure garment use, and splint use. During the baseline phase, the patient is asked to perform the targeted behavior to the point of weakness, fatigue, or pain. Baseline is then the average level tolerated over this 3–5 day period and serves as the basis for determining the initial value in the program phase. To promote early success in therapy, an initial value is chosen that is slightly lower (e.g., 50–80%) than the average performance. Exercises are then increased each day by consistent, predictable, attainable increments (e.g., 5–10% of the initial value) such that increased tolerance is built gradually. The patient is not allowed to exceed any of the quotas, even if he or she feels capable of working beyond tolerance on a given day. Increments can be adjusted up or down if the increment consistently appears too low or high, respectively. Ehde, Patterson, and Fordyce (1998) reported the success of this approach on the burn unit.

Conclusion

The treatment of burn injuries has long been dominated by the medical model, which is certainly warranted given the surgical needs of this population. Over time, an increasing number of people have survived such trauma, only to be faced with pain control and rehabilitation needs that burn teams have been ill equipped to address. Psychologists have only recently become involved in providing care and outcome research with their population. Some of the impact of this profession can be seen in improved outcome research and more sophisticated models of biosocial care. However, conceptualizations of the emotional needs of patients with burns continue to be influenced unduly by oversimplified medical models that do not address rehabilitation needs and the complex interplay of factors involved in adapting to a disability.

Patients with burn injuries present with different issues, depending on whether they are going through intensive, acute, or rehabilitative phases of care. Early psychological care tends to emphasize crisis management and anxiety and pain control. Long-term issues deal more with therapy compliance and disfigurement and self-esteem. Effective psychologists working with this population often benefit by having relatively unique skills (e.g., a systems orientation, consultation, and liaison), because of issues presented by the staff, as well as the patients. Teaming up with well-adjusted burn survivors as a means to promote the emotional recovery of more recent, struggling patients appears to offer great promise.

Burn units face the same health care challenges as other fields of care. Reduced hospital stays and funding for auxiliary staff increasingly test the ability of burn teams to provide optimal care. Just as the value of psychologists in providing burn rehabilitation has become increasingly prominent, the ability to fund such positions has become a greater challenge. However, psychologists should be able to continue to prove their worth in this area by providing sophisticated outcome studies, nonpharmacologic pain control, and management strategies for high-using patients (e.g., recurrent patients with parasuicidal behavior). Many of the challenges to current burn care can be most effectively addressed by the field of psychology.

References

Adcock, R., Goldberg, M., & Patterson, D. (in press). Staff perceptions of emotional distress in patients with burn trauma. *Rehabilitation Psychology*.

American Psychiatric Association. (1987). *Diagnostic and statistical manual of mental disorders* (3rd ed. rev.). Washington, DC: Author.

American Psychiatric Association. (1994). *Diagnostic and statistical manual of mental disorders* (4th ed.). Washington, DC: Author.

Andreasen, N. J. C., & Norris, A. S. (1972). Long-term adjustment and adaptation mechanisms in severely burned adults. *Journal of Nervous and Mental Disease, 154*, 352–362.

Andreasen, N. J. C., Norris, A. S., & Hartford, C. E. (1971). Incidence of long-term psychiatric complications in severely burned adults. *Annals of Surgery, 174*, 785–793.

Avni, J. (1990). The severe burns. *Advances in Psychosomatic Medicine, 10*, 57–77.

Bernstein, N. R. (1976). *Emotional care of the facially burned and disfigured*. Boston: Little, Brown.

Bortz, W. (1984). The disuse syndrome. *Western Journal of Medicine, 141*, 691–694.

Brigham, P. A., & McLoughlin, E. (1996). Burn incidence and medical care use in the United States: Estimates, trends and data sources. *Journal of Burn Care and Rehabilitation, 17*, 95–107.

Caldwell, F. T. J., Wallace, B. H., & Cone, J. B. (1996). Sequential excision and grafting of the burn injuries of 1507 patients treated between 1967 and 1986: End results and the determinants of death. *Journal of Burn Care and Rehabilitation, 17*, 137–146.

Castellani, G., Beghini, D., Barisoni, D., & Marigo, M. (1995). Suicide attempted by burning: A 10-year study of self-immolation deaths. *Burns, 21*, 607–609.

Choiniere, M., Melzack, R., Rondeau, J., Girard, N., & Paquin, M.-J. (1989). The pain of burns: Characteristics and correlates. *Journal of Trauma, 29*, 1531–1539.

Currerie, P. W., Luterman, A., Braun, D. W., & Shires, G. T. (1980). Burn injury: Analysis of survival and hospitalization time for 937 patients. *Annals of Surgery, 192*, 472–478.

Daniels, S. M., Fenley, J. D., Powers, P. S., & Cruse, C. W. (1991). Self-inflicted burns: A ten-year retrospective study. *Journal of Burn Care and Rehabilitation, 12*, 144–147.

Ehde, D. M., Patterson, D. R., & Fordyce, W. E. (1998). The quota system in burn rehabilitation. *Journal of Burn Care and Rehabilitation, 19*, 436–440.

Ehde, D. M., Patterson, D. R., Wiechman, S. A., & Wilson, L. G. (1999). Post traumatic stress symptoms and distress following acute burn injury. *Burns, 25*, 587–592.

Ehde, D. M., Patterson, D. R., Wiechman, S. A., & Wilson, L. G. (in press). Post traumatic stress symptoms and distress one year post burn injury. *Journal of Burn Care and Rehabilitation*.

Everett, J. J., Patterson, D. R., & Chen, A. C. (1990). Cognitive and behavioral treatments for burn pain. *The Pain Clinic, 3*, 133–145.

Ewin, D. (1979). Hypnosis in burn therapy. In G. D. Burrows & L. Dennerstein (Eds.), *Hypnosis* (pp. 210–235). Amsterdam: Elsevier.

Ewin, D. (1986). Emergency room hypnosis for the burned patient. *American Journal of Clinical Hypnosis, 29,* 7–12.

Filkins, S. A., Cosgrav, P., & Marvin, J. A. (1981). Self-administered anesthesia: A method of pain control. *Journal of Burn Care and Rehabilitation, 2,* 33–34.

Foa, E. B., Hearst-Ikeda, D. E., & Perry, K. J. (1995). Evaluation of a brief cognitive–behavioral program for the prevention of chronic PTSD in recent assault victims. *Journal of Consulting and Clinical Psychology, 63,* 948–955.

Fordyce, W. E. (1976). *Behavioral methods for chronic pain and illness.* St. Louis, MO: Mosby–Year Book.

Hamburg, D. A., Hamburg, B., & deGoza, S. (1953). Adaptive problems and mechanisms in severely burned patients. *Psychiatry, 16,* 1–20.

Hurren, J. (1995). Rehabilitation of the burned patient: James Laing Memorial Essay for 1993. *Burns, 21,* 116–126.

Kolman, P. B. R. (1983). The incidence of psychopathology in burned adult patients: A critical review. *Journal of Burn Care and Rehabilitation, 4,* 430–436.

Moss, B. F., Everett, J. J., & Patterson, D. R. (1994). Psychologic support and pain management of the burn patient. In R. L. Richard & M. J. Staley (Eds.), *Burn care and rehabilitation: Principles and practice* (pp. 475–498). Philadelphia: Davis.

Nguyen, T. T., Gilpin, D. D., Meyer, N. A., & Herndon, D. N. (1996). Current treatment of severely burned patients. *Annals of Surgery, 223,* 12–25.

Partridge, J. (1997). *When burns affect the way you look.* London: Changing Faces.

Patterson, D. R. (1987). Psychological care of the burn patient. *Topics in Acute and Trauma Rehabilitation, 1,* 25–39.

Patterson, D. R. (1995). Nonopioid based approaches to burn pain. *Journal of Burn Care and Rehabilitation, 16,* 372–376.

Patterson, D. R., Adcock, R. J., & Bombardier, C. H. (1997). Factors predicting hypnotic analgesia in clinical burn pain. *International Journal of Clinical and Experimental Hypnosis, 45,* 377–394.

Patterson, D. R., Carrigan, L., Robinson, R., & Questad, K. A. (1990). Post-traumatic stress disorder and delirium in hospitalized patients. *Journal of Burn Care and Rehabilitation, 11,* 181–184.

Patterson, D. R., Everett, J. J., Bombardier, C. H., Questad, K. A., Lee, V. K., & Marvin, J. A. (1993). Psychological effects of severe burn injuries. *Psychological Bulletin, 113,* 362–378.

Patterson, D. R., Everett, J. J., Burns, G. L., & Marvin J. A. (1992). Hypnosis for the treatment of burn pain. *Journal of Consulting and Clinical Psychology, 60,* 713–717.

Patterson, D. R., Finch, C. P., Wiechman, S. A., Avery, R., Gibran, N., & Heimbach, D. (in press). Premorbid mental health status of adult burn patients: Comparison with a normative sample. *Journal of Burn Care and Rehabilitation.*

Patterson, D. R., Goldberg, M. L., & Ehde, D. M. (1996). Hypnosis in the treatment of patients with severe burns. *American Journal of Clinical Hypnosis, 38,* 200–212.

Patterson, D. R., Ptacek, J. T., Carrougher, G. J., & Sharar, S. (1997). Lorazepam as an adjunct to opioid analgesics in the treatment of burn pain. *Pain, 72,* 367–374.

Patterson, D. R., Ptacek, J. T., & Esselman, P. C. (1997–1998). Management of suffering in patients with severe burn injury. *Western Journal of Medicine, 166,* 272–273.

Patterson, D. R., & Sharar, S. (1997). Treating pain from severe burn injuries. *Advances in Medical Psychotherapy, 9,* 55–71.

Perry, S., & Blank, K. (1984). Relationship of psychological processes during delirium to outcome. *American Journal of Psychiatry, 141,* 843–847.

Perry, S., Difede, J., Musngi, G., Frances, A. J., & Jacobsberg, L. (1992). Predictors of post-traumatic stress disorder after burn injury. *American Journal of Psychiatry, 149,* 931–935.

Perry, S., Heidrich, G., & Ramos, E. (1981). Assessment of pain in burn patients. *Journal of Burn Care and Rehabilitation, 2,* 322–326.

Perry, S. W. (1984). Undermedication for pain on a burn unit. *General Hospital Psychiatry, 6,* 308–316.

Porter, J., & Jick, H. (1980). Addiction rare in patients treated with narcotics. *New England Journal of Medicine, 302,* 123–124.

Pruzinsky, T., & Cash, T. F. (1990). Integrative themes in body-image development, deviance, and change. In T. F. Cash & T. Pruzinsky (Eds.), *Body images: Development, deviance, and change* (pp. 337–349). New York: Guilford Press.

Ptacek, J. T., Patterson, D. R., & Doctor, J. N. (in press). Describing and predicting the nature of procedural pain following thermal injury. *Journal of Burn Care and Rehabilitation.*

Ptacek, J. T., Patterson, D. R., Montgomery, B. K., Ordonez, N. A., & Heimbach, D. M. (1995). Pain, coping, and adjustment in patients with severe burns: Preliminary findings from a prospective study. *Journal of Pain and Symptom Management, 10,* 446–455.

Seligman, M. E. P. (1975). *Helplessness: On depression, development, and death.* San Francisco: Freeman.

Shelby, J. (1992). Severe burn injury: Effects on psychologic and immunologic function in non-injured close relatives. *Journal of Burn Care and Rehabilitation, 12,* 58–63.

Skully, J. H., & Hutcherson, R. (1983). Suicide by burning. *American Journal of Psychiatry, 140,* 905–906.

Steiner, H., & Clark, W. R. (1977). Psychiatric complications of burned adults: A classification. *Journal of Trauma, 17,* 134–143.

Stoudemire, A., & Thompson, T. L., II. (1982). The borderline personality in the medical setting. *Annals of Internal Medicine, 96,* 76–79.

Tempereau, C. E. (1989). Loss of will to live in patients with burns. *Journal of Burn Care and Rehabilitation, 10,* 464–468.

Trieschmann, R. (1988). *Spinal cord injuries: Psychological, social, and vocational rehabilitation* (2nd ed.). New York: Demos.

Wiechman, S. A., Ehde, D. M., Patterson, D. R., & Wilson, L. (in press). The management of self-inflicted burns in patients diagnosed with borderline personality disorder. *Journal of Burn Care and Rehabilitation.*

8

Multiple Sclerosis

Gerald M. Devins and Zachary M. Shnek

Chronic disabling diseases introduce psychosocial challenges and adaptive demands, threatening quality of life. Clinicians and researchers have long recognized the deleterious psychosocial consequences of such conditions. Yet only recently were effective psychological interventions introduced to facilitate coping and adaptation. Whereas earlier approaches emphasized insight, understanding, and tolerance for the vicissitudes of chronic disease (Viederman & Perry, 1980), more recent approaches emphasize active patient involvement and collaborative partnerships with health care providers (Devins & Binik, 1996a; Devins, Cameron, & Edworthy, in press; Lorig et al., 1994). In the present chapter, we review these issues as they relate to multiple sclerosis (MS), a chronic disabling disease of the central nervous system that can compromise physical and intellectual integrity. After decades of research documenting the psychosocial burden imposed by MS, researchers have begun to emphasize a more proactive orientation to living with and actively managing the symptoms associated with this chronic disabling disease. The goals of these new interventions include minimizing illness-induced lifestyle disruptions (illness intrusiveness), reducing emotional distress, and maximizing quality of life. In this chapter, we provide a brief description of MS and its treatment, review historical developments, describe current assessment and intervention practices, and conclude with a discussion of current issues.

Historical Perspective and Background

Disease Process

MS is a chronic progressive degenerative neurological disease that produces demyelination (destruction of a neuron's myelin sheath) of central nervous system axons, resulting in delayed or blocked nervous impulses.

This work was supported in part by the Medical Research Council of Canada through a Senior Scientist Award and a Fellowship. We would like to express our thanks to Andy Gotowiec for valuable comments and suggestions and to Astrid Mitchell for extensive help in searching the literature, retrieving reference materials, and in preparing the manuscript.

A wide and confusing array of symptoms can be produced, including weakness and fatigability, loss of sensation, visual impairment, lack of coordination, spasticity, bladder disturbances, sexual dysfunction, and cognitive changes. Although the disease is not fatal, life expectancy may be affected by the hazards of chronic invalidism, most commonly respiratory and urinary infections. Suicide accounts for a sizable minority of deaths (Sadovnick, Eisen, Ebers, & Paty, 1991).

MS is more prevalent in the United States and Canada than most other countries. In the United States, it has an estimated incidence of 3.2 new cases per 100,000 and a prevalence of 58.3 cases per 100,000, resulting in an estimated 154,278 individuals with MS in the United States alone (Jacobson, Gange, Rose, & Graham, 1997). In Canada, prevalence estimates have ranged from 55 to 202 per 100,000, with an estimated 35,000 affected individuals overall, a difference consistent with epidemiologic findings of increased prevalence in northern areas of temperate climate (Matthews, Acheson, Batchelor, & Weller, 1985). The ratio of women to men affected ranges from 2:1 to 3:1 (Scheinberg, 1983). Because MS occurs in relatively young people—onset is frequently during the years of young adulthood, age 20–40 years—and has a prolonged course, its lifetime aggregate cost is very high (Asche, Ho, Chen, & Coyte, 1997; Seland, 1984). A recent study indicated that estimated annual costs per patient (in Canadian dollars) rise dramatically with increasing severity of disease: $14,523; $21,698; and $37,024 for "mild," "moderate," and "severe" groups, respectively; the lifetime cost of MS, including institutionalization, was $1,608,000 per person (Canadian Burden of Illness Study Group, 1998).

MS is characterized by an extremely variable progression of relapses (or exacerbations) and remissions, making it difficult to predict the course of the disease. Approximately 65–70% of affected individuals experience a *relapsing-remitting* course, in which symptoms intensify suddenly and subsequently subside, often with little or no residual deficit or effect. Approximately 15–20% experience a *progressive* course of illness (differentiated into primary-, secondary-, and relapsing-progressive variants), in which disease activity is generally uninterrupted. The remainder experience a *benign* course, in which the disease does not progress and neurologic systems remain unaffected long after diagnosis (Lublin & Reingold, 1996). For the vast majority of people with MS, the general trend is one of progressively increasing deterioration and disability. Severely affected individuals eventually require a wheelchair and ultimately may be confined to bed.

Because the disease presents a confusing and transient constellation of symptoms, and given that no definitive test is available, it is frequently misdiagnosed (Salloway, Price, Charney, & Shapiro, 1988; Skegg, Corwin, & Skegg, 1988). Many symptoms cannot be observed directly and can fluctuate markedly (e.g., fatigue, visual and other sensory disturbances). The diagnosis is primarily one of exclusion, depending on the identification of multiple central nervous system lesions over time and the exclusion of other causes (Poser et al., 1983). As a result, definitive diagnosis of MS may occur many years after initial symptoms are experienced and protracted laboratory testing is performed. Recent advances in magnetic resonance imaging techniques have improved the accuracy and efficiency of diagnoses (van Oosten, Truyen, Barkhof, & Polman, 1995). Although many of the complications associated with MS may be amenable to treatment, there is currently no cure and little symptomatic relief through medical or pharmacologic means (van Oosten et al., 1995).

Early Psychological Formulations

Early investigators adopted the perspective of psychosomatic medicine in attempting to delineate the interrelations between psychological factors and the underlying disease process in MS. Much of this work was undertaken in the context of providing psychiatric care and psychoanalytic therapy to people affected by the disease. Early investigators focused on emotional factors as etiologically significant. They highlighted factors such as emotional shock, conflict, and distress as responsible for the induction of unspecified pathological processes resulting in the development or exacerbation of MS. Examples include "vascular dysfunction," "exudative diathesis," and "proliferative" changes "known to be closely bound up with emotional stress or emotional stimuli" (Jelliffe, 1921, p. 667). Philippopoulos, Wittkower, and Cousineau (1958) identified "passive individuals caught in . . . entangling emotional relationships" (p. 459), and others cited these personality organizations as causally implicated in a diathesis-stress etiologic process (Teitelbaum, Hall, & Phillips, 1952). They also characterized people with MS as "immature" and "frustrated, deprived emotionally and trying to conceal their deep need for care" (p. 460). Despite the theoretically rich formulations within which these observations were framed, the research had serious shortcomings. Research participants were selected from clinically referred individuals, and methodologies relied heavily on retrospective subjective reports generated in the context of seeking psychiatric care. Although a number of later psychosomatic studies supplemented patients' subjective reports with psychological test data, these tended to entail projective techniques of unproven reliability. Because appropriate sampling or statistical controls were not included, even researchers using more objective measures (e.g., Minnesota Multiphasic Personality Inventory) could not rule out the competing hypothesis that, rather than inducing or exacerbating the disease, emotional distress and personality problems may arise in response to MS.

Despite these shortcomings, investigators have continued to examine stressful experiences and the disease process in MS. Although results are inconsistent, there is methodologically sound evidence that stressful life events can precipitate the onset of a relapse or exacerbation episode (Foley, LaRocca, Kalb, Caruso, & Shnek, 1993; Grant et al., 1989; Warren, Greenhill, & Warren, 1982). Not surprisingly, stressful life events have also been implicated as determinants of psychosocial well-being and emotional distress in MS, independent of their putative roles in the onset and course of the disease (Devins et al., 1996; Zeldow & Pavlou, 1984).

Early psychosomatic studies may inadvertently have distracted researchers and clinicians from more productive strategies to facilitate adaptation. By focusing on personality and emotional distress as etiologically relevant to the onset and exacerbation of the disease, psychosomatic medicine minimized the importance of the disease process as a stressor with which affected individuals would have to contend in attempting to maintain a productive and satisfying life. The notion that emotional distress, for example, might actually represent a normative response to the highly stressful chronic disease was minimized. The implication for psychological interventions, therefore, was to emphasize the modification of pathological intrapsychic processes through insight-oriented psychotherapy. It was not until recently that serious consideration was given to the alternative perspective that people with MS might better be served by teaching them how to manage their disease and how to cope with its associated psychosocial stressors, thereby minimizing its intrusiveness into psychologically meaningful activities. The self-management perspective is grounded in the premise that affected individuals can and should actively collaborate with service providers in managing symptoms and adhering to treatments. Increased illness- and treatment-related knowledge is combined with a proactive problem-solving orientation so that individuals can minimize the disruptive impact of chronic disease on lifestyles, activities, and interests (i.e., to minimize illness intrusiveness; Devins et al., in press).

Psychosocial Stressors

MS introduces numerous psychosocial challenges (Foley et al., 1993; Mohr & Dick, in press; Walker & Eremin, 1996). Uncertainty is a highly stressful feature of life with MS. Uncertainty is associated with both the diagnosis and the course of the disease. Given that there is no cure and limited medical treatment, the question of to tell or not to tell the patient about a diagnosis of MS has long been debated (Sencer, 1988). Whereas accurate information is generally believed to mitigate stress and anxiety, many have speculated about the possibility that the provision of such information may render affected individuals hopeless, undermining adaptive efforts to cope. Recent evidence, however, appears to favor provision of the diagnosis. At least two independent studies have shown that specific diagnostic and prognostic information can help reduce uncertainty and anxiety, although these benefits may come at the cost of decreased optimism (e.g., about future health; Mushlin, Mooney, Grow, & Phelps, 1994; O'Connor, Detsky, Tansey, Kucharczyk, & Rochester–Toronto MRI Study Group, 1994). Interestingly, whereas theory and research in experimental psychopathology maintain that unpredictability with regard to uncontrollable aversive events is more stressful and, hence, emotionally more destructive than predictability (Seligman & Binik, 1977), evidence in MS indicates that emotional distress is higher among patients with the more predictable chronic–progressive compared with a relapsing–remitting course (McIvor, Riklan, & Reznikoff, 1984; these studies have not ruled out, however, the possibility that this result may be attributable to more severe MS progression among chronic-progressive as compared with relapsing-remitting patients in the experimental samples). Lack of control over the disease process is also a significant stressor (Devins & Seland, 1987), compromising self-efficacy and contributing to learned helplessness (Shnek, Foley, LaRocca, Smith, & Halper, 1995; Shnek et al., 1997). Reduced self-efficacy and increased feelings of helplessness are likely, in turn, to compromise problem-focused coping (Bandura, 1986, 1995), in general, and to limit the individual's willingness and ability to engage in programs designed to bolster self-management knowledge and skills.

Cognitive changes frequently accompany the progression of MS. The literature concerning neuropsychological changes in MS has burgeoned over the past decade, improving the understanding of their nature, extent, and prevalence. A recent state-of-the-art review identifies memory and information-processing changes as most common, affecting 43–59% of people with MS (Fischer et al., 1994). Memory deficits can interfere with the ability to maintain attention for prolonged periods and can occur in both visual and auditory modalities. Deficits in so-called executive functions, such as problem-solving, can also be compromised, as can communication-related abilities, principally verbal fluency (Rao, Leo, Bernardin, & Unverzagt, 1991; Rao, Leo, Ellington, et al., 1991; Ron, Callanan, & Warrington, 1991). Fortunately, a number of memory functions do not appear to be affected by MS: Rate of learning, likelihood of remembering a specific item based on when it was presented, the ability to detect semantic characteristics of learned material, and *incidental* or *implicit memory* (the ability to learn new information or skills without explicitly attending to it) are largely unaffected (Fischer et al., 1994).

MS-induced cognitive changes can be stressful because they interfere with fundamental social and instrumental processes. Communication or problem-solving deficits attributable to the disease process are often misinterpreted, for example, by family and significant others as evidence of emotional or other psychosocial consequences of MS. Failure to recognize these problems as attributable to cognitive changes can create problems if it interferes with effective communication or leads to marginalization of the person with the disease (Foley, 1998a). Difficulties in maintaining concentration, problem-solving, communication, and other cognitive skills essential to social exchange and goal-directed behavior can also be stressful when they compromise interpersonal communication and personal control and interfere significantly with lifestyles (illness intrusiveness; Devins, Seland, Klein, Edworthy, & Saary, 1993).

Fatigue (Krupp, Alvarez, LaRocca, & Scheinberg, 1988; Ritvo, 1996), disability (Devins, Seland, et al., 1993; Wineman, 1990), and other symptoms (e.g., "pathological laughing and weeping"; Feinstein, Feinstein, Gray, & O'Connor, 1997) can also be highly stressful for people affected by MS. Such changes, aversive in themselves; can also be stressful because they introduce significant lifestyle disruptions that further compromise quality of life.

Illness Intrusiveness

Implicit in these and many other chronic conditions are a number of losses and barriers to active involvements in valued activities and interests. The concept of *illness intrusiveness* represents such illness-induced lifestyle disruptions that compromise quality of life (Devins et al., 1983). Self-management approaches are predicated on the assumption that goal-directed coping and self-efficacy to exercise such skills facilitate adaptation to chronic disease by minimizing illness intrusiveness and thereby enhance subjective well-being. Illness intrusiveness is hypothesized to affect psychosocial well-being by reducing (a) positively reinforcing outcomes of participation in psychologically meaningful activities and (b) personal control by limiting the ability to obtain positively valued outcomes or to avoid negative ones (Devins, 1994; Devins, Seland, et al., 1993).

Figure 8.1 illustrates a conceptual model outlining the role of illness intrusiveness in relation to the antecedents, consequences, and moderators of its psychosocial effects in chronic disease. A central hypothesis is that disease (e.g., pain, fatigue, disability) and treatment factors (e.g., time required for treatment, amelioration of symptoms) influence psychosocial well-being and emotional distress indirectly through their effects on illness intrusiveness which, in turn, directly influences these outcomes.

Psychological and social factors are hypothesized to play important roles. Some such factors (e.g., gender, premorbid personality) antedate the onset of disease and moderate the impact of disease and treatment on experienced illness intrusiveness (e.g., the same chronic disease may result in differential lifestyle disruptions for women and men). Other factors

Figure 8.1. Conceptual model outlining relations between illness intrusiveness and the psychosocial impact of chronic disease. Illness intrusiveness acts as a mediating variable through which objective circumstances of disease and treatment influence psychosocial well-being and emotional distress. In addition to their direct effects on psychosocial outcomes, psychological and social factors act as moderators of illness intrusiveness. Direct effects are depicted by solid arrows; moderating effects are depicted by dashed arrows.

(e.g., stigma, disfigurement) occur as a consequence of illness and its treat-ment and may moderate the impact of illness intrusiveness on psychoso-cial outcomes (e.g., the deleterious emotional impact of illness intrusive-ness is greater when individuals feel stigmatized by having to use a walker or a wheelchair). Psychological and social factors also establish the context in which chronic disease is experienced (e.g., culture, age, or stage in the life cycle). Differences in the symbolic significance of ill health or in the developmental challenges faced by the individual may moderate the psy-chosocial impact of illness intrusiveness despite similarities in the objec-tive circumstances of disease. Moderating influences are depicted by dashed arrows in Figure 8.1.

Several lines of evidence across diverse chronic conditions support the model in Figure 8.1. Illness intrusiveness is associated with a number of disease variables, including (a) severity of disease (Bloom, Stewart, John-ston, & Banks, 1998; Devins, 1989; Devins, Edworthy, Guthrie, & Martin, 1992; Devins, Mandin, et al., 1990; Devins, Seland, et al., 1993), (b) co-morbid conditions (Binik, Chowanec, & Devins, 1990; Devins et al., 1983; Devins, Mandin, et al., 1990), (c) sleep disturbances (Devins, Edworthy, et al., 1993), (d) fatigue (Devins, Mandin, et al., 1990; Devins, Styra, et al., 1994), (e) recurrent pain (Devins, Armstrong, et al., 1990), and (f) physical disability (Devins et al., 1992; Devins et al., 1996). Treatment factors also relate to illness intrusiveness. Renal transplant recipients re-port lower illness intrusiveness than do maintenance dialysis patients (De-vins et al., 1983; Devins, Mandin, et al., 1990). Increased time required for treatment is associated with illness intrusiveness (Devins, 1991; De-vins, Mandin, et al., 1990). Illness intrusiveness is also significantly and uniquely related, as hypothesized, to numerous psychosocial outcomes, in-cluding life happiness, positive and negative moods, depressive symptoms, pessimism, mood disturbance, self-esteem, symptoms of psychopathology, marital role strain, marital happiness, and illness-related concerns (Abraido-Lanza, 1997; Binik & Devins, 1986; Binik et al., 1990; Bloom et al., 1998; Devins, 1989, 1991; Devins et al., 1983; Devins et al., 1986; Devins, Mandin, et al., 1990; Eitel, Hatchett, Friend, Griffin, & Wadhwa, 1995; Hatchett, Friend, Symister, & Wadhwa, 1997; Peterson et al., 1991).

The psychosocial impact of illness intrusiveness is not simply reduci-ble to illness- or treatment-related factors. Many disease and treatment variables relate directly to illness intrusiveness but not to well-being or distress, such as severity of disease (Devins et al., 1983, 1992, 1996), phys-ical disability (Devins, Mandin, et al., 1990; Devins et al., 1992; Devins, Seland, et al., 1993), and alternative modes of treatment (Binik et al., 1990; Devins et al., 1983; Devins, Mandin, et al., 1990), whereas illness intrusiveness correlates significantly with numerous psychosocial out-comes (Devins, 1994).

Findings also corroborate the hypothesis that psychological and social factors moderate the impact of illness intrusiveness. Research to date identifies the following moderator variables: (a) stigma as a result of life-threatening illness and disfiguring treatment (Devins, Stam, & Koopmans, 1994), (b) self-concept as a chronic patient (Devins, Beanlands, Mandin,

& Paul, 1997), and (c) stage in the life cycle (Devins et al., 1992; Devins et al., 1996; Devins et al., 1997).

Although not widely discussed, it is important to caution against inadvertent iatrogenic effects attributable to pessimistic communications from service providers about the long-term consequences of MS. Messages from clinicians that the disease is incurable, for example, or that there is little one can do to alter its course, ultimate severity, or the eventual constriction of lifestyles may lead patients to feel helpless and dependent. Well-intended advice to accept the disease or encouragement to "learn to live with it" are not likely to be helpful in the absence of specific behavioral directions about how to achieve an effective adaptation. Informal communications between service providers and recipients can exert a powerful influence on illness-related self-representations (Devins, 1989). To the extent that people construe themselves as "chronic patients," they may be vulnerable to self-imposed constriction of lifestyles with the resulting reduction in quality of life (Devins et al., 1997; Leake, Friend, & Wadhwa, 1999).

Maintenance of hope is also crucial to facilitate adaptation (Eklund & MacDonald, 1991; Scheier et al., 1989). That many people with MS are able to establish a satisfactory quality of life despite the stressors and adaptive challenges imposed by the disease (Bal, Vazquez-Barquero, Pena, Miro, & Berciano, 1991; Devins, Seland, et al., 1993; Joffe, Lippert, Gray, Sawa, & Horvath, 1987; Patten & Metz, 1997) is a testament to resilience of the human spirit and should be pointed out to affected people as a challenge to which they too can aspire. That not all are so fortunate and that a sizeable minority choose not to continue the struggle (Sadovnick et al., 1991), however, is a call to health care providers that more can and must be done. Fortunately, promising psychological and behavioral interventions have begun to produce encouraging results.

Assessment and Intervention

Psychological assessment is a cornerstone of effective intervention. Given the unique biomedical context in which MS occurs, a number of issues must be recognized and addressed. The most striking developments in psychological assessment over the past decade have involved the substantial development of neuropsychological expertise in relation to MS. Given increased awareness of the character and extent of cognitive effects, together with the increasing availability of specialized interventions to minimize these, thorough neuropsychological testing is strongly recommended in all cases. Unfortunately, space limitations do not permit a detailed discussion of these issues. Interested readers are referred to excellent reviews for comprehensive coverage of this important issue (Fischer et al., 1994; Lezak, 1995; Rao, 1986).

Current rehabilitation psychology emphasizes principles of empowerment, mastery, and enhancement of personal control (Gonzalez, Goeppinger, & Lorig, 1990; McLaughlin & Zeeberg, 1993). The overall aim is to help affected individuals compensate for deficits that can be addressed directly and accommodate to those that cannot with the goal of minimizing illness intrusiveness and maximizing quality of life. The rehabilitation psychologist's repertoire of interventions has expanded dramatically in recent years and includes therapeutic methods to assist affected individuals in achieving insight into self-defeating psychological responses to illness and other life stressors (Crawford & McIvor, 1985), exploring important existential issues to achieve acceptance of life with a chronic disabling disease (Yalom, 1980), and engaging in cognitive rehabilitation to restore deficits (Fischer et al., 1994; LaRocca et al., 1998). Incorporating fundamental behavioral and social–cognitive principles, the majority of new interventions have adapted empirically validated cognitive–behavior therapy (CBT) techniques into programs intended to maximize effective adaptation.

A burgeoning interest in the self-management of chronic disease incorporates these ideas into a clinically valuable multicomponent group intervention that can be applied across chronic disease populations (Devins et al., in press; Lorig & Holman, 1993; Lorig et al., 1994). The self-management perspective is predicated on the assumption that goal-directed coping and self-efficacy to exercise such skills facilitate adaptation to chronic disease by minimizing illness-induced interference with valued activities and interests (i.e., illness intrusiveness), thereby enhancing psychosocial well-being and minimizing emotional distress (Devins et al., 1983). Effective self-management of chronic disabling disease entails a number of elements, combining knowledge, skill, and an active orientation toward the treatment process.

Three principles are fundamental (Devins & Binik, 1996b). First, the emphasis is on self-management of disease, implying that the individual must accept responsibility for managing his or her condition to the extent that this is possible. This can take the form of actively monitoring and evaluating physical and psychological well-being and taking appropriate actions as indicated. The emphasis on self-management also implies that people must acquire knowledge relevant to their condition and its treatment.

Second, self-management emphasizes a partnership between service providers and recipients, meaning patient collaboration with health care personnel rather than subservience to them. Activities particularly to be enhanced by active patient participation include communicating with health care professionals, adhering to and implementing therapeutic regimens, reporting adverse reactions, and modifying daily routines to minimize illness intrusiveness.

The third principle is that information acquired through patient education efforts must be implemented through effective coping skills and behavior. Thus, potential benefits of increased illness-related knowledge must be actualized through effective self-management behavior. Relevant skills include maintaining a regular schedule of activity and exercise (e.g., through behavioral contracting), applying a problem-solving orientation to the integration of illness-relevant knowledge into daily practice, managing symptoms and moods effectively, maintaining adequate sleep hygiene, attending to nutrition and medications, and communicating regularly and directly with the treatment team.

The self-management approach addresses the focussed domains of cognitive and behavioral coping skills. It aims to help people acquire skills to cope with or better adapt to their illness and, through a variety of alternative experiential and didactic methods, seeks to enhance self-efficacy to perform these effectively. Commonly targeted tasks include recognizing and responding to symptoms, using medications correctly, managing emergencies, maintaining nutrition and diet, maintaining adequate exercise and activity, giving up smoking, using stress management techniques, interacting with health service providers, seeking information and using community resources, adapting to work, managing relationships with significant others, and managing psychological responses to one's disease (Clark, Becker, Janz, & Lorig, 1991).

Self-management principles have been applied to a variety of chronic conditions with encouraging results (Holroyd & Creer, 1986; Lorig & Holman, 1993). Although the approach has been developed extensively for some conditions (e.g., rheumatic diseases, asthma, and diabetes mellitus), its application to MS is still at an early stage. Nevertheless, its practical and proactive emphasis on symptom self-control, informed problem-solving, collaborative partnerships, and active involvement in personally significant goals and activities combine to make the self-management approach particularly appropriate to facilitate adaptation to life with MS.

Stress Inoculation Training

Stress inoculation training (SIT) was adapted for MS (Foley, Bedell, LaRocca, Scheinberg, & Reznikoff, 1987) from the generic intervention of the same name (Meichenbaum, 1985). SIT seeks to enhance coping by preventing maladaptive psychological responses. As adapted for MS, SIT integrates progressive deep-muscle relaxation training with standard CBT techniques. SIT involves three phases of treatment: education, rehearsal, and application. During the education phase, individuals learn the rationale underlying the SIT model and acquire self-assessment skills (e.g., self-monitoring, identifying dysfunctional thoughts and negative emotions, recognizing maladaptive behaviors such as social withdrawal in response to emotional distress, recognizing physiological arousal). During the rehearsal phase, the therapist and patient identify and bolster coping skills where these already exist in the individual's repertoire (e.g., distraction, prioritization of goals, or cognitive reframing). Coping skills with which the individual may not already be familiar (e.g., progressive muscle relaxation) are also acquired. The rehearsal phase concludes with practice and refinement of new skills during CBT training sessions. When the patient masters these skills "in vitro," the training process enters the (final) application phase, during which individuals are encouraged to apply the skills in their day-to-day lives (under therapist supervision). As originally developed, SIT consists of six 1½-hour individual sessions. In the only study to evaluate this program to date, SIT significantly increased problem-focused coping and reduced depression and anxiety (Foley et al., 1987). Future research must replicate and extend these encouraging results.

Psychoremediation of Communication Skills Training

Psychoremediation of communication skills training was developed to assist people with MS when cognitive deficits interfere with effective communication. The intervention represents an adaptation of the SIT approach. Psychoremediation of communication skills was organized to be delivered within the same educational, rehearsal, and application phases as outlined for SIT. In the education phase, the therapist presents a rationale for enhancing communication skills when individuals experience MS-induced cognitive impairments. Neuropsychological assessment identifies cognitive difficulties and characterizes their effects on communication. Family and patient interviews complement this information by assessing communication in the family system context.

Active treatment is implemented during the rehearsal phase. Skills necessary to improve communication are rehearsed with the therapist. Newly acquired skills are then implemented and refined in everyday social exchange during the application phase. Although therapeutic contact is maintained during this phase, the therapist increasingly takes on the role of "coach" in supporting the consolidation of skillful communication behaviors and in bolstering the confidence to apply these effectively in relevant situations.

A promising example of communication skills training as applied to cognitively impaired people with MS has recently been reported (Foley et al., 1994). At the heart of the program are detailed behavioral templates that, once acquired, help the individual master the following skills: (a) active listening, (b) empathic responding, (c) making "empathic requests" (i.e., assertively ensuring that one's own needs are met while responding to the needs of others), (d) making "empathic requests with feedback" (i.e., assertively providing feedback to others about the effects of their behavior on oneself), and (e) responding directly and assertively to requests from others.

Behavioral templates entail explicit step-by-step articulations of the structural elements that comprise a communication sequence. By requiring the individual to identify and make explicit the situational, cognitive, emotional, behavioral, and somatic components of a communication sequence, the intervention enables the person with MS to rebuild and master basic skills. A workbook format is used to identify and record a detailed communication analysis. Situational cues to be identified include who was present, what took place, and when and where the event occurred. Internal cues include thoughts (images, self-statements), feelings, behaviors (verbal and nonverbal), and physical experience (symptoms). These components are further analyzed and relevant decisions are interleaved to maximize effective exchanges. For example, the "thinking" component requires that one identify what he or she wants from the other person and anticipate (a) the consequences should the request be granted, (b) the other person's likely reciprocal expectations, and (c) the other's likely reaction to the initial request. This is followed by a decision about whether one should modify the initially conceived request or offer a compromise. If a modification or compromise is indicated, the individual is directed to return to the first step (identifying personal wants) and to repeat the thinking process. If no modification or compromise is indicated, the individual is directed to consider a second decision: whether the other's anticipated response is negative or positive. If a negative response is anticipated, the individual is directed to incorporate an empathic element into the request. This first template concludes with an evaluation of whether the MS individual's "want" arose in response to an undesirable behavior by the other person in the exchange. On completion of the thinking template, similarly detailed templates address subsequent communication behaviors, including separate components for making empathic, feedback, request, and consequence statements.

Individuals also learn to attend to and understand nonverbal interpersonal cues, such as body language and facial expressions. The intervention includes self-monitoring of daily interpersonal situations and recording associated thoughts, feelings, behaviors, and physiological reactions. These data are used in the rehearsal and application phases to help determine when to apply communication skills. Although we are aware of no experimental evaluation of psychoremediation of communications skills in MS, a recent case report (Foley et al., 1994) described the application of communication skills training following this protocol.

Behavioral Self-Management of Chronic Disease

A variety of self-management programs have been developed to facilitate adaptation to life with chronic disabling diseases. The Chronic Disease Self-Management Course (Lorig et al., 1994; Lorig, Gonzalez, & Laurent, 1997) is a prototype. It combines a number of component interventions with the objective of training affected individuals to manage symptoms, collaborate with the health care team, minimize illness-induced life-style disruptions, and thereby preserve quality of life. Participants attend 6 weekly 2-hour group sessions (12–20 participants with mixed diagnoses), led by a volunteer lay leader (often a chronically ill individual who has mastered self-management skills). A smorgasbord approach is used to provide course attenders with a broad range of information and skills.

Early emphasis is placed on acquiring knowledge about the illness and its treatment. Fundamentals of behavioral self-management are also covered as these apply to chronic disease. This is complemented by an overview of self-management strategies, including specification of short- and long-term goals, pacing to minimize strain and maximize successful application of skills, behavioral contracting to enhance motivation and maintain performance rates, and a problem-solving orientation in which illness-relevant knowledge and coping skills can be integrated to enhance the effectiveness of self-management efforts. Nutrition and the benefits of maintaining a healthy diet are emphasized. Considerable attention is directed to the importance of adherence to medical regimens and collaboration with health care professionals to maximize the benefits derived from treatment. Physical mobility and well-being are encouraged through exercise, with an emphasis on maintaining fitness, strength, stamina, and mobility through routines that are appropriate to the individual's condition. Pain management is particularly relevant to many chronic diseases, including MS (Moulin, Foley, & Ebers, 1988). The Chronic Disease Self-Management Course provides an overview of the mechanisms responsible for pain, pharmacologic agents to control it, and instruction in behavioral stress management techniques (e.g., progressive-muscle and breathing-control relaxation, guided imagery, and meditation). Specific CBT techniques are also presented, including distraction, relabeling pain-associated sensations, self-talk to enhance self-efficacy, and self-hypnosis. Spirituality and prayer are often encouraged as adjuncts to more structured behavioral or cognitive methods.

A central emphasis is on the application of illness-relevant information in addressing the unique demands of life with a chronic disabling condition. Problem-solving strategies are reviewed, and participants are encouraged to use these in response to day-to-day challenges. Achievement of restorative sleep is emphasized through a focus on sleep hygiene, including basic sleep hygiene principles, the need to maintain a regular sleep–wake schedule, use of analgesic agents (as prescribed) to control pain before retiring, use of relaxation techniques to facilitate falling and staying asleep, avoidance of caffeine or other stimulants and moderation of alcohol consumption before retiring, avoidance of daytime napping, and other tips. Mood management—minimization of distress and maintenance of positive affect—is emphasized by helping participants recognize the vicious cycle in which stress, pain, and depression interact to produce a downward spiral. Self-monitoring and record-keeping of pain and moods are encouraged to facilitate recognition that these phenomena are interdependent. The program emphasizes the behavioral principle that a regular schedule of pleasant activities and active involvement in other valued pursuits helps minimize illness intrusiveness, resulting in enhanced well-being and reduced distress (Devins, 1994). In some cases, recognition and management of other negative affects is also addressed (e.g., anger, fear, frustration).

A crucial element of the program involves communication with health care providers to maximize active collaboration between service providers and recipients. Participants are encouraged to acquire relevant information, to raise questions and concerns with health professionals, to evaluate responses carefully and critically, and to discuss problems in sufficient depth to satisfy their needs. Where appropriate, advance directives and other decisions relevant to the final phases of life are also discussed. Overall, the emphasis on open and direct communication between patients and service providers is summarized by the acronym CAD, which stands for encouraging participants to come prepared, ask questions, and discuss problems.

The Chronic Disease Self-Management Course incorporates a variety of elements to bolster the sense of self-efficacy that one can effectively manage the disease. Tactics include an emphasis on skills mastery, modeling of effective self-management behavior by lay leaders and other group members, and verbal persuasion in providing encouragement and support. Considerable evidence substantiates the therapeutic efficacy of self-management training as applied to a variety of chronic disabling conditions (Devins & Binik, 1996a; Devins et al., in press; Holroyd & Creer, 1986; Lorig & Holman, 1993). Although its usefulness in MS remains to be demonstrated, it is reasonable to speculate that self-management principles and procedures can be equally effective for this patient population (LaRocca, 1990).

Implementation of psychosocial interventions for people affected by chronic disease requires adaptation to address the unique situation presented by each condition. In adapting the self-management approach to MS, it may be useful to modify certain elements. It may be worthwhile, for example, to reduce the pace with which topics are introduced and to extend the number of sessions in which component interventions are delivered, rehearsed, and implemented into daily life. The current schedule of 6 weekly 2-hour group sessions demands a level of efficiency that may not be practical given that MS-induced cognitive impairments can interfere with the acquisition of skills and knowledge. It may also be important to consider group composition carefully. Many chronic disease self-management programs allow for diagnostic heterogeneity across participants. Given the need to modify component interventions to accommodate for cognitive difficulties in MS, however, it may be preferable to limit participation to individuals affected by neurologic diagnoses or traumatic brain injuries. In such cases, it is important to protect less severely affected (or more recently diagnosed) individuals from overgeneralizing about the likely course of their own condition when exposed to more severely affected people.

Bibliotherapy

Facilitating individual and family efforts to live as full and satisfying a life as possible given the constraints imposed by MS is a common goal across supportive psychological interventions (LaRocca, Kalb, & Foley, 1993). Self-help books and other publications represent a valuable adjunct to psychological interventions. In addition to helping people with MS understand the nature, course, and treatment of the disease, educational materials can assist them in anticipating the potential impact of the condition across life domains and can introduce positive steps that can be taken to manage symptoms and adjust lifestyles to minimize illness intrusiveness. These can include learning to discuss the condition more comfortably with health professionals and becoming an informed and active participant in managing the disease. Important life goals involving family, career, and finances also require thoughtful consideration. Educational materials can be highly useful for family members, friends, employers, and others who interact with the individual with MS. Finally, such materials often identify relevant organizations, such as the National Multiple Sclerosis Society, that can provide additional information or mutual aid. A number of useful materials are available (e.g., Kalb, 1996, 1998; Lorig et al., 1994; Schapiro, 1994; Scheinberg, 1983). Self-help materials can be used at a pace determined by the individual and can be read repeatedly. Thus, they are ideal adjuncts to professional intervention.

Current Issues

The literature concerning rehabilitation and quality of life in MS has burgeoned in recent years. In the following section, we highlight some of the issues that merit increased attention in rehabilitation efforts.

Characterization and Management of Fatigue

Fatigue in chronic disabling disease is rapidly gaining recognition as a complex phenomenon with neurologic, neuropsychological, affective, and other psychological determinants (e.g., personality). Fatigue appears to be multifactorial in MS: At least four independent dimensions have been identified, including fatigue attributable to physical exertion, depression, nerve impulse, and idiopathic lassitude ("an abnormal sense of tiredness or lack of energy that is disproportional to the amount of energy expended and to the level of disability"; Schwartz, Coulthard-Morris, & Zeng, 1996, p. 165; see also Schapiro, Harris, Lenling, & Metelak, 1987). Each is hypothesized to occur independently of the others and to be attributable to unique underlying (but as yet unspecified) mechanisms. Recognizing that symptomatic expression and etiologic hypotheses overlap substantially across many conditions in which fatigue is a prominent symptom, investigators have begun to compare neuropsychological, affective, personality, and psychopathological factors across diagnostic groups. A number of recent studies compare these factors between people with MS and others diagnosed with chronic fatigue syndrome (DeLuca, Johnson, & Natelson, 1993; Johnson, Deluca, & Natelson, 1996a, 1996b; Krupp, Sliwinski, Masur, Friedberg, & Coyle, 1994; Schwartz et al., 1996; Vercoulen et al., 1996). Although the severity and extent of fatigue is equivalent across these diverse groups, results indicate that cognitive and other neuropsychological deficits are greater among people with MS and that symptoms of psychopathology (e.g., depression) and personality disturbances (e.g., neuroticism) are more prevalent in chronic fatigue syndrome.

Recognizing that fatigue contributes significantly to illness intrusiveness and compromises quality of life (Aronson, 1997; Devins, Seland, et al., 1993; Devins, Styra, et al., 1994; Krupp et al., 1988; Schwartz et al., 1996), clinicians have begun to describe self-management programs to minimize this disruptive and pervasive symptom. Although still in the very early stages, authors have described programs that incorporate time management, pacing, energy conservation, work simplification, paced relaxation, and modification of lifestyles and environments to minimize illness intrusiveness (Schapiro et al., 1987; Schwartz et al., 1996).

Marital and Family Issues

Just as chronic disease introduces adaptive challenges for those diagnosed, it also presents coping demands for their loved ones, whose own lives are intimately interdependent with the directly affected individual. Because its onset is predominantly during the early and middle adult years, MS is particularly likely to strain marital and family relationships. Physical disabilities and cognitive impairments may impose role reversals (e.g., as physically healthy spouses take on responsibilities, such as child care, formerly handled by the individual with MS) and can disrupt the balance of marital role reciprocations (Aronson, 1997; Devins & Hunsley, 1997). Well spouses also assume increased caregiving responsibilities, including the provision of social support. That these increased contributions to marital and family life may be reciprocated to a lesser extent places additional strain on the physically healthy partner (O'Brien, Wineman, & Nealon, 1995) and can threaten marital happiness (Knight, Devereux, & Godfrey, 1997).

Sexuality is particularly vulnerable in MS. MS can affect sexual experience in many ways (e.g., erectile dysfunction, anorgasmia, and decreased desire) through neurologic and psychological mechanisms. Research currently in progress is adapting sex therapy techniques for people with MS, including the use of mechanical devices (e.g., vacuum pumps for erectile problems), routine behavior therapy (sensate focus), relationship counseling, bibliotherapy, and pharmacologic interventions. A detailed treatment of these issues is beyond the scope of this chapter; they are discussed elsewhere in other publications (Foley, 1998b; Foley & Werner, 1996; Mattson, Petrie, Srivastava, & McDermott, 1995).

Contextual Factors

MS and its treatment occur in a broader context. That context can vary in terms of the life span developmental stage, gender, and cultural heritage of the individual. Such factors are relevant to both the psychosocial impact of chronic disease and to the effective facilitation of coping with chronic conditions in general (Devins, 1993; Devins & Binik, 1996a; Devins et al., in press) and are beginning to receive research attention in MS (Black, Grant, & Lapsley, 1994; Christensen & Clausen, 1977; McLaughlin & Zeeburg, 1993). Differences in life stage can dramatically modify the adaptive challenges associated with MS. Disease onset in the early 20s, for example, would be more likely to threaten the establishment of a career and independence, whereas onset in the 40s might more likely challenge roles and responsibilities related to family (Devins et al., 1996). Similarly, the symbolic significance and psychosocial impact of a chronic disabling condition such as MS is likely to differ considerably in women and men (Dyck, 1995; Foley, 1998a). Finally, increasing international migration is rapidly creating a highly pluralistic society, including people from many lands, speaking different languages, and espousing highly diverse explanatory models of illness and preferred modes of treatment. It is crucial, therefore, to evaluate theories and interventions to maximize cultural appropriateness and sensitivity (Anderson, 1986; Kato & Mann, 1996; Uswatte & Elliott, 1997; Yutrzenka, 1995).

Conclusion

MS is a chronic disabling condition that can affect virtually every aspect of a person's life. Whereas earlier psychological analyses focused on the roles of individual weaknesses in the onset and exacerbation of the condition, more recent perspectives have recognized that the disease and its treatments introduce powerful psychosocial stressors and adapative challenges. Recognizing that a proactive collaborative partnership between health service providers and recipients of care can maximize medical benefit and psychosocial adaptation, rehabilitation psychologists have begun to emphasize a self-management model of intervention. Future efforts in rehabilitation psychology should continue to build on this trend by recognizing that the wide-ranging neurologic and neuropsychological changes produced by this disease require that existing self-management practices be adapted for use with MS patients.

Efforts to facilitate adaptation to life with MS have only recently begun to emerge. Although it is reasonable to expect these interventions to improve quality of life, it is crucial to evaluate them through programmatic scientific research that evaluates efficacy, establishes mechanisms of action, and ensures culturally appropriate models of care.

References

Abraido-Lanza, A. F. (1997). Latinas with arthritis: Effects of illness, role identity, and competence on psychological well-being. *American Journal of Community Psychology, 25,* 601–627.

Anderson, J. M. (1986). Ethnicity and illness experience: Ideological structures and the health care delivery system. *Social Science and Medicine, 22,* 1277–1283.

Aronson, K. J. (1997). Quality of life among persons with multiple sclerosis and their caregivers. *Neurology, 48,* 74–80.

Asche, C. V., Ho, E., Chen, B., & Coyte, P. C. (1997). Economic consequences of multiple sclerosis for Canadians. *Acta Neurologica Scandinavica, 95,* 268–274.

Bal, M. A. A., Vazquez-Barquero, J. L., Pena, C., Miro, J., & Berciano, J. A. (1991). Psychiatric aspects of multiple sclerosis. *Acta Psychiatrica Scandinavica, 83,* 292–296.

Bandura, A. (1986). *Social foundations of thought and action: A social cognitive theory.* Englewood Cliffs, NJ: Prentice Hall.

Bandura, A. (1995). *Self-efficacy in changing societies.* Cambridge, England: Cambridge University Press.

Binik, Y. M., Chowanec, G. D., & Devins, G. M. (1990). Marital role strain, illness intrusiveness, and their impact on marital and individual adjustment in end-stage renal disease. *Psychology and Health, 4,* 245–257.

Binik, Y. M., & Devins, G. M. (1986). Transplant failure does not compromise quality of life in end-stage renal disease. *International Journal of Psychiatry in Medicine, 16,* 281–292.

Black, D. A., Grant, C., & Lapsley, H. M. (1994, October–December). The services and social needs of people with multiple sclerosis in New South Wales, Australia. *Journal of Rehabilitation, 60,* 60–65.

Bloom, J. R., Stewart, S. L., Johnston, M., & Banks, P. (1998). Intrusiveness of illness and quality of life in young women with breast cancer. *Psychooncology, 7,* 89–100.

Canadian Burden of Illness Study Group. (1998). Burden of illness of multiple sclerosis: Part I. Cost of illness. *Canadian Journal of Neurological Sciences, 25,* 23–30.

Christensen, O., & Clausen, J. (1977). Social remedial measures for multiple sclerosis patients in Denmark. *Acta Neurologica Scandinavica, 55,* 394–406.

Clark, N. M., Becker, M. H., Janz, N. K., & Lorig, K. (1991). Self-management of chronic disease by older adults: A review and questions for research. *Journal of Aging and Health, 3,* 3–27.

Crawford, J. D., & McIvor, G. P. (1985). Group psychotherapy: Benefits in multiple sclerosis. *Archives of Physical Medicine and Rehabilitation, 66,* 810–813.

DeLuca, J., Johnson, S. K., & Natelson, B. H. (1993). Information processing efficiency in chronic fatigue syndrome and multiple sclerosis. *Archives of Neurology, 50,* 301–304.

Devins, G. M. (1989). Enhancing personal control and minimizing illness intrusiveness. In N. G. Kutner, D. D. Cardenas, & J. D. Bower (Eds.), *Maximizing rehabilitation in chronic renal disease* (pp. 109–136). New York: PMA.

Devins, G. M. (1991). Illness intrusiveness and the psychosocial impact of end-stage renal disease. In M. A. Hardy, J. Kiernan, A. H. Kutscher, L. Cahill, & A. I. Bevenitsky (Eds.), *Psychosocial aspects of end-stage renal disease: Issues of our times* (pp. 83–102). New York: Haworth Press.

Devins, G. M. (1993). Psychosocial impact of illness from a developmental-systems perspective: New directions for health psychology. *Canadian Journal of Behavioural Science, 25,* 329–331.

Devins, G. M. (1994). Illness intrusiveness and the psychosocial impact of lifestyle disruptions in chronic life-threatening disease. *Advances in Renal Replacement Therapy, 1,* 251–263.

Devins, G. M., Armstrong, S. J., Mandin, H., Paul, L. C., Hons, R. B., Burgess, E. D., Taub, K., Schorr, S., Letourneau, P. K., & Buckle, S. (1990). Recurrent pain, illness intrusiveness, and quality of life in end-stage renal disease. *Pain, 42,* 279–285.

Devins, G. M., Beanlands, H., Mandin, H., & Paul, L. C. (1997). Psychosocial impact of illness intrusiveness moderated by self-concept and age in end-stage renal disease. *Health Psychology, 16,* 529–538.

Devins, G. M., & Binik, Y. M. (1996a). Facilitating coping in chronic physical illness. In M. Zeidner & N. S. Endler (Eds.), *Handbook of coping* (pp. 640–696). New York: Wiley.

Devins, G. M., & Binik, Y. M. (1996b). Predialysis psychoeducational interventions: Establishing collaborative relationships between health service providers and recipients. *Seminars in Dialysis, 9,* 51–55.

Devins, G. M., Binik, Y. M., Hutchinson, T. A., Hollomby, D. J., Barré, P. E., & Guttmann, R. D. (1983). The emotional impact of end-stage renal disease: Importance of patients' perceptions of intrusiveness and control. *International Journal of Psychiatry in Medicine, 13,* 327–343.

Devins, G. M., Binik, Y. M., Mandin, H., Burgess, E. D., Taub, K., Letourneau, P. K., Buckle, S., & Low, G. L. (1986). Denial as a defense against depression in end-stage renal disease: An empirical test. *International Journal of Psychiatry in Medicine, 16,* 151–162.

Devins, G. M., Cameron, J. I., & Edworthy, S. M. (in press). Self-management of chronic disabling disease. In R. Leahy (Ed.), *Cognitive–behavioral interventions for persons with disabilities*. New York: Aronson.

Devins, G. M., Edworthy, S. M., Guthrie, N. G., & Martin, L. (1992). Illness intrusiveness in rheumatoid arthritis: Differential impact on depressive symptoms over the adult lifespan. *Journal of Rheumatology, 19,* 709–715.

Devins, G. M., Edworthy, S. M., Paul, L. C., Mandin, H., Seland, T. P., Klein, G. M., & Shapiro, C. M. (1993). Restless sleep, illness intrusiveness, and depressive symptoms in three chronic illness conditions: Rheumatoid arthritis, end-stage renal disease, and multiple sclerosis. *Journal of Psychosomatic Research, 37,* 163–170.

Devins, G. M., & Hunsley, J. (1997). Coping with chronic disabling illness: The marital context of multiple sclerosis. *Canadian Psychology, 38,* 67–67.

Devins, G. M., Mandin, H., Hons, R. B., Burgess, E. D., Klassen, J., Taub, K., Schorr, S., Letourneau, P. K., & Buckle, S. (1990). Illness intrusiveness and quality of life in end-stage renal disease: Comparison and stability across treatment modalities. *Health Psychology, 9,* 117–142.

Devins, G. M., & Seland, T. P. (1987). Emotional impact of multiple sclerosis: Recent findings and suggestions for future research. *Psychological Bulletin, 101,* 363–375.

Devins, G. M., Seland, T. P., Klein, G. M., Edworthy, S. M., & Saary, M. J. (1993). Stability and determinants of psychosocial well-being in multiple sclerosis. *Rehabilitation Psychology, 38,* 11–26.

Devins, G. M., Stam, H. J., & Koopmans, J. P. (1994). Psychosocial impact of laryngectomy mediated by perceived stigma and illness intrusiveness. *Canadian Journal of Psychiatry, 39,* 608–616.

Devins, G. M., Styra, R., Gray, T., O'Connor, P., Jacobson, M., & Shapiro, C. M. (1994). Nature and psychosocial impact of fatigue in multiple sclerosis. *Psychosomatic Medicine, 56,* 161–162.

Devins, G. M., Styra, R., O'Connor, P., Gray, T., Seland, T. P., Klein, G. M., & Shapiro, C. M. (1996). Psychosocial impact of illness intrusiveness moderated by age in multiple sclerosis. *Psychology, Health & Medicine, 1,* 179–191.

Dyck, I. (1995). Hidden geographies: The changing lifeworlds of women with multiple sclerosis. *Social Science and Medicine, 40,* 307–320.

Eitel, P., Hatchett, L., Friend, R., Griffin, K. W., & Wadhwa, N. K. (1995). Burden of self-care in seriously ill patients: Impact on adjustment. *Health Psychology, 14,* 457–463.

Eklund, V. A., & MacDonald, M. L. (1991). Descriptions of persons with multiple sclerosis, with an emphasis on what is needed from psychologists. *Professional Psychology: Research and Practice, 22,* 277–284.

Feinstein, A., Feinstein, K., Gray, T., & O'Connor, P. (1997). Prevalence and neurobehavioral correlates of pathological laughing and crying in multiple sclerosis. *Archives of Neurology, 54,* 1116–1121.

Fischer, J. S., Foley, F. W., Aikens, J. E., Ericson, G. D., Rao, S. M., & Shindell, S. (1994). What do we really know about cognitive dysfunction, affective disorders, and stress in multiple sclerosis? A practitioner's guide. *Journal of Neurologial Rehabilitation, 8,* 151–164.

Foley, F. W. (1998a). Multiple sclerosis. In E. A. Blechman & K. D. Brownell (Eds.), *Behavioral medicine and women: A comprehensive handbook* (pp. 688–694). New York: Guilford Press.

Foley, F. W. (1998b). Sexuality and intimacy in multiple sclerosis. In R. Kalb (Ed.), *Multiple sclerosis: A guide for families* (pp. 39–60). New York: Demos Vermande.

Foley, F. W., Bedell, J. R., LaRocca, N. G., Scheinberg, L. C., & Reznikoff, M. (1987). Efficacy of stress-inoculation training in coping with multiple sclerosis. *Journal of Consulting and Clinical Psychology, 55,* 919–922.

Foley, F. W., Dince, W. M., Bedell, J. R., LaRocca, N. G., Kalb, R., Caruso, L. S., Smith, C. R., & Shnek, Z. M. (1994). Psychoremediation of communication skills for cognitively impaired persons with multiple sclerosis. *Journal of Neurologic Rehabilitation, 8,* 165–176.

Foley, F. W., LaRocca, N. G., Kalb, R. C., Caruso, L. S., & Shnek, Z. (1993). Stress, multiple sclerosis, and everyday functioning: A review of the literature with implications for intervention. *NeuroRehabilitation, 3,* 57–66.

Foley, F. W., & Werner, M. D. (1996). Sexuality. In R. Kalb (Ed.), *Multiple sclerosis: The questions you have, the answers you need* (pp. 223–247). New York: Demos Vermande.

Gonzalez, V. M., Goeppinger, J., & Lorig, K. (1990). Four psychosocial theories and their application to patient education and clinical practice. *Arthritis Care and Research, 3,* 132–143.

Grant, I., Brown, G. W., Harris, T., McDonald, W. I., Patterson, T., & Trimble, M. R. (1989). Severely threatening events and marked life difficulties preceding onset or exacerbation of multiple sclerosis. *Journal of Neurology, Neurosurgery, and Psychiatry, 52,* 8–13.

Hatchett, L., Friend, R., Symister, P., & Wadhwa, N. (1997). Interpersonal expectations, social support and adjustment to chronic illness. *Journal of Personality and Social Psychology, 73,* 560–573.

Holroyd, K. A., & Creer, T. L. (Eds.). (1986). *Self-management of chronic disease: Handbook of clinical interventions and research.* Orlando, FL: Academic Press.

Jacobson, D. L., Gange, S. J., Rose, N. R., & Graham, N. M. (1997). Epidemiology and estimated population burden of selected autoimmune diseases in the United States. *Clinical Immunology and Immunopathology, 84,* 223–243.

Jelliffe, S. E. (1921). Multiple sclerosis and psychoanalysis: A preliminary statement of a tentative research. *American Journal of Medical Science, 161,* 666–675.

Joffe, R. T., Lippert, G. P., Gray, T. A., Sawa, G., & Horvath, Z. (1987). Mood disorder and multiple sclerosis. *Archives of Neurology, 44,* 376–378.

Johnson, S. K., DeLuca, J., & Natelson, B. H. (1996a). Depression in fatiguing illness: Comparing patients with chronic fatigue syndrome, multiple sclerosis and depression. *Journal of Affective Disorders, 39,* 21–30.

Johnson, S. K., DeLuca, J., & Natelson, B. H. (1996b). Personality dimensions in the chronic fatigue syndrome: Comparison with multiple sclerosis and depression. *Journal of Psychosomatic Research, 30,* 9–20.

Kalb, R. C. (Ed.). (1996). *Multiple sclerosis: The questions you have, the answers you need.* New York: Demos Vermande.

Kalb, R. C. (Ed.). (1998). *Multiple sclerosis: A guide for families.* New York: Demos Vermande.

Kato, P. M., & Mann, T. (1996). *Handbook of diversity issues in health psychology.* New York: Plenum Press.

Knight, R. G., Devereux, R. C., & Godfrey, H. P. (1997). Psychosocial consequences of caring for a spouse with multiple sclerosis. *Journal of Clinical Neuropsychology, 19,* 7–19.

Krupp, L. B., Alvarez, L. A., LaRocca, N. G., & Scheinberg, L. C. (1988). Fatigue in multiple sclerosis. *Archives of Neurology, 45,* 435–437.

Krupp, L. B., Sliwinski, M., Masur, D. M., Friedberg, F., & Coyle, P. K. (1994). Cognitive functioning and depression in patients with chronic fatigue syndrome and multiple sclerosis. *Archives of Neurology, 51,* 705–710.

LaRocca, N. G. (1990). A rehabilitation perspective. In S. M. Rao (Ed.), *Neurobehavioral aspects of multiple sclerosis* (pp. 215–229). New York: Oxford University Press.

LaRocca, N. G., Caruso, L., Kalb, R., Smith, C., Elkin, R., Foley, F. W., Dince, W., & Shnek, Z. (1998, September). *Comprehensive rehabilitation of cognitive dysfunction in multiple sclerosis.* Paper presented at the annual meeting of the Consortium of Multiple Sclerosis Centers, Chicago, IL.

LaRocca, N. G., Kalb, R. C., & Foley, F. W. (1993). Psychosocial, affective, and behavioral consequences of multiple sclerosis: Treatment of the "whole" patient. *NeuroRehabilitation, 3,* 30–38.

Leake, R., Friend, R., & Wadhwa, N. (1999). Improving adjustment to chronic illness through strategic self-presentation: An experimental study on a renal dialysis unit. *Health Psychology, 18,* 54–62.

Lezak, M. D. (1995). *Neuropsychological assessment* (3rd ed.). New York: Oxford University Press.

Lorig, K., Gonzalez, V., & Laurent, D. (1997). *The chronic disease self-management course: Leader's manual.* Palo Alto, CA: Stanford University Press.

Lorig, K., & Holman, H. (1993). Arthritis self-management studies: A twelve-year review. *Health Education Quarterly, 20,* 17–28.

Lorig, K., Holman, H. R., Sobel, D., Laurent, D., Gonzalez, V., & Minor, M. (1994). *Living a healthy life with chronic conditions.* Palo Alto, CA: Bull.

Lublin, F. D., & Reingold, S. C. (1996). Defining the clinical course of multiple sclerosis: Results of an international survey. National Multiple Sclerosis Society (USA) Advisory Committee on Clinical Trials of New Agents in Multiple Sclerosis. *Neurology, 46,* 907–911.

Matthews, W. B., Acheson, E. D., Batchelor, J. R., & Weller, R. O. (1985). *McAlpine's multiple sclerosis.* Endinburgh, Scotland: Churchill Livingston.

Mattson, D., Petrie, M., Srivastava, D. K., & McDermott, M. (1995). Multiple sclerosis: Sexual dysfunction and its response to medications. *Archives of Neurology, 52,* 862–868.

McIvor, G. P., Riklan, M., & Reznikoff, M. (1984). Depression in multiple sclerosis as a function of length and severity of illness, age, remissions, and perceived social support. *Journal of Clinical Psychology, 40,* 1028–1033.

McLaughlin, J., & Zeeberg, I. (1993). Self-care and multiple sclerosis: A view from two cultures. *Social Science and Medicine, 3,* 315–329.

Meichenbaum, D. (1985). *Stress inoculation training.* New York: Pergamon.

Mohr, D. C., & Dick, L. P. (in press). Multiple sclerosis. In P. M. Camic & S. J. Knight (Eds.), *Clinical handbook for health psychology: A practical guide to effective interventions.* Seattle, WA: Hogrefe & Huber.

Moulin, D. E., Foley, K. M., & Ebers, G. C. (1988). Pain syndromes in multiple sclerosis. *Neurology, 38,* 1830–1834.

Mushlin, A. I., Mooney, C., Grow, V., & Phelps, C. E. (1994). The value of diagnostic information to patients with suspected multiple sclerosis. *Archives of Neurology, 51,* 67–72.

O'Brien, R. A., Wineman, N. M., & Nealon, N. R. (1995). Correlates of the caregiving process in multiple sclerosis. *Scholarly Inquiry for Nursing Practice, 9,* 323–338.

O'Connor, P., Detsky, A. S., Tansey, C., Kucharczyk, W., & Rochester–Toronto MRI Study Group. (1994). Effect of diagnostic testing for multiple sclerosis on patient health perceptions. *Archives of Neurology, 51,* 46–51.

Patten, S. B., & Metz, L. M. (1997). Depression in multiple sclerosis. *Psychotherapy and Psychosomatics, 66,* 286–292.

Peterson, R. A., Mesquita, M. L., Kimmel, P. L., Simmens, S. J., Sacks, C. R., & Reiss, D. (1991). Depression, perception of illness and mortality in patients with end-stage renal disease. *International Journal of Psychiatric Medicine, 21,* 343–354.

Philippopoulos, G. S., Wittkower, E. D., & Cousineau, A. (1958). The etiologic significance of emotional factors in onset and exacerbations of multiple sclerosis. *Psychosomatic Medicine, 20,* 458–474.

Poser, C. M., Paty, D. W., Scheinberg, L., McDonald, I., Davis, F. A., Ebers, G. C., Johnson, K. P., Sibley, W. A., Silberberg, D. H., & Tourtellotte, W. W. (1983). New diagnostic criteria for multiple sclerosis: Guidelines for research protocols. *Annals of Neurology, 13,* 227–231.

Rao, S. M. (1986). Neuropsychology of multiple sclerosis: A critical review. *Journal of Clinical and Experimental Neuropsychology, 8,* 503–542.

Rao, S. M., Leo, G. J., Bernardin, L., & Unverzagt, F. (1991). Cognitive dysfunction in multiple sclerosis: I. Frequency, patterns, and prediction. *Neurology, 41,* 685–691.

Rao, S. M., Leo, G. J., Ellington, L., Nauertz, T., Bernardin, L., & Unverzagt, F. (1991). Cognitive dysfunction in multiple sclerosis: II. Impact on employment and social functioning. *Neurology, 41,* 692–696.

Ritvo, P. G. (1996). Psychosocial and neurological predictors of mental health in multiple sclerosis patients. *Journal of Clinical Epidemiology, 49,* 467–472.

Ron, M. A., Callanan, M. M., & Warrington, E. K. (1991). Cognitive abnormalities in multiple sclerosis: A psychometric and MRI study. *Psychological Medicine, 21,* 59–68.

Sadovnick, A. D., Eisen, K., Ebers, G. C., & Paty, D. W. (1991). Cause of death in patients attending multiple sclerosis clinics. *Neurology, 41,* 1193–1198.

Salloway, S., Price, L. H., Charney, D. S., & Shapiro, M. (1988). Multiple sclerosis presenting as major depression: A diagnosis suggested by MRI scan but not CT scan. *Journal of Clinical Psychiatry, 49,* 364–366.

Schapiro, R. T. (1994). *Symptom management in multiple sclerosis* (2nd ed.). New York: Demos.

Schapiro, R. T., Harris, L., Lenling, M., & Metelak, J. (1987). Fatigue. In R. T. Schapiro (Ed.), *Symptom management in multiple sclerosis* (pp. 23–28). New York: Demos.

Scheier, M. F., Magovern, G. J., Abbott, R. A., Matthews, K. A., Owens, J. F., Lefebvre, R. C., & Carver, C. S. (1989). Dispositional optimism and recovery from coronary artery bypass surgery: The beneficial effects on physical and psychological well-being. *Journal of Personality and Social Psychology, 57,* 1024–1040.

Scheinberg, L. (1983). *Multiple sclerosis: A guide for patients and their families.* New York: Raven Press.

Schwartz, C. E., Coulthard-Morris, L., & Zeng, Q. (1996). Psychosocial correlates of fatigue in multiple sclerosis. *Archives of Physical Medicine and Rehabilitation, 77,* 165–170.

Seland, T. P. (1984). The diagnostic challenge of multiple sclerosis. *Canadian Family Physician, 30,* 1499–1502.

Seligman, M. E. P., & Binik, Y. M. (1977). The safety signal hypothesis. In H. Davis & H. Hurwitz (Eds.), *Pavlovian operant interactions* (pp. 165–187). Hillsdale, NJ: Erlbaum.

Sencer, W. (1988). Suspicion of multiple sclerosis: To tell or not to tell. *Archives of Neurology, 45,* 441–442.

Shnek, Z. M., Foley, F. W., LaRocca, N. G., Gordon, W. A., DeLuca, J., Schwartzman, H. G., Halper, J., Lennox, S., & Irvine, J. (1997). Helplessness, self-efficacy, cognitive distortions, and depression in multiple sclerosis and spinal cord injury. *Annals of Behavioral Medicine, 19,* 287–294.

Shnek, Z. M., Foley, F. W., LaRocca, N. G., Smith, C. R., & Halper, J. (1995). Psychological predictors of depression in multiple sclerosis. *Journal of Neurologic Rehabilitation, 9,* 15–23.

Skegg, F., Corwin, P. A., & Skegg, D. C. G. (1988). How often is multiple sclerosis mistaken for a psychiatric disorder? *Psychological Medicine, 18,* 733–736.

Teitelbaum, H. A., Hall, B. H., & Phillips, R. E. (1952). Psychosomatic aspects of multiple sclerosis. *A.M.A. Archives of Neurology and Psychiatry, 67,* 535–544.

Uswatte, G., & Elliott, T. R. (1997). Ethnic and minority issues in rehabilitation psychology. *Rehabilitation Psychology, 42,* 61–71.

van Oosten, B. W., Truyen, L., Barkhof, F., & Polman, C. H. (1995). Multiple sclerosis therapy: A practical guide. *Drugs, 49,* 200–212.

Vercoulen, J. H., Hommes, O. R., Swanink, C. M., Jongen, P. J., Fennis, J. F., Galama, J. M., van der Meer, J. W., & Bleijenberg, G. (1996). The measurement of fatigue in patients with multiple sclerosis: A multidimensional comparison with patients with chronic fatigue syndrome and healthy subjects. *Archives of Neurology, 53,,* 642–649.

Viederman, M., & Perry, S. W. (1980). Use of psychodynamic life narrative in the treatment of depression in the physically ill. *General Hospital Psychiatry, 3,* 177–180.

Walker, L. G., & Eremin, O. (1996). Psychological assessment and intervention: Future prospects for women with breast cancer. *Seminars in Surgical Oncology, 12,* 76–83.

Warren, S., Greenhill, S., & Warren, K. G. (1982). Emotional stress and the development of multiple sclerosis: Case-control evidence of a relationship. *Journal of Chronic Diseases, 35,* 821–831.

Wineman, N. M. (1990). Adaptation to multiple sclerosis: The role of social support, functional disability, and perceived uncertainty. *Nursing Research, 39,* 294–299.

Yalom, I. D. (1980). *Existential psychotherapy.* New York: Basic Books.

Yutrzenka, B. A. (1995). Making a case for training in ethnic and cultural diversity in increasing treatment efficacy. *Journal of Consulting and Clinical Psychology, 63,* 197–206.

Zeldow, P. B., & Pavlou, M. (1984). Physical disability, life stress, and psychosocial adjustment in multiple sclerosis. *Journal of Nervous and Mental Disease, 172,* 80–84.

9

Chronic Pain

Daniel M. Doleys

The definition of *pain* has remained elusive (Feurestein, 1994). Because pain is often considered a subjective phenomenon, some consider it to be whatever an individual says it is. Sarno (1991) believes pain to be a response to maladaptive, repressed, or unresolved negative emotions. Most accept pain as a multidimensional problem having both affective–emotional and sensory–discriminative components as outlined by the International Association for the Study of Pain (IASP; Merskey & Bogduk, 1994). More recently, there has been greater attention to conceptualizing pain as a disease rather than a symptom (Cousins, 1999; Liebeskind, 1991). Clearly, the definition one chooses influences assessment, diagnostic, therapeutic, and outcome measurement strategies.

Pain is frequently divided into two categories, acute and chronic. Acute pain is generally associated with some defined tissue damage or disease process and is short lived. Chronic pain has been thought of in several ways (Feurestein, 1994). On occasion it has been defined by the duration of pain; historically, 6 months has been the cut-off but in some instances 3 months has been applied. In other circumstances, the term *chronicity* has been used to refer to pain complaints and symptoms that were considered to be qualitatively or quantitatively disproportionate to the underlying physical pathology. Some definitions associate the term with the type and degree of comorbidities, and individuals are considered to have chronic pain if they develop concomitant depression, anxiety, disability, or drug abuse.

Pain is further subdivided into cancer and noncancer. *Cancer pain* specifies the etiology as some type of cancer. The assessment and treatment of cancer pain has historically been related to amelioration of the cause or palliation. Although frequently undertreated, pain secondary to cancer has been more widely accepted and less controversial than pain of noncancer origin. Improvement in quality of life and pain control are related to both types of pain. However, restoration of function and what one ordinarily thinks of under the rubric of *rehabilitation* is a more common concern with noncancer pain. This chapter focuses primarily on noncancer pain, although there are similarities in assessment, treatment, and psychosocial issues between cancer and noncancer pain (Long, 1997; Portenoy, 1998; Turk et al., 1998).

Chronic noncancer pain continues to pose a major treatment and financial problem. This appears true whether for the common headache leading to extensive pharmacological and therapeutic interventions or the ever-present and yet elusive nonspecific low back pain. There is no indication that occupational injuries, a common cause of chronic noncancer pain, are lessening in frequency, severity, or subsequent cost (Leigh, Markowitz, Fahs, Shin, & Landrigan, 1997; Linton, 1998). Furthermore, the incidence of fraud in worker's compensation has prompted new concern, actions, and expense (Blakeley, 1998).

Several schema are used to characterize the various components of chronic pain. For example, Loeser (1980) noted chronic pain to be a product of (a) nociception (activity induced in neural pathways by potentially tissue-damaging stimuli; Portenoy, 1998), (b) perception, (c) suffering, and (d) pain behavior. Doleys, Lowery, and Brown (1998) noted that chronic pain is an outcome of (a) organic pathology, (b) muscular deviations and dysfunctions, (c) mechanical deformities and abnormalities, and (d) behavioral and psychological factors. Another possible system includes three major categories: central–neuropathic, musculoskeletal–mechanical, and behavioral–psychological. Central–neuropathic pain is caused by some alteration in the peripheral or central processing. Injury to a major nerve root, postherpetic neuralgia (pain following herpes zoster), and avulsion (tearing apart) are but a few examples. The second category, musculoskeletal–mechanical pain, encompasses those syndromes characterized by mechanical deformities such as lumbar spine instability. Major musculoskeletal difficulties arising from deconditioning, inactivity, and myofascial problems would also be included. The behavioral–psychological category would incorporate psychological such states as depression, anxiety, and somatoform pain disorders. It may be possible to demonstrate that conditioning factors, such as positive reinforcement and "secondary-gain" issues, are etiologically significant in the patient's complaints of pain. It is not uncommon that an acute pain state may be initiated by one factor such as a musculoskeletal strain to the low back, but the chronic pain experience is more strongly associated with the behavioral–psychological factors that emerge in the process of evaluating and treating the acute pain.

These three categories are not mutually exclusive. Patients with complex regional pain syndrome (formerly reflex sympathetic dystrophy) may manifest characteristics from each category; that is, the neuropathic component to pain is contributed to by nerve injury. This component of the pain can lead to musculoskeletal abnormalities that may be an outcome of overprotection and disuse. The psychological sequelae can be remarkable, including depression, insomnia, anxiety, and hypervigilance.

Assessment

Assessment of the patient with pain should and has become a more sophisticated matter (Doleys & Doherty, 2000; Doleys et al., 1998). The goal of assessment should be the articulation of a treatment algorithm. For this to be accomplished, the evaluator must have an appreciation for and the ability to discern the relative contributions of various underlying pathophysiologies (e.g., nerve damage, mechanical instability, myofascial problems, and behavioral–psychological factors). Increased emphasis needs to be applied to the relative effectiveness of various therapies on specific patient populations. Pain should not be regarded as a unidimensional and generic sensation to be approached in a shotgun fashion. This "treat-and-hope" method is not only inefficient but may also render the problem more recalcitrant to treatment by virtue of the patient experiencing repeated failures or medical consequences, such as postsurgical scarring, that further complicates the situation. A well-thought-out and comprehensive assessment is therefore essential.

That behavioral–psychological factors contribute to chronic pain is undeniable (Doleys & Doherty, 2000). Their specific role and etiological significance remain unclear, however, and therefore require detailed investigation. Teasell and Merskey (1997) argued for caution in assigning psychological factors a primary causative role in chronic pain. Doing so may inadvertently discourage a more diligent search for underlying pathology, which when corrected may help alleviate the pain or, if left undetected, may render the pain recalcitrant to treatment. Weisberg and Keefe (1997) suggested that personality disorders, rather than predisposing to the development of chronic pain, may, in fact, emerge in response to stress created by the presence of chronic pain. The debate over the relative contribution of such behavioral–psychological factors is no more evidenced than when investigating the placebo effect (Ader, 1997; Price & Fields, 1997). Such fundamental questions as whether a patient must have prior experience with some therapy to manifest a placebo effect continues to be a source of controversy.

In the process of performing a behavioral–psychological assessment it may be useful to consider behavioral–psychological factors as playing one or more of three roles: mediating, modulating, and maintaining (see Figure 9.1). As a mediating factor, behavioral–psychological states would be considered necessary, if not causative, in the development of chronic pain. Some event would activate acute pain, which would then stimulate

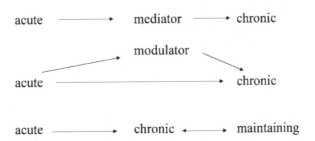

Figure 9.1. Behavioral–psychological factors in chronicity. This figure represents the three possible roles that behavioral–psychological factors can play in the development of chronic pain following an acute pain episode. Behavioral–psychological factors may function as mediators, modulators, or maintainers.

some psychological factors leading to chronicity. For example, one might argue that the presence of acute pain could activate mechanisms of depression and anxiety which, when present, would cause a persistent state of chronic pain through increased sensitivity to pain or alteration in neurotransmitters, such as serotonin, known to be relevant to both emotional states and pain. Theoretically, therefore, two patients could have the same underlying physical pathology, but only one would develop a chronic pain condition. Pain complaints, activity avoidance, levels of depression, drug use, degree of disability, and deactivation would be judged disproportionate to the physical findings.

As a modulating factor, psychological–behavioral states would affect the qualitative and quantitative nature of the pain experience but not necessarily determine its presence or absence. In this scenario, an initiating event such as herpes zoster might produce an acute pain. The subsequent damage to nerve pathways would lead to a persistent and chronic experience of pain (i.e., postherpetic neuralgia). Although psychological factors may influence the severity of the pain and degree of incapacitation, they would not be the primary cause of the chronic pain itself.

In the third instance, maintaining, some event would provoke an experience of acute pain. The pain experience would persist over time. Behavioral–psychological factors would emerge to serve to maintain the chronic pain syndrome. For example, an acute injury might promote the demonstration of pain behaviors such as posturing, wincing, bracing, and guarding, as described by Fordyce (1976) and Keefe and Block (1982). The presence of these pain behaviors may elicit and be reinforced by positive consequences such as attending behavior or activity avoidance. These reinforcement factors would in turn maintain the chronic pain behavior, which again would stimulate the presence of more reinforcement. Thus, even though the acute injury, in total or part, resolves, the chronic pain persists by virtue of its relationship to factors that may be internal or external to the individual.

Given the apparent complexity of performing a comprehensive assessment, including evaluation of the nature of the pain as well as relevant psychological and behavioral factors and their contribution to the experience of pain, the practitioner must use a variety of assessment procedures. Simply administering psychological or pain-oriented tests and questionnaires is likely to prove inadequate. Indeed, a recent article by Robinson et al. (1997) reveals that when asked, individuals without pain were able to respond to commonly used questionnaires such as a Westhaven–Yale Multidimensional Pain Inventory (Kerns, Turk, & Rudy, 1985), the Coping Strategies Questionnaire (Rosenstiel & Keefe, 1983), and the Pain Beliefs and Perception Inventory (Williams & Thorn, 1989) in a fashion almost indistinguishable from pain patients. Furthermore, they were able to present themselves as either coping well or coping poorly. This observation should encourage the use of tests that have validity scales that might identify individuals attempting to misrepresent themselves. Furthermore, psychological tests should be interpreted in the context of detailed interview and behavioral observations. It may be necessary for the clinician to see the patient on more than one occasion to get a reliable picture. Having input from other disciplines, including physical therapy, social work, medicine, and vocational rehabilitation, would be valuable. (A discussion of the details of various psychological tests and questionnaires is beyond the scope of this chapter and can be found elsewhere; Doleys & Doherty, 2000; Doleys, Murray, Klapow, & Colton, 1998.)

In the past decade, researchers have expressed an increased concern and interest in the role of a history of physical and sexual abuse (McMahon, Gatchel, Polatin, & Mayer, 1997) and alcohol or drug addiction in patients with chronic noncancer pain (Portenoy, 1990). Indeed, recent work has shown a correlation between hippocampal volume and a history of sexual abuse in women (Stein, Koverola, Hanna, Torchia, & McClarty, 1997). This same structure appears to be involved in processing noxious (painful) stimulation (Derbyshire et al., 1997). Such patients, therefore, may be less likely than others to have a positive outcome. There has been a tendency to use the presence of such risk factors as contraindications for various therapies. A properly done assessment should not only identify the presence of such risk factors but also posit a hypothesis for their relative contribution to the experience of pain and what alterations may be required to a specific therapy to enhance the outcome. These alterations may include individual therapy to deal with psychological sequelae and enhanced patient education and preparation and may incorporate other disciplines into the planned therapy.

For example, addressing issues of sexual assault and abuse prior to or in combination with other therapies may be beneficial. In the case of an alcohol or drug abuser, consideration should be given to such issues as the length of abuse, the substance of abuse, and the length of recovery. This is particularly true in attempting to determine whether a patient may be a candidate for long-term opioid therapy.

There has also been a good deal of emphasis placed on identifying behavioral–psychological factors that may predispose patients to injury and the subsequent development of chronic pain (Linton & Bradley, 1996; Sanders, 1995). Factors such as job satisfaction seem well documented. One must remain aware, however, of the differences between factors contributing to the development of chronic pain and those contributing to disability. Sanders (1995) noted that these may not be the same. His studies suggest that a history of back pain, job dissatisfaction, and smoking seems to be associated with low back pain, whereas depression, high score on the Hysteria scale of the Minnesota Multiphasic Personality Inventory, and low level of activity combined with high level of pain behaviors correlate well with the development of chronic disability. The behavioral–psychological assessment should also address the impact of the patient's general "personality" style on his or her experience of pain and appropriateness for therapy. Weisberg and Keefe (1997) summarized these various personality types. Clearly, the patient given to flamboyant, exaggerated, and melodramatic behavior poses concerns different from that of the schizoid patient, who may be inclined to be isolated and withdrawn. Such personality types may not be obvious at first contact. A detailed history and input from family members can be extremely useful in making a proper identification and diagnosis. Indeed, some personality types, such as borderline, may not declare themselves until several contacts have been made. Eliminating a particular patient from a treatment option on the basis of a specific label such as *hypochondriacal* is unfair and perhaps even unethical. Whereas it is clear that certain personality characteristics may modulate the individual response to treatment, it is difficult to assume that no treatment would provide any beneficial effect.

Perhaps one of the most intriguing cases to illustrate the complexity of the issues of chronic pain assessment and challenge the time-honored concepts of pain is that of dissociative disorder or multiple personality. Although it is clear that there remains some discussion as to the legitimacy of the diagnosis, it does appear in the *Diagnostic and Statistical Manual of Mental Disorders* (4th ed.; *DSM–IV*; American Psychiatric Association, 1994) under the heading Dissociative Identity Disorder (300.14). I have encountered (as have other clinicians by anecdotal report) the presence of several personalities or "entities," some of which report and demonstrate all of the signs and symptoms characteristic of chronic pain and others that do not. Furthermore, the nonpain entities at times report an inability to understand why other personalities find the condition so painful and disabling. It is remarkable to witness the behavioral patterns of different personalities and the transformation that can occur, sometimes within a matter of minutes. Perhaps this bespeaks of the significant role of the affective component of pain. Although the affective component of pain appears to be related to the sensory component, it seems to be located in different cerebral structures (i.e., anterior cingulate gyrus) and potentially subject to independent manipulation (Rainville, Duncan, Price, Carrier, & Bushnell, 1997). Although these types of patients are clearly the exception rather than the rule, their existence requires attention and may provide more fertile ground for understanding chronic pain than perhaps the more typical patient.

The temporal characteristics of the pain should also be investigated. In some cases the pain, although persistent, is not highly variable in its intensity. Patients report levels of 7–10 (0 = *no pain*; 10 = *most severe pain*) up to 24 hours a day. In other cases the pain may be influenced by certain physical activities (walking, standing, lifting) or psychological states (depression, anxiety, stress). Environmental consequences such as activity avoidance or attention-giving behavior (e.g., back massage) may also influence the experience of pain.

Perhaps one of the more difficult types of pain to evaluate and treat is that of recurrent acute pain. Pain associated with sickle cell anemia is an example of recurrent acute pain and presents a variety of challenges (Ballas, 1998). In such cases allowances must be made for and the practitioner must expect episodes of acute pain, which often requires hospitalization, in addition to the chronic pain symptoms. There may be periods when the pain seems well controlled. Anticipatory anxiety over recurrent episodes of acute pain must be addressed.

There is a growing awareness that male and female patients respond differently to the experience of pain (Fillingim, Maixner, Kincaid, & Silva, 1998; Lamberg, 1998). The role that this difference may play in treatment selection and efficacy is yet to be determined. A comprehensive assessment, however, must take these data into consideration.

Increased acceptance of opioids as legitimate therapy for cancer and noncancer pain has broadened the vistas (Portenoy, 1996). However, it has raised questions regarding patient assessment, selection, and disclosure. For example, what role does a history of drug or alcohol abuse play in determining whether to recommend chronic use of opioids? Are there behavioral–psychological factors that would discriminate between an addict who is appropriate for treatment with opioids and one who is not? When assessing the chronic pain patient who may already be on limited amounts of opioids, it is important to be able to discriminate among physical dependence, tolerance, pseudoaddiction, and addiction. *Physical dependence* is defined by the presence of withdrawal syndrome on discontinuation of the opioid. *Tolerance* is generally defined by the reduction in efficacy at a given dosage or the necessity to increase the dosage to maintain the beneficial effect. Patients who are receiving partial relief and seeking additional medication for the purpose of additional relief, but in whom there is no other evidence of aberrant drug-taking behavior, are thought to evidence *pseudoaddiction*. In general, *addiction* is a term reserved for patients who present with (a) a preoccupation with acquisition of substance, (b) loss of control over use of the substance, and (c) use of the substance despite apparent financial, psychosocial, or physical harm (Portenoy, 1996). An assessment should also determine the type of pain; it is commonly felt that opioid therapy is less effective with nerve-related pathologies than other types of pathologies. Although there is a body of literature supporting the efficacy of long-term opioid therapy, the assessment of the consequences and risks is ongoing (Savage, 1996).

The importance of patient selection and the development of a treatment algorithm would appear to be an obvious goal of a comprehensive assessment. Unfortunately, there continues to be a strong tendency to use behavioral–psychological assessments to screen patients in order to proceed or not proceed with a given procedure. This "go–no go" approach to assessment seems somewhat archaic and unenlightened. Behavioral–psychological knowledge and sophistication have advanced beyond simply attempting to identify patients who meet some statistical formula presumed to provide better than a 50/50 chance of their responding to a specific therapy. This "statistical" approach must be tempered with the realization that patients, as well as their pain states, are dynamic by nature. However appropriate a patient may seem for a particular therapy at a given point in time, things can and often do change. Our task should be one of developing therapeutic approaches to deal with individual patients rather than screening the patient population for those who seem to fit a defined treatment protocol, relegating the remainder of the patients to "living with their pain." In addition, this "statistical approach" to patient assessment and selection does not encourage an ongoing assessment–treat–reassessment–alter treatment–reassessment cycle. It is, after all, the individual patient who is being treated and not a statistically derived group. The more help clinicians can provide each individual patient, the better the group outcome measures are.

Prevention and Management of Acute Pain

Chronic pain occurs only after the individual experiences an episode of acute pain. Prevention remains one of the best mechanisms for "treating" chronic noncancer pain (Linton & Bradley, 1996). Investigations have been carried out as to those factors that may predict or predispose an individual to injury. Some factors are job specific and include jobs with heavy physical demands and repetitive motion and those requiring mechanical strain through a combination of manipulation of heavy objects in mechanically compromising situations. Many individuals report that an accident on the job was "avoidable." In such cases the use of outdated equipment and inadequate training and assistance, combined with an emphasis on productivity rather than safety, contribute to the injury and pain.

The manner in which the patient with acute pain is treated appears to be correlated with the development of chronicity as well. The degree to which chronic nociception (i.e., chronic sensory input from imagery) is allowed to persist unchecked creates fertile ground for the development of anticipatory pain and activity avoidance. Reinforcement factors (Doleys et al., 1998) may play a role; the relative contribution of such factors remains in question. There appears to be a dichotomy. Some (e.g., Fordyce, 1995) have suggested that especially in the case of nonspecific low back pain, the availability of disability compensation, attention, and reinforcement factors may be etiologically significant in chronic pain. Others (e.g., Teasell & Merskey, 1997) have argued that the term *nonspecific* may be more suggestive of diagnostic limitations than descriptive of the disorder. Furthermore, careful examination would reveal sources of nociception.

The general approach to management of acute pain requires consideration (Linton & Bradley, 1996). The use of pain-contingent treatments versus those determined by a fixed schedule has been evaluated. The use of aggressive medical intervention has been debated. The role of self-efficacy as well as patient expectations may also influence the outcome. Some disorders have a lasting impression on central and peripheral processing, such as postherpetic neuralgia following herpes zoster, the effects of which can only be modulated but not eliminated.

Many individuals seek a surgical relief of their pain; some patients experience continued pain postoperatively, whereas others do not. The degree to which this is a problem of patient selection has been debated. A considerable number of researchers (e.g., Block, 1996) has attempted to delineate patient characteristics that may be associated with a better or worse outcome.

This analysis must be examined in the context of the purpose of surgery. In some cases, such as neurocompression or mechanical instability, anatomical deformities form the primary basis for surgical intervention.

Although pain relief is the goal, it is entirely possible to repair the deformity, and therefore have an excellent surgical outcome, but have no subjective relief of pain. The persistence of pain may or may not have an association with the technical adequacy of surgery or the appropriateness of the patient as a surgery candidate.

In a similar vein, efforts have been made to eliminate the chronicity presumed to be a result of acute pain created by surgery. Preemptive analgesia has emphasized the blocking of nociceptive barrages created by surgical intervention so as to interrupt the development of hyperalgesic states. Providing substantial analgesia prior to and after surgery with adequate neuroblockade intraoperatively has been duly considered. The approach is theoretically sound, but the data have not yet suggested any firm conclusions (Niv & Devor, 1996).

Postoperative rehabilitation including physical and psychological care would seem to be of obvious interest. The degree to which a patient should be encouraged to "grin and bear it" or provided analgesic relief during rehabilitation (whether through oral, intravenous, or epidural preparations) is unknown.

Treatments of Chronic Pain

Once the level of chronicity has been achieved, by whatever definition one chooses to apply, the problem remains no less complicated. Many have indicated that, particularly with nonspecific low back pain, the causes are more psychosocial than medical. It is perhaps a mistake to dichotomize and make it an either–or situation. New advances in diagnostic procedures, including the use of epiduroscopy (Saberski, 1996), may give new clues as to the source of nociception. As always, however, one must understand that nociception is not synonymous with pain. The ability to visualize an abnormality, however closely related in proximity to the problem under consideration, does not confirm it as a causative variable. The development of any diagnostic procedure inevitably carries with it the mandatory therapeutic interventions. It is necessary to discriminate between an intervention designed to correct the observed abnormality and that which alters the condition under consideration. The relative contributions of central neuropathic, musculoskeletal–mechanical, and behavioral–psychological variables must be determined. Similarly, the role of behavioral–psychological characteristics as mediators, modulators, or maintainers of chronic pain must be assessed.

The spectrum of therapies for chronic pain runs broad and deep. Most are familiar with the traditional outpatient physical therapy and behavioral–psychological interventions (Klapow, Fillingim, & Doleys, 1998; Turk & Fernandez, 1997). Modality- and exercise-based physical therapy–rehabilitation may play an important role in reactivation. Clear goals should be established and therapies accomplished within the context of these goals. Endless application of modality therapies in the absence of any long-term benefit may reflect a dependency on the patient's part for such therapies. The reinforcing aspects of the therapy may be unrelated to any alteration in nociception or functioning.

Behavioral and cognitive–behavioral therapies have had a long and illustrious history (Compas, Haaga, Keefe, Leitenberg, & Williams, 1998). They have found utility and favor in the treatment of such problems as headache, temporomandibular joint, arthritis, and low back pain. Unfortunately, reimbursement patterns often require substantial financial commitment on the part of the patient, which limits access to these procedures. Time-honored procedures such as relaxation training, goal setting, cognitive restructuring, and biofeedback continue to be effective for a significant segment of the chronic pain population. As our understanding of pain mechanisms is advanced through the use of functional imaging, procedures such as these may be shown to alter the affective component of the pain without affecting the sensory discriminative component. Thus, it may not be uncommon for patients to note that the sensory discriminative aspects of their pain, such as overall intensity, has remained unchanged but that they feel less impaired and more capable of managing their situation. The use of magnetic resonance imaging or positron emission tomography before and after behavioral interventions may provide additional clues as to the mechanism of action and how such therapies may be effective even in situations in which central–neuropathic components dominate.

Medication Management

Continued advances in pharmacological therapeutics have expanded the type and number of preparations potentially beneficial in managing chronic pain (Portenoy, 1996; Portenoy & Kanner, 1996). Categories include muscle relaxers, nonsteroidal anti-inflammatories, opioids, antidepressants, and anticonvulsants. Indeed, the role of methadone has received special attention (Joranson, 1997). *Polypharmacy*, the use of preparations from one or more classes, appears to be the rule rather than the exception. A comprehensive understanding of the risk–benefit ratio is required. Certain behavioral–psychological issues such as psychological dependence and medication administration (i.e., medication given as needed or at regular intervals) cannot be ignored. As mentioned earlier, a distinction between tolerance, dependence, and addiction must be appreciated.

The existence of opiate-responsive pain is well established. Clearly there is a subgroup of patients who can adequately and effectively be managed with long-term opioid therapy. The issue of side effects must remain a serious consideration. Opioids may be delivered by a variety of mechanisms, including orally or by a drug administration system (DAS; Krames, 1997). The use of a medication contract has been recommended. The incidence of addiction in well-supervised patients is rare.

Related issues involve considerations in treating the patient with chronic pain who has a recent or remote history of drug or alcohol abuse.

The risk of activating underlying biological factors that may intensify cravings requires consideration. Other issues revolve around "fitness for duty." Although it is frequently assumed that opioids can negatively affect cognitive functioning and performance, the scientific data are neither convincing nor conclusive (Chesher, 1990; Zacny, 1995). In fact, evidence from published literature and anecdotal reports suggests the opposite. Police officers experiencing chronic pain have been noted to have improved marksmanship once the pain is controlled by opioid management. The effects, however, seem to vary for those on stable and adjusting dosages.

Time-honored misperceptions regarding the impact of opioids, when properly used for treatment of chronic pain, may place this therapy on a collision course with the regulations in the Americans With Disabilities Act (ADA) of 1990 (Office of Equal Opportunity, 1990). For example, a company may have guidelines prohibiting the operation of heavy construction equipment or transportation of vehicles while taking opioids. Nonetheless the ADA would suggest that individuals can be evaluated, queried, and tested only on their ability to perform the essential features of the job. Should they be required to divulge their use of opioids if they clearly are able to perform the relevant tasks and run the risk of being discriminated against? Even more intriguing is the issue of mental or physical health care professionals and the use of opioids. Should physicians be required to inform patients of their use of opioids for control of a pain condition in the absence of any evidence to support impairment in functioning as a result of this therapy?

As this therapy expands in popularity and efficacy, the above questions will require answers. It is the responsibility and obligation of practitioners providing opioid therapy to obtain data supporting the efficacy of this treatment. Information regarding the effects of opioids on pain, general day-to-day functioning, and job-related tasks such as fine motor coordination and cognitive activity should be maintained.

Inpatient and Residential Treatments

By virtue of insurance coverage many inpatient programs have all but disappeared. The lack of medical necessity has frequently been used to deny coverage, forcing patients who could otherwise be treated effectively either to contend with their pain problem without appropriate support or to seek treatments that may be more invasive and carry the potential for irreversible complications. It is ironic that the insurance companies may create the very situation they are concerned about, that is, growing health care costs, by denying coverage for benign procedures and forcing patients to seek more destructive ones. Ongoing pain therapies often occur in response to the side effect of pain following irreversible procedures. Although many carriers purport to be concerned with efficacy, they still remain predisposed to the medical model.

Some residential programs continue (Fishbain, Cutler, Rosomoff, & Steele-Rosomoff, 1997). Such programs may take the form of day treatment, wherein patients come in on a regular basis several hours a day several days a week. Other situations involve motel accommodations where the patient is in residence during a program that may span 2–6 weeks. In a recent report (Doleys et al., 1998), patients accepted into, but not actually receiving, treatment in a 4-week residential program were compared 12–18 months later with those who did participate. Those patients who did not participate in treatment did not show improvement across a variety of parameters but actually acknowledged deterioration in function, mood, and work relative to the treated patients.

Such residential programs may be interdisciplinary or multidisciplinary. The models should not be confused. The multidisciplinary model uses clinicians from various disciplines, each providing input regarding management of the patient. In a truly interdisciplinary model these same individuals interact on a regular basis, using the information to generate a comprehensive and integrated treatment plan. Such programs in fact epitomize the often recommended ideal approach to chronic noncancer pain— that is, the close interaction among multiple disciplines evaluating various aspects of the patient's complaints to generate an appropriate therapeutic algorithm designed with maximum efficiency and efficacy in mind. Such interdisciplinary residential programs also present an excellent forum in which to evaluate therapies such as blocks, spinal cord stimulation (SCS), and DAS, which can be repeated or assessed in clinical trials. One can only speculate on the number of interventions and surgeries that are truly "exploratory" in nature carried out because of the absence of more objective and observational data relevant to the patient's pain complaints and behaviors.

Invasive Therapies

A plethora of invasive procedures to control pain has appeared on the scene (Waldman & Winnie, 1996). Some are designed to be nondestructive in nature and to contain an element of reversibility. Perhaps the best known and most frequently used are various pain blocks (Molloy & Benzon, 1996). These may be diagnostic or therapeutic. Interpreting their effects must be done with caution, however; the temporary disruption of pain by a selective nerve root block does not necessarily define the structure as the pain generator. If this were true, the evidence for permanent denervation through neurolytic procedures as a means of aborting pain would be more compelling. In addition, subsequent treatments often depend on a patient's reports 1–2 weeks after the intervention. Recent studies have shown that less than 60% of patients accurately report 2 weeks after a block the relief obtained immediately after the block (Porzelius, 1995). Their usefulness with acute and subacute pain may be greater than with the chronic noncancer pain.

Attempts to control the experience of pain by disruption of nociception has progressed into implantable technology (Root, Weaver, & Hahn, 1998). Such systems include SCS (Shetter, 1997) and DAS (Krames, 1997; Stangl

& Loeser, 1997). In the case of SCS an electrode of varying configurations is implanted epidurally and programmed to electrically disrupt nociceptive signals, presumably to alter the experience of pain. In general, the technology has been most effective with neuropathic pain. Its continuation as a bona fide therapy appears to be assured, although the specific mechanism of action remains elusive.

DAS involves the implantation of a mechanical device with a reservoir holding approximately 18 milliliters of solution and a mechanism that gradually expels the solution through a catheter to the epidural (or more typically intrathecal) space. Placing medication closer to the suspected "site of action" should (in theory) improve efficacy with fractional amounts compared to those that might be required by oral administration. A variety of preparations have found utility. Morphine is the most commonly used and currently the only Federal Drug Administration-approved opioid, although many patients seem to respond to hydromorphone and sufentanil. Patients with central–neuropathic pain often find the addition of a local anesthetic such as bupivocaine or tetracaine helpful. Baclofen has become an all but indispensable therapy in the treatment of chronic spasticity. Clonidine is being explored and may have analgesic properties. Such therapy is not without its side effects and cost. Its application should best be conceptualized within a multidisciplinary, if not interdisciplinary, model. Ironically, some patients are compelled to pursue this approach to pain management by insurance reimbursement patterns which, if altered, might allow for the emergence of an equally efficacious therapy through much less invasive routes.

Other procedures are more or less destructive in nature. Neurolytic procedures may produce irreversible changes (Blum & Lubenow, 1996). Other approaches, such as radiofrequency denervation, appear to provide temporary disruption of nociception. Patient selection remains a critical factor. Wholesale application of this and other interventional procedures must be guarded against. The application of such techniques should be carried out in patients in whom a clear pattern of nociceptive transmission has been identified and where there is evidence that the disruption of the transmission in fact may alter the long-term experience of pain and may not cause unacceptable side effects.

Issues

Accepting the above, including the IASP definition of pain, the possibility of at least three categories of chronic pain, and the varying role of behavioral–psychological factors, would necessitate and demand a multidisciplinary, if not interdisciplinary, approach to assessment, treatment, and evaluation. Unfortunately, personal preferences, narrowness of vision, conceptual naivete, single-mindedness, and reimbursement patterns may be equally or more influential. However valuable an interdisciplinary approach, its institution is determined by the patient's personal financial resources and insurance company payments (Federico, 1996; Taricco,

1996). We remain a medically oriented society, despite the recent emphasis on alternative medicine. Reimbursement patterns are often determined by diagnosis (*Current Procedural Terminology*; American Medical Association, 1999), codes, and administration of treatment by a physician or nonphysician. The philosophical and practical realities of chronic pain assessment and treatment are rarely influential.

A growing emphasis on outcomes as a compass for reimbursement patterns may or may not have a long-term impact. The effectiveness of noninvasive and primarily behavioral–psychological procedures has been documented repeatedly (Turk, 1996), yet "mental–nervous" and rehabilitation coverage is diminishing in many instances. There is, understandably, a finite pool of financial resources. As medical technology and procedures have advanced in number and cost, funding must come from one of three sources: (a) increase in premiums, (b) reduction in insurance company profits, or (c) reallocation of available monies. Personal and professional influences as well as politics continue to significantly affect reimbursement policy.

In addition, society has continued to be encouraged to seek immediate remedies. Many patients are baffled at the magnitude of the space technology, and yet no one can "cure" their pain. Out of desperation or perhaps faulty but understandable expectations, interventions requiring little of the patient (e.g., surgery, pharmacology) are held in high esteem and seen as holding more promise for a cure. This can lead to the indiscriminate use of procedures that may complicate rather than resolve suspected underlying pathology or promote rather than diminish the pain problem. Attempts to identify a "pain generator" through systematic, or sometimes unsystematic, interruption of peripheral or central nerve activity, thus justifying procedures to alter peripheral or central processing without adequate consideration of behavioral–psychological variables, betray frequently acknowledged advances in the understanding of pain beyond that identified by Descartes centuries ago. This is not to say that such technology and procedures should be abandoned, but only that their application to a primary complaint of pain should be carried out judiciously and only after careful consideration of the multidimensional aspects of the primary complaint.

The demand that "something be done," resulting in a response of "all I know to do is to explore; but there are no guarantees," can be fertile ground for chronicity through postoperative scar tissue or intraoperative damage. The degree to which societal philosophy, medical predilections, and reimbursement policy limit a more multidimensional and interdisciplinary approach may encourage the maintenance or exacerbation of chronicity. It has been noted that undertreatment of acute pain may be the most common cause of chronicity, and overtreatment of chronic pain the greatest problem.

The illusion of a cure beguiles patient and practitioner alike. Perhaps the conceptualization of pain as a disease entity (Liebeskind, 1991) comprising multiple symptoms across physical and psychological domains is necessary. It is clear that many medical problems such as diabetes, hypertension, Alzheimer's, and multiple sclerosis are approached with management and not cure in mind. In many cases, especially diabetes and hypertension, responsibility is shared by the patient with duly noted emphasis on changing lifestyles such as diet, weight, and exercise. In the absence of these changes the expected benefit of medical treatment is diminished.

Changes in health care, society, and the insurance industry have mirrored the technological advances. Faster is seen not only as better but necessary. Technology has replaced, rather than partnered with, self-reliance. Insurance companies seem poised to approve, with less concern, a $30,000 medically invasive procedure as opposed to a much less expensive conservative approach categorized as a rehabilitation or mental health measure. The irony is obvious but has either escaped attention or elicited no response.

Psychology boasts a proud heritage of productive animal and human research in clinical and applied settings. As the demand for outcomes research continues, especially from insurance carriers, efforts in this direction must be expanded. Research-oriented and research-trained clinicians functioning in an applied and clinical setting become a valued commodity. However effective behavioral–psychological approaches alone or in combination with more traditional medical therapies appear to be to the psychological community, their utility must be demonstrated and established on a broader basis. Pain continues to be perceived as an outgrowth of some medical abnormality or disease. For psychology to have parity with more traditional medical interventions, it must continuously establish its clinical and economic efficacy and efficiency.

It would seem only natural in a highly medicalized society that psychology would want to incorporate pharmacological approaches in its armamentarium. If medically trained practitioners can apply psychological therapies, why should psychologists not have the ability to incorporate pharmacological therapies without involving a physician? For example, it would seem logical and useful for a psychologist using behavioral procedures in the treatment of chronic pain to also have the capabilities of prescribing the frequently used and useful analgesics and antidepressants. This would expand the number of practitioners trained to appreciate and address the multifactorial aspects of chronic pain.

Perhaps the proper question is not whether psychologists can or should be licensed to prescribe but, what, in fact, are the educational and training prerequisites. Once these criteria have been established, any clinician satisfying them should be so licensed. This issue has far-reaching philosophical, economical, and practical implications well beyond the scope of this chapter. The issue, however, would clearly suggest that training programs would need to emphasize areas of biochemistry, anatomy, and physiology well beyond the current level.

The viability of psychology in its many forms continues to rely to a certain degree on the business acumen of its practicing clinicians. Marketing strategies, reimbursement protocols, practice management, and liability issues are all part of the business of psychology. The ideal practice would require enough financial resources to support adequate staff and technology not only for patient care but for ongoing analysis of outcomes. As judged by the amount and type of coverage available for psychological therapies, it would appear to have been declared more of a luxury than necessity. Parity with our medical colleagues is more likely to emerge from providing evidence that psychological therapies exceed the notion of "feel-good therapy" and indeed can affect significantly overall disease management, surgical outcomes, and health care costs. All too often the acquisition of practice management and business skills comes from on-the-job training. This, of course, is rather risky; early faulty decisions may have rather dramatic consequences.

The challenges for psychology in many areas, including chronic pain, are obvious. These go beyond the scientific demonstration of the efficacy of psychological therapies. They also include a re-evaluation of what and how graduate students are trained.

Conclusion

The appropriate assessment and treatment of chronic pain, particularly that of noncancer origin, poses a plethora of issues. The spectrum of treatments, both invasive and noninvasive, continues to grow. Debate over their relative effect persists. Patient selection remains paramount. Assessment leading to the development of a treatment algorithm emphasizing the treatment–outcome–reassessment–treatment cycle should be encouraged over a prediction model. In the latter case emphasis is placed not on identifying characteristics of the patient leading to treatment development but on preselecting those individuals thought to evidence a greater statistical probability of a good outcome. A statistical approach should not be undertaken at the expense of an individualized approach (Doleys et al., 1998). Each chronic pain patient requires and deserves individual consideration.

Each new therapy brings with it new hope as well as disappointment. Although the American Pain Society and IASP have been in existence for several decades, our understanding of pain is in its infancy. The relationship between the sensory and affective components remains a mystery. Its definition is clouded by examining a system that is constantly changing. Such plasticity has inherent advantages but complicates understanding. The mechanism by which we appreciate the contribution of behavioral–psychological and nonpsychological factors continues to evolve.

References

Ader, R. (1997). Processes underlying placebo effects: The preeminence of conditioning. *Pain Forum, 6,* 56–58.

American Psychiatric Association. (1994). *Diagnostic and statistical manual of mental disorders* (4th ed.). Washington, DC: Author.

American Medical Association. (1999). *Current procedural terminology*. Chicago, IL: Author.

Ballas, S. K. (1998). *Sickle cell pain: Progress in pain research and management* (Vol. 11). Seattle, WA: International Association for the Study of Pain Press.

Blakely, S. (1998, April) Fighting fraud in worker's comp. *Nation's Business*, pp. 14–22.

Block, A. R. (1996). *Pre-surgical psychological screening in chronic pain syndromes: A guide for the behavioral health practitioner*. Hillsdale, NJ: Erlbaum.

Blum, S. L., & Lubenow, T. (1996). Neurolytic agents. *Current Review of Pain, 1,* 70–78.

Chesher, G. B. (1990). Understanding the opioid analgesics and their effects on skilled performance. *Alcohol, Drugs and Driving, 2,* 111–138.

Compas, B. E., Haaga, D. A., Keefe, F. J., Leitenberg, H., & Williams, D. A. (1998). Sampling of empirical supported psychological treatments from health psychology: Smoking, chronic pain, cancer, and bulimia nervosa. *Journal of Clinical and Consulting Psychology, 66,* 89–112.

Cousins, M. J. (1999). Pain: The past, present, and future of anesthesiology? *Anesthesiology, 91,* 538–551.

Derbyshire, S. W. G., Jones, A. K. P., Guylai, F., Clark, S., Townsend, D., & Firestone, L. L. (1997). Pain processing during 3 levels of noxious stimulation produces differential patterns of central activity. *Pain, 75,* 431–445.

Doleys, D. M., & Doherty, D. C. (2000). Psychological/behavioral assessment. In P. P. Raj (Ed.), *Practical management of pain* (3rd ed.). Philadelphia: Mosby.

Doleys, D. M., Lowery, D., & Brown, J. (1998). *Comparison of treated and untreated worker's compensation patients with chronic pain*. Unpublished manuscript, Pain and Rehabilitation Institute, Birmingham, AL.

Doleys, D. M., Murray, J. B., Klapow, J. C., & Colton, M. A. (1997). Psychological assessment. In M. A. Ashburn & L. J. Rice (Eds.), *The management of pain* (pp. 27–49). New York: Churchill Livingston.

Federico, J. V. (1996). *The cost of pain centers: Where is the return?* In M. J. Cohen & J. N. Campbell (Eds.), *Pain treatment centers at a crossroads: A practical and conceptual reappraisal*. Seattle, WA: International Association for the Study of Pain Press.

Feuerstein, M. (1994). Definition of pain. In C. D. Tollison, J. R. Satterthwaite, & J. W. Tollison (Eds.), *Handbook of pain management* (2nd ed.). Baltimore: Williams & Wilkins.

Fillingim, R. B., Maixner, W., Kincaid, S., & Silva, S. (1998). Sex differences in temporal summation but not sensory-discriminative processing of thermal pain. *Pain, 75,* 121–129.

Fishbain, D. A., Cutler, R. B., Rosomoff, H. L., & Steele-Rosomoff, R. (1997). Pain facilities: A review of their effectiveness and referral selection criteria. *Current Review of Pain, 1,* 107–115.

Fordyce, W. E. (1976). *Behavioral methods in chronic pain and illness*. St. Louis, MO: Mosby.

Fordyce, W. E. (Ed.). (1995). *Back pain in the work place*. Seattle, WA: International Association for the Study of Pain Press.

Joranson, D. E. (1997). Is methadone maintenance the last resort for some chronic pain patients? *American Pain Society Bulletin, 7,* 1–5.

Keefe, F., & Block, A. R. (1982). Development of an observational method of assessing pain behavior in chronic low back pain patients. *Behavior Therapy, 13,* 363–370.

Kerns, R. D., Turk, C. C., & Rudy, T. (1985). The West Haven–Yale Multidimensional Pain Inventory (WHYMPI). *Pain, 23,* 245–256.

Klapow, J. C., Fillingim, R. B., & Doleys, D. M. (1998). *Chronic pain*. In P. M. King (Ed.), *Sourcebook of occupational rehabilitation* (pp. 369–388). New York: Plenum.

Krames, E. S. (1997). Intraspinal opiates for non-malignant pain. *Current Review of Pain, 1,* 198–212.

Lamberg, L. (1998). Venus orbits closer to pain than Mars: Rx for one sex may not benefit the other. *Journal of the American Medical Association, 1280,* 120–124.

Leigh, J. P., Markowitz, S. B., Fahs, M., Shin, C., & Landrigan, P. J. (1997). Occupational injury and illness in the United States; estimates of cost, morbidity and mortality. *Archives of Internal Medicine, 157,* 1557–1568.

Liebeskind, J. C. (1991). Pain can kill. *Pain, 44,* 3–4.

Linton, S. J. (1998). The socioeconomic impact of chronic back pain: Is anyone benefiting? *Pain, 75,* 163–178.

Linton, S. J., & Bradley, L. A. (1996). Strategies for the prevention of chronic pain. In R. J. Gatchel & D. C. Turk (Eds.), *Psychological approaches to pain management: A practitioner's handbook* (pp. 438–457). New York: Guilford Press.

Loeser, J. D. (1980). Perspective on pain. In P. Turner (Ed.), *Proceedings of the first role of congress in clinical pharmacology and therapeutics*. London, England: Macmillan.

Long, D. M. (1997). *Contemporary diagnosis and management of pain*. Neutown, PA: Handbooks in Health Care.

McMahon, M. J., Gatchel, R. J., Polatin, P. B., & Mayer, T. G. (1997). Early childhood abuse in chronic spinal disorder patients. *Spine, 22,* 2408–2415.

Merskey, H., & Bogduk, M. (1994). *Classification of chronic pain: Description of chronic pain syndromes and definition of pain terms* (2nd ed.). Seattle, WA: International Association for the Study of Pain Press.

Molloy, R. E., & Benzon, H. T. (1996). The current status of epidural steroids. *Current Review of Pain, 1,* 61–69.

Niv, D., & Devor, M. (1996). Preemptive analgesia in the relief of post-operative pain. *Current Review of Pain, 1,* 79–91.

Office of Equal Opportunity. (1990). *The Americans With Disabilities Act: Your responsibilities as an employer*. Washington, DC: Author.

Portenoy, R. K. (1990). Opioid therapy in non-malignant pain. *Journal of Pain and Symptom Management, 5,* S46–S62.

Portenoy, R. K. (1996). Opioid analgesics. In R. K. Portenoy & R. M. Kanner (Eds.), *Pain management: Theory and practice* (pp. 248–276). Philadelphia: Davis.

Portenoy, R. K. (1998). *Contemporary diagnosis and management of pain in oncologic and AIDS patients*. Neutown, PA: Handbooks in Health Care.

Portenoy, R. K., & Kanner, R. M. (1996). Non-opioid and adjuvant analgesics. In R. K. Portenoy & R. M. Kanner (Eds.), *Pain management: Theory in practice* (pp. 219–247). Philadelphia: Davis.

Porzelius, J. (1995). Memory for pain after nerve-block injection. *Clinical Journal of Pain, 11,* 112–120.

Price, B. D., & Fields, H. L. (1997). What are the causes of placebo analgesia? A behavioral experiential analysis. *Pain Forum, 6,* 44–52.

Rainville, P., Duncan, G. H., Price, D. D., Carrier, B., & Bushnell, M. C. (1997). Pain affect encoded in human anterior cingulate but not somatosensory cortex. *Science, 277,* 968–971.

Robinson, M. E., Myers, C. D., Sadler, I. J., Riley, J. L., Kvaal, S. A., & Geysser, M. E. (1997). Bias effects in 3 common self report pain assessment measures. *Clinical Journal of Pain, 13,* 74–81.

Root, T. M., Weaver, M. A., & Hahn, M. B. (1998). Implantation therapy for pain management. In M. A. Ashburn & L. J. Rice (Eds.), *The management of pain* (pp. 419–446). New York: Churchill Livingstone.

Rosenstiel, A. K., & Keefe, F. J. (1983). The use of coping strategies in chronic low back pain patients: Relationship of patient characteristics and current adjustment. *Pain, 17,* 33–43.

Saberski, L. R. (1996). Spinal epiduroscopy: Current concepts. In S. D. Waldman & A. P. Winnie (Eds.), *Interventional pain management* (pp. 137–150). Philadelphia: W. B. Sanders.

Sanders, S. H. (1995). Risk factors for the occurrence of low back pain and chronic disability. *American Pain Society Bulletin, 5,* 1–6.

Sarno, J. E. (1991). *Healing back pain: The mind-body connection*. New York: Warner Books.

Savage, S. R. (1996). Long-term opioid therapy (assessment of consequences and risks). *Journal of Pain and Symptom Management, 11,* 274–286.

Shetter, A. G. (1997). Spinal cord stimulation in the treatment of chronic pain. *Current Review of Pain, 1,* 213–222.

Stangl, J. A., & Loeser, J. D. (1997). Intraspinal opiate infusion therapy in the treatment of chronic non-malignant pain. *Current Review of Pain, 1,* 353–360.

Stein, M. B., Koverola, C., Hanna, C., Torchia, M. G., & McClarty, B. (1997). Hippocampal volume in women victimized by childhood sexual abuse. *Psychological Medicine, 27,* 951–959.

Taricco, A. (1996). Perils of payors: A pain center paradigm. In M. J. Cohen & J. N. Campbell (Eds.), *Pain treatment centers at a crossroads: A practical and conceptual reappraisal* (pp. 109–116). Seattle, WA: International Association for the Study of Pain Press.

Teasell, R. W., & Merskey, H. (1997). Chronic pain disability in the work place. *Pain Forum, 6*, 228–238.

Turk, D. C. (1996). Efficacy of multidisciplinary pain centers in the treatment of chronic pain. In M. J. Cohen & J. N. Campbell (Eds.), *Pain treatment centers at a crossroads: A practical and conceptual reappraisal* (pp. 257–273). Seattle, WA: International Association for the Study of Pain Press.

Turk, D. C., & Fernandez, E. (1997). Cognitive–behavioral management strategies for pain and suffering. *Current Review of Pain, 1*, 99–106.

Turk, D. C., Sist, T. C., Okifuji, A., Miner, M. F., Florio, G., Harrison, P., Massey, J., Lema, M. C., & Zevon, M. A. (1998). Adaptation to metastatic cancer pain, regional/local cancer pain, and non-cancer pain: Role of psychological and behavioral factors. *Pain, 74*, 247–256.

Waldman, S. D., & Winnie, A. P. (Eds.). (1996). *Interventional pain management*. Philadelphia: W. B. Sanders.

Weisberg, J. N., & Keefe, F. J. (1997). Personality disorders in the chronic pain population: Basic concepts, empirical findings and critical implications. *Pain Forum, 6*, 1–9.

Williams, D. A., & Thorn, B. E. (1989). An empirical assessment of pain beliefs. *Pain, 36*, 351–358.

Zacny, J. P. (1995). A review of the effects of opioids on psychomotor and cognitive functioning in humans. *Experimental and Clinical Psychopharmacology, 3*, 432–466.

10

Hearing and Vision Loss

Robert Q Pollard, Jr., Ilene D. Miner, and Joe Cioffi

Rehabilitation psychologists traditionally have not served individuals whose primary disability is hearing or vision loss. For the most part, psychological services to these individuals have been delivered within the special education system or by a small number of specialized treatment programs that emerged over the past few decades. This is changing; the Americans With Disabilities Act (ADA) of 1990 (P. L. 101-336) has improved access to higher education, employment settings, and health and mental health services to people with hearing or vision loss. Rehabilitation psychologists are now increasingly expected to have expertise in these disability areas and to competently serve consumers who are deaf, blind, and deaf–blind. As the American population ages, rehabilitation psychologists will also serve an increasing number of individuals who are experiencing hearing and vision loss for the first time in their lives—a different dynamic and service issue in comparison to those who have grown up with deafness or blindness. Scholarship in psychology and hearing and vision loss has also increased greatly over the past few decades, and the well-trained rehabilitation psychologist should be aware of advancements in these areas.

Unless one routinely works or lives with people who have hearing or vision loss, it is difficult to appreciate the many historical, social, and medical–technical factors that shape their experiences and their relationships with professionals. There are great differences between and among people who are deaf, blind, and deaf–blind; however, one common denominator is the degree to which educational, medical, vocational, and other rehabilitative policies and programs, which affect their lives profoundly, are designed and controlled by people who do not share their disability nor often the priorities and values associated with it. The changing balance of power toward consumers with disabilities is uprooting this inequitable heritage as never before. The first step is to listen and learn, with humility and without assumptions, about life in the consumer's world and his or her views on how psychology can contribute to its improvement.

Deafness

What Is Deafness?

Many deaf Americans bristle at the characterization of deafness as a disability at all, preferring to view their hearing status and, more important, the use of American Sign Language (ASL), as just another example of the country's sociolinguistic diversity (Padden & Humphries, 1988). Although the perception of deaf people as a language and cultural minority is becoming more familiar to the general public (Dolnick, 1993), not all people with hearing loss use ASL or consider themselves members of the Deaf community.[1]

Hearing loss affects over 28 million Americans—about 12% of the population. The majority of these individuals, about 93%, are *hard-of-hearing*, that is, they have sufficient residual hearing allowing them to perceive human speech to some effective degree. The remaining 7%, about 2 million Americans, are deaf.

The word *deaf* can have an audiological or sociocultural meaning. Audiologically, it refers to a degree of hearing loss severe enough to render the perception of human speech ineffective for communication. In its sociocultural context, the word deaf (frequently capitalized) indicates association with the Deaf community, its characteristics (e.g., ASL use), and its values. Not all people who are audiologically deaf are Deaf in the sociocultural sense. Many do not know sign language and do not interact with other deaf individuals.

The term *hearing-impaired* has lost favor because of its emphasis on "impairment." In contrast, deaf and *hard-of-hearing* are taken as assertive, unapologetic statements about one's auditory status, leaving open the more important issue of one's broader capacities. Terminology shifts such as this are common among minority groups and reflect important dynamics regarding majority–minority labeling and other social interactions.

Hearing loss affects the older population with much greater frequency than it does young people. Incidence rates rise from 30% to 40% through the 60- and 70-year age brackets. The severity of hearing loss is typically referred to using the terms *mild*, *moderate*, *severe*, and *profound*. Mild hearing loss is typically in the range of 25 to 40 decibels, which would impede the comprehension of more faint speech sounds or speech taking place in noisy environments. Moderate hearing loss of 40 to 65 decibels typically requires use of a hearing aid and close proximity to the speaker or other source of sound for adequate perception. Speech-reading skills become necessary at this level, and knowledge of sign language can be

---

[1]In keeping with contemporary writing practices in the deafness field, the uppercase *D* is used when referring to the deaf population as a specific sociocultural group, and the lowercase *d* is used when a more general reference to people with significant hearing loss is intended. The capitalized term is generally understood as referring to people who have hearing losses in the severe to profound range, prefer to communicate in ASL, and otherwise demonstrate social and cultural affiliation with the American Deaf community.

valuable. Severe hearing loss of 65 to 90 decibels typically causes serious disruption in the ability to perceive speech and identify many sounds. Profound hearing loss of greater than 90 decibels essentially precludes the ability to comprehend speech through audition and even the perception of many loud sounds. There are dozens of hearing-loss etiologies, some congenital and some acquired. Genetic factors, illness, injury, and the normal aging process can lead to various types of hearing loss. Some of these etiologies lead to hearing loss exclusively, whereas others lead to hearing and vision loss in combination or coincident disabilities of many other sorts.

Although knowledge about hearing loss per se is useful, it is knowledge about communication that is most important in interacting with people who are deaf and hard-of-hearing. Communication strategies and preferences differ widely and are not easily predicted by knowledge of an individual's hearing status alone. Residual hearing, visual cues from the environment (including speech reading), sign language (if known), and writing are all potential avenues of communication that the deaf and hard-of-hearing population uses, but the effectiveness of these modalities depends as well on the knowledge and behavior of the other party in the communication exchange. Unfortunately, misinformation abounds in the general public's perceptions about speech reading, sign language, and English fluency in the deaf and hard-of-hearing population.

Communication Assumptions and Realities

"Lip Reading"

The general public assumes that deaf people are adept at understanding human speech by watching lip movements. In the majority of cases, this is a grossly overblown assumption. "Can you read lips?" is not a yes-or-no question. *Speech reading* (a term preferred over *lip reading* because it emphasizes that data other than lip movements contribute to more effective comprehension of what is being said) is a difficult and tiring endeavor that depends as much on the speaker and the situation as on the talents of the deaf individual. A mere 30% of English speech sounds even appear on the lips; the rest is entirely guesswork. That guesswork is enhanced by a good viewing situation, a greater degree of residual hearing, familiarity with the topic, and fluency in English. Unfortunately, childhood deafness is typically associated with limitations in English fluency (see below), making the guesswork of speech reading more difficult.

Sign Language

Common assumptions regarding sign language are that it is a form of mime, a form of English produced manually, concrete in nature and therefore limited in what it can convey, used by deaf people internationally, and easily learned. None of these assumptions is true. The richness and complexity of signed languages are documented in a growing body of linguistic research that began in the 1960s (Valli & Lucas, 1992). Signed languages use the three-dimensional modality in ways that bear no relation to spoken languages. Linguistic elements are represented not only by the signs themselves but also by changes in their speed, placement, and direction of movement. Space around the signer's body can be assigned semantic meaning and incorporated into signed conversations. Facial expressions and body posture add other linguistic (not mime) elements. Different signed languages have evolved in different countries, as different spoken languages have. True signed languages are not "invented" and are not based on a country's spoken language. However, signed representations of spoken languages (e.g., Signed Exact English) have been invented by educators in efforts to teach spoken languages to deaf children. Invented sign systems have not delivered on their initial promises regarding English language acquisition in deaf education for complex reasons (Lane, Hoffmeister, & Bahan, 1996; Walworth, Moores, & O'Rourke, 1992).

ASL is the sign language used by deaf people throughout most of North America. ASL signs represent concepts, whether abstract or concrete; they do not represent English words per se. For example, the various meanings of the English word *run* are expressed by dissimilar signs in ASL. The syntax and grammar of ASL are also unlike English. Like German, ASL verbs are often at the end of sentences; like Spanish, ASL adjectives follow the nouns they modify; like Hebrew, ASL does not use certain forms of the verb "to be"; and like Navajo and Bantu, some subject–verb–object combinations are communicated by single signs. Given such complexities, it is no surprise that it takes as much time and practice to become fluent in ASL as it does to become fluent in any foreign language.

English Fluency

Perhaps the most widespread assumption about deaf people, and the one most difficult to correct, is that most deaf individuals are expected to be fluent in English. In reality, reading and writing are a challenge for many deaf people. The earlier and more profound the hearing loss, the more difficult it is to learn a spoken language, including its written form, because spoken languages are not meant to be acquired through the visual modality. In the primary school years, reading and writing are taught through oral instruction to children who are already proficient, if not fluent, in that spoken language. Competency in (and knowledge about) the spoken language comes first for hearing children; reading and writing comes second. Few deaf children arrive at school fluent in English. How would they have learned it? Speech reading is no adequate means for acquiring early competency in a spoken language. That deaf children would have difficulty mastering reading and writing skills without a solid foundation of English competency would seem to make sense. However, many people wrongly assume that because reading and writing are "visual," they should present no barrier to the deaf student.

More than a century of international deaf education efforts have not yielded truly effective methods for teaching spoken languages to deaf children. The history and intensity of controversy over language education methods are the first things one learns about when entering the deafness field (Marschark, 1997). Research (and arguing) continues, but until advancements in deaf education are more fully realized, the average reading level of deaf adults in the United States remains at about the 4th-grade level, although the distribution of English fluency in the deaf population is wide.

Historical Perspective

Deaf Education

In the world of deaf people or services to deaf people, the legacy and ongoing struggles surrounding deaf education comprise a fundamental, palpable dynamic that must be understood. The central argument has always been whether sign language should have a place in the education and lives of deaf people, especially deaf children.

Aristotle's pronouncement that thought was not possible in the absence of speech, and that deaf people were therefore uneducable (and literally less than human), quashed any thought of the value of deaf education until sporadic efforts began in the 16th century. The first school for the deaf was founded in Paris in 1775 and used manual (signed) methods of instruction. Deaf education in Germany (and later in England) used oral methods exclusively; signed communication was not allowed. Teachers in these countries became rivals, and their differing methods were debated at exhibitions and professional conventions.

Deaf education in the United States began with the founding of the American School for the Deaf in Hartford, Connecticut, in 1817. This school, too, used the manual communication method practiced in France but influenced by the indigenous ASL of the time. Graduates of the American School frequently became teachers of the deaf themselves, and many established other deaf schools that used sign language methods. By the late 1800s, there were over 70 schools for the deaf in the United States, the majority of which employed deaf teachers and used sign language as the primary means of instruction.

The first American oral-method school, the Clarke School, was established in Northampton, Massachusetts, in 1867. This approach, too, began to garner American supporters, the most active being Alexander Graham Bell, who came to lead the international movement for oral deaf education. Bell also published papers on eugenics, advocating that deafness be bred out of the population through legislation prohibiting the marriage of deaf people.

On both sides of the Atlantic, the oral–manual controversy raged. A meeting of professionals was held in Milan, Italy, in 1880 to consider the dispute. Although the Congress of Milan was attended by few proponents of manual education, the attendees voted that oral instruction should be the exclusive method of choice for educating deaf children. Within a short time, virtually all American schools converted to an oral-only philosophy. Deaf teachers were fired and hearing people exclusively employed in the education of deaf children. Students were forbidden to use sign language in most schools, even in the dormitories (although it survived in secret and in adult Deaf communities).

The return of sign language to deaf education classrooms in America has been a slow process and is still nowhere near as widespread as it was in the late 1800s: Deaf teachers remain a rarity because of barriers to higher education and employment that the deaf have historically faced. Ironically, to earn certification as a teacher of the deaf, no sign language skills or knowledge of Deaf history or sociocultural issues are typically required.

Legislative initiatives have been another source of controversy in deaf education. The most significant, the Education for All Handicapped Children's Act of 1975 (usually referred to as P. L. 94-142), required a "free and appropriate public education" for children with disabilities. Although education was available at schools for the deaf long before, it was not mandated. More importantly, the act popularized *mainstreaming*, the practice of educating students in local schools or classrooms (*inclusion*) along with students who do not have disabilities. Mainstreaming was viewed by many as the proper means of achieving the "least restrictive environment" also required by the law. After its passage, enrollment at schools for the deaf across America rapidly and markedly diminished. Some were closed, a trend that continues to this day. The weakening of the traditional deaf school system is an abomination to the Deaf community, for deaf schools are where ASL fluency and Deaf sociocultural values have been passed from generation to generation, not to mention the place where lifelong ties with friends and associates in the Deaf community are first formed.

Although educating children with disabilities alongside children who do not have disabilities remains a popular concept to many, mainstreaming for deaf students raises questions because of the communication and social isolation that frequently result. Opponents of mainstreaming for deaf students emphasize the importance of being able to freely and directly communicate with all of one's peers and teachers. They view a broad and readily accessible communication environment, inside and outside the classroom, as essential to both learning and socialization. They argue that a critical mass of deaf students and educational and extracurricular programs designed for deaf students constitute the only proper definition of a least restrictive environment. Advocates of mainstreaming cite different philosophical values favoring inclusion and point out the frequent need for children at schools for the deaf to reside on campus, away from their families, during the weekdays or sometimes longer. The oral–manual controversy also is close to the surface in most debates about mainstreaming.

The legacy of hearing people's control of the institution of deaf education has left a deep scar on the fabric of deaf–hearing relations that continues to this day. Many deaf people have felt long oppressed by hearing people for reasons that include the prohibition of sign language (and even physical punishment for using it), Bell's eugenics, the sterilization and murder of deaf children (and others with disabilities) in Hitler's Germany, and P.L. 94-142's decimation of the deaf school system (Lane, 1992).

Philosophical and Psychological Perspective

Philosophers and psychologists have written about deaf people for centuries (Pollard, 1993). Aristotle's influential pejorative views were previously noted. Scholars such as psychologist William James eventually began to question the equating of thought with speech, but such radical views took years to win acceptance. This shift was critical in altering hearing people's perceptions of deaf people. Previously described as animalistic and incapable of divine redemption, deaf people's humanity and potential were rapidly "legitimized" by this new thinking, paving the way for deaf education and other advancements.

By the late 1800s, deaf education was widespread, and some psychologists took interest in the field. As more hearing psychologists began to work with deaf children, publications about psychology and deaf people appeared with increasing frequency. Many of these articles were pejorative and were based purely on speculation. Few, if any, authors were fluent in sign language or familiar with well-functioning deaf adults.

After the turn of the century, Rudolf Pintner emerged as the leading psychologist in the deafness field. Pintner and his colleagues at Columbia University developed numerous tests of cognitive and personality functioning for use with deaf children. His interests were wider than deaf education. He lobbied for the psychological study of many aspects of hearing loss and for advancements in psychological services to deaf children and adults (National Research Council, 1929). Soon other psychologists outside deaf education began writing about deaf people. Most had little direct experience with deaf individuals and no knowledge of sign language or healthy deaf adult lifestyles. The growing body of literature was contradictory and unhelpful to deaf education professionals, and their respect for psychological research diminished. Pintner, Helmer Myklebust, and other prominent psychologists writing through the first half of this century also reported that psychological testing methods showed that deaf people were intellectually and psychosocially inferior to hearing people. Harlan Lane (1984, 1988, 1992) is an articulate critic of psychology's contribution to the deaf oppression legacy.

The next generation of psychologists began to view deaf people differently, in light of early investigations into the linguistics of ASL, and took issue with the methods and conclusions of their predecessors. McCay Vernon provided convincing evidence of the normal intellectual abilities of deaf people when unbiased assessment measures were used. He was also a pioneering investigator of variations from normalcy in the deaf population, including psychopathology, learning disabilities, and deaf–blindness. Edna Levine, a rehabilitation psychologist who devoted much of her career to the deafness field, was a tireless advocate for appropriate (including sign fluent) psychological services for deaf people (Levine, 1977). She was instrumental in directing postwar rehabilitation funding to deaf population services and founding the first inpatient psychiatric program for deaf patients in New York City in 1955.

By the late 1960s, five prominent mental health programs for deaf patients had been established in the United States and England. The research emanating from these programs and influential lawsuits and legislative initiatives protecting the rights of deaf psychiatric patients led to wider recognition of the need for specialized inpatient and outpatient services for this population. Many specialized programs now exist (Willigan & King, 1992).

Issues in Psychology Regarding Deaf or Hard-of-Hearing People

Professional Development

The types of psychologists most likely to encounter deaf and hard-of-hearing individuals are school psychologists, clinical psychologists, psychologists who work with vocational rehabilitation agencies, and those who work with elderly populations or people with medical or developmental disabilities commonly associated with hearing loss. Psychologists may be asked to render a broad range of assessment and treatment services to this diverse population. In most cases, doing so requires special expertise, especially when the individual uses sign language, is severely or profoundly deaf, or has visual or other disabilities as well.

The Spartanburg Conference on the Functions, Competencies and Training of Psychological Service Providers to the Deaf (Levine, 1977) specified the knowledge, practical experience, sign fluency, and other qualifications that psychologists ought to have if they seek to serve the deaf population competently. The importance and scarcity of these qualifications have been recently affirmed in another large-scale review of the field (Myers, 1995). Psychologists must weigh carefully their knowledge and communication competencies before providing services to deaf and hard-of-hearing people, in keeping with the ethical mandate not to practice outside of one's areas of expertise. Although some specialized programs have emerged to teach such competencies, the majority of psychologists who come in contact with deaf children and adults lack adequate preparation. There is a growing awareness that psychologists providing services to deaf individuals must not only master the essential knowledge base of their profession but also become proficient in sign language and gain knowledge and experience with the Deaf community that leads to "cross-cultural legitimacy" (Pollard, 1996). The few specialized training programs that exist in the field (e.g., at Gallaudet University in Washington, DC, and the University of Rochester Medical Center in New York) reflect these values and are also training an increasing number of deaf students, a long overdue development.

Continuing education opportunities for psychologists are available through conferences such as the biennial meeting of the American Deafness and Rehabilitation Association (ADARA), the periodic Breakout conferences on psychosocial rehabilitation for deaf people with mental illness, meetings of the European Society on Deafness and Mental Health, and other national and regional conferences. Membership in ADARA and the Special Interest Section on Deafness of the Division of Rehabilitation Psychology (Division 22) of the American Psychological Association are the best means for psychologists to remain abreast of such educational offerings. Meetings of other national organizations, such as the National Association of the Deaf, the American Society for Deaf Children, the Alexander Graham Bell Association, Self Help for Hard of Hearing People (SHHH), and the Convention of American Instructors of the Deaf, also offer valuable learning opportunities for psychologists.

The majority of scholarship in this area appears outside the mainstream psychology press in lesser known publications such as the *American Annals of the Deaf*, *JADARA*, and the *Journal of Deaf Studies and Deaf Education*. Computer searches therefore may not yield references to the majority of articles written by specialists in the deafness field. Newer books and book chapters written by professionals in the field remain a good starting point for professional education (e.g., Braden, 1994; Elliott, Glass, & Evans, 1988; Glickman & Harvey, 1996; Harvey, 1989; Lane, 1992; Lane et al., 1996; Marschark, 1997; Marschark & Clark, 1998; Vernon & Andrews, 1990)

Areas Needing Psychology's Attention

Beyond improvements in professional education for both deaf and hearing psychologists, our field could do much to contribute toward the betterment of the lives of deaf and hard-of-hearing people. Access to quality mental health services remains unavailable to most deaf individuals in this country and inadequate for the rest. Flat rejection from service programs, misdiagnosis, and iatrogenic treatments (treatments that do more harm than good) are common. Interpreter services are often limited, poor in quality, or both and do not adequately substitute for direct communication with providers (Brauer, 1990; Pollard, 1998). Few mental health professionals outside the small deafness field are aware of how diagnosis and treatment interventions need to be adjusted for the sensory, language, and sociocultural variations of this population (Glickman & Harvey, 1996; Harvey, 1989; Pollard, 1998). Change is coming slowly through greater visibility of deaf population issues in professional meetings and organizations (e.g., the Special Interest Section on Deafness in the American Psychological Association and the Caucus of Psychiatrists Working With Deaf and Hard-of-Hearing Persons in the American Psychiatric Association) and through legal interventions such as ADA lawsuits and the consent decree (Pollard, 1996; Raifman & Vernon, 1996a, 1996b).

The struggles that Deaf individuals face in the mental health care arena are arguably overshadowed by the far greater number of hard-of-hearing and late-deafened people who lack access to psychologists knowledgeable about their unique social and mental health needs. When hearing loss first occurs in adulthood, it often stimulates emotional and social adjustment concerns not commonly experienced by people who have been deaf or hard-of-hearing from an early age. Depression symptoms are common, especially when other disabling conditions are present (Pollard, 1998; Trychin, 1991), and family relations are often strained by communication difficulties. The communication and sociocultural characteristics and preferences of late-deafened and hard-of-hearing people also frequently differ from those of the Deaf population. Most do not use sign language, and many are less adept at speech reading than their peers with longer experience with hearing loss. Assertive interpersonal communication strategies and the use of technology (e.g., an array of assistive listening devices) are vital to communication in traditional "hearing" social settings where others are not used to accommodating hearing loss. Through the advocacy of such groups as SHHH and the Association of Late-Deafened Adults (ALDA), rehabilitation and clinical psychologists are beginning to attend to the unique needs of late-deafened and hard-of-hearing people. There is a growing body of literature offering guidance to both consumers and professionals on later onset hearing loss (Dugan, 1997).

Blindness

What Is Blindness?

Difficulties in visual functioning arise from many causes and lead to a variety of conditions and life consequences. The two most commonly disrupted functions are visual acuity and visual field. *Visual acuity* is how clearly one sees in the central area of vision (i.e., looking straight ahead). Acuity can be impaired by nearsightedness, farsightedness, cataracts, and other conditions. *Visual field* refers to peripheral vision in all directions, not just side-to-side as is commonly thought. Normal visual fields are 180° laterally, 70° upward, and 60° downward (with the eyeball stationary). Visual field can be impaired by retinitis pigmentosa (RP; see below), glaucoma, macular degeneration, and other conditions. The severity of impairments of visual acuity and visual field and the degree of disruption they lead to in life activities can be diverse. The terms *blindness*, *visual impairment*, and *vision loss* provide little specific information about such variations in physical and functional experience.

In the United States, an estimated 1.1 million people are *legally blind*; this term implies visual acuity no greater than 20/200 in the better eye, with correction, or visual fields no greater than 20°. Four percent of those who are legally blind are younger than age 20, 31% are between ages 20 and 64, and the remaining 65% are over age 65 (Prevent Blindness America, 1997). As with hearing loss, vision loss can be of congenital onset, resulting from genetic conditions, prenatal infections, or other causes, or it may be acquired later in life through injury or illness. Some genetic etiologies of blindness have a delayed onset (e.g., RP).

The leading causes of blindness worldwide are cataract, *trachoma* (a chronic infection of the eye, common in tropical areas and places with poor sanitation), and glaucoma (World Health Organization, 1997). These three conditions are eminently treatable and, in some cases, preventable. In the United States, glaucoma and diabetic retinopathy are the two leading causes of blindness. They are also partially preventable and treatable. Other common causes of blindness in the United States are age-related macular degeneration and retinal diseases such as RP.

Cataracts cause the lens of the eye to become opaque and are often accompanied by *nystagmus* (involuntary, rhythmic eye movements), leading to poor visual acuity and problems with glare. Cataracts are commonly associated with advancing age (*senile cataracts*). Macular degeneration, another common cause of age-related blindness, results from a retinal disease associated with loss of central visual field, leading to a large central blind spot (*scotoma*). Glaucoma results from dysfunction in the ordinary processes of cleansing the eye and draining toxins. Intraocular pressure builds up, causing tissue damage and pain. Characteristics of glaucoma include acute sensitivity to light and decrease in peripheral visual fields, which can be progressive, leading to total blindness. Injuries or illnesses can result in traumatic cases of blindness at any age. Examples include cataracts stemming from head or eye injury or retinal detachment related to injury or a secondary condition such as diabetes retinopathy. Congenital disorders such as rubella or Marfan's or Down syndromes may also be associated with some degree of blindness.

Although RP is a hereditary condition, its symptoms usually do not appear until childhood or later. RP involves deterioration of retinal cells, beginning with the rods in the periphery and progressing to the cones in the macula. Night vision is affected first, and then decreases in the visual fields become apparent. A worsening degree of *tunnel vision* (narrowed visual fields) continues, often until there is total blindness. When RP occurs with hearing loss of congenital or later onset, this condition is known as Usher syndrome. Usher syndrome, a group of genetic disorders that are the leading cause of adult deaf–blindness in the United States, is discussed at length in the deaf-blindness section of this chapter.

Historical Perspective

From 1830 to 1860, "asylums" and other welfare programs were established across the United States to address the needs of people who were poor and infirm. Schools for the blind were established in nearly every state by the mid-1800s. The first was the Perkins School for the Blind, near Boston, founded in 1829, which became a model for many other schools. However, graduates from these schools were frequently unable to find work. Seeking to assist the employment needs of their graduates, some schools organized sheltered workshop programs, where blind workers were given few options other than simple manual labor such as the production of brooms, brushes, cushions, pillows, and mattresses. The first sheltered workshop was established in 1937; many more followed.

Some of the early developments in vocational rehabilitation for blind people were, in part, a response to blinded veterans who returned home after both World War I and II. Legislation was passed to ensure that rehabilitation and vocational training would be provided to these veterans. Following World War II, the high number of blinded veterans led to the development of more formalized training programs at military hospitals. Blinded soldiers began to receive "foot travel" instruction (later termed *orientation and mobility*). Over time, these instructional efforts led to the establishment of over a dozen teacher-training programs in blindness education at graduate schools across the country. Postwar efforts to instruct blind individuals in orientation and mobility were also influenced by the guide dog movement, which was flourishing in Germany. The Seeing Eye, Inc., the first American guide dog school, was founded in 1929.

Legislation has led to improved services for individuals who are blind. The Vocational Rehabilitation Act of 1920 defined "homemaker" as a legitimate occupation. With this as a formalized (although excessively modest) vocational goal, training and guidance services became more widely available to blind people through vocational rehabilitation funding. In 1936, the Randolph–Sheppard Act authorized states to license qualified blind people to operate vendor stands. This led to further vocational training and fiscal support. The Randolph–Sheppard Act was amended in 1974 (P. L. 93-651) to broaden economic opportunities for individuals who are blind. In the middle and latter parts of this century, the Education for All Handicapped Children Act of 1975 and the ADA led to even more educational, vocational, and social opportunities for the blind population. However, as with deaf education, the mainstreaming emphasis associated with P. L. 94-142 resulted in decreased enrollments at schools for the blind in favor of educational placements in local school district programs, with its attendant consequences.

Service Issues

The educational environment for students who are blind is different than it was in the first half of this century. The mainstreaming–inclusion thrust spurred by P. L. 94-142 has led to many more blind students being served in public schools than in special schools. As in deaf education, there is considerable debate over the appropriateness and effectiveness of mainstreaming as opposed to specialized educational programs for blind students. Although mainstreaming (and inclusion) has its advocates, negative consequences of this shift have included greater isolation of blind students from blind peer and adult role models; less emphasis on Braille literacy, mobility training, and other special services for blind children; and more frequent instruction by teachers who are not specifically trained in the educational needs of blind students. Another consequence of mainstreaming is that it leads more readily accommodated blind students to the public schools, increasing the proportion of students with multiple disabilities enrolling in schools for the blind (and deaf). Then, whether in the mainstream or in special schools, students frequently encounter teachers who are inadequately trained to work with their unique needs, and they rarely encounter blind adult role models.

The legal definition of blindness is a somewhat arbitrary and quantitative measure chosen to help states determine who is eligible to receive vision rehabilitation services. Unfortunately, this definition does not adequately address one's functional capacities or needs. Some people whose vision characteristics do not meet the legal, quantitative definition of blindness nevertheless are unable to use their vision to carry out important life activities. Teenagers with Usher syndrome and severe night blindness often do not qualify as being legally blind yet may have serious accidents under low light conditions and be unable to travel safely alone in the evenings. These and other people whose visual impairments do not meet the acuity and visual field definitions of blindness are precluded from receiving available services (e.g., mobility training) that may assist them greatly. They either disengage from these important functional activities or find alternative ways to accomplish them without training or assistance. Just as the federal government and some states have moved toward a functional rather than quantitative definition (e.g., diagnosis and IQ) of developmental disability, definitions of blindness should reflect one's ability, or lack thereof, to accomplish important life objectives using vision.

Another weakness in the definition of legal blindness is that it does not address progressive conditions that are certain to result in severe visual impairment or total blindness. For individuals with progressive visual disease, an early program of information and education to prepare for the impending loss of vision would be most valuable. Yet such programs are unavailable until the vision loss progresses to a point that satisfies the legal definition of blindness. Each state has a Commission for the Blind (although it may go by another name), which is responsible for providing a range of vision rehabilitation and vocational services to blind youth and adults. Eligibility for these services is determined by one's having met the legal definition of blindness. As might be expected, such policies are most damaging to those of low income, who have no other option but to wait until they meet the restrictive legal criteria for receiving state and federal services; by then, however, a crisis has already developed.

The services that may be appropriate for someone with vision loss require an individualized assessment and cannot be determined simply by a diagnosis or an acuity measurement. Services may include Braille instruction, orientation and mobility training, low-vision services and equipment, the support of role models, professional and peer counseling, and training in alternative techniques for engaging in various tasks ordinarily accomplished through visual means. This training should be provided by qualified professionals.

Sociopolitical Organizations

The National Federation of the Blind (NFB) was founded in 1940 and is the largest organization of blind people in the United States, with an estimated membership of 50,000 and over 700 local chapters. The NFB's mission is "to help blind persons achieve self-confidence and self-respect, and to act as a vehicle for collective self-expression by the blind." One of the early issues taken up by the NFB was the limited and often demeaning vocational options offered by state vocational rehabilitation agencies. For many years, employment for a blind individual meant working at miserably low wages in rote menial labor activities, such as making brooms or mats. Administrators at such work sites received much higher salaries than the workers, who were typically paid less than minimum wage with no benefits. The NFB has led the fight against such unacceptable employment conditions. This advocacy continues to the present day; strikes and other actions still take place as a result of inequities in labor settings that employ blind people. The NFB has also launched many educational campaigns to instruct the public about the facts of blindness and to overcome ignorance, bias, discrimination, and pejorative attitudes commonly found in the general public. The NFB sponsors several publications, including the *Braille Monitor*, *Reflections*, and *Voice of the Diabetic*.

The America Council of the Blind (ACB) was founded in 1961 and reports a membership numbering in the tens of thousands. Its purposes include advocacy, improving the well-being of blind people, and promoting a greater understanding of blindness and the capabilities of blind people. The ACB publishes a monthly magazine, *Braille Forum*, which has a readership of 26,000 people.

The oldest of the national blindness organizations is the American Foundation for the Blind (AFB), established in 1921. AFB is not a membership organization per se but an affiliation of professionals in the blindness field. Its mission focuses on enabling people who are blind to achieve equal access and opportunity in their communities. The AFB is involved in research funding and support and disseminating information and advice to and about blind people. AFB publishes the *Journal of Vision Impairment and Blindness*.

The blind community's struggle to bring the true needs and priorities of blind people to public light mirrors the struggles the Deaf community has experienced. For both communities, accessibility concerns, educational priorities, and service needs have historically been determined by sighted and hearing individuals who have risen to key positions in the education, rehabilitation, and political institutions that serve these populations but who themselves have limited understanding of blindness or deafness. Often, there has been only token representation by deaf and blind people within these systems. As both groups have learned to network and organize their activities within the disability rights movement, this legacy has rapidly begun to change.

There are also broader similarities among deaf and blind people in terms of socialization experiences and community bonding and values. Although blind people do not share a unique language such as ASL and are therefore less commonly referred to as a *community* or *cultural group* than are deaf people, the memories, social significance, and perceived value of residential education are similar. Residential schools are historically where blind children first meet blind adults, learn mobility and other skills, and develop positive, empowering self-perceptions like those modeled by blind adults. Just as hearing people have historically controlled the deaf education system and frequently diminished access to and valuation of ASL, sighted people have controlled the blind education system and diminished access to and valuation of Braille literacy. Like Deaf leaders, blind leaders are increasingly active in regaining control over the policies and institutions of blind education and vocational training and services. A common rallying point is the need to increase Braille literacy and the presence of Braille in society as a key to independence for blind people.

The Blindness Field

Vaughn (1993) noted that the field of "work for the blind" is undergoing professionalization. As a new profession, it is making efforts to gain legitimacy and recognition from the public at large, and it is spawning the creation of various professional organizations. It is only in the past 50 years that this profession has begun to emerge. Yet, in these years of development, the field has not earned a reputation for seeking input and involvement from blind individuals themselves. If one listens to the status quo representatives of the profession, one hears of great advances and improvements in the field, but if one listens to consumer groups, a different perspective is heard.

One reason for these differing views on progress is that blind people have been largely denied access to the blindness profession and that absence has biased the field's development. Consider the field of orientation and mobility. This discipline focuses on the skills (nonvisual or alternative skills) necessary for safe, independent movement (e.g., cane skills, street-crossing skills, and protective skills as one moves physically through space). One might think that a blind individual who has become proficient in safe community travel would have experience to impart to other blind students who have not yet developed such skills. Yet even if a blind person has become a teacher of academic subjects, good vision is a prerequisite for becoming a certified orientation and mobility instructor. At the same time, sighted instructors in training do not have to develop proficiency in cane and travel skills to become certified. They can simply go through a practicum experience with a cane (and remain low in confidence and unable to independently travel under blindfold) and still be given credentials to teach blind students. This illogic and inequity is beginning to change, in part because of advocacy by the NFB.

One area of progress is the greater recognition of the particular needs of people with low vision. Prior to the 1960s, individuals with low vision were treated in much the same way as those with total blindness. Instead of teaching someone to make optimal use of residual vision, rehabilitation practices often involved occluding low-vision rehabilitation clients and even those with "stable" residual vision. In the past 30 years or more, this situation has changed dramatically. An entire low-vision profession has

developed. Not only are there optometrists with a specific focus and certification in low vision, but there are master's programs in vision rehabilitation training as a low-vision specialist

Society and Families

The rhetoric of blindness education and rehabilitation has been that, with
training, one can lead a full and independent life. The reality, however,
has been far different. The view of the blind consumer movement is that
with proper education and training, blindness can be reduced to a "nui-
sance," and full participation in society, including equitable employment
and functional independence, can be achieved. Handicapping societal and
professional attitudes remain the greatest impediment to these goals.
Some 70% of blind people between ages 21 and 64 remain unemployed
(Kuusisto, 1998). Many others work in conditions that are beneath their
ability and are low paying (Chen, 1998).

Low expectations are often rooted in family dynamics. Blind children
and youth are overwhelmingly raised in sighted families that are unfamiliar with vision loss. (The same dynamic occurs with deaf children.)
Movement is a key factor in any child's exploration of the world, but many
blind children are discouraged from navigating their physical environment. Fearful that the child may be injured, parents are often overprotec-
tive and discourage physical exploration, fostering timidness and dependency. The natural entry into social experiences and relationships that
most youngsters experience also is challenging for blind children, especially when overprotection has been a problem. Most blind children grow
up in environments where there are few other blind youths or adults to
provide experienced-based role modeling or information about how to navigate both the physical and social worlds. This isolation has been aggravated by the mainstreaming trend; access that blind youths (and their
families) might otherwise have had to blind youths and adults in special
schools is typically unavailable to blind children educated in local school
districts. In such situations, parents need active guidance on how to fore-
see, encourage, and foster a capable and bright future for their blind child,
including the development of attitudes and skills for dealing with discrimination and bias that people with disabilities encounter in society. When
such guidance is unavailable from blind people themselves, parents often
develop limited and negativistic expectations, which are naturally picked
up by the child. "The behavior of blind people is not a product of blindness,
or the amount of residual vision, but of socialization" (Vaughn, 1993, p. 4).

Role of Psychologists

As noted earlier in regard to deaf children, school psychologists are most
likely to encounter students who are blind, although other psychologists

may be referred blind students as well. Psychologists' roles on Committees on Special Education (convened periodically for all special education students, including those with disabilities) provide an important forum for advocating for appropriate educational and psychosocial services, especially in mainstream settings that may be ill prepared for serving blind students. Assessments and educational service planning for blind students must include contact with the family. Many families have distorted views of their child's capabilities, needs, and characteristics, which negatively affect parental decisions and the child's and parents' well-being. Family members also may have psychological needs of their own pertaining to how the child's blindness has affected them. Psychologists can have a powerful impact on the future of blind students by intervening at a family system level in addition to consulting with the schools.

Psychologists who work with vocational rehabilitation agencies and programs are more likely to encounter blind youths and young adults. Clinical psychology or rehabilitation psychology professionals may be called on to provide various types of assessment or intervention services. Rehabilitation psychologists often have rich experience working with people with disabilities and are more likely to be able to view blind consumers and their needs in a holistic, nonstereotyped manner. One's knowledge base must include familiarity not only with the psychological literature pertaining to blindness and disability but with the consumer-authored literature as well. These additional sources of information broaden the psychologist's understanding of issues and perspectives important to blind people.

A prepared psychologist can likely identify gaps in many blind consumers' education, social and vocational preparation, and self-esteem that would benefit from appropriate training or counseling interventions. Including the family in assessment and treatment planning is critical, as is fostering connections between consumers, families, and groups and organizations of blind adults. Blind people should be encouraged to pursue their dreams and aspirations, not be led into believing that blindness limits them to modest goals such as routine manual labor or lifelong dependence on public assistance.

Consumers are too frequently discouraged from pursuing higher goals by a lifetime of encountering low expectations, by a lack of exposure to successful blind adult role models, and by agencies that are working on limited budgets and are reticent to encourage vocational goals that require higher education and greater accessibility costs. Psychologists can do much to intervene in each of these problem areas, especially when a fair, thorough, and appropriate assessment has been conducted, one that examines the systems affecting the individual as well as the individual himself or herself. The vocational rehabilitation and Commission for the Blind service institutions are a system. The family is a system. The blind community and its organizations are a system. The individual must be understood and counseled in the context of these important systems and what each contributes to problems or resolutions.

Deaf–Blindness

What Is Deaf–Blindness?

The term *deaf–blindness* is an indistinct descriptor for a variety of combinations of hearing and vision loss. Deaf–blindness can range from a mild loss of both senses to complete loss of both senses and may occur with or without coincident disabling conditions. Deaf–blindness may be of congenital or later onset and may be progressive or sudden. These labels convey little specific information regarding the sensory losses themselves and no information regarding the communication preferences or other functional capabilities of the deaf–blind individual, the nature of the individual's psychosocial experiences or needs, or which of several communities—Deaf, blind, deaf–blind, or "hearing sighted"—the person identifies with. Internationally, there is an increasing acceptance of the nonhyphenated term *deafblind* to describe this population as one dealing with a unique condition, not a "combination" of hearing and vision loss.

Historical Perspective

Most people immediately associate deaf–blindness with Helen Keller (1880–1968), who was born with normal hearing and vision but lost both to an illness at the age of 18 months. Her story has been portrayed in movies, on stage and screen, in biographies, and in her own writings. It was not Helen Keller but Laura Bridgman (1829–1889) who was the first deaf–blind person to receive an education in the United States. In 1837, she enrolled at Perkins School for the Blind, where she eventually acquired a modest level of literacy, although not the fame or academic accomplishments of Keller, who did not arrive at Perkins until 50 years later. Bridgman's education was nevertheless pioneering because it involved the use of a system of tactile signs that would later be refined and used successfully with Keller. Keller's famed teacher, Annie Sullivan Macy (1866–1936), who had a vision impairment and was a Perkins student herself, became interested in deaf–blindness because of the presence of Bridgman at the school.

Although clearly a historic and influential figure, Keller is not representative of deaf–blind people generally. In fact, her legacy has arguably been detrimental to societal understanding of the needs of deaf–blind people and the barriers they routinely face in education and employment. Keller had opportunities and services not available to other deaf–blind people, including wealthy benefactors and a full-time teacher–interpreter–personal assistant (Macy) whose entire life was devoted to service provision to Keller alone. Although she earned a degree from Radcliffe College, it was decades before another deaf–blind person had the opportunity to replicate what Keller accomplished—there were no rehabilitation services available to deaf–blind people at that time, and Keller did not choose to focus on this population in her later advocacy work. Throughout her life, she was far more involved in issues affecting blind people than deaf or other deaf–blind people. She never learned to communicate in sign language, unlike many deaf–blind people today.

Keller's primary identification and advocacy work was with the AFB. Her focus on blindness still affects how services to people who are deaf–blind are conceived and delivered today. Such services generally are rendered by agencies whose primary mission is to serve people who are blind and visually impaired. As noted earlier, all states have a Commission on the Blind and vocational rehabilitation offices that provide services to people who are deaf or have other nonvisual disabilities. In most states, people who are deaf–blind must obtain services through the Commission on the Blind; in other words, legal blindness supersedes other issues, including the communication and other unique needs of the deaf–blind population. Tragically, people with Usher syndrome, the most common cause of deaf–blindness and one associated with a progressive loss of vision, must typically await extensive deterioration of their vision before meeting the legal-blindness criteria of these service agencies, even though the prognosis of deaf–blindness was known much earlier, at a time when educational, vocational, social, and psychological interventions may have been far more effective and efficiently rendered. Even in states like New York, where individuals with deaf–blindness can choose between obtaining services from deaf rehabilitation agencies or blind rehabilitation agencies, this either–or choice is not ideal. Counselors and other service providers at the Commission on the Blind generally cannot communicate in sign language, and employees of the deaf rehabilitation agencies usually do not have sufficient knowledge of vision needs.

In retrospect, the remarkable career of Keller can be viewed as something of a missed opportunity. Rather than championing educational and vocational services for a unique and diverse population of individuals with hearing and vision loss, Keller's impact was to further separate the knowledge and service base needed by people who are deaf–blind into separate "camps," neither of which is fully accessible or appropriate to this population.

Etiologies

More than half of all adult cases of deaf–blindness are caused by Usher syndrome, a genetic condition associated with hearing loss and RP (R. J. H. Smith et al., 1994). As noted, RP is a progressive visual condition associated with night blindness and decreasing visual field. A small tunnel of central vision may remain for a long time, but RP may progress to total blindness. Typically, people with Usher syndrome become legally blind by adolescence, although many retain a degree of useful vision well into their 50s. The specific pattern and rate of vision and hearing loss that occur to a given individual with Usher syndrome cannot be predicted with accuracy.

Three subtypes of Usher syndrome have been identified. Type 1 is associated with congenital deafness (severe to profound), RP, and balance problems related to vestibular dysfunction. Type 2 involves a somewhat lesser (mild to severe) degree of congenital hearing loss that remains fairly stable throughout life, with later onset of RP. Type 3, the most recent type identified, involves progressive loss of both vision and hearing (Parakarinen, Karjalainen, Simola, Laippala & Kaitalo, 1995). About 3–6% of children born deaf have Usher syndrome, Type 1 (R. J. H. Smith et al., 1994), and 3–6% of children born hard-of-hearing have Usher syndrome, Type 2. Type 2 had been thought to be rarer than Type 1, but this belief is no longer held. Accordingly, the total population of people with Usher syndrome is thought to be much higher than previously believed. The incidence of Type 3 is not as well documented.

Prenatal rubella infection is another common cause of deaf–blindness. There is a large population of deaf–blind adults in their 30s who were born during the rubella epidemic of the 1960s. Deaf–blindness can be caused by other prenatal infections as well, such as AIDS and herpes. It also can be caused by prematurity and congenital conditions such as CHARGE association. *CHARGE* refers to a pattern of birth defects where each letter of the term stands for one or more types of abnormalities— *c*oloboma (a cleft-in or incompletely closed eyeball), which can lead to impaired visual field and acuity; *h*eart defects; *a*tresia (blockage, or in some cases narrowing, of the passages that make breathing through the nose possible); *r*etardation of growth or later development; *g*enital and urinary abnormalities; and *e*ar abnormalities and hearing loss. Following birth, a child may develop deaf–blindness through a variety of infections and injuries. Although Usher syndrome is not associated with cognitive impairment, a number of these other causes of deaf–blindness often are.

Problems With Epidemiology

The 1990 Individuals With Disabilities Education Act (IDEA; P. L. 101-476) defines *deaf–blindness* as a combination of vision and hearing impairment that "causes such severe communication problems and other . . . needs that the persons cannot be educated . . . in programs solely for children and youth with hearing impairments, visual impairments or severe disabilities, without supplementary assistance." This unusual definition, which focuses on children with severe learning difficulties, has led educational programs to gear their services for deaf–blind children to those with additional cognitive or physical impairments, not the sizable population of children and youths with Usher syndrome or other deaf–blindness etiologies restricted to hearing and vision loss alone.

There is an annual census of deaf–blind children funded by the Office of Special Education and conducted by Western Oregon University. The 1996 census identified more than 10,000 deaf–blind children, but only 270 were noted as having Usher syndrome. Because Usher syndrome is known to cause over 50% of adult cases of deaf–blindness, this finding represents underidentification of the condition in children. These numbers affect how services are planned and delivered, and children with Usher syndrome remain underserved.

The Helen Keller National Center (HKNC) in New York state is mandated to keep a census of deaf–blind Americans ages 16 years and older. However, because reporting is not required, this count is not accurate. Some deaf–blind people are registered with HKNC by early adulthood; others do not come into contact with affiliated service agencies until middle or late adulthood. Again, the delayed diagnosis of Usher syndrome is a significant factor. Some deaf–blind individuals are never counted in the census because they do not receive services. These difficulties make accurate counts and descriptions of the deaf–blind population elusive. The Rehabilitation Services Administration estimates that there are 41,000 deaf–blind individuals in the United States. If the underidentification of individuals with Usher syndrome is as severe as it seems, the actual number of individuals may be twice as many as previously thought.

Communication and Sociocultural Diversity

The communication and socialization preferences of deaf–blind people vary as a function of the degree and age at onset of their hearing and vision losses, and other factors. Many with Usher syndrome Type 1 grew up in the Deaf community and used ASL or other sign communication modalities until their vision began to fail. Subsequently, these individuals continued to communicate expressively in sign language while their receptive communication may include tactile signing or adaptations of regular signing, depending on the acuity and size of their remaining visual field. Tactile signing involves the deaf–blind "recipient" of the communication holding his or her hands lightly on top of those of the signing "speaker." When communicating with a sighted individual who knows sign language, the deaf–blind individual signs normally.

Socialization, even with other signing individuals, becomes markedly narrowed with progressive loss of vision. Many adults report that friends, deaf and hearing, drift away; the result is overwhelming isolation. Comprehension of group conversations is essentially precluded by advancing RP symptoms, and one-to-one conversations require increased effort and dedication, which is often not forthcoming from other parties (Chiccioli et al., 1994). This blocks an important source of information exchange, which is aggravated by a reduction in access to print media (because of the vision loss) and the difficulties of learning Braille for the first time as a deaf–blind adult, especially when one's English proficiency may be limited already. Isolation from people and from information is a major problem for most deaf–blind individuals. Yet in this Type 1 group, the vision loss is the more acutely felt "disability" (Chiccioli et al., 1994). Deafness often remains a cherished aspect of their identity, and the increasing distance from the Deaf community carries special hardship (Miner, 1997a).

Those with Usher syndrome Types 2 and 3 usually grew up outside the Deaf community and did not learn sign language. The loss of vision and hearing in these populations often leads to a more acute communication and socialization crisis. For these groups, both hearing and vision loss are usually perceived as unwelcome, intrusive disabilities, not as an aspect of identity. Those with Type 2 (stable, moderate to severe hearing loss with RP) begin to lose access to the visual cues used for speech reading. Those with Type 3, who grew up with normal vision and hearing or only mild hearing loss, must simultaneously contend with the decline of both senses and, frequently, turmoil in their families and social circles, which are unaccustomed to making communication or mobility accommodations of any sort. Learning to speech read, use sign language or tactile signing, read Braille, and develop adapted mobility skills while simultaneously dealing with the social and emotional aspects of the loss of one's vision and hearing is a tremendous burden. Unfortunately, the delayed diagnosis of Usher syndrome and the scarcity of education, rehabilitation, and other services geared toward helping people adjust to later onset deaf–blindness leaves most unprepared for the adjustment and learning challenges they face.

Unlike deafness, the incidence of deaf–blindness is not high enough for most cities to have a sizable deaf–blind community. There are a few exceptions, most notably Seattle, WA, which has a large and active deaf–blind community and many more appropriate services than other U.S. cities. A deaf–blind center in Seattle offers a variety of social services, and a popular summer camp is attended by deaf–blind people from around the country. Through effective political advocacy, civic leaders and some public services (e.g., the bus system) have become sensitized and more accommodating to Seattle's deaf–blind residents.

Elsewhere in the United States, however, deaf–blind adults typically identify and socialize with either the Deaf community, hearing-sighted people, or the blind community. This division of socialization choices, based on differing communication characteristics for the most part, has the unfortunate consequence of keeping deaf–blind people throughout most of the United States from meeting and sharing their experiences with one another. The exception to this is the biennial meeting of the American Association of Deaf–Blind (AADB). Typically drawing about 250 participants, the AADB convention fosters social and political networking that keeps participants in contact with one another until the next eagerly awaited reunion. This situation is different than the nature of Deaf communities, which exist cohesively in many small geographic regions, bonded by their larger numbers and common use of ASL. Not only does the separation of deaf–blind people from one another preclude the educational and social–emotional benefits of such communion, but it also diminishes the likelihood that the deaf–blind constituency can conduct effective political and social advocacy. This is another reason why educational and social services for deaf people and blind people are better, more widely available, and becoming more consumer driven than services for deaf–blind people.

Sociopolitical Issues

Even more so than deaf and blind individuals, deaf–blind people have been routinely excluded from the decision and policy-making processes that have shaped their lives. The lack of political cohesiveness noted above is a significant factor, as is the greater stigma of deaf–blindness in society, where the average person's image of deaf–blindness is that of Keller's wild tantrums and later "humanization" by a teacher who is deified in the title of the book, play, and movie *The Miracle Worker* (Gibson, 1984).

The AADB seeks a greater impact on deaf–blind affairs. The organization is open to people with any measure of both hearing and vision loss and is largely composed of people with Usher syndrome, especially Type 1. In addition to the biennial convention, AADB publishes a quarterly magazine. State and regional associations of deaf–blind people, such as those in Seattle and Washington, DC, also engage in advocacy at local and national levels.

Tensions between hearing–sighted professionals and deaf–blind consumers and advocacy groups are as common as they are in the deaf and blind populations. Sometimes, this tension arises from the inability or unwillingness of professionals to communicate directly with deaf–blind individuals, especially those who use sign language, finding communication with parents or significant others easier and more likely to result in consensus with the professional's opinions. Disagreements between and among consumers and professionals regarding the benefits and drawbacks of inclusion versus more homogeneous education and work environments are similar to those noted earlier in this chapter. There are disagreements regarding the degree of service focus given to deaf–blind children with congenital or early onset deaf–blindness and, frequently, other disabilities versus the greater number of youths and adults with progressive deaf–blindness. Conflicts between communities of deaf–blind people and the administrations of rehabilitation centers are similar to those described by Vaughn (1991) in relation to blind consumers and sighted rehabilitation program administrators. Such complaints include limited consumer autonomy and decision control, paternalism, and generic rather than individualized rehabilitation plans. Counterarguments are made, including the benefits of deaf–blind people meeting one another, and deaf–blind role models, in such rehabilitation centers. The quality-of-life benefits of providing trained assistants for deaf–blind people, common in Scandinavia but rare in the United States (outside of Seattle), is another controversy.

Perspectives on Services

The lack of specialized services for people who were deaf–blind left the vast majority unable to access education, employment, and independent living until the rubella epidemic of the 1960s, which resulted in the birth of many deaf and deaf–blind children. Subsequently, additional funding for deaf–blind services began to be allocated, especially as schools found themselves serving larger numbers of children with disabilities after the passage of the Education for All Handicapped Children's Act of 1975. The first and only rehabilitation center specifically established for the deaf–blind population is HKNC, founded in Long Island, New York, in 1976.

HKNC now offers or coordinates a wide array of rehabilitation services through the national center and 10 regional offices in other parts of the United States.

The lack of professional training opportunities for careers in rehabilitation services for deaf–blind people poses another problem. Few who work with this population have specific training and preparation for doing so. Professionals serving deaf–blind people often come from backgrounds pertaining to the deaf or blind populations exclusively. The communication skills and knowledge required to serve deaf–blind people well are unique to this population, not merely extensions or combinations of other skills (hence the growing popularity of the singular term *deafblind*). There is still no degree program for aspiring deaf–blindness rehabilitation professionals. Only short-term training courses exist presently, including those offered by HKNC and Northern Illinois University. There are master's programs for teachers who wish to specialize in deaf–blind education, but these programs tend to be geared toward deaf–blind children with multiple disabilities, not the greater proportion of the population with Usher syndrome.

Service Environment for Children

Deaf–blind children today are educated in a variety of settings: schools for the deaf, schools for the blind, deaf or hard-of-hearing programs in regular public schools, and even hearing–sighted classrooms. In many cases, especially those involving Usher syndrome, children do not receive the educational accommodations, counseling, or rehabilitation information that they need to succeed (Miner, 1995, 1996, 1997a, 1997b; Miner & Cioffi, 1997). Even schools for the deaf are frequently lax in screening for deaf–blindness, although improvements are taking place.

For children with Usher syndrome and other progressive forms of hearing and vision loss, these disabilities begin to have a detrimental effect on classroom performance and social–emotional functioning long before the condition is usually detected. Hearing loss, night blindness, reduced visual field and acuity, sensitivity to glare, and other symptoms require differing adaptations in communication, seating, written materials, and other aspects of the educational and social environments. Teachers of the deaf or blind are often not familiar with the proper adaptations for children with deaf–blindness. These children, including those with less severe or slowly progressing conditions, also need orientation and mobility evaluations, which often do not occur until they have left the secondary school setting. The need for counseling by professionals knowledgeable about deaf–blindness is also critical, not only for students' adaptation but for their parents and families as well. Contact with other youths and adults who are deaf–blind can have a powerful and beneficial educational, emotional, and social impact.

In addition to the 10 HKNC regional centers and dozens of smaller HKNC-affiliated programs, each state has a deaf–blind children's program that provides assistance and guidance to families. These programs register families in the deaf–blind children's census, visit and assist families and schools, provide teacher education, and introduce willing families with deaf–blind children to one another. Some states regularly offer workshops on different aspects of deaf–blindness. Although many of these programs do excellent work, they are often focused on special education and the learning and social needs of deaf-blind children with multiple disabilities. Knowledge regarding the needs of children with Usher syndrome is less evident. Psychological services remains a tremendous need.

Each state's vocational rehabilitation (VR) service system generally begins working with identified deaf–blind children and their families when the child reaches the age of 16 and is still in secondary school. The introduction of VR services is often the route by which a deaf–blind person is first referred to a psychologist. As noted, psychologists to whom VR makes such referrals rarely specialize in services to people with sensory disabilities of any sort, much less deaf–blindness. The ability of these providers to offer evaluation or treatment services that are beneficial to this population is questionable.

Rehabilitation Services and Adults

A number of factors and policies influence which agencies and professionals serve deaf–blind adults. Because specialized services for this population are not widely available, most deaf–blind consumers "straddle" traditional deaf or blind services, often with inadequate results. The skills and knowledge gaps evidenced by professionals who serve one or the other population, but not deaf–blind people per se, are conspicuous and common. The rarity of people who are fluent in sign language and also knowledgeable about mobility training and vocational and housing adaptations for people who are blind is just one example. The views and recommendations of professionals experienced in only one of these sensory disabilities are frequently erroneous or ineffective for the deaf–blind consumer.

The vast majority of services to deaf–blind adults are rendered by agencies established to serve people who are blind. As noted, in most cases, people must be legally blind before they qualify for services, even if they have a progressive vision loss that will eventually result in legal blindness. This stunning policy results in even further delay in access to needed training and other services and, arguably, poorer learning as a result, because one's vision and hearing loss are more advanced by the time enrollment and training in Commission on the Blind-sponsored programs finally occurs.

The state commissions contract with rehabilitation agencies to provide a variety of services. Each individual's service plan should vary as a function of his or her unique sensory and communication characteristics, social preferences, cognitive abilities, knowledge and skill patterns, and personal goals. Obviously, the more thorough and competent the initial assessment (which often involves a psychologist), the more helpful and appropriate the resulting service plan is. Common services provided to deaf–blind adults include orientation and mobility training; independent-living-skills instruction; Braille and sign language instruction; computer and other technology training; vocational assessment; and job development, training, and placement. Audiological services, ophthalmologic services, and low-vision services are also important but frequently overlooked by professionals focused on social, educational, and vocational concerns. When post-secondary education is planned, support services may include access to interpreters, notetakers, and special computer equipment, although colleges and universities are increasingly expected to provide such services at their own expense as a function of their responsibilities under the ADA. Conflict and procrastination in providing needed services sometimes occur as the educational institution and the vocational rehabilitation or commission systems argue about fiscal responsibilities.

Although some deaf–blind individuals receive training at HKNC, many states prefer consumers to receive services locally or at nearby rehabilitation centers that serve blind people because of the considerable cost savings involved. The advantage of attending HKNC is that the instructional curriculum and environment are tailored to the deaf–blind population. Classes are taught by experienced teachers, usually several times a week. Perhaps most importantly, this specialized rehabilitation center affords deaf–blind individuals the opportunity to meet others who are deaf–blind, often for the first time, which can be a powerful healing and empowering experience. On the other hand, leaving one's family for an extended period to attend HKNC can impose emotional and financial hardship that may be underappreciated by those making the recommendation for training away from home.

Role of Psychologists

Psychological testing and vocational assessment are often requested in the early stages of rehabilitation service planning, which leads many deaf–blind consumers to psychologists. In addition to lacking the specialized knowledge and assessment tools and procedures necessary to yield valid and helpful results (Vernon & Green, 1980), psychologists frequently lack a sufficiently wide perspective on what evaluations for deaf–blind people should address. Too often, "a psychological" is needed for the records, and insufficient thought goes into formulating referral questions and assessment foci and procedures. These problems are aggravated by communication and attitudinal barriers that can lead psychologists to depend too heavily on information from records and significant others, rather than seeking information directly from the deaf–blind individual.

Conducting a good psychological assessment involves much more than reaching a valid IQ estimate and reporting on vocational interests. The psychosocial and mental health status and needs of the consumer and their family members are critical but are frequently overlooked (Dodd et al., 1994; Hudson, 1994; Miller, 1990; Miner, 1995, 1997a, 1997b). Deaf–blindness can impose tremendous emotional, economic, and social burdens on the consumer and the family. Jobs, marriages, parent–child relations, friendships, and socialization patterns frequently are disrupted by the objective and subjective (e.g., fear, stigma) consequences of the sensory losses. Isolation and dependence become progressively worse, and guilt, fear, pessimism, worry, depression, and anger can reach painful levels in both the deaf–blind individual and the family system. Depression and anxiety disorders are rarely investigated and treated adequately in the chronically ill and disabled populations (Cassem, 1995; Padrone, 1994) because many professionals and nonprofessionals dismiss affective symptoms and social disruption as "normal," given the situation. Communication barriers further diminish the likelihood of consumers receiving a thorough assessment and access to treatment (Pollard, 1994, 1996). The psychologist knowledgeable about deaf–blind issues can have an enormous positive impact on the consumer and the family. Proper assessment of these psychological issues and the initiation of treatment or other appropriate psychosocial interventions can provide life-saving relief and hope for the future to consumers and their families.

Rehabilitation psychologists have been underused in work with deaf–blind people. Their experience in rehabilitation processes and service systems, knowledge of recurrent loss dynamics and recovery from such experiences, and comfort in working with people with a variety of disabilities can open new opportunities for the underserved deaf–blind population. Learning and practicing proper communication accommodations (including using sign language interpreters when necessary) and engaging in outside study and continuing education in this topic area help prepare rehabilitation psychologists to work effectively with deaf–blind people. There is helpful (although limited) literature to which the interested psychologist can turn (Heller, Flohr, & Zegans, 1987; Miner, 1995, 1996, 1997b; Smith, 1993, 1994; Stahlecker, Glass, & Machalow, 1984).

Rehabilitation psychologists are trained to view consumers holistically, even if they are referred for only an assessment, and are less likely to feel inadequacy, distance, or discomfort in the presence of physical disability than psychologists who do not work with such populations. Rehabilitation psychologists are uniquely trained to understand and work with major losses and changes in physical and social functioning (Druss, 1995; Gzesiak & Hicok, 1994). These experiences can help them assist deaf–blind consumers who are moving from lives and communities wholly populated by hearing–sighted people (including themselves prior to the onset of adventitious deaf–blindness) toward different but still vibrant roles and identities as deaf–blind individuals. The complex and multifaceted process associated with adjustment to deaf–blindness has emotional, psychological, familial, social, vocational, fiscal, marital, and even sociopolitical aspects that are familiar to most rehabilitation psychologists, even if their experience has been drawn from other populations.

Conclusion

Although they are vastly different (and diverse) populations, deaf, blind, and deaf–blind people have historically shared the common experience of those who are not disabled controlling most of the decisions and institutions that have shaped their lives. Neither the professionals educated to serve them nor the families they were born into (in most cases) shared their disability or the perspectives and priorities commonly associated with it. This is changing as the broad disability rights movement (Shapiro, 1993), spurred by the proliferation of consumer-directed centers for independent living, the ADA, and disability activist groups and publications, re-educates families, professionals, and society at large about what works for people with disabilities. Psychology has much to contribute to the betterment of the lives of these populations, but only if it brings its knowledge base and methodological skills to the table in partnership with the knowledge base, value systems, and research and service agendas of these consumer populations themselves. There is no better avenue toward forging this partnership than promoting access to professional psychology education for people with disabilities, including those who are deaf, blind, and deaf–blind (Pollard, 1992, 1996).

References

Americans With Disabilities Act of 1990, P. L. 101-336, 104 Stat. 327.

Braden, J. P. (1994). *Deafness, deprivation, and IQ.* New York: Plenum Press.

Brauer, B. (1990, Spring). Caught in the middle: Does interpreting work in a mental health setting? *Gallaudet Today,* 46–49.

Cassem, E. H. (1995). Depressive disorders in the medically ill: An overview. *Psychosomatics, 36*(2), 2–10.

Chen, D. (1998, January 27). Separate jobs for the blind spur a spirited debate. *The New York Times,* pp. B7.

Chiccioli, T., Harrison, S., Kesner, B., LeJeune, J., Stender, A., Tunison, W., Herrada-Benites, R., Levine, F., & Lugo, J. (1994, May). We have Usher syndrome. *Silent News,* p. 3.

Dodd, A., Fergusen, E., Ng, L., Flannigan, H., Hawes, G., & Yates, L. (1994). The concept of adjustment: A structural model. *Journal of Vision Impairment and Blindness, 88,* 487–497.

Dolnick, E. (1993, September). Deafness as culture. *The Atlantic Monthly,* pp. 37–53.

Druss, R. G. (1995). *The psychology of illness, in sickness and in health.* Washington, DC: American Psychiatric Press.

Dugan, M. B. (1997). *Keys to living with hearing loss.* Hauppauge, NY: Baaron's Educational Services.

Education for All Handicapped Children Act of 1975, P. L. 94-142, 89 Stat. 773.

Elliott, H., Glass, L., & Evans, J. W. (1988). *Mental health assessment of deaf clients: A practical manual.* Boston: Little, Brown.

Gibson, W. (1984). *The miracle worker.* New York: Bantam Books.

Glickman, N., & Harvey, M. (1996). *Culturally affirmative psychotherapy with deaf persons.* Mahwah, NJ: Erlbaum.

Gzesiak, R. C., & Hicok, D. A. (1994). A brief history of psychotherapy and physical disability. *American Journal of Psychotherapy, 48*(2), 240–250.

Harvey, M. A. (1989). *Psychotherapy with deaf and hard-of-hearing persons: A systemic model.* Hillsdale, NJ: Erlbaum.

Heller, B. W., Flohr, L. M., & Zegans, L. S. (Eds.). (1987). *Psychosocial interventions with sensorially disabled persons.* Orlando, FL: Grune & Stratton.

Hudson, D. (1994). Causes of emotional and psychological reactions to adventitious blindness. *Journal of Vision Impairment and Blindness, 88,* 498–503.

Individuals With Disabilities Education Act, P. L. 101-476, 104 Stat. 1142.

Kuusisto, S. (1998, April 7). [Radio interview by L. Lopate]. New York and Company National Public Radio (WNC-AM).

Lane, H. (1984). *When the mind hears: A history of the deaf.* New York: Random House.

Lane, H. (1988). Is there "a psychology of the deaf"? *Exceptional Children, 55*(1), 7–19.

Lane, H. (1992). *The mask of benevolence: Disabling the deaf community.* New York: Knopf.

Lane, H., Hoffmeister, R., & Bahan, B. (1996). *A journey into the deaf-world.* San Diego, CA: Dawn Sign Press.

Levine, E. S. (1977, July). The preparation of psychological service providers to the deaf (Monograph No. 4). *Journal of Rehabilitation of the Deaf.*

Marschark, M. (1997). *Raising and educating deaf children.* New York: Oxford University Press.

Marschark, M., & Clark, D. (Eds.). (1998). *Psychological perspectives on deafness* (Vol. 2). Mahwah, NJ: Erlbaum.

Miller, G. (1990). The comprehensive rehabilitation center: Perspectives of clients and implications for professionals. *Journal of Vision Impairment and Blindness, 84,* 177–182.

Miner, I. D. (1995). Psychosocial implications of Usher syndrome, Type I, throughout the life cycle. *Journal of Vision Impairment and Blindness, 89,* 287–296.

Miner, I. D. (1996). The impact of Usher syndrome, Type I, on adolescent development. *Journal of Vocational Rehabilitation, 6,* 159–166.

Miner, I. D. (1997a). Issues of adaptation for people with Usher syndrome, Type 1 and 2: A comparison of process and events. *Proceedings of the Ninth Meeting of the European Usher Syndrome Study Group.* Madrid, Spain: Organizacion Nacional Ciegos Espagnolas.

Miner, I. D. (1997b). People with Usher syndrome, Type II: Issues and adaptation. *Journal of Vision Impairment and Blindness, 91,* 579–589.

Miner, I. D., & Cioffi, J. (1997). *Usher syndrome in the school setting.* Sands Point, NY: Helen Keller National Center.

Myers, R. R. (1995). *Standards of care for the delivery of mental health services to deaf and hard of hearing persons.* Silver Spring, MD: National Association of the Deaf.

National Research Council. (1929). *Research recommendations of the second conference on problems of the deaf and hard of hearing* (Reprint and Circular Series of the National Research Council, No. 88). Washington, DC: Author.

Padden, C., & Humphries, T. (1988). *Deaf in America: Voices from a culture.* Cambridge, MA: Harvard University Press.

Padrone, F. J. (1994). Psychotherapeutic issues with family members of persons with physical disabilities. *American Journal of Psychotherapy, 48*(2), 195–207.

Parakarinen, L., Karjalainen, S., Simola, K. O. J., Laippala, P., & Kaitalo, H. (1995). Usher syndrome, Type 3 in Finland. *Laryngoscope, 105,* 613–617.

Pollard, R. Q (1992). Cross-cultural ethics in the conduct of deafness research. *Rehabilitation Psychology, 37*(2), 87–101.

Pollard, R. Q (1993). 100 years in psychology and deafness: A centennial retrospective. *Journal of the American Deafness and Rehabilitation Association, 26*(3), 32–46.

Pollard, R. Q (1994). Public mental health service and diagnostic trends regarding individuals who are deaf or hard of hearing. *Rehabilitation Psychology, 39*(3), 147–160.

Pollard, R. Q (1996). Professional psychology and deaf people: The emergence of a discipline. *American Psychologist, 51,* 389–396.

Pollard, R. Q (1998). Psychopathology. In M. Marschark & D. Clark (Eds.), *Psychological perspectives on deafness* (Vol. 2, pp. 171–197). Mahwah, NJ: Erlbaum.

Prevent Blindness America. (1997). Demographics update: Legal blindness in the U.S. *Journal of Vision Impairment and Blindness, 91*(4), 413.

Randolph–Sheppard Act, ch. 638, 49 Stat. 1559 (1936).

Randolph–Sheppard Act Amendments of 1974, P. L. 93-651, 89 Stat. 2–7.

Raifman, L. J., & Vernon, M. (1996a). Important implications for psychologists of the Americans with Disabilities Act: Case in point, the patient who is deaf. *Professional Psychology: Research and Practice, 27,* 372–377.

Raifman, L. J., & Vernon, M. (1996b). New rights for deaf patients; new responsibilities for mental hospitals. *Psychiatric Quarterly, 67*(3), 209–220.

Shapiro, J. P. (1993). *No pity: People with disabilities forging a new civil rights movement.* New York: Times Books.

Smith, R. J. H., Berlin, C. I., Hajjtmanick, J. F., Keats, W. J., Lewis, R. A., Moller, C. G., Pelais, M. Z., & Tranebjaerg, L. (1994). Clinical diagnosis of the Usher syndromes. *American Journal of Medical Genetics, 50,* 32–38.

Smith, T. (1993). Psychosocial services: Reaction. In J. Reiman & P. Johnson (Eds.), *Proceedings of the national symposium on children and youth who are deaf–blind* (pp. 113–127). Monmouth, OR: Teaching Research.

Smith, T. B. (1994). *Guidelines: Practical tips for working and socializing with deaf–blind people.* Burtonsville, MD: Sign Media.

Stahlecker, J. E., Glass, L. E., & Machalow, S. (Eds.). (1984). *State-of-the-art research priorities in deaf-blindness.* San Francisco: University of California San Francisco, Center on Mental Health and Deafness.

Trychin, S. (1991). *Manual for mental health professionals: Part II. Psycho-social challenges faced by hard of hearing people.* Washington, DC: Gallaudet University Press.

Valli, C., & Lucas, C. (1992). *Linguistics of American Sign Language: A resource text for ASL users.* Washington, DC: Gallaudet University Press.

Vaughn, C. E. (1991). The social basis of conflict between blind people and agents of rehabilitation. *Disability, Handicap, & Society, 6*(3), 203–217.

Vaughn, C. E. (1993). *The struggle of blind people for self-determination: The dependency-rehabilitation conflict: Empowerment in the blind community.* Springfield, IL: Charles C Thomas.

Vernon, M., & Andrews, J. F. (1990). *The psychology of deafness: Understanding deaf and hard-of-hearing people.* New York: Longman.

Vernon, M., & Green, D. (1980). A guide to the assessment of deaf–blind adults. *Journal of Vision Impairment and Blindness, 74,* 229–231.

Vocational Rehabilitation Act of 1920, P. L. 66-236.

Walworth, M., Moores, F., & O'Rourke, T. J. (1992). *A free hand: Enfranchising the education of deaf children.* Silver Spring, MD: T. J.

Willigan, B. A., & King, S. J. (Eds.). (1992). *Mental health services for deaf people.* Washington, DC: Gallaudet University.

World Health Organization. (1997, February). *Blindness and visual disability. Part II of VII: Major causes worldwide* [Fact sheet]. Geneva, Switzerland: Author. Retrieved from the World Wide Web http://www.who.int/inf-fs/en/fact143.html

11

Psychiatric Rehabilitation

Gary R. Bond and Sandra G. Resnick

This chapter discusses the rehabilitation of adults with persistent and severe mental illness (SMI). Three criteria are used to identify individuals with SMI (Goldman, 1984). The first criterion, diagnosis, can be met by a range of psychiatric diagnoses defined by the *Diagnostic and Statistical Manual of Mental Disorders* (4th ed., *DSM–IV*; American Psychiatric Association, 1994). The second criterion, disability, is manifested in significant role impairments affecting social relationships, work, leisure, and self-care. Although severe impairments in psychosocial functioning are most often present in schizophrenia and major affective disorders, they are also found in other diagnoses, such as obsessive–compulsive disorder and personality disorders. The third criterion, duration, is met by demonstrating chronicity or persistence of the disorder, typically through a history of psychiatric hospitalizations or intensive psychiatric treatment. A liberal estimate is that 4.8 million Americans (3% of the population) can be described as having SMI (Federal Register, 1999).

The treatment of psychiatric disorders was revolutionized during the last half of this century by the discovery and development of psychotropic medications. Neuroleptics, antidepressants, and mood-stabilizing medications have become the mainstay of treatment for patients with SMI, and new discoveries continue with the development of atypical antipsychotics (e.g., clozapine, risperidone, and olanzapine) for schizophrenia (Weiden, Aquila, & Standard, 1996) and the selective serotonin reuptake inhibitors (e.g., fluoxetine) for depression (Glod, 1996). However, despite the potent effects of medications on reducing acute symptoms and decreasing vulnerability to relapse, medications alone are insufficient treatment for severe psychiatric disorders. Some of the psychosocial correlates of SMI not adequately addressed by medications are unemployment, isolation, inadequate social supports, vulnerability to stress, substandard living conditions, homelessness, incarceration in jails and prisons, and the heavy burden of caregiving on relatives (Bond, 1999). The consensus is that medications work best in conjunction with practical psychosocial interventions (Hogarty, Goldberg, & Associates, 1973).

Work on this chapter was supported by National Institute of Mental Health Grant MH00842. We thank Lisa Evans Anderson, Carlos Pratt, and Jeff Picone for their helpful comments.

Psychiatric rehabilitation (also referred to as "psychosocial rehabilitation") addresses psychosocial difficulties associated with SMI. Many definitions of the term have been given (Anthony, Cohen, & Farkas, 1990; Cnaan, Blankertz, Messinger, & Gardner, 1990; Dincin, 1975; Mueser, Drake, & Bond, 1997). One definition in wide use is as follows: "[assisting] persons with long-term psychiatric disabilities to increase their functioning so that they are successful and satisfied in the environments of their choice with the least amount of ongoing professional intervention" (Anthony et al., 1990, p. 2). Psychiatric rehabilitation also has been defined in pragmatic, concrete terms as "giving people with psychiatric disabilities the opportunity to work, live in the community, and enjoy a social life, at their own pace, through planned experiences in a respectful, supportive, and realistic atmosphere" (Rutman, 1993, p. 1). In practice, treatment and rehabilitation are intertwined, although *treatment* often refers specifically to medications and psychotherapy, whereas *rehabilitation* is associated with interventions to assist in employment, housing, and other aspects of community functioning. Labels used for recipients of psychiatric rehabilitation services include "client," "patient," "member," and "consumer." In the absence of a strong preference among service recipients for a particular label (Mueser, Glynn, Corrigan, & Baber, 1996), we use the term *client*, unless the context indicates otherwise.

In this chapter, we discuss fundamental concepts of psychiatric rehabilitation, historical perspectives, client outcomes, competencies of psychiatric rehabilitation practitioners, roles for psychologists, and future directions. Because of space constraints, we have excluded approaches in which clients are not the primary recipient of the interventions. In particular, we exclude family interventions, which are often considered a form of psychiatric rehabilitation—indeed, behavioral family management has a demonstrable effect on clients' psychosocial outcomes (Mueser et al., 1997). We also do not discuss the important literature on interventions for clients with frequently co-occurring conditions, such as substance abuse (Drake, Mercer-McFadden, Mueser, McHugo, & Bond, 1998; see also chapter 19) and posttraumatic stress disorder (Mueser, Goodman, et al., 1998).

Fundamental Concepts

Any discussion of the core ingredients in psychiatric rehabilitation should be prefaced by mention of common ingredients of rehabilitation services in general, regardless of the target population. As is true for all of rehabilitation psychology, psychiatric rehabilitation stresses the importance of individualizing rehabilitation planning, assessment, and intervention and focuses on client strengths and the therapeutic relationship (Rapp, 1998). Many of the specific principles enunciated below also apply to rehabilitation approaches for other client groups. Despite the diversity of psychiatric rehabilitation approaches, most psychiatric rehabilitation practitioners subscribe to a common set of guiding principles (Cnaan et al., 1990). A partial list of these principles is presented below.

Pragmatism

Psychiatric rehabilitation has a focus on practical problems in everyday living (Dincin, 1975). Closely related to this pragmatism is an outcome orientation, wherein services are organized according to specific, tangible goals.

Attention to Client Preferences

Psychiatric rehabilitation programs attend to client preferences, for example, helping clients find jobs in the occupations that they desire (Becker, Drake, Farabaugh, & Bond, 1996) and obtain their preferred types of housing (Carling, 1993).

Situational and Functional Assessment

In addition to shaping services to client preferences, psychiatric rehabilitation programs generally use hands-on approaches to assess client abilities. *Situational assessments*—observing clients in real-life situations—often provide more useful information than standardized paper-and-pencil tests of ability (Anthony & Jansen, 1984). *Functional assessments*—defining skill deficits that need to be addressed to achieve behavioral goals—are used in some psychiatric rehabilitation approaches (Farkas, Cohen, & Nemec, 1988).

Skills Training

All psychiatric rehabilitation approaches emphasize helping clients acquire and apply skills needed to achieve community adjustment. The methods for skills training vary widely, ranging from informal, experiential methods (Vorspan, 1988) to highly structured behavioral approaches (Wallace, Liberman, MacKain, Blackwell, & Eckman, 1992). The locus of training also varies, with some experts arguing that training in vivo, that is, in the specific setting in which the skills are used, is more effective than training in a clinic setting (Stein & Test, 1980).

Environmental Modification

Psychiatric rehabilitation approaches emphasize the importance of selecting and changing environments to maximize the likelihood that clients succeed. For example, staff may place a client with poor hygiene who is looking for work in a recycling center, where hygiene is less critical, rather than attempting to modify deeply ingrained habits (Becker & Drake, 1993). Helping clients move out of emotionally charged living situations is another example of environmental modification. Also pertinent here is the philosophy inherent in the Americans with Disabilities Act (ADA) of 1990

(P.L. 101-336), which directs employers under appropriate circumstances to make "reasonable accommodations" for workers with disabilities (Fabian, Waterworth, & Ripke, 1993).

Integration of Rehabilitation and Treatment

Traditional practice has separated vocational rehabilitation from mental health treatment, leading to fragmented services and poor employment outcomes (Noble, Honberg, Hall, & Flynn, 1997). Many experts agree with Stein and Test (1980) that interventions are most effective when rehabilitation services are closely coordinated with treatment.

Continuity of Services

The importance of maintaining continuity of services over time is another fundamental principle (Test, 1979). Because SMI involves chronic conditions, time-limited interventions are generally ineffective. Maintaining continuity in relationships by providing timely and predictable support is a key element in successful psychiatric rehabilitation programs.

Community Integration

Psychiatric rehabilitation embraces the principle of normalization, helping clients move out of patient roles, treatment centers, segregated housing arrangements, and sheltered work and enabling them to move toward illness self-management and normal adult roles in their communities. Consistent with this principle, studies have shown that day treatment programs can be closed down and replaced with programs that help clients find community jobs, with positive outcomes for clients, families, and mental health staff (Drake, 1998a).

Historical Perspective

Psychiatric rehabilitation developed from many sources. Although some of the better known models have well-articulated program philosophies, in everyday practice most programs include many eclectic, pragmatic elements. The diversity of goals, clients served, community characteristics, funding mandates, staffing patterns, local norms, and many other factors also influence the character of programs as they evolve in particular settings (Bachrach, 1988).

To explain the context for the development of psychiatric rehabilitation, we begin with a brief history of deinstitutionalization. Following in rough chronological sequence of their emergence, we describe several influential approaches. Some describe comprehensive rehabilitation programs that address the entire range of needs of the individual, and others address specific aspects of functioning (such as social skills) and are used in conjunction with other services.

Deinstitutionalization

Beginning in the 1950s, a combination of economic, legal, and humanitarian factors, in addition to the widespread use of psychotropic medications, led to *deinstitutionalization*, that is, the depopulation of psychiatric hospitals. The number of residents in state mental hospitals declined from more than 550,000 to fewer than 90,000 over 4 decades (Torrey, 1995). In 1963, the Mental Retardation Facilities and Community Mental Health Centers Act (P. L. 88-164) authorized the creation of a network of community mental health centers (CMHCs). This legislation eventually led to the funding of 789 CMHCs throughout the United States (Torrey, 1995). Despite initial optimism, CMHCs did not prevent the emergence of revolving-door clients: More than half of all psychiatric patients released from state hospitals returned within 2 years (Anthony, Cohen, & Vitalo, 1978). These trends suggested the need for new approaches to augment traditional CMHC services.

Clubhouse Model

The idea for psychiatric rehabilitation originated with the Fountain House program in New York City. In the 1940s, the precursor to Fountain House was a self-help group for patients discharged from the state psychiatric hospital. With help from a charitable organization, the group acquired a house to serve as its center. Operating outside of the mental health system, the center became known as a "clubhouse," because its identity revolved around a central meeting place for members to socialize. Fountain House pioneered two key vocational concepts: (a) the work-ordered day and (b) transitional employment (Beard, Propst, & Malamud, 1982). With the *work-ordered day*, members participate in work units, performing chores around the clubhouse (e.g., preparing noon meals, cleaning the building). Beard et al. (1982) theorized that a major benefit of work crews is that members feel needed for the successful functioning of the clubhouse, in contrast to their usual feelings of worthlessness in most areas of their lives. *Transitional employment* consists of temporary, part-time community jobs commensurate with members' stamina and stress tolerance, which clubhouse staff workers find for members. These jobs are designed to acclimate members to work and increase their self-confidence. Currently, there are about 230 clubhouses in the United States, with roughly 27,000 active members (Macias, Jackson, Schroeder, & Wang, 1999).

Psychosocial Rehabilitation Centers

Starting in the 1960s, Fountain House's success spawned a national network of independent psychosocial rehabilitation centers, notably in large cities (Dincin, 1975). These comprehensive centers introduced many innovations—in housing, outreach to new populations (e.g., mothers with SMI and their children, hearing impaired and mentally ill populations, young adults), and new program services (e.g., academic tutoring, camping; Dincin, 1995).

Skills-Training Approaches

Behavior modification approaches, such as token economies (Ayllon & Azrin, 1968) and social-learning approaches (Paul & Lentz, 1977), were introduced in psychiatric hospitals in the 1960s. A *token economy* is a therapeutic approach in which staff positively reinforce desirable patient behavior by awarding them points or markers that can later be exchanged for privileges and other things of value. Token economies work best when staff have significant control of the environment. These approaches have declined in popularity partly as a result of the increasingly briefer hospitalizations since the 1960s. Skills training, an offshoot of these inpatient behavior modification techniques, was adopted by many CMHCs and continues to be widely practiced.

The rationale for skills training derives from difficulties often experienced by clients with SMI, especially those with schizophrenia, in many everyday situations, particularly interpersonal situations ranging from intimate relationships to everyday contacts in public settings. The goal of social skills training is to systematically teach the component skills necessary for effective social interactions and thus to improve clients' abilities to achieve interpersonal goals and to improve the quality of their social relationships. Typically, the steps in *skills training* are as follows: (a) explain a rationale for learning the skill, (b) show the skill in a role-play, (c) provide an exercise for the client to role-play the skill, (d) give specific positive and corrective feedback on the client's role-play, (e) practice the skill further, and (f) give a homework assignment to practice the skill in a real-life situation (Mueser et al., 1997). Although skills training is typically centered around interpersonal skills, it also is used for a range of other skills needed for independent living.

Many people have contributed to the skills-training literature and practice. William Anthony was an early leader in the psychiatric rehabilitation field. With his colleagues at the Boston University Center for Psychiatric Rehabilitation, he adapted skills-training techniques for psychiatric rehabilitation practitioners. A clinical research training center at the University of California, Los Angeles, headed by Robert Liberman, has developed and disseminated a series of skills-training modules for people with schizophrenia (Wallace et al., 1992). A number of cognitive–behavioral approaches have been developed and tested recently (Penn & Mueser, 1996). These approaches include *cognitive–behavior therapy*, which aims at changing dysfunctional thoughts and learning new problem-solving skills, and *cognitive retraining*, an approach borrowed from work with individuals with brain injuries that aims at improving attention and cognitive flexibility while reducing paranoia.

Fairweather Lodge

In the 1960s, the prevailing philosophy for helping psychiatric patients return to the community was training them in a gradual, stepwise fashion to gain the skills to function in society. The paradigm was that discharged patients were first transferred to supervised group homes (halfway houses), later to a less supervised setting, and eventually to independent housing. One early transitional-housing approach was the "lodge" model (Fairweather, Sanders, Cressler, & Maynard, 1969). Originally designed as an approach to the transition from psychiatric hospitals, most lodges now in operation are more akin to permanent congregate-housing programs. They are self-contained societies in which people with SMI live, work, and socialize. The lodge model never achieved the national expansion that Fairweather (1980) had thought possible, in part because deinstitutionalization made some elements of the model obsolete. Another factor may have been that the lodge model was supplanted by the ideas of the community support program (CSP).

Community Support Program

A new set of program principles, the CSP approach, was articulated in the 1970s (Turner & TenHoor, 1978). Whereas CMHCs typically provided episodic services, with clients receiving assistance primarily when in crisis, the CSP approach advocated a continuous system of care. CSP features included the identification of a core service agency responsible for the comprehensive needs of clients, outreach to clients not receiving services, assistance in housing and other basic needs, development of permanent supportive networks, vocational rehabilitation, and advocacy. CSP also popularized a new type of mental health worker—the case manager. The case manager's role is to ensure that clients receive services needed for community reintegration, primarily through linking clients to appropriate services (Mueser, Bond, Drake, & Resnick, 1998).

The CSP approach coincided with the expansion of community residential programs, reformulated as an array of housing alternatives with flexible time limits and no fixed linear progression, as assumed in the transitional-housing concept. By the mid-1980s, a national survey identified 4,500 community residential programs for people with SMI (Carling, 1988). Most of these programs were first funded during the 1980s, undoubtedly spurred by the 1975 amendment to the CMHC Act requiring CMHCs to provide residential services.

Assertive Community Treatment

Exemplifying the CSP approach is the *assertive community treatment* (ACT) model (Stein & Test, 1980), a comprehensive individualized approach to treatment and rehabilitation that uses assertive outreach, small client-to-staff ratios, attention to details of everyday living, frequent contact with clients, and provision of service without a time limit. ACT uses a multidisciplinary treatment team that makes most contacts in the client's home and community rather than in agency offices (Test, 1992). A 1996 survey identified 14 states with organized ACT initiatives reporting 397 ACT programs serving an estimated 24,000 clients (Meisler, 1997). Some observers predict further growth of ACT programs, given widespread endorsements by professional and family groups (Drake, 1998b).

Supported Approaches

As a logical extension to the CSP movement, supported approaches to achieving rehabilitation goals were first defined in the literature in the 1980s as more realistic alternatives to transitional approaches, which many practitioners found impractical. Supported approaches address the key areas of housing, employment, and education. In each approach, the strategy is to help clients achieve normal adult roles in integrated settings of their own choosing by providing the professional and informal support needed to succeed in those settings. For example, *supported housing* involves clients living in their own apartments with adequate case management to ensure successful adjustment. Proponents of supported housing have criticized transitional-housing approaches for requiring individuals to complete a series of residential moves that are stressful, artificial, often contrary to personal preferences, and not always culminating in independent living (Carling, 1993).

Supported employment is intended for people with the most severe disabilities; it is defined as paid work that takes place in normal work settings with provision for ongoing support services and was developed originally for people with developmental disabilities as a more effective, humane, and cost-effective alternative to sheltered workshops (Wehman & Moon, 1988). In the 1980s this model was exported to the psychiatric rehabilitation field. Among the various supported employment approaches, the individual placement and support (IPS) model (Becker & Drake, 1993) is the most extensively studied. It is based on the following principles: (a) competitive employment as the goal, (b) rapid job search, (c) integration of rehabilitation and mental health, (d) attention to consumer preferences, (e) continuous and comprehensive assessment, and (f) time-unlimited support.

Supported education helps clients obtain education and training to have the skills and credentials needed to obtain jobs with career potential (Moxley, Mowbray, & Brown, 1993). This concept also has been applied to training clients to work as mental health paraprofessionals. A Denver project training clients with SMI to work as case manager aides (Sherman & Porter, 1991) has been emulated widely (Mowbray, Moxley, Jasper, & Howell, 1997).

Consumer Self-Help

The consumer self-help movement historically has been closely allied to psychiatric rehabilitation. Self-help groups for mental health consumers have been forming in the United States since at least the 1940s, but a 1980 survey found that only 3% of people with schizophrenia had participated in self-help groups (Lieberman & Snowden, 1993). During the 1980s mental health self-help activities started to coalesce into a national movement, with the formation of over 500 groups (Chamberlin, Rogers, & Sneed, 1989). These groups have been active in developing drop-in centers, which provide friendship, social and recreational activities, and practical assistance (Trainor, Shepherd, Boydell, Leff, & Crawford, 1997). The consumer movement stresses the importance of consumer preferences, an element lacking in some professionally run programs. Another difference is that consumers participating in consumer-run organizations may be more likely to turn to peers than to professionals as their primary source of support.

Prosumers

Another trend influenced by the consumer movement has been the role of *prosumers* (consumers who are employed as direct service providers). Prosumers provide treatment alternatives within programs, because peer support may be perceived as more normalizing and less anxiety provoking than that provided by professionals. The role of prosumers appears to be far more accepted in the professional community than even 5 years ago. Prosumers have been used in all aspects of treatment, from members of case management teams (Felton et al., 1995) and counselors on inpatient units (McGill & Patterson, 1990) to staff in supported housing (Besio & Mahler, 1993). The evidence suggests that prosumers provide services somewhat differently but are no less effective than are nonconsumer providers (Solomon & Draine, 1995). The addition of a prosumer to a psychiatric rehabilitation program may have a salutary impact on its effectiveness (Felton et al., 1995). Anecdotal evidence suggests that prosumers who work as service providers experience enhanced self-esteem and identity transformation (Mowbray et al., 1997).

Current State

The practice of psychiatric rehabilitation today reflects the heterogeneity of its diverse roots. One unifying force is the International Association of Psychosocial Rehabilitation Services (IAPSRS), an organization of psychiatric rehabilitation agencies, practitioners, and others that is dedicated to promoting, supporting, and strengthening community-oriented rehabilitation services. Its membership numbers 441 organizations in addition to 1,144 individual members (IAPSRS, 1997a). Recently, IAPSRS developed a formal process for certifying psychiatric rehabilitation practitioners. IAPSRS also has begun to define practice guidelines (IAPSRS, 1997b). In so doing, it has followed the lead of psychiatry (e.g., Herz et al., 1997), as well as other fields of medicine, in attempting to identify effective interventions.

The number of practitioners involved in mental health services in the United States is substantial. Wohlford (1994) reported that, as of 1990, there were 578,000 full-time-equivalent staff in organized mental health settings, of whom 47% had at least bachelor's-level education. A 1993 national survey of 9,437 psychiatric rehabilitation practitioners gives a rough indication of the types of settings in which these practitioners are most commonly found (Blankertz & Robinson, 1996): 32% in day rehabilitation activities (including clubhouses, social rehabilitation programs, and prevocational activities), 36% in residential services, 15% in case management, 9% in vocational services, 2% in administration, and 6% in other activities.

Outcomes

Compared with the psychopharmacological literature, research on psychiatric rehabilitation is still in its infancy (Lehman, 1995; Mueser et al., 1997). Some models of psychiatric rehabilitation, such as ACT and skills training, have been extensively studied, whereas other models, such as the clubhouse model and psychosocial rehabilitation agencies, lack systematic research. An important caveat in evaluating the results of outcome studies is that samples vary widely across studies and to some extent vary systematically according to models. ACT research, for example, has been conducted primarily with clients who are at highest risk for rehospitalization.

This brief section is organized around psychosocial outcome domains, reflecting the outcome orientation in psychiatric rehabilitation. As has been noted often, psychiatric rehabilitation programs focus on small changes, commensurate with the realities of the course of schizophrenia (McGlashan, 1988) and other severe psychiatric disorders. For example, in the vocational area, a typical goal for a client in SMI is part-time competitive employment for a period of at least 6 months. This is a far cry from the long-term goal of permanent recovery and integration into society. A detailed discussion of specific outcome indicators and their measurement is beyond the scope of this chapter. For details on measurement, we refer interested readers to Hargreaves, Shumway, Hu, and Cuffel (1998) and to review articles cited in this section.

Reduction of Hospital Use

The viability of community alternatives to hospitalization is well established (Test, 1984). Many psychiatric rehabilitation approaches have been shown to reduce the use of psychiatric hospitals (both number of admissions and days of hospitalization). The evidence is very strong for ACT (Mueser, Bond, et al., 1998). Crisis housing programs (Stroul, 1988), consumer self-help groups (Trainor et al., 1997), and clubhouses (Stroul, 1986) also may decrease hospital use.

Improvement of Independent-Living Status

The literature on independent living continues to be fragmented and unsystematic. Among rehabilitation approaches, ACT has been shown to increase stability of housing (typically measured as duration at a single residence; Mueser, Bond, et al., 1998). Less documented is the extent to which ACT improves independent-living skills (e.g., cooking and shopping). Dion and Anthony (1987) concluded that psychiatric rehabilitation was effective in improving outcomes in the area of independent living.

Increase in Competitive Employment Outcomes

None of the traditional psychiatric rehabilitation approaches has been shown to be effective in helping people with SMI attain permanent jobs in the community (Bond, 1992). In particular, despite its popularity, there has been little systematic research on the clubhouse model. By contrast, recent findings in the area of supported employment have been encouraging. Combined results from six recent experimental studies found that 58% of supported-employment clients achieved competitive employment, compared with 21% of control participants, with other indicators of vocational success (such as earnings from employment and job tenure) also favoring supported employment. However, these studies did not show that supported-employment programs systematically improved nonvocational outcomes (Bond, Drake, Mueser, & Becker, 1997).

Improvement in Social Skills

In a meta-analysis of 68 studies, Dilk and Bond (1996) found that skills training was strongly effective in helping people with SMI acquire social skills. Unfortunately, these studies rarely examined whether acquired skills were used outside the training setting. Moreover, most studies were confined to inpatient settings. Recently, seven controlled studies of social skills training for outpatients with schizophrenia have suggested benefits of their training in increasing social adjustment (Mueser et al., 1997).

Reduction in Psychiatric Symptoms

As suggested at the beginning of this chapter, psychiatric rehabilitation can be conceptualized as complementary to psychopharmacological interventions, which have a direct effect on psychiatric symptoms. Nonetheless, both ACT (Mueser, Bond, et al., 1998) and skills training (Dilk & Bond, 1996; Mueser et al., 1997) appear to have a measurable impact in reducing symptoms. The mechanisms for improvement may include better medication monitoring and psychoeducational efforts to improve coping with symptoms.

Improvement in Subjective Quality of Life

The research on the impact of psychiatric rehabilitation on quality of life is mixed. About half of the controlled studies of ACT have found an impact on subjective quality of life (Mueser, Bond, et al., 1998). Excluding ACT research, much of the research on psychiatric rehabilitation models has been correlational, precluding strong conclusions. It seems likely that measurement problems associated with self-report instruments and expectation level confound assessment in this domain (e.g., Atkinson, Zibin, & Chuang, 1997).

Empowerment and Recovery

The concepts of empowerment and recovery are currently popular in the literature. As metaphors for positive direction of change in one's life, these constructs are appealing. Psychometrically, however, they may have some of the same limitations as found for subjective quality-of-life and other self-report measures.

Competencies of Practitioners

The preceding sections of this chapter have focused on principles of psychiatric rehabilitation and the features of program models as they relate to client outcomes. However, as important as these factors are, the day-to-day workings of programs are highly dependent on the competencies of practitioners. We examine current thinking in this area and then discuss roles for psychologists.

Efforts to define the competencies needed to be an effective psychiatric rehabilitation practitioner have drawn on expert and consumer panels (Friday & McPheeters, 1985; Gill, Pratt, & Barrett, 1997; Sechrest & Pion, 1990) and reviews of the literature (Jonikas, 1994). Psychiatry, psychology, nursing, and social work all have convened national conferences to identify the training needs for their specific disciplines; two conferences in psychology have been summarized in monographs (Johnson, 1990; Marsh, 1994). Many useful and important ideas have emerged from these efforts. The truth is that there is virtually no empirical literature on the knowledge, attitudes, and skills of practitioners related to successful rehabilitation outcomes. Moreover, the conclusion of one expert panel is telling: It was unable to identify the unique competencies needed to be an effective psychiatric rehabilitation practitioner, as distinct from those needed to be effective in working with any other population (Sechrest & Pion, 1990). Indeed, our current vocabulary for selecting new staff with native talents to work with this population is intuitive and imprecise. Traits often mentioned include high energy, flexibility, persistence, creativity, problem-solving ability, orientation toward growth, and "street smarts" (Engstrom, Brooks, Jonikas, Cook, & Witheridge, 1992).

Given the ambiguities about the competencies needed, it is not surprising that there is little research on the effectiveness of training approaches for developing the skills needed to be an effective psychiatric rehabilitation professional, through either preservice or inservice training. In a survey of 81 mental health employers, 34% rated their bachelor's-level employees as unprepared (Gill et al., 1997). Gill concluded that academic curricula generally do not prepare students to work as psychiatric rehabilitation specialists. Thus, the description in this section is based primarily on clinical opinion. We discuss knowledge, attitudes, and skills in turn.

Knowledge

The knowledge base important for psychiatric rehabilitation practitioners includes both theoretical and practical knowledge. Content domains include abnormal psychology, psychopharmacology, many traditional domains of clinical psychology, and information about psychiatric rehabilitation models and the history of deinstitutionalization. Practical knowledge includes the workings of the service systems (e.g., vocational rehabilitation, Social Security Administration, Medicaid, public housing) and information about local community resources.

Attitudes

Many observers have emphasized the importance of a core set of values and attitudes as a precondition to effectiveness. It is frequently noted that staff who are afraid of mental illness or who do not like people with SMI are poorly suited for this work. Dincin (1975) noted the importance of maintaining an attitude of hopefulness and optimism. Based on a qualitative study of managers of successful case management programs, Rapp (1993) concluded that a particular constellation of values and attitudes facilitated positive client outcomes. Rapp's "principles of client-centered performance management" (p. 175) are as follows: (a) venerate the people called "clients," (b) create and maintain the focus, (c) possess a healthy disrespect for the impossible, and (d) learn for a living.

Skills

Many of the skills taught in clinical psychology programs are believed to be important to being well prepared to work in the psychiatric rehabilitation field. The skill most extensively researched is empathic listening. The rationale is straightforward in that some research suggests that the therapeutic alliance is a critical ingredient in effective psychiatric rehabilitation (Gehrs & Goering, 1994). Therefore, skills that facilitate positive, trusting relationships with clients are important. To this end, the graduate training at Boston University's Center for Psychiatric Rehabilitation emphasizes traditional client-centered counseling skills as one basic building block of training (Farkas, O'Brien, & Nemec, 1988). However, not all forms of training in traditional programs are appropriate for preparing psychiatric rehabilitation practitioners. For example, intensive forms of insight-oriented psychotherapy, as found in psychodynamic approaches, are often ineffective or harmful for clients with schizophrenia (Drake & Sederer, 1986). Thus academic programs stressing this type of training are not suited to prepare students to work with this population.

Roles for Psychologists

In considering discipline-specific roles for psychologists in psychiatric rehabilitation, it is logical to consider the traditional roles in research, assessment, and intervention (Bond, Hellkamp, Dilk, & Eberlein, 1993; Smith, Schwebel, Dunn, & McIver, 1993). We consider these traditional roles in the context of psychologists' contributions to direct service, administration, graduate training, research, and other roles. We preface this by noting that space limitations dictate that any list of major contributors among psychologists to the field of psychiatric rehabilitation will not include many who deserve mention; for example, our list overlaps partially, but not completely, with psychologists featured in a special issue of a magazine for family members (Safarjan, Marsh, & Husted, 1998).

Direct Service and Administration

Estimates of the number of psychologists working in clinical or administrative capacities in the public mental health system are hard to locate. Bachelor's-level practitioners constitute the backbone of the psychiatric rehabilitation workforce. A survey from the early 1980s suggested that there were 24,000 master's-level psychologists in clinical practice, of whom many were working in public mental health (O'Connor & Tucker, 1990). Only a small fraction of doctoral-level psychologists in clinical practice have jobs in public mental health (Kohout & Wicherski, 1996). Stratoudakis (1990) reported employment of 3,000 psychologists in state mental hospitals and 4,900 psychologists (2,100 doctoral level and 2,800 master's level) in CMHCs. Projections from managed care practices suggest that the ratio of master's-level psychologists to doctoral-level psychologists in public mental health will increase (Frank & Johnstone, 1996).

Unlike the situation for almost any other medical disease, the more seriously ill a client with a psychiatric disorder is, the less trained the direct service provider is (Mechanic & Aiken, 1987). Among psychologists working in the public sector, most are peripherally involved in services to people with SMI (Lefley & Cutler, 1988). Psychologists working in CMHCs tend to seek out clients who have the highest likelihood of success within an office-based system of intervention, that is, clients who typically have less serious psychiatric disorders (Bernheim, 1990).

Nationally, many psychologists also have contributed as administrators and planners in federal and state mental health agencies and in service agencies (Johnson, 1990). One example is Jerry Dincin (1995), who for 3 decades has been executive director of Thresholds, a large psychosocial rehabilitation agency in Chicago.

Graduate Training Programs

Although there are important exceptions, graduate psychology programs have a weak record in training psychologists for careers in psychiatric rehabilitation (Johnson, 1990, 1992; Marsh, 1994). A survey of 165 clinical psychology program directors was revealing (Johnson, 1992); only 11% of programs had strengths in SMI, and 26% of the directors of these programs said that they would turn away applicants with interests in SMI (Wohlford, 1994).

Research and Theoretical Contributions

On a more positive note, many psychologists have made major conceptual and empirical contributions to the psychiatric rehabilitation field. Anthony is regarded as the "grandfather" of psychiatric rehabilitation. Along with Leonard Stein (a psychiatrist), Mary Ann Test was codeveloper of the ACT model. Their seminal ACT study (Stein & Test, 1980) was probably the most influential piece of research in the psychiatric rehabilitation field over the past 3 decades. Nathan Azrin, Bill Fairweather, and Gordon Paul were other important early contributors to the field. Carling's articulation of the supported-housing model and his work in developing training programs continue to exert an important influence.

Psychologists also have an important leadership role in articulating program models, implementing them, and evaluating their effectiveness. This tradition dates to the work of Fairweather et al. (1969) and Paul and Lentz (1977). Robert Drake's (1998a) dissemination of an effective supported employment model is an outstanding recent example of this role. Gary Morse's work on case management for homeless people with SMI is another example (Morse et al., 1997).

Other psychologists with current active psychiatric rehabilitation research programs include Alan Bellack and Kim Mueser, whose research includes work on skills training and social competence (e.g., Mueser, Bellack, Morrison, & Wixted, 1990), and Morris Bell and Paul Lysaker, known for research on vocational rehabilitation (e.g., Bell, Lysaker, & Milstein, 1996). Given the cognitive deficits of schizophrenia and other severe psychiatric disorders, neuropsychological assessment has been hypothesized to be a fertile ground for investigation and ultimately to help in tailoring interventions. Psychologists have been in the forefront of advances in this area as well (e.g., Green, 1996; Jaeger & Douglas, 1992; Spaulding, 1992).

Advocacy

Psychologists have also been successful as advocates for individuals with SMI. As former president of the National Alliance for the Mentally Ill, Dale Johnson has played an important advocacy role in shaping the direction of psychiatric rehabilitation services in the United States. Diane Marsh, Kayla Bernheim, and Frederick Frese have helped articulate family and client roles in psychiatric rehabilitation (see Marsh, 1994). Carol Mowbray has made many contributions, including her sustained efforts in defining roles for clients in the service system (e.g., Mowbray et al., 1997).

Future Roles

Certainly the research skills traditionally stressed by the scientist–practitioner model of psychology are much-needed competencies in a field increasingly dominated by managed care-driven outcomes orientation, especially given the dearth of expertise among psychiatric rehabilitation practitioners (Spaniol, 1986). As is true throughout the health care field, doctoral-level psychologists will increasingly become involved in supervising master's-level and bachelor's-level practitioners (Frank & Johnstone, 1996), with increasingly reduced roles as direct service providers. Clinical leadership, informed by a knowledge of the research literature, is crucial for increasing the quality of psychiatric rehabilitation services.

Ultimately, it is this integration of research and clinical training that allows psychologists to forge a new path in psychiatric rehabilitation. Over the past 2 decades, psychologists have proactively created a niche in the areas of health psychology and neuropsychology (Belar, 1998). If psychologists are to have an integral role in psychiatric rehabilitation, we must create that role for ourselves.

Future Directions

Where does psychiatric rehabilitation fit in the current political and economic environment? Managed care is expected to continue to grow in its dominance in the U.S. health care system (McFarland, 1996). Assuming that this trend continues, psychiatric rehabilitation agencies must adapt or else disappear from the scene.

One frequent consequence of managed care is the switch from *fee-for-service*, in which provider agencies are reimbursed for amount of services provided, to *capitation*, in which provider agencies are paid a flat rate for the care of a client. Under traditional funding, psychiatric rehabilitation programs have been partly funded through formulas based on the number of units of service (e.g., reimbursement calculated by multiplying the unit rate by the number of clients enrolled in a particular activity). Under capitation, volume of service is not a factor in reimbursement. Another critical element in managed care concerns the organization that assumes the financial risk for the costs of client services. Two general approaches have been used in managed mental health care. In the *integrated approach*, both physical and mental health are managed by a single organization. In a mental health *carve out*, mental health services are managed separately from general health care (Cutler, McFarland, & Winthrop, 1998).

Proponents argue that capitation offers the possibility for reducing costs without compromising quality of services. The underlying assumption in capitation plans is that organizations paying for services have an incentive to use effective treatment approaches, because ineffective approaches require further (and often more expensive) services. When two approaches are both effective, then the less expensive approach is the logical choice under capitation. Captitation has led to closer attention to identifying and providing services of proven effectiveness, but in the eyes of critics, the use of capitation also led to an excess emphasis on cost containment without careful consideration of the impact on consumer care (Flynn, 1997). Moreover, the knowledge base in many areas of mental health services is woefully incomplete, resulting in decision making based on inadequate information.

During the past decade, capitation has become a prominent feature of public mental health. Since its inception in the 1960s, the federal Medicaid program has been an increasingly important source of funding for public mental health, supplementing state mental health budgets. To date, at least 35 states have experimented with capitation through waivers to their Medicaid programs, with mixed results (McFarland, 1994). Setting appropriate rates has proved to be a vexing problem. Early capitation projects have sometimes shown unexpected adverse consequences for organizations assuming responsibility (and financial risk) for patient care (Christianson, Lurie, Finch, Moscovice, & Hartley, 1992), and some states may have attempted to change too much too fast (Cutler et al., 1998).

Accompanying the movement toward managed care has been the attempt to define best practices (Giesler & Hodge, 1997; IAPSRS, 1997b), with the goal of restricting services to well-defined activities that are effective. Some psychiatric rehabilitation models appear to be compatible with managed care objectives. For example, ACT has been shown to be effective and cost effective in the treatment and rehabilitation of clients with the most challenging psychosocial problems. An example of a managed care company incorporating ACT services into behavioral health care is given by Quinlivan (1997). Other psychiatric rehabilitation program models, such as rehabilitation day treatment services, have less coherent bodies of such evidence. Under capitated models, psychiatric rehabilitation programs no longer have a financial incentive, as they did under fee-for-service models, to provide day treatment activities with large enrollments of clients.

Another managed care issue concerns how long clients remain in psychiatric rehabilitation programs. Although psychiatric rehabilitation stresses the importance of time-unlimited services, managed care organizations look for ways to limit the number of visits. Some observers are predicting a decline in heavily professionalized and expensive time-unlimited day program activities (McFarland, 1996). Others propose restricting rehabilitative day treatment to time-limited programs targeted to specific subgroups that have been found to benefit from such services (Piper, Rosie, Joyce, & Azim, 1996).

Future financing of vocational rehabilitation services for people with SMI is uncertain. Traditionally, the main source of funding has been through the federal–state vocational rehabilitation system. Vocational rehabilitation's budget is clearly not sufficient to fund supported-employment programs on the scale needed to address the needs of the SMI population. Less than 5% of clients with SMI in the public mental health system are receiving supported-employment services (Noble et al., 1997). Mental health dollars are used in some states to partially fund vocational services. Under managed care, mental health providers may not perceive any direct incentives to expand or even continue vocational services (Baron, Rutman, & Hadley, 1996), because vocational services historically have not been considered a "medical necessity," which is the standard for providing managed care services. We hope that research will show that supported employment results in a cost offset in which expensive mental health services are reduced by helping clients gain employment (Clark, 1998).

Related to the need for more compelling outcomes and cost-effectiveness research is the growing need for better definitions of program models (i.e., standardized protocols for psychiatric rehabilitation) and systematic ways to measure program implementation. For much of its history, the field of psychiatric rehabilitation has progressed through trial and error, capitalizing on the ingenuity of its leaders and opportunities as they have presented themselves in different communities. Psychiatric rehabilitation practitioners have celebrated diversity and creativity, perhaps at the expense of developing a cumulative body of knowledge. However, there are exceptions to this characterization, notably in the work of university-based researchers.

In the long run, we believe that the development of standardized protocols is healthy for the psychiatric rehabilitation field, because it leads to greater articulation of how programs are implemented. One tool for developing standardized protocols has been the development of *fidelity scales*, defined as systematic measurement tools for assessing how closely a program adheres to the standards of a program model. These tools have advanced most rapidly for the ACT model (Teague, Bond, & Drake, 1998), which not coincidentally is the best-defined psychiatric rehabilitation model. Only a few examples can be found of well-developed fidelity scales in other psychiatric rehabilitation domains (Bond, Becker, Drake, & Vogler, 1997; Wallace et al., 1992).

Conclusion

The pragmatism, eclecticism, and theoretical pluralism that characterize the psychiatric rehabilitation field is appealing from the standpoint of encouraging experimentation and creativity in the design of programs. However, the lack of an overall framework and common vocabulary has hampered communication, both for program implementation and for advancement of scientific knowledge. Progress is facilitated by grounding approaches in theory, defining them operationally, and using rigorous research protocols (Hogarty, Schooler, & Baker, 1997).

More research is needed to establish direct links between putative critical ingredients of psychiatric rehabilitation and client outcomes. Five characteristics have the most empirical support: (a) Effective interventions tend to be direct and behavioral; (b) rehabilitation programs have specific effects on related outcomes, with limited generalization to other domains; (c) short-term interventions are less effective than long-term interventions; (d) interventions need to be delivered close to clients' natural environments; and (e) effective programs often combine skills training and environmental support (Mueser et al., 1997).

Other aspects of psychiatric rehabilitation are underdeveloped. One element that has been inadequately described and evaluated concerns assessment procedures. Although it is generally acknowledged that setting an overall rehabilitation goal and conducting a functional assessment are critical ingredients in the psychiatric rehabilitation process, the extent to which these procedures are systematically applied in everyday practice is suspect (Farkas, Cohen, & Nemec, 1988). The question can be raised whether valid assessment protocols exist. Another glaring gap concerns empirically validated practitioner competencies.

Reflecting on the psychologists who have made the most significant contributions to psychiatric rehabilitation, they typically have been individuals who have not been rigidly bound to the "psychologist" role. As a discipline, we have been guilty of "role lock," often constraining our contributions to the psychiatric rehabilitation field to standardized psychological tests, behavior modification programs, and statistical analyses. We need to make a conscious effort to expand our domains of expertise to affect the rehabilitation of complex psychiatric disorders.

References

American Psychiatric Association. (1994). *Diagnostic and statistical manual of mental disorders* (4th ed.). Washington, DC: Author.

Anthony, W. A., Cohen, M. R., & Farkas, M. A. (1990). *Psychiatric rehabilitation.* Boston: Center for Psychiatric Rehabilitation.

Anthony, W. A., Cohen, M. R., & Vitalo, R. (1978). The measurement of rehabilitation outcome. *Schizophrenia Bulletin, 4,* 365–383.

Anthony, W. A., & Jansen, M. A. (1984). Predicting the vocational capacity of the chronically mentally ill: Research and implications. *American Psychologist, 39,* 537–544.

Atkinson, M., Zibin, S., & Chuang, H. (1997). Characterizing quality of life among patients with chronic mental illness: A critical examination of the self-report methodology. *American Journal of Psychiatry, 154,* 99–105.

Ayllon, T., & Azrin, N. H. (1968). *The token economy: A motivational system for therapy and rehabilitation.* New York: Appleton-Century-Crofts.

Bachrach, L. L. (1988). The chronic patient: On exporting and importing model programs. *Hospital and Community Psychiatry, 39*, 1257–1258.

Baron, R. C., Rutman, I. D., & Hadley, T. (1996). Rehabilitation services for persons with long term mental illness in the managed behavioral health care system: Stepchild again? *Psychiatric Rehabilitation Journal, 20*(2), 33–38.

Beard, J. H., Propst, R. N., & Malamud, T. J. (1982). The Fountain House model of rehabilitation. *Psychosocial Rehabilitation Journal, 5*(1), 47–53.

Becker, D. R., & Drake, R. E. (1993). *A working life: The Individual Placement and Support (IPS) Program.* Concord: New Hampshire–Dartmouth Psychiatric Research Center.

Becker, D. R., Drake, R. E., Farabaugh, A., & Bond, G. R. (1996). Job preferences of clients with severe psychiatric disorders participating in supported employment programs. *Psychiatric Services, 47*, 1223–1226.

Belar, C. D. (1998). Graduate education in clinical psychology: "We're not in Kansas anymore." *American Psychologist, 53*, 456–464.

Bell, M. D., Lysaker, P. H., & Milstein, R. M. (1996). Clinical benefits of paid work activity in schizophrenia. *Schizophrenia Bulletin, 22*, 51–67.

Bernheim, K. F. (1990). Additional comments to "Key issues in training in psychology for service to the seriously mentally ill." In H. P. Lefley (Ed.), *Clinical training in serious mental illness* (pp. 72–74). Washington, DC: U.S. Government Printing Office.

Besio, S. W., & Mahler, J. (1993). Benefits and challenges of using consumer staff in supported housing services. *Hospital and Community Psychiatry, 44*, 490–491.

Blankertz, L. E., & Robinson, S. E. (1996). Who is the psychosocial rehabilitation worker? *Psychiatric Rehabilitation Journal, 19*(4), 3–13.

Bond, G. R. (1992). Vocational rehabilitation. In R. P. Liberman (Ed.), *Handbook of psychiatric rehabilitation* (pp. 244–275). New York: Macmillan.

Bond, G. R. (1999). Psychiatric disabilities. In M. G. Eisenberg, R. L. Glueckauf, & H. H. Zaretsky (Eds.), *Medical aspects of disability: A handbook for the rehabilitation professional* (rev. ed., pp. 412–434). New York: Springer.

Bond, G. R., Becker, D. R., Drake, R. E., & Vogler, K. M. (1997). A fidelity scale for the Individual Placement and Support model of supported employment. *Rehabilitation Counseling Bulletin, 40*, 265–284.

Bond, G. R., Drake, R. E., Mueser, K. T., & Becker, D. R. (1997). An update on supported employment for people with severe mental illness. *Psychiatric Services, 48*, 335–346.

Bond, G. R., Hellkamp, D. T., Dilk, M. N., & Eberlein, L. (1993). Psychology and psychiatric rehabilitation. In M. A. Farkas & W. A. Anthony (Eds.), *Incorporating psychiatric rehabilitation into graduate training programs: Psychiatry, psychology, nursing and social work* (pp. 35–45). Boston: Center for Psychiatric Rehabilitation.

Carling, P. J. (1988). Directions for the 1990s. In L. G. Perlman & C. E. Hansen (Eds.), *Switzer monograph* (pp. 25–47). Alexandria, VA: National Rehabilitation Association.

Carling, P. J. (1993). Housing and supports for persons with mental illness: Emerging approaches to research and practice. *Hospital and Community Psychiatry, 44*, 439–449.

Chamberlin, J., Rogers, J. A., & Sneed, C. S. (1989). Consumers, families, and community support systems. *Psychosocial Rehabilitation Journal, 12*(3), 93–106.

Christianson, J. B., Lurie, N., Finch, M., Moscovice, I., & Hartley, D. (1992). Use of community-based mental health programs by HMOs: Evidence from a Medicaid demonstration. *American Journal of Public Health, 82*, 790–796.

Clark, R. E. (1998). Supported employment and managed care: Can they co-exist? *Psychiatric Rehabilitation Journal, 22*(1), 62–68.

Cnaan, R. A., Blankertz, L., Messinger, K. W., & Gardner, J. R. (1990). Experts' assessment of psychosocial rehabilitation principles. *Psychosocial Rehabilitation Journal, 13*(3), 59–73.

Cutler, D. L., McFarland, B. H., & Winthrop, K. (1998). Mental health in the Oregon Health Plan: Fragmentation or integration? *Administration and Policy in Mental Health, 25*, 361–386.

Dilk, M. N., & Bond, G. R. (1996). Meta-analytic evaluation of skills training research for individuals with severe mental illness. *Journal of Consulting and Clinical Psychology, 64*, 1337–1346.

Dincin, J. (1975). Psychiatric rehabilitation. *Schizophrenia Bulletin, 1*, 131–147.

Dincin, J. (1995). A pragmatic approach to psychiatric rehabilitation: Lessons from Chicago's Thresholds program. *New Directions for Mental Health Services, 68*(Whole Issue).

Dion, G. L., & Anthony, W. A. (1987). Research in psychiatric rehabilitation: A review of experimental and quasi-experimental studies. *Rehabilitation Counseling Bulletin, 30*, 177–203.

Drake, R. E. (1998a). A brief history of the Individual Placement and Support model. *Psychiatric Rehabilitation Journal, 22*(1), 3–7.

Drake, R. E. (1998b). Brief history, current status, and future place of assertive community treatment. *American Journal of Orthopsychiatry, 68*, 172–175.

Drake, R. E., Mercer-McFadden, C., Mueser, K. T., McHugo, G. J., & Bond, G. R. (1998). Treatment of substance abuse in patients with severe mental illness: A review of recent research. *Schizophrenia Bulletin, 24*, 589–608.

Drake, R. E., & Sederer, L. I. (1986). The adverse effects of intensive treatment of chronic schizophrenia. *Comprehensive Psychiatry, 27*, 313–326.

Engstrom, K., Brooks, E. B., Jonikas, J. A., Cook, J. A., & Witheridge, T. F. (1992). *Creating community linkages: A guide to assertive outreach for homeless persons with severe mental illness.* Chicago: Thresholds.

Fabian, E. S., Waterworth, A., & Ripke, B. (1993). Reasonable accommodations for workers with serious mental illness: Type, frequency, and associated outcomes. *Psychosocial Rehabilitation Journal, 17*(2), 163–172.

Fairweather, G. W. (1980). The Fairweather lodge: A twenty-five year retrospective [Whole issue]. *New Directions for Mental Health Services, 7.*

Fairweather, G. W., Sanders, D., Cressler, D., & Maynard, H. (1969). *Community life for the mentally ill: An alternative to hospitalization.* Chicago, IL: Aldine.

Farkas, M. D., Cohen, M. R., & Nemec, P. B. (1988). Psychiatric rehabilitation programs: Putting concepts into practice? *Community Mental Health Journal, 24*, 7–21.

Farkas, M. D., O'Brien, W. F., & Nemec, P. B. (1988). A graduate level curriculum in psychiatric rehabilitation: Filling a need. *Psychosocial Rehabilitation Journal, 12*(2), 53–66.

Federal Register. (1999). Estimation methodology for adults with serious mental illness (SMI). In *Federal Register* (Vol. 64, pp. 33890–33897). Washington, DC: Center for Mental Health Services, Substance Abuse and Mental Health Services Administration, Health and Human Services.

Felton, C. J., Stastny, P., Shern, D. L., Blanch, A., Donahue, S. A., Knight, E., & Brown, C. (1995). Consumers as peer specialists on intensive case management teams: Impact on client outcomes. *Psychiatric Services, 46*, 1037–1044.

Flynn, L. (1997). Managed care and mental illness. *NAMI Advocate, 18*(4), 4.

Frank, R. G., & Johnstone, B. (1996). Changes in the health work force: Implications for psychologists. In R. L. Glueckauf, R. G. Frank, G. R. Bond, & J. H. McGrew (Eds.), *Psychological practice in a changing health care system: Issues and new directions* (pp. 39–51). New York: Springer.

Friday, J. C., & McPheeters, H. L. (1985). *Assessing and improving the performance of psychosocial rehabilitation staff.* Atlanta, GA: Southern Regional Education Board.

Gehrs, M., & Goering, R. (1994). The relationship between the working alliance and rehabilitation outcomes of schizophrenia. *Psychosocial Rehabilitation Journal, 18*(2), 43–54.

Giesler, L., & Hodge, M. (1997). *Clinical protocols for case management for adults with serious and persistent mental illness.* Cincinnati, OH: National Association of Case Management.

Gill, K. J., Pratt, C. W., & Barrett, N. (1997). Preparing psychiatric rehabilitation specialists through undergraduate education. *Community Mental Health Journal, 33*, 323–329.

Glod, C. A. (1996). Recent advances in the pharmacotherapy of major depression. *Archives of Psychiatric Nursing, 10*, 355–364.

Goldman, H. H. (1984). Epidemiology. In J. A. Talbott (Ed.), *The chronic mental patient: Five years later* (pp. 15–31). Orlando, FL: Grune & Stratton.

Green, M. F. (1996). What are the functional consequences of neurocognitive deficits in schizophrenia? *American Journal of Psychiatry, 153*, 321–330.

Hargreaves, W. A., Shumway, M., Hu, T. W., & Cuffel, B. (1998). *Cost-outcome methods for mental health.* San Diego, CA: Academic Press.

Herz, M. I., Liberman, R. P., Lieberman, J. A., Marder, S. R., McGlashan, T. H., & Wang, P. (1997). Practice guideline for the treatment of patients with schizophrenia. *American Journal of Psychiatry, 154*(Suppl.), 1–63.

Hogarty, G., Goldberg, S., & Associates. (1973). Drug and sociotherapy in the aftercare of schizophrenia patients: One-year relapse rates. *Archives of General Psychiatry, 28*, 54–64.

Hogarty, G. E., Schooler, N. R., & Baker, R. W. (1997). Efficacy versus effectiveness. *Psychiatric Services, 48*, 1107.

International Association of Psychosocial Rehabilitation Services. (1997a). *1996 annual report of the International Association of Psychosocial Rehabilitation Services* [Brochure]. Columbia, MS: Author.

International Association of Psychosocial Rehabilitation Services. (1997b). *Practice guidelines for the psychiatric rehabilitation of persons with severe and persistent mental illness in a managed care environment.* Unpublished manuscript, Columbia, MS.

Jaeger, J., & Douglas, E. (1992). Neuropsychiatric rehabilitation for persistent mental illness. *Psychiatric Quarterly, 63*, 71–94.

Johnson, D. L. (Ed.). (1990). *Service needs of the seriously mentally ill: Training implications for psychology.* Washington, DC: American Psychological Association.

Johnson, D. L. (1992). Training psychologists to work with people with serious mental illness: A survey of directors of clinical psychology training programs. *Innovations and Research, 1*(2), 25–29.

Jonikas, J. A. (1994). *Staff competencies for service delivery staff in psychosocial rehabilitation programs: A review of the literature.* Chicago, IL: UIC National Research and Training Center on Psychiatric Disability.

Kohout, J. L., & Wicherski, M. (1996). Employment settings of psychologists. *Psychiatric Services, 47*, 809.

Lefley, H., & Cutler, D. (1988). Training professionals to work with the chronically mentally ill. *Community Mental Health Journal, 24*, 253–257.

Lehman, A. F. (1995). Vocational rehabilitation in schizophrenia. *Schizophrenia Bulletin, 21*, 645–656.

Lieberman, M. A., & Snowden, L. R. (1993). Problems in assessing prevalence and membership characteristics of self-help group participants. *Journal of Applied Behavioral Science, 29*, 166–180.

Macias, C., Jackson, R., Schroeder, C., & Wang, Q. (1999). What is a clubhouse? Report on the ICCD 1996 survey of USA clubhouses. *Community Mental Health Journal, 35*, 181–190.

Marsh, D. T. (1994). *New directions in the psychological treatment of serious mental illness.* Westport, CT: Praeger.

McFarland, B. H. (1994). Health maintenance organizations and persons with severe mental illness. *Community Mental Health Journal, 30*, 221–242.

McFarland, B. H. (1996). Ending the millennium: Commentary on "HMOs and the seriously mentally ill—A view from the trenches." *Community Mental Health Journal, 32*, 219–222.

McGill, C. W., & Patterson, C. J. (1990). Former patients as peer counselors on locked psychiatric inpatient units. *Hospital and Community Psychiatry, 41*, 1017–1019.

McGlashan, T. H. (1988). A selective review of recent North American long-term followup studies of schizophrenia. *Schizophrenia Bulletin, 14*, 515–542.

Mechanic, D., & Aiken, L. H. (1987). Improving the care of patients with chronic mental illness. *New England Journal of Medicine, 317*, 1634–1638.

Meisler, N. (1997). Assertive community treatment initiatives: Results from a survey of selected state mental health authorities. *Community Support Network News, 11*(4), 3–5.

Mental Retardation Facilities and Community Mental Health Centers Construction Act of 1963. P. L. 88-164, 77 Stat. 282.

Morse, G. A., Calsyn, R. J., Klinkenberg, W. D., Trusty, M. L., Gerber, F., Smith, R., Tempelhoff, B., & Ahmad, L. (1997). An experimental comparison of three types of case management for homeless mentally ill persons. *Psychiatric Services, 48*, 497–509.

Mowbray, C. T., Moxley, D. P., Jasper, C. A., & Howell, L. L. (1997). *Consumers as providers in psychiatric rehabilitation*. Columbia, MD: IAPSRS.

Moxley, D. P., Mowbray, C. T., & Brown, K. S. (1993). Supported education. In R. W. Flexer & P. L. Solomon (Eds.), *Psychiatric rehabilitation in practice* (pp. 137–153). Boston: Andover Medical.

Mueser, K. T., Bellack, A. S., Morrison, R. L., & Wixted, J. T. (1990). Social competence in schizophrenia: Premorbid adjustment, social skill, and domains of functioning. *Journal of Psychiatric Research, 24*, 51–63.

Mueser, K. T., Bond, G. R., Drake, R. E., & Resnick, S. G. (1998). Models of community care for severe mental illness: A review of research on case management. *Schizophrenia Bulletin, 24*, 37–74.

Mueser, K. T., Drake, R. E., & Bond, G. R. (1997). Recent advances in psychiatric rehabilitation for patients with severe mental illness. *Harvard Review of Psychiatry, 5*, 123–137.

Mueser, K. T., Glynn, S. M., Corrigan, P. W., & Baber, W. (1996). A survey of preferred terms for users of mental health services. *Psychiatric Services, 47*, 760–761.

Mueser, K. T., Goodman, L. B., Trumbetta, S. L., Rosenberg, S. D., Osher, F. C., Vidaver, R., Auciello, P., & Foy, D. W. (1998). Trauma and posttraumatic stress disorder in severe mental illness. *Journal of Consulting and Clinical Psychology, 66*, 493–499.

Noble, J. H., Honberg, R. S., Hall, L. L., & Flynn, L. M. (1997). *A legacy of failure: The inability of the federal-state vocational rehabilitation system to serve people with severe mental illness*. Arlington, VA: National Alliance for the Mentally Ill.

O'Connor, P., & Tucker, R. D. (1990). The case for master's degree training in psychology for practice in the public sector. In D. L. Johnson (Ed.), *Service needs of the seriously mentally ill: Training implications for psychology* (pp. 81–85). Washington, DC: American Psychological Association.

Paul, G. L., & Lentz, R. J. (1977). *Psychosocial treatment of chronic mental patients: Milieu versus social learning programs*. Cambridge, MA: Harvard University Press.

Penn, D. L., & Mueser, K. T. (1996). Research update on the psychosocial treatment of schizophrenia. *American Journal of Psychiatry, 153*, 607–617.

Piper, W. E., Rosie, J. S., Joyce, A. S., & Azim, H. F. (1996). *Time-limited day treatment for personality disorders: Integration of research and practice in a group program*. Washington, DC: American Psychological Association.

Quinlivan, R. (1997). Managed care: Cost savings and rehabilitation: Compatible goals in for-profit care for persons with serious mental illness? *Psychiatric Services, 48*, 1269–1271.

Rapp, C. A. (1993). Client-centered performance management for rehabilitation and mental health services. In R. W. Flexer & P. L. Solomon (Eds.), *Psychiatric rehabilitation in practice* (pp. 173–192). Boston: Andover.

Rapp, C. A. (1998). The active ingredients of effective case management: A research synthesis. *Community Mental Health Journal, 34*, 363–380.

Rutman, I. D. (1993). And now, the envelope please. . . . *Psychosocial Rehabilitation Journal, 16*(3), 1–3.

Safarjan, W., Marsh, D. T., & Husted, J. (1998). Psychologists [Entire issue]. *Journal of the California Alliance of the Mentally Ill, 9*(1).

Sechrest, L., & Pion, G. (1990). Developing cross-discipline measures of clinical competencies in diagnosis, treatment, and case management. In D. L. Johnson (Ed.), *Service needs of the seriously mentally ill: Training implications for psychology* (pp. 29–31). Washington, DC: American Psychological Association.

Sherman, P. S., & Porter, R. (1991). Mental health consumers as case management aides. *Hospital and Community Psychiatry, 42*, 494–498.

Smith, G. B., Schwebel, A. I., Dunn, R. L., & McIver, S. D. (1993). The role of psychologists in the treatment, management, and prevention of chronic mental illness. *American Psychologist, 48*, 966–971.

Solomon, P., & Draine, J. (1995). One year outcomes of a randomized controlled trial of consumer case management. *Evaluation and Program Planning, 18*, 117–127.

Spaniol, L. (1986). Program evaluation in psychosocial rehabilitation: A management perspective. *Psychosocial Rehabilitation Journal, 10*(1), 15–26.

Spaulding, W. D. (1992). Design prerequisites for research on cognitive therapy for schizophrenia. *Schizophrenia Bulletin, 18*, 39–42.

Stein, L. I., & Test, M. A. (1980). An alternative to mental health treatment: I. Conceptual model, treatment program, and clinical evaluation. *Archives of General Psychiatry, 37*, 392–397.

Stratoudakis, J. P. (1990). Responsibilities of the states in collaborating with academia to improve the service system. In D. L. Johnson (Ed.), *Service needs of the seriously mentally ill: Training implications for psychology* (pp. 15–18). Washington, DC: American Psychological Association.

Stroul, B. A. (1986). *Models of community support services: Approaches to helping persons with long-term mental illness.* Boston: Center for Psychiatric Rehabilitation.

Stroul, B. A. (1988). Residential crisis services: A review. *Hospital and Community Psychiatry, 39*, 1095–1099.

Teague, G. B., Bond, G. R., & Drake, R. E. (1998). Program fidelity in assertive community treatment: Development and use of a measure. *American Journal of Orthopsychiatry, 68*, 216–232.

Test, M. A. (1979). Continuity of care in community treatment. *New Directions for Mental Health Services, 2*, 15–23.

Test, M. A. (1984). Community support programs. In A. S. Bellack (Ed.), *Schizophrenia: Treatment, management, and rehabilitation* (pp. 347–373). Orlando, FL: Grune & Stratton.

Test, M. A. (1992). Training in community living. In R. P. Liberman (Ed.), *Handbook of psychiatric rehabilitation* (pp. 153–170). New York: Macmillan.

Torrey, E. F. (1995). *Surviving schizophrenia: A manual for families, consumers, and providers* (3rd. ed.). New York: HarperCollins.

Trainor, J., Shepherd, M., Boydell, K. M., Leff, A., & Crawford, E. (1997). Beyond the service paradigm: The impact and implications of consumer/survivor initiatives. *Psychiatric Rehabilitation Journal, 21*(2), 132–140.

Turner, J. C., & TenHoor, W. J. (1978). The NIMH community support program: Pilot approach to a needed social reform. *Schizophrenia Bulletin, 4*, 319–348.

Vorspan, R. (1988). Activities of daily living in the clubhouse: You can't vacuum in a vacuum. *Psychosocial Rehabilitation Journal, 12*(2), 15–21.

Wallace, C. J., Liberman, R. P., MacKain, S. J., Blackwell, G., & Eckman, T. A. (1992). Effectiveness and replicability of modules for teaching social and instrumental skills to the severely mentally ill. *American Journal of Psychiatry, 149*, 654–658.

Wehman, P., & Moon, M. S. (Eds.). (1988). *Vocational rehabilitation and supported employment.* Baltimore: Brookes.

Weiden, P. J., Aquila, R., & Standard, J. (1996). Atypical antipsychotic drugs and long-term outcome in schizophrenia. *Journal of Clinical Psychiatry, 57*(Suppl. 11), 53–60.

Wohlford, P. (1994). National perspectives on clinical training for psychological services. In D. T. Marsh (Ed.), *New directions in the psychological treatment of serious mental illness* (pp. 3–20). Westport, CT: Praeger.

Part II

Critical Factors

12

Functional Status and Quality-of-Life Measures

Allen W. Heinemann

Health care and rehabilitation in the United States are undergoing remarkable transitions. Administrators are consolidating and integrating delivery systems, providers are assuming financial risk for patient outcomes, and patients alone rather than providers alone evaluate interventions. These changes have helped create support for what Ellwood (1988) called "outcomes management." A fundamental premise of this movement is the belief that assessment and monitoring of health outcomes are critical to improving care. Two important aspects of health care outcomes are the recipient's functional status and quality of life (QoL). Whereas *functional status* is widely understood by rehabilitation psychologists in terms of disability severity or independence in activities of daily living (ADL), *quality of life* is apt to be a less familiar term without a shared definition.

Confusion about the term's definition reflects the fact that QoL can mean many things to different people. Material possessions, wealth, body functioning, social relationships, life satisfaction, emotional well-being, and spiritual wholeness are aspects of QoL that many people reference when asked to provide a definition. One central distinction in QoL concerns the perspective one takes (Dijkers, 1997). *Subjective approaches* define QoL in terms of congruence between aspirations and achievements as judged by the person. *Objective approaches* focus on observable characteristics such as income, neighborhood poverty level, life span, education, and disorders. *Health-related QoL*, the focus of this chapter, expounds on those aspects of life that may be affected by health; these characteristics typically include functional status, energy level, pain, participation in social and daily activities, and ability to leave one's home. The importance of assessing both subjective and objective measures of disability and QoL is recognized widely (Hobart, Freeman, & Lamping, 1996; Rothwell, McDowell, Wong, & Dorman, 1997). Although QoL evaluation has been a focus of research in the chronic illness (Kane, 1995) and cancer literature (Cella, Lloyd, & Wright, 1996), it has only recently become a concern of rehabilitation clinicians and researchers (Tate, 1997). Instrument developers have promoted item sets for use in such diverse undertakings as multi-

I appreciate the editorial comments of Rita Bode, William Borden, and Johnnie Berry.

center clinical trials, monitoring of outcomes in various clinical practices (Clark et al., 1997; Epstein & Sherwood, 1996; Werner & Kessler, 1996), severity- or "risk-adjusting" outcomes (Iezzoni, 1994), and development of care protocols (U.S. Department of Health and Human Services [DHHS], 1995).

Accompanying this increased interest in health care outcomes generally and QoL specifically, dozens of instruments have been promoted; their psychometric properties and clinical use vary widely (Berzon, Mauskopf, & Simeon, 1996; Erickson, 1998; Herndon, 1997; Spilker, 1996). A "gold standard" functional status or QoL instrument is unlikely to emerge, given the needs of various users, divergent scaling properties, experiences of different clinical populations, and high level of sophistication needed to understand and interpret these instruments. Proponents of both generic and disease-specific measures seek instruments with a minimum number of items, a high level of precision, clinical relevance, and sensitivity. Aggregation across individuals and comparison of outcomes over time are typical applications. Applicability to people with a variety of chronic illnesses and disabilities is also valued, although it is often at odds with the need to assess disability-specific characteristics.

Rehabilitation professionals generally and rehabilitation psychologists specifically have just begun to enter the health-related QoL discussion. The growth of rehabilitation professionals' interest in QoL is illustrated by the absence of QoL index listings in Marcus Fuhrer's landmark 1987 textbook *Rehabilitation Outcomes*, whereas the 1997 *Assessing Medical Rehabilitation Practices* has extensive listings. Interest in QoL is relatively new for other allied health disciplines too (Jette, 1993). Rehabilitation psychology's fundamental concern with the experiences of people with chronic illness and disability allows for relative ease in grasping the vocabulary of the QoL literature (Livneh & Antonak, 1997; Shontz, 1982; B. A. Wright, 1983). As this chapter demonstrates, parallel developments in health outcomes research are widely applicable to rehabilitation psychologists' work in clinical, research, and policy roles. My purpose here is to summarize work outside of rehabilitation psychology related to measurement of functional status and QoL and to relate it to the concerns of rehabilitation psychologists. Here I do not focus on measures developed for cost effectiveness or cost–benefit analysis, such as quality-adjusted life years, a useful method of characterizing and comparing health states used frequently with surgical (Birkmeyer & Welch, 1997; Rutigliano, 1995), long-term care (Hays et al., 1996), arthritis (Kaplan, Alcaraz, Anderson, & Weisman, 1996), and other medical populations because of the distinct history and assumptions of these measures.

Historical Perspective

Functional status and QoL measures provide a means of comparing (a) changes within an individual over time, (b) groups of individuals defined on the basis of disability or illness, or (c) organizations that provide rehabilitation or health care. Measures of functional status and QoL have varied in whether the recipient, provider, payer, or purchaser was the intended user of the information. The development of functional status and QoL measures allows us to assess (a) functional, psychological, and social improvements experienced by people with impairments; (b) the structure and processes of provider organizations; and (c) the relative value of services received. The history described below focuses on the utility of functional status and QoL measures as they serve the need to describe health care outcomes.

Instruments

Three generations of health-related measurement can be identified. In the first generation, information was collected to improve the quality of acute care hospital processes and outcomes. The Health Care Financing Administration inaugurated a hospital-specific mortality report to monitor and improve surgical outcomes in the mid-1980s (DHHS, 1986). The Joint Commission on Accreditation of Healthcare Organizations (JCAHO; Nadzam, Turpin, Hanold, & White, 1993; Turpin et al., 1996) and the Maryland Hospital Association (Kazandjian, Lawthers, Cernak, & Pipesh, 1993) subsequently developed indicator-monitoring systems that were designed to improve quality of patient care. In medical rehabilitation, the Uniform Data System for Medical Rehabilitation (UDS$_{MR}$; Hamilton, Granger, Sherwin, Zielezny, & Tashman, 1987) and the Medical Outcome System ("Formations in health care," 1998) were developed to provide rehabilitation facilities with a comparative outcomes database for program improvement. The Commission for the Accreditation Rehabilitation Facilities (CARF) strategic outcome initiative is increasing its focus on performance-based information for postacute care (Wilkerson, 1997). Improved functional status, shortened lengths of stay and minimized costs, efficient gains in functional status, and home discharge are the types of rehabilitation outcomes considered by CARF in its development of performance indicators.

Outcome measure development moved from acute hospitals to a variety of settings in the second generation as payers and purchasers came to realize the value of outcomes information in selecting provider groups on the basis of cost effectiveness. The Health Plan Employer Data and Information Set initiative by the National Committee for Quality Assurance (NCQA; Morrissey, 1996c) exemplifies this shift in focus. Large provider groups such as Columbia/HCA Healthcare Corporation (Greene, 1996) and United Healthcare Corporation (McGlynn, 1993) promoted the value of comparative data in marketing to purchasers. A variety of purchaser coalitions continue to support accountability in health care by emphasizing purchasing decisions based on outcomes ("Employer coalitions as a vehicle," 1996).

The third generation is characterized by the development of consumer groups' interest in outcomes. The Foundation for Accountability published summaries of performance measures to help patients select providers on the basis of access and quality (Morrissey, 1995, 1996a, 1996c). State governments have developed reports of provider performance to help consumers make health care decisions. Finally, *Health Pages* provides consumer-oriented comparative information in specific markets.[1] These efforts focus on acute health conditions rather than chronic conditions. One exception is the NCQA, which is developing measures for major depression, childhood asthma, diabetes, and coronary artery disease (Morrissey, 1996b). A consensus about the types of outcomes for which rehabilitation is responsible and can be expected to affect is needed (Batterham, Dunt, & Disler, 1996).

Structure, Process, and Outcome

Donabedian (1966) distinguished three components of health care quality measurement: (a) structure (i.e., the settings in which health care is provided, the adequacy of facilities and equipment, and the qualifications of staff), (b) process (i.e., information obtained from patients, technical competence of staff, extent of preventive management, coordination and continuity of care), and (c) outcomes (i.e., recovery, restoration of function, survival). Early attempts to evaluate health care focused on structure and process because this information was the most readily available. More recently, researchers have argued that outcomes should be the focus of attention because good outcomes are the product that medical care is seeking. Accreditation bodies have added outcome measurement to their traditional focus on structure and process. However, an exclusive focus on outcomes denies the power of organizational attributes and is unable to provide much direction for quality improvement. A comprehensive quality measurement system must include indicators of structure, process, and outcome.

There is considerable evidence that health care processes and outcomes vary across settings (Wennberg, 1982). In medical rehabilitation, variations in outcomes are evident to inpatient rehabilitation subscribers to *Caredata* and UDS$_{MR}$; subscribers receive comparative outcome information nationally and by region. The current movement toward clinical guidelines or protocols is based on the assumption that greater standardization of practice results in greater quality at less cost and helps reduce practice variations. Empirical demonstration of variation in practice and an explanation for why it exists are entirely another matter. Clinicians and researchers are just now achieving consensus about how best to treat certain illnesses or conditions, in part because of the work of patient outcomes research teams and clinical guidelines funded by the Agency for Health Care Policy and Research and other organizations. Current efforts to identify best practices reflect the belief that clinical processes are related to outcomes.

---

[1]For more information, contact M. Schreider (Ed.) at 212/505-0103 or 135 Fifth Avenue, 7th Floor, New York, NY 10010.

Although there are strong theoretical reasons to believe that organizational characteristics influence patient outcomes, little empirical evidence supports this belief. It is unclear whether organizational structures and processes, even those that are believed to be strongly related to patient outcomes, are causal or correlational. For some medical conditions, relationships have been found among organizational characteristics, patient outcomes, and resource utilization (Shortell, Levin, O'Brien, & Hughes, 1995). In Shortell et al.'s study, increased availability of technology, technical level of care, and caregiver interaction with patients reduced hospitals' risk-adjusted mortality and length of stay for patients treated in intensive care units; these results support the importance of evaluating structure, process, and outcome.

Fundamental Measurement Concepts

Recent changes in rehabilitation organization and service delivery have important implications for the science and practice of functional assessment and health services research. What we measure, how we measure, and how well these measures predict outcomes are of concern not only to academics but also to consumers, providers, and payers so as to ensure that rehabilitation is responsive to today's market realities. Summarized below are fundamental issues in how functional status and QoL are measured.

Advances in Conceptualizing and Measuring Disablement and Its Consequences

The World Health Organization's (WHO) definition of *health* refers to physical, mental, and social well-being rather than the absence of disease or infirmity (WHO, 1958). Interest in QoL beyond the absence of disease or infirmity has increased steadily in recent years. Medical rehabilitation is built on a QoL foundation, emphasizing functional, psychological, and social restoration and adjustment to residual disability. Its goal is to maximize QoL, and it uses various medical, physical, psychological, cognitive, and occupational therapies to do so. The WHO's model of disablement provides a fundamental advance in the understanding of what to measure and the relationships among disablement concepts (WHO, 1997). *Disablement* is described as involving complex relationships between health conditions and contextual factors, both environmental and personal; the relationships are potentially bidirectional. *Impairment* is defined as "a loss or abnormality of body structure or of a physiological or psychological function" (WHO, 1997, p. 15). Level or completeness of spinal cord injury resulting in paralysis or extent of visual limitation associated with macular degeneration are examples of impairments. Impairments may result in *activity limitations*, defined as "the nature and extent of functioning at the level of the person" (p. 16). In turn, impairment or activity limitations may result in *participation restrictions*, "the nature and extent of a person's involvement in life situations in relation to Impairments, Activities, Health Conditions and Contextual factor" (p. 17). Social roles such as worker, homemaker, student, and community member are examples of roles that may be limited. The Craig Handicap Assessment and Reporting Technique (CHART; Whiteneck, Charlifue, Gerhart, Overholser, & Richardson, 1992) is a tool developed to assess extent of role limitation or (conversely) societal participation.

Disease classification and impairment category are often combined in rehabilitation research because there is little treatment for the disease (Wade, 1992). The unifying theme among impairment, activities, and participation is that each represents a different level of interest (Turner, 1990). The Donabedian (1966), WHO, and QoL frameworks provide complementary models for QoL measurement.

Most QoL measures are patient centered and depend on individuals' perception of their health. The QoL literature typically distinguishes four essential components: (a) physical function, (b) psychological state, (c) social interaction, and (d) somatic sensation (Schipper, Clinch, & Powell, 1990). In a similar model, Kane (1995) described (a) physiological functioning, (b) ADL, (c) pain, (d) cognition, (e) affect, (f) social activity, (g) social relationships, and (h) satisfaction as generally accepted components for assessment of quality in long-term care.

Outcome measures can be either generic or disease specific. Generic measures, such as QoL and return to work, can be used for many impairment groups, including spinal cord injury, traumatic brain injury, and multiple sclerosis. Yet because the WHO model emphasizes the importance of measuring impairment-level quality, disease-specific measures of health status are important as well.

In summary, perceptions of QoL are typically assessed from the perspective of the care recipient, include functional status as an element, and can monitor outcomes and compare groups or change over time. In the next section I review measurement principles, followed by examples of functional status and QoL measures.

Alternate Conceptual Models for Functional Status

Although the WHO's *International Classification of Impairments, Activity and Participation* (1997) is used worldwide, limitations exist. Wade (1992) noted that the distinctions between conceptual domains can be unclear. Finding an operational definition of participation that is acceptable to consumers, clinicians, and researchers is also challenging, despite the work by Whiteneck et al. (1992). Wade noted that some diagnoses, particularly mental health diagnoses, do not have a clear pathology, and some conditions, such as epilepsy, are characterized by only intermittent impairment.

A U.S. variant of the WHO disablement model has been adopted by the Institute of Medicine and the National Center for Medical Rehabilitation Research (National Institutes of Health, 1993). It is based on Saad

Nagi's (cited in Pope & Tarlov, 1991) terminology, in which *functional limitations* replaces WHO's *activities* and *disability* replaces WHO's *participation*. These terminology differences reflect the U.S. Public Health Service Task Force's organ-level definition of *impairment*, person-level definition of *functional limitations*, and the person–environment interaction-level definition of *disability*. The confusion resulting from the different uses of the same terms requires that users describe the context of their terms.

Conceptual Models

A confusing plethora of definitions and terms abounds in the QoL literature. One of the most authoritative compendiums of QoL measures asserts that there is no agreement on the number and types of "quality of life" (Spilker, 1996). Various levels of QoL components are sometimes viewed in a pyramidal fashion in which multiple, specific components comprise a bottom level, broad domains comprise a higher level, and an overall appraisal of well-being comprises the top level. Domains generally referenced include (a) physical status and functional abilities, (b) psychological status and well-being, (c) social interactions, (d) economic and vocational status and factors, and (e) religious and spiritual status. Spilker categorized the foci of instruments designed to assess QoL into five realms: (a) universally agreed-on aspects of health-related QoL applicable to everyone, (b) components of health-related QoL applicable to everyone, (c) components of health-related QoL applicable to people with specific conditions, (d) components sometimes viewed as an aspect of health-related QoL that are usually classified as clinical measures (e.g., depression, pain, or cognition), and (e) tangential aspects of QoL that are used occasionally. Schipper, Clinch, and Olweny (1996) asserted that QoL is a multifactorial construct, subjectively appraised, and related to a concept of reintegration to normal living. It reflects the "net consequences of disease and its treatment on the patient's perception of his ability to live a useful and fulfilling life" (p. 15). Rubenstein (1996) related severity of impairment and disability to health status limitations, whereas handicap affects and is affected by environmental limitations. In turn, both health status and environmental limitations are viewed as affecting QoL. The variety of QoL measures has led to efforts to equate measures within and across cultures (Cella et al., 1996).

Overview of Functional Status Measurement Issues

The British Medical Council (Wade, 1992) proposed five criteria by which to evaluate the utility of measures:

1. *Context of use.* Who can use the test? Is it appropriate for the purpose of the study? Who can complete the test? Can a proxy

complete the test? What is the method of administration? How long does it take? Is the test acceptable to patients?

2. *Development*. How were the items selected? What populations have been sampled? What is the format of the test? Is the format suitable for the intended population? How is it scored? What are the ceiling and floor of the test? Are normal values or a cut-off score available? Are there distinct subscores?

3. *Validity*. Has construct, concurrent, and predictive validity been established? For which populations?

4. *Reliability*. How consistent are scores across raters? Occasions? Settings? Is there bias?

5. *Sensitivity*. Has the test been used in placebo-controlled trials? Used in a trial of known efficacy? Compared with other measures?

The critical question to consider in test selection is this: Will the test provide the required information? A satisfactory answer requires that one state in advance what one wants to measure to select an appropriate test. Testing for the sake of testing is unlikely to yield useful information.

Wade (1992) suggested the following criteria in evaluating instruments for screening purposes: (a) suitability to one's purpose, (b) relevance and sensibility, (c) validity—does it measure what it purports to measure, (d) reliability—consistency of measurement, (e) sensitivity, (f) simplicity, and (g) ease of communicating results. An evaluation of suitability requires that one consider the reasons for assessment. These reasons may include (a) describing the kind of patient being studied, often for prognostic purposes; (b) measuring aspects of the treatment process, usually at the level of impairment; and (c) measuring outcomes of treatment, usually at the level of disability or handicap. A general discussion of psychometric issues follows and then a discussion of how these criteria can be applied to widely used instruments.

Reliability

Reliability concerns the issue of how consistently a score is obtained. Measurement error can affect repeated measures across time or situations or between raters. Reliability theory distinguishes two components of any score: that which is true and that which is due to error. Noise or imprecision in measurement creates error. Rater bias and other systematic errors are an issue of validity, discussed below. *Reliability of measurement* is defined as the ratio of true variation to observed variance. Internal consistency of tests evaluates how well items cohere. Cronbach's alpha and Kuder–Richardson's formula are traditional ways to assess internal consistency. As noted above, newer psychometric approaches built on Georg Rasch's rating scale extend these ideas by distinguishing item and person fit characteristics (B. D. Wright & Masters, 1982; B. D. Wright & Stone, 1979).

Validity

Validity concerns the meaning of scores derived from an instrument; it is commonly defined as the extent to which a test measures what it purports to measure. A more general definition focuses on the range of interpretations that can be appropriately placed on a score, that is, its meaning. Related concepts are sensitivity and specificity: *Sensitivity* pertains to how well a test identifies people with a certain condition, and *specificity* reflects the extent to which a test identifies only those people with that condition. Validity can be assessed in several ways. *Content validity*, a usual first step, involves comprehensiveness or adequacy of sampling. Relevance of items to the concept being measured is considered in determining content validity. *Sensibility* is a related concept; it refers to the clinical appropriateness of the measure. Critical reviews by patients or experts in the field are ways to assess content validity.

    Criterion validity assesses how well a new instrument is related to a gold standard that measures the same construct. Statistical procedures such as correlational analyses examine how strongly a new measure is associated with established measures and uncorrelated with unrelated measures. Criterion validity is often divided into *concurrent validity* and *predictive validity*, reflecting an interest in contemporaneous or future relationships, respectively. Sensitivity and specificity may reflect a variety of patient background factors, such as gender and education in the case of QoL appraisals.

    Construct validity emerges when sufficient evidence is collected that allows test users to evaluate how well a test measures its intended construct. Correlational evidence (the new test correlates with similar established tests but not dissimilar ones) is useful for such an appraisal. Clearly stated hypotheses about the relationship of a test to other tests are required to evaluate the construct validity of a test.

Level of Measurement

A classical distinction in measurement defines four levels that reflect the properties of the test (Stevens, 1951). *Nominal scales* distinguish the presence or absence of a condition or the ability or inability to complete a task. *Ordinal scales* provide for rank ordering of a condition or phenomenon from more to less (e.g., severity of symptoms or disruption of function). *Interval level of measurement* is defined by equal spacing of responses (e.g., physical measures of length, pressure, and mass in terms of centimeters, millimeters of mercury, and kilograms, respectively). A *ratio level of measurement* extends interval measurement with the addition of an absolute zero point; temperature in degrees kelvin is such an example. Most rating scales of functional status and QoL provide only ordinal data. Assumptions about severity of impairment on the basis of sums of item values are severely limited because the extent of a condition is unknown. Conversion to linear measures is required to properly use parametric statistics such as analysis of variance and regression. That continuous numbers are produced that one can manipulate in seemingly meaningful ways reflects the fact that the relationship between ordinal scores and interval measures are often linear in the midrange of their values. However, the relationship between raw scores and linear measures is necessarily ogival (S shaped) across the entire range of scores because one is attempting to relate a necessarily finite range of raw scores to an infinite range of potential values.

Functional Status Conceptual Models

Linear measurement is crucial to the advancement of rehabilitation practice. The raw score that is obtained by summing item responses is ordinal in nature; its use in parametric statistical comparisons is precluded because these raw data only allow rank ordering of scores. A measurement procedure that can be used to develop interval-scaled measures from ordinal scores is rating scale, or Rasch, analysis (Rasch, 1960/1980), named after the Danish mathematician whose work in the 1950s and 1960s has been widely applied in educational testing and more recently in rehabilitation outcome measurement. Interval-level measures have the advantage of having equal intervals between units of the scale. When distributed in a reasonably normal fashion, measures from an interval scale can be subjected to parametric statistical analyses. Transforming ordinal raw scores to interval measures allows one to quantify an individual's level of functional status or QoL along an equal-interval continuum, make quantitative comparisons within an individual across time, or compare individuals or groups. Rating scale analysis helps evaluate the extent to which responses to a set of items are dominated by the one dimension it purports to measure. This procedure defines items along a continuum that ranges from easy to perform (or endorse) to difficult to perform (or endorse). If functional tasks form a single construct, one would expect individuals to be more able to perform easy tasks and less able to perform difficult tasks. When individuals are unable to perform a task that they would have been expected to perform on the basis of their overall level, their responses do not fit the measurement model. Thus, a patient poststroke who climbs stairs (a harder task) but cannot walk (an easier task) would not fit a model of ambulation recovery. Although individuals do not always respond exactly as expected on a given series of tasks, the finding that a substantial proportion respond unexpectedly to a task provides an indication that the task does not "fit" with the remaining tasks in forming a unidimensional construct. It is often the case that an item set contains "noisy" items or that the definitions of scale categories are vague, which contributes to imprecise measurement. Rating scale analysis provides guidance for fine-tuning an item set to enhance its precision. Strategies include rewording or deleting items, rescoring or combining rating scales, or segregating people into homogeneous subgroups. The derived measure becomes useful in describing and evaluating functional status or QoL when the evidence for unidimensionality is compelling. Attaining a fine-tuned item set allows each person to be characterized by a single, interval-level measure and each item by an estimate of its difficulty.

Several criteria are used to judge and improve the adequacy of a measure. These criteria include (a) *person separation* (the range of function or QoL represented by the people in the sample) and *item separation* (the range of function or QoL covered by the measure), (b) *item fit* (the extent to which the sample as a whole responds unexpectedly to specific items), (c) *person fit* (the extent to which individuals or diagnostic subgroups respond idiosyncratically to the item set), and (d) *scale structure* (the extent to which raters use the steps in the scale consistently). The range of a construct, such as QoL, represented in a given sample is summarized with a *person separation index*, defined as the ratio of the true spread of the measure to its measurement error. The index indicates the spread of a given sample of patients in units of the error in their measures. A clinically useful set of items should define at least three strata of patients (e.g., "high," "moderate," and "low" levels). A related statistic, called *item separation*, indicates the item set's potential range of measurement; larger values indicate a potentially greater range of the construct that the item set can measure. Development of Rasch model computer programs such as BIGSTEPS (B. D. Wright & Linacre, 1998) allows the easy computation of these statistics.

Rating scale analysis provides clinicians and researchers with a valid method of describing the extent of functional status and QoL in people undergoing rehabilitation, of extending scales across a continuum of settings, of identifying people for whom a common scale is not useful, and of identifying items that do not work well to define a unidimensional construct. Preliminary work with functional status measures such as the Functional Independence Measure (FIM) instrument (Heinemann, Linacre, Wright, Hamilton, & Granger, 1994; Linacre, Heinemann, Wright, Granger, & Hamilton, 1994), Patient Evaluation and Conference System (W. P. Fisher, Harvey, Taylor, Kilgore, & Kelly, 1995), Level of Rehabilitation Scale III (Velozo, Magalhaes, Pan, & Leiter, 1995), and participation measure (CHART; Whiteneck et al., 1992) helps clinicians assess WHO's (1997) model of disablement. Additional work is needed to extend the range of measured functional status and QoL from what is observed in single settings to a continuum of treatment settings (Segal, Heinemann, Schall, & Wright, 1997), to equate estimates of functional status and QoL across specific instruments (A. G. Fisher, 1997), and to identify and correct bias introduced by raters with different backgrounds (Bode & Heinemann, 1997; Lai, Velozo & Linacre, 1997).

Strategies for Improving Functional Status

Functional status and QoL measures should be reliable, valid, sensitive to change, and able to discriminate among levels of performance. Few useful instruments exist to measure these characteristics across a range of settings. For example, functional status measures are often targeted at patients in specific settings (e.g., inpatient rehabilitation) and are too easy for patients in other settings (e.g., outpatient facilities). An important task is to cocalibrate items from across tests targeted at low, medium, and high levels of function to provide estimates of performance regardless of which test was administered. A major goal of some functional status and QoL investigators is to create measures that are useful for people in the general community who are receiving treatment for a variety of conditions. A sensible approach is to cocalibrate items from two or more tests and rescore items as necessary to maximize the range of the instrument, item fit, and utility. A typical approach would involve the following:

- defining the clinical population for which one wants to develop a useful measure
- defining the settings from which one wants to sample the population
- conducting a literature review to identify candidate instruments
- selecting instruments on the basis of criteria listed above and the results of a literature review
- training clinicians to administer the instruments consistently
- administering the candidate instrument to the sample
- evaluating the number of strata into which the sample can be distinguished, item reliability, range of item difficulties, item misfit, and person misfit.

Typical questions might include the following:

- How well do items from separate tests work to define a construct?
- Does each item set span a useful range of performance?
- Do any of them fit poorly with the underlying construct?
- Does the addition of items from several tests improve the span of function or QoL that is measured?
- Do any of these items fit poorly with a construct of function or QoL?
- What minimum set of items, drawn perhaps from across several existing instruments, works most efficiently to define functional status or QoL in specific settings, such as the community, a geriatric unit, or a rehabilitation program?

The results of the evaluation phase may require revision of instructions, development of additional items, deletion of items because of poor fit, identification of patients for whom the instrument may usefully be applied, and development of refined scoring criteria.

Relationship Between Functional Status and Quality-of-Life Measures

As this review illustrates, functional status is often viewed in the general health care literature as a component of QoL. For example, the Short

Form-36 Health Survey (SF-36; Ware, 1993) includes a 10-item physical function subscale, which is summed separately or as part of a total score. The Sickness Impact Profile (SIP; Bergner, Bobbitt, Carter, & Gilson, 1981) also includes categories assessing daily activities. This is a different perspective from that of rehabilitation professionals, who usually think of functional status as an aspect of disablement. Both conceptual models are useful, but one must clarify the framework an author is using to communicate clearly. The confidence with which one can sum items from diverse conceptual domains and obtain coherent, unitary measures has been evaluated adequately with only a few instruments.

Developmental level must be considered in selecting instruments. For example, the pediatric version of the FIM, the Wee-FIM (Ottenbacher et al., 1997), has modified item definitions that consider developmental expectations. Similarly, the Pediatric Evaluation of Disability Inventory (PEDI; Haley, Ludlow, & Coster, 1993) was developed to assess children's functional status. As described below, cocalibration of items from different instruments can equate performance levels of individuals, regardless of age, when the items cohere in defining a common construct.

A variety of condition- or disease-specific measures have been developed. Excellent reviews of QoL measures are in Spilker's (1996) and McDowell and Newell's (1996) textbooks. The extent to which a QoL measure is useful and applicable to a specific population must be considered carefully.

Applications and Chronic Health Conditions

Space limitations preclude a thorough review of all instruments. Because rating scale analysis represents a major advancement in methodology, instruments were selected for review on the basis of their evaluation with rating scale analysis and favorable findings. These reviews are intended to provide an overview of commonly used instruments that possess good psychometric properties and are likely to serve clinicians' and researchers' needs well into the 21st century.

Functional Status Measures

Reviews of functional status measures are large and growing. Interested readers are urged to consult comprehensive textbooks such as Dittmar and Gresham (1997); Cole, Finch, Gowland, and Mayo (1995); Wade (1992); Smith (1997); and Bowling (1995, 1997) to appreciate the array of functional status instruments. This section describes three representative functional status measures for which well-developed psychometric properties have been reported; the PEDI, the FIM, and the Assessment of Motor and Process Skills (AMPS; A. G. Fisher, 1997; A. G. Fisher & Fisher, 1993).

Pediatric Evaluation of Disability Inventory

Stephen Haley et al. (1993), at the Health Institute of the New England Medical Center, developed PEDI to assess functional capabilities and performance in children between 6 months and 7 years 6 months of age; it can be used with older children whose disability levels are within this age range. The PEDI was designed for children with both congenital and acquired disorders. Potential uses include identifying goals for individual educational plans; measuring delays in self-care, mobility, and social skills; monitoring children's progress; and describing program outcomes. It was normed on a carefully chosen nondisabled sample to distinguish normal and delayed performance. It is administered by structured interview with the child's parent, clinician, or educator who is familiar with the child; administration typically requires 20–60 minutes.

PEDI focuses on three domains: self-care (15 items; e.g., use of utensils, drinking containers; toileting), mobility (14 items; e.g., transfers, locomotion, stairs), and social function (12 items; e.g., comprehension of words and sentences, expressive communication, orientation). These 41 items are scored on a six-category rating scale that ranges from *total assistance* (0) to *independent* (5). In addition to measuring the child's performance, PEDI measures the amount of caregiver assistance and modifications or equipment required; modifications are rated on a 4-point scale (*no modifications*, *nonspecialized modifications*, *rehabilitation equipment*, *extensive modifications*).

PEDI summary scores are based on a normative sample of 412 children from New England. Normative scores are based on chronological age in 6-month intervals. Rating scale analysis of PEDI items revealed an item difficulty hierarchy that supports the validity of the instrument. For example, relatively easy items on the Functional Skills Mobility Scale (as part of PEDI) include sitting supported by equipment or the caregiver, rising to a sitting position, crawling and creeping on the floor, and changing location purposefully. Harder items include getting in and out of a car, getting in and out of a chair without arms, walking up a flight of stairs, and moving 150 feet or further without difficulty. The item hierarchy is congruent with developmental models. Results are reported as standard scores based on age-based norms, scaled scores, and frequency counts; software is available to assist scoring. Evidence of reliability (internal consistency, interrater reliability) and validity is good. Construct validity is supported by significant correlations with the Wee-FIM (the pediatric version of the FIM instrument) and the Battelle Development Inventory Screening Test. The PEDI is limited to self-care, mobility, and social functioning; the extent to which the normative sample is representative of children from across the nation is unclear.

Functional Independence Measure

The FIM (Hamilton et al., 1987) was designed to rate the severity of patient disability and the outcomes of medical rehabilitation. It grew out of a task force sponsored by the American Congress on Rehabilitation Medicine and the American Academy of Physical Medicine and Rehabilitation. After reviewing a variety of instruments, the task force defined 18 items that assess self-care, sphincter management, mobility (transfers), locomotion, communication, and social cognition on a 7-point scale that ranges from 1 (*total assistance*) to 7 (*complete independence*). Several items have two forms that reflect type of locomotion (walk vs. wheelchair), comprehension (auditory, visual, or both), and expression (vocal, nonvocal, or both). The FIM is part of the UDS$_{MR}$, a format for recording rehabilitation-relevant information, including category of impairment, length of stay and charges, admission and discharge setting and living arrangement, *International Classification of Diseases* 9-CM codes, and vocational participation. It has become the de facto standard for describing medical rehabilitation outcomes in the United States; over 700 facilities use it worldwide. Two subscription services use the FIM and provide a data management service that helps facilities fulfill CARF accreditation requirements.

Reliability evidence is excellent when raters are accredited to use the instrument (Ottenbacher, Hsu, Granger, & Fiedler, 1996). Evidence of construct validity is provided by studies correlating minutes of caregiver assistance with FIM scores. Heinemann, Linacre, Wright, Hamilton, and Granger (1993, 1994) evaluated the extent to which the items cohered to define a measure of disability and a measure of disability that is comparable for patients with differing impairments. They sought to construct an interval-level measure of disability that is useful over as large a range of impairments as possible without losing clear distinctions between patients with different impairments. Ratings from 33,709 rehabilitation inpatients who received services at hospitals subscribing to the UDS$_{MR}$ comprised their sample. They found that the FIM could be scaled as two measures. Motor (self-care, sphincter management, mobility, locomotion) and cognitive (communication, social cognition) aspects of function were important to distinguish. Item difficulties varied slightly across impairment groups, reflecting the unique affects of various impairments, although not usually in a way that distorted uniform measurement. The item hierarchy and results of factor analysis support the validity of the FIM. Discharge expectancies can be established on the basis of these scaling results, and programs can evaluate their outcomes in terms of attainment of discharge performance. Demonstration of patient function as consisting of two distinct aspects of behavior suggests that both domains are important in helping patients live independently and in estimating caregiver requirements. The FIM could be improved by raising the ceiling of the measures to cover patients in outpatient settings, enhancing the sensitivity of the cognitive measure, and by distinguishing sphincter control from hygiene management.

Assessment of Motor and Process Skills

Anne Fisher (1997; Fisher & Fisher, 1993) developed the AMPS to measure the quality of performance of domestic and instrumental ADLs. Performance quality is measured in terms of efficiency, effectiveness, safety, and difficulty of actions. The instrument was designed for occupational therapists to evaluate two domains of occupational performance: motor and process skills. *Motor skills* are defined as the actions that people use to move objects and themselves; the assessment considers posture, mobility, coordination, strength and effort, and energy. Process skills are the actions taken to sequence actions logically, select and use equipment appropriately, and modify performance when problems occur; they include energy, use of knowledge, temporal organization, space and objects, and adaptation. The instrument enhances meaningfulness of the task to the person and takes full advantage of multifaceted rating scale analysis by asking the person to select 2 or 3 tasks from a list of 56 standardized tasks. Sample tasks include making an instant drink, washing clothes, washing dishes, potting a plant, and changing bedsheets. Cultural sensitivity is reflected in flexible methods for evaluating tasks such as brewing tea or coffee.

The therapist observes a client's performance and makes ratings on 16 motor and 20 process skill items using a 4-point rating scale (1 = *deficit*, 2 = *ineffective*, 3 = *questionable*, 4 = *competent*). The scoring guidelines require consideration of a client's need for assistance, level of effort, degree of efficiency, and degree of safety. A training course provides the mechanism to calibrate severity of occupational therapists' ratings. Therapists learn how to use software that provides client and rater measures, including client ability measures, and analysis of ill-fitting ratings. The program converts raw AMPS scores to linear client measures of motor and process ability; the conversion is based on rating scale analysis of 4,689 people with physical, psychiatric, and cognitive limitations as well as people living in the community without impairments. The software also provides calibration of items, tasks, rating scale categories, raters, and clients.

A. G. Fisher (1997) subsequently added personal ADL items to the AMPS to extend its use to children as young as age 5 years. Personal ADL items tend to be easier to rate than instrumental ADL items. Personal ADL items evaluated included eating a meal, brushing teeth, grooming the upper body and bathing, dressing the upper body, and putting on socks and shoes. The fit of the new personal ADL items with the previously calibrated set of instrumental ADL items was good and extended the range of ability measured significantly lower.

A strength of the AMPS is the explicit conceptual model on which it is built. A. G. Fisher (1997) described task performance in terms of a person–task–environment model in which mind–brain–body relationships and cultural and volitional factors are incorporated. Another strength is the large item bank on which the AMPS was built. The 56 tasks rated on 16 motor and 20 process skills yield a total of 896 motor item and 1,120 process item calibrations. AMPS tasks are equated and linked by common skill items, thus allowing comparison of the same client over time on different tasks and comparison of different clients using different tasks. Subsequently, data were collected from more than 12,000 clients worldwide. Updated item calibrations are provided by continuous data collection from the user software.

Validity of the AMPS is supported by the calibration of the tasks and the skill items level of difficulty. For example, "lifts," "endures," and "moves and reaches" were among the easiest motor items, whereas "stabilizes," "aligns," and "walks" were of intermediate difficulty, and "grips," "flows," "bends," "manipulates," "calibrates," and "positions" were the six most difficult items, in accordance with hypothesized skill difficulties. The step calibration of the rating scale also supports the AMPS validity. A. G. Fisher (1997) reported that 97% of raters were able to provide consistent ratings and that 94% of rated clients fit the motor scale model and 95% fit the process scale model. The developmental course of children with and without dyspraxia as reflected in AMPS ability measure also supports the construct validity of the instrument. The AMPS also appears to be free of gender bias. The ability to distinguish measurement error introduced by different raters from clients' ability level is a major benefit of the multifaceted rating scale analysis used by the AMPS. Potential users should consider the lengthy training required to learn the AMPS.

Quality-of-Life Measures

The wealth of QoL instruments makes the task of selecting representative instruments daunting. See the excellent guides of McDowell and Newell (1996), Spilker (1996), and Bowling (1995, 1997) and the official journal of the International Society for Quality of Life Research, *Quality of Life Research*. This section summaries information about two widely used QoL measures for which adequate psychometric information has been reported, the SF-36 and the SIP.

Short Form 36 Health Survey

John Ware et al. at the Rand Corporation developed the SF-36 for use in the Health Insurance Study Experiment/Medical Outcomes Study (1993). Their intent was to develop a generic measure of subjective health status that could be applied widely to people with a variety of conditions. The SF-36 evolved from a factor analysis of responses from over 22,000 people to 149 items. The instrument was distributed initially by the Rand Corporation and by the Health Outcomes Institute; the Medical Outcomes Trust of the Health Institute at the New England Medical Center is the distributor of a slightly revised version after a copyright transfer. Rand distributes the original survey, now called the Rand 36-Item Health Survey, as does the Health Outcomes Institute; the latter version is called the Health Status Questionnaire (Bowling, 1997). An online version with sample scoring is available at http://www.qmetric.com/demo/sf-36v1.shtml from QualityMetric, Inc. The 36 items measure eight dimensions: physical functioning (10 items), social functioning (2), role limitations related to physical problems (4), role limitations related to emotional problems (3), mental health (5), energy–vitality (4), pain (2), and general health perceptions (5); a ninth category, represented by a single item, addresses perceptions of health changes over the past year. Separate versions allow assessment of health perceptions over the past 4 weeks and past week.

A variety of response formats are used, including a dichotomous, "yes–no" format, and 3-, 5-, and 6-category rating scales that indicate frequency of problems, extent of limitations, severity of pain, and extent of agreement with various statements. The eight subscale scores are the product of summing item responses; raw subscale scores are transformed algebraically into a 0 (*poor health*) to 100 (*good health*) continuum by computing where an individual's score resides in the possible raw score continuum. Evidence for reliability and validity is good across a variety of health conditions; the instrument appears sensitive to changes in health status over time. Floor and ceiling effects may be a problem in specific samples.

Haley, McHorney, and Ware (1994) reported rating scale analysis of the 10 physical function (PF-10) items from the SF-36. They examined the hierarchical order of the items, unidimensionality of the item set, and reproducibility of item calibrations. Their results support the unidimensionality of the PF-10 for most patient groups and the reproducibility of item calibrations across patient groups and repeated assessments. Their results also support the content validity of the PF-10 as a measure of physical functioning. Their subsequent publication (McHorney, Haley, & Ware, 1997) evaluated the relative precision of raw scores and linear measures. Differences between raw scores and linear measures were attributed to the logarithmic nature of the linear measures, the uneven distribution of the PF-10 item calibrations, and reduction of within-group variance. The explicit, but perhaps unintended, weighting of items with more response categories could also contribute to their findings. They found that the linear measures discriminated better than raw scores between patients who differed in disease severity. In all comparisons, differences between raw scores and linear measures were most apparent in clinical groups with extreme scores.

Bode (1997) extended the rating scale analysis of Haley by evaluating the fit of all 36 items to an underlying construct of health status in a sample of 526 adults with intermittent claudication, a condition that results from atherosclerosis of the leg arteries and often limits walking (Feinglass, McCarthy, Slavensky, Manheim, & Martin, 2000). The items cohered to define a unidimensional construct of health status and measured four strata of health (*excellent, good, fair, poor*). Rescoring several items and designating "pivot points" between good and poor health improved reliability by increasing the spread of item difficulties. The hierarchy of item difficulties made clinical sense such that people with relatively good health reported few activity limitations, infrequent mood disruption, minimal pain, and a perception that their health was stable. In contrast, people with relatively poor health reported several activity limitations, frequent mood disruption, pain disruption, and an overall perception that their health was declining. These results support the utility of the SF-36, provide a measure that is sensitive to change, provide measures with known measurement error, and help identify individuals whose responses do not fit the underlying construct.

Sickness Impact Profile

The SIP was developed by Marilyn Bergner et al. (1981) as a performance-based measure of perceived health status that is sensitive to changes over time or differences in health status between groups. Intended uses are as (a) a health survey to determine general health levels of a population and to compare groups or communities, (b) an outcome measure to compare treatments and measure patient change in studies of specific disease, and (c) an outcome measure for evaluating various approaches to the delivery of health care services. The SIP contains 136 statements describing sickness-related behavior that are combined in 12 daily activity, behavior, well-being, and social-functioning categories (ambulation, mobility, body care and movement, communication, alertness behavior, social interaction, sleep and rest, eating, work, home management, and recreation and pastimes). In turn, 7 of the 12 categories are collapsed into two dimensions measuring physical and psychosocial health (the remaining five categories are scored separately). Response time is about 20–30 minutes; scoring takes 5–10 minutes. English and Spanish versions are available. The SIP can be self-administered or interviewer administered with people who have acute and chronic conditions; completing the items is sometimes experienced as tedious.

SIP items were developed by asking more than 1,000 professionals and laypeople to describe sickness-related changes in behavior and by reviewing functional assessment instruments for relevant items. More than 1,300 statements were distilled to a group of 312 items that, in turn, were condensed to the final set of 136. Scoring criteria were based on ratings of 25 judges who rated each item on an 11-point scale that ranged from minimally to severely dysfunctional. Items judged to reflect greatest and least dysfunction within each group were rated on a 15-point scale. Validation of the dysfunction construct was provided by four groups of 25 judges, each of whom determined the relationship of SIP scores to a global assessment of dysfunction. High agreement among judges was obtained at both stages. Scores are obtained by adding item weights that reflect the relative severity of limitation derived from judges' ratings. A weighted total score and a score within each dimension is calculated as the percentage of the maximum weighted score possible.

The SIP's reliability evidence is strong (Bowling, 1997). Test–retest reliability estimates range from .88 to .92; internal consistency estimates are in the range of .81 to .97. Evidence of construct validity is provided by substantial correlations between SIP scores and disease-specific measures of disability and QoL in samples with arthritis, Parkinson's disease, urinary incontinence, and brain injury as well as nursing home residents and older veterans (Dittmar & Gresham, 1997). Correlations with physical measures such as grip strength and sedimentation rates also support the SIP's validity. Factor analysis results support the physical and psychosocial dimensions (McDowell & Newell, 1996). The SIP's sensitivity may be limited in samples with relatively few health problems; its utility in samples with stable physical disabilities may also be limited. Moreover, its sensitivity to change with individual cases may be limited; its length may be a deterrent to some potential users. Despite these limitations, the SIP is often viewed as a gold standard against which other measures are compared; its extensive use and long history make it a good choice across a variety of populations. Evaluation with contemporary psychometric approaches is needed.

Clinical and Research Applications

This section provides information about the application of functional status and QoL measures to clinical and research settings and identifies (a) the key skills that clinicians and researchers need to apply these skills, (b) means of developing the skills, and (c) future trends in clinical research.

Application of Concepts and Key Skills

Suitability to the population and sensitivity to change are important considerations in selecting an instrument for clinical purposes. Various instruments have been developed and applied to patients with a variety of conditions, including chronic obstructive pulmonary disease (Lareau, Breslin, & Meek, 1996), head and neck cancer (D'Antonio, Zimmerman, Cella, & Long, 1996), diabetes (Boyer & Earp, 1997), stroke (de Haan, Aaronson, Limburg, Hewer, & van Crevel, 1993; Dorman, Slattery, Farrell, Dennis, & Sandercock, 1998; Kelly-Hayes & Paige, 1995; Wyller, Holmen, Laake, & Laake, 1998), brain injury (Eames, Cotterill, Kneale, Storrar, & Yeomans, 1996), peripheral neuropathy (Molenaar, de Haan, & Vermeulen, 1995), primary hip arthroplasty (Chan & Villar, 1996), and rheumatologic conditions generally (Pioro & Kwoh, 1996) and to working-age adults with disabilities (Mehnert, Krauss, Nadler, & Boyd, 1990) and clients in independent-living centers (Nosek, Fuhrer, & Potter, 1995). Our ability to compare different groups requires the use of generic instruments or instruments that have been cocalibrated. In some situations, the use of condition-specific measures is desired in order to capture the unique aspects of a disability or chronic illness.

Functional status and QoL measures should be widely applicable to studies that examine change in these constructs over time within individuals or groups. They should also be applicable to studies contrasting different interventions or contrasting groups with different conditions. Instruments considered for research purposes should be sensitive to change and have utility with the groups under consideration.

Rehabilitation psychologists are well qualified to evaluate functional status and QoL measures, given a shared scientist–practitioner background and exposure to measurement basics. The literature on functional status and QoL can be evaluated with skills acquired in graduate training. The basics of rating scale analysis can be acquired through the textbooks cited here or through the following online resources:

- MESA Press (http://www.rfi.org/mesa.html)
- Australian Council for Educational Research (http://www.acer.edu.au/)
- Rehabilitation Foundation, Inc. (http://www.rfi.org/)
- Jean Piaget Society (http://www.piaget.org/main.html)
- Assessment Systems Corporation (http://www.assess.com/)
- Information Technology for the Social and Behavioral Sciences (http://www.gamma.rug.nl/iechomfr.html).

Future Trends

The application of sophisticated psychometric methods has allowed a clearer conceptualization of functional status and QoL. In turn, we have benefited from measuring these constructs with improved reliability, validity, and sensitivity. We have only begun to cocalibrate items from different instruments and explore the pattern of fitting items and people poorly to measurement models. Cocalibrated instruments allow clinicians and researchers to describe QoL using different instruments. Understanding patterns of person misfit to measurement models enables clinicians to make more informed choices of instruments. Better generic and condition-specific measures will be developed, and the characteristics of specific impairments and of people that affect QoL perceptions will be understood better. Upgraded QoL measures can, in turn, be used to improve the utilities or values assigned to outcomes by patients in cost effectiveness and decision analysis research that use quality-adjusted life years. Further growth in measurement technology should continue to benefit the users of functional status and QoL measures and, ultimately, the health of people on whom these instruments are used.

Conclusion

The increasing prominence of chronic diseases in the health literature, changing population demography, and growing cost containment concerns all converge to support functional status and QoL as major focuses in rehabilitation. The development of prospective payment for medical rehabilitation (Medicare Payment Advisory Commission, 1998a, 1998b) and the value of functional status in providing a basis for prospective payment (Stineman et al., 1994) underscore the need to understand and apply functional status concepts. In addition, continuing efforts to develop indicators of health providers' performance by the JCAHO and the Rehabilitation Accreditation Commission, as well as managed care organizations' performance by the NCQA, rely heavily on functional status and QoL concepts. A clear understanding of how functional status and QoL as outcomes of rehabilitation are connected to clinical practices (process) and provider organizations (structure) is a prerequisite to improving quality of services. The current focus of health care debates on accountability and quality improvement requires that rehabilitation providers collect and report information about their outcomes so that consumers can make comparative evaluations. Rehabilitation psychologists' skills in assessment, familiarity with disablement concepts, and exposure to measurement processes prepare them to be sophisticated developers and users of functional status and QoL measures. The extension from familiar terms of disablement to the larger health services research focus on outcomes should be a comfortable one for most clinicians and researchers. Readers of this chapter should be better prepared to apply outcomes measurement terminology to a variety of rehabilitation settings, populations, and applications.

References

Batterham, R. W., Dunt, D. R., & Disler, P. B. (1996). Can we achieve accountability for long-term outcomes? *Archives of Physical Medicine and Rehabilitation, 77*, 1219–1225.

Bergner, M., Bobbitt, R. A., Carter, W. B., & Gilson, B. S. (1981). The Sickness Impact Profile: Development and final revision of a health status measure. *Medical Care, 19*, 787–805.

Berzon, R. A., Mauskopf, J. A., & Simeon, G. P. (1996). Choosing a health profile (descriptive) and/or a patient-preference (utility) measure for a clinical trial. In B. Spilker (Ed.), *Quality of life and pharmacoeconomics in clinical trials* (2nd ed., pp. 375–380). Philadelphia: Lippincott-Raven.

Birkmeyer, J. D., & Welch, H. G. (1997). A reader's guide to surgical decision analysis. *Journal of the American College of Surgeons, 184*, 589–595.

Bode, R. (1997). Pivoting items for construct definition. *Rasch Measurement Transactions, 11*, 576–577.

Bode, R. K., & Heinemann, A. W. (1997). An exploration of interdisciplinary ratings of functional assessment items. *Physical Medicine and Rehabilitation: State of the Art Review, 11*, 1–18.

Bowling, A. (1995). *Measuring disease*. Philadelphia: Open University Press.

Bowling, A. (1997). *Measuring health: A review of quality of life measurement scales* (2nd ed.). Philadelphia: Open University Press.

Boyer, J. G., & Earp, J. A. L. (1997). The development of an instrument for assessing the quality of life of people with diabetes (Diabetes 39). *Medical Care, 35*, 440–453.

Cella, D. F., Lloyd, S. R., & Wright, B. D. (1996). Cross-cultural instrument equating: Current research and future directions. In B. Spilker (Ed.), *Quality of life and pharmacoeconomics in clinical trials* (2nd ed., pp. 707–716). Philadelphia: Lippincott-Raven.

Chan, C. L. H., & Villar, R. N. (1996). Obesity and quality of life after primary hip arthroplasty. *Journal of Bone and Joint Surgery, 78*, 78–81.

Clark, F., Azen, S. P., Zemke, R., Jackson, J., Carlson, M., Mandel, D., Hay, J., Josephson, K., Cherry, B., Hessel, C., Palmer, J., & Lipson, L. (1997). Occupational therapy for independent-living older adults. *Journal of the American Medical Association, 278*, 1321–1326.

Cole, B., Finch, E., Gowland, C., & Mayo, N. (1995). *Physical rehabilitation outcome measures*. Baltimore: Williams & Wilkins.

D'Antonio, L. L., Zimmerman, G. J., Cella, D. F., & Long, S. A. (1996). Quality of life and functional status measures in patients with head and neck cancer. *Archives of Otolaryngology, Head and Neck Surgery, 122*, 482–487.

de Haan, R., Aaronson, N., Limburg, M., Hewer, R. L., & van Crevel, H. (1993). Measuring quality of life in stroke. *Stroke, 24*, 320–327.

Dijkers, M. (1997). Quality of life after spinal cord injury: A meta-analysis of the effects of disablement components. *Spinal Cord, 35*, 829–840.

Dittmar, S. S., & Gresham, G. E. (1997). *Functional assessment and outcome measures for the rehabilitation professional.* Gaithersburg, MD: Aspen.

Donabedian, A. (1966). Evaluating the quality of medical care. *Millbank Memorial Fund Quarterly, 44*, 166–206.

Dorman, P., Slattery, J., Farrell, B., Dennis, M., & Sandercock, P. (1998). Qualitative comparison of the reliability of health status assessments with the EuroQol and SF-36 questionnaires after stroke. *Stroke, 29*, 63–68.

Eames, P., Cotterill, G., Kneale, T. A., Storrar, A. L., & Yeomans, P. (1996). Outcome of intensive rehabilitation after severe brain injury: A long-term follow-up study. *Brain Injury, 10*, 631–650.

Ellwood, P. M. (1988). Outcome management: A technology of patient experience. *New England Journal of Medicine, 318*, 1551–1556.

Employer coalitions as a vehicle for health care reform. (1996). *Health Care Financing & Organization News & Progress* [Newsletter], pp. 5–7. [Available from Alpha Center, Washington, DC]

Epstein, R. S., & Sherwood, L. M. (1996). From outcomes research to disease management: A guide for the perplexed. *Annals of Internal Medicine, 124*, 838–842.

Erickson, P. (1998). Evaluation of a population-based measure of quality of life: The Health and Activity Limitation Index (HALEX). *Quality of Life Research, 7*(2), 101–114.

Feinglass, J., McCarthy, W. J., Slavensky, R., Manheim, L. M., & Martin, G. J. (2000). Functional status and walking ability after lower extremity bypass grafting or angioplasty for intermittent claudication: Results from a prospective outcomes study. *Journal of Vascular Surgery, 31*, 93–103.

Fisher, A. G. (1997). Multifaceted measurement of daily life task performance. In R. M. Smith (Ed.), *Outcome Measurement. Physical Medicine and Rehabilitation: State of the Art Reviews, 11*, 289–303.

Fisher, A. G., & Fisher, W. P. (1993). Applications of Rasch analysis to studies in occupational therapy. In C. V. Granger & G. E. Gresham (Eds.), *New developments in functional assessment: Physical Medicine and Rehabilitation Clinics of North America, 4*, 551–569.

Fisher, W. P., Harvey, R. F., Taylor, P., Kilgore, K. M., & Kelly, C. K. (1995). Rehabits: A common language of functional assessment. *Archives of Physical Medicine and Rehabilitation, 76*, 113–122.

Formations in health care. (1998). *Medical outcome system.* Chicago: Author.

Fuhrer, M. J. (Ed.). (1987). *Rehabilitation outcomes: Analysis and measurement.* Baltimore: Brookes.

Fuhrer, M. J. (Ed.). (1997). *Assessing medical rehabilitation practices: The promise of outcomes research.* Baltimore: Brookes.

Greene, J. (1996). Columbia starts quality comparisons. *Modern Healthcare, 26*(16), 6.

Haley, S. M., Ludlow, L. H., & Coster, W. J. (1993). Pediatric Evaluation of Disability Inventory: Clinical interpretation of summary scores using Rasch rating scale methodology. In C. V. Granger & G. E. Gresham (Eds.), *New developments in functional assessment. Physical Medicine and Rehabilitation Clinics of North America, 4*, 551–569.

Haley, S. M., McHorney, C. A., & Ware, J. E., Jr. (1994). Evaluation of the MOS SF-36 Physical Functioning Scale (PF-10): I. Unidimensionality and reproducibility of the Rasch item scale. *Journal of Clinical Epidemiology, 47*, 671–684.

Hamilton, B. B., Granger, C. V., Sherwin, F. S., Zielezny, M., & Tashman, J. S. (1987). A uniform national data system for medical rehabilitation. In M. J. Fuhrer (Ed.), *Rehabilitation outcomes: Analysis and measurement* (Vol. 10, pp. 137–147). Baltimore: Brookes.

284 ALLEN W. HEINEMANN

Hays, R. D., Siu, A. L., Keeler, E., Marshall, G. N., Kaplan, R. M., Simmons, S., el Mouchi, D., & Schnelle, J. F. (1996). Long-term care residents' preferences for health states on the quality of well-being scale. *Medical Decision Making, 16*, 254–261.

Heinemann, A. W., Linacre, J. M., Wright, B. D., Hamilton, B. B., & Granger, C. V. (1993). Relationships between impairment and disability as measured by the Functional Independence Measure. *Archives of Physical Medicine and Rehabilitation, 74*, 566–573.

Heinemann, A. W., Linacre, J. M., Wright, B. D., Hamilton, B. B., & Granger, C. V. (1994). Measurement characteristics of the Functional Independence Measure. *Topics in Stroke Rehabilitation, 1*, 1–15.

Herndon, R. M. (1997). *Handbook of neurologic rating scales.* New York: Demos Vermande.

Hobart, J. C., Freeman, J. A., & Lamping, D. L. (1996). Physician and patient-oriented outcomes in progressive neurological disease: Which to measure? *Current Opinion in Neurology, 9*, 441–444.

Iezzoni, L. (Ed.). (1994). *Risk adjustment for measuring health care outcomes.* Ann Arbor, MI: Health Administration Press.

Jette, A. (1993). Using health-related quality of life measures in physical therapy outcomes research. *Physical Therapy, 73*, 528–537.

Kane, R. L. (1995). Improving the quality of long-term care. *Journal of the American Medical Association, 273*, 1376–1380.

Kaplan, R. M., Alcaraz, J. E., Anderson, J. P., & Weisman, M. (1996). Quality-adjusted life years lost to arthritis: Effects of gender, race, and social class. *Arthritis Care & Research, 9*, 473–482.

Kazandjian, V. A., Lawthers, J., Cernak, C. M., & Pipesh, F. C. (1993). Relating outcomes to processes of care. *Journal of Quality Improvement, 19*, 530–538.

Kelly-Hayes, M., & Paige, C. (1995). Assessment and psychologic factors in stroke rehabilitation. *Neurology, 45*, S29–S32.

Lai, J. S., Velozo, C. A., & Linacre, J. M. (1997). Adjusting for rater severity in an unlinked Functional Independence Measure national database: An application of the many-facets Rasch model. *Physical Medicine and Rehabilitation: State of the Art Reviews, 11*, 325–332.

Lareau, S. C., Breslin, E. H., & Meek, P. M. (1996). Functional status instruments: Outcome measure in the evaluation of patients with chronic obstructive pulmonary disease. *Heart and Lung, 25*, 212–224.

Linacre, J. M., Heinemann, A. W., Wright, B. D., Granger, C. V., & Hamilton, B. B. (1994). The structure and stability of the Functional Independence Measure. *Archives of Physical Medicine and Rehabilitation, 75*, 127–132.

Livneh, H., & Antonak, R. F. (1997). *Psychosocial adaptation to chronic illness and disability.* Gaithersburg, MD: Aspen.

McDowell, I., & Newell, C. (1996). *Measuring health: A guide to rating scales and questionnaires* (2nd ed.). New York: Oxford University Press.

McGlynn, E. A. (1993). Gathering systematic information on health plans: An interview with Sheila Leatherman. *Journal on Quality Improvement, 19*, 266–271.

McHorney, C. A., Haley, S. M., & Ware, J. E., Jr. (1997). Evaluation of the MOS SF-36 Physical Functioning Scale (PF-10): II. Comparison of relative precision using Likert and Rasch scoring methods. *Journal of Clinical Epidemiology, 50*, 451–461.

Medicare Payment Advisory Commission. (1998a). *Report to the Congress: Medicare payment policy: Vol. 1. Recommendations.* Washington, DC: Author.

Medicare Payment Advisory Commission. (1998b). *Report to the Congress: Medicare payment policy: Vol. 2. Analytical papers.* Washington, DC: Author.

Mehnert, T., Krauss, H. H., Nadler, R., & Boyd, M. (1990). Correlates of life satisfaction in those with disabling conditions. *Rehabilitation Psychology, 35*, 3–17.

Molenaar, D. S. M., de Haan, R., & Vermeulen, M. (1995). Impairment, disability, or handicap in peripheral neuropathy: Analysis of the use of outcome measures in clinical trials in patients peripheral neuropathies. *Journal of Neurology, Neurosurgery, and Psychiatry, 59*, 165–169.

Morrissey, J. (1995). Alliance urges patient-oriented measures. *Modern Healthcare, 25*(42), 52–53.

Morrissey, J. (1996a). Alliance prepares to roll out proposed performance measures. *Modern Healthcare, 26*(13), 54.

Morrissey, J. (1996b). Grant to fund NCQA study on chronic care. *Modern Healthcare, 26*(8), 21.

Morrissey, J. (1996c). NCQA database to allow quick HMO comparisons. *Modern Healthcare, 26*(13), 50–51.

Nadzam, D. M., Turpin, R., Hanold, L. S., & White, R. E. (1993). Data-driven performance improvement in health care: The Joint Commission's Indicator Measurement System. *Journal of Quality Improvement, 19*, 492–500.

National Institutes of Health. (1993). *Research plan for the National Center on Medical Rehabilitation Research* (NIH Publication No. 93-3509). Washington, DC: U.S. Department of Health and Human Services.

Nosek, M. A., Fuhrer, M. J., & Potter, C. (1995). Life satisfaction of people with physical disabilities: Relationship to personal assistance, disability status, and handicap. *Rehabilitation Psychology, 40*, 191–202.

Ottenbacher, K. J., Hsu, Y., Granger, C. V., & Fiedler, R. C. (1996). The reliability of the Functional Independence Measure: A quantitative review. *Archives of Physical Medicine and Rehabilitation, 77*, 1226–1232.

Ottenbacher, K. J., Msall, M. E., Lyon, N. R., Duffy, L. C., Granger, C. V., & Braun, S. (1997). Interrater agreement and stability of the Functional Independence Measure for Children (WeeFIM): Use in children with developmental disabilities. *Archives of Physical Medicine and Rehabilitation, 78*, 1309–1315.

Pioro, M. H., & Kwoh, C. K. (1996). Update on measurement of relevant outcomes in rheumatology. *Current Opinion in Rheumatology, 8*, 101–105.

Pope, A., & Tarlov, A. R. (1991). *Disability in America*. Washington, DC: National Academy Press.

Rasch, G. (1980). *Probabilistic models for some intelligence and attainment tests*. Chicago: University of Chicago Press. (Original work published 1960.)

Rothwell, P. M., McDowell, Z., Wong, C. K., & Dorman, P. J. (1997). Doctors and patients don't agree: Cross sectional study of patients' and doctors' perceptions and assessments of disability in multiple sclerosis. *British Medical Journal, 314*, 1580–1583.

Rubenstein, L. V. (1996). Using quality of life tests for patient diagnosis or screening, or to evaluate treatment. In B. Spilker (Ed.), *Quality of life and pharmacoeconomics in clinical trials* (2nd ed., pp. 363–374). Philadelphia: Lippincott-Raven.

Rutigliano, M. J. (1995). Cost effectiveness analysis: A review. *Neurosurgery, 37*, 436–443.

Schipper, H., Clinch, J., & Olweny, C. L. M. (1996). Quality of life studies: Definitions and conceptual issues. In B. Spilker (Ed.), *Quality of life and pharmacoeconomics in clinical trials* (2nd ed., pp. 11–24). Philadelphia: Lippincott-Raven.

Schipper, H., Clinch, J., & Powell, V. (1990). Definitions and conceptual issues. In B. Spilker (Ed.), *Quality of life assessments in clinical trials* (pp. 11–24). New York: Raven Press.

Segal, M., Heinemann, A. W., Schall, R. R., & Wright, B. D. (1997). Rasch analysis of a brief physical ability scale for long-term outcomes of stroke. In R. Smith (Ed.), *Physical medicine and rehabilitation: Vol. 11. State of the art reviews: Outcome measurement* (pp. 385–396). Philadelphia: Hanley & Belfus.

Shontz, F. C. (1982). Adaptation to chronic illness and disability. In T. Millon, C. Green, & R. Meagher (Eds.), *Handbook of clinical health psychology* (pp. 153–172). New York: Plenum.

Shortell, S. M., Levin, D. A., O'Brien, J. L., & Hughes, E. F. X. (1995). Assessing the evidence on CQI: Is the glass half empty or half full? *Hospital and Health Services Administration, 40*, 4–24.

Smith, R. M. (1997). The relationship between goals and functional status in the patient evaluation and conference system. In R. Smith (Ed.), *Physical medicine and rehabilitation: Vol. 11. State of the art reviews: Outcome measurement* (pp. 333–343). Philadelphia: Hanley & Belfus.

Spilker, B. (1996). *Quality of life and pharmacoeconomics in clinical trials* (2nd ed.). Philadelphia: Lippincott-Raven.

Stevens, S. S. (1951). *Handbook of experimental psychology*. New York: Wiley.

Stineman, M. G., Escarce, J. J., Goin, J. E., Hamilton, B. B., Granger, C. V., & Williams, S. V. (1994). A case-mix classification system for medical rehabilitation. *Medical Care, 32,* 366–379.

Tate, D. G. (1997). *Quality of life outcomes measures in cancer: Applications in rehabilitation* (Final project report). Ann Arbor: University of Michigan Press.

Turner, R. (1990). Rehabilitation: In B. Spilker (Ed.), *Quality of life assessment in clinical trials* (pp. 839–851). New York: Raven Press.

Turpin, R. S., Darcy, L. A., Koss, R., McMahill, C., Meyne, K., Morton, D., Rodriguez, J., Schmaltz, S., Schyve, P., & Smith, P. (1996). A model to assess the usefulness of performance indicators. *International Journal for Quality in Health Care, 8,* 321–329.

U.S. Department of Health and Human Services. (1986). *Health Care Financing Administration: Medicare hospital information report.* Washington, DC: Author.

U.S. Department of Health and Human Services. (1995). *Post-stroke rehabilitation* (AHCPR Pub. No. 95-0662). Washington, DC: Agency for Health Care Policy Research.

Velozo, C. A., Magalhaes, L., Pan, A., & Leiter, P. (1995). Differences in functional scale discrimination at admission and discharge: Rasch analysis of the Level of Rehabilitation Scale–III (LORS-III). *Archives of Physical Medicine and Rehabilitation, 76,* 705–712.

Wade, D. T. (1992). *Measurement in neurological rehabilitation.* New York: Oxford University Press.

Ware, J. E. (1993). *SF-36 Health Survey: Manual and interpretation guide.* Boston: Health Institute, New England Medical Center.

Wennberg, J. E. (1982). Should the cost of insurance reflect the cost of use in local hospital markets? *New England Journal of Medicine, 307,* 1374–1381.

Werner, R. A., & Kessler, S. (1996). Effectiveness of an intensive outpatient rehabilitation program for postacute stroke patients. *American Journal of Physical Medicine and Rehabilitation, 75,* 114–120.

Whiteneck, G. G., Charlifue, S. W., Gerhart, K. A., Overholser, J. D., & Richardson, G. N. (1992). Quantifying handicap: A new measure of long-term rehabilitation outcomes. *Archives of Physical Medicine and Rehabilitation, 73,* 519–526.

Wilkerson, D. L. (1997). Accreditation and the use of outcomes-oriented information systems. *Archives of Physical Medicine and Rehabilitation, 78,* S31–S35.

World Health Organization. (1958). *The first ten years of the World Health Organization.* Geneva: Author.

World Health Organization. (1997). *International classification of impairments, activities, and participation: A manual of dimensions of disablement and functioning.* Geneva, Switzerland: Author.

Wright, B. A. (1983). *Physical disability: A psychosocial approach.* New York: Harper & Row.

Wright, B. D., & Linacre, J. M. (1998). *BIGSTEPS: A Rasch program for rating scale analysis.* Chicago: MESA Press.

Wright, B. D., & Masters, G. (1982). *Rating scale analysis: Rasch measurement.* Chicago: MESA Press.

Wright, B. D., & Stone, M. H. (1979). *Best test design.* Chicago: MESA Press.

Wyller, T. B., Holmen, J., Laake, P., & Laake, K. (1998). Correlates of subjective well-being in stroke patients. *Stroke, 29,* 363–367.

13

Assessment of Psychopathology and Personality in People With Physical Disabilities

Cynthia L. Radnitz, Neil Bockian, and Alberto I. Moran

A large extent of the psychology literature includes the psychometric properties of psychopathology and personality measures. A vast array of studies describes the uses of instruments for both the general population and assorted subpopulations. Historically, these subpopulations have been distinguished according to age, gender, ethnicity, nationality, first language, psychiatric diagnosis, medical condition, disability and a host of other characteristics. In one way or another, individuals are members of many subpopulations, and it is important to consider subpopulation issues when contemplating an assessment strategy for a given individual.

In this chapter, we address the issue of assessment for a particular subpopulation, those with physical disabilities. Specifically, we describe issues relevant to assessment of personality and psychopathology in people with physical disabilities. We primarily focus on conceptual issues that underlie the assessment endeavor. In doing so, we have summarized the available research regarding adaptations and renorming of existing instruments. For our purposes, assessment is divided according to the *Diagnostic and Statistical Manual of Mental Disorders* (4th ed.; *DSM–IV*; American Psychiatric Association, 1994) into assessment of Axis I psychopathology and Axis II personality. Although the Minnesota Multiphasic Personality Inventory (MMPI) is often used to diagnose and assess psychopathology, in addition to personality pathology (because its theoretical underpinnings are more trait focused), we discuss its use in the personality section. This section also includes a brief review of the assessment of healthy personality functioning. We conclude by addressing issues such as practical applications, basic competencies for those administering these instruments, implications for treatment and rehabilitation, and the effect of contextual issues (e.g., who is requesting the assessment and the current state of health care reimbursement) on assessment.

Assessment of Psychopathology

People with disabilities are subject to the full range of psychopathology found among people in general. We have chosen to focus on assessment of disorders that may be especially relevant to those with disabilities such as mood, anxiety, substance abuse, and psychotic disorders.

Mood Disorders

Several researchers have suggested that people with acquired and non-acquired disabilities are at risk for a depression spectrum disorder (Davidoff et al., 1990; Feinstein, 1995; Fullerton, Harvey, Klein, & Howell, 1981; Hohmann, 1975). However, the presumption that depression automatically follows the onset of a disability has been shown to be unfounded in numerous studies (Elliott & Frank, 1996). For example, estimates of the prevalence of major depressive episodes following spinal cord injury (SCI) range from 22% (Howell, Fullerton, Harvey, & Klein, 1981) to 44% (Frank, Kashani, Wonderlich, Lising, & Visot, 1985); multiple sclerosis (MS), 27% (Whitlock & Siskind, 1980) to 54% (Minden, Orav, & Reich, 1987); amputation, 35% (Schubert, Burns, Paras, & Sioson, 1992); and stroke, 40% (Schubert et al., 1992). Therefore, determining who is depressed and the severity and quality of that depression is an important task for clinicians working with individuals with disabilities.

The detection and assessment of depression in people with disabilities remain challenging for the clinician and researcher alike. First, somatic and other symptoms of depression may be difficult to distinguish from the sequelae of the disability (Blalock, DeVellis, Brown, & Wallston, 1989; Radnitz et al., 1997). For example, after amputation, individuals may perceive themselves as unattractive, a perception that may be mistaken for a symptom of depression. Similarly, the progression of MS often leads to neurovegetative symptoms such as fatigue, psychomotor retardation, loss of interest in sex, and weight gain (Allen & Goreczny, 1995). Endorsement of these symptoms is likely to elevate depression scales with items that assess these changes and, as a consequence, artificially inflate estimates of both prevalence and severity (Nyenhuis et al., 1995). For those with physical disabilities who have concomitant cognitive impairment, depressionlike symptoms may result from brain disease or insult (Primeau, 1988). Delineating which symptoms are the result of brain damage and which constitute depression requires careful psychological and neuropsychological evaluation.

Second, according to some theories (Bracken & Shephard, 1980; Hohmann, 1975), depression is normal and perhaps necessary in order to come to terms with the onset of a disabling condition. However, these studies do not address depression as a clinical syndrome using standard *DSM* nomenclature; instead, they typically refer to depressed mood or distress. Few would argue against the idea that acquiring a physical disability can be a distressing experience. However, to date, research suggests that there is no universal stage sequence people go through when they become disabled (Elliott & Frank, 1996). In fact, there are a variety of responses that can occur in the wake of a traumatic injury (Overholser, Schubert, Foliart, & Frost, 1993). Not everyone becomes depressed, and for those that do, it may not be healthy. Therefore, what is "normal" in terms of depressive symptomatology becomes a complex issue for those undertaking assessment. Because the development of a major depressive episode does not inevitably follow the acquisition of a disability, it would seem prudent to base diagnosis and treatment of depression on established psychiatric nomenclature without being influenced by disability status.

The most extensive efforts to renorm and validate instruments for people with disabilities have been undertaken in the area of depression. Work has been conducted to establish norms and collect psychometric evaluation data on some measures for some disability groups; however, the existing literature is not comprehensive. Some studies provide new norms, some give means, and others give estimates of reliability and validity (see Table 13.1 for a summary). Having available normative data for individual disability groups may address, in part, some of the concerns that we have highlighted. Specifically, these data can provide an important perspective in the interpretation of scale scores, both in terms of overlap between depressive symptoms and disability sequelae and in terms of normative reactions. Knowing what is normative within a particular subpopulation can provide a context for interpretation. However, what is typical in those with a given disability may still constitute depression and warrant intervention. The clinician is advised to consider both general population and subpopulation norms when forming judgments about the existence and severity of depression.

Anxiety Disorders

A few measures of anxiety have norms for those with disabilities. There have been studies of the Symptom Checklist 90 (SCL-90; Buckelew, Baumstark, Frank, & Hewett, 1990) and the Brief Symptom Inventory (BSI; Heinrich, Tate, & Buckelew, 1994; Tate, Kewman, & Maynard, 1990) in individuals with SCI, which show higher scores on anxiety scales. Although there may be significant differences in scale scores between those with SCI and comparison samples, in one study, the elevation in the SCI sample did not exceed the cutoff of .65 that denotes a clinically significant problem (Elliott & Umlauf, 1995).

In attempting to assess anxiety in those with disabilities, there are issues that should be considered. First, as with depression, the endorsement of physical symptoms secondary to a disability may elevate scale scores. To date, with a few exceptions, norms for disability groups are nonexistent, which makes the interpretation of an individual's score difficult. Second, there may be some question as to whether anxiety in some disability groups where there is significant brain or spinal involvement is the same as in those without these kinds of disabilities. For example, Rad-

Table 13.1. Psychometric Properties of Depression Measures in People With Disabilities

Measure	Disability			
	Rheumatoid arthritis (RA)	Amputation	Spinal cord injury (SCI)	Multiple sclerosis (MS)
Center for Epidemiological Studies–Depression Scale (CES-D)	Analysis of items showed that 4 were influenced by aspects of the disease and may not necessarily reflect depression. Results suggest the CES-D may modestly overestimate depression severity in RA (Blalock et al., 1989).	In a sample with amputations, the mean CES-D score was 11.3 ± 9.7. This is higher than the mean found in the general population (9.2 ± 8.6; Rybarczyk et al., 1992).	The mean CES-D score was 14.5 ± 11.2 in a sample with SCI. The CES-D was found to possess adequate construct validity when assessing people with physical disability, including SCI (Coyle & Roberge, 1992). The mean CES-D score found in a sample with SCI (12.1 ± 9.6) was higher than that reported in an earlier study of the general population (9.2 ± 8.6). The mean score for women with SCI (14.7 ± 8.9) was significantly higher than that found for men (11.1 ± 9.7; $p < .05$ (Fuhrer et al., 1993).	The mean CES-D score was 16.7 ± 11.2 in a sample with MS. The CES-D was found to possess adequate construct validity when assessing people with physical disability, including MS (Coyle & Roberge, 1992).

Inventory to Diagnose Depression (IDD)	The sample with RA had significantly higher mean scores (16.4) than both a student (12.1) and community sample (9.4), but did not differ significantly from a sample with SCI (13.3). Factor analysis revealed a 4-factor solution where the main factor, accounting for 33% of the common variance, was consistent across RA, SCI, and nonpatient groups (Frank et al., 1992).	In a study using Bayesian analysis in people with SCI, neurovegetative symptoms (appetite, sleep, and psychomotor disturbance) were significant predictors of diagnosable depression. Lack of interest or pleasure best predicted depression in those with paraplegia, whereas poor concentration was the best predictor in those with quadriplegia (Clay et al., 1995).	
Beck Depression Inventory (BDI)	Mean BDI score was 11.8 ± 7.7. The correlation between the BDI and HRSD was significantly higher than the correlation between the BDI and measures of disability, providing good evidence of convergent and divergent validity (Peck et al., 1989).	Mean BDI score of a sample of amputees was 12.8 ± 9.6. No significant differences in BDI scores were found among people with amputations, strokes, or Parkinson's disease (Langer, 1994).	Of 21 BDI items, only 3 were poor discriminators of depressed and nondepressed veterans with SCI (Radnitz et al., 1997).	The BDI was found to overestimate the prevalence and severity of depression in patients with MS (Nyenhuis et al., 1995). Compared with a sample with other progressive, chronic, neurological syndromes, patients with MS reported significantly higher BDI scores ($p < .001$; Whitlock & Siskind, 1980).

Table 13.1 continues

Table 13.1. (*Continued*)

| | Disability | | | |
Measure	Rheumatoid arthritis (RA)	Amputation	Spinal cord injury (SCI)	Multiple sclerosis (MS)
Multiple Affect Adjective Check List (MAACL)		Mean MAACL score for a sample of amputees was 13.9 ± 9.2. They were not found to score higher on the MAACL than stroke or Parkinson's patients (Langer, 1994).		
Zung Self-Rating Depression Scale			The Zung has been found to be a reliable and valid measure of depression in SCI. Factor analytic results, normative data, estimates of sensitivity and specificity, and correlations between the Zung and BSI are provided. The Zung was superior to the BSI for identifying people with SCI at risk for depression (Tate et al., 1993). For individuals with acute SCI, the mean Zung score was 49.0 ± 1.3 compared with that of healthy volunteers, 37.1 ± 1.1 (p < .0001; Davidoff et al., 1990).	

HRSD	Mean HRSD score was 5.1 ± 4.5. The correlation between the HRSD and the BDI was significantly higher than the correlation between the HRSD and measures of disability, providing good evidence of convergent and divergent validity (Peck et al., 1989).	The mean depression score obtained using the HRSD was 13.1 ± 6 in relapsing–remitting MS (Noy et al., 1995).
Symptom Checklist 90–Revised	Coefficient alphas were .62 for the somatic depression subscale and .89 for the cognitive depression subscale. The sample with SCI reported significantly less cognitive depression than did both chronic pain patients and college students and significantly less somatic depression than the pain sample (Buckelew et al., 1988).	
Multiscale Depression Inventory (MDI)		The MDI Mood subscale was found to reliably separate mood and nonmood depression symptoms (Nyenhuis et al., 1995).

Note. HRSD = Hamilton Rating Scale for Depression; BSI = Brief Symptom Inventory.

nitz, Hsu, Tirch, et al. (1998) found that posttraumatic stress disorder (PTSD) in those with quadriplegia was less prevalent than in those with paraplegia. To further explore this finding, Radnitz, Hsu, Willard, et al. (1998) compared both samples with paraplegia and quadriplegia with a control sample composed of veterans with other traumatic injuries who were also seeking medical care. They found that veterans with quadriplegia had more severe current PTSD symptoms and were more likely to be diagnosed with current PTSD compared with the control sample. Having a quadriplegic SCI was associated with decreased risk of having chronic PTSD if they defined *chronic* as having a syndrome that persisted to the time of assessment. The best explanation for this finding was that in veterans with quadriplegia, SCI interfered with the peripheral nervous system activity that is an important part of PTSD. Although these results have yet to be replicated, they nonetheless suggest that PTSD is manifested differently in those with quadriplegia.

In work examining PTSD in people with SCI, other issues related to assessment emerged. First, some individuals declined to participate in the study because they did not want to revisit the trauma that left them paralyzed. Avoidance of trauma-related stimuli (which can include assessment) is a core symptom of PTSD. Therefore, if a patient declines to undergo assessment, the clinician is left with the decision as to what extent he or she should try to convince the patient to be assessed. Persistent entreaties may harm the therapeutic relationship; on the other hand, failure to address PTSD means that the problem may go unabated. Asking to what extent the trauma distresses the individual and interferes with functioning can help in guiding this decision. It may also be helpful to educate the patient about avoidance symptoms of PTSD, the manner in which symptoms maintain the disorder, and the importance of assessment in guiding treatment.

Another issue was the extent to which reported symptoms were specific to PTSD and the traumatic injury. Although Radnitz and colleagues used structured interviews, which asked specifically about the trauma that led to the SCI, it is possible that participants had difficulties delineating whether some symptoms, especially nonspecific symptoms, were the result of the trauma. Similarly, there was some overlap between symptoms of PTSD and those of other disorders, particularly depression (Green, Lindy, Grace, & Leonard, 1992; Southwick, Yehuda, & Giller, 1991). Again, there may be some difficulty in determining whether these symptoms are the result of PTSD or another syndrome.

Substance Use Disorders

In the area of substance abuse, efforts to renorm and validate established instruments for populations with disabilities have yet to be undertaken. Nonetheless, there are important factors to consider when assessing substance abuse in those with a disability. Prescription of psychoactive medications (e.g., for spasticity and pain) is common. Assessing whether there is misuse of these medications or even dependence can be challenging.

Before this assessment is undertaken, it is important to determine what constitutes misuse and dependence. *Misuse* is defined as not taking medication as prescribed (Heinemann, McGraw, Brandt, Roth, & Dell'Oliver, 1992). In *DSM–IV*, indications of *dependence* include tolerance, withdrawal, taking larger amounts or for a longer period of time than intended, difficulty cutting down, spending a great deal of time in substance-related activities, giving up other activities, and continued substance use despite adverse consequences (American Psychiatric Association, 1994).

Clues suggestive of misuse or dependence include manipulative behavior (i.e., running out of medication early, seeking medication from multiple physicians, persistently requesting increased dosages, persistently requesting more psychoactively potent medications, and concealing important facts about usage), use at levels above "ceiling doses," simultaneous use of nonmedical drugs, adverse life consequences, an irregular pattern of use (i.e., at parties or other social settings), a poor therapeutic response, and a history of substance misuse (Dupont, 1989; Dupont & Saylor, 1991). A preexisting history is an important clue because studies have shown that those without a history have a low probability of becoming addicted (Hoffmann, Olofsson, Salen, & Wickstrom, 1995).

Assessment should include corroborative information because there is a disincentive for addicted individuals to be truthful if honesty results in the discontinuation of medication, the discovery of their addiction, or some other perceived negative consequence (Verebey & Turner, 1991). This information can include collateral reports from friends, family members, or caregivers. Physiological measures such as urine toxicology screenings, breath analysis, blood tests (e.g., tests of gamma-glutamyl transferase, mean corpuscular volume, high-density lipoproteins, and carbohydrate-deficient transferrins), and radioimmunoassay of hair can also confirm or contradict patient reports.

When using urine toxicology, which is a common method of detecting drug abuse, certain considerations are germane to those with disabilities. First, prescribed medications may test positive on a toxicology report. Records of medication prescriptions should be consulted before judgments are made. Second, several nonprescription medications may give false-positive results as well, so that the clinician must be informed about the nonprescription medications that the individual is taking as well as which ones may be mistaken for addictive drugs. Third, if prescribed medications, particularly benzodiazepines or opiates, do not come up positive on a toxicology report, this suggests that either the patient is not taking medication as prescribed or the report is invalid. Finally, standardized procedures should be followed for the collection, identification, transport, analysis, and reporting of urine toxicology screenings because sloppy handling can lead to mistakes or security breaches (Blanke, 1986).

Psychotic Disorders

Few published studies describe the use of measures of psychosis in treating people with physical disabilities. The SCL-90-R and BSI have psychosis scales; in two studies of the BSI (Heinrich et al., 1994; Tate et al., 1990), significant elevations were found in individuals with SCI versus control groups. Items that comprise this scale reflect retribution, isolation, and withdrawal as well as non-reality-based content. We can speculate that elevations on the scale in individuals with SCI result from endorsement of the items suggesting loneliness and the feeling of being punished for past wrongdoing. In contrast, no significant differences were obtained on the SCL-90-R Psychosis scale between a sample with amputations and the SCL-90 normative sample (Frank et al., 1984). The most likely explanations for the seeming discrepancy between these results may be either measurement variance (SCL-90 vs. BSI) or sample variance (SCI vs. amputation); however, other explanations are possible. Depending on the instrument and the group for whom it is being used, new norms may need to be developed to ensure the valid interpretation of individual scores.

Depending on the type of disability and the manifestation and extent of symptoms, there may be other important issues to consider. For example, in those with MS, florid psychiatric symptoms may obscure signs of MS and interfere with detection, diagnosis, and evaluation of symptoms (Pine, Douglas, Charles, Davies, & Kahn, 1995). Pine et al. (1995) suggested that because psychiatric symptoms occur simultaneously or immediately following MS exacerbation, they may be, in fact, the result of the central nervous system disease that underlies MS. In a similar vein, specific brain lesions in individuals with MS have been associated with elation and psychosis (Ron & Logsdail, 1989). If future research supports the association between specific brain abnormalities in MS and psychiatric disturbance, there may be important implications for treatment, thus making careful assessment more critical.

Assessment of Personality

Personality assessment is extremely important to the overall rehabilitation endeavor. Individuals with personality problems can disrupt their treatment environment (Stewart, 1994). For example, an individual with borderline personality disorder can undermine his or her rehabilitation while creating dissension (e.g., provoking disagreements) among staff (Bockian, 1994). Reich and Green (1991) showed that individuals with personality problems have poorer treatment outcomes. Conversely, personality strengths such as perseverance, a positive attitude, and extroversion can facilitate rehabilitation as well as adjustment to the changes brought on by the acquisition of a disability (Krause & Rohe, 1998; Mann, 1994). To discover such strengths and liabilities, accurate assessment is necessary.

Personality Patterns

Despite great variability, certain personality patterns occur with regularity in populations of individuals with disabilities. Mean profiles on the

MMPI include significant elevations on scales 1, 2, and 3 (McDaniel, 1976) and scales 7, 8, and 0, depending on the disability under evaluation (Harper & Richman, 1978). These findings suggest concern with somatic issues (scale 1) that would be natural in a group with medical conditions. Coping with such conditions may lead to denial or putting on a "good front" (scale 3), anxiety/worry (scale 7), and depression (scale 2). Disfiguring conditions (e.g., cleft palate) may lead to social withdrawal (scale 0; Williamson, 1995). Spergel, Erlich, and Glass (1978) found elevations on scales 1, 2, 3, and 7 for a sample with rheumatoid arthritis, a profile similar to those found in samples with ulcers, low back pain, MS, and pulmonary disease. In a similar vein, Wilson, Olson, Gascon, and Brumback (1982) found subclinical mean elevations on scales 1, 2, and 3 in a sample with MS, in a slight conversion V pattern, a profile corresponding to that found in a group with rheumatoid arthritis.

The manner of onset of the disability can have a substantial impact on personality findings. Fordyce (1964) and Taylor (1970) found patients with SCI to have impulse-dominated characteristics (impulsivity, acting out, and a subjective sense of high energy and personal drive) based on elevations of MMPI scales 4, 9, or both. Fordyce's analysis revealed that compared with those whose injury onset was not judged to be "imprudent," those judged to be imprudent were more likely to have impulse-dominated behavior. Using a case control design, Mawson et al. (1996) found that SCI was associated with sensation-seeking prior to injury. Using the Eysenck Personality Inventory (Eysenck & Eysenck, 1968) and SCL-90, Malec (1985) found that people with SCI appeared more extroverted than those with nontraumatic injuries or injuries resulting in chronic pain. On the Strong Vocational Interest Blank, individuals whose behavior led to their injury were characterized by adventurousness, boldness, and assertiveness (Kunce & Worley, 1966). A sample with paraplegia evaluated with the Rorschach test showed characteristics such as impulsiveness, body image concerns, and interpersonal distancing (Mattlar, Tarkkanen, Carlsson, Aaltonen, & Helenius, 1993). In his extensive literature review, Woodbury (1978) also reported similar findings, noting that increased risk taking and impulsivity may have an etiologic role in SCI.

Elevations on personality instrument scales found in those with traumatic injuries may not translate into diagnosable conditions. In a study using *DSM–IV* Axis II diagnoses, 28% of participants with SCI and a similar number of control participants were found to have personality disorders. Unexpectedly, the prevalence of impulsive–externalizing disorders (histrionic, narcissistic, antisocial, and borderline) was not unusually high in those with SCI and was not higher than that found in control participants. Avoidant, schizoid, and depressive disorders were unexpectedly frequent. Because of the small sample size and limited geographical and ethnic diversity of the sample, the findings must be considered preliminary; nonetheless, the study does imply that further research into the range and frequency of personality disorders in populations with disabilities is warranted (Bockian, 1997).

An alternative approach to mean profile elevations is to use cluster analysis and other multivariate techniques. Supporters of this approach criticize mean profile analyses as tending to gloss over individual differences, creating a "one size fits all" prototype, and providing little clinically useful information. Such studies have generally identified 3–4 naturally occurring patterns. For example, Berven, Habeck, and Malec (1985) found 4 MMPI clusters. The *adaptive coper* pattern, with no mean elevations in the clinical range, accounted for 50% of the sample. Cluster 2, labeled *depression*, was marked by a pronounced elevation on scale 2; approximately 16% of the sample had this pattern. The third cluster, *somatic focusing* (12% of the sample), had high elevations on scales 1 and 3 in a conversion V configuration. Cluster 4, *personality disorganization* (20%), had extreme elevations on scales 2, 7, 8, and F and moderate elevations on most of the remaining scales; this pattern suggests being emotionally overwhelmed or psychotic.

If the disability assessment involves litigation, various complications ensue because the client may be motivated to attempt to manipulate the assessment in a variety of ways:

> Many malingerers paradoxically present a combined mixture of fake good and fake bad self-reports. This mixture of reports is not so contradictory when considered in context. These reports can be described as analogous to goal directed behavior oriented toward ends such as: (1) to appear honest, (2) to appear psychologically normal except for the influence of the alleged cause of injury, (3) to avoid admitting pre-existing psychopathology, (4) where pre-existing complaints are known or suspected to have been disclosed to the examining clinician or likely to be disclosed to judge or jury, to attempt to minimize those complaints, (5) to hide preinjury behavior which is antisocial or illegal or to minimize this if it appears that the behavior will be discovered independently, (6) to present an extent of injury or disability within perceived plausibility [these limits vary widely], (7) related ends. (Lees-Haley, English, & Glenn, 1991, pp. 204–205)

The authors studied 25 known malingerers (confirmed by surveillance tapes that showed them performing behaviors for which they claimed to be disabled) and 20 nonmalingerers. Using a cutoff score of 20, their 43-item MMPI subscale accurately identified 96% of the malingerers and ruled out 90% of the nonmalingerers. The relative clarity of the cases involved probably contributed to these excellent results. Another study of 123 cases showed hit rates of approximately 80% using either the MMPI (scale 1 or scale 3 > 70) or a specially constructed 52-item subscale (Rosen, Johnson, & Frymoyer, 1983). The criterion was a surgeon's determination of appropriate or inappropriate disability (see Butcher, 1985, and Meloy, 1989, for more information on forensic assessment of disability).

Scale Corrections

A limited number of scale corrections are available in the literature. Marsh, Hirsh, and Leung (1982) found 27 items on MMPI scales 1, 2, 3, and 8 that were directly related to MS symptomatology. When these items were removed, scores on scales 1, 3, and 8 declined substantially, although scores on scale 2 did not. Mueller and Girace (1988), following Marsh et al.'s work, found that when MS-related items were removed, psychopathology was reduced more in the MS group than in the control group. Mueller and Girace concluded that both scores, with and without removing the potentially biased items, should be evaluated when performing an assessment.

Taylor (1970) developed an MMPI correction scale for SCI. Ten items (273, 330, 9, 192, 63, 310, 51, 179, 20, and 62) were removed, resulting in significant reductions on scales 1, 2, 3, 4, and 8 relative to a nondisabled sample. Kendall, Edinger, and Eberly (1978) replicated Taylor's work, using both a medical and a nondisabled control group, with essentially identical results. More recently, a novel approach to renorming the second edition of the MMPI (MMPI-2) for people with SCI was undertaken by Rodevich and Wanlass (1995). The authors had physiatrists rate items that seemed directly related to the physical sequelae of SCI. A total of 28 items were rated as having at least a moderate impact. Individuals with SCI were then asked to take the MMPI-2 in a standard administration and then substitute answers for how they were prior to their SCI for the 28 affected items. Using this correction procedure, the authors noted a dramatic change in interpretation of the profiles. However, in a subsequent three-part study, they examined the validity of this correction procedure and concluded that it was not valid (Barncord & Wanlass, 1998). The authors developed a new correction based on responses from both health care and mental health professionals familiar with SCI and validated this correction in 10 individuals with SCI. Although this correction seems promising, the validation requires further study with a larger sample.

The broader issue of norming is complex. Renorming should not a priori be assumed to be the optimal strategy for interpreting scale scores. It is difficult to tease out which problems are more frequent in a population (e.g., PTSD in traumatic SCI; Radnitz et al., 1995) and which elevations are a product of test bias. Renorming studies should include semistructured interviews, which allow the clinician to determine the meaning of item responses in the context of the person's disability.

Non-Pathology-Based Assessment of Personality

The majority of individuals with disabilities do not have personality disorders (Bockian, 1997). Personality assessment can provide information regarding how to interact with a patient in a way that maximizes the effectiveness of medical and psychological rehabilitation interventions. The Millon Behavioral Health Inventory (MBHI; Millon, Green, & Meagher, 1982) consists of eight scales that measure personality (called "coping styles") and 12 scales that measure attitudes related to medical treatment (e.g., Future Despair), psychosomatic problems (e.g., Cardiovascular Tendency), and prognosis (e.g., Pain Treatment Response, to predict patient outcome in pain management programs). The personality styles are seen as "normal" variants of the more familiar *DSM* personality disorder categories. The MBHI is useful for a variety of purposes, such as indicating the type of relationship that the patient will respond to and will try to establish with health care providers. For example, the "cooperative" patient may respond well to explicit instructions from the health care provider(s), whereas a "forceful" individual may require a high degree of independence in directing his or her care. These instruments also yield information regarding strengths that can be integrated into treatment planning.

The Neuroticism Extraversion Openness–Personality Inventory (NEO-PI) and the revised version (NEO-PI-R) have demonstrated utility with a variety of populations, including people with chronic pain (Wade, Dougherty, Hart, & Cook, 1992) and people with Parkinson's disease (Glosser et al., 1995). In rehabilitation, the NEO-PI-R has been used to investigate the relationship between personality change and the onset of a traumatic disability using twin methodology (Hollick et al., 1998). Scores on NEO-PI-R facet scales were compared in 13 pairs of monozygotic twins where one of each pair had sustained an SCI. Results supported the hypothesis that personality is relatively stable and largely unaffected by traumatic incidents such as the acquisition of a disabling condition. The NEO-PI-R has also been used to predict outcomes in people with SCI (Krause & Rohe, 1998). Neuroticism was correlated with emotional distress and negatively correlated with adjustment, whereas extraversion was positively correlated with general satisfaction and adjustment. The hostility facet was associated with emotional distress, skill deficits, and financial limitations and negatively correlated with adjustment. The warmth and positive emotion facets were positively associated with general satisfaction and positive emotions. The authors concluded that personality, as measured by the NEO-PI-R, is related to life adjustment.

Costa and McCrae (1992a) listed several areas in which they believe that the NEO can be of particular use. It can help one understand the client's strengths and weaknesses, and some of the facets may be of diagnostic value. The therapist can gain a better understanding of the client, leading to better empathy and rapport, and the NEO-PI-R's nonpathological focus helps to direct the therapist toward more strengths. Feedback is easier because the client is unlikely to feel hurt or belittled by the results; in fact, a nontechnical sheet, "Your NEO Summary," can be given to the client. In addition, the instrument may be of use in matching clients to treatments, such as noting that patients high in "O" are more open to novel approaches to therapy.

Non-pathology-based personality assessment has been much less heavily studied with individuals with disabilities and presumably less widely used than pathological personality assessment. Therefore, specific issues regarding renorming scales, biases from item content, pattern analysis based on factor or cluster analyses, and other important issues have not yet been addressed. Nonetheless, the logic of using nonpathological instruments is compelling. The individual with a disability is most often a "normal" person in an "abnormal" situation; thus, assessing normal traits would make the most sense. From a philosophical standpoint, much of the pathology of individuals with disabilities is a function of societal stigma; to add to that by searching for internalized pathology may unwittingly further that process. The goals of rehabilitation are consistent with finding and building on strengths.

Practical Application

To enable those with disabilities to complete assessment measures independently, adaptations to standard administration procedures have been made using technological advances. For example, individuals with mobility impairments can often take self-administered tests such as the Millon Clinical Multi-Axial Inventory (3rd ed., MCMI-III; Millon, 1997) or MMPI-2 online, using special keyboards, head-mounted pointing systems, or voice command systems. Alternate keyboards can be reconfigured to have a small number of available responses (e.g., the left side of the keyboard is "true," and the right side is "false"). Using head-mounting devices and voice entry systems may require from 30 minutes to several hours of training and numerous sessions of trial and error. Errors are often encountered initially; for example, accidentally pressing a key may exit one from a program, which the client does not know how to restart. A head-mounted pointing device can slip or be knocked askew, especially with an inexperienced user. On the other hand, voice technology is rapidly improving. Voice systems are likely to become the entry method of choice in the near future (except, of course, for individuals with vocal impairments).

Most instruments are not separately normed for individuals with disabilities; furthermore different outcomes on measures are possible if an examiner reads and records the responses to items. The presence of an administrator may increase demand characteristics and social desirability effects. On the other hand, if the adaptation to allow self-administration makes the process too lengthy or arduous, especially with a poorly motivated patient, random responding may occur. Moreover, the presence of the administrator may provide attention, support, and other social reinforcers, increasing motivation to undergo assessment.

Alternate forms of administration are necessary for individuals with certain impairments. The MMPI is available on tape, in large-print format, and in Braille. The Millon instruments (MBHI, MCMI-III, Millon Adolescent Clinical Inventory [Millon, 1982]) are all available on tape.

Fundamental Competencies and Skills

To competently conduct assessments of people with disabilities, psychologists should know how to administer and interpret these tests for individuals in the general population and be familiar with psychometric considerations and other issues pertinent to administering them to people with disabilities. Clinicians who lack these skills should educate themselves and obtain supervision from someone who is both experienced and knowledgeable in these areas. Moreover, depending on the context of the assessment, other skills may be required. For assessments administered as part of a research study, the researcher should possess knowledge of the topic being investigated and knowledge of research design. In studies of acquired disabilities, the purpose is often to distinguish pre-existing characteristics from those present after onset in order to delineate a causal connection (or lack thereof) between the presence of a disability and psychological characteristics, feeling states, cognitions, or behaviors. For conditions in which there are changes over time, how these changes correlate with the aforementioned psychological variables may constitute the purpose of the study. However, regardless of the purpose and design of the study, these considerations influence the choice of assessment measures and how study results are interpreted.

The role of a consultant in conducting an assessment is typically to make a psychiatric diagnosis; suggest a theoretical formulation; and give recommendations for disposition, management, and intervention. Often, the consultant possesses knowledge of assessment beyond that of the treating clinician and is considered by those requesting the assessment to be an expert in the field. Therefore, in filling this role, the consultant should possess both advanced and current knowledge of the field of disability assessment as well as a great deal of practical experience. In conducting assessments in clinical settings, psychologists, whether in consulting roles or as treatment providers, should be cognizant of how patterns of results affect treatment decisions.

In addition to obtaining education about conducting assessments for those with disabilities, psychologists must confront their own prejudices and reactions. These may include the belief that those in wheelchairs are helpless, pitiful, asexual, subhuman, or possess little quality of life (Connally, Roberts, & Gold, 1992). People conducting psychological assessments may be uncomfortable discussing certain issues (e.g., sexuality and bowel and urinary tract dysfunction). This discomfort may become apparent to patients and potentially damage the quality of the assessment as well as the therapeutic relationship. To avoid this potential pitfall, it is important that prejudices and uncomfortable reactions be discussed with a competent supervisor. Ideally, then, these feelings can be dealt with in a way that would prevent them from adversely affecting the assessment.

Implications for Treatment

Several studies reveal linkages between psychopathology, personality pathology, and outcomes among those with disabilities. For example, people with SCI who have a history of drinking problems and current illicit drug use have an increased risk of pressure ulcers and urinary tract infections, respectively (Heinemann & Hawkins, 1995). In another study of individuals with SCI, those scoring higher on measures of distress (i.e., BDI and MMPI) needed longer rehabilitation and engaged in fewer self-care behaviors (Malec & Neimeyer, 1983). Even indicators of so-called "normal" personality, such as the NEO-PI-R (Costa & McCrae, 1992b), have predictive value for identifying difficulties in several areas of adjustment, including general satisfaction, career satisfaction, emotional distress, skills deficits, and financial limitations (Krause & Rohe, 1998). These studies represent only a few examples of how assessment of psychopathology and personality can have important implications for outcomes. As to the mechanisms that underlie these linkages (e.g., poor self-care regimens, difficulty working with health care professionals, impoverished social support networks), there has been speculation regarding which may be operating (e.g., Elliott, Jackson, Layfield, & Kendall, 1996), but these have yet to be fully delineated. In one of the few studies to explore these linkages, Herrick, Elliott, and Crow (1994) found that self-appraised problem-solving deficits predicted secondary complications in individuals with SCI. Although the performance of self-care regimens and the existence of psychopathology and personality pathology were not the focus of the study (and therefore were not assessed), this study is significant because it is one of the few to explore potential mechanisms.

Current Issues

Psychological assessment does not occur in a vacuum. Consideration of contextual issues is always necessary when assessing a patient. Contextual issues include the purpose of assessment, the party who is requesting the assessment, and who is paying for the assessment.

Traditionally, the purpose of psychological assessment has been to determine psychiatric diagnosis and render treatment recommendations. However, for those with disabilities, it may also be used for disability determinations and as a basis of recommendations for state and federal disability services (Elliott & Umlauf, 1995). Moreover, with the explosion of personal injury litigation during the past 20 years, assessment of personality and psychopathology may be performed by either side to bolster a case. Obviously depending on the purpose, demand characteristics of the situation may affect responses, leading to potential biases. Even if steps are taken to address these biases, contextual factors may affect the interpretation of test results and their use. Especially in litigation, test results are susceptible to slanted interpretations, depending on the intent of the party using them (Dyer, 1997).

Whoever requests the assessment should also be considered throughout the assessment process. Parties asking for psychological assessment can include health care staff, family members, attorneys, assorted agencies, or the individuals themselves. If the request originates from someone other than the patient, it is incumbent on the clinician to explain the request to the patient and ensure that results are used appropriately.

One last contextual issue to consider is method of payment. The proliferation of managed care organizations has substantially affected how mental health services are delivered. Limitation in reimbursement has meant that assessment strategies that formerly were covered by insurance may no longer be covered. For some individuals in these plans, extensive or expensive testing may be beyond their means, even though these tests are indicated. However, many managed care corporations require continuous assessment to demonstrate the effectiveness of psychological interventions. This can substantially affect the provider's choice of assessment measures. Moreover, issues of confidentiality of assessment findings are raised because disclosure of assessment results and progress in therapy often are prerequisites for reimbursement. In this atmosphere, the clinician is forced to strike a balance between complying with the requirements of the managed care corporation to secure remuneration and adhering to the ethical tenets to which psychologists are bound. To do so, the clinician must be familiar with assessment options to provide the client with meaningful choices. Then, he or she should clearly explain the situation to patients, clarify options, and assist them in making an informed choice.

Conclusion

Assessing individuals with physical disabilities is an extremely important task in rehabilitation. To achieve rehabilitation goals as effectively as possible, the clinician must understand the respective strengths and difficulties of a given patient. Detection and treatment of psychopathology leads to improved patient care and improved rehabilitation outcomes. Early detection can also prevent misunderstandings and the ensuing distress engendered in both patients and staff. The psychologist, armed with appropriate assessment data, can be an essential liaison for the rehabilitation team.

Appropriate assessment can also detect strengths that empower the patient while providing a balanced perspective for the treatment team. Providing patients with feedback about their areas of competence fosters improved therapeutic relationships and creates a context of encouragement and respect. Interventions can be designed to draw on the individual's most efficacious coping strategies, thereby increasing the chances of success and helping the client feel more skilled and competent.

Despite the importance of the endeavor, however, numerous challenges confront the clinician who is assessing the individual with a disability. Psychological variables may be difficult to distinguish from the sequelae of the physical condition itself. Few instruments are explicitly designed with individuals with disabilities in mind; therefore, the most common practice is to adapt existing instruments. The degree to which instruments have been examined, adapted, or renormed is highly variable. The process by which instruments are adapted can also have implications for interpretation. Thus, the clinician is often required to make inferences concerning the meaning of the test data in the context of the disability.

Contextual issues extend beyond the disability. The clinician must consider who is requesting the assessment and the purpose of the assessment. Moreover, the sociocultural atmosphere, including the health care delivery environment and the assessor's own competencies and prejudices, may substantially affect the assessment endeavor. Thus, psychological and personality assessment encompasses a vast array of considerations that can affect the assessment process and the decisions that stem from it.

References

Allen, D. N., & Goreczny, A. J. (1995). Multiple sclerosis. In A. J. Goreczny (Ed.), *Handbook of health and rehabilitation psychology* (pp. 389–429). New York: Plenum Press.

American Psychiatric Association. (1994). *Diagnostic and statistical manual of mental disorders* (4th ed.). Washington, DC: Author.

Barncord, S. W., & Wanlass, R. L. (1998, September). *Construct validity of a MMPI-2 correction procedure and development of an alternate correction method.* Paper presented at the annual meeting of the American Association of Spinal Cord Injury Psychologists and Social Workers, Las Vegas, NV.

Berven, N. L., Habeck, R. V., & Malec, J. F. (1985). Predominant MMPI-168 profile clusters in a rehabilitation medicine sample. *Rehabilitation Psychology, 30,* 209–219.

Blalock, S. J., DeVellis, R., Brown, G., & Wallston, K. A. (1989). Validity of the Center for Epidemiological Studies Depression Scale and arthritis population. *Arthritis and Rheumatism, 32,* 991–997.

Blanke, R. V. (1986). Accuracy in urinalysis. In R. L. Hawks & N. C. Chiang (Eds.), *Urine testing for drugs of abuse* (NIDA Research Monograph No. 73, pp. 43–53). Washington, DC: U.S. Government Printing Office.

Bockian, N. (1994). Systemic–behavioral treatment of a personality disorder and abusive behavior on a spinal cord injury unit: A case illustration. *SCI Psychosocial Process, 7,* 153–160.

Bockian, N. (1997, September). *Personality disorders and spinal cord injury: A controlled study.* Paper presented at the annual meeting of the American Association of Spinal Cord Injury Psychologists and Social Workers, Las Vegas, NV.

Bracken, M. B., & Shephard, M. J. (1980). Coping and adaptation following acute spinal cord injury: A theoretical analysis. *Paraplegia, 18,* 74–85.

Buckelew, S. P., Baumstark, D., Frank, R. G., & Hewett, J. (1990). Adjustment following spinal cord injury. *Rehabilitation Psychology, 35,* 101–109.

Buckelew, S. P., Burk, J., Brownlee-Duffeck, M., Frank, R. G., & DeGood, D. (1988). Cognitive and somatic aspects of depression among a rehabilitation sample: Reliability and validity of SCL-90-R research sub-scales. *Rehabilitation Psychology, 33,* 67–75.

Butcher, J. N. (1985). Assessing psychological characteristics of personal injury or worker's compensation litigants. *The Clinical Psychologist, 38*(4), 84–87.

Clay, D. L., Hagglund, K. J., Frank, R. G., Elliott, T. R., & Chaney, J. (1995). Enhancing the accuracy of depression diagnosis in patients with spinal cord injury using Bayesian analysis. *Rehabilitation Psychology, 40,* 171–180.

Connally, P., Roberts, E. V., & Gold, J. (1992). Old attitudes, new attitudes, and disability policy. *SCI Psychosocial Process, 5,* 124–130.

Costa, P. T., Jr., & McCrae, R. R. (1992a). Normal personality assessment in clinical practice: The NEO Personality Inventory [Special section]. *Psychological Assessment, 4,* 5–13.

Costa, P. T., Jr., & McCrae, R. R. (1992b). *NEO-PI-R professional manual.* Odessa, FL: Psychological Assessment Resources.

Coyle, C. P., & Roberge, J. J. (1992). The psychometric properties of the Center for Epidemiological Studies-Depression Scale (CES-D) when used with adults with physical disabilities. *Psychology and Health, 7,* 69–81.

Davidoff, G., Roth, E., Thomas, P., Doljanac, R., Dijkers, M., Berent, S., Wolf, L., Morris, J., & Yarkony, G. (1990). Depression among acute spinal cord injury patients: A study utilizing the Zung Self-Rating Depression Scale. *Rehabilitation Psychology, 35,* 171–179.

Dupont, R. L. (1989, October). Addiction, withdrawal, and the role of BZs. *The Psychiatric Times,* vi.

Dupont, R. L., & Saylor, K. E. (1991). Sedatives/hypnotics and benzodiazepines. In R. J. Frances & S. I. Miller (Eds.), *Clinical textbook of addictive disorders* (pp. 69–102). New York: Guilford Press.

Dyer, F. J. (1997). Application of the Millon inventories in forensic psychology. In T. Millon (Ed.), *The Millon inventories* (pp. 124–139). New York: Guilford Press.

Elliott, T. R., & Frank, R. G. (1996). Depression following spinal cord injury. *Archives of Physical Medicine and Rehabilitation, 77,* 816–823.

Elliott, T. R., Jackson, W. T., Layfield, M., & Kendall, D. (1996). Personality disorders and response to outpatient treatment of chronic pain. *Journal of Clinical Psychology in Medical Settings, 3,* 219–234.

Elliott, T. R., & Umlauf, R. (1995). Measurement of personality and psychopathology following acquired physical disability. In L. Cushman & M. Scherer (Eds.), *Psychological assessment in medical rehabilitation settings* (pp. 325–358). Washington, DC: American Psychological Association.

Eysenck, H. J., & Eysenck, S. B. G. (1968). *Manual for the Eysenck Personality Inventory.* San Diego, CA: Educational and Industrial Testing Service.

Feinstein, A. (1995). Depression associated with multiple sclerosis: An etilogical conundrum. *Canadian Journal of Psychiatry, 40,* 573–576.

Fordyce, W. (1964). Personality characteristics of men with spinal cord injury as related to manner of onset of disability. *Archives of Physical Medicine and Rehabilitation, 45,* 321–325.

Frank, R. G., Chaney, J. M., Clay, D. L., Shutty, M. S., Beck, N. C., Kay, D. R., Elliott, T. R., & Grambling, S. (1992). Dysphoria: A major symptom factor in persons with disability or chronic illness. *Psychiatry Research, 43,* 231–241.

Frank, R. G., Kashani, J. H., Kashani, S. R., Wonderlich, S. A., Umlauf, R. L., & Ashkanazi, G. S. (1984). Psychological response to amputation as a function of age and time since amputation. *British Journal of Psychiatry, 144,* 493–497.

Frank, R. G., Kashani, J. H., Wonderlich, S., Lising, A., & Visot, L. (1985). Depression and adrenal function in spinal cord injury. *American Journal of Psychiatry, 142,* 252–253.

Fuhrer, M. J., Rintala, D. H., Hart, K. A., Clearman, R., & Young, N. E. (1993). Depressive symptomatology in persons with spinal cord injury who reside in a community. *Archives of Physical Medicine and Rehabilitation, 74,* 255–260.

Fullerton, D. T., Harvey, R. F., Klein, M. C., & Howell, T. (1981). Psychiatric disorders in patients with spinal cord injuries. *Archives of General Psychiatry, 38,* 1369–1371.

Glosser, G., Clark, C., Freundlich, B., Kliner-Krenzel, L., Flaherty, P., & Stern, M. (1995). A controlled study of current and premorbid personality: Characteristics of Parkinson's disease patients. *Movement Disorders, 10,* 201–206.

Green, B. L., Lindy, J. D., Grace, M. C., & Leonard, A. C. (1992). Chronic posttraumatic stress disorder and diagnostic comorbidity in a disaster sample. *Journal of Nervous and Mental Disease, 180,* 760–766.

Harper, D. C., & Richman, L. C. (1978). Personality profiles of physically impaired adolescents. *Journal of Clinical Psychology, 34,* 636–642.

Heinemann, A. W., & Hawkins, D. (1995). Substance abuse and medical complications following spinal cord injury. *Rehabilitation Psychology, 40,* 125–140.

Heinemann, A. W., McGraw, T. E., Brandt, M. J., Roth, E., & Dell'Oliver, C. (1992). Prescription medication misuse among persons with spinal cord injuries. *International Journal of the Addictions, 27,* 301–316.

Heinrich, R. K., Tate, D. G., & Buckelew, S. P. (1994). Brief symptom inventory norms for spinal cord injury. *Rehabilitation Psychology, 35,* 217–228.

Herrick, S., Elliott, T. R., & Crow, F. (1994). Self-appraised problem-solving skills and the prediction of secondary complications among persons with spinal cord injuries. *Journal of Clinical Psychology in Medical Settings, 1,* 269–283.

Hoffmann, N. G., Olofsson, O., Salen, B., & Wickstrom, L. (1995). Prevalence of abuse and dependency in chronic pain patients. *International Journal of the Addictions, 30*, 919–927.

Hohmann, G. W. (1975). Psychological aspects of treatment and rehabilitation of the spinal cord injured person. *Clinical Orthopedics, 112*, 81–88.

Hollick, C., Radnitz, C. L., Tirch, D. D., Silverman, J., Birstein, S., & Bauman, W. A. (1998, September). *Personality and spinal cord injury: A study of monozygotic twins*. Poster presented at the annual conference of the American Association of Spinal Cord Injury Psychologists and Social Workers, Las Vegas, NV.

Howell, T., Fullerton, D. T., Harvey, R., & Klein, M. (1981). Depression in spinal cord injured patients. *Paraplegia, 19*, 284–288.

Kendall, P. C., Edinger, J., & Eberly, C. (1978). Taylor's MMPI correction factor for spinal cord injury: Empirical endorsement. *Journal of Consulting and Clinical Psychology, 46*, 370–371.

Krause, J. S., & Rohe, D. E. (1998). Personality and life adjustment after spinal cord injury: An exploratory study. *Rehabilitation Psychology, 43*, 118–130.

Kunce, J. T., & Worley, B. H. (1966). Interest patterns, accidents, and disability. *Journal of Clinical Psychology, 22*, 105–107.

Langer, K. G. (1994). Depression in disabling illness: Severity and patterns of self-reported symptoms in three groups. *Journal of Geriatric Psychiatry and Neurology, 7*, 121–128.

Lees-Haley, P. R., English, L. T., & Glenn, W. J. (1991). A fake bad scale on the MMPI-2 for personal injury claimants. *Psychological Reports, 68*, 203–210.

Malec, J. (1985). Personality factors associated with severe traumatic disability. *Rehabilitation Psychology, 3*, 165–172.

Malec, J., & Neimeyer, R. (1983). Psychologic prediction of duration of inpatient spinal cord injury rehabilitation and performance of self-care. *Archives of Physical Medicine and Rehabilitation, 64*, 359–363.

Mann, K. (1994). Winners: Characteristics of highly successful rehabilitation clients. *Vocational Evaluation and Work Adjustment Bulletin, 27*(1), 15–18.

Marsh, G. G., Hirsh, S. H., & Leung, G. (1982). Use and misuse of the MMPI in multiple sclerosis. *Psychological Reports, 51*, 1127–1134.

Mattlar, C. E., Tarkkanen, P., Carlsson, A., Aaltonen, T., & Helenius, H. (1993). Personality characteristics for 83 paraplegic patients evaluated by the Rorschach method using the comprehensive system. *British Journal of Projective Psychology, 38*(2), 20–30.

Mawson, A. R., Biundo, J. J., Clemmer, D. I., Jacobs, K. W., Ktsanes, V. K., & Rice, J. C. (1996). Sensation-seeking, criminality, and spinal cord injury: A case-control study. *American Journal of Epidemiology, 144*, 463–472.

McDaniel, J. W. (1976). *Physical disability and human behavior* (2nd ed.). New York: Pergamon Press.

Meloy, R. (1989). The forensic interview. In R. J. Craig (Ed.), *Clinical and diagnostic interviewing* (pp. 323–344). London: Aronson.

Millon, T. (1982). *Millon Adolescent Clinical Inventory manual*. Minneapolis, MN: National Computer Systems.

Millon, T. (1997). *Millon Clinical Multiaxial Inventory—III manual* (2nd ed.). Minneapolis, MN: National Computer Systems.

Millon, T., Green, C. J., & Meagher, R. (1982). *Millon Behavioral Health Inventory manual*. Minneapolis, MN: National Computer Systems.

Minden, S. L., Orav, J., & Reich, P. (1987). Depression in multiple sclerosis. *General Hospital Psychiatry, 9*, 426–434.

Mueller, S. R., & Girace, M. (1988). Use and misuse of the MMPI: A reconsideration. *Psychological Reports, 6*, 483–491.

Noy, S., Achiron, A., Gabbay, U., Barak, Y., Rotstein, Z., Laor, N., & Sarova-Pinhas, I. (1995). A new approach to affective symptoms in relapsing-remitting multiple sclerosis. *Comprehensive Psychiatry, 36*, 390–395.

Nyenhuis, D. L., Rao, S. M., Zajecka, J. M., Luchetta, T., Bernardin, L., & Garron, D. C. (1995). Mood disturbance versus other symptoms of depression in multiple sclerosis. *Journal of the International Neuropsychological Society, 1*, 291–296.

Overholser, J. C., Schubert, D. S. P., Foliart, R., & Frost, F. (1993). Assesment of emotional distress following spinal cord injury. *Rehabilitation Psychology, 38*, 187–189.

Peck, J., Smith, T. W., Ward, J., & Milano, R. (1989). Disability and depression in rheumatoid arthritis. *Arthritis and Rheumatism, 32*, 1100–1106.

Pine, D. S., Douglas, C. J., Charles, E., Davies, M., & Kahn, D. (1995). Patients with multiple sclerosis presenting to psychiatric hospitals. *Journal of Clinical Psychiatry, 56*, 297–306.

Primeau, F. (1988). Post-stroke depression: A critical review of the literature. *Canadian Journal of Psychiatry, 33*, 757–765.

Radnitz, C. L., Hsu, L., Tirch, D. D., Willard, J., Lillian, L. B., Walczak, S., Festa, J., Perez-Strumolo, L., Broderick, C., Binks, M., Schlein, I. S., Bockian, N., Green, L., & Cytryn, A. (1998). A comparison of posttraumatic stress disorder in veterans with and without spinal cord injury. *Journal of Abnormal Psychology, 107*, 676–680.

Radnitz, C. L., Hsu, L., Willard, J., Perez-Strumolo, L., Festa, J., Lillian, L. B., Walczak, S., Tirch, D. D., Schlein, I. S., Binks, M., & Broderick, C. P. (1998). Posttraumatic stress disorder in veterans with spinal cord injury: Trauma-related risk factors. *Journal of Traumatic Stress, 11*, 505–520.

Radnitz, C. L., McGrath, R. E., Tirch, D. D., Willard, J., Perez-Strumolo, L., Festa, J., Binks, M., Broderick, C. P., Schlein, I. S., Walczak, S., & Lillian, L. B. (1997). Use of the Beck Depression Inventory in veterans with spinal cord injury. *Rehabilitation Psychology, 42*, 93–101.

Radnitz, C. L., Schlein, I. S., Walczak, S., Broderick, C. P., Binks, M., Tirch, D. D., Willard, J., Perez-Strumolo, L., Festa, J., Lillian, L. B., Bockian, N., Cytryn, A., & Green, L. (1995). The prevalence of posttraumatic stress disorder in veterans with spinal cord injury. *SCI Psychosocial Process, 8*(4), 145–149.

Reich, J. H., & Green, A. I. (1991). Effect of personality disorders on outcome of treatment. *Journal of Nervous and Mental Disease, 179*(2), 74–82.

Rodevich, M. A., & Wanlass, R. L. (1995). A moderating effect of spinal cord injury on MMPI-2 profiles: A clinically derived *t* score correction procedure. *Rehabilitation Psychology, 40*, 181–190.

Ron, M. A., & Logsdail, S. J. (1989). Psychiatric morbidity in multiple sclerosis: A clinical and MRI study. *Psychological Medicine, 19*, 887–895.

Rosen, J. C., Johnson, C., & Frymoyer, J. W. (1983). Identification of excessive back disability with the Faschingbaur Abbreviated MMPI. *Journal of Clinical Psychology, 39*, 71–74.

Rybarczyk, B. D., Nyenhuis, D. L., Nicholas, J. J., Schulz, R., Alioto, R. J., & Blair, C. (1992). Social discomfort and depression in a sample of adults with leg amputations. *Archives of Physical Medicine and Rehabilitation, 73*, 1169–1173.

Schubert, D. S. P., Burns, R., Paras, W., & Sioson, E. (1992). Decrease of depression during stroke and amputation rehabilitation. *General Hospital Psychiatry, 14*, 135–141.

Southwick, S. M., Yehuda, R., & Giller, E. L. (1991). Characterization of depression in war-related posttraumatic stress disorder. *American Journal of Psychiatry, 148*, 179–183.

Spergel, P., Erlich, G. E., & Glass, D. (1978). The rheumatoid arthritic personality: A psychodiagnostic myth. *Psychosomatics, 19*(2), 79–86.

Stewart, J. R. (1994). Denial of disabling conditions and specific interventions in the rehabilitation counseling setting. *Journal of Applied Rehabilitation Counseling, 25*(3), 7–15.

Tate, D. G., Forchheimer, M., Maynard, F., Davidoff, G., & Dijkers, M. (1993). Comparing two measures of depression in spinal cord injury. *Rehabilitation Psychology, 38*, 53–61.

Tate, D. G., Kewman, D. G., & Maynard, F. (1990). The brief symptom inventory: Measuring psychological distress in spinal cord injury. *Rehabilitation Psychology, 35*, 211–216.

Taylor, G. P. (1970). Moderator-variable effects on personality-test-item endorsements of physically disabled patients. *Journal of Consulting and Clinical Psychology, 35*, 183–188.

Verebey, K., & Turner, C. E. (1991). Laboratory testing. In R. J. Frances & S. I. Miller (Eds.), *Clinical textbook of addictive disorders* (pp. 221–236). New York: Guilford Press.

Wade, J. B., Dougherty, L. M., Hart, R. P., & Cook, D. B. (1992). Patterns of normal personality structure among chronic pain patients. *Pain, 48*(2), 37–43

Whitlock, F. A., & Siskind, M. M. (1980). Depression as a major symptom of multiple sclerosis. *Journal of Neurology, Neurosurgery & Psychiatry, 43*, 861–865.

Williamson, G. (1995). Restriction of normal activities among older adult amputees: The role of public self-consciousness. *Journal of Clinical Geropsychology, 1*, 229–242.

Wilson, H., Olson, W. H., Gascon, G. G., & Brumback, R. A. (1982). Personality characteristics and multiple sclerosis. *Psychological Reports, 51*, 791–806.

Woodbury, B. (1978). Psychological adjustment to spinal cord injury: A literature review, 1950–1977. *Rehabilitation Psychology, 25*, 119–134.

14

Evaluating Outcomes Research: Statistical Concerns and Clinical Relevance

Mary McAweeney and Nancy Crewe

A substantial proportion of rehabilitation psychology research has been devoted to assessment of treatment interventions and clinically relevant outcomes such as depression and adaptation. Rehabilitation psychologists have attempted to answer questions about the value of such diverse interventions as providing social skills training to people with spinal cord injury (SCI; Dunn, 1981), teaching consumers to write letters of self-advocacy (White, Thomson, & Nary, 1997), and training attendant service users in effective interview skills (Ulicny, Adler, & Jones, 1990). They have examined the effectiveness of counseling and psychotherapy for individuals with disabilities and their families (White et al., 1997), of sexual counseling with individuals with developmental disabilities (Lund, 1992), and many other interventions.

The roots of psychological practice are found in science, so it is not surprising that many psychologists have long expected to evaluate the efficacy of their work. Curiosity and the desire for information that might guide clinical practice are only surface reasons for studying outcomes, however. Increasingly, third-party payers are requiring evidence of treatment effectiveness before they provide referrals and reimbursement for services, and providers are conducting research to generate such data.

Unlike many clinical and counseling psychologists who work alone or in small group practices, rehabilitation psychologists typically function in complex interdisciplinary settings. As a result, they have played a pivotal role in the increasingly urgent efforts to document outcomes of heterogeneous medical and vocational rehabilitation programs. Because psychologists are often the team members with the most specific training in research methodology, they have been among the leaders in developing and testing outcome measures and creating assessment systems. Because rehabilitation psychology outcomes are so often intertwined with interdis-

We acknowledge the support of the Paralyzed Veterans of America, Eastern Paralyzed Veterans of America, and American Association of Spinal Cord Injury Psychologists and Social Workers.

ciplinary rehabilitation medicine, we address the broad issues of rehabilitation outcome measurement rather than the evaluation of psychological services in isolation.

There are four sections to this chapter. The first section provides a historical overview of research that has been conducted in rehabilitation psychology over the past two decades. The second section investigates the practice of using null hypothesis statistical testing for evaluating outcome studies and its common pitfalls, misuses, and limitations related to rehabilitation psychology. The third section furnishes a tool in which rehabilitation psychology research can be evaluated as well as examples of using the tool. The final section includes recommendations for future research practice in rehabilitation psychology.

History

Federal accreditation requirements provided an early impetus for the collection of programmatic outcome data in rehabilitation. The Joint Commission on Accreditation of Healthcare Organizations (JCAHO) has required outcomes data from rehabilitation hospitals since 1973 (Brooks, 1995), and the Commission on the Accreditation of Rehabilitation Facilities (CARF) has also required program evaluation data (including consumer satisfaction and patient follow-up) for some 20 years (American Health Consultants, 1994). Over the years, different kinds of data have been collected, and there is still disagreement about what kind of information can best document the quality of rehabilitation services. In the past, much of the data have focused on the kinds of resources available in the institutions and on the treatment processes provided to patients.

In recent years, increasing emphasis is being placed on outcomes, the results of the services rather than the content of the services themselves. Jean Welsh, clinical programs vice president for Advanced Rehabilitation Systems, summed up the point: The essential measure of rehabilitation's value is how the patient feels and functions at the end of treatment; process measures simply tell how that end was achieved. What sounds like a straightforward proposition, however, is far from simple. Given the diversity of patients and conditions treated by rehabilitation professionals, the varied kinds of treatment settings, and the wide range of financial and social resources available to patients, finding outcome measures that can be standardized and that provide appropriate data across the board is a challenge, indeed. As a result, dozens of homegrown measurement tools have been created to suit the needs of a particular setting but do not provide a basis for comparison with other programs. Norms have been lacking, compounding the difficulty with interpreting outcome data (American Health Consultants, 1994). Furthermore, determining the clinical relevance of data produced by such heterogeneous methodologies is tenuous.

The field has been moving toward a degree of consensus, however, with two or three systems gaining increased use and visibility. The Functional Independence Measure (FIM), which stands at the heart of the uniform data system for medical rehabilitation (UDS$_{MR}$), is probably the most widely used measure in rehabilitation at this time (Granger & Hamilton, 1992). The FIM consists of 18 functional limitation items, each rated on a 7-point scale. It is stronger in its ability to capture information about mobility and activities of daily living than it is in cognitive or psychosocial areas. It was devised as a minimum data set, and some rehabilitation organizations supplement it with one or more data collection instruments, such as the Rehabilitation Institute of Chicago's (1996) Functional Assessment Scale (FAS), which includes items such as transportation, housing, work, leisure, support systems, and medical status.

The JCAHO has been developing another system that is likely to achieve wide usage. The indicator measurement system is intended to be used at all levels of rehabilitation, from acute rehabilitation hospitals through subacute and long-term care (Brooks, 1995). Other measurement systems that have achieved substantial recognition include the Level of Rehabilitation Scale (LORS; Carey & Prosovac, 1982), the Patient Evaluation and Conference System (PECS; Harvey & Jellineck, 1981), and the Functional Assessment Measure (FAM; Hall, Hamilton, Gordon, & Zasler, 1993). The LORS and PECS have shared databases (American Health Consultants, 1994).

Although these systems represent a step forward in standardization of rehabilitation outcomes, they nevertheless are limited in some respects. They cannot address the important circumstances and needs of all individuals receiving rehabilitation services. In particular, the FIM provides little information about psychosocial outcomes. Furthermore, because the instruments are based on ratings, there is inherent subjectivity in the data produced. Interrater reliability is satisfactory when collected under neutral research conditions, but the results may be different if the motivation exists to skew data. For example, to rate patients who are on the borderline of categories as somewhat more impaired at admission or somewhat less impaired at discharge would skew the data toward more positive change or improvement (Mermis et al., 1998).

Many rehabilitation providers are also concerned that third-party payers may misuse outcome data, particularly the simplified data provided by a minimum data set such as the FIM. If case managers focus on a total FIM score without appropriate understanding of the characteristics of the patient population being served by a particular facility, they may reach inappropriate conclusions about the effectiveness of treatment being provided by the organization.

The global outcome measures may not be appropriate for measuring the impact of specific interventions (e.g., a problem-solving group for individuals with traumatic brain injury [TBI]). Similarly, they may be of minimal value in guiding individual treatment decisions. The Goal Attainment Scale system, a different approach to outcome assessment (Kiresuk, 1982), involves defining specific goals that are individualized for each patient. Data can be aggregated to some extent (e.g., to determine what proportion of patients are meeting or exceeding their personal goals in the area of independent living compared with psychosocial adjustment), but the results would be of minimal use in comparing one facility with another.

Whiteneck (1992) proposed a conceptual model for investigating outcomes for individuals with SCI that examines six dimensions. Three of the dimensions are based on the World Health Organization's (1980) ICIDH system: impairment (organ-system-level loss of structure or function), disability (person-level loss of the ability to function in typical ways), and handicap (societal-level disadvantage, created by an interaction between the impairment and the environment). To these he added outcome dimensions of health, personal satisfaction, and costs. For each dimension, specific measurement tools would have to be defined. The model is an interesting contrast to the UDS_{MR} with respect to its breadth and its inclusion of the dimensions of handicap and personal satisfaction.

A great deal of work has gone into the task of outcome measurement during the past two decades, and it is apparent that more remains to be done. In all likelihood, no single system will meet all of the needs associated with decisions made at clinical, programmatic, institutional, and industry levels. Nevertheless, the field is clearly becoming more serious and sophisticated about the need for accountability.

Uses, Misuses, and Limitations of the Null Hypothesis Statistical Testing Model

The underpinnings of quantitative research are in null hypothesis statistical testing (NHST); this model has been used by psychological research and rehabilitation psychology as well. Over the years, there has been an ongoing debate concerning the dubious value of NHST in general (Brewer, 1974; Cohen, 1990; Dayton, Schafer, & Rogers, 1973; Hagan, 1997; Hubbard, 1995) and, in particular, with rehabilitation psychology (McAweeney, Tate, & McAweeney, 1997a; Ottenbacher, 1995; Ottenbacher & Barrett, 1991; Schafer, 1993). The following review of NHST illustrates the shortcomings and limitations of this paradigm within rehabilitation psychology. We use a two-group outcome design as a template.

In statistical practice, a theoretical hypothesis should guide the design, analysis, and interpretation of results (Serlin, 1987). As its name suggests, NHST must be preceded by a theoretical hypothesis to be meaningful. The goal in developing a research hypothesis is to state a decision rule about the nature of selected parameters. Ultimately, a researcher's objective is to infer from a random sample to the general population. Therefore, the statistical hypothesis is defined with regard to a population that the sampled individuals represent. In a treatment–control group study, the statistical hypothesis is typically defined as $H_o : \mu_1 - \mu_2 = 0$ or $H_o : \mu_1 = \mu_2$, where μ_1 and μ_2 are the population means of the treatment and control groups, and H_o is the null hypothesis. The null hypothesis states that the two sample means come from the same population and that no difference exists between them except those caused by chance (Kirk, 1982; Serlin, 1987). The alternative hypothesis is that the means are not equal and come from different populations; in other words, $H_o : \mu_1 - \mu_2$ is not equal to 0 or $H_o : \mu_1$ is not equal to μ_2.

As described, NHST results in a decision that is correct—not rejecting the null hypothesis when it is true (true negative) or rejecting the null hypothesis when it is false (true positive)—or a decision that is incorrect that results in a Type I or Type II error. In outcome studies a Type I error occurs when the researcher concludes that there is a significant treatment effect, rejecting the null hypothesis, when actually the rejection is caused by chance variability (false positive). The probability of this happening is equal to the significance level, or alpha (α), selected by the researcher. Generally, a widely accepted value of α is .05. The level of tolerable error that is set is important because it determines the degree of conservatism and is central in interpreting results obtained from statistical analysis (McNamara, 1990).

The failure to reject a false null hypothesis is a Type II or β error (false negative). If a difference between the treatment and control group exists in the population but is unlikely to be identified, conducting the research study is likely to be an inefficient use of time and resources (Cole, 1988; Freiman, Chalmers, Smith, & Kuebler, 1978; McAweeney, Forchheimer, & Tate, 1996; Olejnik, 1984).

As stated above, a correct decision is made when the null hypothesis is false and it is rejected (true positive). The probability of rejecting the null hypothesis when a true population difference exists is statistical power (ϕ). The four factors affecting the ϕ of a study are the level of α, sample size (n), error variance (σ_ε^2), and effect size (Δ). For our purposes, it is sufficient to say that the relationship among these four factors (α, $\Sigma\Delta^2$, n, σ_ε^2) is intertwined such that if one or more are increased or decreased, the ϕ for a particular study changes (Kirk, 1982; Olejnik, 1984).

The ϕ of a study is often calculated prior to conducting a study to determine sample size requirements. Power can range from 0.0 to 1.0. A ϕ of .8 or higher is often considered desirable and acceptable in rehabilitation psychology (Kirk, 1982; Maxwell, Cole, Arvey, & Salas, 1991; McAweeney, Forchheimer, & Tate, 1997). This value reflects the view that Type I error is more serious than Type II error. The ratio of Type II error to Type I error when $\phi =. 8$ is $(1 - \beta/\alpha)$ or $.20/.05 = 4$. In this case, the probability of committing a Type II error is four times larger than that for a Type I error.

Although a Type I error is generally viewed as being more serious than a Type II error, there are situations in outcomes research in which a Type II error may be regarded as more serious.[1] For example, a researcher may be investigating the effectiveness of a newly developed computer learning strategy for people with TBI and unwittingly commits a Type II error. The error may cause the researcher to abandon further research on this strategy even though it may be an effective strategy for people with TBI. The statistically nonsignificant results may be due to a number of factors that are discussed below.

---

[1]For further information, see Brewer and Sindelar (1988), Casio and Sedeck (1983), Cohen (1990), Cole (1988), Goodwin and Goodwin (1989), Kirk (1982), McNamara (1990), Olejnik (1984), and Ottenbacher (1995).

Because outcomes are paramount, researchers in rehabilitation psychology cannot afford to conduct studies wherein significant methodological shortcomings compromise the validity of the results. Hence, rehabilitation psychologists cannot overlook the inherent limitations and common misuses of NHST.

Many of the limitations and misuses of NHST have been sufficiently described in the literature (Cohen, 1990; Hubbard, 1995; McAweeney et al., 1997; Meyer, 1974; Olejnik, 1984; Ottenbacher, 1995; Shaver, 1993).[2] However, deficiencies in outcome research in rehabilitation have not been sufficiently explored (McAweeney et al., 1997; Ottenbacher & Barrett, 1991). These deficiencies include (a) the inability to draw conclusions about clinical significance, (b) a rigid adherence to a set α, (c) the arbitrariness of choosing Type I error, (d) the misinterpretation of p values, (e) the choice of two- versus one-tailed tests, (f) typically small sample sizes, (g) failure to report results that are not statistically significant, and (h) a lack of control over Type I error. We examine each of these limitations.

Drawing Conclusions About Clinical Significance

As discussed above, NHST provides a means of determining whether evidence is sufficient to conclude that a sample fails to conform to a specified model or null hypothesis (Fisher, 1956). NHST has become the predominant means of conducting rehabilitation psychology research, but it was not developed for this purpose (Meyer, 1974). Rather, it was developed for use in the "hard" sciences (Fisher, 1956). Although NHST is straightforward, the conclusions that can be drawn from NHST do not provide information pertinent to assess the magnitude of group differences. Thus, whereas NHST can be used to address statistical significance, it is inherently unable to shed light on issues of clinical significance, which are the ultimate questions of interest in outcomes research (Cohen, 1990; McAweeney et al., 1997; Ottenbacher & Barrett, 1991).

For example, rehabilitation psychologists working with people with SCI may believe that cognitive restructuring therapy will work for some of their patients, despite research indicating that the therapy does not reach the standard level of statistical significance. They may choose to ignore the lack of statistical significance and provide the therapy to some of their patients because their own clinical experiences have demonstrated its utility. Thus, an intervention that does not reach a point of statistical significance may still be clinically relevant, and a clinically relevant intervention may not reach statistical significance.

To determine the strength of a rehabilitation intervention, an index is needed that is responsive to the strength of the association between the

---

[2]For further discussion on the interrelationship of these factors and the trade-offs associated with altering them, see Bird and Hall (1986), Brewer and Sindelar (1988), Casio and Sedeck (1983), Cohen (1990), Cole (1988), Goodwin and Goodwin (1989), Kirk (1982), McAweeney et al. (1997), McNamara (1990), Olejnik (1984), and Ottenbacher (1995).

treatment and the outcomes and is independent of sample size. Such an index—effect size—is discussed in the "Recommendations" section of this chapter. Effect size can be used to help resolve the conflict between statistical significance and clinical relevance.

Rigid Adherence to Alpha Set at .05

A second limitation of NHST is that α is nearly universally set at .05, meaning that the probability of committing a Type I error is 5%. This rigid adherence to .05 disregards the relative importance of Type I and Type II errors, for which there is a trade-off (Casio & Sedeck, 1983; McAweeney et al., 1997; Olejnik, 1984; Ottenbacher, 1995). Depending on the nature of the outcome of interest, either a higher or lower level of α may be more suitable. For example, studies investigating the effectiveness of medications generally use a smaller α than .05 because the risk of a Type I error is of great concern. Regardless of whether α is chosen implicitly or explicitly, this choice about the relative importance of different types of errors is not a statistical one but rather a function of value judgments.

Arbitrariness of Choosing Type I Error

Even if researchers do give careful consideration to the level of α that they choose, the decision is innately arbitrary. For example, in the case of assessing the effectiveness of a newly developed intervention for the treatment of chronic depression, two researchers may both conclude that a "high" level should be selected for α to decrease the possibility of a Type II error. In this context, *high* has no precise definition. Thus, if Researcher X chooses to use .10 and Researcher Y chooses .20, the conclusions that they draw from their NHSTs are the opposite if the p value is between .10 and .20, even though both researchers may have similar clinical concerns about the importance of the intervention. Because NHST provides only information regarding whether analysis supports or rejects a dichotomous decision and this decision rule is inherently arbitrary, it can result in the drawing of conflicting conclusions, none of which is wrong.

Misinterpretation of p Values

Although NHST provides dichotomous decision rules rather than probabilities, it is frequently misinterpreted as having utility for assessing probabilities and the strength of relationships. In the example given above, if the p value were .15, it would not be uncommon for Researcher Y to report the results as being "almost significant" (Cohen, 1990). This term is not meaningful (McAweeney et al., 1997). Similarly, although NHST does not provide information concerning the strength of relationships, it is common for manuscripts to inappropriately refer to small p values as "highly significant" and as such, clinically pertinent. The reporting of p values in any way other than as not significant or small enough to reject the null hypothesis is misleading at best (McAweeney et al., 1997). Significance level alone should not be used as an index of the strength of an experimental effect.

Two-Tailed Versus One-Tailed Tests

Most questions of interest in rehabilitation psychology research tend to be of the form, "Do subjects taking part in intervention Z have substantially better outcomes than controls?" Although insubstantial differences are not of clinical interest, NHST does not address the issue of magnitude. This is an inherent limitation. NHST is unable to address questions of the substantiveness of differences; moreover, in attempting to address these questions with NHST, null hypotheses are invariably stated as "experimental subjects do not have different outcomes from control ones." Although this two-tailed test is almost always used, it is inappropriate to answer the question of interest: "Does the treatment group have substantially better outcomes than control?" If NHST is to be used, a one-tailed test should be conducted. The common failure to appropriately choose between one- and two-tailed significance tests is indicative of frequent misinterpretation of NHST results, by both authors and reviewers.

Typically Small Samples

If the sample size used to conduct NHST is too small, study findings frequently are erroneous, suggesting that the null hypothesis cannot be rejected when if samples of appropriate size were used, they would be rejected (Ottenbacher & Barrett, 1991; Parker, 1995). Unfortunately it has been shown that the vast majority of rehabilitation research is conducted with insufficient sample sizes (McAweeney, Tate, & McAweeney, 1997b; Ottenbacher & Barrett, 1991). To determine the appropriate sample size, one needs to calculate ϕ before the beginning of a study. The fact that considerations of ϕ cannot be ignored in conducting NHST is direct proof that whereas the technique may be straightforward, it is not sufficient for the conduct of outcome research.

Research in rehabilitation shows low levels of ϕ, commonly as a result of small samples. Ottenbacher and Barrett (1991) conducted a post hoc power analysis of 100 studies that explored the effectiveness of rehabilitation procedures. Whereas a ϕ of .80 is generally considered sufficient, indicating a 20% chance of a Type II error and a 5% chance of Type I error, the median ϕ to detect small treatment effects in the studies that they reviewed was .08. This is equivalent to an 8% chance of finding a treatment effect when it is present or a 92% chance of committing a Type II error. The median ϕs to detect medium and large treatment effects were .26 and .56, respectively. Thus, even among those studies with large treatment effects, the average study had almost a 50% chance of not detecting true treatment effects when they were present because of the inadequacy of the study's φ. Ottenbacher and Barrett's findings should alert rehabilitation researchers to the likely scenario that many treatments that have produced "no significant differences" may have been deemed to be ineffective, not because of their inherent ineffectiveness, but rather because of the low φ of the study that evaluated them. In general, sample sizes in rehabilitation are too small to adequately use NHST.

Failure to Report Results That Are Not Statistically Significant

Because there is a tendency among researchers to refrain from submitting manuscripts that do not report statistically significant findings, this problem is likely to be even more severe than that noted by Ottenbacher and Barrett (1991), who analyzed only published studies. One can only guess how many studies have had findings that were clinically significant yet were not submitted (or accepted by editors of professional journals) because of the lack of sufficient φ. Conversely, findings may be statistically significant when φ is excessively high but wholly irrelevant from a clinical perspective.

Some researchers may conduct their studies appropriately but choose not to report findings that are not statistically significant, either because they feel that these are not acceptable for publication or because they conclude their studies to be failures. This calls into question their beliefs about whether interventions are of utility. This failure to report NHSTs that do not result in rejection skew the body of knowledge accumulated in the literature; their finding may be just as important as those resulting in NHST rejection.

Lack of Control Over Type I Error

Researchers may opt to conduct multiple NHSTs to be able to report statistical significance. This can be a result of the culture of "publish or perish" in the academic community. Regardless of the motivation for conducting multiple tests, this process results in additive Type I errors (e.g., if 10 tests of statistical significance are conducted using an α of .05, there is a 50% chance of error). Although "corrections" such as Bonferroni (Brooks, 1995) can be used to adjust for the conduct of multiple tests, these are rarely conducted. Moreover, readers and reviewers have no way of determining how many statistical tests were conducted; thus the magnitude of the effective inflation of Type I error is unknown.

More fundamentally, by running multiple significance tests, one essentially tests multiple hypotheses. The NHST of theoretical interest is discarded and replaced with the discussion of findings concerning a hypothesis chosen only after the "test" of its significance has been conducted and found to converge with the interests of the researcher. As stated above, the logic behind NHST depends on the existence of an a priori hypothesis. The conduct and reporting of findings and conclusions concerning alternative hypotheses is a gross violation of the underlying logic of NHST. In many cases, researchers study issues for which they have no a priori theory. In these cases, conducting multiple tests is acceptable. Although these studies can be of value, they should be reported as being exploratory, and because they were not directed by hypotheses, NHST should not be used.

Appropriate use and interpretation of statistical analysis in rehabilitation psychology research is critical for the body of knowledge to be furthered.

Tools and Procedures for Evaluating Research

McAweeney et al. (1997b) developed an evaluation tool for assessing the literature related to psychosocial outcomes in the rehabilitation of people with SCI.[3] Although this tool was specifically developed for a project sponsored by the AASCIPSW, it can easily be applied to evaluating other literature in rehabilitation. The tool is divided into three broad sections, each containing separate criteria.

Part 1 consists of descriptive data, including variables that are related to psychosocial outcomes, measures used for the assessment of those outcomes, study design, retrieval form, and article type. Part 2 consists of 11 quantitative categories addressing a specific aspect of methodological standards: significance of problem or theoretical relevance, clarity of problem definition, scope of the literature review, adequacy of the research design, control of variables, sample selection and sample size, psychometric properties of the instruments, analysis techniques, interpretations and generalizations from the results, limitations of the study, and adequacy of the research report. Each quantitative category contains items rated on a 0–5-point scale (0 = *none of the criteria met*, 1 = *very few criteria met*, 2 = *few criteria met*, 3 = *sufficient criteria met*, 4 = *more than sufficient criteria met*, and 5 = *all criteria met*). These scores are summed, and each article receives a score.

Table 14.1 gives an example of the specific evaluation criteria that are included in this tool. Mean scores and percentages of studies with a score of 3 or greater, for the AASCIPSW study mentioned above, are provided for illustrative purposes. The scores are listed in ascending order based on percentages; a score of three or greater was chosen because it indicated sufficient criteria met. A total of 100 articles were reviewed for this study (McAweeney et al., 1997b).

The third part of this tool consists of calculating effect sizes for experimental and quasi-experimental studies that have an effect size that can accurately be evaluated. Examples of effect sizes found in McAweeney et al. (1997b) are provided in Table 14.2. As mentioned above, effect size

[3]The project by McAweeney et al. (1997b), *The Status of Psychosocial Interventions in the Rehabilitation of Persons With Spinal Cord Injury: Implications for Practitioners, Researchers, and Health Care Reform*, was sponsored by the American Association of Spinal Cord Injury Psychologists and Social Workers (AASCIPSW) and was published by Eastern Paralyzed Veterans of America. Mary McAweeney, Denise Tate, and William McAweeney are extremely grateful to these two groups for their support.

Table 14.1. Study Responses for Items on the Evaluation Tool

Research evaluation criteria	Mean scores	% of studies with a score of 3 or greater
Adequate statistical power	0.03	1
Effect size calculated	0.50	1
Confidence intervals stated	0.08	2
Type I error reported	0.30	7
Adequate description of nonparticipants	0.63	15
Clinical limitations stated	1.04	25
Hypothesis stated	1.49	31
Reported the validity of measures	1.42	38
Measurement limitations stated	1.77	43
Control of error attempted	2.38	50
Reported the reliability of measures	1.95	50
Method limitations stated	2.30	55
Control of environment	2.43	59
Adequate criteria for entry	2.74	62
Discuss generalizations of the results	2.68	62
Adequate selection of participants	2.67	65
Discuss limitations of the results	2.97	69
Variables defined	3.11	70
Contribution to SCI literature	3.18	72
Completeness of study	3.08	74
Hypothesis matches the design	3.51	75
Overall summary rating	3.11	76
Adequate review of the literature	3.40	78
Reported the study measures used	3.21	79
Practical significance of the results	3.35	79
Cutting edge of available research	3.51	80
Descriptive statistics provided	3.90	81
Conceptualization	3.49	81
Administration of measures	3.14	83
Design matches hypothesis	3.67	84
Concise review	3.66	85
Methods clear	3.44	85
Clear problem stated	3.61	87
Purpose stated	4.02	90
Appropriate statistics	4.24	90
Use of p values	3.64	91

Note. Each criterion was measured on a 6-point scale (0 = *none of the criteria met*, 5 = *all criteria met*). SCI = spinal cord injury.

can be used as an index of strength of relationship between a treatment and an outcome. Specifically, effect sizes can assist researchers in determining the practical versus statistical significance of results. A conclusion that was drawn from Table 14.2 was that the effect sizes found in the rehabilitation of people with SCI was consistent with other effect sizes found in psychotherapeutic rehabilitation (McAweeney, Tate, & Mc-

Table 14.2. Intervention Studies in the Rehabilitation of People With Spinal
cord Injury

Study	Effect size	Evaluation score	N
Frank (1993)	.63	129	29
Riggin (1976)	.65	90	42
	.32[a]		
Melnyk et al. (1979)	.37	86	34
Miller et al. (1975)	.73	103	31
	.81[a]		
Richards et al. (1992)	.71	92	17
Rohrer et al. (1983)	.731	71	160
	.74[a]		
Moore (1990)	.71	134	34
Ginsberg (1978)	.56	119	12
Dunn (1981)	—[b]	—	—

Note. [a]More than one effect size was created for studies that had more than one intervention. [b]This article was identified after completion of the American Association of Spinal
cord Injury Psychologists and Social Workers Study, so no evaluation results are included.

Aweeney, 1997a, 1997b) which were deemed clinically significant effects.
This finding provided evidence to support the clinical value of psychosocial
interventions in the rehabilitation of people with SCI.

The information gathered from using this tool (evaluation scores and
effect sizes), review articles on the same topic, and clinical expertise can
be used in conjunction to enhance the determination of the clinical relevance of a study. For example, a comprehensive review article on depression following SCI (Elliott & Frank, 1996) was used in addition to the
above-mentioned evaluation tool to assist an expert panel in the development of clinical practice guidelines for primary care physicians (Eastern
Paralyzed Veterans of America, 1998).[4]

Recommendations for the Assessment of Outcomes

Structure and Execution

The following recommendations are for grant reviewers.

1. If assessing the outcome of a specific intervention, explicitly state
    the hypothesis that is to be addressed. Refrain from conducting
    analyses of alternative hypotheses within the context of a singular
    study unless they are all developed a priori.

---

[4]The cited project was completed by PVA and involved the development of *Clinical
Practice Guidelines in the Treatment of Depression in Persons with Spinal Cord Injury.* Mary
McAweeney completed a review and evaluation of the literature on depression in people
with SCI. Using the results of this evaluation, as well as clinical expertise from a selected
panel, guidelines for primary care physicians were created.

2. Based on the nature of the outcome of interest, decide on the smallest clinically relevant effect. This is the most fundamental decision because the assessment of clinically irrelevant differences does not provide insights pertinent to outcome research.

3. Consider the relative importance of Type I and Type II errors, and choose levels of ϕ and α that reflect the importance of these two types of errors.

4. After determining levels for Δ, α, and ϕ a priori, determine the sample size that needs to be obtained.

5. Because it is often untenable to obtain large samples in rehabilitation psychology research, explore other ways of reducing error variance. These can include careful selection of measures and statistical techniques (e.g., analysis of covariance accounts for more error variance than analysis of variance).

6. Based on these choices, calculate the level of ϕ that is expected. If the ϕ is below the desired level, reevaluate the trade-off of Type I and II error. When Type II error is of primary concern, it may be justifiable to increase α. If the ϕ is much lower than the level chosen, it is questionable whether the study merits conducting. The decision to discard a study as being untenable should be made cautiously, because ϕ as calculated prior to the conduct of a study is only a best guess.

Evaluation and Presentation

The following recommendations are generally for researchers, clinicians, grant reviewers, and journal editors.

1. Report the study's observed ϕ. Whereas a priori ϕ calculations are essential to evaluate the appropriateness of a study design, they are only best guesses. To interpret findings, the actual ϕ needs to be calculated. Unfortunately, this is rarely reported. The a priori calculation should not be labeled as such but rather used as an estimate. To do otherwise is to pretend that one has more information than is available. Similarly, to think of the a priori estimate of Δ as factual makes the study tautological. The Δ computed from the a priori power calculation is an estimate; therefore, the actual Δ from the study should be reported.

2. Similar to the arbitrariness of selecting an α level, the level of adequate ϕ chosen is arbitrary. A level of .80 has become standard, but there is no reason why this should be appropriate regardless of the research question. When ϕ is excessively high, findings may be statistically significant but wholly irrelevant from a clinical perspective. Although .80 has become a standard for ϕ, it is not nearly as entrenched as an α level of .05.

3. Report Δs, not p values. p values measure the likelihood of associations and not their magnitudes. Like the choice of α, conclu-

sions about the substantiveness of Δ are subjective, a function of clinical and value judgments. The researcher states that "I found a difference of magnitude X, which is moderately (or nominally, or very) substantial." By their very nature, analyses focusing on Δ and ϕ provide readers with the information necessary to draw their own value judgments about the clinical significance of the outcome. By contrast, the value judgment implicit in setting a null hypothesis is established at a more fundamental level: Readers cannot simply determine whether a conclusion about accepting or rejecting is based on value judgments in accordance with their own.

4. In conjunction with reporting Δs, calculate and report confidence intervals for them. It may be preferable to select and present results concerning more than one set of confidence intervals. Selection of a 95% level answers the question of statistical significance posed by NHST, without loss of information concerning the outcome's magnitude. Although the choice of the 95% confidence interval around the observed Δ allows for conclusions to be drawn about the values above and below 95%, smaller confidence intervals (such as 70%) provide a better depiction of the range in which the true Δ is likely to reside.

5. Use various forms of information (i.e., evaluation tools, review articles, clinical expertise) to assist in the determination of the clinical relevance of an intervention.

Conclusion

The research community is responsible for improving the quality of research in rehabilitation. Journal editors should demonstrate a greater willingness to accept manuscripts that do not reject their null hypotheses, especially if they provide evidence of small Δs, indicating that replications with larger samples are warranted. Reviewers of grant applications and manuscripts should demand that a discussion of the trade-off between Type I and Type II errors be included in submissions. Analogously, they should accept studies that use levels for α and ϕ other than .05 and .80, if justification is provided.

References

American Health Consultants. (1994). Outcomes measurement: Who is measuring what and what does it mean? *Hospital Rehabilitation, 3,* 14–20.

Bird, D. K., & Hall, W. (1986). Statistical power in psychiatric research. *Australian and New Zealand Journal of Psychiatry, 20,* 189–200.

Brewer, J. K. (1974). Issues of power: Clarification. *American Educational Research Journal, 11,* 189–192.

Brewer, J. K., & Sindelar, P. T. (1988). Adequate sample size: *A priori* and post hoc considerations. *Journal of Special Education, 21,* 74–84.

Brooks, S. (1995). Chasing the holy grail of outcomes. *Subacute Care*, 22–26.

Carey, R. G., & Prosovac, E. J. (1982). Rehabilitation program evaluation using a revised Level of Rehabilitation Scale. *Archives of Physical Medicine & Rehabilitation, 63*, 367–370.

Casio, W. F., & Sedeck, S. (1983). Open a new window in rational research planning: Adjusting alpha to maximize statistical power. *Personnel Psychology, 36*, 517–526.

Cohen, J. (1990). Things I have learned (so far). *American Psychologist, 45*, 1304–1312.

Cole, D. A. (1988). Statistics for small groups: The power of the pretest. *Journal of the Association for Persons with Severe Handicaps, 13*, 142–146.

Dayton, C. M., Schafer, W. D., & Rogers, B. G. (1973). On appropriate uses and interpretations of power analysis: A comment. *American Educational Research Journal, 10*, 231–234.

Dunn, M. (1981). Social skills and spinal cord injury: A comparison of three training procedures. *Behavior Therapy, 12*, 153–164.

Eastern Paralyzed Veterans of America. (1998). *Guidelines for depression in persons with spinal cord injury*. Jackson Heights, NY: Author.

Elliott, T., & Frank, R. (1996). Depression following spinal cord injury. *Archives of Physical Medicine and Rehabilitation, 77*, 816–823.

Fisher, R. A. (1956). *Statistical methods and scientific inference*. London: Oliver & Boyd.

Frank, R. A. (1993). Structured group psychotherapy for individuals with SCI. *Dissertation Abstracts International*, p. 23.

Freiman, J. A., Chalmers, M. D., Smith, H., & Kuebler, R. R. (1978). The importance of beta, the Type II error and sample size in the design and interpretation of the randomized control trial. *New England Journal of Medicine, 9*, 690–694.

Ginsberg, M. L. (1978). Assertion with the wheelchair-bound: Measurement and training. *Dissertation Abstracts International*, p. 41.

Goodwin, L. D., & Goodwin, W. L. (1989). The use of power estimation in early childhood special education research. *Journal of Early Intervention, 13*, 365–373.

Granger, C. V., & Hamilton, B. B. (1992). UDS report: The uniform data system for medical rehabilitation report for first admissions for 1990. *American Journal of Physical Medicine & Rehabilitation, 71*, 108–113.

Hagan, R. L. (1997). In praise of the null hypothesis statistical test. *American Psychologist, 52*, 15–25.

Hall, K. M., Hamilton, B. B., Gordon, W. A., & Zasler, N. D. (1993). Characteristics and comparisons of functional assessment indices: Disability Rating Scale, Functional Independence Measure, and Functional Assessment Measure. *Journal of Head Trauma Rehabilitation, 8*(2), 60–74.

Harvey, R. F., & Jellineck, H. M. (1981). Functional performance assessment: A program approach. *Archives of Physical Medicine and Rehabilitation, 62*, 456–461.

Hubbard, R. (1995). The earth is highly significantly round ($p < .0001$). *American Psychologist, 50*, 1094–1098.

Kiresuk, T. J. (1982). Quality assurance and goal attainment scaling. *Professional Psychology, 13*, 145–152.

Kirk, R. E. (1982). *Experimental design. Procedures for the behavioral sciences*. Monterey, CA: Brooks/Cole.

Lund, C. A. (1992). Long-term treatment of sexual behavior problems in adolescent and adult developmentally disabled persons. *Annals of Sex Research, 5*, 5–31.

Maxwell, S. E., Cole, D. A., Arvey, R. D., & Salas, E. (1991). A comparison of methods for increasing power in randomized between-subjects designs. *Psychological Bulletin, 110*, 328–337.

McAweeney, M. J., Forchheimer, M., & Tate, D. G. (1996). Methodological issues in outcomes research. *Rehabilitation Outlook, 1*, 1–4.

McAweeney, M. J., Forchheimer, M., & Tate, D. G. (1997). Improving outcome research in rehabilitation psychology: Some methodological recommendations. *Rehabilitation Psychology, 42*, 125–135.

McAweeney, M. J., Tate, D. G., & McAweeney, W. J. (1997a). Psychosocial interventions in the rehabilitation of persons with spinal cord injury: A comprehensive methodological inquiry. *SCI Psychosocial Process, 10*, 58–63.

McAweeney, M. J., Tate, D. G., & McAweeney, W. J. (1997b). *The status of psychosocial interventions in the rehabilitation of persons with spinal cord injury: Implications for practitioners, researchers, and health care reform* [Monograph]. Jackson Heights, NY: Eastern Paralyzed Veterans of America.

McNamara, J. F. (1990). Statistical power in educational research. *National Forum of Applied Educational Research Journal, 3,* 23–36.

Melnyk, R., Montgomery, R., & Over, P. (1979). Attitude change following a sexual counseling program for SCI persons. *Archives of Physical Medicine and Rehabilitation, 60,* 601–605.

Mermis, B., Bosshart, H., Evans, B., Freedman, J. N., Hansen, N., Heinemann, A., Hendricks, R., Merbitz, C., & Richards, S. (1998). Outcomes Task Force white paper. *SCI Psychosocial Process, 10,* 139–140.

Meyer, D. (1974). Statistical tests and surveys of power: A critique. *American Educational Research Journal, 11,* 179–188.

Miller, D. K., Wolfe, M., & Spiegel, M. H. (1975). Therepeutic groups in patients with SCI. *Archives of Physical Medicare and Rehabilitation, 56,* 130–135.

Moore, L. I. (1990). Behavioral changes in male spinal cord-injured following two types of psychosocial rehabilitation experience. *Dissertation Abstracts International, 51*(3-B), 1537.

Olejnik, S. F. (1984). Planning educational research: Determining the necessary sample size. *Journal of Experimental Education, 53,* 40–48.

Ottenbacher, K. J. (1995). Why rehabilitation research does not work (as well as we think it should). *Archives of Physical Medicine and Rehabilitation, 76,* 123–129.

Ottenbacher, K. J., & Barrett, K. A. (1991). Statistical conclusion validity of rehabilitation research, a quantitative analysis. *American Journal of Physical Medicine & Rehabilitation, 70,* 5138–5143.

Parker, S. (1995). The "difference of means" may not be the "effect size." *American Psychologist, 50,* 1101–1109.

Rehabilitation Institute of Chicago. (1996). *Rehabilitation Institute of Chicago Functional Assessment System Manual, Version 4.* Chicago: Author.

Richards, J. S., Lloyd, L. K., James, J. W., & Brown, J. (1992). Treatment of erectile dysfunction secondary to SCI: Sexual and psychosocial impact on couples. *Rehabilitation Psychology, 41,* 55–66.

Riggin, O. Z. (1976). A comparison of individual and group therapy on self-concept and depression of patients with spinal cord injury. *Dissertation Abstracts International, 37*(6-A), 3528–3529.

Rohrer, K., Adelman, B., Puckett, J., Toomey, T., Talbert, D., & Johnson, E. W. (1983). Rehabilitation in the spinal cord injury: Use of patient–family group. *Archives of Physical Medicine and Rehabilitation, 61,* 225–229.

Schafer, W. (1993). Interpreting statistical significance and nonsignificance. *Journal of Experimental Education, 61,* 383–387.

Serlin, R. C. (1987). Hypothesis testing, theory building, and the philosophy of science. *Journal of Counseling Psychology, 34,* 365–371.

Shaver, J. P. (1993). What statistical testing is, and what it is not. *Journal of Experimental Education, 61,* 293–316.

Ulicny, G. R., Adler, A. B., & Jones, M. L. (1990). Training effective interview skills to attendant service users. *Rehabilitation Psychology, 35,* 55–66.

White, G. W., Thomson, R. J., & Nary, D. E. (1997). An empirical analysis of the effects of a self-administered advocacy letter training program. *Rehabilitation Counseling Bulletin, 41,* 74–87.

Whiteneck, G. G. (1992). Outcome evaluation and spinal cord injury. *NeuroRehabilitation, 2,* 31–44.

World Health Organization. (1980). *International classification of impairments, disabilities, and handicaps: A manual of classification relating to the consequences of disease.* Geneva, Switzerland: Author.

15

Neuropsychological Assessment

Tim Conway and Bruce Crosson

Historically, the assessment of cognitive and behavioral functions in people with brain injury or central nervous system disease has served a variety of purposes. These purposes have included diagnosis of injury or disease state, description of cognitive or behavioral sequelae, and description of functional limitations and strengths. Prior to the advent of modern structural neuroimaging techniques (i.e., X-ray computed tomography [CT] and magnetic resonance imaging [MRI]), neuropsychological assessment was used extensively in the diagnostic arena to assist in evaluating the nature and location of disturbances in brain function. Although there are still significant uses for neuropsychological assessment in this area (e.g., localizing seizure foci in epilepsy surgery candidates or diagnosing dementia), this type of diagnostic application has declined since the mid- to late 1970s as better neuroimaging techniques became available. At roughly the same time, the use of neuropsychological evaluation to assist in rehabilitation planning experienced a rapid rise. The application of neuropsychological assessment to the rehabilitation arena was driven in part by the increasing numbers of long-term survivors of traumatic brain injury (TBI). This latter phenomenon, in turn, was precipitated by advances in technology and procedures for acute management of TBI since World War II and even to some extent by improvements in systems for transporting acute TBI patients to the trauma center.

Because of the rapid developments of TBI rehabilitation programs in the 1980s and the incorporation of neuropsychologists into the treatment teams, the application of neuropsychological and neurobehavioral assessment to neurorehabilitation is seen in some circles as a relatively new development, when in fact it has older and deeper roots in rehabilitation. Individuals as revered in neuropsychology as Goldstein and Luria used their extensive experience to comceptualize the role of neurobehavioral assessment in rehabilitation. Nonetheless, the shift in emphasis within the specialty of clinical neuropsychology to rehabilitation in the United States during the 1980s resulted in the adaptation of techniques developed for neurological diagnosis or delineation of cognitive deficits to rehabilitation endeavors. These techniques have provided valuable information for rehabilitation teams, but they were not developed specifically to address the range of functional issues in neurorehabilitation cases. More functionally oriented neuropsychological instruments have been developed, but typically inference is used in applying neuropsychological assessment findings to the functional tasks in a rehabilitation environment.

It should be obvious from this discussion that the rehabilitation neuropsychologist or the neuropsychologically oriented rehabilitation psychologist must develop competencies specific to translating findings from the neuropsychological laboratory to the everyday problems patients encounter. A further challenge for neuropsychology, in an era of managed care, is to measure rehabilitation outcomes in a way that provides useful feedback regarding the success of a course of rehabilitation and the continuing cognitive and functional limitations of the patient. In the current environment, the justification for neuropsychological assessment rests on its ability to contribute to the efficiency of treatment; guide treatment planning and community reentry; improve rehabilitation outcomes; provide useful information to the patient, family, or treatment team; and contribute to the patient's quality of life.

Thus, we begin our review by addressing the history of neurobehavioral assessment in rehabilitation settings. Review of previous assessment methods offers insights that continue to have applicability to present endeavors. Current methods of neuropsychological assessment and their applicability to rehabilitation are presented. The basic competencies of a neuropsychologist working in a rehabilitation setting are highlighted by comparing prominent approaches to neuropsychological assessment for neurorehabilitation settings and by discussing the nature of neuropsychological assessment, the role of the neuropsychologist on the rehabilitation team, and the needs of neurorehabilitation patients. We discuss how neuropsychological methods can bridge the gaps among diagnosing cognitive deficits, predicting functional outcomes, and evaluating the effectiveness of rehabilitation. We conclude by summarizing the main points and potential future directions for neuropsychological assessment in rehabilitation. Because the application of neuropsychological assessment techniques to the rehabilitation environment has been heavily influenced by the emergence of TBI programs, this chapter reflects that influence. However, our main points are also applicable to other traditional and emerging rehabilitation populations, including those diagnosed with dementia, epilepsy, neurodegenerative diseases, stroke, tumor, and learning disabilities. Furthermore, we do not focus on individual assessment instruments but on more general issues faced by the neuropsychologically oriented psychologist practicing in the rehabilitation setting.

Historical Perspectives and Systems

The history of modern neuropsychological assessments in rehabilitation settings can be traced at least as far back as World War I. Throughout this history, the purposes of such evaluations have extended beyond the simple definition of cognitive deficits. Other goals have included developing standardized assessment instruments, predicting functional outcomes, guiding treatment plans, and measuring the effects of rehabilitation on specific cognitive processes and functional outcomes. We highlight the works of Walter Poppelreuter, Kurt Goldstein, Alexander R. Luria, Oliver Zangwill, Leonard Diller, Yehuda Ben-Yishay, George Prigatano, Anne-Lise Christensen, and Barbara Wilson to demonstrate these principles. For additional examples, the reader is referred to the neurorehabilitation works of a growing number of authors, such as Mitchell Rosenthal, Robert Frank, and Patrick Corrigan.

Walter Poppelreuter has been called "one of the founders of neuro-psychology" (Poppelreuter, 1917/1990, p. xv) because of his significant contributions to neurorehabilitation in Cologne in 1914 (Poser, Kohler, & Schönle, 1996). Poppelreuter was one of the first to use techniques from experimental psychology when assessing the neuropsychological functioning of individuals with brain injuries. For example, he developed his own instruments, such as his well-known overlapping figures test (Lezak, 1995), to identify cognitive deficits and measure progress in rehabilitation (Poser et al., 1996). Poppelreuter advocated the use and development of such standardized, quantitative tests to facilitate systematic assessment and treatment of brain injuries. Although he focused primarily on quantitative assessment techniques, he advocated qualitative observations of a patient's performance during reeducation and rehabilitation classes and performance in a workshop.[1] Poppelreuter was so committed to this method of assessment and rehabilitation that his secretary was a graduate of his rehabilitation program (Poppelreuter, 1917/1990). His assessment was multidisciplinary and was based on the most current models of brain function from experimental psychology, neurology, and psychiatry.

Kurt Goldstein has been regarded as the father of brain injury rehabilitation (Boake, 1991). He stressed the importance of a neurobehavioral assessment that included assessing psychosocial effects as well as cognitive deficits (Wilson, 1997a). However, Goldstein believed that the assessment of individual cognitive skills was inadequate for predicting performance levels of complex cognitive functions. He advocated combining two assessment approaches to predict vocational potential, namely, abstract performance testing and concrete labor testing. Abstract performance testing involved measuring basic cognitive skills for vocational purposes, such as reaction time. Concrete labor testing included real work performance in hospital-based vocational workshops (Boake, 1991). Therefore, Goldstein's approach to rehabilitation and neurobehavioral assessment in-

---

[1]The terms *qualitative* and *quantitative* have been applied to describe different approaches to neuropsychological assessment. Approaches classified as *quantitative* have tended to emphasize a summary score for each neuropsychological test, with some emphasis on the standing of the patient's summary score relative to some normative sample. Approaches classified as *qualitative* have emphasized the process of how patients approach a task, in particular, what errors they have made and what strategies they have applied in completing the task. Proponents of qualitative approaches maintain that the neuropsychologist learns more about the nature of cognitive impairment from observing the processes used during tests than from the summary score. It should be noted that common processes involved in completing tests can be quantified. One trend in neuropsychological assessment is to unify qualitative and quantitative approaches by both providing summary scores and scoring process components of a test.

cluded evaluating underlying cognitive deficits, psychosocial impairments, and personality factors in relation to functional goals for rehabilitation.

Alexander R. Luria's systems approach to higher cortical function (Luria, 1963, 1980) has been described (Uzzell, 1997) as providing the only "sound and all inclusive" (p. 42) theory of neurorehabilitation. Christensen and Caetano (1996) stated that Luria believed "that the basic units of psychological analysis were functions, each of which represented systems of elementary acts that controlled organism−environment relations" (p. 283). A model of brain functioning with three functional systems guided Luria's assessment and rehabilitation methods. The activation system was described as controlling arousal and vigilance. The input system was responsible for registering, analyzing, and storing information. The output system involved the organizing and planning of all behaviors. By assessing a patient's performance in each system, Luria identified dissociable cognitive and sensory deficits and determined whether they existed across a group of behaviors. Luria used his extensive knowledge of neuroanatomy and physiology along with his three-system model of brain functions to determine whether a common deficit across a group of behaviors represented a functional area of cortex that had been impaired. Unlike Goldstein, Luria's assessment methods were mostly subjective and based on clinical experience, and patient performance guided his individualized, hypothesis-driven evaluation.

Oliver Zangwill advocated using an interdisciplinary, functional approach to neurorehabilitation. His patients received neuropsychological, occupational therapy, and speech language assessments. In addition, patients participated in supervised work trials to determine their functional vocational status and to guide rehabilitation. Zangwill performed systematic evaluations to measure the effectiveness of rehabilitation as well as the relationships between assessment and rehabilitation outcome (Boake, 1991). Like Poppelreuter, Goldstein, and Luria, Zangwill used neurobehavioral and functional assessments to guide the rehabilitation of patients with a TBI.

More recently, Yehuda Ben-Yishay (1996) and George Prigatano (1997) led the development of a holistic approach to neurorehabilitation. Although there are some differences between the approaches of Ben-Yishay and Prigatano, there are many similarities because Prigatano incorporated many aspects of Ben-Yishay's program into this rehabilitation system. Their approach includes a neuropsychological assessment with standardized measures as well as specially developed information-processing and motor measures. Aspects of their holistic approach include a therapeutic, social milieu format for rehabilitation as well as assessing the patient's psychological adjustment to the new deficits, teaching skills for coping with the psychosocial consequences of brain impairment, and controlling environmental conditions that may affect adjustment. They contended that the cognitions and emotions of an individual with a brain injury perform interactive roles in the process of rehabilitation as expressed through the patient's psychological reactions to the acquired behavioral and cognitive disabilities. The holistic approach simultaneously treats and assesses cognitive and emotional processes through cognitive rehabilitation, psychotherapy, and a therapeutic milieu. Thus, although formal assessments are performed, assessment is also a process that continues throughout rehabilitation. Within these program components, input from the patient concerning the rehabilitation program is actively sought. In addition, this approach includes supervised work trials, education, and a work alliance among the rehabilitation program staff, the patient, and the patient's family members (Ben-Yishay & Prigatano, 1990). Ben-Yishay and Prigatano's approach to neurorehabilitation is comprehensive, contains a social milieu format, treats the patient's psychological reactions to the acquired disabilities, and includes ongoing assessments within all components of the rehabilitation program.

Anne-Lise Christensen (1989) combined Luria's theory of rehabilitation and his hypothesis-driven assessment methods (Christensen, 1984) with Goldstein's (1942) emphasis on the psychosocial aspects of rehabilitation. She advocated a qualitative, individualized, hypothesis-testing approach to cognitive retraining, psychosocial training, and vocational goals. Integrated within these treatment components, Christensen used an expanded neuropsychological assessment that includes qualitative and quantitative evaluations of the patient by program staff, program peers, significant family members, and a self-evaluation by the patient. The patient plays an active role in rehabilitation through interactive feedback sessions that use assessment and observational data. This dynamic interaction among the patient, staff, and family members is the product of Christensen's assimilation of Luria's emphasis "on a collaborative, problem-solving, working relationship" (Caetano & Christensen, 1997, p. 66). The comprehensiveness of Christensen's approach to neurorehabilitation is similar to that of Ben-Yishay and colleagues; however, Christensen placed more emphasis on qualitative assessments of neuropsychological processes throughout the rehabilitation program and less emphasis on a therapeutic milieu format. Her approach to neuropsychological assessment is dynamic, hypothesis driven, qualitative, and highly integrated with functional assessments and goals.

Barbara Wilson (1987) advocated a behaviorally based approach to cognitive rehabilitation that combines neuropsychology, cognitive psychology, and behavioral psychology. She advocated a comprehensive neurorehabilitation approach, that is, the treatment of cognitive, emotional, behavioral, personality, and motor deficits (Wilson, 1997b), rather than the rehabilitation of only specific cognitive deficits. Wilson (1989) stated that the primary contributions of neuropsychology to cognitive rehabilitation are elucidating brain–behavior relationships that may affect a patient's response to treatment, providing an empirical base for effective rehabilitation strategies, and identifying the optimum time to initiate specific strategies. Wilson relied on cognitive psychology for theoretical models of normal and impaired brain functioning, which she used to guide case conceptualization and diagnosis.

However, Wilson (1997a) noted that whereas the diagnosis and conceptualization of disorders is based on the identification of cognitive impairments, they do not guide treatment of the patient's functional disabilities that result from these cognitive impairments. The assessment and rehabilitation of functional disabilities are enhanced by the systematic principles of behavioral psychology, providing ongoing monitoring and evaluation of the cognitive rehabilitation program. Moreover, Wilson (1997b) advocated using experimental designs within the rehabilitation program for a thorough, ongoing assessment of impairments and evaluation of treatment effectiveness. Therefore, her approach to rehabilitation is functionally oriented and systematic and is based on theoretical models of brain–behavior relationships that focus specifically on cognitive deficits. She viewed the role of a neuropsychological assessment as primarily diagnostic, whereas neuropsychological research may provide an empirical basis for the selection and initiation of specific treatment strategies.

Although Poppelreuter, Goldstein, Luria, and others may have different conceptual frameworks or models of neuropsychology, the needs of their patient population have been similar. The common themes are worth noting. One involves the assessment of cognitive and behavioral deficits as a basis for neurorehabilitation. Yet few models suggest that rehabilitation focused only on cognitive deficits is an adequate basis for meeting the needs of patients with brain injuries. In particular, almost every model describes the need for assessment and treatment of functional deficits in true-to-life functional environments, most frequently emphasizing vocational skills. Unique skills for functioning in home, family, and avocational environments may have been compromised, and many programs emphasize assessment and rehabilitation of these skills as well. Finally, many models, particularly those labeled "holistic," emphasize the assessment and treatment of psychosocial functions. They contend that patients' ability to interact effectively with other people in their family, community, and work environments may have been compromised by their injury and that functional outcomes cannot be optimized without addressing this issue. In both functional activities and social milieus, behavioral principles can be used to facilitate rehabilitation of psychosocial functions. These commonalities among models provide the basis for considering neuropsychological assessment needs in the rehabilitation environment.

Methods

On the basis of this analysis, we can set forth the following parameters for neuropsychological assessment in rehabilitation settings. Neuropsychological assessments should evaluate cognitive functions in a manner that addresses the unique demands of the rehabilitation setting. Emphasizing the links between strengths and weaknesses of cognition and functional abilities and disabilities makes the neuropsychological evaluation useful for treatment planning. Although occupational therapists, physical therapists, speech and language pathologists, and vocational rehabilitation specialists perform functional evaluations in various arenas, the neuropsychologist should state the probable implications of cognitive deficits for various target functional activities. To accomplish this goal, test selection for neuropsychological batteries should be based on an understanding of treatment goals and activities, as well as patient deficits. Neuropsychological assessments typically are either a fixed-battery or hypothesis-testing approach (sometimes referred to as a *flexible-battery approach*). Both methods have strengths and weaknesses relative to a rehabilitation setting.

Fixed Battery

For fixed batteries, Bauer (1994) noted that tests are selected prior to learning the patient's presenting complaints. Fixed batteries that target the most common deficits in a disorder are becoming more prevalent. For example, in closed head injury, frontal and temporal contusions and diffuse white-matter injuries are common (Jennett & Teasdale, 1981). Therefore, the relevant fixed battery may include tests of executive functions, memory, and attention (Reitan & Wolfson, 1993).

Fixed-battery approaches have some strengths in a rehabilitation environment. A clinician can compare performance across patients on the most common variables when the strategic, a priori selection of tests occurs. This sharpens the focus on a patient's cognitive strengths and weaknesses. Test selection also can be connected to treatment components that address the common problems of a specific disorder. For example, memory testing can determine whether and how to emphasize compensation for memory deficits. A weakness of fixed-battery approaches is their failure to address a patient's unique problems. The fixed-battery approach assumes that a limited range of deficits and rehabilitation goals is likely. The test results may highlight general areas of cognitive strengths and weaknesses but lack the necessary detail for determining remediation or compensation techniques.

Hypothesis Testing (Flexible Battery)

In hypothesis-testing (flexible-battery) approaches, the selection of assessment instruments is based on the patient's presenting problems. During the assessment, the discovery of specific deficit areas suggests further tests for defining the precise nature of the difficulty. Strengths of hypothesis-testing approaches are that the assessment is designed to address the patient's presenting problems. Thus, evaluating a particular deficit defines the specific reasons for impairment, which may identify restitutive or compensatory strategies. However, lengthy administration time can be a weakness of hypothesis-testing approaches. Furthermore, although instruments are being developed that closely explore deficit areas (e.g., the work of Delis, Kaplan, & Kramer, in press, in executive functions), standardized instruments designed to break down deficits into their possible components generally do not exist. Although methods for assessing aspects of a deficit area can be developed during the evaluation, as demonstrated by Luria, they lack an adequate normative basis to compare performances among various tasks. As implied above, one trend in the development of neuropsychological instruments is the use of cognitive models to break down complex functions, such as memory and executive functions, so that deficits in more fundamental underlying cognitive processes can be defined. The development of such instruments may be accompanied by increasing sophistication in addressing cognitive deficits during rehabilitation.

Despite the claims of some proponents of fixed-battery and hypothesis-testing approaches, the two methods are not necessarily incompatible. The resolution of the two approaches lies in the realization that assessment of patients' cognitive deficits is a continuous process in rehabilitation that should permeate therapeutic endeavors on a daily basis. A formal, neuropsychological assessment targets deficit areas for beginning rehabilitation; however, the patient's success and failure on the treatment tasks determine the next step for rehabilitation. The interplay between assessment of specific deficits and ongoing assessment of functional capacities is necessary to develop an optimal rehabilitation plan with realistic goals. Thus, it is necessary to determine how a specific cognitive deficit prevents adequate performance of a particular functional activity (e.g., Corrigan & Yudofsky, 1996). Such relationships may become apparent only as treatment progresses; treatment plans are continuously refined as the patient's abilities and disabilities are clearly defined through the treatment process.

Identifying the Most Effective Approach

Many individuals (Ben-Yishay, 1996; Crosson, 1987; Farmer, Clippard, Luehr-Wiemann, Wright, & Owings, 1997; McLellan, 1997; Prigatano, 1997) have noted the need for integration of the interdisciplinary rehabilitation team. In most rehabilitation settings the neuropsychologically oriented psychologist does not perform all treatments. Yet he or she may be the team member in the best position to elucidate the cognitive processes that underlie functional deficits or devise procedures to define the underlying cognitive processes. Holland, Hogg, and Farmer (1997) described "community standards" that facilitate team communication and cooperation within an interdisciplinary rehabilitation environment. In an integrated team, such standards can assist the neuropsychologist in using his or her knowledge of cognition and skills in assessment to consult with other members of the rehabilitation team to define optimal assessment and rehabilitation procedures during the course of treatment. These ideals for neuropsychological assessment are highlighted in the rehabilitation philosophies of Luria (Christensen, 1989) and Sohlberg and Mateer (1989).

Assessment of psychological issues in patients with TBI is covered in detail elsewhere in this volume (see chapter 3); however, comprehensive discussion of neuropsychological assessment in the rehabilitation setting demands brief mention of the issue here. An effective assessment must include evaluation of a patient's interpersonal strengths and deficits (i.e., personality functioning). As noted by Crosson (1987), three causes of interpersonal deficits must be assessed: (a) premorbid factors, (b) reaction to injury, and (c) changes induced by neurological injury. Assessment techniques in this arena may include standardized instruments, clinician observation, patient and family interviews, and correlation with structural imaging and cognitive findings.

To summarize, a neuropsychological assessment provides a starting point for cognitive rehabilitation by defining a patient's deficit areas. Although an initial neuropsychological evaluation may not identify a single component process that causes a particular deficit, a patient's response to treatment clarifies where a cognitive process is breaking down. Indeed, many veterans of neurorehabilitation settings have noted that successful cognitive rehabilitation requires continuous assessment of patients' abilities and disabilities in order to refine the treatment plan. Although such ongoing assessment does not always lend itself to standardized neuropsychological tests, the knowledge and skills of the neuropsychologist are often useful for incorporating measurement of target behaviors into treatment regimens. Overall, these issues enhance the determination of treatment progress and conceptualization of the patient's deficits. It is also important to assess interpersonal functioning (see chapter 3).

Competencies for the Neuropsychologist

Assessment and treatment needs in rehabilitation settings require neuropsychologists to have a broad range of competencies that are a function of patient population characteristics. Broadly speaking, the neuropsychologist must skillfully diagnose psychological as well as neurobehavioral deficits and function as an interdisciplinary team member.

Regarding assessment in general, rehabilitation neuropsychologists must have a sound grounding in psychometric theory and applications. The selection of instruments and the interpretation of findings require a knowledge of reliability and validity issues and the relevance of normative samples. Furthermore, establishing good rapport with patients, administering tests to patients whose behavior may interfere with the examination, and making observations regarding how the patient's behavior deviates from normative expectations are essential skills.

To assess cognitive functions, rehabilitation neuropsychologists must have a firm grounding in cognitive psychology and the neural systems underlying cognition. If they are to have an impact on cognitive rehabilitation, they must understand how brain systems produce cognition and behavior. This knowledge assists in identifying the specific stages at which cognition breaks down and in selecting instruments and procedures to identify the adequacy of cognitive processing at the various stages. Furthermore, it is necessary to evaluate a patient's cognitive strengths and to know how such strengths can help compensate for specific deficits. Related knowledge regarding neurological syndromes, neuropathological processes, and neuroanatomy is a prerequisite. The site of the injury or the nature of a disease process or underlying injury frequently helps determine which cognitive processes are most likely to be disrupted.

The goal of rehabilitation is to improve patients' ability to function in their home, job, and community. Improving their ability to perform tasks in the neuropsychological laboratory is useful only if it contributes to some functional goal. There is some variability in the degree to which neuropsychologists may become involved in assessment and treatment of functional activities such as cooking, balancing a checkbook, or performing various vocational activities. However, even if neuropsychologists have a small role in these endeavors, they must be able to relate cognitive assessment findings to functional activities. Crosson (1994) discussed the reasons why the correspondence between cognitive evaluation results and functional abilities is often less than perfect: Cognitive skills must be isolated from complex functional activities to pinpoint cognitive deficits; testing is done in an optimal environment, whereas patients' home, work, and community environments do not elicit optimal cognitive performance; and test instruments rarely assess the ability to compensate for deficits. The strength of cognitive assessment ideally is to specify how a cognitive process breaks down, but the assessment procedures designed to accomplish this goal are reductionistic and not inherently functional in nature. This property of cognitive assessment means that, at the very least, rehabilitation neuropsychologists must have a firm grounding in functional assessment and treatment. With this knowledge, they can use results of cognitive assessment to participate in designing a treatment program that most efficiently reaches the functional goals of rehabilitation.

Rehabilitation neuropsychologists also must be able to assess interpersonal deficits. Prigatano et al. (1986) noted that personality change after brain injury is difficult to measure objectively. Assessment of interpersonal deficits generally requires good interviewing skills because information must be gathered from both the patient and close family members. To assess the contribution of premorbid disturbances or emotional reactions to injury, neuropsychologists must be familiar with a broad range of psychopathology, including personality disorders. Because history and observations may be essential for making accurate diagnoses, it is desirable to have considerable firsthand experience in the diagnosis of psychopathology. In addition, there must be an ability to recognize personality change caused by brain injury. Here, too, it is necessary to understand thoroughly how brain systems work and what sites of injury are likely to lead to different types of interpersonal deficits. Neuropsychologists also should know what cognitive deficits correlate highly with personality change. The distinctions in evaluating interpersonal deficits are often subtle, and multiple etiologies for interpersonal deficits are often present. Because accurate diagnosis is essential for determining the best intervention strategy, these skills are key.

Interpersonal deficits also have functional implications. Interpersonal deficits are a frequent source of distress in families and are among the most disabling aspects of closed head injury (Lezak, 1978). Jennett, Snoek,

Bond, and Brooks (1981) found that over 60% of patients with severe closed head injury experience significant personality change, even when physical and cognitive changes are minimal. Thus, the patient who cannot adequately relate to coworkers is less employable. Because other professionals usually have less training than psychologists in dealing with interpersonal deficits, the psychologist is often best suited to address the interpersonal deficits in the social milieu of rehabilitation (e.g., Ben-Yishay, 1996; Prigatano, 1997). Frequently, as a patient interacts with staff and other patients, the etiology of interpersonal deficits becomes more obvious. Thus, rehabilitation neuropsychologists should consult with other team members regarding these issues. Because a firm grounding in brain systems is necessary to identify the etiology of an interpersonal deficit, rehabilitation neuropsychologists ideally should be involved in the treatment of interpersonal deficits. Their grounding in brain systems and social behavior should leave them less confused about the source of a particular behavior and thus in a better position to select the most appropriate treatment.

Consultation with treatment team members is essential in a rehabilitation setting. Only through this process can the relationship between cognitive deficits and functional activities be optimally understood. Rehabilitation neuropsychologists must listen to other team members describe functional deficits and determine how cognitive functioning might contribute to the deficits. Occasionally, direct observation by neuropsychologists may assist in accurately determining the relationship between cognitive deficits and the functional problems. Once the relationship between cognitive and functional deficits has been determined, neuropsychologists may aid in devising and monitoring a treatment strategy. Furthermore, it may be necessary to consult with other treatment team members to devise treatment strategies for interpersonal deficits that the team can implement. Consultation in a rehabilitation environment can require a great deal of tact and diplomacy. Rehabilitation neuropsychologists must be aware of and respect the training and knowledge of other professions in the rehabilitation environment. They should know that there is much to learn from other professionals that increases their ability to function in rehabilitation settings.

A rehabilitation environment should include active program evaluation. The purpose of program evaluation is to monitor the progress of individual patients and the effectiveness of the program over time. Thus, the program evaluation skills of rehabilitation neuropsychologists are often a valuable asset. We discuss program evaluation in the next section.

To summarize, the rehabilitation arena is a complex and demanding environment. To be effective, rehabilitation neuropsychologists need a variety of skills. Not only must they have a firm grounding in personality and diagnostic assessment as well as neurocognitive assessment, but they also must be able to interact and consult with members of the interdisciplinary rehabilitation treatment team. The following is a brief recap of the requisite skills: interviewing, performing personality and diagnostic assessment (including identifying interpersonal deficits caused by brain injury), setting treatment strategies for interpersonal deficits, performing neurocognitive assessment, translating cognitive assessment findings into functional implications, developing cognitive treatments on the basis of assessment findings, consulting with rehabilitation team members, and evaluating the program.

Acquiring these skills requires a broad-based training in applied psychology as well as specific training in neuropsychology. The 1997 Houston Conference on Specialty Education and Training in Clinical Neuropsychology (Hannay et al., 1998) describes the knowledge base as including a generic psychology core, a generic clinical core, study of brain–behavior relationships, and foundations for practice of clinical neuropsychology. Skills include assessment, treatment, consultation, research, and teaching. The training begins at the level of the doctoral program, continues during internship, and is completed after a 2-year residency. However, training in applied psychology and neuropsychology is inadequate for practice in a rehabilitation environment without knowledge about and specific training in rehabilitation. Guidelines for such training at the graduate and postgraduate level have been suggested by Johnstone and Farmer (1997). Their guidelines include requiring experience with several rehabilitation populations, training in multiple functional outcome content areas, and experiential site visits at a variety of rehabilitation settings.

Demonstration of competence for the rehabilitation neuropsychologist is a complex issue. From the viewpoint of Bruce Crosson, an adequate solution has not been reached. Ideally, the profession should move toward a model in which a diplomate from the American Board of Professional Psychology is accepted as the best indicator of competence. The current dilemma is that acquiring a diplomate in clinical neuropsychology does not require as much depth in rehabilitation issues as obtaining a diplomate in rehabilitation psychology, and obtaining a diplomate in rehabilitation psychology does not require as much depth in neuropsychological knowledge and skills as obtaining a diplomate in clinical neuropsychology. Perhaps this dilemma can be resolved by some cross-fertilization between the clinical neuropsychology and rehabilitation psychology boards in the future, such as an examination procedure jointly administered by both boards and evaluating competence in both areas.

Evaluating Outcomes

The skills of the rehabilitation neuropsychologist can be useful in evaluating changes in cognitive functioning following neurorehabilitation. Ultimately, the success of rehabilitation programs is dependent on the degree to which improved cognitive functioning results in functional goals being met. A number of functional assessment instruments (Boake, 1996; Corrigan, Arnett, Houck, & Jackson, 1985; Keith, Granger, Hamilton, & Sherwin, 1987; Rappaport, Hall, Hopkins, Belleza, & Cope, 1982) have been developed and are used in neurorehabilitation settings. Traditional neuropsychological assessments, such as those discussed in this chapter, can be of some use in determining whether significant cognitive changes have occurred across the course of a patient's rehabilitation program. This can be determined by reevaluating the patient toward the end of his or her rehabilitation program, and the results of the exit evaluation can be compared with the assessment at the beginning of treatment. However, the rehabilitation neuropsychologist frequently has scientific training that is unique among rehabilitation team members.

Incorporating the basic principles of research design and methodology into neurorehabilitation facilitates the evaluation of both cognitive and functional outcomes. However, the utility of such principles is influenced by the theoretical basis of the rehabilitation model, the hypotheses to be tested, the outcome variables, and specific problems with outcome data from neurorehabilitation programs. Only a few experimental and quasi-experimental designs are appropriate for evaluating neuropsychological and functional changes. Wilson (1997a) advocated incorporating systematic elements of single-subject designs into individual treatment regimens within a treatment program. McReynolds and Kearns (1983) provided an extensive resource on the variety of single-subject designs and their implementation with clinical populations, whereas Morales (1997) discussed research designs in the context of program evaluation. For example, Sohlberg and Mateer (1987) reported on the use of a multiple-baseline design to evaluate the effectiveness of an attention-training program. Conway et al. (1998) reported on the use of a multiple-probe design to assess the effectiveness of a treatment for a case of phonological alexia with agraphia. In the multiple-probe design, the patient's performance is tested on both target and nontarget skills of treatment. Different probes measure both types of skills at critical points of the treatment to determine its impact on functional target skills and hence the underlying cognitive abilities. Thus, treatment effects are separated from spontaneous recovery, and probes of nontargeted skills indicate the treatment's specificity. Although such single-subject designs can be used effectively in rehabilitation, some single-subject designs are ethically inappropriate for neurorehabilitation studies, such as removing a treatment or extinguishing an adaptive behavior.

Small-group designs can also be used to evaluate changes in neuropsychological functioning following treatment in neurorehabilitation programs. However, small-group designs tend to mask differential responses to treatment among the group members; require a homogenous group of patients, which is rarely present in a neurorehabilitation program; and focus on statistical significance of the outcomes rather than on clinical significance (Morales, 1997). Nevertheless, additional studies with either single-case studies or small-group designs are needed to establish an empirical basis for neurorehabilitation as well as to compare the effectiveness of neurorehabilitation programs with differing theoretical bases.

Regardless of whether a single-object or small-group design is selected, additional considerations involve the research variables and neuropsychological assessment instruments. Morales (1997) stated that statistically significant changes in test scores do not always coincide with clinically significant changes in behaviors, and the reverse scenario is likely to occur as well. Wilson (1997a) further examined this issue by asking whether the assessment instruments measure impairments in cognitive functioning or a functional disability. Measurement of specific cognitive skills may be useful when they are the target of a treatment and the majority of neuropsychological assessment tools focus on cognitive skills. Nonetheless, treatments that focus on specific cognitive skills must contribute to the ultimate goal of rehabilitation—improvement in functional activities. Functional behaviors should be the research variables that are evaluated, and they should be clearly operationalized. Thus, focusing only on cognitive performance or neuropsychological test scores as an outcome measure is problematic because neuropsychological tests have been reported to account for not more than 40% of the explained variance in outcome measures (Sbordone, 1997).

In summary, some single-subject designs can be built into rehabilitation to monitor a patient's performance. When such a philosophy is used consistently within a rehabilitation program, it can serve the needs of program evaluation. In this day of increasing demands for accountability in treatment, these designs can serve as a powerful justification for treatment or perhaps act as an indicator to terminate an ineffective treatment strategy. The therapist must carefully select measures that reflect the specific goals of treatment. Although measurement of specific cognitive skills may be useful when they are the targets of treatment, we must be mindful that the ultimate goal of rehabilitation is to increase the patient's ability to perform functional activities. Thus, measurement of functional behaviors should be included at some point to verify that cognitive treatments have had the desired impact. Regarding the evaluation of treatment outcomes, Wilson (1989) noted that

> the point to stress is that without rigorous recording, monitoring and evaluation, cognitive rehabilitation could become nothing more than a passing fad and go the way of phrenology or sleep-teaching machines. We owe it to the patients to make sure our discipline is properly supported by strong theoretical frameworks, sound research, and detailed scrutiny of practice. (p. 138)

Conclusion

Rehabilitation neuropsychologists can perform a variety of tasks in neurorehabilitation. One of the most time-honored roles is that of neuropsychological assessment. Neurobehavioral assessment has a long history in neurorehabilitation, dating back to Poppelreuter (1917/1990), Goldstein (1942), and Luria (1963). This assessment must involve evaluation of both cognitive skills and interpersonal behaviors. A major difference between traditional neuropsychological assessment and neuropsychological assessment in a rehabilitation setting is that rehabilitation neuropsychologists must be skilled at translating neuropsychological assessment findings into functional implications. However, neuropsychological assessment is only a starting point for rehabilitation planning. During treatment implementation, the team must constantly assess the patient's skills and abilities, and this assessment refines the conceptualization of the patient, treatment goals, and treatment plan. Some elements of single-subject designs (McReynolds & Kearns, 1983) may be extraordinarily useful in monitoring patient skills and treatment progress. The research skills and knowledge of brain systems possessed by rehabilitation neuropsychologists are valuable in the design and implementation of single-subject studies.

To maximize their impact in the rehabilitation setting, neuropsychologists must be skilled at consultation. In this way, they can assist rehabilitation team members in understanding where the breakdown in cognitive processing is and designing ways to address it. Neuropsychological consultation may be particularly useful in defining and addressing interpersonal deficits, because other professionals often are not taught how to treat these problems. In consultation with other treatment team members, rehabilitation neuropsychologists must be familiar with the skills and competencies of other team members and be sure the team's communication relies on a common set of definitions, conceptions, and cognitive constructs (Holland et al., 1997).

To function in these capacities, rehabilitation neuropsychologists must receive training in a number of areas. Good basic clinical skills, including diagnosis and treatment of psychopathology, are the foundation. In neuropsychological training, knowledge of brain systems, cognitive processes, neuropathological processes, and neuropsychological assessment must be acquired. However, a firm grounding in clinical neuropsychology is not enough. Individuals training to be rehabilitation neuropsychologists must receive education relevant to rehabilitation issues and training in rehabilitation settings. For those willing to avail themselves of such training, the rewards can be satisfying in terms of furthering the empirical validity of neurorehabilitation and having a visible and positive impact on patient care.

References

Bauer, R. M. (1994). The flexible battery approach to neuropsychological assessment. In R. D. Vanderploeg (Ed.), *Clinician's guide to neuropsychological assessment* (pp. 259–290). Hillsdale, NJ: Erlbaum.

Ben-Yishay, Y. (1996). Reflections on the evolution of the therapeutic milieu concept. *Neuropsychological Rehabilitation, 6,* 327–343.

Ben-Yishay, Y., & Prigatano, G. (1990). Cognitive remediation. In M. Rosenthal, M. Bond, E. R. Griffith, & J. D. Miller (Eds.), *Rehabilitation of the adult and child with traumatic brain injury* (pp. 393–409). Philadelphia: Davis.

Boake, C. (1991). History of cognitive rehabilitation. In J. S. Kreutzer & P. H. Wehman (Eds.), *Cognitive rehabilitation for persons with traumatic brain injury—A functional approach* (pp. 3–12). Baltimore: Brookes.

Boake, C. (1996). Supervision Rating Scale: A measure of functional outcome from brain injury. *Archives of Physical Medicine and Rehabilitation, 77,* 765–772.

Caetano, C., & Christensen, A.-L. (1997). The design of neuropsychological rehabilitation: The role of the neuropsychological assessment. In J. Leon-Carrion (Ed.), *Neuropsychological rehabilitation: Fundamentals, innovations and directions* (pp. 63–72). Delray Beach, FL: GR/St. Lucie Press.

Christensen, A. L. (1984). The Luria method of examination of the brain-impaired patient. In P. E. Logue & J. M. Schear (Eds.), *Clinical neuropsychology—A multi-disciplinary approach* (pp. 5–28). Springfield, IL: Charles C Thomas.

Christensen, A. L. (1989). The neuropsychological investigation as a therapeutic and rehabilitative technique. In D. W. Ellis & A.-L. Christensen (Eds.), *Neuropsychological treatment after brain injury* (pp. 127–153). Norwell, MA: Kluwer Academic.

Christensen, A. L., & Caetano, C. (1996). Alexandr R. Luria (1902–1977): Contributions to neuropsychological rehabilitation. *Neuropsychological Rehabilitation, 6,* 279–303.

Conway, T. W., Heilman, P., Rothi, L. J. G., Alexander, A. W., Adair, J., Crosson, B. A., Heilman, K. M. (1998). Treatment of a case of phonological alexia with agraphia using the Auditory Discrimination in Depth (ADD) Program. *Journal of the International Neuropsychological Society, 4,* 608–620.

Corrigan, J. D., Arnett, J. A., Houck, L. J., & Jackson, R. D. (1985). Reality orientation for brain injured patients: Group treatment and monitoring of recovery. *Archives of Physical Medicine and Rehabilitation, 66,* 626–630.

Corrigan, P. W., & Yudofsky, S. C. (1996). What is cognitive rehabilitation? In P. W. Corrigan & S. C. Yudofsky (Eds.), *Cognitive rehabilitation for neuropsychiatric disorders* (pp. 53–69). Washington, DC: American Psychiatric Press.

Crosson, B. (1987). Treatment of interpersonal deficits for head-trauma patients in inpatient rehabilitation settings. *The Clinical Neuropsychologist, 1,* 335–352.

Crosson, B. (1994). Application of neuropsychological assessment results. In R. D. Vanderploeg (Ed.), *Clinician's guide to neuropsychological assessment* (pp. 113–163). Hillsdale, NJ: Erlbaum.

Delis, D. C., Kaplan, E., & Kramer, J. H. (in press). *Delis–Kaplan executive function system.* San Antonio, TX: The Psychological Corporation.

Farmer, J. L., Clippard, D. S., Luehr-Wiemann, Y., Wright, E., & Owings, S. (1997). Assessing children with traumatic brain injury during rehabilitation: Promoting school and community reentry. In E. Bigler, E. Clark, & J. E. Farmer (Eds.), *Childhood traumatic brain injury: Diagnosis, assessment and intervention* (pp. 33–61). Austin, TX: PRO-Ed.

Goldstein, K. (1942). *After-effects of brain injury in war.* New York: Grune & Stratton.

Hannay, H. J., Bieliauskas, L. A., Crosson, B., Hammeke, T. A., Hamsher, K. D., & Koffler, S. P. (1998). Proceedings of the Houston Conference on Specialty Education and Training in Clinical Neuropsychology. *Archives of Clinical Neuropsychology, 13,* 157–250.

Holland, D., Hogg, J., & Farmer, J. E. (1997). Fostering effective team cooperation and communication: Developing community standards within interdisciplinary cognitive rehabilitation settings. *NeuroRehabilitation, 8,* 21–29.

Jennett, B., Snoek, J., Bond, M. R., & Brooks, D. N. (1981). Disability after severe head injury: Observations on the use of the Glasgow Outcome Scale. *Journal of Neurology, Neurosurgery, and Psychiatry, 44,* 285–293.

Jennett, B., & Teasdale, B. (1981). *Management of head injury.* Philadelphia: F. A. Davis.

Johnstone, B., & Farmer, J. E. (1997). Preparing neuropsychologists for the future: The need for additional training guidelines. *Archives of Clinical Neuropsychology, 12,* 523–530.

Keith, R. A., Granger, C. V., Hamilton, B. B., & Sherwin, F. A. (1987). The Functional Independence Measure: A new tool for rehabilitation. In M. G. Eisenberg & R. C. Grzesiak (Eds.), *Advances in clinical rehabilitation* (Vol. 1, pp. 6–18). New York: Springer-Verlag.

Lezak, M. D. (1978). Living with the characterologically altered brain injured patient. *Journal of Clinical Psychiatry, 39,* 592–598.

Lezak, M. D. (1995). *Neuropsychological assessment* (3rd ed.). New York: Oxford University Press.

Luria, A. R. (1963). *Restoration of function after brain injury* (B. Haigh, Trans.). London: Pergamon Press. (Original work published in 1948)

Luria, A. R. (1980). *Higher cortical functions in man* (2nd ed.). New York: Basic Books.

McLellan, L. (1997). Introduction to rehabilitation. In J. Leon-Carrion (Ed.), *Neuropsychological rehabilitation: Fundamentals, innovations and directions* (pp. 1–19). Delray Beach, FL: GR/St. Lucie Press.

McReynolds, L. V., & Kearns, K. (1983). *Single-subject experimental designs in communicative disorders*. Baltimore: University Park Press.

Morales, M. (1997). Evaluation of neuropsychological rehabilitation programs. In J. Leon-Carrion (Ed.), *Neuropsychological rehabilitation: Fundamentals, innovations and directions* (p. 109–123). Delray Beach, FL: GR/St. Lucie Press.

Poppelreuter, W. (1990). *Disturbances of lower and higher visual capacities caused by occipital damage* (J. Zihl & L. Weiskrantz, Trans.). Oxford, England: Clarendon Press. (Original work published 1917)

Poser, U., Kohler, J. A., & Schönle, P. W. (1996). Historical review of neuropsychological rehabilitation in Germany. *Neuropsychological Rehabilitation, 6,* 257–278.

Prigatano, G. P. (1997). The problem of impaired self-awareness in neuropsychological rehabilitation. In J. Leòn-Carriòn (Ed.), *Neuropsychological rehabilitation: Fundamentals, innovations, and directions* (pp. 301–311). Delray Beach, FL: GR/St. Lucie Press.

Prigatano, G. P., Fordyce, D. J., Zeiner, H. K., Roueche, J. R., Pepping, M., & Wood, B. C. (1986). *Neuropsychological rehabilitation after brain injury*. Baltimore: Johns Hopkins University Press.

Rappaport, M., Hall, K. M., Hopkins, K., Belleza, T., & Cope, D. N. (1982). Disability Rating Scale for severe head trauma: Coma to community. *Archives of Physical Medicine and Rehabilitation, 63,* 118–123.

Reitan, R. M., & Wolfson, D. (1993). *The Halstead–Reitan Neuropsychological Test Battery: Theory and clinical interpretation*. Tucson, AZ: Neuropsychology Press.

Sbordone, R. J. (1997). The ecological validity of neuropsychological testing. In A. M. Horton, D. Wedding, & J. Webster (Eds.), *The neuropsychology handbook: Vol. 1. Foundations and assessment* (pp. 365–392). New York: Springer.

Sohlberg, M. M., & Mateer, C. A. (1987). Effectiveness of an attention training program. *Journal of Clinical and Experimental Neuropsychology, 19,* 117–130.

Sohlberg, M. M., & Mateer, C. A. (1989). *Introduction to cognitive rehabilitation: Theory and practice* (pp. 18–36). New York: Guilford Press.

Uzzell, B. P. (1997). Neuropsychological rehabilitation models. In J. Leòn-Carriòn (Ed.), *Neuropsychological rehabilitation: Fundamentals, innovations, and directions* (pp. 41–56). Delray Beach, FL: GR/St. Lucie Press.

Wilson, B. A. (1987). *Rehabilitation of memory*. New York: Guilford Press.

Wilson, B. A. (1989). Models of rehabilitation. In R. L. Wood & P. Eames (Eds.), *Models of brain injury rehabilitation* (pp. 117–141). Baltimore: Johns Hopkins University Press.

Wilson, B. A. (1997a). Cognitive rehabilitation: How it is and how it might be. *Journal of International Neuropsychological Society, 3,* 487–496.

Wilson, B. A. (1997b). Management of acquired cognitive disorders. In B. A. Wilson & D. L. McLellan (Eds.), *Rehabilitation studies handbook* (pp. 243–261). New York: Cambridge University Press.

16

Forensic Psychological Evaluation

Brick Johnstone, Laura H. Schopp, and Cheryl L. Shigaki

In criminal and civil proceedings, psychologists are frequently asked to address such issues as competency to stand trial, psychological damages suffered by a plaintiff, child custody issues, jury selection, criminal responsibility, and disability determination. Psychologists have a unique role to play; they offer predictions and measurements of behavior, using psychometrically sound tests and normative data to assess cognitive functioning and personality. These skills and tools separate psychologists' expertise from that of other mental health professionals such as psychiatrists, vocational counselors, or social workers.

Within the past several decades psychologists working in rehabilitation settings have increasingly participated in the legal arena as experts on psychological impairments associated with physical and mental disabilities. Historically, psychologists working in rehabilitation have been trained in content areas primarily pertaining to direct patient care, such as diagnosing and treating psychological disorders associated with disabilities. However, because many individuals with disabilities are involved in civil litigation related to the cause of their disability, rehabilitation psychologists must be knowledgeable about the legal system and their role in it. In most civil litigation cases, psychologists' testimonies are not based on their perceptions of the patient's disorders and needs, but rather on attorneys' decisions on how to present facts best suited to argue their case. Given that psychologists are increasingly involved in civil litigation (and are actively promoting their services to attorneys), it is difficult to imagine that a psychologist can wholly avoid interactions with attorneys, disability boards, or the courts over the course of a career in rehabilitation. Indeed, the American Psychological Association's (APA) Committee on Ethical Guidelines for Forensic Psychologists (1991) clearly suggested that any psychologist involved in evaluating or treating a client with an injury-related problem should assume that information from such an evaluation will become part of a legal action.

The focus of this chapter is largely on the forensic evaluation of traumatic brain injury (TBI). Although other physical disorders (e.g., spinal cord injuries, musculoskeletal disorders) are evaluated and treated by rehabilitation psychologists, physicians more commonly testify as to the degree of physical impairment in these cases. This chapter is relevant for rehabilitation, clinical, counseling, forensic, and neuropsychologists working in rehabilitation settings.

Growth

The growing need for forensic psychological evaluations for individuals with disabilities has been based on several factors, including increased understanding of brain injury, higher survival rates of individuals with brain injuries and their associated chronic disabilities, enhanced recognition of psychology's unique role in evaluating brain injury, and growth of civil litigation involving brain injuries. In highlighting the increased use of psychological evaluation in the legal arena, Puente (1987) reported that 41% of all applicants for Social Security assistance each year (nearly 150,000 individuals) have organic brain syndromes or related disorders.

Along with high rates of prevalence for brain injuries in the United States, there is increasing understanding of the mechanisms of brain injury that frequently take place at a microscopic level and cannot always be visualized even by modern neurodiagnostic techniques. This results in some patients showing indications of disrupted cognitive and behavioral functions in the absence of clear evidence of structural neurological damage (Guilmette & Giuliano, 1991; Salmon & Meyer, 1986). As neuropsychological research in the 1980s began to suggest that long-standing impairments in these domains may follow even mild brain injury (e.g., Raskin, Mateer, & Tweeten, 1998; Rimel, Bruno, Barth, Boll, & Jane, 1981; Sorenson & Krause, 1991), psychologists have become more active in the courtroom (Laing & Fisher, 1997; Puente & Gillespie, 1991).

Statistics are not available regarding the practice of rehabilitation psychologists who engage in forensic activity, most likely because rehabilitation psychology training guidelines were only recently established in 1995. However, neuropsychologists Guilmette, Faust, Hart, and Arkes (1990) found that of 449 psychologists who offer neuropsychological services, 50% have testified at least once in forensic neuropsychology cases, and nearly 20% have testified more than 10 times. Similarly, Putnam, DeLuca, and Anderson (1994) reported on a 1993 survey of APA Division 40 (Clinical Neuropsychology) members, which indicated that over half of respondents (51%) reported some involvement in forensic activities.

History of Psychology in the Legal System

Psychology has a long history of involvement with the American legal system. During the first decade of the 20th century, both experimental psychologists (e.g., Munsterberg, 1908) and clinical psychiatrists (e.g., Freud, 1906/1959) spoke of psychology's potential for assisting lawyers seeking to establish the truth (Kurke, 1986). One of the first indicators of the developing relationship between psychology and law was the establishment of a psychological clinic attached to the juvenile court in Chicago in the early 1900s (Kurke, 1986), which was provided data from the courts for psychological research (Healy, 1915).

Mid-century progress toward further collaboration between psychology and law was generally slow. However, as early as 1921, a West Virginia psychologist was recorded as serving as an expert witness in the courtroom (*State v. Driver*), although his testimony was ultimately rejected (Giuliano, Barth, Hawk, & Ryan, 1997). In 1962, a benchmark ruling (*Jenkins v. United States*) by the District of Columbia Court of Appeals held that a lower federal court had erred in excluding psychological testimony and that psychologists could be qualified as experts when providing testimony about criminal responsibility, despite their lack of a medical degree (Giuliano et al., 1997). Since that time, the direction of both legislation and court decisions generally has been to affirm and expand the role of psychologists as expert witnesses within their field of expertise in criminal and civil cases (Barth, Ryan, & Hawk, 1992).

The first seminal forensic testimony of a neuropsychologist occurred in 1974 (Puente, 1997), when Ralph Reitan testified in a brain injury case (*Indianapolis Union Railway v. Walker*). Reitan's original testimony was not considered admissible because he was not a physician. However, the decision was eventually overturned in the Indiana Court of Appeals because of the usefulness of the neuropsychological evidence provided. Similarly, in the mid-1980s, Antonio Puente gave testimony on brain injury in *Horne v. Goodson* (1986). Puente's testimony was originally ruled not admissible on the grounds that Puente was not a physician, but the ruling was reversed by the North Carolina Court of Appeals on the basis of information about neurocognitive changes that could be detected by neuropsychological testing (Puente, 1997). By the end of the 1970s, the relationship between psychology and law had gained significant momentum. Interdisciplinary groups such as the American Psychology–Law Society and the American Board of Forensic Psychology were established; the latter certified eligible professionals in the specialty of forensic psychology (Kurke, 1986).

Admissibility of Testimony

Until the 1950s, psychologists examined and debated empirical findings among other psychologists, primarily through scientific journals. However, given the surge of forensic activity in the profession of psychology, the validity and reliability of psychological assessment also has begun to be questioned in the legal arena (Matarazzo, 1987). In the late 1980s and early 1990s many questions were raised about the scientific merit (or lack thereof) of neuropsychological evidence and (consequently) its admissibility in the courts. A few psychologists have argued that the discipline "has not reached the state of scientific development or knowledge that permits legal questions to be answered with reasonable certainty" (Faust, Ziskin, & Hiers, 1991, p. 2).

Despite the reservations expressed by some neuropsychologists, neuropsychological testing procedures have achieved increasing prominence from a legal perspective (Gilandas & Touyz, 1983) and have been generally accepted as being a viable adjunct or alternative to medical testimony in disability determinations and personal-injury litigation (Anchor, Rogers, Solomon, Barth, & Peacock, 1983). Given legal precedent regarding the use of expert testimony, it is evident that the courts are aware of the scientific limitations within the behavioral health fields (and other scientific disciplines) yet continue to seek out and welcome testimony from psychologists (Barth, Ryan, & Hawk, 1992).

From the legal perspective, the *Federal Rules of Evidence 702–705* govern the admissibility of opinions and expert testimony. These rules (established in 1975) permit the admission of a qualified expert's opinion into evidence if it is based on specialized knowledge and assists the judge or the jury (*Federal Rule of Evidence 702*; Green, Nesson, & Murray, 1997). The *Federal Rules of Evidence* do not require perfection of scientific evidence and expert opinion, and they clearly frame the question of admissibility as one of incremental rather than absolute validity (Green et al., 1997; Melton, 1994). Experts are expected to be open about the bases of their evaluations, limitations of their data, and uncertainty in their opinions (Guilmette & Giuliano, 1991; Hawk & Benedek, 1989). In turn, the law relies on cross-examination (*Federal Rule of Evidence 705*) to illuminate the strengths and weaknesses of opinion evidence and the capacity of the jury to perceive and weigh it fairly (Green et al., 1997; Melton, 1994).

Prior to the *Federal Rules of Evidence*, the admissibility of expert opinion and scientific evidence had long been based on what is referred to as the *Frye* standard (Broun et al., 1992), which was adopted in the 1920s by the U.S. Court of Appeals for the District of Columbia Circuit and required that admissible evidence had to be "sufficiently established to have gained general acceptance in the particular field to which it belongs" (*Frye v. United States*, 1923, p. 1014). In the 1990s, however, the U.S. Supreme Court ultimately superseded *Frye* (regarding federal law) in favor of *Daubert vs. Merrell Dow Pharmaceuticals* (1993). The *Daubert* standard was adopted in an effort to establish a standard for the admissibility of scientific evidence that could be implemented more consistently with the *Federal Rules of Evidence* (Cohen, 1996; Livingood, 1994). *Daubert* focuses on the admissibility of unpublished research indicating that the use of Bendectin could cause birth defects. In settling *Daubert*, the U.S. Supreme Court suggested factors to consider to aid the lower courts in their review of scientific evidence. These factors include the "general acceptance" concept of *Frye* and the concepts of empirical substantiveness of the techniques used, including error rates and the use of control groups in the technique's operation (Reed, 1996).

Although it allows breadth by the inclusion of scientifically derived but unpublished data, *Daubert* may lead to stricter scrutiny of scientific evidence in courts (Laing & Fisher, 1997). In fact, the *Daubert* standard has been applied to neuropsychological evidence in this manner in *Chap-

ple v. Ganger (1994), a case that has important implications for the practice of forensic psychologists. In *Chapple*, three neuropsychological batteries were offered as evidence to determine the status of a closed brain injury sustained by a child involved in an automobile accident. In considering the conflicting interpretations of these neuropsychological assessments, the court chose to accept "fixed" or standardized battery results (in this case most of the Halstead–Reitan Battery was administered) in toto, but not "flexible" (nonstandardized) battery results (see Chapter 15, this volume). Thus, *Chapple* has set a precedent that likely favors the use of fixed-battery assessments as admissible neuropsychological evidence. However, it is important to note that in *Chapple* the court also accepted some of the individual tests used in the flexible batteries (or as supplements to the fixed battery) as meeting the *Daubert* requirements of scientific validity, reliability, methodology, and procedure (Reed, 1996).

It is important to note that the *Chapple* decision does not question the admissibility of neuropsychological evidence in and of itself. In fact, Richardson and Adams (1992) reviewed nearly 200 appellate case decisions regarding the use of clinical psychologists and neuropsychologists as expert witnesses concerning brain damage since 1980. They reported that of all cases reviewed, the courts have supported the right of neuropsychologists to testify concerning the presence of brain dysfunction. However, the courts have been somewhat divided regarding the admissibility of neuropsychological testimony regarding the cause of brain damage or dysfunction. For example, Florida and Ohio appellate courts have held that the etiology of brain damage is a medical issue and (therefore) that only physicians are qualified to testify regarding causality (Richardson & Adams, 1992). Although little is available to determine the eligibility of neuropsychologists to testify regarding the prognosis of a patient following brain injury, these authors have speculated that jurisdictions are most likely to follow the precedents set in the causality cases.

What to Expect in Courtroom Testimony

It is essential for psychologists working in the legal system to be aware of the norms, orientation, goals, and procedures of the legal system. Legal proceedings can appear alien to the clinician, whose work in rehabilitation often focuses on entirely different aims and values. The rehabilitation psychologist is primarily concerned with assessing and treating injury sequelae, maximizing coping skills, assisting family members, facilitating community reintegration, and assisting the rehabilitation team in functioning optimally.

In contrast, the primary role of the forensic rehabilitation psychologist as expert witness is to provide information or specialized knowledge that assists the trier of fact (i.e., the jury or the judge) in its deliberations (Melton, 1994). The psychologist as expert witness may be called on to make what seem to be unduly dichotomous distinctions between organic and psychological factors influencing outcomes. Faced with such different demand characteristics and role expectations, the psychologist may be tempted either to qualify remarks excessively or to overstate findings. Either extreme can be problematic and can increase the likelihood of clinician judgment errors (Wedding, 1991). Finally, there may be minimal scientific evidence that pertains directly to the concerns of the court, and psychologists may often be put in a position to extrapolate from studies that may be less than optimally relevant to the legal question at hand (Faust, 1991).

The rehabilitation psychologist entering the forensic setting also faces potential conflicting demands on the scope of his or her concern. The psychologist is permitted under *Federal Rule of Evidence 704* to offer opinions on "ultimate issue" questions such as the dangerousness and specific prognosis of the individual in question. However, the dictates of professional ethics discourage such speculation, leaving it to the trier of fact to decide these matters (Melton, 1994). The APA's Committee on Ethical Guidelines for Forensic Psychologists (1991) further suggested that psychologists withhold testimony on questions lying outside their realm of specialized knowledge. Although it is desirable both in clinical and legal settings to avoid broad speculation and to limit conclusions to those drawn from expert knowledge, the line is drawn more sharply in the forensic context, and the psychologist must be more than usually vigilant about role constraints because nonscientific conjecture can carry especially serious consequences for a litigant's independence, finances, and reputation.

Although practicing psychologists are accustomed to providing a rationale for the conclusions they reach, few are routinely called on to withstand rigorous cross-examination about their findings. Although such vociferous questioning is rarely personal in nature (Adams & Rankin, 1996), it can certainly pose a challenge to the psychologist in maintaining composure and avoiding argument. Fortunately, there are some excellent guides to the rehabilitation psychologist working in the legal arena. Many works have been written to familiarize psychologists with pragmatic strategies to cope with personal injury, disability determination, worker's compensation (Barth, Ryan, Schear, & Puente, 1992), direct and cross-examination (Adams & Rankin, 1996), and common pitfalls in testimony (Guilmette & Giuliano, 1991). Also available are updates on case law; descriptions of forensic publications (Schwartz, 1991); and discussions of reliability, validity, and standard error of measurement as they pertain to psychological testimony (Matarazzo, 1987). Expert witnesses in rehabilitation psychology should also become familiar with works challenging neuropsychological testimony (Faust, 1991; Wedding, 1991) and publications written for attorneys, especially those that pertain to challenging neuropsychological testimony (Faust et al., 1991).

Although many cases settle out of court and do not proceed to trial, the forensic rehabilitation psychologist may be called on to give testimony on the impact of injury. As such, the psychologist must be aware of litigation procedures, common mistakes, and testimony skills that help articulate an expert opinion and prevent one's views from being misconstrued.

The forensic psychologist may be involved in several types of cases; those most relevant to the rehabilitation psychologist include personal injury, malpractice, competency, and disability determination. Whatever the nature of the case, psychologists must be familiar with legal protocol and strategy. Several excellent and specific guides to the legal process are available, from the initial telephone contact with the attorney through the deposition and trial phases (see Adams & Rankin, 1996). In the preassessment and assessment phases, the psychologist must communicate clearly and honestly with the attorney about how psychological testimony may be helpful or damaging to the plaintiff or defendant's case. In this phase, communication also pertains to the nature of the case, fees, expectations, and testing procedures.

In the deposition or "discovery" phase, the psychologist gives information under oath that offers the plaintiff's and the defense's attorneys a view of the psychologist's testimony and testimonial skills. Anything the psychologist says, as well as any written materials used during the deposition, may be used in court. The deposition may be videotaped.

Although most cases settle out of court (Adams & Rankin, 1996), some cases proceed to trial. In a trial, the attorneys may or may not elect to introduce neuropsychological testimony. If neuropsychological testimony is used, the psychologist is subject to direct examination, cross-examination, and redirect and recross-examination.

The attorney employing the psychologist calls on the psychologist for testimony during direct examination, beginning with questions qualifying the psychologist as an expert. The attorney portrays the psychologist as favorably as possible and presents aspects of the psychological evaluation that support that attorney's case. Ultimately, in brain injury litigation the psychologist is usually asked to provide, with a reasonable degree of certainty, an opinion as to whether the client suffered brain damage as a result of the incident in question and the extent to which that injury is likely to affect the patient's prognosis. The direct examination represents the period of explication of the case under sympathetic questioning.

In contrast, the cross-examination by the opposing attorney seeks to cast doubt on the psychologist's testimony, often by the use of numerous debunking tactics. Such tactics may include trying to detect the psychologist's lack of knowledge about obscure facts or studies, asking questions that are unanswerable given the present state of the art in psychology, using yes-or-no questions in a way calculated to undermine the psychologist's credibility, accusing the psychologist of being a "hired gun," and attacking the reliability and validity of tests (Adams & Rankin, 1996). The psychologist is well advised to become familiar with these ploys and with strategies to cope with them before entering the courtroom (Adams & Rankin, 1996; Guilmette & Giuliano, 1991).

The redirect and recross-examination phases are attempts by the employing and opposing attorneys, respectively, to undo damage done by the opposite side and to recast testimony in the light most favorable to their own purposes.

In civil cases, the plaintiff must prove the case on the basis of a preponderance of evidence, which in essence means that those deciding the case find the allegation more likely to be true than not true. The standard for the psychologist who is an expert witness is one of "reasonable certainty," which suggests that the psychologist believes, based on expertise derived from training and clinical experience, that the opinion he or she offers the court is reasonable and true.

Those charged with deciding cases may be swayed by skilled attorney cross-examination that undermines a psychologist's testimony. Psychologists are vulnerable to such attack because of the lack of a universal assessment standard, poor correlation between training and experience and diagnostic accuracy, limited ecological validity of neuropsychological tests, the inability to rule out malingering definitively, and the fallibility of clinical judgment even in the face of relevant information (Guilmette & Giuliano, 1991; Matarazzo, 1987; Wedding, 1983; Ziskin & Faust, 1988). Psychologists need to be aware of the actual and apparent vulnerabilities of their testimony and should prepare to be confronted on these matters by the opposing attorney.

Content Areas

Because of the likelihood that rehabilitation psychologists may be asked to testify in court, they are advised to familiarize themselves with the issues that are likely to be raised in litigation. Psychologists working in rehabilitation settings should be knowledgeable about issues relevant in forensic evaluations: accepted assessment measures, estimation of premorbid abilities, reliability and validity of psychological tests, developmental issues and injury outcome, and malingering. An understanding of these issues may help them avoid common courtroom pitfalls and provide sound scientific testimony.

Accepted Assessment Measures

Chapple v. Ganger (1994) set a precedent for accepting fixed-battery approaches in civil litigation. However, psychologists assessing brain dysfunction are notorious for using a variety of tests and batteries. For example, Lees-Haley, Smith, Williams, and Dunn (1996) reviewed the forensic neuropsychological reports of 100 examiners in over 20 states. Results indicated that, on average, 11.73 (SD = 6.70) tests were administered per assessment. Five tests were administered most frequently: Wechsler Adult Intelligence Scale—Revised (WAIS-R; 76% of evaluations); the original and second editions of the Minnesota Multiphase Personality Inventory (MMPI and MMPI-2; 68%); Wechsler Memory Scale—Revised (Wechsler, 51%); and the Trailmaking Test parts A and B (48% and 47%, respectively). Ten percent of evaluations included part or all of the Luria–Nebraska Neuropsychological Battery. Although Halstead–Reitan Neuropsychological Test Battery (HRNB) subtests were found to be pervasive, few clinicians used the entire battery. Batteries characterized by examiners as the HRNB varied from five to eight procedures or more of those described by Reitan and Wolfson (1985). Not surprisingly, these authors found that few neuropsychologists used precisely the same battery as other neuropsychologists. When using different tests and batteries to evaluate brain dysfunction, psychologists need to be familiar with those tests most likely to be permitted as evidence in trial and with examples of previous cases in which these tests were used.

Estimation of Premorbid Functioning

One of the hallmarks of personal-injury litigation is the need to establish a decrement in physical, vocational, neuropsychological, academic, or social abilities associated with injury. Assessment of functional decline necessitates a comparison of current abilities to some estimate of premorbid abilities. In turn, documenting decline presupposes an adequate standard for estimating previous abilities. To document decline, psychologists must correctly differentiate preexisting developmental weaknesses from actual injury-related decline and do so on the basis of intra-individual comparisons and comparisons with others in relevant population subgroups.

If possible, psychologists need to obtain preinjury testing or examples of premorbid level of functioning, including intelligence and academic tests, standardized educational testing, and work evaluations. If this information is not available, as is commonly the case, it is necessary to estimate premorbid levels of functioning. Several standards of premorbid comparison have been proposed in the literature, with the most common being level of education, reading ability, and demographically based regression equations. Education is assumed to be a good estimate of premorbid intelligence, given the high correlation between education and intelligence (Lezak, 1995). Reading ability is also believed to be a reliable indicator of premorbid abilities, on the assumption that it is an overlearned ability and is therefore relatively spared following brain injury (e.g., Crawford, Besson, & Parker, 1988; Johnstone & Wilhelm, 1996; Ryan & Paolo, 1992). Others have argued that demographic prediction equations, such as the Barona Index (Barona, Reynolds, & Chastain, 1984) and its multiple revisions, are the best predictors of premorbid skills. The articles in a special issue of *Archives of Clinical Neuropsychology* (Hannay et al., 1997) provide an overview of the current state of the art in estimating premorbid functions.

Reliability and Validity of Data

In testimony regarding psychological functioning, an area of critical importance is the reliability and validity of psychological data. In the past, validity and reliability were issues debated among psychologists, with decisions about the appropriateness of instruments left to scholarly investigation. Increasingly, such decisions have come to the fore in the public arena, both legislatively and in the courtroom. For example, legislative action has been taken to prevent the use of the MMPI in federal hiring, and psychologists must present proof of the validity of instruments used for educational placement decisions (Matarazzo, 1987).

Reliable and valid testimony rests on the objectivity of the examiner. If the expert witness is perceived by the judge or jury as biased, either because of a strong advocacy role or because the psychologist is a hired gun intent on secondary gain, both the client and the profession suffer. Several suggestions are made for reducing expert witness bias. Adhering strictly to available scientific evidence introduces a corrective tendency because of the scientific method's disconfirmation bias. A disciplined approach of attending to all relevant data (e.g., history, medication effects, alternative explanations for dysfunction) also attenuates clinician bias. Limiting exposure to others' impressions of the case has resulted in less confirmatory bias, and deliberately challenging hypotheses about other possible causes may lessen clinicians' susceptibility to such confirmatory bias (Williams, 1997).

Developmental Issues and Injury Outcome

Expert witnesses help a jury assess the extent to which injury affects future functioning, and damages are awarded in part on the basis of a life care plan detailing a client's future care needs. The need to project the course of disability and recovery becomes especially acute in cases involving children, in which costs related to care and lost future educational and vocational opportunities are anticipated. Psychologists are often called on to speculate on the prognosis of younger clients with brain injury.

In the past, it was largely assumed that individuals sustaining brain injury at earlier ages had more favorable outcomes than individuals with similar injuries sustained at a later age, presumably because of the brain's early plasticity. However, several limitations are associated with neuroplasticity theories, and rehabilitation psychologists testifying in child injury cases should be thoroughly familiar with them. For example, recent research suggests that damage sustained in the 1st year of life is associated with more severe deficits than damage sustained later, largely because of arrested neuroanatomical development during that time (Kolb & Fantie, 1997). It is also true that children's deficits may not be evident until later in their development, when more complex skills would normally be expected to develop (Kolb & Fantie, 1997). These issues are complex, and the rehabilitation psychologist must help the judge and jury anticipate the likely course of future deficits on the basis of limited current information. It is easy to see why such speculation, although necessary and valid, could place the psychologist on uncertain ground. Although it is difficult to predict a client's ultimate level of recovery at any point, it is especially difficult to do so during the 1st year after injury. Fortunately, few cases involving brain injury go to trial within the 1st year after injury; the psychologist is thereby able to refrain from making prognostic statements until a client's neuropsychological functioning has stabilized.

Malingering

From a legal perspective, a key role of the rehabilitation psychologist as expert witness involves the detection of malingering. Malingering is the deliberate presentation of "false or grossly exaggerated physical or psychological symptoms" (American Psychiatric Association, 1994, p. 683) to achieve secondary gain, often for an external incentive (e.g., money, drugs, avoiding work or punishment). Whenever the psychologist evaluates a litigant in a civil suit, financial and other incentives should be investigated, and the possibility of malingering should be considered.

There are several well-known indicators of malingering. Among those cited in the literature are a history of antisocial personality disorder, recent substance abuse (American Psychiatric Association, 1994), very brief tenure at the job where one was allegedly injured (Adams & Rankin, 1996), and potential for financial gain. Other indicators include a wide discrepancy between physical findings and functional impairment, reports of bizarre and unrelated symptoms, and obvious response bias in favor of endorsing any symptoms about which one is questioned. Other unusual features noted in a clinical interview, such as a course inconsistent with that expected from the injury, as well as patterns of equal decline across all areas, should arouse the evaluator's concern.

Objective testing for malingering is a task made difficult by the absence of ideal measures. Most measures err on the conservative side. In real terms, this suggests that malingering is more likely to go undetected than to be overdiagnosed (Etcoff & Kampfer, 1996). However, some psychologists are reluctant even to raise the specter of malingering (Pankratz & Erickson, 1990) because it is not at all clear that psychologists make those determinations of intent better than others. However, these and other professional criticisms aside, malingering is an issue of significant legal interest, and psychologists should be prepared to address the question of secondary gain when giving testimony.

A recent review of methods used to evaluate symptom exaggeration and malingering outlines legal standards for various malingering tests (Etcoff & Kampfer, 1996). Citing Rogers's (1988) proposed levels of certainty in malingering evaluation, five levels of certainty were outlined. A "definite" standard of malingering is defined as one in which 90% of individuals are correctly classified as malingering or nonmalingering on the basis of a broad body of research. "Probable" methods correctly classify at least 75% of individuals, and "tentative" methods have some empirical support but may not be useful in classifying particular individuals. The research methods for measuring malingering in laboratory settings have been debated in the scholarly literature. However, leaving aside arguments of whether individuals instructed to "fake bad" in the lab actually do so in a way that is similar to actual malingering, these levels of certainty offer at least some guidance for the clinician in evaluating tests of malingering against a broad, if somewhat vague, standard.

Using this framework, symptom validity tests have been rated according to level of certainty. Only a few tests met the criteria for *definite*, including the Hiscock Digit Recognition Test (72-item version and 36-item version; Hiscock & Hiscock, 1989), the Portland Digit Recognition Test (full 72-item version and 54-item version with conservative scoring; Binder, 1993), the MMPI-2 F scale and $F - K$ Index, WAIS-R age-corrected scaled scores of less than four on the Digit Span subtest, and an error score of 24 or more on the Speech Sounds Perception Test (Etcoff & Kampfer, 1996). The authors emphasized that even in using measures that have empirical support, clinicians should not rely solely on one instrument to make definitive statements regarding malingering or symptom exaggeration.

Conclusion

It is incumbent on the rehabilitation psychologist to develop a familiarity with forensic issues and the legal system, largely because injury cases are likely to enter the legal system for redress. It is also important for psychologists to understand the different roles that psychologists play in legal versus clinical settings, what to expect in depositions and courtroom testimony, and how best to present clinically relevant information to judges, juries, and attorneys. A familiarity with diagnostic problems, psychometric properties of instruments, symptom courses and recovery curves, and questions of secondary gain is the *sine qua non* of ethical forensic rehabilitation practice.

References

Adams, R. L., & Rankin, E. J. (1996). A practical guide to forensic neuropsychological evaluations and testimony. In R. L. Adams, O. A. Parsons, J. L. Culbertson, & S. J. Nixon (Eds.), *Neuropsychology for clinical practice* (pp. 455–487). Washington, DC: American Psychological Association.

American Psychiatric Association. (1994). *Diagnostic and statistical manual of mental disorders* (4th Ed). Washington, DC: Author.

Anchor, K. N., Rogers, J. P., Solomon, G. S., Barth, J. T., & Peacock, C. (1983). Alternatives to medical testimony in determining vocational and industrial disability. *American Journal of Trial Advocacy, 6*, 443–480.

Barona, A., Reynolds, C. R., & Chastain, R. (1984). A demographically based index of premorbid intelligence for the WAIS-R. *Journal of Consulting and Clinical Psychology, 52*, 885–887.

Barth, J. T., Ryan, T. V., & Hawk, G. L. (1992). Forensic neuropsychology: A reply to the method skeptics. *Neuropsychology Review, 2*, 251–266.

Barth, J. T., Ryan, T. V., Schear, J. M., & Puente, A. E. (1992). Forensic assessment and expert testimony in neuropsychology. In S. L. Hanson & D. M. Tucker (Eds.): *Physical medicine & rehabilitation: Vol. 6. State of the art reviews: Neuropsychological assessment* (pp. 531–546). Philadelphia: Hanley & Belfus.

Binder, L. M. (1993). An abbreviated form of the Portland Digit Recognition Test. *The Clinical Neuropsychologist, 7*, 104–107.

Broun, K. S., Dix, G. E., Graham, M. H., Kaye, D. H., Mosteller, R. P., & Roberts, E. F. (Eds.). (1992). *McCormick on evidence* (4th ed., pp. 362–364). St. Paul, MN: West.

Chapple v. Ganger, 851 F. Supp. 1481 (E. D. Wash, 1994).

Cohen, L. E. (1996). The Daubert decision: Gatekeeper or executioner? *Trial, 32*, 52.

Committee on Ethical Guidelines for Forensic Psychologists. (1991). Specialty guidelines for forensic psychologists. *Law and Human Behavior, 15*, 655–665.

Crawford, J. R., Besson, J. A. O., & Parker, D. M. (1988). Estimation of premorbid intelligence in organic conditions. *British Journal of Psychiatry, 153,* 178–181.

Daubert v. Merrell Dow Pharmaceuticals, 113 S. Ct. 2786 (1993).

Etcoff, L. M., & Kampfer, K. M. (1996). Practical guidelines in the use of symptom validity and other psychological tests to measure malingering and symptom exaggeration in traumatic brain injury cases. *Neuropsychology Review, 6,* 171–201.

Faust, D. (1991). Forensic neuropsychology: The art of practicing a science that does not yet exist. *Neuropsychology Review, 2,* 205–231.

Faust, D., Ziskin, J., & Hiers, J. B. (1991). *Brain damage claims: Coping with neuropsychological evidence* (Vol. 2). Los Angeles, CA: Law and Psychology Press.

Freud, S. (1959). Psycho-analysis and the ascertaining of truth in courts of law. In *Clinical papers and papers on technique, collected papers* (Vol. 2, pp. 13–14). New York: Basic Books. (Original work published 1906)

Frye v. United States, 293 Fed. 1013 (D.C. Cir. 1923).

Gilandas, A. J., & Touyz, S. W. (1983). Forensic neuropsychology: A selective introduction. *Journal of Forensic Sciences, 28,* 713–723.

Giuliano, A. J., Barth, J. T., Hawk, G. L., & Ryan, T. V. (1997). The forensic neuropsychologists: Precedents, roles, and problems. In R. J. McCaffrey, A. D. Williams, J. M. Fisher, & L. C. Laing (Eds.), *The practice of forensic neuropsychology: Meeting challenges in the courtroom* (pp. 1–35). New York: Plenum Press.

Green, E. D., Nesson, C. R., & Murray, P. L. (1997). *Federal Rules of Evidence: With selected legislative history, California Evidence Code, and case supplement* (pp. 156–163). New York: Aspen Law & Business.

Guilmette, T. J., Faust, D., Hart, K., & Arkes, H. R. (1990). A national survey of psychologists who offer neuropsychological services. *Archives of Clinical Neuropsychology, 5,* 373–392.

Guilmette, T. J., & Giuliano, A. J. (1991). Taking the stand: Issues and strategies in forensic neuropsychology. *The Clinical Neuropsychologist, 5,* 197–219.

Hannay, H. J., Bieliauskas, L., Crosson, B. A., Hammeke, T. A., Hamser, K. D., & Koffler, S. (Eds.). (1997). Estimation of premorbid neuropsychological ability [Special issue]. *Archives of Clinical Neuropsychology, 12.*

Hawk, G., & Benedek, E. P. (1989). The forensic evaluation in the criminal justice system. In R. Michels (Ed.), *Psychiatry* (pp. 1–15). Philadelphia: Lippincott.

Healy, W. (1915). *Honesty: A study of the causes and treatment of dishonest among children.* Indianapolis, IN: Bobbs-Merrill.

Hiscock, M., & Hiscock, C. K. (1989). Refining the forced-choice method for the detection of malingering. *Journal of Clinical and Experimental Neuropsychology, 11,* 967–974.

Horne v. Goodson. North Carolina Court of Appeals. (NC 1986, October).

Indianapolis Union Railway v. Walker. Court of Appeals of Indiana, First District, 578–590. (IN 1974, November 12).

Jenkins v. United States, 113 U.S. App. D.C. 300, 307 F.2d 637 (1962).

Johnstone, B., & Wilhelm, K. L. (1996). The longitudinal stability of the WRAT-R reading subtest: Is it an appropriate estimate of premorbid intelligence? *Journal of the International Neuropsychology Society, 2,* 282–285.

Kolb, B., & Fantie, B. (1997). Development of the child's brain and behavior. In C. R. Reynolds & E. Fletcher-Janzen (Eds.), *Handbook of clinical child neuropsychology* (2nd ed., pp. 17–41). New York: Plenum Press.

Kurke, M. I. (1986). Anatomy of product liability/personal injury litigation. In M. I. Kurke & R. G. Meyer (Eds.), *Psychology in product liability and personal injury litigation* (pp. 3–15). Washington, DC: Hemisphere.

Laing, L. C., & Fisher, J. M. (1997). Neuropsychology in civil proceedings. In R. J. McCaffrey, A. D. Williams, J. M. Fisher, & L. C. Laing (Eds.), *The practice of forensic neuropsychology: Meeting challenges in the courtroom* (pp. 117–133). New York: Plenum Press.

Lees-Haley, P. R., Smith, H. H., Williams, C. W., & Dunn, J. T. (1996). Forensic neuropsychological test usage: An empirical study. *Archives of Clinical Neuropsychology, 11,* 45–51.

Lezak, M. D. (1995). *Neuropsychological assessment* (2nd ed.). New York: Oxford University Press.

Livingood, J. A. (1994). Admissibility and reliability of expert scientific testimony after Daubert. *Defense Counsel Journal, 61,* 19–21.

Matarazzo, J. D. (1987). Validity of psychological assessment: From the clinic to the courtroom. *The Clinical Neuropsychologist, 1,* 307–314.

Melton, G. B. (1994). Expert opinions: "Not for cosmic understanding. " In B. D. Sales & G. R. VandenBos (Eds.), *Psychology in litigation and legislation: Master lectures in psychology* (pp. 59–99). Washington, DC: American Psychological Association.

Munsterberg, H. (1908). *On the witness stand.* New York: Doubleday.

Pankratz, L., & Erickson, R. C. (1990). Two views of malingering. *The Clinical Neuropsychologist, 4,* 379–389.

Puente, A. (1987). Social Security Disability and clinical neuropsychological assessment. *The Clinical Neuropsychologist, 1,* 353–363.

Puente, A. E. (1997). Forensic clinical neuropsychology as a paradigm for clinical neuropsychological assessment: Basic and emerging issues. In R. J. McCaffrey, A. D. Williams, J. M. Fisher, & L. C. Laing (Eds.), *The practice of forensic neuropsychology: Meeting challenges in the courtroom* (pp. 165–175). New York: Plenum Press.

Puente, A. E., & Gillespie, J. B. (1991). Workers' compensation and clinical neuropsychological assessment. In J. Dywan, R. D. Kaplan, & F. J. Pirozzolo (Eds.), *Neuropsychology and the law* (pp. 39–63). New York: Springer-Verlag.

Putnam, S. H., DeLuca, J. W., & Anderson, C. (1994). The second TCN salary survey: A survey of neuropsychologists. Part II. *The Clinical Neuropsychologist, 8,* 245–282.

Raskin, S. A., Mateer, C. A., & Tweeten, R. (1998). Neuropsychological assessment of individuals with mild traumatic brain injury. *The Clinical Neuropsychologist, 12,* 21–30.

Reed, J. E. (1996). Fixed vs. flexible neuropsychological test batteries under the Daubert Standard for the admissibility of scientific evidence. *Behavioral Sciences and the Law, 14,* 315–322.

Reitan, R. M., & Wolfson, D. (1985). *The Halstead–Reitan Neuropsychological Test Battery.* Tucson, AZ: Neuropsychology Press.

Richardson, R. E., & Adams, R. L. (1992). Neuropsychologists as expert witnesses: Issues of admissibility. *The Clinical Neuropsychologist, 6,* 295–308.

Rimel, R. W., Bruno, G., Barth, J. T., Boll, T. J., & Jane, J. A. (1981). Disability caused by minor head injury. *Neurosurgery, 9,* 221–228.

Rogers, R. (1988). Introduction. In R. Rogers (Ed.), *Clinical assessment of malingering and deception* (p. 19). New York: Guilford Press.

Ryan, J. J., & Paolo, A. M. (1992). A screening procedure for estimating premorbid intelligence in the elderly. *The Clinical Neuropsychologist, 6*(1), 53–62.

Salmon, P. G., & Meyer, R. G. (1986). Neuropsychology and its implications for personal injury assessment: Adults. In M. I. Kurke & R. G. Meyer (Eds.), *Psychology in product liability and personal injury litigation* (pp. 157–184). Washington, DC: Hemisphere.

Schwartz, M. L. (1991). Sometimes safe, sometimes out: Umpire gives split decision. *The Clinical Neuropsychologist, 5,* 89–99.

Sorenson, S., & Krause, J. F. (1991). Occurrence, severity, and outcomes of brain injury. *Journal of Head Trauma Rehabilitation, 6,* 1–10.

State v. Driver, 88 W. Va. 479, 107 S.E. 189 (1921).

Wedding, D. (1983). Clinical and statistical prediction in neuropsychology. *Clinical Neuropsychology, 5,* 49–55.

Wedding, D. (1991). Clinical judgement in forensic neuropsychology: A comment on the risks of claiming more than can be delivered. *Neuropsychology Review, 2,* 223–239.

Williams, A. D. (1997). The forensic evaluation of adult traumatic brain injury. In R. J. McCaffrey, A. D. Williams, J. M. Fisher, & L. C. Craig (Eds.), *The practice of forensic neuropsychology* (pp. 37–56). New York: Plenum Press.

Ziskin, J., & Faust, D. (1988). Challenging clinical judgement. In J. Ziskin & D. Faust (Eds.), *Coping with psychiatric and psychological testimony* (Vol. 1, 4th ed., pp. 220–295). Marina del Rey, CA: Law & Psychology Press.

17

Brain Tumors

Marc W. Haut, Stephen M. Bloomfield,
Jody Kashden, and Jennifer S. Haut

Brain tumor often conjures up a bleak outcome. Our goal in this chapter is to emphasize the high degree of variability associated with brain tumors in terms of deficits, prognosis, and rehabilitation potential. To successfully work with individuals with brain tumors, one must have a healthy respect for the design of individual treatment plans in the context of patient-specific disease variables, treatment variables, current functioning, prognosis, and patient and family goals. We review tumor types, treatments, skills needed for working with this population, quality of life, and rehabilitation. We also address developmental issues.

Patients with brain tumors have played a significant role in the development of current understandings of human cognition. The lesion model of human cognition contains examples of specific deficits associated with brain tumors localized to different brain areas. The medical literature contains recent studies on the neuropsychological and quality-of-life aspects of brain tumors. Unfortunately, there has been little systematic study of the rehabilitation of patients with brain tumors. We located only two outcome studies of rehabilitation for patients with brain tumors (Philip, Ayyangar, Vanderbilt, & Gaebler-Spira, 1994; Sherer, Meyers, & Bergloff, 1997). We are not certain of the reasons, but there are two plausible explanations. Until recently, many health professionals may not have seen the value of providing rehabilitation to someone with a death sentence. This is a mistake for two reasons. As one outcome study points out, patients with primary malignant tumors benefit from rehabilitation. Moreover, not all brain tumors result in certain death. Another explanation for the lack of research on rehabilitation outcome in patients with brain tumors is that the patients may often be treated within the general rubric of "brain injury." This is a population that is both different from and similar to those with stroke and head injury.

This chapter provides the background on the issues unique to that population. We believe that an understanding of the unique characteristic of the population enables treatment of patients with brain tumors within established brain injury rehabilitation programs. With advances in treatment and thus survival time, the need for rehabilitation increases.

Epidemiology

In 1983, 12,000 adult patients died in the United States because of primary brain tumors; among an estimated 400,000 deaths from systemic cancer, 100,000 had some type of brain involvement (Adams, Victor, & Ropper, 1997). Recent epidemiological research indicates that the incidence of patients with brain tumors is rapidly increasing (Davis, Ahlbom, Hole, & Percy, 1991), largely because patients with metastatic brain tumors are living longer with more effective treatment of their primary cancers. Primary brain tumors may also be increasing because of the increase in incidence of patients with cerebral lymphoma. In 1994, the estimated annual incidence of newly diagnosed primary central nervous system (CNS) tumors in the United States was 17,500, with more than 85,000 patients diagnosed with metastatic brain tumors (Boring, Squires, Tong, & Montagomery, 1994). In adults, brain tumors are the third leading cause of cancer-related death in men younger than 55 and the fourth leading cause in women younger than 35 (Posner, 1993). In children, brain tumors are the most common solid neoplasm and the second most common cause of death (Cogen & Nolan, 1996). The prevalence of brain tumors in children is between 2.2 and 2.5 per 100,000 (Dennis, Spiegler, Hoffman et al., 1991; Spreen, Risser, & Edgell, 1995). The annual incidence of all types of patients with brain tumors is 46 per 100,000 people in the United States (Posner, 1993).

Pathology

When a brain tumor is identified, a common concern is whether it is benign or malignant. The term *malignant* often invokes emotional reactions, whereas the term *benign* seems to have a comforting ring of security. However, all neoplasms are cancerous and are made up of abnormal tissue that grows over time. The terms *malignant* and *benign* refer to the ends of a spectrum of conditions that influence the biological behavior of the brain tumor. The characteristics of malignant lesions include rapid growth rates, microscopic infiltration into the brain, the tendency to spread throughout the brain, and relative resistance to treatment efforts. The characteristics of benign lesions include relatively slow growth rates and a circumscribed nature without direct invasion of the brain, and they are amenable to surgical removal or responsive to other treatments. However, even low-grade or slow-growing gliomas are associated with significant changes in cognitive functions (e.g., Taphoorn et al., 1994).

Brain tumors evolve from the different tissues within and around the brain. Table 17.1 describes the frequency of the various tumor types in a large combined series consisting of over 15,000 patients between 1920 and 1970 (Adams et al., 1997). The prognosis and clinical outcomes of patients with different brain tumors is best described by the 5-year survival rate, which indicates the percentage of patients surviving 5 years after diagnosis. The Victorian Cancer Registry identified over 4,000 patients diag-

Table 17.1. Tumor Incidence and Survival Rates

Brain tumor type	Incidence (%)	Outcome (%)[a]
Glioblastoma multiforme	20[b]	4[c]
Astrocytoma	10[b]	43[c]
Medulloblastoma	4[b]	41[c]
Oligodendroglioma	5[b]	47[c]
Ependymoma	6[b]	59[c]
Meningioma	15–30[d]	83[e]

[a]Percentage of patients who are alive 5 years after diagnosis. [b]Adams, Victor, & Ropper (1997). [c]Giles & Gonzales (1995). [d]DeMonte & Al-Mefty (1995). [e]Simpson (1957).

nosed with brain tumors in Australia between 1982 and 1991 (Giles & Gonzales, 1995). The column on the right in Table 17.1 identifies the 5-year survival rates of patients with various types of brain tumors.

Primary Brain Tumors

Gliomas are malignant tumors representing a family of brain tumors that arise from various cells in the brain. These cells include astrocytes that maintain homeostasis for the neurons, ependymal cells that line the ventricles, and oligodendroglia cells that form the myelin. The most common glioma is composed of astrocytes, which have been subclassified into grades that predict growth rates. Low-grade astrocytomas microscopically invade the brain and tend to mingle with functioning brain tissue. Higher grade astrocytomas, glioblastoma multiforme and anaplastic astrocytomas, typically occur in the cerebrum and are very infiltrative. Edema is commonly associated with these tumors, and a cystic component may be present. Oligodendrogliomas are typically low-grade tumors. Ependymomas grow into the ventricle or surrounding brain tissue. Medulloblastomas arise in the cerebellum and are a developmental tumor affecting children ages 4–8. Primary cerebral lymphoma is observed most commonly around the ventricles but can occur in any location in the brain and is multifocal. Primary cerebral lymphoma may occur in immunosuppressed patients.

Meningiomas are usually benign tumors that arise from the coverings of the brain, falx, or tentorium. They rarely invade the brain and are potentially curable with surgery. Meningiomas grow very slowly. The presenting clinical syndrome depends on the location of the lesion and the function of the surrounding brain areas that become compressed. Almost half of meningiomas arise from the top or lateral convexity surfaces of the brain, making them relatively amenable to surgical resection. Cerebral edema of the brain adjacent to meningiomas has been demonstrated in the majority of patients leading to increased intracranial pressure and neurological symptoms (Go, Wilmink, & Molenaar, 1988). Patients with convexity meningiomas usually have more complete excisions and better outcomes than patients with base-of-skull meningiomas, who tend to fare less well because it is difficult to completely resect the tumor and the dural attachments.

Metastatic Brain Tumors

Cancers in the body usually spread to the brain by the bloodstream. Hematogenous spread of cancer typically follows the blood flow patterns to the brain, with the tumor seed usually coming to rest in the cortex at the gray–white matter junction. The tumor seed begins to grow radially outward within the brain, leading to pressure on surrounding brain structures. Blood vessels formed by the metastatic brain tumors have an imperfect blood–brain barrier, which leads to significant swelling and mass effect around the tumor. The cerebral cortex is the site of 80–85% of metastatic brain tumors (Delattre, Krol, Thaler, & Posner, 1988). At the time of initial presentation 37–50% of patients are found to have a single metastatic lesion, but on autopsy 60–85% of patients who died from systemic cancer had multiple brain metastases (Delattre et al., 1988; Takakura, Sano, Hojo, Fujimaki, & Nakamura, 1982).

Treatment

In terms of treatment, neurodevelopmental factors add variability in that children of the same age often vary in their developmental progress, particularly when a tumor adds unpredictable effects on brain development. Response to treatment and even treatment choice may differ, depending on the neurodevelopmental stage of the child. Clinical lore used to maintain that the earlier the neurological insult, the better the outcome, but recent research has shown that there appear to be significant limits to the idea that neurodevelopmental plasticity engenders better recovery. It may be most appropriate to consider the developing brain as vulnerable to early insult with the potential for sparing of function relative to the adult brain. Early acquired brain injuries may result in more significant long-term deficits in the survivor, whereas older children and adolescents with similar injuires seem to show less significant cognitive sequelae (Levin et al., 1993).

Surgery

In general, the surgical treatment of tumors provides the best option in terms of survival time. For example, surgical resection is the primary treatment for meningiomas. However, not all tumors are surgical candidates. Lymphoma is not typically resected; given its diffuse nature, surgery would result in substantial amounts of good tissue being resected. Some high-grade gliomas are not resected because of their location (dominant hemisphere or brain stem) or if they spread across the midline through the corpus callosum. Some low-grade tumors are not resected because they are in eloquent cortex, and the diffuse infiltrative nature means that functional tissue would be resected to capture the lesion. Surgical strategies balance the desire to remove the maximal amount of tumor burden with minimal impact on brain function. This balance is significantly influenced by the location of the tumor. The main neuropsychological side effects from surgery result from the resection of functional tissue, so the residual deficits are a product of surgery at a specific site.

The prevalence of tumors in children varies from that in adults, and many are amenable to a surgical cure (Cogen & Nolan, 1996). For example, cystic cerebellar astrocytomas occur almost exclusively in children and are considered to be surgically curable. Pontine gliomas are observed rarely in adults; they are not surgical candidates, have a poorer prognosis, and are treated with chemotherapy and radiation (Cogen & Nolan, 1996). However, even in children who have been treated surgically for a benign brain tumor, there is an increase in behavioral and adjustment difficulties, perhaps because of increased stress on the family (Harbeck-Weber & Conaway, 1994) or continuing subtle disruption to neurodevelopmental processes that clinicians are unable to detect or quantify. We are aware of several children who have had benign cerebellar tumors surgically removed, requiring no further medical intervention, and later met the criteria for a diagnosis of attention deficit hyperactivity disorder (ADHD). Although these may have been unrelated events, there may be some connection between a relatively silent brain area with regard to cognitive skills and the manifestation of behavioral difficulties. Cerebellar involvement has recently been linked to the development of appropriate executive functioning and frontal-lobe skills (Ciesielski, Harris, Hart, & Pabst, 1997) and may be related to ADHD, given reports of executive dysfunction in this disorder. This point illustrates that surgical cure of brain tumors in children may not necessarily indicate the absence of cognitive–behavioral sequelae in the future.

Radiation Therapy

Radiation therapy has been a mainstay of treatment for malignant CNS tumors and even for benign lesions that are not curable by surgery (Karim, 1995). Radiation therapy applies an ionizing high-energy beam that attacks the tumor cells on a cellular level, destroying the metabolic machinery of many cells and leading to significant cell death and tumor shrinkage. Frequently, cellular destruction is limited to the genetic machinery, making it impossible for the tumor cell to divide, thereby impeding any further growth of the tumor. The probability of tumor cure or control increases with dose, but the dose that can be delivered is usually limited by tolerance of the surrounding brain tissue to the radiation effects. Radiation damage at high enough doses can lead to necrosis of normal brain tissue. Normal brain tissue is highly differentiated, has a low metabolic rate, no longer divides, and is inherently less susceptible to radiation damage than are rapidly dividing tumor cells. The relationship between the probability of tumor control and the probability of radiation injury defines the therapeutic ratio. Computer-guided convergent beam radiation therapy reduces the exposure of the surrounding brain while increasing the total dose to the tumor by the use of computers to accurately aim many radiation therapy beams to a prescribed target volume.

Adverse reactions of the brain to radiation therapy have been divided into three phases according to when the reaction occurs (Sheline, 1980). Acute radiation injury occurs during the course of radiation therapy; it results in dry desquamation (peeling) of the scalp, hair loss, headaches, nausea, lethargy, otitis media, and edema leading to both an increase in focal neurological deficits and increased intracranial pressure. Early-delayed radiation injury, which develops a few months after treatment, leads to a diffuse encephalopathy and somnolence. Late-delayed radiation injury is a major clinical hazard appearing several months to a year or more after treatment. It is thought to be due to damage to the microcirculation of the brain that can lead to white matter change, loss of cortical volume, or cell death. It is generally an irreversible, progressive, dose-related process, which can be fatal. Patients develop signs and symptoms of both increasing focal neurological deficits and diffuse encephalopathy. The incidence and severity of damage to the brain have increased with the advent of more aggressive radiotherapy techniques, such as the direct implantation of radioactive seeds into the tumor and radiosurgery (Karim, 1995). In terms of neuropsychological effects, an abundance of the data comes from childhood survivors of leukemia.

Research into the effects of radiation therapy for CNS tumors generally shows poorer cognitive outcome in children who are younger than 6 (Silverman et al., 1984) or 8 years at the time of treatment (Mulhern & Kun, 1985). Children older than 6 years showed more improvement and less deterioration in cognitive functioning than younger children. Greater impairment was also associated with supratentorial compared with posterior fossa tumors (Mulhern & Kun, 1985). Other researchers (Spreen et al., 1995) have noted that children under 5 years and particularly under 3 years are more susceptible to cognitive deficit and decline caused by radiation therapy. In a review of this issue, Dennis et al. (1992) noted that the "critical" age for cognitive vulnerability after radiation treatment has been found to be anywhere between 3 and 8 years. Most of the research investigating cognitive functioning in children and adolescents with brain tumors has been limited to intellectual and academic skills (Baron, Fennell, & Voeller, 1995). However, a series of studies focuses on memory in addition to intellectual functioning (Dennis, Spiegler, Hoffman et al., 1991; Dennis, Spiegler, Fitz et al., 1991; Dennis et al., 1992). This reveals evidence for a more complex relationship between age at time of radiation and cognitive functioning; specifically, verbal but not nonverbal intellectual functioning varied positively with age at the time of radiation treatment (Dennis et al., 1992). Thus, verbally based intellectual functioning appears to be more susceptible to radiation at younger ages. Memory performance was not associated with radiation, even when analyses included possible variation related to the age at treatment (Dennis et al., 1992).

Two complicating factors in these results are the presence of closed head injury (20%) in the sample (Spreen et al., 1995) and varying location and tumor types, in some cases resulting in small experimental cell size. Clearly, more specific investigation is indicated, and cooperative research groups are currently studying these issues (Baron et al., 1995).

The effects of radiation on quality of life and cognitive functions are being studied in clinical trials in adults (Vigliani, Sichez, Poisson, & Delattre, 1996). It has been reported that radiation treatment does not produce changes in cognition above and beyond changes associated with the tumor in patients with low-grade gliomas (Taphoorn et al., 1994). There is some evidence that treatment of low-grade gliomas does not cause long-term risk of significant cognitive change at 2-year follow-up and that the initial early delayed effects are reversible (Vigliani et al., 1996). This is supported by a study that demonstrated little loss of higher cortical skills, with only motor slowing noted (Glosser et al., 1997). This study is important because the participants were patients with skull-based lesions, so the complications of an intracranial process were removed from the effect of radiation on cognitive functions. However, the initial recovery of function from early-delayed effects can be followed by a decline in memory function representing late-delayed effects (Armstrong, Ruffer, Corn, DeVries, & Mollman, 1995) secondary to microvascular changes. Finally, whole-brain radiation has a greater impact on cognitive functioning than more focal radiation (Gregor et al., 1996).

Chemotherapy

Chemotherapy is typically administered to patients with malignant gliomas, medulloblastoma, lymphoma, and some metastatic brain tumors, resulting in a prolonging of survival (Flowers & Levin, 1995). Tumor shrinkage occurs with chemotherapy for medulloblastoma and lymphoma. There are some reports of changes in cognition associated with chemotherapy with brain involvement (Scheibel, Meyers, & Levin, 1996) and in patients without CNS disease (Meyers & Abbruzzese, 1992). Toxicity to the brain from standard intravenous chemotherapy is limited by the blood–brain barrier, which reduces the absorption of the drug into the brain. The barrier unfortunately limits the benefits of chemotherapy by also reducing absorption into the brain tumor. Techniques that increase the concentrations of chemotherapy in the tumor, such as implantation of wafers soaked with drugs into the tumor bed and intra-arterial infusion or intrathecal infusion into the ventricles, can be associated with diffuse encephalopathy (Flowers & Levin, 1995).

Skills for Psychologists

Competent practice as a rehabilitation neuropsychologist begins with specialization in neuropsychology. The standard guidelines for specialized neuropsychological training at the doctoral, internship, and postdoctoral levels were established by the INS–Division 40 (International Neuropsychological Association and American Psychological Association's Division 40) Task Force on Education, Accreditation, and Credentialing (1987). More recently, the Houston Conference on Specialty Education and Training in Clinical Neuropsychology (1998) updated and expanded the INS–Division 40 guidelines and published comprehensive guidelines from graduate school beyond postdoctoral training. Both sets of guidelines are geared toward preparing an individual to qualify as a diplomate in clinical neuropsychology by the American Board of Professional Psychology.

A clinical neuropsychologist must be able to function in a variety of settings, including a rehabilitation setting. The special demands in a rehabilitation setting may be best addressed through the purposeful cultivation of skills designed to fit a rehabilitation setting. Division 22 of the American Psychological Association in conjunction with the American Congress of Rehabilitation Medicine have developed guidelines for training in rehabilitation psychology (Patterson & Hanson, 1995). The merging of the training guidelines for neuropsychology and rehabilitation may at present be best captured by the suggestions of Johnstone and Farmer (1997), who recommended training and experiences in functional outcome to complement traditional neuropsychological skills. A neuropsychologist working with patients with brain tumors in a rehabilitation setting needs a strong knowledge of brain behavior relationships and an appreciation of the philosophy of rehabilitation. Treating children with brain tumors requires a strong appreciation of neurodevelopmental issues.

Ability to Perform a Neuropsychological Assessment

The areas assessed neuropsychologically in patients with brain tumors are really no different than what would be assessed in any patient with suspected brain dysfunction. A comprehensive evaluation is helpful in the delineation of strengths and weaknesses. This is particularly relevant because many factors influence brain function, such as tumor location, tumor type, edema, treatment effects, and developmental stage.

A comprehensive neuropsychological evaluation must include a thorough clinical interview. The clinical interview can provide key information regarding issues such as appearance, level of alertness, insight, interpersonal skills, humor, disposition, and psychological status. It is important to ascertain whether the patient has symptoms that might best be managed by medication (e.g., depression, disinhibition) so that appropriate treatment decisions can be made. The clinical interview can be useful in providing samples of behavior problems identified through more objective testing. Standardized, psychometrically sound testing instruments are used to illustrate cognitive functioning in a systematic manner. In our experience, a flexible-battery approach with emphasis on process (Kaplan, 1988) leads to the most useful data for rehabilitation and treatment planning. Brain tumor effects on cognition are controlled by numerous variables. An evaluation that focuses on the individual is most appropriate. For example, not all patients with frontal-lobe lesions demonstrate frontal–executive dysfunction, and those who do show deficits on different tasks. One should be prepared to alter the battery, depending on the history obtained in the interview and performance during the evaluation.

The assessment strategy should be largely directed by the tumor location. Practioners are referred to classic texts that fully address specific deficits associated with specific lesion locations (e.g., Heilman & Valenstein, 1993). The degree of focal deficits seen in patients with a brain tumor is not the same as that seen in patients who have had a stroke (Anderson, Damasio, & Tranel, 1990), but patients with brain tumors do show signs consistent with the effects on a specific hemisphere (Scheibel et al., 1996). The lack of focal deficits in some patients maybe an additional reason why patients with brain tumors do not receive rehabilitation (Meyers, Boake, Levin, & Ratliff, 1996). Table 17.2 lists tumor locations and tests of particular interest for specific functions. Given the variability of functioning encountered with patients with brain tumors, these tests should be considered only as suggestions. Measures should be matched to ability, and we have attempted to provide examples of the tests that we have found most helpful. In many cases, a good bedside neurobehavioral examination is all that the patient can tolerate and provides more than enough information to assist with treatment planning and rehabilitation. We encourage clinicians to use experimentally based tasks, such as procedural learning, to find strengths when developing a treatment program.

Assessment of frontal-lobe lesions should focus on tests of abstraction, flexibility, or planning. If a dominant hemisphere frontal lesion is present, language production skills should be emphasized and apraxia is ruled out. With patients having temporal-lobe lesions, clinicians should focus on measure of memory, with emphasis on material-specific differentiation of skills. Measures that allow a clinician to differentiate between the different aspects of memory dysfunction (e.g., encoding) have great relevance for treatment planning. With patients having parietal-lobe lesions, clinicians should focus on tactile sensation and spatial and visual perceptual skills, with an emphasis on language comprehension, reading, or writing if the lesion is in the dominant hemisphere. The focus for occipital-lobe lesions should be visual processing of language for the left hemisphere and perception for the right one. Syndromes such as alexia, agraphia, and visual–spatial neglect should always be checked when patients have lesions of the parietal as well as occipital lobes. Finally, lesions of subcortical structures result in emphasis on many of the areas described above, depending on which connections to cortical areas are disrupted. Lesions involving the thalamus or basal ganglia can produce language and memory impairment (Crosson, 1992), whereas lesions of the third ventricle can produce severe amnesia (McMackin, Cockburn, Anslow, & Gaffan, 1995). Regardless of the location, we believe that all patients should receive measures of memory, processing, and abstraction because these skills are most likely to have the greatest effect on functioning, in addition to the focal effects produced by a lesion (e.g., hemispatial neglect).

Table 17.2. Neuropsychological Measures

Lesion location	Assessment area	Measure
Frontal lobe	Abstraction	Wisconsin Card Sorting Test[a]
		Booklet Category Test[b]
	Flexibility	Trail Making Test[c]
		Stroop Color Word Test[d]
	Planning	Rey Osterrieth Figure-Copy[e]
		Picture Arrangement subtest of the WAIS–III[f]
	Language (nonfluent aphasia)	Boston Naming Test[g]
		Controlled Oral Word Association Test[h]
		Animal Naming[i]
Temporal lobe	Verbal memory	California Verbal Learning Test[j]
		Hopkins Verbal Learning Test[k]
		CERAD Word List[l]
		Logical Memory subtest of the WMS–III[m]
		Recognition Memory Test—Word Subtest[n]
	Visual memory	Rey Osterrieth Figure[e]
		Visual Reproduction subtest of the WMS–III[m]
		Recognition Memory Test—Faces Subtest[n]
Parietal lobe	Language (alexia, agraphia, fluent aphasia)	Boston Diagnostic Aphasia Examination[o]
	Visual perceptual	Visual Form Discrimination[p]
		Judgment of Line Orientation[o]
		Facial Recognition[o]
		Hooper Visual Organization Test[p]
	Tactile	Double Simultaneous Stimulation
		Finger Recognition
		Grahathesia
Occipital lobe	Perceptual	Line Bisection
	Language (alexia, agraphia)	Boston Diagnostic Aphasia Examination[q]
General measures	Attention	Digit Span subtest of the WAIS–III[f]
	Processing	Digit Symbol subtest of the WAIS–III[f]

Note. WMS–III = Wechsler Memory Scale (3rd ed.); WAIS–III = Wechsler Adult Intelligence Scale (3rd ed.); CERAD = Center to Establish a Registry for Alzheimer's Disease. [a]Heaton (1981). [b]Defilippis et al. (1979). [c]Reitan and Wolfson (1985). [d]Golden (1978). [e]Lezak (1995). [f]Wechsler (1997a). [g]Kaplan et al. (1983). [h]Benton and Hamsher (1978). [i]Goodglass and Kaplan (1983). [j]Delis et al. (1987). [k]Benedict et al. (1998). [l]Morris et al. (1989). [m]Wechsler (1997b). [n]Warrington (1984). [o]Benton et al. (1994). [p]Hooper (1983). [q]Goodglass and Kaplan (1983).

Psychological Skills and Psychotherapy

Psychological functioning can be directly affected by brain tumors (e.g., Price, Goetz, & Lovell, 1992). Although many patients with brain tumors do show evidence of cognitive and psychological dysfunction, there is no absolute relationship.

Providing care to patients with brain tumors requires strong general clinical skills. Patients and their caretakers often require psychotherapy to facilitate management of their condition and its associated stressors. Therapy involving the patient must take into consideration factors such as physical status and cognitive functioning. The stress of having a brain tumor may exacerbate long-standing dysfunction and introduce new areas of dysfunction. Psychotherapy targeting specific psychopathology may be warranted to teach the patient more effective coping skills and ways of managing new behavioral tendencies and thought patterns. Denial is a common coping mechanism that initially may be successful in reducing fears, especially in the early stage of the illness (Price et al., 1992). As the illness progresses, denial can cause problems for patients and families in coping effectively, complying with treatment, and making timely decisions. Denial as a coping mechanism should be differentiated from anosagnosia, or unawareness of deficits as a result of changes to the CNS. Supportive psychotherapy can be extremely helpful for the patient and caretakers in providing a forum to deal with difficult issues and stresses on the patient's support system. Supportive psychotherapy ideally is reality based, with a strong educational component, and focuses on issues such as diagnosis, prognosis, impact of the illness, and dealing with loss (Price et al., 1992). We cannot overemphasize the importance of education for the patient and the family (Haut, Haut, & Bloomfield, 1991). This is particularly helpful in addressing symptoms such as anosagnosia to help the family understand the patient's behavior. A wealth of information is available from the National Brain Tumor Foundation. An important issue to address with patients is the inability to do the tasks that previously provided positive reinforcement. Finding alternative activities to maintain self-esteem is important to the psychological well-being of patients.

Children with brain tumors may also benefit from psychotherapy, as was demonstrated in a group of boys who participated in a treatment program targeting social skills (Die-Trill et al., 1996). During psychotherapy, children with brain tumors can address the social pressures that they may experience related to changes in physical appearance, stamina, and cognitive functioning. Families may benefit as well. Initial recovery from treatment for a brain tumor in children and adolescents is likely to change the focus of family functioning; this may lead to secondary consequences, such as another child vying for attention through behavioral transgressions. Patients often have difficulty adjusting to a return to normalcy when they no longer receive increased attention or when the attention shifts into more demanding activities, such as return to school.

The child recovering from a brain tumor and returning to school often faces special challenges. Compromised cognitive and behavioral functioning may be coupled with more generalized effects, such as fatigue. One patient treated in our clinic demonstrated a dramatic drop in school performance, eventually obtaining failing grades. Her fatigue limited her ability to gather her books at the end of the day, so she stopped bringing them home, doing little homework as a result. The problem was solved by asking the school for a second set of books that she could keep at home. Peers may be initially curious about the child's experience, but with time they may become less tolerant of the child's cognitive or behavioral difficulties. For example, impulsive behavior or increased aggressiveness may interfere with a friendship. Children are more likely to be subjected to inappropriate remarks from peers than are adults, and the psychosocial consequences may be most difficult for adolescents, who experience an increased emphasis on appearance. Changes in appearance may be primary to the tumor (e.g., hemiplegia) or secondary to its treatment (e.g., hair loss). Depending on the child's stamina and cognitive status, return to school should be accomplished in a gradual fashion, with consideration being given for home-bound tutoring and partial-day attendance at the outset. This is particularly relevant for children undergoing radiation and chemotherapy. Attempts should be made to maximize success so that the child is not overwhelmed by frustration.

More concrete, behaviorally based treatments may be more effective than insight-oriented therapy in treating patients with brain tumor because cognitive impairment is often associated with brain tumors. Pharmacotherapy can be a helpful supplement to effective psychotherapy and should be considered for patients who show psychological dysfunction, which affects a patient's quality of life.

In cancer patients, quality of life as a measurable and important outcome parameter has become increasingly recognized (Trojanowski et al., 1989). There have been several recent studies highlighting quality of life as a key outcome parameter in the treatment of brain tumor patients (e.g., Weitzner & Meyers, 1996). Although many physicians rely on patient interview to obtain a general sense of their patient's quality of life, there now exists a variety of psychometrically sound quality-of-life instruments to be used with cancer patients (see chapter 12, this volume). Several articles provide comprehensive reviews of such instruments (e.g., Cella & Tulsky, 1990). The Functional Assessment of Cancer Therapy Scale (Cella et al., 1993) has been modified to include a subscale for brain tumor patients (Weitzner et al., 1995). In addition, the Medical Outcome Study SF-36 (Ware, Snow, Kosinski, & Gandek, 1993) is widely used with medical populations.

Brain tumors, like all significant medical illnesses, affect more than the patient. Families and support systems are stressed any time a major illness affects a member. Educating the patient and family on treatment issues and cognitive and behavioral changes eases their burden and diminishes their worry. It is easier to deal with a difficult known than an easy unknown. Families and patients do better when they understand the reason for their symptoms and know what the symptoms mean. When clinicians check mental status, the patient and family receive immediate feedback and interpretation. Family variables appear to be related to outcomes in pediatric patients with a brain tumor, and a combination of family and illness variables is the best predictor of intellectual outcome (Carlson-Green, Morris, & Krawiecki, 1995). In our experience patients and their families benefit greatly from a friendly, familiar face and quality listening in the complex world of medical treatment of brain tumors.

Outcome

We are aware of two outcome studies of rehabilitation of patients with brain tumor. One study examined adults with primary malignant brain tumors (Sherer et al., 1997). Thirteen patients were examined, 9 of whom had anaplastic astrocytomas. The patients received typical medical treatment, including surgical debulking and radiation therapy. Twelve of the patients received chemotherapy. The patients were an average of 75 months postdiagnosis. Rehabilitation occurred in a postacute outpatient clinic for patients with traumatic brain injury (TBI). Treatment was individualized to the patient's deficits and directed toward functional limitations. Patients were treated in the clinic first and were then transferred to a community setting. After treatment, the number of independent patients increased from 1 to 5, and 6 were independent at follow-up. Eight of the patients had an increase in productivity, with 4 working competitively, 1 working a modified job, and 3 returning to school. The authors noted the methodological limitations of sample size and lack of blind clinician ratings. In addition, there was no control or comparison group. Despite these limits, this study does provide support for involving patients with primary brain tumors in outpatient rehabilitation programs using strategies developed for patients with TBI.

A second study examined inpatient rehabilitation for children and adolescents (Philip et al., 1994). Thirty children and adolescents (mean age = 10.8 years) underwent an average of 41 days of inpatient rehabilitation. The majority of patients had medulloblastomas and cerebellar astrocytomas. Twenty-three patients had surgery, 22 had radiation, and 7 underwent chemotherapy. Improvement was documented at discharge for overall functional ability, self-care, locomotion, communication, and social cognition. For a sample of 20 patients available for follow-up, functioning showed further improvement. The lack of a control group limits the specific conclusions regarding the efficacy of rehabilitation.

Rehabilitation services provided to individuals with brain tumors are limited. Sixty-two percent of acute and postacute rehabilitation treatment centers provided services to fewer than 10 patients with brain tumors per year (Meyers et al., 1996). One group dedicated to researching, promoting, and supporting rehabilitation services for patients with brain tumors is Christina Meyers and her colleagues at M. D. Andersen Cancer Center in Houston, TX (Meyers et al., 1996). They emphasize that patients with brain tumors differ from those with stroke and that rehabilitation should account for the differences. With recognition of the differences, clinicians can treat patients with brain tumors within existing brain injury programs.

The following are the issues that need to be considered. Prognosis depends greatly on the tumor pathology. Patients with more malignant primary gliomas often survive 2 years from diagnosis to death. Rehabilitation should focus on maximizing the patients' quality of life during that time. We find that brief inpatient rehabilitation stays that focus on providing a rapid transition to home care is often the most feasible and practical in the context of the patient's quality of life. Complicated treatment schedules and fatigue from treatment often prevent full participation in comprehensive rehabilitation. If treatment can be accomplished to some degree in the home, the patient can receive the benefits of treatment and rehabilitation. The goals for treatment may be maintaining function. With lower grade tumors or benign lesions such as meningiomas, there can be a period of gradual recovery and no decline for many years, a course similar to that experienced by patients who have had a stroke or TBI.

The second consideration is understanding the influence of treatment variables. For example, radiation therapy may produce an initial decline of cognition followed by a rebound of functioning. Patients with high-grade malignant lesions are more susceptible to variations in brain function. The flu or a urinary tract infection may produce an exaggerated effect on functioning. In addition, steroids are used to treat edema and can have an immediate effect on focal neurological symptoms by decreasing swelling and a very positive short-term effect on quality of life.

The third consideration is family issues and support, particularly for patients with highly malignant lesions. It is appropriate to discuss death and dying issues, but we firmly believe in and suggest a model of rehabilitation that does not assume that all patients and families go through a series of stages that include depression or grieving. Patients and families should be treated individually, and symptoms that interfere with functioning, such as depression, should be addressed up front. The use of psychoactive medication to improve mood, increase energy, or control disinhibition are strongly encouraged. The aim is to enhance the quality of remaining time.

Conclusion

In summary, there is a paucity of outcome literature on the rehabilitation of patients with brain tumors. Most clinicians have either not provided rehabilitation to individuals with brain tumors or, when doing so, have provided treatment within the context of a standard brain injury program. We believe that it is appropriate to use the existing rehabilitation structure to provide treatment to patients with brain tumors as long as their individual needs are met in the context of the type of brain tumor, the treatment being performed, and the goals of the patient and family. Clearly more research is needed on the benefits of rehabilitation with patients with brain tumors. As treatment advances and life is prolonged, greater numbers of individuals will require rehabilitation.

References

Adams, R. D., Victor, M., & Ropper, A. H. (1997). Intracranial neoplasms and paraneoplastic disorders. (1997). In R. D. Adams, M. Victor, & A. H. Ropper (Eds.), *Principles of neurology* (6th ed., pp. 642–694). New York: McGraw-Hill.

Anderson, S. W., Damasio, H., & Tranel, D. (1990). Neuropsychological impairments associated with lesions caused by tumor or stroke. *Archives of Neurology, 47*, 397–405.

Armstrong, C., Ruffer, J., Corn, B., DeVries, K., & Mollman, J. (1995). Biphasic patterns of memory deficits following moderate-dose partial-brain irradiation: Neuropsychologic outcome and proposed mechanisms. *Journal of Clinical Oncology, 13*, 2263–2271.

Baron, I. S., Fennell, E. B., & Voeller, K. K. S. (1995). *Pediatric neuropsychology in the medical setting.* New York: Oxford University Press.

Benedict, R. H., Schretlen, D., Groniger, L., & Brandt, J. (1998). Hopkins Verbal Learning Test—Revised: Normative data and analysis of inter-form and test-retest reliability. *Clinical Neuropsychologist, 12*, 43–55.

Benton, A. L., & Hamsher, K. (1978). *Multilingual aphasia examination.* Iowa City: University of Iowa Press.

Benton, A. L., Sivan, A. B., Hamsher, K., Varney, N. R., & Spreen, O. (1994). *Contributions to neuropsychological assessment* (2nd ed.). New York: Oxford University Press.

Boring, C. C., Squires, T. S., Tong, T., & Montagomery, S. (1994). Cancer statistics, 1994. *CA Cancer Journal Clinical, 44*, 7–26.

Carlson-Green, B., Morris, R. D., & Krawiecki, N. (1995). Family and illness predictors of outcome in pediatric brain tumors. *Journal of Pediatric Psychology, 20*, 769–784.

Cella, D. F., & Tulsky, D. S. (1990). Measuring quality of life today: Methodological aspects. *Oncology, 4*, 29–38.

Cella, D. F., Tulsky, D. S., Gray, G., Sarafian, B., Linn, E., Bonomi, A., Silberman, M., Yellen, S. B., & Brannon, J. (1993). The functional assessment of cancer therapy scale: Development and validation of the general measure. *Journal of Clinical Oncology, 11*, 570–579.

Ciesielski, K. T., Harris, R. J., Hart, B. L., & Pabst, H. F. (1997). Cerebellar hypoplasia and frontal lobe cognitive deficits in disorders of early childhood. *Neuropsychologia, 35*, 643–655.

Cogen, P. H., & Nolan, C. P. (1996). Intracranial and intraspinal tumors of children. In B. O. Berg (Ed.), *Principles of child neurology* (pp. 731–748). New York: McGraw Hill.

Crosson, B. (1992). *Subcortical functions in language and memory.* New York: Guilford Press.

Davis, D. L., Ahlbom, A., Hole, D., & Percy, C. (1991). Is brain cancer mortality increasing in industrial countries? *American Journal of Internal Medicine, 19*, 421–431.

DeFilippis, N. A., McCampbell, E., & Rogers, P. (1979). Development of a booklet form of the Category Test: Normative and validity data. *Journal of Clinical Neuropsychology, 1*, 339–342.

Delattre, J., Krol, G., Thaler, H., & Posner, J. B. (1988). Distribution of brain metastases. *Archives of Neurology, 45*, 741–744.

Delis, D. C., Kramer, J. H., Kaplan, E., & Ober, B. A. (1987). *The California Verbal Learning Test.* San Antonio, TX: The Psychological Corporation.

DeMonte, F., & Al-Mefty, O. (1995). Meningiomas. In A. Kaye & E. R. Laws, Jr. (Eds.), *Brain tumors: An encyclopedic approach* (pp. 675–704). New York: Churchill Livingston.

Dennis, M., Spiegler, B. J., Fitz, C. R., Hoffman, H. J., Hendrick, E. B., Humphreys, R. P., & Chuang, S. (1991). Brain tumors in children and adolescents: II. The neuroanatomy of deficits in working, associative, and serial-order memory. *Neuropsychologia, 29*, 829–847.

Dennis, M., Spiegler, B. J., Hoffman, H. J., Hendrick, E. B., Humphreys, R. P., & Becker, L. E. (1991). Brain tumors in children and adolescents: I. Effects on working, associative and serial-order memory of IQ, age at tumor onset and age of tumor. *Neuropsychologia, 29*, 813–827.

Dennis, M., Spiegler, B. J., Obonsawin, M. C., Maria, B. L., Cowell, C., Hoffman, H. J., Hendrick, E. B., Humphreys, R. P., Bailey, J. D., & Erlich, R. M. (1992). Brain tumors in children and adolescents: III. Effects of radiation and hormone status on intelligence and on working, associative and serial-order memory. *Neuropsychologia, 30*, 257–275.

Die-Trill, M., Bromberg, J., LaVally, B., Portales, L. A., SanFeliz, A., & Patenaude, A. F. (1996). Development of social skills in boys with brain tumors: A group approach. *Journal of Psychosocial Oncology, 14*, 23–41.

Flowers, A., & Levin, V. A. (1995). Chemotherapy for brain tumors. In A. Kay & E. R Laws (Eds.), *Brain tumors: An encyclopedic approach* (pp. 349–360). New York: Churchill Livingstone.

Giles, G. G., & Gonzales, M. F. (1995). Epidemiology of brain tumors and factors in prognosis. In A. Kaye & E. Laws (Eds.), *Brain tumors: An encyclopedic approach* (pp. 31–67). New York: Churchill Livingston.

Glosser, G., McManus, P., Munzenrider, J., Austin-Seymour, M., Fullerton, B., Asams, J., & Urie, M. M. (1997). Neuropsychological function in adults after high dose fractionated radiation therapy of skull base tumors. *International Journal of Radiation Oncology and Biological Physics, 38*, 231–239.

Go, K. G., Wilmink, J. T., & Molenaar, W. M. (1988). Peritumoral edema associated with meningiomas. *Neurosurgery, 23*, 175–179.

Golden, C. J. (1978). *Stroop Color–Word Test*. Chicago: Stoeling.

Goodglass, H., & Kaplan, E. (1983). *Assessment of aphasia and related disorders* (2nd ed.). Philadelphia: Lea & Febiger.

Gregor, A., Cull, A., Traynor, E., Stewart, M., Lander, F., & Love, S. (1996). Neuropsychometric evaluation of long-term survivors of adult brain tumors: Relationship with tumor and treatment parameters. *Radiotherapy & Oncology, 41*, 55–59.

Harbeck-Weber, C., & Conaway, L.P. (1994). Childhood cancers: Psychological issues. In R. A. Olson, L. L. Mullins, J. B. Gillman, J. M. Chaney (Eds.), *The sourcebook of pediatric psychology* (pp. 98–110). Boston: Allyn & Bacon.

Haut, M. W., Haut, J. S., & Bloomfield, S. M. (1991). Family issues in rehabilitation of patients with malignant brain tumors. *Neurorehabilitation, 1*, 39–47.

Heaton, R. K. (1981). *A manual for the Wisconsin Card Sorting Test*. Odessa, FL: Psychological Assessment Resources.

Heilman, K. M., & Valenstein, E. (1993). *Clinical neuropsychology* (3rd ed.). New York: Oxford University Press.

Hooper, H. E. (1983). *Hooper Visual Organization Test (VOT)*. Los Angeles, CA: Western Psychological Services.

Houston Conference on Specialty Education and Training in Clinical Neuropsychology. (1998). Proceedings of the Houston Conference on Specialty Education and Training in Clinical Neuropsychology. *Archives of Clinical Neuropsychology, 13*, 157–249.

INS–Division 40 Task Force on Education, Accreditation, and Credentialing. (1987). Report of the INS–Division 40 Task Force on Education, Accreditation, and Credentialing. *The Clinical Neuropsychologist, 1*, 20–34.

Johnstone, B., & Farmer, J. E. (1997). Preparing neuropsychologists for the future: The need for additional training guidelines. *Archives of Clinical Neuropsychology, 12*, 523–530.

Kaplan, E. (1988). A process approach to neuropsychological assessment. In T. Boll & B. K. Bryant (Eds.), *Clinical neuropsychology and brain function: Research measurement and practice* (pp. 125–167). Washington, DC: American Psychological Association.

Kaplan, E., Goodglass, H., & Weintraub, S. (1983). *The Boston Naming Test*. Philadelphia: Lea & Febiger.

Karim, A. B. M. F. (1995). Radiation therapy and radiosurgery for brain tumors. In A. Kaye & E. Laws (Eds.), *Brain tumors: An encyclopedic approach* (pp. 331–348). New York: Churchill Livingston.

Levin, H. S., Culhane, K. A., Mendelsohn, D., Lilly, M. A., Bruce, D., Fletcher, J. M., Chapman, S. B., Harward, H., & Eisenberg, H. M. (1993). Cognition in relation to magnetic resonance imaging in head-injured children and adolescents. *Archives of Neurology, 50*, 897–905.

Lezak, M. D. (1995). *Neuropsychological assessment* (3rd ed.). New York: Oxford University Press.

McMackin, D., Cockburn, J., Anslow, P., & Gaffan, D. (1995). Correlation of fornix damage with memory impairment in six cases of colloid cyst removal. *Acta Neurochirurgica, 135*, 12–18.

Meyers, C. A., & Abbruzzese, J. L. (1992). Cognitive functioning in cancer patients: Effects of previous treatments. *Neurology, 42*, 434–436.

Meyers, C. A., Boake, C., Levin, V. A., & Ratliff, D. D. (1996). Symptom management, rehabilitation strategies, and improved quality of life for patients with brain tumors. In V. A. Levin (Ed.), *Cancer in the nervous system* (pp. 449–462). New York: Churchill Livingstone.

Morris, J. C., Heyman, A., Mohs, R. C., Hughes, J. P., van Belle, G., Fillenbaum, G., Mellitis, E. D., Clark, C., and the CERAD investigators. (1989). The Consortium to Establish a Registry for Alzheimer's Disease (CERAD). Part I. Clinical and neuropsychological assessment of Alzheimer's disease. *Neurology, 39*, 1159–1165.

Mulhern, R. K., & Kun, L. E. (1985). Neuropsychologic function in children with brain tumors: III. Interval changes in the six months following treatment. *Medical and Pediatric Oncology, 13*, 318–324.

Patterson, D. R., & Hanson, S. L. (1995). Joint division 22 and ACRM guidelines for postdoctoral training in rehabilitation psychology. *Rehabilitation Psychology, 40*, 299–310.

Philip, P. A., Ayyangar, R., Vanderbilt, J., & Gaebler-Spira, D. J. (1994). Rehabilitation outcome in children after treatment of primary brain tumor. *Archives of Physical Medicine and Rehabilitation, 75*, 36–39.

Posner, J. B. (1993). Brain tumors. *CA Cancer Journal Clinical, 43*, 261–262.

Price, T. R., Goetz, K. L., & Lovell, M. R. (1992). Neuropsychiatric aspects of brain tumors. In S. C. Yudofsky & R. E. Hales (Eds.), *Textbook of neuropsychiatry* (2nd ed., pp. 473–497). Washington, DC: American Psychiatric Press.

Reitan, R. M., & Wolfson, D. (1985). *The Halstead–Reitan Neuropsychological Test Battery: Theory and clinical interpretation*. Tucson, AZ: Neuropsychology Press.

Scheibel, R. S., Meyers, C. A., & Levin, V. A. (1996). Cognitive dysfunction following surgery for intracerebral glioma: Influence of histopathology, lesion location, and treatment. *Journal of Neuro-oncology, 30*, 61–69.

Sheline, G. E. (1980). Irradiation injury of the human brain: A review of clinical experience. In H. A. Gilert & A. R. Kagan (Eds.), *Radiation damage to the nervous system* (pp. 39–52). New York: Raven Press.

Sherer, M., Meyers, C. A., & Bergloff, P. (1997). Efficacy of postacute brain injury rehabilitation for patients with primary malignant brain tumors. *Cancer, 80*, 250–257.

Silverman, C. L., Palkes, H., Talent, B. A., Kovnar, E., Clouse, J. W., & Thomas, P. R. M. (1984). Late effects of radiotherapy on patients with cerebellar medulloblastoma. *Cancer, 54*, 825–829.

Simpson, D. (1957). The recurrence of intracranial meningiomas after surgical treatment. *Journal of Neurology, Neurosurgery, and Psychiatry, 20*, 22–39.

Spreen, O., Risser, A. H., & Edgell, D. (1995). *Developmental neuropsychology*. New York: Oxford University Press.

Takakura, K., Sano, K., Hojo, S., Fujimaki, T., & Nakamura, O. (1982). *Metastatic tumors of the nervous system*. New York: Igaku-Shoin.

Taphoorn, M. J. B., Schiphorst, A. K., Snoek, F. J., Lindeboom, J., Wolbers, J. G., Karim, A. B. M. F., Hujgens, P. C., & Heimans, J. J. (1994). Cognitive functions and quality of life in patients with low-grade gliomas: The impact of radiotherapy. *Annals of Neurology, 36*, 48–54.

Trojanowski, T., Peszynski, J., Turowski, K., Markiewicz, P., Goscinski, I., Bielawski, A., Bendarzewska, B., Szymona, J., Dabrowska, A., Lopatkiewicz, J., Czochra, T., Jeziernicka, B., Basinska, G., & Kozniewska, H. (1989). Quality of survival of patients with brain gliomas treated with postoperative CCNU and radiation therapy. *Journal of Neurosurgery, 70,* 18–23.

Vigliani, M. C., Sichez, N., Poisson, M., & Delattre, J. Y. (1996). Prospective study of cognitive functions following conventional radiotherapy for supratentorial gliomas in young adults: 4 year results. *International Journal of Radiation Oncology and Biological Physics, 35,* 527–533.

Ware, J. E., Snow, K. K., Kosinski, M., & Gandek, B. (1993). *SF-36 Health Survey Manual and Interpretation Guide.* Boston: New England Medical Center, Health Institute.

Warrington, E. K. (1984). *Recognition Memory Test.* Windsor, Derks, England: NFER-Nelson.

Wechsler, D. A. (1997a). *Wechsler Adult Intelligence Scale—III.* New York: The Psychological Corporation.

Wechsler, D. A. (1997b). *Wechsler Memory Scale—III.* New York: The Psychological Corporation.

Weitzner, M. A., & Meyers, C. A. (1996). Cognitive functioning and quality of life in malignant glioma patients: A review of the literature. *Psychooncology, 6,* 169–177.

Weitzner, M. A., Meyers, C. A., Gelke, C. K., Byrne, K. S., Cella, D. F., & Levin, V. A. (1995). The Functional Assessment of Cancer Therapy (FACT) Scale: Development of a brain subscale and revalidation of the general version (FACT-G) in patients with primary brain tumors. *Cancer, 75,* 1151–1161.

18

Pediatric Neuropsychology

Janet E. Farmer and Laura Muhlenbruck

The number of children who survive life-threatening illnesses, injuries, and congenital disorders has increased steadily with advances in medical technology (Wallander & Thompson, 1995). Neurological impairments are common among survivors and can result in physical, cognitive, and behavioral disabilities. These children and their families often require medical rehabilitation services to optimize functional outcomes and improve quality of life. The primary role of the pediatric neuropsychologist on the rehabilitation team is to assess each child's level of cognitive and behavioral functioning in order to assist with treatment planning.

Children treated in medical rehabilitation vary widely in the nature and complexity of their presenting problems (Richards, Elliott, Cotliar, & Stevenson, 1995). From a neuropsychological perspective, children can be classified into four main groups. Many children experience sudden onset, acquired brain injury as a result of events such as head trauma, stroke, viral and infectious diseases, and hypoxic injuries. Some youngsters experience more gradual, insidious declines in functioning because of diseases affecting the central nervous system (CNS), such as brain tumors, leukemia, and other forms of cancer; they often receive rehabilitation services following debilitating treatment regimens. Others have neurodevelopmental disorders, including cerebral palsy and spina bifida (see chapter 6), with primary physical dysfunction and increased risk of cognitive deficits. A fourth group consists of children receiving rehabilitation services for injury- or illness-related physical disabilities that are not typically associated with cerebral damage (e.g., burns, amputation, juvenile rheumatoid arthritis), among whom a subgroup of children have learning problems similar to those that occur in the general population (e.g., developmental delays and learning disabilities).

Our purpose in this chapter is to discuss the application of pediatric neuropsychology to meet the various needs of these children during the rehabilitation process. Children may be referred during the course of an inpatient hospitalization or as the result of concerns raised during outpatient clinic visits or therapies. Because most young people with disabilities and chronic illnesses return to school, questions for the pediatric neuropsychologist are often raised by educators as well. The neuropsychologist frequently interacts with both the rehabilitation and educational treatment teams, allowing a unique opportunity to support continuity of care across systems.

Historical Perspective

As a field, pediatric neuropsychology is still in its infancy. Contributions to the assessment and understanding of brain–behavior relationships in children have come from many disciplines, including child clinical psychology, school psychology, adult neuropsychology, developmental psychology, cognitive psychology, neurolinguistics, psychobiology, and neurology (Baron, Fennell, & Voeller, 1995; Bigler, 1996). However, research on brain–behavior relationships in children has lagged behind such study in adults for several reasons. First, many clinicians have been influenced heavily by early evidence that youth offers protection against the negative effects of brain injury (Ryan, LaMarche, Barth, & Boll, 1996). This belief was driven by researchers who examined brain plasticity during development and found a remarkable potential for cerebral reorganization and recovery of function in the immature brain (e.g., Kennard, 1940). In addition, subsequent studies such as those of Bruce et al. (1979) suggest a relatively low mortality rate of children with serious neurological injury compared to adults. These studies provided important insights into the resilient aspects of the developing brain, but they did not capture the full scope of morbidity associated with childhood brain injury (Kolb & Fantie, 1997; Taylor & Alden, 1997) and may have inadvertently discouraged examination of brain-based changes in child functioning.

A second reason that pediatric neuropsychology has developed more slowly is the lack of adequate measurement strategies for assessment of cognition in youth at varying stages of development. Early measures were often downward extensions of adult neuropsychological tests that were not normed by age and that did not capture key areas of vulnerability such as memory and learning (e.g., Halstead–Reitan Neuropsychological Battery for Children 9 to 14; Reitan & Davison, 1974). Finally, the complex relationship between brain structure and function was poorly understood in the normally developing brain, making it difficult to document changes associated with neurological insult during childhood and adolescence.

Several factors worked synergistically to create contemporary patterns of growth in the field of pediatric neuropsychology. Public policy decisions in the 1960s and 1970s such as the Education for All Handicapped Children Act of 1975 (P. L. 94-142) placed value on the needs of children with disabilities in the United States and led to increased funding for research. A growing number of researchers began to document the link between neurologic aberrations and childhood disorders of learning and behavior (e.g., Galaburda & Kemper, 1979; Levin & Eisenberg, 1979; Rutter, Chadwick, Shaffer, & Brown, 1980). Despite their methodological limitations, neuropsychological batteries and related tests for children became more widely available in the 1970s and 1980s (Golden, 1986; Kaufman & Kaufman, 1983; Reitan & Davison, 1974).

At the same time as awareness of the needs of children with neurological dysfunction increased, rapid developments in allied neuroscience fields produced new neurodiagnostic imaging techniques and advanced methodology for understanding microanatomical changes at the cellular level (Bigler, 1997). These refinements have led to greater knowledge about normal brain growth and development; more specific questions about developmental pathology following brain injury; expansion of the instrumentation used by clinicians to assess neurodevelopmental functioning; and accumulating evidence of the impact of physical disease, injury, and congenital brain abnormalities on children's learning and behavioral adaptation (Baron et al., 1995; Batchelor & Dean, 1996; Reynolds & Fletcher-Janzen, 1997; Spreen, Risser, & Edgell, 1995). In the past 5–10 years, there has been steady growth in publication outlets for pediatric neuropsychology research, including journals such as *Child Neuropsychology*, *Journal of Learning Disabilities*, *Journal of Pediatric Psychology*, *Developmental Neuropsychology*, and *Pediatric Rehabilitation*. In 1995, the growth of this subspecialty resulted in the formation of the Pediatric Neuropsychology Interest Group within Division 40 of the American Psychological Association (Yeates & Shapiro, 1997).

Parallel to these events, continuing evidence of the potential for enhancing brain development and recovery through enriching and supportive environments (Bigler, 1996; Taylor, 1996) has fueled the growth of pediatric rehabilitation and educational interventions for children with neurological disorders. However, descriptions of clinical applications of pediatric neuropsychology to medical rehabilitation are relatively few, and treatment outcomes research is minimal (Batchelor, 1996a). The number of psychologists conducting such child neuropsychological assessments is unknown, and specific training standards have not been established (Shapiro & Ziegler, 1997). Despite these challenges to the field, there is great potential for psychologists to use emerging neuropsychological measurement strategies and research about brain–behavior relationships in children to improve child rehabilitation outcomes.

Fundamental Concepts

Pediatric neuropsychologists in rehabilitation settings adhere to the basic premises of general neuropsychological assessment: Brain functioning and behavior are causally related, and cognitive or behavioral deficits resulting from cerebral damage can be identified and treated. However, three factors shape service provision by pediatric neuropsychologists in rehabilitation settings: (a) the importance of development as a determinant of brain–behavior relationships in children; (b) the emphasis in rehabilitation on treatment goals and functional outcomes, as opposed to diagnosis; and (c) the interdisciplinary team approach to assessment.

Role of Development

A fundamental concept in pediatric neuropsychology is that children are not simply small adults (Baron et al., 1995); they have a developing CNS and a constantly changing skills level. Behaviors that are normal and expected at one age level can be abnormal and unexpected at subsequent ages (e.g., falling on the floor in a temper tantrum is normal in a 2-year-old but unusual in a 12-year-old). Furthermore, developmental milestones typically emerge unevenly, with substantial variability in rate of skills acquisition both within and across children.

Assessment of children with neurological impairments must consider two parallel processes that influence behavior: normal maturational changes and adaptations associated with recovery from cerebral damage. The task of the child neuropsychologist is to tease out the impact of known or suspected cerebral injury on an already complex and changing system. This can be a daunting assignment for a number of reasons. The behavioral expression of brain injury in young people varies greatly, depending not only on the location and extent of neurologic damage, but also on the age at injury. Like adults, children can show full or partial recovery of functioning after loss of ability caused by neurological insults. On the other hand, children are unique because cerebral damage can also lead to delayed emergence of new skills or the failure of such skills to emerge at all. A child may exhibit generally age-appropriate functioning shortly after injury, followed by the late onset of impairments as more mature abilities fail to develop. Although brain plasticity and the capacity for cerebral reorganization may be greater in children than adults, a growing body of literature documents that younger age at injury is associated with poorer developmental outcomes (Kolb & Fantie, 1997; Taylor & Alden, 1997). Early brain injury can exact a toll on new learning abilities and developing cognitive skills, which in turn interferes with subsequent maturation.

Other factors also make the process of child assessment challenging. For instance, brain–behavior relationships identified in adult neuropsychology often do not apply to children and youth, making it difficult to draw conclusions about the localization of brain injury on the basis of test results (Baron et al., 1995; Batchelor, 1996b; Taylor & Fletcher, 1990). The rules that allow inferences about brain localization in adults may be disrupted because of the child's stage of brain development or because of idiopathic patterns of cerebral reorganization resulting from early brain lesions. Test interpretation is also confounded by factors such as the lack of premorbid baseline data in young injured children; error variance caused by children's easy fatigability, limited attention span, and motivational fluctuations; and the increased influence of social and environmental factors on rate of early development. Thus, maturational level is a central concept in pediatric neuropsychology and in its application to rehabilitation. It shapes the biological response to injury, the presenting problems, the methods of assessment, the interpretation of test performance, and treatment options.

Focus on Treatment Goals and Functional Outcomes

Neuropsychology as a field developed from a tradition of diagnostic assessments aimed at localizing lesions and describing structure–function relationships. Tests were designed to accurately measure CNS integrity and emphasized "neurological" validity (Taylor & Schatschneider, 1992). Pediatric neuropsychologists in rehabilitation settings may focus on diagnosis at times, such as when they are asked to determine whether a child's learning problems are related to his or her early history of brain injury. However, neuropsychological assessment in rehabilitation settings is primarily treatment oriented (Johnstone & Farmer, 1997). That is, the ultimate purpose of assessment during rehabilitation is to determine ways to increase everyday functioning in real-world settings. The assessment process must provide data that have "ecological" validity, that is, the ability to describe the child's capabilities, predict level of functioning in daily activities, and define a treatment plan (Sbordone & Long, 1996). Specific assessment goals during rehabilitation treatment may be the following:

- to determine the child's cognitive, behavioral, social, and emotional competencies
- to document changes in functioning over time
- to indicate to what extent presenting problems are related to neurological dysfunction
- to make prescriptive statements regarding the child's ability to engage in daily activities
- to identify the types of intervention strategies that are most likely to be effective
- to help plan child-focused rehabilitation and educational programs
- to describe environmental and social factors that influence everyday functioning
- to recommend interventions that optimize environmental and social supports.

Depending on the child's individual needs, some goals are likely to be prioritized over others. For example, in the case of a child who is hospitalized after severe traumatic brain injury, the focus might be on assessment of posttraumatic amnesia and on caregiver education about behavioral management strategies for agitation. Once the child has returned home, the focus typically shifts to tracking the course of recovery through outpatient assessments, consultation with the educational team, and identification of family supports in the community.

Assessment that contributes to treatment planning involves more than interpretation of standardized tests. This approach requires ecological assessment of children and their families in a context of multiple systems or levels of influence (Farmer, 1997; Fletcher, Levin, & Butler, 1995; Kazak, 1997; Singer, 1996; Teeter, 1997). Cognitive ability as measured by neuropsychological tests remains a central aspect of assessment and an important indicator of CNS integrity. However, as Taylor and Fletcher

(1990) pointed out, impairments identified by such tests only estimate the upper limits of the child's basic behavioral competencies. The actual level of disability and handicap is more broadly determined over time by interactions between the child and the environment. Because functional outcomes are multiply determined, both child and contextual variables must be assessed to identify a range of treatment options. Exhibit 18.1 depicts variables that influence treatment planning and child outcomes following neurological injury.

Exhibit 18.1. Factors Influencing Outcomes in Children With Neurological Disorders

Child Characteristics
Age at the time of neurologic injury
Severity of injury
Type and persistence of impairments
Time since onset
General health
Premorbid functioning
Postinjury adjustment

Family Characteristics
Socioeconomic status
Family size and structure
Level of education
Cultural background
Stage of family life cycle
Premorbid functioning
Postinjury adjustment
Coping resources
Social supports
Other life stressors
Advocacy skills

Community Characteristics
Educational services
   Teacher knowledge about neurologic injury
   Support from school administrators
   Availability of ancillary services
Formal community support services
   Medical and rehabilitation services
   Mental health services
   Social services (housing, transportation, financial assistance)
   Vocational rehabilitation
   Support groups
   Interagency service coordination
Public and private funding resources
Informal support networks (e.g., relatives, friends, coworkers, church and service
   groups)
Attitudes toward disability
Public policy

To illustrate, the neuropsychological assessment of an 8-year-old girl with a history of spina bifida, hydrocephalus, and multiple shunt revisions is likely to identify cognitive impairments in nonverbal processing and oral discourse and significant sensorimotor problems (Baron & Goldberger, 1993; Dennis & Barnes, 1993). This girl undoubtedly needs specialized, child-focused interventions to maximize learning, social integration, and long-term level of independence. However, the extent of her disability may vary considerably, depending on social and environmental circumstances, such as whether she lives with an uninsured single mother in an isolated rural town or with an insured, middle-class family in an area with medical, rehabilitation, and educational resources. Specific treatment recommendations by the neuropsychologist must take such circumstances into account.

Interdisciplinary Team Approach

A third principal shaping assessment strategy in rehabilitation settings is a philosophical commitment to teamwork and interdisciplinary collaboration. Children treated in rehabilitation typically have complex needs that extend beyond the expertise of any single discipline. Furthermore, cognitive assessments are conducted by several disciplines, including the neuropsychologist, the speech–language pathologist, the occupational therapist, and sometimes an educational specialist. Poor communication among these specialists can result in extensive testing with either an incorrect or incomplete picture of the child's abilities, inadequate treatment goals, and less-than-optimal child outcomes (Ylvisaker et al., 1990).

Coordinated team assessments can be more efficient and effective. For example, to assess the cognition of an adolescent boy with severe spastic cerebral palsy, the occupational therapist may check the child's positioning prior to the assessment to optimize his ease of responding, and the speech–language therapist may facilitate his use of an augmentative communication device. While these preparations are underway, the neuropsychologist may observe attentional and motivational factors that suggest a clear limit to the amount of assessment that can be conducted. As a team, these specialists can then decide how to organize and prioritize measurement of perceptual–motor, speech–language, and higher order cognitive functioning. Treatment recommendations are then made on the basis of pooled expertise.

Another aspect of this team model of service delivery is the importance of including input from family members, school personnel, and other community-based professionals in the assessment process. This greatly extends knowledge about the child's presenting problems, behaviors in real-life settings, and the social–environmental context for treatment.

Professional Skills

The pediatric neuropsychologist requires a broad range of clinical knowledge and skills to function effectively in rehabilitation settings. The clinician must have a fund of knowledge about normal child development and brain maturation; understand common changes in child functioning associated with various neurological problems; identify strategies to measure factors that affect child outcomes; integrate multiple viewpoints about the child's abilities and concerns; help plan treatment strategies; and communicate these plans to other professionals and family members. Exhibit 18.2 presents a more detailed list of competencies for pediatric neuropsychologists in rehabilitation settings that are intended to supplement existing Division 40 training guidelines (Hartlage & Long, 1997).

The skills needed to work in rehabilitation overlap considerably with those needed to practice child neuropsychology in other medical and educational settings. However, during rehabilitation, cognitive deficits are rarely the only concern. Children are often physically impaired because of illness, injury, or congenital motor dysfunction. Stressors such as hospitalization, pain, changes in medication, new onset of disability, disfigurement, and disruption of normal routines can tax the coping resources of

Exhibit 18.2.   Core Competencies for the Pediatric Neuropsychologist in Rehabilitation Settings

---

 I. Assessment procedures
   A. Strategies for obtaining background information from parents, therapists, and educators
   B. Selection and administration of children's standardized tests, coordinated with other testing conducted by cognitive therapists or educators
   C. Qualitative assessment strategies
   D. Methods of test interpretation, including integration of neuropsychological results with other team members' assessments
 II. Communication skills
   A. Report writing, with inclusion of data needed for educational diagnosis and treatment
   B. Feedback to child, family, and professionals
III. Intervention skills for children with neurological disorders
   A. Cognitive, behavioral, and multisystems treatment strategies
   B. Consultation with health and education professionals
   C. Interdisciplinary and interagency collaboration skills
   D. Child and family advocacy
IV. Knowledge base
   A. Normal child development
   B. Neuroanatomy of the developing brain
   C. Neuroimaging techniques
   D. The effect of neurological insults on brain development and behavior
   E. Common cognitive and behavioral sequelae of childhood central nervous system disorders
   F. Child and family coping with brain-based disorders
   G. Educational policies and procedures, special education service delivery options
   H. Other state agencies and local community resources for children and their families
   I. Ethical and legal concerns (e.g., child abuse reporting)
   J. Disability mandates and concepts (e.g., inclusive education)

---

even the most well-adjusted child and family. The following sections address assessment procedures and treatment considerations that are applicable to children treated in rehabilitation settings.

Assessment Procedures

An individualized, flexible approach to child neuropsychological assessment is needed during rehabilitation (Farmer, Clippard, Luehr-Wiemann, Wright, & Owings, 1997; Ylvisaker et al., 1990). The first step is to formulate an assessment plan based on the unique characteristics of the child. Important variables to consider are the child's age and general developmental level; the nature of the injury or illness, including time since onset and course; the child's presenting problems; the child's ability to participate in standardized testing (e.g., may have limited response modalities); the length of time the child is available for testing (e.g., may be shortened by decreased child endurance or by plans for rapid discharge from an inpatient rehabilitation setting); recent testing by other therapists and educators; and whether the child needs to participate in serial assessments to track change. Valuable sources of such background information include medical and school records, the child, family members, teachers, and other rehabilitation specialists.

Test selection is the next step in assessment planning. Neuropsychologists have specified domains of functioning that are often affected in children with known neurological disorders and that therefore must be evaluated. These domains are as follows: (a) sensory–perceptual, (b) motor, (c) intellectual–cognitive (e.g., orientation, attention, memory and learning, speed of processing, abstract reasoning, executive functions), (d) academic achievement, (e) communication–language, and (f) personality–behavior (e.g., emotional coping, adaptive behaviors, social integration, behavioral self-regulation). Within these domains, no universally accepted, age-standardized battery of neuropsychological tests exists that is applicable to all children (Bigler, 1996). Instead, clinicians select assessment instruments from a "menu" of tests available in each domain, taking into account child characteristics and using as many standardized tests as possible to answer the specific referral question (for sample menus, see Baron et al., 1995; D'Amato & Rothlisberg, 1997).

Both quantitative, standardized measures and qualitative clinical data contribute to a comprehensive assessment of child functioning during rehabilitation (Batchelor, 1996b; Ylvisaker et al., 1990). Each approach has pros and cons. Standardized measures have the advantage of offering normative age-based comparisons, uniformity of procedure, and the ability to track performance over time. Age-normed measures can provide a frame of reference to help the child, parents, and other professionals understand the child's level of functioning relative to peers. However, children seen in rehabilitation settings often have such significant cognitive and physical impairments that they cannot participate in standardized tests. In addition, such tests sample isolated bits of behavior in a highly regulated testing environment, generally without benefit of any helpful compensatory strategies. This may overestimate the functional skills of children who have difficulty with higher order planning and organization or underestimate the skills of those who function well with supportive accommodations (e.g., assignment notebook, extra time for work completion). Furthermore, simply having a product, such as a low score on a math achievement measure, may not provide sufficient information about how to intervene.

Because of the limits of quantitative tests, qualitative or nonstandardized measures of child functioning are particularly important during rehabilitation. Such assessments might be as simple as altering nonessential features on a standardized test (e.g., the response modality) so that a child with sensory or motor limitations can respond to its content or essential features (Sattler, 1992). However, most qualitative testing relies heavily on the examiner's knowledge base about normal brain development and behavior and about common sequelae of specific neurological disorders. Given a broad fund of such knowledge, the examiner can formulate hypotheses about expected competencies at the child's developmental level and then devise diagnostic tasks to assess the child's ability to meet the expectations (see Ylvisaker, Hartwick, Ross, & Nussbaum, 1994, for a listing of informal probes to use during cognitive assessments).

Using informal assessments, clinicians can examine the process, or how a task is performed, as well as the product, or what is achieved, in both controlled and real-life situations. In addition to noting basic skill levels, the examiner can observe the child's endurance and stamina, ability to initiate and sustain goal-directed behavior, rate of processing complex or lengthy material, retention and generalization of new learning, and awareness of deficits. Aspects of the learning environment (e.g., length of training session, number of distractors) can be manipulated to determine their effect on performance. Data may be collected by directly observing the child or by consulting with other rehabilitation staff, family members, and teachers to obtain their observations. These informal assessments provide rich opportunities to identify functional deficits and the effective use of compensatory strategies and thus have strong implications for treatment. Drawbacks to qualitative assessment include subjectivity and potential examiner bias that can interfere with the reliability and validity of results. Interdisciplinary team assessments may offset some of these drawbacks; drawing on the observations of multiple professionals may decrease the likelihood of error.

To illustrate this assessment approach using a case example, a neuropsychologist was asked to evaluate an 8-year-old inpatient boy following a motor vehicle accident injury that resulted in severe diffuse axonal injury and a 4-week coma. Three weeks after admission to rehabilitation, at the time of consultation, the child had recovered many basic language skills and was dressing and feeding himself with set-up and standby assistance. He was still dependent in mobility because of right-side hemiparesis, and he had toileting accidents throughout the day that were without known medical cause. His parents were frustrated because they thought that he was not trying hard enough to achieve toileting goals. They noted that he could tell them if he needed to use the toilet when they asked. The nursing staff expressed concern that the child might simply be using toileting accidents to gain adult attention because the family visited him infrequently during the course of his hospital stay.

Although the parents and nurses identified behavioral and psychosocial concerns, the neuropsychologist raised questions about attention, orientation, and general level of cognitive functioning at this early stage of recovery. Screening with tests such as those listed in Exhibit 18.3, combined with observation and informal mental status testing, revealed that the child showed a 10–15 minute attention span under highly structured conditions. In addition, he displayed marked impairments in orientation to place and time, memory functioning, oral word fluency, speed of processing, motor dexterity, planning and problem solving, and initiation. His strengths were in one-word receptive language, conversational speech, and visual perception. Interactions with therapists confirmed these observations across treatment settings.

The neuropsychologist provided feedback about the child's cognitive functioning to the parents and rehabilitation team. During the feedback session, the parents expressed distress over their child's slow rate of recovery, their uncertainty about how to help him, and their problems juggling the demands of work and their other children. In response, additional family supports were arranged through the team social worker. An orientation notebook was devised for the child by the rehabilitation team, and the parents were instructed in its use. The nursing staff was educated about this child's cognitive limits, and an externally structured toileting program was successfully implemented. Rehabilitation staff contacted school personnel to provide an update about the child's cognitive status

Exhibit 18.3. Sample Assessment Tools for Screening Children and Adolescents in the Early Stages of Recovery From Moderate to Severe Acquired Brain Injury

---

Children's Orientation and Amnesia Test (Ewing-Cobbs et al., 1990; Iverson et al., 1994)

Kaufman Brief Intelligence Test (Kaufman & Kaufman, 1990)

Test of Nonverbal Intelligence–2 (Brown et al., 1990)

Leiter International Performance Scales–Revised (Roid & Miller, 1997)

Peabody Picture Vocabulary Test–III (Dunn & Dunn, 1997)

Expressive One-Word Picture Vocabulary Test–Revised (Gardner, 1990)

Token Test (Spreen & Strauss, 1998)

Motor-Free Visual Perception Test–Revised (Colarusso & Hummill, 1996)

Bracken Basic Concepts Scale (Bracken, 1984)

Peabody Individual Achievement Test–Revised (Markwardt, 1989)

Selected memory and attention subtests from the Wide Range Assessment of Memory and Learning (Sheslow & Adams, 1990), Test of Memory and Learning (Reynolds & Bigler, 1994), or Children's Memory Scale (Cohen, 1997)

Battelle Developmental Inventory Screening Test (Svinicki, 1984)

NEPSY (Korkman et al., 1998)

---

and to discuss the need to meet closer to the time of discharge to design a school re-entry plan. Thus, the assessment process led directly to multidimensional treatment strategies.

In summary, neuropsychological assessment during rehabilitation must be individually tailored to identify each child's neurocognitive and neurobehavioral strengths and impairments, functional skills in various environments, and social and environmental moderators of disability. This remains an evaluative process that relies heavily on imperfect measures of child functioning and on clinical judgment about relationships among variables (Batchelor, 1996b; Fennell & Bauer, 1997), particularly for children who are recovering from acute brain injury or who have severe impairments. However, when integrated with observations from other team members, results of such assessments yield much useful information for treatment planning.

Treatment Strategies

Assessment results should lead directly to formulations or hypotheses about how to improve the child's level of functioning and prevent secondary disability (e.g., school failure and maladaptive emotional and social adjustment). The goals of treatment vary depending on the child's specific needs. However, Blosser and DePompei (1994) provided a useful guideline; they proposed that child treatment should be designed to achieve four major long-term outcomes: (a) maximum participation in the learning process; (b) development of independent-living skills; (c) competence in social skills needed for communication at home, school, and work; and (d) development of vocational skills. To accomplish these broad objectives, the pediatric neuropsychologist may act primarily as a consultant to rehabilitation and educational teams or may provide direct treatment interventions. Regardless of the exact treatment role, the clinician must be aware of a range of cognitive, behavioral, and systemic interventions to promote well-being in children with neurological impairments.

Cognitive Interventions

There is a small but growing body of literature about the use of cognitive rehabilitation strategies with children (for reviews, see Mateer, Kerns, & Eso, 1997; McCoy, Gelder, VanHorn, & Dean, 1997; Teeter, 1997; Ylvisaker, 1998). Ylvisaker, Szekeres, Hartwick, and Tworek (1994) identified six goals of cognitive rehabilitation:

1. to improve spontaneous recovery through general stimulation
2. to remediate impaired cognitive processes through direct retraining
3. to develop compensatory strategies for residual deficit areas
4. to devise environmental accommodations that promote adequate performance

5. to use instructional procedures that focus on cognitive strengths
6. to increase metacognitive awareness.

These goals reflect three broad approaches to cognitive rehabilitation (Mateer et al., 1997): (a) remediation, (b) compensation, and (c) environmental supports. The first two are focused on the child. *Remediation* involves interventions that attempt to restore or build the child's cognitive-processing capabilities in areas of deficit. Although restorative techniques are often used to support spontaneous recovery immediately following acquired brain injury, such process-training approaches are not generally accepted for children with stable cognitive deficits (Ylvisaker, Szekeres, et al., 1994). Mental-muscle-building strategies, such as rote memory drills, typically are not effective, and improvements do not generalize to functional applications of the skill.

There may be some exceptions to this rule. Mateer et al. (1997) reported evidence of improved attentional abilities following computerized "attention process training" in children. In contrast, Light et al. (1996) did not find similar effects for an attention training module in the Neuro-Cognitive Re-Education Project, a comprehensive program for children with head injuries that provided remediation in attention, memory, behavior, and executive functioning. They did, however, identify significant improvements in children's overall functional skills. Research on cognitive remediation is incomplete. More data are needed to identify which children benefit under various conditions.

Compensation, another child-focused intervention, teaches the child strategies that increase performance on cognitively effortful tasks, without attempting to change the underlying cognitive deficit. Such strategies range from those that are simple and concrete to those that require a fairly high level of general cognitive ability. For example, the child may be taught to use external aides (e.g., daily schedules, calendar, memory notebook, calculator), behavioral strategies (e.g., asking for clarification, using paraphrasing to improve memory and comprehension in social interactions), or metacognitive procedures (e.g., mental self-cuing about steps for problem solving, organizational procedures, mnemonic strategies). There is stronger research support for the use of compensation training than for remediation strategies, particularly among older children and those who are cognitively more intact (Ylvisaker, Szekeres, et al., 1994). The data are mixed, however. For example, the use of self-directed strategies has not resulted in consistent improvements in behavioral or academic performance in children with attention problems (e.g., Abikoff, 1991). There remains much to be learned about how compensatory strategies affect overall learning outcomes and adaptive behaviors.

Finally, externally focused interventions can be used to improve the child's cognitive functioning (Mateer et al., 1997). These include modifying the environment (e.g., removing distractors, increasing the size of print for a child with visual deficits), changing others' expectations regarding the child's performance, or using specialized instructional strategies (e.g., Glang, Singer, Cooley, & Tish, 1992). This approach designs materials and sets up procedures that use the child's cognitive strengths to achieve therapeutic goals (Reynolds & Fletcher-Janzen, 1997).

Neuropsychological assessments can be especially helpful in defining external supports for cognitive remediation. For example, an 11-year-old boy with severe burns to the face and arms and hypoxia caused by inhalation injury was referred by the outpatient occupational therapist and physical therapist because of concerns over the child's memory problems during therapies. Neuropsychological screening revealed significant verbal memory and language-processing problems but also identified generally intact nonverbal functioning. After sharing these findings with the therapists, the neuropsychologist helped the team develop a plan to reach rehabilitation goals by relying primarily on the child's visual-processing strengths (e.g., through visual cuing, pictorial directions, and modeling of new skills). The child's participation and cooperation in therapies improved, as did his learning and level of independence.

Behavioral Interventions

Children with brain-based disorders are at increased risk of both cognitive and behavioral problems, including internalizing and externalizing problems and decreased social competence (Butler, Rourke, Fuerst, & Fisk, 1997; Fletcher et al., 1995; Horton, 1997). Pediatric neuropsychologists in rehabilitation settings must be keenly aware of the association between cognition and behavioral concerns because there will be opportunities to recommend behavioral treatments for children referred for cognitive problems and cognitive treatments for those referred for behavioral problems. Children with neurological impairments are often seen as noncompliant or unmotivated, when in fact their cognitive deficits interfere with task completion or work production. Cognitive problems may be simply underestimated, especially when basic language abilities are intact, or executive functioning problems may interfere with the child's ability to access intact abilities. Cognitive interventions can improve behavioral problems. For instance, Glang et al. (1992) demonstrated that teaching a child with brain injury a metacognitive problem-solving strategy increased frustration tolerance and on-task behavior during math instruction and generalized to other instructional periods.

In other cases, the rehabilitation staff may assume that the behavioral problems of a child with severe cognitive impairments cannot be treated. For example, a 5-year-old boy with a genetic syndrome that caused severe growth delays and mental retardation was admitted to rehabilitation for evaluation after physical abuse by his mother. The youngster was so inattentive and overactive that it was difficult for therapists to assess his level of functioning, even during one-on-one interactions in quiet settings. The neuropsychologist recognized that this level of hyperactivity was not typical for children at his estimated level of cognitive functioning, pharmacological treatment was instituted, and the child's behavior and ability to interact with others improved substantially.

Other researchers have reviewed specific approaches to behavioral interventions for children who have neurological impairments (Horton, 1997; Ylvisaker, 1998). In addition, Fletcher-Janzen and Kade (1997) described a pediatric brain injury rehabilitation program that assesses neuropsychological functioning and uses a therapeutic social milieu to improve child cognitive and behavioral functioning. Although such comprehensive programs are promising, outcome data are limited, so their efficacy remains to be demonstrated.

Systemic Interventions

As discussed previously, outcomes for children with neurological impairments are multiply determined. The pediatric neuropsychologist is often in the unique position of consulting with others in many systems that influence child outcomes. Therefore, treatment recommendations should be considered in the following domains: medical (e.g., review of pharmacological treatment), rehabilitation (e.g., cognitive–behavioral treatments to be implemented by the rehabilitation staff), education (e.g., goals and interventions for academic programming), family (e.g., information about ways to manage behavioral problems), and community (e.g., referrals for additional services from public agencies). These can be communicated either directly through face-to-face feedback and team meetings or indirectly through a written report.

An example of a systemic intervention occurs when a child makes a transition from the rehabilitation hospital to school following a moderate to severe brain injury. This time of transition is a prime opportunity for the pediatric neuropsychologist and other rehabilitation team members to provide information to educators about the child's strengths and needs and to problem solve with representatives from the school about the optimal strategies for school re-entry. There have been protocols developed to aid communication across the rehabilitation and educational systems (e.g., Ylvisaker & Feeney, 1998).

Despite the strong rationale for exchange of information, there are substantial barriers to interdisciplinary and interagency interactions. Team members often lack a common vocabulary and a unified conceptual framework for evaluation and planning. Schedules must be coordinated and time set aside for collaboration. Professional turf issues may impede interactions. Such barriers must be addressed systematically if a team is to become truly efficient and effective. Improvements in team functioning involve adopting a philosophy of collaboration; increasing awareness and appreciation of other members' knowledge base and roles; improving communication through decreased use of professional jargon; structuring in time for interactions; and engaging in joint problem-solving efforts (DePompei & Blosser, 1993; Holland, Hogg, & Farmer, 1997). It is particularly important to include family members in team planning efforts, because they often provide continuity for the child across settings and systems of care.

Functional Outcomes in Children

Because the role of pediatric neuropsychology is so poorly defined in rehabilitation settings, there has been little information about its impact on long-term functional outcomes. It is clear that young people with disabilities are at greatly increased risk of poor educational and vocational outcomes (Farmer & Clippard, 1995; Phelps & Hanley-Maxwell, 1997). Despite equal access to educational services under laws such as the Individuals With Disabilities Education Act (P. L. 101-476, 1990), they are much more likely to live with their parents, less likely to participate in postsecondary education, and more likely to have lower employment rates than their nondisabled peers.

Neuropsychologists can play an important role in improving the functional outcomes of young people with neurological impairments. However, in the world of managed health care, pediatric neuropsychologists must demonstrate that their skills affect children and families in positive ways. For instance, Farmer and Brazeal (1998) conducted a study of parental satisfaction with the process and outcomes of their child's outpatient neuropsychological assessment. As part of the assessment, the family received written reports and verbal feedback about ways to achieve functional goals through interventions at multiple levels (e.g., child, family, school). Parents indicated that the assessment made a difference for their child. They reported increased understanding of their child's impairments and strengths, greater knowledge about treatment strategies and community resources, and a high level of overall satisfaction with the evaluation. This was accomplished without increasing parental distress or negative feelings toward the child. More research on the impact of neuropsychological assessment and intervention is needed to determine how best to improve child and family well-being.

Conclusion

Pediatric neuropsychological assessment in rehabilitation settings must be developmentally sensitive, treatment oriented, and integrated into the continuum of interdisciplinary and interagency services for children with neurodevelopmental disorders. Its conceptual roots are in the understanding of brain–behavior relationships in children, but its branches have extended into applications of that knowledge to treatments involving the child, the rehabilitation team, the family, the school, and the community. This type of assessment is designed not only to diagnose brain-based disorders, but also to produce a positive change in the child's level of functioning and to prevent secondary disability.

There is much to be done to refine this clinical practice. Research is needed to develop additional psychometrically sound and ecologically valid measures of children's cognitive and behavioral functioning, particularly for children who are young, have multiple disabilities, or are in the early stages of recovery from brain insult. Studies must delve inward, to increase understanding of patterns of behavior resulting from specific types of brain injury and to identify biologically based prognostic indicators for long-term outcome. Others must focus more on treatment of the outward manifestations of neurological impairments, carefully defining how best to individualize treatment strategies and support caregivers. Research method problems, including heterogeneity within similar disorders, small sample sizes, nonrepresentative samples, and difficulties establishing an appropriate control group, must be overcome (cf. Taylor & Fletcher, 1995).

In parallel to these efforts, models of service delivery must be created and evaluated to ensure that they are efficient, cost effective, and family centered. New aspects of service delivery are already emerging. First, there is a mounting national effort to see that increasing numbers of children receive rehabilitation services and follow-up care after acute hospitalization (Christopher, 1997). Second, there is a growing trend toward integration of rehabilitation and education services for children with brain-based disorders. Savage (1997) speculated that managed health care pressures and decreasing lengths of hospitalization may encourage greater provision of rehabilitation services in school-based clinics, with service partnerships based on blended funding from public and private sources. Pediatric neuropsychologists must be aware of such trends, as they provide opportunities to participate in a continuum of care for children with neurological disorders and to advocate for improved long-term outcomes.

References

Abikoff, A. (1991). Cognitive training in ADHD children: Less to it than meets the eye. *Journal of Learning Disabilities, 24,* 205–209.

Baron, I. S., Fennell, E. B., & Voeller, K. K. S. (1995). *Pediatric neuropsychology in the medical setting.* New York: Oxford University Press.

Baron, I. S., & Goldberger, E. (1993). Neuropsychological disturbances of hydrocephalic children with implications for special education and rehabilitation. *Neuropsychological Rehabilitation, 3,* 389–410.

Batchelor, E. S. (1996a). Future considerations for rehabilitation research and outcome studies. In E. S. Batchelor & R. S. Dean (Eds.), *Pediatric neuropsychology: Interfacing assessment and treatment for rehabilitation* (pp. 347–352). Boston: Allyn & Bacon.

Batchelor, E. S. (1996b). Neuropsychological assessment of children. In E. S. Batchelor & R. S. Dean (Eds.), *Pediatric neuropsychology: Interfacing assessment and treatment for rehabilitation* (pp. 9–26). Boston: Allyn & Bacon.

Batchelor, E. S., & Dean, R. S. (1996). *Pediatric neuropsychology: Interfacing assessment and treatment for rehabilitation.* Boston: Allyn & Bacon.

Bigler, E. D. (1996). Bridging the gap between psychology and neurology: Future trends in pediatric neuropsychology. In E. S. Batchelor & R. S. Dean (Eds.), *Pediatric neuropsychology: Interfacing assessment and treatment for rehabilitation* (pp. 27–54). Boston: Allyn & Bacon.

Bigler, E. D. (1997). Brain imaging and behavioral outcome in traumatic brain injury. In E. D. Bigler, E. Clark, & J. E. Farmer (Eds.), *Childhood traumatic brain injury* (pp. 7–29). Austin, TX: PRO-Ed.

Blosser, J., & DePompei, R. (1994). *Pediatric traumatic brain injury: Proactive intervention.* San Diego, CA: Singular.

Bracken, B. A. (1984). *Bracken Basic Concepts Scale.* San Antonio, TX: The Psychological Corporation.

Brown, L., Sherbenou, R. J., & Johnsen, S. K. (1990). *Test of Nonverbal Intelligence* (2nd ed.). Austin, TX: PRO-Ed.

Bruce, D. A., Raphaely, R. C., Goldberg, A. I., Zimmerman, R. A., Bilaniuk, L. T., Schut, L., & Kuhl, D. E. (1979). Pathophysiology, treatment, and outcome following severe head injury in children. *Child's Brain, 2*, 174–191.

Butler, K., Rourke, B. P., Fuerst, D. R., & Fisk, J. L. (1997). A typology of psychosocial functioning in pediatric closed-head injury. *Child Neuropsychology, 3*, 98–133.

Christopher, R. P. (1997). Emergency medical services for children: Early referral to physical medicine and rehabilitation. *Archives of Physical Medicine and Rehabilitation, 78*, 339.

Cohen, M. J. (1997). *Children's Memory Scale.* San Antonio, TX: The Psychological Corporation.

Colarusso, R. P., & Hummill, D. D. (1996). *Motor-Free Visual Perception Test—Revised.* Novato, CA: Academic Therapy.

D'Amato, R. C., & Rothlisberg, B. A. (1997). How education should respond to students with traumatic brain injury. In E. D. Bigler, E. Clark, & J. E. Farmer (Eds.), *Childhood traumatic brain injury* (pp. 213–237). Austin, TX: PRO-Ed.

Dennis, M., & Barnes, M. A. (1993). Oral discourse after early-onset hydrocephalus: Linguistic ambiguity, figurative language, speech acts, and script-based inferences. *Journal of Pediatric Psychology, 18*, 639–652.

DePompei, R., & Blosser, J. L. (1993). Professional training and development for pediatric rehabilitation. In C. J. Durgin, M. D. Schmidt, & L. J. Fryer (Eds.), *Staff development and clinical intervention in brain injury rehabilitation* (pp. 229–253). Gaithersburg, MD: Aspen.

Dunn, L. M., & Dunn, E. S. (1997). *Peabody Picture Vocabulary Test—III.* Circle Pines, MN: American Guidance Service.

Education for All Handicapped Children Act of 1975, P.L. 94-142, 89 Stat. 773.

Ewing-Cobbs, L., Levin, H. S., Fletcher, J. M., Miner, M. E., & Eisenberg, H. M. (1990). The Children's Orientation and Amnesia Test: Relationship to severity of acute head injury and to recovery of memory. *NeuroSurgery, 25*, 683–691.

Farmer, J. E. (1997). Epilogue: An ecological-systems approach to childhood traumatic brain injury. In E. D. Bigler, E. Clarke, & J. E. Farmer (Eds.), *Childhood traumatic brain injury* (pp. 261–275). Austin, TX: PRO-Ed.

Farmer, J. E., & Brazeal, T. J. (1998). Parent perceptions about the process and outcomes of child neuropsychological assessment. *Applied Neuropsychology, 5*, 194–201.

Farmer, J. E., & Clippard, D. S. (1995). Educational outcomes in children with disabilities: Linking hospitals and schools. *NeuroRehabilitation, 5*, 49–56.

Farmer, J. E., Clippard, D. S., Luehr-Wiemann, Y., Wright, E., & Owings, S. (1997). Assessing children with traumatic brain injury during rehabilitation: Promoting school and community reentry. In E. D. Bigler, E. Clarke, & J. E. Farmer (Eds.), *Childhood traumatic brain injury* (pp. 33–61). Austin, TX: PRO-Ed.

Fennell, E. B., and Bauer, R. M. (1997). Models of inference and evaluating brain-behavioral relationships in children. In C. R. Reynolds & E. Fletcher-Janzen (Eds.), *Handbook of clinical child neuropsychology* (2nd ed., pp. 204–215). New York: Plenum Press.

Fletcher, J. M., Levin, H. S., & Butler, I. J. (1995). Neurobehavioral effects of brain injury in children: Hydrocephalus, traumatic brain injury, and cerebral palsy. In M. C. Roberts (Ed.), *Handbook of pediatric psychology* (2nd ed., pp. 362–383). New York: Guilford Press.

Fletcher-Janzen, E., & Kade, H. D. (1997). Pediatric brain injury rehabilitation in a neurodevelopmental milieu. In C. R. Reynolds & E. Fletcher-Janzen (Eds.), *Handbook of clinical child neuropsychology* (2nd ed., pp. 452–481). New York: Plenum Press.

Galaburda, A. M., & Kemper, T. L. (1979). Cytoarchitectonic abnormalities in developmental dyslexia: A case study. *Annals of Neurology, 6*, 94–100.

Gardner, M. F. (1990). *Expressive One-Word Picture Vocabulary Test—Revised.* Novato, CA: Academic Therapy.

Glang, A., Singer, G., Cooley, E., & Tish, N. (1992). Tailoring direct instruction techniques for use with elementary students with brain injury. *Journal of Head Trauma Rehabilitation, 7*(4), 93–108.

Golden, C. J. (1986). *Manual for the Luria–Nebraska Neuropsychological Battery: Children's revision.* Los Angeles, CA: Western Psychological Services.

Hartlage, L. C., & Long, C. J. (1997). Development of neuropsychology as a professional psychological speciality: History, training, and credentialing. In C. R. Reynolds & E. Fletcher-Janzen (Eds.), *Handbook of clinical child neuropsychology* (2nd ed., pp. 3–16). New York: Plenum Press.

Holland, D. C., Hogg, J. R., & Farmer, J. E. (1997). Fostering effective team communication: Developing community standards within interdisciplinary cognitive rehabilitation settings. *NeuroRehabilitation, 8,* 21–29.

Horton, A. M. (1997). Child behavioral neuropsychology: Update and further considerations. In C. R. Reynolds & E. Fletcher-Janzen (Eds.), *Handbook of clinical child neuropsychology* (2nd ed., pp. 651–662). New York: Plenum Press.

Individuals With Disabilities Education Act, P. L. 101-476, 104 Stat. 1142.

Iverson, G. L., Iverson, A. M., & Barton, E. A. (1994). The Children's Orientation and Amnesia Test: Educational status is a moderator variable in tracking recovery from TBI. *Brain Injury, 8,* 685–688.

Johnstone, B., & Farmer, J. E. (1997). Preparing neuropsychologists for the future: The need for additional training guidelines. *Archives of Clinical Neuropsychology, 12,* 523–530.

Kaufman, A. S., & Kaufman, N. L. (1983). *Kaufman Assessment Battery for Children (K-ABC) administration and scoring manual.* Circle Pines, MN: American Guidance Service.

Kaufman, A. S., & Kaufman, J. L. (1990). *Kaufman Brief Intelligence Test manual.* Circle Pines, MN: American Guidance Service.

Kazak, A. E. (1997). A contextual family/systems approach to pediatric psychology: Introduction to the special issue. *Journal of Pediatric Psychology, 22,* 141–148.

Kennard, M. A. (1940). Relation of age to motor impairment in man and in subhuman primates. *Archives of Neurology and Psychiatry, 44,* 377–397.

Kolb, B., & Fantie, B. (1997). Development of the child's brain and behavior. In C. R. Reynolds & E. Fletcher-Janzen (Eds.), *Handbook of clinical child neuropsychology* (2nd ed., pp. 17–41). New York: Plenum Press.

Korkman, M., Kirk, U., & Kemp, S. (1998). *NEPSY: A developmental neuropsychological assessment.* San Antonio, TX: The Psychological Corporation.

Levin, H. S., & Eisenberg, H. M. (1979). Neuropsychological impairment after closed head injury in children and adolescents. *Journal of Pediatric Psychology, 4,* 389–402.

Light, R., Satz, P., Asarnow, R. F., Lewis, R., Ribbler, A., & Neumann, E. (1996). Disorders of attention. In E. S. Batchelor & R. S. Dean (Eds.), *Pediatric neuropsychology: Interfacing assessment and treatment for rehabilitation* (pp. 269–302). Boston: Allyn & Bacon.

Markwardt, F. C. (1989). *Peabody Individual Achievement Test—Revised.* Circle Pines, MN: American Guidance Service.

Mateer, C. A., Kerns, K. A., & Eso, K. L. (1997). Management of attention and memory disorders following traumatic brain injury. In E. D. Bigler, E. Clark, & J. E. Farmer (Eds.), *Childhood traumatic brain injury* (pp. 153–175). Austin, TX: PRO-Ed.

McCoy, K. D., Gelder, B. C., VanHorn, R. E., & Dean, R. S. (1997). Approaches to the cognitive rehabilitation of children with neuropsychological impairment. In C. R. Reynolds & E. Fletcher-Janzen (Eds.), *Handbook of clinical child neuropsychology* (2nd ed., pp. 439–451). New York: Plenum Press.

Phelps, L. A. & Hanley-Maxwell, C. (1997). School-to-work transitions for youth with disabilities: A review of outcomes and practices. *Review of Educational Research, 67,* 197–226.

Reitan, R. M., & Davison, L. A. (Eds.). (1974). *Clinical neuropsychology: Current status and applications.* Washington, DC: Winston.

Reynolds, C., & Bigler, E. D. (1994). *The Test of Memory and Learning.* Austin, TX: PRO-Ed.

Reynolds, C. R., & Fletcher-Janzen, E. (Eds.). (1997). *Handbook of clinical child neuropsychology* (2nd ed.). New York: Plenum Press.

Richards, J. S., Elliott, T. R., Cotliar, R., & Stevenson, V. (1995). Pediatric medical rehabilitation. In M. C. Roberts (Ed.) *Handbook of pediatric psychology* (2nd ed., pp. 703–722). New York: Guilford Press.

Roid, G. H., & Miller, L. J. (1997). *Leiter International Performance Scales—Revised*. Wood Dale, IL: Stoelting.

Rutter, M., Chadwick, O., Shaffer, D., & Brown, C. (1980). A prospective study of children with head injuries: I. Description and methods. *Psychological Medicine, 10,* 633–645.

Ryan, T. B., LaMarche, J. A., Barth, J. T., & Boll, T. J. (1996). Neuropsychological consequences in treatment of pediatric head trauma. In E. S. Batchelor & R. S. Dean (Eds.), *Pediatric neuropsychology: Interfacing assessment and treatment for rehabilitation* (pp. 117–138). Boston: Allyn & Bacon.

Sattler, J. M. (1992). *Assessment of children* (3rd ed. rev.). San Diego, CA: Sattler.

Savage, R. C. (1997). Integrating rehabilitation and education services for school-age children with brain injuries. *Journal of Head Trauma Rehabilitation, 12*(2), 11–20.

Sbordone, R. J., & Long, C. (Eds.). (1996). *Ecological validity of neuropsychological testing*. Delray Beach, FL: St. Lucie Press.

Shapiro, E. G., & Ziegler, R. (1997). Training issues in pediatric neuropsychology. *Child Neuropsychology, 3,* 227–229.

Sheslow, D. V., & Adams, W. (1990). *The Wide Range Assessment of Memory and Learning*. Wilmington, DE: Jastak.

Singer, G. H. S. (1996). Constructing supports: Helping families of children with acquired brain injury. In G. H. S. Singer, A. Glang, & J. M. Williams (Eds.), *Children with acquired brain injury: Educating and supporting families* (pp. 1–22). Baltimore: Brookes.

Spreen, O., Risser, A. T., & Edgell, D. (1995). *Developmental neuropsychology*. New York: Oxford University Press.

Spreen, O., & Strauss, E. (1998). *A compendium of neuropsychological tests* (2nd ed.). New York: Oxford University Press.

Svinicki, J. (1984). *Battelle Developmental Inventory Screening Test*. Itasca, IL: Riverside.

Taylor, H. G. (1996). Critical issues and future directions in the development of theories, models, and measurements for attention, memory, and executive function. In G. R. Lyon & N. A. Krasnegor (Eds.), *Attention, memory, and executive function* (pp. 399–412). Baltimore: Brookes.

Taylor, H. G., & Alden, J. (1997). Age-related differences in outcomes following childhood brain insults: An introduction and overview. *Journal of the International Neuropsychological Society, 3,* 555–567.

Taylor, H. G., and Fletcher, J. M. (1990). Neuropsychological assessment of children. In M. Hersen & G. Goldstein (Eds.), *Handbook of psychological assessment* (2nd ed., pp. 228–255). New York: Plenum Press.

Taylor, H. G., & Fletcher, J. M. (1995). Editorial: Progress in pediatric neuropsychology. *Journal of Pediatric Psychology, 20,* 695–701.

Taylor, H. G., & Schatschneider, C. (1992). Child neuropsychological assessment: A test of basic assumptions. *The Clinical Neuropsychologist, 6,* 259–275.

Teeter, P. A. (1997). Neurocognitive interventions for childhood and adolescent disorders: A transactional model. In C. R. Reynolds & E. Fletcher-Janzen (Eds.), *Handbook of clinical child neuropsychology* (2nd ed., pp. 387–417). New York: Plenum Press.

Wallander, J. L., & Thompson, R. J. (1995). Psychosocial adjustment of children with chronic physical conditions. In M. C. Roberts (Ed.), *Handbook of pediatric psychology* (2nd ed., pp. 124–141). New York: Guilford Press.

Yeates, K. O., & Shapiro, E. G. (1997). Introduction to the special section. *Child Neuropsychology, 3,* 226.

Ylvisaker, M. (Ed.). (1998). *Traumatic brain injury rehabilitation: Children and adolescents*. Boston: Butterworth-Heinemann.

Ylvisaker, M., Chorazy, A. J. L., Cohen, S. B., Mastrilli, J. P., Molitor, C. B., Nelson, J., Szekeres, S. F., Valko, A. S., & Jaffe, K. M. (1990). Rehabilitative assessment following head injury in children. In M. Rosenthal, E. R. Griffith, M. R. Bond, & J. D. Miller (Eds.), *Rehabilitation of the adult and child with traumatic brain injury* (2nd ed., pp 558–592). Philadelphia: Davis.

Ylvisaker, M., & Feeney, T. (1998). School reentry after traumatic brain injury. In M. Ylvisaker (Ed.), *Traumatic brain injury rehabilitation: Children and adolescents* (pp. 369–387). Boston: Butterworth-Heinemann.

Ylvisaker, M., Hartwick, P., Ross, B., & Nussbaum, N. (1994). Cognitive assessment. In R. C. Savage & G. F. Wolcott (Eds.), *Educational dimensions of acquired brain injury* (pp. 69–119). Austin, TX: PRO-Ed.

Ylvisaker, M., Szekeres, S. F., Hartwick, P., & Tworek, P. (1994). Cognitive intervention. In R. C. Savage & G. F. Wolcott (Eds.), *Educational dimensions of acquired brain injury* (pp. 121–184). Austin, TX: PRO-Ed.

19

Alcohol and Traumatic Disability

Charles H. Bombardier

Alcohol is arguably the most used and abused drug in the United States. Although most people manage to use alcohol safely without incurring significant harm, 1 in 10 American adults has significant problems related to the use of alcohol (Miller & Brown, 1997). In this chapter I argue that alcohol use and abuse is of particular concern among people with disabilities and that rehabilitation psychologists should become more knowledgeable about these issues. Rates of alcohol problems are particularly high among people with traumatic injuries, including traumatic brain injury (TBI; Corrigan, 1995) and spinal cord injury (SCI; Heinemann, Keen, Donohue, & Schnoll, 1988). Therefore, TBI and SCI are used as examples of disabling conditions in which alcohol-related problems play a significant role. The links between alcohol problems and these two forms of acquired disability are described in terms of the prevalence and effects on outcome. Also described are the major ways in which alcohol problems and models of treatment are conceptualized. Practical strategies for screening, assessing, and intervening in alcohol-related problems are discussed, with an emphasis on promoting improved access to treatment for people with disabilities. Rehabilitation psychologists are in a good position to identify alcohol-related problems and to intervene when problems are present.

Prevalence and Impact of Alcohol Problems

Alcohol problems merit special attention among people with TBI and SCI for two major reasons: (a) the prevalence of alcohol-related problems in these populations and (b) the potential that alcohol may contribute to poor recovery or secondary complications. In the following sections prevalence is described in terms of preinjury alcohol problems, intoxication at the time of injury, and postinjury alcohol problems.

Preparation of this chapter was supported by Grant R49/CCR011714-02, funded by the National Center for Injury Prevention and Control and the Office on Disability and Health, National Center for Environmental Health, and by the Northwest Regional Spinal Cord Injury System Grant, funded by the National Institute of Disability and Rehabilitation Research. I thank David Patterson, Tracy Simpson, Aaron Turner, and Heather Zintel for comments on an earlier version of this chapter.

Preinjury Alcohol Problems

Corrigan (1995) reviewed the literature on alcohol and TBI and found that preinjury alcohol abuse or dependence ranged from 16 to 66%. The most rigorous studies and those conducted in rehabilitation settings produced the highest prevalence rates, between 44 and 66%. People with SCI reported greater than average preinjury alcohol consumption, and 35–49% reported a history of significant alcohol problems (Bombardier & Rimmele, 1998a).

Much larger studies of preinjury alcohol problems have been conducted on general trauma patients. Rivara et al. (1993) found that 44% of consecutive trauma admissions scored in the "alcoholic" range on a brief screening measure. In another study, 24% of all admissions met diagnostic criteria for current alcohol dependence (28% for men and 15% for women; Soderstrom et al., 1997).

Alcohol Intoxication

Another indication of alcohol-related problems among people with TBI or SCI is alcohol intoxication (blood alcohol level greater than 100 mg/dL) at the time of injury. In the seven studies he reviewed, Corrigan (1995) found that rates of alcohol intoxication ranged from 36% to 51% among patients with TBI. Alcohol intoxication rates for SCI reported in the literature are 40% (Heinemann, Schnoll, Brandt, Maltz, & Keen, 1988) and 36% (Kiwerski & Krasuski, 1992). Among general trauma patients, Rivara et al. (1993) found that 47% had a positive blood alcohol level and that 36% were intoxicated.

Postinjury Alcohol Problems

Longitudinal surveys of alcohol use and alcohol problems among people with TBI and SCI show that drinking declines during the months immediately following injury followed by increased drinking during the 1st and 2nd years after injury (Dikmen, Machmer, Donovan, Winn, & Temkin, 1995; Heinemann, Keen, et al., 1988). Drinking problems after injury typically represent a continuation of a preinjury pattern, although some appear to develop alcohol problems for the first time following their injury (Corrigan, Rust, & Lamb-Hart, 1995; Heinemann, Doll, & Schnoll, 1989). Alcohol consumption after TBI and SCI may be somewhat higher than in the general population (Kreutzer, Witol, & Marwitz, 1996; Young, Rintala, Rossi, Hart, & Fuhrer, 1995). Drinking rates may be particularly high among selected groups, such as vocational rehabilitation clients (Kreutzer, Wehman, Harris, Burns, & Young, 1991), those in postacute rehabilitation programs (National Head Injury Foundation [NHIF], 1988; now the Brain Injury Association), and veterans with SCI (Kirubakaran, Kumar, Powell, Tyler, & Armatas, 1986).

Taken together, these studies provide considerable support for the idea that a prior history of alcohol problems is common among people who sustain an SCI or TBI. Rates of lifetime alcohol abuse or dependence approach 50%, whereas current dependence is nearly 25%, or three to six times higher than the general population. Men are at higher risk than women. Drinking declines soon after injury but increases over time, probably as the person resumes greater independence. There is little known about who resumes drinking or why or when they resume drinking. People in postacute and vocational rehabilitation settings may have especially high rates of alcohol abuse, possibly because alcohol problems interfere with the achievement of community integration goals and necessitate additional psychosocial services.

Effect of Alcohol-Related Factors on Outcome

Alcohol Intoxication

Studies of the effects of alcohol intoxication on neurological outcomes provide mixed results. Some studies have shown that alcohol intoxication at the time of TBI is associated with poorer short-term outcomes, such as longer length of coma, longer period of agitation (Corrigan, 1995), and greater cognitive impairment 1–2 months postinjury (Bombardier & Thurber, 1998). In other studies of people with TBI, researchers found no relationship between blood alcohol level and neurological outcome (Kaplan & Corrigan, 1992). Alcohol may have both neuroprotective and neurotoxic effects in the context of acute TBI (Kelly, 1995). However, both animal (Halt, Swanson, & Faden, 1992) and human studies (Kiwerski & Krasuski, 1992) suggest that alcohol intoxication may be associated with more severe SCI.

Preinjury Alcohol Problems

A preinjury pattern of chronic alcohol abuse or dependence is predictive of numerous negative outcomes after TBI and SCI. Preinjury alcohol abuse is associated with increased risk of mortality and more severe brain lesions (Corrigan, 1995). Patients with a history of alcohol abuse demonstrate poorer neuropsychological test performance 1-month and 1-year postinjury (Dikmen, Donovan, Loberg, Machamer, & Temkin, 1993), are at higher risk for emotional and behavioral problems, are less likely to successfully integrate back into the community, and are at higher risk for recurrent TBI (Corrigan, 1995). Because many of these studies did not completely control for potential confounding factors, the precise role alcohol plays in poorer outcomes merits further study (Dikmen et al., 1993). People with SCI who had premorbid alcohol problems were found to spend less time in productive activities such as rehabilitation therapies (Heinemann, Goranson, Ginsburg, & Schnoll, 1989) and to have higher rates of suicide (Charlifue & Gerhart, 1991) than SCI patients who did not have a history of alcohol problems.

Postinjury Alcohol Use or Abuse

It is widely suspected that even moderate alcohol consumption after TBI may dampen neurological recovery and magnify cognitive impairments (NHIF, 1988). Yet there is surprisingly little empirical research in this area. Clearly, alcoholism can cause cognitive impairment, including permanent brain damage (Rourke & Loberg, 1996). Cognitive impairment also can develop in heavy "social drinkers," and the effects are roughly dose dependent (Parsons & Nixon, 1998). In the only study of brain functioning influenced by drinking after TBI, event-related potentials were found to be more impaired among people with TBI who also abused alcohol than among people who only had a TBI or who only abused alcohol (Baguley et al., 1997). Support for the idea that TBI magnifies the acute neurocognitive effects of alcohol comes from self-reports of increased sensitivity to alcohol (Oddy, Coughlan, Tyerman, & Jenkins, 1985) and the finding that alcohol intoxication and TBI produce similar neuropsychological impairments (Peterson, Rothfleisch, Zelazo, & Pihl, 1990).

Regarding people with SCI, Krause (1992) speculated that return to drinking may interfere with health maintenance behaviors secondary to impaired judgment, coordination, and memory. Curiously, people with preinjury alcohol problems who abstained from alcohol after injury have been found to be at increased risk for developing pressure sores (Heinemann & Hawkins, 1995).

Taken together, the relevant literature could be interpreted to suggest that alcohol intoxication at the time of injury is most likely to affect early indicators of cognitive function, but that with time and physical recovery the influence of intoxication on cognitive functioning diminishes. The effect of preinjury alcohol abuse on postinjury outcomes is the most well-established finding. However, even this relationship remains controversial because of the potential confounding effects of numerous variables, including education level and preinjury socioeconomic status as well as postinjury drinking. Extremely little is known about the additional risks attributable to alcohol use or abuse that occurs after TBI or SCI. Studies are needed that examine the differential impact of preinjury alcohol abuse, intoxication at the time of injury, and postinjury alcohol use on outcomes. The effects of alcohol on cognition, behavior, complications (e.g., seizures), and recovery after TBI merit further research. Studies are needed on the effects of alcohol on immune functioning, sexual functioning, depression, and self-care after SCI.

Historical Perspective

Competing Models of Alcoholism

Alcoholism can be conceptualized in categorical terms as a disease or as a continuum of alcohol-related problems. The prevailing disease model is represented by the *Diagnostic and Statistical Manual of Mental Disorders* (4th ed.; *DSM–IV*; American Psychiatric Association, 1994) definition of *alcohol dependence*. The disease model views alcoholic individuals as qualitatively different from nonalcoholic individuals. That is, people with alcoholism are thought to have a medical or psychological defect resulting in behaviors such as excessive consumption. Alcoholism is believed to be progressive and can be put in remission only through abstinence. Nonalcoholic individuals are assumed to have no such defect and to experience no adverse consequences from alcohol.

The emphasis on alcoholism as a disease follows a historical pattern similar to that of other medical conditions:

> The historical record also suggests that treatment for any problem tends to originate as a result of attention being drawn to severe cases. Initially, treatment consists of applying to these cases the existing remedies that are available when the problem is first recognized. As time passes, however, it becomes increasingly clear that *(a) cases other than severe cases exist and (b) other methods can be used to deal with them.* . . . Thus, it is not surprising to find the same progression in the treatment of persons with alcohol problems. (Institute of Medicine [IOM], 1990, p. 59, emphasis added)

Many contemporary researchers on alcoholism have moved away from the categorical disease model and toward a continuum model, which holds that alcohol-related problems occur along a spectrum of severity (Miller & Brown, 1997). Although it is predicated on the disease model, the *DSM–IV* recognizes gradations of alcoholism other than dependence through the diagnosis of alcohol abuse (American Psychiatric Association, 1994). The IOM report (1990) is notable for moving even farther from the disease model by explicitly adopting a terminology of "alcohol problems" that are expressed along numerous dimensions.

In the IOM report (1990) a triangle diagram was developed to represent this continuum of alcohol problems (see Figure 19.1). The area of the triangle depicts the U.S. population with regard to alcohol consumption and alcohol-related problems. The figure illustrates a number of important conceptual shifts that are relevant to the issue of alcohol and disability.

First, prototypical alcoholic individuals represent a minority of Americans with alcohol problems. A large proportion of Americans consume hazardous amounts of alcohol and incur significant harm from alcohol use without meeting the criteria for alcoholism or seeking help. Second, the IOM model emphasizes that there are no clear boundaries between normal use and abuse of alcohol or between alcohol abuse and dependence. Third, individuals seem to shift back and forth along the continuum. Among people with alcoholism, consumption and the degree of alcohol-related problems vary significantly over the course of the person's lifetime (Valliant, 1983). Moreover, the majority of the shifting that occurs is probably not attributable to treatment (Sobell, Cunningham, & Sobell, 1996). Finally, the continuum model provides a more appropriate framework through which to view the modal person with alcoholism whom rehabilitation psy-

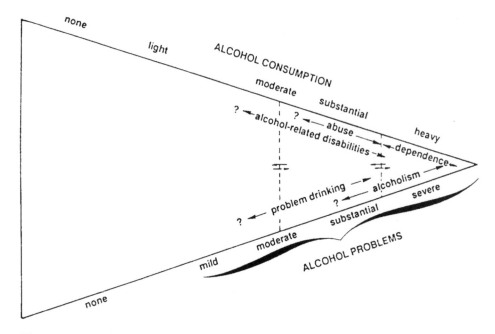

Figure 19.1. A terminological map. From *Broadening the Base of Treatment for Alcohol Problems* (p. 30), by the Institute of Medicine, 1990, Washington, DC: National Academy Press. Copyright 1990 by the National Academy Press. Reprinted with permssion.

chologists will encounter, someone with mild to moderate problems with alcohol.

Common Assumptions Associated With the Disease Model

The treatment assumptions of the disease model deserve examination. Some common assumptions appear to conflict with the contemporary literature on addictive behaviors and interfere with potential innovations in clinical care. First, there is the belief that patients must acknowledge that they have an alcohol problem before treatment can begin. Requiring patients to admit they are alcoholic individuals, however, is not only unnecessary for therapeutic change but may actually generate resistance (Miller & Rollnick, 1991). A nonjudgmental attitude on the part of the therapist and the avoidance of labels is thought to facilitate greater motivation to change and more valid self-report (Miller & Rollnick, 1991).

A second belief is that not wanting professional help is a sign of "denial." Yet, most people with addictive behaviors or other psychological problems do not seek professional help (Prochaska, DiClemente, & Norcross, 1992). The term *denial* pathologizes and blames the individual for a condition most of us seem to have: preferring to change on our own. Staff also may believe that denial is a personality trait of the alcoholic individual and must be confronted. Numerous studies have not found differences between alcoholic and nonalcoholic individuals on measures of denial (Miller & Rollnick, 1991). Rather, denial has been shown to be an interpersonal phenomenon (Miller, Benefield, & Tonigan, 1993). Therapist confrontation increases patient resistive behaviors, whereas empathic listening decreases resistance. Confrontation has been shown to be positively correlated with greater alcohol consumption 1 year later (Miller et al., 1993).

A widely held belief is that specialized treatment is always necessary to address alcohol problems. In fact, the literature suggests other routes to recovery. For example, a review of at least 44 controlled studies shows that brief interventions of 1–3 sessions produce significant change and are often as effective as more intensive treatment (Bien, Miller, & Tonigan, 1993). In fact, there is more evidence for the efficacy of brief interventions than any other treatment modality (Miller, Brown, et al., 1995). People with alcohol problems have been shown to benefit as much from a self-help guide as from formal treatment (Miller, Gribskov, & Mortell, 1981). Surprisingly, studies of people with alcoholism residing in the community show that the majority seem to recover on their own. Two independent population surveys of problem drinkers who recovered from their alcohol problem for at least 1 year found that 77% of those who recovered did so without treatment, other professional help, or Alcoholics Anonymous (AA; Sobell et al., 1996).

Finally, there is the belief that lifetime abstinence is the only acceptable goal. There is little question that lifetime abstinence is the best option for many people with alcohol problems. However, there are also good reasons to support moderate drinking when this is the person's treatment goal. Engaging the person in setting treatment goals is considered more therapeutic than imposing treatment goals, and the practice of requiring a commitment to abstinence at the outset may unnecessarily exclude individuals who could make meaningful changes in their drinking (Dimeff & Marlatt, 1995). Many patients who initially refuse abstinence reconsider it after a trial of moderate drinking fails (Miller & Page, 1991).

In summary, common disease model assumptions have little support when one considers research on the broader population of people with alcohol problems. What emerges is a sense that alcohol-related problems are more treatable and have more in common with other psychological disorders. In fact, the most effective way to address alcohol-related problems for many rehabilitation patients may be to identify and treat them like any other psychosocial problem and to do so in the context of the rehabilitation setting.

Screening for Alcohol Problems

General Considerations

Universal alcoholism screening is needed to address the underlying cause of nearly half of the trauma patients in the United States (Gentilello,

Donovan, Dunn, & Rivara, 1995). Numerous studies have shown that alcohol screening is possible, even in the context of acute medical and surgical or primary care practice (Gentilello et al., 1995). Most screening can be conducted in minutes by clinical or nonclinical staff using face-to-face interviews, paper-and-pencil self-report, or computer-guided self-report. Before undertaking alcohol screening, the psychologist should become familiar with federal law (United States Public Health Service, 1989) that requires special protection for information related to alcohol and drug abuse.

Some clinicians may be reluctant to institute alcohol-screening and assessment procedures because they are doubtful that the results are valid. Reviews of the literature have concluded that people with alcohol problems generally provide reliable and valid reports if proper measures and procedures are used (Cooney, Zweben, & Fleming, 1995). These authors also described numerous ways of maximizing the validity of self-reports. Interviews should be conducted in clinical settings when the individual is alcohol free and after he or she is given reassurances of confidentiality. Alcohol-screening measures should be imbedded within the context of a larger battery of health-related assessments, and emphasis should be placed on alcohol use as one of several behavioral risk factors that might affect health or well-being. Adjunctive biomedical data such as blood alcohol levels or liver function tests can enhance validity. All alcohol-related assessments should be conducted in a nonjudgmental fashion, avoiding terms such as *alcoholism* or similar labels. Screening batteries should always include a measure of recent alcohol use to distinguish patients with current versus lifetime alcohol-related problems.

Practical Measures

A number of brief screening measures have been found to be reliable and valid indicators of significant alcohol-related problems. One valid tool for identifying people with alcohol dependence is the CAGE questionnaire (Ewing, 1984). The CAGE acronym stands for four questions: Have you ever felt you should *c*ut down on your drinking? Have you ever felt *a*nnoyed by someone criticizing your drinking? Have you ever felt bad or *g*uilty about your drinking? Have you ever had a drink first thing in the morning to steady your nerves or to get rid of a hangover (*e*ye opener)? Each affirmative response is scored as one point, and a total score of 2 points or greater is considered clinically significant. The CAGE has been used extensively in medical settings, requires less than 1 minute to administer, and has documented internal consistency and criterion-related validity with sensitivity and specificity ranging from 60 to 95% and 40 to 95%, respectively (Cooney et al., 1995).

The Michigan Alcoholism Screening Test (MAST; Selzer, 1971) is a 25-item list of common signs and symptoms of generic alcoholism that can be administered in about 10 minutes. The traditional cutoff score of 5 or more is thought to result in unacceptably high false-positive rates (21–34%); a cutoff of 12 is recommended (Jacobson, 1989). The 13-item Short MAST (Selzer, Vinokur, & van Rooijen, 1975) has been found to be nearly as sensitive as the complete MAST among patients with TBI (Bombardier, Kilmer, & Ehde, 1997).

The Alcohol Use Disorders Identification Test (AUDIT) was developed by the World Health Organization to promote early identification of problem drinking in primary care medical settings (Allen, Litten, Fertig, & Babor, 1997). The AUDIT consists of 10 items: 3 questions on alcohol consumption, 4 questions on alcohol-related life problems, and 3 questions on alcohol dependence symptoms. A cutoff score of 8 is recommended (Allen et al., 1997). The AUDIT requires 2 minutes to administer and approximately 1 minute to score. Reported sensitivities have typically been above 90%, with specificities in the 80–90% range (Allen et al., 1997).

In summary, universal screening for alcohol-related problems is widely recommended, can be conducted with little investment in clinical time, and can be used to predict a variety of clinical outcomes among people with recent TBI and SCI. Both drinking problems and recent alcohol consumption should be measured, especially when neuropsychological testing is conducted (Bombardier & Thurber, 1998). Conducted skillfully, screening procedures produce valid results and can be conducted with nearly every interviewable person.

Assessing Alcohol Problems

Assessment should include at least three dimensions: (a) drinking patterns, (b) symptoms of dependence, and (c) alcohol-related life problems (IOM, 1990). Assessment frequently covers diagnosis, motivation to change, and other factors related to tailoring treatment. Selected measures for assessing each of the aforementioned areas are reviewed below. Measures were chosen primarily on the basis of good psychometric properties as well as brevity and ease of use.

Patterns

Four general procedures can be used to elicit information on alcohol use: the Quantity Frequency Variability Index (QFVI), the grid method, timeline follow-back, and drinking diaries (see Miller, Westerberg, & Waldron, 1995). The QFVI measures the number of drinking occasions that occur over a fixed time interval and the number of drinks consumed on a typical drinking occasion. Separate questions may be used to cover beer, wine, and distilled spirits and the frequency of binge drinking episodes. In the grid method a typical drinking week is reconstructed by assessing alcohol consumption during the morning, afternoon, and evening of each day. The timeline follow-back method samples drinking during a specific time period by using a calendar and specific memory anchor points to prompt recall of daily drinking. Finally, alcohol use can be measured through a daily drinking diary. An advantage of this method is that it minimizes reliance on memory and the subjective averaging needed to respond to "typical-day" drinking questions (Miller, Westerberg, & Waldron, 1995).

Dependence

The Alcohol Dependence Scale (ADS; Skinner & Horn, 1984) consists of 25 questions that can be self-administered in less than 10 minutes. The ADS, which focuses on symptoms of dependence over the past year, is the most psychometrically sound measure of dependence, with established reliability, validity, and normative data (Miller, Westerberg, et al., 1995). The Severity of Alcohol Dependence Questionnaire (Stockwell, Hodgson, Edwards, Taylor, & Rankin, 1979), a 20-item measure that takes about 5 minutes to complete, measures the frequency of dependence symptoms associated with a 30-day period of heavy drinking. The briefest recommended measure is the Short Alcohol Dependence Data (Davidson & Raistrick, 1986) questionnaire, which includes only 15 items. This measure has established validity and is sensitive to early signs of dependence (Heather, 1995).

Life Problems

The Drinker's Inventory of Consequences (DrInC; Miller, Tonigan, & Longabaugh, 1994) is a 50-item scale designed to assess negative life events that are specifically attributable to alcohol. This measure has good psychometric properties and detailed norms on people seeking help for alcohol-related problems. The DrInC has five subscales: physical, interpersonal, intrapersonal, impulse control, and social responsibility. The measure includes a control scale to check on unreliable reporting.

Diagnosis

One of the most widely used diagnostic measures is the alcohol section from the Structured Clinical Interview for DSM, Patient Edition (Spitzer, Williams, Gibbon, & First, 1990). The interview requires training, takes 15–20 minutes, and permits a diagnosis of alcohol abuse as well as mild, moderate, or severe dependence (Miller, Westerberg, et al., 1995). An alternative diagnostic measure is the alcohol section of the National Institute of Mental Health, Diagnostic Interview Schedule (Robins, Cottler, & Keating, 1989), which contains 30 questions to be asked exactly as written, requires about 15–20 minutes to administer, and captures mild to moderate symptoms (Miller, Westerberg, et al., 1995).

Readiness to Change

Several measures of readiness to change are based on the transtheoretical stages-of-change model (Prochaska et al., 1992). These measures are designed to predict acceptance of treatment as well as to help tailor the initial treatment approach. The University of Rhode Island Change Assessment Scale (McConnaughy, Prochaska, & Velicer, 1983) is composed of 32-items that measure readiness to change "your problem." The measure has been used in a number of studies and has a stable factor structure (Miller, Westerberg, et al., 1995). The Stages of Change and Treatment Eagerness Scale (Miller, 1993) is available in longer (40-item) and shorter (20-item) forms with good internal consistency, factor structure, and test–retest reliability (Miller, Westerberg, et al., 1995). Finally, the shortest measure is the 12-item Readiness to Change Questionnaire (Rollnick, Heather, Gold, & Hall, 1992), which was designed to be used in medical settings as part of a brief opportunistic intervention for problem drinkers. This measure has been used successfully among people with TBI and SCI (Bombardier, Ehde, & Kilmer, 1997; Bombardier & Rimmele, 1998a, 1998b).

Comprehensive Measures

The strongest, most researched comprehensive measure is the Alcohol Use Inventory (AUI; Horn, Wanberg, & Foster, 1987). The AUI has 228 items yielding 17 primary scales on such dimensions as motivation for and styles of drinking, physical dependence, loss of behavioral control, and readiness for change (Miller, Westerberg, et al., 1995). The AUI can be completed in about 1 hour and scored by hand or computer. Another well-regarded omnibus measure is the Addiction Severity Index (McLellan, Luborski, O'Brien, & Woody, 1980), a structured interview comprising 8 subscales that takes about 40 minutes to complete. Subscales include life problems, medical, legal, employment/support, alcohol, other drugs, family/social, and psychiatric status.

A range of measures exists to assess alcohol problems. Choice of measures depend on clinical needs, time constraints, staffing, and level of staff training. Attention should be paid to the time frame referred to in the measure (typically lifetime or recent). In people with TBI, memory impairment may complicate recall, depending on the time frame (Corrigan et al., 1995). Unfortunately, most measures have no psychometric data to support their use among people with cognitive impairment. Research is needed in this area.

Selected Effective Interventions

There are at least three broad approaches to providing alcohol treatment in health care settings. One is to develop expertise in a single effective treatment modality and treat all at-risk patients with that model. Another is to attempt to match patients to different levels or types of treatment, depending on the severity of their alcohol problem. A third approach is to use a "stepped-care" model. Stepped care involves providing a small dose of therapy (e.g., brief intervention) to all at-risk patients, followed by reassessment and more intensive treatment only for those who do not meet a predetermined clinical goal (Marlatt & Tapert, 1993).

In the United States, treatment for alcoholism has developed largely independent of scientific scrutiny. As a result, the most commonly used therapies (confrontation and general alcoholism counseling) are the ones with the least empirical support, and effectiveness is inversely related to cost (Miller, Brown, et al., 1995). Fortunately, empirical reviews and meta-analyses (e.g., Miller, Brown, et al., 1995) are available as a rational guide to clinical care. In the following sections, several effective alcohol interventions are described with an emphasis on how they may be used in rehabilitation settings. Therapies with the highest cumulative evidence for their efficacy are (in rank order): brief interventions, social-skills training, motivational enhancement, and the community reinforcement approach (Miller, Brown, et al., 1995). AA has not been studied in a way that permits conclusions about its efficacy (Miller, Brown, et al., 1995). Many believe that AA and other similar treatments are not effective for people with TBI (NHIF, 1988); however, it can be difficult to find treatment programs in the community that offer something else (Langley & Kiley, 1992). The documented ineffectiveness of a number of therapies—educational lectures and films, general psychotherapy, general alcohol counseling, relaxation therapy, and anti-anxiety medications—is worth noting (Miller, Brown, et al., 1995).

Advice

Giving at-risk patients brief advice to abstain from or reduce drinking is possible for any psychologist who works with these patient populations. Numerous controlled studies in medical settings have shown that brief physician advice results in significant, lasting decreases in drinking (Cooney et al., 1995). For example, a recent study showed that two 10–15 minute interactions with a primary care physician resulted in a 40% reduction in alcohol consumption among problem drinkers measured 1 year later (Fleming, Barry, Manwell, Johnson, & London, 1997). Advice may be more effective when it is combined with self-help materials or personalized feedback and information about the adverse health effects of alcohol (Cooney et al., 1995). Several self-help guides are available (Kishline, 1994; Miller & Munoz, 1982), including one written specifically for people with TBI (Karol & Sparadeo, 1991).

Brief Interventions

Brief interventions have been used in a variety of settings, both as a stand-alone treatment and as a means of enhancing the effects of subsequent treatments (Heather, 1995). The most widely known model of brief interventions is "motivational interviewing" (Miller & Rollnick, 1991); detailed training manuals and workshops are available for clinicians to learn this model. The effective elements of brief interventions have been summarized by the acronym FRAMES (Bien et al., 1993). These key elements are *feed-back*, *responsibility*, *advice*, a *menu* of options, *empathy*, and *self-efficacy*. Typically, after an assessment is made, the patient is provided with personally relevant feedback, which includes the impairment or risks associated with past and future drinking. The therapist emphasizes the patient's personal responsibility for change, provides clear advice to make a change in drinking, and gives a menu of alternative strategies for changing problem drinking. This information is provided with empathy and understanding, not confrontation, in such a way as to reinforce the patient's hope, self-efficacy, and optimism. Motivational interviewing has been adapted for use during inpatient rehabilitation (Bombardier & Rimmele, 1998a). Preliminary outcome data obtained from 9 of 12 patients with TBI and problem drinking show that 89% reported consuming no alcohol during a typical week 1 year after treatment, compared with 50% abstinence in a control group (Bombardier & Rimmele, 1998b).

Coping and Social-Skills Training

This approach to alcohol treatment has evolved from a social-learning perspective on alcoholism (Monti, Rohsenow, Colby, & Abrams, 1995). The underlying assumption is that people with alcohol problems lack adequate skills to regulate positive and negative mood and to cope with social and interpersonal situations such as work, marriage, and parenting. Core interpersonal treatment modules include enhancing drink refusal skills, giving positive feedback and giving criticism, receiving criticism about substance use, enhancing listening and conversation skills, developing sober supports, and improving conflict resolution skills. Core mood regulation topics include managing negative thinking and coping with drinking-related beliefs, triggers, and cravings. Coping and social skills training has been adapted for people with TBI and is highly recommended for those with significant alcohol dependence (Langley & Kiley, 1992).

Community Reinforcement Approach

The CRA is a behaviorally based intervention that emphasizes the use of natural reinforcers in the patient's environment (e.g., family, spouse, friends, work, leisure activities) to facilitate change in drinking behavior (Smith & Meyers, 1995). The CRA begins with a traditional functional analysis of drinking and nondrinking behaviors (Smith & Meyers, 1995). Rather than requiring clients to make a commitment to lifelong abstinence, CRA therapists negotiate a period of "time out" from drinking that may include the use of Disulfiram (Antabuse). The CRA includes special procedures to address marital and relationship issues, vocational training, lack of social support, and the absence of nondrinking recreational alternatives (Smith & Meyers, 1995). This approach has been shown to be effective in four out of four outcome studies (Miller, Brown, et al., 1995).

A promising application of CRA is when it is used with the concerned friends or family members of a person with alcoholism who refuses to seek treatment (Meyers, Dominguez, & Smith, 1996). Concerned others are trained to use behavior management skills, communication skills, and assertiveness to help the person with alcoholism seek treatment. Studies show a dramatic increase in treatment participation and decreased drinking before treatment as well as decreased distress among the concerned others with this treatment (Meyers et al., 1996).

Relapse Prevention

Relapse prevention is an influential cognitive–behavioral self-management program originally designed to complement traditional treatments by anticipating and planning to cope with relapse (Dimeff & Marlatt, 1995). The relapse prevention model includes three major components: (a) behavioral-skills training, (b) cognitive interventions, and (c) lifestyle change. Alcoholism is reconceptualized as an overlearned maladaptive habit, and relapse becomes a natural phase of behavior change that can be anticipated. This model involves the use of abstract and metaphorical content that may be difficult for people with cognitive impairment.

In summary, recent innovations in theory and treatment should make it possible for every rehabilitation program to provide on-site interventions. The types and intensity of interventions as well as the staff who provide treatment vary, depending on the individual site or program. Legitimate, potentially efficacious interventions range from brief advice provided by a rehabilitation psychologist or physician to intensive interdisciplinary coping-skills treatment tailored for people with neurological impairments. Alcohol interventions are likely to be more effective to the extent that they are woven into the daily fabric of a given rehabilitation program and to the extent that the substance abuse intervention focuses on enhancing rehabilitation outcomes, general health, and well-being rather than solely on reducing alcohol or drug use.

Conclusion

A key to providing better alcohol-related services for people with disabilities is improving access to effective treatment. Perhaps the best way that rehabilitation psychologists can promote access to treatment is to bring empirically based treatment approaches into the medical, vocational, rehabilitation, and independent-living settings in which people with disabilities are usually seen. Rehabilitation psychologists can facilitate this process in several ways. We can become more familiar with current thinking in the area of addictive behavior. In doing so, we can help dispel myths and shed new light on these problems for our colleagues as well. We can expand our clinical expertise to include alcohol- and drug-related problems. Psychologists frequently have had little training in the area of substance abuse and tend to think that treating addictions requires unique skills and experiences (Miller & Brown, 1997). However, current theory and practice emphasize that alcohol and drug problems are behaviors that respond to the same psychological principles as other disorders, such as anxiety and depression. Using empirically validated treatments, psychologists can tailor treatment programs to meet the needs of people with disabilities where they are, physically, cognitively, and motivationally. Research can help determine if the treatment approaches that we have tailored are effective.

References

Allen, J., Litten, R., Fertig, J., & Babor, T. (1997). A review of research on the Alcohol Use Disorders Identification Test (AUDIT). *Alcoholism: Clinical and Experimental Research, 21,* 613–619.

American Psychiatric Association. (1994). *Diagnostic and statistical manual of mental disorders* (4th ed.). Washington, DC: Author.

Baguley, I., Felmingham, K., Lahz, S., Gordon, E., Lazzarl, H., & Schote, D. (1997). Alcohol abuse and traumatic brain injury: Effect on event-related potentials. *Archives of Physical Medicine and Rehabilitation, 78,* 1248–1253.

Bien, T. H., Miller, W. R., & Tonigan, J. S. (1993). Brief interventions for alcohol problems: A review. *Addiction, 88,* 315–335.

Bombardier, C., Ehde, D., & Kilmer, J. (1997). Readiness to change alcohol use after traumatic brain injury. *Archives of Physical Medicine and Rehabilitation, 78,* 592–596.

Bombardier, C., Kilmer, J., & Ehde, D. (1997). Screening for alcoholism among persons with recent traumatic brain injury. *Rehabilitation Psychology, 42,* 259–271.

Bombardier, C., & Rimmele, C. (1998a). Alcohol use and readiness to change after spinal cord injury. *Archives of Physical Medicine and Rehabilitation, 79,* 1110–1115.

Bombardier, C., & Rimmele, C. (1998b, January). *Preventing alcohol abuse after traumatic brain injury: A case series.* Poster session presented at the 8th International Conference on Treatment of Addictive Behaviors, Santa Fe, NM.

Bombardier, C., & Thurber, C. (1998). Blood alcohol level and early cognitive status after traumatic brain injury. *Brain Injury, 12,* 725–734.

Charlifue, S., & Gerhart, K. (1991). Behavioral and demographic predictors of suicide after spinal cord injury. *Archives of Physical Medicine and Rehabilitation, 72,* 488–492.

Cooney, N., Zweben, A., & Fleming, M. (1995). Screening for alcohol problems and at-risk drinking in health-care settings. In R. Hester & W. Miller (Eds.), *Handbook of alcoholism treatment approaches: Effective alternatives* (pp. 45–60). Boston: Allyn & Bacon.

Corrigan, J. D. (1995). Substance abuse as a mediating factor in outcome from traumatic brain injury. *Archives of Physical and Medical Rehabilitation, 76,* 302–309.

Corrigan, J., Rust, E., & Lamb-Hart, G. (1995). The nature and extent of substance abuse problems in persons with traumatic brain injury. *Journal of Head Trauma Rehabilitation, 10,* 29–46.

Davidson, R., & Raistrick, D. (1986). The validity of the Short Alcohol Dependence Data (SADD) questionnaire. *British Journal of Addictions; 81,* 217–222.

Dikmen, S., Donovan, D., Loberg, T., Machmer, J., & Temkin, N. (1993). Alcohol use and its effects on neuropsychological outcome in head injury. *Neuropsychology, 7,* 296–305.

Dikmen, S., Machmer, J., Donovan, D., Winn, R., & Temkin, N. (1995). Alcohol use before and after traumatic head injury. *Annals of Emergency Medicine, 26,* 167–176.

Dimeff, L., & Marlatt, A. (1995). Relapse prevention. In R. Hester & W. Miller (Eds.), *Handbook of alcoholism treatment approaches: Effective alternatives* (pp. 148–159). Boston: Allyn & Bacon.

Ewing, J. (1984). Detecting alcoholism: The CAGE Questionnaire. *Journal of the American Medical Association, 252,* 1905–1907.

Fleming, M., Barry, K., Manwell, L., Johnson, M., & London, R. (1997). Brief physician advice for problem alcohol drinkers. *Journal of the American Medical Association, 277*, 1039–1045.

Gentilello, L., Donovan, D., Dunn, C., & Rivara, F. (1995). Alcohol interventions in trauma centers. *Journal of the American Medical Association, 274*, 1043–1048.

Halt, P., Swanson, R., & Faden, A. (1992). Alcohol exacerbates behavioral and neurochemical effects of rat spinal cord trauma. *Archives of Neurology, 49*, 1178–1184.

Heather, N. (1995). Brief intervention strategies. In R. Hester & W. Miller (Eds.), *Handbook of alcoholism treatment approaches: Effective alternatives* (pp. 105–122). Elmsford, NY: Pergamon Press.

Heinemann, A., Doll, M., & Schnoll, S. (1989). Treatment of alcohol abuse in persons with recent spinal cord injuries. *Alcohol Health and Research World, 13*, 110–117.

Heinemann, A., Goranson, N., Ginsburg, K., & Schnoll, S. (1989). Alcohol use and activity patterns following spinal cord injury. *Rehabilitation Psychology, 34*, 191–206.

Heinemann, A., & Hawkins, D. (1995). Substance abuse and medical complications following spinal cord injury. *Rehabilitation Psychology, 40*, 125–141.

Heinemann, A., Keen, M., Donohue, R., & Schnoll, S. (1988). Alcohol use in persons with recent spinal cord injuries. *Archives of Physical Medicine and Rehabilitation, 69*, 619–624.

Heinemann, A., Schnoll, S., Brandt, M., Maltz, R., & Keen, M. (1988). Toxicology screening in acute spinal cord injury. *Alcoholism: Clinical and Experimental Research, 12*, 815–819.

Horn, J., Wanberg, K., & Foster, F. (1987). *Guide to the Alcohol Use Inventory*. Minneapolis, MN: National Computer Systems.

Institute of Medicine. (1990). *Broadening the base of treatment for alcohol problems*. Washington, DC: National Academy Press.

Jacobson, G. (1989). A comprehensive approach to pre-treatment evaluation: I. Detection, assessment and diagnosis of alcohol. In R. Heather & W. Miller (Eds.), *Handbook of alcoholism treatment approaches: Effective alternatives* (pp. 53–71). Elmsford, NY: Pergamon Press.

Kaplan, C., & Corrigan, J. (1992). Effect of blood alcohol level on recovery from severe closed head injury. *Brain Injury, 6*, 337–349.

Karol, R., & Sparadeo, F. (1991). *Alcohol, drugs and brain injury: A survivor's workbook*. Lynn, MA: Mew Medico Head Injury System.

Kelly, D. (1995). Alcohol and head injury: An issue revisited. *Journal of Neurotrauma, 12*, 883–890.

Kirubakaran, V., Kumar, V., Powell, B., Tyler, A., & Armatas, P. (1986). Survey of alcohol and drug misuse in spinal cord injured veterans. *Journal of Studies on Alcohol, 47*, 223–227.

Kishline, A. (1994). *Moderate drinking: The moderation management guide*. New York: Random House.

Kiwerski, J., & Krasuski, M. (1992). Influence of alcohol intake on the course and consequences of spinal cord injury. *International Journal of Rehabilitation Research, 15*, 240–245.

Krause, J. S. (1992). Delivery of substance abuse services during spinal cord injury rehabilitation. *Neurorehabilitation, 2*, 45–51.

Kreutzer, J., Wehman, P., Harris, J., Burns, C., & Young, H. (1991). Substance abuse and crime patterns among persons with traumatic brain injury referred for supported employment. *Brain Injury, 5*, 177–187.

Kreutzer J., Witol, A., & Marwitz, J. (1996). Alcohol and drug use among young persons with traumatic brain injury. *Journal of Learning Disabilities, 29*, 643–651.

Langley, M., & Kiley, D. (1992). Prevention of substance abuse in persons with neurological disabilities. *NeuroRehabilitation, 2*, 52–64.

Marlatt, G. A., & Tapert, S. F. (1993). Harm reduction: Reducing the risk of addictive behaviors. In J. S. Baer & G. A. Marlatt (Eds.), *Addictive behaviors across the life span: Prevention, treatment, and policy issues* (pp. 243–273). Newbury Park, CA: Sage.

McConnaughy, E., Prochaska, J., & Velicer, W. (1983). Stages of change in psychotherapy: Measurement and sample profiles. *Psychotherapy: Theory, Research and Practice, 20,* 368–375.

McLellan, A., Luborski, L., O'Brien, C., & Woody, G. (1980). An improved evaluation instrument for substance abuse patients: The Addiction Severity Index. *Journal of Nervous and Mental Disease, 168,* 26–33.

Meyers, R., Dominguez, T., & Smith, J. (1996). Community reinforcement training with concerned others. In V. Van Hasselt & M. Hersen (Eds.), *Sourcebook of psychological treatment manuals for adult disorders* (pp. 257–294). New York: Plenum Press.

Miller, W. (1993). *The Stages of Change Readiness and Treatment Eagerness Scale* (SOCRATES, Version 6.0). Unpublished instrument, University of New Mexico.

Miller, W., Benefield, G., & Tonigan, J. (1993). Enhancing motivation for change in problem drinking: A controlled comparison of two therapist styles. *Journal of Consulting and Clinical Psychology, 61,* 455–461.

Miller, W., & Brown, S. (1997). Why psychologists should treat alcohol and drug problems. *American Psychologist, 52,* 1269–1279.

Miller, W., Brown, J., Simpson, T., Handmaker, N., Bien, T., Luckie, L., Montgomery, H., Hester, R., & Tonigan, S. (1995). What works? A methodological analysis of the alcohol treatment outcome literature. In R. Hester & W. Miller (Eds.), *Handbook of alcoholism treatment approaches: Effective alternatives* (pp. 12–44). Boston: Allyn & Bacon.

Miller, W., Gribskov, C., & Mortell, R. (1981). Effectiveness of a self-control manual for problem drinkers with and without therapist contact. *International Journal of the Addictions, 16,* 1247–1254.

Miller, W., & Munoz, R. (1982). *How to control your drinking* (rev. ed.). Albuquerque: University of New Mexico Press.

Miller, W., & Page, A. (1991). Warm turkey: Other routes to abstinence. *Journal of Substance Abuse, 8,* 227–232.

Miller, W., & Rollnick, S. (1991). *Motivational interviewing: Preparing people to change addictive behavior.* New York: Guilford Press.

Miller, W., Tonigan, J. S., & Longabaugh, R. (1994). *The drinker's inventory of consequences: An instrument for assessing the adverse consequences of alcohol abuse* [Project MATCH Monograph Series]. Rockville, MD: National Institute on Alcohol Abuse and Alcoholism.

Miller, W., Westerberg, V., & Waldron, H. (1995). Evaluating alcohol problems in adults and adolescents. In R. Hester & W. Miller (Eds.), *Handbook of alcoholism treatment approaches: Effective alternatives* (pp. 61–88). Boston: Allyn & Bacon.

Monti, P., Rohsenow, D., Colby, S., & Abrams, D. (1995). Coping and social skills training. In R. Hester & W. Miller (Eds.), *Handbook of alcoholism treatment approaches: Effective alternatives* (pp. 221–241). Boston: Allyn & Bacon.

National Head Injury Foundation. (1988). *Substance abuse task force white paper.* Southborough, MA: Author.

Oddy, M., Coughlan, T., Tyerman, A., & Jenkins, D. (1985). Social adjustment after closed head injury. *Journal of Neurology, Neurosurgery and Psychiatry, 48,* 564–568.

Parsons, O., & Nixon, S. (1998). Cognitive functioning in sober social drinkers: A review of the research since 1986. *Journal of Studies on Alcohol, 59,* 180–190.

Peterson, J., Rothfleisch, J., Zelazo, P., & Pihl, R. (1990). Acute alcohol intoxication and cognitive functioning. *Journal of Studies on Alcohol, 51,* 114–122.

Prochaska, J., DiClemente, C., & Norcross, J. (1992). In search of how people change. *American Psychologist, 47,* 1102–1114.

Rivara, F., Jurkovich, G., Gurney, J., Seguin, D., Flinger, C., Ries, R., Raisys, V., & Copass, M. (1993). The magnitude of acute and chronic alcohol abuse in trauma patients. *Archives of Surgery, 128,* 907–913.

Robins, L., Cottler, L., & Keating, S. (1989). *NIMH Diagnostic Schedule: Version III— Revised (DIS–III–R).* St. Louis, MO: Washington University Press.

Rollnick, S., Heather, N., Gold, R., & Hall, W. (1992). Development of a short "readiness to change" questionnaire for use in brief, opportunistic interventions among excessive drinkers. *British Journal of Addiction, 87,* 743–754.

Rourke, S., & Loberg, T. (1996). The neurobehavioral correlates of alcoholism. In I. Grant & K. Adams (Eds.), *Neuropsychological assessment of neuropsychiatric disorders* (pp. 423–485). New York: Oxford University Press.

Selzer, M. (1971). The Michigan Alcoholism Screening Test. *American Journal of Psychiatry, 127,* 1653–1658.

Selzer, M., Vinokur, A., & van Rooijen, L. (1975). A self-administered Short Michigan Alcoholism Screening Test (SMAST). *Journal of Studies on Alcohol, 36,* 127–132.

Skinner, H., & Horn, J. (1984). *Alcohol Dependence Scale (ADS) user's guide.* Toronto, Ontario, Canada: Addiction Research Foundation.

Smith, J., & Meyers, R. (1995). The community reinforcement approach. In R. Hester & W. Miller (Eds.), *Handbook of alcoholism treatment approaches: Effective alternatives* (2nd ed., pp. 251–266). Boston, MA: Allyn & Bacon.

Sobell, L., Cunningham, J., & Sobell, M. (1996). Recovery from alcohol problems with and without treatment: Prevalence in two population surveys. *American Journal of Public Health, 86,* 966–972.

Soderstrom, C., Smith, G., Dischinger, P., McDuff, D., Hebel, J., Gorlick, D., Kerns, T., Ho, S., & Read, K. (1997). Psychoactive substance use disorders among seriously injured trauma center patients. *Journal of the American Medical Association, 277,* 1769–1774.

Spitzer, R., Williams, J., Gibbon, M., & First, M. (1990). *Structured Clinical Interview for DSM–III–R—Patient Edition* (Version 1.0). Washington, DC: American Psychiatric Press.

Stockwell, T., Hodgson, R., Edwards, G., Taylor, C., & Rankin, H. (1979). The development of a questionnaire to measure severity of alcohol dependence. *British Journal of Addiction, 74,* 79–87.

United States Public Health Service. (1989). *Code of Federal Regulations, Part II: Confidentiality of alcohol and drug abuse patient records.* Washington, DC: Author.

Valliant, G. (1983). *The natural history of alcoholism: Causes, patterns and paths to recovery.* Cambridge, MA: Harvard University Press.

Young, M., Rintala, D., Rossi, C., Hart, K., & Fuhrer, M. (1995). Alcohol and marijuana use in a community-based sample with spinal cord injury. *Archives of Physical Medicine and Rehabilitation, 76,* 525–532.

20

Postacute Brain Injury

James F. Malec and Jennie L. Ponsford

Both economic and humanistic forces encouraged the development of post-acute brain injury rehabilitation (PABIR). The need for brain injury rehabilitation services of any kind arose in the late 1970s as the advent of emergency medical services and improved neurosurgical techniques allowed for rapid and effective medical intervention in cases of severe brain injury. Mortality following brain injury declined dramatically. Early survivors of brain injury were routinely admitted to inpatient rehabilitation units.

Inpatient rehabilitation models had been developed for people with primarily physical disabilities, such as spinal cord injury, cerebral palsy, and polio. Consequently, inpatient rehabilitation units since the late 1970s have emphasized physical medicine and physical therapy interventions directed at restoring or developing adaptations to allow the performance of basic self-care activities, bowel and bladder management, other activities of daily living (ADLs), and independent mobility.

As this model of inpatient rehabilitation was applied to early survivors of brain injury, it rapidly became apparent that specified approaches did not meet their needs. Physical disabilities were present for some individuals following brain injury, but the more prominent and common impairments were psychological in nature: impairments of attention, memory, reasoning, and other cognitive abilities; changes in the capacity for behavioral self-regulation that resulted in impulsive behavior or, conversely, impaired initiation; other changes in personality; and severe stress among family and close others as they recognized the sometimes dramatic changes in their loved one resulting from brain injury.

Early rehabilitation psychology approaches also missed the mark with people with brain injury. In the 1970s, rehabilitation psychology interventions focused on facilitating adjustment to disability, addressing sexuality and intimacy issues, and assisting in vocational reintegration among people with significant physical disabilities but normal cognitive capacities. Adjustment counseling with people following brain injury, however, often proved futile, particularly among those for whom severe brain damage resulted in impaired self-awareness. Impaired self-awareness made this group oblivious to adjustment issues and behavioral problems apparent to staff and to their close others. Sexuality and intimacy were often problematic, not because of physical sexual dysfunction, but because of reduced libido, relationship problems resulting from personality changes, or disinhibited and inappropriate sexual and interpersonal behaviors resulting from frontal cerebral damage. Primary barriers to vocational reintegration were cognitive and behavioral impairments that are not easily addressed by environmental adaptations or rehabilitation engineering as in the case of physical disabilities.

One of the initial (and in retrospect, naive) attempts to address the unique impairments of the survivor of brain injury was through cognitive rehabilitation. The thinking at the time was that, if cognitive capacities could be retrained or restored, then many of the disabilities associated with cognitive impairment would be eliminated (Malec, 1984). In the field of psychology, cognitive–behavioral psychology was also becoming prominent in the late 1970s. The message of cognitive–behavioral psychology was that clear thinking led to effective behavior. Meichenbaum (1977) reported that another group of people with organic brain dysfunction (attention deficit disorder) could improve their behavioral self-regulation by learning goal-directed self-talk. Like cognitive–behavioral psychotherapy, one of the basic premises of cognitive rehabilitation was that relearning how to remember and how to regulate attention and behavior through internal verbalizations should greatly improve adjustment after brain injury.

Cognitive rehabilitation techniques continue to be developed and may be effective in addressing specific goals for individuals following brain injury (Benedict, 1989; Gianutsos, 1991; Malec, 1996; Mateer & Sohlberg, 1988; Matthews, Harley, & Malec, 1991; Rimmele & Hester, 1987). Cognitive rehabilitation also continues to play a role in most PABIR programs. However, it became rapidly apparent during the 1980s that one of the primary barriers to adjustment after brain injury—poor memory—could not be restored through learning-based interventions (Mateer & Sohlberg, 1988; Schacter, Rich, & Stampp, 1985). Through extended repetitive practice, people with memory impairment could learn specific skills, procedures, and new information (Glisky, Schacter, & Tulving, 1986). However, their basic memory capacity could not be increased. Also associated with memory impairment was the impaired capacity to generalize new learning from one situation to another. So, whereas individuals with memory impairment may learn to apply a set of new skills in the environment in which they were trained, it is unlikely that they can apply these skills in a new situation or setting without additional training in that setting. Along these same lines, people with brain injury can learn age-old mnemonic techniques (e.g., imagery, peg words) to improve their limited memory, but seldom are they able to transfer this learning to everyday life (Schacter & Glisky, 1986; Sloan & Ponsford, 1995).

A second major set of obstacles to a circumscribed cognitive rehabilitation approach to brain injury rehabilitation was the impaired self-awareness that commonly resulted from brain injury and the catastrophic emotional reactions that occurred as more accurate self-awareness of deficits began to emerge. Some people are difficult to engage in any type of rehabilitation after brain injury because they do not recognize the deficits that are the focus of rehabilitation efforts. Impaired self-awareness may be the direct result of cerebral dysfunction (McGlynn & Schachter, 1989). Self-awareness of deficits may improve after brain injury. However, increased self-awareness of deficits is commonly associated with the onset of depression or other negative emotional reactions (Bond, 1984; Fordyce, Roueche, & Prigatano, 1983; Godfrey, Partridge, Knight, & Bishara, 1993). These negative emotional reactions also interfere with participation in rehabilitation as well as with adaptation and adjustment.

Two major PABIR approaches were developed in response to these two primary barriers to rehabilitation and adaptation: (a) impaired memory and transfer of training and (b) impaired self-awareness−emotional upheaval. To circumvent the obstacle of impaired memory and transfer of training, community reintegration programs were developed that brought training to the environments in which people with brain injury must learn to live. Holistic or comprehensive-integrated programs focused on improving self-awareness and increasing emotional self-regulation through innovative group approaches. A third type of program—the neurobehavioral program—developed in response to the needs of the small proportion of people with extremely severe and often destructive behavioral disorders following brain injury.

In the United States, concurrent with the development of these new approaches to the clinical needs of people with brain injury was the increasing pressure beginning in the 1980s to reduce health care costs, including expensive inpatient rehabilitation stays. Because patients with brain injury frequently had few medical or physical care needs after acute hospital care, they were prime candidates for early discharge from the hospital to postacute programs. Although PABIR is not inexpensive, the cost of even a comprehensive outpatient day treatment program can be one-half to one-third of the cost of inpatient rehabilitation. Unfortunately, some PABIR providers in the United States in the late 1980s inflated their charges to whatever the market would bear, obviating the cost−benefit of postacute services and raising questions for insurance companies about the cost-effectiveness of such services. Outright dishonest and unethical practices among some PABIR providers ("Centers for head injuries," 1992) during this period raised additional concerns about the value of PABIR among payers as well as among brain injury advocates (National Head Injury Association, 1989).

Fundamental Models and Approaches

In this section we describe fundamental concepts underlying PABIR as they have developed in the United States and in Australia. These approaches have striking similarities in terms of origins, issues to be addressed, and emphasis on the development of skills and behaviors that are relevant to social and vocational re-engagement. Despite the emphasis on community reintegration in all types of PABIR, the more recently developed programs in Australia tend to be more community based in contrast to more institution-based programs in the United States.

Programs

Approaches to PABIR may be roughly divided into three major types: (a) comprehensive integrated, (b) community reintegration, and (c) neurobehavioral. Each approach focuses on reducing disability and handicap caused by cognitive, emotional, and behavioral impairments. In contrast to acute inpatient rehabilitation, these approaches include significantly less emphasis on medical concerns and physical impairments. In recent years, another alternative to inpatient or postacute rehabilitation— subacute rehabilitation—has developed. People admitted to subacute programs typically require regular nursing care and benefit from continuing daily physical or other rehabilitation therapy. However, because of severe impairments or chronic medical problems, these individuals are unable to participate in the intensive program of therapy (usually 5–6 hours per day) offered in inpatient rehabilitation programs.

Teams

PABIR programs typically differ from inpatient or subacute rehabilitation programs in the configuration of the rehabilitation team. It has long been recognized that rehabilitation services require a team of experts from medicine, physical therapy, occupational therapy, recreational therapy, speech pathology, psychology, nursing, social services, and pastoral care. This team is multidisciplinary; it consists of an appropriate array of experts from different health disciplines who provide their individual services to the patient. In traditional psychiatric settings and probably in most subacute rehabilitation settings for brain injury, when services are provided by a team, the team is multidisciplinary. In contrast, most inpatient rehabilitation teams are interdisciplinary; the experts on the team coordinate their services through both formal and informal meetings to pursue common goals and reinforce each other's individual efforts.

In PABIR settings, however, the ideal configuration of the team is neither multidisciplinary nor interdisciplinary but transdisciplinary. The transdisciplinary team members not only coordinate their individual services, but they also assume the roles of other members in appropriate situations. A transdisciplinary approach is required in PABIR because the participants' cognitive problems preclude their being effectively directed to address an issue at a later time. For example, a participant with brain injury indicates during a leisure skills session that she is very angry that she can no longer drive. If the recreational therapist directing that session were to suggest that she discuss her feelings in a later session with the psychologist, the participant is likely to forget to do so or to forget the saliency of the experience precipitated by the leisure skills discussion. For maximum overall therapeutic impact of the program, the recreational therapist must be able to respond to the patient's anger therapeutically in the same way that the psychologist would. In a well-coordinated transdisciplinary program, a discussion led by the psychologist would have occurred previously describing how best to respond to this participant's anger about her losses. Similarly, in a transdisciplinary team, the psychologists with instruction from other therapists must be able to assume their roles at critical times and, for instance, assist participants in using the bus schedule; prompt them to make appropriate entries into their memory notebooks; and counsel them about the purposes of assistive devices, orthoses, and medications.

Approaches

The transdisciplinary team approach is distinct to PABIR programs and contrasts with the approaches taken in many psychology, neuropsychology, and psychiatric treatment programs, which tend to focus on change within the individual served. Both contemporary psychiatry and clinical psychology typically attempt to change behavior through interventions that are directed by a sole practitioner to an individual patient. Significant others may be brought into therapy as therapeutic allies or additional clients. However, in clinical psychology, the basic model of intervention continues to be one of facilitating adaptive learning within clients in therapy sessions that is expected to transfer into the client's real life.

Psychologists trained in neuropsychology have adapted cognitive–behavioral approaches to allow application to people with brain injury despite their memory and other cognitive problems (Schefft, Malec, Lehr, & Kanfer, 1996). These modified approaches may be beneficial to some but not all people with brain injury. Other individuals with brain injury, because of cognitive impairments, are able to make only small gains in developing internalized and transferable skills that improve adjustment and adaptation. To successfully reintegrate into the community, these individuals require training that assists them in developing self-management and social skills and also in developing methods to compensate for cognitive impairments and in changing their social and physical environments to prompt, support, and reinforce adaptive and successful behavior. This comprehensive approach characterizes comprehensive-integrated and community reintegration PABIR programs.

Principles and methods of comprehensive-integrated PABIR have been extensively described by Ben-Yishay and Prigatano (Ben-Yishay & Prigatano, 1990; Prigatano et al., 1986). Essential features of comprehensive-integrated rehabilitation are outlined in Exhibit 20.1. Comprehensive-integrated rehabilitation uses group processes to improve self-awareness and address emotional reactions associated with more accurate self-assessments. Typically specific interventions are included to improve social skills and to develop compensation techniques (e.g., the use of a sys-

Exhibit 20.1. Defining Features of Comprehensive (holistic) Day Treatment

I. Neuropsychological orientation
   A. cognitive and metacognitive impairments
   B. neurobehavioral impairments
   C. interpersonal and psychosocial issues
   D. affective issues
II. Integrated treatment
   A. formal staff meetings with core team in attendance four times a week
   B. a team leader or manager for each patient
   C. a program leader or manager with at least 3 years' experience in brain injury rehabilitation
   D. integrated goal setting and monitoring
   E. transdisciplinary staff roles
III. Group interventions
   A. awareness
   B. acceptance
   C. social pragmatics
IV. Dedicated resources
   A. an identified core team
   B. dedicated space
   C. a patient-to-staff ratio no greater than 2:1
V. A neuropsychologist as part of the treatment team, not just a consultant
VI. Formal and informal opportunities for involvement of close others, including systematic inclusion of close others on a weekly basis
VII. Inclusion of a dedicated vocational or independent-living trial
VIII. Assessment of multiple outcomes
   A. productive activity
   B. independent living
   C. psychosocial adjustment
   D. emotional adjustment

Note. From "Postacute Brain Injury Rehabilitation," by J. F. Malec and J. S. Basford, *Archives of Physical Medicine and Rehabilitation, 77,* 1996, p. 199. Copyright 1996 by W. B. Saunders. Adapted with permission by the copyright holder and the original authors: Trexler et al. (1994).

tematized notebook) for cognitive problems. Family members and close friends are included to assist in transfer of training, to develop prompts and supports for developing skills, and to address emotional issues that involve these close others. Transfer of training is also assisted by starting training in work and independent living in community settings while the participant is still involved in the comprehensive-integrated program.

The community reintegration approach is less well articulated in terms of specific interventions and techniques. This approach emphasizes training people with cognitive impairment in necessary skills for independent living and work in the settings in which they will use these skills. Training in the community reintegration program tends to be functional; practical skills, such as learning how to use a bus schedule, are favored over more abstract skills, such as reading or telling time. Supported employment represents a specific type of community reintegration programming that has been highly successful in facilitating return to work for people following brain injury (Wehman et al., 1993; Wehman et al., 1990). In supported employment, people with brain injury are trained to perform specific job tasks in the work setting in which they will be employed. Supports for successful employment, such as a job coach, may be permanent or, if the client is able to eventually master a series of routine work procedures, temporary.

Another type of community reintegration rehabilitation is offered by the Clubhouse (see chapter 11, this volume). Jacobs (1979; Jacobs & DeMello, 1996) introduced the Clubhouse concept into brain injury rehabilitation. The Clubhouse concept originally evolved in response to needs of individuals with chronic mental illnesses who live in the community. A Clubhouse typically provides the kinds of functional skills training and development of community supports that are offered by most community reintegration programs. In the Clubhouse, however, services are developed largely through an internal governmental structure that is directed by the participants themselves. Professional staff in the Clubhouse support this participant-directed governance and provide services as specified by the participants.

Despite varying emphases, both comprehensive-integrated and community reintegration programs tend to address the needs of the individual client comprehensively. For instance, a hallmark of comprehensive-integrated programs is involvement in vocational and independent-living activities prior to discharge to facilitate transfer of learning from rehabilitation to real life. Successful community reintegration programs, on the other hand, encourage more accurate self-awareness through participants' involvement in a variety of life experiences with program support.

Neurobehavioral programs are a third type of PABIR designed to address the severely uncontrolled and frequently aggressive behaviors of a small proportion of people with brain injury. These residential programs provide specialized treatment and supervision to people with brain injury who are often dangerous to themselves or others. Neurobehavioral programs have shown some success in reducing severely disruptive and uncontrolled behaviors following brain injury with a combination of behavioral and pharmacologic interventions (Burke, Wesolowski, & Guth, 1988; Eames & Wood, 1985).

Not all people require PABIR programming after brain injury. Our examination of a small series of 58 patients with moderate to severe traumatic brain injury (TBI) admitted to the hospital from the Level I Trauma Center in the Mayo Medical Center in Rochester, Minnesota, suggests that only about 25% require an intensive comprehensive-integrated day treatment program. Another 10% or so are transferred from acute care to subacute facilities, and only a small number of these require intensive neurobehavioral programming. The remainder typically benefit from limited community reintegration services or individual outpatient rehabilitation therapies following acute medical and inpatient rehabilitation care. Nonmedical services to assist people with brain injury, including support and advocacy groups, federally funded vocational programs and independent-living services, and state social services, also provide significant assistance for community reintegration to people with brain injury. In some cases, these community programs obviate the need for professional rehabilitation services.

Decision making about the level and type of service is complex and typically requires input from a rehabilitation team, survivor, and family. Several factors, however, figure prominently in this decision making: ability to function safely with minimal supervision, self-awareness of deficits, and identifiable goals for rehabilitation. People with brain injury who are unable to function safely, either because of extremely imprudent and inattentive behavior (danger to self) or very severely aggressive behavior (danger to others), are probably best served in residential treatment settings. In cases of severe and aggressive behavioral disturbance, consideration is given to treatment in a neurobehavioral program.

Another factor in the decision between residential and outpatient settings is the availability of services. Some people who could safely function in an outpatient setting enter residential programs simply because an appropriate outpatient program is not available close to their home. Although the ideal may be to provide PABIR services in the home community of each person served, this is unrealistic in many of the more rural regions of the United States and other countries. Participation in a PABIR program at a distance from the home community of the person served involves additional challenges in assisting the person to successfully transfer training and skills back to that community. Transfer and generalization of training are enhanced by the early inclusion of social, vocational, and other professional service providers as well as family and close others from the home community in treatment program development and planning. The transition from program to home is facilitated by educating these potentially supportive individuals about brain injury, about the specific barriers to community reintegration encountered by the individual served, and about specific techniques and interventions that help level these barriers.

People with brain injury whose limited self-awareness of deficits interferes with sustained participation in rehabilitation are probably best served in a comprehensive-integrated program, where issues related to limited self-awareness are emphasized. Those whose self-awareness is not severely impaired may benefit from community reintegration programming, the extent of programming dependent on the range of identified goals. A number of people with a history of moderate to severe brain injury struggle with a single area of impairment, such as memory. Many are able to accurately identify their deficit without severe distress and, in consultation with a rehabilitation therapist, set reasonable goals for learning compensatory strategies to reduce disability associated with the impairment. The more involved individual who requires a comprehensive-integrated, community reintegrated, or neurobehavioral treatment is much more capable of memory. However, it is important to keep in mind that the majority of people served after brain injury require a relatively circumscribed and inexpensive course of a single or small number of specific therapeutic services to be successfully reintegrated into work, independent living, and social networks.

Considerations for rehabilitative treatment options following acute medical and rehabilitation care are illustrated in Figure 20.1. The figure also indicates that a re-evaluation should occur following each level of service implementation. This is particularly significant following neurobehavioral rehabilitation. As we review in the "Outcomes" section, neurobehavioral rehabilitation can improve the ability to live independently without supervision, but rarely does it adequately address vocational needs. It seems appropriate that those individuals who have successfully eliminated severely maladaptive behaviors through neurobehavioral rehabilitation should be advanced to comprehensive-integrated or community reintegration treatment to further develop skills and community supports for vocational reentry.

Funding

Access to PABIR services in the United States has become increasingly restricted in recent years by limitations in funding. Many individuals discover after brain injury that their private health insurance provides very limited, if any, benefits for outpatient or postacute rehabilitation. Those who have exhausted their private insurance benefits for acute medical care can obtain funding for further rehabilitation through governmental programs, such as Medical Assistance or Medicare. However, because Medical Assistance and Medicare pay only a fraction of the actual fees for these services, some rehabilitation providers avoid or limit the provision of services to people supported by these agencies. In Minnesota, funding is less problematic than in other states. A special social services program in Minnesota, the TBI Waiver, provides additional funds for community-based services to people with brain injury.

Private insurers routinely deny initial requests for funding for postacute rehabilitation services. However, through a process of reciprocal communication and education between insurers and clinicians, many private insurers can understand the value of PABIR for their clients and provide coverage to pursue specific concrete goals that may ultimately increase the health maintenance and financial independence of their clients. On the negative side, this process of communication and education can take 6 months to a year. We have worked with people with brain injury who have regressed and developed severe depressive disorders and whose family members have also become significantly depressed during this stressful waiting period without professional services or support. In some areas, PABIR has become nonexistent because of an absence of funding streams for these programs. Recent legislative and administrative actions may mark the beginning of a reversal of this trend. Federal appropriations through the Traumatic Brain Injury Act of 1996 grant funding to states to study improved access to health and human services for people with brain injury. Increased funding through the National Institute of Disability and Rehabilitation Research (NIDRR) has recently expanded the num-

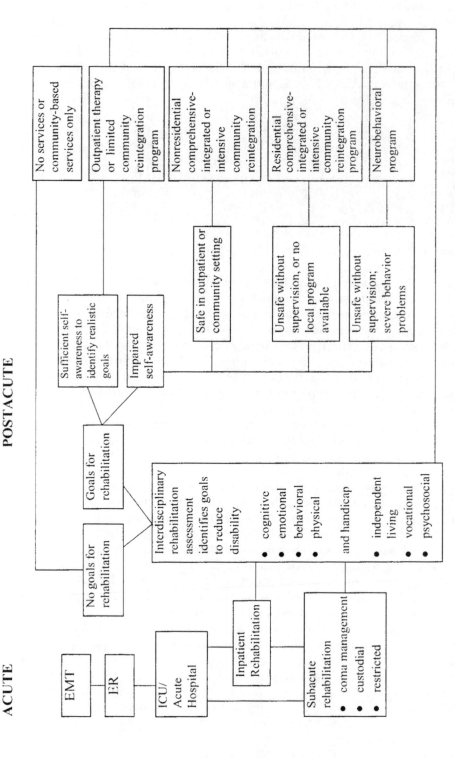

Figure 20.1. Treatment options and decision making in brain injury rehabilitation. EMT = emergency medical technician; ER = emergency room; ICU = intensive care unit. From "Postacute Brain Injury Rehabilitation," by J. F. Malec and J. S. Basford, 1996, *Archives of Physical Medicine and Rehabilitation, 77,* p. 199. Copyright 1996 by W. B. Saunders. Adapted with permission.

ber of TBI Model Center from 4 to 17, with a priority for evaluating the effectiveness of various postacute rehabilitation pathways and interventions to improve vocational outcomes and community integration after brain injury.

Programs in Australia

Over the past 2 decades in Australia a number of models of delivery of PABIR services have been developed that have, to a large extent, paralleled those in the United States. However, there are significant differences in the funding systems for rehabilitation in Australia, and these differences affect the nature and availability of services. Most Australians do not receive rehabilitation funded by private health insurance. They are treated either in government-funded programs or in private programs funded by the no-fault accident insurance plans that exist in some states, such as Victoria. Under the plans in Victoria, which are administered by the Transport Accident Commission and the Victorian Workcover Authority, individuals who sustain injuries in motor vehicle or work-related accidents have all hospital and rehabilitation costs, as well as loss of earnings, paid by the plan. This has allowed the development of specialized services for brain injury rehabilitation. Moreover, access to services is more readily available close to home and without monetary cost to the family. Services also tend to be somewhat less time limited than in the United States and are better integrated. However, there are wide variations in the quality and availability of programs in different parts of the country. Some individuals receive only standard inpatient and outpatient therapy in a general neurologic rehabilitation setting. Availability of follow-up support also varies greatly. Compared with patients in urban areas, those in rural areas have greater difficulty accessing services.

In the 1980s and in some centers up to the present time, services in Australia tended to be provided in traditional outpatient rehabilitation settings, usually attached to an inpatient program. These programs were multidisciplinary and emphasized cognitive rehabilitation. As mentioned previously, there has been no clear evidence that circumscribed cognitive rehabilitation affects the everyday functioning of the person with brain injury (Sloan & Ponsford, 1995). Over the past decade there has been a growing awareness in Australia that many people with brain injury, particularly those with associated executive or adaptive problems, have great difficulty in generalizing what they learn in one situation to another. Follow-up studies have identified a significant number of individuals who continue to experience numerous difficulties in their daily lives after they leave the rehabilitation setting. This has led many programs to alter their focus toward working with people with brain injury within the context of their daily life rather than within the rehabilitation center.

These programs differ from the traditional center-based model in essential ways. For instance, the emphasis has shifted from ameliorating impairments and disabilities toward re-establishing life roles, that is, reducing handicap. The process of assessment no longer involves the standardized administration of a number of neuropsychological or vocational tests or scales of ADLs. Rather, it involves identifying, within the community context, the roles that are important to the individual with brain injury as assessed from the perspective of that individual, close others, employers, educators, and other involved parties, and the skills required to fulfill these roles. In this way, the individual with brain injury and close others are actively involved in the process of goal setting and are empowered to play a key role in their rehabilitation. Assessment and therapy occur, as far as possible, in the context in which a given role is normally performed. Education of the injured person's network of contacts, including family, friends, and employers or teachers, is another key aspect of this model because the use and adaptation of strategies continue through the person's lifetime, far beyond the availability of therapeutic input. Psychological support is required to assist the person with brain injury and close others in coming to terms with lasting personality and lifestyle changes. Follow-up contact ideally is maintained over an extended period to provide support in dealing with new problems as they arise with changing circumstances. Examples of these service models include transitional-living programs and community teams.

Transitional-Living Programs

Transitional-living programs, such as that run by Bethesda Hospital, have been established to provide individuals with brain injury with the experience of living in a shared house or an apartment within a residential community (Olver & Harrington, 1996; Ponsford, 1995). Staff are available to observe performance of all activities, including personal care, domestic tasks (e.g., cooking, cleaning, laundry, gardening, home maintenance, household planning and budgeting), community-based tasks (e.g., shopping, banking, paying bills, using public transport, keeping appointments, getting to work or school), and generally planning and carrying through with a daily routine. Performance of each task is carefully assessed. Where there are difficulties, a detailed analysis is carried out to identify why the task is not being performed adequately. This provides the basis for the intervention, which involves repeated practice of different components under supervision with feedback. Tasks are broken into steps. Initially, the execution of each step is prompted, and then over time the prompts are faded. In this way, routines can be shaped gradually. Task modification, or the introduction of certain aids, may be necessary to maximize performance. In the longer term, it may become apparent that certain tasks require ongoing supervision or assistance. Plans for future living arrangements incorporate this ongoing support.

In addition to retraining ADLs, such programs can also facilitate awareness of limitations to allow for realistic planning in which the person with brain injury is actively involved. There is an opportunity to deal with interpersonal difficulties and to develop and practice anger management strategies and other interpersonal problem-solving skills. In most cases, considerable effort is devoted to developing social skills and use of leisure time. Above all, psychological support is provided for coming to terms with major changes in lifestyle and ability levels and dealing with adjustment difficulties and substance abuse problems. Group therapy may assist in achieving many of these goals.

The most important step is the planning and implementation of the move to a permanent place of living. This may involve searching for suitable accommodations, negotiating with agents or fellow tenants, organizing furniture—all of the multiple chores involved in independent living. When the person is returning to a previous place of living, roles in the household need to be renegotiated, family members or fellow tenants need to be educated, and myriad practical and relationship issues must be addressed. A great deal of energy is required to establish the individual's ability to function independently and to develop social and recreational activities and emotional supports within the local community network.

If funding is available, an attendant caregiver may be employed and trained to support the person with brain injury to live independently. Attendant caregiver roles may vary from the provision of assistance or supervision with personal, domestic, or community activities to assistance in accessing work, study, or recreational activities to facilitating the development of a social network. Often regular contact must be maintained over an extended period, and the caregiver should be prepared to deal with new problems as they arise.

Community Team

Although many more traditional center-based outpatient brain injury programs still exist, along the lines of the community reintegration model, community teams have replaced center-based outpatient services in a number of programs in Australia and New Zealand (Henry & McGarry, 1996; Sloan, Balicki, & Winkler, 1996). The composition of such teams depends on its focus. Most include a case manager, coordinating the services of occupational therapy, speech pathology, clinical and neuropsychology, physical therapy, and social work, as needed. Vocational counseling and educational assessment are also typically available. The entire team is not necessarily involved with a given individual, and generic services in the local community may be used. Assessment, goal setting, and interventions are carried out within the relevant settings in the community. As in the transitional-living center, performance of tasks needed to fulfill specific roles is observed. Intervention may involve repeated practice to establish routines, develop compensatory strategies, or modify the task or environment to maximize successful task performance. The role of the team is to harness a broad range of community resources and natural supports to assist the individual with brain injury to attain self-determined goals. The establishment of a support network of family, friends, and others is also facilitated by the community team. The long-term aim of intervention is to have the person with brain injury and family supported within their local community. Nonetheless, the case manager or specific team members typically maintain follow-up contact to ensure that the network is maintained and to deal with any difficulties that arise.

A similar approach is applied to the process of return to work or school. Early contact is made with the school or employer to keep them informed of the progress of the person with brain injury. A detailed analysis of job or study requirements is carried out to determine what limitations the person with brain injury may have in fulfilling these and what modifications need to be made to the work or study regime to accommodate these limitations. Education of employers and teachers is a vital component of this process. Usually the employee returns to work initially on a part-time, trial basis with his or her salary paid by the insurer. A therapist may spend time in the workplace facilitating job performance and assisting in the development of strategies to overcome difficulties (Ponsford, 1995).

For those who do not have a job to return to, the process is more complex. Assistance is required in evaluating work skills, developing a résumé and job interview skills, networking suitable employers, and supporting the employee in learning to cope with the job. These individuals are frequently referred to a government-funded vocational service for this purpose. For those who are unable to return to work or study, the focus of intervention is on the development of meaningful avocational activities, which may include voluntary work, recreational pursuits, and social activities.

In Victoria, a government-funded community-based support team, known as the Acquired Brain Injury Behaviour Consultancy, assists individuals with severe behavior problems. This team of clinical psychologists and neuropsychologists offers education and secondary and tertiary consultation to institutions (e.g., nursing homes, schools) or caregivers, as well as direct intervention in relevant community settings.

Skills Required of the Rehabilitation Psychologist

People served in PABIR programs are highly complex. Typically the behavioral presentation of these individuals reflects a combination of impairments in cognitive and metacognitive abilities involved in the self-management of behavior and emotions; stress created by multiple factors, including brain injury–related disabilities; social role changes, personal losses, and the reactions of close others to these changes and losses; and preinjury personality and social factors. Psychologists working with this group must consequently possess a complementarily complex set of personal qualities and skills. Among the most important personal qualities for successful work in PABIR is the flexibility to consider multiple avenues for treatment and to shift the treatment plan when initial efforts are unsuccessful. Flexibility is also required to consider potential treatment goals from multiple perspectives. In the social milieu of PABIR, several parties often hold distinct sets of treatment goals for the person with brain injury. These goals may be realistic or unrealistic. Initially the goals of the person with brain injury and family may simply be to return the person to his or her preinjury level of functioning. In many cases, this is an un-realistic goal that requires substantial and extensive discussion to refor-mulate in more realistic terms. As this discussion ensues, family and sur-vivor goals may diverge. The psychologist is often in the role of negotiator and counselor to assist the person with brain injury and the family in identifying realistic goals and in reconciling discrepant goals. Personal flexibility by the psychologist supports this therapeutic process of negoti-ation and an ultimately successful adjustment for the person with brain injury.

A less flexible approach would be to favor the goals of the person with brain injury over those of the family or vice versa. Responding to the wishes of the identified client is clearly an appropriate response to the requests of competent individuals and, in some cases, may be forced by those who request that their treatment exclude their family. However, for most, ignoring the wishes of the family only increases the stress within the family for the person with brain injury. Efforts to involve close others in the goal-setting process offer an opportunity to uncover and resolve discrepant expectations of both the person with brain injury and close others, which may underlie tensions among them.

Unfortunately, the social system in which PABIR occurs is more com-plex than that of the person with brain injury and his or her close others. A wide range of professionals that includes both members of the medical rehabilitation team and community-based professionals are likely to be involved and to hold their own agendas and goals for rehabilitation. These professional perspectives need to be considered because they frequently hold additional information relevant to life planning for the person with brain injury. The viewpoints of other professionals (as well as funding sources) also should be appropriately processed to gain support for pur-suing the final treatment plan. In negotiating with funding sources, the first step is to demonstrate their responsibility for paying for the proposed treatment. Once this is determined, the funding source may require ad-ditional evidence, including evaluation reports and outcome data, that the proposed treatment has been found effective with people like the individ-ual for whom treatment is proposed.

This complex process of negotiation and goal setting is particularly challenging with the person with brain injury with impaired self-awareness. Those who are largely unaware of their deficits may be brought into treatment by identifying a broad goal that is generally valued by the person with brain injury, close others, and professionals, such as indepen-dent living. An important part of the treatment process involves defining this goal more specifically and, through this process, assisting the person with brain injury to increase awareness of deficits by identifying concrete steps to approach the more abstract goal. The process of realistic goal setting is itself an intervention to increase appreciation of impairments by the person with brain injury. In the Mayo PABIR program, we have found the technique of goal attainment scaling (a method for quantifying individualized goals) to be helpful in defining concrete program goals with the person served (Malec, 1999; Malec, Smigielski, & DePompolo, 1991). In the long term, involving the person served in the goal-setting process reinforces the therapeutic alliance between the person and the treatment team. Prigatano and colleagues (1994) have shown that the quality of this therapeutic alliance is an important determiner of outcome in PABIR.

A capacity for flexibility may be important for psychologists to tolerate the complex and shifting parameters of the PABIR arena, but specific skills are required to translate this flexibility into effective therapeutic interventions. The psychologist must possess basic psychotherapeutic skills required for accurate listening, synthesizing information, developing a therapeutic alliance, and appreciating the emotional overtones of expectations and appraisals of the person served and involved others. The psychologist should have a strong background in behavioral and cognitive–behavioral assessment and intervention strategies. An appreciation of interpersonal and family dynamics is essential, as are skills in working with these dynamics toward realistic goal setting and future planning. The psychologist must possess skills in negotiating goals and treatment plans based on the multiple perspectives of the person served, close others, and involved professionals.

Psychologists working in PABIR should understand basic brain–behavior relationships relevant to the neurologic groups with whom they work. They should be able to conduct a standardized neurocognitive assessment to identify cognitive strengths and weaknesses and be able to translate this profile, in consultation with other involved parties, into realistic treatment, vocational goals, and life plans. The psychologist working in PABIR should also understand the types of adjustment reactions that occur in response to disabling medical conditions, as well as psychological and personality disorders that may occur after or that have been present prior to brain injury. The psychologist should have an understanding of substance abuse issues that may arise among people with brain injury. He or she should have an appreciation of when pharmacologic treatment may be beneficial in addressing cognitive, emotional, or behavioral problems and should have identified an appropriate physician to respond to referrals in such cases.

The psychologist working in PABIR must be comfortable sharing responsibility with other professionals involved with the person with brain injury. He or she must be able to work effectively with the rehabilitation team as well as to coordinate interventions with the community service network. To the degree that the psychologist is an effective team player, he or she may rely on other members of the team to provide cognitive and behavioral rehabilitation services and other services that enhance community reintegration. The PABIR psychologist may also depend on other psychologists to provide specialty services, for instance, in neuropsychological assessment, substance abuse treatment, or marital and family therapy.

In the United States, competency in the psychological skills required for PABIR practice is probably best verified by diplomate status through the American Board of Rehabilitation Psychology (ABRP) of the American Board of Professional Psychology. Examination through ABRP assesses the rehabilitation psychologist's competencies in the areas outlined previously as essential skills. By comparison, diplomate status through the American Board of Clinical Neuropsychology (ABCN) of the American Board of Professional Psychology provides evidence of the psychologist's competency primarily as a diagnostic neuropsychologist. Competency in the field of diagnostic clinical neuropsychology is required of psychologists whose practices involve the evaluation of people with brain disorders for differential diagnosis (e.g., neurologic vs. psychiatric disorders, TBI vs. other neurologic disorders affecting cognition, medicolegal determination of brain dysfunction). However, in the rehabilitation setting where people with brain injury are referred for treatment without diagnostic question, the psychologist's neuropsychological knowledge may be more circumscribed. Rehabilitation psychologists should be able to evaluate cognitive strengths and weaknesses using neuropsychometric measures for rehabilitation and life planning. They should also have a basic knowledge of brain–behavior relationships to be able to educate people with brain injury and their close others about the effects of brain injury on cognitive, behavioral, and emotional functioning. Rehabilitation psychologists whose practices are primarily devoted to the cognitive–behavioral rehabilitation of people with brain injury and are not neurodiagnostic may choose to refer more complex diagnostic neuropsychological evaluations to a clinical neuropsychologist who is board certified through ABCN. In Australia, most PABIR programs employ a registered clinical neuropsychologist and in some cases also a clinical psychologist. Their ability to function successfully within the rehabilitation team depends very much on their ability to adopt all of the roles outlined above.

Outcomes

Controversy persists regarding appropriate tools for measuring outcomes of PABIR. Recommendations for a PABIR outcome measurement system typically include measures of living independence, vocational status, and social–behavioral adjustment (Evans, 1997; Johnston, Hall, & Banja, 1994; Malec & Basford, 1996). Most indicators of living independence attempt to quantify the degree of support or supervision that the person with brain injury requires for residence in the community. Indicators of vocational outcome also attempt to describe the degree to which support or supervision is required for work (i.e., sheltered vs. supported vs. independent). Another dimension of work adjustment that merits evaluation is the economic benefit of returning to work both for the individual and for society. For instance, Dikmen, Machamer, and Temkin (1993) reported that survivors of brain injury often return to jobs that pay significantly less than those of their same-age peers. Harrick, Krefting, Johnston, Carlson, and Minnes (1994) reported that 73% of the graduates of their outpatient PABIR program who were employed continued to require other financial supports in addition to earned income.

Determination of measures of changes in self-awareness, other behaviors, and social adjustment after brain injury eludes consensus. Generally accepted methods with unquestioned validity are not available, and further development and evaluation of methodologies are needed (Malec & Basford, 1996). Various measures, such as the Community Integration Questionnaire (Willer, Rosenthal, Kreutzer, Gordon, & Rempel, 1993) and the Mayo–Portland Adaptability Inventory (MPAI; Malec & Thompson, 1994), have been developed to assess the types of functional, self-management, and social behaviors that are addressed in PABIR. At Mayo, we have developed three forms of the MPAI: one for staff, one for people with brain injury, and one for close others (Malec, Machulda, & Moessner, 1997). Comparisons of independent administration of these forms may provide insights into differing perceptions among each of these sources regarding significant problems and strengths of the person with brain injury. Comparison of the person with brain injury's self-ratings with those of staff may also be an indicator of the person's self-awareness. Goal attainment scaling is another method that can be useful in measuring change toward the highly individualized goals that are often the focus of PABIR. Goal attainment scaling has been shown to be more sensitive to change as a function of rehabilitation than are standard functional impairment indicators (Rockwood, Joyce, & Stolee, 1997; Rockwood, Stolee, & Fox, 1993).

The absence of a consistent metric for describing PABIR outcomes across studies frustrates summarization of outcome results. A previous review of PABIR outcome studies (Malec & Basford, 1996) showed that most studies indicated the percentage of people served who were either unemployed or in independent community-based employment after program completion. Overall comprehensive-integrated (Ben-Yishay, Silver, Piasetsky, & Rattok, 1987; Christensen, 1992; Malec, Smigielski, DePompolo, & Thompson, 1993; Namerow, 1987; Prigatano et al., 1984; Prigatano et al., 1994; Rattok et al., 1992; Scherzer, 1986; Stern et al., 1985) and community reintegration (Cope, Cole, Hall, & Barkan, 1991; Fryer & Haffey, 1987; Harrick et al., 1994; Johnston & Lewis, 1991; Jones & Evans, 1992; Lyons & Morse, 1988) programs reviewed reported 56% of program participants in independent work, school, or homemaking at follow-up (typically 6–12 months after program completion). The samples included a small percentage of students and a negligible percentage of homemakers. Only 29% were unemployed at follow-up. Presumably the remaining 16% were in sheltered, supported, or volunteer work. Comprehensive-integrated programs showed somewhat better vocational outcomes, in the range of 60–80% in independent community-based work at follow-up.

Previously reviewed studies (Malec & Basford, 1996) document that 36–86% of participants in comprehensive-integrated or community reintegration programs are in unsupervised living at follow-up, with most studies showing greater than 50% living independently in the community. Outcome data from the Transitional Living Centre at Bethesda Hospital

(Olver & Harrington, 1996) in Australia have demonstrated that, whereas 85% of clients required assistance with domestic and community activities on commencement of the program, on completion more than 80% were independent in light domestic tasks, cooking, laundry, shopping, banking, and public transport, and more than 50% were independent in heavy domestic tasks, household organization, and financial management. Although only 2% were able to live independently on entry to the program, 58% were able to live independently afterward, 22% required some supervision, and 19% continued to need active assistance.

Outcome data from community team and community reintegration programs in Australia suggest that there is a need for ongoing, intermittent follow-up to maintain stable employment and to provide further assistance when there is a change in circumstances, for example, when a student leaves school and needs to find work or avocational pursuits (Olver, Ponsford, & Curran, 1996). Coping styles also have a demonstrated influence on long-term psychological adjustment (Curran, Crowe, & Ponsford, 1997). Programs are now being established to focus on the facilitation of more adaptive active problem-solving coping styles rather than the more maladaptive styles, such as avoidance and substance abuse.

Neurobehavioral programs report significant changes in independent-living status. For instance, Eames and Wood (1985) reported a reduction from 79 to 33% in people requiring 24-hour supervision and an increase from 8 to 17% of those who could live without supervision as a result of neurobehavioral treatment. Burke and associates (1988) reported a reduction from 77 to 13% in need of 24-hour supervision and an increase from 23 to 51% in unsupervised living following participation in their neurobehavioral program.

Such cohort studies consistently support the effectiveness of various types of PABIR. Individuals with more severe impairments and disabilities typically require more intensive and sustained intervention to make substantial changes in independent living, social, and vocational adjustment (Cope et al., 1991; Fryer & Haffey, 1987; Johnston, 1991; Malec et al., 1993). Because of the absence of strong scientific evidence (i.e., randomized controlled studies) for the effectiveness of PABIR, requests for third-party funding of these programs are often met with skepticism and reluctance. Outcome data for the specific program proposed and a demonstration that the proposed participant has similar impairments and disabilities to other people successfully served in the program is helpful to third-party payers in appreciating the benefit of these types of programs to their clients. More extensive and better controlled studies of PABIR that include some assessment of level of service required by various levels of impairment and disability would assist rehabilitation professionals in making optimal treatment recommendations to people served and would assist third-party payers in evaluating the cost–benefit of PABIR.

Funding for this type of research, however, is also elusive. Because research in PABIR defies examination through the traditional randomized controlled trial format favored by the National Institutes of Health, funding for multicenter studies from this source in the United States is unlikely. On a more optimistic note, initial studies of postacute rehabilitation pathways through the expanded TBI Model Systems funded by NIDRR may serve as the foundation for more systematic research evaluations of specific PABIR methods in the next funding cycle. Because of the significant benefit to both providers and payers, a partnership approach in which research funded by payers is conducted by providers to answer the efficacy questions of both parties may also merit careful consideration and discussion.

References

Ben-Yishay, Y., & Prigatano, G. P. (1990). Cognitive remediation. In M. Rosenthal, E. R. Griffith, M. R. Bond, & J. D. Miller (Eds.), *Rehabilitation of the adult and child with traumatic brain injury* (2nd ed., pp. 393–400). Philadelphia: Davis.

Ben-Yishay, Y., Silver, S. M., Piasetsky, E., & Rattok, J. (1987). Relationship between employability and vocational outcome after intensive holistic cognitive rehabilitation. *Journal of Head Trauma Rehabilitation, 2*(1), 35–48.

Benedict, R. H. (1989). The effectiveness of cognitive remediation strategies for victims of traumatic head-injury: A review of the literature. *Clinical Psychology Review, 9*, 605–626.

Bond, M. (1984). The psychiatry of closed head injury. In N. Brooks (Ed.), *Closed head injury. Psychological, social and family consequences* (pp. 148–178). London: Oxford University Press.

Burke, W. H., Wesolowski, M. D., & Guth, M. L. (1988). Comprehensive head injury rehabilitation: An outcome evaluation. *Brain Injury, 2*, 313–322.

Centers for head injury accused of earning millions for neglect. (1992, March 16). *New York Times*, p. A1.

Christensen, A. L. (1992). Outpatient management and outcome in relation to work in traumatic brain injury patients. *Scandinavian Journal of Rehabilitation Medicine, 26*(Suppl.), 34–42.

Cope, D. N., Cole, J. R., Hall, K. M., & Barkan, H. (1991). Brain injury: Analysis of outcome in a post-acute rehabilitation system: Part 1. General analysis. *Brain Injury, 5*(2), 111–125.

Curran, C., Crowe, S., & Ponsford, J. (1997). Coping strategies and emotional outcome: A comparison between traumatic brain injury and orthopaedic subjects [Abstract]. *Australian Journal of Psychology, 49*(Suppl.), 136.

Dikmen, S., Machamer, J., & Temkin, N. (1993). Psychosocial outcome in patients with moderate to severe head injury: 2-year follow-up. *Brain Injury, 7*, 113–124.

Eames, P., & Wood, R. (1985). Rehabilitation after severe brain injury: A follow-up study of a behaviour modification approach. *Journal of Neurology, Neurosurgery, and Psychiatry, 48*, 613–619.

Evans, R. W. (1997). Postacute neurorehabilitation: Roles and responsibilities within a national information system. *Archives of Physical Medicine and Rehabilitation, 78*(Suppl.), S17–S25.

Fordyce, D. J., Roueche, J. R., & Prigatano, G. P. (1983). Enhanced emotional reactions in chronic head trauma patients. *Journal of Neurology, Neurosurgery and Psychiatry, 46*, 620–624.

Fryer, L. J., & Haffey, W. J. (1987). Cognitive rehabilitation and community readaptation: Outcomes of two program models. *Journal of Head Trauma Rehabilitation, 2*(3), 51–63.

Gianutsos, R. (1991). Cognitive rehabilitation: A neuropsychological specialty comes of age. *Brain Injury, 5*, 353–368.

Glisky, E. L., Schacter, D. L., & Tulving, E. (1986). Computer learning by memory-impaired patients: Acquisition and retention of complex knowledge. *Neuropsychologia, 24*(3), 313–328.

Godfrey, H. P. D., Partridge, F. M., Knight, R. G., & Bishara, S. (1993). Course of insight disorder and emotional dysfunction following closed head injury: A controlled cross-sectional follow-up study. *Journal of Clinical and Experimental Neuropsychology, 15,* 503–515.

Harrick, L., Krefting, L., Johnston, J., Carlson, P., & Minnes, P. (1994). Stability of functional outcomes following transitional living programme participation: 3-year follow-up. *Brain Injury, 8,* 439–447.

Henry, J., & McGarry, P. (1996). Community-based neuro-rehabilitation. In J. Ponsford, P. Snow, & V. Anderson (Eds.), *International perspectives in traumatic brain injury* (pp. 362–366). Bowen Hills, Queensland, Australia: Australian Academic Press.

Jacobs, H. E. (1979). The Clubhouse: Addressing work-related behavioral challenges through a supportive social community. *Journal of Head Trauma Rehabilitation, 12*(5), 14–27.

Jacobs, H. E., & DeMello, C. (1996). The Clubhouse model and employment following brain injury. *Journal of Vocational Rehabilitation, 7,* 169–179.

Johnston, M. V. (1991). Outcomes of community re-entry programmes for brain injury survivors. Part 2: Further investigations. *Brain Injury, 5*(2), 155–168.

Johnston, M. V., Hall, K. M., & Banja, J. (1994). Outcomes evaluation in traumatic brain injury rehabilitation [Special issue]. *Archives of Physical Medicine and Rehabilitation,* 12(Suppl.).

Johnston, M. V., & Lewis, F. D. (1991). Outcomes of community re-entry programmes for brain injury survivors: Part 1. Independent living and productive activities. *Brain Injury, 5*(2), 141–154.

Jones, M. L., & Evans, R. W. (1992). Outcome validation in post-acute rehabilitation: Trends and correlates in treatment and outcome. *Journal of Insurance Medicine, 24*(3), 186–192.

Lyons, J. L., & Morse, A. R. (1988). A therapeutic work program for head-injured adults. *American Journal of Occupational Therapy, 42*(6), 364–370.

Malec, J. (1984). Training the brain-injured client in behavioral self-management skills. In B. A. Edelstein, & E. T. Couture (Eds.), *Behavioral assessment and rehabilitation of the traumatically brain-damaged* (pp. 121–150). New York: Plenum Press.

Malec, J. F. (1996). Cognitive rehabilitation. In R. W. Evans (Ed.), *Neurology and trauma* (pp. 231–248). Philadelphia: Saunders.

Malec, J. F. (1999). Goal attainment scaling in rehabilitation. *Neuropsychological Rehabilitation, 9*(3–4), 253–275.

Malec, J. F., & Basford, J. S. (1996). Postacute brain injury rehabilitation. *Archives of Physical Medicine and Rehabilitation, 77,* 198–207.

Malec, J. F., Machulda, M. M., & Moessner, A. M. (1997). Assessment of the differing problem perceptions of staff, survivors, and significant others after brain injury. *Journal of Head Trauma Rehabilitation, 12*(3), 1–13.

Malec, J. F., Smigielski, J. S., & DePompolo, R. W. (1991). Goal Attainment Scaling and outcome measurement in postacute brain injury rehabilitation. *Archives of Physical Medicine and Rehabilitation, 72,* 138–143.

Malec, J. F., Smigielski, J. S., DePompolo, R. W., & Thompson, J. M. (1993). Outcome evaluation and prediction in a comprehensive-integrated post-acute outpatient brain injury rehabilitation programme. *Brain Injury, 7*(1), 15–29.

Malec, J. F., & Thompson, J. M. (1994). Relationship of the Mayo-Portland Adaptability Inventory to functional outcome and cognitive performance measures. *Journal of Head Trauma Rehabilitation, 9*(4), 1–15.

Mateer, C. A., & Sohlberg, M. M. (1988). A paradigm shift in memory rehabilitation. In H. A. Whitaker (Ed.), *Neuropsychological studies of nonfocal brain damage* (pp. 202–225). New York: Springer-Verlag.

Matthews, C. G., Harley, J. P., & Malec, J. F. (1991). Guidelines for computer-assisted cognitive neuropsychological rehabilitation and cognitive rehabilitation. *The Clinical Neuropsychologist, 5*(1), 3–19.

McGlynn, S. M., & Schacter, D. L. (1989). Unawareness of deficits in neuropsychological syndromes. *Journal of Clinical and Experimental Neuropsychology, 11,* 143–205.

Meichenbaum, D. (1977). *Cognitive–behavior modification.* New York: Plenum.

Namerow, N. S. (1987). Cognitive and behavioral aspects of brain-injury rehabilitation. *Neurological Clinics, 5,* 569–583.

National Head Injury Association. (1989). *Ethical marketing practices for health care providers engaged in head injury management.* Washington, DC: Author.

Olver, J., & Harrington, H. (1996). Functional outcome after a transitional living programme for adults with traumatic brain injury. In J. Ponsford, P. Snow, & V. Anderson (Eds.), *International perspectives in traumatic brain injury* (pp. 359–361). Bowen Hills, Queensland: Australian Academic Press.

Olver, J. H., Ponsford, J. L, & Curran, C.A. (1996). Outcome following traumatic brain injury: A comparison between 2 and 5 years after injury. *Brain Injury, 10,* 841–848.

Ponsford, J. (1995). Returning to the community. In J. Ponsford, S. Sloan, & P. Snow (Eds.), *Traumatic brain injury: Rehabilitation for everyday adaptive living* (pp. 195–229). Hove, UK: Lawrence Erlbaum.

Prigatano, G. P., Fordyce, D. J., Zeiner, H. K., Roueche, J. R., Pepping, M., & Wood, B. C. (1984). Neuropsychological rehabilitation after closed head injury in young adults. *Journal of Neurology, Neurosurgery, and Psychiatry, 47,* 505–513.

Prigatano, G. P., Klonoff, P. S., O'Brien, K. P., Altman, I. M., Amin, K., Chiapello, D., Shepherd, J., Cunningham, M., & Mora, M. (1994). Productivity after neuropsychologically oriented milieu rehabilitation. *Journal of Head Trauma Rehabilitation, 9*(1), 91–102.

Prigatano, G. P., Fordyce, D. J., Zeiner, H. K., Roueche, J. R., Pepping, M., & Wood, B.C. (1986). *Neuropsychological rehabilitation after brain injury.* Baltimore: Johns Hopkins University Press.

Rattok, J., Ben-Yishay, Y., Ezrachi, O., Lakin, P., Piasetsky, E., Ross, B., Silver, S., Vakil, E., Zide, E., & Diller, L. (1992). Outcome of different treatment mixes in a multidimensional neuropsychological rehabilitation program. *Neuropsychology, 6,* 395–415.

Rimmele, C. T., & Hester, R. K. (1987). Cognitive rehabilitation after traumatic head injury. *Archives of Clinical Neuropsychology, 2,* 353–384.

Rockwood, K., Joyce, B., & Stolee, P. (1997). Use of Goal Attainment Scaling in measuring clinically important change in cognitive rehabilitation patients. *Journal of Clinical Epidemiology, 50,* 581–588.

Rockwood, K., Stolee, P., & Fox, R. A. (1993). Use of Goal Attainment Scaling in measuring clinically important change in the frail elderly. *Journal of Clinical Epidemiology, 46,* 1113–1118.

Schacter, D. L., & Glisky, E. L. (1986). Memory remediation: Restoration, alleviation, and the acquisition of domain-specific knowledge. In B. Uzzell, & Y. Gross (Eds.), *Clinical neuropsychology of intervention* (pp. 257–282). Boston: Martinus Nijhoff.

Schacter, D. L., Rich, S. A., & Stampp, M. S. (1985). Remediation of memory disorders: Experimental evaluation of the spaced retrieval technique. *Journal of Clinical and Experimental Neuropsychology, 7,* 79–96.

Schefft, B. K., Malec, J. F., Lehr, B. K., & Kanfer, F. H. (1996). The role of self-regulation therapy with the brain-injured patient. In M. Maruish, & J. A. Moses, (Eds), *Theoretical foundations of clinical neuropsychology for clinical practitioners* (pp. 237–282). New York: Erlbaum.

Scherzer, B. P. (1986). Rehabilitation following severe head trauma: Results of a three-year program. *Archives of Physical Medicine and Rehabilitation, 67,* 366–374.

Sloan, S., Balicki, S., & Winkler, D. (1996). Community reintegration of people with severe traumatic brain injuries: Keys to success. In J. Ponsford, P. Snow, & V. Anderson (Eds.), *International perspectives in traumatic brain injury* (pp. 346–349). Bowen Hills, Queensland: Australian Academic Press.

Sloan, S., & Ponsford, J. (1995). Managing cognitive problems following TBI. In J. Ponsford, S. Sloan, & P. Snow (Eds.), *Traumatic brain injury: Rehabilitation for everyday adaptive living* (pp. 103–135). Hove, UK: Erlbaum.

Stern, J. M., Groswasser, Z., Alis, R., Geva, N., Hochberg, J., Stern, B., & Yardeni, Y. (1985). Day center experience in rehabilitation of craniocerebral injured patients. *Scandinavian Journal of Rehabilitation Medicine, 12*(Suppl.), 53–58.

Trexler, L. E., Diller, L., Gleuckauf, R., Tomusk, A., Anrieter, B., Ben-Yishay, Y., Bucking-
ham, D., Christensen, A. L., Erant, M., Klonoff, P., Malec, J., Mauer, B., & Seller, S.
(1994). *Consensus conference on the development of a multi-center study on the efficacy
of neuropsychological rehabilitation,* Unpublished manuscript, Zionsville, IN.

Traumatic Brain Injury Act of 1996, P. L. 104-166 (H.R., S. 96), 110 Stat. 1445.

Wehman, P., Kregel, J., Sherron, P., Ngyen, S., Kreutzer, J., Fry, R., & Zasler, N. (1993).
Critical factors associated with the successful supported employment placement of patients with severe traumatic brain injury. *Brain Injury, 7,* 31–44.

Wehman, P., Kreutzer, J., West, M., Sherron, P., Zasler, N., Groah, C., Stonnington, H. H.,
Burns, C., & Sale, P. (1990). Return to work for persons with traumatic brain injury: A
supported employment approach. *Archives of Physical Medicine and Rehabilitation, 71,*
1047–1052.

Willer, B., Rosenthal, M., Kreutzer, J. S., Gordon, W. A., & Rempel, R. (1993). Assessment
of community integration following rehabilitation for traumatic brain injury. *Journal of
Head Trauma Rehabilitation, 8*(2), 75–87.

21

Neuroimaging and Outcome

Erin D. Bigler

In the history of neuroscience, Leonardo Da Vinci somewhere in the early 1500s and Vesalius in 1543 are credited with the first proportional and perceptually accurate drawings of the postmortem human brain (Clarke & Dewhurst, 1996). By the 17th century, greater and greater interest in neuroanatomy had been kindled, yet little was known about brain function related to anatomy (Corsi, 1991). By the 19th century, primitive studies began where postmortem pathological findings of brain anatomy were related to facets of human brain function. Even for most of the 20th century, any relationship between brain structure and function was relegated to the autopsy table and retrospective analysis—not much help for the living patient with a neurological injury or disease. However, that dramatically changed in the 1970s with the advent of the first noninvasive method to image the brain in the living individual, namely, the computerized tomographic (CT) scan. This revolutionized the understanding of injury to the brain and how it relates to rehabilitation outcome. This chapter reviews some contemporary neuroimaging methods and how these techniques provide critical clinical information about rehabilitation. Because much of neuroimaging deals with technical issues concerning the physics of image acquisition, including the technical jargon, for more background in these areas, see Papanicolaou (1998).

The ability to image the human brain in vivo revolutionized neurodiagnostics (Bigler, 1996a, 1996b). The rapid developments in neuroimaging in the past 2 decades have produced methods by which human brain structure (both brain and blood vessels) can be visualized, regions of metabolic activity and blood flow outlined, and some basic neurochemical compositions determined (see Figures 21.1–21.4). Neuropsychological assessment methods have been advanced and interfaced with neuroimaging findings to enhance diagnostic accuracy (Bigler & Clement, 1997). With these impressive methods, diagnostic decision making in the assessment of neurological and neurobehavioral disorders has become more refined and straightforward. For example, Figure 21.3 presents similar levels of magnetic resonance imaging (MRI) of a patient who sustained a severe traumatic brain injury and the brain of a nontraumatized individual. At each level anatomic abnormalities can be clearly identified when compared with the normal anatomy of the noninjured brain. Figure 21.4 presents an image from the same patient using single-photon emission computed to-

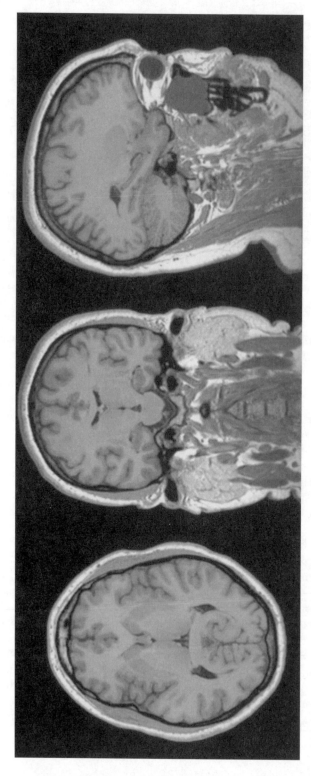

Figure 21.1. The three common planes of an MRI scan: (left) axial or horizontal, (middle) coronal, and (right) sagittal. Note the clarity of the images and the distinction between white- and gray-matter structures.

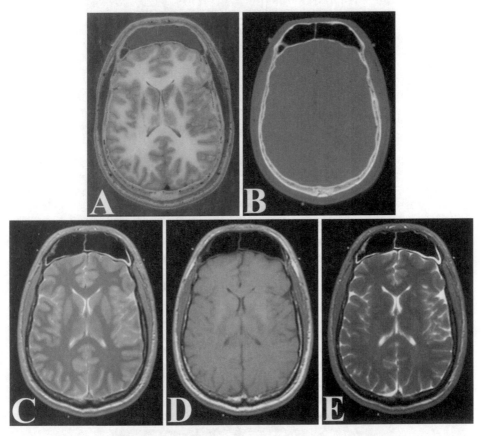

Figure 21.2. (A) Postmortem axial section of the brain at the level of the caudate and anterior horns of the lateral ventricular system, depicting the clear distinction between white and gray matter and bone. (B) Axial computerized tomography (CT) scan using a "bone window" setting at the identical level to A. Note the ability of CT imaging to perfectly capture the bone depicted in the postmortem subject shown in A. The bottom row depicts three types of MRIs based on the "weighting" of the image: (C) mixed weighted or proton density, (D) T1, and (E) T2. As can be readily visualized, the mixed weighted image (C) closely resembles the actual postmortem specimen, where white matter is depicted in darker shades of gray, gray matter represented by lighter gray, and cerebral spinal fluid spaces depicted in white. Each of these weightings has a different sensitivity in the detection of pathological changes. This illustration demonstrates that contemporary imaging methods closely approximate actual anatomy. For information about techniques and nomenclature, see Papanicolau (1998).

mography (SPECT) imaging. SPECT imaging provides a method for investigating blood flow by measuring the perfusion of an injected radiotracer transported by the blood as it is taken up in the brain. Both methods demonstrate abnormalities and are complementary techniques: The SPECT image actually demonstrates a greater area of abnormal perfusion than is defined by the MRI. If the question is whether the patient has

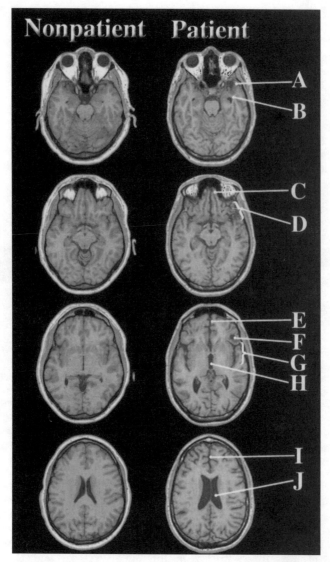

Figure 21.3. Neuroimaging in a patient who sustained frontal-lobe damage secondary to a high-speed motor vehicle accident. The multiple abnormalities identified become apparent when the patient's images are compared with the images of the non-brain-damaged control patient presented on the left. Particularly evident is the enlargement of the ventricular system. (A) Encephalomalacia of right temporal lobe secondary to contusion; (B) dilated temporal horn; (C) focal injury (dark area) to anterior aspect of gyrus rectus, a lesion that typically results in alteration in sense of smell; (D) atrophy in the peris-Sylvian area; (E) widening of the interhemispheric fissure, a sign of frontal atrophy; (F) focal, cystic lesion in the right frontal area, the residual consequence of a prior hemorrhagic contusion, and prominence of the Sylvian fissure, an indication of frontal and temporal lobe atrophy of the right hemisphere; (G) region of Sylvian fissure exhibiting atrophy; (H) dilated third ventricle; (I) reduced size of the cingulate gyrus; and (J) dilated lateral ventricle. From "Neuroimaging in Pediatric Traumatic Brain Injury: Diagnostic Considerations and Relationships to Neurobehavioral Outcome," by E. D. Bigler, 1999, *Journal of Head Trauma Rehabilitation, 14*(4), p. 414. Copyright 1999 by Aspen. Adapted with permission.

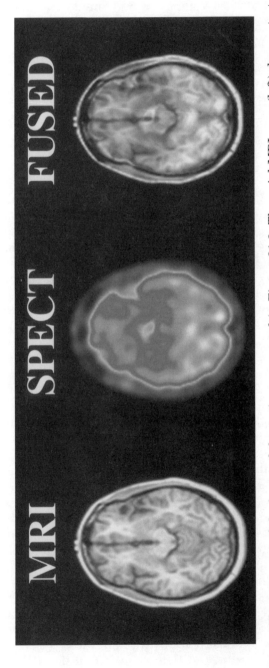

Figure 21.4. Three images of the brain of the patient presented in Figure 21.3. The axial MRI scan (left) demonstrates a focal lesion in the right frontal region of the brain. The midpoint of the lesion is cerebrospinal fluid because there is complete dissolution of brain tissue in that area. The single-photon emission computed tomography (SPECT) imaging (middle) in approximately the same area demonstrates perfusion abnormalities that are greater than the structural defects observed in the MRI scan. This illustration demonstrates how the "functional" imaging of SPECT complements the structural imaging of the MRI scan. The image to the right is the fusion of the MRI scan with the SPECT to provide a composite representation of both images.

sustained an injury and where that injury is located, these two imaging modalities provide an opportunity to visualize gross pathology. Likewise, the neuropsychological and neurobehavioral deficits exhibited by this individual were straightforward—impaired judgment, executive deficits, and dysfunctional memory. In general, however, how well do the abnormalities viewed on neuroimaging studies match the neuropsychological deficits, the course of rehabilitation, and the recovery achieved by patients with neurological disorders? An attempt to answer these questions is the objective of this chapter and represents the next major challenge to neuroimaging because up to this point neuroimaging has focused almost exclusively on diagnostic accuracy (Osborn, 1994).

Background

Without a defined classification of what is abnormal, there would be little utility in even the most elegant of imaging methods. Accordingly, the first 25 years of contemporary neuroimaging have been primarily dedicated to diagnostic issues and emergent medical care, with little emphasis placed on rehabilitative outcome. The other problem over the past two decades of neuroimaging research is that technology has changed so rapidly that it has been impossible for researchers (and clinicians) to keep up with systematic studies examining topics other than diagnostic accuracy. However, as some level of standardization and diagnostic precision (especially with MRI) has been reached, intense interest has focused on issues of rehabilitative treatment and outcome based on imaging studies (Barber et al., 1998; Cwik, Hanstock, Allen, & Martin, 1998; Davis, Bigler, Valdivia, Chong, & Lewine, 1999; De Stefano et al., 1998; Godefroy et al., 1998; Malm et al., 1998; Riahi et al., 1998). In addition, exciting new MRI and other neuroimaging applications on the horizon are likely to contribute to the detection of brain abnormalities as they apply to diagnosis and rehabilitation prediction (see McKinstry & Feinberg, 1998).

The issue of rehabilitative outcome from a neuroimaging perspective is an extremely complex question. On the surface, it may seem straightforward—the larger the lesion, the greater the deficit, and large structural and physiological deficits lead to poor outcomes. In reality, it is not that simple. The old concepts of lesion localization dominated neurology, neuropsychology, and rehabilitative medicine for the better part of this century and still do for some clinicians (see Bigler, 1991). Perusal of neurology texts prior to the advent of contemporary neuroimaging (circa 1975) exemplifies the domination of lesion-localization conceptualizations, particularly for aphasic and apraxic disorders. Figure 21.5 illustrates this point. Prior to the advent of contemporary imaging, clinical case studies, postmortem investigations, and observations through direct visual inspection during neurosurgical procedures all led to various lesion-localization inferences being made concerning regional control over language function (see Figure 21.5; Benson, 1979). Thus, according to this older lesion-localization version of brain–behavior relationships, a lesion in the pos-

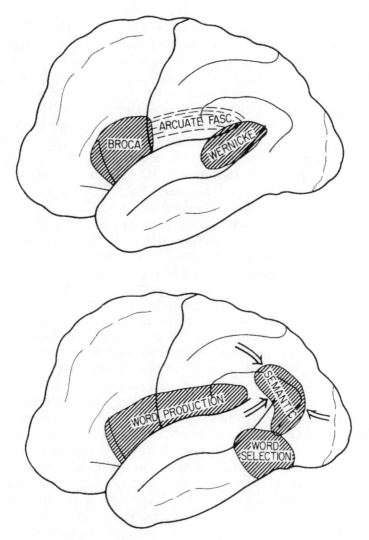

Figure 21.5.   Lateral view schematic of brain regions formerly considered to control certain language functions, based primarily on clinical case studies and postmortem analyses (circa 1980 and earlier). From *Aphasia, Alexia, and Agraphia* (p. 77), by D. F. Benson, 1979, New York: Churchill Livingstone. Copyright 1979 by Churchill Livingstone. Adapted with permission.

terior aspect of the superior temporal gyrus (houses Wernicke's area; see Figure 21.5) would lead to a specific language disorder—Wernicke's or receptive aphasia. So clinicians believed that all they had to do was examine some neuroimaging technique, typically a computerized tomograph (CT) or MRI scan, and the diagnosis along with prognosis would be made. In Figure 21.5, for example, in the upper right corner are the boundaries for producing syntactic and sequential problems. However, problems with language production occur outside of those boundaries on the schematic.

The same holds true for various receptive functions. The outline of these functions is where subcortical pathology produces a pure word deafness, a perceptive area on the cortical surface associated with Wernicke's aphasia, and a semantic area. In the lower right corner are areas outlining regions that produce reading deficits, which were referred to as parietal–temporal alexia, occipital alexia, or frontal alexia. Aphasiologists soon realized, even with the earliest applications of initial-generation CT, that language disturbance following cerebral insult could only be grossly approximated by the location and size of the lesion (see Kertesz, 1994).

This is exemplified in Figure 21.6, in which two patients, approximately the same age, both sustained massive left-hemisphere damage as a consequence of a left middle cerebral artery stroke. One might expect that both patients should have global language deficits and that because these scans exhibit permanent structural damage (in fact, entire areas are simply nonexistent), the deficits should be permanent. Likewise, because the damage is relatively in the same areas (infarction along the distribution of the middle cerebral artery but sparing the caudate and thalamus), one might expect the deficits to be similar. Although the entire left hemisphere was compromised in both individuals, only the patient on the left has a global aphasia—complete loss of both receptive and expressive ability along with loss of reading, spelling, writing, and mathematical ability. His aphasia did not modify or improve over time, despite extensive rehabilitative efforts. In the patient presented on the right, the MRI displays extensive encephalomalacic changes throughout the frontal and temporal regions, with a large area of hemosiderin (blood by-product from previous hemorrhage in the frontal area, depicted by the dark blob). Despite extensive damage—he had far more of the left hemisphere obliterated than just the arcuate fasiculus—clinically this patient exhibited only a conduction aphasia with intact receptive, writing (grammatically correct), and spelling abilities. From an outcome prediction standpoint, the knowledge of the size and location of structural damage predicts one patient's outcome but completely misses the other. These limitations of lesion-localization theory to language function actually generalize to all cognitive functions. With the exception of some dedicated motor and sensorineural systems, which have more predictable and pathognomic neurological sequelae when injured (e.g., hemiplegia), no precise lesion-localization algorithm exists to explain cognitive or neurobehavioral deficits or to guide or predict rehabilitation outcome solely on the basis of neuroimaging studies.

Unlike some aspects of diagnostic medicine where a specific laboratory finding leads to prescriptive treatment with a predictable outcome, neuroimaging as well as neuropsychological findings in the rehabilitation patient do not fully predict outcome in most situations. As shown in Figure 21.6, outcome is determined by more than simply the location, size, or type of the lesion. Psychologists involved in rehabilitative therapies must therefore be careful about making recommendations solely on the basis of neuroimaging findings. Unlike all other bodily systems, the complexity of the brain renders any simplistic lesion-location modeling completely untena-

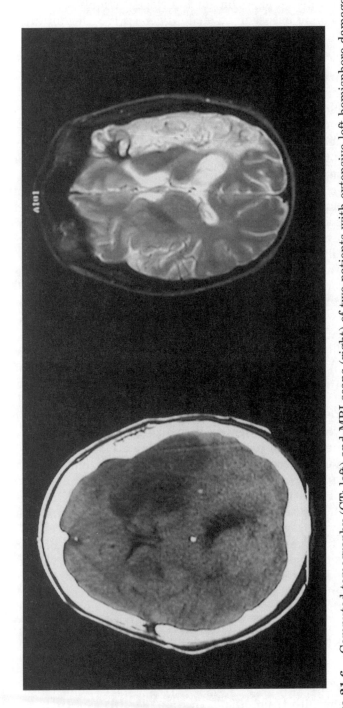

Figure 21.6.   Computed tomography (CT; left) and MRI scans (right) of two patients with extensive left-hemisphere damage but different outcomes. In both scans the patient's left side is on the viewer's right, the standard radiological perspective. In the CT scan the dark area on the left side of the brain represents extensive infarction of the left cerebral hemisphere. Note that the subcortical structures of the head of the caudate nucleus and the thalamus were both preserved. Reviewing the diagrams presented in Figure 21.5, one might predict that both patients would have global language deficits. Although extensive damage is present to the left hemisphere in both patients, only the patient on the left developed a global aphasia.

ble, when it comes to prescribing neurological rehabilitation and predicting outcome. The brain—mind—behavior interface is simply too complex to be captured by a single assessment modality, even the elegant anatomic clarity achieved by contemporary MRI.

Brain Complexity: Challenges for Neuroimaging

Another factor that leads to this complexity relates to the uniqueness of each brain. Each central nervous system (CNS) is an individualized composition of experience and genetic endowment. Thus, no two brains or neural systems or the functions they subserve are alike. This uniqueness is the basis of human identity and diversity. If each brain were identical and each injury or disease exactly the same, humans would be nothing more than little automatons, with all aspects of behavior fully predicted just by brain structure—function relationships. Because of the complexity of the brain—behavior interface, earlier prima facie acceptance of certain neuropsychological tenets has been called into question. For example, neuropsychology has a rich tradition of discussing frontal-lobe damage and frontal-lobe syndrome (FLS; lack of insight, poor judgment, impaired learning and executive function, emotional lability), typically referring to the famous case of Phinneas P. Gage (the first fully described case in the medical literature about FLS; see Damasio, Grabowski, Frank, Galaburda, & Damasio, 1994). In the rehabilitation setting the FLS patient is common and often a significant management problem. Thus, when neuroimaging became sophisticated enough to identify and examine in vivo structural pathology, the assumption was that the presence of a frontal-lobe lesion would be associated with FLS. However, Anderson, Bigler, and Blatter (1996) demonstrated FLS in patients with no demonstrable frontal-lobe lesions on MRI and no FLS in patients with clearly documented frontal pathology. Furthermore, although it would seem intuitive that the presence of well-identified frontal- and temporal-lobe lesions as a consequence of trauma would lead to a specific neuropsychological profile, Kurth, Bigler, and Blatter (1994) demonstrated no relationship between location of acute, focal lesions and neuropsychological outcome. When the same issue is examined in regard to long-term structural sequelae (i.e., static location and size of chronic lesions), only modest relations are often observed (Bigler, Blatter, et al., 1997; Bigler et al., 1996; Mitchener et al., 1997; Wilson et al., 1988), but even the best correlations rarely exceed .6, indicating that less than 40% of the variance is explained by the neuroimaging findings.

Another major reason for the complexity of neuroimaging as it relates to neuropsychological rehabilitation and outcome depends on which neuroimaging techniques are used, when they are done, and a host of patient and demographic issues. An excellent example of this is presented in the case study shown in Figure 21.7. This is a CT and MRI comparison from a 2-year-old patient with traumatic brain injury (TBI) who sustained the severe injury from a fall off a balcony. The acute imaging demonstrates areas of contusion to the right frontal region with small areas of intrinsic

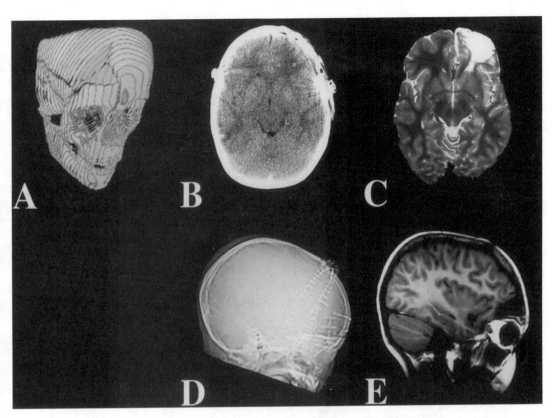

Figure 21.7. CTs and MRIs of a 2-year-old girl with a traumatic brain injury. Top left: Three-dimensional composite of computed tomography imaging depicting the right frontal skull fractures. Top middle: Axial CT scan taken shortly after the fall demonstrating an area of frontal contusion. The right frontal area has a focal white "dot," which represents a focal shear and hemorrhage, with surrounding edema. Note that the surrounding area of the focal hemorrhage is darker than its homologous, right-hemisphere counterpart. Also note a small area of surface contusion (the white area just adjacent to the skull) in the posterior temporal region on the left. Top right: Axial MRI depicting a large porencephalic cyst (white area) in the right frontal region. Bottom right: Sagittal view of the right hemisphere showing a large dark area in the anterior and inferior right frontal lobe indicating a cystic formation where brain tissue used to reside. Bottom left: Lateral skull film showing position of fracture and surrounding surgical clips.

hemorrhage beneath where a depressed skull fracture occurred. By all standards, the child had sustained a severe TBI—loss of consciousness, pediatric Glasgow Coma Scale (GCS; Jennett & Teasdale, 1981) less than 7, multiple areas of skull fractures requiring neurosurgical treatment, and hemorrhagic brain contusions (see Bigler, Clark, & Farmer, 1997). Despite the severity of the acute injury, she responded excellently to emergent medical and neurosurgical care, spent less than 2 weeks in the hospital, and required only limited outpatient rehabilitative services. On the basis of this positive initial outcome, the parents assumed that their daughter had been spared a major debilitating injury. Throughout the remainder of her childhood until about age 8, she was "asymptomatic." However, as time progressed in public school, it became apparent that her higher language ability, including reading, spelling, and mathematical applications, was not developing at a proper pace. When seen in neuropsychological consultation at age 8, obvious deficits in phonetic processing were evident, along with spelling dyspraxia and dyscalculia. It was discovered at this time in the consultation process that the child had never received any follow-up neuroimaging studies after leaving the hospital at age 2. Because she recovered so rapidly she only had the day-of-injury (DOI) scan and a similar scan performed the day after neurosurgical correction for the fracture. MRI studies were requested at age 8 and revealed major structural damage (including a large porencephalic cyst in the right frontal lobe) that far exceeded what was expected based on the DOI scan. Thus, if no other imaging had been performed than the DOI CT scan, by history this would be considered only a case of "frontal contusion," with a few small areas of punctate hemorrhage in frontal brain parenchyma that were observed in the DOI scan. In stark contrast, the follow-up MRI scan depicted a major structural defect of the right frontal lobe, but no other abnormalities elsewhere. At the time of initial injury, the frontal contusion was so severe that tissue disintegrated, forming a porencephalic cyst the size of a fist and leaving no tissue in the anterior right frontal region.

Examples of Brain Complexity

Looking at Figure 21.7, with a huge right-frontal-lobe lesion, one wonders why the language-based symptoms occurred in a predominantly right-hemisphere-damaged child who is right handed. In this child, what likely happened at the time of trauma was a coup-contrecoup injury (directly opposite the site of impact; Bigler, 1990) pattern (see Bigler & Clement, 1997). The point of initial impact was clearly in the right frontal region (an area controlling nonverbal executive and left body side motor function) where the skull fracture occurred, but a contrecoup injury took place in a linear fashion just opposite the focal point of impact, thereby involving the left temporal-parietal cortex. In fact, with careful review of the DOI CT scan in Figure 21.7, a small area of contusion can be visualized in the posterior-left-temporal-lobe region. Because of an immature nervous system and developmental plasticity (see Bigler, Yeo, & Turkheimer, 1989), at the time of injury this infant's brain made immediate adaptations around clearly damaged and dysfunctional brain tissue, and neurobehavioral improvement progressed at a rapid rate where developmental stages were met at appropriate intervals. Unfortunately, later in maturation, when higher level cortical integration was needed for verbal abilities, particularly those associated with reading, spelling, and mathematics, latent deficits from the original contrecoup injury (and probably not the frontal region) were expressed. Obviously, any function that was preprogrammed for the right frontal region was completely transferred, because there is no tissue in the cystic region of the right frontal lesion. One look at the size of the frontal lesion suggests that by traditional standards, this child should have prominent FLS. However, her only manifestation of a residual deficit was in higher order language, typically functions thought to involve the left hemisphere, where MRI demonstrated no lesion (even though the DOI CT was abnormal). Only the DOI CT at age 2 offered information that was clinically relevant to her neuropsychological rehabilitative status at age 8. This entire diagnostic scenario underscores the need for clinical integration of all relevant neuroimaging information. In some cases, imaging performed closest to the onset of symptoms is most predictive of outcome, despite what may be observed in subsequent imaging.

In contrast, the patient presented in Figure 21.8, who as an adult sustained a severe skull fracture and TBI from a fall, had a similar traumatically induced porencephalic (a large hole filled with cerebrospinal fluid [CSF]) cyst in the right frontal region (like the child in Figure 21.7). However, he does have a prominent FLS (dysexecutive features or impaired complex reasoning, judgment, and learning; temperament and personality changes; problematic judgment; and impaired memory). Similarly, the patient presented in Figures 21.3 and 21.4 had a prominent FLS, even though the frontal lesions are relatively small compared to the area of damage present in the patients depicted in Figures 21.7 and 21.8. So why does FLS develop in some and not in others? When it occurs, why is it not dependent on lesion size or precise location? Why do no MRI-identified lesions result in fully predictable (i.e., 100%) neurobehavioral outcomes? The reasons may be related to the limitation of image analysis techniques. Does the application of qualitative ratings and quantitative methods to image analysis add to understanding rehabilitation outcome? The next sections address these topics.

Qualitative and Quantitative Image Analysis and Outcome

In the early days of image analysis with first-generation CT imaging, deciphering the image was truly an art (Eisenberg, 1991). However, as technology improved, the two-dimensional axial images more closely approximated gross anatomic resolution, but technology was lacking on how to quantify such images. The earliest quantitative studies were performed by hand, where tracing of a structure or region of interest was performed. Because of technical limitations with CT imaging (i.e., bone artifact that clouds some regions of bone–brain interface) and the lack of tissue definition (i.e., white vs. gray vs. CSF), application of quantitative methods to CT imaging was of limited value.

However, CT is typically the imaging of choice in any medical emergency, and accordingly, it usually is the scan that provides baseline information. In such situations, research has shown that rating scales are an excellent method for establishing certain characteristics of acute pathology. For example, Marshall et al. (1991) established a clinical rating

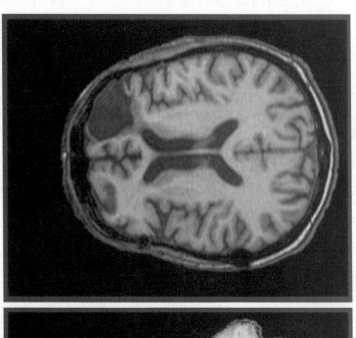

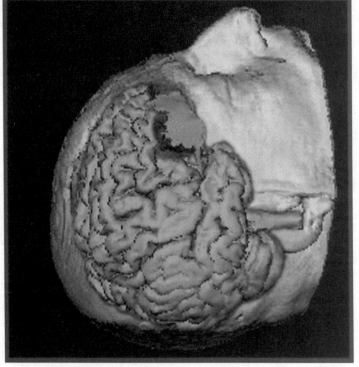

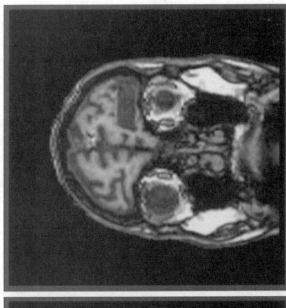

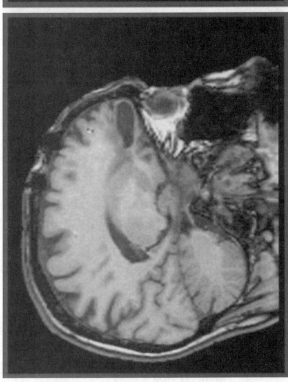

Figure 21.8. Porencephaly (cystic formation in the brain filled with cerebrospinal fluid) associated with traumatic brain injury secondary to a fall that produces frontal-lobe syndrome. The cystic lesion is readily viewed in the standard three planes (axial, top right; coronal, bottom right; and sagittal, bottom left). This imaging information can then be represented in three dimensions, as depicted in the upper left where the light gray region in the inferior right frontal pole represents the cystic lesion and the darker area represents the white-matter degeneration associated with the frontal pole damage.

method for CT classification of head injury. Presence of TBI is first established by history and medical presentation of the patient (i.e., impaired GCS; acute neurologic findings such as aphasia, paralysis, or specific sensory deficit). Once presence of TBI is established, this CT/TBI rating method categorizes three levels of diffuse injury: no visible intracranial pathology (Diffuse Injury Level I), presence of lesions and some edema (brain swelling, Diffuse Injury Level II), and extensive swelling with significant midline shift (Diffuse Injury Level III). The application of this type of rating is discussed further in the next section.

Although the rating system proposed by Marshall et al. (1991) provides a qualitative rating of cerebral pathology, it does not provide a quantitative description of specific anatomical changes associated with brain trauma. With the advent of sophisticated image analysis programs (Rasband, 1993; Robb, 1995), quantitative methods now can be applied in addition to any type of qualitative analysis or rating method. Figure 21.9 summarizes a common quantitative method. The computer screen image of the brain obtained by MRI is merely a constellation of different pixel values, presented on a 256-point "gray scale" ranging from white at one end to dark at the other. Because brain tissue is either white matter or gray matter and these tissues have different physical characteristics, the tissue types have different MRI signals, as represented by values on the gray-scale continuum, and therefore are represented by different pixel vales. The image analysis technique presented in Figure 21.9 is based on a computer algorithm that uses differences in pixel values that permit differentiating white matter, gray matter, and CSF-filled spaces. This segmentation or isolation of tissue is important, because in the most basic analysis, all brain tissue can be categorized as white matter (pathways in the brain; white because of the myelin or fat coating), gray matter (darker-appearing tissue where neuronal cell bodies reside), or cavities or spaces filled by CSF. Such techniques allow the quantification of nearly any brain structure that can be visualized, and normative standards now exist (see Blatter et al., 1995; Blatter et al., 1997). The application of such quantitative analyses is just now being established, as described below.

Although much of the discussion above has centered on TBI imaging studies, the principles of image interpretation and quantitative image analysis apply to all CNS disorders and diseases where neuroimaging displays demonstrable abnormalities. For example, multiple sclerosis (MS) is a common neurological disorder seen in the context of rehabilitation. MS has characteristic lesions of the white matter (demyelination) that can be observed by MRI (Osborn, 1994). However, the mere detection of a lesion may have little relationship to actual disability. Even when multiple factors are considered, such as demyelination "load" by quantifying the number of lesions, their volume or location, and even the integrity of white matter through spectroscopy, only limited success in predicting the course of MS has been achieved (De Stefano et al., 1998; Riahi et al., 1998). This is not unique to MS and applies to all neurological disorders. Simply stated, despite the very sophisticated and refined detection of anatomic and physiological abnormalities by contemporary imaging, the interpre-

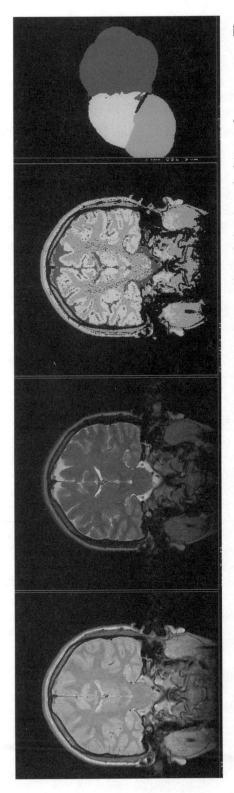

Figure 21.9. The mixed-weighted or proton density scan on the left provides excellent definition of white and gray matter. The T2-weighted image, second from the left, clearly outlines cerebrospinal fluid (CSF) space. The images are coregistered. By using the best features of each protocol, a feature space map can be generated (far right) where the proton density image is represented by the Y axis and the T2 images by the X axis. This feature space map can be manipulated to enhance the likelihood of a given pixel to be either white matter, gray matter, or CSF space. This information can then be used to "segment" the brain into its three components—white and gray matter and cerebrospinal fluid-filled spaces, as shown in the second image from the right. This information can be used to calculate the volume of any structure or region of the brain. See Papanicolau (1998) for more information on procedures.

tation of the significance of those abnormalities in the context of rehabilitation outcome is complex. Nonetheless, research into this neuroimaging conundrum provides some important insights into how imaging findings may be useful in predicting outcome; this topic is discussed in the next section.

Prediction of Outcome for Patients With Multiple Sclerosis

It was once thought that there should be a linear relationship between presence of white-matter abnormalities (i.e., their number and size) on the MRI and level of impairment in the MS patient. The assumption was that the number of white-matter abnormalities would result in an accumulative pathological "loading" effect that would relate directly to disability. Another way of stating this would be the simple (although incorrect) axiom that the more brain damage, the greater the disability, and with greater disability, the less positive the outcome. Because MS may be treated with pharmaceutical and rehabilitation methods, considerable research has focused on attempting to establish some type of standard based on MRI-identified white-matter abnormalities, because these are so objective and reproducible.

However, all of the problems discussed in the TBI examples given above apply to this problem. For example, the study by Riahi et al. (1998) examined the total load of white-matter abnormality defined by three-dimensional (3-D) MRI analysis in individuals with MS. The highest correlation (.67) between disability (i.e., motor disability) and any other variable was with the total white-matter lesion load in a specific area, the corticospinal track. Lesions elsewhere correlated either modestly or minimally with any other type of disability. Because the corticospinal track is a small bilateral and well-defined pathway with dedicated motor fibers, it is not surprising that lesions detected there relate to motor disability. What is surprising is that a clearly visible and distinctly localized lesion in the corticospinal track, the only pathway projecting from motor cortex directly to spinal motor neurons, accounts for less than 50% of the variance associated with motor disability. With such imperfect relationships, it is obvious that simply knowing a lesion's location and loading factor does not tell the whole picture, even when the lesion is precisely located in a dedicated motor tract and clearly identifiable region. Furthermore, with such imperfect relationships, it is virtually impossible to simply use one neuroimaging finding to predict rehabilitative outcome.

What has just been discussed with motor deficits in MS also applies to cognitive deficits (Rao, 1996). However, Hohol et al. (1997) have demonstrated some improvement in predicting overall cognitive performance in MS patients when MRI-identified lesion burden is monitored over time. Here again, it appears that simplistic views of brain pathology to neurobehavioral status must be avoided in the rehabilitation of neurologically compromised patients. Camp et al. (1999) summarized this as follows: "the cognitive dysfunction . . . in MS has a complex and mutifactorial etiology, which is not adequately explained by pathology as demonstrated on conventional MRI" (p. 1341).

Clinical correlation by the clinician remains an extremely important part of rehabilitation psychology, and this has to be done by the clinician. Thus, knowing that an MS patient has an identifiable lesion, knowing where the lesion is and whether there is any change over time combined with the psychological, neuropsychological, and pertinent medical information about a patient does permit the clinician to make some reasonable inferences about treatment and outcome. The point here is that rehabilitation decision making is affected by the integration of all of this information, not just one test, no matter how sophisticated or elegant the imaging procedure.

Prediction of Outcome for Patients With Traumatic Brain Injury

The conclusion of the previous section should not be interpreted to mean that brain-imaging methods are fraught with too many problems to yield definitive empirical findings applicable to rehabilitation. Contemporary neuroimaging is a new field, and it is merely taking time, combined with trial and error, to develop proper databases to yield the anticipated clinical usefulness of neuroimaging information in rehabilitation. Superior and futuristic technology supplants the old, and the amazing technological advances of the past 2 decades give one reason to believe that imaging of the brain will only improve over time. Thus, applications of various types of imaging and image analysis methods to explore ways to improve the prediction of rehabilitation outcome remain a most worthwhile endeavor, with the expected outcome of enormous clinical potential.

A study by Ryser, Bigler, and Blatter (1996) demonstrates the limits of current imaging technology. This study examined 79 patients with moderate to severe TBI in the context of qualitative neuroimaging information (i.e., clinical rating of DOI CT scans according to the protocol proposed by Marshall et al. (1991), combined with quantitative magnetic resonance (QMR) findings (based on follow-up MRI scans obtained at least 6 weeks postinjury) and rehabilitative and neuropsychological outcome. All patients received comprehensive in- and outpatient rehabilitative services. To measure rehabilitation outcome, all patients received the Disability Rating Scale (DRS; Rappaport, Hall, Hopkins, Belleza, & Cope, 1982) and the Rancho Los Amigos Cognitive Functioning Scale (RLAS; Duncan, 1990), along with the Functional Independent Measure (FIM; Research Foundation–State University of New York, 1990) on admission and at discharge from the rehabilitation unit. For both the DRS and RLAS, levels of disability and cognitive impairment, as expected, were at their maximum at the time of injury and gradually decreased over time. The FIM score demonstrated the most significant limitations in levels of independence, as is expected, in the acute and subacute phase of injury and gradually improved over time. Thus, as a group, these patients responded to the rehabilitative milieu and improved in various domains of function, although in any such study no control over spontaneous recovery can be made.

From a qualitative neuroimaging standpoint, the majority of these TBI patients had a Level II diffuse injury as determined by DOI CT ratings outlined by Marshall et al. (1991). However, despite well-defined and observed abnormalities on CT imaging, only a few modest relationships (typically $r < .3$) were significant between qualitative CT ratings and outcome. Consequently, even though distinct abnormalities were observable at the time of brain injury, little systematic relationship between qualitative markers of cerebral trauma and rehabilitation outcome were observed.

Similarly, applying QMR image analysis to this same group of TBI patients yielded somewhat parallel results. It is important to understand that when the brain is traumatically injured, it progresses through some well-defined stages characterized by degeneration (Bigler, 1990, 1997). This progression that culminates in brain atrophy presents a paradox: Subsequent to injury the noncomatose surviving patient with TBI passes through various stages of improvement, but brain morphology based on QMR measures (see Blatter et al., 1997) shows an ever-increasing degree of cerebral atrophy during the same passage of time. Such observations of the dynamically changing brain in response to trauma during the first 6–18 months postinjury probably further complicate the clinical picture between QMR neuroimaging status and rehabilitation outcome. DRS, RLAS, and FIM scores distinctly improve in the same time frame that the brain goes through substantial degenerative changes, culminating in significant loss of brain volume and more than doubling of CSF space. Thus, brain morphology changes, in some cases dramatically, over time even as the patient is improving. So is there a time when brain imaging should be performed to maximize brain–behavior relations in the rehabilitative patient?

Figure 21.10 shows a normal MRI scan compared with a "normal" clinical CT scan at the time of injury compared with the MRI-identified significant changes in this TBI patient over the next 18 months. Such an observation clearly demonstrates the need to monitor neuroimaging changes over time postinjury or symptom–disease onset (i.e., tumor, cerebrovascular accident, degenerative disease). Perhaps the relationship between brain imaging and rehabilitative outcome is limited because most studies have used a single scan, not uniformly taken at some arbitrary point postinjury without reference to the dynamic changes that occur over time in the brain once it is injured. This is research that needs to be done. For example, in the patient whose scans are presented in Figure 21.10, had the second scan not been obtained, the clinician would have been left with the impression that although the patient had a serious acute head injury (i.e., GCS < 11), no major structural damage had been sustained (because the acute CT was negative). By performing the follow-up scan, it is obvious that considerable structural damage has taken place, and this is consistent with the persistence of cognitive and behavioral sequelae observed in this patient. Neuroimaging analysis has not yet analyzed scan

Normal   04-Jul-96   25-Feb-98

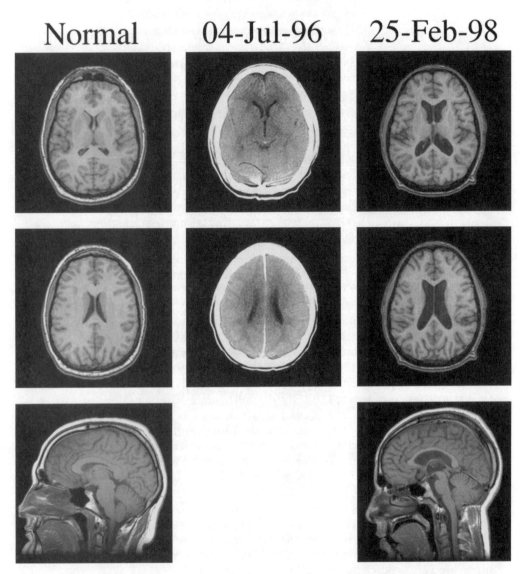

Figure 21.10. Comparison of change in neuroimaging studies following traumatic brain injury, where the days-of-injury (DOI) scan is interpreted as normal.
On July 4, 1996, the patient sustained a severe closed head injury (Glasgow Coma
Scale = 6), but the DOI scan was interpreted as normal. The radiologist circled a
region in the posterior skull area where a congenital skull deformity was corrected,
but this was unrelated to the injury. MRI follow-up more than 2 years later showed
significant ventricular dilation, a sign of generalized brain atrophy in response to
trauma. The thinning of the corpus callosum is another index of cerebral atrophy.
This case demonstrates that the key to pathological changes may be the degree
that a brain changes from baseline rather than static abnormalities viewed on a
given day postinjury.

sequences sufficiently well to be able to infer the optimal time to image for predicting outcomes.

In the Ryser et al. (1996) study, despite distinct and measurable qualitative changes on neuroimaging findings, the relationship of quantitative neuroimaging outcomes to neuropsychological and rehabilitation outcomes was only modestly better than qualitative analyses. Three quantitative brain measures were found to have the most prominent relationship to neuropsychological outcome following TBI. The significant relationships were all associated with changes in the ventricular system—third-ventricle and temporal-horn measures of the lateral ventricular system along with a ventricle-to-brain ratio (VBR). The third ventricle is likely sensitive because it sits at midline and is responsive to subcortical as well as cortical degenerative changes. Reider-Groswasser, Cohen, Costeff, and Groswasser (1993) have demonstrated the importance of the third-ventricle measurement to rehabilitative outcome, where it has been assumed that third-ventricle expansion is an indicator of nonspecific neuronal degeneration at the subcortical and cortical levels (also see Anderson, Wood, Bigler, & Blatter, 1996; Wood & Bigler, 1995). Thus, third-ventricle size represents a relatively good index of overall brain pathology: The larger the size, the worse the rehabilitation outcome. The VBR also is a measure of global brain integrity and demonstrates a negative relationship to outcome. A larger VBR is an index of greater cerebral atrophy.

Temporal-horn dilation was negatively correlated with neuropsychological and rehabilitative outcome. Because the temporal lobe is critical to the integration of so many human cognitive functions, it is not surprising that it relates to outcome (see Bigler, Johnson, & Blatter, 1999). However, none of these measures achieved a correlation higher than .45 with rehabilitation outcome. Consequently, despite significant relationships between QMR and neuropsychological and rehabilitative outcome, applying quantitative assessment to the scan accounted for less than 20% of the variance. Thus, even with very accurate measurements of specific brain structures and regions distinctly affected by traumatic injury, quantitative neuroimaging findings account for only a limited amount of variance associated with rehabilitation outcome. Despite the lure of exquisite precision captured by contemporary neuroimaging of brain structure, knowing the degree of damage provides only partial information to the clinician interested in predicting rehabilitation outcome.

Obviously, knowing about structural damage through neuroimaging analysis provides some important information but yields only one piece of the diagnostic and predictive puzzle. What seems to be the next step is to integrate structural neuroimaging data with other characteristics of the patient's diagnostic and rehabilitation profile to better predict outcome. As a logical application of this principle, what is the outcome when QMR and neuropsychological data and injury severity along with some premorbid indicators are examined in terms of their interaction? Using a subset of the Ryser et al. (1996) data, Lowry (1996) examined the interactive nature of a marker of injury severity (GCS), neuropathologic impairment (QMR), and degree of neuropsychological impairment (standard score on the Trail Making Test; Reitan & Davison, 1974). The interaction of these three variables was examined using principal component analysis. Simple linear modeling between any two of these variables revealed only minimal relationships, but the interaction of these three variables does provide important information about the relative value of each parameter. Thus, TBI patients who function in the normal range on the Trail Making Test (indicating normal visual scanning and visual–verbal discrimination, motor speed, and planning) and have a high GCS score (indicating injury in the mild range) tended to have minimal or no QMR change associated with injury. Similarly, those who had a mild injury and had the least neuropsychological deficit had the least brain atrophy, or those with the least brain atrophy had the least neuropsychological deficit and the mildest rating of injury. Thus, if two variables were known (e.g., impaired Trail Making performance and low GCS), then QMR abnormalities were likely. The presence of just a low GCS score or just an impaired Trail Making score was not necessarily associated with QMR findings. Thus, the interaction on these three factors was the key.

So much of the neuroimaging research in the past has been looking at two dimensions—presence or absence of a lesion or localization findings compared to some index of rehabilitation outcome. Much of the discussion of this chapter has shown the limited utility for such research. More important and instructive future research is likely to deal with the interaction of neuroimaging indicators with measures of neuropsychological function and rehabilitation status. Moreover, the new imaging techniques discussed below, which provide more of a physiological index to brain function, are likely to improve the understanding of the significance of structural lesions.

New Technologies to Solve Old Problems

Most neuroimaging research of the past, and a major focus of this chapter, has been on structural imaging. Multiple avenues of measuring metabolic, blood flow, or other "activation" measures of cerebral function recently have been applied to the problem of evaluating the patient in neurological rehabilitation. Figure 21.11 depicts the type of neurochemical analysis that can be achieved with contemporary magnetic resonance spectroscopy. These chemical constituents of the brain may be critical markers for CNS integrity. For example, N-acetyl-L-aspartate (NAA) is found in neurons and therefore is considered to be a neuronal marker. Reduced NAA probably indicates damaged, biochemically abnormal, or dysfunctional neurons. Using MRS-identified NAA, Friedman, Brooks, Jung, Hart, and Yeo (1998) and Ross and Ernst (1998) demonstrated promising findings in showing NAA abnormalities associated with the severity of brain injury. Friedman et al. also demonstrated that reduced NAA was strongly related to worse neuropsychological outcome. It may be that in TBI, reduced NAA is an indicator of the degree of diffuse axonal injury, a main substrate of pathology in cerebral trauma (Bigler, 1997).

Another area with great promise is functional magnetic resonance im-

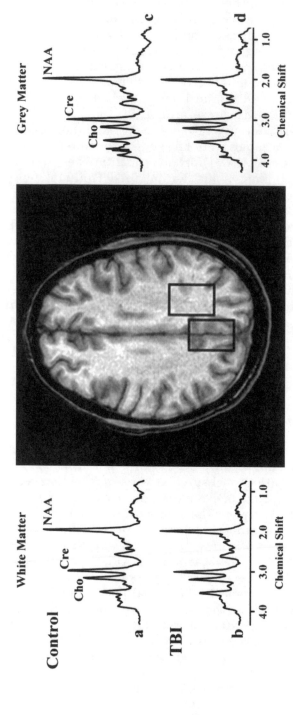

Figure 21.11. MRIs of a patient with a traumatic brain injury (TBI). The MRI scan in the axial plane is presented in the middle, where the right region of interest (ROI) defines the area where white-matter spectroscopic values were obtained, and the centrally located ROI defines the region where gray matter was assessed. The chemical shift analysis is presented on the left for white matter and the right for gray matter. Although the differences are subtle to the naked eye, the TBI patient's MRIs findings differ significantly from that of a non-TBI patient. NAA = N-acetyl-L-aspartate, cre = creatine; cho = choline; a = white matter chemical shift in control; b = white matter chemical shift in TBI patient; c = gray matter chemical shift in control; d = gray matter chemical shift in TBI patient. From "Proton MR Spectroscopic Findings Correspond to Neuropsychological Function in Traumatic Brain Injury," by S. D. Friedman, W. M. Brooks, R. E. Jung, B. L. Hart, and R. A. Yeo, 1999, *American Journal of Neuroradiology, 19,* p. 1881. Copyright 1999 by the American Society of Neuroradiology. Adapted with permission.

aging (fMRI; see Figure 21.12), a measure of cell activation based on the paramagnetic properties of deoxyhemoglobin and its concentration. Prichard (1998) and Prichard and Cummings (1997) reviewed potential rehabilitation applications of fMRI. In regions of cerebral activation there is increased oxygen use, which induces a rise deoxyhemoglobin that can be detected by MRI techniques. Widespread research on fMRI has been ongoing for several years. Although it is too early to make inferences about the rehabilitation potential of fMRI findings, fMRI provides the exquisite anatomic detail and precision of MRI combined with an index of functional activation. Accordingly, this technique has considerable promise for evaluating neurobehavioral deficits.

A third area of research is with magnetoencephalography (MEG). This procedure assesses magnetic field potentials and their alterations in various behavioral and pathological states (Lewine & Orrison, 1995; Lewine, Davis, Sloan, Kodituwakku, & Orrison 1999). Figure 21.13 depicts the application of MEG to the more traditional MRI and SPECT imaging observed in the patient presented in Figures 21.3 and 21.4. What this figure illustrates is the greater sensitivity and range of abnormality detected by MEG than MRI or SPECT combined. This patient's MRI presents excellent anatomic detail of the pathology, but the SPECT imaging, in this case based on blood flow characteristics, demonstrates that the perfusion of the radiotracer is considerably more extensive than the boundaries defined by the structural pathology seen with the MRI. Moreover, MEG abnormalities, which are based on the physiological properties of underlying brain tissue, exhibit an even greater distribution of pathology.

With the improvement in imaging modalities, another obvious application is to monitor functional changes in the brain over time during the recovery process. For example, Laatsch et al. (Laatsch, Jobe, Sychra, Lin, & Blend, 1997; Laatsch, Pavel, Jobe, Lin, & Quintana, 1999) followed patients with TBI with SPECT imaging and neuropsychological testing while they received intense cognitive rehabilitation therapy. Improved cognitive function was associated with improved cerebral blood flow determined by SPECT imaging and matched improved neuropsychological test performance and rehabilitation outcome. This type of research design obviously is contaminated by spontaneous recovery and the passage of time, but conceptually, the idea that someday clinicians will be able to functionally monitor changes during the rehabilitation process and actually predict outcomes has intriguing possibilities.

The integration of this information with other clinical and demographic data is vital to understanding the ultimate outcome in brain injury. At some point workable algorithms may be developed that include quantitative measures of brain structures and various combinations of functional brain imaging data (some that may be unanticipated and unknown at this time) along with neuropsychological findings and clinical observation that will be powerfully predictive of outcome. Being predictive of outcome, this information is likely to guide rehabilitation.

Part of the art and science of neuroimaging interpretation has been the ability to take two-dimensional information and, through the "minds

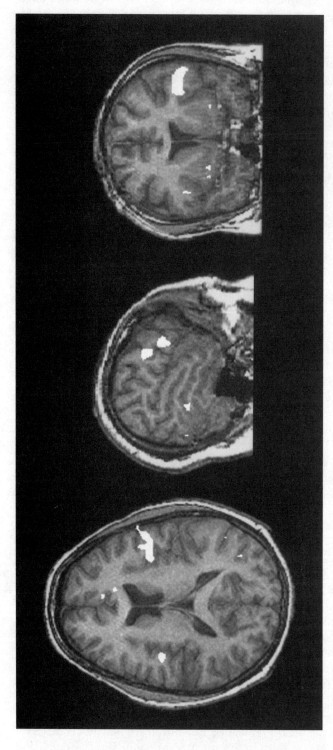

Figure 21.12. A functional magnetic resonance imaging. In this sequence of axial, sagittal, and coronal images, the activation pattern from a language task is mapped out on the brain. (From a patient of Robert Burr, University of Utah). From "Neuroimaging in Pediatric Traumatic Brain Injury: Diagnostic Considerations and Relationships to Neurobehavioral Outcome," by E. D. Bigler, 1999, *Journal of Head Trauma Rehabilitation, 14*(4), p. 419. Copyright 1999 by Aspen. Adapted with permission.

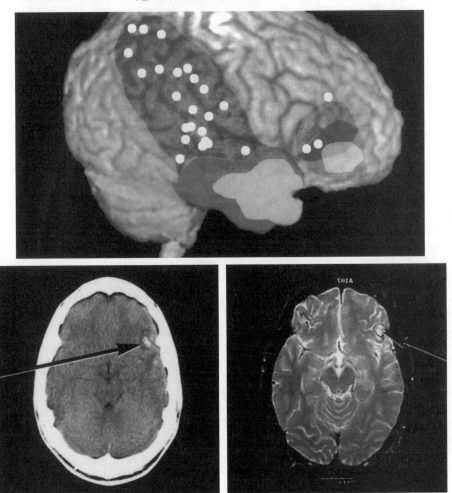

Figure 21.13. Integration of MRI, single-photon emission computed tomography (SPECT), and magnetoencephalography (MEG) images. This is the same patient as depicted in Figures 21.3 and 21.4; however, the MRI has been rendered in lateral three-dimensional perspective with the focal lesions depicted in Figures 21.3 and 21.4 superimposed over the damaged areas with SPECT (see Figure 21.4) superimposed on MRI abnormalities and, finally, points of MEG (dots) also superimposed. Note that the structural imaging of MRI only classifies part of the damage and that MEG and SPECT, which are both more sensitive to the physiological abnormalities, show much larger areas of dysfunction. I thank Jeffrey Lewine, whose laboratory performed the MEG. The CT in the lower left shows the area of acute contusion (arrow) on the day of injury, and the MRI in the lower right shows the residual structural damage (arrow) in the frontal and temporal lobe regions. ALFMA = abnormal low-frequency magnetic activity, representing an area of physiological damage and dysfunction.

eye," translate that information into 3-D space. Most neural structures, such as the hippocampus, amygdala, or ventricular system, have irregular shapes, with projections coursing in various directions and sizes. Similarly, brain lesions are almost always irregular in size, shape, and configuration. However, with the application of current MRI technology, the brain and any structure can be presented in 3-D (e.g., see Hopkins, Abildskov, Bigler, & Weaver, 1997). This imaging permits in one view observation of multiple brain structures simultaneously. Existing pathology or other imaging modalities (i.e., SPECT, MEG, fMRI, MRI) can then be mapped onto these 3-D images, as presented in Figure 21.14. Three-dimensional image analysis holds great promise for further detailed assessment of brain structure and also provides the rehabilitation patient and family more informative (i.e., user-friendly) images for viewing. Significant improvements are rapidly occurring in automated imaging (Webb et al., 1999) and new MRI protocols that even permit the detection of fiber tracks (Virta, Barnett, & Pierpaoli, 1999). The implications of such research are that MRI will be capable of detecting abnormalities at an even more sensitive resolution level, and almost the entire brain and all of its constituent parts will be automatically displayed in 3-D.

Assessment Implications for the Future

As reviewed in this chapter, incredible accomplishments have been reached in the past 2 decades of brain imaging research. The ability to safely and noninvasively image with MRI (Kangarlu et al., 1999) and visualize the brain in 3-D along with functional assessment provides detailed image analysis of brain pathology in the living individual. With intense research and improved pathological detection by neuroimaging, clinicians will acquire a better understanding of brain imaging findings in the context of rehabilitation. In fact, this line of research will likely change all of neuropsychological assessment. I (Bigler, 1966) predicted that neuropsychological assessment will move directly into the imaging environment. For example, in the near future a patient with memory disorder will be tested online using MRI with neuropsychological probes of memory function while undergoing fMRI followed by MRI of the hippocampus. With such integration of brain image with brain function, much of what is currently done in the neuropsychological assessment of memory will become obsolete. Likewise, there will undoubtedly be neurobehavioral probes developed that will permit direct assessment of a wide spectrum of behaviors.

Neuroimaging will likely change the face of neuropsychology, rehabilitation psychology, and clinical psychology. Almost all doctoral programs in psychology currently require some course work in the biological basis of behavior. However, what will likely be required in the future is a much more detailed neuroscience education of basic and advanced brain anatomy, physiology, and pathology, as well as applied experience in understanding neuroimaging and neuroradiology (see Papanicolaou, 1998). Some

Figure 21.14. Various 3-D orientations illustrate different perspectives of how the brain can be generated in a 3-D view. The image on the left shows the frontal and temporal lobes with the spinal cord in a saggital cut and with the skin, skull, and meninges intact behind the coronal break. The middle view shows the partial face with a horizontal and saggital transection, exposing the temporal and inferior frontal lobe, and the horizontal cut allows visualization of the lateral ventricles. The image on the far right is a midsaggital cut, showing the left lateral ventricle intact as it meets the horizontal surface cut at the peri-Sylvian level. This type of imaging graphically displays the fact that the 3-D presentation is almost limitless and essentially any perspective desired can be portrayed. Various functional imaging findings can then be superimposed on the 3-D imaging.

of this training will be eased by the virtual classroom, where real-time 3-D training programs are now available to visualize and learn about brain structure and function.

Psychology students and psychologists in training who want to remain current with developments in cognitive neuroscience need to take heed: In the span of a single decade, science has managed to assess brain function in ways that had been simply speculated about (Bigler et al., 1989, p. 344). In the context of neuroimaging it is now possible simultaneously to view a structure, apply various physiological and metabolic analyses, and use neurobehavioral probes to assess function. Soon rapid measures that automatically compare normal anatomy with pathological changes will be available. Algorithms will use and integrate this information to make predictions about behavior, treatment, and recovery for all neurological diseases and disorders. Thus, for the future, what psychologists need to know is how to integrate this information with a patient's symptoms and behavior to guide neuropsychology and rehabilitation psychology.

The 100-year-old tradition of paper-and-pencil tests and questionnaires in psychology will give way to computer- and virtual-reality-based test programs. The clinical practice of psychology had its origin in personal contact, compassion, and understanding of the human condition, and the need for understanding and professional person-to-person interaction and leadership will continue. Psychologists involved in rehabilitation, regardless of their specialty, will require this human commitment, but they will receive more extensive neuroscience training.

The issues around neuroimaging also have implications for the costs of such integrated procedures. Unfortunately, the services of clinical psychologists, neuropsychologists, and rehabilitation psychologists have become less reimbursable over the past decade. This trend is likely to continue. However, if the diagnostic power of integrated neuroimaging and computer-based assessment methods become appropriately standardized and predictive, the costs of such assessments are likely to be economical, because they will be fast and accurate and provide important information to guide rehabilitation decisions. Thus, economics will be another factor that will probably eliminate many traditional assessment practices.

For example, traditional evaluation of just verbal abilities typically takes a minimum of an hour and a maximum of several hours. Neurobehavioral probes are being established that provide for reliable and rapid in vivo assessment with fMRI. As this research progresses and clinical application is reached, these probes will provide rapid neuroimaging information about basic auditory and language reception, language comprehension, and speech production. Fluency will not be assessed by the clinician writing down the patients' generated word production for the number of words produced in 1 minute that begin with a certain consonant. The next-generation assessment will have a voice-activated computer that not only records the actual fluency but also examines activation patterns from regions involved in word generation (prespeech) compared with actual speech production (including quality of articulation). The MRI scan will be automatically compared with a normative database not only for morphology (standardized for age, sex, body size, education, and vocation as well as certain medical variables) but also for standard activation patterns (the fMRI component). There will be no need for a standard sensory–perceptual examination because all basic sensory functions will be directly visualized through tactile, auditory, visual, olfactory, and gustatory probes. Executive, memory, spatial–perceptual, and perceptual–motor functions will be assessed as well. Part of the algorithm in these futuristic systems will be to determine when a threshold for normalcy or pathology is passed rather than administering the whole procedure.

A major limitation of current assessment techniques is their requirement that all aspects of the test be administered. Using the speech example above, the clinician may be fully aware of language deficits shortly into the assessment process, but the entire battery must be administered to maintain psychometric reliability and validity. In the future, much of this will be obviated by the integration of neuroimaging with neurobehavioral assessment because direct measures of brain activation will be combined with behavioral assessment, all under the integration and scrutiny of powerful databases. Speed and accuracy will be the key to assessment in the future. These factors will keep costs down. Because neurological and rehabilitation patients must have neuroimaging performed, during standard neuroimaging neurobehavioral probes may become part of that protocol. In the early days of MRI considerable time was required to obtain imaging. What took minutes in the past can now be achieved in seconds. Computer hardware and software will only become faster, which translates into less patient time in the scanner. Less time typically equates to less cost. Likewise, because fMRI is noninvasive and has minimal risks, there will not be the medical limitations associated with other neuroimaging procedures (e.g., positron emission tomography), thereby increasing the availability of fMRI procedures for determining brain structure–function relationships. If science is at the brink of revealing the entire human genome, methods of (neuro)psychological assessment in rehabilitation can and will undergo similar profound changes of understanding as new technology is applied to these clinical issues.

Conclusion

Neuroimaging studies provide rich qualitative and quantitative information about the brain. Exactly how this information relates to rehabilitation remains an area of active investigation. Simple lesion-localization-outcome paradigms of the past must be abandoned. More integrative approaches using multiple neuroimaging methods (and methods for image analysis) combined with neuropsychological, medical, and demographic data will probably yield important insights into rehabilitation outcome in a variety of neurological disorders. It is likely that some greater success in prescriptive rehabilitative outcome will come from neuroimaging studies that take this integrative approach. In fact, I predict that neuroimaging will radically alter the neuropsychological and rehabilitative assessment of the neurological patient and that many current clinical practice techniques will simply become passé within a few years.

References

Anderson, C. V., Bigler, E. D., & Blatter, D. D. (1996). Frontal lobe lesions, diffuse damage, and neuropsychological functioning in traumatic brain-injured patients. *Journal of Clinical and Experimental Neuropsychology, 18*(1), 1–9.

Anderson, C. V., Wood, D. G., Bigler, E. D., & Blatter, D. D. (1996). Lesion volume, injury severity, and thalamic integrity following head injury. *Journal of Neurotrauma, 13*(1), 35–40.

Barber, P. A., Darby, D. G., Desmond, P. M., Yang, Q., Gerraty, R. P., Jolley, D., Donnan, G. A., Tress, B. M., & Davis, S. M. (1998). Prediction of stroke outcome with echoplanar perfusion- and diffusion-weighted MRI. *Neurology, 51*, 418–426.

Benson, D. F. (1979). *Aphasia, alexia, and agraphia.* New York: Churchill Livingstone.

Bigler, E. D. (1990). *Traumatic brain injury: Mechanisms of damage, assessment, intervention and outcome.* Austin, TX: Pro-ED.

Bigler, E. D. (1991). Neuropsychological assessment, neuroimaging, and clinical neuropsychology: A synthesis. *Archives of Clinical Neuropsychology, 6*, 113–132.

Bigler, E. D. (1996a). *Handbook of human brain function: Neuroimaging II: Clinical applications* (Vol. 1). New York: Plenum Press.

Bigler, E. D. (1996b). *Handbook of human brain function: Neuroimaging II. Clinical applications* (Vol. 2). New York: Plenum Press.

Bigler, E. D. (1997). Brain imaging and behavioral outcome in traumatic brain injury. In E. D. Bigler, E. Clark, & J. E. Farmer (Eds.), *Childhood traumatic brain injury: Diagnosis, assessment, and intervention* (pp. 7–29). Austin, TX: Pro-ED.

Bigler, E. D. (1999). Neuroimaging in pediatric traumatic brain injury: Diagnostic considerations and relationships to neurobehavioral outcome. *Journal of Head Trauma Rehabilitation, 14*(4), 70–87.

Bigler, E. D., Blatter, D. D., Anderson, C. V., Johnson, S. C., Gale, S. D., Hopkins, R. O., & Burnett, B. (1997). Hippocampal volume in normal aging and traumatic brain injury. *American Journal of Neuroradiology, 18*, 11–23.

Bigler, E. D., Clark, E., & Farmer, J. E. (Eds.). (1997). *Childhood traumatic brain injury: Diagnosis, assessment, and intervention.* Austin, TX: Pro-ED.

Bigler, E. D., & Clement, P. (1997). *Diagnostic clinical neuropsychology* (3rd ed.). Austin: University of Texas Press.

Bigler, E. D., Johnson, S. C., Anderson, C. V., Blatter, D. D., Gale, S. D., Russo, A. A., Ryser, D. K., Macnamara, S. E., Bailey, B. J., Hopkins, R. O., & Abildskov, T. J. (1996). Traumatic brain injury and memory: The role of hippocampal atrophy. *Neuropsychology, 10*, 333–342.

Bigler, E. D., Johnson, S. C., & Blatter, D. D. (1999). Head trauma and intellectual status: Relation to quantitative magnetic resonnance imaging findings. *Applied Neuropsychology, 6*, 217–225.

Bigler, E. D., Yeo, R. A., & Turkheimer, E. (1989). *Neuropsychological function and brain imaging.* New York: Plenum Press.

Blatter, D. D., Bigler, E. D., Gale, S. D., Johnson, S. C., Anderson, C. V., Burnett, B. M., Parker, N., Kurth, S., & Horn, S. (1995). Quantitative volumetric analysis of brain MR: Normative database spanning five decades of life. *American Journal of Neuroradiology, 16*(1), 241–251.

Blatter, D. D., Bigler, E. D., Gale, S. D., Johnson, S. C., Anderson, C. V., Burnett, B. M., Ryser, D., Macnamara, S. E., & Bailey, B. J. (1997). MR-based brain and cerebrospinal fluid measurement after traumatic brain injury: Correlation with neuropsychological outcome. *American Journal of Neuroradiology, 18*, 1–10.

Camp, S. J., Stevenson, V. L., Thompson, A. J., Miller, D. H., Borras, C., Auriacombe, S., Brochet, B., Falautano, M., Filippi, M., Herisse-Dulo, L., Montalban, X., Parrcira, E., Polyman, C. H., De Su, J., & Langdon, D. W. (1999). Cognitive function in primary progressive and transitional progressive multiple sclerosis: A controlled study with MRI correlates. *Brain, 122*, 1341–1348.

Clarke, E., & Dewhurst, K. (1996). *Illustrated history of brain function*. San Francisco, CA: Norman.

Corsi, P. (1991). *The enchanted loom*. New York: Oxford University Press.

Cwik, V. A., Hanstock, C. C., Allen, P. S., & Martin, W. R. (1998). Estimation of brainstem neuronal loss in amyotrophic lateral sclerosis with in vivo proton magnetic resonance spectroscopy. *Neurology, 50*, 72–77.

Damasio, H., Grabowski, T., Frank, R., Galaburda, A. M., & Damasio, A. R. (1994). The return of Phineas Gage: Clues about the brain from the skull of a famous patient. *Science, 264*, 1101–1105.

Davis, J. T., Bigler, E. D., Valdivia, S., Chong, B. W., & Lewine, J. D. (1999). *Multimodal imaging in the evaluation of traumatic brain injury*. Manuscript submitted for publication.

De Stefano, N., Matthews, P. M., Fu, L., Narayanan, S., Stanley, J., Francis, G. S., Antel, J. P., & Arnold, D. L. (1998). Axonal damage correlates with disability in patients with relapsing-remitting multipsclerosis. Results of a longitudinal magnetic resonance spectroscopy study. *Brain, 121*, 1469–1477.

Duncan, P. W. (1990). Physical therapy assessment. In M. Rosenthal, E. R. Griffith, M. R. Bond, & J. D. Miller (Eds.), *Rehabilitation of the adult and child with traumatic brain injury* (pp. 264–283). Philadelphia: Davis.

Eisenberg, R. L. (1991). *Radiology: An illustrated history*. St. Louis, MO: Mosby.

Friedman, S. D., Brooks, W. M., Jung, R. E., Hart, B. L., & Yeo, R. A. (1998). Proton MR spectroscopic findings correspond to neuropsychological function in traumatic brain injury. *American Journal of Neuroradiology, 19*, 1879–1885.

Godefroy, O., Duhamel, A., Leclerc, X., Saint Michel, T., Hénon, H., & Leys, D. (1998). Brain–behaviour relationships: Some models and related statistical procedures for the study of brain-damaged patients. *Brain, 121*, 1545–1556.

Hohol, M. J., Guttmann, C. R. G., Orav, J., Mackin, G. A., Kikinis, R., Khoury, S. J., Jolesz, F. A., & Weiner, H. L. (1997). Serial neuropsychological assessment and magnetic resonance imaging analysis in multiple sclerosis. *Archives of Neurology, 54*, 1018–1025.

Hopkins, R. O., Abildskov, T. J., Bigler, E. D., & Weaver, L. K. (1997). Three dimensional image reconstruction of neuroanatomical structures: Methods for isolation of the cortex, ventricular system, hippocampus, and fornix. *Neuropsychology Review, 7*(2), 87–104.

Jennett, B., & Teasdale, G. (1981). *Management of head injuries*. Philadelphia: Davis.

Kangarlu, A., Burgess, R. E., Zhu, H., Hakayama, T., Hamlin, R. L., Abduljalil, A. M., & Robitaille, P. M. L. (1999). Cognitive, cardiac, and physiological safety in ultra high field magnetic resonance imaging. *Magnetic Resonance Imaging, 17*, 1407–1416.

Kertesz, A. (1994). Recovery in aphasia and language networks. *NeuroRehabilitation, 5*, 103–113.

Kurth, S. M., Bigler, E. D., & Blatter, D. D. (1994). Neuropsychological outcome and quantitative image analysis of acute hemorrhage in traumatic brain injury: Preliminary findings. *Brain Injury, 8*, 489–500.

Laatsch, L., Jobe, T., Sychra, J., Lin, Q., & Blend, M. (1997). Impact of cognitive rehabilitation therapy on neuropsychological impairments as measured by brain perfusion SPECT: A longitudinal study. *Brain Injury, 11*, 851–863.

Laatsch, L., Pavel, D., Jobe, T., Lin, Q., & Quintana, J.-C. (1999). Incorporation of SPECT imaging in a longitudinal cognitive rehabilitation therapy programme. *Brain Injury, 13*, 555–570.

Lewine, J. D., Davis, J. T., Sloan, J. H., Kodituwakku, P. W., & Orrison, W. W. (1999). Neuromagnetic assessment of pathophysiologic brain activity induced by minor head trauma. *American Journal of Neuroradiology, 20*, 857–866.

Lewine, J. D., & Orrison, W. W. (1995). Magnetoencephalography and magnetic source imaging. In W. W. Orrison, J. D. Lewine, J. A. Sanders, & M. F. Hartshorne (Eds.), *Functional brain imaging* (pp. 369–417). St. Louis, MO: Mosby.

Lowry, C. M. (1996). *A multivariate analysis of ventricular dilation and visuomotor performance*. Unpublished master's thesis, Brigham Young University, Provo, UT.

Malm, J., Krstensen, B., Karlsson, T., Carlberg, B., Fagerlund, M., & Olsson, T. (1998). Cognitive impairment in young adults with infratentorial infarcts. *Neurology, 51*, 433–440.

Marshall, L. F., Marshall, S. B., Klauber, M. R., Clark, M., Eisenberg, H. M., Jane, J. A., Luerssen, T. G., Marmarou, A., & Foulkes, M. A. (1991). A new classification of head injury on computerized tomography. *Journal of Neurosurgery, 75,* S14–S20.

McKinstry, R. C., & Feinberg, D. A. (1998). A new window on brain research: Ultrafast magnetic resonance imaging. *Science, 279,* 1965–1966.

Mitchener, A., Wyper, D. J., Patterson, J., Hadley, D. M., Matthew, P., Wilson, J. T. L., Scott, L. C., Jones, M., & Teasdale, G. M. (1997). SPECT, CT and MR imaging in head injury: Acute abnormalaties followed up at 6 months. *Journal of Neurology, Neurosurgery, and Psychiatry, 62,* 633–636.

Osborn, A. G. (1994). *Diagnostic neuroradiology.* St. Louis, MO: Mosby.

Papanicolaou, A. C. (1998). *Fundamentals of functional brain imaging: A guide to the methods and their applications to psychology and behavioral neuroscience.* Lisse, The Netherlands: Swets & Zeitlinger.

Prichard, J. W. (1998). Neurorehabilitation: Three new NMR tools. *The Neuroscientist, 4*(4), 231–235.

Prichard, J. W., & Cummings, J. L. (1997). The insistent call from functional MRI. *Neurology, 48,* 797–800.

Rao, S. M. (1996). White matter disease and dementia. *Brain and Cognition, 31,* 250–268.

Rappaport, M., Hall, K. M., Hopkins, K., Belleza, T., & Cope, D. N. (1982). Disability rating scale for severe head trauma: Coma to community. *Archives of Physical Medicine and Rehabilitation, 63,* 118–123.

Rasband, W. (1993). *IMAGE (Version 1.52).* Washington, DC: National Institutes of Health.

Reider-Groswasser, I., Cohen, M., Costeff, H., & Groswasser, Z. (1993). Late CT findings in brain trauma: Relationship to cognitive and behavioral sequelae and to vocational outcome. *American Journal of Neuroradiology, 160,* 147–152.

Reitan, R. M., & Davison, L. A. (1974). *Clinical neuropsychology: Current status and applications.* Washington, DC: Winston.

Research Foundation–State University of New York. (1990). *Functional Independence Measure (FIM).* Buffalo, NY: Author.

Riahi, F., Zijdenbos, A., Narayanan, S., Arnold, D., Francis, G., Antel, J., & Evans, A. C. (1998). Improved correlation between scores on the expanded Disability Status Scale and cerebral lesion load in relapsing-remitting multiple sclerosis. Results of the application of new imaging methods. *Brain, 121,* 1305–1312.

Robb, R. (1995). *Three-dimensional biomedical imaging.* New York: VCH.

Ross, B. D., & Ernst, T. (1998). 1H MRS in acute traumatic brain injury. *Journal of Magnetic Resonance Imaging, 8,* 829–840.

Ryser, D. K., Bigler, E. D., & Blatter, D. (1996). Clinical and neuroimaging predictors of post TBI outcome. In J. Ponsford, P. Snow, & V. Anderson (Eds.), *International perspectives in traumatic brain injury* (pp. 79–83). Bowen Hills, Australia: Australian Academic Press.

Virta, A., Barnett, A., & Pierpaoli, C. (1999). Visualizing and characterizing white matter fiber structure and architecture in the human pyramidal tract using Diffusion Tensor MRI. *Magnetic Resonance Imaging, 17,* 1121–1133.

Webb, J., Guimond, A., Eldridge, P., Chadwick, D., Meunier, J., Thirion, J.-P., & Roberts, N. (1999). Automatic detection of hippocampal atrophy on magnetic resonance images. *Magnetic Resonance Imaging, 17,* 1149–1161.

Wilson, J. T. L., Wiedmann, K. D., Hadley, D. M., Condon, B., Teasdale, G., & Brooks, D. (1988). Early and late magnetic resonance imaging and neuropsychological outcome after head injury. *Journal of Neurology, Neurosurgery, and Psychiatry, 51*(3), 391–396.

Wood, D. G., & Bigler, E. D. (1995). Diencephalic changes in traumatic brain injury: Relationship to sensory perceptual function. *Brain Research Bulletin, 38,* 545–549.

22

Constraint-Induced Movement Therapy Based on Behavioral Neuroscience

Edward Taub and Gitendra Uswatte

Constraint-induced (CI) movement therapy is a new approach to physical rehabilitation (Taub, 1980) elaborated from basic research in behavioral psychology and neuroscience. It has been shown in controlled experiments to greatly increase the amount of use of an impaired upper extremity in patients with chronic stroke (see Chapter 4, this volume) in both the laboratory (Wolf, Lecraw, Barton, & Jann, 1989) and the real world (Morris, Crago, DeLuca, Pidikiti, & Taub, 1997; Taub et al., 1993; Taub, Pidikiti, DeLuca, & Crago, 1996; Taub & Wolf, 1997). CI therapy includes a family of treatments that involve repeatedly practicing use of the stroke-affected arm in the clinic and, in most variants, constraining use of the unaffected arm both in the clinic and at home. These treatments emerged directly from research that used operant-conditioning techniques to change the arm use of deafferented monkeys, animals from whose forelimbs somatic sensation had been surgically abolished (Taub, 1977).

We start with a brief exploration of reasons why psychologists are not regularly involved in motor rehabilitation research and practice, a discussion of the importance of basic research for progress in rehabilitation, and a sketch of the contributions of basic behavioral psychology and neuroscience research to rehabilitation psychology. We review the basic re-

Portions of this chapter appeared in E. Taub, J. E. Crago, & G. Uswatte, 1998. "Constraint-Induced Movement Therapy: A New Approach to Treatment in Physical Rehabilitation," *Rehabilitation Psychology, 43*, 152–170. Copyright 1998 by the Educational Publishing Foundation. Adapted with permission. Research was supported by National Institutes of Health Grant HD34273; Retirement Research Foundation Grant 94-172; a grant from the Center for Aging, University of Alabama at Birmingham; Rehabilitation Research and Development Service, U.S. Department of Veterans Affairs Grants B93-629AP and B95-975R; and James S. McDonnell Foundation Grant 97-41. We thank the following collaborators: Jean E. Crago, Rama D. Pidikiti, Anjan Chatterjee, Stephanie C. DeLuca, David Morris, Sharon Shaw, Danna Kay King, Michelle Spear, Edwin W. Cook, Wolfgang H. R. Miltner, Sherry Yakley, Francilla Allen, Jennifer Glasscock, Christy Willcutt, Maneesh Varma, Scott Moran, Seth Spraggins, Harrison Walker, Ben Foo, Jesse Calhoun, Kim Rudolph, Louis D. Burgio, Thomas Novack, Donna M. Bearden, Thomas E. Groomes, William D. Fleming, Cecil S. Nepomuceno, and Neal E. Miller.

search on which CI therapy is founded, provide a model explaining the operation of CI therapy in terms of learning followed by use-dependent cortical reorganization, summarize the research on the application of CI therapy to chronic upper- and lower-extremity hemiparesis in patients with chronic stroke, and describe new methods in treatment outcome measurement that our laboratory has developed. We conclude with a discussion of the implications of this research for the participation of psychologists in the development and practice of this and other novel interventions for the motor behavior of rehabilitation patients.

Contributions From Psychology to Motor Rehabilitation

Psychologists have not traditionally been involved in the development or conduct of treatments for motor impairments. This absence is curious given that the ultimate aim of such treatments is to teach individuals with motor impairments new patterns of movement that help them negotiate their daily environment. It appears that this aim—modifying their behavior—would fall within the purview of psychology. Operant conditioning, a branch of behavioral psychology, has developed empirically validated and highly effective methods for modifying human behavior. Furthermore, the organ system that is the source of dysfunction in rehabilitation, the central nervous system (CNS), is the object of study of neuroscience, a basic natural science closely associated with psychology.

The most important and successful contribution from psychology to rehabilitation to date has arguably been the development of behavioral modification programs for patients with chronic pain. Behavioral modification programs essentially involve conducting functional analyses of patients' pain-related behaviors (identifying behaviors that need to be increased or decreased and the reinforcers that control their frequency) and applying operant-conditioning techniques (e.g., positive and negative reinforcement, shaping, and modeling) to increase the frequency of desirable behaviors or decrease the frequency of undesirable ones (Fordyce, 1991; Skinner, 1953). These assessment and treatment methods are based on research by Skinner (1938) and Thorndike (1898) that established how to control the frequency of behaviors in animals. The clinical methods for increasing patients' activity and participation in treatment advocated by Ince (1980), which have not been adopted by the field, are also based on the work of these pioneering behaviorists. Similarly, treatments to improve strength and other motor parameters using biofeedback (e.g., Brucker & Bulaeva, 1996) are based on research by physiological psychologists who established that animals (e.g., Engel & Gottlieb, 1970; Gruber & Taub, 1998) and humans (e.g., Taub & Emurian, 1976) can control some physiological functions when provided with information about their operation.

Behavioral psychology has had little impact on motor rehabilitation, in part because of the failure of biofeedback techniques to consistently effect changes in functional activity when applied to the treatment of movement disorders. In the 1970s, a strong interest developed in the application of operant-conditioning techniques to the area of rehabilitation (Ince, 1980). Initial experiments involving the application of biofeedback procedures as a type of operant conditioning were promising; studies reported improvements in range of movement (ROM), manual muscle test scores, and muscle tension as measured by electromyography (EMG) techniques (Wolf, 1983). Later work, however, did not show that these physiological changes were persistent and related to changes in functional activity, so biofeedback techniques came to be viewed as having questionable clinical significance (Duncan, 1997; Wolf, 1983). The disappointment engendered by the biofeedback research appears to have spread to all operant-conditioning techniques. Consequently, there has been little interest in recent years in the application of operant-conditioning techniques to the rehabilitation of movement.

The limited practical influence of neuroscience on motor rehabilitation to date may be because the findings, until recently, have been restricted to areas that are distant from obvious application to clinical practice. Recent discoveries about the processes of injury and CNS recovery, such as findings on nervous system damage in the early postinjury phase (reviewed in Novack, Dillon, & Jackson, 1996), spinal cord regeneration (reviewed in Schwab & Bartholdi, 1996), and cortical reorganization (e.g., Elbert, Pantev, Wienbruch, Rockstroh, & Taub, 1995; Flor et al., 1995; Taub, Flor, Knecht, & Elbert, 1995), have generated considerable interest. We hope that these findings lead more behavioral neuroscientists to investigate problems of clinical relevance and lead to new and effective rehabilitation interventions.

A Scarcity of Empirically Validated Treatments for Impaired Movement

A major review of stroke rehabilitation interventions noted that CI therapy provided the most promising evidence that motor recovery can be facilitated in stroke patients with some purposive movement of the hand and that CI therapy is one of the few treatment modalities for which there is sound evidence of transfer of therapeutic effect from the clinic to everyday situations (Duncan, 1997). Other reviewers (Dobkin, 1989; Ernst, 1990) have shared Duncan's view that traditional neurorehabilitation interventions have not been demonstrated to be effective in controlled studies. In a 1992 review of the stroke rehabilitation literature, de Pedro-Cuesta, Widen-Holmqvist, and Bach-y-Rita wrote that "as regards activities of daily life and motor function, differences between . . . rehabilitation in stroke units . . . and non-rehabilitation . . . were detected in relatively few quality studies and remained particularly inconclusive insofar as life in the home environment was concerned" (p. 433).

The scarcity of effective interventions may be directly attributable to the weak contribution from behavioral psychology and neuroscience, and other basic sciences, to physical rehabilitation. In rehabilitation psychology and other health-related fields, basic research has been of inestimable value in developing new therapeutic approaches. It uncovers new, general mechanisms or parameters that can be manipulated to benefit patients in a variety of specific contexts in which the general mechanism operates.

Behavioral and Neurological Bases

Animal Model of Learned Nonuse

When a single forelimb is deafferented in a monkey, the animal does not use it in the life situation (Lassek, 1953; Mott & Sherrington, 1895). However, by restricting movement of the intact limb for several days, the monkey can be induced to use the deafferented extremity permanently. Training of deafferented limb use also proved to be an effective technique. Conditioned response techniques initially were used to train limb use (Knapp, Taub, & Berman, 1958, 1963; Taub, 1977; Taub, Bacon, & Berman, 1965; Taub, Ellman, & Berman, 1966; Taub, Williams, Barro, & Steiner, 1978). Subsequently, it was found that shaping techniques, which involve increasing behavioral requirements by very small steps (Morgan, 1974; Panyan, 1980; Skinner, 1938, 1968), are considerably more effective (Taub, 1976, 1977). Several converging lines of evidence suggest that nonuse of a single deafferented limb is a learning phenomenon involving a conditioned suppression of movement (Taub, 1977, 1980). The restraint and shaping techniques appear to be effective because they overcome learned nonuse.

Background for the learned nonuse formulation is that substantial neurological injury usually leads to an initial depression in motor and perceptual function that is considerably greater than the impairment that remains after spontaneous recovery has taken place. The processes responsible for the initial depression and the later recovery of function, which occur both at the level of the spinal cord and brain, are incompletely understood at present. Regardless of the mechanism, recovery processes that enable movements at least potentially to be expressed come into operation in monkeys 2–6 months after deafferentation (Taub, 1977).

The initial inability of the monkeys to use the deafferented limb leads to conditioned suppression of use of that limb. Animals with one deafferented limb try to use that extremity in the immediate postoperative situation, but they cannot. Attempts to use the deafferented limb often lead to painful and otherwise aversive consequences, such as falls and loss of food. These failures constitute punishments that suppress arm use (Azrin & Holz, 1966; Catania, 1998; Estes, 1944). Meanwhile, the monkeys get along well in the laboratory environment on three limbs and are therefore positively reinforced for this pattern of behavior, which as a result is strengthened. These contingencies of reinforcement lead to a persistence of the nonuse of the affected extremity, and consequently the monkeys never learn that, several months after the operation, it had become possible to use the limb.

The restraint of the intact limb several months after unilateral deafferentation serves to overcome this conditioned suppression of movement or "learned nonuse." Restriction of the intact limb induces animals to use the deafferented limb or forego feeding, locomotion, and other important daily activities with any degree of efficiency. This change in motivation overcomes the learned nonuse of the deafferented limb, and consequently the animals use it.

An experiment was carried out to test the learned nonuse formulation directly (Taub, 1977, 1980). Movement of a unilaterally deafferented forelimb was prevented with a restraining device in several animals so that they could not attempt to use that extremity for a period of 3-months following surgery. The reasoning was that by preventing an animal from trying to use the deafferented limb during the period before spontaneous recovery of function had taken place, one should prevent the animal from learning that the limb could not be used during that interval. In conformity with this prediction, the animals were able to use their deafferented extremity in the free situation after the restraint was removed. Suggestive evidence in support of the learned nonuse formulation was also obtained during the course of deafferentation experiments carried out on the day of birth (Taub, Perrella, Miller, & Barro, 1973) and prenatally (Taub, 1980; Taub et al., 1975).

Learned nonuse was hypothesized to develop in some humans after stroke by similar mechanisms to those that operate after deafferentation in monkeys, with the difference that the initial period of motor incapacitation was primarily due to cortical rather than spinal mechanisms. It was therefore felt that the techniques that overcome learned nonuse in monkeys following unilateral deafferentation also constituted a potential treatment to increase the amount of limb use in patients with an upper-extremity hemiparesis associated with stroke (Taub, 1980, 1994). Multiple experiments that have applied the unaffected-arm constraint and affected-arm training techniques directly to chronic stroke patients have supported this hypothesis; these experiments are summarized in later sections.

There was no prior commitment to the use of a behavioral mechanism, learned nonuse, to account for a motor deficit associated with neurological injury, paresis of an arm. The concept of learned nonuse was originally proposed and tested only when a neural mechanism, crossed inhibition (Taub, 1977, 1980), had been disconfirmed experimentally. The learned nonuse formulation has survived because it has continued to explain the data. If an alternate mechanism were proposed that explained the data gathered to date adequately, it would be considered and experimentally evaluated. Similarly, if plausible alternate mechanisms to use-dependent cortical reorganization were proposed, they also would be considered and evaluated.

Use-Dependent Cortical Reorganization

Magnetic source imaging studies with humans, carried out by groups of investigators including one of the authors (Taub), and an intracortical microstimulation (ICMS) study with monkeys suggest that cortical reorganization may be associated with the therapeutic effect of CI therapy. The human magnetic source imaging studies followed the seminal work of Recanzone, Merzenich, and co-workers on use-dependent cortical reorganization in monkeys (e.g., Recanzone, Merzenich, Jenkins, Grajski, & Dinse, 1992). One human imaging study showed that the cortical somatosensory representation of the digits of the left hand was larger in stringed-instrument players, who use their left hand in the dexterity-demanding task of fingering the strings, than in a nonmusician control group (Elbert et al., 1995). Another study found that the representation of the fingers of blind Braille readers, who use several fingers simultaneously to read, was enlarged (Sterr et al., 1998). These results, in conjunction with research on cortical reorganization in adult patients with phantom limb pain (Flor et al., 1995), suggest that the area devoted to the cortical representation of a body part in adult humans depends on the amount of use of that part. The ICMS study tested this hypothesis in adult squirrel monkeys. It demonstrated that in monkeys who were surgically given an ischemic infarct in the cortical area controlling the movements of a hand, training of the affected limb results in cortical reorganization so that the area surrounding the infarct, which is not normally involved in control of the hand, starts to participate in that function (Nudo, Wise, SiFuentes, & Milliken, 1996).

The hypothesis that CI therapy produces a large use-dependent cortical reorganization in humans with stroke-related hemiparesis of an upper extremity was recently confirmed in two studies. One study used focal transcranial magnetic stimulation (TMS) to map the areas of the brain that control arm movement in 6 patients with a chronic upper-extremity hemiparesis (mean chronicity = 6 years) before and after CI therapy (Liepert et al., 1998). The investigators found that CI therapy produced a significant increase in the patients' amount of arm use in the home over the 2-week treatment period. Over the same period, they found that the cortical region from which EMG responses of a hand muscle can be elicited by TMS was more than doubled. Kopp et al. (1999) carried out a current source density analysis of the steady-state electroencephalographic motor potential of CI therapy patients. They found that 3 months after treatment the motor cortex ipsilateral to the affected arm, which normally controls movements of the contralateral arm, had been recruited to generate movements of the affected arm. This effect was not in evidence immediately after treatment and was presumably due to the sustained increase in affected arm use over the 3-month follow-up period produced by CI therapy.

The findings of Liepert et al. (1998) and Kopp et al. (1999) suggest that CI therapy produces a permanent increase in arm use (Taub et al., 1993) by two independent mechanisms. First, CI therapy changes the contingencies of reinforcement (provides opportunities for reinforcement of use of the affected arm by constraining the unaffected arm) so that the learned nonuse of the stroke-affected arm conditioned in the acute and early subacute periods is counterconditioned or lifted. Second, the consequent increase in use, involving sustained and repeated practice of functional arm movements, induces expansion of the contralateral cortical area controlling movement of the affected arm and recruitment of new ipsilat-eral areas. This use-dependent cortical reorganization may serve as the neural basis for the permanent increase in use of the affected arm. More-over, to the best of our knowledge, these recent studies are the first to demonstrate an alteration in brain structure or function associated with a therapy-induced improvement in movement after CNS damage.

Application to Stroke Patients With an Upper-Extremity Hemiparesis

Development of Therapy

The initial studies of the application of CI therapy to humans were carried out by Ince (1969) and Halberstam, Zaretsky, Brucker, and Guttman (1971). Ince transferred the conditioned response techniques used with the deafferented monkeys directly to the rehabilitation of movement of the paretic upper extremity of three chronic stroke patients. He tied the un-affected upper extremity of the patients to the arm of a chair and asked them to flex their affected arm to avoid an electric shock. The motor status of two of the patients did not change; the third patient, however, improved substantially in the training and life situations (Ince, 1969). Halberstam et al. used a similar treatment protocol with a sample of 20 elderly stroke patients and 20 age-matched control patients. Those in the treatment group were asked to flex their affected arm and also to make a lateral movement at the elbow to avoid electric shocks; the unaffected arm was not tied down. Most of the patients in the treatment group increased the amplitude of their movements in the two conditioned-response tasks; some showed very large improvements. There was no report of whether this improvement transferred to activities of daily living (ADLs).

Steven Wolf and coworkers (Ostendorf & Wolf, 1981; Wolf et al., 1989) applied the unaffected limb constraint portion, but not the affected limb training component, of the treatment protocol published by Taub (1980) to the rehabilitation of movement in chronic neurologically impaired patients with an upper-extremity hemiparesis. The 1989 study included 25 stroke and traumatic brain injury patients who were more than 1-year postinjury and who possessed a minimum of 10° extension at the metacarpophalan-geal and interphalangeal joints and 20° extension at the wrist of the af-fected arm (minimum motor criterion). The patients were asked to wear a sling on the unaffected arm all day for 2 weeks, except during a 30-minute exercise period and sleeping hours. The patients demonstrated sig-nificant but small improvements in speed or force of movement, depending on the task, on 19 out of 21 tasks on the Wolf Motor Function Test (WMFT; Morris, Uswatte, Crago, Cook, & Taub, 2000; Taub et al., 1993; Uswatte & Taub, 1999; Wolf et al., 1989), a laboratory test involving simple upper-extremity movements. There was no report of whether the improvements transferred to everyday situations.

Taub et al. (1993) applied both the paretic arm training and contralateral arm restraint portions of the treatment protocol (Taub, 1980) to the rehabilitation of chronic stroke patients with an upper-extremity hemiparesis in a study that used an attention-placebo control group and emphasized transfer of therapeutic gains in the laboratory to the life situation. Four treatment patients signed a behavioral contract in which they agreed to wear a sling on their unaffected arm for 90% of waking hours for 14 days. On 10 of those days, they received 6 hours of supervised task practice using their affected arm (e.g., eating lunch; throwing a ball; playing dominoes, Chinese checkers, or card games; writing; pushing a broom; using the Purdue Pegboard; and completing the Minnesota Rate of Manipulation Test; Smith, 1993) interspersed with 1 hour of rest. Five control patients were told that they had much greater movement in their affected limb than they were exhibiting, were led through a series of passive movement exercises in the treatment center, and were given passive movement exercises to perform at home. All experimental and control participants were at least 1 year poststroke (M = 4 years) and had passed the minimum motor criterion before they were accepted into the study. Treatment efficacy was evaluated using the WMFT and the Arm Motor Ability Test (AMAT; Kopp et al., 1997; McCulloch et al., 1988). All participants also exhibited a substantial lack of use of their more affected arm in their daily life, as defined by a score of 2.5 (less than half as much use of the more impaired extremity as before the stroke) or less on the Motor Activity Log (MAL; a semistructured interview of real-world arm use; Taub et al., 1993; Uswatte & Taub, 1999). The treatment group demonstrated a significant increase in motor ability as measured by both laboratory motor tests (WMFT, AMAT) over the treatment period, whereas the control patients showed no change or showed a decline in arm motor ability. On the MAL, the treatment group showed a very large increase in real-world arm use over the 2-week period and demonstrated a further small increase in use when tested 2 years after treatment; the control group exhibited no change or showed a decline in real-world arm use over the same period.

These results have since been confirmed in an experiment using unaffected arm constraint and shaping (Morgan, 1974; Panyan, 1980; Skinner, 1938, 1968) of the affected arm, instead of task practice, with a larger sample (41 participants) and a more credible control-group procedure than was used in the first study. The shaping procedure involved selecting tasks that were tailored to address the motor deficits of the individual patient, helping patients carry out parts of a movement sequence if they were incapable of completing the movement on their own at first, and providing explicit verbal feedback for small improvements in task performance (Taub, Pidikiti, DeLuca, & Crago, 1996). Modeling and prompting of task performance were also used. The control group was designed to control for the duration and intensity of the therapist–patient interaction and the duration and intensity of the therapeutic activities. The control group received a general fitness program in which patients performed strength, balance, and stamina training exercises; played games that stimulated cognitive activity; and practiced relaxation skills for 10 days. As in the first experiment, the treatment group (n = 21) demonstrated a significant increase in motor ability as measured by the WMFT over the intervention period, whereas the control group ($n = 20$) did not. On the MAL, the treatment group showed a very large increase in real-world arm use from pre- to posttreatment; the control group did not exhibit a significant change. The control group's answers to an expectancy and self-efficacy questionnaire about their expectations for rehabilitation prior to the control intervention and their reported increase in quality of life after the intervention, as measured by the Medical Outcome Study 36-Item Short-Form Health Survey (Ware & Sherbourne, 1992), suggest that they found the control intervention to be credible.

The results from the sling-plus-task-practice and sling-plus-shaping experiments have been replicated in over 10 laboratories in the United States, Germany, and Sweden. The sling-plus-shaping results have been replicated in published studies by the laboratories of Wolfgang Miltner (Miltner, Bauder, Sommer, Dettmers, & Taub, 1999) and Herta Flor (Kunkel et al., 1999) and in pilot data elsewhere (Desai, 1991; Koelbel et al., 1997; G. Lavinder, J. Charles, & A. Gordon, personal communication, June–August 1997; Tries, 1991). The sling-plus-task-practice results have been replicated in pilot studies with subacute stroke patients who were 3–6 months poststroke (personal communications, C. Giuliani, K. Light, D. Nichols, C. Winstein, & S. L. Wolf, September–December 1997). It remains to be determined whether CI therapy techniques produce similar positive results in acute stroke inpatients.

Other experiments have indicated that a family of techniques can overcome learned nonuse (Taub, Pidikiti, DeLuca, & Crago, 1996; Taub & Wolf, 1997). Other interventions that have been tested are (a) placement of a half-glove on the less-affected arm as a reminder not to use it and shaping of the paretic arm, (b) shaping of the paretic arm only, and (c) intensive physical therapy (e.g., aquatic therapy, neurophysiological facilitation, and task practice) of the paretic arm for 5 hours a day for 10 consecutive weekdays. Our laboratory designed the half-glove intervention so that CI therapy could be used with patients who have balance problems and might be at risk for falls when wearing a sling; this intervention expands the population of stroke patients amenable to CI therapy threefold. We currently use a padded safety mitt that leaves the unaffected arm free, so as not to compromise safety, but safety also prevents use of the hand and fingers in ADLs. The shaping-only intervention was tested to evaluate the relative importance of the constraint and task practice components of the intervention. The intensive physical therapy intervention did not involve physical constraint of the unaffected arm; however, the study participants were asked not to use their unaffected arm, and this regimen was monitored. To our knowledge, such a concentrated application of physical therapy had not been evaluated before this trial. All of these groups showed very large increases in arm use in the life situation over the treatment period equivalent to that observed for the sling-plus-task-practice and the sling-plus-shaping groups. Two years after treatment, however, these three groups showed some decrement in arm use, whereas the sling-plus-task-practice and sling-plus-shaping groups did not.

Common Therapeutic Factors

Although most of the CI therapy techniques tested involved constraining movement of the less affected arm, the shaping-only and intensive physical therapy interventions did not. Yet, all of the techniques produced similar gains in arm use over the treatment period. There is thus nothing talismanic about the use of a sling or other constraining device on the less-affected extremity. The common therapeutic factor appears to be providing opportunities for the reinforcement of use of the paretic arm by forcing or encouraging use of that extremity. This change in the contingencies of reinforcement results in massed or repetitive practice of paretic arm use, which in turn appears to give rise to the use-dependent cortical reorganization observed by Liepert et al. (1998) and Kopp et al. (1999). The change in brain function is presumed to be the basis for the long-term increase in the amount of more-affected extremity use. Mauritz and coworkers (Butefisch, Hummelsheim, Denzler, & Mauritz, 1995; Hesse, Bertelt, Schaffrin, Malezic, & Mauritz, 1994) have also shown that repetitive practice is an important factor in stroke rehabilitation interventions.

Lower Functioning Patients

Until recently, the patients with whom we worked all met or exceeded a minimum motor criterion of 20° of extension at the wrist and 10° of extension of each finger. This represents a relatively high initial level of motor ability. It is estimated that approximately 20–25% of the chronic stroke population meet this motor criterion (Wolf & Binder-Macleod, 1983). However, work conducted with lower functioning patients has been promising, suggesting that CI therapy may be applicable to up to 50–75% of the stroke population with a chronic unilateral motor deficit. The minimum motor criterion for inclusion of the first group of lower functioning patients into therapy was 10° extension of the wrist, 10° abduction of the thumb, and 10° extension of any two other digits. Eleven patients whose initial motor ability fell below the minimum motor criterion for the higher functioning group and above the minimum criteria for this lower functioning group have been given CI therapy to date. All 11 of these lower functioning patients exhibited substantial improvement; the gain was about 75% of that shown in higher functioning patients. Therapy with a group of 11 even lower functioning patients was recently evaluated. The minimum motor criterion for this subgroup was that they were able to lift a wash rag off a tabletop using any type of prehension they could manage and then release it. The gain in arm use for the group was about 60% of that for the higher functioning patients. Although the benefit of CI therapy does appear to diminish as the initial level of motor ability decreases, these data suggest that the motor capacity of chronic patients is modifiable in a larger percentage of the population than our research originally indicated (Taub, Pidikiti, Uswatte, Shaw, & Yakley, 1998).

Application to Stroke Patients With a Lower-Extremity Hemiparesis

The learned-nonuse formulation predicts that stroke patients with paresis of a lower extremity are also liable to develop deficits in use. These deficits, however, are probably better characterized as learned misuse than learned nonuse. Whereas patients with an upper-extremity paresis can function using one arm, patients with a lower-extremity paresis cannot walk using just their less-affected leg. Patients with a lower-extremity paresis must use both legs to ambulate, but they develop degraded gait patterns in the acute and subacute phases to adjust to their unilateral deficit in motor ability. Because most patients are able to carry out some progression in their environment, as opposed to being entirely nonambulatory, these abnormal patterns of coordination are reinforced and, consequently, persist in the chronic phase, even when some of the motor deficits that made them necessary have resolved. The gait patterns that are unnecessarily exaggerated include (a) hip flexion, knee extension, ankle plantar flexion, and lower-limb circumduction during swing; (b) hip flexion, limited knee flexion, and ankle plantar flexion during loading; (c) knee hyperextension during midstance; and (d) lack of roll-off at toe-off (Perry, 1969). They produce inefficient ambulation and cause damage to bone, ligament, and muscle tissue (Giuliani, 1990). The use of the maladaptive lower-extremity coordination can be overcome by repeated practice of improved gait patterns in the laboratory and attention in the home to the use of new gait patterns acquired in the laboratory. Learned nonuse per se may occur in stroke patients with a lower-extremity paresis who are nonambulatory in the acute and subacute phases; this condition of greatly reduced walking may persist into the chronic phase even when the underlying neurological recovery makes substantial walking possible. However, only a relatively small percentage of chronic stroke patients do not walk at all. Learned misuse is thus a much more common condition.

To date, our laboratory has treated the lower extremity of 23 patients with chronic stroke (3 received combined lower- and upper-extremity therapy) with substantial success (Taub et al., 1999). These patients have had a wide range of disability extending from close to nonambulatory to moderately impaired coordination. The treatment has involved shaping and practice of improved coordination for 7 hours per day for 2 or 3 weeks. Initially, we thought that it might be more difficult to overcome learned misuse than learned nonuse because in the former case, bad habits of coordination need to be overcome before more appropriate patterns of coordination can be substituted, whereas in the latter case there is simply an absence of use in the life situation. Surprisingly, this expectation proved to be incorrect. We have obtained improvements in the quality of movement of the lower extremity on laboratory motor tests in some patients that are approximately equivalent to those that we have obtained for the upper extremity. We still have insufficient lower-extremity MAL data to draw conclusions about the permanence of the transfer of these gains in motor ability to use in the real world. We recently treated 5 people with a spinal cord injury and obtained substantial improvements in the quality of movement of the lower extremity with these patients also.

New Methods in Treatment Outcome Measurement

CI therapy successfully transfers improvement in the quality and amount of arm use from the clinic to the life setting (Duncan, 1997; Taub et al., 1993). The current consensus in the rehabilitation field, including the perspectives of patients, researchers, clinicians, and health care payers, is that functional activity in the life situation is the most important outcome to pursue and measure (Keith, 1995). Physical rehabilitation outcome evaluation instruments, however, do not provide a direct measure of motor function in the real world (Uswatte & Taub, 1999). Traditional instruments in physical rehabilitation focus on measuring strength, flexibility, and coordination in the clinic or laboratory situation (D. S. Smith & Clark, 1995). More recent instruments measure functional ability in the home indirectly by clinician observation of ADLs performed in the laboratory or clinic (e.g., Cress et al., 1996), but the relationship between performance on these instruments and performance in the life situation has not been rigorously tested (Keith, 1995). When investigators have attempted to measure behavior in the home, they have relied on retrospective, self-report questionnaires and focused on functional independence rather than extremity function (e.g., Keith, Granger, Hamilton, & Sherwin, 1987). The experimental work conducted by this laboratory and the observations of others (Andrews & Stewart, 1979) suggest that laboratory motor tests indicate a rehabilitation patient's maximum motor ability but that patients frequently do not make full use of that ability in the life setting. There is frequently a large gap between the two. Our laboratory group, consequently, has developed two new instruments and is working on a third method for measuring upper-extremity function in the life situation. Our group has also developed two new laboratory motor tests and has collaborated on making a device for measuring compliance with the unaffected arm constraint protocol when patients are out of the laboratory.

Real-World Upper-Extremity Use

Motor Activity Log

The semistructured MAL interview measures how much and how well patients use their affected arm for ADLs in the home over a specified period. The MAL is administered independently to the patient and a significant other or informant. In the interview, the patient or caregiver is asked to rate how much and how well the patient has used the affected arm for 14 ADL tasks in the past day, week, or year. Patients and caregivers use a 6-point Amount of Use (AOU; Uswatte & Taub, 1999) Scale to rate how much they use their affected arm and a 6-point Quality of Movement

(QOM; Uswatte & Taub, 1999) Scale to rate how well they use it. The tasks include such activities as brushing teeth, buttoning a shirt or blouse, and eating with a fork or spoon (Uswatte & Taub, 1999). A 30-item version of the MAL, which includes a wider range of activities, is used with lower functioning patients.

The CI therapy patients treated in this laboratory improved from a mean of 1.2 (1 = *very little use*, 2 = *slight use*) 1 year before treatment to 3.2 (3 = *moderate use*, 4 = *almost normal amount of use*) 4 weeks after treatment on the AOU scale and improved from 1.1 (1 = *very poor quality of movement*, 2 = *poor quality of movement*) to 3.4 (3 = *moderate quality of movement*, 4 = *almost normal quality of movement*) on the QOM scale. The caregiver reports indicated similar improvements: from 1.1 to 3.1 on the AOU scale and from 0.8 to 3.0 on the QOM Scale. The interrater reliability within patient and caregiver pairs on both scales was very high; mean intraclass correlation Type 3,1 (Shrout & Fleiss, 1979) = .90. An attention-placebo control group did not show significant changes; mean patient-rated QOM remained constant at 1.6 rating points (Uswatte & Taub, 1999).

The MAL has drawbacks that are typically associated with self-report instruments. Patients' ratings may be influenced by experimenter bias or demand characteristics, or patients simply may not be able to accurately recall how they used their affected extremity. However, no other instrument is available for assessing the actual amount of use of impaired extremities in the life setting. Although there are several global measures of functional independence (e.g., Functional Independence Measure; Keith, Granger, Hamilton, & Sherwin, 1987), these are "burden-of-care" assessments that determine to what extent patients can carry out ADLs independently, regardless of the function of their affected arm (Uswatte & Taub, 1999).

Actual Amount of Use Test

The AAUT (Uswatte & Taub, 1999) is an observational test that measures how much patients spontaneously use their affected arm to perform a set of tasks in the laboratory. The AAUT is administered on first entrance into the laboratory before pretreatment testing and just prior to posttreatment testing. Patients are videotaped as they are unobtrusively led through a standardized scenario of 19 tasks that they might encounter in the clinic on a regular basis (e.g., remove coat, place project card in wallet, fill out form). Patients give informed consent to be videotaped when they enter the CI therapy project. The patients are not prompted as to what arm to use to accomplish the tasks, and they are not informed that they are being tested. Independent clinicians use the videotape to rate the patients' behavior on the amount of arm use and functional ability (Taub, De Luca, & Crago, 1996). The patients' performance on the AAUT is believed to be more closely related to how much they actually use their affected arms in their daily lives than to their performance on tests of motor ability, where they are asked to perform tasks specifically with their affected arm (Uswatte & Taub, 1999).

Although the AAUT is not subject to the problems associated with self-report measures, the relationship between performance on this in-lab test and actual use of the limb in the home has yet to be evaluated experimentally. Preliminary results indicate a large increase in the percentage of activities carried out spontaneously by the affected arm with treatment. Five patients in the sling constraint and shaping group who have taken the AAUT so far performed 34% of the tasks attempted with the affected arm before treatment and 64% after treatment. This increase is congruent with the increase in the amount of use reported on the MAL (Uswatte & Taub, 1999). Furthermore, there was an almost perfect correlation, r (5) = .99, between the change in quality of movement rated by patients on the MAL and the change in functional ability observed by clinicians on the AAUT.

Accelerometers

Accelerometers can provide a more objective, direct, and detailed measure of how much patients use their affected arm in the home situation than interview or in-lab observational measures. In physical rehabilitation, accelerometers have been used with initial success to measure overall physical activity in the laboratory and the home (Kochersberger, McConnell, Kuchibhatla, & Pieper, 1996; Veltnic, Bussmann, de Vries, Martens, & Van Lummel, 1996), the use of a prosthetic device in the home by individuals with a transtibial amputation (Stam, Eijskoot, & Bussman, 1995), and the use of the arm to propel a wheelchair in the laboratory (Tajima, Ogata, Lee, Ookawa, & Piciulo, 1994). Keil, Elbert, and Taub (1999) evaluated the validity of uniaxial accelerometers (Koelner Vitaport System, Vitaport GmbH, Erftstadt, Germany) for measuring arm movement involved in standardized ADLs in the laboratory and the home by examining the relationship between accelerometer and EMG recordings taken from the arm. They found statistically significant but modest correlations between the accelerometer recordings taken from the wrist and a combination of EMG recordings taken from the upper and lower arm for the standardized tasks (mean R = .34, p < .01) and for the ADL tasks (mean R = .53, p < .01); they concluded that the EMG and accelerometer recordings measure different aspects of arm movement.

The accelerometers used in our laboratory are Computer Science Application Inc. (Shalimar, FL) Model 7164 Activity Monitors, which are plastic, uniaxial, piezoelectric crystal technology-based units about the size and weight of a large wristwatch. When the piezoelectric crystal in the Activity Monitors is subject to acceleration, it deforms and produces a charge. This charge is digitized at a 10-Hz sampling rate, summed over a user-specified epoch, and reported as a whole number every epoch (Computer Science Applications Inc., 1996; Tryon & Williams, 1996).

We propose that patients wear activity monitors on each arm, the chest, and one leg during waking hours for weeklong periods before and after treatment. The acceleration recordings from these devices indicate how much the patient is moving the affected arm, the unaffected arm, and the whole body. Acceleration recordings from the affected arm unit are compared before and after treatment to evaluate the change in arm use as a result of treatment. Acceleration recordings from the unaffected arm unit are used to compare the change in affected arm use relative to the unaffected arm. Acceleration recordings from the chest and leg units are used to assess the impact of the intervention on general physical activity.

We conducted a series of experiments to provide reliability and validity data for using Activity Monitors to measure arm use. The results from two experiments with college students performing simple, standardized arm movements and standardized arm movements involved in ADLs suggested that the raw Activity Monitor recordings provided highly reliable measures of arm movement with high sensitivity to movement parallel to the x and y axes of the units, low sensitivity to movement parallel to the z axis, and higher sensitivity to changes in movement, speed, and duration than distance (Uswatte, Miltner, et al., 1997; Uswatte, Spraggins, Walker, Calhoun, & Taub, 1997). However, there was a large amount of error in the measurement of changes in the speed and duration of arm movement (median error = 21%). In two subsequent experiments with college students performing similar types of arm movements, the recording epoch was set to 2 seconds and the raw accelerometer recordings were transformed using a threshold filter. The filter set the value of epochs containing raw recordings greater than a low threshold to 2 and set others to 0; the sum of the threshold-filtered values over the recording period thus represented the duration of movement in seconds. These threshold-transformed values provided a measure of the duration of simple and ADL arm movements with low error (median error = 0%; Uswatte, Varma, Sharma, Spraggins, & Taub, 1998). In a third study, 9 stroke patients and 1 healthy individual wore the proposed set of four accelerometers and were videotaped while they performed their regular therapeutic activities in the clinic or daily activities at home. From the videotapes, two teams of observers independently rated whether the participants moved their affected arm and torso and whether the participants walked in 2-second intervals. The correlations between the threshold-filtered accelerometer recordings and the observers' judgments of the duration of arm, torso, and ambulatory movements were .93, .93, and .99, respectively (Uswatte et al., 2000). We are now exploring the application of digital filtering technology (Cook & Miller, 1992) to the accelerometer recordings to obtain an accurate measure of the speed of arm movement and exploring, with the laboratory of Wolfgang Miltner, the use of a neural network analysis of the pattern of recordings (Kiani, Snijders, & Gelsema, 1998) from the arm, chest, and leg to identify functional arm activity.

Laboratory Upper-Extremity Motor Ability

The laboratory has developed two tests of upper-extremity motor ability of specific value for evaluating the population of chronic stroke patients that we study. The WMFT was first developed in the laboratory of Steven Wolf and has been modified (Morris et al., 2000; Taub et al., 1993). The WMFT measures the ability of patients to perform 19 simple limb movements and tasks with the affected arm. Two of the items measure strength and 17 items are timed and scored by raters blinded to the pre- or post-treatment status of the patient. The items include activities such as lifting the affected arm from the test table surface to a box, extending the elbow past a line 40 cm from the initial position, turning over playing cards, and picking up a pencil. The AMAT (Kopp et al., 1997; McCulloch et al., 1988; Taub et al., 1993) measures the ability of patients to perform 13 ADLs with the affected arm. Each of the 13 tasks of ADLs commonly carried out in the life setting, such as putting on a sweater, dialing a telephone number, and unscrewing a jar cap.

Relationship Between Motor Ability and Real-World Use

Laboratory motor tests and real-world outcome measures provide complementary information about patient motor status. On laboratory motor tests, clinicians observe the best a patient is able to achieve when explicitly asked to carry out a movement or task in the laboratory; the results indicate a patient's maximum motor ability. However, this performance does not indicate whether the patient is actually using the extremity for the tested purpose in the life situation. In a study of 29 stroke patients who were consecutive admissions to a rehabilitation facility (Andrews & Stewart, 1979), primary caregivers reported that in 25–45% of cases, ADLs were performed less well in the home situation than in the laboratory. This observation has been confirmed by every clinician that we have contacted. Among the patients treated in our laboratory, there were no significant correlations between performance on the pretreatment motor ability tests and the baseline measure of arm use. These observations and our results confirm that the transfer from the laboratory to the home needs to be tested directly (Uswatte & Taub, 1999).

Indeed, the gap between performance on laboratory tests and the actual amount of extremity use in the home is an index of learned nonuse. CI therapy operates in this window. It provides a bridge between the laboratory or clinic and the life setting so that the therapeutic gains made in the clinic transfer maximally and contribute to the functional independence of the patient in the real world (Uswatte & Taub, 1999).

Among the patients treated in this laboratory, there has been a moderately strong, positive relationship between the initial level of arm motor ability and the improvement in arm use produced by CI therapy ($.48 < r < .57, p < .01$); patients with a high initial level of motor ability have shown larger gains in arm use than patients with a low initial motor ability level. Given that there was no significant relationship between the initial level of arm use and arm ability, this result is congruent with the hypothesis that CI therapy operates in the gap between arm motor ability and arm use; patients with high motor ability have more room to improve. The relationship between changes in arm motor ability and changes in arm use with treatment is not yet clear (Uswatte & Taub, 1999).

Compliance

The Daily Home Treatment Diary provides an estimate of how well the patient has complied with the main intervention in the home environment. During treatment, patients are instructed to wear a sling, which includes a resting hand splint to restrict hand movement, or safety mitt, which also restricts hand movement, on the less-affected arm for more than 90% of the time when they are at home and awake. The sling and safety mitt prevent use of the less-affected arm and thereby induce use of the more-affected arm. Patients record when the constraint device is on and what activities they engage in during the day. If patients do not fill out the diary, because of forgetfulness, difficulty writing with the affected hand, or functional illiteracy, the experimenter helps them fill it out on arrival in the laboratory the next day. If there has been substantial noncompliance with wearing the constraint device, the experimenter attempts to determine the reasons and then problem-solves with the patients to help increase compliance. The experimenter calculates the percentage of patient compliance with the constraint protocol on the basis of the diary account. Patients, on average, reported a 74% compliance rate at home (Uswatte & Taub, 1999). The diary is subject to the same problems as the MAL: experimenter bias, demand characteristics, and inaccurate recall.

Miltner's laboratory, in collaboration with Taub, developed a timing device for objectively recording compliance with the sling and resting hand splint home protocol (Miltner, Franz, & Taub, 2000). The device is activated when the pressure of the hand on the upper surface of the splint alters the capacitance of two separated rectangles of conducting lacquer painted on the inner surface of the splint. In addition to measuring real-world treatment outcome, measuring compliance with home exercise programs is another area of physical rehabilitation in which there is a lack of accurate instruments (Perkins & Epstein, 1988; Robinson & Rogers, 1994). The resting hand splint compliance device represents an example of how the need to measure compliance with home interventions, which are becoming progressively more important for treatment in the current cost-conscious health care climate, can be addressed.

Implications for Research and Practice

The success and potentially wide application of CI therapy reopens a large area of rehabilitation, the treatment of impaired movement, for research and practice by rehabilitation psychologists. As described, CI therapy is based on research in behavioral neuroscience and involves (a) the application of operant-conditioning techniques to overcome the learned nonuse or learned misuse of an extremity and (b) repetitive practice of movement to induce cortical reorganization, which may be responsible for the long-term improvement in extremity use (Taub, 1980; Taub, Crago, & Uswatte, 1998). In our laboratory, the treatment for the more-impaired upper extremity after stroke is administered by research assistants with undergraduate degrees in psychology. Rehabilitation psychologists can administer this treatment in clinical practice with adequate medical participation. Psychologists can take a leading role in helping devise treatment plans, educating families and encouraging their participation, and identifying aspects of the patients' environments that may encourage or hinder their extremity use. Following the advent of behavioral management techniques for the treatment of chronic pain (Fordyce, 1976), many psychologists were instrumental in developing multidisciplinary chronic pain treatment programs. We envision a similar role for rehabilitation psychologists in CI therapy treatment programs; rehabilitation psychologists can assume an active role in developing and managing interdisciplinary programs that incorporate CI therapy treatments.

With regard to research, CI therapy provides a model for psychologists to engage in the development of new interventions for impaired movement and new instruments to measure compliance and treatment outcomes in real-world environments. In addition, it points to the importance of studying behavioral variables, such as the schedule of delivery of treatment, that operate across all types of physical therapy interventions.

References

Andrews, K., & Stewart, J. (1979). Stroke recovery: He can but does he? *Rheumatology and Rehabilitation, 18,* 43–48.

Azrin, N. H., & Holz, W. C. (1966). Punishment. In W. K. Honig (Ed.), *Operant behavior: Areas of research and application* (pp. 380–447). New York: Appleton-Century-Crofts.

Brucker, B. S., & Bulaeva, N. V. (1996). Biofeedback effect on electromyography responses in patients with spinal cord injury. *Archives of Physical Medicine & Rehabilitation, 77,* 133–137.

Butefisch, C., Hummelsheim, H., Denzler, P., & Mauritz, K.-H. (1995). Repetitive training of isolated movements improves the outcome of motor rehabilitation of the centrally paretic hand. *Journal of the Neurological Sciences, 130,* 59–68.

Catania, A. C. (1998). *Learning* (4th ed., pp. 88–110). Upper Saddle River, NJ: Prentice Hall.

Computer Science Applications, Inc. (1996). *Activity Monitor Model 7164* [Manual]. Shalimar, FL: Author.

Cook, E. W., & Miller, G. A. (1992). Digital filtering: Background and tutorial for psychologists. *Psychophysiology, 29,* 350–367.

Cress, M. E., Buchner, D. M., Questad, K. A., Esselman, P. C., deLateur, B. J., & Schwartz, R. S. (1996). Continuous-scale physical functional performance in healthy older adults: A validation study. *Archives of Physical Medicine and Rehabilitation, 77,* 1243–1250.

Desai, V. (1991, March). Report on functional utility score change in nine chronic stroke or closed head injury patients receiving a training program for overcoming learned nonuse as part of a multi modality treatment program. In N. E. Miller (Chair), *Overcoming learned nonuse and the release of covert behavior as a new approach to physical medicine.* Symposium conducted at the meeting of the Association of Applied Psychophysiology and Biofeedback, Dallas, TX.

Dobkin, B. H. (1989). Focused stroke rehabilitation programs do not improve outcome. *Archives of Neurology, 46,* 701–703.

Duncan, P. W. (1997). Synthesis of intervention trails to improve motor recovery following stroke. *Topics in Stroke Rehabilitation, 3,* 1–20.

Elbert, T., Pantev, C., Wienbruch, C., Rockstroh, B., & Taub, E. (1995). Increased use of the left hand in string players associated with increased cortical representation of the fingers. *Science, 270,* 305–307.

Engel, B. T., & Gottlieb, S. H. (1970). Differential operant conditioning of heart rate in the restrained monkey. *Journal of Comparative and Physiological Psychology, 73,* 217–225.

Ernst, E. (1990). A review of stroke rehabilitation and physiotherapy. *Stroke, 21,* 1081–1085.

Estes, W. K. (1944). An experimental study of punishment. *Psychological Monographs, 57*(Serial No. 263).

Flor, H., Elbert, T., Knecht, C., Wienbruch, C., Pantev, C., Birbaumer, N., Larbig, W., & Taub, E. (1995). Phantom limb pain as a perceptual correlate of massive cortical reorganization in upper limb amputees. *Nature, 375,* 482–484.

Fordyce, W. E. (1976). *Behavioral methods for chronic pain and illness.* St. Louis, MO: Mosby.

Fordyce, W. E. (1991). Behavioral factors in pain. *Neurosurgery Clinics of North America, 2,* 749–759.

Giuliani, C. A. (1990). Adult hemiplegic gait. In G. Smidt (Ed.), *Normal and abnormal human gait* (pp. 253–266). New York: Churchill Livingston.

Gruber, B. L., & Taub, E. (1998). Thermal and EMG biofeedback learning in nonhuman primates. *Applied Psychophysiology and Biofeedback, 23,* 1–12.

Halberstam, J. L., Zaretsky, H. H., Brucker, B. S., & Gutman, A. (1971). Avoidance conditioning of motor responses in elderly brain-damaged patients. *Archives of Physical Medicine and Rehabilitation, 52,* 318–328.

Hesse, S., Bertelt, C., Schaffrin, A., Malezic, M., & Mauritz, K.-H. (1994). Restoration of gait in nonambulatory hemiparetic patients by treadmill training with partial body-weight support. *Archives of Physical Medicine and Rehabilitation, 75,* 1087–1093.

Ince, L. P. (1969). Escape and avoidance conditioning of response in the plegic arm of stroke patients: A preliminary study. *Psychonomic Science, 16,* 49–50.

Ince, L. P. (1980). *Behavioral psychology in rehabilitation medicine: Clinical applications.* Baltimore: Williams & Wilkins.

Keil, A., Elbert, T., & Taub, E. (1999). Relation of accelerometer and EMG recordings for measurement of upper extremity movement. *Psychophysiology, 13,* 77–82.

Keith, R. A. (1995). Conceptual basis of outcome measures. *American Journal of Physical Medicine and Rehabilitation, 74,* 73–80.

Keith, R. A., Granger, C. V., Hamilton, B. B., & Sherwin, F. S. (1987). The functional independence measure: A new tool for rehabilitation. In M. G. Eisenberg & R. C. Grzesiak (Eds.), *Advances in clinical rehabilitation* (Vol. 1, pp. 6–18). New York: Springer-Verlag.

Kiani, K., Snijders, C. J., & Gelsema, E. S. (1998). Recognition of daily life motor activity classes using an artificial neural network. *Archives of Physical Medicine and Rehabilitation, 79,* 147–154.

Knapp, H. D., Taub, E., & Berman, A. J. (1958). Effect of deafferentation on a conditioned avoidance response. *Science, 128,* 842–843.

Knapp, H. D., Taub, E., & Berman, A. J. (1963). Movements in monkeys with deafferented forelimbs. *Experimental Neurology, 7,* 305–315.

Kochersberger, G., McConnell, E., Kuchibhatla, M. N., & Pieper, C. (1996). The reliability, validity, and stability of a measure of physical activity in the elderly. *Archives of Physical Medicine and Rehabilitation, 77,* 793–795.

Koelbel, S., Elbert, T., Rockstroh, B., Sterr, A., Jahn, T., & Taub, E. (1997, May). *Constraint-induced movement therapy under German conditions.* Paper read at the meeting of the European Congress of Psychophysiology, Konstanz, Germany.

Kopp, B., Kunkel, A., Flor, H., Platz, T., Rose, U., Mauritz, K. H., Gresser, K., McCulloch, K. L., & Taub, E. (1997). The Arm Motor Ability Test (AMAT): Reliability, validity, and sensitivity to change of an instrument for assessing ADL disability. *Archives of Physical Medicine and Rehabilitation, 78,* 615–620.

Kopp, B., Kunkel, A., Muehlnickel, W., Villringer, K., Taub, E., & Flor, H. (1999). Plasticity in the motor system related to therapy-induced improvement of movement after stroke. *Neuroreport, 10*, 807–810.

Kunkel, A., Kopp, B., Muller, G., Villringer, K., Villringer, A., Taub, E., & Flor, H. (1999). Constraint-induced movement therapy for motor recovery in chronic stroke patients. *Archives of Physical Medicine and Rehabilitation, 80*, 624–628.

Lassek, A. M. (1953). Inactivation of voluntary motor function following rhizotomy. *Journal of Neuropathology and Experimental Neurology, 2*, 83–87.

Liepert, J., Bauder, H., Sommer, M., Miltner, W. H. R., Dettmers, C., Weiller, C., & Taub, E. (1998). Motor cortex plasticity during constraint-induced movement therapy in chronic stroke patients. *Neuroscience Letters, 250*, 5–8.

McCulloch, K., Cook, E. W., III, Fleming, W. C., Novack, T. A., Nepomuceno, C. S., & Taub, E. (1988). A reliable test of upper extremity ADL function [Abstract]. *Archives of Physical Medicine and Rehabilitation, 69*, 755.

Miltner, W. H. R., Bauder, H., Sommer, M., Dettmers, C., & Taub, E. (1999). Effects of constraint-induced movement therapy on chronic stroke patients: A replication. *Stroke, 30*, 586–592.

Miltner, W. H. R., Franz, S., & Taub, E. (2000). *A device for objectively determining patient compliance with home training.* Manuscript submitted for publication.

Morgan, W. G. (1974). The shaping game: A teaching technique. *Behavior Therapy, 5*, 271–272.

Morris, D. M., Crago, J. E., DeLuca, S. C., Pidikiti, R. D., & Taub, E. (1997). Constraint-induced movement therapy for motor recovery after stroke. *NeuroRehabilitation, 9*, 29–43.

Morris, D. M., Uswatte, G., Crago, J., Cook, E., & Taub, E. (2000). *The reliability of the Wolf Motor Function Test for assessing upper extremity function following stroke.* Manuscript submitted for publication, University of Alabama at Birmingham.

Mott, P. W., & Sherrington, C. S. (1895). Experiments upon the influence of sensory nerves upon the movement and nutrition of limbs. *Proceedings of the Royal Society of London, 57*, 481–488.

Novack, T. A., Dillon, M. C., & Jackson, W. T. (1996). Neurochemical mechanisms in brain injury and treatment: A review. *Journal of Clinical and Experimental Neuropsychology, 18*, 685–706.

Nudo, R. J., Wise, B. M., SiFuentes, F., & Milliken, G. W. (1996). Neural substrates for the effects of rehabilitative training on motor recovery following ischemic infarct. *Science, 272*, 1791–1794.

Ostendorf, C. G., & Wolf, S. L. (1981). Effect of forced use of the upper extremity of a hemiplegic patient on changes in function. *Physical Therapy, 61*, 1022–1028.

Panyan, M. V. (1980). *How to use shaping.* Lawrence, KS: H & H Enterprises.

de Pedro-Cuesta, J., Widen-Holmqvist, L., & Bach-y-Rita, P. (1992). Evaluation of stroke rehabilitation by randomized controlled studies: A review. *Acta Neurologica Scandinavia, 86*, 433–439.

Perkins, K. A., & Epstein, T. H. (1988). Methodology in exercise adherence research. In R. K. Dishman (Ed.), *Exercise adherence: Its impacts on public health* (pp. 399–416). Champaign, IL: Human Kinetics.

Perry, J. (1969). The mechanics of walking in hemiplegia. *Clinical Orthopaedics & Related Research, 63*, 23–31.

Recanzone, G. H., Merzenich, M. M., Jenkins, W. M., Grajski, A., & Dinse, H. R. (1992). Topographic reorganization of the hand representation in area 3b of owl monkeys trained in a frequency discrimination task. *Journal of Neurophysiology, 67*, 1031–1056.

Robinson, J. I., & Rogers, M. A. (1994). Adherence to exercise programmes. Recommendations. *Sports Medicine, 17*, 39–52.

Schwab, M. E., & Bartholdi, D. (1996). Degeneration and regeneration of axons in the lesioned spinal cord. *Psychological Reviews, 76*, 319–370.

Shrout, P. E., & Fleiss, J. L. (1979). Intraclass correlations: Uses in assessing rater reliability. *Psychological Bulletin, 86*, 420–428.

Skinner, B. F. (1938). *The behavior of organisms.* New York: Appleton-Century-Crofts.

Skinner, B. F. (1953). *Science and human behavior.* New York: Macmillan.

Skinner, B. F. (1968). *The technology of teaching*. New York: Appleton-Century-Crofts.

Smith, D. S., & Clark, M. S. (1995). Competence and performance in activities of daily living in patients following rehabilitation from stroke. *Disability and Rehabilitation, 17,* 15–23.

Smith, H. D. (1993). Assessment and evaluation: An overview. In H. L. Hopkins & H. D. Smith (Eds.), *Willard and Spackman's occupational therapy* (8th ed.). Philadelphia: Lippincott.

Stam, H. J., Eijskoot, F., & Bussmann, J. B. (1995). A device for long-term ambulatory monitoring in trans-tibial amputees. *Prosthetics & Orthotics International, 19,* 53–55.

Sterr, A., Mueller, M. M., Elbert, T., Rockstroh, B., Pantev, C., & Taub, E. (1998). Changed perceptions in Braille readers. *Nature, 391,* 134–135.

Tajima, F., Ogata, H., Lee, K. H., Ookawa, H., & Piciulo, C. M. (1994). Use of an accelerometer in evaluating arm movement during wheelchair propulsion. *Sangyo Ika Daigaku Zasshi, 16,* 219–226.

Taub, E. (1976). Motor behavior following deafferentation in the developing and motorically mature monkey. In R. Herman, S. Grillner, H. J. Ralston, P. S. G. Stein, & D. Stuart (Eds.), *Neural control of locomotion* (pp. 675–705). New York: Plenum Press.

Taub, E. (1977). Movement in nonhuman primates deprived of somatosensory feedback. *Exercise and Sports Science Reviews* (Vol. 4, pp. 335–374). Santa Barbara, CA: Journal Publishing Affiliates.

Taub, E. (1980). Somatosensory deafferentation research with monkeys: Implications for rehabilitation medicine. In L. P. Ince (Ed.), *Behavioral psychology in rehabilitation medicine: Clinical applications* (pp. 371–401). Baltimore: Williams & Wilkins.

Taub, E. (1994). Overcoming learned nonuse: A new approach to treatment in physical medicine. In J. G. Carlson, A. R. Seifert, & N. Birbaumer (Eds.), *Clinical applied psychophysiology* (pp. 185–220). New York: Plenum Press.

Taub, E., Bacon, R., & Berman, A. J. (1965). The acquisition of a trace-conditioned response after deafferentation of the responding limb. *Journal of Comparative and Physiological Psychology, 58,* 275–279.

Taub, E., Crago, J. E., & Uswatte, G. (1998). Constraint-induced movement therapy: A new approach to treatment in physical rehabilitation. *Rehabilitation Psychology, 43,* 152–170.

Taub, E., DeLuca, S., & Crago, J. E. (1996). *Actual Amount of Use Test (AAUT)* [Manual]. (Available from Edward Taub, Psychology Department, UAB, CH415, 1300 8th Avenue South, Birmingham, AL 35294)

Taub, E., Ellman, S. J., & Berman, A. J. (1966). Deafferentation in monkeys: Effect on conditioned grasp response. *Science, 151,* 593–594.

Taub, E., & Emurian, C. E. (1976). Feedback-aided self-regulation of skin temperature with a single feedback locus: I. Acquisition and reversal training. *Biofeedback and Self-Regulation, 1,* 147–167.

Taub, E., Flor, H., Knecht, S., & Elbert, T. (1995). Correlation between phantom limb pain and cortical reorganization. *The Journal of NIH Research, 7,* 49–50.

Taub, E., Miller, N. E., Novack, T. A., Cook, E. W., III, Fleming, W. D., Nepomuceno, C. S., Connell, J. S., & Crago, J. E. (1993). Technique to improve chronic motor deficit after stroke. *Archives of Physical Medicine and Rehabilitation, 74,* 347–354.

Taub, E., Perrella, P. N., Miller, N. E., & Barro, G. (1973). Behavioral development following forelimb deafferentation on day of birth in monkeys with and without blinding. *Science, 181,* 959–960.

Taub, E., Perrella, P. N., Miller, N. E., & Barro, G. (1975). Diminution of early environmental control through perinatal and prenatal somatosensory deafferentation. *Biological Psychiatry, 10,* 609–626.

Taub, E., Pidikiti, R. D., Chatterjee, A., Uswatte, G., King, D. K., Bryson, C., Willcutt, C., Jannett, T., Yakley, S., & Spear, M. (1999). CI therapy extended from upper to lower extremity in stroke patients. *Society for Neuroscience Abstracts, 25,* 320.

Taub, E., Pidikiti, R. D., DeLuca, S. C., & Crago, J. E. (1996). Effects of motor restriction of an unimpaired upper extremity and training on improving functional tasks and altering brain/behaviors. In J. Toole (Ed.), *Imaging and neurologic rehabilitation* (pp. 133–154). New York: Demos.

Taub, E., Pidikiti, R. D., Uswatte, G., Shaw, S., & Yakley, S. (1998). Constraint induced (CI) movement therapy: Application to lower functioning stroke patients. *Society for Neuroscience Abstracts, 24,* 1769.

Taub, E., Williams, M., Barro, G., & Steiner, S. S. (1978). Comparison of the performance of deafferented and intact monkeys on continuous and fixed ratio schedules of reinforcement. *Experimental Neurology, 58,* 1–13.

Taub, E., & Wolf, S. (1997). Constraint induction techniques to facilitate upper extremity use in stroke patients. *Topics in Stroke Rehabilitation, 3,* 38–61.

Thorndike, E. L. (1898). Animal intelligence: An experimental study of the associative processes in animals. *Psychological Monographs, 2,* 1–109.

Tries, J. M. (1991, March). Learned nonuse: A factor in incontinence. In N. E. Miller (Chair), *Overcoming learned nonuse and the release of covert behavior as a new approach to physical medicine.* Symposium conducted at the meeting of the Association for Applied Psychophysiology and Biofeedback, Dallas, TX.

Tryon, W., & Williams, R. (1996). Fully proportional actigraphy: A new instrument. *Behavior Research Methods, Instruments, & Computers, 28,* 392–403.

Uswatte, G., Miltner, W. H. R., Foo, B., Varma, M., Moran, S., & Taub, E. (2000). Objective measurement of functional upper extremity movement using accelerometer recordings transformed with a threshold filter. *Stroke, 31,* 662–667.

Uswatte, G., Miltner, W., Walker, H., Spraggins, S., Moran, S., Calhoun, J., Beatty, C., & Taub, E. (1997). Accelerometers in rehabilitation: Objective measurement of extremity use at home [Abstract]. *Rehabilitation Psychology, 42,* 139.

Uswatte, G., Spraggins, S., Walker, H., Calhoun, J., & Taub, E. (1997). Validity and reliability of accelerometry as an objective measure of upper extremity use at home [Abstract]. *Archives of Physical Medicine and Rehabilitation, 78,* 904.

Uswatte, G., & Taub, E. (1999). Constraint-induced movement therapy: New approaches to measurement in physical rehabilitation. In D. T. Stuss, G. Winocur, & I. H. Robertson (Eds.), *Cognitive neurorehabilitation* (pp. 215–229). Cambridge, England: Cambridge University Press.

Uswatte, G., Varma, M., Sharma, V., Spraggins, S., & Taub, E. (1998). Validity and reliability of accelerometry as an objective measure of upper extremity use at home [Abstract]. *Archives of Physical Medicine and Rehabilitation, 78,* 1334–1335.

Veltnic, P. H., Bussmann, H. B., de Vries, W., Martens, W. L., & Van Lummel, R. C. (1996). Detection of static and dynamic activities using uniaxial accelerometers. *IEEE Transactions on Rehabilitation Engineering, 4,* 375–385.

Ware, J. E., & Sherbourne, C. D. (1992). The MOS 36-Item Short-Form Health Survey (SF-36). I. Conceptual framework and item selection. *Medical Care, 30,* 473–483.

Wolf, S. L. (1983). Electromyographic biofeedback applications to stroke patients: A critical review. *Physical Therapy, 63,* 1148–1155.

Wolf, S. L., & Binder-Macleod, S. A. (1983). Electromyographic biofeedback applications to the hemiplegic patient: Changes in upper extremity neuromuscular and functional status. *Physical Therapy, 63,* 1393–1403.

Wolf, S. L., Lecraw, D. E., Barton, L. A., & Jann, B. B. (1989). Forced use of hemiplegic upper extremities to reverse the effect of learned nonuse among chronic stroke and head-injured patients. *Experimental Neurology, 104,* 125–132.

Part III

Social Interpersonal Issues

23

Disability and Vocational Behavior

Edna Mora Szymanski

Work, a central activity of humans, may be affected by disability. Thus, vocational behavior is an important consideration in the practice of rehabilitation psychology. In this chapter, I provide an overview of theories and practices relating to vocational behavior and disability and address the following topics: (a) work and its changing nature, (b) vocational behavior, (c) disability and vocational behavior, (d) interventions, and (e) challenges.

Work and Its Changing Nature

Work is a complex social activity that is deeply connected to psychological well-being (Quick, Murphy, Hurrell, & Orman, 1992). The complexity of work derives from its multifaceted nature and implies that changes in the context in which it is performed can have considerable psychological impact.

The Nature of Work

Strictly speaking, work is "an activity performed to produce goods or services of value to others" (Rothman, 1987, p. 5). In essence, then, work can be considered a goal-directed activity (Szymanski, Ryan, Merz, Treviño, & Johnston-Rodriguez, 1996).

Work is social, cultural, psychological, and economic in nature. It is a social endeavor; "its meaning and value [are] determined by social values and beliefs" (Rothman, 1987, p. 5). Work is culturally constructed in that its meaning is intertwined with the culture of the organization in which it is performed (Quick, Murphy, Hurrell, & Orman, 1992) and the cultural heritage of the worker (Leong, 1995; Quintanilla, 1990). It is also psychological in nature. Work affects and is affected by personality (Hershenson, 1996; Kohn, 1990); "the process of developing a vocational identity is an integral part of the process of overall identity development" (Vondracek & Skorikov, 1997, p. 322). Finally, work is an economic endeavor (Millington, Asner, Linkowski, & Der-Stepanian, 1996).

The value of work can be intrinsic, instrumental, or both (Quick, Murphy, Hurrell, & Orman, 1992):

> Intrinsically, the value of work is found in its central role as one important aspect of a person's psychological well-being. The intrinsic value of work is the value an individual finds in performing the work, in and of itself, outside of its utilitarian function. Instrumentally, the value of work is found in its identity-defining characteristic; its basis for providing the necessities of life; its role in giving meaning and structure to the adulthood years; and serving as a channel for the individual's talents, abilities, and knowledge. (p. 4)

Changes in Work

Both the nature of work and the context in which it is performed have changed in many ways in recent years. The number of tasks within individual jobs has increased, jobs now involve more teamwork and computer skills, and continuing education is a necessity (Ryan, 1996).

The global economy has changed the pace at which the workplace evolves. Many jobs have been cut as a result of restructuring and reengineering (D. T. Hall & Mirvis, 1996; Schein, 1995). As a result, firms consist of a core of full-time employees complemented by a group of part-time workers and by contract or contingent workers (D. T. Hall & Mirvis). The once-traditional contract, that is, the perceived agreement between workers and their employers, is now "short term and performance based. . . . The company's commitment to the employee extends only to the current need for that person's skill and performance" (D. T. Hall & Mirvis, 1996, p. 17). In other words, job security, for most people, is a thing of the past.

Vocational Behavior

The human aspect of work is the topic of vocational behavior. A wide range of theories exists across a variety of disciplines (e.g., counseling, vocational psychology, sociology; Szymanski & Hershenson, 1998). The development of these theories has been somewhat divergent: "Each academic discipline happily develops its own concepts but does not feel obligated to connect them to the concepts that flow from other disciplines" (Schein, 1986, pp. 315–316). Recently, however, there has been an effort to examine convergence of the theories in counseling and vocational psychology (Savickas & Lent, 1994a).

Some theory convergence has occurred naturally over time (Osipow, 1994). However, differences among theories remain. This diverse theoretical landscape affords multiple perspectives from which to plan and interpret research (Savickas & Lent, 1994b). Nonetheless, it does complicate assessment and intervention.

My colleagues and I recently developed an ecological model of vocational behavior, including career development, that encompasses the constructs and processes of the major theories (Szymanski & Hershenson, 1998; Szymanski, Hershenson, Enright, & Ettinger, 1996). The model is generic, in that it is not limited to people with disabilities; rather, it is designed to address the behavior of people with and without disabilities as well as people of diverse ethnic backgrounds. Simply stated, the model postulates that career development is a result of the interaction of five groups of constructs (context, individual, mediating, work environmental, and outcome) and six groups of processes (development, decision making, congruence, socialization, allocation, and chance). *Constructs* are concepts used for a scientific or explanatory purpose (Kerlinger, 1985), whereas *processes* are a series of activities or events. They are described in Figure 23.1. Szymanski and Hershenson (1998) provided an in-depth discussion of theories, the model and its relationship to the theories, related literature, and application to people with disabilities.

There is no special theory of career development or vocational behavior for people with disabilities, nor should there be. Theories depend in part on some homogeneity of target populations. People with disabilities are heterogeneous, and it is likely that their within-group variation is far greater than the difference between them and the general population. Under these circumstances, therefore, there can be no simple application or nonapplication of theories to people with disabilities (Szymanski, Hershenson, Enright, & Ettinger, 1996).

Although theories are neither fully applicable or nonapplicable to individuals, their constructs and processes, as depicted in Figure 23.1, do offer some insights for clinical consideration. The following section provides a discussion of disability and vocational behavior with connection to the ecological model. Later in the chapter, the elements of the model are connected with interventions.

Disability and Vocational Behavior

The interrelationship of disability and vocational behavior has been of interest to a variety of disciplines, including rehabilitation psychology (e.g., Bruyere & O'Keefe, 1994; Crewe & Krause, 1990), vocational psychology (e.g., Super, 1990), rehabilitation counseling (e.g., Szymanski & Hershenson, 1998), industrial engineering (e.g., Carayon, 1992; Luczak, 1992), health psychology (e.g., Gatchel, Polatin, & Kinney, 1995), nursing (e.g., Gulick, 1992), and industrial and organizational psychology (e.g., Muchinsky, 1997). It has been a multidisciplinary area of inquiry focused on the following topics: (a) preventing potential disability, (b) returning workers with disabilities to employment, (c) introducing people with disabilities into the labor force, and (d) keeping workers with illness and disability employed.

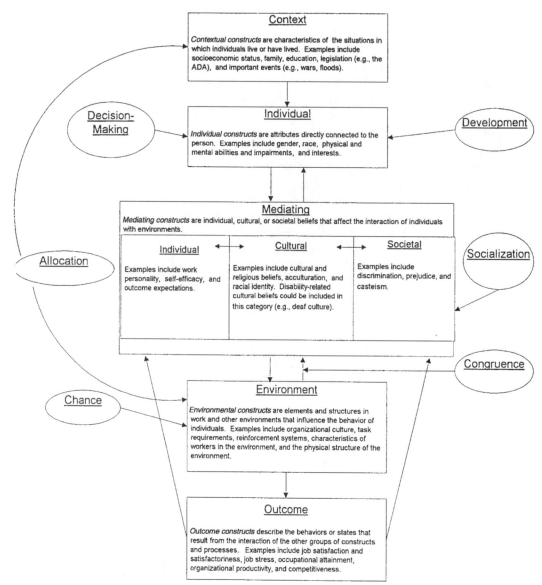

Figure 23.1. An ecological model of the vocational behavior of people with disabilities. *Congruence* is the process of relative match or mismatch between individuals and their environments. *Development* describes the process that produces systematic changes over time, which are interwoven with characteristics and perceptions of individuals and reciprocally influenced by the environment. *Decision making* is the process by which individuals consider career-related alternatives and formulate decisions. *Socialization* is the process by which people learn work and life roles. *Allocation* is the process by which societal gatekeepers use external criteria to channel individuals into or exclude them from specific directions. *Chance* is the occurrence of unforeseen events or encounters. ADA = Americans With Disabilities Act. From "Career Development of People With Disabilities: An Ecological Model" by E. M. Szymanski & D. B. Hershenson, 1998, in R. M. Parker & E. M. Szymanski (Eds.), *Rehabilitation Counseling: Basics and Beyond* (3rd ed., p. 3). Austin, TX: PRO-Ed. Copyright 1998 by PRO-Ed. Adapted with permission.

Preventing Potential Disability

Work can cause both physical and psychological disability (Fitzgerald, 1992; Quick, Murphy, Hurrell, & Orman, 1992). It can directly cause musculoskeletal disability through injury, cumulative trauma, or repetitive-motion disorders (e.g., carpal tunnel syndrome). Similarly, work can cause unhealthy job stress, which can result in psychological and physical disease (e.g., anxiety, cardiovascular disease; Karasek & Theorell, 1990).

Stress is a key concept in many mechanisms that connect work and disability. There are a variety of definitions of *stress*. For example, according to Lazarus and Folkman (1984), "psychological stress is a particular relationship between the person and the environment that is appraised by the person as tasking or exceeding his or her resources and endangering his or her well-being" (p. 19). Similarly, "stress is a systemic concept referring to a disequilibrium of the system as a whole, in particular of the system's control capabilities" (Karasek & Theorell, 1990, p. 87).

Stress appears to be a mechanism by which work causes psychological and some physical harm. It has been related to a variety of workplace conditions, including lack of control, uncertainty, and dysfunctional conflict, which have, in turn, been linked to physical and psychological distress (Landy, 1992; Quick, Murphy, Hurrell, & Orman, 1992) and work disability (Romanov, Appelberg, Heikkilä, Honkasalo, & Koskenvuo, 1996). Results of stress can include coronary heart disease and other physical illness, fatigue, anxiety, and depression (Karasek & Theorell, 1990). The work, stress, and disability connection is extremely important to rehabilitation psychology. For a more comprehensive discussion of the topic, readers are referred to Karasek and Theorell (1990); Keita and Sauter (1992); Quick, Murphy, and Hurrell (1992); Keita and Hurrell (1994); Quick, Quick, Nelson, and Hurrell (1997); and Sauter and Murphy (1995).

Additional individual and environmental variables appear to affect the connection between work and disability. From a review of the research, Fitzgerald (1992) proposed the following relational patterns for musculoskeletal disability:

1. Although most demographic variables have proven to be poor predictors of work disability, age is a notable exception. . . .
2. Musculoskeletal "injury" may be precipitated by a mismatch between the physical capabilities or work style of the individual and the biomechanical demands of the job. . . .
3. Mood-related appraisals and behaviors may inhibit adaptive coping and prolong musculoskeletal disability. . . .
4. Perceptions of the work environment may influence the likelihood of disability. . . .
5. Work-related musculoskeletal disability is most likely a multivariate phenomenon maintained by interactions among physical, ergonomic, and psychological factors. (pp. 121–122)

Current changes in the labor market may influence the connection between work and disability. Uncertainty, which is prevalent with restructuring and the change in the traditional perceived work contract, is related to job stress. Similarly, many service industry jobs, which are on the rise, also present increased risk for psychological disorders (Keita & Hurrell, 1994). These changes may be particularly important considerations for rehabilitation psychology, because people with disabilities are often placed in stress-prone jobs (e.g., service sector jobs, jobs with low levels of individual control) because they often are members of the surplus labor market.

According to the model presented in Figure 23.1, work can cause disability (in this case, an outcome construct) through the interaction of contextual (e.g., the labor market), individual (e.g., physical and mental abilities), mediating (e.g., appraisals, perceptions), and environmental (e.g., the structure of the job) constructs. This relationship is influenced by a variety of processes, especially chance (e.g., uncertainty), allocation (e.g., lack of control), and decision making, which may mitigate some of the uncertainty.

Returning Workers With Disabilities to Employment

The return of injured workers to employment is not solely determined by physical factors. Rather, it is a more complex phenomenon influenced by individual, contextual, and environmental constructs.

Although physical factors generally have been expected to influence return to work, a number of studies of workers with low back pain have identified psychological and work environment factors. For example, Dozois, Dobson, Wong, Hughes, and Long (1995) related both physical and psychological factors (e.g., coping strategies, depression, general psychological distress) to return to work. Similarly, Härkäpää (1992) reported that early retirement was predicted by the following factors: status as a wage earner rather than a self-employed individual, anxiety, weaker beliefs of personal control over back pain, belief in control by others, and lack of accomplishment of back exercises. In addition, Gatchel et al. (1995) reported that remaining out of work at 6 months postinjury was predicted by self-reported pain and disability, and personality disorder.

Psychological and demographic factors have been associated with return to work in a number of other disabilities. For example, in myocardial infarction, the following factors were associated with return to work at 6 months: in-hospital expectations of future work capacity, more anxiety and depression during hospitalization, and lower level of cardiac life-style knowledge (Maeland & Havik, 1987). Similarly, in a review of research, Boll, Klatt, Koch, and Langbehn (1987) found that the following factors were related to return to work after coronary artery bypass surgery: younger age, higher levels of education, lower physical demands, self-employment, and psychological variables. In spinal cord injury, being White, being male, having higher education, and having more functional independence were related to employment (Young, Alfred, Rintala, Hart, & Fuhrer, 1994), as was personality (Krause, 1997).

In addition to psychological factors, two contextual factors are believed to affect return to work. First, disability compensation is believed to impede return to work (Aarts & de Jong, 1996; Leonard, 1991). Second, the structure of the labor market appears to affect the return or lack of return of people with disabilities to work (Yelin, 1992; Yelin & Cisternas, 1996). In fact, Yelin (1992) suggested that

> the rise in work disability rates is concentrated among workers in industries undergoing contraction and has occurred because firms in these industries fail to make the accommodations necessary for persons with impairments to continue working and because the firms and their employees can call upon the disability compensation system to buffer unemployment. (p. 13)

Again, returning to the model in Figure 23.1, return to work (an outcome construct) can be related to individual constructs (e.g., physical, psychological, and demographic factors), contextual constructs (e.g., benefits, labor market), mediating constructs (e.g., coping strategies, belief in control by others, expectations of future work capacity), and environmental constructs (e.g., the nature of the job).

Introducing People With Disabilities Into the Labor Force

School-to-work transition is one part of the lifelong process of career development (Szymanski, 1994). In addition, it is the focal point for the entry of many people with disabilities into the labor market. Phelps and Hanley-Maxwell (1997) and Szymanski (1998) provide a comprehensive discussion of this topic.

A potent predictor of postschool employment for students with disabilities has been employment experiences while in school. Other predictors include skills, family characteristics, socioeconomic status, disability, ethnicity, gender (Phelps & Hanley-Maxwell, 1997), type and level of postsecondary education (DeLoach, 1992; Victor, McCarthy, & Palmer, 1986), and self-perceived functional independence (Victor et al., 1986).

Again, in a school-to-work transition, there is evidence that individual constructs (disability, ethnicity, gender, type and level of education), contextual constructs (family, socioeconomic status), mediating constructs (self-perceived functional independence), and outcome constructs (in-school work experiences) are related to employment. In-school work experiences could also be considered to contribute to a socialization process.

Keeping Workers With Illness and Disability Employed

A somewhat different, but nonetheless important, form of relationship between work and disability relates to keeping workers with illness and disability in the labor market. Interestingly, work cannot only be considered evidence of an adjustment outcome (e.g., Krause, 1997); it can also

be part of the adjustment mechanism. For example, employment was as-
sociated with more positive adjustment in people with leukemia (Magid &
Golomb, 1989) and AIDS (B. A. Hall, 1994; Massagli, Weissman, Seage, &
Epstein, 1994).

As noted in the discussion on return to work, the nature of the job
and work environment also appear to play an important part in enabling
individuals to remain employed.

> Those whose jobs required higher mental effort were more likely to
> continue working, perhaps because these jobs allow more discretion
> over the pace of work or offer flexible work arrangements. Alternatively,
> such jobs may also hold enough intrinsic interest to stimulate contin-
> ued employment even among patients with severe physical dysfunction.
> (Massagli et al., 1994, p. 1980)

A similar, albeit more complex, relationship between the nature of the
work environment has been found for workers with multiple sclerosis
(Gulick, 1992). Thus, it appears that the work environment (an environmental construct) can facilitate or impede the overall adjustment (outcome
construct) of workers with chronic illness or disability.

Summary

The relationship of disability and vocational behavior is only just beginning to be understood. In this section, I have presented a cursory overview
of some facets of the relationship. However, from that review, it is apparent
that this area of inquiry is truly multidisciplinary. Rehabilitation psychologists working in the area need to attend to developments in industrial, health, occupational, and vocational psychology as well as human
factors engineering, nursing, and rehabilitation counseling.

Interventions

People with disabilities are not all that different from people without disabilities. Therefore, many general work-related interventions or treatments can be used to assist them in obtaining and maintaining employment. For a description of some of these interventions, see Herr and
Cramer (1992); Isaacson and Brown (1993); Phillips (1992); Szymanski,
Hershenson, Ettinger, and Enright (1996); and Walsh and Osipow (1988).
This section provides an overview of some vocational behavior interventions that may be useful in working with people with disabilities and is
organized according to the constructs and processes in Figure 23.1.

Context

Contextual interventions are usually long term and address the context
in which individuals live and work. The primary contextual intervention

of this century has been the passage of the Americans With Disabilities Act (ADA) of 1990 (P.L. 101-336). This act directly addressed access to educational programs, work, transportation, and accommodations (Danek et al., 1996) and had specific implications for rehabilitation psychologists (Bruyere & O'Keeffe, 1994; Crewe, 1994).

Other contextual interventions have included rehabilitation and special education legislation (Danek et al., 1996). Laws in these areas have established service delivery systems to address the educational and rehabilitation needs of people with disabilities.

Individual

Individual interventions are primarily directed toward changes in personal attributes or skills. Examples include skills training, career counseling, and work hardening. Skills training addresses work competencies, which are an individual construct (Hershenson, 1996; Szymanski, Hershenson, Enright, & Ettinger, 1996). Examples include providing a college education or training in word processing or as a dental technician.

Career counseling addresses individual understanding and planning skills by helping clients to do the following:

1. Understand one's self (e.g., identity and related issues).
2. Understand the world of work and other relevant environments.
3. Understand the decision-making process.
4. Implement career and educational decisions.
5. Adjust and adapt to the world of work and school (Salomone, 1996, p. 369).

Work hardening, a multidisciplinary approach to returning individuals to work by improving physical and psychological function, uses actual or simulated work activities to build up tolerance (Hanley-Maxwell, Bordieri, & Merz, 1996).

Mediating

Mediating interventions address beliefs and the ways individuals relate to environments. Examples include portfolios and stress inoculation training (SIT).

Portfolios, which address the cognitive nature of career development, are tangible organizations of information and products relating to career decision making. Among other things, they may include information on individual abilities and accomplishments, goal-related job requirements, decision-making tools, and vocational plans (Koch & Johnston-Rodriguez, 1997; Szymanski, Fernandez, Koch, & Merz, 1996).

SIT "a flexible, individually tailored, multifaceted form of cognitive–behavioral therapy. . . . The central notion is that bolstering an individual's repertoire of coping responses to milder stressors can . . . defuse maladaptive responses or susceptibility to more severe forms of distress and persuasion" (Meichenbaum, 1993, p. 378). SIT has been used to treat job stress (Lowman, 1993).

Individual and Mediating

A group of interventions addresses both individual and mediating constructs and teaches skills and changes individual beliefs. This group includes brief career workshops, longer career-skills-training programs, and psychoeducational interventions.

Short-term career workshops have been shown to improve career decision making, vocational identity, and career decision-making self-efficacy in college students with disabilities (Conyers & Szymanski, 1998). Similar workshops have been shown to improve vocational identity, vocational exploration, and commitment in vocational rehabilitation clients with low scores on those measures (Merz & Szymanski, 1997).

Longer term career skills programs that include a strong emphasis on skills training have been a mainstay in vocational rehabilitation (see, e.g., Azrin & Besalel, 1980). These programs continue to be effective, as evidenced by a recent meta-analysis of interventions provided by the Arkansas Rehabilitation Research and Training Center (Bolton & Akridge, 1995).

Psychoeducational interventions can address both the psychosocial nature of disability and career planning. They help individuals deal with their disability and take control of career planning. This type of workshop has been successful with young adults with end-stage renal disease (Ericson & Riordan, 1993).

Environment

A key determinant of vocational behavior is the work environment. Examples of environmental interventions include job placement and disability management. Most job placement approaches include a strong focus on employers and the work environment (Hagner, Fesko, Cadigan, Kiernan, & Butterworth, 1996). New models of placement include marketing, team networking and mentoring, and demand-side placement (Stensrud, Millington, & Gilbride, 1997). These interventions focus on the employer, and the goal is to secure a job for an individual with a disability.

Disability management also focuses on employers but reflects a somewhat different level of interest. "*Disability management* is a proactive, employer-based approach developed to (a) prevent the occurrence of injuries and disability, (b) intervene early for disability risk factors, and (c) coordinate services for cost effective restoration and return to work" (Habeck, Kress, Scully, & Kirchner, 1994, p. 199, emphasis added). Although disability management can be compatible with rehabilitation, the approach is more focused on the employer than on the individual (Habeck, 1996).

Individual and Environment

The last group of interventions addresses the interaction of individuals with environments. Examples include ergonomics, accommodation, assistive technology, and supported employment. Whereas ergonomics addresses the needs of the general population, the other three interventions pertain to people with disabilities.

Ergonomics is "the study of the interface between individuals and their work environment" (Muchinsky, 1997, p. 449). It involves a major focus on designing safer work environments for all workers and is used to prevent or ameliorate disability. Examples might include good chair design or a wrist rest for a keyboard. *Accommodation* is the adjustment of a job or work environment to enable a person with a disability to perform the job (Brodwin, Parker, & DeLaGarza, 1996). Accommodation can include assistive technology or ergonomics

Assistive technology involves the provision of equipment or products to assist people with disabilities or chronic illness in employment or independent living (Merbitz, Lam, Chan, & Thomas, 1999). "Assistive technologies help individuals with disabilities live more independent lives in their communities my minimizing 'disability' and the need for assistance from other people" (Sherer & Galvin, 1996, p. 1). Examples of assistive technology include screen-reading programs and augmentative communication devices.

"Supported employment is a time-enduring (ongoing) service for persons with severe disabilities who without this service would be unable to obtain or maintain competitive employment" (Hanley-Maxwell et al., 1996, p. 344). It has been used with individuals with developmental disabilities as well as those with traumatic brain injury, chronic mental illness, and a variety of other disabilities (Hanley-Maxwell, Szymanski, & Owens-Johnson, 1998). In fact, supported employment has grown into a major service option for people with severe disabilities over the past decade (Schalock & Kiernan, 1997). It can provide support to the individual (e.g., job coaching), the environment (e.g., identifying or enhancing natural supports), or both (Szymanski & Parker, 1989).

Processes

Although the interventions presented in this section were organized according to the constructs, they also address one or more processes of vocational behavior. Table 23.1 illustrates the relationship of the interventions to both the constructs and processes of vocational behavior. It should be noted that an intervention may be related to more than those constructs and processes shown in the table.

A few explanations are warranted regarding career counseling, portfolios, and disability management. These broad-based interventions can address a variety of constructs and processes. All three address chance. Career counseling and portfolios assist individuals in preparing to take

Table 23.1. Interventions, Constructs, and Processes

Intervention	Constructs					Processes					
	Ind.	Con.	Med.	Env.	Out.	Dev.	DM	Cng.	Soc.	All.	Chnc.
ADA		X								X	
Skills training	X							X			
Career counseling	X					X	X	X			X
Work hardening	X					X		X			
Portfolios			X			X	X				X
SIT			X		X			X			
Career workshops	X		X				X		X		
Psychoeducational interventions	X		X				X		X		
Job placement	X			X				X			
Disability management	X		X	X				X	X		X
Ergonomics	X			X				X			
Accommodation	X			X				X			
Assistive technology	X			X				X			
Supported employment	X			X				X	X		

Note. ADA = Americans With Disabilities Act; All. = allocation; Chnc. = chance; Cng. = congruence; Con. = context; Dev. = development; DM = decision making; Env. = environment; Ind. = individual; Med. = mediating; Out. = outcome; SIT = stress inoculation training; Soc. = socialization.

advantage of chance opportunities, whereas disability management helps organizations and individuals avoid the chance occurrence of disability.

The interventions presented in this section are examples, described without much elaboration. The purpose is to illustrate the multidimensional nature of interventions addressing vocational behavior of people with disabilities. These interventions are linked to individuals and environments through assessment (Parker & Schaller, 1996).

Challenges

Major points are summarized in the following paragraphs.

- Work is a complex and changing activity.
- There are many theories of vocational behavior. These theories can be distilled into an ecological model, which postulates that vocational behavior is the result of the interaction of individual, contextual, mediating, environmental, and outcome constructs with developmental, decision-making, congruence, socialization, allocation, and chance processes.
- No individual theory is fully applicable or nonapplicable to people with disabilities. The constructs and processes of the theories are, nonetheless, important for clinical consideration.
- The study of disability and vocational behavior is a multidisciplinary area of inquiry with four points of focus: (a) preventing potential disability, (b) returning workers with disabilities to employment, (c) introducing people with disabilities into the labor force, and (d) keeping workers with illness and disability employed.
- A wide variety of interventions can be used to address the vocational behavior of individuals with disabilities. These can be conceptually organized according to the constructs and processes of the ecological model.

The area of vocational behavior presents some major challenges for rehabilitation psychology. Some suggest considerations for practice and others relate to research.

The Interdisciplinary Nature of the Topic

As the reference list of this chapter illustrates, vocational behavior and disability make up a truly interdisciplinary area of inquiry. From the content of the journal articles and book chapters that were reviewed, blurring of disciplinary lines was obvious, both within psychological disciplines (e.g., rehabilitation psychology, health psychology, industrial and organizational psychology) and with related disciplines (e.g., rehabilitation counseling, human factors engineering, nursing).

This situation presents a challenge for both research and practice in rehabilitation psychology. Both must be informed by research and theory within and outside of the discipline.

The Changing Nature of Work

The changing nature of work suggests some different approaches to the traditional, individual, and advocacy-oriented rehabilitation models. Two such approaches are the protean career and disability management.

As a result of the changing nature of work, D. T. Hall and Mirvis (1996) suggested a protean model of career that is analogous to the free-agent model in sports. "Organizations provide a context, a medium in which individuals pursue their personal aspirations" (D. T. Hall & Mirvis, 1996, p. 21). This model dictates a supportive and competency-building, rather than advocacy-oriented, approach for rehabilitation professionals. The goal is for the individual to learn how to identify and build the skills and decision-making competencies necessary to navigate the complex employment landscape. Portfolios can serve as individual navigational tools.

Employers cannot afford to lose money on work disability, and rehabilitation providers cannot afford to be seen as part of the problem. To that end, Habeck (1996) identified the following principles for disability management practice.

1. Focus on the workplace as the locus of intervention activities. . . .
2. Develop a problem-solving versus advocacy perspective.
3. Acquire organizational competencies to augment clinical skills.
4. Move the target of services upstream to disability prevention. . . .
5. Use data to analyze needs and evaluate performance. (pp. 11–12)

The Challenging Current Context

Vocational interventions are influenced by the current context of professional practice in rehabilitation psychology and related fields, which restricts the consumers served and the types of services that they receive. Two major forces have converged to challenge practice: managed care and the vocational rehabilitation order of selection.

The managed care approach to cost containment and resource management is spreading through health care and health-related vocational services (Lui, Chan, Kwok, & Thorson, 1999). As a result, rehabilitation professionals no longer have complete control over whom they see and what services they deliver. This poses considerable challenges for rehabilitation psychologists and related professionals (Hagglund & Frank, 1996).

At the same time, vocational rehabilitation agencies continue to use a priority-of-service approach to determining who is served. State vocational rehabilitation resources are determined by a fixed level of matching federal and state funds. When resources are not sufficient, states must determine who will and will not receive service. The law stipulates that priority must be given to those with the most severe disabilities (Brabham, Mandeville, & Koch, 1998).

Conclusion

The connections of stress, work, and disability warrant immediate research. Work can cause stress, which can cause disability. In addition, people with disabilities, who are part of the surplus labor market, often enter jobs that have high stress risks.

Some questions should be addressed: How are people with disabilities faring in high-stress jobs? Do they have higher rates of turnover, or do they have more longevity because their options are limited? Is stress exacerbating disability?

In addition, it has been suggested that disability contributes to chronic stress (Gulick, 1992; Turner & McLean, 1989). Does this mean that individuals with certain disabilities may have heightened vulnerabilities to job stress? If so, what supports can be provided to lessen such vulnerability?

How does stress relate to (a) returning injured workers to employment and (b) retaining workers with disabilities or chronic illness in the workplace? With the advent of the ADA, there are more opportunities for accommodations in work environments. Nonetheless, some physical and psychological job characteristics contribute to early retirement. Identifying these factors may help inform interventions.

In summary, the combination of the multidisciplinary venue, the changes in work, and developments in the area of job stress make this an exciting time for rehabilitation psychologists interested in vocational behavior. The research and innovations occurring across disciplines should increase the effectiveness and the repertoire of services that rehabilitation psychologists can offer to people with disabilities. However, these advances are coupled with a changing context of service delivery, which poses many challenges for rehabilitation psychologists and other professionals.

References

Aarts, L. J. M., & de Jong, P. R. (1996). European experiences with disability policy. In J. L. Nashua, V. Reno, R. Purchaser, & M. Berkowitz (Eds.), *Disability, work, and cash benefits* (pp. 129–166). Kalamazoo, MI: Upjohn Institute for Employment Research.

Americans With Disabilities Act of 1990, P. L. 101-336, 42 U.S.C.A. § 12101 *et seq.* (West 1993).

Azrin, N. H., & Besalel, V. A. (1980). *Job club counselors manual: A behavioral approach to vocational counseling.* Austin, TX: PRO-Ed.

Boll, A., Klatt, L., Koch, J., & Langbehn, A. F. (1987). Psychosocial factors influencing return to work after coronary artery bypass surgery (CABS). *International Journal of Rehabilitation Research, 4,* 145–154.

Bolton, B., & Akridge, R. L. (1995). A meta-analysis of skills training programs for rehabilitation clients. *Rehabilitation Counseling Bulletin, 38,* 262–273.

Brabham, R., Mandeville, K. A., & Koch, L. (1998). The state-federal vocational rehabilitation program. In R. M. Parker & E. M. Szymanski (Eds.), *Rehabilitation counseling: Basics and beyond* (3rd. ed.; pp. 41–70). Austin, TX: PRO-Ed.

Brodwin, M., Parker, R. M., & DeLaGarza, D. (1996). Disability and accommodation. In E. M. Szymanski & R. M. Parker (Eds.), *Work and disability: Issues and strategies in career development and job placement* (pp. 165–207). Austin, TX: PRO-Ed.

Bruyere, S. M., & O'Keeffe, J. (Eds.). (1994). *Implications of the Americans With Disabilities Act for psychology*. New York: Springer.

Carayon, P. (1992). A longitudinal study of job design and worker strain: Preliminary results. In J. C. Quick, L. R. Murphy, & J. J. Hurrell, Jr. (Eds.), *Stress and well-being at work: Assessments and interventions for occupational mental health* (pp. 19–32). Washington, DC: American Psychological Association.

Conyers, L., & Szymanski, E. M. (1998). The effectiveness of an integrated career intervention on college students with and without disabilities. *Journal of Postsecondary Education and Disability, 13*(1), 23–34.

Crewe, N. M. (1994). Implications of the ADA for the training of psychologists. In S. M. Bruyere & J. O'Keeffe (Eds.), *Implications of the Americans With Disabilities Act for psychology* (pp. 15–23). New York: Springer.

Crewe, N. M., & Krause, J. S. (1990). An eleven-year follow-up of adjustment to spinal cord injury. *Rehabilitation Psychology, 35,* 205–210.

Danek, M. M., Conyers, L. M., Enright, M. S., Munson, M., Brodwin, M., Hanley-Maxwell, C., & Gugerty, J. (1996). Legislation concerning career counseling and job placement for people with disabilities. In E. M. Szymanski & R. M. Parker (Eds.), *Work and disability: Issues and strategies in career development and job placement* (pp. 39–78). Austin, TX: PRO-Ed.

DeLoach, C. P. (1992). Career outcomes for college students with severe physical and sensory disabilities. *Journal of Rehabilitation, 58*(1), 57–63.

Dozois, D. J. A., Dobson, K. S., Wong, M., Hughes, D., & Long, A. (1995). Factors associated with rehabilitation outcome in patients with low back pain (LBP): Prediction of employment at 9-month follow up. *Rehabilitation Psychology, 40,* 243–259.

Ericson, G. D., & Riordan, R. J. (1993). Effects of a psychosocial and vocational intervention on the rehabilitation potential of young adults with end-stage renal disease. *Rehabilitation Counseling Bulletin, 37,* 146–162.

Fitzgerald, T. E. (1992). Psychological aspects of work-related musculoskeletal disability. In J. C. Quick, L. R. Murphy, & J. J. Hurrell, Jr. (Eds.), *Stress and well-being at work: Assessments and interventions for occupational mental health* (pp. 117–133). Washington, DC: American Psychological Association.

Gatchel, R. J., Polatin, P. B., & Kinney, R. K. (1995). Predicting outcome of chronic back pain using clinical predictors of psychopathology: A prospective analysis. *Health Psychology, 14,* 415–420.

Gulick, E. E. (1992). Model for predicting work performance among persons with multiple sclerosis. *Nursing Research, 5,* 266–272.

Habeck, R. V. (1996). Differentiating disability management and rehabilitation: A distinction worth making. *NARPPS Journal, 11*(2), 8–20.

Habeck, R. V., Kress, M., Scully, S., & Kirchner, K. (1994). Determining the significance of the disability management movement for rehabilitation counselor education. *Rehabilitation Education, 8,* 195–240.

Hagglund, K., & Frank, R. G. (1996). Rehabilitation psychology practice, ethics, and a changing health care environment. *Rehabilitation Psychology, 41,* 19–32.

Hagner, D., Fesko, S. L., Cadigan, M., Kiernan, W., & Butterworth, J. (1996). Securing employment: Job search and employer negotiation strategies in rehabilitation. In E. M. Szymanski & R. M. Parker (Eds.), *Work and disability: Issues and strategies in career development and job placement* (pp. 309–340). Austin, TX: PRO-Ed.

Hall, B. A. (1994). Ways of maintaining hope in HIV disease. *Research in Nursing and Health, 17,* 283–293.

Hall, D. T., & Mirvis, P. H. (1996). The new protean career: Psychological success and the path with a heart. In D. T. Hall (Ed.), *The career is dead: Long live the career: A relational approach to careers* (pp. 1–45). San Francisco: Jossey-Bass.

Hanley-Maxwell, C., Bordieri, J., & Merz, M. A. (1996). Supporting placement. In E. M. Szymanski & R. M. Parker (Eds.), *Work and disability: Issues and strategies in career development and job placement* (pp. 341–364). Austin, TX: PRO-Ed.

Hanley-Maxwell, C., Szymanski, E. M., & Owens-Johnson, L. (1998). School-to-adult life transition and supported employment. In R. M. Parker & E. M. Szymanski (Eds.), *Rehabilitation counseling: Basics and beyond* (3rd ed., pp. 143–179). Austin, TX: Pro-Ed.

Härkäpää, K. (1992). Psychosocial factors as predictors for early retirement in patients with chronic low back pain. *Journal of Psychosomatic Research, 36,* 553–559.

Herr, E. L., & Cramer, S. H. (1992). *Career guidance and counseling through the lifespan: Systematic approaches* (4th ed.). New York: HarperCollins.

Hershenson, D. B. (1996). A systems reformulation of a developmental model of work adjustment. *Rehabilitation Counseling Bulletin, 40,* 2–10.

Isaacson, L. E., & Brown, D. (1993). *Career information, career counseling, and career development* (5th ed.). Boston: Allyn & Bacon.

Karasek, R., & Theorell, T. (1990). *Healthy work: Stress, productivity, and the reconstruction of working life.* New York: Basic Books.

Keita, G. P., & Hurrell, J. J., Jr. (Eds.). (1994). *Job stress in a changing workforce: Investigating gender, diversity, and family issues.* Washington, DC: American Psychological Association.

Keita, G. P., & Sauter, S. L. (Eds.). (1992). *Work and well being: An agenda for the 1990s.* Washington, DC: American Psychological Association.

Kerlinger, F. N. (1985). *Foundations of behavioral research* (3rd ed.). New York: Holt, Rinehart, & Wilson.

Koch, L., & Johnston-Rodriguez, S. (1997). The career portfolio: A vocational rehabilitation tool for assessment, planning, and placement. *Journal of Job Placement, 13*(1), 19–22.

Kohn, M. L. (1990). Unresolved issues in the relationship between work and personality. In K. Erickson & S. P. Vallas (Eds.), *The nature of work: Sociological perspectives* (pp. 36–68). New Haven, CT: Yale University Press.

Krause, J. S. (1997). Personality and traumatic spinal cord injury: Relationship to participation in productive activities. *Journal of Applied Rehabilitation Counseling, 28*(2), 15–20.

Landy, F. J. (1992). Work design and stress. In G. P. Keita & S. L. Sauter (Eds.), *Work and well being: An agenda for the 1990s* (pp. 119–158). Washington, DC: American Psychological Association.

Lazarus, R. S., & Folkman, S. (1984). *Stress, appraisal, and coping.* New York: Springer.

Leonard, J. S. (1991). Disability policy and the return to work. In C. L. Weaver (Ed.), *Disability and work: Incentives, rights, and opportunities* (pp. 46–55). Washington, DC: AEI Press.

Leong, F. T. L. (Ed.). (1995). *Career development and vocational behavior of racial and ethnic minorities.* Mahwah, NJ: Erlbaum.

Lowman, R. L. (1993). *Counseling and psychotherapy of work dysfunctions.* Washington, DC: American Psychological Association.

Luczak, H. (1992). "Good work" design: An ergonomic, industrial engineering perspective. In J. C. Quick, L. R. Murphy, & J. J. Hurrell, Jr. (Eds.), *Stress and well-being at work: Assessments and interventions for occupational mental health* (pp. 96–112). Washington, DC: American Psychological Association.

Lui, J., Chan, F., Kwok, J., & Thorson, R. (1999). Managed care concepts in the delivery of case management services. In F. Chan & M. Leahy (Eds.), *Disability and health care case managers' desk reference* (pp. 99–119). Lake Zurich, IL: Vocational Consultants.

Maeland, J. G., & Havik, O. E. (1987). Psychological predictors for return to work after myocardial infarction. *Journal of Psychosomatic Research, 31,* 471–481.

Magid, D. M., & Golomb, H. (1989). The effect of employment on coping with chronic illness among patients with hairy cell leukemia. *Journal of Psychosocial Oncology, 7,* 1–17.

Massagli, M. P., Weissman, J. S., Seage, G. R., III, & Epstein, A. M. (1994). Correlates of employment after AIDS diagnosis in the Boston Health Study. *American Journal of Public Health, 84,* 1976–1981.

Meichenbaum, D. (1993). Stress inoculation: A 20-year update. In P. M. Lehrer & R. L. Woolfolk (Eds.), *Principles and practice of stress management* (2nd ed., pp. 373–406). New York: Guilford Press.

Merbitz, C., Lam, C., Chan, F., & Thomas, K. R. (1999). Assistive technology for case managers. In F. Chan & M. Leahy (Eds.), *Disability and health care case managers' desk reference* (pp. 379–413). Lake Zurich, IL: Vocational Consultants.

Merz, M. A., & Szymanski, E. M. (1997). The effects of a vocational rehabilitation based career workshop on commitment to career choice. *Rehabilitation Counseling Bulletin, 41,* 88–104

Millington, M. J., Asner, K. K., Linkowski, D. C., & Der-Stepanian, J. (1996). Employers and job development: The business perspective. In E. M. Szymanski & R. M. Parker (Eds.), *Work and disability: Issues and strategies in career development and job placement* (pp. 277–308). Austin, TX: PRO-Ed.

Muchinsky, P. M. (1997). *Psychology applied to work* (5th ed.). Pacific Grove, CA: Brooks/ Cole.

Osipow, S. H. (1994). Moving career theory into the twenty-first century. In M. L. Savickas & R. W. Lent (Eds.), *Convergence in career development theories: Implications for science and practice* (pp. 217–224). Palo Alto, CA: Counseling Psychologists Press.

Parker, R. M., & Schaller, J. L. (1996). Issues in vocational assessment and disability. In E. M. Szymanski & R. M. Parker (Eds.), *Work and disability: Issues and strategies in career development and job placement* (pp. 127–164). Austin, TX: PRO-Ed.

Phelps, L. A., & Hanley-Maxwell, C. (1997). School-to-work transition for youth with disabilities: A review of outcomes and practices. *Review of Educational Research, 67,* 197–226.

Phillips, S. D. (1992). Career counseling: Choice and implementation. In S. D. Brown & R. W. Lent (Eds.), *Handbook of counseling psychology* (2nd ed., pp. 513–547). New York: Wiley.

Quick, J. C., Murphy, L. R., & Hurrell, J. J., Jr. (Eds.). (1992). *Stress and well-being at work: Assessments and interventions for occupational mental health.* Washington, DC: American Psychological Association.

Quick, J. C., Murphy, L. R., Hurrell, J. J., Jr., & Orman, D. (1992). The value of work, the risk of distress, and the power of prevention. In J. C. Quick, L. R. Murphy, & J. J. Hurrell, Jr. (Eds.), *Stress and well-being at work: Assessments and interventions for occupational mental health* (pp. 3–13). Washington, DC: American Psychological Association.

Quick, J. C., Quick, J. D., Nelson, D. L., & Hurrell, J. J. (1997). *Preventive stress management in organizations.* Washington, DC: American Psychological Association.

Quintanilla, S. A. R. (1990). Major work meaning patterns toward a holistic picture. In U. Kleinbeck, H. Quast, H. Thiery, & H. Hacker (Eds.), *Work motivation* (pp. 257–272). Hillsdale, NJ: Erlbaum.

Romanov, K., Appelberg, K., Heikkilä, K., Honkasalo, M., & Koskenvuo, M. (1996). Interpersonal conflict as a predictor of work disability: A follow-up study of 15,348 Finnish employees. *Journal of Psychosomatic Research, 40,* 157–167.

Rothman, R. A. (1987). *Working: Sociological perspectives.* Englewood Cliffs, NJ: Prentice-Hall.

Ryan, C. P. (1996). Work isn't what it used to be: Implications, recommendations, and strategies for vocational rehabilitation. *Journal of Rehabilitation, 61*(4), 8–15.

Salomone, P. (1996). Career counseling and job placement: Theory and practice. In E. M. Szymanski & R. M. Parker (Eds.), *Work and disability: Issues and strategies in career development and job placement* (pp. 365–420). Austin, TX: PRO-Ed.

Sauter, S. L., & Murphy, L. R. (Eds.). (1995). *Organizational risk factors for job stress.* Washington, DC: American Psychological Association.

Savickas, M. L., & Lent, R. W. (Eds.). (1994a). *Convergence in career development theories: Implications for science and practice.* Palo Alto, CA: Counseling Psychologists Press.

Savickas, M. L., & Lent, R. W. (1994b). Introduction: A convergence project for career psychology. In M. L. Savickas & R. W. Lent (Eds.), *Convergence in career development theories: Implications for science and practice* (pp. 1–6). Palo Alto, CA: Counseling Psychologists Press.

Schalock, R. L., & Kiernan, W. E. (1997). How we got to where we are. In W. E. Kiernan & R. L. Schalock (Eds.), *Integrated employment: Current status and future directions* (pp. 5–16). Washington, DC: American Association on Mental Retardation.

Schein, E. H. (1986). A critical look at current career development theory and research. In D. T. Hall (Ed.), *Career development in organizations* (pp. 310–331). San Francisco: Jossey-Bass.

Schein, E. H. (1995). *Career survival: Strategic job and role planning.* San Diego, CA: Pfeiffer.

Scherer, M. J., & Galvin, J. C. (1996). An outcomes perspective of quality pathways to most appropriate technology. In J. C. Galvin & M. J. Scherer (Eds.), *Evaluating, selecting, and using appropriate assistive technology* (pp. 1–26). Gaithersburg, MD: Aspen Medical.

Stensrud, R., Millington, M., & Gilbride, D. (1997). Professional practice: Placement. In D. R. Maki & T. F. Riggar (Eds.), *Rehabilitation counseling: Profession and practice* (pp. 197–213). New York: Springer.

Super, D. E. (1990). A life-span, life-space approach to career development. In D. Brown, L. Brooks, & Associates (Eds.), *Career choice and development: Applying contemporary theories to practice* (2nd ed., pp. 197–261). San Francisco: Jossey-Bass.

Szymanski, E. M. (1994). Transition: Life-span, life-space considerations for empowerment. *Exceptional Children, 60,* 402–410.

Szymanski, E. M. (1998). Career development, school to work transition, and diversity: An ecological approach. In F. R. Rusch & J. Chadsey-Rusch (Eds.), *Beyond high school: Transition from school to work* (pp. 127–145). Belmont, CA: Wadsworth.

Szymanski, E. M., Fernandez, D., Koch, L., & Merz, M. A. (1996). *Career development: Planning for placement* (training materials). Madison: University of Wisconsin—Madison, Rehabilitation Research and Training Center on Career Development and Advancement.

Szymanski, E. M., & Hershenson, D. B. (1998). Career development of people with disabilities: An ecological model. In R. M. Parker & E. M. Szymanski (Eds.), *Rehabilitation counseling: Basics and beyond* (3rd ed., pp. 327–378). Austin, TX: PRO-Ed.

Szymanski, E. M., Hershenson, D. B., Enright, M. S., & Ettinger, J. (1996). Career development theories, constructs, and research: Implications for people with disabilities. In E. M. Szymanski & R. M. Parker (Eds.), *Work and disability: Issues and strategies in career development and job placement* (pp. 79–126). Austin, TX: PRO-Ed.

Szymanski, E. M., Hershenson, D. B., Ettinger, J., & Enright, M. S. (1996). Career development interventions for people with disabilities. In E. M. Szymanski & R. M. Parker (Eds.), *Work and disability: Issues and strategies in career development and job placement* (pp. 255–276). Austin, TX: PRO-Ed.

Szymanski, E. M., & Parker, R. M. (1989). Rehabilitation counseling in supported employment. *Journal of Applied Rehabilitation Counseling, 20*(3), 65–72.

Szymanski, E. M., Ryan, C., Merz, M. A., Treviño, B., & Johnston-Rodriguez, S. (1996). Psychosocial and economic aspects of work: Implications for people with disabilities. In E. M. Szymanski & R. M. Parker (Eds.), *Work and disability: Issues and strategies in career development and job placement* (pp. 9–38). Austin, TX: PRO-Ed.

Turner, R. J., & McLean, P. D. (1989). Physical disability and psychological distress. *Rehabilitation Psychology, 34,* 225–242.

Victor, J., McCarthy, H., & Palmer, J. T. (1986). Career development of physically disabled youth. In E. L. Pan, S. Newman, T. Becker, & C. Vash (Eds.), *Annual review of rehabilitation* (Vol. 5; pp. 97–150). New York: Springer.

Vondracek, F. W., & Skorikov, V. B. (1997). Leisure, school, and work activity preferences and their role in vocational identity development. *Career Development Quarterly, 45,* 322–340.

Walsh, W. B., & Osipow, S. H. (Eds.). (1988). *Career decision making.* Hillsdale, NJ: Erlbaum.

Yelin, E. H. (1992). *Disability and the displaced worker.* New Brunswick, NJ: Rutgers University Press.

Yelin, E. H., & Cisternas, M. (1996). The contemporary labor market and the employment prospects of persons with disabilities. In J. L. Mashaw, V. Reno, R. Burkhauser, & M. Berkowitz (Eds.), *Disability, work, and cash benefits* (pp. 33–58). Kalamazoo, MI: Upjohn Institute for Employment Research.

Young, M. E., Alfred, W. G., Rintala, D. H., Hart, K. A., & Fuhrer, M. J. (1994). Vocational status of persons with spinal cord injury living in the community. *Rehabilitation Counseling Bulletin, 37,* 229–243.

24

Injury Prevention

Frank A. Fee, Dawn E. Bouman, and Pamela A. Corbin

Injury is probably the most under recognized major public health problem facing the nation today. (National Academy of Sciences, 1988)

Throughout history, the two major causes of early death have been infectious disease and injury. Prior to 1900, epidemics of infectious disease were the most critical health problem for the majority of Americans. Since the early 20th century, injury has been the principal public health problem in the United States; it will affect the life of one of every three Americans in any given year. Deaths caused by injuries outnumber deaths from any other cause for individuals younger than age 44 in the United States (Committee on Trauma Research, 1985). Injury is also a leading cause of short- and long-term disability (Lescohier & Gallagher, 1996).

Approximately 62.5 million injuries serious enough to require medical attention occurred in 1985. The cost of injuries for that year has been estimated at more than $107 billion (National Safety Council, 1986). Although the greatest cost of injury is in human suffering and loss, the financial cost of injury is estimated at more than $224 billion for 1994, an increase of more than 42% in the past decade. These costs include direct medical care and rehabilitation costs as well as individual lost wages and national productivity losses (National Center for Injury Prevention and Control [NCIPC], 1996). Although enormous, the numbers are neither well publicized nor widely appreciated (NCIPC, 1996).

Motor vehicle crashes cause more deaths among people ages 1–64 than any other type of injury (NCIPC, 1996). Other leading causes of death from unintentional injuries include fires, burns, falls, drownings, and poisonings. For every death from unintentional injury, there are about 19 hospitalizations, 233 emergency room (ER) visits, and 450 office-based physician visits for injuries (Burt, 1995). Alcohol is involved in many injuries, including 40% of all deaths caused by motor vehicle crashes and about 40% of deaths in residential fires (National Highway Traffic Safety Administration, 1998; Runyan, Bangdiwala, Linzer, Sacks, & Butts, 1992). Injuries affect all segments of the population, but the burden is borne disproportionately by poor and minority populations. Underlying social, environmental, and economic conditions exacerbate these disparities (NCIPC, 1989).

Each year, an estimated 600,000 children are hospitalized for preventable injuries, and almost 16 million children are seen in ERs for their injuries. More than 30,000 children are permanently disabled from injuries each year. The costs of injuries to children are estimated to exceed $7.5 billion each year (Division of Injury Control, Centers for Disease Control [CDC], 1990; Rodriguez, 1990).

Childhood death rates in the United States are considerably higher than in other industrialized countries. Excess mortality among children in the United States is attributable to unintentional injury and violence (Fingerhut & Kleinman, 1989). Because cognitive, motor, and psychosocial functioning influence the risk for certain injuries at specific ages, development must be taken into account in the study of injury risk in children (Finney et al., 1993; Maddux, Brawley, & Boykin, 1995).

Even the former Centers for Disease Control updated its name to more accurately reflect current health problems; it is now officially the Centers for Disease Control and Prevention. In June 1992, CDC established the NCIPC. As the lead federal agency for injury prevention, NCIPC works closely with other federal agencies; national, state, and local organizations; state and local health departments; and research institutions. As the CDC's domain has expanded to include "an even wider scope of health problems, such as environmental health, chronic disease, injury, and violence" (Snider & Satcher, 1997, p. 141), behavioral and social scientists have become increasingly involved in this organization. In the past, the CDC focused on controlling the spread of infectious diseases, but now it also addresses diseases and injuries resulting from "behavioral as well as infectious sources" (G. W. Roberts, Banspach, & Peacock, 1997, p. 143). The NCIPC is proposing a new initiative, Safe America, which encompasses a comprehensive approach to injury prevention and control (CDC, 1997).

Prevention is also a major focus of the U.S. Department of Health and Human Service's (DHHS; 1990) health objectives, *Healthy People 2000*. This document delineates the main health challenges for Americans in terms of measurable objectives in 22 areas of health promotion, health protection, and disease prevention. The goals of this national effort are to increase the healthy life span, reduce health disparities among segments of the population, and achieve access to preventive services for all Americans. Although numerous areas of prevention are included, injury prevention is identified as a separate priority area.

Unfortunately, many view injuries as inevitable, random, and not amenable to prevention efforts because they are caused by accidents. Viewing injuries as preventable is one of the first steps in eliminating them or at least reducing their occurrence. Current convention in the field of injury prevention uses the term *unintentional injury* rather than *accident* to avoid reinforcing the belief that injuries cannot be prevented. Because many injuries are largely a result of modifiable human behavior, it is logical that psychologists who are expert in promoting behavior change should intervene (Fowler, 1990). We examine various frameworks that organize injury prevention efforts.

In this chapter, we provide a review of the important issues related to injury prevention and examine various frameworks that organize injury prevention efforts. After an overview of the theoretical frameworks relevant to any type of prevention, we describe conceptual models specific to the injury prevention literature. Prominent examples of specific injury prevention programs are described. Factors affecting successful prevention efforts are discussed. The chapter concludes with a description of potential roles for rehabilitation psychologists.

Framework of Prevention

The most common way of describing preventive activities is to divide them into primary, secondary, and tertiary prevention. Primary prevention typically occurs before the onset of a disease or disorder and is a population-wide approach (e.g., THINK FIRST assemblies presented to schools, general media campaigns to increase seat belt use). Secondary prevention involves early intervention with specified risk factors (e.g., specialized driving training for male adolescents who have received a DUI, distribution of smoke detectors to low-income families with young children). Tertiary prevention is "prevention in name only" (Winett, 1995, p. 343) because it involves improving treatment and restoring function following the initial injury (e.g., collaborative treatment by a rehabilitation professional to foster safer home discharges for older people with disabilities who are at increased risk of falling, education of patients and families of patients with TBI regarding the increased risk of subsequent TBI following the initial one).

Another basic method for categorizing injury prevention is the dichotomization of prevention into the active (e.g., seat belts and car seats that require fastening every time they are used, proper lifting techniques for moving heavy loads, wearing bicycle and motorcycle helmets) and the passive (e.g., automatic airbags installed on a vehicle, divided highways, child-resistant medicine containers). The schema of preventive activities is concerned with the extent to which a certain measure requires the active participation of the person in question to have an effect and the extent to which the measure is built into the environment, having an effect regardless of human activation. Although these categories are useful for considering types of intervention, in reality many allegedly "passive" measures can be enhanced by individual effort or even thwarted by individuals who do not accept the passive approach. Countless anecdotes exist of people who refuse childproof caps on their medicine containers or who disable automatic seat belts. Even the effectiveness of purportedly "passive" measures should be evaluated to ensure that humans accept the intervention as intended because a basic level of acceptance is necessary before passive measures are implemented.

Even passive measures with proven effectiveness are frequently thwarted because of economic and political pressures. In an enlightening discussion, Michael Roberts (1994) described numerous delays in implementing standard manufacture of automobile safety devices. Ironically, the same safety devices that manufacturers initially rejected because of cost and lack of public approval (e.g., air bags) are now marketed as desirable features. It is interesting to contemplate the role that prevention messages had in fostering this societal value change.

Although psychologists involved in rehabilitation are typically accustomed to intervening at the individual and family levels, we argue that injury prevention is most effective when all levels are addressed (Frank, Bouman, Cain, & Watts, 1992b). Individuals, groups, organizations, entire communities, and the nation are appropriate targets for psychologists' injury prevention interventions. Health habits are learned and maintained in social groups, and therefore attempts to alter these habits must also address these groups. The aforementioned theoretical frameworks are relevant to any type of prevention effort. We now turn our attention to conceptual models specific to injury prevention.

Conceptual Models Underpinning Prevention

We now describe several theoretical models of injury prevention. In one of the early classic works on injury prevention, Haddon (1980) described 10 approaches to eliminating or decreasing the energy transfer that results in injuries by focusing on vectors or vehicles of energy (e.g., cars or guns) and the physical environment rather than on individuals' behavior. His approach is a foundation on which many current efforts build, particularly ergonomic approaches. Haddon's suggestions include general directives that can be applied to a variety of prevention situations. Basic premises include abstract recommendations to prevent the creation of the hazard (e.g., stop producing poisons), modify the rate or spatial distribution of the hazard (e.g., require automobiles to have air bags), and make what is to be protected more resistant to damage from the hazard (e.g., appropriate nutrition and exercise; NCIPC, 1989, pp. 9–10). Although this model has value, alone it does not offer specific advice for maximizing the effectiveness of prevention efforts.

In contrast to Haddon's (1980) physical emphasis, the PRECEDE model was developed for planning health education programs (Green & Kreuter, 1991; Green, Kreuter, Deeds, & Partridge, 1980). The acronym PRECEDE stands for "predisposing, reinforcing, and enabling causes in educational diagnosis and evaluation" (DeJoy, 1996, p. 64). Three sets of diagnostic or behavioral factors drive the development of prevention strategies. *Predisposing* factors are the characteristics of the individual (beliefs, attitudes, values) that motivate or hinder self-protective behavior. *Enabling* factors refer to objective aspects of the environment or system that block or promote self-protective action. *Reinforcing* factors involve any reward or punishment that follows or is anticipated as a consequence of the behavior (DeJoy, 1996). The revised version of the PRECEDE model proposes that an environmental diagnosis should be included with the behavioral diagnosis and that special attention should be given to the interaction of behavioral and environmental factors (Green & Kreuter, 1991). This encourages the selection of both behavioral and environmental targets for change within the intervention program (DeJoy, 1996).

Another comprehensive model for categorizing injury prevention involves careful attention to tactics, methods, targets, and contingencies (Peterson & Mori, 1985; Peterson, Zink, & Downing, 1993). *Tactic* refers to the way in which the program consumer is contacted (e.g., populationwide vs. high-risk-behavior group). *Method* refers to the type of prevention required of the consumer, such as active versus passive. In Peterson's model, *target* refers to the recipient of the intervention, which ranges from the injury vector (the injury-causing agent, e.g., a car) to the person driving the vehicle. *Contingency* refers to the extent to which the prevention effort uses a direct and discernable consequence following compliance. Examples of contingencies include financial charges to manufacturers who do not comply with safety regulations or rewards for children who wear bike helmets.

Numerous theories that influence the current delivery of health education are described well by Freudenberg et al. (1995). One of the most prominent is summarized here. The health belief model (HBM; Rosenstock, 1966) has four basic components: (a) perceived susceptibility to the health problem in question, (b) perceived seriousness of the problem, (c) perceived benefits associated with taking a particular action, and (d) perceived barriers associated with taking the action. Published reviews of the HBM literature reveal support for the model and offer some general conclusions about the relative importance of its major components (Becker, 1974; Harrison, Mullen, & Green, 1992; Janz & Becker, 1984). Perceived barriers have been shown to be the most powerful single predictor across all studies and behaviors. In terms of the total literature, perceived severity appears to be the weakest of the four dimensions (DeJoy, 1996). The predictive ability of this well-known model is variable, yet it continues to serve as a widely used heuristic model in much of health education. Specific dimensions of this model are the focus of several injury prevention interventions.

The THINK FIRST Brain Injury and Spinal Cord Injury Prevention Program, which is described later in this chapter, attempts to heighten viewers' perceived vulnerability and increase their awareness of the severity of traumatic brain injury (TBI) and spinal cord injury (SCI). It appears that such beliefs are resistant to change or at least cannot be expected to be easily altered by brief interventions. Strong beliefs of personal invulnerability probably serve a protective role and are therefore difficult to alter. For instance, in reference to a variety of health risks, Weinstein (1984) stated that students consistently described personal actions and psychological attributes as decreasing, but not increasing, their risks. Several educational, technological, and regulatory methods of injury prevention are described. We now move from a discussion of specific models to a description of typical selected methods of injury prevention.

Selected Methods of Prevention

Most early efforts to reduce the incidence of injuries involved educational approaches. Despite much evidence to the contrary, even many psychologists assumed that people act in reasonable, rational ways to maximize their good health. Although some brief educational methods have been proven effective, and others may serve as a useful adjunct to laws and passive compliance measures, it is clear that "you get what you pay for." It is unreasonable to expect a brief intervention to result in dramatic behavior changes. Christophersen (1993, pp. 223–225) indicated that more comprehensive educational approaches yield more promising results. Peterson et al. (1993) also noted that extensive practice is essential to foster the maintenance of safety skills. Pless and Arsenault (1987) asserted that health education is "necessary but insufficient" (p. 100). Jones and Zaharopoulous (1994) also concurred that educational tactics, including those using the media, have not led to consistent behavior change. Finney et al. (1993) asserted that psychological principles have been used to enhance the effectiveness of health education strategies.

Another major method of injury prevention involves technological changes in design. *Ergonomics,* the study of how people respond to and interact with the environment, has fostered vital improvements such as automatic seat belts, safer automobile designs, guard plates on power saws, and discharge protectors on lawnmowers. Major strides in prevention were made with relatively simple changes such as reducing the space between crib slats, increasing the size of infant toys, and manufacturing child-resistant cigarette lighters.

Government regulations can also have a major influence on some safety behavior, as evidenced by seat belt use. However, not all areas are as amenable to regulation as seat belt use. For instance, in-home safety cannot be fully legislated and enforced. As a result, a variety of prevention efforts are necessary and work synergistically to alter beliefs and behavior. Interventions involving seat belt use serve as good examples of regulatory, ergonomic, and educational methods of prevention.

The use of lap and shoulder belts reduces fatal injuries by 45% and reduces risk for moderate to critical injury by 45–55% (National Highway Traffic Safety Administration [NHTSA], 1996). Despite their clear value, seat belts remain underused. Increased seat belt use is clearly linked to state laws requiring their use. Although many influences likely contribute to seat belt use, laws are more effective in increasing use than other programs (Johnston, Hendricks, & Fike, 1994). In 1984, when only one state had a mandatory seat belt law, only 14% of the population used seat belts. By 1991, 41 states had mandatory seat belt use laws, and seat belt use had risen to 54% (Datta & Guzek, 1991). National rates of seat belt use had further risen to 66% by 1993. Police officers' authority to enforce existing laws is paramount; states with primary laws that permit officers to stop motorists solely for not wearing seat belts have greater compliance than states with only secondary laws (Lescohier & Gallagher, 1996).

Educational programs that also include a reinforcement component have also been shown to effectively increase seat belt use in a variety of school, work, and community settings. However, despite the effectiveness of such interventions in initially increasing belt use, some argue that such interventions are not warranted because belt use declines following withdrawal of the incentive (Robertson, 1986). Although use does decrease, seat belt use remains at a level higher than the initial baseline and therefore represents an overall positive effect (Grant, 1990; M. C. Roberts & Fanurik, 1986). We now describe several educational and regulatory methods of injury prevention, including model programs with specific foci for prevention efforts.

THINK FIRST

Because rehabilitation psychologists are well acquainted with the sequelae of TBI and SCI, we describe in detail the THINK FIRST Brain Injury and Spinal Cord Injury Prevention Program. Each year approximately 2 million people in the United States sustain TBIs (Brain Injury Association, Inc., 1999) and another 10,000 sustain SCI (Stover, DeLisa, & Whiteneck, 1995). In response to the devastating impact of these injuries, more than 200 sites (primarily rehabilitation centers and hospitals) have sponsored the THINK FIRST program. The original program, developed in 1986, is geared toward teenagers and young adults. By using speakers who have sustained TBIs or SCIs, an action-packed film, and factual information regarding the occurrence of TBI and SCI (and an optional paramedic demonstration and wheelchair obstacle course), the 45–60 minute program stresses "using your mind to protect your body" (Susan Morton, personal communication, July 3, 1997).

One prevention program that has been empirically evaluated is the Missouri Head and Spinal Cord Injury Prevention Program, a chapter of the THINK FIRST program. This multicomponent program based on the HBM introduces adolescents to their vulnerability to injury, models injury effects, and educates them about reducing risk and preventing injury. When first evaluated, the program discussed only SCI. At that time, general improvements in knowledge, attitudes, and behaviors were found 1 week after the program was presented (Lechman & Bonwich, 1981). After the program was expanded to address both brain injuries and SCI, another large-scale evaluation compared high school students exposed to the program with students who were not exposed. Three years after exposure, students who viewed the program scored significantly higher on measures of knowledge, attitudes, and self-reported safety behaviors than students who had never seen the program (Frank et al., 1992a). In a similar evaluation of another THINK FIRST program, increased belief that personal actions could prevent injuries was found, but no self-reported behavior changes were noted (Avolio, Ramsey, & Neuwelt, 1992). Englander, Cleary, O'Hara, Hall, and Lehmkuhl (1993) also demonstrated THINK FIRST's effectiveness at increasing teens' awareness, but they reported only minimal behavioral changes. Although these studies demonstrated promising preliminary results, they did not address which students were most receptive to the program message, whether the program affected perceived vulnerability, and which risky behaviors were affected by the program.

A more methodologically rigorous evaluation of the Missouri program used an effective deception method to decrease demand characteristics (Bouman & Frank, 1992). Contrary to the hypotheses, those who viewed the program did not report improved driving habits or increased perceptions of vulnerability to injury. However, interesting gender differences were found. Male individuals reported less safe driving habits than female individuals, but they believed they were safer drivers and less vulnerable to injury than female individuals. Unfortunately, students at highest risk for injury responded to this educational prevention intervention with the most negative cognitions, suggesting that alternative models that do not rely on traditional educational methods must be considered if high-risk students are to be influenced.

Recognizing that safety behaviors must be taught early in life and recognizing that children have different risk factors than do adolescents, a program aimed at children, THINK FIRST for KIDS, was started in 1996. Six safety modules, including vehicular, bicycle, water, sports, recreational, and violence, are designed for children ages 6–8. Interventions are designed to be presented by classroom teachers through the use of a curriculum that is integrated across academic subjects. Another curriculum for children was developed at the University of Alabama (Richards & Hendricks, 1991) and is also presented by classroom teachers. In addition to the presentation of factual information, activities in both programs are designed to involve children as active learners. Innovative reinforcement strategies include "ticketing" students who are spotted wearing helmets or seat belts; tickets are for free ice cream and conducting bike safety rodeos.

HeadSmart

Another injury prevention program developed for children, HeadSmart, was created in 1994 by the Brain Injury Association (1999) for elementary and preschool-age children. Already used at 200 schools, this comprehensive program addresses brain injury and violence prevention by training educators to integrate prevention messages into their regular curriculum. HeadSmart provides lessons and materials for a variety of classroom subjects so that prevention can be taught "across the school and throughout the year" (Mary-Garrett Bodel, personal communication, November 14, 1997). Strategies and materials are also available to provide outreach to parents and the larger community. In addition to a focus on helmets, seat belts, and car seats, conflict resolution and social perspective taking are also addressed. Evaluation is presently under way to assess parents', students', and teachers' views of this program.

Home Injury Prevention Project

The Home Injury Prevention Project (HIPP) is a child-oriented intervention that took place within participants' homes (Gallagher, Hunter, & Guyer, 1985). Educational and technological strategies designed to prevent injuries in children younger than age 6 were pilot tested. Participants' homes were inspected to identify and correct state sanitary code violations (e.g., structural soundness, electrical safety, and hot water temperature), parents were educated about other hazards not covered by the code (e.g., storage of cleaners), and safety devices were provided and installed in the homes. Follow-up evaluation visits found a decrease in household hazards for both code and noncode hazards. Education was found to be the least effective strategy for change, whereas safety counseling with installation of safety equipment was most efficacious. The authors hypothesized that the perceived threat of litigation may have increased compliance, suggesting health department roles for preventing injury (Gallagher et al., 1985).

SAFEKIDS

The SAFEKIDS Campaign, a national program initiated in 1988, is devoted to child injury prevention and composed of over 270 state and local coalitions across the country (SAFEKIDS, 1999). Its goals include educating families about the human element involved in injury, decreasing the availability of dangerous products in the environment to lessen the risk of injury to children, and making child injury prevention a public priority at all levels of government (Jones & Zaharopoulos, 1994). One program developed out of the SAFEKIDS campaign is Get Alarmed, a residential fire detection strategy. This program was developed to increase the number of working smoke detectors in low-income homes with young children and to raise awareness of the need to maintain these smoke detectors. Another SAFEKIDS project involves a partnership with General Motors to promote correct car seat and safety belt use.

Although many professionals believe that it is more effective to intervene with caregivers rather than with children themselves (Peterson & Roberts, 1992), the literature lacks an empirical basis for prevention efforts focusing solely on caregiver behavior. An example of the effectiveness of targeting children is offered by M. C. Roberts and Layfield (1987), who reported that the rate of children in safety restraints doubled as a result of rewarding them with scented stickers when arriving at day care in their safety restraints. Although it is important to target parents for prevention interventions (Kronefeld & Glik, 1995), targeting the behavior of children is appropriate because as many injuries occur when parents are not present. In response to the growing number of "latchkey" children in the 1980s, Peterson (1984) developed a behaviorally focused, manualized program for training children ages 8–10 years from low-income families in self-care activities, dealing with strangers, handling emergencies, and caring for younger children. Comparison of the behavioral training strategy with a pre-existing discussion-oriented strategy revealed that behavioral train-ing strategies were superior to discussion-oriented strategies.

Factors Affecting Successful Prevention

Age

At the other end of the age continuum, injury prevention efforts have in-creasingly been directed at the aging population. The public health com-munity now recognizes that injuries and the events associated with them are not the result of chance, nor are they an inevitable consequence of the aging process. Falls are a leading cause of injury and death in older adults. One-third of community-dwelling older people fall each year, and up to 50% of nursing home residents fall annually (Wolter & Studenski, 1996). Numerous studies have identified risk factors associated with falling: age, female gender, medications, weakness, cognitive impairment, poor vision, foot problems, acute illness, chronic neuromuscular conditions, environ-mental factors, and risky behaviors. Fall risk increases with the number of risk factors present (Tinetti & Speechley, 1989). The Frailty and Inju-ries: Cooperative Studies of Intervention Techniques trials established that exercise, particularly balance training, reduces fall incidence (Prov-ince, Hadley, & Hornbrook, 1995).

Minority Status

Individuals belonging to minority and disenfranchised populations are un-derrepresented in the injury prevention literature. The Hispanic popula-tion is of special concern because of its higher rate of death resulting from motor vehicle crashes compared with African Americans and White people (DHHS, 1990). The national Coalition of Hispanic Health and Human Ser-vices Organizations (COSSMHO, 1999), a private and nonprofit nation-wide agency, is now collaborating with NHTSA to pilot interventions in seven Hispanic communities.

Native Americans have also been neglected in the prevention litera-ture, even though Native American children ages 1–4 are three times more likely to have an injury-related death compared with children in the general U.S. population (Berger & Kitzer, 1989). Hsu and Williams (1991) asserted that knowledge deficits and increased risk of injury-related deaths in Native American children may be related to economic conditions. This assertion is consistent with the association between poverty and the increased rate of injury-related deaths reported by Wise, Kotelchuck, Wil-son, and Mills (1985).

Socioeconomic Status

The Safe Kids/Healthy Neighborhoods Injury Prevention Program was implemented in Harlem in 1988, where 40% of the residents lived below the poverty level in 1990. The goal of the program was to decrease outdoor injuries (Davidson et al., 1994). Playgrounds were renovated; safety equipment such as bicycle helmets were provided at reasonable cost; children and adolescents were involved in safe, supervised activities such as dance and art; and injury and violence prevention education was provided. In this community as well as a nearby community, injury rates fell from 1983 through 1991. Although the researchers consider the results mixed, they found a 44% decrease in injuries in Harlem in the targeted age groups as a result of cooperation of government officials and members of the community. This program has expanded and is now referred to as Injury Free in Harlem: Harlem Hospital Injury Prevention Program (2000).

Challenges of Program Implementation and Evaluation

Most injury prevention efforts are undertaken without any program evaluation. Although improvements are being made to correct this deficiency, several understandable difficulties contribute to the problem. Because severe injuries are relatively rare events, very large sample sizes are necessary to detect effects of interventions. Behavioral compliance with safety recommendations is often difficult to monitor except by self-report, which is often inaccurately inflated. Research is complicated by difficulty in obtaining accurate data of nonfatal injuries, including causes and incidence (Kronefeld & Glik, 1995). Many prevention messages exist in the media and probably confound any hope of a perfectly clean laboratory design occurring in a natural setting.

Peterson et al. (1993) presented a practical description of difficulties encountered when attempting to implement and evaluate prevention interventions; the suggestions they offered to counter such difficulties are both useful and encouraging. Those who work in the area of prevention must remember that behavior change is "usually characterized by a slow process of erosion and accretion rather than by one of sudden upheaval and conversion" (D. Roberts & Maccoby, 1985, p. 547) and be prepared to invest much effort in prevention before drastic changes are evident.

In addition, it may be more difficult to obtain financial support for injury prevention activities because the goal is intangible, namely the non-occurrence of injuries. This is in sharp contrast to the widely publicized funding for already diagnosed and existing conditions such as cancer or AIDS. Preventionists must ultimately demonstrate the preferability of reducing the incidence of injuries versus expanding services to deal with the aftermath of these preventable events. This opportunity may become more readily available with the current proliferation of managed care health services.

Approximately 56 million Americans who are insured through their employment are in managed care, accounting for about 25% of the population. A nationwide penetration at 50% is anticipated within the next 5 years. In Minneapolis, 80% of the insured population is enrolled (Smith, 1997). Medicaid and Medicare recipients are increasingly moving into the managed care market. In the area of prevention, health maintenance organizations enter the picture by making access to preventive measures easy through special programs, extended hours, and increased availability. Occasionally, employers assist by offering incentives to employees to access preventive services.

According to senior analysts, managed care evolves through three stages (Slomski, 1995). In Stage 1, intensive utilization review controls expenditures through rules that limit physicians' decisions. Stage 2 replaces this costly, intrusive monitoring with economic incentives. Physicians regain clinical autonomy by assuming financial risk. Stage 3 is dubbed "true managed care": Health plans "actually reduce the health risks of their enrollees. Plans' competitive advantages will not come from premiums, which are already nearly the same, but from proving that . . . they actually did something about health care risks" (Slomski, 1995, p. 56). Health plans' main vehicle for reducing health care risks is, of course, to reduce health risks. That inevitably means addressing patients' lifestyles. When managed care organizations are integrated delivery systems, they provide all the health care that patients need. Reducing need is thus crucial to containing costs (Morreim, 1995).

Economic responses to lifestyle-induced costs are becoming more common. Some employers and insurers charge higher premiums for people with unhealthy habits (Schwartz, 1993) or deny benefits if injuries were caused by reckless behavior, such as drunk driving (*Hoag Memorial Hosp. v. Managed Care Administrators,* 1993). One analyst predicts that managed care organizations will eventually require enrollees to pay a portion of their medical bills if they neglect their health; for example, people involved in a motorcycle accident will be responsible for part of their medical bills if they were not wearing a helmet (Slomski, 1995). As managed care organizations provide an increasing proportion of citizen's health care, the move toward asking individuals to help control costs by taking more responsibility for their health is likely to intensify. Economic, medical, and legal responses to lifestyle-induced health care costs raise concerns as well as possibilities for using resources responsibly (Morreim, 1995).

Recommended Roles for Psychologists

We have attempted to provide a review of some of the important issues related to injury prevention and to discuss several models and programs that are currently active. We challenge readers to become familiar with the injury prevention literature in their own area of practice and to become preventionists in addition to being clinical practitioners.

Psychologists have been repeatedly charged with the responsibility of contributing to the enhancement of quality of life through prevention of injuries. Because of their expertise in bringing about behavior change through feedback, rewards, and behavioral rehearsal, psychologists are particularly suited to prevention (Finney et al., 1993; Peterson, 1988). They are called on to dispel the belief that injuries are unavoidable and to shift the focus to individual behavior to explain injuries. This is particularly important because environmental or passive interventions have been shown to be insufficient (Peterson, 1988).

Within the CDC, psychologists have been involved in investigating factors putting individuals at increased risk for injury or disease and have worked in areas including neurobehavioral toxicology, occupational stress, and ergonomics to facilitate behavior change and decrease injury risk. This role is consistent with the goal of health psychologists, who study the influence of factors such as coping style, attitudes or beliefs, and personality characteristics on disease processes (Galavotti, Saltzman, Sauter, & Sumartojo, 1997). We are encouraged to become more involved with the CDC, particularly with activities including surveillance, risk factor identification, and intervention evaluation for which we have been well trained. As educators, psychologists are also in prime position to assist the CDC with the dissemination of information regarding the causes and consequences of various diseases and injuries (Galavotti et al., 1997).

Rugg, Levinson, DiClemente, and Fishbein (1997) asserted that the challenge to behavioral and social scientists is "to effectively introduce new topics and methods of study and analysis to traditional public health practice" (p. 147). We must develop research projects and identify targets, methods, tactics, and contingencies regarding prevention strategies in our efforts to decrease the risk of injury. We must also accept the responsibility of lobbying for legal changes that protect people of all ages and ethnic backgrounds (Finney et al., 1993).

Conclusion

An examination of the various theoretical prevention models and specific prevention programs described here clearly points to multilevel approaches as most efficacious. Attention to both passive and active intervention at all levels—individual, group, community, state, and national—is crucial. Comprehensive consideration of tactics, methods, targets, and contingencies for prevention increases the impact of prevention efforts. Collaborative integration of prevention goals further enhances program success. Even if dramatic behavior change is not evident immediately following a specific prevention effort, exposure to the program may increase receptivity to future prevention information encountered in other settings (Bouman & Frank, 1992). Cumulative effects of prevention efforts work together to alter community norms about appropriate safety devices and behaviors. As Winett, King, and Altman (1989) explained, "behavior is affected as much by political, economic, legislative, and cultural influences as by personality, behavioral, and medical (i.e., individual) factors. As a result, the focus of intervention must be multi-faceted" (p. 141).

Effective psychologists are already accustomed to intervening on a variety of levels. In addition, because of psychologists' varied organizational affiliations, it is natural for them to serve as proponents of injury prevention efforts in settings as diverse as hospitals, schools, and the government. Psychologists possess the skills and training to design and implement interventions and evaluations that can prevent much human suffering. Numerous resources are available for the psychologist interested in injury prevention. A recent search for "injury prevention" on the Internet revealed 257,888 sites. Several resources and Web sites are listed in the "Resource" section at the end of this volume.

References

Avolio, A. E. C., Ramsey, F. L., & Neuwelt, E. A. (1992). Evaluation of a program to prevent head and spinal cord injuries: A comparison between middle school and high school. *Neurosurgery, 31,* 557–562.

Becker, M. H. (1974). *The health belief model and personal health behavior.* Thorofare, NJ: Slack Press.

Berger, L. R., & Kitzer, J. (1989). Injuries to children in a native American community. *Pediatrics, 84,* 152–156.

Bouman, D. E., & Frank, R. G. (1992, August). *Examination of a traumatic injury prevention program: Adolescents' reactions and program efficacy.* Paper presented at the 100th Annual Convention of the American Psychological Association, Washington, DC.

Brain Injury Association, Inc. (1999a). *The costs and causes of traumatic brain injury.* Retrieved March 8, 2000, from the World Wide Web: http://www.biausa.org/costsand.htm

Brain Injury Association, Inc. (1999b). *Prevention: The Violence and Brain Injury Institute.* Retrieved March 8, 2000, from the World Wide Web: http://www.biausa.org/preventi.htm

Burt, C. W. (1995). *Injury-related visits to hospital emergency departments: United States* (Advance Data, No. 261). Hyattsville, MD: National Center for Health Statistics.

Centers for Disease Control and Prevention. (1997). *Injury Control Update, 2*(1), 2–4.

Christophersen, E. R. (1993). Improving compliance in childhood injury control. In N. A. Krasnegor, L. H. Epstein, S. B. Johnson, & S. J. Yaffe (Eds.), *Developmental aspects of health compliance behavior* (pp. 219–231). Hillsdale, NJ: Erlbaum.

Coalition of Hispanic Health and Human Services Organization. (1999). *COSSMHO Hispanic HealthLink.* Retrieved March 8, 2000, from the World Wide Web: http://www.cossmho.org

Committee on Trauma Research. (1985). *Injury in America: A continuing public health problem.* Washington, DC: National Academy Press.

Datta, T. K., & Guzek, P. (1991). *Restraint systems used in 19 U.S. cities—1990 Annual Report* (U.S. Department of Transportation Report DTNH22-89-C-070034). Washington, DC: U.S. Department of Transportation.

Davidson, L. L., Durkin, M. S., Kuhn, L., O'Connor, P., Barlow, B., & Heagarty, M. C. (1994). The impact of the safe kids/healthy neighborhood injury prevention program in Harlem, 1988 through 1991. *American Journal of Public Health, 84,* 580–586.

DeJoy, D. M. (1996). Theoretical models of health behavior and workplace self-protective behavior. *Journal of Safety Research, 27*(2), 61–72.

Division of Injury Control, Centers for Disease Control. (1990). Childhood injuries in the United States. *American Journal of Diseases of Children, 144,* 627–646.

Englander, J., Cleary, S., O'Hara, P., Hall, K. M., & Lehmkuhl, L. D. (1993). Implementing and evaluating injury prevention programs in the traumatic brain injury model systems of care. *Journal of Head Trauma Rehabilitation, 8*(2), 101–113.

Fingerhut, L., & Kleinman, J. (1989). Trends and current status in childhood mortality, United States, 1900–1985, *Vital Health Statistics, 26,* 1–44.

Finney, J. W., Christophersen, E. R., Friman, P. C., Kalnins, I. V., Maddux, J. E., Peterson, L., Roberts, M. C., & Wolraich, M. (1993). Society of Pediatric Psychology Task Force report: Pediatric psychology and injury control. *Journal of Pediatric Psychology, 18,* 499–526.

Fowler, R. D. (1990). Psychology: The core discipline. *American Psychologist, 45,* 1–6.

Frank, R. G., Bouman, D. E., Cain, K., & Watts, C. (1992a). A preliminary study of a traumatic injury prevention program. *Psychology and Health, 6,* 129–140.

Frank, R. G., Bouman, D. E., Cain, K., & Watts, C. (1992b). Primary prevention of catastrophic injury. *American Psychologist, 47,* 1045–1049.

Freudenberg, N., Eng, E., Flay, B., Parcel, G., Rogers, T., & Wallerstein, N. (1995). *Health Education Quarterly, 22,* 290–306.

Gallagher, S. S., Hunter, P., & Guyer, B. (1985). A home prevention program for children. *Pediatric Clinics of North America, 32,* 95–112.

Galavotti, C., Saltzman, L. E., Sauter, S. L., & Sumartojo, E. (1997). Behavioral science activities at the Centers for Disease Control and Prevention. *American Psychologist, 52,* 154–166.

Grant, B. A. (1990). Effectiveness of feedback and education in an employment based seat belt program. *Health Education Research, 5*(2), 197–205.

Green, L. W., & Kreuter, M. W. (1991). *Health promotion planning: An educational and environmental approach* (2nd ed.). Mountain View, CA: Mayfield.

Green, L. W., Kreuter, M. W., Deeds, S. G., & Partridge, K. B. (1980). *Health education planning: A diagnostic approach.* Palo Alto, CA: Mayfield.

Haddon, W., Jr. (1980). Advances in the epidemiology of injuries as a basis for public policy. *Public Health Report, 95,* 411–421.

Harrison, J. A., Mullen, P. D., & Green, L. W. (1992). A meta-analysis of studies of the health belief model with adults. *Health Education Research, 7*(1), 107–116.

Hoag Memorial Hospital v. Managed Care Administrators, 820 F.Supp. 1232 (C.D. Cal 1993).

Hsu, J. S. J., & Williams, S. D. (1991). Injury prevention awareness in an urban Native American population. *American Journal of Public Health, 81,* 1466–1468.

Injury Free in Harlem. (2000). *Harlem Hospital Injury Prevention Program.* Retrieved date from the World Wide Web: http://www.injuryfree.org/harlem.htm

Janz, N. K., & Becker, M. H. (1984). The health belief model: A decade later. *Health Education Quarterly, 11*(1), 1–47.

Johnston, J. J., Hendricks, S. A., & Fike, J. M. (1994). Effectiveness of behavioral safety belt interventions. *Accident Analysis and Prevention, 26,* 315–323.

Jones, R. T., & Zaharopoulos, V. (1994). Prevention. In K. K. Tarnowski (Ed.), *Behavioral aspects of pediatric burns: Issues in clinical child psychology* (pp. 243–264). New York: Plenum Press.

Kronefeld, J. J., & Glik, D. C. (1995). Unintentional injury: A major health problem for young children and youth. *Journal of Family and Economic Issues, 16,* 365–393.

Lechman, B. C., & Bonwich, E. B. (1981, Winter). Evaluation of an education program for spinal cord injury prevention: Some preliminary findings. *SCI Digest,* pp. 27–34.

Lescohier, I., & Gallagher, S. S. (1996). Unintentional injury. In R. J. DiClemente, W. B. Hansen, & L. E. Ponton (Eds.), *Handbook of adolescent health risk behavior* (pp. 225–258). New York: Plenum Press.

Maddux, J. E., Brawley, L., & Boykin, A. (1995). Self-efficacy and healthy behavior: Prevention, promotion, and detection. In J. E. Maddux (Ed.), *Self-efficacy, adaptation, and adjustment: Theory, research, and application* (pp. 173–202). New York: Plenum Press.

Morreim, E. H. (1995). Lifestyles of the risky and infamous: From managed care to managed lives. *Hastings Center Report, 25*(6), 5–12.

National Academy of Sciences. (1988). *Injury control.* Washington, DC: National Academy Press.

National Center for Injury Prevention and Control. (1996). *Major causes of unintentional injuries among older persons: An annotated bibliography.* Atlanta, GA: Centers for Disease Control and Prevention.

National Highway Traffic Safety Administration. (1996). *Third report to Congress: Effectiveness of occupant protection systems and their use.* Washington, DC: U.S. Department of Transportation.

National Highway Traffic Safety Administration. (1998). *Traffic safety facts 1997: Alcohol.* Washington, DC: Author.

National Safety Council. (1986). *Accident facts.* Chicago: Author.

Peterson, L. (1984). Teaching home safety and survival skills to latch key children: A comparison of two manuals and methods. *Journal of Applied Behavioral Analysis, 17,* 279–293.

Peterson, L. (1988). Preventing the leading killer of children: The role of the school psychologist in injury prevention. *School Psychology Review, 17,* 593–600.

Peterson, L., & Mori, L. (1985). Prevention of child injury: An overview of targets, methods, and tactics for psychologists. *Journal of Consulting and Clinical Psychology, 53,* 586–595.

Peterson, L., & Roberts, M. C. (1992). Complacency, misdirection, and effective prevention of children's injuries. *American Psychologist, 47,* 1040–1044.

Peterson, L., Zink, M., & Downing, J. (1993). Childhood injury prevention. In D. S. Glenwick & L. A. Jason (Eds.), *Promoting health and mental health in children, youth, and families* (pp. 51–73). New York: Plenum Press.

Pless, I. B., & Arsenault, L. (1987). The role of health education in the prevention of injuries to children. *Journal of Social Issues, 43,* 87–104.

Province, M. A., Hadley, E. C., & Hornbrook, M. C. (1995). The effects of exercise on falls in elderly patients: A preplanned meta-analysis of the FICSIT trials. *Journal of the American Medical Association, 273,* 1341–1347.

Richards, J. S., & Hendricks, C. (1991). Prevention of spinal cord injury: An elementary education approach. *Journal of Pediatric Psychology, 16,* 595–609.

Roberts, D., & Maccoby, N. (1985). Effects of mass communication. In G. Lindzey & E. Aronson (Eds.), *Handbook of social psychology: Vol. 2. Special fields and applications* (pp. 505–547). New York: Random House.

Roberts, G. W., Banspach, S. W., & Peacock, N. (1997). Behavioral scientists at the Centers for Disease Control and Prevention: Evolving and integrated roles. *American Psychologist, 52,* 143–146.

Roberts, M. C. (1994). Prevention/promotion in America: Still spitting on the sidewalk. *Journal of Pediatric Psychology, 19,* 267–281.

Roberts, M. C., & Fanurik, D. (1986). Rewarding elementary school children for their use of safety belts. *Health Psychology, 5,* 185–186.

Roberts, M. C., & Layfield, D. A. (1987). Promoting child passenger safety: A comparison of two positive methods. *Journal of Pediatric Psychology, 12,* 257–271.

Robertson, L. S. (1986). Injury. In B. A. Edelstein & L. Michelson (Eds.), *Handbook of prevention* (pp. 343–360). New York: Plenum Press.

Rodriguez, J. G. (1990). Childhood injuries in the United States: A priority issue. *American Journal of Diseases of Children, 144,* 625–626.

Rosenstock, I. M. (1966). Why people use health services. *Milbank Memorial Fund Quarterly, 44,* 94–127.

Rugg, D. L., Levinson, R., DiClemente, R., & Fishbein, M. (1997). Centers for disease control and prevention partnerships with external behavioral and social scientists. *American Psychologist, 52,* 147–153.

Runyan, C. W., Bangdiwala, S., Linzer, M. A., Sacks, J., & Butts, J. (1992). Risk factors for fatal residential fires. *New Journal of Medicine, 327,* 859–863.

SAFEKIDS. (1999). *National SAFEKIDS Campaign.* Retrieved March 8, 2000, from the World Wide Web: http://www.safekids.org

Schwartz, R. L. (1993). Life style, health status, and distributive justice. *Health Matrix, 3,* 195–217.

Slomski, A. J. (1995). Maybe bigger isn't better after all. *Medical Economics, 72*(4), 55–58.

Smith, R. B. (1997). Managed health care: An overview. *Proceedings of the Managed Health Care Conference, Cancer, 79*(Suppl.), 648–652.

Snider, D. E., & Satcher, D. (1997). Behavioral and social sciences at the Centers for Disease Control and Prevention. *American Psychologist, 52,* 140–142.

Stover, S. L., DeLisa, J. A., & Whiteneck, G. G. (1995). *Spinal cord injury: Clinical outcomes from the model systems*. Gaithersburg, MD: Aspen.

Tinetti, M. E., & Speechley, M. (1989). Current concepts—Geriatrics: Prevention of falls among the elderly. *New England Journal of Medicine, 320,* 1055–1059.

U.S. Department of Health and Human Services. (1990). *Healthy People 2000: National health promotion and disease prevention objectives*. Washington, DC: U.S. Government Printing Office.

Weinstein, N. D. (1984). Why it won't happen to me: Perceptions of risk factors and susceptibility. *Health Psychology, 3,* 431–457.

Winett, R. A. (1995). A framework for health promotion and disease prevention programs. *American Psychologist, 50,* 341–350.

Winett, R. A., King, A. C., & Altman, D. G. (1989). *Health psychology and public health: An integrative approach*. New York: Pergamon Press.

Wise, P. H., Kotelchuck, M., Wilson, M. L., & Mills, M. (1985). Racial and socioeconomic disparities in childhood mortality in Boston. *New England Journal of Medicine, 313,* 360–366.

Wolter, L. L., & Studenski, S. A. (1996). A clinical synthesis of falls intervention trials. *Topics in Geriatric Rehabilitation, 11*(3), 9–19.

25 _____

Social Support and Adjustment to Disability

Kathleen Chwalisz and Alan Vaux

"Rehabilitation psychology is concerned with the life problems of persons who have suffered deprivation because of a value loss due to disability or other condition such as old age and poverty" (Shontz & Wright, 1980, p. 919), and societal and interpersonal barriers are a major source of such deprivation. Social support is an important asset in combating barriers faced by people with disabilities, and thus social support has received a great deal of attention in the rehabilitation literature. However, much more could be done to incorporate more general advances in the understanding of social support. Furthermore, the nature of illnesses or injuries that result in functional limitations and disability may interfere with one's ability to maintain or use social support, suggesting that this area may warrant some new formulations in the manner in which social support theory is applied.

Fundamental Concepts

The importance of social ties to individual well-being has been a topic of interest since the beginning of psychology and the social sciences. Yet the current interest in social support has recent origins in social epidemiological work of the mid-1970s (Caplan, 1974; Cassel, 1974; Cobb, 1976). The volume of research on the topic, generated by several disciplines, has been extraordinary, yet it has not always been enlightening. The sheer scope and richness of the topic have impeded systematic scientific study. The resultant diversity of perspective and focus has made it difficult to organize the literature, synthesize findings, and conduct research that systematically extends knowledge. Much of the variety in perspective surrounds three issues: (a) the range of relevant social ties (e.g., intimate relationships, friends, acquaintances through organizational affiliation, professional assistance), (b) the relative importance of objective features of social relationships versus the individual's perception or appraisal of these, and (c) the wide variety of forms that support might take (e.g., emotional support, practical assistance).

Metaconstruct

Building on the work of numerous scholars, Vaux (1988) sought to more explicitly differentiate various foci and articulate important social support concepts. He proposed viewing social support as a metaconstruct comprising three theoretically distinct constructs: (a) support network resources, (b) supportive behavior, and (c) support appraisals. The support network is that subset of the social network to which a person routinely turns or could turn for assistance in managing demands and achieving goals. *Support network resources* include features of the support network (e.g., size, structure, composition, and relationship quality) that likely contribute to its value as a resource (i.e., its sensitivity, accessibility, and capacity as a source of assistance).

Supportive behaviors are those acts generally recognized as efforts to help a person, either spontaneously or on request. Note that supportive behavior, despite best intentions, may or may not be helpful. The outcome likely depends on the amount, timing, and fit of supportive activity relative to the recipient's needs in a given context. Supportive behavior may be a good or a poor fit to need: A rope would be more helpful than sympathy to a drowning man, but the reverse would be true for his widow. Moreover, supportive behavior may have multiple outcomes that differ, in the short and long term, on affect or performance. For example, comforting an individual may ameliorate distress in the short term but undermine efforts to face a chronic difficulty.

In rehabilitation situations in particular, supportive behaviors may actually have a negative effect on functioning. In a study of 148 married patients with chronic pain, Turk, Kerns, and Rosenberg (1992) found that solicitous spouse responses to pain-related expressions were associated with increased experience of pain and disability. Similarly, in a study of social support among 179 individuals with spinal cord injury (SCI), interaction effects were found between various dimensions of social support and psychosocial functioning by time since injury (Elliott, Herrick, Witty, Godshall, & Spruell, 1992).

Support appraisals are "subjective evaluative assessments of a person's supportive relationships and the supportive behavior that occurs within them" (Vaux, 1988, p. 29). These appraisals (often termed *perceived support*) may reflect somewhat independent facets such as satisfaction; feeling cared for, respected, or involved (e.g., Cobb, 1976); or having a sense of attachment, belonging, or reliable alliance (e.g., Cutrona & Russell, 1987). Support appraisals may be general (i.e., with respect to the entire network) or specific to a particular tie or type of relationship (e.g., romantic partner, friends, family, work supervisors), or they may be focused on a particular mode of support (e.g., emotional, practical). Thus, an individual with a disability might feel that he or she is deeply cared for by immediate family but lacks extrafamilial friends, or that practical assistance is abundant but emotional support sparse, or that people care but do not know how to help overcome functional limitations.

Support appraisals have been shown to reflect supportive behavior and network resources (Vaux & Athanassopoulou, 1987), but the association is moderate. Moreover, appraisals routinely show stronger associations with well-being compared with supportive behavior or network resources (Turner, Frankel, & Levin, 1983). This has led to a focus on support appraisals as though they are independent of support resources or experiences. Indeed, some researchers view appraisals as aspects of personality (Sarason, Sarason, & Shearin, 1986). Yet, we can readily explain why support appraisals do not match resources or behaviors and why they show stronger associations with well-being by recognizing that they are an evaluative synthesis sampling numerous and diverse experiences, in multiple relationships, incorporating a host of features regarding quality, fit, and so forth (Hobfoll, 1988; Vaux, 1988).

Models of Support

Supportive behavior may take many forms (e.g., listening, making suggestions, sharing tasks) and serve many functions (e.g., giving tangible assistance, expressing love). Building on five typologies of supportive functions (e.g., Cobb, 1976; Lin, 1986) and seven typologies of supportive activities (e.g., Barrera & Ainlay, 1983; Caplan, 1974; Foa & Foa, 1980), Vaux and colleagues (Vaux, 1988; Vaux, Riedel, & Stewart, 1987) proposed a synthesis involving six modes of support: emotional, feedback, advice–guidance, practical, financial–material, and socializing. Such distinctions are not always explicit in social support research. Indeed, many measures of support—whether of resources, behavior, or appraisals—either do not adequately sample or do not properly distinguish these modes (see review by Vaux, 1988). Distinguishing support modes is pertinent in the rehabilitation area in which practical and material support may play as important a role as the emotional support and guidance that have occupied so much research attention to date.

Dynamic Process in Ecological Context

Independently, Vaux (1988) and Hobfoll (1988) proposed theories that mesh well to advance the understanding of social support and stress, and they are particularly relevant to the rehabilitation area. Vaux emphasized that social support involves a dynamic process of transaction between people and their social networks that takes place in an often changing ecological context. Some key propositions of this view follow.

Social support processes not only fulfill basic social needs but also enhance the person's capacity to cope with demands, to negotiate transitions, and to achieve goals. At their best, supportive relationships constitute a rich and reliable source of resources (e.g., affection, comfort, expertise, information, energy) that can profoundly expand the individual's functional capacity.

Most individuals actively develop and maintain support resources to supplement their personal capacities. Support networks that are large and diverse likely offer advantages such as accessibility, stamina in the face of chronic demand, varied expertise, breadth of information, and diverse perspectives on life's problems and challenges. Intimate and close relationships are more likely to respond to need, to be motivated to expend energy to help, to be accurate in reading the nature and extent of one's difficulties, and to provide help that fits the need. The individual with rich support resources not only receives more and more appropriate assistance, but through enhanced supportive appraisals is also able to sustain morale and effort in the face of difficulty even without direct intervention by network members.

These support processes do not occur in a vacuum but rather in a changing ecological context. There is an interplay of personal assets and liabilities, social contexts that facilitate or impede support processes, environmental demands and opportunities, and so forth. Personal assets such as attractiveness, social skills, or agreeableness may facilitate the development and use of support resources, whereas liabilities such as stigma, neuroticism, or a negative network orientation may impede them (Vaux, 1988). Social context factors (e.g., social roles occupied, interaction opportunities, privacy) facilitate or impede support processes.

Paradoxically, individuals with substantial personal and social assets also are likely to maintain substantial support resources with a high sustainable yield and to have relatively less need for support, thus allowing further accumulation of resources. On the other hand, those with limited personal and social assets also are more likely not only to have more ongoing need for support (e.g., need to deal with more stressors) but also to have limited and vulnerable support resources (e.g., small networks, few intimates, unreliable friends, with fewer resources to share). Life events, whether planned role changes (e.g., employment, marriage, relocation) or unplanned trauma (e.g., illness, accident, bereavement), involve transitions that must be negotiated. They involve the risk of a vicious cycle of accumuluating stressors, support resource strain or loss, and demoralization, especially for those with limited resources initially.

Hobfoll's (1988) theory of conservation of resources begins with the tenet that people actively strive to obtain, retain, and protect what they value—specifically, resources such as objects (e.g., possessions), personal characteristics (e.g., sense of mastery, skills), conditions (e.g., seniority, good relationships), and energies (e.g., money, knowledge). Stress results when resources are lost, threatened, or invested without gain. Individuals cope by using resources to offset losses and strive by using resources to enhance gains. Social support clearly is an integral part of this process. People strive to develop relationships that have value, and they use those relationships both to help them enhance resources and to cope with threat or loss.

Both models highlight the risk that impairment might trigger a loss spiral or impede escape from a state of resource impoverishment. For example, an accident might lead to impairment that both dramatically increases demands on the individual (e.g., coping with impairment, job loss, reappraisal of life aspirations) and simultaneously reduces support resources (e.g., isolation from friends, workmates) or strains those resources beyond sustainable yield (e.g., friends cannot meet all support needs), damaging the relationships (e.g., friends drop away). The result may be a disabled individual who is demoralized and friendless.

Buffer and Direct Models

Considering the volume of research on social support, models of its effects on well-being have advanced relatively little. Early on, Cobb (1976) proposed that social support acted to protect individuals from stressful events. This *buffer model* was interpreted as a reduced association between stressors and distress under conditions of relatively greater support. A *direct effect model* stated that social support had a positive effect on well-being independently of the stress process. Virtually all social support research has focused on these models, particularly the former. Moreover, they seem straightforward and easily tested, respectively implying an interactive or main effect of social support and stress on well-being.

However, the simplicity of the buffer and direct effects models is deceptive. Many studies purporting to test them were flawed by conceptual confusion, methodological problems, or inappropriate statistical tests (see discussions by Dooley, 1985; and Kessler & McLeod, 1985; and Wheaton, 1985). Reviews of the literature on the buffer model reached different conclusions that were not easily reconciled (e.g., Cohen & Wills, 1985; Kessler & McLeod, 1985; Lin, 1986; Vaux, 1988). The most thorough reviews suggest revisions that resolve some inconsistencies. Cohen and McKay (1984) proposed a modified buffer hypothesis: Support buffers stress when it matches the functional coping requirements of the stressor. Kessler and McLeod (1985) conducted perhaps the most systematic review to date, although it was limited to studies involving community samples experiencing life stressors. They found buffer effects primarily for tests involving emotional support and support appraisal measures, not for those involving support network measures. The latter yielded evidence for direct effects in several strong studies.

Hobfoll and Vaux (1993) noted that although these reviews begin the task of synthesizing findings of numerous studies, a number of problems persist. Why do only some types of support measures yield buffer effects? What do tests of a "pervasive" buffer effect, involving heterogeneous life events, tell us about how support buffers specific stressors? What are the implications of the very poor measurement of support in many studies? (A third of the tests reviewed by Kessler & McLeod, 1985, involved three or fewer items as support measures.) Finally, Vaux (1988) reviewed some 20 studies conducted after these reviews and found that results did not conform to the revised models. Some studies yielded evidence of buffer effects not only for just some support measures but also for just some subsamples or for just some distress measures. As Hobfoll and Vaux concluded, the general buffer model may have outlived its usefulness: An ecological model suggests specification of stressors, support, process, outcome, and context.

Specificity Models

Cohen and McKay (1984) proposed the first explicit statement of a stressor-support specificity model. They suggested that stressors generate particular coping demands and will be effectively buffered only by modes of support that meet those demands. Thus, what they term *tangible, appraisal, esteem,* and *belonging support* would buffer stressors involving resource deficits, subjective interpretations of events, internal attributions of inadequacy, and loss of important relationships, respectively. Early evidence for specificity models, however, was limited.

Cutrona (1990; Cutrona & Russell, 1990) proposed a model of optimal matching that distinguished stressors on the basis of controllability and life domain. According to the model, controllable stressors are best buffered by instrumental support but also by esteem support to sustain efficacy. In contrast, uncontrollable stressors allow only palliative coping and are best buffered by emotional support. The life domain distinctions are based in part on Hobfoll's (1988) conservation-of-resources theory. Losses of assets, relationships, achievements, and roles are best buffered by tangible support, attachment or network support, esteem support, and network support, respectively. Cutrona and Russell (1990) reviewed about 40 studies and concluded that, in two-thirds of the studies, findings were consistent with optimal matching predictions.

Another aspect of specificity, of particular relevance to rehabilitation, is *outcome specificity*. Social support is hypothesized to have a variety of positive outcomes, yet most research has focused on psychological distress. Quite likely, specific modes of support have differential impact on various outcomes. For example, practical assistance may lead to instrumental success, whereas emotional support may be more likely to lead to reduced negative affect and emotional calm (Vaux, 1988). The interplay of various support modes and instrumental and affective outcomes would seem particularly pertinent in the context of an individual negotiating impairment-related functional limitations.

These issues highlight the need to address mechanisms of support: How does support influence well-being? With respect to stress, support might prevent a stressor from occurring, inoculate the individual against it, promote accurate appraisals of it, aid reappraisal as the stress encounter unfolds, involve direct action to counter the stressor, suggest coping options, maintain efficacy, or facilitate recovery of emotional equilibrium (Thoits, 1986; Vaux, 1988). A variety of models have been articulated but rarely tested.

If rehabilitation specialists and psychologists are to use social support theory in understanding and reducing disability, they would do well to take note of the issues discussed above. The ecological model of social support (i.e., dynamic process in a changing ecological context) seems particularly pertinent to understanding how individuals and their networks deal with such trauma as the dramatic life-changing sequelae of injury or the onset of chronic debilitating illness. The rehabilitation process is greatly facilitated by our ability to distinguish support network resources, behavior, and appraisals, differentiating modes of support, examining specificity models, and attending to mechanisms of support effects.

Disability Literature

Social support appears extensively in the disability literature. However, much of the research has been atheoretical, ignoring developments in social support theory and research. Social support has been examined in a variety of contexts, suggesting a variety of mechanisms from which support might affect people with disabilities.

Social Support as a Predictor of Outcomes

Most of the research on social support and disability has simply included social support among predictors of a variety of outcomes, presumably conceptualizing support in terms of the buffer model. Social support appraisals have most often been examined in conjunction with coping strategies to predict depression (e.g., Zea, Belgrave, Townsend, Jarama, & Banks, 1996), acceptance of disability (Coca, 1991), and psychosocial adjustment (e.g., Brenner, Melamed, & Panush, 1994) among people with a variety of disabling conditions.

Elliott and Shewchuk (1995) examined perceived social support and depression as predictors of leisure activities among people with disabilities. Perceived social support has also been examined along with stress in predicting functional status (Weinberger, Tierney, Booher, & Hiner (1990) and with self-efficacy in predicting health status and adherence with health recommendations (Taal, Rasker, Seydel, & Wiegman, 1993) among people with rheumatoid arthritis.

Models Including Social Support

A few studies involve social support and disability in the context of more sophisticated theoretical models using more advanced statistical procedures, although support is still conceptualized from a buffering perspective. For example, McNett (1987) tested a theoretical model, in which perceived availability of social support, perceived effectiveness of social support, and personal constraints on the use of social support were predictors of degree of threat and use of social support and coping to predict coping effectiveness among people who were wheelchair bound as a result of SCI or stroke. Perceived availability of social support was a significant predictor of threat appraisals, use of social support, and coping. Perceived effectiveness of social support only predicted use of social support, and personal constraints did not predict any support or coping variables. Despite a number of limitations, McNett (1987) explored some of the ecological model propositions and support mechanisms discussed earlier.

Ben Sira (1983) included emotional support and resource-enhancing support (e.g., vocational training) in a structural equation model of readjustment to traumatic loss. Support affected the subsequent experience of stress and distress and was associated with decreased cardiac symptoms in a longitudinal model of recovery from myocardial infarction or coronary artery bypass surgery (Fontana, Kerns, Rosenberg, & Colonese, 1989). Hoen (1991) examined a model of continuity of leisure, self-esteem, and social support predicting well-being among older people with physical disabilities and found that social support had a strong positive effect on well-being for women and a strong negative effect for men. Brown, Wallston, and Nicassio (1989) used structural equation modeling to examine the relationships among social support, chronic pain, and depression over time.

One of the most sophisticated model studies we found was conducted by McColl, Lef, and Skinner (1995). Covariance structural modeling was used to examine the relationships among different dimensions of social support (informational, instrumental, emotional) and coping (problem oriented, perception oriented, emotion oriented) among people with SCI at 1, 4, and 12 months postdischarge. The structure of social support was found to change over time, with informational support most salient at 1 month and emotional support most important at 4 and 12 months postdischarge. Social support was also found to differentially influence coping over time. Studies such as this one are exemplary, because they not only examine social support as a dynamic process but also provide for the influence of other ecological factors relevant to the support process.

Social Support Predicting Disability

A few studies look at the buffering role of social support between illness and disability. In a study of older people who had experienced hip fracture, stroke, or myocardial infarction, Wilcox, Kasl, and Berkman (1994) obtained measures of social support and physical disability before and after illness and during the recovery period. These authors found that illness was associated with changes in both qualitative and quantitative aspects of support, and the relationship between social support and recovery from illness depended on the type of support measured. Task support adequacy was associated with less disability 6 months after the onset of illness, whereas individuals with no premorbid need for emotional support fared better than those who needed and received adequate emotional support. This finding is consistent with the ecological model's "rich get richer" hypothesis.

Hallberg, Lillemor, Johnsson, and Axelsson (1993) identified social support as one of a number of individual, environmental, and socioeconomic predictors of perceived disability among middle-aged men with noise-induced hearing loss. The nature of one's social network was found by Richmond (1997) to influence disability indirectly through its effects on psychological distress in a longitudinal study of people with non-central-nervous-system traumatic injuries. Whereas social support has been identified as a predictor of disability, it has typically been included in studies along with a plethora of other predictors. However, the findings of the more focused Wilcox et al. (1994) study suggest that the role of social support warrants investigation in its own right.

Effects of Disability on Support

A few researchers have examined the effects of disability status on social support with mixed results. Orr and Aronson (1990) found no direct relationship between orthopedic disability status and social support. However, Orr, Thein, and Aronson (1995) found that people with physical disabilities were less likely to receive social support than people without disabilities, and the relationship was moderated by conformity behavior. In a study of community residents with a variety of physical disabilities, Burkart (1992) found that personality factors were related to social support, whereas disability-related factors were not. In contrast, Davis (1985) found that adolescents with visible disabilities were more likely to have smaller peer support networks and that individuals with neurological impairments were significantly more likely to be isolated from peers. These mixed findings suggest that direct effects of disability on social support are less likely than effects mediated or moderated by personality, behavioral, and cognitive factors or by developmental stage or ecological context.

Nature of Social Support Among People With Disabilities

Some researchers have merely attempted to describe the nature of social support among people with disabilities, and these studies have focused primarily on the composition and quality of their social networks. In a study of the social networks of 30 college students with disabilities and 15 students without disabilities, students with disabilities were found to have (a) more friends in their networks, (b) more relationships involving casual conversation and entertainment, and (c) more relationships providing transportation and housekeeping assistance (Parris Stephens & Norris-Baker, 1984). Using a participant observation technique, Knox and Parmenter (1993) examined the nature of social networks and how support was provided for 9 individuals with mild intellectual disabilities in a competitive employment situation. Family and organizations for people with disabilities were found to be the major sources of support. Such studies provide an interesting picture of social support as it is manifested for people with disabilities, but they contribute little to the theoretical understanding or applied research on social support and disability.

Interventions

A logical outgrowth of research on social support and disability is research on social support interventions with people with various illnesses and injuries. Lanza and Revenson (1993) reviewed the literature on social support interventions with individuals with rheumatoid arthritis, and their review appears representative of the social support intervention literature in general. Social support interventions were categorized in terms of (a) counseling and group therapy interventions, some of which were combined with more systematic education or skills training (e.g., relaxation and assertion training); (b) multimodal interventions, which generally have involved comparing social support against support combined with other types of interventions (e.g., cognitive–behavioral therapy) or a no-treatment control condition; and (c) supportive contexts, which are inadvertently created supportive environments associated with other types of interventions (e.g., participants in an educational intervention feeling that others in the group cared about them). These authors noted a number of methodological limitations to research on support interventions, including small sample sizes, high attrition rates, pretest effects, failing to account for characteristics of the participants' illness, lack of evaluation, and failure to adequately document the components of the interventions. In many ways, the development of social support interventions appears premature, given the state of knowledge regarding the relationship between social support and disability.

Summary

This research provides at least some evidence that social support of various types appears to be associated with coping and a variety of outcomes (e.g., depression, adjustment, self-esteem) for individuals with potentially disabling conditions. Social support also appears to affect disability status, at least indirectly, following illness or injury, although social support has often been included among many potential predictors. The nature of support networks and supportive relationships may be different for people with disabilities, although this research is still in the exploratory stages. Disability appears to affect both quality and quantity of social support; however, this relationship may be mediated or moderated by other factors (e.g., personality, conformity behavior). Finally, social support interventions have yielded mixed results, perhaps attributable to methodological and conceptual problems with such interventions.

Existing research on social support and disability manifests a number of limitations, some reflecting problems in the social support literature more generally, some specific to disability and rehabilitation. A major limitation of this research is a lack of clarity in how support is defined and operationalized. In particular, distinctions between network resources, supportive behaviors, and support appraisals are not recognized. Different modes of support are also ignored by some researchers. Given the lack of conceptual clarity, weak measures of support are sometimes used. Most of the research on social support and disability has been based on the general buffer model, which has been found to have little utility in the general social support literature. Finally, little or no attention has been given to the ecological context in which support occurs for people with disabilities.

Current Issues

A substantial body of theory and research suggests that social support processes serve not only to fulfill basic social needs for affection, esteem, and belonging but also to enhance the person's capacity to cope with demands, to negotiate transitions, and to achieve goals. Clearly this work has great potential for understanding and shaping the rehabilitation process. What issues are most pertinent for the rehabilitation psychologist— in terms of research and intervention—and what roles are such professionals suited to play?

Research

As noted above, there is a substantial gap between the complexity of social support theory and existing work on social support in the rehabilitation context. A dedicated scholar could advance a lengthy research agenda. We highlight a few key issues, propositions, and hypotheses.

Loss is central to most disability, which involves life-changing injury or disease. Often losses are not limited to functional capacity but involve loss of roles, esteem, and social ties. For example, essay accounts of family members of people with brain injuries included injury-related losses involving life purpose, personality traits, intellectual capacity, income and earning potential, quality of life, sexual functioning, capacity to love, and family relationships (Chwalisz, 1998; Chwalisz & Stark-Wroblewski, 1996).

Individuals with disabilities clearly are at risk for the debilitating loss spirals described earlier: When do these occur, and when do they not? Are there rich longitudinal descriptions of how these ecological transitions are negotiated? We can advance some illustrative propositions.

- Acute injury or illness that leads to impairment results in a dramatic contraction of support network resources (e.g., size, quality, diversity).
- Loss of support resources is (a) proportional to the number and centrality of lost roles and (b) inversely proportional to initial resources.
- Compared with other losses, loss of core support resources such as spousal support (a) is more likely to result from illnesses or injuries that alter the fundamental character of the individual with a disability and (b) has the most detrimental effects on the disability process.
- Support resource loss varies across types of acute disability.
- Loss spirals predict functional limitations and poor disability outcomes.
- Emotional support predicts psychological distress and well-being.
- Practical support predicts instrumental—functional capacity— outcomes. However, the association between social support and

functional capacity may not always be positive (e.g., Turk et al., 1992).

Conceptualizing social support as a dynamic process in ecological context (Hobfoll, 1988; Vaux, 1988) highlights the importance of the individual's role in maintaining his or her social network. Illness, injury, and disability can drastically alter one's assets and liabilities with regard to developing, maintaining, and using one's social network. For example, physical attractiveness or social skill may change, altering one's ability to attract new network members. Access to certain aspects of one's social network may change (e.g., being disabled from work decreases access to network interactions that typically occurred in the workplace). Increases in needs and distress may decrease one's capacity to provide support for others in the network.

A number of writers have discussed the importance of reciprocity in social support among people with disabilities; however, we were unable to locate much empirical research in the area. In one empirical study of social support reciprocity among 140 persons with SCI, participants reported being more satisfied with relationships in which others provided more support, and parents and professional helpers were most likely to fall into that category (Rintala, Young, Hart, & Fuhrer, 1994). Ell (1996) suggested that a family systems model should be used to conceptualize social support following illness or disability, focusing on the nature of the everyday interactions and support exchange between family members.

Intervention

Much of the interest in social support rests on its promise as a framework for psychosocial interventions. This promise has yet to be fully realized (see Lanza & Revenson, 1993; Rook & Dooley, 1985; Vaux, 1988). Relatively few support interventions have built on a sophisticated theoretical framework, identified a deficit in the support process, clearly specified a target of change, crafted an appropriate enhancement of support, and carefully evaluated the intervention through appropriate measures collected in a robust design.

Vaux (1988) proposed several strategies for enhancing support processes. These include (a) improving the use of existing resources by countering negative network orientation; (b) facilitating the development and maintenance of resources (e.g., identifying strengths and weaknesses, containing costs, establishing new relationships); (c) enhancing the skills involved in managing support incidents (e.g., identifying and articulating needs, selecting a helper and a suitable time and place, showing appreciation); and (d) enhancing support appraisals (e.g., helping the person collect evidence that he or she is cared for, esteemed, and involved). A few key issues in the rehabilitation area include the following:

- Can professionals or paraprofessionals serve important emotional support functions?

- Can family members and friends learn to perform technical practical assistance functions?
- If so, what impact does this have on their expressive support functions?
- What factors contribute to (a) loss spirals resulting in a dramatic contraction of resources and (b) the redevelopment of adequate support network resources?
- What support processes allow successful negotiation of an ecological transition that entails a complete reassessment of an individual's identity and future (e.g., in the case of an individual with severe brain injury)?

Roles

Rehabilitation psychologists play a key function in patient assessment. No effort to intervene in terms of support should be attempted without adequate assessment. Premorbid social support needs and resources should be assessed. Given that the general buffer model has been replaced by specificity conceptualizations, an individual's current support needs and resources should be assessed in terms of specific modes of support and desired outcomes. In all cases, social support can be assessed in terms of network resources, supportive behaviors, or the individual's support appraisals.

The ecological context in which support occurs must also be assessed. Noting a positive relationship among instrumental, informational, and emotional support over time, McColl et al. (1995) suggested that social support may be a characteristic of the individual rather than the support system. What ecological assets and liabilities exist that might facilitate or obstruct the support process? For example, does transportation allow the individual access to friends? Are socialization settings capable of making appropriate accommodations? Is privacy available for close relationships? The ecological context for each individual is unique and highly complex, requiring thorough assessment.

With the development of empirical and theoretical models of the social support in the disability process and with thorough assessment of individuals' social support needs and resources, it is then possible to design and implement support-based intervention programs. Such programs could be designed to maximize or acquire assets and minimize or eliminate support liabilities. Rehabilitation psychologists' skills regarding program evaluation may also be applied, compensating for limitations of the previous social support intervention research (e.g., small sample sizes, atheoretical interventions, failure to adequately document aspects of the intervention).

Conclusion

A great deal has been accomplished in terms of examining the role of social support in the disability process and attempting to influence the disability process through social support. In many ways, however, this work has been plagued by some of the same problems, particularly diversity of perspective and focus, that have obstructed progress in more general knowledge of social support. It is time for rehabilitation psychologists to refocus their efforts in a more systematic fashion, capitalizing on more recent developments in the area of social support and recognizing unique aspects of support in rehabilitation, to enhance research, assessment, and, ultimately, intervention.

References

Barrerra, M., Jr., & Ainlay, S. L. (1983). The structure of social support: A conceptual and empirical analysis. *Journal of Community Psychology, 11,* 133–143.

Ben Sira, Z. (1983). Loss, stress, and readjustment: The structure of coping with bereavement and disability. *Social Science and Medicine, 17,* 1619–1632.

Brenner, G. F., Melamed, B. G., & Panush, R. S. (1994). Optimism and coping as determinants of psychosocial adjustment to rheumatoid arthritis. *Journal of Clinical Psychology in Medical Settings, 1,* 115–134.

Brown, G. K, Wallston, K. A., & Nicassio, P. M. (1989). Social support and depression in rheumatoid arthritis: A one-year prospective study. *Journal of Applied Social Psychology, 19,* 1164–1181.

Burkart, D. F. (1992). *An exploratory study of the correlates of coping in community residents with physical disabilities.* Unpublished doctoral dissertation, University of Missouri—Columbia.

Caplan, C. (1974). *Support systems and community mental health.* New York: Human Sciences Press.

Cassel, J. (1974). Psychosocial processes and "stress": Theoretical formulations. *International Journal of Health Services, 4,* 471–482.

Chwalisz, K. (1998). Brain injury: A tapestry of loss. In J. H. Harvey (Ed.), *Perspectives on loss: A sourcebook* (pp. 189–200). Philadelphia: Taylor & Francis.

Chwalisz, K., & Stark-Wroblewski, K. (1996). The subjective experience of spouse caregivers of persons with brain injuries: A qualitative analysis. *Applied Neuropsychology, 3,* 28–40.

Cobb, S. (1976). Social support as a moderator of life stress. *Psychosomatic Medicine, 38,* 300–314.

Coca, B. (1991). *Coping strategies, social support and acceptance of disability among persons with spinal cord injury.* Unpublished doctoral dissertation, California School of Professional Psychology, Los Angeles.

Cohen, S., & McKay, G. (1984). Social support, stress, and the buffering hypothesis: A theoretical analysis. In A. Baum, S. E. Taylor, & J. E. Singer (Eds.), *Handbook of psychology and health: Vol. 4. Social psychological aspects of health* (pp. 253–267). Hillsdale, NJ: Erlbaum.

Cohen, S., & Wills, T. A. (1985). Stress, social support, and the buffering hypothesis. *Psychological Bulletin, 98,* 310–357.

Cutrona, C. E. (1990). Stress and social support: In search of optimal matching. *Journal of Social and Clinical Psychology, 9,* 3–14.

Cutrona, C. E., & Russell, D. (1987). The provisions of social relationships and adaptation to stress. In W. H. Jones & D. Perlman (Eds.), *Advances in personal relationships* (pp. 37–67). Greenwich, CT: JAI Press.

Cutrona, C. E., & Russell, D. (1990). Type of social support and specific stress: Toward a theory of optimal matching. In B. R. Sarason, I. G. Sarason, & G. R. Pierce (Eds.), *Social support: An interactional view* (pp. 319–366). New York: Wiley.

Davis, S. E. (1985). *The relationships amongst peer support networks, intorversion/extraversion, visibility of illness, and psychological functioning in chronically ill/disabled adolescents.* Unpublished doctoral dissertation, University of Maryland—College Park.

Dooley, D. (1985). Causal inference in the study of social support. In S. Cohen & L. Syme (Eds.), *Social support and health* (pp. 109–125). Orlando, FL: Academic Press.

Ell, K. (1996). Social networks, social support, and coping with serious illness: The family connection. *Social Science and Medicine, 42,* 173–183.

Elliott, T. R., Herrick, S. M., Witty, T. E., Godshall, F., & Spruell, M. (1992). Social relationships and psychosocial impairment of persons with spinal cord injury. *Psychology and Health, 7,* 55–67.

Elliott, T. R., & Shewchuk, R. M. (1995). Social support and leisure activities following severe physical disability: Testing the mediating effects of depression. *Basic and Applied Social Psychology, 16,* 471–487.

Foa, E. B., & Foa, U. G. (1980). Resource theory: Interpersonal behavior as an exchange. In K. J. Gergens, M. S. Greenberg, & R. H. Wills (Eds.), *Social exchange: Advances in theory and research* (pp. 77–94). New York: Plenum.

Fontana, A. F., Kerns, R. D., Rosenberg, R. L., & Colonese, K. L. (1989). Support, stress, and recovery from coronary heart disease: A longitudinal causal model. *Health Psychology, 8,* 175–193.

Hallberg, L. R., Lillemor, R., Johnsson, T., & Axelsson, A. (1993). Structure of perceived handicap in middle-aged males with noise-induced hearing loss, with and without tinnitus. *Audiology, 32,* 137–152.

Hobfoll, S. E. (1988). *The ecology of stress.* New York: Hemisphere.

Hobfall, S. E., & Vaux, A. (1993). Social support: Support resources and social context. In L. Goldberger & S. Breznitz (Eds.), *Handbook of stress: Theoretical and clinical aspects* (2nd ed., pp. 685–705). New York: Free Press.

Hoen, P. A. (1991). *The effects of continuity of leisure, informal social support, and self-esteem on the psychological well-being of aged, physically disabled persons (disengagement theory).* Unpublished doctoral dissertation, State University of New York at Buffalo.

Kessler, R. C., & McLeod, J. D. (1985). Social support and mental health in community samples. In S. Cohen & S. L. Syme (Eds.), *Social support and health* (pp. 219–240). Orlando, FL: Academic Press.

Knox, M., & Parmenter, T. R. (1993). Social networks and support mechanisms for people with mild intellectual disability in competitive employment. *International Journal of Rehabilitation Research, 16,* 1–12.

Lanza, A. F., & Revenson, T. A. (1993). Social support interventions for rheumatoid arthritis patients: The cart before the horse? *Health Education Quarterly, 20,* 97–117.

Lin, N. (1986). Modeling the effects of social support. In N. Lin, A. Dean, & W. Ensel (Eds.), *Social support, life events, and depression* (pp. 173–209). Orlando, FL: Academic Press.

McColl, M. A., Lef, H., & Skinner, H. (1995). Structural relationships between social support and coping. *Social Science and Medicine, 41,* 395–407.

McNett, S. C. (1987). Social support, threat, and coping responses and effective in the functionally disabled. *Nursing Research, 36*(2), 98–103.

Orr, E., & Aronson, E. (1990). Relationships between orthopedic disability and perceived social support: Four theoretical hypotheses. *Rehabilitation Psychology, 35,* 29–41.

Orr, E., Thein, R. D., & Aronson, E. (1995). Othopedic disability, conformity, and social support. *Journal of Psychology, 129,* 203–219.

Parris Stephens, M. A., & Norris-Baker, C. (1984). Social support in college life for disabled students. *Rehabilitation Psychology, 29,* 107–111.

Richmond, T. S. (1997). An explanatory model of variables influencing postinjury disability. *Nursing Research, 46*(5), 262–269.

Rintala, D. H., Young, M. E., Hart, K. A., & Fuhrer, M. J. (1994). The relationship between the extent of reciprocity with social supporters and measures of depressive symptomatology, impairment, disability, and handicap in persons with spinal cord injury. *Rehabilitation Psychology, 39,* 15–27.

Rook, K. S., & Dooley, D. (1985). Applying social support research: Theoretical problems and future directions. *Journal of Social Issues, 41*(1), 5–28.

Sarason, I. G., Sarason, B. R., & Shearin, E. N. (1986). Social support as an individual difference variable: Its stability, origins, and relational aspects. *Journal of Personality and Social Psychology, 50,* 845–855.

Shontz, F. C., & Wright, B. A. (1980). The distinctiveness of rehabilitation psychology. *Professional Psychology, 11,* 919–924.

Taal, E., Rasker, J. J., Seydel, E. R., & Wiegman, O. (1993). Health status, adherence with health recommendations, self-efficacy and social support in patients with rheumatoid arthritis. *Patient Education and Counseling, 20*(2–3), 63–76.

Thoits, P. A. (1986). Social support as coping assistance. *Journal of Consulting and Clinical Psychology, 54,* 416–425.

Turk, D. C., Kerns, R. D., & Rosenberg, R. (1992). Effects of marital interaction on chronic pain and disability: Examining the down side of social support. *Rehabilitation Psychology, 37,* 259–274.

Turner, R., Frankel, B. G., & Levin, D. M. (1983). Social support: Conceptualization, measurement, and implications for mental health. *Research in Community and Mental Health, 3,* 67–111.

Vaux, A. (1988). *Social support: Theory, research, and intervention.* New York: Praeger.

Vaux, A., & Athanassopoulou, M. (1987). Social support appraisals and network resources. *Journal of Community Psychology, 15,* 537–556.

Vaux, A., Riedel, S., & Stewart, D. (1987). Modes of social support: The Social Support Behaviors (SSB) Scale. *American Journal of Community Psychology, 15,* 209–327.

Weinberger, M., Tierney, W. M., Booher, P., & Hiner, S. L. (1990). Social support, stress, and functional status in patients with osteoarthritis. *Social Science and Medicine, 30,* 503–508.

Wheaton, B. (1985). Models for the stress-buffering functions of coping resources. *Journal of Health and Social Behavior, 5,* 139–184.

Wilcox, V. L., Kasl, S. V., & Berkman, L. F. (1994). Social support and physical disability in older people after hospitalization: A prospective study. *Health Psychology, 13,* 170–179.

Zea, M. C., Belgrave, F. Z., Townsend, T. G., Jarama, S. L., & Banks, S. R. (1996). The influence of social support and active coping on depression among African Americans and Latinos with disabilities. *Rehabilitation Psychology, 41,* 225–242.

26

Family Caregiving in Chronic Disease and Disability

Richard Shewchuk and Timothy R. Elliott

And it ought to be remembered that there is nothing more difficult to take in hand, more perilous to conduct, or more uncertain in its success, than to take the lead in the introduction of a new order of things. Because the innovator has for enemies all those who have done well under the old conditions, and lukewarm defenders in those who may do well under the new. (Nicolo Machiavelli, *The Prince*)

Over the past decade the traditional landscape of health care has shifted dramatically as public and private-sector initiatives were developed in an effort to slow the growth of health care costs that were increasing more rapidly than annual rates of inflation and the consumer price index. The most noticeable shift has resulted from expanding penetration of managed care organizations into the health care market. Inherent in the concept of managed care is some form of capitated reimbursement, increased involvement of primary care physicians, better integration of services, and a shift in emphasis from illness to health maintenance. Increasingly, managed care organizations have been expected to control costs and have found it necessary under fixed capitation formulas to limit service utilization. There is growing recognition that this strategy is largely inefficient because health care systems continue to focus on acute care and the treatment of episodic illness at the expense of the care and management of chronic health conditions.

The reasons for this historical and pervasive focus on acute medical care are varied and complex (Counte, 1998). Some suggest that key and vocal stakeholders such as physicians, hospitals, and indemnity insurers shape policies that maintain this focus (Shewchuk & O'Connor, 2000). Kiesler (1992) sardonically observed that most health care programs in the United States are less concerned with health care per se and more concerned with hospital care. This limited vision has immense consequences for people with disability and their families and warrants concern

This work was supported by Grant R49/CCR412718-01 from the National Center for Injury Prevention and Control (NCIPC) and the Disabilities Prevention Program, National Center for Environmental Health. Its contents are solely the responsibility of the authors and do not necessarily represent the official views of the NCIPC.

about the extent to which these consumers are marginalized by health care systems and left to navigate through the maze of fractionated and piecemeal health services.

In 1995 approximately 100 million Americans of all ages had at least one chronic physical condition, and it is projected that this number will grow to 167 million by 2050. Chronic conditions include long-term illnesses (e.g., AIDS, cancer, Alzheimer's disease, emphysema, heart disease, diabetes), impairments that result from either a developmental disability (e.g., cerebral palsy, autism) or structural birth defects (e.g., spina bifida), and traumatic injuries (e.g., head injuries, spinal cord injuries) that produce significant physical and neurological damage (Hoffman, Rice, & Sung, 1996; Robert Wood Johnson Foundation, 1996). It is important to note that chronic conditions are positively related to levels of morbidity, mortality, and disability and to health care expenditures. Although people who are older and economically impoverished are more at risk than others, chronic conditions affect men, women, and children of all races and socio-economic strata. These conditions can significantly impair work and quality of life, and they place individuals at risk for secondary complications and further disability (Hoffman et al., 1996; Robert Wood Johnson Foundation, 1996; Scharlach, 1994).

As the number of people with chronic conditions increases over the coming decades, health care expenditures will increase dramatically as well. The estimated annual direct medical costs of providing care to people with chronic conditions are expected to grow from an estimated $503 billion in 2000 to approximately $906 billion in 2050 (Robert Wood Johnson Foundation, 1996). However, given the cost pressures experienced by various payers of health care services and the possible Medicare trust fund insolvency, it is unlikely that society can sustain projected growth in expenditures needed to provide adequate treatment and care for the expanding population with chronic conditions (Sofaer, 1998).

Unless significant changes are made to an American health care system that has been characterized as "not particularly efficient or effective" (Counte, 1998, p. 404), a sizeable population of people with chronic conditions will be at considerable risk of receiving inadequate care. As currently configured, the financing and delivery of health care services in the United States are focused almost exclusively on the treatment of acute episodic illnesses. Moreover, there is an institutional bias inherent in the medical model of acute care intervention that is patently unsuited for managing the care needs of people with chronic conditions. Sofaer (1998) noted that the "delivery system's structure, professional training, assumptions about the roles of patients and families, and financing and reimbursement all have been built on the assumption that healthcare needs arise from acute episodes of illness, rather than from longer-term chronic conditions" (p. 304). As currently organized, these services are woefully inadequate (Robert Wood Johnson Foundation, 1996).

Although many features of the organization and delivery of health care services clearly require reconceptualization and restructuring to address the needs of those with chronic conditions, here we address issues concerning the role of family members and friends as providers of care. We briefly review the status of family caregiving and outline the dominant theoretical framework that has been used to guide research efforts. Critical substantive and methodological directions for caregiving research are also identified. We conclude with a brief discussion of policies and interventions relating to family caregiving and the potential for rehabilitation psychologists and other behavioral scientists to make contributions in this area.

Management of Chronic Conditions

Over the past 2 decades, psychologists and other social scientists have demonstrated a growing interest in a variety of issues that concern family caregiving. There is keen interest, for example, in those types of activities and experiences that a family member encounters when providing care and other forms of functional assistance to an incapacitated family member. More recently, biological and health science investigators have added their caregiving research findings to what some have called "one of the largest and most conceptually sophisticated literatures in health psychology" (Williamson, Shaffer, & Schulz, 1998, p. 152).

With constricting availability of formal services, family members—spouses, parents, daughters, sons, or "fictive kin"—are required to function as primary caregivers for relatives who have incurred chronic and disabling conditions. A family caregiver is typically defined as one who "without financial compensation, regularly assists a care recipient in carrying out one or more activities or instrumental activities of daily living" (H. Res. 2081 [did not pass], 1997). In this capacity, family providers assume responsibility for a variety of services that were formerly and formally provided by traditional health service professions. The changing health care system and an increasing emphasis on self-care has forced caregivers to take an active role in promoting care recipient adherence to behavioral self-care regimens (Elliott & Shewchuk, 1998). When caregivers are unable to meet the role demands as de facto health care providers in the home, the risk of disability and secondary complications increases for the care recipient (Elliott, Shewchuk, & Richards, 1999). Regardless of the quality of care provided, we know that caregivers are susceptible to a variety of emotional and physical health problems. When caregivers are unable to effectively manage the demands and challenges of their career, we can expect health care expenditures to increase for both caregiver and care recipient.

Theoretical Model

Pearlin and colleagues formulated the preeminent model of the caregiving process. According to their perspective, individuals who assume caregiver roles embark on a career that is defined by the tasks in which they engage and the relationships that they have with people who have ongoing or chronic diseases or disabilities (Aneshensel, Pearlin, Mullan, Zarit, & Whitlatch, 1995; Moen, Robison, & Dempster-McClain, 1995). In this model, caregiving is not construed as a stressful situation in and of itself, although it may be associated with a variety of outcomes. Caregiver adjustment—in terms of depression, anxiety, and health—is a function of the complex interplay between personal and environmental characteristics over time. These characteristics include primary stressors (e.g., role overload) and secondary stressors (e.g., loss of self in the caregiving role), coping strategies (e.g., management of meaning), and social support (Pearlin, Mullan, Semple, & Skaff, 1990). These elements are not static, and changes in any one element effects changes in another, which in turn alter the functional relationships that determine the experience and trajectory of the caregiving career. Stress proliferation can occur when carry-over effects from one or more stressors impinge on other ongoing role demands or create new ones for the caregiver (Thoits, 1995). Furthermore, the stress proliferation process may be mediated or moderated by the social support and coping resources of the caregiver and the care recipient (Aneshensel et al., 1995; Pearlin, Aneshensel, Mullan, & Whitlatch, 1996).

This elegant model emphasizes the need to understand the dynamic processes that affect the trajectory of the caregiving career. The contextual setting in which caregiving is embedded (e.g., biological relationship of caregiver to the recipient, personality characteristics, ethnic and racial background, type of condition or disability) forms only the backdrop of the caregiving experience. Nevertheless, the caregiving context is theoretically subordinate to the dynamic, time-ordered nature of the relationships that unfold during the course of caregiving.

The Need for an Expanded Research Paradigm

Opportunities to examine both the theoretical and applied aspects of family caregiving increasingly have attracted the efforts of psychologists and other researchers to what has been termed "a veritable growth industry since the 1960s" (Avison, Turner, Noh, & Speechley, 1993, p. 75). As a "flourishing enterprise," family caregiving research has produced an enormous literature base and much insight into the experiences encountered by those who provide ongoing care and assistance to relatives with chronic physical conditions (Pearlin et al., 1990). Collectively, many studies address the pernicious effects that prolonged family caregiving is likely to have on the physical and emotional well-being of care providers.

The extant literature generally indicates that caregivers are at an increased risk for problems with distress, depression, and well-being (for reviews, see Schulz et al., 1997; and Schulz & Quittner, 1998). Descriptive research reveals that differences in distress exist between caregivers of people with physical disability and noncaregivers (e.g., Weitzenkamp, Gerhart, Charlifue, Whiteneck, & Savic, 1997). More elaborate research designs reveal that over time the health of the caregiver may be compromised by disruptions in cardiovascular and immune functioning (see Vitaliano, 1997), and these psychological and physical problems may be exacerbated as caregivers neglect their own health and care (Burton, Newsom, Schulz, Hirsch, & German 1997). We have found that anxiety, health, and depression are interrelated over the 1st year of the caregiver career and that these outcomes are sensitive to changes in social support experienced by the caregiver (Shewchuk, Richards, & Elliott, 1998).

Yet the deleterious effects of caregiving are by no means uniform, as is evidenced by the differential display of distress among those who have been subjected to similar caregiving demands. Many studies now acknowledge that caregiver adjustment may be influenced by myriad individual difference and environmental variables (Elliott & Shewchuk, 1998). Paradoxically, some research shows that a number of caregivers may not experience any appreciable degree of elevated distress and may in fact derive a sense of well-being and personal meaning in providing care (Kramer, 1997; Miller & Lawton, 1997). Rehabilitation psychologists have yet to develop screening devices to identify those at risk for problems and those who are likely to handle the caregiving role without incident.

The developmental chronology of caregiving research parallels the evolutionary process that characterizes most areas of psychosocial inquiry. Early caregiving studies were concerned primarily with the identification and description of caregiving burdens and their effects on the physical and emotional well-being of those in caregiving roles. As the descriptive foundations and basic relationships were established, researchers increasingly focused their collective attention on explanations of the mechanisms or processes that generate the set of stress-related behavior often observed among care providers at some point during their involvement in the course of this activity. In particular, caregiving studies over the past decade have been dominated by efforts to explain the variability in caregiving outcomes that are commonly seen among different caregivers who seem to have been subjected to comparable demands.

Although the actual causal sequencing of various caregiving antecedents and consequences are not fully understood, there is clear consensus that family caregiving is not a static event or a single behavior but is instead a complex dynamic process that unfolds over time. Not surprisingly, the situational variations observed in the interplay among constructs defining these processes contribute to the heterogeneity of caregiving experiences. The differential patterns of experiences regularly observed between and within caregivers at different points in time further underscore the dynamic complexities of caregiving processes (Shewchuk et al., 1998).

Our understanding of the mechanisms that determine the different career trajectories observed among caregivers (or "the multiple pathways to the same illness"; Thoits, 1995, p. 69) will benefit from statistical approaches and research designs that uncover sequential patterns of causal relationships among variables. Analytic techniques that may help explain the different combinations of variables that influence caregiver health and well-being at various junctures include qualitative comparative analysis or stochastic models (e.g., first-order Markov processes, hierarchical linear modeling, event history methods). Event-structure analysis, a method based on the analysis of narrative content, also has been identified as an approach that will "handle, in formal and replicable ways, data that are detailed, chronological, and qualitative" (Thoits, 1995, p. 69).

The stress process model posits a viable explanation for how caregiving experiences are transacted over time and what outcomes might be expected from these transactions. Although the broad scope of this model enhances its heuristic value, it also has made empirical validation of the model difficult. Researchers generally have confined their investigations to relatively circumscribed relationships outlined by the model's theoretical framework and most often have used cross-sectional data in their validation efforts. Validation attempts also have been inhibited by the use of a narrow range of statistical procedures roughly based on the general linear model.

Given the inherent process orientation of the Pearlin model, it is not surprising that the analysis of non-time-ordered data contributes to findings in which the "explained variance in physical and psychological outcomes has remained relatively modest" (Thoits, 1995, p. 68). Scientific and clinical appreciation of the caregiving experience is enriched by the utility of theoretical models that define variables and specify relationships in an a priori fashion, as Pearlin et al. (1990) did. Nonetheless, theory-driven research may show statistical associations between variables of interest and outcomes without revealing the mechanisms by which these constructs are linked. We assert that contextual variables such as demographic characteristics of the family, the type of disability, and the type of family tie of caregiver to the recipient (e.g., mother, spouse, child) do little to help explain what occurs within the "black box" (i.e., mechanisms of change; Lipsey, 1990) of the caregiving experience.

Traditional data collection and analytic techniques provide little understanding of the different experiential journeys that individual caregivers negotiate over their careers. Matthews (1993) correctly noted that we ultimately "know comparatively little about the trajectory of caregiving" (p. 115). We do not know—nor do we routinely solicit—caregiver perspectives and input in our research and clinical endeavors. For us to understand the black box between characteristics and outcomes (and to develop ecologically valid interventions), we must acknowledge caregivers as experts on the "realities of their daily lives" (Mechanic, 1998, p. 284). Thus, research and clinical intervention programs must incorporate strategies that embrace the unique, phenomenological experience of each individual caregiver.

Policy Concerns

As we observed, many intellectually compelling questions concerning the caregiving process as it unfolds over time and differentially impinges on the emotional, physical, and social well-being of care providers and recipients remain to be addressed. Behavioral and social scientists who have chosen to examine questions about family caregiving processes appear to have little difficulty in finding an audience—or a market—for their work. In addition to the academic currency to be gained from these efforts, researchers have an opportunity and perhaps an obligation to expand their roles by becoming active members of a "policy community" (Kingdon, 1995). According to Kingdon, membership in a policy community is composed of different "specialists" (p. 117; e.g., congressional staff members, interest group consultants, academicians) whose interests and ongoing efforts tend to coalesce around specific policy problems. Through a complex pattern of interactions, the ideas generated and shared among the members of a policy community may result in proposed solutions that are then considered at another level of the policy-making process. To date, psychologists and other behavioral–social scientists have been relatively inactive members of this policy community.

The brisk pace of research activity and accumulating evidence that shows the negative health impact of caregiving have prompted "some to consider reliance on family caregivers to be a major, although *unstated* part of national health care policy" (Council on Scientific Affairs, 1993, p. 1282, emphasis added). Notwithstanding the growing prevalence of chronic physical conditions and the acknowledged value of family members as care providers, it is somewhat surprising that the topic has not figured more prominently on the federal policy-making agenda.

The apparent indifference of the federal government to an increasingly important element of the health care delivery matrix contrasts sharply with the intense focus directed toward other health care concerns (e.g., Medicare, Medicaid). A number of reasons may account for the relatively conspicuous absence of family caregiving issues from the U.S. health policy agenda.

Some suggest that family caregiving issues have been ignored in the agenda-setting process because they would seem to be antithetical to policies that reflect the vested interests of health care providers and hospitals. Strong institutional bias clearly is evident in U.S. health care delivery and reimbursement strategies. This bias derives in part from a political process shaped by special-interest groups (e.g., American Medical Association, American Hospital Association, and American Health Care Association, which represents nursing homes and providers of long-term care) that provide substantial financial contributions in the form of political action committee spending (Weissert & Weissert, 1996). In a strongly worded criticism, Kiesler (1992) argued that the fundamental failings of U.S. health care exist because policies are developed without "effective national planning . . . leaving doctors alone and providing them with enhanced hospital and diagnostic facilities" (p. 1080). He added that policies supporting these "doctors' workshops" are narrowly focused on typical hospital service offerings and not on patient health care. Given these patterns in health care policy, it should not be surprising that rehabilitation issues generally and family caregiving issues in particular have not been integrated into service delivery offerings.

Implications

Rehabilitation psychologists can participate with other behavioral and social scientists in making meaningful contributions at different points in the health care policy formation process. Although the policy agenda fundamentally is determined by problems that impinge on elements of the political process, it is reasonable to assume that the accumulated findings from relevant research also may have some effect on the agenda. Furthermore, as Kingdon (1995) has observed, academic research may profoundly influence the specification of alternatives in proposed solutions to identified problems. Therefore, it is incumbent on rehabilitation psychology to develop solutions that can be used by policy makers: The development, execution, and verification of efficacious caregiver intervention programs are of the highest priority.

Unfortunately, no intervention study has had much more than a moderate impact because most problems are not formulated with a complete knowledge of the caregiving process and its expression among individual caregivers. Consequently, caregiver intervention studies to date have been unable to demonstrate the sort of clinical efficacy and cost-effectiveness that would engender interest among policymakers (George, 1990; Thoits, 1995). Atheoretical and cross-sectional "snapshot" studies and analytic techniques insensitive to the unique phenomenological perspectives of the caregiver have limited utility in developing meaningful intervention programs.

Ideally, effective interventions for caregivers address the problems experienced by individuals and help them become more active and expert in their own self-management and to operate competently as formal extensions of health care systems (Wagner, Austin, & Von Korff, 1996). Intervention programs should balance the needs of the caregiver with those of the care recipient (Niederehe, 1993). Promising interventions for caregivers that embody these features emphasize a problem-solving approach to identify the unique problems experienced by caregivers (and care recipients) and can be implemented in community and home settings with multidisciplinary and low-cost service providers (Elliott & Shewchuk, in press; Houts, Nezu, Nezu, & Bucher, 1996).

Although the integrated delivery structure of managed care organizations would seem more conducive to the care needs of those with chronic physical conditions than traditional fee-for-service reimbursement services, the literature generally does not bear this out (see Wagner et al., 1996). In some cases, the opposite may be true: Ware, Bayliss, Rogers, Kosinski, and Tarlov (1996) found that frail older individuals and people with disabilities tended to have worse health outcomes in managed care programs than was observed among those in fee-for-service programs. Successful management and care of chronic disease and disability can help families engage in health-promoting behaviors and make appropriate life-style changes to adhere to treatment protocols.

To develop and implement integrated, flexible, and ecologically valid health care programs for caregivers and care recipients, rehabilitation psychologists must critically evaluate the relative contributions and roles of each professional stakeholder in the health care delivery process. Physicians, for example, are high-cost service providers who account for a significant amount of health care expenditures; their utility in long-term and home-based prevention and health maintenance programs may have a "lower payoff" for family caregivers than behaviorally based intervention programs (Zarit & Pearlin, 1993, p. 314). Similarly, policymakers often view behavioral intervention—as typically described and prescribed by psychologists—"as prohibitively labor intensive, because they equate it with one-to-one counseling by highly trained and expensive staff" (Leviton, 1996, p. 47). It is possible that the delivery of interventions best suited for these consumers may be provided by low-cost, nonphysician personnel who are able to conduct routine evaluations and provide guidance for self-management (Wagner et al., 1996).

Rehabilitation psychologists need to take the lead in developing, implementing, and evaluating the utility of home-based health care programs for caregivers and care recipients with disabilities and other chronic health conditions. This requires framing research efforts in a manner consistent with the needs of policymakers and consumers. Intervention research that demonstrates efficacy is necessary before policymakers incorporate these programs as viable approaches to health care problems experienced by caregivers and care recipients. Furthermore, it is incumbent on rehabilitation psychologists to communicate and translate this research in a fashion that speaks directly to policymakers and their constituents. This is necessary for these stakeholders to appreciate and understand the utility of rehabilitation psychology research, theory, and practice in that particular arena. Publishing this kind of research in professional outlets and journals is insufficient to the task (Kingdon, 1995; Lee, 1991). In addition to our disciplinary responsibilities to advance the professional literature base, rehabilitation psychologists must also establish and maintain open lines of communication with policymakers and consumer groups if we are to have a voice in restructuring health care programs for caregivers and care recipients with disabling conditions.

References

Aneshensel, C. S., Pearlin, L. I., Mullan, J. T., Zarit, S. H., & Whitlatch, C. J. (1995). *Profiles in caregiving: The unexpected career.* San Diego, CA: Academic Press.

Avison, W. R., Turner, R. J., Noh, S., & Speechley, K. N. (1993). The impact of caregiving: Comparisons of different family contexts and experiences. In S. H. Zarit, L. I. Pearlin, & K. W. Schaie (Eds.), *Caregiving systems: Informal and formal helpers* (pp. 75–105). Hillsdale, NJ: Erlbaum.

Burton, L. C., Newsom, J. T., Schulz, R., Hirsch, C., & German, P. S. (1997). Preventive health behaviors among spousal caregivers. *Preventive Medicine, 26,* 162–169.

Council on Scientific Affairs. (1993). Physicians and family caregivers; A model for partnership. *Journal of the American Medical Association, 269,* 1282–1284.

Counte, M. A. (1998). The emerging role of the client in the delivery of primary care to older Americans. *Health Services Research, 33,* 402–423.

Elliott, T. R., & Shewchuk, R. M. (1998). Recognizing the family caregiver: Integral and formal members of the rehabilitation process. *Journal of Vocational Rehabilitation, 10,* 123–132.

Elliott, T., & Shewchuk, R. (in press). Problem solving therapy for family caregivers of persons with severe physical disabilities. In C. Radnitz (Ed.), *Cognitive–behavioral interventions for persons with disabilities.* New York: Aronson.

Elliott, T., Shewchuk, R., & Richards, J. S. (1999). Caregiver social problem solving abilities and family member adjustment to recent-onset physical disability. *Rehabilitation Psychology, 44,* 104–123.

Family Caregiver Enumeration Act. H. R. 2081, 105th Cong., 1st Sess. Charles. T. Canady, Florida 12th District. (1997).

George, L. K. (1990). Caregiver stress studies—there really is more to learn. *The Gerontologist, 30,* 580–581.

Hoffman, C., Rice, D., & Sung, H. (1996). Persons with chronic conditions: Their prevalence and costs. *Journal of the American Medical Association, 276,* 1473–1479.

Houts, P. S., Nezu, A. M., Nezu, C. M., & Bucher, J. A. (1996). The prepared family caregiver: A problem-solving approach to family caregiver education. *Patient Education and Counseling, 27,* 63–73.

Kiesler, C. A. (1992). U.S. mental health policy: Doomed to fail. *American Psychologist, 47,* 1077–1082.

Kingdon, J. W. (1995). *Agendas, alternatives, and public policies* (2nd ed.). New York: HarperCollins.

Kramer, B. J. (1997). Gain in the caregiving experience: Where are we? What next? *The Gerontologist, 37,* 218–232.

Lee, P. R. (1991). The public policy perspective on health policy and primary care. In M. L. Grady (Ed.), *AHCPR conference proceedings—Primary care research: Theory and methods* (pp. 5–12). Washington, DC: U.S. Department of Health and Human Services.

Leviton, L. C. (1996). Integrating psychology and public health: Challenges and opportunities. *American Psychologist, 51,* 42–51.

Lipsey, M. W. (1990). Theory as method: Small theories of treatments. In L. Sechrest, E. Perrin, & J. Bunker (Eds.), *Research methodology: Strengthening causal interpretations of nonexperimental data* (pp. 33–51). Washington, DC: U.S. Department of Health and Human Services.

Matthews, A. M. (1993). Issues in the examination of the caregiving relationship. In S. H. Zarit, L. I. Pearlin, & K. W. Schaie (Eds.), *Caregiving systems: Informal and formal helpers* (pp. 107–118). Hillsdale, NJ: Erlbaum.

Mechanic, D. (1998). Public trust and initiatives for new health care partnerships. *The Milbank Quarterly, 76,* 281–302.

Miller, B., & Lawton, M. P. (1997). Positive aspects of caregiving; Introduction: Finding balance in caregiver research. *The Gerontologist, 37,* 216–217.

Moen, P., Robison, J., & Dempster-McClain, D. (1995). Caregiving and women's well-being: A life course approach. *Journal of Health and Social Behavior, 36,* 259–273.

Niederehe, G. (1993). Public policy issues related to the SHMO demonstrations and Alzheimer's disease. In S. H. Zarit, L. I. Pearlin, & K. W. Schaie (Eds.), *Caregiving systems: Informal and formal helpers* (pp. 201–216). Hillsdale, NJ: Erlbaum.

Pearlin, L., Aneshensel, C. S., Mullan, J. T., & Whitlatch, C. (1996). Caregiving and its social support. In R. H. Binstock & L. K. George (Eds.), *Handbook of aging and the social sciences* (pp. 283–302). San Diego, CA: Academic Press.

Pearlin, L. I., Mullan, J. T., Semple, S. J., & Skaff, M. (1990). Caregiving and the stress process: An overview of concepts and their measures. *The Gerontologist, 30,* 583–594.

Robert Wood Johnson Foundation. (1996). *Chronic care in America: A 21st century challenge.* Princeton, NJ: Author.

Scharlach, A. E. (1994). Caregiving and employment: Competing or complementary roles? *The Gerontologist, 34,* 378–385.

Schulz, R., Newsom, J., Mittelmark, M., Burton, L., Hirsch, C., & Jackson, S. (1997). Health effects of caregiving: The caregiver health effects study: An ancillary study of the cardiovascular health study. *Annals of Behavior Medicine, 19,* 110–116.

Schulz, R., & Quittner, A. L. (1998). Caregiving for children and adults with chronic conditions: Introduction to the special issue. *Health Psychology, 17,* 107–111.

Shewchuk, R., & O'Connor, S. J. (2000). *Using cognitive concept mapping to understand what health care means to elderly persons.* Manuscript submitted for publication, University of Alabama at Birmingham.

Shewchuk, R., Richards, J. S., & Elliott, T. (1998). Dynamic processes in health outcomes among caregivers of patients with spinal cord injuries. *Health Psychology, 17,* 125–129.

Sofaer, S. (1998). Aging and primary care: An overview of organizational and behavioral issues in the delivery of health care services to older Americans. *Health Services Research, 33,* 298–321.

Thoits, P. A. (1995). Stress, coping, and social support processes: Where are we? What next? *Journal of Health and Social Behavior* [Suppl.], pp. 53–79.

Vitaliano, P. P. (Ed.). (1997). Physiological and physical concomitants of caregiving: Introduction to the special issue [Special issue]. *Annuals of Behavioral Medicine, 19*(2).

Wagner, E. H., Austin, B. T., & Von Korff, M. (1996). Organizing care for patients with chronic illness. *The Milbank Quarterly, 74,* 511–544.

Ware, J. E., Bayliss, M. S., Rogers, W. H., Kosinski, M., & Tarlov, A. R. (1996). Differences in 4-year health outcomes for elderly and poor chronically ill patients treated in HMO and fee-for-service systems. *Journal of the American Medical Association, 276,* 1039–1047.

Weissert, C. S., & Weissert, W. G. (1996). *Governing health: The politics of health policy.* Baltimore: Johns Hopkins University Press.

Weitzenkamp, D. A., Gerhart, K. A., Charlifue, S. W., Whiteneck, G. G., & Savic, G. (1997). Spouses of spinal cord injury survivors: The added impact of caregiving. *Archives of Physical Medicine and Rehabilitation, 78,* 822–827.

Williamson, G. M., Shaffer, D., & Schulz, R. (1998). Activity restriction and prior relationship history as contributors to mental health outcomes among middle-aged and older spousal caregivers. *Health Psychology, 17,* 152–162.

Zarit, S. H., & Pearlin, L. I. (1993). Family caregiving: Integrating informal and formal systems for care. In S. H. Zarit, L. I. Pearlin, & K. W. Schaie (Eds.), *Caregiving systems: Informal and formal helpers* (pp. 303–316). Hillsdale, NJ: Erlbaum.

27

Social Psychological Issues
in Disability

Dana S. Dunn

There is general agreement in the literature on physical disability that the problems of the handicapped are not physical, but social and psychological. (Meyerson, 1948a, p. 2)

* * *

An analysis in Rehabilitation Psychology should not only clarify the problems but also indicate their possible solution. This raises the question: Who is the person who judges what the problem is, and in what way does he or she think it can be solved? (Dembo, 1982, p. 135)

As these epigraphs attest, social psychological factors are inextricably linked with rehabilitative issues because they concern the social perception, judgment, and action of the perceiver and the perceived. The social psychological processes affecting people with disabilities, those receiving rehabilitative services, and nondisabled observers are undeniable. I review several social psychological theories and key factors identified within them that inform the rehabilitative process and the understanding of the experience of disability as a matter of perspective. Although both social and rehabilitation psychology share some similar psychological assumptions, interests, and theoretical stances, communication between the two areas is somewhat limited; but hope for a constructive rapprochement remains nonetheless (see Asch & Fine, 1988b; Dunn, 1994b; and Leary & Maddux, 1987, for related views).

Overview

Definitions for the field of social psychology abound. Generally, most contain variations on a basic theme: the scientific examination of how people

This chapter is dedicated to the memory of Harold E. Yuker. Preparation of this chapter was partially supported by a Moravian College Summer Faculty Development and Research Award. I thank Sarah Dunn, Stacey Zaremba, and the editors for their thoughtful comments on an earlier draft.

think and feel about, influence, and relate to actual, imagined, or assumed others (e.g., Allport, 1985). To explore this theme, social psychologists systematically examine personal or situational factors that affect social perception, expectation, and interaction when two or more persons gather together. Personal factors include the physical or dispositional characteristics of people, their affective states, and the role of individuals as perceivers or as objects of others' perceptions. Variables or constants outside people in perceived or real environments are considered situational factors, and these can be tangible (e.g., other people, physical boundaries), intangible (e.g., cultural norms, social roles), and even transient (e.g., temperature, crowding).

The study of groups and group processes, too, represents a grand tradition in social psychology, one that examines the combined influence of personal and situational factors on thought and behavior. Groups consist of two or more people interacting with each other in interdependent relationships; that is, individuals in groups rely on one another in the course of satisfying needs, advancing or achieving goals, and engaging in mutual social influence (e.g., Cartwright & Zander, 1968). Groups are basic, essential parts of social life, as they imply dynamic relationships among people, highlighting issues such as real or perceived group membership, identity, majority–minority relations, and socialization. Moreover, group dynamics can have profound effects on the psychological adjustment or dysfunction of individuals belonging to groups (Forsyth & Elliott, 1999).

The empirical focus is necessarily narrower in rehabilitation psychology than in social psychology because behavior is seen through a rehabilitative lens; that is, personal and situational factors are evaluated on the basis of their potential to promote the assessment, amelioration, and treatment of chronic physical or mental disorders. Whether disabilities are acquired, induced by trauma, or developmental in origin, some of the same personal and situational factors examined by social psychologists come into play, but these factors are usually evaluated from exclusively clinical or therapeutic vantage points. As a result, the bulk of research within rehabilitation psychology is directed toward reducing societal barriers preventing people with disabilities from achieving life goals, often creating an amalgam of knowledge from psychology, medicine, physical therapy, and education in the process (Fenderson, 1984). Similarly, aside from research dealing with disability as a stigmatizing condition or attitudes toward people with disabilities (topics reviewed below), broader questions concerning groups and group process have been virtually ignored in rehabilitation psychology (but see Wright, 1983).

As disciplines, both social psychology and rehabilitation psychology posit that personal and situational factors have profound effects on behavior. Quite properly, both disciplines trace this focus and its lineage to the social–personality psychologist Kurt Lewin and his colleagues and students, some of whom explored questions incorporating these disciplinary foci (see, e.g., Barker, Wright, Meyerson, & Gonick, 1953; Dembo, 1982; Dembo, Leviton, & Wright, 1956; G. Lewin, 1957; Meyerson, 1948a, 1948b, 1988; Wright, 1980). K. A. Lewin (1935) suggested that behavior is a function of both the person and the situation or, interchangeably, the environment. Indeed, the formula Lewin used to express this relation, $B = f(P, E)$, is often cited in the psychological literature, and the reciprocal wisdom it poses has found its way into related theoretical formulations (e.g., Bandura, 1978).

Social psychological research assumes that an adequate understanding of behavior can be achieved only when factors affecting people and situations are studied together. In practice, traditional social psychological research takes place in the controlled setting of the laboratory, which does not always allow K. A. Lewin's (1935) dynamic interplay of social forces. Some contemporary social psychologists take note of this fact (e.g., Barone, Maddux, & Snyder, 1997; Ross & Nisbett, 1991), but it is something akin to an article of faith among researchers interested in psychosocial factors in the arena of rehabilitation (e.g., Shontz, 1977; Wright, 1983), possibly because the field has always had a pronounced interdisciplinary focus (Stubbins, 1989). That is, rehabilitation researchers routinely find themselves working out in the world and across disciplinary boundaries because disability affects the whole person, from social milieu to psychological and physical process.

The Lewinian tradition represented in much of the research in rehabilitation psychology concerns the interplay of situational forces and perceived dispositions. Specifically, rehabilitation researchers have long recognized that environmental constraints—a building's architecture, for example—are more influential as behavioral constraints than are most disabilities (Barker, 1948; Dembo, 1982; Wright, 1983). K. A. Lewin (1935) realized, however, that social perceivers downplay the power of situations and, instead, assume that aspects of the person (e.g., personality traits, physical or mental disabilities) drive behavior. Behavior engulfs the field precisely because people are salient actors within it—they warrant our attention—and our attributions about them allow us to enjoy a modicum of prediction and a sense of control (Heider, 1958).

More to the point in rehabilitative contexts is that behavior is often compared to some normative "ideal" by observers because people with disabilities are evaluated almost exclusively in terms of their disabilities (Goffman, 1963; Jones et al., 1984). Even a single personal characteristic (e.g., disability, race, gender, ethnicity) is sufficient to drive inferences about a target person, a phenomenon labeled *spread* in rehabilitation research (Dembo et al., 1956). To casual observers, people with disabilities are often different in character or trait—the physical, social, emotional, or cognitive constraints common to situations are overlooked. Lay perceivers often discount this more diagnostic situational information in favor of dispositional attributions (e.g., Ross, 1977), which can lead to biases, errors, or exaggerations in social judgment. Workers in the Lewinian tradition in rehabilitation, as well as people with disabilities themselves, have gone to great lengths to argue and demonstrate that self and ability cannot be equated with physique or with a disability per se; people cannot be equated with conditions (e.g., Shontz, 1977; Wright, 1983). As I demonstrate in subsequent sections, this psychosocial realization and its relevance to the person–situation relation has important implications for social psychological theorizing about rehabilitation and related issues.

History, Theories, and Background

The social–clinical interface existing between social psychology and rehabilitation psychology leads to research efforts centered in two main areas: attitudes toward people with disabilities and reactions to disabling experiences. I introduce the scope of each area and then present representative theory and data.

Attitudes Toward People With Disabilities

The attitude literatures within social psychology and rehabilitation psychology are extensive. The attitude construct has been an essential tool for the American psychological community since the 1920s (Allport, 1935; Eagly & Chaiken, 1993). Most research explores variations on a main theme: The conditions under which an expressed attitude predicts future behavior. Topics emanating from or related to this theme include attitude formation, stability, accessibility, and change; measurement issues; and attitude structure.

Within social psychology, most researchers treat attitudes as individual tendencies toward favorable or unfavorable evaluations of an entity (Eagly & Chaiken, 1993). Attitudes have cognitive, affective, and behavioral components (Breckler, 1984), that is, collections of beliefs, feelings, and actions that guide approach toward or avoidance of some entity, or in social psychological parlance, the attitude object. Knowing that a person likes liberal politicians or that someone dislikes a particular food, for instance, allows for prediction of a probable vote and proper menu planning, respectively.

The attitude literature pertaining to disability developed independently of research in social psychology, and it focuses largely on identifying variables influencing attitudes toward people with disabilities (see Yuker, 1988, 1994, for reviews). Over several decades, various attitude measures were designed to achieve this end (e.g., Gething, 1994; Yuker & Block, 1986; Yuker, Block, & Young, 1966). Regrettably, disability attitude research is rarely studied, let alone cited, by mainstream social psychology. There are exceptions to this rule in the social psychological community (e.g., Esses & Beaufoy, 1994), but they are few indeed, possibly because social psychologists tend to read and publish in social–personality journals (e.g., *Journal of Personality and Social Psychology*), whereas rehabilitation psychologists write for and read periodicals aimed specifically at researchers and practitioners (e.g., *Rehabilitation Psychology*).

Furthermore, within the past 25 years or so, research focus on attitudes has diverged within the respective literatures. The social psychological literature has emphasized theory development, theory testing, and the examination of boundary conditions within various models of attitude formation, structure, and change. In contrast, the literature in rehabilitation psychology tends to be pragmatic, focused on measurement issues and clinical application. This practical concern is understandable and certainly justified, given the social, educational, and vocational reforms—both before and after the Americans With Disabilities Act (ADA) of 1990 (P. L. 101-336)—encouraging people with disabilities to enter the classroom (Individuals With Disabilities Education Act of 1990 [P. L. 101-336]) and the workplace in increasing numbers.

Research interest in attitudes toward people with disabilities is well over half a century old (Antonak, 1988). In that time, research generally emphasized nondisabled people's reactions to people with disabilities, although recent efforts have examined the attitudes of people with disabilities themselves (Weinberg, 1988). A reason for the primary emphasis on the reactions of people without disabilities is the stigmatized role that people with disabilities are assumed to fill in society. Whether congenital or acquired, physical or mental impairments often lead people without disabilities to stigmatize, marginalize, or otherwise respond in a discriminatory manner toward people with disabilities (e.g., Wright, 1983). Such reactions suggest that when disability is treated as a social problem, it has clear links to the study of minority groups, prejudice, and stereotyping (Fine & Asch, 1988a).

People without disabilities tend to hold unfavorable attitudes toward those with disabilities (e.g., Farina, 1982; Yuker, 1988), although some authors have suggested that societal opinion is more ambivalent than prejudicial (Katz, Haas, & Bailey, 1988; Soder, 1990). The sources of these stigmatizing attitudes range from curiosity to simple ignorance about the nature of disability, but psychological investigations naturally consider affective and cognitive explanations. Many people without disabilities intentionally ignore those with disabilities for emotional reasons. They may fear saying the wrong thing or drawing attention to a disability, for example, or they may experience anxiety, tension, or general unease when encountering people with disabilities (Gething, 1991; Heinemann, 1990). Unfortunately, ignoring people or characteristics that they possess only creates a climate for rejection and isolation, or at least ambiguous, even stilted, communication.

A prominent social psychological theory that has been used to explain negative reactions to people with disabilities is the *just-world hypothesis* (Lerner, 1980); people believe that good things should happen to good people and, consequently, when bad events—including disability—befall individuals, they must somehow be deserving of them. To maintain a view of the world as consistent, thereby preserving their place in it, people without disabilities must devalue, even derogate, people with disabilities. In a related vein, competence and other desirable personal traits are linked to ascriptions of interpersonal attractiveness, so that differences in physique (e.g., missing a limb, facial disfigurement) can influence perceptions negatively (Berscheid & Walster, 1974; Hahn, 1988). Perceived responsibility for one's condition, too, is a relevant factor (Weiner, 1993).

Not all attitudes regarding disability are negative in content, nor are they the result of social stigma. Some perceivers attribute highly favorable traits to people with disabilities because they view coping with a mental or physical impairment as somehow ennobling or otherwise indicative of outstanding personal success (e.g., Esses & Beaufoy, 1994; Wright, 1983). Such attitudes miss the mark, however, because they are distorted in the opposite direction, placing undue emphasis (again) on people's disabilities rather than on their abilities (Yuker, 1994). Nondisabled perceivers rarely recognize that disability is merely one aspect of an individual's experience or personality and that people with disabilities do not wish to be seen as either saints or victims; disability is another part of one's life (Fine & Asch, 1988a; Wright, 1983).

Other research efforts point to several interpersonal behaviors that can ameliorate negative social reactions to disability and modify accompanying attitudes. People with disabilities can establish positive social interactions by casually explaining a disability (Hastorf, Wildfogel, & Cassman, 1979), being assertive when requesting assistance (Mills, Belgrave, & Boyer, 1984), expressing interest in other people and common topics (Belgrave, 1984), or displaying adaptive emotional adjustment to a disability (Elliott & Frank, 1990). Each strategy promotes social acceptance of disability by reducing discomfort in real or potential social encounters; in turn, people without disabilities may come to evaluate people with disabilities (and perhaps disability generally) in more positive ways.

A recent, critical review of the literature argues that information about disability and contact with people with disabilities have important influences on attitudes (Yuker, 1994). Assuming that it is accurate, information gleaned from contact with people with disabilities, the opinions of others, or the media can educate those without disabilities in positive ways. Information can also reduce stereotypes by individuating people with disabilities (e.g., Hamilton, Sherman, & Ruvolo, 1990). In turn, the oft-researched *contact hypothesis*—that sustained, equal, supported, and cooperative interaction between those with and without disabilities leads to positive attitudes in the latter group—remains a viable proposition (e.g., Rothbart & John, 1985), although empirical results are sometimes mixed (e.g., Horne, 1988).

As for other cognitive accounts regarding attitudes, the aforementioned Lewinian analysis can be extended by considering attributional processes from the social cognition literature (Fiske & Taylor, 1991). Like all social targets, people with disabilities are subject to the categorization processes used by social perceivers—the expectation-driven knowledge structures (e.g., schemas, stereotypes, scripts) that efficiently guide judgment and behavior but often neglect detail (e.g., Langer & Chanowitz, 1988). As noted previously, the atypicality of disability can lead to extreme judgments, but work on a novel stimulus hypothesis (Langer, Fiske, Taylor, & Chanowitz, 1976) suggests a different interpretation of the reactions of people without disabilities.

The novel stimulus hypothesis advocates that perceivers experience a conflict when encountering people with disabilities—they wish to stare at them because disability is novel or unusual in their experience, but they fear transgressing the cultural norm against staring at people (Langer et al., 1976). This intrapsychic conflict leads perceivers to engage in avoidance behavior, which people with disabilities, in turn, interpret negatively. Stimulus novelty is reduced as observers become familiar with people and their disabilities by having the chance to view them in a socially sanctioned manner; social avoidance, in turn, is reduced. It is regrettable that little follow-up research on the novel stimulus hypothesis has been conducted (but see Fichten, Amsel, Robillard, Sabourin, & Wright, 1997).

Coping With Disability

Where attitudinal studies largely focus on reactions to people with disabilities, research on coping processes emphasizes the reactions of people with disabilities to their conditions and social worlds. Historically, this area of research has undergone a variety of shifts in perspective and received substantial criticism on social, psychological, and even political grounds (e.g., Asch, 1984; Fine & Asch, 1988a; Shontz, 1977; Vash, 1981). In Vash's view, for example, the idea of accepting disability was understood in different ways across the past 60 or so years—from functionally acknowledging the reality of disability (i.e., absence of psychological denial) and accepting one's "limitations," to an activist orientation portraying disability as one facet of many in the lives of people with disabilities. As Fine and Asch (1988a) succinctly put it, "what needs to be stated is that disability—while never wished for—may simply not be as wholly disastrous as imagined" (p. 11).

Considered from the latter perspective, terms such as *coping, adjustment*, and *adaptation* sometimes take on a pejorative tinge because they intimate that people with disabilities are never wholly satisfied with their situations and that in any case, "rational" people would never see their circumstances as positive. Such views are naive at best, prejudiced at worst. In point of fact, dissatisfaction is more often apt to be directed at aforementioned environmental and social constraints, not the self (e.g., Wright, 1983), and undue negativity is a judgment of observers (including researchers) and not people with disabilities themselves.

Both social and rehabilitation psychologists have shown a great deal of interest in subjective reactions to disability. For instance, there is substantial overlap between the literatures where the issue of searching for meaning in disability is concerned (Dunn, 1994a). Rehabilitation psychologists have been interested in how individual reactions to disability affect well-being in the context of rehabilitative experiences (e.g., Dembo et al., 1956; Elliott, Witty, Herrick, & Hoffman, 1991). Social psychologists study disability as a negative or threatening event, how it is integrated into people's lives and thoughts, and the affective consequences (if any) of that integration (e.g., Tait & Silver, 1989; Taylor, 1983).

Conceptual agreement diverges, however, regarding how people with disabilities are sometimes portrayed within the respective literatures.

Some social psychological approaches apply the terms *victim* and *victimization* to people who experience traumas, including the onset of disability (e.g., Janoff-Bulman & Frieze, 1983). Practitioners and researchers in the rehabilitation tradition are quick to criticize this nomenclature on the grounds that it characterizes people with disabilities as helpless and dependent, objects instead of actors where their fate is concerned (Fine & Asch, 1988a; Shontz, 1982).

The best example of this conceptual disagreement is a well-intentioned study by Bulman and Wortman (1977) on adjustment to spinal cord injury (for related discussions, see Dunn, 1996; Janoff-Bulman & Frieze, 1983; and Taylor, Wood, & Lichtman, 1983). These researchers have noted that many of the people in their sample re-evaluated the injury as positive after asking "why me" questions (see Heinemann, Bulka, & Smetak, 1988, for a conceptual replication; Schulz & Decker, 1985). Bulman and Wortman concluded that such defensive attributions were adaptive under the circumstances, but at least one rehabilitation researcher noted that the term *re-evaluation* elicited images of rationalizations that did not accurately reflect the reality of the situation (Shontz, 1982). Besides highlighting sensitivity in semantics, an important issue emerging from this border dispute is the status of self-report: Are people with disabilities' self-reports trustworthy, reflective accounts of the experience of disability, or are they simply biased, self-serving attributions? Debate over the status of such self-insight is not new in the context of disability (Dunn, 1994a), and more research on its salutary implications is clearly needed (for a novel, related approach, see Rybarczyk & Bellg, 1997).

A potentially fruitful approach to the study of salutary effects integrating social and rehabilitation psychology is *reality negotiation* (Snyder, 1989; see also Dunn, 1994a, 1996; Elliott et al., 1991). Reality negotiation is contextual and occurs when individuals rely on cognitive strategies that promote favorable beliefs about the self in situations that threaten self-esteem and well-being (Elliott et al., 1991; Snyder, 1989). To maintain consistent and positive theories about themselves, individuals distort self-relevant information in beneficial ways (Barone et al., 1997). When people negotiate their realities, they tend to engage in two activities: protective behaviors and self-enhancing behaviors (Snyder, 1989). Protective behaviors, such as making an excuse for the inability to perform some action, lead people away from situations that threaten their self-image. In contrast, self-enhancing behaviors direct people to situations that are positive in content or outcome. Reality negotiation may be conceptually and semantically acceptable to rehabilitation researchers precisely because it does not deny the perspectives of people with disabilities (Dunn, 1994a).

A final, even classical, area of coping with disability should be mentioned: value change following a disabling event. Values and worldviews, principles that are important in any person's life, sometimes undergo dramatic change with the onset of disability (Keany & Glueckauf, 1993). The working assumption in various models of rehabilitation is that adjustment to a disabling event is augmented when the disability is accepted by the individual (Dembo et al., 1956; Wright, 1983). Affected individuals adjust their value systems so that any change or loss does not diminish other perceived abilities (Wright, 1983). Vision loss should not influence self-perceptions regarding intelligence or sociability, for example, once the disability is accepted. Acceptance can be accomplished through expanding one's pool of values while decreasing emphasis on physique relative to other values (Wright, 1983). The empirical problem is that satisfactory measurement of value systems following disability has not been achieved, although one method of redress was recently proposed (Keany & Glueckauf, 1993).

Summary

Whether focused on attitudes toward or coping reactions of people with disabilities, empirical efforts are rarely contextual; that is, investigations are Lewinian in spirit but rarely in practice (e.g., Kerr & Bodman, 1994). Within both lines of inquiry, the focus is on people with disabilities and not on the environmental constraints that they encounter. To date, few researchers adequately study how person variables and environmental characteristics mutually affect one another (for one example, see Williamson, Schulz, Bridges, & Behan, 1994).

Fundamental Psychosocial Concepts

A hallmark of rehabilitation research and practice is a focus on the experience of the individual, whereas mainstream social psychological approaches emphasize individual behavior within the larger social world by focusing on response similarities across people. Rehabilitation psychology's appreciation of individual experience in the assessment, amelioration, and treatment of disability has identified useful psychosocial concepts for understanding and treating people with disabilities. These concepts can inform all facets of the rehabilitative process, whether it takes place in the laboratory, clinic, or community. Following the points made in the earlier sections of this chapter, the overarching issue is how point of view interacts with the experience of disability.

Somatopsychology

Research and practice concerned with the social psychological aspects of disability rely on what traditionally is called the *somatopsychological relation* (Barker et al., 1953). This relation exists between physique and its influence over an individual's psychology, especially where body image and action, as well as the reactions of other people, are concerned (Wright, 1983). What is the impact of this relation? Having difficulty navigating through the physical environment or being unable to engage in activities of daily living without assistance (e.g., meal preparation, housekeeping, dressing) has a social basis as well as a personal reality. Reactions (or the lack thereof) from observers and environmental constraints affect how people with disabilities think about themselves and their situations. Somatopsychology, then, is important, if implicit, in the development of social psychological theorizing about and concern for people with disabilities. It stands in contrast to psychosomatic relations, which attempt to link people's psychological characteristics to physical or organic disorders (e.g., Wright, 1983).

Insider–Outsider Distinction

In attributional terms, the *insider–outsider distinction* is straightforward: Insiders (people with disabilities) know what disability is like, whereas outsiders (people without disabilities) make assumptions, including erroneous ones, about it. Because of the salience of disability, for example, there is a pronounced tendency to view disability as illness, creating the perception that people with disabilities are preoccupied with their physical states. To the contrary, insiders see their situations more favorably than do outsiders (Hamera & Shontz, 1978; Mason & Muhlenkamp, 1976). Little thought, then, is given to the possibility that insiders do not view their disabilities as salient personal characteristics unless they are directed to do so by outsiders, including researchers and practitioners. Several researcher–practitioners have advocated that those who work with people with disabilities pay close attention to the implied judgments that occur when the insider–outsider distinction is ignored (Dembo, 1969, 1970; Shontz, 1982; Wright, 1991).

Within social psychology, the *actor–observer difference* is a well-established line of empirical inquiry within the attribution literature (e.g., Jones & Nisbett, 1972) that should have close links to the insider–outsider distinction, yet this connection is rarely made. Like insiders, actors have some private knowledge about what drives their behavior, but they generally look to the situation when making causal ascriptions about themselves. Similar to outsiders, observers downplay situational constraints in favor of dispositional accounts, so that personality is inferred from action, resulting in what has been dubbed the *fundamental attribution error* (Ross, 1977) or *correspondence bias* (Gilbert & Jones, 1986). The error is fundamental because observers adopt almost exclusively dispositional explanations for an actor's behavior; potential situational influences are discounted.

Where an understanding of the experience of disability is concerned, one author constructively extended this attributional error to whole groups of people. Pettigrew (1979) argued for an *ultimate attribution error*, where the negative behavior of people outside one's own group is attributed to a shared disposition (e.g., one thief renders all group members potential thieves), and any positive behavior is discounted (e.g., a public service is attributed to individual, not group, initiative). Attributional clemency is granted by giving the benefit of the doubt to in-group members. To be sure, some prejudicial judgments regarding people with disabilities as a group probably operate in this fashion; however, the finer point raised by the ultimate attribution error is one of deindividuation.[1] When people are perceived as members of a group—as people with disabilities or any minority group are—individual characteristics or behaviors have little effect on social perceivers; group membership is *deindividuating*; that is, it leads to a loss of perceived individuality from the perspective of others (Wright, 1991). I turn now to the importance of individuation and its link to language and disability.

Individuation and Labeling

Language is a powerful social tool. Rehabilitation psychology has pioneered efforts to create individuating situations for people with disabilities, and care with language plays a large part in this effort. The use of terms such as *schizophrenics, the disabled*, or *amputees*, for example, refers to and consequently relates to people as a group and not as individuals. Disability, a personal characteristic, is thereby rendered impersonal and, in turn, interpersonal—everything from recognition of a disability to social interaction is related back to a physical or mental condition. Understandably, perhaps, the link between a language of referral and stereotyping appears strong.

Wright (1991) called attention to the problem of labeling by arguing for greater person–environment individuation. In general, labels engender negative reactions, resulting in what Wright called the "fundamental negative bias" (Wright, 1988, p. 5). Because disability is salient and given pejorative value by people without disabilities, a negative bias is apt to guide perception unless contextual information is positive or otherwise individuating (Wright, 1991). Because of their shared experiences, then, a friend of a person with a disability should be less likely to subscribe to a negative group stereotype about disability than a stranger (Wright, 1983). More to the point, labels are of consequence to those who are labeled. Labels highlighting people ("blind people") rather than emphasizing conditions ("blindness") are rated more favorably (Whiteman & Lukoff, 1965). This demonstration is simple but powerful, and it fits in well with other instances of group categorization (e.g., Linville & Jones, 1980; Tajfel, 1981) and illusory correlation (e.g., Hamilton, 1981).

Individuating circumstances can be created in research and clinical contexts by attending to language considerations and involving rehabilitation clients in their own case management. The American Psychological Association (1994) now eschews the use of monolithic, objectifying language to describe the participants (not "subjects") who take part in research projects. Broad categorization, often a hallmark of scientific writing, is now discouraged in favor of a style of presentation that promotes individuality.

---

[1]Note that the use of the term *deindividuation* in rehabilitation contexts differs from its application in mainstream social psychology, where it refers to a loss of self-awareness coupled with a potential for antisocial behavior (e.g., Zimbardo, 1970).

Conceptions of Well-Being

Rehabilitation researchers and practitioners share one major psychosocial goal: enhancing or maintaining the psychological well-being of people with disabilities. A perusal of the rehabilitation literature reveals that various indices of well-being, chiefly depression or self-esteem scales, are used as dependent measures in research. As part of the rehabilitation experience, too, clients routinely complete these and related indicators of mental and physical health. In both contexts, focus was traditionally on the absence of well-being among people with disabilities; that is, the guiding assumption was that disability results in negative outcomes (e.g., higher levels of depression, lower levels of self-esteem). To be sure, there is ample evidence that disability is associated with physical, emotional, social, economic, and employment challenges that can affect psychosocial well-being, but any individual's problems should be considered in concert with his or her abilities (Wright, 1983).

Over the past several years, however, there has been a sea change in how subjective affective experience is conceived, and this change has decided consequences for the study of subjective well-being. Both social and clinical psychologists have adopted the view that positive and negative affect are often uncorrelated (Diener & Emmons, 1984; Watson & Tellegen, 1985). This view complements a similar trend in the field of health psychology, where the dominant pathogenic focus has gradually become more salutogenic—instead of exclusively searching for the causes of illness, greater attention is now given to factors preventing it (e.g., Antonovsky, 1987). In the present context, it is not sufficient to treat depression, a negative outcome, as the only dimension of experience for disability; many people with disabilities exhibit no depressive symptomatology, for example, but the factors responsible for creating and maintaining their beneficial psychological states go unexplored (for exceptions, see Dunn, 1996; Elliott et al., 1991; Rybarczyk, Nicholas, & Nyenhuis, 1997; Schulz & Decker, 1985; Taylor & Brown, 1988). Minimally, then, researchers should necessarily treat positive and negative affectivity as discrete and resolve to use both sorts of measures in their research designs.

The irony in this new emphasis in the study of health and well-being is that the focus on positive rather than negative outcomes is not new to rehabilitation psychology. Rehabilitation psychologists have consistently sought to guarantee that people with disabilities are treated with respect and that societal and environmental barriers to their full participation in daily living are eliminated. To do so, researchers have been repeatedly exhorted to retain a human focus in their work and to ensure that the integrity of each research participant is maintained (Wright, 1980, 1983). Others have argued that any social psychology of rehabilitation must move away from its traditional anchorage, the study of stigma (Fine & Asch, 1988a). Practitioners, too, have been urged to retreat from their natural inclination to examine pathology or dysfunction in favor of understanding clients' problem-solving abilities or personal and social assets in the face of disability (Wright & Fletcher, 1982). Of course, the aforementioned Lewinian analysis of person–environment relations features large in the adoption of positive vantage points in rehabilitation psychology as well.

Future Research

As this review illustrates, perspective is powerful, touching on many social psychological issues in the study of disability and rehabilitation. Four nascent candidates for future research inquiry stand out, however, and should be briefly noted: (a) occupational burnout among health care providers of people with disabilities, (b) women and disability, (c) group processes, and (d) the function of attitudes toward people with disabilities in community settings.

Burnout and Health Provider Stress

Despite popular wisdom, health care providers, including medical and rehabilitative professionals, are not immune to the physical and emotional cost of caring for people with disabilities. The most common stress reaction found among these professionals is occupational burnout. The risk for burnout in human services professions is high because providers become emotionally involved in their work, yet the work outcomes are usually independent of the effort they exert (e.g., Maslach & Jackson, 1982).

Given the demands and involving nature of the work, burnout appears to be ubiquitous in rehabilitation settings (e.g., Stav & Florian, 1986; Ursprung, 1986). A few predictive factors associated with the presence or absence of burnout have been identified. For example, susceptibility to burnout appears to be higher among rehabilitation staff members who have fewer sources of social support (Clanton, Rude, & Taylor, 1992). However, reliance on positive social–cognitive processes, such as self-efficacy (Chwalisz, Altmaier, & Russell, 1992) and hope (Sherwin et al., 1992), appears to protect some providers from burnout (see also Elliott, Shewchuk, Hagglund, Rybarczyk, & Harkins, 1996). More research is clearly needed, because psychology's understanding of the burnout construct and its implications remains incomplete (Elliott et al., 1996).

Women and Disability

Gender is a long-neglected topic in the social psychology of disability and rehabilitation. Brief reflection on the content of this chapter so far reveals that gender, a prominent social as well as demographic factor, receives little attention in the published literature. Various explanations for this paucity of scholarship can be identified, but it may simply be that the relevant literatures have chosen to emphasize commonalities, not differences, among people with disabilities (Asch & Fine, 1988a). Indeed, what little focus that has been placed on gender in disability is apt to have been on the disabled male individual, possibly because a high percentage of men acquire disabilities in industrial accidents. A less charitable view suggests that inattention to women's issues in this context is another case of assuming that male experiences are defining for both genders (e.g., Thurer, 1982).

To date, there are few psychological references on women and disabilities (Fine & Asch, 1988b), but many questions. Do women and men with disabilities have different perspectives on the role disability plays in their lives? Do one's gender and having a disability interact? Body image is a sensitive, if not reactive, issue for many women; in what ways does it affect on women with disabilities? Do men with disabilities receive more favorable treatment in society than women with disabilities? How do women understand the experience of having a disability? Some important topics, such as employment (e.g., Vash, 1982) and intimacy (e.g., Vash, 1981), have been studied, but much remains to be done.

Scholars routinely note that women with disabilities experience an unusual dilemma in American culture—they experience traditional sexism without being placed on the "pedestal" of femininity (Fine & Asch, 1981). Women with disabilities are said to lead lives at society's margins (e.g., Britt, 1988; Fine & Asch, 1988b; Hanna & Rogovsky, 1991), and research and practice must address their personal as well as social status. Previous efforts leaned toward anecdotal, even inspirational, accounts of women with disabling conditions. Such portrayals drew needed attention to women's issues, but future efforts must adopt a more systematic, interpretive approach to understanding women with disabilities. There is ample room for researchers and practitioners to make a contribution to our understanding of women, disability, and the rehabilitative process.

Focus Group Processes

Groups and group processes are a focus in social rather than rehabilitation psychology. How can researchers and practitioners in rehabilitation psychology use group dynamics or issues of group membership toward understanding as well as treating disabilities? One potentially fruitful possibility is to use focus group techniques to examine perspectives and concerns expressed by people from different groups with specific disabilities.

A focus group is essentially a formal, structured setting wherein an interviewer asks group members specific questions about a topical area that has already been heavily researched (e.g., Merton, Fiske, & Kendall, 1956; see also Fontana & Frey, 1994). The interviewer within a focus group is directive about asking questions, and the group's responses should verify what is already understood while serving an exploratory function—to consider what critical information regarding a topic may have been missed in the present or prior research inquiries. There is a tradition in focus group research of interviewing a select group of participants who act as astute observers and a valuable resource for the researcher, who is apt to sacrifice representative samples and quantitative assumptions for detailed insights in a qualitative vein (e.g., Blumer, 1969).

The implications of the insider–outsider distinction are particularly applicable to focus group outcomes: Researchers and practitioners no doubt learn a great deal about the phenomenology of disability by asking and then listening to what people with disabilities disclose regarding the experience of specific disabilities, their treatment histories, and resulting perspectives on research and practice issues (e.g., Renwick, Brown, Rootman, & Nagler, 1996). Such qualitative use of focus groups bring rehabilitation professionals closer to the ideal of learning from—rather than studying—people with disabilities. A slogan from disabilities studies applies well here: "Nothing about us without us."

Community Perspectives

Many empirical researchers sought to understand the attitudes of people without disabilities toward people with disabilities, whereas a much smaller literature addressed ways that the latter group can foster positive relationships with the former. Although clearly important, these two research foci neglect what is increasingly a concern for people with disabilities and the communities that they inhabit—the relatively seamless integration of people with disabilities into educational and business settings. Research on attitudes and attitude change regarding disability must change perspective with the times by being more functional.

Legal barriers regarding disability are largely gone, and political activism is on the rise; however, some key social barriers remain. Note that *social barriers* does not refer to traditional issues such as prejudice and stigma; rather, the term is meant to encompass the uncertainty that teachers, educational administrators, and employers feel about working with people with disabilities who have been mainstreamed into the community. These professionals must learn to relate to and understand people with disabilities within community contexts in social and professional domains. Despite required course work and occasional in-service programs, for example, many teachers feel unprepared to adequately work with mainstreamed students with disabilities. For their parts, employers worry about the inherent ambiguities and potential liability issues associated with the ADA and its implementation in the workplace.

Heretofore, research on attitudes and attitude change has generally targeted issues of acceptance and prejudice reduction, but it has ignored ways to promote cooperation, interdependence, and mutual respect. A change in perspective is warranted: Social psychologists, especially those interested in applied social psychology, should develop ways to reduce the potential uncertainties existing between people without and those with disabilities in community settings. To be sure, researchers and practitioners can build on existing research and tradition within rehabilitation psychology and, by doing so, address issues of value to community experience and public policy. The reality is not a social problem per se needing to be solved but, instead, existing community diversity to be constructively acknowledged and engaged.

Conclusion

There is a clear need to recognize and capitalize on the interdisciplinary links between social psychology and rehabilitation psychology. An emphasis on person–environment interaction is common to both areas. As demonstrated in this chapter, one's perspective—one's literal and figurative point of view—matters a great deal where disability and people with disabilities are concerned. Perspective is social psychological because it implies the reactions of both the perceiver and the perceived, the one to the other. Researchers, practitioners, and those whom they serve benefit by remembering how perceptions of people and their situations can promote or inhibit accurate understanding of social psychological issues in disability and rehabilitation.

References

Allport, G. W. (1935). Attitudes. In C. W. Murchison (Ed.), *Handbook of social psychology* (pp. 798–844). Worcester, MA: Clark University Press.

Allport, G. W. (1985). The historical background of social psychology. In G. Lindzey & E. Aronson (Eds.), *Handbook of social psychology: Vol. 1. Theory and methods* (3rd ed., pp. 1–46). New York: Random House.

American Psychological Association. (1994). *Publication manual of the American Psychological Association* (4th ed.). Washington, DC: Author.

Americans with Disabilities Act of 1990, P. L. 101-336, 104 Stat. 327.

Antonak, R. F. (1988). Methods to measure attitudes toward people who are disabled. In H. Yuker (Ed.), *Attitudes toward persons with disabilities* (pp. 109–126). New York: Springer.

Antonovsky, A. (1987). *Unraveling the mystery of health: How people manage stress and stay well*. San Francisco: Jossey-Bass.

Asch, A. (1984). The experience of disability: A challenge for psychology. *American Psychologist, 39,* 529–536.

Asch, A., & Fine, M. (1988a). Introduction: Beyond pedestals. In M. Fine & A. Asch (Eds.), *Women with disabilities: Essays in psychology, culture, and politics* (pp. 1–37). Philadelphia: Temple University Press.

Asch, A., & Fine, M. (Eds.). (1988b). Moving disability beyond "stigma." *Journal of Social Issues, 44*(1, whole issue).

Bandura, A. (1978). The self system in reciprocal determinism. *American Psychologist, 33,* 344–358.

Barker, R. (1948). The social psychology of physical disability. *Journal of Social Issues, 4,* 28–38.

Barker, R. G., Wright, B. A., Meyerson, L., & Gonick, M. R. (1953). *Adjustment to physical handicap and illness: A survey of the social psychology of physique and disability* (2nd ed.). New York: Social Science Research Council.

Barone, D. F., Maddux, J. E., & Snyder, C. R. (1997). *Social cognitive psychology: History and current domains*. New York: Plenum Press.

Belgrave, F. Z. (1984). The effectiveness of strategies for increasing social interaction with a physically disabled person. *Journal of Applied Social Psychology, 14,* 147–161.

Berscheid, E., & Walster, E. (1974). Physical attractiveness. In L. Berkowitz (Ed.), *Advances in experimental social psychology* (Vol. 7, pp. 157–215). New York: Academic Press.

Blumer, H. (1969). *Symbolic interactionism: Perspective and method*. Englewood Cliffs, NJ: Prentice Hall.

Breckler, S. J. (1984). Empirical validation of affect, behavior, and cognition as distinct components of attitude. *Journal of Personality and Social Psychology, 47,* 1191–1205.

Britt, J. H. (1988). Psychosocial aspects of being female and disabled. *Journal of Applied Rehabilitation Counseling, 19,* 19–23.

Bulman, R., & Wortman, C. B. (1977). Attributions of blame and coping in the "real world": Severe accident victims respond to their lot. *Journal of Personality and Social Psychology, 35,* 351–363.

Cartwright, D., & Zander, A. (Eds.). (1968). *Group dynamics: Research and theory* (3rd ed.). New York: Harper & Row.

Clanton, L. D., Rude, S., & Taylor, C. (1992). Learned resourcefulness as a moderator of burnout in a sample of rehabilitation providers. *Rehabilitation Psychology, 37,* 131–140.

Chwalisz, K., Altmaier, E., & Russell, D. (1992). Causal attributions, self-efficacy cognitions, and coping with stress. *Journal of Social and Clinical Psychology, 11,* 377–400.

Dembo, T. (1969). Rehabilitation psychology and its immediate future: A problem of utilization of psychological knowledge. *Rehabilitation Psychology, 16,* 63–72.

Dembo, T. (1970). The utilization of psychological knowledge in rehabilitation. *Welfare Review, 8,* 1–7.

Dembo, T. (1982). Some problems in rehabilitation as seen by a Lewinian. *Journal of Social Issues, 38,* 131–139.

Dembo, T., Leviton, G. L., & Wright, B. A. (1956). Adjustment to misfortune: A problem of social-psychological rehabilitation. *Artificial Limbs, 3,* 4–62.

Diener, E., & Emmons, R. A. (1984). The independence of positive and negative affect. *Journal of Personality and Social Psychology, 47,* 1105–1117.

Dunn, D. S. (1994a). Positive meaning and illusions following disability: Reality negotiation, normative interpretation, and value change. *Journal of Social Behavior and Personality, 9,* 123–138.

Dunn, D. S. (Ed.). (1994b). Psychosocial perspectives on disability [Special issue]. *Journal of Social Behavior and Personality, 9*(5, Whole issue).

Dunn, D. S. (1996). Well-being following amputation: Salutary effects of positive meaning, optimism, and control. *Rehabilitation Psychology, 41,* 285–302.

Eagly, A. H., & Chaiken, S. (1993). *The psychology of attitudes.* Fort Worth, TX: Harcourt Brace Jovanovich.

Elliott, T. R., & Frank, R. G. (1990). Social and interpersonal responses to depression and disability. *Rehabilitation Psychology, 35,* 135–147.

Elliott, T. R., Shewchuk, R., Hagglund, K., Rybarczyk, B., & Harkins, S. (1996). Occupational burnout, tolerance for stress, and coping among nurses in rehabilitation units. *Rehabilitation Psychology, 41,* 267–284.

Elliott, T. R., Witty, T. E., Herrick, S. M., & Hoffman, J. T. (1991). Negotiating reality after physical loss: Hope, depression, and disability. *Journal of Personality and Social Psychology, 61,* 608–613.

Esses, V. M., & Beaufoy, S. L. (1994). Determinants of attitudes toward people with disabilities. *Journal of Social Behavior and Personality, 9,* 43–64.

Farina, A. (1982). The stigma of mental disorders. In A. G. Miller (Ed.), *In the eye of the beholder* (pp. 305–363). New York: Praeger.

Fenderson, D. A. (1984). Opportunities for psychologists in disability research. *American Psychologist, 39,* 524–528.

Fichten, C. S., Amsel, R., Robillard, K., Sabourin, S., & Wright, J. (1997). Personality, attentional focus, and novelty effects: Reactions to peers with disabilities. *Rehabilitation Psychology, 42,* 209–230.

Fine, M., & Asch, A. (1981). Disabled women: Sexism without the pedestal. *Journal of Sociology and Social Welfare, 8,* 233–248.

Fine, M., & Asch, A. (1988a). Disability beyond stigma: Social interaction, discrimination, and activism. *Journal of Social Issues, 44,* 3–21.

Fine, M., & Asch, A. (Eds.). (1988b). *Women with disabilities: Essays in psychology, culture, and politics.* Philadelphia: Temple University Press.

Fiske, S. T., & Taylor, S. E. (1991). *Social cognition* (2nd ed.). New York: McGraw-Hill.

Fontana, A., & Frey, J. H. (1994). Interviewing: The art of science. In N. K. Denzin & Y. S. Lincoln (Eds.), *Handbook of qualitative research* (pp. 361–376). Thousand Oaks, CA: Sage.

Forsyth, D. R., & Elliott, T. R. (1999). Group dynamics and psychological well-being: The impact of groups on adjustment and dysfunction. In R. Kowalski & M. R. Leary (Eds.), *The social psychology of emotional and behavioral problems: Interfaces of social and clinical psychology* (pp. 339–361). Washington, DC: American Psychological Association.

Gething, L. (1991). Generality versus specificity of attitudes toward people with disabilities. *British Journal of Medical Psychology, 64,* 55–64.

Gething, L. (1994). The Interaction With Disabled Persons Scale. *Journal of Social Behavior and Personality, 9,* 23–42.

Gilbert, D. T., & Jones, E. E. (1986). Perceiver-induced constraint: Interpretations of self-generated reality. *Journal of Personality and Social Psychology, 50,* 269–280.

Goffman, E. (1963). *Stigma: Notes on the management of spoiled identity.* Englewood Cliffs, NJ: Prentice-Hall.

Hahn, H. (1988). The politics of physical differences: Disability and discrimination. *Journal of Social Issues, 44,* 39–48.

Hamera, E. K., & Shontz, F. C. (1978). Perceived positive and negative effects of life-threatening illness. *Journal of Psychosomatic Research, 22,* 419–424.

Hamilton, D. L. (1981). Illusory correlation as a basis for stereotyping. In D. L. Hamilton (Ed.), *Cognitive processes in stereotyping and intergroup behavior* (pp. 115–144). Hillsdale, NJ: Erlbaum.

Hamilton, D. L., Sherman, S. J., & Ruvolo, C. M. (1990). Stereotype-based expectancies: Effects on information processing and social behavior. *Journal of Social Issues, 46,* 35–60.

Hanna, W. J., & Rogovsky, B. (1991). Women with disabilities: Two handicaps plus. *Disability, Handicap, & Society, 6,* 49–63.

Hastorf, A. H., Wildfogel, J., & Cassman, T. (1979). Acknowledgement of handicap as a tactic on social interaction. *Journal of Personality and Social Psychology, 37,* 1790–1797.

Heider, F. (1958). *The psychology of interpersonal relations.* New York: Wiley.

Heinemann, A. W. (1990). Meeting the handicapped: A case of affective-cognitive inconsistency. In W. Stroebe & M. Hewstone (Eds.), *European review of social psychology* (Vol. 1, pp. 323–338). Chichester, England: John Wiley.

Heinemann, A. W., Bulka, M., & Smetak, S. (1988). Attributions and disability acceptance following traumatic injury: A replication and extension. *Rehabilitation Psychology, 33,* 195–206.

Horne, M. D. (1988). Modifying peer attitudes toward the handicapped: Procedures and research issues. In H. E. Yuker (Ed.), *Attitudes toward persons with disabilities* (pp. 203–222). New York: Springer.

Individuals With Disabilities Education Act of 1990, P. L. 101-476, 104 Stat. 1142.

Janoff-Bulman, R., & Frieze, I. H. (1983). A theoretical perspective for understanding reactions to victimization. *Journal of Social Issues, 39,* 1–17.

Jones, E. E., Farina, A., Hastorf, A. H., Markus, H., Miller, D. T., Scott, R. A., & French, R. de S. (1984). *Social stigma: The psychology of marked relationships.* New York: Freeman.

Jones, E. E., & Nisbett, R. E. (1972). The actor and the observer: Divergent perceptions of the cause of behavior. In E. E. Jones, D. E. Kanouse, H. H. Kelley, R. E. Nisbett, S. Valins, & B. Weiner (Eds.), *Attribution: Perceiving the causes of behavior* (pp. 79–94). Morristown, NJ: General Learning Press.

Katz, I., Haas, R. G., & Bailey, J. (1988). Attitudinal ambivalence and behavior toward people with disabilities. In H. Yuker (Ed.), *Attitudes toward persons with disabilities* (pp. 47–57). New York: Springer.

Keany, K. C. M.-H., & Glueckauf, R. L. (1993). Disability and value change: An overview and reanalysis of acceptance of loss theory. *Rehabilitation Psychology, 38,* 199–210.

Kerr, N., & Bodman, D. A. (1994). Disability research methods: An argument for the use of Galileian modes of thought in disability research. *Journal of Social Behavior and Personality, 9,* 99–122.

Langer, E. J., & Chanowitz, B. (1988). Mindfulness/mindlessness: A new perspective for the study of disability. In H. E. Yuker (Ed.), *Attitudes toward persons with disabilities* (pp. 68–81). New York: Springer.

Langer, E. J., Fiske, S. T., Taylor, S. E., & Chanowitz, B. (1976). Stigma, staring, and discomfort: A novel-stimulus hypothesis. *Journal of Experimental Social Psychology, 12,* 451–463.

Leary, M. R., & Maddux, J. F. (1987). Progress toward a viable interface between social and clinical-counseling psychology. *American Psychologist, 42,* 904–911.

Lerner, M. J. (1980). *The belief in a just world: A fundamental delusion.* New York: Plenum Press.

Lewin, G. W. (1957). Some characteristics of the socio-psychological life space of the epileptic patient. *Human Relations, 10,* 249–256.

Lewin, K. A. (1935). *A dynamic theory of personality.* New York: McGraw-Hill.

Linville, P. W., & Jones, E. E. (1980). Polarized appraisals of out-group members. *Journal of Personality and Social Psychology, 38,* 689–703.

Maslach, C., & Jackson, S. E. (1982). Burnout in health professions: A social psychological analysis. In G. Sanders & J. Suls (Eds.), *Social psychology of health and illness* (pp. 227–251). Hillsdale, NJ: Erlbaum.

Mason, L., & Muhlenkamp, A. (1976). Patients' self-reported affective states following loss and caregivers' expectations of patients' affective states. *Rehabilitation Psychology, 23,* 72–76.

Merton, R. K., Fiske, M., & Kendall, P. L. (1956). *The focused interview.* Glencoe, IL: Free Press.

Meyerson, L. (1948a). Physical disability as a social psychological problem. *Journal of Social Issues, 4,* 2–10.

Meyerson, L. (Ed.) (1948b). The social psychology of physical disability. *Journal of Social Issues, 4*(4, Whole issue).

Meyerson, L. (1988). The social psychology of physical disability: 1948 and 1988. *Journal of Social Issues, 44,* 173–188.

Mills, J., Belgrave, F. Z., & Boyer, K. M. (1984). Reducing avoidance of social interaction with a physically disabled person by mentioning the disability following a request for aid. *Journal of Applied Social Psychology, 14,* 1–11.

Pettigrew, T. F. (1979). The ultimate attribution error: Extending Allport's cognitive analysis of prejudice. *Personality and Social Psychology Bulletin, 5,* 461–476.

Renwick, R., Brown, I., Rootman, I., & Nagler, M. (1996). Conceptualization, research, and applications: Future directions. In R. Renwick, I. Brown, & M. Nagler (Eds.), *Quality of life in health promotion and rehabilitation* (pp. 357–367). Thousand Oaks, CA: Sage.

Ross, L. (1977). The intuitive psychologist and his shortcomings: Distortions in the attribution process. In L. Berkowitz (Ed.), *Advances in experimental social psychology* (Vol. 10, pp. 174–221). New York: Academic Press.

Ross, L., & Nisbett, R. E. (1991). *The person and the situation: Perspectives of social psychology.* New York: McGraw Hill.

Rothbart, M., & John, O. P. (1985). Social categorization and behavioral episodes: A cognitive analysis of the effects of intergroup contact. *Journal of Social Issues, 41,* 81–104.

Rybarczyk, B., & Bellg, A. (1997). *Listening to life stories: A new approach to stress intervention in health care.* New York: Springer.

Rybarczyk, B., Nicholas, J. J., & Nyenhuis, D. L. (1997). Coping with a leg amputation: Integrating research and clinical practice. *Rehabilitation Psychology, 42,* 241–256.

Schulz, R., & Decker, S. (1985). Long-term adjustment to physical disability: The role of social support, perceived control, and self-blame. *Journal of Personality and Social Psychology, 48,* 1162–1172.

Sherwin, E. D., Elliott, T. R., Rybarczyk, B., Frank, R. G., Hanson, S., & Hoffman, J. (1992). Negotiating the reality of caregiving: Hope, burnout, and nursing. *Journal of Social and Clinical Psychology, 11,* 129–139.

Shontz, F. C. (1977). Six principles relating disability and psychological adjustment. *Rehabilitation Psychology, 24,* 207–210.

Shontz, F. C. (1982). Adaptation to chronic illness. In T. Millon, C. Green, & R. Meagher (Eds.), *Handbook of clinical health psychology* (pp. 157–171). New York: Plenum Press.

Snyder, C. R. (1989). Reality negotiation: From excuses to hope and beyond. *Journal of Social and Clinical Psychology, 8,* 130–157.

Soder, M. (1990). Prejudice or ambivalence? Attitudes toward people with disabilities. *Disability, Handicap, and Society, 5,* 227–241.

Stav, A., & Florian, V. (1986). Burnout among social workers working with physically disabled persons and bereaved families. *Journal of Social Service Research, 10,* 81–94.

Stubbins, J. (1989). The interdisciplinary status of rehabilitation psychology. *Rehabilitation Psychology, 34,* 207–215.

Tait, R., & Silver, R. C. (1989). Coming to terms with major negative events. In J. S. Uleman & J. A. Bargh (Eds.), *Unintended thought* (pp. 351–382). New York: Guilford Press.

Tajfel, H. (1981). *Human groups and social categories: Studies in social psychology.* London: Cambridge University Press.

Taylor, S. E. (1983). Adjustment to threatening events: A theory of cognitive adaptation. *American Psychologist, 38,* 1161–1173.

Taylor, S. E., & Brown, J. D. (1988). Illusion and well-being: A social psychological perspective on mental health. *Psychological Bulletin, 103,* 193–210.

Taylor, S. E., Wood, J. V., & Lichtman, R. R. (1983). "It could be worse": Selective evaluation as a response to victimization. *Journal of Social Issues, 39,* 19–40.

Thurer, S. L. (1982). Women and rehabilitation. *Rehabilitation Literature, 43,* 194–197.

Ursprung, A. W. (1986). Burnout in the human services: A review of the literature. *Rehabilitation Counseling Bulletin, 29,* 190–199.

Vash, C. L. (1981). *The psychology of disability.* New York: Springer.

Vash, C. L. (1982). Employment issues for women with disabilities. *Rehabilitation Literature, 43,* 198–207.

Watson, D., & Tellegen, A. (1985). Toward a consensual structure of mood. *Psychological Bulletin, 98,* 219–235.

Weinberg, N. (1988). Another perspective: Attitudes of persons with disabilities. In H. Yuker (Ed.), *Attitudes toward persons with disabilities* (pp. 141–153). New York: Springer.

Weiner, B. (1993). On sin versus sickness: A theory of perceived responsibility and social motivation. *American Psychologist, 48,* 957–965.

Whiteman, M., & Lukoff, I. F. (1965). Attitudes toward blindness and other physical handicaps. *Journal of Social Psychology, 66,* 135–145.

Williamson, G. M., Schulz, R., Bridges, M. W., & Behan, A. M. (1994). Social and psychological factors in adjustment to limb amputation. *Journal of Social Behavior and Personality, 9,* 249–268.

Wright, B. A. (1980). Person and situation: Adjusting the rehabilitation focus. *Archives of Physical and Medical Rehabilitation, 61,* 59–64.

Wright, B. A. (1983). *Physical disability: A psychosocial approach* (2nd ed.). New York: Harper & Row.

Wright, B. A. (1988). Attitudes and the fundamental negative bias: Conditions and corrections. In H. E. Yuker (Ed.), *Attitudes toward persons with disabilities* (pp. 3–21). New York: Springer.

Wright, B. A. (1991). Labeling: The need for greater person–environment individuation. In C. R. Snyder & D. R. Forsyth (Eds.), *Handbook of social and clinical psychology: The health perspective* (pp. 469–487). New York: Pergamon.

Wright, B. A., & Fletcher, B. L. (1982). Uncovering hidden resources: A challenge in assessment. *Professional Psychology: Research and Practice, 13,* 229–235.

Yuker, H. E. (Ed.). (1988). *Attitudes toward persons with disabilities.* New York: Springer.

Yuker, H. E. (1994). Variables that influence attitudes toward people with disabilities: Conclusions from the data. *Journal of Social Behavior and Personality, 9,* 3–22.

Yuker, H. E., & Block, J. R. (1986). *Research with the Attitude Toward Disabled People Scales: 1960–1985.* West Hempstead, NY: Hofstra University Center for the Study of Attitudes Toward People With Disabilities.

Yuker, H. E., Block, J. R., & Young, J. H. (1966). *The measurement of attitudes toward disabled persons.* Albertson, NY: Human Resources Center.

Zimbardo, P. G. (1970). The human choice: Individuation, reason, and order versus deindividuation, impulse, and chaos. In W. J. Arnold & D. Levine (Eds.), *Nebraska Symposium on Motivation, 1969* (pp. 237–307). Lincoln: University of Nebraska Press.

28

Culture and the Disability and Rehabilitation Experience: An African American Example

Faye Z. Belgrave and S. Lisbeth Jarama

Culture influences disability prevalence, the experience of disability, participation in rehabilitation, and one's overall level of functioning and adaptation to a disability. We refer to these processes as the "disability experience." In this chapter, we draw on our programs and research with African Americans with disabilities to illustrate the pervasive influence of culture in the experience of disability. A fuller discussion of the role of culture on the disability experience of African Americans can be found in *Psychosocial Aspects of Chronic Illness and Disability Among African Americans* (Belgrave, 1998). For a discussion of Latino culture and the disability experience, see the works of Zea and colleagues (Zea, Garcia, Belgrave, & Quezada, 1997; Zea, Quezada, & Belgrave, 1994). Cook, Cook, Tran, and Tu (1997) and Fatimilehin and Nadirshaw (1994) provided examples of how Asian culture affects the disability experience. Although other cultural and ethnic groups could have been used to illustrate the role of culture, we chose to focus on African American culture because most of our work has been with this cultural group.

We begin with definitions and distinctions between culture, ethnicity, and race. The next section provides an overview of the role of culture and ethnicity in disability prevalence. Cultural factors that influence health care and rehabilitation utilization patterns are discussed next. The African American worldview provides an appropriate cultural context in which to understand the experiences of African Americans. Cultural values including "Africentric" values are discussed next. In the final section of the chapter, we provide an illustration of how Africentric beliefs affect outcomes and functioning among African Americans with disabilities and chronic illnesses.

Definitions

There are many definitions of *culture*. Culture informs its members how to process, evaluate, and interpret the world and their experiences (Landrine & Klonoff, 1996). Culture may be considered the sum total of a society's customs, habits, beliefs, and values (Kroeber & Cluckhohm, 1963). These customs, values, thoughts, and actions are overarching and affect all aspects of one's life, including how one experiences disability. For African Americans in this country, both the African and American cultures shape core values, beliefs, and behaviors.

Concepts related to culture are ethnicity and race. Ethnicity is based on membership and is defined as a sense of common historical origins, which may include a shared culture, religion, or language. Jalali (1988) defined ethnicity as the values, attitudes, perceptions, needs, modes of expression, behavior, and identity of a cultural group. An ethnic group such as African Americans holds shared values and customs. Race, in contrast to ethnicity, is biologically determined. Landrine and Klonoff (1996) defined *race* as an ethnic group that has been socially defined as such on the basis of physical criteria.

Disability is defined as any restriction on normal functioning or lack of ability to perform activities because of an impairment (World Health Organization, 1980). Whether disability is a result of physical or psychological impairment, it implies constraints on an individual's daily functioning.

Incidence of and Factors Contributing to Disability Prevalence

Of the estimated 13.4 million working-age adults with a disability, approximately 2.4 million (18%) are African Americans, although African Americans comprise only 12% of the population in this country. This represents approximately 14% of African Americans in the 16–64-year age group (Asbury, Walker, Maholmes, Rackley, & White, 1991; Bowe, 1991).

Approximately 24.4% or 1.8 million of the working-age population with a severe disability are African Americans, which indicates a substantially high incidence of severe disability among African Americans. These figures show that African Americans with a disability are much more likely to have functional limitations. Individuals with severe disabilities are less likely to work, attend school, take care of a household, or participate in community activities compared with those without.

Overall, disability among African Americans is associated with a decreased standard of living (Asbury et al., 1991). Only 13% of working-age African Americans with a disability are employed. Education is also compromised: Among African Americans with disabilities, about 43% of women and 27% of men have less than a high school level of education. The level of poverty is also high among African Americans with disabilities, with 41% living on or below the poverty line. Although these statistics suggest that many African Americans with disabilities have low socioeconomic standards of living, variability is large, and many African Americans with disabilities function well at home and work and in the community.

Several reasons explain the increased prevalence of disability among

African Americans and their poorer functional outcomes compared to White Americans. Many of these factors are socioeconomic in origin. A history of discrimination and oppression, which continues today, has resulted in a lower socioeconomic status for African Americans compared to White Americans. However, even when socioeconomic factors are controlled for, disability prevalence rates are higher and outcomes are more negative for African Americans than White Americans. Cultural factors operate in conjunction with socioeconomic factors to increase disability prevalence among African Americans.

Statistics show that African Americans are less likely than White Americans to visit physicians and engage in routine medical care (Horner, 1995). However, when hospitalized, the length of stay is longer for African Americans and they are more likely to be seen in emergency rooms compared with White Americans, which suggests that when African Americans do go for medical treatment they are "sicker."

Access to medical care is contingent on socioeconomic status. Lower rates of employment and underemployment for African Americans make preventive care and treatment of medical problems less likely if medical insurance is not available. Other factors that limit access to prevention and treatment health services include limited transportation and inconvenient location of health care facilities. Most health care facilities are not located within inner cities where many African Americans reside, and public transportation may not be accessible. Even when medical care and treatment are accessible for African Americans, there may be less attention devoted to preventive care against the backdrop of the many other problems and concerns faced by African Americans. These are discussed in greater detail later in this chapter.

Cultural beliefs about the etiology of a particular condition may affect whether or not treatment is sought. For example, beliefs that one's wellbeing is determined by fate or that little can be done to change one's situation may contribute to the decision not to seek treatment. An emphasis on communal relationships and interdependence may prevent people from taking the time to engage in preventive health care and treatment if significant others are negatively affected by these actions. The facilitative and inhibitory roles of cultural factors on disability and illness are discussed in greater detail later in the chapter.

Increased stress among African Americans is also a contributor to disability prevalence. There is extensive evidence of a link between stress, disease, disability, and mortality. Stress affects the immune system and one's overall health status through reduced behavioral responses to health care behaviors, by limiting one's cognitive capability of thinking about health and medical needs, and physiologically through a depression of one's immune functioning (Maier, Watkins, & Flesher, 1994). Many African Americans live and work under conditions of high environmental stress. High levels of unemployment and underemployment, financial and economic problems, and racism are sources of increased environmental stress for African Americans (Anderson, 1991). Racism, a major stressor for many

African Americans, has been implicated as a contributor to poor mental and physical health outcomes (Landrine & Klonoff, 1996).

Compared with White Americans, African Americans are also more likely to experience stress because of where they live. They are more likely to live in urban environments than rural or suburban environments. Inner-city environments with increased drugs and violence can be stressful and contribute to a poor quality of living (G. Y. Phillips, 1996). Living in neighborhoods with high levels of criminal activity and drugs also increases one's daily risk of disability morbidity. For example, the violence associated with the drug trade in many inner-city neighborhoods has contributed to increased levels of trauma, including brain and spinal cord injuries, especially among young male African Americans. Many of the traumatic injuries among male African Americans are due to gunshot wounds, high-speed police chases, and related criminal factors (Gordon & Lewis, 1993). All too often, these traumatic injuries are inflicted on innocent bystanders who live in these communities. Another reason for the increased disability morbidity of African Americans is that they are more likely to work under conditions in which they are at increased risk for injury or environmental health hazards (Asbury et al., 1991). Employment in low-skilled jobs increases the risk of disability through accidental injury.

Western and Non-Western Conceptualizations

Influence of Culture on Beliefs About Health and Illness

One's conceptualization of disability is derived from one's cultural experiences. Landrine and Klonoff (1992) examined the influence of culture on health and illness schema of ethnic and cultural groups in the United States and other countries and noted that the schema of non-White Americans differs from that of White Americans. Although Landrine and Klonoff focused on health and illness schemas, their analysis can be applied to disability.

A *schema* is an organized collection of beliefs or information about someone or something (Fiske & Taylor, 1991). Schema guide us in the interpretation of our world, including ourselves. An *illness schema* is an organized collection of beliefs about illness, whereas a *disability schema* would include organized beliefs and ways of thinking about disability or a particular type of disability. The Western view of illness tends to focus on illness as person centered and as an interpersonal condition caused by microlevel, natural, and etiological agents such as genes, viruses, bacteria, and stress. Illness or disease then may be seen as discrete or episodic (Landrine & Klonoff, 1992). From this perspective, disability is also likely to be seen as an isolated, person-centered condition, and treatment is likely to be more targeted and episodic. Rehabilitation may be treated in isolation of spirituality, community, nature, or the family.

In contrast to the more person-centered approach of Western culture regarding illness and disability, Landrine and Klonoff (1992) noted that many non-Western groups, including some ethnic minority groups in the United States, view illness as a long-term, fluid, and continuous manifestation of longtime and dynamic relationships within the family, community, or nature. The schema of these individuals regarding illness would include macrolevel, interpersonal, and supernatural causes as explanations for illness or disease. From this perspective, illness would be seen as something that is more integrative and something that extends outside of the affected individual.

Extending this analogy, disability within many cultures may not be seen as a condition limited to the individual. One implication of this conceptualization is that some African Americans who do not hold the Westernized schema of disability may not comply with Western treatment or recommendations. Hence, participation in rehabilitation is related to the schema one has regarding the etiology of the disabling condition. We will return to this point later when we discuss Africentric culture.

In a review of explanations for illness, Murdock (1989, cited in Landrine & Klonoff, 1992) found that theories about the causes of illness can be categorized into two major types: theories of natural causation and of supernatural causation. Theories of natural causation include viruses, infection, aging, accidents, homicides, and stress as the causes of illness. Theories of supernatural causation include mystical retribution (punishment by God for violating rules), animistic causation (soul loss or spirit aggression for violating rules), and magical causation (witchcraft, "evil eye"). In an examination of 189 cultures, Murdock found that the beliefs of only 4 cultures included natural explanations for illness.

Some minority ethnic and cultural groups in the United States may also hold supernatural beliefs about the causes of illness. There is anecdotal evidence of the beliefs of African Americans that illness, disease, and disability may be caused by forces outside of the individual. We are reminded of conversations with African Americans who held beliefs that certain people have the power to put a "hex" or a "spell" causing illness or disability on them or someone else. Beliefs about the causes of illness and disease promote supernatural explanations for the treatment of illness and disease.

For example, within African American Southern communities, healers known as "root doctors" were used to cure illness and disease. Root doctors used roots and herbs to treat physical, mental, and social conditions, and they were the only ones who could break a spell cast on a person. In some parts of the United States, root doctors held positions of high status and prestige in their community. Although root doctors are no longer prevalent within the African American community, anecdotal accounts suggest that they still exist, especially in certain areas of the South. It is interesting to note that individuals from other ethnic groups, including White Americans, are increasing their use of herbs and roots for enhancing health and treating disease.

In addition to root doctors, there have always been other types of nonmedical healers. Although not unique to the African American community, these healers served several functions (i.e., psychological, medical, spiritual) and were numerous in the African American community during the first half of the 20th century. Sometimes referred to as "faith healers" or "divine healers," they served the needs of the African American community in varying ways. They offered hope through faith that one would get better and that one's circumstances would improve. They lived within the community and were accessible and relatively inexpensive, and they acknowledged and involved the family in the treatment regimen. Although faith healers and divine healers are not prevalent within the African American community today, remnants of their methods are still used. This is evidenced by present-day testimonials, witnessing, and other expressions of spirituality and faith as a requisite for mental and physical healing.

The power of faith and divine healers makes intuitive sense when one considers the powerful influence that beliefs have on behavior. There is historical and theoretical support for the role of faith and spirituality in affecting outcomes. The power of faith and meditation has been documented since antiquity. If one has strong beliefs that one will improve or function adaptively, the likelihood of such is enhanced. This is akin to self-efficacy beliefs, which have been associated with improved functioning across many domains (Bandura, 1986).

One other adaptive aspect of faith is that it provides an adaptive coping strategy so that individuals are better able to deal with and accept the challenge or limitations of their health status, disability, or impairment. Faith is a by-product of spirituality, which is a key Africentric value; we discuss this in more detail later.

In summary, views of illness, disease, and disability are influenced by culture. In Western conceptualizations, disability is regarded as person centered, whereas in non-Western cultures it may be seen as caused by forces outside of the individual. Some of these beliefs may be operative although in a more subtle fashion today. Given these beliefs, African Americans may be more receptive to nontraditional healers and treatment sources. Faith and spirituality are important for treatment and rehabilitation. These beliefs are likely to be mediated by socioeconomic status, demographic factors, such as the region of the country where a person resides, and age.

Cultural Values

A central assumption throughout this chapter is that the beliefs and values of African Americans affect their disability experience and participation in rehabilitation. We present a brief overview of the African American worldview followed by a discussion of the Africentric framework. African Americans have core values rooted in West African culture and modified by experiences in the United States. African American values and beliefs have also been shaped by a history of slavery and oppression in this country. However, this is not to suggest that the history and present-day circumstances of African Americans have been exclusively one of victimization and helplessness. Quite the contrary: The oppressive institutions of this country have in fact provided an opportunity for many African Americans to demonstrate resiliency and strength. As we discuss later in this chapter, these circumstances have led many African Americans to "make a way out of no way" (Randolph & Banks, 1993, p. 204) and to reinterpret a negative situation favorably.

Some of the cultural values among African Americans (e.g., collectiveness, spirituality) are shared among other non-Western cultures, including other ethnic minority groups in this country. Although not all African Americans endorse these values and some White Americans do, it is assumed that substantial numbers of African Americans endorse such values to varying degrees. These values are contrasted with Eurocentric values found most often among people of European descent, including White Americans (and some African Americans). Whereas Africentric values may be considered universal, they are found among people of African descent more so than people of European descent (Logan & Belgrave, 1999; Myers, 1988). What are these values, and how do they influence the disability experience? We provide an example and then return to a more in-depth discussion of those values. Among African Americans, an interpersonal orientation may take precedence over materialistic and achievement-related orientations. Within this context, the relationship one has with another person is of the highest value. This means that the relationship is significant in its own right regardless of whether the person has a disability that might limit (at least in the perceiver's eyes) the ability to achieve and produce in a materialistic sense (Myers, 1988). Within this context, Africentric values could be considered adaptive for African Americans with disabilities.

When Africans were brought to this country, the institution of slavery contributed to the evolution of systems that augmented Africentric values to meet the needs of Africans in America. These systems and values continue today. One such system is the extended family. African American extended kin networks have been a central structure in African and African American family life (Martin & Martin, 1978) and crucial to the survival and adaptation of African Americans in this country (Wilson, 1989).

McAdoo (1981) described the extended family as a "help network" in which there is reciprocal obligation to help biological or nonbiological relatives. This network provides not only a bond and an emotional connection but economical and financial support as well. Members of the family who are able are expected to help the less able. The African American family network is further characterized by frequent contact; close relationships are developed with cousins and other relatives. Relationships may also be developed with *fictive kin*, individuals who are treated as if they are members of the family, although they are not biologically related or related through marriage. The interdependence and connection among American families is an extension of Africentric values, which emphasize interpersonal, communal, and affiliative relationships. The extended kin reciprocity has been reinforced by a legacy of discrimination and oppression, which dictated that African Americans look out for and help one another.

Respect for elders is another characteristic of African American families, which originated in Africa. Children are responsible for the care and welfare of their parents, and older relatives are expected to spend their last years in the homes of relatives rather than in nursing homes (Toliver-Weddington, 1990). This same respect and sharing of responsibilities may also be evidenced among African Americans who may assist in caring for people who are physically or mentally not able to take care of themselves.

Africentric Framework

Several scholars have written on the Africentric worldview, values, and beliefs (Akbar, 1990; Asante, 1988; Azibo, 1989, 1996; Baldwin, 1981, 1990; Myers, 1988; Nobles, 1986, 1990; F. B. Phillips, 1990). According to these scholars, the Africentric worldview is generally the appropriate framework for understanding behaviors of people of African descent. Thus, the Africentric framework is useful for providing a framework in which to understand the influence of culture on the disability experience of African Americans. An *Africentric worldview* may be defined as the values, beliefs, and ways of behavior that characterize people of African descent. African American scholars maintain that this worldview is adaptive and necessary for optimal functioning for African Americans (Azibo, 1989, 1996; Myers, 1988; Nobles, 1986). In his thesis on African American personality, Azibo (1989) noted that deviation from core Africentric values may lead to pathology.

The assumption made here is that adherence to Africentric values can facilitate functioning and positive outcomes among African Americans with disabilities. However, as we demonstrate, these values and beliefs may be deleterious when they are in contrast with the values and beliefs of the mainstream culture.

Randolph and Banks (1993) summarized nine dimensions or qualities of the African worldview that have been articulated by several African American scholars, including Na'im Akbar, Daudi Azibo, Joseph Baldwin, Wade Boykins, Asa Hilliard, Linda J. Myers, Edwin Nichols, and Wade Nobles.

- *Spirituality*. Spirituality is the acknowledgment that there is a presence or force greater than oneself and that there is a relationship with God or some other "supernatural being." This orientation emphasizes the spiritual over the material. Spirituality provides the foundation for meaning and direction to one's life and permeates every aspect of one's being. Spirituality is often (but not always) manifested by worship, prayers, and other rituals. These symbolic rituals strengthen one's spiritual connection. In short, a belief in spirituality provides a reason for being on this earth and a framework for accepting one's disability experiences.

- *Interpersonal orientation–communalism.* Interrelatedness and connection to others characterize this orientation. Interpersonal and affiliative relationships may be valued over materialistic, production, or achievement-oriented activities. This worldview emphasizes a belief in the importance of the group over the individual and cooperation rather than competition. The self is viewed as part of a collective phenomenon. The principle "I am because we are" typifies this dimension. An interpersonal communal orientation recognizes the value of the person within the rehabilitation setting. The relationship with the rehabilitation professional is central, and the lack of a meaningful connection or relationship might impede progress.
- *Harmony.* This is the belief that all aspects of one's life must be integrated. Such a belief assumes that all aspects of one's being—physical, spiritual, and emotional—are linked. For people holding this belief, optimal functioning is not possible unless all aspects of one's life are in balance. Imbalance occurs when one's physical self is not integrated with one's spiritual and emotional self. This orientation would support the belief that one's physical self, including one's disability, is an important part of who one is. This integration of all aspects of one's self should encourage favorable self-acceptance. It is important to acknowledge and treat all aspects of the person in the rehabilitation process.
- *Time as a social phenomenon.* This dimension relates to the previous one in that all things flow into one another, and events are not discrete and unconnected. The clock or calendar does not dictate when something begins or ends; the occurrence of events is dictated by the will of the people. This is exemplified by the saying "the party starts when the people arrive." The African worldview regarding time differs from a European worldview. European time is much more mathematical and ordered than African time. For Europeans, there is an appropriate place and time in which things are supposed to happen (e.g., one's physical therapy session is held at 4:00 p.m. every Wednesday, not anytime during the late afternoon). Conflict may occur when African Americans and European Americans are on different time rhythms within a rehabilitation environment.
- *Affect sensitivity to emotional cues (synthesis of the verbal and nonverbal).* This involves sensitivity to the feelings and the emotional needs of others. The expression and perception of feelings is seen in nonverbal as well as verbal behavior, and it is important to be in tune with how others feel. If the person one is interacting with is feeling bad, this is likely to rub off and interfere with interactions—at least until the emotional and affective states can be addressed. When rehabilitation professionals and African American consumers interact, the affective states of each may affect the quality of the interaction.
- *Expressive communication–orality.* This dimension recognizes that

oral expression is a preferred means of communication. Information transmitted orally carries weight equal to, if not greater than, that which is written. Communication may be less direct but expressive and fluid. Art, dance, speech, music, and body movements and position may be used to convey thoughts and ideas. This orientation has implications for communicating with an African American with a disability. A personal conversation regarding adherence instructions may be more effective than an impersonal written list of instructions.

- *Rhythmic movement and stylistic expressiveness.* This orientation recognizes the uniqueness of each person's flair, style, and manner of expression. Spontaneity and improvisation are emphasized to the extent that they facilitate individual and group goals. This unique manner of expression can be seen in African Americans' way of walking, dressing, and communicating with others. Regardless of one's circumstances (e.g., amount of money, physical state), style and flair are maintained. The rhythmic mode of being should be acknowledged in rehabilitation settings when consumers are encouraged to maintain their natural rhythm and manner of expressing themselves.

- *Multidimensional perception and verve (multimodal perception and learning).* This dimension recognizes the need for different ways of learning. The means of acquiring information are multidimensional and may include visual, auditory, tactile, and motor channels simultaneously. This orientation would support the notion that various methods are necessary for encouraging preventive and treatment adherence.

- *Negativity to positivity.* This orientation reflects the ability to turn a bad situation into a positive one, to see something good derived from something bad. This positive orientation has a favorable influence on the acceptance of disability and conditions that others may perceive as potentially adverse. Within a rehabilitation setting, a disability limitation may provide an opportunity for positive reinterpretation.

Randolph and Banks (1993) were not suggesting that all African Americans adhere to all of these dimensions and that all White Americans do not. A great deal of diversity exists among both ethnic groups. The assumption is that these values exist more or less among many people of African descent throughout the Diaspora. The transmission of Africentric values modified by experiences in America has shaped the values, behaviors, and beliefs of African Americans today.

Illustrations

Cultural values affect the experiences of African Americans and can both facilitate and impede adaptive functioning among African Americans with disabilities. The following provides some illustrations of how this may occur.

Extended Family Network

The extended family can be an asset for a person with a disability who may need support in a number of areas. Some mental and physical limitations may isolate some individuals and limit their participation in activities outside of the home. However, within African American extended families, there may be less isolation because of ties to people within and outside of the immediate family, thereby increasing the number of individuals who are a part of the immediate network structure. The presence of an extended family among African Americans with disabilities was seen in a study by Belgrave, Davis, and Vadja (1994). In a study of providers of social support for African and White Americans with disabilities, Belgrave et al. found that African Americans listed more extended kin than White Americans, although there was no difference between the two groups in the number of immediate family members listed. The findings from this study suggest that the networks of African Americans with disabilities are more likely to include more significant others outside of the immediate family. This extended network may provide emotional support as well as material support.

An understanding of who is in the extended family and what functions these individuals serve may help explain why and how medical and rehabilitation services are accessed. For example, when working with consumers, it may be helpful to know who will assist them in coming to their appointments and who will provide transportation.

The importance of the extended family in employment outcomes of African Americans with disabilities was demonstrated in a study by Walker and Belgrave (1995). In this study, the investigators examined the relationship between support from various sources and employment efficacy. Employment efficacy beliefs are important insofar as they contribute to actual employment. Using a mostly African American sample, the authors found that support from family was related to one's efficacy beliefs that he or she would secure employment. Support from professionals was not related to efficacy employment beliefs. This finding encourages the involvement of family members in rehabilitation activities.

Communal and Group Orientation

Having a communal and group orientation may be adaptive among African Americans with disabilities for several reasons. The achievement of the individual is subordinate to the achievement of the group. Thus, an individual is respected because he or she is a member of a group rather than for individual achievements. As noted previously, success is not necessarily defined by the acquisition of material goods, education, or status but by the viability of the group or family. When a person with physical or mental limitations is not able to achieve material success, his or her status within the community would not diminish.

An Africentric worldview assumes that a communal or group approach is useful when working with African Americans with disabilities. Here, support groups and self-help groups might be more effective than services and interventions that are individually focused. In our work, we have found this to be true. In groups composed of African Americans with disabilities, the goal of each group member is defined by the group, with a central task being that group members help each other. In more individualistic and competitive environments, the accomplishments of individuals are often pitted against each other.

Spirituality

Belief in a power or force greater than oneself is adaptive for those undergoing stress and turmoil. Spirituality provides a framework for that which is incomprehensible. It also provides hope and faith for a better life. Turning one's life over to God facilitates acceptance of adversity and hard times because there is the acknowledgment that there is a purpose and reason to all things. This sentiment is expressed in Beatrice Wright's (1983) writings on acceptance of disability. According to Wright, acceptance of disability involves recognition of the decreasing importance of one's physical self relative to one's spiritual self.

Some research shows that spirituality is an adaptive coping response for African Americans. Cheung and Snowden (1990) identified religion, prayer, and spirituality as key ways of coping among African Americans. According to Cheung and Snowden, African Americans use prayer more often than White Americans as a response to problems. In a study on stress and coping among African Americans, Neighbors, Jackson, Bowman, and Gurin (1983) confirmed the extensive use of prayer and noted that as the seriousness of the problems increased, so did the number of African Americans who felt that prayer helped them the most.

Being part of a spiritual and religious network also serves a practical function of increasing the number of people in the network. Ministers, deacons, and other church members fulfill many of the support functions of the extended family and, in effect, become members of the extended family. Spirituality also likely contributes to one's acceptance of self, including any limitations that one may have. However, acceptance of one's condition without critical assessment or with the belief that this is God's will may limit the person's ability to optimize rehabilitation.

Negativity to Positivity

The view that good can come from something bad can be adaptive in getting people through tough times and is related to spirituality. In interviews with African American women who were HIV positive, Belgrave found that the women frequently mentioned that their diagnosis helped turn their lives around, made them stop and reassess their priorities, and put them in touch with God and their faith. In other words, they had turned a negative into a positive.

Similarly, when African Americans or members of their families acquire a disabling condition, there is often a positive reinterpretation of this condition. In a study of parents of children with disabilities, Walker and Belgrave (1995) found that African American parents were likely to report the use of positive reinterpretation as a coping strategy. In interviews with these parents, several reported that very favorable outcomes had resulted from having a child with a disability. For example, they reported that they became stronger and that the experience strengthened their faith and made them grow stronger as a family.

Harmony

An orientation toward harmony can affect how a disability is perceived. A functional limitation is not seen as discrete and separate from other aspects of one's life. The implication here is that the physical, spiritual, and emotional aspect of the individual must be considered when rehabilitative services are provided. Physical rehabilitation may not be useful if in fact one is not dealing with other aspects of the individual. The authors conducted an intervention aimed at enhancing adjustment to disability and vocational outcomes among African Americans with disabilities (Banks, 1998). Participants requested that each session start with a prayer and other affirmations of spirituality. Although the focus was on vocational rehabilitation, consumers needed to connect to their spiritual selves to move forward.

Conclusion

The culture of African Americans influences their disability experience. Compared with White Americans, African Americans may have schemas about disability that are more congruent with a non-Western conceptualization than a Western conceptualization. Disability is seen not as a concrete individualistic condition but as a condition that is much more integrated within other aspects of the individual's life and social group. It is likely that the schema of other ethnic minority groups in this country also differ from that of White Americans and may be similar to that of African Americans.

The values and beliefs of African Americans are derived from West African culture and shaped by American socialization. Values of communalism, harmony, time as a social phenomenon, affect and sensitivity, orality, rhythmic movement, multidimensional perception, extended family, and respect for elders shape the disability experience for African Americans. When these values are not considered, consumers' ability to receive full benefits from rehabilitation may be compromised. Thus, it is necessary to consider such values when conducting research and developing programs for African Americans with disabilities.

We have chosen to focus on how cultural values can be used to facilitate optimal functioning. Under certain conditions, however, this will not be the case; that is, African American values may in fact undermine optimal functioning, especially when those values are incongruent with the values of those in power.

The potential maladaptive effects of cultural values should be investigated. For example, an extreme reliance on spirituality may result in relinquishing control over one's life circumstances and one's motivation and beliefs about one's ability to change. Although a communal orientation that ranks the group over the individual may serve various supportive functions (e.g., provide emotional, instrumental, or financial assistance), it may at the same time foster dependency and intrusiveness of network members. More research is necessary to explicate the conditions under which cultural values are adaptive and maladaptive.

The impact of culture on the disability experience opens the door for further research on the nature and aspects of culture that are critical for a successful rehabilitation. It is of interest, for instance, to learn how cultural values may differently influence the responses of African Americans of different age groups to the disability and rehabilitation experience. Whereas spirituality and positive reinterpretations of the disability may be emphasized in the rehabilitation process among older people, a different approach may be more effective with younger individuals. Encouraging participation in support groups and connecting with family, kin, and friends might prove more beneficial for younger African Americans with disabilities. The potential for the favorable effects of culture as a tool to facilitate rehabilitation to disability warrants further examination.

References

Akbar, N. (1990). The evolution of human psychology for African Americans. In R. L. Jones (Ed.), *Black psychology* (pp. 99–123). Berkeley, CA: Cobb & Henry.

Anderson, L. (1991). Acculturative stress: A theory of relevance to Black Americans. *Clinical Psychology, 11,* 685–702.

Asante, M. K. (1988). *Afrocentricity.* Trenton, NJ: Africa World Press.

Asbury, C. A., Walker, S., Maholmes, V., Rackley, R., & White, S. (1991). *Prevalence and demographic associations among race/ethnic minority populations in the United States: Implications for the 21st century,* Washington, DC: Howard University Research and Training Center for Access to Rehabilitation and Economic Opportunity.

Azibo, D. A. (1989). African-centered theses on mental health and a nosology of Black/African personality disorder. *Journal of Black Psychology, 15*(2), 173–214.

Azibo, D. A. (1996). *African psychology in historical perspective related commentary.* Trenton, NJ: Africa World Press.

Baldwin, J. A. (1981). Notes on an Africentric theory of Black personality testing. *Western Journal of Black Studies, 5*(3), 172–179.

Baldwin, J. A. (1990). African (Black) psychology: Issues and synthesis. In R. L. Jones (Ed.), *Black psychology* (pp. 125–135). Berkeley, CA: Cobb & Henry.

Bandura, A. (1986). *Social foundations of thought and action: A social cognitive theory.* Englewood Cliffs, NJ: Prentice Hall.

Banks, S. R. (1998). *The impact of social support and active coping on enhancing mental health and employability outcomes among African Americans and Latinos with disabilities: A community-based group intervention.* Unpublished doctoral dissertation, George Washington University, Washington, DC.

Belgrave, F. Z. (1998). *Psychosocial aspects of chronic illness and disability among African Americans.* Westport, CT: Greenwood.

Belgrave, F. Z., Davis, A., & Vadja, J. (1994). An examination of social support source, type, and satisfaction among African Americans and White Americans with disabilities. *Journal of Social Behavior and Personality, 9*(5), 307–320.

Bowe, F. (1991). *Black adults with disabilities: A portrait.* Report prepared for the President's Committee on Employment of People With Disabilities, Washington, DC.

Cheung, F. K., & Snowden, L. R. (1990). Community mental health and ethnic minority populations. *Community Mental Health Journal, 26,* 277–291.

Cook, P., Cook, M., Tran, L., & Tu, W. (1997). Children enabling change: A multicultural, participatory, community-based rehabilitation research project involving Chinese children with disabilities and their families. *Child and Youth Care Forum, 26*(3), 205–219.

Fatimilehin, I. A., & Nadirshaw, Z. (1994). A cross-cultural study of parental attitudes and beliefs about learning disability (mental handicap). *Mental Handicap Research, 7*(3), 202–227.

Fiske, S., & Taylor, S. F. (1991). *Social cognition.* New York: McGraw-Hill.

Gordon, S., & Lewis, D. (1993). Psychological challenges of drugs, violence and spinal cord injury among African American inner-city males. *Psychosocial Process, 6,* 53–60.

Horner, L. L. (1995). *Black Americans: A statistical sourcebook.* Palo Alto, CA: Information.

Jalali, B. (1988). Ethnicity, cultural adjustment, and behavior: Implications for family therapy. In L. Comas-Diaz & E. E. H. Griffith (Eds.), *Clinical guidelines in cross-cultural mental health* (pp. 9–32). New York: Wiley.

Kroeber, A. L., & Cluckhohm, C. (1963). *Culture: A critical review of concepts and definitions.* New York: Vintage.

Landrine, H., & Klonoff, E. A. (1992). Culture and health-related schema: A review and proposal for interdisciplinary integration. *Health Psychology, 11,* 267–276.

Landrine, H., & Klonoff, E. A. (1996). *African American acculturation.* Thousand Oaks, CA: Sage.

Logan, D. D., & Belgrave, F. Z. (1999, August). *Relationship between level of Africentricity and stress, self-esteem, and drug use among African Americans.* Paper presented at the 31st Annual Conference of the Association of Black Psychologists, Charleston, S. C.

Maier, S. F., Watkins, L. R., & Flesher, M. (1994). Psychoimmuneurology. *American Psychologists, 49,* 1004–1017.

Martin, E., & Martin, J. M. (1978). *The Black extended family.* Chicago: University of Chicago Press.

McAdoo, H. P. (1981). *Black families.* Beverly Hills, CA: Sage.

Myers, L. J. (1988). *An Afrocentric worldview: Introduction to an optimal psychology.* Dubuque, IA: Quintal-Hunt.

Neighbors, H. W., Jackson, J. S., Bowman, P., & Gurin, G. (1983). Stress, coping and black mental health: Preliminary findings from a national study. *Prevention in Human Services, 2,* 979–983.

Nobles, W. W. (1986). *African psychology: Towards its reclamation, reascension, and revitalization.* Oakland, CA: Black Family Institute.

Nobles, W. W. (1990). African philosophy: Foundations of Black psychology. In R. L. Jones (Ed.), *Black psychology* (pp. 47–63). Berkeley, CA: Cobb & Henry.

Phillips, F. B. (1990). NTU psychotherapy: An Afrocentric approach. *Journal of Black Psychology, 17,* 55–74.

Phillips, G. Y. (1996). Stress and residential well-being. In H. W. Neighbors & J. S. Jackson (Eds.), *Mental health in Black America* (pp. 27–44). Thousand Oaks, CA: Sage.

Randolph, S. M., & Banks, H. D. (1993). Making a way out of no way: The promise of Africentric approaches to HIV prevention. *Journal of Black Psychology, 19,* 204–214.

Toliver-Weddington, G. (1990). Cultural considerations in the treatment of craniofacial malformations in African Americans. *Cleft Palate Journal, 27,* 289–293.

Walker, S., & Belgrave, F. Z. (1995). *Coping patterns among families with children with disabilities* [Technical report]. Washington, DC: Howard University Research and Training Center for Access to Rehabilitation and Economic Opportunity.

Wilson, M. N. (1989). Child development in the context of the Black extended family. *American Psychologist, 44,* 380–385.

World Health Organization. (1980). *International classification of impairments, disabilities, and handicaps: A manual of classification relating to the consequences of disease.* Geneva, Switzerland: Author.

Wright, B. (1983). *Physical disability: A psychosocial approach.* New York: Harper & Row.

Zea, M. C., Garcia, J. G., Belgrave, F. Z., & Quezada, T. (1997). Socioeconomic and cultural factors in rehabilitation of Latinos with disabilities. In J. G. Garcia & M. C. Zea (Eds.), *Psychological interventions and research with Latino populations* (pp. 217–234). Boston: Allyn & Bacon.

Zea, M. C., Quezada, T., & Belgrave, F. Z. (1994). Latino cultural values: Their role in adjustment to disability. *Journal of Social Behavior and Personality, 9,* 185–200.

Part IV

Professional Issues

29

Medicare and Prospective Payment Systems

Kristofer J. Hagglund, Donald G. Kewman, and Glenn S. Ashkanazi

Payment systems for rehabilitation health care services are undergoing a revolution that directly affects rehabilitation hospitals, skilled-nursing facilities (SNFs) and nursing homes, and home health care agencies. During the previous 18 years, these rehabilitation facilities received payment for treating Medicare patients in a formula loosely based on the costs of providing the services. Insurance companies also generally followed this payment model for their patients, although they often negotiated discounts. With the Balanced Budget Act of 1997 (P. L. 105-33) and the subsequent refinement (P. L. 106-113), payment for services to Medicare patients are "prospective." That is, rehabilitation facilities will be paid a lump sum for each patient, and it will be up to the facility to control costs. This shift in payment method is likely to be a watershed event for rehabilitation health care.

The shift in payment indirectly but powerfully affects health care providers, including psychologists. We summarize the recent and anticipated changes in payment systems, with an emphasis on the changes instituted for Medicare. We also discuss the potential effects on psychologists and other health care providers and offer recommendations for continued clinical participation in rehabilitation health care.

Medicare

Medicare is the federally directed social insurance program for elderly people and people with disabilities and is the largest public purchaser of health care services in the United States. As of 1995, approximately 12% of Medicare beneficiaries (14.4 million people) had a disability and were younger than age 65 (Davis & O'Brien, 1996). These beneficiaries, combined with the large population of people older than age 65 requiring rehabilitation, make Medicare a frequent payer for rehabilitation services.

We thank Steve Riggert for his helpful critique of a draft of this chapter.

In fact, approximately 70% of admissions to rehabilitation hospitals and rehabilitation units are Medicare patients (Aitchisin, 1999). Eligible health care services are paid for under Medicare's two systems, Part A and Part B. Part A covers inpatient hospitalization, SNF care, home health care, and hospice as well as outpatient physical therapy, occupational therapy, and speech pathology delivered in some settings. Part B, the optional Supplemental Medical Insurance, pays for the costs of physician and psychological services and other services such as durable medical equipment, laboratory tests, medical supplies, and outpatient rehabilitation therapies delivered in some nonhospital settings (Health Care Financing Administration [HCFA], 1998b).

In 1996, Medicare financed $203.1 billion in health care services, an increase of 8.1% over the previous year. In fact, Medicare expenditure growth has outpaced growth in other public programs and the private sector for several consecutive years. This growth rate has significant ramifications for future generations. Most people assume that when Medicare recipients were wage earners, sufficient funds were deducted from their wages to pay for their current Medicare benefits. Contrary to this popular belief, Medicare Part A expenditures are derived from mandatory 1.45% payroll deduction from current wage earners and an identical amount paid by employers (Rovner, 1995). As health care costs rise and the eligible Medicare population grows, Medicare Part A grows increasingly closer to financial insolvency. This situation has triggered action by HCFA and Congress to slow Medicare costs, especially those in Part A. Legislation has been passed that limits payment to providers, and increased fraud and abuse detection activities have been initiated. Combined with a short-term dip in the Medicare population and slowing health care service prices, these efforts have contributed to a slight downturn in Medicare expenditures growth (Levit, Lazenby, & Braden, 1998). Moreover, expenditures in the form of capitation payments to managed care organizations (MCOs) have been increasing, reflecting the growth of enrollment of Medicare beneficiaries in managed care systems. These relatively modest federal initiatives are likely only the initial steps in controlling Medicare cost growth; more sweeping legislation may be needed for financial salvage of Medicare Part A.

Prospective payment systems (PPSs) represent the type of sweeping legislative change designed to guarantee reduced financial outlays. PPSs have proven to be moderately successful when applied to acute care hospitals. The principal effect on rehabilitation is a slowing of the rate of new facilities opening and possibly a reduction in SNFs, home health agencies, and rehabilitation hospitals.

History of Payment Systems

Rehabilitation medicine has experienced unparalleled growth over several decades. For example, between 1965 and 1993, the number of freestanding rehabilitation hospitals increased from 68 to 195 (Frederickson & Cannon, 1995). Between 1990 and 1993, federal payments for rehabilitation therapies across all settings increased 167%, to $10.4 billion (Shriver, 1996). Several factors have contributed to this explosive growth, including advances in medical technology and clinical practice that have increased the number of people surviving traumatic injuries (Buchanan, Rumpel, & Hoenig, 1996). Perhaps the most powerful factor, however, has been the favorable reimbursement for rehabilitation services (Buchanan et al., 1996). The steady stream of reimbursement for inpatient services was augmented by rehabilitation's exemption from Medicare's diagnosis-related groups (DRGs) form of PPS that was applied to acute hospitals in 1983. Prior to that, hospitals had been reimbursed under a fee-for-service system—the more care patients received, the more a facility was reimbursed. In the DRG payment method, diagnoses and procedures are organized into payment groups. An acute care hospital receives a single lump sum payment for an individual's inpatient stay based on the grouping assigned from information abstracted from medical records. In other words, a hospital treating a patient with an uncomplicated myocardial infarction is reimbursed a designated amount irrespective of how long the person is in the hospital and, to some extent, the amount of services provided.

The shift to a DRG-based PPS for Medicare was a watershed event for health care in the United States (Frank, 1999). This switch by the federal government to lump sum "payments" for specific episodes of care for a specific diagnosis fueled conversion to prepaid–capitated health care purchasing, such as health maintenance organizations in the private sector. Rehabilitation and psychiatric services were exempted from PPS under the Tax Equity and Fiscal Responsibility Act (TEFRA) of 1982 (P. L. 97-248) because of the variability in rehabilitation patients' clinical needs, making cost projections for these patients unreliable. TEFRA protected the rehabilitation industry and its patients from financial distortions that would likely have developed had DRGs been applied to rehabilitation in 1982. The unexpected consequence of this protection, however, was the explosive growth in rehabilitation. With the PPSs title in the Balanced Budget Act of 1997, Congress essentially stated that Medicare would not continue to financially support this rate of growth. A field that was previously "psychology's greatest opportunity" (Frank, Gluck, & Buckelew, 1990, p. 757) may now be one of its greatest challenges.

Under TEFRA, rehabilitation and psychiatric facilities were reimbursed on a cost-based formula. Each facility seeks to establish a "not-to-exceed" case rate on the basis of its cost per Medicare patient discharge during the first 2 years of operation. This method created incentives for new hospitals to maximize their costs for the period when their base rate was established to maximize later payments (testimony of B. Wynn, 1997). During the base-rate setting period, facilities would maximize qualifying services to patients and complete capital improvement projects. Subsequent to the establishment of the case rate, rehabilitation facilities received their case-rate plus incentives payments if their costs remained under their established rate. Therefore, facilities were enticed to discontinue "extra" services that were provided when the base rate was being established to lower costs and enhance profits. This aspect of the TEFRA reimbursement method also contributed to reductions in lengths of stay

and increased numbers of discharges to other settings in order for rehabilitation hospitals and units to avoid surpassing their TEFRA limit
(Wynn, 1997). In the TEFRA cost-based reimbursement system, facilities
received the same level of reimbursement for each day of service for all
patients, irrespective of the level of care needed by the individual or provided by the facility. This resulted in a perverse incentive for facilities to
refuse to accept "sicker" patients and to offer fewer services to patients
they do accept.

TEFRA payment methods have not served HCFA well in holding the
line on total costs to all Medicare providers. Between 1991 and 1996,
growth in Medicare payments per discharge increased 22% for acute hospital patients and 11% for acute rehabilitation hospital inpatients. However, payments per discharge for home health care increased 84% and
132% for SNFs (Balsano, 1998). These increases in per discharge costs
were partly due to increasingly earlier discharges from rehabilitation facilities. Aggregate Medicare payments to freestanding home health care
increased 219%, to $13.6 billion between 1991 and 1996. Similarly, aggre-
gate payments to freestanding nursing homes increased 334%, to $8.9 bil-
lion during the same time period (HCFA, 1998a).

Implementation of PPS represents a significant step toward controlling future cost growth. PPS is capable of reducing financial distortions in
clinical care decisions by adjusting payments according to the patient's
rehabilitation needs and level of services provided. Theoretically, this better aligns payment incentives with actual levels of care (Fries et al., 1994).

A PPS was initially instituted in 1998 for SNFs—nursing homes,
hospital-affiliated skilled nursing units, and similar facilities where patients require skilled nursing care but no daily interventions by physicians. PPSs are scheduled to be implemented for home health agencies on
October 1, 2000. *Home health agencies* are companies that provide therapeutic services in patients' homes. Inpatient rehabilitation hospitals and
rehabilitation units within hospitals are also scheduled to begin receiving
PPS reimbursement beginning October 1, 2000, although there have been
indications that this time line may not be followed (Olsen, 1998). Rehabilitation patients have complex medical problems, and associated costs
are not as predictable as people with other conditions; the range of costs
is substantial. Therefore, HCFA is challenged to develop a reimbursement
system that accounts for this variability and pays providers accurately. To
help alleviate any unanticipated negative financial impact on rehabilitation facilities, a transition in payment method was planned that phases
in the financial impact on facilities over a 2-year period.

Prospective Payment Systems

During the initial federal deliberations of PPSs in the fall of 1997, long-
term care industry representatives lobbied for a fixed, case-rate payment
method for approximately 100 functionally related groups (FRGs). However, HCFA voiced its desire to develop a payment method that disre-

garded the site of care and to avoid using a patient evaluation system with intellectual property rights (DeJong & Sutton, 1998; discussed in more detail later in the chapter). This spawned the multistate Nursing Home Case-Mix and Quality (NHCMQ) Demonstration Project in Kansas, Maine, Mississippi, New York, South Dakota, and Texas for the Medicare Part A SNF program. In addition to developing the tools necessary to create a payment system based on patients' needs, the NHCMQ also attempted to define longitudinal quality outcome measures that could be linked to payment incentives. Out of the NHCMQ came the classification system (resource utilization groups; RUGs), the Minimum Data Set (MDS) assessment tool, and 30 quality indicators. When the Congress passed the Balanced Budget Act of 1997, it mandated the implementation of a prospective case-mix system for Medicare Part A SNF care, which began in 1998. The system uses the RUGs classification system and a version of the MDS as the classification tool. The RUGs method for SNFs identifies resources associated with a patient's care and establishes a per diem payment for that level of resource utilization. RUGs are only indirectly related to diagnoses. The 44 mutually exclusive RUGs are divided into 7 major categories (listed here in order of intensity): (a) rehabilitation, (b) extensive care services, (c) special care, (d) clinically complex, (e) impaired cognition, (f) behavior problems, and (g) physical functions reduced.

The rehabilitation category features five subcategories (ultrahigh, very high, high, medium, and low). Designation is determined by number of minutes of therapy provided, activities of daily living (ADL) index score on the MDS, and number of disciplines involved. Although the facility must score the patient for all of the areas of ADL listed on the MDS, only the scores for bed mobility, transfer, eating, and toileting are used to determine the RUG. Patients who are assigned to any of the top 26 RUGs (i.e., all rehabilitation, extensive care services, special care, and clinically complex care patients) are automatically deemed eligible for a skilled level of care. Patients assigned to any of the bottom 18 RUGs (i.e., impaired cognition, behavior problems, and physical functions reduced) are not automatically classified as meeting a skilled-nursing level of care.

Periodic assessments using the MDS determine into which classification group a patient falls and, hence, the SNF's reimbursement rate for that time period. Facilities send the completed MDS assessments to designated state agencies, which review them for quality control and then forward them to HCFA. This system has resulted in marked reductions in reimbursement and, consequently, layoffs of rehabilitation personnel such as occupational therapists and physical therapists working in these facilities. This financial crisis also caused stock prices of publically traded SNF companies to plummet, and one major company has declared bankruptcy (Vencor, Incorporated, 2000).

Evaluation and Classification System

Based on concerns that a similar system could cause financial ruin for rehabilitation hospitals, organizations representing rehabilitation facilities advocated for an alternative system. The advocacy efforts cited the approximately 90% of rehabilitation facilities that used the Functional Independence Measure (FIM; Stineman et al., 1996) to assess patients' functional abilities and to implement an effective plan for clinical rehabilitative services. Moreover, the rehabilitation industry has noted that HCFA had already commissioned the RAND Corporation to construct a classification system. The rehabilitation industry stated explicitly that the MDS–RUG system does not accurately classify patients and leads to both severe financial losses to facilities and to facilities not admitting patients with the most severe conditions. After receiving support from Rep. William Thomas (R-CA), HCFA agreed to develop a PPS that uses the FIM to create FRGs for rehabilitation hospitals and units (American Medical Rehabilitation Providers Association, 1999). Analyses of the FIM suggest that it is psychometrically sound and that the FIM–FRG system could accurately classify patients (who vary by type and severity of injury) for a PPS (Stineman et al., 1994; Stineman et al., 1996). HCFA plans to use the MDS, however, to collect data for the development of treatment planning protocols and as a possible quality indicator.

Another critical element in the PPS is the decision to pay facilities on a per discharge basis instead of a per diem basis. A per diem payment would potentially provide a financial incentive for facilities to extend patients' stays in the rehabilitation unit. In the face of decreasing lengths of stay over the previous decade, some rehabilitation professionals, including rehabilitation psychologists, favor this type of reimbursement because they believe that the current average lengths of stay are not adequate to prepare patients to return to their homes and communities safely and effectively. Available evidence suggests that some groups of patients are being discharged to nursing homes at a higher rate with shortened lengths of stay (National Spinal Cord Injury Statistical Center, 1998). Concerns about per diem payments, however, are that hospitals may extend lengths of stay but provide only the minimally required therapies instead of the types and amounts of therapies required for a more efficient stay, resulting in greater costs to Medicare. Undoubtedly, this would lead to further restructuring of the system and negative consequences for rehabilitation facilities, providers, and patients (Aitchisin, 1999). HCFA has stated its intention to implement the PPS for rehabilitation hospitals using a per discharge payment method. HCFA believes that this type of reimbursement is more consistent with the rationale underlying prospective payment and encourages efficiency. The potential drawback for patients is that rehabilitation facilities are motivated to collect the lump sum payment and increase profits by discharging patients earlier than what may be in their best interests. HCFA stated its intention to use the PPS to eliminate financial incentives that distort the timing and appropriateness of acute and rehabilitative medical care for patients, perhaps by a transfer rule for rehabilitation facilities. Ultimately, HCFA would like to see a "seamless continuum" of care, where patients receive the most efficient care in the least restrictive setting.

Transfer Rule

HCFA developed a "transfer rule" because of its concern that acute care hospitals were collecting their DRG payments for patients and discharging them too quickly to postacute care facilities (e.g., SNFs, rehabilitation hospitals). Under a transfer rule, acute care hospitals would be reimbursed less for discharging patients with specific diagnoses to postacute care settings prior to the average length of stay for certain DRGs. HCFA's intent with a rule of this sort is to reduce the incentive to discharge patients prematurely to other settings, especially those that are reimbursed under TEFRA or owned by the hospital or health system. With the implementation of a transfer rule, lengths of stay in acute care hospitals may increase. If true, patients may likely be at a higher level of functioning at discharge, thus requiring less postacute care. Some patients may be able to bypass inpatient rehabilitation as they improve enough in the acute care setting to be discharged home. Congressional opposition to the implementation of a transfer rule has been building in response to lobbying and advocacy by provider groups and rehabilitation facilities.

Interestingly, increasing lengths of stay are contrary to the fundamental discharge strategy adopted by acute care hospitals on the implementation of the DRG reimbursement method. For hospitals within an integrated delivery system (e.g., an acute care hospital that offers rehabilitation; i.e., linked health care services to avoid a disruption in care), the question is "Does the system gain more than it loses by transferring the patient before the geometric mean length of stay?"

Skilled Nursing Facilities' Response

The response to the implementation of PPS for SNFs has been mixed. The Office of the Inspector General (OIG) for the U.S. Department of Health and Human Services (DHHS, 1999a) concluded in a preliminary report on PPS for SNFs that there is no direct evidence that Medicare patients are not receiving the care that they require. The OIG report acknowledges that transferring the most complex patients (e.g., those who require ventilator support) to SNFs was more difficult for rehabilitation facilities but that most patients were easier to place in SNFs under the PPS system. The OIG also noted in similar reports that its audit of SNF bills found substantial errors, accounting for over $1 billion for fiscal year 1998. These errors included "markups," where services were provided by nonlicensed assistants or technicians, but were billed as if provided by a licensed therapist (DHHS, 1999b).

The SNF and nursing home industry has claimed that PPS and its transition payment system is not reimbursomg facilities for the costs of care for patients with Medicare. Other experts point to a reduction in the number of individuals using nursing home care (Bishop, 1999) and growth in alternatives to nursing home care, such as community-assisted living (Fubini, 1999), as a reason for the distress in this industry. Further analyses are needed to disentangle the various factors leading to the financial distress in the skilled-nursing industry and to determine whether consumers' needs are being met (Bishop, 1999).

The Horizon for Rehabilitation

With the Balanced Budget Act of 1997 and subsequent refinements, the federal government fired the PPS shot over the bow of rehabilitation. The DRG PPS for acute hospitals and rehabilitation's exemption under TEFRA contributed to a substantially increased volume in patients admitted to rehabilitation facilities; often these patients were transferred "sicker and quicker." These factors fueled the rapid proliferation of rehabilitation facilities and the growth of for-profit rehabilitation corporations. HCFA believes that the growth in rehabilitation hospitals, SNFs, and home health agencies has contributed to the rapid increases in overall expenditures. HCFA sees the PPS as a method to slow this growth and to ensure that patients are more likely to be receiving care in the most appropriate setting (Wynn, 1997). In her testimony to the Subcommittee on Health of the House Committee on Ways and Means, Barbara Wynn of HCFA described the administration's desire to create an "integrated post-acute payment system" that was "site neutral." HCFA would like to remove incentives that maximize reimbursement at the expense of patient care. "Our long-term goal is to create a beneficiary-centered system of post-acute services that promotes quality of care, access to care, and continuity of care while adequately controlling costs" (Wynn, 1997, p. 5). The current PPS payment models are an effort to unify the reimbursement structure across different kinds of facilities. This may well be an interim step toward bundling payment for all postacute services similar to what has been done for acute services under the DRG system.

Implications

The most problematic implication for quality of care for rehabilitation patients under the new PPS is the incentive to reduce services that do not qualify for payment. If services such as psychology or recreation therapy are not acounted for when determining patients' classification or payment group, hospital administrators may begin to view such services as expendable. Even those hospitals with directors who place a high priority on providing high-quality comprehensive rehabilitation will find it hard to justify maintaining rehabilitation services beyond nursing, physical, occupational, and speech and language therapy. Rehabilitation hospitals may abandon accreditation if the criteria require them to provide services for which there is no payment. These decisions may be influenced by payer mix, market strength, and (potentially) quality indicator reports. Rehabilitation facilities with a high percentage of Medicare reimbursement will be motivated to provide only "qualifying services," especially if they have good market strength. Conversely, facilities with a lower percentage of Medicare patients but a higher percentage of patients with private insurance may find it beneficial to provide additional services, such as recreation therapy, to be able to market a "value-added" product. This is most likely in a highly competitive market.

A related concern is the use of less trained personnel providing multiple kinds of therapeutic services ("multiskilling") under the guidance of professional personnel. A PPS may create incentives for rehabilitation facilities to deliver care with the use of multiple assistants under the supervision of licensed professionals. There are few guidelines for the appropriate ratio of assistants to professionals for such services. In theory, many assistants could work in a therapeutic setting under the supervision of one physical, occupational, or speech therapist or nurse, who may have only minimal direct contact with the patients. There will also be strong incentives to treat patients in groups to decrease costs by reducing the number of providers needed to deliver care.

The implications for psychology are less clear. At the least, facilities that include psychology services as part of their Medicare Part A daily charge will begin to bill for these services as professional charges under Medicare Part B. Psychological services that can be billed as professional services under Medicare Part B will enhance revenue beyond what the facility can collect under Part A. The implications are especially dire for psychological or neuropsychological technicians, master's-level trained psychologists, or social workers because of their inability to bill separately under Medicare Part B. Moreover, the current trend for social workers to become "case managers" and provide less counseling to patients and families is likely to accelerate.

Rehabilitation PPS may create opportunities for psychologists. If initial patient evaluations by occupational therapists, physical therapists, and speech and language therapists are not credited toward therapy hours (which is currently the case for SNFs under their PPS), psychology evaluations that can be billed under Medicare Part B may become more sought after for team planning and treatment. For example, psychologists may position themselves to take on more cognitive, speech, and related evaluations and to provide recommendations for the treatment team. Efficiencies are maximized when psychologists complete the evaluations, freeing the therapists to conduct interventions that count toward higher reimbursement levels for facilities. Psychologists may take on the roles of evaluators and treatment team supervisors. In addition, as PPS is implemented for rehabilitation, facilities will work to develop the most efficient treatment protocols possible. Psychologists should continue to be involved in developing clinical practice guidelines and critical pathways because their role may be critical to efficient treatment. One possible method for obtaining a PPS patient classification that accurately predicts cost is to combine measurements of patient care time by staff (especially nurses) from the MDS with the FIM. The use of these measures when combined with other data from the MDS, such as medical complications, mental and behavioral status, and diagnoses, may provide the most accurate prediction of costs.

A PPS using the FIM–FRG allows for outcome evaluations across rehabilitation facilities for Medicare patients because costs are known. Whether and how such analyses will be conducted or the results distributed are unknown. Rehabilitation facilities could benefit or suffer from market forces based on their results from the outcomes evaluations. Establishing the reliability and validity of such evaluations will be critical to their successful application to outcomes evaluation. If the evaluations are psychometrically sound, analyses of costs as related to the effectiveness of outcome in rehabilitation may be more easily examined using such a system. If the evaluations are combined with patient satisfaction data, rehabilitation facilities would have powerful tools for developing effective and efficient services and for marketing. Psychological services may become part of a "value-added" package of services available at "aggressive" rehabilitation facilities. Furthermore, psychologists have the evaluation and research skills to substantially contribute to and lead these types of clinical outcome research efforts.

Increasing numbers of Medicare recipients are moving into managed care arrangements. The degree to which MCOs will adopt a PPS form of reimbursement is not clear, and therefore the degree to which a PPS system will affect how facilities operate is uncertain. Private insurers are expected to follow Medicare's lead in prospective payment, however. For the first time, Medicare's payment system for a rehabilitation service is aligned with the methods and goals of managed care systems. MCOs will watch these developments closely and adopt the most cost-efficient aspects of a Medicare PPS. As DeJong (1997) pointed out, the sweeping changes induced by PPS in rehabilitation demand a restructuring of traditional rehabilitation. Rehabilitation institutions and providers need to develop systems to deliver comprehensive services under capitated, full-risk payment systems. Psychologists have a good understanding of the long-term needs and costs of people with disabilities. This knowledge may prove vital as new payment systems evolve. A PPS for rehabilitation patients is one step toward a unified payment system across all types of settings for measuring postacute patient needs. In addition, HCFA is studying other indicators for determining quality of care across settings.

Future payment systems may bring about a bundled payment. That is, a rehabilitation or postacute system may be paid one sum for providing all of a patient's postacute care, including inpatient and outpatient rehabilitation, home care, and SNF services. When full-risk payment systems are implemented for the continuum of rehabilitation, community-based programs emphasizing prevention and health promotion will be integral to patients' long-term success and to cost control (DeJong, 1997). Most rehabilitation providers are poised to move toward alternative rehabilitation settings, such as subacute, outpatient, and home care, if there are opportunities for growth (DeJong, 1997). Psychologists' ability to join forces with hospital administrators and payers to develop high-quality, cost-efficient services has yet to be determined. Success depends on psychologists facilitating the development of and participating in integrated health delivery systems (Frank, 1999).

References

Aitchisin, K. (1999). An update on rehab PPS. *American Medical Rehabilitation Providers Association Magazine, 2*(2), 24–27.

American Medical Rehabilitation Providers Association. (1999). *PPS-15*. Retrieved on March 8, 2000, from the World Wide Web http://ampra.firminc.com/pps-15.htm

Balanced Budget Act of 1997, P. L. 105-33, 111 Stat. 251.

Balanced Budget Refinement Act of 1999, P. L. 106-113, 113 Stat. 1501.

Balsano, A. (1998, February). *Financial implications of Medicare reform for hospitals and freestanding skilled nursing facilities.* Paper presented at the Executive Summit on the New Perspective Payment Systems for Skilled Nursing Facilities and Subacute Care, Orlando, FL.

Bishop, C. E. (1999). Where are the missing elders? The decline in nursing home use, 1985 and 1995. *Health Affairs, 18*(4), 146–155.

Buchanan, J. L., Rumpel, J. D., & Hoenig, H. (1996). Changes for outpatient rehabilitation: Growth and differences in provider types. *Archives of Physical Medicine and Rehabilitation, 77,* 320–328.

Davis, M. H., & O'Brien, E. (1996). Profile of persons with disabilities in Medicare and Medicaid. *Health Care Financing Review, 17*(4), 179–211.

DeJong, G. (1997). Primary care for persons with disabilities. *American Journal of Physical Medicine and Rehabilitation, 76*(3, Suppl.), 52–58.

DeJong, G., & Sutton, J. P. (1998). HCFA proposes RUGs as basis for rehabilitation prospective payment system. *Rehabilitation Outlook, 3*(2), 1, 7.

Frank, R. G. (1999). Rehabilitation psychology: We zigged when we should have zagged. *Rehabilitation Psychology, 44*(1), 36–51.

Frank, R. G., Gluck, J. P., & Buckelew, S. P. (1990). Rehabilitation: Psychology's greatest opportunity? *American Psychologist, 45,* 757–761.

Frederickson, M., & Cannon, N. L. (1995). The role of the rehabilitation physician in the postacute continuum. *Archives of Physical Medicine and Rehabilitation, 76*(Suppl.), sc5–sc9.

Fries, B. E., Schneider, D. P., Foley, W. J., Gavazzi, M., Burke, R., & Cornelius, E. (1994). Refining a case-mix for nursing homes: Resource utilization groups (RUG-III). *Medical Care, 32,* 668–685.

Fubini, S. (1999). Are nursing homes becoming dinosaurs? *Healthcare Trends Reports, 13*(8), 1–2, 15–16.

Health Care Financing Administration. (1998a). *National health expenditures by type of service and source of funds: Calendar years 1960–1996.* Washington, DC: Author. Retreived February 26, 2000 from the World Wide Web http://www.hcfa.gov/stats/nhe-oact/tables/nhe96.txt

Health Care Financing Administration (1998b). *Overview of the Medicare program.* Washington, DC: Author. Retreived February 25, 2000 from the World Wide Web http://www.hcfa.gov/Medicare.careover.htm

Levit, K. R., Lazenby, H. C., & Braden, B. R. (1998). National health spending trends in 1996. *Health Affairs, 17*(1), 35–51.

National Spinal Cord Injury Statistical Center. (1998). *Annual report for the model spinal cord injury care systems.* Birmingham, AL: Author.

Olsen, G. G. (1998, August/September). 42K's impact on Medicare. *Rehabilitation Management,* pp. 93–94.

On rehabilitation and long-term care hospital payments: Bureau of Policy Development, Health Care Financing Administration, House Committee on Ways and Means, Subcommittee on Health, 105th Cong., 1st Sess. (1997). (testimony of B. Wynn).

Rovner, J. (1995). Congress's "catastrophic" attempt to fix Medicare. In T. E. Mann & N. J. Ornstein (Eds.), *Intensive care: How Congress shapes health policy* (pp. 145–178). Washington, DC: American Enterprise Institute and the Brookings Institution.

Shriver, K. (1996). Rehabilitation providers fight HCFA data. *Modern Health Care, 26*(10), 130–132.

Stineman, M. G., Escarce, J. E., Goin, J. E., Hamilton, B. B., Granger, C. V., & Williams, S. V. (1994). A case-mix classification system for medical rehabilitation. *Medical Care, 32,* 366–379.

Stineman, M. G., Shea, J. A., Jette, A., Tassoni, C. J., Ottenbacher, K. J., Fiedler, R., & Granger, C. V. (1996). The Functional Independence Measure: Tests of scaling assumptions, structure, and reliability across 20 diverse impairment categories. *Archives of Physical Medicine and Rehabilitation, 77,* 1101–1108.

Tax Equity and Fiscal Responsibility Act of 1982, P. L. 92-248, 96 Stat. 324.

U.S. Department of Health and Human Services. (1999a). *Early effects of the prospective payment system on access to skilled nursing facilities* (Office of the Inspector General Publ. No. OEI-02-99-00400). New York: Author.

U.S. Department of Health and Human Services. (1999b). *Physical and occupational therapy in nursing homes: Cost of improper billings to Medicare* (office of the Inspector General No. OEI-09-97-00122). San Francisco: Author.

Vencor, Incorporated. (2000). *Vencor, Inc. files for chapter 11 protection; $100 million debter in possession financing secured; normal operations to continue in all facilities* [Press release]. Louisville, KY: Author. Retrieved February 18, 2000 from the World Wide Web http://www.vencor.com/press/prhtml/pr091399.asp

30

Doctoral Education in Rehabilitation and Health Care Psychology: Principles and Strategies for Unifying Subspecialty Training

Robert L. Glueckauf

One of the greatest challenges facing rehabilitation psychology today is ensuring the viability and marketability of doctoral training in the discipline. The marketplace for psychological services in rehabilitation and health care settings has undergone rapid transformation in the past decade. Third-party payers now expect psychologists to provide services that are brief, cost effective, and beneficial, regardless of the complexity of the presenting problems and the need for follow-up intervention. Intensive psychological assessment procedures that were standard 5–10 years ago (e.g., fixed neuropsychological and vocational assessment batteries) are no longer supported in the current health reform climate (Benton, 1992; Bond & Dietzen, 1993; Faust, 1993). Time available for case consultation with staff members and graduate trainees has dwindled. The pressure to engage in activities that "pay" comes from all sides.

Ironically, these developments have come at a time of remarkable growth of specialty programs in health care psychology, including clinical neuropsychology, pediatric psychology, health psychology, and rehabilitation psychology (Johnstone et al., 1995). Psychology departments are now faced with the daunting task of preparing increasing numbers of psychology doctoral students for a health care marketplace with, at best, uncertain economic opportunity and (at worst) increasing levels of unemployment (Frank & Johnstone, 1996).

Rehabilitation psychologists must confront this challenge directly; this requires taking a hard look at our vision for rehabilitation psychology and educational mission. Do we have a common philosophy to impart to our doctoral students? Are we adequately preparing them for the diverse and multiple roles within the health care marketplace? Are we imparting the

I thank Tim Elliott and Jordanna Glueckauf for their comments and suggestions on earlier drafts of this chapter.

skills and attitudes that future rehabilitation psychologists need to ensure their survival and well-being in the workplace?

In the first part of this chapter, I provide an overview of doctoral training in rehabilitation psychology and highlight current controversies in the field. I then focus on the need for a unified vision across health-oriented doctoral training programs. I describe why a unified approach is needed in training doctoral students for work in rehabilitation and health settings and outline the basic philosophical underpinnings of this unified vision. In the second part of the chapter, I offer specific strategies for increasing the viability and utility of doctoral training in rehabilitation and health-oriented psychology programs. Finally, I propose a plan for encouraging the adoption of a common set of philosophical principles, goals, and educational standards among health care psychology's specialty programs.

Doctoral Training

Most psychologists working in rehabilitation settings today have taken limited or no formal predoctoral course work and practicum training in rehabilitation psychology. As a rule, doctoral programs have not offered rehabilitation psychology courses (e.g., medical and psychosocial aspects of disability, vocational evaluation) and practicum training experiences (e.g., working on a stroke rehabilitation unit). Although this trend has changed over the past few years (because of the growing interest in aging, health promotion, and chronic illness), still only a minority of psychology doctoral students obtain comprehensive training in rehabilitation psychology. Current course offerings in clinical and counseling graduate programs may include one or two specialty courses in geropsychology, health psychology, neuropsychology, or rehabilitation psychology.

Parker and Chan's (1990) survey of psychology service directors in accredited rehabilitation hospitals and specialized settings highlights the dominance of broad-based predoctoral preparation in clinical and counseling psychology. They found that 62% of respondents identified clinical psychology as their degree specialty area; an additional 20% identified counseling psychology as their degree specialty. The training of these clinical service directors was generic in nature; most of their rehabilitation knowledge and clinical expertise was acquired through postdoctoral work or on-the-job training. Only 2% of the sample indicated that they were graduates of doctoral rehabilitation psychology specialty programs. The latter differed from clinical or counseling psychologists in at least one major respect: They had decided that rehabilitation issues and practice would be their primary career goal. Furthermore, their graduate education included a variety of courses on the vocational, psychosocial, and legislative aspects of disability, as well as practicum training in rehabilitation settings.

Thus, predoctoral preparation of psychologists in rehabilitation settings typically has been generic in nature, drawing heavily from traditional clinical or counseling psychology assessment and intervention course work and, in some cases, specialty courses in geropsychology, health psychology, neuropsychology, or rehabilitation psychology.

This brings us to a key question: If most doctoral programs in professional psychology offer only limited exposure to rehabilitation, where does the bulk of training occur? Most clinical and counseling psychology students are first exposed to the principles and practice of rehabilitation psychology during the internship year or during formal postdoctoral training. It has become more commonplace for clinical psychology internships approved by the American Psychological Association (APA) to offer rehabilitation rotations on stroke, traumatic brain injury, renal dialysis, and pain management units, particularly those programs located in hospital settings or having consortium arrangements with medical centers. Although the 1-year internship may provide important introductory experiences in rehabilitation assessment and intervention, as well as the multidisciplinary team approach, postdoctoral programs in rehabilitation psychology are the primary locus for systematic and comprehensive training in this subspecialty area (Patterson & Hanson, 1995). Currently 19 postdoctoral programs offer comprehensive training in rehabilitation psychology (Patterson, 1997).

Controversies

Over the past several years, the academic preparation of psychologists for work in rehabilitation settings has been the subject of considerable debate (e.g., Elliott, 1993; Elliott & Gramling, 1990; Elliott & Klapow, 1997; Kelley & Schiro-Geist, 1992; Olshansky & Hart, 1967; Pape & Tarvydas, 1993; Walker, 1992; Wegener, Hagglund & Elliott, 1998). The primary focus of the debate is on the primacy of training in psychological science versus core training in rehabilitation psychology principles, concepts, and functions. Elliott and colleagues (e.g., Elliott & Klapow, 1997; Wegener et al., 1998) have argued that the primary mission of predoctoral training is to provide a rigorous foundation in psychological science, particularly research design, statistics, psychometric theory, learning theories, and psychotherapeutic intervention. Their position is consistent with the basic tenets of the scientist–practitioner or Boulder model (Raimy, 1950) of professional training, affirming the preeminence of course preparation in the core areas of psychological science (e.g., social–psychological and biological bases of human behavior) and the integration of science and professional practice. Accordingly, specific course work on the psychosocial aspects of disability, vocational rehabilitation, and the Americans With Disability Act (ADA) of 1990 (P. L. 101-336) legislation as well as rehabilitation practicum experiences represents secondary areas of concentration "best suited for advanced seminars . . . internship and postdoctoral fellowships" (Wegener et al., 1998, p. 21). Elliott and colleagues have asserted that rehabilitation psychologists whose training is firmly rooted in psychological science and applied research methods have the best chance of positively influencing the quality of life of people with disabilities.

In contrast, Pape and Tarvydas (1993) and others (e.g., Kelley & Schiro-Geist, 1992; Walker, 1992) have questioned the adequacy of the traditional Boulder model in preparing rehabilitation psychologists to provide services to consumers in the ADA era. Of particular concern is the failure of most clinical and counseling psychology doctoral programs to recognize the paradigm shift created by the ADA. As Pape and Tarvydas suggested, psychology graduate training programs continue to perpetuate the view that "disability is a problem located within the individual" rather than interpreting "the problem as located within the social political environment in which the person with the disability is embedded" (p. 118). This paradigm clash (i.e., the traditional clinical vs. the minority group model of disability) forms the basis of Pape, Tarvydas, and others' (see above) argument for the primacy of course work in rehabilitation principles and practice. Following their line of thinking, the optimal preparation of rehabilitation psychologists is through doctoral course work and practicum experiences that emphasize the perspectives, functional capacities, and legislative rights of people with disabilities. They argued that training in psychological science is important to the extent that it promotes the larger interests of individuals with disabilities. Course work in research design and methodology is considered essential but should be linked to the needs and priorities of people with disabilities.

Reformulation of Controversy and the Need for a Broader Vision

Although the generic scientist–practitioner and rehabilitation specialty proponents appear to have adopted antithetical positions, they actually have more in common than they do unique differences. Both camps recognize the importance of rehabilitation psychology course work, practicum experiences, and the scientific method. They both are concerned about the role of psychologists in advocating for social change. The primary differences lie in the timing of rehabilitation course work and in the inculcation of the minority group perspective into the fabric of doctoral education. Thus, the current controversy is one of emphasis and concentration rather than of severely contrasting philosophies and training methods.

Although debate about the merits of different training models helps sharpen thinking about rehabilitation education, it is my contention that we can no longer afford to dwell on single, subspecialty controversies. The recent wave of managed care has altered the landscape of psychological practice for a wide range of health-related subspecialties, such as rehabilitation psychology, clinical neuropsychology, health psychology, pediatric psychology, and clinical geropsychology. This revolution has forced psychologists across all health-related subspecialties to rethink their assumptions about the viability of current models of professional practice, health care research, and doctoral education and training (Glueckauf, Frank, Bond, & McGrew, 1996; Johnstone et al., 1995). The livelihood of health care psychology practitioners, researchers, and educators and the future of the profession are at stake.

Thus, one of the most daunting tasks facing psychologists in rehabilitation and health settings today is the need for unification on critical issues of workforce oversupply, access to psychology services, outcomes evaluation, and education and training. Ironically, the need for unified action comes at a time of remarkable growth of specialization in health care psychology (Frank, Gluck, & Buckelew, 1990; Frank & Ross, 1995). This is particularly evident by the rapid expansion of pre- and postdoctoral training programs in rehabilitation psychology, health psychology, clinical neuropsychology, geropsychology, and pediatric psychology. Although these subspecialty programs share a common core curriculum, similar practicum training methods, and common research interests, to date they generally have behaved as if they were separate entities (Johnstone et al., 1995, pp. 352–354).

Before articulating the need for a unified training curriculum across subspecialty areas, I define the terms health care psychology and health care psychologist. *Health care psychology*, a term originally coined by Ronald Fox (1986), refers to the domain of professional psychology whose ultimate goal is to provide high-quality and effective preventive, health-promoting, and rehabilitative services. Treatment involves both the individual as well as the family and community support systems with whom he or she interacts. Health care psychologists' knowledge base and practice methods are grounded in psychological science, and many of their intervention strategies have been empirically validated.

Health care psychologists provide a "broad array of services to children and adults with acute and chronic medical conditions, such as neuropsychological and functional assessments, health promotion and intervention strategies, independent living and vocational consultations" (McGrew, Glueckauf, Bond, & Frank, 1996, p. 3). Currently, within the framework of APA, health care psychology is represented by (but is not limited to) Divisions 38 (Health Psychology), 40 (Clinical Neuropsychology), 22 (Rehabilitation Psychology), 54 (Pediatric Psychology), and 12-2 (Clinical Geropsychology). As noted, training programs in these areas are typically sections of or concentration areas within overarching clinical or counseling psychology doctoral programs (Elliott & Gramling, 1990).

Why Is a Unified Vision Needed?

DiCowden, Crosson, and McSweeny (1996) delineated the consequences of the failure to find common ground among health care psychology specialties; they noted that "we have inadvertently created an identity crisis: we are not able to articulate who we are and our potential clientele often is not able to formulate a clear idea regarding what to expect from our services" (pp. 178–179).

This failure in articulating common goals and aspirations also has had a deleterious effect on practitioners in the field, especially recent graduates. It has deprived them of one of the most powerful buffers against discouragement in tough times, that is, a larger vision of professional role and purpose. This is especially important in light of the high expectations for employment and for high quality-of-work life fostered by proponents of psychology's health specialties during the heyday of the late 1980s. Of course, the failure to articulate a common educational and professional vision is not unique to health care psychology; this dilemma pervades graduate training across a variety of health disciplines. Nonetheless, a set of unifying principles and goals may help guard against disillusionment in times of uncertainty and rapid change.

Fundamental Principles for a Unified Health Care Psychology

The fundamental principles of health care psychology are grounded in the seminal theorizing of Beatrice A. Wright (1972, 1983) and later works, such as the "Report of the National Working Conference on Education and Training in Health Psychology" (Olbrisch, Weiss, Stone, & Schwartz, 1985) and the "Report of the INS–Division 40 Task Force on Education, Accreditation, and Credentialing" (1987).

Principle 1: Client as the Hub of the Wheel

Psychological practice and applied research in health care psychology should serve the interests of people with health concerns and their families. This makes active consultation with expert clients or consumers a prerequisite for intervention and program evaluation efforts (Glueckauf, 1990; Wright, 1983). Assessment and intervention strategies guided by the priorities of expert consumers not only are more likely to be relevant to the needs of the target populations but also are more likely to affect positively clients' daily functioning (Wax, 1993).

This principle directly applies to doctoral research and clinical training. One distinguishing feature of health care psychology is the "humanity of its science" and research products. We do not engage in scientific investigation for science's sake but rather use science as a vehicle for improving the quality of life of people with health concerns and their families.

Principle 1 is the raison d'être of graduate training in health care psychology. It is easy to lose sight of a commitment to the welfare of people with health care problems, particularly in a health care system whose bottom line is cost containment. Nonetheless, the success of the profession and the viability of graduate training are inextricably linked to the public's perception that we sensitively and effectively represent their priorities and interests.

Principle 2: Dynamic Role Orientation

Principle 2 emphasizes the dynamic role orientation of health care psychology. The discipline is rooted in the Lewinian tradition that emphasizes the dynamic interplay among organismic factors, behavior, and the social environment (Lewin, 1935). It is therefore well equipped, theoretically and practically, to adapt to changing role demands and work contexts. Psychologists' roles have changed considerably over the past two decades, beginning with more traditional delivery of frontline, diagnostic, and intervention services in the 1970s and 1980s to contemporary clinical team managers, part-time consultants to nursing homes, and clinical research directors of for-profit medical care companies.

However, most health care psychology doctoral programs continue to prepare students for classical research and service roles in health care settings. Traditional positions in academic psychology programs, medical school research and, more recently, staff psychologist jobs in rehabilitation centers have dwindled, particularly in large metropolitan areas (Johnstone et al., 1995). Furthermore, they may not represent the most optimal roles for health care psychologists, particularly if they plan to exert greater influence on health behaviors at the community and societal levels.

To have maximum impact, health care psychologists must fully embrace the dynamic nature of their discipline and the range of vocational roles that we can effectively assume. Faculty members need to take a more active role in imparting this principle to graduate students, not only in terms of course development, but also by modeling it. They should endeavor to free themselves from their current, narrow conceptualizations as in-house, clinical scientists or medical school clinicians and to pursue options in government policy making, behavioral consultation to extended care facilities, community health program evaluation, and coordinators of rural, telehealth (i.e., information and services using telecommunications, such as the Internet and email) networks.

Principle 3: Research Training Linked to Effective Care

Most health care psychology doctoral programs provide didactic instruction and practice in clinical methods that are grounded in empirical research. The reports of the National Working Conference on Education and Training in Health Psychology (Olbrisch et al., 1985) and that of the INS–Division 40 Task Force on Education, Accreditation, and Credentialing (1987) strongly endorsed the scientist–practitioner model, with its emphasis on the use of empirically based treatments in resolving health problems. Leaders across psychology's health specialties have also asserted that predoctoral preparation should include the acquisition of the "basic science" that underlies health problems.

Although most programs have affirmed the preeminence of the scientific method in guiding clinical practice, training in research on the effectiveness of psychological intervention in routine health care settings and with typical health care providers has not been emphasized. Limited attention also has been given to the cost effectiveness of psychological interventions, as well as instruction in the development and evaluation of clinical practice guidelines, an extension of effectiveness research (Di-Cowden et al., 1996). These research activities are closely linked to the practical health care concerns of the public and third-party payers and thus represent highly valued and marketable competencies for psychology doctoral students.

Research on effectiveness is concerned with whether an intervention will generally improve health and health-related quality of life under everyday circumstances and in typical practice settings. This contrasts with traditional efficacy research that is carried out under ideal circumstances in controlled settings (O'Keeffe, Quittner, & Melamed, 1996; Office of Technology Assessment [OTA], 1994). The findings of cost-effectiveness analyses help determine whether an intervention's combined economic and health value justifies its further use compared with the alternatives (OTA, 1994). Clinical practice guidelines are an extension of effectiveness research because they integrate the findings of existing empirical research and use the informed judgment of specialists where research evidence is either lacking or controversial. They are promising tools to promote cost-effectiveness and appropriate care by a variety of psychological practitioners. In summary, research training in health care psychology should focus on the practical concerns of people with health problems, especially the effectiveness of interventions in routine settings and cost-effectiveness analysis.

Principle 4: Diversity

Changing national demographics have made training in ethnic and cultural diversity a top priority for graduate programs in health care psychology. Compared with the White majority in the United States, ethnic minority groups show disproportionately higher rates of chronic disabilities (e.g., diabetes and stroke) and unemployment (Giordano & D'Alonzo, 1995). The viability of health care psychology may well depend on the ability to effectively address the concerns of this rapidly growing sector of the U.S. population (Johnstone et al., 1995, p. 362).

Psychological practice involving minority populations with health problems introduces many challenges to health care psychology doctoral programs. Suzuki, Meller, and Ponterotto (1996) and Leung (1990) identified three major training needs for serving ethnic populations: (a) increasing students' understanding of behavior and values within diverse ethnic frameworks as well as of similarities among groups; (b) practicing using assessment and intervention procedures that are culturally valid; and (c) training in research methods that includes the frame of reference of ethnic minority clients.

Providing course work and practicum training in cultural diversity is only one facet of the diversity principle. Programs must strive to actively recruit and train psychologists from minority backgrounds. Research on ethnicity and rehabilitation (Douzinas & Carpenter, 1981) suggests that matching backgrounds of therapists and clients improves treatment outcome. Furthermore, such matching may reduce the level of burnout among staff working with clients who have severe disabilities (Salyers, 1996).

It is also critical to increase the number of ethnic minority faculty in health care psychology programs. The hiring of minority psychologists not only provides expert role models for graduate students and contributes to increasing their cultural competencies but also may be a crucial component in retaining minority students (Myers, Echemendia, & Trimble, 1991).

Strategies for Increasing Viability

Within the framework of the four core principles, I propose specific strategies to enhance the viability of graduate training in health care psychology.

Advisory Panel Input

Consistent with the principles of a client focus and diversity, input from a regional advisory board, consisting of expert consumers, community-based psychologists, graduate students, health care administrators, and medical professionals, should be sought in guiding the design of course curricula and practicum training experiences. The skills of this panel should be used in generating a list of issues that health care psychologists currently face and how they might be effectively addressed. These issues and their solutions should be incorporated into the classroom and in practicum training. Recruitment of advisors should show a strong preference for professionals who have successfully addressed the challenges of tailoring services to the needs of people with chronic disabilities and to underserved populations (e.g., minority groups). Furthermore, selection of advisors should be guided by the goal of appropriate representation by individuals from diverse ethnic backgrounds.

Innovative Psychologist Role Models

To foster the development of a dynamic role orientation, programs should integrate community-based psychologists who have carved out innovative clinical and research roles into the fabric of doctoral training. This can be accomplished in three major ways:

1.   Psychologists working in nontraditional health care settings (e.g., hospice centers and nursing homes) should be included in practicum training. Considerable emphasis should be placed on the practical aspects of health care delivery, such as third-party re-

imbursement strategies, quality assurance mechanisms, and strategies for successful multidisciplinary interaction.

2. Community-based health care researchers should be actively recruited to develop research assistantships at both the early apprenticeship and more senior student levels.

3. Health care planners, administrators, and policymakers should be encouraged to serve as supervisors for assistantships in public health. Training should be provided on the nature and organization of the health care system and health policy decision making and on ethical and legal issues in health policy (Olbrisch et al., 1985, p. 1040).

Grant Writing and Cost-Effectiveness Analysis

To ensure the viability of research training in health care psychology, instruction in grant writing, cost-effectiveness analysis, and health outcomes should be strongly emphasized. Grant writing should be incorporated within the course curriculum or within the preliminary exam structure. Training in cost-effectiveness analyses and the development of clinical practice guidelines is critical as well. Cost-offset analysis, a type of cost-effectiveness research, is especially important to psychological practice in health care settings. As Friedman, Sobel, Myers, Caudill, and Benson (1995) have noted, behavioral and psychosocial variables significantly influence the needs and demands for health care services. Recent research shows interventions that directly address these variables reduce demand and, in turn, cost, without compromising clinical outcomes (Caudill, Schnable, Zuttermeister, Benson, & Friedman, 1991; Lorig, Mazonson, & Holman, 1993; Vickery et al., 1983).

Training in the development of clinical practice guidelines is strongly recommended. Clinical practice guidelines are promising tools to enhance quality control and to contain costs. They have become increasingly important to professional societies and government health care agencies (DeLeon, Frank, & Wedding, 1995). The development of guidelines may be a key factor to the broad acceptance of psychological intervention in health care and, potentially, to establishing the importance of doctoral-level providers.

Implementing a Unified Vision

All health care psychologists would agree that ensuring the viability and marketability of doctoral training in the discipline is a top priority. It is my contention that economic viability has its foundation in consensual agreement about mission, standards, and goals. Despite the importance of this issue, doctoral programs in psychology's health care specialties have not developed a common set of guiding principles or a clear course curriculum, nor have they established a set of essential competencies. If health care psychology training programs are to have any leverage on the claim that they are preparing students for diverse scientist–practitioner roles, the movement toward increased specialization and fractionation must be halted.

Fortunately, there now exists a vehicle for developing a unified vision for health care psychology training. In response to the Indianapolis Conference on Psychological Practice in Health Care Settings (Glueckauf, 1993), the Interdivisional Healthcare Committee (IHC) was formed. Leaders across APA's health care divisions are for the first time crafting a common health care psychology agenda. The guiding premise of the IHC is that psychology is a health profession and within psychology, there is a domain of expertise recognized as health care psychology. A number of APA divisions represent this expertise, including (but not limited to) Clinical Geropsychology (Division 12-3), Clinical Neuropsychology (Division 40), Health Psychology (Division 38), Pediatric Psychology (Division 12-5), and Rehabilitation Psychology (Division 22). The IHC was formed to address the professional concerns of psychologists working in health care settings and the evolution of psychology as a health care profession.

One of the key focal points of collaboration is the need for crosscutting doctoral training standards. Over the next 2 years, the IHC is likely to pursue three major doctoral training objectives: (a) the development of a common set of philosophical assumptions about the purpose, educational mission, and goals of doctoral training in health care psychology, (b) the establishment of course requirements across health care psychology subspecialty programs, and (c) the development of a specific set of essential competencies for all health care psychology doctoral students (Glueckauf, 1999).

Conclusion

Doctoral training in health care psychology is currently at a crossroads in its development. We can continue to take the well-trodden path of insularity and "parallel operations" among subspecialty areas, or we can develop a unified philosophy and curriculum to maximize our capacity to achieve important ideals. It is essential for the well-being of new graduates and the viability of the profession that we articulate a unified vision for education and training in health care psychology.

References

Americans With Disabilities Act of 1990, P. L. 101-336, 104 Stat. 327.

Benton, A. (1992). Clinical neuropsychology: 1960–1990. *Journal of Clinical and Experimental Neuropsychology, 14,* 407–417.

Bond, G. R., & Dietzen, L. L. (1993). Predictive validity and vocational assessment: Reframing the question. In R. L. Glueckauf, L. B. Sechrest, G. R. Bond, & E. C. McDonel (Eds.), *Improving assessment in rehabilitation and health* (pp. 61–86). Newbury Park, CA: Sage.

Caudill, M., Schnable, R., Zuttermeister, P., Benson, H., & Friedman, R. (1991). Decreased clinic use by chronic pain patients: Response to behavioral medicine interventions. *Clinical Journal of Pain, 7,* 305–310.

DeLeon, P. H., Frank, R. G., & Wedding, D. (1995). Health psychology and public policy: The political press. *Health Psychology, 14,* 493–499.

DiCowden, M. A., Crosson, B. A., & McSweeny, A. J. (1996). Education and training. In R. L. Glueckauf, R. G. Frank, G. R. Bond, & J. H. McGrew (Eds.), *Psychological practice in a changing health care system: Issues and new directions* (pp. 178–189). New York: Springer.

Douzinas, N., & Carpenter, M. D. (1981). Predicting the community performance of vocational rehabilitation clients. *Hospital and Community Psychiatry, 32,* 409–413.

Elliott, T. (1993). Training psychology students in assessment for rehabilitation settings. In R. L. Glueckauf, L. B. Sechrest, G. R. Bond, & E. C. McDonel (Eds.), *Improving assessment in rehabilitation and health* (pp. 196–211). Newbury Park, CA: Sage.

Elliott, T. R., & Gramling, S. E. (1990). Psychologists and rehabilitation: New roles and old training models. *American Psychologist, 45,* 762–765.

Elliott, T. R., & Klapow, J. C. (1997). Training psychologists for a future in evolving health care delivery systems: Building a better Boulder model. *Journal of Clinical Psychology in Medical Settings, 4,* 255–267.

Faust, D. (1993). The use of traditional neuropsychological tests to describe and prescribe: Why polishing the crystal ball won't help. In R. L. Glueckauf, L. B. Sechrest, G. R. Bond, & E. C. McDonel (Eds.), *Improving assessment in rehabilitation and health* (pp. 87–108). Newbury Park, CA: Sage.

Fox, R. (1986). Professional preparation: Closing the gap between education and practice. In H. Dorken and Associates (Eds.), *Professional psychology in transition* (pp. 121–140). San Francisco: Jossey-Bass.

Frank, R. G., Gluck, J. P., & Buckelew, S. P. (1990). Rehabilitation: Psychology's greatest opportunity? *American Psychologist, 45,* 757–761.

Frank, R. G., & Johnstone, B. (1996). Changes in the health work force: Implications for psychologists. In R. L. Glueckauf, R. G. Frank, G. R. Bond, & J. H. McGrew (Eds.), *Psychological practice in a changing health care system: Issues and new directions* (pp. 39–51). New York: Springer.

Frank, R. G., & Ross, M. J. (1995). The changing workforce: The role of health psychology. *Health Psychology, 14,* 519–525.

Friedman, R., Sobel, D., Myers, P., Caudill, M., & Benson, H. (1995). Behavioral medicine, clinical health psychology, and cost offset. *Health Psychology, 14,* 509–518.

Giordano, G., & D'Alonzo, B. J. (1995). Challenge and progress in rehabilitation: A review of the past 25 years and a preview of the future. *American Rehabilitation, 21*(3), 14–21.

Glueckauf, R. L. (1990). Program evaluation guidelines for the rehabilitation professional. In M. G. Eisenberg & R. Grzesiak (Eds.), *Advances in clinical rehabilitation* (Vol. 3, pp. 250–266). New York: Springer.

Glueckauf, R. L. (1993, Winter). Health care reform and psychological practice in rehabilitation and health care settings. *Rehabilitation Psychology News, 21*(2), 1–3.

Glueckauf, R. L. (1999). Interdivisional Healthcare Committee: Speaking with one voice on crosscutting issues in health care psychology. *Journal of Clinical Psychology in Medical Settings, 6,* 171–181.

Glueckauf, R. L., Frank, R. G., Bond, G. R., & McGrew, J. H. (Eds.). (1996). *Psychological practice in a changing health care system: Issues and new directions.* New York: Springer.

INS–Division 40 Task Force on Education, Accreditation, and Credentialing. (1987). Report of the INS–Division Task Force on Education, Accreditation, and Credentialing. *The Clinical Neuropsychologist, 1,* 29–34.

Johnstone, B., Frank, R. G., Belar, C., Berk, S., Bieliauskas, L. A., Bigler, E. D., Caplan, B., Elliott, T. R., Glueckauf, R. L., Kaplan, R. M., Kreutzer, J. S., Mateer, C. A., Patterson, D., Puente, A. E., Richards, J. S., Rosenthal, M., Sherer, M., Shewchuk, R., Siegel, L. J., & Sweet, J. J. (1995). Psychology is health care: Future directions. *Professional Psychology: Research and Practice, 26,* 341–365.

Kelley, D. G., & Schiro-Geist, C. (1992). An analysis of rehabilitation psychologists trained in clinical, counseling, and rehabilitation psychology doctoral programs: Recommendations for future training. *Rehabilitation Education, 6,* 67–73.

Leung, P. (1990). Position openings in rehabilitation psychology: A ten-year survey. *Rehabilitation Psychology, 35,* 157–160.

Lewin, K. (1935). *A dynamic theory of personality.* New York: McGraw Hill.

Lorig, K., Mazonson, P. D., & Holman, H. R. (1993). Evidence suggesting that health education for self-management in patients with chronic arthritis has sustained health benefits while reducing health care costs. *Arthritis and Rheumatism, 36,* 439–446.

McGrew, J. H., Glueckauf, R. L., Bond, G. R., & Frank, R. G. (1996). Health care reform and professional psychology: Overview of key issues and background of book. In R. L. Glueckauf, R. G. Frank, G. R. Bond, & J. H. McGrew (Eds.), *Psychological practice in a changing health care system: Issues and new directions* (pp. 3–13). New York: Springer.

Myers, H. F., Echemendia, R. J., & Trimble, J. E. (1991). The need for training ethnic minority psychologists. In H. F. Myers, P. Wohlford, L. P. Guzman, & R. J. Echemendia (Eds.), *Ethnic minority perspectives on clinical training and services in psychology* (pp. 3–11). Washington, DC: American Psychological Association.

Office of Technology Assessment. (1994). *Identifying health technologies that work: Searching for evidence* (Pub. No. OTA-H-608). Washington, DC: U.S. Government Printing Office.

O'Keeffe, J., Quittner, A. L., & Melamed, B. (1996). Quality and outcome indicators. In R. L. Glueckauf, R. G. Frank, G. R. Bond, & J. H. McGrew (Eds.), *Psychological practice in a changing health care system: Issues and new directions* (pp. 134–149). New York: Springer.

Olbrisch, M. E., Weiss, S. M., Stone, G. C., & Schwartz, G. E. (1985). Report of the national working conference on education and training in health psychology. *American Psychologist, 40,* 1038–1041.

Olshansky, S., & Hart, W. (1967). Psychologists in vocational rehabilitation or vocational rehabilitation counselors? *Journal of Rehabilitation, 33*(2), 28–29.

Pape, D. A., & Tarvydas, V. M. (1993). Responsible and responsive rehabilitation consultation on the ADA: The importance of training for psychologists. *Rehabilitation Psychology, 38,* 117–131.

Parker, H. J., & Chan, F. (1990). Psychologists in rehabilitation: Preparation and experience. *Rehabilitation Psychology, 35,* 239–248.

Patterson, D. (1997). Training programs in rehabilitation psychology. *Rehabilitation Psychology News, 24*(2), 7.

Patterson, D. R., & Hanson, S. (1995). Joint Division 22 and American College of Rehabilitation Medicine guidelines for postdoctoral training in rehabilitation psychology. *Rehabilitation Psychology, 40,* 299–310.

Raimy, V. C. (1950). *Training in clinical psychology.* New York: Prentice-Hall.

Salyers, M. P. (1996). *Predictors and consequences of staff burnout: A longitudinal study of assertive community treatment case managers.* Unpublished doctoral dissertation, Indiana University/Purdue University Indianapolis.

Suzuki, L. A., Meller, P. J., & Ponterotto, J. G. (1996). Multicultural assessment: Present trends and future directions. In L. A. Suzuki, P. J. Meller, & J. G. Ponterotto (Eds.), *Handbook of multicultural assessment: Clinical, psychological, and educational applications* (pp. 673–684). San Francisco: Jossey Bass.

Vickery, D. M., Kalmer, H., Lowry, D., Constantine, M., Wright, E., & Loren, W. (1983). Effect of a self-care education program on medical visits. *Journal of the American Medical Association, 250,* 2952–2956.

Walker, M. L. (1992). Rehabilitating a philosophy of rehabilitation. *Journal of Vocational Rehabilitation, 2*(4), 12–19.

Wax, T. M. (1993). Matchmaking among cultures: Disability culture and the larger marketplace. In R. L. Glueckauf, L. B. Sechrest, G. R. Bond, & E. C. McDonel (Eds.), *Improving assessment in rehabilitation and health* (pp. 156–175). Newbury Park, CA: Sage.

Wegener, S. T., Hagglund, K., & Elliott, T. R. (1998). On psychological identity and training: Boulder is better for rehabilitation psychology. *Rehabilitation Psychology, 43,* 17–29.

Wright, B. A. (1972). Value-laden beliefs and principles for rehabilitation psychology. *Rehabilitation Psychology, 19,* 38–45.

Wright, B. A. (1983). *Physical disability: A psychosocial approach* (2nd ed.). New York: Harper & Row.

31

Ethics: Historical Foundations, Basic Principles, and Contemporary Issues

Stephanie L. Hanson, Robert Guenther, Thomas Kerkhoff, and Marcia Liss

The complexities of ethical practice and debate lie at the intersection of wondrous health-related discoveries, evolving health care delivery systems, and daily health care experience. Ethics has a rich history, basic principles that form its core, and attainable skills that require ongoing study and application. In this chapter, we discuss (a) part of the historical context in which formal ethical principles in psychology evolved, (b) basic bioethical principles relevant to rehabilitation psychology, and (c) a training model for ethics skills development. We hope that this chapter helps raise awareness regarding the responsibility that all rehabilitation psychologists bear for ethical practice.

Historical Foundations of Ethical Practice

Some of the parameters on which the recognition of ethical issues in rehabilitation has evolved include (a) the establishment and revisions of the Ethical Principles of Psychologists and Code of Conduct of the American Psychological Association (APA), (b) the development of the rehabilitation field, (c) legal decisions interfacing with an individual's health care rights, and (d) the impact of managed health care on rehabilitation service delivery.

Perhaps the most obvious historical context in which to think about rehabilitation psychology ethics is the development of the APA ethics code itself. Initial ethics complaints had been predominantly concerned with academics and research and were managed under existing academic standards (Hobbs, 1948). In 1938, with the rapidly expanding psychology field and the recognition that informal case review was becoming inadequate, APA formed the temporary Committee on Scientific and Professional Ethics to consider developing an ethics code. Although the committee recommended that a standing APA committee be created to review complaints and to periodically formulate ethics rules for adoption by the association (Olson, 1940), formal guidelines governing conduct were not established at that time.

By 1947, with the continuing growth of psychology, it became apparent that a formal "Code Governing the Professional Practice of Psychology" was needed (Peak, 1947, p. 490). "These rules should do much more than help the unethical psychologist keep out of trouble; they should be of palpable aid to the ethical psychologist in making daily decisions" (Hobbs, 1948, p. 81). Hobbs suggested formulating the code on the basis of widespread participation by psychologists, from which the code might then provide both effective help with ethical decision making and increase the likelihood of influencing practice behavior, something previous codes developed from committee-based approaches had apparently not done.

Based on Hobbs's (1948) recommendation, the Committee on Ethical Standards for Psychology requested that the 7,500 APA members provide information on ethical situations they had experienced, highlighting the ethical issues involved (Canter, Bennett, Jones, & Nagy, 1994). Through revision and classification of the ethical issues identified through this critical incident method, the inaugural ethics code was born. At the 60th Annual Business Meeting of the APA in 1952, the "ethical standards for psychologists" was adopted (Adkins, 1952).

Since that time, the ethics code has undergone several revisions, which Canter et al. (1994) discussed in detail. Some of the more notable changes include adding principles related to drug use in therapy and research (1965), research with human participants (1972), and prohibition of sexual intimacy with clients (1977); adding a major section on resolving ethical violations (1992); and resolving the Federal Trade Commission's challenge to the 1981 ethics code, part of which was not finalized until December 1992 (Clark, 1994). Although most revisions of the APA ethics code have not been based on the critical incident method, Pope and Vetter (1992) suggested that obtaining recent critical incidents from membership rather than relying solely on committee input for code revisions would maintain the code's richness and relevance to professional practice.

Around the same time that the APA ethics code was established, the field of rehabilitation was growing. Advances in medicine had resulted in better survival rates for individuals sustaining catastrophic injury. In addition, veterans with catastrophic injuries from World War II presented unique health care needs that the traditional model of acute hospital care was not designed to address. Psychologists, who had traditionally played only marginal roles in general hospital care, responded to this emerging market for rehabilitation services. In addition to clinical care, rehabilitation psychologists had the opportunity to contribute to a new knowledge base regarding rehabilitation through research development related to clinical practice (i.e., the scientist–practitioner model). Recognizing the need to organize psychologists "concerned with the psychological and social consequences of disability and with ways to prevent and solve problems associated with disability," the Division of Rehabilitation Psychology within APA (1998) was established in 1956.

The unprecedented growth of rehabilitation has resulted in diversified opportunities for rehabilitation psychologists. It was not until the 1980s, however, with the legitimization of bioethics as a field of study, the rapidly changing health care market, and the explosion of rehabilitation hospitals and outpatient centers, that ethical issues received significant attention. There has been a slowly developing recognition of the need for discussion and more specific guidelines and training around ethical practice in the context of modern health care (Kerkhoff, Hanson, Guenther, & Ashkanazi, 1997). This is reflected in the number of publications dedicated to rehabilitation ethics in the past 10 years (Banja & Rosenthal, 1996; Deaton & Hanson, 1996; Haas, Caplan, & Callahan, 1988; Herbison, 1988). Each of the volumes cited highlights core rehabilitation ethics issues, such as procuring informed consent from individuals with neurological impairment, maintaining confidentiality in the team environment, and rationing limited resources.

The boundaries of ethical practice around these types of issues have also been influenced by the interpretation of health care law. Consider the following legal parameters relevant to rehabilitation. Decision-making capacity depends on the individual having (a) a set of values and goals (i.e., to make consistent decisions), (b) the ability to communicate and understand information, and (c) the ability to make informed choices by weighing the alternatives and potential consequences. Courts have fairly consistently held since 1978 that "a patient who fluctuates between competence and incompetence can not be denied opportunity to make decisions regarding medical care" (Furrow, Johnson, Jost, & Schwartz, 1991, p. 262). The practitioner is therefore obligated to determine the previously expressed preferences of an individual with fluctuating mental status (a common presentation in rehabilitation). Although the team or family may have good intentions, substituting their goals for the patient's is not generally acceptable practice. Similarly, a patient can be competent in specific areas and not others (Rosenthal & Lourie, 1996). Therefore, if the individual is capable of providing informed consent in specific rehabilitation situations, the psychologist needs to understand under what circumstances the patient is capable of providing informed consent and how to assess that consent. Miller (1997) suggested that health care law may increasingly address the issue of managed care and its influence over who makes health care decisions.

Perhaps one of the most significant factors contributing to the modern ethics debate in rehabilitation has been the penetration of managed care, resulting in the rationing of health care dollars. This is particularly troubling given the high cost of health care for individuals with disabilities (Hagglund & Frank, 1996). Penetration of managed care has resulted in shorter lengths of stays, fewer approved visits, and the use of lower cost and unqualified providers. In addition, reimbursement restrictions have seemingly forced some psychologists to consider how they can use diagnostic codes to their advantage, and how or whether to provide treatment when the number of approved sessions is insufficient to achieve the desired goal. Although the basic bioethical principles—autonomy, beneficence, and justice—have been the foundation of the modern ethics debate, this principle-based approach is being challenged as "unnecessarily narrow" (Furrow, Johnson, Jost, & Schwartz, 1996, p. 1; Tarvydas & Shaw,

1996). Continuing changes in health care challenge the strict application of bioethics to rehabilitation psychology and the ability to practice ethically in an increasingly restrictive rehabilitation environment. However, this does not argue against the importance of understanding the bioethical principles in conjunction with the discipline code on which the ethical practice of psychology is founded. An understanding of both is critical to ethical skills development.

Basic Principles in Bioethics

Respect for people is often viewed as the fundamental principle on which other principles are based (Ross et al., 1993; see also Banja, 1998; Beauchamp & Childress, 1994). Autonomy, nonmaleficence or beneficence, and justice as individual core ethical principles are then derived from respect for people. Respect for autonomy requires health care providers to respect the following individual rights: (a) the right to receive accurate information about diagnosis, prognosis, possible treatments and alternatives, and their costs—benefits; (b) the right to accept or reject recommended treatments; and (c) the right to choose other people to act on the individual's behalf if and when the individual is rendered unable to make decisions for herself or himself. Autonomy must be respected when exercised by a competent informed person, except when undue harm may accrue to innocent related parties (e.g., bodily injury), at which point the state may intervene. A constitutional right to privacy and the ethical obligation to obtain informed consent for psychological services are both based fundamentally on the principle of respect for autonomy.

Nonmaleficence and beneficence are closely related principles and include several aspects, admonishing health care providers to (a) not cause harm to another, (b) prevent harm to another, (c) remove sources of harm to others, and (d) promote that which is good. Ross et al. (1993) noted that this list of subprinciples is in the generally accepted order of importance.

The ethical principle of justice in health care usually concerns distributive justice; that is, the responsibility of society to equitably distribute the burdens and benefits of care. Among the three principles, respect for autonomy is usually ranked as more important than justice and nonmaleficence and beneficence in health care decisions if other considerations are generally equal.

Although respect for autonomy may be a dominant concern in ethical dilemmas affecting individuals, organizations and agencies may shape policy decisions based on a higher ranking of justice or beneficence (Ross et al., 1993). For example, Durgin (1998) included the principles of professional advocacy and organizational morality as fundamental to the ethics of admissions criteria in rehabilitation. These principles are related to the overarching principle of justice.

Application of the Basic Bioethical Principles

Ethical areas specific to rehabilitation include (a) informed consent to and ongoing participation in rehabilitation, (b) costs of services relative to the individual's ability to benefit from those services, (c) issues of justice that result from unequal access to rehabilitation, (d) confidentiality, and (e) caregiver issues (Haas, 1995b; Jennings, 1995).

Informed Consent and Respect for Autonomy

Negative stereotypes about people with disabilities and the patient's initial reaction to injury may limit the individual's ability to make an informed decision to participate in rehabilitation (Hamilton, Sherman, & Ruvolo, 1990). Caplan (1988) argued for an educational model of informed consent in which respect for autonomy is initially suspended until the patient refusing services is better informed about the true nature of disability and the value of rehabilitation. From this widely held perspective, patients are best served by preserving their potential to reacquire full autonomy by first paternalistically overriding impaired decision making (Caplan, Callahan, & Haas, 1987). As rehabilitation progresses and the patient can take more responsibility for decision making and direction of care, paternalism is no longer acceptable, and respect for autonomy is restored. Thus, a power shift occurs from rehabilitation provider to patient.

At one end of the debate about informed consent lies the ethically defensible position that people with a strong prejudice against living their lives with a disability have a fundamental right to decline rehabilitation services. At the other extreme exists a tradition within rehabilitation of subjecting reluctant patients to rehabilitation until they are "educated" and agree that it is worthwhile. The need to think differently about informed consent in rehabilitation practice may be overstated. It would be difficult to paternalistically force ongoing participation in a rehabilitation program in which new learning and behavioral change occur. Rehabilitation candidates have a fundamental right to accept or reject services. Therefore, they should be given complete relevant information needed to reach a decision.

The principle of respect for autonomy becomes more complicated when an individual has sustained cognitive or emotional impairment as a result of injury. Because reduced cognitive or emotional abilities do not automatically suspend an individual's right to self-determination, special measures (e.g., the appointment of a surrogate decision maker) are required to safeguard the rights of people with newly acquired deficits to hold unconventional beliefs or values and to protect patients' general right to participate in decision making (Beauchamp & Childress, 1994). Post, Ripich, and Whitehouse (1994) made a compelling argument for using discourse ethics and offered methods to address legal and ethical parameters regarding individuals with cognitive impairment. In addition, Rosenthal and Lourie (1996) reviewed the history of determination of competency, and

Auerbach and Banja (1996) presented a competency assessment tool. Although valuable resources exist to assist clinicians (e.g., Venesy, 1995), complicated, ambiguous cases continue to defy straightforward management. In these situations, collegial consultation and a systematic approach to decision making are critical.

It is the entire rehabilitation team's ethical responsibility to ensure that the patient's and family's autonomy is respected. In an effective rehabilitation team, the needs of the patient and family should drive the system, and all members, including the patient, should actively participate in decision making (Eisenberg, 1992). Unfortunately, team reports on which goals are based are often fraught with professional jargon (e.g., *don, doff, mental status exam*) and are offered within severe time constraints. If a patient does not participate in the team process, the team may inappropriately assume that the patient accepts the goals presented when it may be just as likely that the patient does not or cannot process what the conference represents. Conversely, Childress and Campbell (1989) reported that health care professionals most often question decision-making capacity when the patient disagrees with recommendations. This is particularly true if the patient's goals are deemed unsafe (Watts, Cassel, & Howell, 1989). As Wright (1981) and others (e.g., Eisenberg, 1992) have discussed and rehabilitation regulatory bodies (e.g., Committee on Accreditation of Rehabilitation Facilities) have echoed, procedures must be "built in" to elicit patient concerns, treatment goals, and decisions regarding rehabilitation.

Justice

Difficult issues regarding justice reside in considerations of who might benefit from rehabilitation, how much rehabilitation is required to achieve a benefit, and how much benefit is justifiable given limited resources that are unevenly distributed. Rehabilitation service providers must be increasingly aware that their time and expertise are limited resources that must be available to many people in need. One cannot ethically defend providing any one person with every service that might be beneficial (Fleck, 1990). Managed care may demand that care providers provide less intensive service to more people in need (Morreim, 1988). Although no one person reaches optimal recovery, many more people benefit at least minimally. However, in attempting to serve more people, those who are most vulnerable are at risk for neglect. It therefore falls to rehabilitation service providers to advocate for the community of people with disabilities, who deserve a sufficient range of basic services to meet their basic and special health care needs (Caplan, 1997). Fortunately, rehabilitation, unlike most other areas of health care, has a wonderful tradition of advocacy for the people it serves.

A related ethical imperative is to demonstrate the efficacy of one's services. Because limited resources are consumed in health care, harm in the form of wasting resources results from the provision of ineffective services. Although rehabilitation is probably as successful as other areas of contemporary health care in empirically demonstrating efficacy (DeJong, 1997), rehabilitation psychology could benefit greatly from better demonstrations of both efficacy and cost effectiveness of service delivery, supporting the investment of limited dollars.

Rehabilitation service providers must also be aware that ethical quandaries reside in seemingly pristine areas such as goal setting. Unpopular patient choices may be experienced by rehabilitation professionals as contrary to the traditional goals of rehabilitation (Haas, 1995a). A difficult balance must be found between resource utilization, which may seem to rigidly disregard individual values, and the pursuit of idiosyncratic patient goals at society's expense. The greatest risks are that, at one extreme, valuable rehabilitation resources may inappropriately be wasted in pursuit of relatively trivial goals, while at the other extreme personal preferences may be disregarded or individuals who devalue traditional rehabilitation goals may be punitively discharged before they can achieve even marginal benefit (Gans, 1983).

Rehabilitation specialists working within systems that encourage inequality in health care availability may be frustrated by such injustice (Purtilo & Meier, 1995). They may be tempted to "even the score" by falsifying records or exaggerating a deficit or benefit. However, providers are bound by both their professionalism and organizational contracts to practice ethically within unjust systems. Providers not only have a responsibility to the individuals they serve; they should also be informed advocates of a more equitable and adequate health care system to help prevent harm to people with disabilities at risk in the unjust system (Callahan, 1995).

Confidentiality

Pope and Vetter (1992) found confidentiality to be the most frequently described ethical concern among psychologists. Conversely, psychotherapy patients treated by psychologists seem to understand the general concept of confidentiality, but not its limits, in the treatment process (Clairborn, Berberoglu, Nerison, & Somberg, 1994). Compared with psychotherapy patients, rehabilitation patients frequently navigate more treacherous waters regarding their privacy, given the team milieu and the daily routines of rehabilitation practice. Team members routinely share information about patients. The medical record, in particular, may contain entries and information that patients insist be kept confidential (e.g., positive drug screens at admission, HIV status, high-risk sexual behavior, history of mental illness). Yet patients may be unaware that state statutes dictate reporting information regarding threat or harm and that attorneys, case managers, and insurance representatives commonly acquire access to medical records and other relevant information.

Team members may also insist on sharing a great deal of information with caregivers. Although the patient may indicate that caregivers not be informed of the severity of the patient's limitations or level of potential independence, such information may be considered essential for caregivers to know if their training is to be medically adequate. Rehabilitation service providers can draw on discussions of the nature and limits of confidentiality in health care to assist them in clearly stating throughout the rehabilitation process that the "unit of treatment" may legitimately be defined to include essential caregivers (Wear, 1988).

In all of these situations, the boundaries of confidentiality must be clarified if the rehabilitation team is to effectively manage complex and often dysfunctional relationships toward the goal of safe patient discharge. Patients must be fully informed prior to and during rehabilitation of the practical limits of confidentiality. Similarly, team members benefit from reminders that unnecessary violations of patient confidentiality (e.g., discussions of patients in public areas) must be avoided. The rehabilitation psychologist clearly has an ethical responsibility to balance confidentiality with the essential nature of information to rehabilitation treatment and patient safety.

Caregiver Issues

Caregiver issues can present rehabilitation professionals with difficult ethical dilemmas, particularly if the caregiver is unreliable. Inadequate caregiving can cause complications limiting functioning or even threatening the patient's life, necessitating team intervention. Although the patient may be reluctant to consent to team intervention (e.g., he or she may be fearful of jeopardizing caregiver support), such refusal may be extremely difficult for the team to respect if the patient has cognitive or emotional deficits exacerbating vulnerability to neglect or abuse. An alternative to neglect might be to consider a skilled-nursing facility against the individual's preferences in violation of respect for the person's autonomy. In these situations, the team must be careful not to abuse its authoritative position in helping the patient make a discharge decision.

At the other extreme is the caregiver who insists on giving unnecessary care. Some patients fear that the caregiver will resent them if they reject the care offered. Others may welcome unnecessary care, undermining their independence. The role of being "disabled" can be as limiting as neurologic insult. Other people may autonomously choose where they invest their limited energy, avoiding exhausting self-care activities. The rehabilitation service provider risks violating respect for the individual's autonomy if she or he overreacts to such situations. However, neglect is risked if no action is taken (Callahan, 1988).

Clearly, the pitfalls are many and deep for the contemporary health care provider who must embrace the additional roles of advocate, scientist, gatekeeper, and entrepreneur. The requirements for the ethical provision of care are far higher than legal standards. One must maintain an awareness that she or he is obliged to respect the autonomy of patients regardless of their limitations. Complete information about treatment alternatives and their costs and benefits must be provided to the patient or a surrogate. Complete information includes clear information about the limits of confidentiality. Choices that reflect the patient's values, beliefs, and preferences should usually be respected. This is difficult and important when the patient is opposed to team recommendations. The health care provider's responsibility to avoid causing harm usually takes precedence over the desire to promote the patient's welfare. People with new disabling conditions may have the right to refuse rehabilitation based on firmly held but unpopular values and prejudice. However, a temporary suspension of respect for autonomy may be justifiable if intense emotional reactions are believed to be impairing the patient's judgment. Rehabilitation service providers must be advocates not only for individuals but also for the patient's caregivers and for the community of people with disabilities. Caregivers may frequently be considered part of the "target" for treatment, with rights and responsibilities similar to those of the patient. Health care professionals simultaneously must demonstrate efficacy and distribute efficacious care in a just manner and an awareness of resource limitations throughout all of the health care industry. These high expectations require skills development beginning in graduate school and continuing beyond the graduate to the postgraduate level.

Ethical Skills Development

Ethical discernment can be construed as a skill to be enhanced throughout one's professional lifetime. Effectively developing and applying ethics skill necessitates several assumptions: an academic fund of information regarding the conceptual foundations; understanding the historical development and current iteration of the APA (1992) ethics code; the existence of personal moral development and a related values system consonant with the ethics code; and in-vivo experience in ethical decision making.

Eberlein (1987) observed that personal values often play an important role in ethical decision making when ethical standards provide equivocal guidance in a specific dilemma. This tendency to resort to personal values is increased when one is unsure of how to use the ethics code. The profession can afford no substitute for thorough knowledge of ethical standards. Yet addressing the challenge of variability in psychologists' personal values systems also lends itself to constructive ethics training. Interweaving perspectives such as virtue ethics (Jordan & Meara, 1990) and the influences of philosophical thought (Fine & Ulrich, 1988) during formal ethics training may concurrently facilitate personal moral development, complementing training in the ethics code. "While the discipline of ethics itself may not provide answers ... practice that is tempered with such reflection, that is grounded in character and virtue, and that takes moral issues seriously, can make a moral difference" (Furrow et al., 1991, p. 6).

Beyond these fundamentals, however, it is paramount that professionally relevant ethical experience and related competence be attained in the practice setting. The challenge for rehabilitation psychologists lies in the environment in which we practice—the interdisciplinary team milieu. Although the learning process begins with the individual clinician, we are one member of a team of professionals, each with his or her own set of practice standards. Tarvydas and Shaw (1996) showed that different types of professionals vary in their ratings of the importance of specific ethical issues. Familiarity with different disciplines' ethics codes may help in the process of reaching ethical consensus when dilemmas arise within the team (see Veatch & Flack, 1997, for a compilation of several codes). In addition, the consequences of ethical decisions may involve the family, the team of rehabilitation professionals, and the health care facility. Opportunities for ethics skills building and practice occur during team case conferences, clinical rounds, family conferences, and program planning—in essence, in the global treatment context. Banja (1998) construed the whole rehabilitation process as a moral relationship between the server (i.e., psychologist, individual rehabilitation team members) and the people served, one that is played out in every facet of clinical and organizational interaction.

Fortunately, working in a professionally diverse environment can prepare the student of rehabilitation psychology for the culminating step in rounding out training—serving on a health care institutional ethics committee. The committee format provides a rich example of the effect of member personalities and group dynamics on the process of ethical choice. The psychology intern and resident should develop a sense of how psychology's ethical principles interface with those of colleagues from other health care heritages and contribute a valuable perspective on practice ethics.

Competence in applying the APA ethics code has been assessed traditionally by national and state boards (Bersoff, 1995). The focus has been broad-based sampling of ethical issues within the discipline of psychology. This oral examination tradition regarding ethical dilemmas has helped fuel formal ethics education nationally. The advent of the American Board of Rehabilitation Psychology, Inc., undoubtedly reinforces the necessity of refocusing on the special needs of individuals with disabilities as they affect ethical issues against the wider background of health care.

Rehabilitation clearly presents challenging issues, such as those reflected in informed consent, balancing patient and family needs, respect for autonomy within the context of patient safety, and protection of records in a team setting. These examples reflect the importance of ethically guided behavior within rehabilitation psychology. Developing a systematic, multifactorial methodology to approach ethical conflicts helps minimize stereotypes, personality differences, situational biases, and negative aspects of group dynamics, which can be exacerbated in rehabilitation. We suggest the following 10 components in constructing an effective ethics skills-building program for rehabilitation psychology students and practitioners:

1. Combine the study of historical ethical thought in philosophy and psychology with a thorough working knowledge of the current APA (1992) ethics code.

2. Ensure recognition and understanding of the impact of biases, values, and professional boundaries on rational decision making.
3. Establish referential familiarity with federal and state legal statutes, particularly legal precedents in health care law, that provide a counterpoint to applying the ethics code and affect the boundaries of professional practice.
4. Gain thorough familiarity with societal issues affecting people with disabilities.
5. Provide structured practice in applying the psychology standards through case examples and discussion.
6. Provide structured practice in weighing the consequences of different potential decisions from the standpoint of the individual, team, and broader system.
7. Incorporate collegial consultation to thoroughly consider available options in dilemma resolution from a discipline perspective.
8. Gain familiarity with the ethics codes of other health care disciplines and then provide an educational consortium in which students from related health care fields address ethical cases from a broader perspective and with consideration of values of the health care milieu, such as universal access and patient–provider choice.
9. Provide a simulation of an ethics committee in a classroom context to experience the effects of group dynamics on the process and outcome of decision making.
10. Provide supervised experience on a multidisciplinary bioethics committee.

Ethical skills are not the sole purview of professional ethicists, to be relegated to the practice of this group of specialists. Aspiring to achieve the ethical principles remains central to all psychology practice. Ethical skills must be integral to each practitioner's armamentarium, coincident with conceptual foundations of psychology, and routinely exercised in all professional activities. Ethically guided behavior is the sine qua non to preserving the welfare of the people that we serve, our profession, and ourselves.

Conclusion

Initial ethics training should lay the foundation for both the recognition of professional boundaries (i.e., the ethics of establishing a professional relationship) and the ethical decision-making process once a relationship is established. Although accreditation requirements dictate that graduate students receive ethics training, many students are not adequately prepared for "the basics" from which to evaluate ethical dilemmas. As Belar (1998) argued, graduate training programs must adapt to the marketplace; as psychologists, we fear that our graduate training programs have lagged behind the market in preparing students for practice complexities. Practicing psychologists have significant concerns regarding the ethical complexities created by managed care (Newman & Taylor, 1996).

Ethical problem solving in rehabilitation requires unique skills and knowledge because of the environment in which we practice. Psychologists working in health care settings must have a grasp of health care law and clearly understand issues such as variable competency, patients' and families' legal rights, justice as it relates to limited resource allocation, and confidentiality in the context of the rehabilitation team. Although case examples in graduate training can help shape students' critical thinking, ethical judgment is a skill that must be maintained. Consider, for example, Whitler's (1996) observation that nurses in long-term care facilities recognize the importance of autonomy within patient care but typically do not consistently demonstrate these behaviors within their daily routine. This may suggest that rehabilitation psychologists have a seemingly untapped behavioral research arena—to assess if and how ethics training translates into ethical practice. In addition, the recent development of generic guidelines around practice with specific rehabilitation populations, such as standards in spinal cord injury rehabilitation and guidelines for working with individuals with Alzheimer's disease (Small et.al., 1997), suggest that as rehabilitation service providers, we need more specific discussion regarding ethical practice with identified rehabilitation populations.

Rehabilitation psychologists also face strong challenges because of cost and access issues across health care settings. When challenged by limited resources, equitable distribution (of service, funding, organs) becomes central to the ethics debate. Although the aspiration of managed care changes might have been to create equitability in an environment of limited dollars, these changes have magnified the discrepancies for the professional practice of psychology. Rehabilitation psychologists have reached a critical juncture: redesigning rehabilitation in an environment of cost containment, which concretely translates into fewer assessment and treatment sessions. What becomes too little to matter and therefore unethical to put forth as a "reasonable" assessment or treatment? Must rehabilitation psychologists shift service to training families and lower cost providers, which then might threaten the very existence of the specialty (or perhaps the lower cost providers might then become our advocates)? Is it ethical to improve access to psychological services through Internet-based assessment and intervention?

Telehealth presents one of the greatest emerging opportunities and ethical challenges for rehabilitation psychology. Its opportunities include improving access and frequency of service to individuals living long distances from rehabilitation facilities, increasing family involvement in outpatient treatment programs, and designing realistic interventions applicable to the patient's home environment. Its ethical challenges lie in protecting patient and family privacy, maintaining the confidentiality of electronic records, controlling task demands given the structure required in many rehabilitation interventions, determining the boundaries of appropriate assessment, controlling access so that telehealth does not encourage dependency, determining efficacy, and settling licensure issues so that individuals living in different states can participate in rehabilitation activities. These are the types of issues that rehabilitation psychologists are grappling with in the new millennium. One of the greatest challenges in the 21st century is to ensure that we as rehabilitation psychologists believe in our own value strongly enough and can demonstrate that value in rehabilitation effectively enough to regain practice ground that has been slipping through our hands.

References

Adkins, D. C. (1952). Proceedings of the Sixtieth Annual Business Meeting of the American Psychological Association, Inc., Washington, D. C. *American Psychologist, 7,* 645–670.

American Psychological Association. (1992). Ethical principles of psychologists and code of conduct. *American Psychologist, 47,* 1597–1611.

American Psychological Association. (1998). *Our purpose.* Washington, DC: Author. Retrieved on February 3, 2000 from the World Wide Web http://www.apa.org/divisions/div22/

Auerbach, V. S., & Banja, J. D. (1996). Assessing client competence to participate in rehabilitation decision-making. *NeuroRehabilitation, 6*(2), 123–132.

Banja, J. D. (1998). The persons served: Ethical perspectives on CARF's accreditation standards and guidelines. Tucson, AZ, Commission on the Accreditation of Rehabilitation Facilities.

Banja, J. D., & Rosenthal, M. (Eds.). (1996). Ethics [Special issue]. *NeuroRehabilitation: An Interdisciplinary Journal, 6*(2), 95–162.

Beauchamp, T. L., & Childress, J. F. (1994). *Principles of biomedical ethics* (4th ed.). New York: Oxford University Press.

Belar, C. D. (1998). Graduate education in clinical psychology: "We're not in Kansas anymore." *American Psychologist, 53,* 456–464.

Bersoff, D. (Ed.). (1995). Ethical conflicts in psychology. Washington, DC: American Psychological Association.

Callahan, D. (1988). Families as caregivers: The limits of morality. *Archives of Physical Medicine and Rehabilitation 69,* 13–18.

Callahan, D. (1995). Allocating health care resources: The vexing case of rehabilitation. *American Journal of Physical Medicine and Rehabilitation, 74*(1, Suppl.), S3–S6.

Canter, M. B., Bennett, B. E., Jones, S. E., & Nagy, T. F. (1994). *Ethics for psychologists: A commentary on the APA ethics code.* Washington, DC: American Psychological Association.

Caplan, A. L. (1988). Informed consent and provider–patient relationships in rehabilitation medicine. *Archives of Physical Medicine and Rehabilitation, 69,* 2–7.

Caplan, A. L. (1997). The ethics of gatekeeping in rehabilitation medicine. *Journal of Head Trauma Rehabilitation, 12*(1), 29–36.

Caplan, A. L., Callahan, D., & Haas, J. (1987). *Ethical & policy issues in rehabilitation medicine: A Hastings Center report.* Briarcliff Manor, NY: Hastings Center.

Childress, J. F., & Campbell, C. C. (1989). "Who is a doctor to decide whether a person lives or dies?" Reflections on Dax's case. In L. D. Kliever (Ed.), *Dax's case: Essays in medical ethics & human meaning* (pp. 23–41). Levittown, PA: Phoenix Society.

Clairborn, C. D., Berberoglu, L. S., Nerison, R. M., & Somberg, D. R. (1994). The client's perspective: Ethical judgments and perceptions of therapist practices. *Professional Psychology: Research and Practice, 25,* 268–274.

Clark, C. R. (1994). Report of the Ethics Committee, 1993. *American Psychologist, 49,* 659–666.

Deaton, A. V., & Hanson, S. (Eds.). (1996). Ethics and rehabilitation psychology: Exploring the issues [Special issue]. *Rehabilitation Psychology, 41*(1), 3–86.

DeJong, G. (1997, May). *State of the science in medical rehabilitation effectiveness research.* Keynote address at the 3rd Annual Del Harder Rehabilitation Research Day, Rehabilitation Institute of Michigan, Detroit.

Durgin, C. J. (1998). Admission criteria. In J. D. Banja (Ed.), *The persons served: Ethical perspectives on CARF's accreditation standards and guidelines* (pp. 11–31). Tucson, AZ: Commission on the Accreditation of Rehabilitation Facilities.

Eberlein, L. (1987). Introducing ethics to beginning psychologists: A problem-solving approach. Professional Psychology: *Research and Practice, 18,* 353–359.

Eisenberg, M. G. (1992). *Guide to interdisciplinary practice in rehabilitation settings.* Skokie, IL: American Congress of Rehabilitation Medicine.

Fine, M., & Ulrich, L. (1988). Integrating psychology and philosophy in teaching a graduate course in ethics. *Professional Psychology: Research and Practice, 19,* 542–546.

Fleck, L. M. (1990). Pricing human life: The moral costs of medical progress. *Centennial Review, 34*(2), 227–254.

Furrow, B. R., Johnson, S. H., Jost, T. S., & Schwartz, R. L. (1991). *Bioethics: Health care law and ethics.* St. Paul, MN: West.

Furrow, B. R., Johnson, S. H., Jost, T. S., & Schwartz, R. L. (1996). *1996–1997 Supplement to bioethics: Health care law and ethics.* St. Paul, MN: West.

Gans, J. S. (1983). Hate in the rehabilitation setting. *Archives of Physical Medicine and Rehabilitation, 64,* 176–179.

Haas, J. F. (1995a). Ethical considerations of goal setting for patient care in rehabilitation medicine. *American Journal of Physical Medicine and Rehabilitation, 74*(1, Suppl.), S16–S20.

Haas, J. F. (1995b). Ethical issues in physical medicine and rehabilitation: Conclusion to a series. *American Journal of Physical Medicine and Rehabilitation, 74*(1, Suppl.), S54–S58.

Haas, J., Caplan, A. L., & Callahan, D. (Eds.). (1988). *Case studies in ethics and medical rehabilitation.* Briarcliff Manor, NY: Hastings Center.

Hagglund, K., & Frank, R. G. (1996). Rehabilitation psychology practice, ethics, and a changing health care environment. *Rehabilitation Psychology, 41*(1), 19–32.

Hamilton, D. L., Sherman, S. J., & Ruvolo, C. M. (1990). Stereotype based expectancies: Effects on information processing and social behavior. *Journal of Social Issues, 46,* 35–60.

Herbison, G. J. (Ed.). (1988). Ethics and rehabilitation: Introduction. *Archives of Physical Medicine and Rehabilitation, 69,* 1.

Hobbs, N. (1948). The development of a code of ethical standards for psychology. *American Psychologist, 3,* 80–84.

Jennings, B. (1995). Healing the self: The moral meaning of relationships in rehabilitation. *American Journal of Physical Medicine and Rehabilitation, 74*(1, Suppl.), S25–S28.

Jordan, A., & Meara, N. (1990). Ethics and the professional practice of psychologists: The role of virtue ethics and principles. *Professional Psychology: Research and Practice, 21,* 107–114.

Kerkhoff, T., Hanson, S., Guenther, R., & Ashkanazi, G. (1997). The foundation and application of ethical principles in rehabilitation psychology. *Rehabilitation Psychology, 42*(1), 17–30.

Miller, T. E. (1997). Managed care regulation in the laboratory of the states. *Journal of the American Medical Association, 278,* 1102–1109.

Morreim, E. H. (1988, December). Cost containment: Challenging fidelity and justice. *Hastings Center Report,* 20–25.

Newman, R., & Taylor, G. (1996). Practitioner survey results offer comprehensive view of psychology practice. *Practitioner Update, 4*(2), 2–4.

Olson, W. C. (1940). Proceedings of the forty-eighth annual meeting of the American Psychological Association, Inc., Pennsylvania State College, September 4–7, 1940. *Psychological Bulletin, 37,* 699–741.

Peak, H. (Chair). (1947). Proceedings of the fifty-fifth annual business meeting of the American Psychological Association, Inc., Detroit, Michigan. *American Psychologist, 2,* 468–515.

Pope, K. S., & Vetter, V. A. (1992). Ethical dilemmas encountered by members of the American Psychological Association: A national survey. *American Psychologist, 47,* 397–411.

Post, S., Ripich, D., & Whitehouse, P. (1994). Discourse ethics: Research, dementia and communication. *Alzheimer Disease and Associated Disorders, 8*(Suppl. 4), 58–65.

Purtilo, R. B., & Meier, R. H. (1995). Team challenges: Regulatory constraints and patient empowerment. *American Journal of Physical Medicine and Rehabilitation, 74*(1, Suppl.), S21–S24.

Rosenthal, M., & Lourie, I. (1996). Ethical issues in the evaluation of competence in persons with acquired brain injury. *NeuroRehabilitation, 6*(2), 113–121.

Ross, J. W., Glaser, I. W., Rasinski-Gregory, D., Gibson, J. M., & Bayley, C. (1993). *Health care ethics committees: The next generation.* Chicago: American Hospital.

Small, G. W., Rabins, P. V., Barry, P. P., Buckholtz, N. S., DeKosky, S. T., Ferris, S. H., Sanford, F. I., Gwyther, L. P., Khachaturian, Z. S., Lebowitz, B. D., McRae, T. D., Morris, J. C., Oakley, F., Schneider, L. S., Streim, J. E., Sunderland, T., Teri, L. A., & Tune, L. E. (1997). Diagnosis and treatment of Alzheimer disease and related disorders: Consensus statement of the American Association for Geriatric Psychiatry, the Alzheimer's Association, and the American Geriatrics Society. *Journal of the American Medical Association, 278,* 1363–1369.

Tarvydas, V. M., & Shaw, L. (1996). Interdisciplinary team member perceptions of ethical issues in traumatic brain injury rehabilitation. *NeuroRehabilitation, 6*(2), 97–111.

Veatch, R. M., & Flack, H. E. (1997). *Case studies in allied health ethics.* Upper Saddle River, NJ: Prentice-Hall.

Venesy, B. A. (1995). A clinician's guide to decision-making capacity and ethically sound medical decisions. *American Journal of Physical Medicine and Rehabilitation, 74*(1, Suppl.), S41–S48.

Watts, D. T., Cassel, C. K., & Howell, T. (1989). Dangerous behavior in a demented patient: Preserving autonomy in a patient with diminished competence. *Journal of the American Geriatric Society, 37,* 658–662.

Wear, S. (1988). Commentary on the case of Tony. In J. Haas, A. L. Caplan, & D. Callahan (Eds.), *Case studies in ethics and medical rehabilitation* (pp. 3–6). Briarcliff Manor, NY: Hastings Center.

Whitler, J. M. (1996). Ethics of assisted autonomy in the nursing home: Types of assisting among long-term care nurses. *Nursing Ethics, 3,* 224–235.

Wright, B. A. (1981). Value-laden beliefs and principles for rehabilitation. *Rehabilitation Literature, 42,* 9–10, 266–269. (Original work published 1972).

Afterword: Drawing New Horizons

Timothy R. Elliott and Robert G. Frank

And this is a universal law: a living thing can be healthy, strong, and fruitful only when bounded by a horizon; if it is incapable of drawing a horizon around itself . . . it will pine away slowly or hasten to its timely end. Cheerfulness, the good conscience, the joyful deed, confidence in the future . . . all of them depend . . . on a line dividing the bright and the discernible from the unilluminable and dark; on one's being just as able to forget at the right time as to remember at the right time. (Nietzsche, 1873–1876/1983)

The chapters in this book attest to the emergence of rehabilitation psychology as a comprehensive discipline providing care to people with chronic health conditions. Rehabilitation psychology has moved far beyond its initial emphasis on the medical and vocational problems experienced by people with physical disabilities to encompass the entire realm of psychological factors associated with chronic health conditions that limit activities (Frank, 1999). The current generation of rehabilitation psychologists now must contend with problems of a historic nature and others that stem from "growing pains." At these times, it is imperative to remember key elements in our heritage as scientist–practitioners and mull over some problems that may constrain our future.

Wielding the Tools of Science

The Scientist–Practitioner Model

Probably the greatest current and future flashpoint for rehabilitation psychology concerns the inevitable conflict between scientific advancement and clinical practice in health care generally and in rehabilitation specifically. Ideally, scientific research progresses at a steady and nonpartisan pace, building on converging evidence and benefiting from new technologies, methodologies, and theoretical insights (Popper, 1963). Like Henry

We are grateful to Richard Shewchuk and Monica Kurylo for their comments and criticisms of an earlier draft.

Ford's apparent disregard for the blacksmiths of his day, effective innovations that meet with favorable market conditions can easily push aside common practices and render them obsolete. Many policy makers and administrators are likewise looking to empirical evidence—however convenient or controversial it may be—to aid decisions about resources, services, and their distribution.

Professional psychology has awkwardly grappled with the scant support for the presumed superiority of the doctoral-trained psychologists over those in other mental health professions and those with master's-level degrees with respect to psychotherapy and counseling outcomes (Hayes, 1998). The resulting protests seem to be a melding of cognitive dissonance and union stump speeches with little appreciation for the larger scientific issues at stake. Rather than seize on the scientific, theoretical, and clinical implications for practice from these data, the economic self-interests of the guild wash away any objectivity. Subsequently, professional psychology debates endlessly the veracity of equivocal findings regarding therapeutic outcomes and misses opportunities to advance the profession in light of them.

To a certain extent, rehabilitation psychology is vulnerable to the whims of the scientific blade and empirical scrutiny. Despite the long involvement of rehabilitation psychology in programs sponsored by the National Institute of Disability Rehabilitation and Research (including the model systems, research and training center, and field-initiated projects), an unbiased scholar would be hard pressed to find more than a few research programs funded by these agencies that systematically demonstrates the efficacy of psychological interventions in any area of rehabilitation. Too often rehabilitation psychologists have loaned their research skill and expertise to the atheoretical enterprise of data gathering and description for the multidisciplinary enterprise of rehabilitation. In this process, psychologists ironically ignored the need to demonstrate the worth and cost-effectiveness of psychological interventions while nurturing medical databases. Rehabilitation psychologists have been instrumental in setting priorities and refining a medically oriented research agenda. Unfortunately, rehabilitation psychologists may have abdicated psychological explanations of behavior while advancing a medical model of rehabilitation.

Work that demonstrates the effectiveness of psychological interventions in rehabilitation has often resulted from projects outside the realm of funded research per se. In fact, the best demonstrations of psychological interventions among people with spinal cord injury (SCI; and the only ones with true experimental designs) have been doctoral dissertations. Moreover, careful examination of these studies and their findings reveals that these works cannot be used to demonstrate any unique role or impact strictly attributable to the clinical expertise of a doctoral-level psychologist. The interventions described in these studies were devised in such a way that they could be replicated and implemented by nondoctoral personnel.

As argued in a series of articles by Elliott and colleagues (Elliott & Klapow, 1997; Elliott & Shewchuk, 1996; Johnstone et al., 1995), behavioral science research is needed at all levels of the health care spectrum. Psychological research was thought to primarily inform and guide the clinical activities of the practitioner and the academic theorists (Strupp & Hadley, 1977). However, at the administrative and policy-making levels of private and public health care systems, decisions are made concerning resource allocation, the identification of service priorities, and the development, administration, and evaluation of programs. Psychological research and expertise are needed at these higher levels to ensure rational and empirical distribution and services (Kaplan, 1994).

Current Health Care Trends

The industrialization of American health care has forced all service professions to evaluate their role in providing cost-effective, efficacious services. Thus, physicians are often eschewed in favor of advanced practice nurses or physician assistants, and money allocated to mental health is divided among providers from counseling, social work, nursing, and psychology. Doctoral training programs in psychology have carelessly contributed to this problem by producing more graduates than the market can support, forcing the rate and amount of reimbursement down and perpetuating a "buyer's market" (Frank & Johnstone, 1996; Frank & Ross, 1995). Hayes (1998) and Cummings (1996) argued that doctoral-level psychologists should be more concerned with treatment development, administration, and evaluation; evolving health care systems need innovative, cost-efficient programs at all levels of service delivery (Sanderson, Riley, & Eshun, 1997). Policy makers often view "behavioral intervention as prohibitively labor intensive, because they equate it with one-to-one counseling by highly trained and expensive staff" (Leviton, 1996, p. 47). This may be particularly true in the provision of services to people with disabilities, whose health care is often paid by Medicaid, and the coverage for psychological services varies widely between states (Frank, 1997; O'Keeffe, 1996).

    Therefore, it is prudent that we determine when and under what circumstances high-cost providers (e.g., doctoral-level psychologists) provide efficacious interventions and when and under what circumstances low-cost service providers would be more efficacious in these roles. It may be that the doctoral-level psychologist is best suited for roles in research, treatment planning and development, program evaluation, and administration of services. There seems to be little logic in using high-cost service providers (e.g., doctoral-level psychologists) to deliver face-to-face therapeutic interventions if in fact low-cost service providers deliver these services effectively. Research is needed to identify the conditions when low-cost service providers deliver efficacious behavioral interventions, and the development, implementation, and evaluation of these programs is certainly within the domain of the rehabilitation psychologist. Furthermore, such programs could take advantage of emerging technologies (such as tele-counseling and telehealth) to deliver in-house programs to people with disabilities and their families. In this manner, rehabilitation psychologists may effectively assume the professional "primary caregiver" and "general practitioner" roles that have been advocated for professional psychology (Cummings, 1996; Frank, 1999).

Recent trends in medicine focus on the evaluations of treatments. This evidence-based approach is consonant with the heritage and ideals of psychology (Johnstone et al., 1995). In rehabilitation, Rosenthal and Ricker (see chapter 3) observe that psychological interventions are among the few interventions that have demonstrated effects. For rehabilitation psychologists, future opportunities may be in the evaluation of treatment effects.

The recent movement toward prescription authority for psychologists might usher in several unique challenges and opportunities for rehabilitation psychologists. Proponents of the prescription authority movement believe this privilege could augment the skills, services, and autonomy of those at the front line of service delivery and might eventually obviate the need for referrals to physicians for medical management. This might be particularly cost effective in outpatient, community-based, and home-based programs and to people in rural, inner-city, and other underserved areas.

Most in the prescription authority movement are concerned chiefly with psychotropic medications for people with more traditionally defined psychological disorders (DeLeon et al., 1996; Ivey, Scheffler, & Zazzali, 1998). Rehabilitation psychologists serve clientele with physical and neuromuscular disabilities who often have considerable pharmacological needs other than psychotropic medication. More importantly, other professionals vying for prescription authority (and those that already have it in many states, such as nurse practitioners) often assume the role of a "physician extender." Rehabilitation psychologists should not compete with these professions by pursuing an identity as a "physician extender" when other opportunities have greater merit and potential influence.

Prescription authority offers psychologists the ability to extend services for the consumer. If these skills enhance the delivery of rehabilitation services in a cost-effective fashion, they could prove to be a great boon to the discipline. Evolving payment methods for rehabilitation recognize cardinal symptoms that designate as primary those syndromes that most influence the health of the individual (Frank, 1996). In this model of care, rehabilitation psychologists could assume the role of a primary care manager in providing the majority of service to people with disabilities reintegrating into the community. Clients receiving care in this type of model may benefit from a more centralized coordinated care if the psychologist has prescription authority.

Harnessing Research With Theory

If scientific endeavors are truly nonpartisan, then a good theory—to paraphrase Lewin—is quite egalitarian. Outstanding contributions to everyday rehabilitation practice can be grounded in sound theoretical frameworks that feature sound internal logic, a clear connection to a larger theoretical system in behavioral science, and logical hypotheses that are testable and potentially falsifiable (e.g., Fordyce, 1976; Taub & Uswatte, chapter 22). These are elements of any good theory in established science (Popper, 1963). Although many other professions in rehabilitation can offer advanced research expertise, psychologists offer the best theoretical insights into and explanations of behavior that can be translated into testable propositions, useful predictions, and meaningful interventions. Intervention programs based on theory-driven, empirical research can then be implemented and evaluated in a cost-effective manner.

Theory gives meaning to facts and allows researchers to advance and refine established theories in field settings. Without theory to guide research programs, we are left with an accumulation of data points unconnected to larger bodies of knowledge, and we are unable to make meaningful predictions about future events or make logical choices about intervention strategies. Applications such as the Fordyce (1976) and Taub and Uswatte (chapter 22) models illustrate how psychological theories can be used to develop and refine models of human behavior that help the science understand generalizable principles of human behavior across a wide array of settings and situations. Without theory to guide research, a discipline is left to endlessly debate technology and methodology without any clear direction.

Unfortunately, the bulk of rehabilitation psychology research is disconnected from larger theoretical perspectives of behavior. Consequently, much of the data collected and produced from years of collaborative, funded projects is descriptive and devoid of any theoretical explanation. This reliance on naïve empiricism provides essentially no theoretical direction for efficacious psychological interventions, and it fails us when we need to make predictions about behavioral phenomena under general and specific conditions. Moreover, the atheoretical enterprise of data gathering and description has produced reams of means and standard deviations divorced from any theoretical context, severely hampering the ability to make meaningful comparisons with propositions that could be refuted or confirmed. These conditions must be rectified so that psychologists can propose and implement large-scale intervention programs.

Elliott (1994) argued that the lack of theory in rehabilitation psychology creates an untenable dilemma. Rehabilitation psychologists are trained to develop, test, and apply theoretical explanations of behavior that advance knowledge and guide interventions. Repeated attention on demographic variables (e.g., type of disability, type of lesion, gender, race, age, time since disability onset) in the absence of behavioral theories does nothing to advance the knowledge of human behavior or meaningful interventions.

It is imperative that we conduct research to determine who benefits from what kinds of psychosocial and medical interventions in rehabilitation practice. It is particularly important that these inquiries include all procedures, interventions, and practices; this work should not be confined to interventions that are strictly psychological per se. All standard medical and psychosocial practices in rehabilitation that are currently guided by nothing more than clinical lore should be especially open to empirical scrutiny. For example, what evidence is there to indicate that antidepressant medication is required for a person with a recent-onset SCI admitted to an inpatient SCI rehabilitation program? These medications are prescribed routinely to inpatients with recent-onset SCI with no empirical support at cost to the person, the clinic, and health care system (Elliott & Frank, 1996). In an attempt to justify and manage formulary costs, then, rehabilitation psychologists should assume the lead in examining the efficacy of pharmacological agents in everyday clinical practice.

New Horizons and New Roles

When a call for a return to the old paths of science goes out among psychologists, it typically emanates from a fairly traditional training program and extols the virtues of a science-based agenda in the fairly traditional roles of counseling and psychotherapy (e.g., McFall, 1991). Adhering to these old paths may be the best way to carefully cultivate obsolescence. Professions that evolve with increased relevance, applied skill, and critical vision flourish. Their focus should entail the rational distribution of health care services generally and in rehabilitation specifically (Kaplan, 1996). Psychologists must address issues of accessibility to service; the timing of service delivery; the accountability of providers for services, practices, and expenditures; and the affordability of services to the system, patients, and payers (Kaplan, 1996). Therefore, rehabilitation psychologists must be involved at the highest levels of all health care service delivery systems, using research and clinical expertise to inform the rational use and allocation of resources that support clinical activity (Elliott & Klapow, 1997; Elliott & Shewchuk, 1996). Theory-based science serves psychologists well in this regard; they cannot, however, be held hostage by tradition to limited, parochial roles at the lowest levels of any health care service delivery system (Elliott & Shewchuk, 1996).

More important, the current generation of rehabilitation psychologists should thoughtfully reconsider their roles in multidisciplinary teams. As noted earlier, rehabilitation psychologists can develop and execute the role of primary care manager of service delivery programs for people with chronic physical conditions or disability in a cardinal symptom management model (Frank, 1999). Most managed care programs for people with disability are more concerned with saving costs than with providing expert care (Frank, 1997). Rehabilitation psychologists have the skills and ability to lead rehabilitation teams in the primary care for people with disability or chronic physical problems. Physiatrists can provide the primary medical expertise in this model; however, psychologists or nurse practitioners with prescription privileges may be efficacious in basic management of ongoing pharmaceutical needs. This would not nullify expert consultation with physiatrists—or any other medical specialty, for that matter—when indicated. Rehabilitation psychologists can assume the lead, as they possess the research, clinical, and policy expertise prerequisite for the cost-efficient, strategic, and timely dispersion of resources and services.

Furthermore, this role could allow rehabilitation psychologists to implement many programs congruent with our knowledge of our clients' fundamental individual and social processes. Rehabilitation psychologists could manage advanced options and programs for those motivated and able to make informed choices, work at their own pace, and pursue their personal, vocational, and rehabilitation goals on their own recognizance. In contrast, those clients at risk for secondary complications, additional expense, and less optimal outcomes could be selectively handled in more conservative, strategic programs that minimize cost to the clinic, staff, and community. This integrated approach could result in considerable savings to all stakeholders involved in the health care of people with chronic physical problems or disability.

To realize these roles, rehabilitation psychologists must remember their primary identity as scientists in the pursuit of refining clinical practice. However, they must critically examine our roles in health care and on multidisciplinary teams. Traditional practices in physical medicine and rehabilitation still insist on traditionally defined roles for most psychologists. Changes in payment systems lead professions to grapple over the "ownership" of clinical skills. In particular, strain between rehabilitation psychology and physiatry might result. Experiments with alternative service delivery models that focus on psychologists as leaders or managers in the provision of primary care for people with chronic health conditions are needed. For example, psychologists may collaborate with nurse practitioners and pharmacists to create a comprehensive, low-cost delivery system that may be highly efficacious and beneficial to consumers and other stakeholders. In these pursuits, psychologists must maintain their heritage as scientist–practitioners to develop, advance, and apply knowledge in these programs of care.

Changes in technology also affect health care; as described by Bigler (chapter 21), there is a revolution in the neuroimaging of brain function, and the potential for tying imaging methods to psychological assessment is immense but relatively unexamined. Psychologists may be instrumental in integrating information learned in functional magnetic resonance imaging and other neuroimaging methods to the understanding of large segments and chains of behavior. There will be an explosion of information from the interface of neuroimaging and behavior. Psychologists may be able to take the lead in applying this information to develop interventions that improve the quality of life for people with debilitating conditions.

Psychologists have a bright future as catalysts of change in health care. Maintenance of the current paradigm inevitably weakens the profession. Recognizing the importance of chronic health issues, developing theory-driven models of psychological health, and harnessing innovation all provide the keys to success for the discipline.

References

Cummings, N. A. (1996). The new structure of health care and a role for psychology. In R. Resnick & R. H. Rozensky (Eds.), *Health psychology through the life span: Practice and research opportunities* (pp. 27–38). Washington, DC: American Psychological Association.

DeLeon, P. H., Howell, W. C., Newman, R., Brown, A. B., Keita, G. P., & Sexton, J. L. (1996). Expanding roles in the twenty-first century. In R. Resnick & R. H. Rozensky (Eds.), *Health psychology through the life span: Practice and research opportunities* (pp. 427–453). Washington, DC: American Psychological Association.

Elliott, T. (1994). A place for theory in the study of psychological adjustment among persons with neuromuscular disorders: A reply to Livneh and Antonak. *Journal of Social Behavior and Personality, 9*(5), 231–236.

Elliott, T., & Frank, R. G. (1996). Depression after spinal cord injury. *Archives of Physical Medicine and Rehabilitation, 77,* 816–823.

Elliott, T., & Klapow, J. (1997). Training psychologists for a future in evolving health care delivery systems: Building a better Boulder model. *Journal of Clinical Psychology in Medical Settings, 4,* 255–267.

Elliott, T., & Shewchuk, R. (1996). Defining health and well-being for the future of counseling psychology. *The Counseling Psychologist, 24,* 743–750.

Fordyce, W. E. (1976). *Behavioral methods for chronic pain and illness.* St. Louis, MO: Mosby.

Frank, R. G. (1996). Changes in the post-acute health delivery system in the United States: International implications. *Proceedings of the 5th Conference of the IATSBI and 20th Conference of the Australian Society for the Study of Brain Impairment* (pp. 498–502). Bowen Hills, Queensland. Australian Society for the Study of Brain Impairment.

Frank, R. G. (1997). Lessons from the great battle: Health care reform 1992–1994. *Archives of Physical Medicine and Rehabilitation, 78,* 120–124.

Frank, R. G. (1999). Organized delivery systems: Implications for clinical psychology services or we zigged when we should have zagged. *Rehabilitation Psychology, 44*(1), 36–51.

Frank, R. G., & Johnstone, B. (1996). Changes in health work force: Implications for psychologists. In R. L. Glueckauf, R. G. Frank, G. R. Bond, & J. H. McGrew (Eds.), *Psychological practice in a changing health care system* (pp. 39–51). New York: Springer.

Frank, R. G., & Ross, M. (1995). The changing workforce: The role of health psychology. *Health Psychology, 14,* 519–525.

Hayes, S. C. (1998). Market-driven treatment development. *The Behavior Therapist, 21,* 32–33.

Ivey, S. L., Scheffler, R., & Zazzali, J. L. (1998). Supply dynamics of the mental health workforce: Implications for health policy. *Milbank Quarterly, 76,* 25–58.

Johnstone, B., Frank, R. G., Belar, C., Berk, S., Bieliauskas, L. A., Bigler, E. D., Caplan, B., Elliott, T. R., Glueckauf, R. L., Kaplan, R. M., Kreutzer, J. S., Mateer, C. A., Patterson, D., Puente, A. E., Richards, J. S., Rosenthal, M., Sherer, M., Shewchuk, R., Siegel, L. J., & Sweet, J. J. (1995). Psychology in health care: Future directions. *Professional Psychology: Research and Practice, 26,* 341–365.

Kaplan, R. M. (1994). The Ziggy theorem: Toward an outcomes-focused health psychology. *Health Psychology, 13,* 451–460.

Kaplan, R. M. (1996). Measuring health outcomes for resource allocation. In R. L. Glueckauf, R. G. Frank, G. R. Bond, & J. H. McGrew (Eds.), *Psychological practice in a changing health care system* (pp. 101–133). New York: Springer.

Leviton, L. C. (1996). Integrating psychology and public health: Challenges and opportunities. *American Psychologist, 51,* 42–51.

McFall, R. M. (1991). Manifesto for a science of clinical psychology. *The Clinical Psychologist, 44*(6), 75–88.

Nietzsche, F. (1983). On the uses and disadvantages of history for life. In C. Taylor (Ed.), *Untimely meditations* (pp. 59–123). Cambridge, England: Cambridge University Press. (Original work published 1873–1876).

O'Keeffe, J. (1996). The American health care system. In R. L. Glueckauf, R. G. Frank, G. R. Bond, & J. H. McGrew (Eds.), *Psychological practice in a changing health care system* (pp. 14–34). New York: Springer.

Popper, K. R. (1963). *Conjectures and refutations: The growth of scientific knowledge.* New York: Harper & Row.

Sanderson, W. C., Riley, W. T., & Eshun, S. (1997). Report of the working group on clinical services. *Journal of Clinical Psychology in Medical Settings, 4,* 3–12.

Strupp, H. H., & Hadley, S. W. (1977). A tripartite model of mental health and therapeutic outcomes. *American Psychologist, 32,* 187–196.

Resources

ADARA (formerly known as the
American Deafness and
Rehabilitation Association)
P.O. Box 727
Lusby, MD 20657
410/495-8440
http://www.adara.org/

Administration for Children and
Families (ACF; divided by region;
part of the U.S. Department of
Health and Human Services)
370 L'Enfant Promenade SW
Washington, DC 20447
http://www.acf.dhhs.gov/

Agency for Health Care Policy and
Research (AHCPR; *also see* Agency
for Health Care Research and
Quality)
Office of Health Care Information,
Executive Office Center,
2101 East Jefferson Street, Suite 501
Rockville, MD 20852

Agency for Health Care Research and
Quality (AHCRQ; formerly Agency
for Health Care Policy and
Research)
AHCRQ Publications Clearinghouse
P.O. Box 8547
Silver Spring, MD 20907
800/358-9295
http://www.ahcpr.gov/

Alexander Graham Bell Association for
the Deaf and Hard of Hearing
3417 Volta Place NW
Washington, DC 20007-2778
202/337-5220
http://www.agbell.org/

American Academy for Cerebral Palsy
and Developmental Medicine
6300 North River Road, Suite 727
Rosemont, IL 60018
847/698-1635, 847/823-0536 (fax)
http://www.aacpdm.org/

American Academy of Clinical
Neuropsychology
http://www.med.umich.edu/abcn/
aacn.html

American Academy of Physical
Medicine and Rehabilitation
One IBM Plaza, Suite 2500
Chicago, IL 60611-3604
312/464-9700, 312/464-0227 (fax)
http://www.aapmr.org/

American Amputee Foundation, Inc.
(AAF)
P.O. Box 250218, Hillcrest Station
Little Rock, AK 72225-0218
501/666-2523, 501/666-8367 (fax)

American Association of the Deaf–
Blind (AADB)
814 Thayer Avenue
Silver Spring, MD 20910
800/735-2258 (voice), 301/588-8705
(fax), 301/588-6545 (TTY)
http://www.tr.wou.edu/dblink/aadb.htm

American Association of Sex
Educators, Counselors and
Therapists
P.O. Box 238
Mount Vernon, IA 52314
319/895-6203 (fax)
http://www.aasect.org/

American Association of Spinal Cord
Nurses (AASCIN)
75-20 Astoria Blvd.
Jackson Heights, NY 11370
718/803-3782
http://www.aascin.org/

American Association of Spinal Cord
Injury Psychologists and Social
Workers (AASCIPSW)
75-20 Astoria Blvd.
Jackson Heights, NY 11370
718/803-3782
http://www.aascipsw.org/

American Association of University
Affiliated Programs for Persons with
Developmental Disabilities
8630 Fenton Street, Suite 410
Silver Spring, MD 20910
301/588-8252, 301/588-2842 (fax)
http://www.aauap.org/

American Board of Clinical
Neuropsychology
University of Michigan Hospitals
1500 East Medical Center Drive
Ann Arbor, MI 48109-0704
734/936-8269
http://www.med.umich.edu/abcn/

American Board of Forensic
Psychology (ABFP, part of the
American Board of Professional
Psychology)
128 North Craig Street
Pittsburgh, PA 15213
412/681-3000, 412/681-1471 (fax)
http://www.abfp.com/board.html

American Board of Professional
Psychology, Inc. (ABPP)
514 East Capitol Avenue
Jefferson City, MO 65101
573/634-5607, 573/634-7157 (fax)
http://www.abpp.org/

American Board of Rehabilitation
Psychology (ABRP)
% David R. Cox
1555 Howell Branch Road, Suite C-210
Winter Park, FL 32789
http://www.apa.org/divisions/div22/
ABRP.html

American College of Forensic
Examiners (ACFE)
2750 East Sunshine
Springfield, MO 65804
417/881-3818, 417/881-4702 (fax)
http://www.acfe.com/

American Congress of Rehabilitation
Medicine (ACRM)
5987 East 71st Street, Suite 111
Indianapolis, IN 46220
317/915-2250, 317/915-2245 (fax)
http://www.acrm.org/

American Council of the Blind (ACB)
1155 15th Street NW, Suite 720
Washington, DC 20005
800/424-8666, 202/467-5081, 202/467-
5085 (fax)
http://www.acb.org/

American Foundation for the Blind
(AFB)
11 Penn Plaza, Suite 300
New York, NY 10001
800/232-5463, 212/502-7661, 212/502-
7777 (fax), 212/502-7662 (TDD)
afbinfo@afb.net (email)
http://www.afb.org/

American Heart Association
National Center
7272 Greenville Avenue
Dallas, TX 75231
800/AHA-USA1
http://www.americanheart.org/

American Medical Rehabilitation
Providers Association
1606 20th Street NW, Suite 300
Washington, DC 20009
888/346-4624
http://www.amrpa.firminc.com/

American Pain Society
4700 West Lake Avenue
Glenville, IL 60025-1489
847/375-4715, 847/375-6315 (fax)
info@ampainsoc.org (email)
http://www.ampainsoc.org/

American Psychological Association
(APA)
http://www.apa.org/
    American Psychology–Law Society
    (Division 41)
    http://www.unl.edu/ap-ls/
    Division 22 Rehabilitation
    Psychology
    http://www.apa.org/divisions/div22/
    Division 40 Clinical
    Neuropsychology
    http://www.div40.org/

American Society for Deaf Children
P.O. Box 3355
Gettysburg, PA 17325
800/942-ASDC
http://www.deafchildren.org/

Americans With Disabilities Act of
   1990
800/514-0301, 800/514-0383 (TDD)
http://www.usdoj.gov/crt/ada/

Amputee Coalition of America
900 East Hill Avenue, Suite 285
Knoxville, TN 37915-2568
423/525-7917 (fax)
http://www.amputee-coalition.org/

Assessment Systems Corporation
2233 University Avenue, Suite 200
St. Paul, MN 55114
651/647-9220, 651/647-0412 (fax)
http://www.assess.com/

Association of Late-Deafened Adults,
   Inc. (ALDA)
1145 Westgate Street, Suite 206
Oak Park, IL 60301
877/348-7537 (voice and fax), 877/358-
   0125 (TTY)
http://www.alda.org/

Association of Postdoctoral Programs
   in Clinical Neuropsychology
1D-SMH-Mayo
Rochester, MN 55905
http://www.appcn.org/

Australian Council for Educational
   Research
19 Prospect Hill Road
Private Mail Bag 55
Camberwell, Victoria, Australia 3124
61/3/9277-5500, 61/3/92744-5555 (fax)
http://www.acer.edu.au/

Beach Center on Families and
   Disabilities
University of Kansas
3111 Haworth Hall
Lawrence, KS 66045
785/864-7600 (voice and TDD),
   785/864-7605 (fax)
http://www.lsi.ukans.edu/beach/
   beachhp.htm

Bioethics for Beginners
University of Pennsylvania
3401 Market Street, Suite 320
Philadelphia, PA 19104-3308
215/898-7136, 215/573-3036 (fax)
http://www.med.upenn.edu/bioethics/
   bioforbegin/

Brain Injury Association, Inc. (BIA)
105 North Alfred Street
Alexandria, VA 22314
703/236-6000, 703/236-6001 (fax)
http://www.biausa.org/

Caredata
Two Piedmont Center, Suite 400
3565 Piedmont Road
Atlanta, GA 30305-1502
800/955-5056, 404/364-6700
http://www.caredata.com/

Center for Alcohol and Addiction
   Studies
Brown University
Box G-BH
Providence, RI 02912
401/444-1800, 401/444-1850 (fax)
http://center.butler.brown.edu/
   index.htm

Center for Outcome Measurement in
   Brain Injury (COMBI)
http://www.tbims.org/combi.html

Center for Psychiatric Rehabilitation
   (part of Boston University)
940 Commonwealth Avenue West
Boston, MA 02215
617/353-3549, 617-353-7700 (fax),
   617-353-7701 (TTY)
http://www.bu.edu/sarpsych/

Centers for Disease Control and
   Prevention (CDC; part of the U.S.
   Department of Health and Human
   Services)
1600 Clifton Road
Atlanta, GA 30333
404/639-3311, 800/311-3435
http://www.cdc.gov/

Changing Faces
1 and 2 Junction Mews
London, England W2 1PN
020/7706-4232, 020/7706-4234 (fax)
info@changingfaces.co.uk
http://www.cfaces.demon.co.uk/

Clinical Neuropsychology
Division 40 of the American
  Psychological Association
% William B. Meneese
4912 Clairmont Avenue
Birmingham, AL 35222
205/591-8992
http://www.div40.org/

Coalition of Hispanic Health and
  Human Services Organization
  (COSSMHO)
1501 16th Street NW
Washington, DC 20036
202/387-5000, 202/797-4353 (fax)
http://www.cossmho.org/

Commission on Accreditation of
  Rehabilitation Facilities (CARF)
4891 East Grant Road
Tucson, AZ 85712
520/325-1044 (voice and TDD)

Constraint-Induced (CI) Movement
  Therapy Research Group at the
  University of Alabama at
  Birmingham
518 Spain Rehabilitation Center
619 19th Street South
Birmingham, AL 35249-7201
205/975-9799
excite@uab.edu (email)
http://www.neuroguide.com/
  pharmatransfer.htm

Convention of American Instructors of
  the Deaf (CAID)
P.O. Box 377
Bedford, TX 76095-0377
817/354-8414
http://www.gallaudet.edu/~pcnmpaad/
  caid.html

Eastern Paralyzed Veterans of
  American (EPVA)
75-20 Astoria Blvd.
Jackson Heights, NY 11370
718/803-3782, 718/803-0414 (fax)
info@epva.org (email)
http://www.epva.org/

Empowerment Zone
http://www.empowermentzone.com (in
  Miscellaneous and then
  Rehabilitation)

ERIC at Catholic University
http://www.lib.utulsa.edu/guides/
  educeric.htm

European Society for Mental Health
  and Deafness (ESMHD)
% Lars von der Lieth
University of Copenhagen
Njalsgade 86
2300 Copenhagen, Denmark
45/3532-8655, 45/3532-8635 (fax)
http://www.esmhd.org/

FindLaw
http://www.findlaw.com/

HeadSmart School Program (see also
  the Brain Injury Association)
Violence in Brain Injury Institute
105 North Alfred Street
Alexandria, VA 22314
703/235-6000
http://www.biausa.org/prevention.htm

Health Care Financing Administration
  (HCFA; part of the U.S. Department
  of Health and Human Services;
  multiple locations depending on
  state)
Clearinghouse: 7500 Security Blvd.
Baltimore, MD 21244
410/786-3000
http://www.hcfa.gov/

Helen Keller National Center (HKNC)
  for Death–Blind Youths and Adults
111 Middle Neck Road
Sands Point, NY 11050
516/944-8900, 516/944-7302 (fax),
  516/944-8637 (TTY)
http://www.helenkeller.org/national/

Houston Conference on Specialty
  Education and Training in Clinical
  Neuropsychology
http://www.nanonline.org/nan/
  subpages/general/houstn.html

Howard University Research and
  Training Center for Access to
  Rehabilitation and Economic
  Opportunity (HURTC)
Holy Cross Hall, Suite 100
2900 Van Ness Street NW
Washington, DC 20008
202/806-8086, 202/806-8148 (fax),
  202/244-7628 (TDD)
http://www.law.howard.edu/HURTC/
  HURTC.html

Information Technology for the Social
  and Behavioral Sciences (SSIT;
  online server)
http://www.gamma.rug.nl/
  iechomfr.html

International Association for the
  Scientific Study of Intellectual
  Disabilities (IASSID)
% Trevor Parmenter
Centre for Developmental Disability
  Studies
P.O. Box 6
Ryde New South Wales 1680
Australia
61/2/9807-7062, 61/2/9807-7053 (fax)
http://www.waisman.wisc.edu/iassid/
  index.html

International Association for the Study
  of Pain (IASP)
909 NE 43rd Street, Suite 306
Seattle, WA 98105-6020
206/547-6409, 206/547-1703 (fax)
http://www.halcyon.com/iasp/

International Association of
  Psychosocial Rehabilitation Services
  (IAPSRS)
10025 Governor Warfield Parkway,
  Suite 301
Columbia, MD 21044-3357
401/730-7190, 410/730-5965 (fax)
general@iapsrs.org (email)
http://www.iapsrs.org

International Neuropsychological
  Society (INS)
700 Ackerman Road, Suite 550
Columbus, OH 43202
614/263-4200, 614/263-4366 (fax)
http://www.ohio-state.edu/ins/

International Society for Quality of
  Life Research (ISOQOL)
6728 Old McLean Village Drive
McLean, VA 22101-3906
703/556-9222, 703/556-8729 (fax)
http://www.isoqol.org/

Institute of Medicine (IOM; part of the
  U.S. National Academy of Sciences)
2101 Constitution Avenue NW
Washington, DC 20418
202/334-3300
http://www.iom.edu/

Jean Piaget Society
http://www.piaget.org/main.html

Joint Commission on Accreditation of
  Healthcare Organizations (JCAHO)
One Renaissance Blvd.
Oakbrook Terrace, IL 60181
630/792-5000, 630/792-5006 (fax)
http://www.jcaho.org/

Laurent Clerc National Deaf
  Education Center
Gallaudet University
800 Florida Avenue NE
Washington, DC 20002
202/651-5340 (voice and TTY)
clearinghouse.infotogo@gallaudet.edu
  (email)
http://clerccenter.gallaudet.edu/

Let's Face It (for people with facial
  differences)
P.O. Box 29972
Bellingham, WA 98228-1972
360/676-7325
http://www.faceit.org/letsfaceit/

Maryland Hospital Association
410/379-6200
http://www.mdhospitals.org/

MESA Press
5835 South Kimbark Avenue
Chicago, IL 60637-1609
312/702-1596, 312/288-5680, 312/834-
   0326 (fax)
http://www.rfi.org/mesa.htm

Medirisk (*see* Caredata)

Model Spinal Cord Injury Systems
% Arnie B. Jackson
University of Alabama at Birmingham
Spain Rehabilitation Center
619 19th Street South, Room 190
Birmingham, AL 35249-7330
205/934-3330, 205/975-9754 (fax)
http://www.spinalcord.uab.edu/
   show.asp?durki=21392/

Motivational Interviewing,
   Rehabilitation Research and
   Training Center (RRTC) on Drugs
   and Disability
New York University
35 West 4th Street, Suite 1200
New York, NY 10012
212/998-5294, 212/995-4192 (fax)
http://www.nyu.edu/projects/wolkstein/
   about/index.htm

National Academy of Neuropsychology
   (NAN)
2125 South Oneida Street, Suite 500
Denver, CO 80224-2594
303/691-3694, 303/691-5983 (fax)
http://nanonline.org/

National Association of the Deaf
814 Thayer Avenue
Silver Spring, MD 20910-4500
301/587-7789 (voice), 301/587-1789
   (TTY), 301/587-1791 (fax)
nadinfo@nad.org (email)
http://www.nad.org/

National Alliance for the Mentally Ill
   (NAMI)
Colonial Place Three
2107 Wilson Blvd., Suite 300
Arlington, VA 22201-3042
800/950-NAMI, 703/524-7600
http://www.nami.org/

National Association for Home Care
228 7th Street SE
Washington, DC 20003
202/547-7424, 202/547-3540 (fax)
http://www.nahc.org/

National Brain Tumor Foundation
414 13th Street, Suite 700
Oakland, CA 94612-2603
510/839-9777, 510/839-9779 (fax)
nbtf@braintumor.org/

National Center for Injury Prevention
   and Control (NCIPC)
4770 Buford Highway NE, Mailstop
   F41
Atlanta, GA 30341-3724
770/488-4265, 770/488-1662 (fax)
http://www.cdc.gov/ncipc/

National Center for Medical
   Rehabilitation Research
9000 Rockville Pike
Bldg. 61E, Room 2A03
Rockville, MD 20892
301/402-2242, 301/402-2554 (TTY),
   303/402-0832 (fax)
http://silk.nih.gov/silk/NCMRR

National Center for the Dissemination
   of Disability Research
211 East 7th Street, Room 400
Austin, TX 78701-3281
800/266-1832, 512/476-6861, 512/476-
   2286 (fax)
http://www.ncddr.org/

National Family Caregivers
   Association
10400 Connecticut Avenue #500
Bethesda, MD 20895-3944
800/896-3650, 301/942-2302 (fax)
info@nfcacares.org (email)
http://www.nfcacares.org/

National Federation of the Blind
   (NFB)
1800 Johnson Street
Baltimore, MD 21230
410/659-9314
http://www.nfb.org/

National Head Injury Foundation
  (NHIF)
333 Turnpike Road
Southborough, MA 01772
800/444-NHIF

National Highway Traffic Safety
  Administration (NHTSA, part of the
  U.S. Department of Transportation)
400 7th Street SW
Washington, DC 20590
Auto Safety Hotline: 800/424-9393
http://www.nhtsa.dot.gov/

National Information Center for
  Children and Youth With
  Disabilities
http://www.nichcy.org/

National Institute of Mental Health
  (NIMH)
Public Inquiries
6001 Executive Blvd.
Room 8184, MSC 9663
Bethesda, MD 20892-9663
301/443-4513, 301/443-4279 (fax)
nihminfo@nih.gov (email)
http://www.nimh.nih.gov/

National Institute of Neurological
  Disorders and Stroke (NINDS)
National Institutes of Health
Bethesda, MD 20892
http://www.ninds.nih.gov/patients/
  default.htm

National Institute on Alcohol Abuse
  and Alcoholism
6000 Executive Blvd., Willco Bldg.
Bethesda, MD 20892-7003
http://www.niaaa.nih.gov

National Institute on Disability and
  Rehabilitation Research (NIDRR)
205/934-5359
http://www.ed.gov/offices/OSERS/
  NIDRR/

National Institutes of Health (NIH)
http://www.nih.gov/

National Multiple Sclerosis Society
733 Third Avenue
New York, NY 10017
800/Fight-MS
info@nmss.org (email)
http://www.nmss.org/

National Parent Information Network
ERIC Clearinghouse on Elementary
  and Early Childhood Education
University of Illinois at Urbana–
  Champaign
Children's Research Center
51 Gerty Drive
Champaign, IL 61820-7469
http://ericps.crc.uiuc.edu/npin/

National Reference Center for
  Bioethics Literature (NRCBL)
http://www.georgetown.edu/research/
  nrcbl/

National Rehabilitation Association
  (NRA)
633 South Washington Street
Alexandria, VA 22314
703/836-0850, 703/836-0848 (fax),
  703/836-0849 (TTY)
http://www.nationalrehab.org/

National Rehabilitation Information
  Center (NARIC)
1010 Wayne Avenue, Suite 800
Silver Spring, MD 20910
800/346-2742, 301/562-2400, 301/562-
  2401 (fax), 301/495-5626 (TT)
http://www.naric.com/

National Resource Center for
  Traumatic Brain Injury
Medical College of Virginia
Richmond, VA
http://www.tbi.pmr.vcu.edu/

National SAFEKIDS Campaign
1301 Pennsylvania Avenue NW, Suite
  1000
Washington, DC 20004-1707
202/662-0600, 202/393-2072 (fax)
info@safekids.org (email)
http://www.safekids.org/

National Safety Council
1121 Spring Lake Drive
Itasca, IL 60143-3201
630/285-1121, 630/285-1315 (fax)
http://www.nsc.org/

National Spinal Cord Injury
    Association
8701 Georgia Avenue, Suite 500
Silver Spring, MD 20910
301/588-6959, 301/588-9414
http://www.spinalcord.org/

National Stroke Association
96 Inverness Drive East, Suite I
Englewood, CO 80112-5112
800/STROKES, 303/649-9299, 303/649-
    1328 (fax)
http://www.stroke.org/

National Technical Assistance
    Consortium for Children and Young
    Adults Who Are Deaf–Blind (NTAC;
    also see Helen Keller National
    Center)
Teaching Research Division
Western Oregon University
Monmouth, OR
http://www.tr.wasc.osshe.edu/ntac/

New Hampshire–Dartmouth
    Psychiatric Research Center
2 Whipple Place, Suite 202
Lebanon, NH 03766
603/448-0126
105 Pleasant Street
Concord, NH 03301,
603/271-5747, 603/271-5265 (fax)
http://www.dartmouth.edu/dms/
    psychrc/

NRH Research Center (information
    service and bibliographies)
http://www.nrhrc.org/

Office of Special Education and
    Rehabilitation Services (part of the
    U.S. Department of Education)
http://www.ed.gov/offices/OSERS/

Ohio Valley Center for Brain Injury
    Prevention and Rehabilitation
Ohio State University
Department of Physical Medicine and
    Rehabilitation
Lima, OH
http://www.ohiovalley.org/

Paralyzed Veterans of America (PVA)
http://www.pva.org/

Phoenix Society for Burn Survivors,
    Inc.
2153 Wealthy Street SE, Suite 215
East Grand Rapids, MI 49506
603/889-3000, 800/888-BURN, 603/889-
    4688 (fax)
http://www.phoenix-society.org/

Prevent Blindness America
500 East Remington Road
Schaumburg, IL 60173
800/331-2020
http://www.preventblindness.org/

Prevention Online
National Clearinghouse for Alcohol
    and Drug Information (NCADI)
Center for Substance Abuse
5600 Fishers Lane, Rockwall II
Rockville, MD 20857
301/443-0365
http://www.health.org/

Rehabilitation Accreditation
    Commission
4891 East Grant Street
Tucson, AZ 85712
520/325-1044 (voice and TDD),
    520/318-1129 (fax)
http://www.carf.org

Rehabilitation Foundation, Inc.
P.O. Box 675
Wheaton, IL 60189
800/462-5655, 630/462-4547 (fax)
http://www.rfi.org/

Rehabilitation Psychology (Division 22
  of APA)
% Bernard Brucker
Department of Ortho/Rehab (D-27)
University of Miami School of
  Medicine
P.O. Box 016960
Miami, FL 33101
305/585-6919
bbrucker@mednet.med.miami.edu
  (email)
http://www.apa.org/divisions/div22/

Rehabilitation Services Administration
  (RSA)
U.S. Department of Education
400 Maryland Avenue SW
Washington, DC 20202-0498
800/USA-LEARN
http://www.ed.gov/offices/OSERS/RSA/

Resourceful Caregiver: Helping Family
  Caregivers Help Themselves
National Family Caregivers
  Association
800/667-2968
http://www.nfcacare.org/

Self Help for Hard of Hearing People,
  Inc. (SHHH)
7910 Woodmont Avenue, Suite 1200
Bethesda, MD 20814
301/657-2248, 301/657-2249 (TTY),
  301/913-9413 (fax)
http://www.shhh.org/

Spinal Cord Injury Information
  Network
National SCI Statistical Center
619 19th Street South, SRC 544
Birmingham, AL 35249-7330
205/934-3320, 205/934-2709 (fax),
  205/934-4642 (TDD)
http://www.spinalcord.uab.edu

THINK FIRST
22 South Washington Street
Park Ridge, IL 60068
800/THINK56
http://www.thinkfirst.org/

Traumatic Brain Injury Model
  Systems
Kessler Medical Rehabilitation
  Research and Education Corporation
1199 Pleasant Valley Way
West Orange, NJ 07052
http://www.tbims.org/

University of Iowa Hospitals and
  Clinics (disability-related
  information)
University Hospital School
100 Hawkins Drive
Iowa City, IA 52232-1101
319/353-6900
http://www.uiowa.edu/uhs/

U.S. Department of Health and
  Human Services (DHHS)
http://www.hhs.gov/

Waisman Center (Family Village,
  Cognitive and Developmental
  Disabilities Resources)
University of Wisconsin—Madison
1500 Highland Avenue
Madison, WI 53705-2280
608/263-5776, 608/263-0529 (fax),
  608/263-0802 (TDD)
http://www.waisman.wisc.edu/
  waisman.html

World Health Organization (WHO)
Geneva, Switzerland
http://www.who.org

Acronyms

AA	Alcoholics Anonymous
AADB	American Association of Deaf–Blind
AASCIPSW	American Association of Spinal Cord Injury Psychologists and Social Workers
AAUT	Actual Amount of Use Test
ABCN	American Board of Clinical Neuropsychology
ABRP	American Board of Rehabilitation Psychology
ACB	American Council of the Blind
ACAs	anterior cerebral arteries
ACRM	American Congress of Rehabilitation Medicine
ACT	assertive community treatment
ADA	Americans With Disabilities Act of 1990
ADARA	American Deafness and Rehabilitation Association
ADHD	attention deficit hyperactivity disorder
ADLs	activities of daily living
ADS	Alcohol Dependence Scale
AFB	American Foundation for the Blind
AHCRQ	Agency for Health Care Research and Quality
ALDA	Association of Late-Deafened Adults
AMAT	Arm Motor Ability Test
AMPS	Assessment of Motor and Process Skills
AOU scale	Amount of Use Scale
APA	American Psychological Association
ARS	Advanced Rehabilitation Systems
ASD	acute stress disorder
ASL	American Sign Language
AUI	Alcohol Use Inventory
AUDIT	Alcohol Use Disorders Identification Test
BDI	Beck Depression Inventory
BSI	Brief Symptom Inventory
CAGE	*c*ut down, *a*nnoyed, *g*uilty, *e*ye opener (questionnaire)
CARF	Commission on the Accreditation of Rehabilitation Facilities
CBT	cognitive–behavior therapy
CDC	Centers for Disease Control and Prevention
CES-D	Center for Epidemiological Studies–Depression Scale
CHART	Craig handicap assessment and reporting technique
CI therapy	constraint-induced movement therapy
CIQ	Community Integration Questionnaire
CMHC	community mental health center
CNS	central nervous system
CRA	community reinforcement approach
CSF	cerebrospinal fluid
CSP	community support program
CT	computed tomography
DAI	diffuse axonal injury

DAS	drug administration system
DHHS	U.S. Department of Health and Human Services
DOI scan	date-of-injury scan
DRGs	diagnosis-related groups
DrInC	Drinker's Inventory of Consequences
DRS	Disability Rating Scale; Dementia Rating Scale
DSM	*Diagnostic and Statistical Manual of Mental Disorders*
EMG	electromyography
ER	emergency room
FAM	Functional Assessment Measure
FAS	Functional Assessment Scale
FIM	Functional Independence Measure
FLS	frontal-lobe syndrome
fMRI	functional magnetic resonance imaging
FRGs	functionally related groups
GAD	generalized anxiety disorder
GCS	Glasgow Coma Scale
GDS	Geriatric Depression Scale
GOAT	Galveston Orientation and Amnesia Test
GOS	Glasgow Outcome Scale
HBM	health belief model
HCFA	Health Care Financing Administration
HIPP	Home Injury Prevention Project
HKNC	Helen Keller National Center
HRNB	Halstead–Reitan Neuropsychological Test Battery
HRSD	Hamilton Rating Scale for Depression
IAPSRS	International Association of Psychosocial Rehabilitation Services
ICA	internal cartoid artery
ICH	intracerebral hemorrhage
ICMS	intracortical microstimulation
ICP	intracranial pressure
IDEA	Individuals With Disabilities Education Act
IDD	Inventory to Diagnose Depression
IHC	Interdivisional Healthcare Committee
ILC	independent-living center
INS	International Neuropsychological Society
IOM	Institute of Medicine
IPS	individual placement and support
JCAHO	Joint Commission on Accreditation of Healthcare Organizations
JRA	juvenile rheumatoid arthritis
LORS	Level of Rehabilitation Scale III
MAACL	Multiple Affect Adjective Checklist
MAL	Motor Activity Log
MAST	Michigan Alcoholism Screening Test

MBHI	Millon Behavioral Health Inventory
MCA	middle cerebral artery
MCMI	Millon Clinical Multi-Axial Inventory
MCOs	managed care organizations
MDS	Minimum data set
MEG	magnetoencephalography
MMPI	Minnesota Multiphasic Personality Inventory
MMSE	Mini-Mental State Examination
MPAI	Mayo–Portland Adaptability Inventory
MRI	magnetic resonance imaging
MS	multiple sclerosis
NAA	N-acetyl-L-aspartate
NCIPC	National Center for Injury Prevention and Control
NCQA	National Committee for Quality Assurance
NCSE	Neurobehavioral Cognitive Status Examination
NEO-PI-R	Neuroticism Extraversion Openness Personality Inventory Revised
NFB	National Federation of the Blind
NHCMQ	Nursing Home Case-Mix and Quality Project
NHIF	National Head Injury Foundation
NHIS	National Health Interview Survey
NHST	null hypothesis statistical testing
NHTSA	National Highway Traffic Safety Administration
NIDRR	National Institute on Disability and Rehabilitation Research
NIH	National Institutes of Health
NRA	National Rehabilitation Association
NSRP	Normative Studies Research Project Test Battery
OT	occupational therapy
OIG	Office of the Inspector General
OTA	Office of Technology Assessment
PABIR	postacute brain injury rehabilitation
PCA	posterior cerebral artery
PECS	patient evaluation and conference system
PEDI	Pediatric Evaluation of Disability Inventory
PLISSIT	*p*ermission, *l*imited *i*nformation, *s*pecific *s*uggestions, *i*ntensive *t*herapy (framework)
PLP	phantom limb pain
PPS	prospective payment system
PSD	poststroke depression
PT	physical therapy
PTA	posttraumatic amnesia
PTSD	posttraumatic stress disorder
PVA	Paralyzed Veterans of America
PVS	persistent vegetative state
QFVI	Quantity Frequency Variability Index
QoL	quality of life
RA	rheumatoid arthritis

RINDS	reversible ischemic neurologic deficits
RLAS	Rancho Los Amigos Levels of Cognitive Functioning Scale
RP	retinitis pigmentosa
RUGs	resource utilization groups
SAH	subarachnoid hemorrhage
SCI	spinal cord injury
SCL-90	Symptom Checklist 90
SCS	spinal cord stimulation
SF-36	Short Form-36 Health Survey
SHHH	Self Help for Hard of Hearing People, Inc.
SIP	Sickness Impact Profile
SIT	stress inoculation training
SNF	skilled-nursing facility
SPECT	single photon emission computed tomography
SMI	severe mental illness
SR	subacute rehabilitation
SSRIs	selective serotonin reuptake inhibitors
STDs	sexually transmitted diseases
TBI	traumatic brain injury
TEFRA	Tax Equity and Fiscal Responsibility Act of 1982
TIAs	transient ischemic attacks
TMS	transcranial magnetic stimulation
UDS_{MR}	Uniform data system for medical rehabilitation
VBR	ventricle:brain ratio
VR	vocational rehabilitation
WAIS	Wechsler Adult Intelligence Scale
WHO	World Health Organization
WMFT	Wolf Motor Function Test

Glossary

AMYGDALA an almond-shaped mass that is a key structure of the limbic system

ANOXIA oxygen deprivation

APHASIC language disorder affecting receptive or expressive abilities (or both), ranging from mild to severe difficulties in understanding spoken and written language and in using language for oral or written communications

APRAXIC having difficulty or loss of ability in performing well-learned skills

ARCUATE FASICULUS connects Wernicke's area to Broca's area; a bundle of association fibers in the cerebrum extending from the frontal-lobe to the posterior end of the lateral sulcus and interrelating the cortex of the frontal, temporal, parietal, and occipital lobes

ASSERTIVE COMMUNITY TREATMENT a comprehensive individualized approach to treatment and rehabilitation using assertive outreach, small client: staff ratios, attention to details of everyday living, frequent contact with clients, and provision of service without a timelimit

AXIAL horizontal plane

CAGE QUESTIONNAIRE *cut* down on drinking, *a*nnoyed anyone, felt *g*uilty, or *e*ver had a hangover; one of the most commonly used alcoholism screening measures used in medical settings

CAUDATE NUCLEUS part of the basal ganglia; an elongated, arched gray mass closely related to the lateral ventricle throughout its entire extent and consisting of a head, body, and tail

COMMUNITY MENTAL HEALTH CENTER a center providing community mental health services, as authorized by the Community Mental Health Center Act of 1963

COMMUNITY REINFORCEMENT APPROACH a form of effective alcoholism treatment based on a functional analysis of alcohol-related behaviors and a behavioral approach to treatment

COMMUNITY SUPPORT PROGRAM a set of program principles developed by the National Institute of Mental Health in the 1980s to make services more relevant for people with severe mental illness

COMPUTERIZED TOMOGRAPHY X-ray technique for imaging the brain

CONDUCTION APHASIA fluent but paraphasic speech with nearly perfect comprehension of spoken or written language, but an inability to repeat spoken words

CONTRECOUP INJURY injury to the brain to its rebound opposite from a direct blow (the coup lesion)

CONTUSION a bruise

CORTICOSPINAL TRACK direct white matter track from motor cortex projecting to the spine; provides speed, discrete movements, strength, and agility to limb movements

COUP INJURY the point of direct impact injury widespread disruption of axonal tracts that is caused by external mechanical trauma or rapid deceleration of the head against an external surface

DIFFUSE AXONAL INJURY widespread disruption of axonal tracts that is caused by external mechanical trauma or rapid deceleration of the head against an external surface

DEMYELINATION destruction, removal, or loss of the myelin sheath (part of the "white" matter) of a nerve or nerves

DEOXYHEMOGLOBIN hemoglobin not combined with oxygen, formed when oxyhemoglobin releases its oxygen; called also deoxygenated or reduced hemoglobin

DYSCALCULIA inability to perform math

ENCEPHALOMALACIA softening of the brain

EXECUTIVE FUNCTIONS four components: (a) goal formulation, (b) planning, (c) carrying out goal-directed plans, and (d) effective performance in complex problem solving

FUNCTIONAL MAGNETIC RESONANCE IMAGING a new technique that capitalizes on changes that occur when homoglobin is attached to oxygen rather than carbon dioxide, which gives an indirect measure of hemodynamics

FRAILTY AND INJURIES Cooperative studies of intervention techniques trials established that exercise reduces incidence of falls

GLOBAL APHASIA inability either to speak or comprehend

GRAY MATTER mixture of capillary blood vessels and cell bodies of neurons; masses of cell bodies and dendrites in various parts of the central nervous system, which appear "gray" because they are not myelinated

HEMIPLEGIA paralysis or weakness of one side of the body

HEMOSIDERIN an intracellular storage form of iron; the granules consist of an ill-defined complex of ferric hydroxides, polysaccharides, and proteins having an iron content of about 33% by weight

HIPPOCAMPUS a nucleus of densely packed pyramidal cells in the medial temporal lobe of each cerebral hemisphere, lying in the floor of the inferior horn of the lateral ventricles, thought to be involved in the processing of short-term memory

INDIVIDUAL PLACEMENT AND SUPPORT a vocational approach based on the following principles: (a) goal of competitive employment, (b) rapid job search, (c) integration of rehabilitation and mental health, (d) attention to consumer preferences, (e) continuous and comprehensive assessment, and (f) unlimited time support

INTERNATIONAL ASSOCIATION OF PSYCHOSOCIAL REHABILITATION SERVICES an organization of psychiatric rehabilitation agencies, practitioners, and others dedicated to promoting, supporting, and strengthening community-oriented rehabilitation services

INTRACRANIAL MIDLINE SHIFT the distortion and swelling that occur when a mass effect such as a tumor, brain swelling, or large hemorrhage occupies an extensive part of a cerebral hemisphere; the swelling or increasing size of the mass pushes across the midline, distorting the falx cerebri

LATERAL VENTRICLE the cavity in each hemisphere, derived from the cavity of the embryonic neural tube; it consists of a pars centralis and three horns: frontal (anterior), temporal (inferior), and occipital in the frontal, temporal, and occipital lobes, respectively

MAGNETOENCEPHALOGRAPHY a recording of magnetic signals related to magnetic field potentials of living tissue

MIDDLE CEREBRAL ARTERY one or two major divisions of the internal carotid artery; the other division is the anterior cerebral artery; irrigates the anterior and middle portions of the cortex as well as the subcortical structures of this same area; joins with the anterior cerebral artery to form the anterior communicating artery

MODEL SYSTEMS OF CARE National Institute of Disability Rehabilitation and Research administers these programs that have become world renowned for people with spinal cord injuries, burns, and traumatic brain injuries; these programs establish innovative projects for the delivery, demonstration, and evaluation of comprehensive medical, vocational, and other rehabilitation services; the work of the systems begins at the point of injury and ends with successful re-entry into full community life

MOTIVATIONAL INTERVIEWING OR MOTIVATION ENHANCEMENT THERAPY a form of brief therapy based on empathetic listening skills and other therapeutic strategies found to be effective in an analysis of brief intervention studies

MYELIN the substance of the cell membrane that coils to form the myelin sheath; it has a high proportion of lipid to protein and serves as an electrical insulator

NOCICEPTION activity induced in neural pathways by potentially tissue-damaging stimuli

PATHOGNOMONIC specifically distinctive or characteristic of a disease or pathologic condition; a sign or symptom on which a diagnosis or pathologic condition; a sign or symptom on which a diagnosis can be made

PHANTOM LIMB PAIN the perception of painful sensations seemingly present in a missing limb or segment

PIXEL basic computer unit for image display

PORENCEPHALLIC CYST cavity in the brain that communicates with the lateral ventricle

PREDISPOSING, REINFORCING, AND ENABLING CAUSES IN EDUCATIONAL DIAGNOSIS AND EVALUATION (PRECEDE) model developed for planning health education programs

PUNCTUATE resembling or marked with points or dots

RADIOTRACER biological chemical injected that has a radioactive tracer that can be monitored

SAGGITAL midline plane

SEQUELA the consequence of a lesion or disease

SEVERE MENTAL ILLNESS three criteria are used to identify individual with this illness: (a) diagnosis can be met by a range of psychiatric diagnoses; (b) disability is met by having a severe disability, as manifested in significant role impairments affecting social relationships, work, leisure, and self-care; (c) duration is met by demonstrating chronicity or persistence of the disorder, typically through a history of psychiatric hospitalizations or intensive psychiatric treatment

SINGLE PHOTON EMISSION COMPUTED TOMOGRAPHY an imaging procedure where the uptake of a radiotracer is tracked in the brain

SPECTROSCOPY the propogation and analysis of chemical spectra, in the brain this permits identification of the chemical constituents of brain tissue

SPELLING DYSPRAXIA inability to form words and spell

SUPERIOR TEMPORAL GYRUS the superior most temporal gyrus; at the posterior extension of the superior temporal gyrus is Wernicke's Area, the primary auditory receptive area of the brain

TEMPORAL HORN OF LATERAL VENTRICLE the downward extension of the lateral ventricle into the temporal lobe forms the temporal home; the hippocampus is situated at the flour of the temporal horn and the amygdala provides the anterior boundary

THALAMUS large centrally located subcortical nucleus critical as a sensory relay station of the brain

THIRD VENTRICLE part of the lateral ventricular system situated between the two thalamic lobes

VENTRICLE:BRAIN RATIO a ratio score based on total ventricular volume divided by total brain volume

VENTRICULAR SYSTEM the cerebral spinal fluid-filled spaces of the brain

VOCATIONAL REHABILITATION the federal–state vocational rehabilitation system established by the Rehabilitation Act of 1973

WERNICKE'S AREA (BRODMANN'S AREA 22) an area that lies next to the primary auditory cortex and involves the understanding of auditory input as language and monitors speech output transforms auditory input into meaningful units (words); if this area has a lesion, comprehension of both spoken and written language is impaired

WHITE MATTER area of the nervous system rich in axons covered with glial cells, the conducting portion of the brain and spinal cord; it is composed mostly of myelinated nerve fibers, commissural fibers, and projection fibers

Author Index

Numbers in italics refer to listings in the reference sections.

Subject Index

AA. *See* Alcoholics Anonymous

AADB. *See* American Association of the Deaf–Blind

AAUT. *See* Actual Amount of Use Test

ABCP. *See* American Clinical Board of Professional Psychology

ACB. *See* American Council of the Blind

ACBPN. *See* American Clinical Board of Professional Neuropsychology

American Clinical Board of Professional Psychology (ABCP), 433

Academic reintegration, following traumatic brain injury, 64–65

Acalculia, 86

ACT. *See* Assertive community treatment

Activity limitations, 265

Actor–observer difference, 574

Actual Amount of Use Test (AAUT), 487–488

Acute pain
  prevention–management of, 192–193
  recurrent, 190

Acute stress disorder (ASD), 149, 150, 153–154

ADA. *See* Americans With Disabilities Act of 1990

ADARA. *See* American Deafness and Rehabilitation Association

ADHD. *See* Attention deficit hyperactivity disorder

Adolescents
  with chronic physical disorders, 133
  limb amputation in, 34

ADS. *See* Alcohol Dependence Scale

AFB. *See* American Federation for the Blind

African Americans, 585–586
  and Africentric worldview, 592–594
  beliefs of, about health–illness, 588–590
  communal–group orientation among, 595–596
  and conversion of negativity into positivity, 596–597
  cultural values of, 590–592
  and extended family network, 595
  factors affecting prevalence of disability among, 586–588
  incidence of disability among, 586
  and injury prevention, 528
  orientation of, toward harmony, 597
  with spinal cord injury, 11

and spirituality, 596

Age
  See also Geriatric issues
  and injury prevention, 528
  and stroke, 76–77

Agency for Health Care Research and Quality (AHCRQ), 82, 84

Agnosia, 86

Agraphia, 86

AHCRQ. *See* Agency for Health Care Research and Quality

AIDS, 39, 224

Alcohol Dependence Scale (ADS), 408

Alcoholics Anonymous (AA), 405

Alcohol problems, 399–413
  assessment of, 407–409
  brief interventions, 410–411
  community reinforcement approach to, 411–412
  coping–social-skills training approach to, 411
  and disease model of alcoholism, 402–405
  outcome, effects on, 401–402
  postinjury, 400–402
  preinjury, 400, 401
  prevalence–impact of, 399–401
  relapse prevention with, 412
  screening for, 405–407
  treatment approaches, 409–412

Alcohol use
  and spinal cord injury, 12
  and stroke, 77

Alcohol Use Disorders Identification Test (AUDIT), 407

Alcohol Use Inventory (AUI), 409

ALDA. *See* Association of Late-Deafened Adults

Alexander Graham Bell Association, 213

Alexia, 86

Alzheimer's disease, 112–113

Amantadine, 59

AMAT. *See* Arm Motor Ability Test

American Association of Spinal Cord Injury Psychologists and Social Workers, 4

American Association of the Deaf–Blind (AADB), 226

American Board of Professional Psychology, 3

American Clinical Board of Professional Neuropsychology (ABCN), 433

American Clinical Board of Professional Psychology (ABCP), 433

About the Editors

Robert G. Frank, PhD, is a professor and dean of the College of Health Professions at the University of Florida. He has a doctorate in clinical psychology from the University of New Mexico. He joined the faculty of the Department of Physical Medicine and Rehabilitation at the University of Missouri—Columbia's School of Medicine in 1979, where he established the Division of Clinical Health Psychology and Neuropsychology. From 1991 to 1995, Frank worked on federal and state health policy. As a Robert Wood Johnson Health Policy Fellow, he worked for Senator Jeff Bingaman (D-NM). After completing his fellowship, he returned to the University of Missouri, where as an assistant to the dean for health policy, he continued to work with Senator Bingaman and managed the ShowMe Health Reform Initiative, Missouri's health reform effort. He is a diplomate in clinical psychology of the American Board of Professional Psychology. He is also a past president of the Division of Rehabilitation Psychology of the American Psychological Association (APA) and a Fellow in APA's Divisions of Rehabilitation Psychology (22) and Health Psychology (38). His empirical publications focus on coping with chronic illness.

Timothy R. Elliott, PhD, is an associate professor in the Department of Physical Medicine and Rehabilitation at the University of Alabama at Birmingham. He received his PhD in counseling psychology from the University of Missouri—Columbia in 1987. He is a diplomate of the American Board of Professional Psychology and has been named a Fellow by three divisions (Rehabilitation, Health, and Counseling Psychology) of APA. He was recently elected president (2000–2001) of the Division of Rehabilitation Psychology. He serves as an associate editor for the *Journal of Social and Clinical Psychology, Journal of Clinical Psychology in Medical Settings,* and *Rehabilitation Psychology.* He has authored over 100 empirical articles and numerous book chapters.

newmobility.com
Baylor College of Med.
1 800-422-7693
Research on Women